Tulsian's

ACCOUNTANCY
for
CA-IPC (Group-II)

With Quick Revision Book

CA (Dr) P C TULSIAN

M.Com., PhD, FCA, PGDFM
Additional Director (Former)
Board of Studies
The Institute of Chartered Accountants of India, New Delhi
Head
Department of Commerce
Ramjas College
University of Delhi
DELHI
Recipient of an Award for ***Exemplary Services Contributed to the Cause of Profession***
by The Institute of Chartered Accountants of India, New Delhi

CA BHARAT TULSIAN

Chartered Accountant
Manager, KPMG
Alumnus of Sri Ram College of Commerce (SRCC)
University of Delhi
DELHI
Recipient of an Award for the ***Best Article on Foreign Exchange*** *at the all-India level*
by The Institute of Chartered Accountants of India, New Delhi

S. CHAND & COMPANY PVT. LTD.
(AN ISO 9001 : 2008 COMPANY)
RAM NAGAR, NEW DELHI - 110 055

S. CHAND & COMPANY PVT. LTD.

(An ISO 9001 : 2008 Company)

Head Office: 7361, RAM NAGAR, NEW DELHI - 110 055

Phone: 23672080-81-82, 9899107446, 9911310888 Fax: 91-11-23677446

www.schandpublishing.com; e-mail: helpdesk@schandpublishing.com

Branches

Ahmedabad : Ph: 27541965, 27542369, ahmedabad@schandpublishing.com
Bengaluru : Ph: 22268048, 22354008, bangalore@schandpublishing.com
Bhopal : Ph: 4274723, 4209587, bhopal@schandpublishing.com
Chandigarh : Ph: 2625356, 2625546, chandigarh@schandpublishing.com
Chennai : Ph: 28410027, 28410058, chennai@schandpublishing.com
Coimbatore : Ph: 2323620, 4217136, coimbatore@schandpublishing.com (Marketing Office)
Cuttack : Ph: 2332580, 2332581, cuttack@schandpublishing.com
Dehradun : Ph: 2711101, 2710861, dehradun@schandpublishing.com
Guwahati : Ph: 2738811, 2735640, guwahati@schandpublishing.com
Hyderabad : Ph: 27550194, 27550195, hyderabad@schandpublishing.com
Jaipur : Ph: 2219175, 2219176, jaipur@schandpublishing.com
Jalandhar : Ph: 2401630, 5000630, jalandhar@schandpublishing.com
Kochi : Ph: 2378740, 2378207-08, cochin@schandpublishing.com
Kolkata : Ph: 22367459, 22373914, kolkata@schandpublishing.com
Lucknow : Ph: 4026791, 4065646, lucknow@schandpublishing.com
Mumbai : Ph: 22690881, 22610885, mumbai@schandpublishing.com
Nagpur : Ph: 6451311, 2720523, 2777666, nagpur@schandpublishing.com
Patna : Ph: 2300489, 2302100, patna@schandpublishing.com
Pune : Ph: 64017298, pune@schandpublishing.com
Raipur : Ph: 2443142, raipur@schandpublishing.com (Marketing Office)
Ranchi : Ph: 2361178, ranchi@schandpublishing.com
Siliguri : Ph: 2520750, siliguri@schandpublishing.com (Marketing Office)
Visakhapatnam : Ph: 2782609, visakhapatnam@schandpublishing.com (Marketing Office)

First Edition 2009; Subsequent Editions and Reprints 2010, 2011 (Twice), 2012, 2013 (Twice), 2014, 2015
Tenth Revised Edition 2016, *Reprint with updates 2016*

ISBN : 978-93-525-3147-9

PRINTED IN INDIA

By Nirja Publishers & Printers Pvt. Ltd., 54/3/2, Jindal Paddy Compound, Kashipur Road, Rudrapur-263153, Uttarakhand and published by S. Chand & Company Pvt. Ltd., 7361, Ram Nagar, New Delhi -110 055.

PREFACE TO THE TENTH EDITION

We are thankful to the readers and teachers for their response and encouragement given to the Ninth Edition. This edition is thoroughly revised and substantially expanded; all chapters have been updated and expanded.

Salient Features

The book adopts a fresh and novel approach to the study of Accountancy for the students of CA Integrated Professional Competence Course (IPC) Group-II. It has been written in a teach yourself style strictly following a student-friendly approach, and is essentially meant to serve as a tutor at home.

PEDAGOGICAL FEATURES

Simple Language	The text is presented in the simplest language "meant to serve beginners"
Heading for each Paragraph	Each paragraph has been arranged under a suitable heading for easy retention of concepts
Tabular form	Wherever possible, the text matter relating to a particular topic/ sub-topic has been presented in a tabular form
Eye-catching Screens	All important equations, formulae, figures and practical steps have been presented in screen format to catch the eye
Uniform Format of Chapter	Each chapter has been uniformly organised under suitable headings, viz., text supported by suitable illustrations, solved problems

DISTINCTIVE FEATURES

Exhibits	Over 120 exhibits to acquaint students with various accounting treatment and formats
Illustrations	Over 600 illustrations have been provided for a better understanding of the text
Solved Problems	Over 250 solved problems along with necessary working notes and alternative solution have been provided throughout the text

Tulsian's Quick Revision for Accountancy for CA-IPC (Group-II)

Section 1	**Fully Solved Scanner Chapterwise (C.A. Professional Examination Problems with Authentic Solutions)**
Section 2	**Revision One Day Before Examination**
Section 3	**Tulsian's Model Test Papers**
Section 4	**IPC Examination Papers**

CA (Dr) P C Tulsian
pctulsian@gmail.com

CA Bharat Tulsian
bharattulsian88@gmail.com

ACKNOWLEDGEMENTS

We wish to express our sincere thanks to several individuals who have been a source of inspiration and support, personally and professionally, including Dr. R P Tulsian, Dr. M M Goyal, Dr. S C Garg, Dr. Tanushree Jain, Ms. Madhu Aggarwal, Dr. Rajeev Goyal, Dr. S N Gupta, Dr. S S Lamba, Dr. Sarita Jain, Dr. Usha Jain, Dr. V K Aggarwal, Dr. V P Bansal, Dr. Vibha Jain, Dr. Savita Gopal, Dr. S C Gupta, Dr. S P Gupta, Dr. Naresh Gupta, Dr. Amit Singhal, Dr. J B Gupta, Dr. Madhu Gupta, Dr. Sushma Aggarwal, Dr. Renu Gupta, Dr. Manju Gupta, Dr. C P Gupta Dr. S Z H Zaidi. CA M K Aggarwal, CA S K Aggarwal, CA N D Gupta, CA Naveen Gupta, CA Anil Jindal, CA Madhu Sudan Goyal, CA Vinod Aggarwal, CA Sunil Gupta, CA Arun Jain, CA Virender Aggarwal, CA S K Gupta, CA Ishwar Khemka, CA Prem Bansal, CA Ashish Gupta, CA M K Sharda, CA Rajeev Rastogi. CA Atul Gupta, CA Kuldeep Bhardwaj, CA Neeraj Chabra, CA Kishore Paul, CA Pradeep Narang, CA S K Gupta, CA R Devarajan, CA Tapas Dutta, CA Arnav Chakrabarty, CA Seema Gupta, CA Shilpa Aggarwal, CA Vishal Pandey, Ms. Nidhi Singh, Dr. N N Sen Gupta, Prof. J P Sharma, CA Pallavi, CA Antima Jain, CA Piyush Tulsian, CA Swati Tulsian, CA Piyush and CA Prarthana Mittal.

Special word of thanks is also due to our favourite students **Piyush, Pranav, Arushi and Aman Mittal** who provided incisive comments and useful feedback.

We must conclude that this book would have never been written without the support, encouragement and prodding of our family members. Many thanks to them.

Any criticisms or suggestions for further improvement of the book will be gratefully acknowledged and appreciated.

CA (Dr) P C Tulsian
pctulsian@gmail.com

CA Bharat Tulsian
bharattulsian88@gmail.com

SYLLABUS

INTEGRATED PROFESSIONAL COMPETENCE COURSE (IPC) SYLLABUS

Paper 5: Advanced Accounting (Group II)

Time: 3 Hours **Marks-100**

Level of Knowledge: Working Knowledge

Objectives:

(a) To have an understanding of the conceptual framework for the preparation and presentation of financial statements

(b) To gain working knowledge of the professional standards and application of accounting principles to different practical situations

(c) To gain the ability to solve advanced problems in the case of different entities

S.No.	*Contents*	*Relevant Chapter of the Book*
1.	**Conceptual Framework for Preparation and Presentation of Financial Statements**	**Sec. B**
2.	**Accounting Standards** Working knowledge of: AS 4: Contingencies and Events occurring after the Balance Sheet Date AS 5: Net Profit or Loss for the Period, Prior Period Items and Changes in Accounting Policies AS 11: The Effects of Changes in Foreign Exchange Rates (Revised 2003) AS 12: Accounting for Government Grants AS 16: Borrowing Costs AS 19: Leases AS 20: Earnings Per Share AS 26: Intangible Assets AS 29: Provisions, Contingent Liabilities and Contingent Assets.	**Sec. B**
3.	**Advanced Issues in Partnership Accounts** Dissolution of partnership firms including piecemeal distribution of assets; Amalgamation of partnership	**1, 2, 2A**
4.	**Company Accounts** (a) Accounting for employee stock option plan, Buy-back of securities, Equity shares with differential rights, Underwriting of shares and debentures, Redemption of debentures	**3, 4, 5, 6**
	(b) Advanced problems for business acquisition, Amalgamation and reconstruction (excluding problems of amalgamation of inter-company holding)	**7, 8**

	(c) Accounting involved in liquidation of companies, Statement of Affairs (including deficiency/surplus accounts) and liquidator's statement of account of the winding up	9
	(d) Financial Statements of Banking, Insurance and Electricity Companies	10, 11, 12, 13
5.	**Accounting for Special Transactions** Departmental and branch accounts including foreign branches	**14, 15, 15A**

Note: *If either old Accounting Standards (ASs), Announcements and Limited Revisions to ASs are withdrawn or new ASs, Announcements and Limited Revisions to ASs are issued by the Institute of Chartered Accountants of India in place of existing ASs, Announcements and Limited Revisions to ASs, the syllabus will accordingly include/exclude such new developments in place of the existing ones with effect from the date to be notified by the Institute.*

Tulsian's

ACCOUNTANCY

for

CA-IPC (Group-II)

CONTENTS

PAPER 5: ADVANCED ACCOUNTING (GROUP II) (One Paper – Three hours – 100 Marks)

SECTION A – TEXTBOOK

SECTION B – ACCOUNTING STANDARDS

SECTION C – QUESTIONS BASED ON SCHEDULE III TO THE COMPANIES ACT, 2013

Supplement to Textbook

Tulsian's Quick Revision for ACCOUNTANCY CA-IPC (Group-II)

CONTENTS

SECTION 1

FULLY-SOLVED SCANNER CHAPTERWISE

[CA PROFESSIONAL EXAMINATION PROBLEMS WITH AUTHENTIC SOLUTIONS]

SCANNER FOR CA EXAMINATION PROBLEMS

SHORT ANSWER CARRYING 4-6 MARKS &
LONG ANSWER CARRYING 8-16 MARKS

SCANNER FOR ACCOUNTING STANDARDS

CA EXAMINATION PROBLEMS CARRYING 4-6 MARKS

SECTION 2

REVISION ONE DAY BEFORE EXAMINATION

SECTION 3

TULSIAN'S MODEL TEST PAPERS WITH ANSWERS

SECTION 4

IPC EXAMINATION PAPERS

SECTION A

PAPER 5: ADVANCED ACCOUNTING [GROUP-II]

Textbook

1 DISSOLUTION OF A FIRM

LEARNING OBJECTIVES

After studying this chapter, you should be able to understand:

- Meaning of Dissolution
- Meaning of Dissolution of Partner
- Meaning of Dissolution of a Firm
- Modes of Dissolution of a Firm
- Distinction between Dissolution of Partnership and Dissolution of Firm
- Settlement of Accounts [Section 48]
- Treatment of Firm's Debts and Private Debts [Section 49]
- Realisation Account
- Accounting Entries
- Treatment of Goodwill preparation of Balance Sheet as at Date of Dissolution
- Calculation of Remuneration Payable to Incharge of Realisation

1.0 MEANING OF DISSOLUTION

The term 'dissolution' stands for discontinuation. Under the Indian Partnership Act, 1932, the dissolution may be *either* of partnership *or* of a firm.

2.0 MEANING OF DISSOLUTION OF PARTNERSHIP

Dissolution of partnership refers to the change in the existing relations of the partners. The firm continues its business. It may take place on admission/retirement/ death/expulsion/insolvency of a partner *or* on change in the profit sharing ratio.

3.0 MEANING OF DISSOLUTION OF A FIRM

Dissolution of a firm means the dissolution of partnership between all the partners of the firm alongwith the termination of firm's business.

4.0 MODES OF DISSOLUTION OF A FIRM

It may take place in any of the following ways:

1. **By Mutual Agreement**	When all the partners agree to dissolve the firm
2. **Compulsory Dissolution**	(i) on the insolvency of all the partners *or* all except one partner; (ii) on business becoming unlawful.

3. On happening of Certain Contingencies	Dissolution on the happening of certain contingencies. Subject to contract between the partners. A firm is dissolved by — (i) the expiry of the term for which the firm was formed; (ii) the completion of the venture(s) for which the firm was formed; (iii) the death of a partner; (iv) the adjudication of a partner as insolvent.
4. By Notice	When any one of the partners gives a notice in writing to other partners in case of partnership at will
5. Dissolution by Court	A court may dissolve a firm on any of the following grounds: (a) Insanity of a partner, (b) Permanent incapacity of a partner, (c) Misconduct of/by a partner, (d) Persistent breach of agreement by a partner, (e) Transfer of interest by a partner, (f) Improbability of carrying on the business except at a loss, (g) any other ground on which court is satisfied that it would be just and equitable to dissolve the firm.

5.0 DISTINCTION BETWEEN DISSOLUTION OF PARTNERSHIP AND DISSOLUTION OF FIRM

Dissolution of Partnership differ from Dissolution of Firm in the following respects:

Basis of Distinction	Dissolution of Partnership	Dissolution of Firm
1. Termination of business	The business is not terminated.	The business of the firm is closed.
2. Settlement of assets and liabilities	Assets and liabilities are revalued and new balance sheet is drawn.	Assets are realized and liabilities are paid off.
3. Account to determine Profit/Loss	Revaluation Account is prepared to determine the profit/ loss on revaluation.	Realisation Account is prepared to determine the profit/loss on realization.
4. Court's Intervention	Court does not intervene because partnership is dissolved by mutual agreement.	A firm can be dissolved by the court's order.
5. Economic Relationship	Economic relationship between the partners changes.	Economic relationship between the partners comes to an end forever.
6. Closure of books	It does not require closure of books because the business is not terminated	All books of accounts are closed.

6.0 SETTLEMENT OF ACCOUNTS [SECTION 48]

The provisions of Sec 48 relating to settlement of accounts at the time of dissolution of firm are given below:

1. Treatment of Losses	Losses including deficiencies of capital are to be paid in the following manner: (a) First out of profits; (b) Then out of capital; (c) Lastly by partners individually in their profit-sharing ratio. [Sec. 48 (a)]
2. Application of Assets	The assets of the firm (including the sums, if any, contributed by the partners to make up the deficiencies of capital) shall be applied in the following manner and order: (a) First to pay off firm's debts due to the third parties; **Note:** Secured creditors are to be paid off first out of the proceeds of secured assets before anything is paid to unsecured creditors. (b) Then to pay off loans from partners. (c) Then to pay off capitals of partners. (d) Lastly the surplus, (if any), shall be divided among the partners in their profit-sharing ratio. [Sec. 48 (b)]

ILLUSTRATION 1

All the partners want to dissolve the firm. Y, a partner wants that his loan of ₹ 16,000 must be paid off before the payment of capitals of the partners. But X, another partner wants that capitals must be paid before the payment of Y's loan. Who is correct?

SOLUTION

Y is correct as per sec. 48 since partner's loan is to be paid first before the payment of partners' capitals.

ILLUSTRATION 2

All the partners want to dissolve the firm. Y, a partner wants that his loan of ₹ 16,000 must be paid off before the payment of Mrs X's loan. But X, another partner wants that Mrs. X's loan must be paid before the payment of Y's loan. Who is correct?

SOLUTION

X is correct as per sec. 48 since third party's debts are to be paid first before the payment of partner's loan.

ILLUSTRATION 3

A and B are partners in a firm sharing profits in the ratio of 3 : 2. Mrs. A has given a loan of ₹ 20,000 to the firm and the firm also obtained a loan of ₹ 10,000 from B. The firm was dissolved and its assets were realised for ₹ 25,000. State the order of payment of Mrs. A's Loan and B's Loan with reason, if there were no other creditors of the firm.

SOLUTION

According to the Section 48 of the Indian Partnership Act, 1932, Mrs. A's Loan of ₹ 20,000 will be paid first and after that B's Loan will be paid up to the available cash ₹ 5,000.

7.0 TREATMENT OF FIRM'S DEBTS AND PRIVATE DEBTS [SECTION 49]

Where there are firm's debts and partners' private debts, the following provisions shall apply:

1. Application of Firm's Property	Firm's property shall be applied first in payment of firm's debts then the surplus, (if any), shall be applied in the payment of partner's private debts to the extent to which the concerned partner is entitled to share in the surplus; and
2. Application of Partner's Pvt property	Partner's private property shall be applied first in payment of his private debts and the surplus, (if any), in payment of firm's debts if the firm's liabilities exceed the firm's assets. [Sec. 49] If the assets of the firm are not sufficient to pay off the firm's creditors, the partners are required to make contribution out of their net private assets (i.e. private assets minus private liabilities) because of the unlimited nature of the liability of partner.

DISTINCTION BETWEEN FIRM'S DEBTS AND PRIVATE DEBTS

Basis of Distinction	Firm's Debts	Private Debts
1. Who incurs	Firm's debts are incurred by the **firm**.	Private debts are incurred by a **partner** in the individual capacity of a household and not in the capacity of a partner of a firm.
2. Who is liable	For firm's debts, **all partners** are jointly and severally liable.	For private debts, **only the concerned partner** is liable.
3. Application of firm's property	**For firm's debts,** firm's Property shall be applied first.	**For private debts, only the share of** concerned **partner in the excess** of firm's property over firm's debts can be applied.
4. Application of private property	**For firm's debts, only the excess of partner's private property over his private** debts can be applied.	**For private debts,** private property shall be applied **first.**

8.0 REALISATION ACCOUNT

OBJECT OF A REALISATION ACCOUNT

The object of Realisation Account is to close the books of account of a dissolved firm and to compute the net effect of realisation various assets and payments of various liabilities.

DISTINCTION BETWEEN REALISATION ACCOUNT AND REVALUATION ACCOUNT

Realisation Account is different from the Revaluation account in the following respects:

Basis of Distinction	Revaluation Account	Realisation Account
1. Meaning	It records the **effect of revaluation of assets and liabilities.**	It records the **realisation of various assets and payments of various liabilities.**
2. Purpose	It is prepared **to determine the net Profit/loss on revaluation.**	It is prepared **to determine the net profit/loss on realisation.**

3. **When prepared**	It Is prepared **at the time of constitution of partnership** (e.g., on admission of a new partner on retirement/death of a partner).	It is prepared **at the time of dissolution of the firm.**
4. **Transfer of Balance**	Its balance is transferred only to **old partners' capital accounts.**	Its balance is transferred **to all partners' capital accounts.**
5. **Basis of entries relating to the assets and liabilities**	Entries relating to assets and liabilities are made on the basis of **difference between the book values and revalued figures.**	Entries relating to assets and liabilities are made on the basis of their **book values and actual payments.**
6. **Effect of entries on accounts relating to assets and liabilities**	As a result of entries passed in this account, the **accounts** of assets and liabilities revalued, are **not closed.**	As a result of entries passed in this account, the **accounts** of assets and liabilities are **closed.**
7. **Preparation of account during the life time of the firm**	This account may be required to be prepared **at a number of occasions** during the lifetime of a firm.	This account is prepared only **once during the lifetime of a firm.**

9.0 ACCOUNTING ENTRIES

The various journal entries to close the books of a dissolved firm are summarized as under:

JOURNAL ENTRY ON TRANSFER OF ASSETS TO REALISATION ACCOUNT

Open Realisation Account and transfer **all the recorded assets** *[including Goodwill, Joint Life Policy but* ***excluding*** *the fictitious assets, Cash Balance, Bank Balance, Current account (Debit balance/ Capital account (Debit balance) of a partner]* to the debit of Realisation Account at their respective **book values** (i.e. the values at which they are appearing in the books of the firm). The following journal entry is passed to record such transfer:

JOURNAL

Date	*Particulars*		*L.F.*	*Dr. (₹)*	*Cr. (₹)*
	Realisation A/c	Dr.		(With the Total)	
	To Sundry Assets *(Individually)*				(With their Individual Book Values)
	(Being the transfer of Assets to Realisation A/c)				

TUTORIAL NOTES

1. An Asset against which a provision *or* reserve has been created, should be transferred at its gross figure and not at its net figure e.g., Debtors.
2. Provision/Reserve against a liability is a separate account and thus, it should be transferred to Realisation A/c separately like other assets, e.g., Provision for Discount on Creditors.
3. The balance at bank is not transferred to the Realization Account because it is not to be realised but instead distributed in its present form. However, In case of dissolution of a firm on account of 'Sale of Business to another firm *or* a company', unless otherwise stated, Cash & Bank balances shall also be transferred to the Realisation A/c.

ILLUSTRATION 4

A and B sharing profits and losses in the ratio of 3: 2 agreed upon the dissolution of the firm on 31st March, 2016 on which date their Balance Sheet was as follows:—

Liabilities	₹	*Assets*		₹
Trade Creditors	1,60,000	Cash		12,000
Bills Payable	40,000	Bank		60,000
Loan from A	10,000	Stock		1,60,000
Loan from Mrs A	30,000	Book Debts	1,32,000	
Employees' Provident Fund	10,000	*Less:* Provisions	12,000	1,20,000
Workmen Compensation Reserve	4,000	Plant and Machinery		60,000
Machinery Replacement Reserve	16,000	Land and Building		66,000
General Reserve	48,000	Joint Life Policy (at Surrender Value)		10,000
Profit and Loss A/c	22,000	Investments (Face Value ₹ 4,000)		20,000
A's Capital	1,68,000	Goodwill		30,000
B's Capital	52,000	Prepaid Insurance		2,000
		Deferred Revenue Advt. Expenditure		20,000
	5,60,000			5,60,000

Note: Their is a bill for ₹ 2,000 under discount. The bill was received from Z.

Required: Pass the necessary journal entry to record the transfer of assets to Realisation Account.

SOLUTION

JOURNAL

Date	*Particulars*	*L.F.*	*Dr. (₹)*	*Cr. (₹)*
	Realisation A/c Dr.		4,80,000	
	To Stock			1,60,000
	To Book Debts			1,32,000
	To Plant & Machinery			60,000
	To Land & Building			66,000
	To Joint Life Policy			10,000
	To Investments			20,000
	To Goodwill			30,000
	To Prepaid Insurance			2,000
	(Being the transfer of assets to Realisation A/c)			

JOURNAL ENTRY ON TRANSFER OF OUTSIDERS' LIABILITIES, PROVISION FOR DOUBTFUL DEBTS & PROVISION FOR DEPRECIATION TO REALISATION ACCOUNT

Transfer all the recorded outsiders' liabilities [e.g. creditors, B/P, O/S Expenses, Employees' Provident Fund, Loan from relative of a partner) and the Provision for Doubtful Debts & Provision for Depreciation to the credit of Realisation Account, at their respective book values. The following journal entry is passed to record such transfer.

JOURNAL ENTRY

Date	Particulars		L.F.	Dr. (₹)	Cr. (₹)
	Outsiders' Liabilities (Individually)	Dr.		With Individual	
	Provision for Doubtful Debt A/c	Dr.		Book Figures)	
	Provision for Depreciation A/c	Dr.			
	To Realisation A/c			(With the Total)	
	(Being the transfer of Liabilities to Realisation A/c)				

TUTORIAL NOTES

1. A liability against which a provision *or* reserve has been created, should be transferred at its gross figure and not at its net figure, e.g., Creditors.
2. Provision/Reserve against an asset is a separate account and thus, it should be transferred to Realisation Account separately like other liabilities, e.g., Provision for Doubtful Debts A/c, Machinery Replacement Reserve.
3. That portion of any provision/fund which represents a liability expected to arise in future, should also be transferred to Realisation A/c.
4. Loan from a relative of a partner is an external liability whereas loan from any partner is not an external liability since its payment can be made only after the repayment of outsiders' liabilities. No doubt, loan from partner is having priority as to repayment over the repayment of any part of capital.

ILLUSTRATION 5

Taking the same information as given in Illustration I, give the necessary journal entry to record the transfer of liabilities to Realisation Account.

SOLUTION

JOURNAL

Date	Particulars		L.F.	Dr. (₹)	Cr. (₹)
	Provision for Doubtful Debts A/c	Dr.		12,000	
	Creditors	Dr.		1,60,000	
	Bills Payable	Dr.		40,000	
	Loan from Mrs A	Dr.		30,000	
	Employees' Provident Fund	Dr.		10,000	
	Machinery Replacement Reserve A/c	Dr.		16,000	
	To Realisation A/c				2,68,000
	(Being the transfer of liabilities, provisions & reserves to Realisation A/c)				

JOURNAL ENTRY ON REALISATION OF ALL ASSETS (WHETHER RECORDED OR UNRECORDED)

Mode of Realisation	Accounting Entry to be Passed
(a) When the assets are sold for cash	Cash/Bank A/c Dr. To Realisation A/c
(b) When the assets are taken away by any of the partners	Concerned Partner's Capital A/c Dr. To Realisation A/c
(c) When the assets are given away to any of the creditors towards the full/partial payment of his dues.	No journal entry may be passed.

Note: Firm's assets which are not appearing in its books, are called firm's unrecorded assets.

tutorial Note: *If the ouestion is silent about the realisation of any asset (except life insurance policy appearing at surrender value), it is reasonable to assume that such asset has not realised any amount.*

ILLUSTRATION 6

Pass the necessary Journal Entries for the following transactions on the disolution of the firm of X and Y after the various assets (other than cash) and outside liabilities have been transferred to Realisation Account:

1. Stock ₹ 1,60,000 'X' took over 50% of the Stock at a discount of 20%. Remaining Stock was sold off at a profit of 30% on cost.
2. Debtors ₹ 1,32,000. Provision for Doubtful Debts ₹ 12,000. ₹ 24,000 of the book debts proved bad.
3. Land and Building (Book Value ₹ 66,000) sold for ₹ 3,00,000 through a broker who charged 2%.
4. Plant and Machinery (Book Value ₹ 60,000) was handed over to a creditor at a discount of 10%.
5. Investments (Book Value ₹ 4,000) realised 150%.
6. Goodwill of ₹. 30,000, Prepaid Fire Insurance of ₹ 2,000 and Joint Life Policy having a surrender value of ₹ 10,000.

SOLUTION

JOURNAL

Date	*Particulars*	*L.F.*	*Dr. (₹)*	*Cr. (₹)*
1(a)	X's Capital A/c [(1,60,000 × 50%) – (20% of 80,000)] Dr.		64,000	
	To Realisation A/c			64,000
	(Being 50% of Stock taken over by X at a discount of 20%)			
1(b)	Bank A/c [(1,60,000 × 50%) + (30% of 80,000)] Dr.		1,04,000	
	To Realisation A/c			1,04,000
	[Being the balance Stock realised at a profit of 30%]			
2	Bank A/c [₹ 1,32,000 – ₹ 24,000] Dr.		1,08,000	
	To Realisation A/c			1,08,000
	[Being the Good Debtors realised]			

3	Bank A/c [₹ 3,00,000 – (2% of ₹ 3,00,000)] Dr. To Realisation A/c [Being Land & Building realised]		2,94,000	2,94,000
4	No Journal Entry			
5	Bank A/c [₹ 4,000 × 150/100] Dr. To Realisation A/c [Being the Investments realised]		6,000	6,000
6(a)	Bank A/c Dr. To Realisation A/c [Being the surrender Value of JLP realised]		10,000	10,000
6(b)	For Goodwill. No Journal Entry assuming that Goodwill has not realised anything.			
6(c)	For Prepaid Fire Insurance, No Journal Entry because it is not realised at all.			

ILLUSTRATION 7

Pass the necessary journal entries to record the realisation of following unrecorded assets in the books of X and Y.

(a) There was an old furniture in the firm which had been written off completely in the books. This was sold for ₹ 3,000.

(b) 'Z' an old customer whose account for ₹ 1,000 was written off as bad in the previous year, paid 60%.

(c) A partner Mr 'X' agreed to takeover the firm's goodwill (Not recorded in the books of the firm) at a valuation of ₹ 30,000.

(d) A joint life policy having a surrender value of ₹ 10,000 remained unrecorded.

(e) There was an old typewriter which had been written off completely from the books. It was estimated to realise ₹ 400. It was taken away by 'Y' a partner at the estimated price *less* 25%.

(f) There were 100 shares of ₹ 10 each in Star Ltd. acquired at a cost of ₹ 2,000 which had been written off completely from the books. There shares are valued @ ₹ 6 each and divided among the partners in their profit sharing ratio.

SOLUTION

JOURNAL

Date	*Particulars*	*L.F.*	*Dr. (₹)*	*Cr. (₹)*
	Bank A/c Dr. To Realisation A/c (Being an unrecorded furniture realised)		3,000	3,000
	Bank A/c Dr. To Realisation A/c (Being a debt already written off recovered)		600	600
	X's Capital A/c Dr. To Realisation A/c (Being an unrecorded goodwill taken over by X)		30,000	30,000

	Bank A/c Dr. To Realisation A/c (Being an unrecorded life policy realised)	10,000	10,000
	Y's Capital A/c Dr. To Realisation A/c (Being an unrecorded typewriter taken away by Y)	300	300
	X's Capital A/c Dr. Y's Capital A/c Dr. To Realisation A/c (Being the unrecorded shares taken away by X and Y in their profit sharing ratio)	300 300	600

JOURNAL ENTRY ON DISCHARGE OF OUTSIDERS' LIABILITIES (WHETHER RECORDED *or* UNRECORDED)

Mode of Discharging	Accounting Entry to be Passed
(a) When the liabilities are discharged in cash	Realisation A/c Dr. To Cash/Bank A/c
(b) When any of the partners agree to discharge a liability	Realisation A/c Dr. To Concerned Partner's Capital A/c

Note: Firm's liabilities which are not appearing in its books are called unrecorded liabilities.

tutorial Note: *If the Question is silent about the payment of any liability (e.g. Creditors, Loan from a Relative of a Partner, Employees Provident Fund, Outstanging Expenses), it is always assumed that such liability has been paid at its book value.*

ILLUSTRATION 8

Pass the necessary Journal entries for the following transactions on the dissolution of the firm of X and Y after the various assets (other than cash) and outside liabilities have been transferred to Realisation Account:

1. 'Y' undertook to pay Mrs Y 's loan of ₹ 30,000.
2. Trade Creditors ₹ 1,60,000. Half the Trade Creditors accepted plant and machinery at an agreed valuation of ₹ 54,000 and Cash in full settlement of their claims after allowing a discount of ₹ 16,000. Remaining Trade Creditors were paid 95% in final settlement.
3. Bills Payable of ₹ 40,000 falling due after 1 month were discharged at a discount of 18% p.a.
4. Employees Provident Fund ₹ 10,000.

SOLUTION

JOURNAL

Date	Particulars	L.F.	Dr. (₹)	Cr. (₹)
1.	Realisation A/c Dr. To Y's Capital A/c (Being the payment of Mrs Y's loan by Y)		30,000	30,000
2(a)	Realisation A/c [(50% of 1,60,000) – 54,000 – 16,000] Dr. To Bank A/c		10,000	10,000

	[Being the Cash payment made to half creditors of value of ₹ 80,000]			
2(b)	Realisation A/c [(50% of 1,60,000) × 95/100] Dr.		76,000	
	To Bank A/c			76,000
	[Being the remaining half creditors discharged at 95%]			
3.	Realisation A/c [40,000 – (40,000 × 18% × 1/12)] Dr.		39,400	
	To Bank A/c			39,400
	[Being the B/P discharged at a discount of ₹ 600]			
4.	Realisation A/c Dr.		10,000	
	To Bank A/c			10,000
	[Being the Employees Providened Fund paid]			

ILLUSTRATION 9

Pass the necessary journal entries to record the discharge of following unrecorded liabilities:

(a) There was a contingent liability in respect of bills discounted but not matured of ₹ 3,700. An acceptor of one bill of ₹ 500 became insolvent and fifty paise in a rupee was recovered. The liability of the firm on account of this bill discounted and dishonoured has not so far been recorded.

(b) There was a contingent liability in respect of a claim for damages for ₹ 37,500. Such liability was settled for ₹ 18,000 and was undertaken by a partner Mr X to pay.

(c) The firm was required to pay ₹ 5,000 as compensation to an employee for an injury suffered by him, which was a contingent liability not accepted by the firm.

(d) ₹ 2,000 for damages claimed by a customer had been disputed by the firm. It was agreed at 75% by a compromise between the customer and the firm.

SOLUTION

JOURNAL

Date	*Particulars*	*L.F.*	*Dr. (₹)*	*Cr. (₹)*
	Realisation A/c Dr.		500	
	To Bank A/c			500
	(Being the payment made to the bank from whom the bill was discounted)			
	Bank A/c Dr.		250	
	To Realisation A/c			250
	(Being 50% of the dishonoured bill recovered)			
	Realisation A/c Dr.		18,000	
	To X's Capital A/c			18,000
	(Being an unrecorded liability for damages undertaken by Mr X)			

	Realisation A/c Dr. To Bank A/c (Being an unrecorded liability for compensation discharged)		5,000	5,000
	Realisation A/c Dr. To Bank A/c (Being an unrecorded liability for damages discharged)		1,500	1,500

ILLUSTRATION 10

There was one unrecorded asset estimated at ₹ 3,000, half of which was handed over to an unrecorded liability of ₹ 5,000 in settlement of a claim of ₹ 2,500 and remaining half was sold in the market at a discount of ₹ 200. Give the necessary journal entries:

SOLUTION

JOURNAL

Date	*Particulars*	*L.F.*	*Dr. (₹)*	*Cr. (₹)*
	Bank A/c Dr. To Realisation A/c (Being the remaining half of unrecorded asset realised)		1,300	1,300
	Realisation A/c Dr. To Bank A/c (Being the remaining half of unrecorded liability discharged)		2,500	2,500

JOURNAL ENTRY ON PAYMENT OF REALISATION EXPENSES

Mode of Payment	Accounting Entry to be Passed
(a) When expenses are paid by the firm on its own behalf	Realisation A/c Dr. To Cash/Bank A/c
(b) When expenses are paid by a partner on firm's behalf	Realisation A/c Dr. To Partner's Capital A/c
(c) When any of the partners agrees to do dissolution work for an agreed remuneration	Realisation A/c Dr. To Concerned Partner's Capital A/c
(d) When expenses are paid by a partner who has to bear such expenses	No entry
(e) When expenses. are paid by the firm on behalf of a partner who has to bear such expenses	Concerned Partner's Capital A/c Dr. To Cash/Bank A/c

ILLUSTRATION 11

Give the necessary journal entries in each of the following alternative cases:

(a) Realisation expenses were ₹ 1,000

(b) Realisation expenses amounting to ₹ 1,000 paid by a partner 'X';

(c) 'X' a partner agreed to take over the responsibility of completing dissolution at an agreed remuneration of ₹ 1,000. and to bear all realization expenses. Actual realization expenses amounted to ₹ 800 were paid by X out of his private funds.

(d) 'X' a partner agreed to take over the responsibility of completing dissolution at an agreed remuneration of ₹ 1,000 and to bear all realization expenses. Actual realization expenses amounted to ₹ 800 were paid by the firm.

SOLUTION

JOURNAL

Date	*Particulars*		*L.F.*	*Dr. (₹)*	*Cr. (₹)*
	Case (a)				
	Realisation A/c	Dr.		1,000	
	To Bank A/c				1,000
	(Being the expenses paid by firm)				
	Case (b)				
	Realisation A/c	Dr.		1,000	
	To X's Capital A/c				1,000
	(Being the expenses paid by X)				
	Case (c)				
	Realisation A/c	Dr.		1,000	
	To X's Capital A/c				1,000
	(Being the remuneration due to X)				
	Case (d)				
	(i) Realisation A/c	Dr.		1,000	
	To X's Capital A/c				1,000
	(Being the remuneration due to X)				
	(ii) X's Capital A/c	Dr.		800	
	To Bank A/c				800
	(Being the realisation expenses paid on behalf of X)				

ILLUSTRATION 12

Give the necessary journal entries in each of the following alternative cases:

Case (a) X, one of the partners was to receive ₹ 3,000 as remuneration for completing the dissolution work and was to bear realisation expenses. Realisation expenses were ₹ 1,000 paid by the firm.

Case (b) 'X', one of the partners was to receive 2% of the value of assets realised as remuneration for completing the dissolution work and was to bear realization expenses. Realisation expenses were ₹ 1,000 paid by X. The assets (including cash at Bank ₹ 3,000) realised ₹ 1,53,000.

Case (c) X, one of the partners was to receive 2% of the net cash realised from dissolution and was to bear realisation expenses. Realization expenses were ₹ 1,000. The assets (including Cash at Bank ₹ 3,000) realised ₹ 1,53,000 and cash paid for outsiders' liabilities amounted to ₹ 40,000.

SOLUTION

JOURNAL

Date	Particulars		L.F.	Dr. (₹)	Cr. (₹)
(a)	Realisation A/c	Dr.		3,000	
	To X's Capital A/c				3,000
	(Being the remuneration for dissolution work due to X)				
	X's Capital A/c	Dr.		1,000	
	To Cash A/c				1,000
	(Being the expenses paid on X's behalf)				
(b)	Realisation A/c	Dr.		3,000	
	To X's Capital A/c				3,000
	(Being the remuneration for dissolution work due to X i.e. 2% of ₹ 1,50,000 (i.e. ₹ 1,53,000 – ₹ 3,000)				
(c)	Realisation A/c	Dr.		2,200	
	To X's Capital A/c				2,200
	(Being the remuneration for dissolution work due to X i.e. 2% of ₹ 1,10,000 (i.e. ₹ 1,50,000 – ₹ 40,000) No entry for realisation expenses assuming that X has paid the same out of his private funds.				

Dr. **FORMAT OF REALISATION ACCOUNT [ASSUMING THAT X & Y ARE PARTNERS]** *Cr.*

Particulars		₹	Particulars		₹
To Assets Transferred:			By Provision for Doubtful Debts		XXXX
Stock		XXXX	By Creditors		XXXX
Book Debts		XXXX	By Bills Payable		XXXX
Plant & Machinery		XXXX	By Mrs X's Loan		XXXX
Land & buildings		XXXX	By Employees P.F.		XXXX
Joint Life Policy		XXXX	By Commission received in advance		XXXX
Goodwill		XXXX	By Machinery Replacement Reserve		XXXX
Investment		XXXX	By Y's Capital A/c (Stock)		XXXX
Prepaid Insurance		XXXX	By Bank A/c:		
To X's Capital A/c (Mrs X Loan)		XXXX	Stock	XXXX	
To Bank A/c:			Debtors	XXXX	
Creditors	XXXX		Land & Building	XXXX	
B/P	XXXX		Joint Life Policy	XXXX	
EPF	XXXX		Investments	XXXX	XXXX
Commission	XXXX		By Bank A/c (Bad debt recovered)		XXXX
Workmen Comp. Claim	XXXX	XXXX			
To X's Capital A/c (Realisation Exp.)		XXXX			
To Bank A/c (Discounted B/R)		XXXX			

To Profit on Realisation t/f to:			
X's Capital A/c	XXXX		
Y's Capital A/c	XXXX		
	XXXX		XXXX

JOURNAL ENTRY ON TRANSFER OF THE BALANCE IN REALISATION ACCOUNT TO ALL PARTNERS IN THEIR PROFIT SHARING RATIO

Nature of Balance in Realisation Account	Accounting Entry to be Passed
(a) In case of Profit on Realisation	Realisation A/c Dr. To All Partners' Capital A/cs
(b) In case of Loss on Realisation	All Partners' Capital A/cs Dr. To Realisation A/c

JOURNAL ENTRY ON PAYMENT OF PARTNER'S LOAN/ADVANCE

Partner's Loan/Advance to Partner A/c Dr.	
To Capital A/c	[Only to the extent of Dr. Balance in Capital A/c]
To Cash/Bank A/c	[With the Balance]

Tutorial Note: Where a Partner's Capital account shows a debit balance, his loan (to firm) account should be transferred to his capital account to the extent of debit balance and the balance, if any, in his loan account (to firm) should always be paid off separately.

ILLUSTRATION 13

Give the necessary journal entries to account for loan in each of the following alternative cases:

Case (a) Loan from X (a partner) ₹ 15,000

Case (b) Loan from X (a partner) ₹ 15,000, X's Capital Account (debit balance) ₹ 16,000

Case (c) Loan from X (a partner) ₹ 15,000, X's Capital Account (debit balance) ₹ 6,000.

SOLUTION

JOURNAL

Date	*Particulars*	*L.F.*	*Dr. (₹)*	*Cr. (₹)*
	Loan from X Dr.		15,000	
	To Bank A/c			15,000
	(Being loan from X discharged separately)			
	Loan from X Dr.		15,000	
	To X's Capital A/c			15,000
	(Being loan from X transferred to his capital account to set off debit balance)			
	Loan from X Dr.		15,000	
	To X's Capital A/c			6,000
	To Bank A/c			9,000
	(Being loan from X transferred to his capital account to set off debit balance)			

JOURNAL ENTRY ON TRANSFER OF THE ACCUMULATED PROFITS AND LOSSES TO ALL PARTNERS IN THEIR PROFIT SHARING RATIO

Accumulated Profits/Losses	Accounting Entry to be Passed
(a) In case of accumulated profits & reserves (e.g., Credit Balance in P & L A/c, General Reserve)	Profit & Loss A/c Dr. General Reserve Dr. To All Partners' Capital A/cs
(b) In case of accumulated losses, (e.g. debit balance in P & L A/c, Deferred Revenue Expenditure)	All Partners' Capital A/cs Dr. To Profit & Loss A/c To Deferred Revenue Expenditure A/c

TUTORIAL NOTES

1. *Machinery Replacement Fund is in the nature of accumulated depreciation and not in nature of accumulated profits and hence is not distributed among the partners.*
2. *Employees' Provident Fund represents statutory liability due to employees towards Provident Fund and is not an accumulated profit, hence it is not distributed among the partners.*

ILLUSTRATION 14

X, Y and Z sharing profits and losses in the ratio of 5 : 3: 2: decided to dissolve the firm on which date following balances appeared:

Particulars	₹
Contingency Reserve	5,000
General Reserve	10,000
P&L A/c	6,900
Investment Fluctuation Reserve	3,000
Machinery Replacement Reserve	2,000
Workmen's Compensation Reserve	2,400
Joint Life Policy Reserve	1,000
Advertisement Expenditure (Deferred Revenue)	2,000
Employees Provident Fund	700

Required: Pass the necessary journal entries relating to the treatment of accumulated profits and losses.

SOLUTION

JOURNAL

Date	*Particulars*		*L.F.*	*Dr. (₹)*	*Cr. (₹)*
	Contingency Reserve	Dr.		5,000	
	General Reserve	Dr.		10,000	
	P & L A/c	Dr.		6,900	
	Investment Fluctuation Reserve A/c	Dr.		3,000	
	Workmen's Compensation Reserve A/c	Dr.		2,400	
	Joint Life Policy Reserve A/c	Dr.		.1,000	
	To A's Capital A/c				14,150

	To B's Capital A/c			8,490
	To C's Capital A/c			5,660
	(Being the transfer of accumulated profits to all the partners in their profit-sharing ratio)			
	A's Capital A/c Dr.		1,000	
	B's Capital A/c Dr.		600	
	C's Capital A/c Dr.		400	
	To Advertisement Expenditure A/c			2,000
	(Being the transfer of accumulated losses to all the partners in their profit-sharing ratio)			

Notes:

1. *Machinery Replacement Fund is in the nature of accumulated depreciation and not in nature of accumulated profits and hence is not distributed among the partners.*
2. *Employees' Provident Fund represents statutory liability due to employees towards Provident Fund and is not an accumulated profit, hence it is not distributed among the partners.*

JOURNAL ENTRY ON TRANSFER OF THE BALANCE IN CURRENT ACCOUNT(S) (IF ANY)

Nature of Balance In Current Account	Accounting Entry to be Passed
(a) In case of debit balance in a Current Account of a partner	Concerned Partner's Capital A/c Dr. To Concerned Partner's Current A/c
(b) In case of credit balance in a Current Account of a partner	Concerned Partner's Current A/c Dr. To Concerned Partner's Capital A/c

JOURNAL ENTRY ON MAKING PAYMENT TO/BY A PARTNER

Payment to/by a Partner	Accounting Entry to be Passed
(a) In case of payment by a partner having a debit balance in his Capital Account	Cash/Bank A/c Dr. To Concerned Partner's Capital A/c
(b) In case of payment to a partner having a credit balance in his Capital Account	Concerned Partner's Capital A/c Dr. To Cash/Bank A/c

10.0 TREATMENT OF GOODWILL

The treatment of goodwill in case of dissolution of a firm may be summarized as follows:

Particulars	If Goodwill is Already appearing in the Books	If Goodwill is not Appearing in the Books
(a) On Transfer to Realisation A/c	Realisation A/c Dr. To Goodwill A/c	The question of transfer does not arise at all.
(b) On Sale for cash	Cash/Bank A/c Dr. To Realisation A/c	Cash/Bank A/c Dr. To Realisation A/c
(c) On being taken over by any of the partners	Concerned Partner's Capital A/c Dr. To Realisation A/c	Concerned Partner's Capital A/c Dr. To Realisation A/c

Note: *If the question is silent about the realisation of Goodwill, it is assumed that it has realised nothing.*

ILLUSTRATION 14

What journal entries are made in the books of a firm at the time of dissolution:

(a) When payment is made for an unrecorded liability.

(b) When a partner takes over the responsibility to pay off an unrecorded liability.

(c) When an unrecorded asset is taken over by a partner.

(d) When an unrecorded asset is taken over by a creditor.

(e) When a partner has to bear the realisation expenses but the payment of such expenses is made by the firm.

SOLUTION

JOURNAL

Date	*Particulars*		*L.F.*	*Dr. (₹)*	*Cr. (₹)*
(a)	Realisation A/c	Dr.			
	To Bank/Cash A/c				
	(Being for payment of unrecorded liability)				
(b)	Realisation A/c	Dr.			
	To Partner's Capital A/c				
	(Being an unrecorded liability taken over by a partner)				
(c)	Partner's Capital A/c	Dr.			
	To Realisation A/c				
	(Being an unrecorded asset taken over by a partner)				
(d)	No Entry				
(e)	Partner's Capital A/c	Dr.			
	To Cash or Bank A/c				
	(Being the payment of expenses made on partners' behalf)				

ILLUSTRATION 15

What Journal entries would be passed in the books of X and Y sharing profits & losses in the ratio of 5:2, for the following transactions on the dissolution of a firm, after various assets (other than cash) and third party liabilities have been transferred to Realisation Account?

1. Bank Loan ₹ 12,000 is paid.
2. Stock worth ₹ 6,000 is taken over by partner Y.
3. Expenses on dissolution amounted to ₹ 1,500 and were paid by partner X.
4. A typewriter completely written off in the books of accounts was sold for ₹200.
5. Loss on Realisation ₹ 14,000
6. The firm had a joint life policy of ₹ 1,00,000 on which the premium paid was considered as an ordinary business expenses. The surrender value of the policy was ₹ 10,000 on dissolution.
7. There was a balance of ₹ 21,000 in the General Reserve Account on the date of dissolution.

SOLUTION

JOURNAL

Date	*Particulars*		*L.F.*	*Dr.* (₹)	*Cr.* (₹)
1.	Realisation A/c	Dr.		12,000	
	To Bank A/c				12,000
	(Being the payment of Bank loan)				
2.	Y's Capital A/c	Dr.		6,000	
	To Realisation A/c				6,000
	(Being the stock taken over by Y)				
3.	Realisation A/c	Dr.		1,500	
	To X's Capital A/c				1,500
	(Being the payment of dissolution expenses by X)				
4.	Bank A/c	Dr.		200	
	To Realisation A/c				200
	(Being an unrecorded asset realised)				
5.	X's Capital A/c	Dr.		10,000	
	Y's Capital A/c	Dr.		4,000	
	To Realisation A/c				14,000
	(Being the transfer of loss on realisation)				
6.	Bank A/c	Dr.		10,000	
	To Realisation A/c				10,000
	(Being surrender value of JLP realised)				
7.	General Reserve A/c	Dr.		21,000	
	To X's Capital A/c				15,000
	To Y's Capital A/c				6,000
	(Being the t/f of Cr. Balance of General Reserve A/c)				

ILLUSTRATION 16

What Journal entries would be passed in the books of X and Y sharing profits & losses in the ratio of 5:2, for the following transactions on the dissolution of a firm, after various assets (other than cash) and third party liabilities have been transferred to Realisation Account?

1. Realization Expenses amounted to ₹ 2,000. Y one of the partners has to bear these expenses.
2. Y, one of the partners agreed to take over the creditor of ₹ 30,000 for ₹ 20,000.
3. X, one of the partners has given loan to the firm of ₹ 10,000. It was paid back to him at the time of dissolution.
4. Profit and Loss Account balance of ₹ 56,000 appeared on the assets side of the Balance Sheet.
5. Deferred Revenue Advertising Expenditure appeared at ₹ 28,000,
6. An unrecorded Investment of ₹ 7,000.
7. X, one of the partners was to bear all the realisation expenses for which he was given a commission of 2% of net cash realised from dissolution. Cash realised from assets was ₹ 25,000 and cash paid for liabilities amounted to ₹ 5,000.

SOLUTION

JOURNAL

Date	Particulars		L.F.	Dr. (₹)	Cr. (₹)
1.	Y's Capital A/c	Dr.		2,000	
	To Cash A/c				2,000
	(Being the payment of realisation expenses on Y's behalf)				
2.	Realisation A/c	Dr.		20,000	
	To Y's Capital A/c				20,000
	(Being the Creditors paid by Y)				
3.	X's Loan A/c	Dr.		10,000	
	To Cash A/c				10,000
	(Being the payment of X's Loan)				
4.	X's Capital A/c	Dr.		40,000	
	Y's Capital A/c	Dr.		16,000	
	To Profit & Loss A/c				56,000
	(Being the loss transferred to Partners' Capitals)				
5.	X's Capital A/c	Dr.		20,000	
	Y's Capital A/c	Dr.		8,000	
	To Deferred Revenue Advertising Exp. A/c				28,000
	(Being the transfer oi deferred advertising Exp. to capitals)				
6.	Bank A/c	Dr.		7,000	
	To Realisation A/c				7,000
	(Being the unrecorded investment realised)				
7.	Realisation A/c	Dr.		400	
	To X's Capital A/c				400
	(Being the commission due to X @ 2% of ₹. 20,000 (i.e., ₹ 25,000 – ₹ 5,000)				

ILLUSTRATION 17

O and P were partners in a firm sharing profits and losses equally. Their firm was dissolved which resulted in a loss of ₹ 50,000. On that date the capital account of O showed a credit balance of ₹ 40,000 and Capital Account of P showed a credit balance of ₹ 50,000. There was a cash balance of ₹ 40,000 on the date of dissolution.

You are required to pass the necessary journal entries for the (i) transfer of loss to the capital accounts of the partners and (ii) making final payment to the partners.

SOLUTION

JOURNAL

Date	Particulars		L.F.	Dr. (₹)	Cr. (₹)
(a)	O's Capital A/c	Dr.		25,000	
	Ps Capital A/c	Dr.		25,000	
	To Realisation A/c				50,000
	(Being the transfer of Loss on realisation)				

(b)	O's Capital A/c Dr.		15,000	
	P's Capital A/c Dr.		25,000	
	To Cash A/c			40,000
	(Being the final Payment made to partners)			

ILLUSTRATION 18

Pass the necessary Journal entries for the following transactions at the time of dissolution of the firm:

(i) Loan of ₹ 10,000 advanced by a partner to the firm was refunded.

(ii) X, a partner, takes over an unrecorded asset (Typewriter) at ₹ 300.

(iii) Undistributed balance (Debit) of Profit and Loss Account ₹ 30,000. The firm has three partners X, Y and Z.

(iv) The assets of the firm realised ₹ 1,25,000.

(v) Y who undertakes to carry out the dissolution proceedings is paid ₹ 2,000 for the same.

(vi) Creditors paid ₹ 28,000 in full settlement of their account of ₹ 30,000.

SOLUTION

JOURNAL

Date	*Particulars*	*L.F.*	*Dr. (₹)*	*Cr. (₹)*
(i)	Partner's Loan A/c Dr.		10,000	
	To Bank A/c			10,000
	(Being the partner's loan discharged)			
(ii)	X's Capital A/c Dr.		300	
	To Realisation A/c			300
	(Being the unrecorded typewriter taken away by X)			
(iii)	X's Capital A/c Dr.		10,000	
	Y's Capital A/c Dr.		10,000	
	Z's Capital A/c Dr.		10,000	
	To Profit and Loss A/c			30,000
	(Being the debit balance of Profit and Loss Account transferred to Partners' Capital Accounts)			
(iv)	Bank A/c Dr.		1,25,000	
	To Realisation A/c			1,25,000
	(Being the assets of the firm realised)			
(v)	Realisation A/c Dr.		2,000	
	To Y's Capital A/c			2,000
	(Being the remuneration due to Y)			
(vi)	Realisation A/c Dr.		28,000	
	To Bank A/c			28,000
	(Being the creditors paid ₹ 28,000 in full settlement of their account of ₹ 30,000)			

ILLUSTRATION 19

Pass the necessary Journal entries for the following transactions on the dissolution of the firm of T and P after the various assets (other than cash) and outside liabilities have been transferred to Realisation Account:

(i) Bank Loan ₹ 34,000 was paid.

(ii) Furniture work ₹ 70,000 was taken over by partner T at ₹ 43,000.

(iii) Partner P agreed to pay a creditor ₹ 7,500.

(iv) A computer previously written off fully, realised ₹ 3,900.

(v) Expenses of realisation ₹ 3,200 were paid by partner T.

(vi) Profit on realisation ₹ 4,800 was distributed between T and P in 5 : 3 ratio.

SOLUTION

JOURNAL

Date	*Particulars*	*L.F.*	*Dr. (₹)*	*Cr. (₹)*
(i)	Realisation A/c Dr.		34,000	
	To Bank A/c			34,000
	(Being the payment of Bank loan made)			
(ii)	T's Capital A/c Dr.		43,000	
	To Realisation A/c			43,000
	(Being the furniture taken over by T)			
(iii)	Realisation A/c Dr.		7,500	
	To P's Capital A/c			7,500
	(Being credit paid by P credited to his Capital Account)			
(iv)	Bank A/c Dr.		3,900	
	To Realisation A/c			3,900
	(Being the computer realised previously written off fully)			
(v)	Realisation A/c Dr.		3,200	
	To T's Capital A/c			3,200
	(Being the dissolution expenses paid by T credited to his Capital Account)			
(vi)	Realisation A/c Dr.		4,800	
	To T's Capital A/c			3,000
	To P's Capital A/c			1,800
	(Being the profit on realisation transferred to the Capital Accounts of Partners)			

ILLUSTRATION 20

Pass the necessary Journal entries for the following transactions on the dissolution of the firm of Sudha and Shiva after the various assets (other than cash) and outside liabilities have been transferred to Realisation Account:

(i) Sudha agreed to pay off her husband's loan ₹ 19,000.

(ii) A debtor whose debt of ₹ 9,300 was written off as bad in the books paid ₹ 7,500 in full settlement.

(iii) Shiva took over all investments at ₹ 13,300.

(iv) Sundry creditors ₹ 10,000 were paid at 9% discount.

(v) Realisation expenses ₹ 3,400 were paid by Sudha for which she was allowed ₹ 3,000.

(vi) Loss on realisation ₹ 9,400 was divided between Sudha and Shiva in 3 : 2 ratio.

SOLUTION

JOURNAL

Date	*Particulars*		*L.F.*	*Dr. (₹)*	*Cr. (₹)*
(i)	Realisation A/c	Dr.		19,000	
	To Sudha's Capital A/c				19,000
	(Being Sudha's husband loan taken over by Sudha)				
(ii)	Bank A/c	Dr.		7,500	
	To Realisation A/c				7,500
	(Being the Debtors realised)				
(iii)	Shiva's Capital A/c	Dr.		13,300	
	To Realisation A/c				13,300
	(Being the Investment taken over by Shiva)				
(iv)	Realisation A/c	Dr.		9,100	
	To Bank A/c				9,100
	(Being Creditors settled)				
(v)	Realisation A/c	Dr.		3,000	
	To Sudha's Capital A/c				3,000
	(Being the realisation expenses borne by Sudha)				
(vi)	Sudha's Capital A/c	Dr.		5,640	
	Shiva's Capital A/c	Dr.		3,760	
	To Realisation A/c				9,400
	(Being the loss on realisation transferred to Partner's Capital Accounts)				

ILLUSTRATION 21

Disha, Mohit and Nandan are partners. They decided to dissolve the firm.Pass the necessary Journal entries for the following after the various assets (other than Cash & Bank) and outside liabilities have been transferred to Realisation Account:

(a) An old typewriter which was not recorded in the books was sold for ₹ 2,000 whereas its expected value was ₹ 5,000.

(b) Stock of ₹ 70,000 was taken by Disha at a discount of 30%.

(c) Total creditors of the firm were ₹ 20,000. A creditors for ₹ 2,000 was untraceable and other creditors accepted payment allowing 10% discount.

(d) Mohit paid realisation expenses of ₹ 18,000 out of his private funds, who was to get remuneration of ₹ 13,000 for completing the dissolution process and was responsible to bear all the realisation expenses.

(e) Nandan had taken a loan of ₹ 50,000 from the firm, which was paid fully by him to the firm.

(f) ₹ 12,000 were recovered from a debtor which was written off as Bad debts last year.

SOLUTION

JOURNAL

Date	*Particulars*		*L.F.*	*Dr. (₹)*	*Cr. (₹)*
(a)	Bank A/c	Dr.		2,000	
	To Realisation A/c				2,000
	(Being the Unrecorded Asset realized)				
(b)	Disha's Capital A/c	Dr.		49,000	
	To Realisation A/c				49,000
	(Being the Stock taken over by partner)				
(c)	Realisation A/c	Dr.		16,200	
	To Bank A/c				16,200
	(Being the Creditors paid off) [(20,000 – 2,000) × 90/100]				
(d)	Realisation A/c	Dr.		13,000	
	To Mohit's Capital A/c				13,000
	(Being the remuneration for dissolution work due to Mohit)				
(e)	Bank A/c	Dr.		50,000	
	To Realisation A/c				50,000
	(Being Nandan's Loan realized)				
(f)	Bank A/c	Dr.		12,000	
	To Realisation A/c				12,000
	(Being Bad Debts recovered)				

ILLUSTRATION 22

Parul, Payal and Priyanka are partners. They decided to dissolve the firm. Pass the necessary Journal entries for the following after the various assets (other than Cash & Bank) and outside liabilities have been transferred to Realisation Account:

(a) There were total debtors of ₹ 76,000. A provision of Bad and doubtful debts also stood in the books at ₹ 6,000. ₹ 12,000 debtors proved bad and rest paid the amount due.

(b) Parul agreed to pay off her husband's loan of ₹ 7,000 at a discount of 5%.

(c) Total creditors of the firm were ₹ 40,000. Creditors worth ₹ 10,000 were given a piece of furniture costing ₹ 8,000 in full and final settlement. Remaining creditors allowed a discount of 10%.

(d) Payal had given a loan of ₹ 70,000 to the firm which was duly paid.

(e) A contingent liability (not provided for) of ₹ 4,000 was also discharged.

(f) The firm had a debit balance of ₹ 27,000 in the Profit and Loss Account on the date of dissolution.

SOLUTION

JOURNAL

Date	*Particulars*		*L.F.*	*Dr. (₹)*	*Cr. (₹)*
(a)	Bank A/c	Dr.		64,000	
	To Realisation A/c				64,000
	(Being the Debtors realized)				
(b)	Realisation A/c	Dr.		6,650	
	To Parul's Capital A/c				6,650
	(Being husband's loan taken over by Parul)				
(c)	Realisation A/c	Dr.		27,000	
	To Bank A/c				27,000
	(Being the Creditors paid off) [(40,000 – 10,000) × 90/100]				
(d)	Payal's Loan A/c	Dr.		70,000	
	To Bank A/c				70,000
	(Being Payal's loan paid off)				
(e)	Realisation A/c	Dr.		4,000	
	To Bank A/c				4,000
	(Being the Contingent liability paid off)				
(f)	Parul's Capital A/c	Dr.		9,000	
	Payal's Capital A/c	Dr.		9,000	
	Priyanka's Capital A/c	Dr.		9,000	
	To Profit and Loss A/c				27,000
	(Being the t/f of Dr.balance of P & L A/c to Partners' Capital A/cs)				

ILLUSTRATION 23

Pass the necessary Journal Entries for the following transactions on the dissolution of firm of A, B and C (who were sharing profits in the ratio of 4 : 3 : 3) after the transfer of all assets (other than cash) and external liabilities to Realisation Account.

(a) K, a creditor, to whom ₹ 6,000 were due to be paid, accepted office equipment at ₹ 4,000 and the balance was paid to him in cash.

(b) L, a creditor, to whom ₹ 16,000 were due to be paid, took over machinery at ₹ 20,000. Balance was paid by him in cash.

(c) M, an unrecorded creditor of ₹ 9,000 was paid by A at a discount of 10%.

(d) The amount of Sundry Liabilities (including creditors) was ₹ 2,00,000 appearing in the Balance Sheet.

(e) An unrecorded computer of ₹ 5,000 was taken over by B at discount of 10%.

(f) C's Loan of ₹ 10,000 was discharged alongwith Accrued Interest of ₹ 200 (Not yet recorded).

(g) The loss on dissolution was ₹ 10,000.

SOLUTION

JOURNAL

Date	Particulars		L.F.	Dr. (₹)	Cr. (₹)
(a)	Realisation A/c	Dr.		2,000	
	To Cash A/c				2,000
	(Being cash paid to a creditor)				
(b)	Cash A/c	Dr.		4,000	
	To Realisation A/c				4,000
	(Being cash received from a creditor)				
(c)	Realisation A/c	Dr.		8,100	
	To A's Capital A/c				8,100
	(Being an unrecorded liability taken over by A at a discount of 10%)				
(d)	Realisation A/c	Dr.		1,78,000	
	To Bank A/c				1,78,000
	(Being the payment made to remaining creditor) (i.e. ₹ 2,00,000 – ₹ 6,000 – ₹ 16,000)				
(e)	B's Capital A/c	Dr.		4,500	
	To Realisation A/c				4,500
	(Being an unrecorded asset taken over by B at a discount of 10%)				
(f)	C's Loan A/c	Dr.		10,000	
	Realisation A/c	Dr.		200	
	To Bank A/c				10,200
	(Being C's loan discharged alongwith Accrued Interest)				
(g)	A's Capital A/c	Dr.		4,000	
	B's Capital A/c	Dr.		3,000	
	C's Capital A/c	Dr.		3,000	
	To Realisation A/c				10,000
	(Being the transfer of Loss on Realisations)				

ILLUSTRATION 24

Pass the necessary journal entries for the following transactions on the dissolution of the firm of X and Y (who were sharing profits in the ratio of 3:1) after the transfer of all assets (other than Cash) and external liabilities to Realisation Account:

(a) An Unrecorded Furniture of ₹ 50,000 is taken over by X at a discount of 60%

(b) An Unrecorded Liability of ₹ 30,000 is settled and paid by Y at a discount of 40%.

(c) A Machine having a book value of ₹ 30,000 is given away to W, a firm's creditor of ₹ 44,000 at an agreed valuation of 80% towards full & final payment of his dues,

(d) A Furniture having a book value of ₹ 30,000 is given away to Z, a firm's creditor of ₹ 44,000 at a discount of 20% towards partial payment of his dues,

(e) P, a creditor to whom ₹ 20,000 were due, took over Patents having a book value of ₹ 30,000 at 80%. Balance was paid by him in Cash.

(f) X pays the Realisation Expenses of ₹ 20,000 on behalf of the firm,

(g) Firm pays actual Realisation Expenses of ₹ 18,000 on behalf of Y, a partner who has to bear the expenses,

(h) Loan from X,a partner of ₹ 22,000 appears on the liabilities side of the Balance Sheet of the firm and the X's Capital Account has a debit balance of ₹ 2,000.

SOLUTION

JOURNAL

Date	*Particulars*		*L.F.*	*Dr. (₹)*	*Cr. (₹)*
(a)	X's Capital A/c [₹ 50,000 – (₹ 50,000 × 60/100)]	Dr.		20,000	
	To Realisation A/c				20,000
	(Being the Unrecorded Furniture taken over by X)				
(b)	Realisation A/c [₹ 30,000 – (₹ 30,000 × 40/100)]	Dr.		18,000	
	To Y's Capital A/c				18,000
	(Being the Unrecorded Liability paid by Y)				
(c)	No journal entry may be passed.				
(d)	Realisation A/c	Dr.		20,000	
	To Cash/Bank A/c				20,000
	(Being the Balance paid to Creditor)				
(e)	Cash A/c	Dr.		4,000	
	To Realisation A/c				4,000
	(Being cash received from a Creditor)				
(f)	Realisation A/c	Dr.		20,000	
	To X's Capital A/c				20,000
	(Being the Realisation Expenses paid by X on behalf of the firm)				
(g)	Y's Capital A/c	Dr.		18,000	
	To Cash/Bank A/c				18,000
	(Being the Realisation Expenses paid by firm on behalf of the Y)				
(h)	Loan from X A/c	Dr.		22,000	
	To Capital A/c				2,000
	To Cash/Bank A/c				20,000
	(Being the loan from X transferred to his capital account to set off debit balance of ₹ 2,000 and the Balance paid)				

ILLUSTRATION 25

Pass the necessary journal entries for the following transactions on the dissolution of the firm of X,Y and Z (who were sharing profits in the ratio of 2 : 2 : 1) after the transfer of all assets (other than Cash) and external liabilities to Realisation Account:

(a) Debtors were of ₹ 1,24,200. X takes over debtors amounted to ₹ 1,20,000 at ₹ 1,17,200 and the remaining debtors were sold to a debt collecting agency at 50% of the value.

(b) Sundry Assets were of ₹ 1,17,000. Y is to take over some Sundry Assets at ₹ 72,000 (being 10% less than the book value). Z is to take over remaining Sundry Assets at 80% of the book value.

(c) Z assumes the responsibility of discharge of Mrs Z' Loan of ₹ 11,500 together with accrued interest of ₹ 2,300.

SOLUTION

JOURNAL

Date	Particulars		L.F.	Dr. (₹)	Cr. (₹)
(a) (i)	X's Capital A/c	Dr.		1,17,200	
	To Realisation A/c				1,17,200
	(Being some Debtors taken over by X)				
(a) (ii)	Cash/Bank A/c [(1,24,200 – 1,20,000) x 50/100]	Dr.		2,100	
	To Realisation A/c				2,100
	(Being the remaining debtors sold to a debt collecting agency)				
(b) (i)	Y's Capital A/c	Dr.		72,000	
	To Realisation A/c				72,000
	(Being some Sundry Assets taken over by Y)				
(b) (ii)	Z's Capital A/c [(1,17,000 – 80,000) x 80/100]	Dr.		29,600	
	To Realisation A/c				29,600
	(Be ing the remaining Sundry Assets taken over by Z)				
(c)	Realisation A/c	Dr.		13,800	
	To Z's Capital A/c				13,800
	(Being Mrs Z' Loan assumed by Z)				

ILLUSTRATION 26

Pass the necessary journal entries for the following transactions on the dissolution of the firm of A,B and C (who were sharing profits in the ratio of 4:3:3) after the transfer of all assets (other than Cash) and external liabilities to Realisation Account:

(a) A, one of the partners was to bear all the realisation expenses for which he was given a commission of 2% of net cash realised from dissolution. Cash realised from assets was ₹ 25,000 and cash paid for liabilities amounted to ₹ 5,000. Expenses of Realisation ₹ 1,000 paid by A.

(b) Workmen Compensation Reserve ₹ 30,000, Workmen Compensation paid ₹ 10,000.

(c) Commission received in advance (₹ 1,000) was returned to customers after deducting ₹ 200.

(d) There was a bill for ₹ 1,000 under discount. The bill was received from Z who proved insolvent and a first & final dividend of 25% was received from his estate.

(e) Bankers (who granted loan of ₹ 7,000) accepted stock of 6,000 at a discount of 20% and the balance in cash.

(f) On surrender of JLP Insurance Company paid ₹ 11,500 after deducting an amount of ₹ 6,500 towards loan and interest thereon by B against the policy.

(g) Prepaid Insurance of ₹ 5,000 and Goodwill of ₹ 50,000 were also appearing in the Balance Sheet but no other additional information was given with regard to these two items.

SOLUTION

JOURNAL

Date	*Particulars*		*L.F.*	*Dr. (₹)*	*Cr. (₹)*
(a)	Realisation A/c	Dr.		400	
	To A's Capital A/c				400
	[Being the commission due to A @ 2% of ₹ 20,000,(i.e. 25,000 – 5,000)]				
(b) (i)	Realisation A/c	Dr.		10,000	
	To Bank A/c				10,000
	(Being the liability discharged)				
(b) (ii)	Workmen Compersation Fund	Dr.			20,000
	To A's Capital A/c				8,000
	To B's Capital A/c				6,000
	To C's Capital A/c				6,000
	Being the transfer of excess (WCF)				
(c)	Realisation A/c	Dr.		800	
	To Bank A/c				800
	(Being the payment made for commission received in advance)				
(d) (i)	Realisation A/c	Dr.		1,000	
	To Bank A/c				1,000
	(Being the payment of dishonoured discounted B/R)				
(d) (ii)	Bank A/c	Dr.		250	
	To Realisation A/c				250
	(Being a first and final dividend of 25% received from the estate of Z)				
(e)	Realisation A/c	Dr.		2,200	
	To Bank A/c				2,200
	(Being the payment made to Bankers)				
(f)	Bank A/c	Dr.		11,500	
	B's Capital A/c	Dr.		6,500	
	To Realisation A/c				18,000
	(Being the JLP realised)				
(g)	No Journal Entry is required since there is no realisation.				

ILLUSTRATION 27

The following is the Balance-sheet of X and Y as at 31st March, 2016:

Liabilities	₹	*Assets*		₹
Sundry Creditors	20,000	Goodwill		10,000
Bills Payable	20,000	Buildings		25,000
Bank Overdraft	8,000	Plant		25,000
Outstanding Expenses	2,000	Investments		15,300
X's brother's Loan	20,000	Stock		8,700
Y's Loan	10,000	Debtors	17,000	
Plant Replacement Reserve	2,800	*Less:* Provision	2,000	15,000
Employees' Provident Fund	1,200	Bills Receivable		10,000
General Reserve	2,000	Cash & Bank		13,000
X's Capital	20,000	Profit & Loss A/c (Dr. Balance)		2,000
Y's Capital	20,000	Advertisement Suspense A/c		2,000
	1,26,000			1,26,000

The firm was dissolved on 31st March 2016 and the following arrangement were decided upon:

(a) X agreed to pay off his brother's loan.

(b) Debtors of ₹ 5,000 proved bad.

(c) Other assets realised as follows: Plant ₹ 20,000, Building 100% more, Goodwill 60%.

(d) Sundry Creditors and bills payable were settled at 5% discount.

(e) Y accepted Stock at ₹ 8,000 and all investments at ₹ 12,000 and X took over Bills Receivable at 20% discount.

(f) Realisation Expenses amounted to ₹ 2,000. Pass Journal Entries.

SOLUTION

JOURNAL

Particulars		*L.F.*	*Dr.* (₹)	*Cr.* (₹)
Realisation A/c	Dr.		1,11,000	
To Stock				8,700
To Book debts				17,000
To Plant & Machinery				25,000
To Land & Buildings				25,000
To Investments				15,300
To Goodwill				10,000
To B/R				10,000
(Being the transfer of assets to Realisation A/c)				
Provision for Doubtful Debts A/c	Dr.		2,000	
Creditors	Dr.		20,000	
Bills Payable	Dr.		20,000	

Mr. X's Brothers Loan	Dr.	20,000	
Bank Overdraft	Dr.	8,000	
Outstanding Expenses	Dr.	2,000	
Employees' P.F.	Dr.	1,200	
Machinery Replacement Reserve	Dr.	2,800	
To Realisation A/c			76,000
(Being the transfer of liabilities & provisions to Realisation A/c)			
X's Capital A/c	Dr.	8,000	
To Realisation A/c			8,000
(Being B/R taken over by X at a discount of 20%)			
Bank A/c	Dr.	88,000	
To Realisation A/c			88,000
(Being the assets realized)			
Realisation A/c	Dr.	20,000	
To X's Capital A/c			20,000
(Being the payment of X's Brother's Loan)			
Y's Capital A/c	Dr.	20,000	
To Realisation A/c			20,000
(Being investment & Stock taken over by Y)			
Realisation A/c	Dr.	2,000	
To Bank A/c			2,000
(Being the payment of realisation Expenses)			
Realisation A/c	Dr.	38,000	
To Bank A/c			38,000
(Being the payment made to Creditors & B/P)			
Realisation A/c	Dr.	11,200	
To Bank A/c			11,200
(Being the payment of other debts)			
Realisation A/c	Dr.	9,800	
To X's Capital A/c			4,900
To Y's Capital A/c			4,900
(Being the transfer of profit on realisation)			
Y's Loan A/c	Dr.	10,000	
To Bank A/c			10,000
(Being the payment of Y's loan)			
General Reserve	Dr.	2,000	
To X's Capital A/c			1,000
To Y's Capital A/c			1,000
(Being the transfer of General Reserve)			

X's Capital A/c	Dr.	1,000	
Y's Capital A/c	Dr.	1,000	
To Profit & Loss A/c			2,000
(Being the transfers of the debit balance in P & L A/c)			
X's Capital A/c	Dr.	1,000	
Y's Capital A/c	Dr.	1,000	
To Advertisement Suspense A/c			2,000
(Being the transfer of Advertisement Suspense A/c)			
X's Capital A/c	Dr.	35,900	
Y's Capital A/c	Dr.	3,900	
To Bank A/c			39,800
(Being the final payment made to partners)			

ILLUSTRATION 28

The following is the Balance Sheet of X and Y as 31st March 2016.

Liabilities	₹	*Assets*		₹
Creditors	38,000	Cash & Bank Balance		8,500
Loan from Mrs. X	5,000	Stock		5,000
Loan from Mrs. Y	10,000	Investments		10,000
Workmen Compensation Reserve	10,000	Debtors	20,000	
Fixed Assets Replacement Reserve	1,000	*Less:* Provision	2,000	18,000
X's Capital	10,000	Fixed Assets		39,000
Y's Capital	10,000	Profit and Loss A/c		3,000
		Advertisement Suspense A/c		500
	84,000			84,000

The firm was dissolved on 31st March 2016 and the following was found:

(a) X promised to pay off Mrs. X's Loan and took away the stock at 20% discount;
(b) Y took away half the investments at 10% discount;
(c) Debtors falling due on 1st Feb., 2014 were realised at a discount of 6% p.a.
(d) Creditors falling due on 30th April, 2016 were paid @ 6% discount p.a.;
(e) Fixed Assets realised ₹ 71,000 and remaining investment realised ₹ 4,500.
(f) There was an old furniture which has been written off completely from the books. Y agreed to take away the same at the price of ₹ 300.
(g) Realisation expenses were ₹ 1,000 paid by X.

Required: Prepare Realisation A/c, Cash & Bank A/c and Partners' Capital A/cs.

SOLUTION

Dr. **REALISATION ACCOUNT** *Cr.*

Particulars	₹	*Particulars*	₹
To Assets transferred:		By Provision for Doubtful Debtors	2,000
Stock	5,000	By Fixed Assets Replacem. Reserve	1,000

Investment	10,000	By Creditors		38,000
Debtors	20,000	By Mrs. X's Loan		5,000
Fixed Assets	39,000	By Mrs. Y's Loan		10,000
To Bank A/c: (Creditors)	37,810	By X's Capital A/c (Stock)		4,000
To X's Capital A/c (Expenses)	1,000	By Y's Capital A/c (Investments)		4,500
To X's Capital A/c (Mrs. X's Loan)	5,000	By Bank A/c:		
To Bank A/c (Mrs. Y's Loan A/c)	10,000	Debtors	19,000	
To Profit on realisation t/f to:		Fixed Assets	71,000	
X's Capital A/c	15,745	Investments	4,500	94,500
Y's Capital A/c	15,745	By Y's Capital A/c (Furniture)		300
	1,59,300			1,59,300

Dr. **PARTNERS' CAPITAL ACCOUNTS** Cr.

Particulars	*X* ₹	*Y* ₹	*Particulars*	*X* ₹	*Y* ₹
To P & L A/c	1,500	1,500	By Balance b/d	10,000	10,000
To Advertisement			By W. Comp. Reserve	5,000	5,000
Suspense A/c	250	250	By Realisation A/c	5,000	—
To Realisation A/c			By Realisation A/c	1,000	—
(Investment)	—	4,500	By Realisation A/c	15,745	15,745
To Realisation A/c					
(Furniture)	—	300			
To Realisation A/c	4,000	—			
To Bank A/c	30,995	24,195			
	36,745	30,745		36,745	30,745

Dr. **CASH & BANK ACCOUNT** Cr.

Particulars	₹	*Particulars*	₹
To Balance b/d	8,500	By Realisation A/c	37,810
To Realisation A/c	94,500	By Realisation A/c	10,000
		By X's Capital A/c	30,995
		By Y's Capital A/c	24,195
	1,03,000		1,03,000

ILLUSTRATION 29

A, B and C, who were sharing the profits and losses in the ratio of 3 : 1 : 1 respectively decided to dissolve the firm on 31st March, 2016 on which date their Balance Sheet was as follows:

Liabilities	₹	*Assets*		₹
Sundry Creditors	6,000	Cash at Bank		3,200
Loan from Mrs. B	1,500	Debtors	24,200	

Joint Policy Reserve	10,000	*Less:* Provision	1,200	23,000
A's Capital	24,500	Stock		7,800
B's Capital	9,000	Investments		17,000
C's Capital	6,000	Fixed Assets		1,000
		Advertisement Suspense A/c		5,000
	57,000			57,000

It is agreed as follows:

(a) Goodwill is to be ignored.

(b) 'A' is to take over all the fixed assets at ₹ 200 less, debtors amounting to ₹ 20,000 at ₹ 17,200. The creditors of ₹ 6,000 to be assumed by 'A' at that figure.

(c) 'B' is to take over all stocks at ₹ 7,000 and certain of the investment at ₹ 7,200 (being book value *less* 10%).

(d) 'C' is to take over the remaining investments at 90% of book value *less* ₹ 100 allowances and to assume responsibility for the discharge of the Mrs B's loan, together with accruing interest of ₹ 30 which has not been recorded in the books of the firm.

(e) The remaining debtors were sold to a debt collecting agency for 50% of book values.

(f) A was entitled to receive ₹ 270 as remuneration for completing the dissolution work and was to bear the realisation expenses. The expenses of realisation ₹ 170 were paid by A out of his private funds.

Required: Prepare Realisation Account, Bank Account and the Capital Accounts of the Partners.

SOLUTION

Dr. **REALISATION ACCOUNT** *Cr.*

Particulars	₹	*Particulars*		₹
To Investments	17,000	By Creditors		6,000
To Debtors	24,200	By Loan from Mrs. B		1,500
To Stock	7,800	By Prov. for Doubtful Debts		1,200
To Fixed Assets	1,000	By A's Capital A/c:		
To A's Capital A/c (Creditors)	6,000	Fixed Assets	800	
To C's Capital A/c (Loan + Interest)	1,530	Debtors	17,200	18,000
To A's Capital A/c (Expenses)	270	By B's Capital A/c:		
		Stock	7,000	
		Investments	7,200	14,200
		By C's Capital A/c (Investment)		8,000
		By Bank A/c (Debtors)		2,100
		By Loss on Realisation t/f to:		
		A's Capital A/c	4,080	
		B's Capital A/c	1,360	
		C's Capital A/c	1,360	6,800
	57,800			57,800

Dr. **PARTNERS' CAPITAL ACCOUNTS** Cr.

Particulars	A (₹)	B (₹)	C (₹)	Particulars	A (₹)	B (₹)	C (₹)
To Realisation A/c	18,000	14,200	8,000	By Balance b/d	24,500	9,000	6,000
To Realisation A/c	4,080	1,360	1,360	By Realisation A/c	6,000	—	1,530
To Advertisement Suspense A/c	3,000	1,000	1,000	By Realisation A/c	270	—	—
To Bank A/c	11,690	—	—	By Bank A/c	—	5,560	830
				By JLP Reserve	6,000	2,000	2,000
	36,770	16,560	10,360		36,770	16,560	10,360

Dr. **CASH AT BANK ACCOUNT** Cr.

Particulars	₹	Particulars	₹
To Balance b/d	3,200	By A's Capital A/c	11,690
To Realisation A/c	2,100		
To B's Capital A/c	5,560		
To Cs Capital A/c	830		
	11,690		11,690

Working Notes:

(i) Book value of Investment taken over by 'B' = ₹ 7,200 × 10/9 = ₹ 8,000

(ii) Remaining Investment = ₹ 17,000 – ₹ 8,000 = ₹ 9,000

(iii) Book Value of investment taken over by 'C' = 90% of ₹ 9,000 = ₹ 8,100

(iv) Agreed value of Investment taken over by 'C' = ₹ 8,100 – ₹ 100 = 8,000.

ILLUSTRATION 30

A, B and C who were sharing profits in the ratio of 5 : 3 : 2 decided to dissolve the firm whose Balance Sheet is given below:

Liabilities	₹	Assets	₹
A's Capital	2.00,000	Bank	70,000
B's Capital	1,50,000	Debtors	50,000
C's Capital	1.50,000	Stock	60,000
A's Current A/c	25,000	Furniture	1,25,000
B's Current A/c	17,000	Patents	35,000
P & L A/c	50,000	Building	3,20,000
Trade Creditors	60,000	C's Current A/c	12,000
Workmen Compensation Fund	10,000		
employees' P.F.	5,000		
Loan from Mrs A	5,000		
	6,72,000		6,72,000

Following transactions took place at the time of dissolution:

(a) Realisation expenses were to be fully borne by A for which he is to get a credit of ₹ 10,000.

Actual realisation expenses paid out of firm's Bank Account amounted to ₹ 12,000.

(b) B took over Stock for ₹ 55,000 and C took over Buildings for ₹ 4,00,000.

(c) Other assets realised as follows:
Debtors ₹ 48,000; Furniture ₹ 97,000.

(d) Patents didn't realise anything and Trade Creditors were settled in full by paying them ₹ 55,000.

(e) Accounts of Partners were settled after realising assets and paying outside liabilities.

Required: Prepare Realisation A/c, Partners' Current A/cs and Capital A/cs and Bank A/c.

SOLUTION

Dr. **REALISATION ACCOUNT** *Cr.*

Particulars		₹	*Particulars*		₹
To Debtors		50,000	By Trade Creditors		60,000
To Stock		60,000	By Employees' P.F.		5,000
To Furniture		1,25,000	By Loan from Mrs A		5,000
To Patents		35,000	By B's Current A/c (Stock)		55,000
To Building		3,20,000	By C's Current A/c (Building)		4,00,000
To A's Current A/c (Expenses)		10,000	By Bank A/c:		
To Bank (Creditors)		55,000	Debtors	48,000	
To Bank A/c (P.F.)		5,000	Furniture	97,000	1,45,000
To Bank A/c (Loan)		5,000			
To Profit on Realisation t/t to:					
A's Current A/c	2,500				
B's Current A'c	1,500				
C's Current A/c	1,000	5,000			
		6,70,000			6,70,000

Dr. **PARTNERS' CURRENT ACCOUNTS** *Cr.*

Particulars	*A (₹)*	*B (₹)*	*C (₹)*	*Particulars*	*A (₹)*	*B (₹)*	*C (₹)*
To Balance b/d	—	—	12,000	By Balance b/d	25,000	17,000	—
To Realisation A/c	—	55,000	4,00,000	By P & L A/c	25,000	15,000	10,000
To Bank A/c	12,000	—	—	By Workmen			
To Capital A/c	55,500			Comp. Fund	5,000	3,000	2,000
				By Realisation A/c	2,500	1,500	1,000
				By Realisation A/c	10,000	—	—
				By Capital A/c	—	18,500	3,99,000
	67,500	55,000	4,12,000		67,500	55,000	4,12,000

Dr. **PARTNER'S CAPITAL ACCOUNTS** Cr.

Particulars	A (₹)	B (₹)	C (₹)	Particulars	A (₹)	B (₹)	C (₹)
To Current A/c	—	18,500	3,99,000	By Balance b/d	2,00,000	1,50,000	1,50,000
To Bank (Final Payment)	2,55,500	1,31,500	—	By Current A/c	55,500	—	—
				By Bank A/c	—	—	2,49,000
	2,55,500	1,50,000	3,99,000		2,55,500	1,50,000	3,99,000

Dr. **BANK ACCOUNT** Cr.

Particulars	₹	Particulars	₹
To Balance b/d	70,000	By Realisation A/c (Creditors)	65,000
To Realisation A/c	1,45,000	By A's Current A/c (Drawings)	12,000
To C's Capital A/c	2,49,000	By A's Capital A/c	2,55,500
		By B's Capital A/c	1,31,500
	4,64.000		4,64,000

ILLUSTRATION 31

Anju, Manju and Sanju who were sharing profits in the ratio of 2 : 2 :1 decided to dissolve the firm when their Balance Sheet was as follows:

Liabilities	₹	Assets	₹
Creditors	50,000	Cash	60,000
Bank Loan	35,000	Debtors	75,000
Employees' Provident Fund	15,000	Stock	40,000
Investment Fluctuation Fund	10,000	Investments	20,000
Commission received in Advance	8,000	Plant	50,000
Anju's Capital A/c	50,000	Profit and Loss A/c	3,000
Manju's Capital A/c	50,000		
Sanju's Capital A/c	30,000		
	2,48,000		2,48,000

Anju was appointed to realise the assets. Anju was to receive 5% commission on the sale of assets (except cash) and was to bear all expense of realisation. Anju realised the assets as follows:

Debtors 20% less, Stock ₹ 35,500, Investments 80%, Plant 90% of the book value.

Expense of realisation amounted to ₹ 7,500 paid by the firm on Anju's behalf. Commission received in advance was returned to the customers after deducting ₹ 3,000.

Firm had to pay ₹ 8,500 fo outstanding salary not provided for earlier. Compensation pair to employees amounted to ₹ 17,000. This liability was not provided for in the above Balance Sheet ₹ 20,000 has to be paid for provident fund.

Required: Prepare Realisation ccount, Capital Accounts of Partners and Cash Account.

SOLUTION

Dr. **REALISATION ACCOUNT** Cr.

Particulars	₹	Particulars	₹
To Debtors	75,000	By Creditors	50,000
To Stock	40,000	By Bank Loan	35,000

To Investments		20,000	By Provident Fund		15,000
To Plant		50,000	By Investment		
To Cash A/c:			Fluctuation Fund		10,000
Creditors	50,000		By Commission		
Bank Loan	35,000		Received in Advance		8,000
Provident Fund	20,000		By Cash A/c:		
Commission			Debtors	60,000	
Received in Advance	5,000		Stock	35,500	
O/s Salaries	8,500		Investments	16,000	
Compensation	17,000	1,35,500	Plant	45,000	1,56,500
To Anju's Capital A/c (Commission)		7,825	By Realisation Loss t/f to:		
			Anju's Capital A/c		21,530
			Manju'Capital A/c		21,530
			Sanju's Capital A/c		10,765
		3,28,325			3,28,325

Dr. **CASH ACCOUNT** *Cr.*

Particulars	₹	*Particulars*	₹
To Balance b/d	60,000	By Realisation A/c	1,35,500
To Realisation A/c	1,56,500	By Anju's Capital A/c	7,500
		By Anju's Capital A/c	27,595
		By Manju's Capital A/c	27,270
		By Sanju's Capital A/c	18,635
	2,16,500		2,16,500

Dr. **PARTNERS' CAPITAL ACCOUNTS** *Cr.*

Particulars	*Anju* ₹	*Manju* ₹	*Sanju* ₹	*Particulars*	*Anju* ₹	*Manju* ₹	*Sanju* ₹
To P & L A/c	1,200	1,200	600	By Balance b/d	50,000	50,000	30,000
To Realisation A/c	21,530	21,530	10,765	By Realisation A/c	7,825	—	—
To Cash A/c	7,500	—					
To Cash A/c	27,595	27,270	18,635				
	57,825	50,000	30,000		57,825	50,000	30,000

ILLUSTRATION 32

Following was the Balance Sheet of D, G and T:

Liabilities	₹	*Assets*	₹
Creditors	50,000	Bank	20,000
Bills Payable	10,000	Debtors	30,000
G's Loan	8,000	Stock	20,000

R's Loan	12,000	Furniture	15,000
General Reserve	20,000	Land and Building	2,45,000
D's Capital	1,00,000	G's Capital	20,000
T's Capital	1,50,000		
	3,50,000		3,50,000

The firm was dissolved on the above date on the following terms:

(i) Debtors realized ₹ 28,000; and Creditors and Bills Payable were paid at a discount of 10%.

(ii) Stock was taken over by T for ₹ 15,000 and furniture was sold to N for ₹ 12,000.

(iii) Land and Building was sold for ₹ 2,80,000.

(iv) R's loan was paid by a cheque for the same amount.

(v) The firm had a joint life policy of ₹ 5,00,000 with a surrender value of ₹ 1,00,000. The policy was surrendered at its surrender value.

Prepare Realisation Account, Bank Account and Capital Accounts of D, G and T.

SOLUTION

Dr. **REALISATION ACCOUNT** *Cr.*

Particulars		₹	*Particulars*		₹
To Debtors		30,000	By Creditors		50,000
To Stock		20,000	By Bills Payable		10,000
To Furniture		15,000	By R's Loan		12,000
To Land & Building		2,45,000	By Bank A/c (Realisations)		
To Bank A/c (Payments):			Debtors	28,000	
Creditors	45,000		Land & Building	2,80,000	
B/P	9,000		Furnitures	12,000	
R's Loan	12,000	66,000	JLP	1,00,000	4,20,000
To Profit on Realisation t/f to:			By T's Capital A/c (Stock)		15,000
D's Capital A/c		43,667			
G's Capital A/c		43,667			
T's Capital A/c		43,666			
		5,07,000			5,07,000

Dr. **BANK ACCOUNT** *Cr.*

Particulars	₹	*Particulars*	₹
To Balance b/d	20,000	By Realisation A/c	66,000
To Realisation A/c	4,20,000	By G's Loan A/c	8,000
		By D's Capital A/c	1,50,334
		By G's Capital A/c	30,333
		By T's Capital A/c	1,85,333
	4,40,000		4,40,000

Dr. **CAPITAL ACCOUNTS OF PARTNERS** Cr.

Particulars	D (₹)	G (₹)	T (₹)	Particulars	D (₹)	G (₹)	T (₹)
To Balance c/d	—	20,000	—	By Balance b/d	1,00,000	—	1,50,000
To Realisation A/c	—	—	15,000	By Realisation A/c	43,637	43,667	43,666
To Bank A/c	1,50,334	30,333	1,85,333	By General Reserve	6,667	6,666	6,667
	1,50,334	50,333	2,00,333		1,50,334	50,333	2,00,333

ILLUSTRATION 33

Following is the Balance Sheet of A and B who share profits and losses in the ratio of 3 : 2:

Liabilities	₹	Assets		₹
Sundry Creditors	75,000	Cash at Bank		4,500
Bills Payable	30,000	Stock		25,000
Mrs. A's Loan	25,000	Debtors	40,500	
Workmen's Compensation Fund	8,000	Less: Provision	1,000	39,500
Employers' Provident Fund	50,000	Bills Receivable		15,000
General Reserve	27,000	Investments		60,000
A's Capital	30,000	Plant and Machinery		80,000
B's Capital	40,000	Building		61,000
	2,85,000			2,85,000

The firm was dissolved on the same date and the following transactions took place:

(i) A promised to pay Mrs. A's Loan and took half of the Investments @ 10% discount.

(ii) Stock and remaining Investments were sold @ 10% discount.

(iii) Goodwill was taken by B for ₹ 40,000. He also agreed to pay Bills Payable at a discount of 10%.

(iv) Assets realised Debtors ₹ 5,500 less; Bills Receivable at 10% discount; Plant and Machinery at 50% and Building ₹ 1,18,900.

(v) There was a car in the firm, which was completely written off from the books. It was taken over by A for ₹ 24,400. He also agreed to pay Outstanding Salary of ₹ 1,000 not provided in books.

(vi) Creditors were paid 90% in full and final settlement of their dues.

(vii) The expenses of dissolution amounted to ₹ 1,700.

Required: Prepare the realisation Account, Capital Accounts of Partners and Bank Account in the Books of the firm.

SOLUTION

Dr. **REALISATION ACCOUNT** Cr.

Particulars		₹	Particulars	₹
To Sundry Assets:			By Provisions for Doubtful Debts	1,000
Stock	25,000		By Sundry Creditors	75,000
Debtors	40,500		By Bills Payable	30,000
Bills Receivable	15,000		By Mrs. A's Loan	25,000

Investments	60,000		By Employees' Provident Fund		50,000
Plant and Machinery	80,000		By A's Capital A/c (Investments)		27,000
Building	61,000	2,81,500	(₹ 30,000 – ₹ 3,000)		
To A's Capital A/c (Mrs. A's Loan)		25,000	By Bank A/c (Assets Realised)		
To B's Capital A/c (Bills Payable)		27,000	–Stock (25,000 – 2,500)	22,500	
To Bank A/c (Creditors)			–Investments	27,000	
[75,000 – 7,500]		67,500	(30,000 – 3,000)		
To Bank A/c (EPF)		50,000	–Debtors (40,500 – 5,500)	35,000	
To Bank A/c (Expenses)		1,700	–Bills Receivable	13,500	
To A's Capital A/c (o/s Salary)		1,000	(15,000 – 1,500)		
To Profit on Realisation t/f to:			–P&M (80,000 – 40,000)	40,000	
A's Capital A/c	45,360		–Building	1,18,900	2,56,900
B's Capital A/c	30,240	75,600	By B's Capital A/c (Goodwill)		40,000
			By A's Capital A/c (Car)		24,400
		5,29,300			5,29,300

Dr. **PARTNERS' CAPITAL ACCOUNTS** *Cr.*

Particulars	*A (₹)*	*B (₹)*	*Particulars*	*A (₹)*	*B (₹)*
To Realisation A/c	27,000	40,000	By Balance b/d	30,000	40,000
To Realisation A/c	24,400	—	By Realisation A/c (Profit)	45,360	30,240
To Bank A/c	70,960	71,240	By Realisation A/c	25,000	27,000
(Final Payment)			(Liabilities)		
			By General Reserve	16,200	10,800
			By Workmen's		
			Compensation Fund A/c	4,800	3,200
			By Realisation A/c		
			(O/s Salary)	1,000	—
	1,22,360	1,11,240		1,22,360	1,11,240

Dr. **BANK ACCOUNT** *Cr.*

Particulars	₹	*Particulars*	₹
To Balance b/d	4,500	By Realisation A/c (Creditors)	67,500
To Realisation A/c	2,56,900	By Realisation A/c (EPF)	50,000
(Assets Realised)		By Realisation A/c (Expenses)	1,700
		By A's Capital A/c (Final Payment)	70,960
		By B's Capital A/c (Final Payment)	71,240
	2,61,400		2,61,400

ILLUSTRATION 34

X, Y and Z who were sharing profits in the ratio of 2 : 2 : 1 decided to dissolve the firm when the Balance Sheet was as follows:

Liabilities	₹	*Assets*		₹
X's Capital	1,27,500	Other Sundry Assets		1,17,000
Y's Capital	1,10,000	Furniture		11,000
Z's Capital	17,000	Debtors	1,24,200	
Loan	11,500	*Less*: Provision	1,200	1,23,000
Creditors	16,000	Stock		17,800
		Cash		13,200
	2,82,000			2,82,000

It was agreed that:

(i) X to take over furniture at ₹ 8,000 and debtors amounted to ₹ 1,20,000 at ₹ 1,17,200 and the creditors of ₹ 16,000 were to be paid by him at this figure.

(ii) Y is to take over all Stocks for ₹ 17,000 and some sundry assets at ₹ 72,000 (being 10% less than the book value).

(iii) Z to take over remaining sundry assets at 80% of the book value and assume the responsibility of discharge of loan together with accrued interest of ₹ 2,300.

(iv) The expenses of realisation were ₹ 2,700. The remaining debtors were sold to a debt collecting agency at 50% of the value.

Required: Prepare the necessary accounts to close the books of the firm.

SOLUTION

Dr. **REALISATION ACCOUNT** *Cr.*

Particulars	₹	*Particulars*		₹
To Other Sundry Assets	1,17,000	By Provision for Doubtful Debts		1,200
To Furniture	11,000	By Loan		11,500
To Debtors	1,24,200	By Creditors		16,000
To Stock	17,800	By X's Capital A/c:		
To X's Capital A/c (Creditors)	16,000	Furniture	8,000	
To Z's Capital A/c (Loan with Interest)	13,800	Debtors	1,17,200	1,25,200
		By Y's Capital A/c:		
To Cash A/c(Expenses)	2,700	Stock	17,000	
		Sundry Assets	72,000	89,000
		By Z's Capital A/c:		
		Sundry Assets [(1,17,000 – 80,000)80/100]		29,600
		By Cash A/c – (Debtors) [(1,24,200 – 1,20,000)50/100]		2,100
		By Loss transferred to:		
		X's Capital A/c	11,160	
		Y's Capital A/c	11,160	
		Z's Capital A/c	5,580	27,900
	3,02,500			3,02,500

Dr. **PARTNERS' CAPITAL ACCOUNTS** Cr.

Particulars	X (₹)	Y (₹)	Z (₹)	Particulars	X (₹)	Y (₹)	Z (₹)
To Realisation A/c	1,25,200	89,000	29,600	By Balance b/d	1,27,500	1,10,000	17,000
To Realisation A/c (Loss)	11,160	11,160	5,580	By Realisation A/c	16,000	—	13,800
To Cash A/c (b.f)	7,140	9,840	—	By Cash A/c (b.f)	—	—	4,380
	1,43,500	1,10,000	35,180		1,43,500	1,10,000	35,180

Dr. **CASH ACCOUNT** Cr.

Particulars	₹	Particulars	₹
To Balance b/d	13,200	By Realisation A/c (Expenses)	2,700
To Realisation A/c–(Debtors)	2,100	By X's Capital A/c	7,140
To Z's Capital A/c	4,380	By Y's Capital A/c	9,840
	19,680		19,680

ILLUSTRATION 35

Following is the Balance Sheet of A,B,C and D who were sharing in the ratio of 3: 3: 2: 2 as at 31st March, 2016, when they decided to dissolve the firm:

Liabilities	₹	Assets		₹
Loan from Bank (Secured on Other Tangible Fixed Assets)	50,000	Cash at Bank		27,500
		Trade Debtors	40,000	
Mrs. B's Loan (Secured on Stock)	3,000	*Less:* Provision	(8,500)	31,500
Trade Creditors	30,000	Stock		5,000
A's Loan	30,000	Prepaid Insurance		3,000
A's Capital	60,000	Goodwill		5,000
B's Capital	49,000	Machinery		60,000
General Reserve	20,000	Other Tangible Fixed Assets		50,000
Machinery Replacement Reserve	20,000	B's Drawings		4,000
		C 's Capital		48,000
		D's Capital		18,000
		Profit & Loss A/c		10,000
	2,62,000			2,62,000

(a) After preparing the Balance Sheet as at 31st March, it was discovered that purchases amounting to ₹ 10,000 in March, were not recorded in books, though the goods were received during March.

(b) Trade Debtors realized 12.5%. Stock realized 20%, Machinery realised at a loss of 50%. Some Other Tangible Fixed Assets realized ₹ 15,000(being 40% less than the book value) and the remaining Other Tangible Fixed Assets realized 8% more than the book value, Expenses of realisation amounted to ₹ 7,500.

Required: Prepare Realisation A/c, Partners' Capital A/cs and Bank A/c.

SOLUTION

Dr. **REALISATION ACCOUNT** Cr.

Particulars	₹	Particulars	₹
To Assets Transferred:		By Provision for Doubtful Debts	8,500
Stock	5,000	By Machinery Replacement Reserve	20,000
Debtors	40,000	By Loan from Bank	50,000
Prepaid Insurance	3,000	By Mrs. B's Loan	3,000
Goodwill	5,000	By Trade Creditors (30,000 + 10,000)	40,000
Machinery	60,000	By Bank A/c:	
Other Tangible Fixed Assets	50,000	Machinery	
To Bank A/c (Expenses)	7,500	[40,000 – (100/200 × 40,000)]	20,000
To Bank A/c (Loan from Bank)	50,000	Debtors (₹ 40,000 × 12.5%)	5,000
To Bank A/c (Mrs. B's Loan)	3,000	Stock (₹ 5,000 × 20%)	1,000
To Bank A/c (Trade Creditors)	40,000	Other Tangible Fixed Assets	
		[₹ 15,000 +(₹ 25,000) × 108%]	42,000
		By Loss on Realisation t/f to:	
		A's Capital A/c	22,200
		B's Capital A/c	22,200
		C 's Capital A/c	14,800
		D 's Capital A/c	14,800
	2,63,500		2,63,500

Dr. **PARTNERS' CAPITAL ACCOUNTS** Cr.

Particulars	A	B	C	D	Particulars	A	B	C	D
To Balance b/d	—	—	48,000	18,000	By Balance b/d	60,000	49,000	—	—
To Drawings	—	4,000	—	—	By General Reserve	6,000	6,000	4,000	4,000
To P&L A/c (Goods)	3,000	3,000	2,000	2,000	By Bank A/c	—	—	62,800	32,800
To P&L A/c (Loss)	3,000	3,000	2,000	2,000					
To Realisation A/c	22,200	22,200	14,800	14,800					
To Bank A/c	37,800	22,800	—	—					
	66,000	55,000	66,800	36,800		66,000	55,000	66,800	36,800

Dr. **BANK ACCOUNT** Cr.

Particulars	₹	Particulars	₹
To Balance b/d	27,500	By Realisation A/c (Expenses)	7,500
To Realisation A/c (Assets)	68,000	By Realisation A/c (Loan from Bank)	50,000
To C's Capital A/c	62,800	By Realisation A/c (Mrs B's Loan)	3,000
To D's Capital A/c	32,800	By Realisation A/c (Trade Creditors)	40,000
		By A's Loan A/c	30,000
		By A's Capital A/c	37,800

		By B's Capital A/c	22,800
	1,91,100		1,91,100

Working Notes:

1. Total Trade Creditors = ₹30,000 + ₹10,000 (Ommited Purchases) = ₹40,000
2. Book Value of Machinery = Machinery – Machinery Replacement Reserve
   =₹ 60,000 – ₹ 20,000 = ₹ 40,000

CALCULATION OF REMUNERATION PAYABLE TO INCHARGE OF REALISATION

ILLUSTRATION 36

Given below is the Balance Sheet of A, B and C as on 31st March, 2016 on which date they dissolved their partnership. They shared profits and losses in the ratio of 4 : 3 : 3. It was decided that C shall be incharge of realisation and distribution. For this purpose, he was to get as his remuneration, 1% of the value of assets realised other than Cash at Bank and 10% of the amount distributed to the partners.

BALANCE SHEET AS AT 31ST MARCH, 2016

Liabilities	₹	*Assets*	₹
A's Capital	11,000	Cash at Bank	275
B's Capital	4,500	Sundry Assets	53,725
C's Capital	12,000		
Sundry Creditors	15,000		
Employees' Provident Fund	1,500		
Joint Life Policy Reserve	10,000		
	54,000		54,000

Sundry Assets were realised for ₹ 46,500 and Creditors were paid in full.

Required: Prepare a Realisation Account, Cash at Bank Account and Partners' Capital Accounts.

SOLUTION

Dr. **REALISATION ACCOUNT** *Cr.*

Particulars	₹	*Particulars*		₹
To Sundry Assets	53,725	By Sundry Creditors		15,000
To Bank A/c (Sundry Creditors)	15,000	By Employees' P.F.		1,500
To Bank A/c (P.F.)	1,500	By Bank A/c (Sundry Assets)		46,500
To C's Capital A/c (₹ 465 + ₹ 2,710)	3,175	By Loss on Realisation t/f to:		
		A's Capital A/c	4,160	
		B's Capital A/c	3,120	
		C's Capital A/c	3,120	10,400
	73,400			73,400

Dr. **CASH AT BANK ACCOUNT** Cr.

Particulars	₹	Particulars	₹
To Balance b/d	275	By Realisation A/c (S. Creditors)	16,500
To Realisation A/c (S. Assets)	46,500	By A's Capital A/c	10,840
		By B's Capital A/c	4,380
		By C's Capital A/c	15,055
	46,775		46,775

Dr. **PARTNERS' CAPITAL ACCOUNTS** Cr.

Particulars	A (₹)	B (₹)	C (₹)	Particulars	A (₹)	B (₹)	C (₹)
To Realisation A/c	4,160	3,120	3,120	By Balance b/d	11,000	4,500	12,000
To Bank A/c	10,840	4,380	15,055	By JLP Reserve	4,000	3,000	3,000
				By Realisation A/c	—	—	3,175
	15,000	7,500	18,175		15,000	7,500	18,175

Working Notes:

(i) *Calculation of Total Cash available towards payment of commission on amount distributed and Payment to partners*

Particulars	₹	₹
(a) Total cash available		
(a) Balance in hand	275	
(b) Sale proceeds of assets	46,500	46,775
(b) Total payment except payment of commission on amount distributed and payment to partners		
(a) Payment to Sundry Creditors	16,500	
(b) Commission on value of assets realised (1% of ₹ 46,500)	465	16,965
		29,810
(c) Commission on account distributed to the partners (₹ 29,810 × 10/110)		2,710

11.0 PREPARATION OF BALANCE SHEET AS AT DATE OF DISSOLUTION

In examination problems, sometimes the information on book values of assets/ liabilities is missing, in such a case first of all, a Balance Sheet as at the date of dissolution of the firm should be prepared in order to ascertain the missing information. Whenever the dissolution of a firm takes place on a date other than the date on which the accounting year of the firm ends, the balance sheet as at the date of dissolution is required to be prepared. The balance sheet as at the date of dissolution should be carefully drafted after taking into account the balances given in the given balance sheet and the transactions which took place between the date of given balance sheet and the date of dissolution.

ILLUSTRATION 37

X's Capital ₹ 30,000, Advance to Y ₹ 20,000, Loan from X ₹ 20,000, Profits and Loss A/c (debit) ₹ 80,000, X's Current A/c (credit) ₹ 30,000, Y's Capital ₹ 40,000, Loan from Mrs X ₹ 1,20,000, Trade Creditors ₹ 1,20,000, Cash and Bank Balance ₹ 10,000. Prepare the Balance Sheet of the firm as at 31st March 2016 being the date of dissolution of a loss incurring firm.

SOLUTION

BALANCE SHEET AS AT 31ST MARCH, 2016

Liabilities	₹	*Assets*	₹
Trade Creditors	1,20,000	Cash & Bank Balance	10,000
Loan from Mrs X	1,20,000	Advance to Y	20,000
Loan from X	20,000	Profit & Loss A/c (Debit)	80,000
X's Capital	30,000	Sundry Other Assets (b.f.)	2,50,000
Y's Capital	40,000		
X's Current A/c	30,000		
	3,60,000		3,60,000

ILLUSTRATION 38

X's Capital ₹ 20,000, Y's Capital ₹ 10,000, Amount owed by Y to the firm ₹ 6,400, Loan by X ₹ 8,000, Creditors ₹ 5,000, Cash and Bank Balance ₹ 5,400, Fixed and other Current Assets ₹ 30,000. Prepare the Balance Sheet of the firm as at 31st March 2016 being the date of dissolution of a loss incurring firm in.

SOLUTION

BALANCE SHEET AS AT 31ST MARCH, 2016

Liabilities	₹	*Assets*	₹
X's Capital	20,000	Advance to Y	6,400
Y's Capital	10,000	Cash & Bank Balance	5,400
Loan from X	8,000	Fixed & other current assets	30,000
Creditors	5,000	Profit & Loss A/c (Dr.) (b.f.)	1,200
	43,000		43,000

ILLUSTRATION 39

X's Capital (debit) ₹ 30,000, Loan from Y ₹ 20,000, Advance to X ₹ 20,000, Profit and Loss A/c (debit) ₹ 80,000, Y's Current A/c (Credit) ₹ 30,000, Y's Capital ₹ 40,000, Loan from Mrs Y ₹ 1,20,000, Trade Creditors ₹ 1,20,000, Fixed and Current Assets other than Cash and Bank Balance ₹ 1,70,000. Prepare the Balance Sheet of the firm as at 31st March 2016 being the date of dissolution of a loss incurring firm in.

SOLUTION

BALANCE SHEET AS AT 31ST MARCH 2016

Liabilities	₹	*Assets*	₹
Y's Capital	40,000	Advance to X	20,000
Y's Current A/c	30,000	Fixed & Other current Assets	1,70,000
Loan from Mrs. Y	1,20,000	Profit & Loss A/c (Debit)	80,000
Trade Creditors	1,20,000	X's Capital	30,000
Loan from Y	20,000	Cash & Bank Balance (b.f.)	30,000
	3,30,000		3,30,000

ILLUSTRATION 40

On 1st April, 2014, X, Y & Z commenced business in partnership sharing the profits and losses in the ratio of 4 : 3 : 3 respectively with capitals of ₹ 25,000, ₹ 20,000, ₹ 15,000 respectively. During 2014-2015 and 2015-2016, they made profits of ₹ 20,000 and ₹ 25,000 (before allowing interest on capital @ 10%) respectively. Drawings of each partner were ₹ 5,000 per year. The creditors amounted to ₹ 12,000 as on 31st March 2016. Prepare the Balance Sheet as at 31st March 2016.

SOLUTION

BALANCE SHEET AS AT 31ST MARCH, 2016

Liabilities	₹	*Assets*	₹
X's Capital	33,310	Sundry Assets (b.f.)	87,000
Y's Capital	23,870		
Z's Capital	17,820		
Creditors	12,000		
	87,000		87,000

Working Notes:

STATEMENT SHOWING CAPITALS AS ON 31ST MARCH, 2016

	Particulars	X ₹	Y ₹	Z ₹	*Total* ₹
A.	Balance as on 01.04.2014	25,000	20,000	15,000	60,000
B.	*Add:* Interest on Capital @ 10%	2,500	2,000	1,500	6,000
C.	*Add:* Share of Profit [(₹ 20,000 – ₹ 6,000) in the ratio of 4 : 3 : 3]	5,600	4,200	4,200	14,000
D.	*Less:* Drawings	5,000	5,000	5,000	15,000
E.	Balance as on 01.04.2015 [A + B + C – D]	28,100	21,200	15,700	65,000
F.	*Add:* Interest on Capital @ 10%	2,810	2,120	1,570	6,500
G.	*Add:* Share of Profit [(₹ 25,000 – ₹ 6,500) in the ratio of 4:3:3]	7,400	5,550	5,550	18,500
H.	*Less:* Drawings	5,000	5,000	5,000	15,000
I.	Balance as on 31.03.2016	33,310	23,870	17,820	75,000

ILLUSTRATION 41

A and B were partners from 1.4.2014 with capitals of ₹ 60,000 and ₹ 40,000 respectively. They shared profits in the ratio of 3 : 2. They carried on business for two years. In the first year ending on 31.03.2015, they made a profit of ₹ 50,000 but in the second year ending on 31.03.2016. a loss of ₹ 20,000 was incurred. As the business was no longer profitable, they dissolved the firm on 31.03.2016. Creditors on that date were ₹ 20,000. Each partner withdrew for personal use, ₹ 8,000 per year. The expenses of realisation were ₹ 3,000. The assets realised ₹ 1,00,000. Prepare a Realisation Account, Capital Accounts and Cash Accounts.

SOLUTION

Dr. **REALISATION ACCOUNT** Cr.

Particulars	₹	Particulars	₹
To Sundry Assets	1,18,000	By Creditors	20,000
To Cash A/c (Creditors)	20,000	By Cash A/c	1,00,000
To Cash A/c (Expenses)	3,000	By Loss on Realisation t/f to:	
		A's Capital A/c	12,600
		B's Capital A/c	8,400
	1,41,000		1,41,000

Dr. **CASH ACCOUNT** Cr.

Particulars	₹	Particulars	₹
To Realisation A/c (S. Assets)	1,00,000	By Realisation A/c (Creditors)	20,000
		By Realisation (Expenses)	3,000
		By A's Capital A/c	49,400
		By B's Capital A/c	27,600
	1,00,000		1,00,000

Dr. **PARTNER'S CAPITAL ACCOUNTS** Cr.

Particulars	X (₹)	Y (₹)	Particulars	X (₹)	Y (₹)
To Realsation A/c	12,600	8,400	By Balance b/d	62,000	36,000
To Cash A/c	49,400	27,600			
	62,000	36,000		62,000	36,000

Working Notes:

1. Calculation of Capitals as on date of dissolution

Dr. **PARTNER'S CAPITAL ACCOUNTS** Cr.

Date	Particulars	A (₹)	B (₹)	Date	Particulars	A (₹)	B (₹)
2014-2015	To Cash A/c	8,000	8,000	01.04.2014	By Cash A/c	60,000	40,000
31.03.2015	To Balance c/d	82,000	52,000		By P & L A/c	30,000	20,000
		90,000	60,000			90,000	60,000
2015-2016	To Cash A/c	8,000	8,000	01.04.2015	By Balance b/d	82,000	52,000
31.03.2016	To P & L A/c	12,000	8,000				
	To Balance c/d	62,000	36,000				
		82,000	52,000			82,000	52,000

2. Calculation of Sundry Assets as on date of dissolution

BALANCE SHEET AS AT 31st MARCH, 2016

Liabilities	₹	*Assets*	₹
A's Capital	62,000	Sundry Assets *(Balancing figure)*	1,18,000
B's Current A/c	36,000		
Creditors	20,000		
	1,18,000		1,18,000

ILLUSTRATION 42

P, Q and R commenced business on 1st April, 2016 with capitals of: P – ₹ 2,00,000; Q–₹ 2,00,000 and R–₹ 1,00,000.

Profits are shared in the ratio of 4 : 3 : 3. Capital carried interest @ 5% p.a. During the year 2016-2014, the firm suffered a loss of ₹ 1,50,000 before allowing interest on capital. Drawings of each partner during the year were ₹ 20,000.

On 31st March, 2014, the partners agreed to dissolve the firm as it was no longer profitable. The creditors on that date were ₹ 40,000. The assets realised a net value of ₹ 3,20,000 and the expenses of realisation were ₹ 7,000.

Required: Prepare the Realisation Account, Partners' Capital Accounts and Cash Account along with necessary working to close the books of the firm.

SOLUTION

Dr. **REALISATION ACCOUNT** *Cr.*

Particulars	₹	*Particulars*		₹
To Sundry Assets A/c	3,30,000	By Creditors		40,000
To Cash A/c (Expenses)	7,000	By Cash A/c (Assets Realised)		3,20,000
To Cash A/c (Creditors)	40,000	By Loss on Realisation t/f to:		
		P's Capital A/c (4/10)	6,800	
		Q's Capital A/c (3/10)	5,100	
		R's Capital A/c (3/10)	5,100	17,000
	3,77,000			3,77,000

Dr. **PARTNER'S CAPITAL ACCOUNTS (AFTER DISSOLUTION)** *Cr.*

Particulars	A (₹)	B (₹)	C (₹)	*Particulars*	A (₹)	B (₹)	C (₹)
To P&L A/c	6,800	5,100	5,100	By Balance b/d	1,20,000	1,35,000	35,000
To Cash A/c (b.f.)	1,13,200	1,29,900	29,900				
	1,20,000	1,35,000	35,000		1,20,000	1,35,000	35,000

Dr. **CASH ACCOUNT** *Cr.*

Particulars	₹	*Particulars*	₹
To Realisation A/c	3,20,000	By Realisation A/c (Expenses)	7,000
(Assets Realised)		By Realisation A/c (Creditors)	40,000

		By P's Capital A/c (Final Payment)	1,13,200
		By Q's Capital A/c (Final Payment)	1,29,900
		By R's Capital A/c (Final Payment)	29,900
	3,20,000		3,20,000

Working Notes:

1. Calculation of Partners' Capitals as on date of dissolution.

Dr. **PARTNERS' CAPITAL ACCOUNTS (BEFORE DISSOLUTION)** **Cr.**

Particulars	*P (₹)*	*Q (₹)*	*R (₹)*	*Particulars*	*P (₹)*	*Q (₹)*	*R (₹)*
To P & L A/c	60,000	45,000	45,000	By Balance b/d	2,00,000	2,00,000	1,00,000
To Drawings A/c	20,000	20,000	20,000				
To Balance c/d	1,20,000	1,35,000	35,000				
	2,00,000	2,00,000	1,00,000		2,00,000	2,00,000	1,00,000

2. No interest on capital is allowed In case of loss.

3. Calculation of Sundry Assets as on date of dissolution.

MEMORANDUM BALANCE SHEET

Liabilities	₹	*Assets*	₹
Creditors	40,000	Sundry Assets (Bal. Fig.)	3,30,000
P's Capital A/c	1,20,000		
Q's Capital A/c	1,35,000		
R's Capital A/c	35,000		
	3,30,000		3,30,000

ILLUSTRATION 43

X, Y, and Z commenced business on 1st April 2014, with capitals of ₹ 1,00,000, ₹ 80,000 and ₹ 60,000 respectively. Profits and Losses were shared in the ratio of 4 : 3 : 3. Capitals carried interest at 5% p.a. During 2014-2015 and 2015-2016, they made profits of ₹ 40,000 and ₹ 50,000 (before allowing interest on capitals). Drawings of each partner were ₹ 10,000 per year. On 31st March, 2016, the firm was dissolved. Creditors on that date were ₹ 24,000. The assets realised were ₹ 2,60,000 net. Give the necessary accounts to close the books of the firm.

SOLUTION

Dr. **REALISATION ACCOUNT** *Cr.*

Particulars	₹	*Particulars*	₹
To Sundry Assets	2,94,000	By Sundry Creditors	24,000
To Bank A/c (Creditors)	24,000	By Bank A/c (Assets)	2,60,000
		By Loss on Realisation t/f to:	
		X's Capital A/c	13,600
		Y's Capital A/c	10,200
		Z's Capital A/c	10,200
	3,18,000		3,18,000

Dr. **CAPITAL ACCOUNTS OF PARTNERS** Cr.

Particulars	X (₹)	Y (₹)	Z (₹)	Particulars	X (₹)	Y (₹)	Z (₹)
To Realisation A/c (Loss)	13,600	10,200	10,200	By Balance b/d	1,16,510	87,770	65,720
To Bank A/c	1,02,910	77,570	55,520				
	1,16,510	87,770	65,720		1,16,510	87,770	65,720

Dr. **BANK ACCOUNT** Cr.

Particulars	₹	Particulars	₹
To Realisation A/c (Assets)	2,60,000	By Realisation A/c (Creditors)	24,000
		By X's Capital A/c	1,02,910
		By Y's Capital A/c	77,570
		By Z's Capital A/c	55,520
	2,60,000		2,60,000

Working Notes:

(I) STATEMENT SHOWING CAPITALS AS ON 31.3.2016

Particulars	X (₹)	Y (₹)	Z (₹)
A. Balance as on 1.4.2014	1,00,000	80,000	60,000
B. *Add:* Interest on Capital @ 5%	5,000	4,000	3,000
C. *Add:* Share of Profit [(₹ 40,000 – ₹ 12,000) in the ratio of 4 : 3 : 3]	11,200	8,400	8,400
D. *Less:* Drawings	10,000	10,000	10,000
E. Balance as on 1.4.2015 [A + B + C – D]	1,06,200	82,400	61,400
F. *Add:* Interest on capital @ 5%	5,310	4,120	3,070
G. *Add:* Share of Profit [(₹ 50,000 – ₹ 12,500) in the ratio of 4 : 3 : 3]	15,000	11,250	11,250
H. *Less:* Drawings	10,000	10,000	10,000
I. Balance as on 31.3.2016 [E + F + G – H]	1,16,510	87,770	65,720

(II) CALCULATION OF SUNDRY ASSETS AS ON 31.3.2016
BALANCE SHEET AS AT 31st MARCH, 2016

Liabilities	₹	Assets	₹
Sundry Creditors	24,000	Sundry Assets (b.f.) (assumed there is no Cash *or* Bank Balance)	2,94,000
X's Capital	1,16,510		
Y's Capital	87,770		
Z's Capital	65,720		
	2,94,000		2,94,000

SOLVED PROBLEMS

PROBLEM 1

X, Y and Z sharing profits in the ratio of 2 : 2 : 1 agreed upon dissolution of their partnership on 31st March, 2016 on which date their Balance Sheet was as under:

Liabilities		₹	*Assets*		₹
Capital: X		40,000	Fixed Assets		50,000
Y		30,000	Joint Life Policy (at surrender value)		10,000
Reserve Fund		10,000	Debtors	10,000	
Joint Life Policy Fund		10,000	*Less:* Provision	500	9,500
Creditors	19,000		Stock at invoice price	10,000	
Less: Reserve for Discount	500	18,500	*Less:* Price unloading	2,000	8,000
Salary outstanding		2,000	Investments	8,000	
			Less: Fluctuation Fund	500	7,500
			Capital account—Z		2,000
			Bank		23,500
		1,10,500			1,10,500

Investments were taken over by X at 75%; creditors of ₹ 10,000 were taken over by Y who has ageed to settle amount with them at ₹ 9,900. Remaining creditors were paid at at a discount of 16%. Joint life policy was surrendered and fixed assets realised 140%. Stock and debtors realised ₹ 7,000 and 90% respectively. One customer, whose account was written off as bad, now paid ₹ 800 which is not included in ₹ 9,000 above. There was one unrecorded asset estimated at ₹ 3,000, half of which was handed over to an unrecorded liability of ₹ 5,000 in settlement of claim of ₹ 2,500 and remaining half was sold in the market which realised ₹ 200 less.

Y took over the responsibility of completing the dissolution and he is granted a salary of ₹ 400 per month. Actual realisation expenses amounted to ₹ 1,100. Dissolution was completed and final payments were made on 31st July, 2016.

Required: Prepare the Realisation Account, Capital Accounts and the Bank Account.

SOLUTION

Dr. **REALISATION ACCOUNT** *Cr.*

Particulars	₹	*Particulars*		₹
To Fixed assets	50,000	By Creditors		19,000
To Joint Life Policy	10,000	By Salary Outstanding		2,000
To Debtors	10,000	By Joint life Policy Reserve		10,000
To Stock at invoice price	10,000	By Provision for Doubtful Debts		500
To Investment	8,000	By Provision for Stock		2,000
To Provision for discount on creditors	500	By Investment Fluctuation Fund		500
To Y (creditors)	9,900	By X (investment)		6,000
To Bank A/c (creditors)	7,500	By Bank A/c—		
To Bank A/c —		Joint Life policy	10,000	

unrecorded creditors	5,000		Fixed assets	70,000	
Less: Unrecorded asset	2,500	2,500	Stock	7,000	
To Y (realisation expenses)		1,600	Debtors	9,000	
To Bank A/c (salary outstanding)		2,000	Bad debt recovered	800	
To Profit on Realisation t/f to:			Unrecorded asset	1,300	98,100
X's Capital A/c	10,440				
Y's Capital A/c	10,440				
Z's Capital A/c	5,220	26,100			
		1,38,100			1,38,100

Dr. **CAPITAL ACCOUNTS OF PARTNERS** *Cr.*

Particulars	*X* ₹	*Y* ₹	*Z* ₹	*Particulars*	*X* ₹	*Y* ₹	*Z* ₹
To Balance b/d	—	—	2,000	By Balance b/d	40,000	30,000	—
To Realisation A/c	6,000	—		By Reserve Fund	4,000	4,000	2,000
To Bank A/c	—	1,100	—	By Realisation A/c	10,440	10,440	5,220
To Bank A/c	48,440	54,840	5,220	By Realisation A/c	—	9,900	—
				By Realisation A/c	—	1,600	—
	54,440	55,940	7,220		54,440	55,940	7,220

Dr. **BANK ACCOUNT** *Cr.*

Particulars	₹	*Particulars*	₹
To Balance b/d	23,500	By Realisation A/c	7,500
To Realisation A/c	98,100	By Realisation A/c (Unrecorded liability)	2,500
(Assets realisation)		By Realisation A/c (Salary outstanding)	2,000
		By Y (expenses)	1,100
		By X's Capital A/c	48,440
		By Ys Capital A/c	54,840
		By Zs Capital A/c	5,220
	1,21,600		1,21,600

Note: *Actual expenses borne by Y are presumed to have been paid by firm on Y's behalf. If it is presumed that he has paid out of his own private bank balance then this entry will not appear. In the latter case Y's final settlement will be increased by this amount.*

PROBLEM 2

Ram and Hanuman are partners in a firm. They share profits and losses in the ratio of 1 : 2. On 1st April 2016, they decided to dissolve the partnership and on that date the Balance Sheet of the firm was as under:

Liabilities	₹	*Assets*		₹
Sundry Creditors	50,000	Cash at Bank		10,000
General Reserve	60,000	Sundry Debtors	50,000	

Hanuman's Loan	30,000	*Less:* Provision	2,000	48,000
Capital Accounts:		Stock		1,02,000
Ram	1,50,000	Furniture		30,000
Hanuman	1,00,000	Machinery and Plant		80,000
		Land and Building		1,20,000
	3,90,000			3,90,000

The sales of firm's properties realised ₹ 1,00,000 from stock, ₹ 34,000 from furniture and ₹ 1,00,000 from Land and Building. ₹ 45,000 were collected from Debtors and Creditors were paid off at a discount of ₹ 1,000. Machinery and Plant are taken over by Ram at their book value. The expenses of realisation amounted to ₹ 4,000. Pass Journal Entries to close the books of the firm and prepare necessary ledger accounts.

SOLUTION

JOURNAL

Particulars		*L.F.*	*Dr. (₹)*	*Cr. (₹)*
Realisation A/c	Dr.		3,82,000	
To Sundry Debtors				50,000
To Stock				1,02,000
To Furniture				30,000
To Machinery & Plant				80,000
To Land & Building				1,20,000
(Being the transfer of various assets to Realisation Account)				
Provision for Doubtful Debts A/c	Dr.		2,000	
Sundry Creditors	Dr.		50,000	
To Realisation A/c				52,000
(Being the t/f of various liabilities & Provisions to Realisation A/c)				
Bank A/c	Dr.		2,79,000	
To Realisation A/c				2,79,000
(Being the Stock, Furniture, Land & Building and Debtors realised)				
Ram's Capital A/c	Dr.		80,000	
To Realisation A/c				80,000
(Being the Machinery & Plant taken over by Ram)				
Realisation A/c	Dr.		4,000	
To Bank A/c				4,000
(Being the realisation expenses paid)				
Realisation A/c	Dr.		49,000	
To Bank A/c				49,000
(Being the payment made to creditors)				
Ram's Capital A/c	Dr.		8,000	
Hanuman's Capital A/c	Dr.		16,000	

To Realisation A/c			24,000
(Being the transfer of loss on Realisation)			
Hanuman's Loan A/c	Dr.	30,000	
To Bank A/c			30,000
(Being the payment of Hanuman's Loan)			
General Reserve A/c	Dr.	60,000	
To Ram's Capital A/c			20,000
To Hanuman's Capital A/c			40,000
(Being the transfer of General Reserve)			
Ram's Capital A/c	Dr.	82,000	
Hanuman's Capital A/c	Dr.	1,24,000	
To Bank A/c			2,06,000
(Being the final claims of the partners discharged)			

Ledger Accounts:

Dr. **REALISATION ACCOUNT** Cr.

Particulars	₹	Particulars		₹
To Sundry Debtors	50,000	By Provision for Doubtful Debts A/c		2,000
To Stock	1,02,000	By Sundry Creditors		50,000
To Furniture	30,000	By Bank A/c:		
To Machinery & Plant	80,000	Stock	1,00,000	
To Land & Building	1,20,000	Furniture	34,000	
To Bank A/c (Realisation Exp.)	4,000	Land & Building	1,00,000	
To Bank A/c (Creditors)	49,000	Debtors	45,000	2,79,000
		By Ram's Capital A/c (Machinery & Plant)		80,000
		By Loss on Realisation t/f to:		
		Ram's Capital A/c		8,000
		Hanuman's Capital A/c		16,000
	4,35,000			4,35,000

Dr. **BANK ACCOUNT** Cr.

Particulars	₹	Particulars	₹
To Balance b/d	10,000	By Realisation A/c	4,000
To Realisation A/c	2,79,000	By Realisation A/c	49,000
		By Hanuman's Loan A/c	30,000
		By Ram's Capital A/c	82,000
		By Hanuman's Capital A/c	1,24,000
	2,89,000		2,89,000

Dr. **CAPITAL ACCOUNTS OF PARTNERS** Cr.

Particulars	*Ram* ₹	*Hanuman* ₹	*Particulars*	*Ram* ₹	*Hanuman* ₹
To Realisation A/c	80,000	—	By Balance b/d	1,50,000	1,00,000
To Realisation A/c	8,000	16,000	By General Reserve	20,000	40,000
To Bank A/c	82,000	1,24,000			
	1,70,000	1,40,000		1,70,000	1,40,000

PROBLEM 3

X, Y and Z were in partnership sharing profits and losses in the ratio of 3 : 2 : 1. No interest was to be allowed on current *or* capital accounts of the partners but their loan accounts were to carry interest of 10% p.a.

Due to persistent losses and the continued illness of X, the firm decided to get dissolved on 30th June, 2016. Its accounts were closed for the last time on 31st March, 2016 on which date its Balance Sheet was as under:

Liabilities	₹	*Assets*	₹
Capital accounts:		Plant and Machinery	60,000
X	48,000	Furniture and Fittings	10,000
Y	33,000	Motor Cars	40,000
Loan from X	22,000	Stock	55,000
Trade creditors	80,000	Sundry Debtors	40,000
Bank overdraft	30,000	Capital account Z	8,000
	2,13,000		2,13,000

Between 31st March, 2016 and 30th June, 2016 goods of the value of ₹ 30,000 were purchased for cash and cash sales amounted to ₹ 45,000. In addition to payment to trade creditors payments made were for salaries and wages ₹ 12,000 and for general and office expenses ₹ 6,000. Drawings of each partner were ₹ 800 p.m. On 30th June, 2016, debtors, creditors and stock-in-trade were ₹ 60,000, ₹ 70,000 and ₹ 45,000 respectively.

In dissolution proceedings the partners agreed to transfer the entire business (with all assets and liabilities including partner's loan) as a going concern to D for a consideration of ₹ 90,000. Cost of dissolution amounted to ₹ 2,800 which were met by X.

Required: Show the necessary accounts for the dissolution of firm and also the capital accounts of the partners, assuming that all of them are solvent.

SOLUTION

BALANCE SHEET AS AT 30TH JUNE, 2016

Liabilities		₹	*Assets*	₹
Loan X	22,000		Plant and Machinery	60,000
Accrued Interest for 3 months	550	22,550	Furniture and Fittings	10,000
Trade Creditors		70,000	Motor Car	40,000
X	48,000		Stock	45,000
Add: Net Profit	3,225		Debtors	60,000

	51,225		Z	8,000	
Less: Drawings	2,400	48,825	*Add:* Drawings	2,400	
Y	33,000			10,400	
Add: Net Profit	2,150		*Less:* Net Profit	1,075	9,325
	35,150				
Less: Drawings	2,400	32,750			
Bank overdraft		50,200			
		2,24,325			2,24,325

Dr. **REALISATION ACCOUNT** *Cr.*

Particulars		₹	*Particulars*	₹
To Plant and Machinery		60,000	By Loan from X	22,550
To Furniture and Fittings		10,000	By Trade Creditors	70,000
To Motor Car		40,000	By Bank overdraft	50,200
To Stock		45,000	By D (purchase consideration)	90,000
To Debtors		60,000		
To X (cost of dissolution)		2,800		
To Net Profit t/f to:				
X	7,475			
Y	4,983			
Z	2,492	14,950		
		2,32,750		2,32,750

Dr. **CAPITAL ACCOUNTS OF PARTNERS** *Cr.*

Particulars	*X*	*Y*	*Z*	*Particulars*	*X*	*Y*	*Z*
To Balance b/d	—	—	9,325	By Balance b/d	48,825	32,750	—
To Cash A/c				By Realisation A/c	2,800	—	—
—final payment	59,100	37,733	—	By Realisation A/c	7,475	4,983	2,492
				By Cash A/c			
				(brought in)	—	—	6,833
	59,100	37,733	9,325		59,100	37,733	9,325

Dr. **CASH ACCOUNT** *Cr.*

Particulars	₹	*Particulars*	₹
To D	90,000	By X's Capital A/c	59,100
To Z 's Capital A/c	6,833	By Y's Capital A/c	37,733
	96,833		96,833

Working Notes:

(I) TRADING AND PROFIT AND LOSS ACCOUNT
for three months ending on 30th June, 2016

Dr. *Cr.*

Particulars		₹	*Particulars*		₹
To Opening Stock		55,000	By Sales:		
To Purchases		30,000	Cash	45,000	
To Salaries & Wages		12,000	Credit	20,000	65,000
To Office Expenses		6,000	By Closing Stock		45,000
To Interest on Loan		550			
To X	3,225				
Y	2,150				
Z	1,075	6,450			
		1,10,000			1,10,000

(II) TOTAL DEBTORS ACCOUNT

Dr. *Cr.*

Particulars	₹	*Particulars*	₹
To Balance b/d	40,000	By Balance c/d	60,000
To Credit Sales (b.f.)	20,000		
	60,000		60,000

(III) CASH AND BANK ACCOUNT

Dr. *Cr.*

Particulars	₹	*Particulars*		₹
To Sales	45,000	By Balance b/d		30,000
To Balance c/d	50,200	By Salaries & Wages		12,000
		By Office Expenses		6,000
		By Drawings:		
		X	2,400	
		Y	2,400	
		Z	2,400	7,200
		By Creditors (₹ 80,000 – 70,000)		10,000
		By Cash Purchases		30,000
	95,200			95,200

PROBLEM 4

Neel, Neha and Neeraj are partners in a firm M/s NHJ & Co. sharing profits and losses in the ratio 3 : 2 : 1. They are also entitled to interest on loan at 10% p.a., but not interest on Capital.

The partners decided to dissolve the firm on 30.06.2016. The following is their Balance Sheet which was drawn upto 31.03.2016.

M/S. NHJ & CO.

Liabilities	₹	*Assets*	₹
Capital Accounts:		Building	2,10,000
Neel	1,68,000	Furniture	35,000
Neha	1,15,500	Motor cycle	1,40,000
Neel's Loan	77,000	Stock	1,92,500
Sundry Creditors	2,80,000	Sundry Debtors	1,40,000
Bank Overdraft	1,05,000	Neeraj's Capital A/c	28,000
	7,45,500		7,45,500

Between the Balance Sheet date and the date of dissolution, purchases amounted to ₹ 1,05,000 and sales ₹ 1,57,500. In addition to payments made to Creditors, a sum of ₹ 42,000 and ₹ 21,000 were paid on account of Salaries and general expenses.

Each partner withdrew ₹ 2,800 per month. On 30.06.2016, Debtors, Creditors and Stock amounted to ₹ 2,10,000, ₹ 2,45,500 and ₹ 1,57,500 respectively. During course of proceedings the partners decided to transfer the entire business to a private limited company with all assets, liabilities and partner's loan for a consideration of ₹ 3,15,000. Dissolution expenses amounted to ₹ 9,800 and were borne by Neel.

Required: Prepare necessary Ledger Accounts, Profit and Loss Account, Partners Capital Account and Balance Sheet as at 30.06.2016 of the firm M/s. NHJ & Co. Also ascertain the amount of profit on realisation.

SOLUTION

Dr. **SUNDRY DEBTORS ACCOUNT** *Cr.*

Particulars	₹	*Particulars*	₹
To Balance b/d	1,40,000	By Bank A/c (b.f.)	87,500
To Sales	1,57,500	By Balance c/d	2,10,000
	2,97,500		2,97,500

Dr. **SUNDRY CREDITORS ACCOUNT** *Cr.*

Particulars	₹	*Particulars*	₹
To Bank A/c (b.f.)	1,39,500	By Balance b/d	2,80,000
To Balance	2,45,500	By Purchases	1,05,000
	3,85,000		3,85,000

Dr. **BANK ACCOUNT** *Cr.*

Particulars	₹	*Particulars*	₹
To Sundry Debtors	87,500	By Balance b/d	1,05,000
To Balance c/d	2,45,200	By Sundry Creditors	1,39,500
		By Salaries	42,000
		By General Expenses	21,000
		By Drawings	25,200
	3,32,700		3,32,700

Dr. **PROFIT & LOSS ACCOUNT FOR THE QUARTER ENDED 30.06.2016** Cr.

Particulars	₹	Particulars	₹
To Opening Stock	1,92,500	By Sales	1,57,500
To Purchases	1,05,000	By Closing Stock	1,57,500
To Salaries	42,000	By Balance c/d (Loss)	45,500
To General Expenses	21,000		
	3,60,500		3,60,500
To Balance b/d	45,500	By Net Loss:	
To Interest on loan	1,925	Neel	23,712
		Neha	15,808
		Neeraj	7,905
	47,425		47,425

Dr. **PARTNERS' CAPITAL ACCOUNTS** Cr.

Particulars	Neel ₹	Neha ₹	Neeraj ₹	Particulars	Neel ₹	Neha ₹	Neeraj ₹
To Balance b/d	—	—	28,000	By Balance b/d	1,68,000	1,15,500	—
To P & L A/c (Share of loss)	23,712	15,808	7,905				
To Drawings	8,400	8,400	8,400				
To Balance c/d	1,35,888	91,292	—	By Balance c/d	—	—	44,305
	1,68,000	1,15,500	44,305		1,68,000	1,15,500	44,305

NHJ & CO.
BALANCE SHEET AS AT 30.06.2016

Liabilities		₹	Assets	₹
Capital A/c:			Building	2,10,000
Neel	1,35,888		Furniture	35,000
Neha	91,292	2,27,180	Motor Cycle	1,40,000
Sundry Creditors		2,45,500	Stock-in-trade	1,57,500
Bank Overdraft		2,45,200	Sundry Debtors	2,10,000
Neel's Loan A/c	77,000		Neeraj's Capital A/c	44,305
Add: Interest on loan	1,925	78,925		
		7,96,805		7,96,805

PROFIT ON REALIZATION

Particulars	₹	₹
Total Consideration		3,15,000
Less: Net Assets		
Capital A/c Neel	1,35,888	
Capital A/c. Neha	91,292	
	2,27,180	

Capital A/c Neeraj	44,305*	1,82,875
		1,32,125
Less: Realisation Expenses (borne by Neel)		9,800
		1,22,325

PROBLEM 5

X, Y and Z who were sharing profits and losses in the ratio of 2 : 2 : 1, decided to dissolve the partnership on 31st March, 2016 on which date their Balance Sheet was as under:

Liabilities	₹	*Assets*	₹
X 's Capital	24,000	Fixed Assets	27,000
Y 's Capital	20,000	Stock	20,000
Z 's Capital	15,000	Debtors	28,000
Creditors	9,000	Bank Balance	5,000
Mrs X 's Loan	12,000		
	80,000		80,000

Y and Z continued the business, agreeing to purchase X's share in the capital of the firm in the proportion in which they shared profits and losses. Mrs X agreed to allow her loan to remain in the business. Y and Z utilised available bank balance to pay X and contributed the balance. Assets were valued as under:

Fixed Assets ₹ 36,400, Stocks ₹ 18,000, Debtors as in the Balance Sheet, subject to ₹ 2,200 as Provision for Doubtful Debts and an allowance of 5% for discounts. The liability of creditors is taken over by Y and Z subject to an allowance of ₹ 400 for discount. Y and Z continue to share profits and losses in the same proportion as before.

Required: Prepare Realisation A/c, Bank A/c, Partners' Capital Accounts and Opening Balance Sheet of M/s Y and Z together with opening entries.

SOLUTION

Dr. **REALISATION ACCOUNT** *Cr.*

Particulars		₹	*Particulars*		₹
To Fixed Assets		27,000	By Creditors		9,000
To Stock		20,000	By Mrs X 's Loan		12,000
To Debtors		28,000	By Y and Z Joint A/c:		
To Y and Z Joint A/c:			Fixed Assets	36,400	
Creditors	8,600		Stock	18,000	
Mrs X 's Loan	12,000	20,600	Debtors	24,510	78,910
To Profit on Realisation t/f to:					
X – 2/5	1,724				
Y – 2/5	1,724				
Z – 1/5	862	4,310			
		99,910			99,910

Dr. **CAPITAL ACCOUNTS OF PARTNERS** Cr.

Particulars	X ₹	Y ₹	Z ₹	Particulars	X ₹	Y ₹	Z ₹
To Bank A/c	25,724	—	—	By Balance b/d	24,000	20,000	15,000
To Y and Z Joint A/c	—	35,540	22,770	By Realisation A/c	1,724	1,724	862
				By Bank A/c	—	13,816	6,908
	25,724	35,540	22,770		25,724	35,540	22,770

Dr. **Y AND Z JOINT ACCOUNT** Cr.

Particulars	₹	Particulars	₹
To Realisation A/c	78,910	By Realisation A/c	20,600
		By Y 's Capital A/c	35,540
		By Z 's Capital A/c	22,770
	78,910		78,910

BOOKS OF M/S Y AND Z
JOURNAL

Particulars	L.F.	Dr. (₹)	Cr. (₹)
Fixed Assets Dr.		36,400	
Stock Dr.		18,000	
Debtors Dr.		28,000	
Reserve for Discount against Creditors Dr.		400	
To Creditors			9,000
To Mrs X 's Loan			12,000
To Provision for Doubtful Debts			2,200
To Provision for Discount			1,290
To Y's Capital A/c			35,540
To Z's Capital A/c			22,770
(Being the various assets and liabilities taken over from M/s X, Y & Z)			

BALANCE SHEET OF M/S Y AND Z AS ON 31.03.2016

Liabilities		₹	Assets		₹
Y's Capital		35,540	Fixed Assets		36,400
Z's Capital		22,770	Stock		18,000
Mrs X's Loan		12,000	Debtors	28,000	
Creditors	9,000		*Less:* Provision for Doubtful		
Less: Reserve for Discount	400	8,600	Debts	2,200	
				25,800	
			Less: Provision for Discount	1,290	24,510
		78,910			78,910

Working Notes:

		Particulars	₹
(i)		*Calculation of Net Debtors*	
	A	As per Balance Sheet	28,000
	B	*Less:* Provision for Doubtful Debts	2,200
	C	Good Debts (A – B)	25,800
	D	*Less:* 5% allowance for discount	1,290
	E	Net Debtors (C – D)	24,510
(ii)		*Calculation of the amount to be brought in by Y and Z*	
	A	Total Amount payable to X	25,724
	B	Available Bank Balance	5,000
	C	Shortage (A – B) to be contributed by Y & Z in their profit sharing ratio which is 2 : 1	20,724
		Therefore, Y brings — ₹ 13,816, Z brings — ₹ 6,908	

PROBLEM 6

A, B and C are partners sharing profit in the ratio of 2 : 3 : 1 respectively. The position of the firm at 1st April, 2012 was as under:

Liabilities	₹	Assets	₹
A's Capital	20,000	Fixed Assets	30,000
B's Capital	40,000	Current Assets	92,000
C's Capital	10,000		
General Reserve	30,000		
Capital Reserve	12,000		
Bank Overdraft	10,000		
	1,22,000		1,22,000

On this date, the partners decided to change their profit and loss sharing ratio to 2 : 2 : 1. Goodwill was valued at ₹ 30,000. No entries were however passed to give effect to this change. On 31st March, 2016, the Balance Sheet of the firm was as under:

Liabilities	₹	Assets	₹
A's Capital	20,000	Fixed Assets	28,000
B's Capital	40,000	Current Assets	1,24,000
C's Capital	10,000	Drawings:	
General Reserve	72,000	A	2,000
Capital Reserve	12,000	B	4,000
Bank Overdraft	5,000	C	1,000
	1,59,000		1,59,000

On the same date, the firm was as a going concern to C for a total value of ₹ 1,70,000. C brought in sufficient cash to pay out A and B.

Required: Give the necessary Journal entries in the books of the firm as on 31st March 2016 assuming that the same set of books are not continued after the take-over.

SOLUTION

JOURNAL

Particulars		L.F.	Dr. (₹)	Cr. (₹)
A's Capital A/c	Dr.		2,000	
C's Capital A/c	Dr.		1,000	
To B's Capital A/c				3,000
(Being the adjustment made on account of changes in old profit sharing ratio)				
General Reserve	Dr.		30,000	
Capital Reserve	Dr.		12,000	
To A's A/c				14,000
To B 's A/c				21,000
To C 's A/c				7,000
(Being the General Reserve & Capital Reserve as on April 1 t/f to partners' Capital Accounts in the old profit sharing ratio)				
General Reserve A/c	Dr.		42,000	
To A's Capital A/c				16,800
To B's Capital A/c				16,800
To C's Capital A/c				8,400
(Being the General Reserve after change in profit sharing ratio transferred to partners in their new profit sharing ratio)				
Realisation A/c	Dr.		1,52,000	
To Fixed Assets				28,000
To Current Assets				1,24,000
(Being the sundry assets transferred to Realisation A/c)				
Bank Overdraft	Dr.		5,000	
To Realisation A/c				5,000
(Being the overdraft transferred to Realisation A/c)				
C's Personal (Business Purchase) A/c	Dr.		1,70,000	
To Realisation A/c				1,70,000
(Being the amount of purchase consideration due from C as per agreement dated .....)				
Realisation A/c	Dr.		23,000	
To A's Capital A/c				9,200
To B's Capital A/c				9,200
To C's Capital A/c				4,600
(Being the transfer of Profit on realisation)				
C's Capital A/c	Dr.		28,000	
To C's Personal (Business Purchase) A/c				28,000
(Being the transfer of balance in the Capital A/c of C to his Personal (Business Purchase) A/c)				

Cash A/c	Dr.	1,42,000	
To C 's Personal (Business Purchase) A/c			1,42,000
(Being the amount brought in by C)			
A's Capital A/c	Dr.	56,000	
B's Capital A/c	Dr.	86,000	
To Cash A/c			1,42,000
(Being the amounts paid to A and B in final settlement)			

Working Notes:

Dr. **(I) CAPITAL ACCOUNTS OF PARTNERS** Cr.

Particulars	*A* ₹	*B* ₹	*C* ₹	*Particulars*	*A* ₹	*B* ₹	*C* ₹
To Drawings A/c	2,000	4,000	1,000	By Balance c/d	20,000	40,000	10,000
To B's Capital A/c	2,000	—	1,000	By General Reserve & Capital Reserve	14,000	21,000	7,000
To C's Personal (B.P.) A/c	—	—	28,000	By General Reserve	16,800	16,800	8,400
To Cash A/c	56,000	86,000	—	By A 's Capital	—	2,000	—
				By C 's Captal	—	1,000	—
				By Realisation	9,200	9,200	4,600
	60,000	90,000	30,000		60,000	90,000	30,000

(II) DISTRIBUTION OF GENERAL RESERVE

	Particulars	*A* ₹	*B* ₹	*C* ₹
I	General Reserve rate in the beginning (in the ratio of 2 : 3 : 1)	10,000	15,000	5,000
II	Capital Reserve in the beginning (in the ratio of 2 : 3 : 1)	4,000	6,000	2,000
		14,000	21,000	7,000

PROBLEM 7

X, Y and Z carrying on business since 2001 decided to end their partnership on 31st March, 2016 when their Balance Sheet was as under:

Liabilities	₹	*Assets*	₹
Creditors	34,000	Cash	25,000
Capital Accounts:		Debtors	62,000
X	1,20,000	Stock	37,000
Y	90,000	Tools	8,000
Z	60,000	Motor Cars	12,000
		Machinery	60,000
		Freehold Building	1,00,000
	3,04,000		3,04,000

Y and Z agreed to form a new partnership to carry on the business and it was agreed that they shall acquire from the old firm the following assets at amounts shown below:

Stock ₹ 40,000, Tools ₹ 5,000, Motor Cars ₹ 25,000, Machineries ₹ 78,000, Freehold Building ₹ 84,000, Goodwill ₹ 60,000. The partnership agreement of X, Y and Z provided that trading profits *or* losses shall be divided in the ratio of 3 : 2 : 1 and that capital profits *or* losses shall be divided in proportion of their capital. Debtors realised ₹ 59,000 and discounts amounting to ₹ 720 were secured on payments due to creditors.

Required: Prepare the necessary accounts of X, Y and Z giving effect to these transactions and prepare the Opening Balance Sheet of Y and Z who bring the necessary cash in the ratio of 3 : 2 to pay off X.

SOLUTION

Dr. **CAPITAL ACCOUNTS OF PARTNERS** *Cr.*

Particulars	*X* ₹	*Y* ₹	*Z* ₹	*Particulars*	*X* ₹	*Y* ₹	*Z* ₹
To Cash A/c	1,52,320	—	—	By Balance b/d	1,20,000	90,000	60,000
To M/s Y & Z	—	1,75,200	1,16,800	By Realisation A/c	32,320	24,240	16,160
				By Cash A/c	—	60,960	40,640
	1,52,320	1,75,200	1,16,800		1,52,320	1,75,200	1,16,800

OPENING BALANCE SHEET OF M/S Y AND Z AS AT 31ST MARCH, 2016

Liabilities	₹	*Assets*	₹
Capital Accounts:		Goodwill	60,000
Y	1,75,200	Freehold Building	84,000
Z	1,16,800	Machinery	78,000
		Motor Car	25,000
		Tools	5,000
		Stock	40,000
		Cash	—
	2,92,000		2,92,000

Note: *It has been assumed that total profit on realisation including that on stock, debtors and tools and settlement of creditors is a capital profit, as it relates to sale of business. Alternatively, profit on aforesaid items may be treated as revenue profit. Strictly speaking it is not normal 'trading profit' which accrues during the day to day operation of a firm.*

Working Notes:

Dr. **(I) REALISATION ACCOUNT** *Cr.*

Particulars	₹	*Particulars*	₹
To Debtors	62,000	By Creditors	34,000
To Stock	37,000	By Cash A/c (Debtors)	59,000
To Tools	8,000	By M/s Y & Z	2,92,000
To Motor Cars	12,000	(Purchase consideration)	
To Machinery	60,000		
To Freehold Building	1,00,000		

To Cash A/c (Creditors)		33,280		
To Profit on Realisation t/f to:				
X's Capital A/c	32,320			
Y's Capital A/c	24,240			
Z's Capital A/c	16,160	72,720		
		3,85,000		3,85,000

(ii) Purchase Consideration = (Stock) 40,000 + (Tools) 5,000 + (Motor Car) 25,000 + (Machinery) 78,000 + (Freehold Building) 84,000 + (Goodwill) 60,000 = ₹ 2,92,000.

Dr. **(III) CASH ACCOUNT** *Cr.*

Particulars	₹	*Particulars*	₹
To Balance b/d	25,000	By Realisation A/c (Creditors)	33,280
To Realisation A/c (Debtors)	59,000	By X's Capital A/c	1,52,320
To Y's Capital A/c	60,960		
To Z's Capital A/c	40,640		
	1,85,600		1,85,600

PROBLEM 8

Ram, Rahim and Auntony were in partnership sharing profits and losses in the ratio of 1/2, 1/3 and 1/6 respectively. They decided to dissolve the partnership firm on 31.3.2016, when the Balance Sheet of the firm appeared as under:

Liabilities	₹	*Assets*	₹
Sundry Creditors	5,67,000	Goodwill	4,56,300
Bank Overdraft	6,06,450	Plant and Machinery	6,07,500
Joint Life Policy Reserve	2,65,500	Furniture	64,650
Loan from Mrs. Ram	1,50,000	Stock	2,36,700
Capital Accounts:		Sundry Debtors	5,34,000
Ram	4,20,000	Joint Life Policy	2,65,500
Rahim	2,25,000	Commission Receivable	1,40,550
Auntony	1,20,000	Cash on Hand	48,750
	23,53,950		23,53,950

The following details are relevant for dissolution:

(i) The joint life policy was surrendered for ₹ 2,32,500.
(ii) Ram took over goodwill and plant and machinery for ₹ 9,00,000.
(iii) Ram also agreed to discharge bank overdraft and loan from Mrs. Ram.
(iv) Furniture and stocks were divided equally between Ram and Rahim at an agreed valuation of ₹ 3,60,000.
(v) Sundry debtors were assigned to firm's creditors in full satisfaction of their claims.
(vi) Commission receivable was received in toto in time.
(vii) A bill discounted was subsequently returned dishonoured and proved valueless ₹ 30,750 (including ₹ 500 noting charges).

(viii) Ram paid the expenses of dissolution amounting to ₹ 18,000.

(ix) Auntony agreed to receive ₹ 1,50,000 in full satisfaction of his rights, title and interest in the firm.

You are required to show the accounts relating to closing of books on dissolution of the firm.

SOLUTION

Dr. **REALISATION ACCOUNT** *Cr.*

Particulars	₹	*Particulars*		₹
To Goodwill	4,56,300	By Sundry Creditors		5,67,000
To Plant & Machinery	6,07,500	By Joint Life Policy Reserve		2,65,500
To Furniture	64,650	By Cash (Joint Life Policy)		2,32,500
To Stock	2,36,700	By Ram's Capital A/c:		
To Sundry Debtors	5,34,000	Goodwill and		
To Joint Life Policy	2,65,500	Plant & Machinery	9,00,000	
To Cash		Furniture & Stock	1,80,000	1,80,000
(Bills Receivable dishonoured)	30,750	By Rahim's Capital A/c:		
To Ram's Capital A/c:		Furniture & Stock		1,80,000
(dissolution expenses)	18,000			
To Auntony's Capital A/c:				
(₹ 1,50,000 – ₹ 1,20,000)	30,000			
To Profit on Realisation t/f to:				
Ram (3/5)	48,960			
Rahim (2/5)	32,640			
	23,25,000			23,25,000

Note: *No entry is required in settlement of accounts to Sundry Creditors as they have agreed to take up Sundry Debtors in full satisfaction.*

Dr. **CASH ACCOUNT** *Cr.*

Particulars	₹	*Particulars*	₹
To Balance b/d	48,750	By Realisation A/c:	
To Commission Receivable	1,40,550	Bills Receivable Dishonoured	30,750
To Realisation A/c:		By Ram's Capital A/c	1,63,410
Joint Life Policy	2,32,500	By Rahim's Capital A/c	77,640
		By Auntony's Capital A/c	1,50,000
	4,21,800		4,21,800

Dr. **COMMISSION RECEIVABLE ACCOUNT** *Cr.*

Particulars	₹	*Particulars*	₹
To Balance b/d	1,40,550	By Cash	1,40,550
	1,40,550		1,40,550

Dr. **BANK OVER DRAFT ACCOUNT** Cr.

Particulars	₹	Particulars	₹
To Ram's Capital A/c	6,06,450	By Balance b/d	6,06,450
	6,06,450		6,06,450

Dr. **MRS. RAM'S LOAN ACCOUNT** Cr.

Particulars	₹	Particulars	₹
To Ram's Loan A/c	1,50,000	By Balance b/d	1,50,000
	1,50,000		1,50,000

Dr. **CAPITAL ACCOUNT OF PARTNERS** Cr.

Particulars	Ram ₹	Rahim ₹	Auntony ₹	Particulars	Ram ₹	Rahim ₹	Auntony ₹
To Realisation A/c	10,80,000	1,80,000	—	By Balance b/d	4,20,000	2,25,000	1,20,000
To Cash A/c	1,63,410	77,640	1,50,000	By Realisation	18,000	—	—
				By Realisation	48,960	32,640	30,000
				By Mrs. Ram's Loan A/c	1,50,000	—	—
				By Bank Overdraft	6,06,450	—	—
	12,43,410	2,57,640	1,50,000		12,43,410	2,57,640	1,50,000

Notes: *The student may find out the profit on realisation without considering the amount of profit payable to Auntony. Thus profit on realisation will be ₹ 1,11,600 which will be divided between Ram, Rahim and Auntony in the ratio of 3 : 2 : 1 i.e. ₹ 55,800, ₹ 37,200 and ₹ 18,600 respectively. The amount of excess payment to Auntony (₹ 1,50,000 less ₹ 1,38,600 i.e. ₹ 11,400) will be borne by Rahim in the ratio of 3 : 2. The Capital Accounts will be changed accordingly.*

PROBLEM 9

Following is the Balance Sheet of A,B,C and D who were sharing in the ratio of 3:3:2:2 as at 31st March, 2016, when they decided to dissolve the firm:

Liabilities	₹	Assets		₹
Trade Creditors	70,000	Cash at Bank		27,500
Bank Overdraft (Secured on Stock)	15,000	Sundry Debtors	50,000	
A's Loan	30,000	*Less:* Provision	(8,500)	41,500
Mrs. B's Loan	3,000	Stock		25,000
A's Capital	66,000	Prepaid Insurance		3,000
B's Capital	51,000	Goodwill		5,000
Employee's Provident Fund	5,000	Tangible Fixed Assets		80,000
Machinery Replacement Reserve	20,000	C's Capital		44,000
		D's Capital		14,000
		Profit & Loss A/c		20,000
	2,60,000			2,60,000

(a) *Half the Trade Creditors accepted half the Tangible Fixed Assets at an agreed valuation of 80%, an unrecorded furniture of ₹ 2,000 at a discount of 50% and the balance in cash in full settlement of their claims after allowing a discount of ₹ 2,000; Remaining Trade Creditors accepted the Remaining Tangible Fixed Assets at an agreed valuation of 110% after allowing a discount of ₹ 4,000 and the Balance was paid by him in Cash.*

(b) *60% of Sundry Debtors realized 34% less; B is to take over the balance of Sundry Debtors at 70%. Further, he is to be allowed ₹ 800 to cover future losses.*

(c) *Stock was taken over by the banker, and it realised 80%. Bank paid back ₹ 4,000 after recovering its overdraft and interest due thereon.*

(d) *Also, there was a joint life policy for ₹ 90,000. The Joint Life Policy was surrendered to the insurance company. The company paid a sum of ₹ 4,000 after deducting an amount of ₹ 6,500 towards loan and interest thereon by B against the policy.*

(e) *A debtor whose debt of ' 5,000 was written off as bad in the books paid 40% in full settlement.*

(f) *There were unrecorded investments of ₹ 40,000. There were Unrecorded Creditors of ₹ 80,000. Half of such Creditors accepted half the unrecorded investments at an agreed valuation of 60% in full settlement of their claims and the Remaining such Creditors were settled and paid by A at a discount of 20%. Remaining Unrecorded Investments were taken over by B at an agreed valuation of 20%*

(g) *B was appointed to realise the assets and to pay off the liabilities. He was entitled to receive ' 2,000 as remuneration for completing the dissolution work and was to bear the realisation expenses. The expenses of realisation' 1,500 were paid by B out of his private funds.*

Required: Prepare Realisation Account, Partners' Capital Accounts and Bank Account.

SOLUTION

REALISATION ACCOUNT

Particulars	₹	*Particulars*	₹
To Assets Transferred:		By Provision for Doubtful Debts	8,500
Stock	25,000	By Trade Creditors	70,000
Debtors	50,000	By Bank Overdraft	15,000
Prepaid Insurance	3,000	By Mrs. B's Loan	3,000
Goodwill	5,000	By Employees' Provident Fund	5,000
Tangible Fixed Assets	80,000	By Machinery Replacement Reserve	20,000
To Bank A/c (Trade Creditors)	8,000	By Bank A/c:	
		Stock	4,000
To Bank A/c (EPF)	5,000	Debtors(50000 × 60% × 66%)	19,800
To Bank A/c (Mrs B's Loan)	3,000	Tangible Fixed Assets	
To A [Unrecorded Creditors]	32,000	[35,000 – 5,000 – 32,000]	2,000
To B [remuneration]	2,000	Joint Life Policy	4,000
		By B's Capital A/c (Debtors)	
		[(50,000 × 40% × 70%) – 800]	13,200
		By B's Capital A/c (JLP)	6,500
		By Bank A/c [Bad Debts recovered]	2,000
		By B's Capital A/c (Investments)	4,000
		By Loss on Realisation t/f to:	
		A's Capital A/c	10,800
		B's Capital A/c	10,800

		C's Capital A/c	7,200
		D's Capital A/c	7,200
	2,13,000		2,13,000

Dr. **PARTNERS' CAPITAL ACCOUNTS** Cr.

Particulars	*A*	*B*	*C*	*D*	*Particulars*	*A*	*B*	*C*	*D*
To Balance b/d	—	—	44,000	14,000	By Balance b/d	66,000	51,000	—	—
To P&L A/c	6,000	6,000	4,000	4,000	By Bank A/c	—	—	55,200	25,200
To Realisation A/c	—	6,500	—	—	By Realisation A/c	32,000	2,000	—	—
To Realisation A/c	—	13,200							
To Realisation A/c	—	4,000	—	—					
To Realisation A/c	10,800	10,800	7,200	7,200					
To Bank A/c	81,200	12,500	—	—					
	98,000	53,000	55,200	25,200		98,000	53,000	55,200	25,200

Dr. **BANK ACCOUNT** Cr.

Particulars	₹	*Particulars*	₹
To Balance b/d	27,500	By Realisation A/c (Trade Creditors)	8,000
To Realisation A/c	29,800	By Realisation A/c (EPF)	5,000
To Realisation A/c	2,000	By Realisation A/c (Mrs B's Loan)	3,000
To C's Capital A/c	55,200	By A's Loan A/c	30,000
To D's Capital A/c	25,200	By A's Capital A/c	81,200
		By B's Capital A/c	12,500
	1,39,700		1,39,700

PROBLEM 10

Following is the Balance Sheet of A,B,C and D who were sharing in the ratio of 3:3:2:2 as at 31st March, 2016, when they decided to dissolve the firm:

Liabilities	₹	*Assets*		₹
Trade Creditors	60,000	Cash at Bank		27,500
Bank Overdraft (Secured on Stock)	15,000	Sundry Debtors	50,000	
A's Loan	30,000	*Less:* Provision	(8,500)	41,500
Mrs. B's Loan	3,000	Stock		25,000
A's Capital	66,000	Prepaid Insurance		3,000
B's Capital	51,000	Goodwill		5,000
Employee's Provident Fund	5,000	Tangible Fixed Assets		80,000
Machinery Replacement Reserve	20,000	C's Capital		44,000
		D's Capital		14,000
		Profit & Loss A/c		10,000
	2,50,000			2,50,000

Note: *There was a bill for ₹ 23,750 under discount. The bill was received from Z.*

(a) *After preparing the Balance Sheet as at 31st March, it was discovered that purchases amounting to ₹ 10,000 in March, were not recorded in books, though the goods were received during March.*

(b) *Half the Trade Creditors accepted half the Net Tangible Fixed Assets at an agreed valuation of ₹ 25,000 and cash in full settlement of their claims after allowing a discount of ₹ 2,000; Remaining Trade Creditors were paid ₹ 32,000 in final settlement including an investment worth ₹ 2,000 unrecorded in the books.*

(c) *Remaining Net Tangible Fixed Assets realised at a loss of 100% on net collection.*

(d) *60% of Sundry Debtors realized 34% less; B is to take over the balance of Sundry Debtors at 70%. Further, he is to be allowed ₹ 800 to cover future losses.*

(e) *Stock was taken over by the banker, and it realised 80%. Bank paid back ₹ 4,000 after recovering its overdraft and interest due thereon.*

(f) *Also, there was a joint life policy for ₹ 90,000. The Joint Life Policy was surrendered to the insurance company. The company paid a sum of ₹ 2,500 after deducting an amount of ₹ 6,500 towards loan and interest thereon by B against the policy.*

(g) *Z proved insolvent and a first and final dividend of 60% was received from his estate.*

(h) *B was appointed to realise the assets and to pay off the liabilities. He was entitled to receive 5% commission on the amount finally paid to other partners as capital. He was to bear the expenses of realisation. Expenses of realisation amounted to ₹ 1,500.*

(i) *The private position of the partners was as follows:*

Particulars	*A*	*B*	*C*	*D*
Private Estate	1,00,000	2,00,000	3,00,000	4,00,000
Private Liabilities	89,200	1,95,600	2,44,800	3,70,000

Required: Prepare Realisation Account, Partners' Capital Accounts and Bank Account.

SOLUTION

Dr. **REALISATION ACCOUNT** *Cr.*

Particulars	₹	*Particulars*	₹
To Assets Transferred:		By Provision for Doubtful Debts	8,500
Stock	25,000	By Trade Creditors (60,000+10,000)	70,000
Debtors	50,000	By Bank Overdraft	15,000
Prepaid Insurance	3,000	By Mrs. B's Loan	3,000
Goodwill	5,000	By Employee's Provident Fund	5,000
Tangible Fixed Assets	80,000	By Machinery Replacement Reserve	20,000
To Bank A/c (Trade Creditors)		By Bank A/c:	
(8,000 + 30,000)	38,000	Stock	4,000
To Bank A/c (EPF)	5,000	Debtors(50000 × 60% × 66%)	19,800
To Bank A/c (Mrs B's Loan)	3,000	Tangible Fixed Assets	
To Bank A/c		[30,000 – (100/200 × 30,000)]	15,000
(Discounted B/R)	23,750	Joint Life Policy	2,500
		from Z	14,250
		By B's Capital A/c (Debtors)	
		[(50,000 × 40% × 70%) – 800]	13,200

		By B's Capital A/c (JLP)	6,500
		By Loss on Realisation t/f to:	
		A's Capital A/c	10,800
		B's Capital A/c	10,800
		C's Capital A/c	7,200
		D's Capital A/c	7,200
	2,32,750		2,32,750

Dr. **PARTNERS' CAPITAL ACCOUNTS** Cr.

Particulars	A	B	C	D	Particulars	A	B	C	D
To Balance b/d	—	—	44,000	14,000	By Balance b/d	66,000	51,000	—	—
To P&L A/c	3,000	3,000	2,000	2,000	By Bank A/c	—	—	55,200	25,200
To P&L A/c	3,000	3,000	2,000	2,000	By A's Capital A/c	—	2,343	—	—
To Realisation A/c	—	6,500	—	—					
To Realisation A/c	—	13,200	—	—					
To Realisation A/c	10,800	10,800	7,200	7,200					
To B's Capital A/c	2,343	—	—	—					
To Bank A/c	46,857	16,843	—	—					
	66,000	53,343	55,200	25,200		66,000	53,343	55,200	25,200

Dr. **BANK ACCOUNT** Cr.

Particulars	₹	Particulars	₹
To Balance b/d	27,500	By Realisation A/c (Trade Creditors)	38,000
To Realisation A/c	55,550	By Realisation A/c (Bills).	23,750
To C's Capital A/c	55,200	By Realisation A/c (EPF)	5,000
To D's Capital A/c	25,200	By Realisation A/c (Mrs B's Loan)	3,000
		By A's Loan A/c	30,000
		By A's Capital A/c	46,857
		By B's Capital A/c	16,843
	1,63,450		1,63,450

2 PARTNERSHIP—INSOLVENCY, PIECEMEAL DISTRIBUTION AND SALE

LEARNING OBJECTIVES

After studying this chapter, you should be able to understand:

- ◇ Introduction
- ◇ Decision in Garner VS Murray
- ◇ Applicability of the Decision in Garner VS Murray in India
- ◇ Insolvency of a Firm
- ◇ Piecemeal Distribution
- ◇ Basis of Distribution of Cash Among Partners Towards Their Capitals
- ◇ Sale of a Firm To a Company

1.0 INTRODUCTION

The Capital Account of a partner may show a debit balance after making all adjustments (including the share of any profit *or* loss on realisation and the receipts from his private estate, if any). It may be noted that the private estate of each partner is applied first to pay off his private debts and the surplus (i.e. excess of private estate over private debts), if any, is applied to pay off the firm's debts. If a partner having a debit balance in his Capital Account is unable to bring in the necessary cash to make up the deficiency, he is said to be an insolvent partner. The irrecovered debit balance is called the loss arising due to the insolvency of a partner. Now the question arises should this loss be regarded as an ordinary loss (which is shared by the partners in their profit-sharing ratio) *or* an extra ordinary one? This issue was involved in the leading case of *Garner* vs *Murray* (1904).

2.0 DECISION IN GARNER VS MURRAY

Justice Joyee held that the loss arising due to the insolvency of a partner must be distinguished from an ordinary loss (including realisation loss). Unless otherwise agreed, the decision in *Garner* vs *Murray* requires—

(a) That the solvent partners should bring in cash equal to their respective shares of the loss on realisation;

(b) That the solvent partners should bear the loss arising due to the insolvency of a partner in the ratio of their Last Agreed Capitals.

The Last Agreed Capital should be interpreted as under:

Case	***Meaning of Last Agreed Capital***
(a) In case of Fixed Capitals	Last Agreed Capital means the Fixed Capital (given in the Balance Sheet) without any adjustment.

(b) In case of Fluctuating Capitals	Last Agreed Capital means the Capital after making adjustments for past accumulated reserves, profits *or* losses, drawings, interest on capitals, interest on drawings, remuneration to a partner etc. to the date of dissolution but before making adjustment for profit *or* loss on realisation.

3.0 APPLICABILITY OF THE DECISION IN GARNER VS MURRAY IN INDIA

There is nothing which prevents to assume that the decision in Garner vs Murray will also apply in India on the following two grounds:

(a) Section 48 of the Indian Partnership Act is almost a copy of Section 44 of the English Partnership Act upon which the decision in Garner vs Murray is based,

(b) There has been no case law in India which has examined this issue.

Some of the Accountants contend that the above decision is contrary to Sec. 48(a) of the Indian Partnership Act. They contend that unless agreed otherwise, all losses of the firm should be borne by the partners in their profit-sharing ratio.

In order to avoid the aforesaid controversy, it is recommended that while drafting a Partnership Deed, the partners should specify the manner in which the losses arising due to the insolvency of a partner, are to be borne by the solvent partners. While preparing a solution to a problem, the students should also indicate whether *or* not the ruling in Garner vs Murray has been applied.

The practical guidelines in case of an insolvency of a partner according to the decision in Garner vs Murray are given below:

PRACTICAL GUIDELINES IN CASE OF INSOLVENCY OF A PARTNER ACCORDING TO THE DECISION IN GARNER VS MURRAY

(a) Realisation Account should be prepared in the usual manner and its profit or loss should be transferred to the Capital Accounts of all the partners (including insolvent partner) in the profit- sharing ratio.

(b) Solvent partners should bring in cash equal to their respective shares of the loss (if any) on realisation.

(c) The ratio of the Last Agreed Capitals of the solvent partners should be calculated.

(d) If any amount is received from the private estate of an insolvent partner, it should be credited to his Capital Account.

(e) The irrecovered debit balance after making all adjustments (including the share of any profit or loss on realisation) should be transferred to the Capital Accounts of solvent partners (other than one having a debit balance in his Capital Account as on the date of dissolution), in the ratio of their Last Agreed Capitals [as calculated above in (c)].

(f) The solvent partner having a debit balance in his Capital Account should bring in the necessary cash to balance off his account.

(g) The solvent partner having a credit balance in his Capital Account should draw out the necessary cash to balance off his account.

Notes:

(i) If an examination problem specifies that the rule in Garner vs Murray is to be applied, the solvent partners should be required to bring in cash equal to their respective shares of the loss on realisation. In other cases, the solvent partners may not be required to bring their shares of loss on realisation in cash.

(ii) A solvent partner having a debit balance is his Capital Account as at the date of dissolution shall not share any loss arising due to the insolvency of a partner.

ILLUSTRATION 1

Following is the Balance Sheet of A,B,C and D who were sharing in the ratio of 3:3:2:2 as at 31st March, 2016, when they decided to dissolve the firm:

Liabilities	₹	*Assets*	₹
Trade Creditors	1,21,000	Sundry Assets	1,70,000
A's Capital	60,000	C's Capital	48,000
B's Capital	49,000	D's Capital	18,000
General Reserve	20,000	B's Drawings	4,000
		Profit & Loss A/c	10,000
	2,50,000		2,50,000

C is insolvent but ₹ 11,100 is realized from his estate. Sundry Assets realized 80%. Realization Expenses ₹ 2,000. State who will bear C's deficiency and in which ratio.

SOLUTION

CALCULATION OF CAPITAL RATIO

Particulars	*A* ₹	*B* ₹
Capital	60,000	49,000
Less: B's Drawings	–	(4,000)
Less: Share of Debit balance of Profit & Loss A/c	(3,000)	(3,000)
Add: Share of General Reserve	6,000	6,000
	63,000	48,000

C's deficiency is to be borne by A and B in the ratio of 63,000: 48,000 *or* 21: 16.

D will not bear C's deficiency since he had a debit balance in his Capital Account.

ILLUSTRATION 2

Following is the Balance Sheet of A,B,C and D who were sharing in the ratio of 3:3:2:2 as at 31st March, 2016, when they decided to dissolve the firm:

Liabilities	₹	*Assets*	₹
Trade Creditors	1,21,000	Sundry Assets	1,70,000
A's Capital	60,000	C's Capital	48,000
B's Capital	49,000	D's Capital	18,000
General Reserve	20,000	B's Drawings	4,000
		Profit & Loss A/c	10,000
	2,50,000		2,50,000

After preparing the Balance Sheet as at 31st March, it was discovered that purchases amounting to ₹ 10,000 in March, were not recorded in books, though the goods were received during March. C is insolvent but ₹ 11,100 is realized from his estate. Sundry Assets realized 86%. Realization Expenses ₹ 2,200. State who will bear C's deficiency and in which ratio.

SOLUTION

CALCULATION OF CAPITAL RATIO

Particulars	*A* ₹	*B* ₹
Capital	60,000	49,000
Less: B's Drawings	–	(4,000)
Less: Share of Debit balance of Profit & Loss A/c [10,000 + 10,000 (Ommited purchases)]	(6,000)	(6,000)
Add: Share of General Reserve	6,000	6,000
	60,000	45,000

C's deficiency is to be borne by A and B in the ratio of 60,000: 45,000 *or* 4: 3.

D will not bear C's deficiency since he had a debit balance in his Caoital Account.

ILLUSTRATION 3

Following is the Balance Sheet of A,B,C and D who were sharing in the ratio of 3:3:2:2 as at 31st March, 2016, when they decided to dissolve the firm:

Liabilities	₹	*Assets*	₹
Trade Creditors	1,21,000	Sundry Assets	1,70,000
A's Capital	60,000	C's Current	78,000
B's Capital	45,000	D's Current	33,000
C's Capital	30,000	Profit & Loss A/c	10,000
D's Capital	15,000		
General Reserve	20,000		
	2,91,000		2,91,000

After preparing the Balance Sheet as at 31st March, it was discovered that purchases amounting to ₹ 10,000 in March, were not recorded in books, though the goods were received during March. C is insolvent but ₹ 11,100 is realized from his estate. Sundry Assets realized 86%. Realization Expenses ₹ 2,200. State who will bear C's deficiency and in which ratio.

SOLUTION

C's deficiency is to be borne by A, B, C and D in the ratio of their fixed capitals i.e. 60,000 : 45,000 : 30,000 : 15,000 *or* 4 : 3 : 2 : 1.

ILLUSTRATION 4

Following is the Balance Sheet of A,B,C and D who were sharing in the ratio of 3: 3: 2: 2 as at 31st March, 2016, when they decided to dissolve the firm:

Liabilities	₹	*Assets*		₹
Loan from Bank (Secured on Other Tangible Fixed Assets)	50,000	Cash at Bank		27,500
		Trade Debtors	40,000	
Mrs. B's Loan (Secured on Stock)	3,000	*Less:* Provision	(8,500)	31,500
Trade Creditors	30,000	Stock		5,000

A's Loan	30,000	Prepaid Insurance	3,000
A's Capital	60,000	Goodwill	5,000
B's Capital	49,000	Machinery	60,000
General Reserve	20,000	Other Tangible Fixed Assets	50,000
Machinery Replacement Reserve	20,000	B's Drawings	4,000
		C's Capital	48,000
		D's Capital	18,000
		Profit & Loss A/c	10,000
	2,62,000		2,62,000

(a) After preparing the Balance Sheet as at 31st March, it was discovered that purchases amounting to ₹ 10,000 in March, were not recorded in books, though the goods were received during March.

(b) Trade Debtors realized 12.5%. Stock realized 20%, Machinery realised at a loss of 100% on net collection. Other Tangible Fixed Assets realized 84%, Expenses of realisation amounted to ₹ 7,500. Only ₹ 18,700 could be recovered from partner "C".

Required: Prepare Realisation A/c, Partners' Capital A/cs and Bank A/c.

SOLUTION

Dr. **REALISATION ACCOUNT** *Cr.*

Particulars	₹	*Particulars*	₹
To Assets Transferred:		By Provision for Doubtful Debts	8,500
Stock	5,000	By Machinery Replacement Reserve	20,000
Debtors	40,000	By Loan from Bank	50,000
Prepaid Insurance	3,000	By Mrs. B's Loan	3,000
Goodwill	5,000	By Trade Creditors (30,000 + 10,000)	40,000
Machinery	60,000	By Bank A/c:	
Other Tangible Fixed Assets	50,000	Machinery	
To Bank A/c (Expenses)	7,500	[40,000 – (100/200 × 40,000)]	20,000
To Bank A/c (Loan from Bank)	50,000	Debtors (₹ 40,000 × 12.5%)	5,000
To Bank A/c (Mrs. B's Loan)	3,000	Stock (₹ 5,000 × 20%)	1,000
To Bank A/c (Trade Creditors)	40,000	Other Tangible Fixed Assets	
		(₹ 50,000 × 84%)	42,000
		By Loss on Realisation t/f to:	
		A's Capital A/c	22,200
		B's Capital A/c	22,200
		C's Capital A/c	14,800
		D's Capital A/c	14,800
	2,63,500		2,63,500

Dr. **PARTNERS' CAPITAL ACCOUNTS** *Cr.*

Particulars	*A*	*B*	*C*	*D*	*Particulars*	*A*	*B*	*C*	*D*
To Balance b/d	—	—	48,000	18,000	By Balance b/d	60,000	49,000	—	—
To Drawings	—	4,000	—	—	By General Reserve	6,000	6,000	4,000	4,000
To P&L A/c (Goods)	3,000	3,000	2,000	2,000	By Bank A/c	—	—	18,700	32,800
To P&L A/c (Loss)	3,000	3,000	2,000	2,000	By A's Capital A/c	—	—	25,200	—
To Realisation A/c	22,200	22,200	14,800	14,800	By B's Capital A/c	—	—	18,900	—
To C's Capital A/c	25,200	18,900	—						
To Bank A/c	12,600	3,900	—						
	66,000	55,000	66,800	36,800		66,000	55,000	66,800	36,800

Dr. **BANK ACCOUNT** *Cr.*

Particulars	₹	*Particulars*	₹
To Balance b/d	27,500	By Realisation A/c (Expenses)	7,500
To Realisation A/c (Assets)	68,000	By Realisation A/c (Loan from Bank)	50,000
To C's Capital A/c	18,700	By Realisation A/c (Mrs B's Loan)	3,000
To D's Capital A/c	32,800	By Realisation A/c (Trade Creditors)	40,000
		By A's Loan A/c	30,000
		By A's Capital A/c	12,600
		By B's Capital A/c	3,900
	1,47,000		1,47,000

Working Notes:

1. Total Trade Creditors = 30,000 + 10,000 (Ommited Purchases) = 40,000
2. Book Value of Machinery = Machinery – Machinery Replacement Reserve
   = 60,000 – 20,000 = 40,000

3. CALCULATION OF CAPITAL RATIO

Particulars	*A* ₹	*B* ₹
Capital	60,000	49,000
Less: B's Drawings	–	(4,000)
Less: Share of Debit Balance of Profit & Loss A/c [10,000 + 10,000 (Ommited Purchases)]	(6,000)	(6,000)
Add: Share of General Reserve	6,000	6,000
	60,000	45,000

C's Deficiency is to be borne by A and B in the ratio of 60,000 : 45,000 *or* 4 : 3.

A's Capital A/c [₹ 44,100 × 4/7]	Dr.	₹ 25,200	
B's Capital A/c [₹ 44,100 × 3/7]	Dr.	₹ 11,100	
To C's Capital A/c [₹55,200 – ₹ 11,100]			₹ 44,100

4. D will not bear any portion of the loss due to C's insolvency since he had a debit balance in his capital account at the time of Insolvency.

ILLUSTRATION 5

What shall be the change in the solution of the previous problem if C could bring in ₹ 18,700 only and the Rule of Garmer Vs Murray is to be followed?

SOLUTION

As per Rule of Garmer Vs Murray, all solvent partners are required to bring in their shares of loss on realisation in cash.

Dr. **REALISATION ACCOUNT** Cr.

Particulars	₹	Particulars	₹
To Assets Transferred:		By Provision for Doubtful Debts	8,500
Stock	5,000	By Machinery Replacement Reserve	20,000
Debtors	40,000	By Loan from Bank	50,000
Prepaid Insurance	3,000	By Mrs. B's Loan	3,000
Goodwill	5,000	By Trade Creditors (30,000 + 10,000)	40,000
Machinery	60,000	By Bank A/c:	
Other Tangible Fixed Assets	50,000	Machinery	
To Bank A/c (Expenses)	7,500	[40,000 – (100/200 × 40,000)]	20,000
To Bank A/c (Loan from Bank)	50,000	Debtors (₹ 40,000 × 12.5%)	5,000
To Bank A/c (Mrs. B's Loan)	3,000	Stock (₹ 5,000 × 20%)	1,000
To Bank A/c (Trade Creditors)	40,000	Other Tangible Fixed Assets	
		(₹ 50,000 × 84%)	42,000
		By Loss on Realisation t/f to:	
		A's Capital A/c	22,200
		B's Capital A/c	22,200
		C 's Capital A/c	14,800
		D 's Capital A/c	14,800
	2,63,500		2,63,500

Dr. **PARTNERS' CAPITAL ACCOUNTS** Cr.

Particulars	A	B	C	D	Particulars	A	B	C	D
To Balance b/d	—	—	48,000	18,000	By Balance b/d	60,000	49,000	—	—
To Drawings	—	4,000	—	—	By General Reserve	6,000	6,000	4,000	4,000
To P&L A/c (Goods)	3,000	3,000	2,000	2,000	By Bank A/c (Loss)	22,200	22,200	18,700	14,800
To P&L A/c (Loss)	3,000	3,000	2,000	2,000	By Bank A/c	—	—	—	18,000
To Realisation A/c	22,200	22,200	14,800	14,800	By A's Capital A/c	—	—	25,200	—
To C's Capital A/c	25,200	18,900	—	—	By B's Capital A/c	—	—	18,900	—
To Bank A/c	34,800	26,100	—	—					
	88,200	77,200	66,800	36,800		88,200	77,200	66,800	36,800

Dr. **BANK ACCOUNT** Cr.

Particulars	₹	Particulars	₹
To Balance b/d	27,500	By Realisation A/c (Expenses)	7,500
To Realisation A/c (Assets)	68,000	By Realisation A/c (Loan from Bank)	50,000
To A's Capital A/c (Loss)	22,200	By Realisation A/c (Mrs B's Loan)	3,000

To B's Capital A/c (Loss)	22,200	By Realisation A/c (Trade Creditors)	40,000
To D's Capital A/c (Loss)	14,800	By A's Loan A/c	30,000
To D's Capital A/c	18,000	By A's Capital A/c	34,800
To C's Capital A/c	18,700	By B's Capital A/c	26,100
	1,91,400		1,91,400

Working Notes:

1. Total Trade Creditors = 30,000 + 10,000 (Ommited Purchases) = 40,000.
2. Book Value of Machinery = Machinery – Machinery Replacement Reserve
   = 60,000 – 20,000 = 40,000.

3. CALCULATION OF CAPITAL RATIO

Particulars	*A* ₹	*B* ₹
Capital	60,000	49,000
Less: B's Drawings	–	(4,000)
Less: Share of Debit Balance of Profit & Loss A/c [10,000 + 10,000 (Ommited Purchases)]	(6,000)	(6,000)
Add: Share of General Reserve	6,000	6,000
	60,000	45,000

C's Deficiency is to be borne by A and B in the ratio of 60,000 : 45,000 *or* 4 : 3.

A's Capital A/c [₹ 44,100 × 4/7]	Dr.	₹ 25,200	
B's Capital A/c [₹ 44,100 × 3/7]	Dr.	₹ 11,100	
To C's Capital A/c [₹55,200 – ₹ 11,100]			₹ 44,100

4. D will not bear any portion of the loss due to C's insolvency since he had a debit balance in his capital account at the time of Insolvency.

ILLUSTRATION 6

Following is the Balance Sheet of A,B,C and D who were sharing in the ratio of 3: 3: 2: 2 as at 31st March, 2016, when they decided to dissolve the firm:

Liabilities	₹	*Assets*		₹
Loan from Bank (Secured on Other Tangible Fixed Assets)	50,000	Cash at Bank		27,500
		Trade Debtors	40,000	
Mrs. B's Loan (Secured on Stock)	3,000	*Less:* Provision	(8,500)	31,500
Trade Creditors	30,000	Stock		5,000
A's Loan	30,000	Prepaid Insurance		3,000
A's Capital	60,000	Goodwill		5,000
B's Capital	48,000	Machinery		60,000
C's Capital	10,000	Other Tangible Fixed Assets		50,000
D's Capital	12,000	B's Current A/c		3,000
General Reserve	20,000	C's Current A/c		58,000
Machinery Replacement Reserve	20,000	D's Current A/c		30,000

		Profit & Loss A/c	10,000
	2,83,000		2,83,000

(a) After preparing the Balance Sheet as at 31st March, it was discovered that purchases amounting to ₹ 10,000 in March, were not recorded in books, though the goods were received during March.

(b) Trade Debtors realized 12.5%. Stock realized 20%, Machinery realised at a loss of 100% on net collection. Other Tangible Fixed Assets realized 84%, Expenses of realisation amounted to ₹ 7,500. Only ₹ 18,700 could be recovered from partner "C". The Rule of Garmer Vs Murray is to be followed.

Required: Prepare Realisation A/c, Partners' Capital A/cs and Bank A/c.

SOLUTION

As per Rule of Garmer Vs Murray, all solvent partners are required to bring in their shares of loss on realisation in cash.

Dr. **REALISATION ACCOUNT** *Cr.*

Particulars	₹	*Particulars*	₹
To Assets Transferred:		By Provision for Doubtful Debts	8,500
Stock	5,000	By Machinery Replacement Reserve	20,000
Debtors	40,000	By Loan from Bank	50,000
Prepaid Insurance	3,000	By Mrs. B's Loan	3,000
Goodwill	5,000	By Trade Creditors (30,000 + 10,000)	40,000
Machinery	60,000	By Bank A/c:	
Other Tangible Fixed Assets	50,000	Machinery	
To Bank A/c (Expenses)	7,500	[40,000 – (100/200 × 40,000)]	20,000
To Bank A/c (Loan from Bank)	50,000	Debtors (₹ 40,000 × 12.5%)	5,000
To Bank A/c (Mrs. B's Loan)	3,000	Stock (₹ 5,000 × 20%)	1,000
To Bank A/c (Trade Creditors)	40,000	Other Tangible Fixed Assets	
		(₹ 50,000 × 84%)	42,000
		By Loss on Realisation t/f to:	
		A's Current A/c	22,200
		B's Current A/c	22,200
		C's Current A/c	14,800
		D's Current A/c	14,800
	2,63,500		2,63,500

Dr. **PARTNERS' CURRENT ACCOUNTS** *Cr.*

Particulars	A	B	C	D	*Particulars*	A	B	C	D
To Balance b/d	—	3,000	58,000	30,000	By General Reserve	6,000	6,000	4,000	4,000
To P&L A/c (Goods)	3,000	3,000	2,000	2,000	By A's Capital A/c	22,200	—	—	—
To P&L A/c (Loss)	3,000	3,000	2,000	2,000	By B's Capital A/c	—	25,200	—	—
To Realisation A/c	22,200	22,200	14,800	14,800	By C's Capital A/c	—	—	72,800	—
					By D's Capital A/c	—	—	—	44,800
	28,200	31,200	76,800	48,800		28,200	31,200	76,800	48,800

Dr. **PARTNERS' CAPITAL ACCOUNTS** Cr.

Particulars	A	B	C	D	Particulars	A	B	C	D
To Current A/c (T/f)	22,200	25,200	72,800	44,800	By Balance b/d	60,000	48,000	10,000	12,000
To C's Capital A/c	22,050	17,640	—	4,410	By Bank A/c (Loss)	22,200	22,200	18,700	14,800
To Bank A/c	37,950	27,360	—	—	By Bank A/c	—	—	—	22,410
					By A's Capital A/c	—	—	22,050	—
					By B's Capital A/c	—	—	17,640	—
					By D's Capital A/c	—	—	4,410	—
	82,200	70,200	72,800	49,210		82,200	70,200	72,800	49,210

Dr. **BANK ACCOUNT** Cr.

Particulars	₹	Particulars	₹
To Balance b/d	27,500	By Realisation A/c (Expenses)	7,500
To Realisation A/c (Assets)	68,000	By Realisation A/c (Loan from Bank)	50,000
To A's Capital A/c (Loss)	22,200	By Realisation A/c (Mrs B's Loan)	3,000
To B's Capital A/c (Loss)	22,200	By Realisation A/c (Trade Creditors)	40,000
To D's Capital A/c (Loss)	14,800	By A's Loan A/c	30,000
To D's Capital A/c	22,410	By A's Capital A/c	37,950
To C's Capital A/c	18,700	By B's Capital A/c	27,360
	1,95,810		1,95,810

Working Notes:

1. Total Trade Creditors = 30,000 + 10,000 (Ommited Purchases) = 40,000
2. Book Value of Machinery = Machinery – Machinery Replacement Reserve
   = 60,000 – 20,000 = 40,000
3. Capital Ratio of solvent partners (A, B and D) = 60,000 : 48,000 : 12,000 = 5 : 4 : 1
   C's Deficiency is to be borne by A, B and D in the ratio of 5 : 4 : 1

A's Capital A/c [₹ 44,100 × 5/10]	Dr.	₹ 22,050	
B's Capital A/c [₹ 44,100 × 4/10]	Dr.	₹ 17,640	
D's Capital A/c [₹ 44,100 × 1/10]	Dr.	₹ 4,410	
To C's Capital A/c			₹ 44,100

ILLUSTRATION 7

The following is the Balance Sheet of a firm as at 31st March, 2016:

Liabilities	₹	Assets	₹
Creditors	1,02,400	Bank	5,500
Loans:		Debtors	96,060
P	30,000	Stock	64,000
Q	12,000	Machinery	28,600
Current Accounts:		Land	84,000
P	21,200	R's Current Account	9,940
Q	2,500		

Capital Accounts:			
P	60,000		
Q	40,000		
R	20,000		
	2,88,100		2,88,100

Owing to heavy losses in the past two years, it was decided to close the business. The assets, with the exception of bank balance, realised ₹ 2,26,880. The firm has to pay ₹ 1,500 for an outstanding bill, not recorded in the books. R becomes insolvent and ₹ 1,000 is realised from his estate. Prepare the necessary accounts to close the books of the firm.

SOLUTION

Dr. **REALISATION ACCOUNT** *Cr.*

Particulars	₹	*Particulars*		₹
To Debtors	96,060	By Creditors		1,02,400
To Stock	64,000	By Bank (assets realised)		2,26,880
To Machinery	28,600	By Loss on Realisation t/f to:		
To Land	84,000	P's Current A/c	15,760	
To Bank (Outstanding Bill)	1,500	Q's Current A/c	15,760	
To Bank (Creditors)	1,02,400	R's Current A/c	15,760	47,280
	3,76,560			3,76,560

Dr. **BANK ACCOUNT** *Cr.*

Particulars	₹	*Particulars*	₹
To Balance b/d	5,500	By Realisation A/c	1,500
To Realisation A/c	2,26,880	By Realisation A/c	1,02,400
To R's Capital A/c	1,000	By P's Loan A/c	30,000
		By Q's Loan A/c	12,000
		By P's Capital A/c	62,620
		By Q's Capital A/c	24,860
	2,33,380		2,33,380

Dr. **PARTNERS' LOAN ACCOUNTS** *Cr.*

Particulars	*P* ₹	*Q* ₹	*Particulars*	*P* ₹	*Q* ₹
To Bank A/c	30,000	12,000	By Balance b/d	30,000	12,000
	30,000	12,000		30,000	12,000

Dr. **PARTNERS' CAPITAL ACCOUNTS** *Cr.*

Particulars	*P* ₹	*Q* ₹	*R* ₹	*Particulars*	*P* ₹	*Q* ₹	*R* ₹
To Current A/c (Transfer)	—	13,260	25,700	By Balance b/d	60,000	40,000	20,000
				By Current A/c (T/f)	5,440	—	—

To R's Capital A/c	2,820	1,880	—	By Bank A/c	—	—	1,000
To Bank A/c	62,620	24,860	—	By P's Capital A/c	—	—	2,820
				By Q's Capital A/c	—	—	1,880
	65,440	40,000	25,700		65,440	40,000	25,700

Dr. **PARTNERS' CURRENT ACCOUNTS** *Cr.*

Particulars	*P* ₹	*Q* ₹	*R* ₹	*Particulars*	*P* ₹	*Q* ₹	*R* ₹
To Balance b/d	—	—	9,940	By Balance b/d	21,200	2,500	—
To Realisation A/c	15,760	15,760	15,760	By Capital A/c (Transfer)	—	13,260	25,700
To Capital A/c (Transfer)	5,440	—	—				
	21,200	15,760	25,700		21,200	15,760	25,700

Note: *R's Deficiency has been debited to P and Q in the ratio of fixed capitals i.e. 60,000 : 40,000.*

ILLUSTRATION 8

A, B and C are partners sharing profits and losses in the ratio of 4 : 3 : 2. Their Balance Sheet as at 31.3.2016 stood as follows:

Liabilities	₹	*Assets*		₹
Sundry Creditors	20,000	Cash at Bank		2,000
Bank Overdraft		Debtors	18,000	
(secured against stock)	15,000	*Less:* Provision	1,000	17,000
Loan (against the mortgage		Machinery		40,000
of machinery)	25,000	Stock		25,000
Capitals: A	20,000	Profit and Loss A/c		9,000
B	10,000			
C	3,000			
	93,000			93,000

The firm was dissolved on that date. Stock was taken over by the banker, and it realised 80%. Bank paid back ₹ 4,000 after recovering its overdraft and interest due thereon. Machinery was disposed off for 60% and debtors realised ₹ 14,000 only. Loan was fully paid off along with interest due ₹ 1,000. Sundry creditors were discharged at 10% discount. Expenses amounted to ₹ 300, which were paid by A. C became insolvent and only ₹ 950 could be recovered from his private assets. Prepare the necessary ledger accounts to close the books of the firm. Apply Garner vs Murray rule.

SOLUTION

Dr. **REALISATION ACCOUNT** *Cr.*

Particulars	₹	*Particulars*	₹
To Debtors	18,000	By Provision for Doubtful Debts	1,000
To Stock	25,000	By Sundry Creditors	20,000
To Machinery	40,000	By Bank Overdraft	15,000

To Bank (Loan)	26,000	By Loan		25,000
To Bank (Creditors)		By Bank (Surplus from Stock)		4,000
[₹ 20,000 – ₹ 2,000]	18,000	By Bank (Machinery)		24,000
To A (Expenses)	300	By Bank (Debtors)		14,000
		By Loss on Realisation t/f to:		
		A's Capital A/c	10,800	
		B's Capital A/c	8,100	
		C's Capital A/c	5,400	24,300
	1,27,300			1,27,300

Dr. **BANK ACCOUNT** *Cr.*

Particulars	₹	*Particulars*	₹
To Balance b/d	2,000	By Realisation A/c	26,000
To A's Capital A/c		By Realisation A/c	18,000
(Share of Loss on Realization)	10,800	By A's Capital A/c	13,900
To B's Capital A/c		By B's Capital A/c	5,950
(Share of Loss on Realization)	8,100		
To C's Capital A/c	950		
To Realisation A/c	4,000		
To Realisation A/c	24,000		
To Realisation A/c	14,000		
	63,850		63,850

Dr. **CAPITAL ACCOUNTS OF PARTNERS** *Cr.*

Particulars	*A* ₹	*B* ₹	*C* ₹	*Particulars*	*A* ₹	*B* ₹	*C* ₹
To P & L A/c	4,000	3,000	2,000	By Balance b/d	20,000	10,000	3,000
To Realisation A/c	10,800	8,100	5,400	By Bank A/c	10,800	8,100	950
To C's Capital A/c	2,400	1,050	—	By Realisation A/c	300	—	—
To Bank A/c	13,900	5,950	—	By A's Capital A/c	—	—	2,400
				By B's Capital A/c	—	—	1,050
	31,100	18,100	7,400		31,100	18,100	7,400

Working Note:

CALCULATION OF RATIO OF LAST AGREED CAPITAL

Particulars	*A* ₹	*B* ₹
Capital	20,000	10,000
Less: Share of Accumulated Loss (Debit balance of P & L A/c)	4,000	3,000
	16,000	7,000

C's deficiency has been debited to A and B in the ratio of their last agreed capitals i.e. 16,000 : 7,000.

ILLUSTRATION 9

Ram, Indra, Triveni and Umesh were partners, sharing profits and losses in the ratio of 3 : 3 : 2 : 2. Following is their Balance Sheet as at 31st March, 2016:

Liabilities		₹	Assets		₹
Sundry Creditors		46,500	Cash at Bank		6,000
Ram's Loan		30,000	Sundry Debtors	48,000	
Capital Accounts:			*Less:* Provision	1,500	46,500
Ram	60,000		Stock		30,000
Indra	45,000	1,05,000	Furniture and Fittings		12,000
			Trademarks		21,000
			Capital Accounts:		
			Triveni	48,000	
			Umesh	18,000	66,000
		1,81,500			1,81,500

On the same date, the firm was dissolved and Indra was appointed to realise the assets and to pay off the liabilities. He was entitled to receive 5% commission on the amount finally paid to other partners as capital. He was to bear the expenses of realisation. The assets realised: Sundry Debtors: 31.25% less; Stock: 80%; Furniture: 25%; Trademarks: ₹ 9,000 less. Creditors were paid off in full and, in addition to it, a contingent liability for Bills Receivable discounted materialised to the extent of ₹ 7,500. Also, there was a joint life policy for ₹ 90,000. This was surrendered for ₹ 9,000. Expenses of realisation amounted to ₹ 1,500. Triveni was insolvent, but ₹ 11,100 were recovered from his estate.

Required: Write up the necessary accounts to close the books of the firm according to Garners vs. Murray rule. (Ignore Commission while determining Realisation Loss).

SOLUTION

Dr. **REALISATION ACCOUNT** *Cr.*

Particulars	₹	Particulars		₹
To Sundry Debtors	48,000	By Sundry Creditors		46,500
To Stock	30,000	By Provision for Doubtful Debts		1,500
To Furniture and Fittings	12,000	By Bank (Realisation of Assets):		
To Trademarks	21,000	Debtors	33,000	
To Bank (Creditors)	46,500	Stock	24,000	
To Bank (Bill dishonoured)	7,500	Furniture	3,000	
		Trademarks	12,000	
		Joint Life Policy	9,000	81,000
		By Loss on realisation t/f to:		
		Ram's Capital A/c		10,800
		Indra's Capital A/c		10,800
		Triveni's Capital A/c		7,200
		Umesh's Capital A/c		7,200
	1,65,000			1,65,000

Dr. **BANK ACCOUNT** Cr.

Particulars	₹	Particulars	₹
To Balance b/d	6,000	By Realisation A/c (Creditors)	46,500
To Realisation A/c	81,000	By Realisation A/c (Bills)	7,500
To Ram's Capital A/c		By Ram's Loan A/c	30,000
(Share of Loss on Realisation)	10,800	By Ram's Capital A/c	33,657
To Indira's Capital A/c		By Indra's Capital A/c	27,243
(Share of Loss on Realisation)	10,800		
To Triveni's Capital A/c	11,100		
To Umesh's Capital A/c			
(Share of Loss on Realisation)	25,200		
	1,44,900		1,44,900

Dr. **PARTNERS' CAPITAL ACCOUNTS** Cr.

Particulars	Ram ₹	Indra ₹	Triveni ₹	Umesh ₹	Particulars	Ram ₹	Indra ₹	Triveni ₹	Umesh ₹
To Balance b/d	—	—	48,000	18,000	By Balance b/d	60,000	45,000	—	—
To Realisation A/c	10,800	10,800	7,200	7,200	By Bank A/c	10,800	10,800	11,100	25,200
To Triveni's Capital	25,200	18,900	—	—	By Ram's Capital	—	—	25,200	—
To Indra's Capital	1,143	—	—	—	By Indra's Capital	—	—	18,900	—
To Bank A/c	33,657	27,243	—	—	By Ram's Capital	—	1,143	—	—
	70,800	56,943	55,200	25,200		70,800	56,943	55,200	25,200

Notes:

(i) ***Triveni's deficiency has been debited to Ram and Indra in the ratio of 60,000 : 45,000 or 4 : 3.***

(ii) ***Umesh will not bear any portion of the loss due to Triveni's insolvency since he had a debit balance in his capital account to begin with.***

(iii) ***The amount due to Ram, before commission payable to Indira is ₹ 24,000, ignoring the amount brought in by him on account of his share of the loss on realisation. The commission is 5/105 of ₹ 24,000.***

(iv) ***It has been assumed that the realisation expenses have been met by Indra out of his private funds.***

ILLUSTRATION 10

Kay, Ell, Emm and Enn are partners in a firm sharing profits and losses in the ratio of 4 : 1 : 2 : 3. The following is their Balance Sheet as at 31st March, 2016.

Liabilities		₹	Assets		₹
Sundry creditors		30,000	Cash in hand		14,000
Capital Accounts:			Sundry debtors	35,000	
Kay	70,000		*Less:* Provision	5,000	30,000
Enn	30,000	1,00,000	Other Assets		51,000
			Capital Accounts:		
			Ell	20,000	

		Emm	15,000	35,000
	1,30,000			1,30,000

On the same date, the firm is dissolved. The partnership agreement provides that the deficiency of an insolvent partner will be borne by the solvent partners in the ratio of capitals as they stand just before dissolution. The following arrangements are agreed upon:

(a) Kay is to take over 60% of book debts at 70% and Enn is to take over the balance at 75%. Further, they are to be allowed ₹ 2,100 and ₹ 1,100 respectively to cover future losses.

(b) Enn is to realise other assets and to pay off the creditors. He is to receive 5% gross commission on the amounts finally payable to other partners but to bear expenses of realisation. He reports as follows :

Other assets realised at a loss of 2% on net collection, and the creditors were paid off at a discount of 30%. Realisation expenses amounted to ₹ 3,000 but the same is paid by the firm. Ell is declared insolvent and a dividend of 20% in a rupee is realised from his estate.

Required: Prepare Cash Account, Realisation Account, Capital Accounts. (Ignore Commission while determining Realisation Loss).

SOLUTION

Dr. **REALISATION ACCOUNT** *Cr.*

Particulars	₹	*Particulars*	₹
To Sundry debtors	35,000	By Provision for doubtful debts	5,000
To Other assets	51,000	By Sundry creditors	30,000
To Cash (Creditors)	21,000	By Cash (other assets)	50,000
		By Kay's Capital A/c (Sundry debtors)	12,600
		By Enn's Capital A/c (Sundry debtors)	9,400
	1,07,000		1,07,000

Dr. **CAPITAL ACCOUNTS OF PARTNERS** *Cr.*

Particulars	*Kay* ₹	*Ell* ₹	*Emm* ₹	*Enn* ₹	*Particulars*	*Kay* ₹	*Ell* ₹	*Emm* ₹	*Enn* ₹
To Balance b/d	—	20,000	15,000	—	By Balance b/d	70,000	—	—	30,000
To Realisation A/c	12,600	—	—	9,400	By Kay's Capital A/c	—	—	—	2,200
To Cash A/c	—	—	—	3,000	By Cash A/c	—	4,000	15,000	—
To Ell's Capital A/c	11,200	—	—	4,800	By Kay's Capital A/c	—	11,200	—	—
To Enn's Capital A/c	2,200	—	—	—	By Enn's Capital A/c	—	4,800	—	—
To Cash A/c	44,000	—	—	15,000					
	70,000	20,000	15,000	32,200		70,000	20,000	15,000	32,200

Dr. **CASH ACCOUNT** *Cr.*

Particulars	₹	*Particulars*	₹
To Balance b/d	14,000	By Realisation (creditors)	21,000
To Realisation A/c (other assets)	50,000	By Enn's Capital A/c (expenses)	3,000

To Ell's Capital Ac (dividend)	4,000	By Kay's Capital A/c	44,000
To Emm's Capital A/c	15,000	By Enn's Capital A/c	15,000
	83,000		83,000

Working Notes:

(i) Net collection from other assets = ₹ 51,000 – (₹ 51,000 × 2/102) = ₹ 50,000.

(ii) Ell's deficiency (₹ 16,000) has been debited to Kay and Enn in the ratio of their capitals i.e., 7:3.

(iii) Emm will not bear any portion of the loss due to Ell's insolvency since he had a debit balance in his capital account prior to the date of insolvency.

(iv) Enn's commission = 5/105 of the amount due to Kay before commission payable to Enn
= 5/105 of ₹ 46,200 = ₹ 2,200.

ILLUSTRATION 11

The following Balance Sheet of M/s Raja (India) is presented to you:

Liabilities	₹	*Assets*	₹
Creditors	20,000	Sundry assets	31,000
B's loan	5,000	Cash at bank	1,000
Capitals:		Profit and Loss A/c	15,000
A	9,000		
B	6,000		
C	4,000		
D	3,000		
	47,000		47,000

The partners share profits and losses at A 2/10, B 3/10, C 3/10 and D 2/10. The position of partners was as follows:

Particulars	*Private Estate* ₹	*Private Liabilities* ₹
A	10,000	15,000
B	20,000	6,000
C	5,000	4,000
D	8,000	9,000

The assets realised ₹ 27,000 and expenses of dissolution came to ₹ 1,000. Prepare ledger accounts, giving effect to the dissolution.

SOLUTION

Dr. **REALISATION ACCOUNT** *Cr.*

Particulars	₹	*Particulars*	₹
To Sundry assets	31,000	By Creditors	20,000
To Bank (expenses)	1,000	By Bank A/c (Assets realised)	27,000
To Bank A/c (Creditors—paid)	20,000	By Loss on Realisation t/f to A's Capital A/c	1,000

		B 's Capital A/c	1,500
		C 's Capital A/c	1,500
		D 's Capital A/c	1,000
	52,000		52,000

Dr. **BANK ACCOUNT** Cr.

Particulars	₹	Particulars	₹
To Balance b/d	1,000	By Realisation A/c (Expenses)	1,000
To Realisation A/c (Assets)	27,000	By Realisation A/c (Creditors)	20,000
To C's Capital A/c	1,000	By B's Loan A/c	5,000
To B's Capital A/c	400	By A's Capital A/c	3,400
	29,400		29,400

Dr. **CAPITAL ACCOUNTS OF PARTNERS** Cr.

Particulars	A	B	C	D	Particulars	A	B	C	D
To P & L A/c	3,000	4,500	4,500	3,000	By Balance b/d	9,000	6,000	4,000	3,000
To Realisation A/c	1,000	1,500	1,500	1,000	By Bank A/c	—	—	1,000	—
To C's & D's Capital	1,600	400	—	—	By A 's Capital	—	—	800	800
To Bank A/c	3,400	—	—	—	By B 's Capital	—	—	200	200
					By Bank A/c	—	400	—	—
	9,000	6,400	6,000	4,000		9,000	6,400	6,000	4,000

Working Note:

CALCULATION OF RATIO OF LAST AGREED CAPITAL

Particulars	A	B
Capital	9,000	6,000
Less: Share of Accumulated Loss	3,000	4,500
	6,000	1,500

The deficiency of C and D have been debited to A and B in the ratio of their last agreed capitals, i.e. ₹ 6,000 : ₹ 1,500.

ILLUSTRATION 12

A, B and C are partners in a firm sharing profits and losses in the ratio of 2 : 2 : 1. They decide to dissolve and appoint B to realise the assets and distribute the proceeds for which he is to receive, as his remuneration, 5% of the amounts ultimately paid to A and C, but in lieu of this, he is to bear all the expenses of realisation. The Balance Sheet of the firm on the date of dissolution is as under:

Liabilities	₹	Assets		₹
Creditors	1,317	Debtors	4,229	
A's Capital	3,960	*Less:* Provision	211	4,018
B's Capital	2,970	Stock		1,872
		Cash		290
		Other Assets		1,710

		C (Over drawn)	357
	8,247		8,247

B informs about the following realisations:

Debtors: ₹ 3,462, Stock: ₹ 1,444, Goodwill: ₹ 50, Other assets: ₹ 914.

Creditors which were not recorded in books are now paid ₹ 100. The expenses of realisation amounted to ₹ 310. C is able to contribute only ₹ 100 beyond which he expresses his insolvency. Close the books of the firm.

SOLUTION

Dr. **REALISATION ACCOUNT** *Cr.*

Particulars	₹	*Particulars*		₹
To Debtors	4,229	By Creditors		1,317
To Stock	1,872	By Provision for Doubtful Debts		211
To Other Assets	1,710	By Cash A/c:		
To Cash A/c (Creditors)	1,417	Debtors	3,462	
(₹ 1,317 + ₹ 100)		Stock	1,444	
To B's Capital A/c (Commission)	140	Goodwill	50	
		Other Assets	914	5,870
		By Loss on Realisation t/f to:		
		A's Capital A/c	788	
		B's Capital A/c	788	
		C's Capital A/c	394	1,970
	9,368			9,368

Dr. **PARTNERS' CAPITAL ACCOUNTS** *Cr.*

Particulars	A ₹	B ₹	C ₹	*Particulars*	A ₹	B ₹	C ₹
To Balance b/d	—	—	357	By Balance b/d	3,960	2,970	—
To Realisation A/c	788	788	394	By Cash A/c	—	—	100
To C's Capital A/c				By Realisation A/c		140	—
(Insolvency loss)	372	279	—	(Commission)			
To Cash A/c	2,800	2,043	—	By A's Capital A/c			372
(final payment)				By B's Capital A/c	—	—	279
	3,960	3,110	751		3,960	3,110	751

Working Note: *Calculation of commission payable to B:*

B's commission is 5% of amount ultimately paid to A and C.

Here ultimately nothing is being paid to C, hence B's commission is to be 5% of the amount finally paid to A.

Let B's commission be denoted by 'x'.

We can find the realisation loss before taking into account B's commission. It is ₹ 1,830.

Therefore, loss after B's commission is = 1,830 + 'x'.

A's Share of this loss = 732 + (2x/5), B's Share of this loss = 732 + (2x/5).

C's Share of this loss = 366 + (x/5).

C's deficiency borne by A and B in their capital ratio i.e., 3,960 : 2,970 *or* 4 : 3 (Garner vs. Murray).

MEMORANDUM PARTNERS' CAPITAL ACCOUNTS OF A AND C

Particulars	*A* ₹	*C* ₹	*Particulars*	*A*	*C*
To Balance b/d	—	357	By Balance b/d	3,960	—
To Realisation A/c			By Cash A/c	—	100
(Loss)	732 + (2x/5)	366 + (x/5)	By A and B	—	623 + (x/5)
To C's Capital A/c	356 + (4x/35)	—			
To Final Payment	2,872 – (18x/35)	—			
	3,960	723 + (x/5)		3,960	723 + (x/5)

$$5\% \text{ of } [2{,}872 - (18x/35)] = x$$
$$5/100 \times [2{,}872 - (18x/35)] = x$$
$$[2{,}872 - (18x/35)] = 20x$$
$$(2{,}872 \times 35) - 18x = 20x \times 35$$
$$718x = ₹\ 1{,}00{,}520$$
$$x = ₹\ 140$$

Note: *It has been assumed that the realisation expenses have been met by B out of his private funds.*

4.0 INSOLVENCY OF A FIRM

MEANING OF INSOLVENCY OF A FIRM

When the assets of a firm [including the surplus (i.e. excess of private estate over Private Debts) received from insolvent partners] are inadequate to meet the firm's liabilities, the firm is said to be insolvent.

EFFECT OF INSOLVENCY OF A FIRM

In case of insolvency of a firm, the creditors of the firm cannot be paid in full. An unpaid amount of creditors represents the partners' capital deficiencies borne by creditors.

WHETHER CREDITORS ARE T/F TO REALISATION ACCOUNT OR NOT?

If the loss on realisation is to be determined before considering the amount ultimately paid to creditors, the creditors are not transferred to Realisation Account. If the loss on realisation is to be determined after considering the amount ultimately paid to creditors, the creditors are transferred to Realisation Account.

PRACTICAL GUIDELINES IN CASE OF INSOLVENCY OF A FIRM WHEN THE CREDITORS ARE NOT TRANSFERRED TO REALISATION ACCOUNT

Step 1: *Prepare Cash and Bank Account to ascertain the cash available for creditors.*

Step 2: *Prepare Realisation Account (without transferring creditors) in the usual manner and transfer its profit/loss to the capital accounts of all the partners in the profit-sharing ratio.*

Step 3: *Prepare Creditors' Accounts to ascertain the unpaid credit balance which should be transferred to the credit of Deficiency Account.*

Step 4: *Prepare Partners' Capital Accounts to ascertain the irrecovered debit balance which should be transferred to the debit of Deficiency Account.*

ILLUSTRATION 13

The Balance Sheet of A, B and C, who are sharing profits and losses in the ratio of 2 : 2 : 1, was as follows as at 31st March, 2016, the date of dissolution:

Liabilities	₹	*Assets*	₹
Sundry Creditors	1,20,000	Cash	1,000
Bank Loan (with a charge on Stock)	50,000	Stock	60,000
Capital:		Other Assets	1,09,000
A	30,000	Goodwill	30,000
B	20,000	Capital: C	20,000
	2,20,000		2,20,000

Stock realised ₹ 52,000 and other assets were sold for ₹ 90,000. Expenses on realisation amounted to ₹ 3,000.

Required: Assuming that all the partners are insolvent, prepare the necessary ledger accounts to close the books of the firm.

SOLUTION

Dr. **REALISATION ACCOUNT** *Cr.*

Particulars	₹	*Particulars*		₹
To Stock	60,000	By Cash A/c:		
To Other Assets	1,09,000	Stock	52,000	
To Goodwill	30,000	Other Assets	90,000	1,42,000
To Cash A/c (Expenses)	3,000	By Loss on Realisation t/f to:		
		A's Capital A/c		24,000
		B's Capital A/c		24,000
		C's Capital A/c		12,000
	2,02,000			2,02,000

Dr. **CASH ACCOUNT** *Cr.*

Particulars	₹	*Particulars*	₹
To Balance b/d	1,000	By Realisation A/c (Expenses)	3,000
To Realisation A/c	1,42,000	By Bank Loan	50,000
		By Sundry Creditors A/c	90,000
	1,43,000		1,43,000

Dr. **BANK LOAN ACCOUNT** *Cr.*

Particulars	₹	*Particulars*	₹
To Cash A/c	50,000	By Balance b/d	50,000

Dr. **SUNDRY CREDITORS' ACCOUNT** Cr.

Particulars	₹	*Particulars*	₹
To Cash A/c	90,000	By Balance b/d	1,20,000
To Deficiency A/c	30,000		
	1,20,000		1,20,000

Dr. **CAPITAL ACCOUNTS OF PARTNERS** Cr.

Particulars	*A* ₹	*B* ₹	*C* ₹	*Particulars*	*A* ₹	*B* ₹	*C* ₹
To Balance c/d	—	—	20,000	By Balance b/d	30,000	20,000	—
To Realisation A/c	24,000	24,000	12,000	By Deficiency A/c	—	4,000	32,000
To Deficiency A/c	6,000	—	—				
	30,000	24,000	32,000		30,000	24,000	32,000

Dr. **DEFICIENCY ACCOUNT** Cr.

Particulars	₹	*Particulars*	₹
To B's Capital A/c	4,000	By Sundry Creditors A/c	30,000
To C's Capital A/c	32,000	By A's Capital A/c	6,000
	36,000		36,000

ILLUSTRATION 14

Following is the balance sheet as at 31st March, 2013 of a firm, having three partners, Alfa, Beta and Gama sharing profits and losses equally:

Particulars	₹	*Particulars*	₹
Sundry Creditors	20,000	Cash	3,120
Loan (secured by Machinery)	10,000	Stock	14,630
Capital accounts:		Debtors	4,720
Alfa	8,000	Machinery	10,530
Beta	6,000	Profit and Loss Account	12,000
Gama	1,000		
	45,000		45,000

The firm was dissolved due to insolvency of all the partners. Stock was sold for ₹ 9,900 while Machinery fetched ₹ 5,000. ₹ 4,100 were received from debtors. Realisation expenses totalled ₹ 220. Nothing could be recovered from Beta and Gama, but ₹ 600 could be collected from Alfa's private estate.

Required: Close the books of the firm.

SOLUTION

Dr. **REALISATION ACCOUNT** Cr.

Particulars	₹	*Particulars*	₹
To Stock	14,630	By Cash A/c (assets)	19,000

To Debtors	4,720	By Alfa's Capital A/c	3,700
To Machinery	10,530	By Beta's Capital A/c	3,700
To Cash A/c (expenses)	220	By Gama's Capital A/c	3,700
	30,100		30,100

Dr. **CASH ACCOUNT** Cr.

Particulars	₹	*Particulars*	₹
To Balance b/d	3,120	By Realisation A/c (Expenses)	220
To Realisation A/c (assets)	19,000	By Loan (Upto realisable	
To Alfa's Capital A/c	600	value of Machinery) A/c	5,000
		By Loan A/c (₹ 17,500 × 1/5)	3,500
		By Sundry Creditors (₹ 17,500 × 4/5)	14,000
	22,720		22,720

Dr. **LOAN ACCOUNT** Cr.

Particulars	₹	*Particulars*	₹
To Cash A/c (Up to realisable		By Balance b/d	10,000
value of Machinery)	5,000		
To Cash A/c (Share with			
creditors in proportion of 1 : 4)	3,500		
To Deficiency A/c	1,500		
	10,000		10,000

Dr. **SUNDRY CREDITORS' ACCOUNT** Cr.

Particulars	₹	*Particulars*	₹
To Cash A/c (4/5 of cash available)	14,000	By Balance b/d	20,000
To Deficiency A/c	6,000		
	20,000		20,000

Dr. **CAPITAL ACCOUNTS OF PARTNERS** Cr.

Particulars	*Alfa* ₹	*Beta* ₹	*Gama* ₹	*Particulars*	*Alfa* ₹	*Beta* ₹	*Gama* ₹
To P & L A/c	4,000	4,000	4,000	By Balance b/d	8,000	6,000	1,000
To Realisation A/c	3,700	3,700	3,700	By Cash A/c	600	—	—
To Deficiency	900	—	—	By Deficiency A/c	—	1,700	6,700
	8,600	7,700	7,700		8,600	7,700	7,700

Dr. **DEFICIENCY ACCOUNT** Cr.

Particulars	₹	*Particulars*	₹
To Beta's Capital A/c	1,700	By Loan A/c	1,500
To Gama's Capital A/c	6,700	By Sundry Creditors	6,000

		By Alfa's Capital A/c	900
	8,400		8,400

ILLUSTRATION 15

Following is the Balance Sheet of A,B,C and D who were sharing in the ratio of 3: 3: 2: 2 as at 31st March, 2016, when they decided to dissolve the firm:

Liabilities	₹	*Assets*		₹
Loan from Bank (Secured on Other Tangible Fixed Assets)	50,000	Cash at Bank		27,500
		Trade Debtors	40,000	
Mrs. B's Loan (Secured on Stock)	3,000	*Less:* Provision	(8,500)	31,500
Trade Creditors	30,000	Stock		5,000
A's Loan	30,000	Prepaid Insurance		3,000
A's Capital	60,000	Goodwill		5,000
B's Capital	49,000	Machinery		60,000
General Reserve	20,000	Other Tangible Fixed Assets		50,000
Machinery Replacement Reserve	20,000	B's Drawings		4,000
		C's Capital		48,000
		D's Capital		18,000
		Profit & Loss A/c		10,000
	2,62,000			2,62,000

(a) After preparing the Balance Sheet as at 31st March, it was discovered that purchases amounting to ₹ 10,000 in March, were not recorded in books, though the goods were received during March.

(b) Trade Debtors realized 12.5%. Stock realized 20%, Machinery realised at a loss of 100% on net collection. Other Tangible Fixed Assets realized 84%, Expenses of realisation amounted to ₹ 7,500. Nothing could be recovered from any partner.

Required: Prepare Realisation A/c, Partners' Capital A/cs , Bank A/c, Loan from Bank A/c, Mrs. B's Loan A/c and Trade Creditors A/c.

SOLUTION

Dr. **REALISATION ACCOUNT** *Cr.*

Particulars	₹	*Particulars*	₹
To Assets Transferred:		By Provision for Doubtful Debts	8,500
Stock	5,000	By Machinery Replacement Reserve	20,000
Debtors	40,000	By Bank A/c:	
Prepaid Insurance	3,000	Machinery	
Goodwill	5,000	[40,000 – (100/200 × 40,000)]	20,000
Machinery	60,000	Debtors (₹ 40,000 × 12.5%)	5,000
Other Tangible Fixed Assets	50,000	Stock (₹ 5,000 × 20%)	1,000
To Bank A/c (Expenses)	7,500	Other Tangible Fixed Assets	
		(₹ 50,000 × 84%)	42,000

		By Loss on Realisation t/f to:	
		A's Capital A/c	22,200
		B's Capital A/c	22,200
		C 's Capital A/c	14,800
		D 's Capital A/c	14,800
	1,70,500		1,70,500

Dr. **PARTNERS' CAPITAL ACCOUNTS** Cr.

Particulars	*A*	*B*	*C*	*D*	*Particulars*	*A*	*B*	*C*	*D*
To Balance b/d	—	—	48,000	18,000	By Balance b/d	60,000	49,000	—	—
To Drawings	—	4,000	—	—	By General Reserve	6,000	6,000	4,000	4,000
To P&L A/c (Goods)	3,000	3,000	2,000	2,000	By A's Loan A/c	30,000			
To P&L A/c (Loss)	3,000	3,000	2,000	2,000	By Deficiency A/c			62,800	32,800
To Realisation A/c	22,200	22,200	14,800	14,800					
To Deficiency A/c	67,800	22,800	—	—					
	96,000	55,000	66,800	36,800		96,000	55,000	66,800	36,800

Dr. **BANK ACCOUNT** Cr.

Particulars	₹	*Particulars*	₹
To Balance b/d	27,500	By Realisation A/c (Expenses)	7,500
To Realisation A/c (Assets)	68,000	By Loan from Bank A/c	42,000
		By Mrs B's Loan A/c	1,000
		By Loan from Bank A/c	7,200
		By Mrs B's Loan A/c	1,800
		By Trade Creditors A/c	36,000
	95,500		95,500

Dr. LOAN FROM BANK ACCOUNT Cr.

Particulars	₹	*Particulars*	₹
To Bank A/c (Up to realisable value of Other Tangible Fixed Assets)	42,000	By Balance b/d	50,000
To Bank A/c (45,000 × 8/50)	7,200		
To Deficiency A/c	800		
	50,000		50,000

Dr. LOAN FROM MRS B ACCOUNT Cr.

Particulars	₹	*Particulars*	₹
To Bank A/c (Up to realisable value of Stock)	1,000	By Balance b/d	3,000
To Bank A/c (45,000 × 2/50)	1,800		
To Deficiency A/c	200		
	3,000		3,000

Dr. **TRADE CREDITORS' ACCOUNT** Cr.

Particulars	₹	Particulars	₹
To Bank A/c (45,000 × 40/50)	36,000	By Balance b/d	30,000
To Deficiency A/c	4,000	By P & L A/c (ommited purchases)	10,000
	40,000		40,000

Dr. **DEFICIENCY ACCOUNT** Cr.

Particulars	₹	Particulars	₹
To C's Capital A/c	62,800	By Loan from Bank A/c	800
To D's Capital A/c	32,800	By Loan from Mrs B A/c	200
		By Trade Creditors	4,000
		By A's Capital A/c	67,800
		By B's Capital A/c	22,800
	95,600		95,600

Working Notes:

1. Total Trade Creditors = 30,000 + 10,000 (Ommited Purchases) = 40,000
2. Book Value of Machinery = Machinery – Machinery Replacement Reserve
   = 60,000 – 20,000 = 40,000

PRACTICAL GUIDELINES WHEN CREDITORS ARE TRANSFERRED TO REALISATION A/C

Where loss on realisation is to be determined after considering the amount ultimately paid to creditors, all partners are insolvent and a partner can bring only a proportion of what is due from him, the solution can be obtained with the help of algebraic equation since two inter-dependent figures (i.e. amount to be brought in by a partner and total amount due from that partner) are missing. The following practical guidelines are suggested to follow in this case:

Step 1: *Treat the amount to be brought in by that partner be 'X '.*

Step 2: *Prepare 'Cash & Bank Account' after considering 'X ' as a receipt on its debit side to ascertain the amount available for all outside creditors.*

Step 3: *Prepare Realisation Account to ascertain the share of loss on realisation of that partner.*

Step 4: *Prepare the Capital Account of that partner to ascertain total amount due from him.*

Step 5: *Form the algebraic equation and solve it for value of X.*

Step 6: *Prepare Cash and Bank Account to ascertain the cash available for creditors.*

Step 7: *Prepare Realisation Account in the usual manner and transfer its profit/loss to the capital accounts of all partners in the profit sharing ratio.*

Step 8: *Prepare Partners' Capital Accounts in the usual manner.*

Example: "Suppose 'C' can bring only 50% of what is due from him and total amount due from him comes to 10,000 + 5x/10

X = 50% of (10,000 + 5x/10) = 5,000 + 5x/20

20X = 1,00,000 + 5X → X = 1,00,000/15 = ₹ 6666.67

ILLUSTRATION 16

A, B and C were in partnership sharing profits and losses in the ratio of 2:3:5. They prepared the following balance sheet as at 31st March 2016, when they decided to dissolve:

Liabilities	₹	*Assets*	₹
Loan from Bank (against the security of Plant and Machinery)	3,00,000	Plant and Machinery	5,00,000
		Debtors	50,000
Loan from C	40,000	Stock	50,000
Trade Creditors	2,50,000	Advance to A	40,000
Bills Payable	10,000	Cash	10,000
Capitals:		Profit and Loss A/c	
A	60,000	(Dr. Balance)	1,50,000
B	80,000		
C	60,000		
	8,00,000		8,00,000

Plant and Machinery realised 70%; Debtors 40% *less* and Stock, 80%. A has a private estate, valued at ₹ 1,00,000 and his liabilities amounted to ₹ 40,000. The private estate realised only ₹ 60,000, B is insolvent. C can pay only 50 paise in the rupee of what is payable on his own account to the firm.

Required: Prepare the necessary ledger accounts, assuming that the loss on realisation is to be determined after considering the amount ultimately paid to the creditors.

SOLUTION

Dr. **REALISATION ACCOUNT** *Cr.*

Particulars		₹	*Particulars*		₹
To Cash A/c			By Loan from Bank		3,00,000
To Plant and Machinery		5,00,000	By Trade Creditors		2,50,000
To Debtors		50,000	By Bills Payable A/c		10,000
To Stock		50,000	By Cash A/c:		
To Cash A/c:			Plant and Machinery	3,50,000	
Bank Loan	3,00,000		Debtors	30,000	
Creditors & Bills Payable	1,56,667	4,56,667	Stock	40,000	4,20,000
			By Loss on realisation t/f to:		
			A's Capital A/c		15,333
			B's Capital A/c		23,000
			C's Capital A/c		38,334
		10,56,667			10,56,667

Dr. **CAPITAL ACCOUNTS OF PARTNERS** *Cr.*

Particulars	*A* ₹	*B* ₹	*C* ₹	*Particulars*	*A* ₹	*B* ₹	*C* ₹
To Realisation A/c	15,333	23,000	38,334	By Balance b/d	60,000	80,000	60,000
To P and L A/c	30,000	45,000	75,000	By C 's Loan A/c	—	—	40,000

To A's Advance	40,000	—	—	By Cash A/c	20,000	—	6,667
To A's Capital	—	5,333		By B's Capital A/c	5,333		6,667
To C's Capital	—	6,667	—				
	85,333	80,000	1,13,334		85,333	80,000	1,13,334

Dr. **CASH ACCOUNT** Cr.

Particulars	₹	*Particulars*		₹
To Balance b/d	10,000	By Realisation A/c:		
To Realisation A/c (Assets realised)	4,20,000	Bank Loan	3,00,000	
To A's Capital A/c	20,000	Other Liabilities	1,56,667	4,56,667
To C's Capital A/c	6,667			
	4,56,667			4,56,667

Working Notes:

Let the amount to be brought in by C be x.

Dr. **(I) MEMORANDUM CASH ACCOUNT** Cr.

Particulars	₹	*Particulars*	₹
To Balance b/d	10,000	By Realisation A/c (Bank Loan)	3,00,000
To Realisation A/c (Assets)	4,20,000	By Realisation A/c (Creditors)	1,50,000 + X
To A	20,000		
To C	X		
	4,50,000 + X		4,50,000 + X

Dr. **(II) MEMORANDUM REALISATION ACCOUNT** Cr.

Particulars	₹	*Particulars*	₹
To Sundry Assets	6,00,000	By Sundry Liabilities	5,60,000
To Cash (Bank Loan)	3,00,000	By Cash (Assets)	4,20,000
To Cash (Creditors)	1,50,000 + X	By Loss: A	14,000 + 2X/10
		B	21,000 + 3X/10
		C	35,000 + 5X/10
	10,50,000 + X		10,50,000 + 5X/10

Dr. **(III) C'S CAPITAL ACCOUNT** Cr.

Particulars	₹	*Particulars*	₹
To Realisation A/c (loss)	35,000 + 5X/10	By Balance b/d	60,000
To P & L A/c	75,000	By C's Loan A/c	40,000
		By Finally due	10,000 + 5X/10
	1,10,000 + 5X/10		1,10,000 + 5X/10

Thus, X = 50% of (₹ 10,000 + 5X/10) = 5,000 + 5X/20 or,
20X = 1,00,000 + 5X, *or* 15X = ₹ 1,00,000 *or* X = ₹ 6,667.

ILLUSTRATION 17

A, B and C had the following Balance Sheet as at 31st March, 2016

Liabilities	₹	*Assets*	₹
Trade Creditors	40,000	Fixed Assets	40,000
Loan from Mrs A		Debtors	24,000
(with a charge on Stock)	15,000	Stock	20,000
Loan from A	10,000	Cash at Bank	1,000
Capital Accounts:		Profit and Loss A/c	30,000
A	20,000		
B	20,000		
C	10,000		
	1,15,000		1,15,000

The firm was dissolved. Stock realised 50% and fixed assets and debtors realised ₹ 30,000 in all. The private position of the partners was as under:

Particulars	*Private Estate* ₹	*Private Liabilities* ₹
A	10,000	15,000
B	8,000	6,000

C was able to pay 50 paise in the rupee of what was payable on his own account to the partnership. The partners shared profits and losses in the ratio of 4 : 3 : 3 for A, B and C respectively. The loss on realisation is to be determined after considering the amount finally paid to the creditors. You are required to close the books of the firm by preparing the necessary ledger accounts.

SOLUTION

Dr. **REALISATION ACCOUNT** *Cr.*

Particulars	₹	*Particulars*		₹
To Fixed Assets A/c	40,000	By Creditors A/c		40,000
To Debtors A/c	24,000	By Loan from Mrs A A/c		15.000
To Stock A/c	20,000	By Bank A/c—Sale of assets		
To Bank A/c (Mrs A's Loan)	10,000	(30,000 + 10,000)		40,000
To Bank A/c (Mrs A's Loan		By Loss on Realisation t/f to:		
and Trade Creditors)	38,059	A 's Capital A/c	14,823	
		B 's Capital A/c	11,118	
		C 's Capital A/c	11,118	37,059
	1,32,059			1,32,059

Dr. **CASH AT BANK ACCOUNT** *Cr.*

Particulars	₹	*Particulars*	₹
To Balance b/d	1,000	By Realisation A/c	10,000
To Realisation A/c	40,000	By Realisation A/c	38,059
To B's Capital A/c	2,000		

To C's Capital A/c	5,059		
	48,059		48,059

Dr. **CAPITAL ACCOUNTS OF PARTNERS** Cr.

Particulars	A ₹	B ₹	C ₹	Particulars	A ₹	B ₹	C ₹
To Realisation A/c	14,823	11,118	11,118	By Balance b/d	20,000	20,000	10,000
To Pand L A/c	12,000	9,000	9,000	By A's Loan	10,000	—	—
To C's Capital A/c	3,177	1,882	—	By Bank A/c	—	2,000	5,059
				By A's Capital	—	—	3,177
				By B's capital	—	—	1,882
	30,000	22,000	20,118		30,000	22,000	20,118

Working Note: *Calculation of the amount to be brought in by C.*

Let the amount to be brought in by C be X.

Dr. **(I) MEMORANDUM CASH AT BANK ACCOUNT** Cr.

Particulars	₹	Particulars	₹
To Balance b/d	1,000	By Realisation A/c	
To Realisation A/c (Assets)	40,000	(Mrs A's Loan)	10,000
To B's Capital A/c	2,000	By Realisation A/c	
To C's Capital A/c	X	(Loan from Mrs A	
		and Trade Creditors)	33,000 + X
	43,000 + X		43,000 + X

Dr. **(II) MEMORANDUM REALISATION ACCOUNT** Cr.

Particulars	₹	Particulars	₹
To Sundry Assets	84,000	By Sundry Liabilities	55,000
To Bank A/c (Mrs A's Loan)	10,000	By Bank A/c (Assets)	40,000
To Bank A/c (Mrs A's Loan		By Loss on Realisation t/f to:	
& Trade Creditors)	33,000 + X	A's Capital A/c	12,800 + 4X/10
		B's Capital A/c	9,600 + 3X/10
		C's Capital A/c	9,600 + 3X/10
	1,27,000 + X		1,27,000 + X

Dr. **(III) C'S CAPITAL ACCOUNT** Cr.

Particulars	₹	Particulars	₹
To P & L A/c	9,000	By Balance b/d	10,000
To Realisation A/c	9,600 + 3X/10	By Finally due	8,600 + 3X/10
	18,600 + 3X/10		18,600 + 3X/10

Thus, X = 50% of [8,600 + 3X/10] = 4,300 + 3X/20

20X = 86,000 + 3X *or* 17X = 86,000 *or* X = ₹ 5,059.

5.0 PIECEMEAL DISTRIBUTION

The assumption of realisation of all the assets and the payments of all the liabilities as on the date of dissolution is far away from practice. In actual practice the assets are realised gradually and the cash available is applied in following order:

ORDER OF PAYMENT OUT OF ASSETS

Step 1: *First,* ***realisation expenses*** *are paid or provided for.*

Step 2: *Then* ***outside creditors*** *are paid. The point to be noted here is that whenever an asset charged (i.e. an asset provided by way of security to a creditor) is realised the payment is made first to the concerned creditor (i.e., to whom that asset has been provided by way of security). Whenever 'an asset not charged' is realised, payment is made to all the creditors (whether secured or unsecured) in proportion to their respective claims.*

Step 3: *After the payment of all outside liabilities, the* ***partners' loans*** *are discharged in proportion to their respective loans.*

Step 4: *After the payment of all partners' loan but before the partners' capitals are paid off, as a prudent measure, an adequate* ***provision*** *should be made* ***for a contingent liability*** *(if any) (e.g. Discounted Bills Receivable the maturity date of which has not yet fallen due).*

Step 5: ***Lastly, the partners' capitals*** *are paid.*

6.0 BASIS OF DISTRIBUTION OF CASH AMONG PARTNERS TOWARDS THEIR CAPITALS

In case the capitals of partners are in the profit-sharing ratio, distribution of cash can be made in the profit-sharing ratio among the partners. However, in case the capitals of the partners are not in the profit sharing ratio, distribution of cash can be made according to Maximum Loss Method *or* Proportionate Capital Method.

MAXIMUM LOSS METHOD

The basic presumption of this method at every state of realisation is that there will be no further realisation of assets. The practical steps to be followed are given below:

PRACTICAL STEPS IN CASE OF MAXIMUM LOSS METHOD

Step 1: *Calculate the ratio of capitals just before the date of dissolution.*

Step 2: *Calculate the balances of capital accounts of all partners (after making adjustments for accumulated profits/reserves/losses, transfer of balances of current accounts etc.)*

Step 3: *Calculate the Maximum Loss assuming that the remaining assets will realise nothing.*

Note: *Maximum Loss = Total of Balances of capital Accounts less Cash available.*

Step 4: *Distribute the Maximum Loss among the partners in their profit sharing ratio,*

Step 5: *Calculate the balances of capital accounts after distributing the Maximum Loss.*

Step 6: *If no capital account shows a negative balance (i.e., debit balance), distribute the available cash among the partners, exactly equal to their respective capital balances.*

OR

If any capital account shows a negative balance (i.e., debit balance), transfer the same to the capital accounts of other partners (having credit balance), in the ratio of their capitals (as calculated in Step 1) assuming the partner having a negative balance as insolvent and the application of Garner vs Murray ruling. Repeat this process till the negative balance is abolished.

Step 7: *Go to Step 3 on next realisation.*

ILLUSTRATION 18

Following is the Balance Sheet of X, Y and Z who were sharing in the ratio of 2:3:5 as at 31st March, 2016, when they decided to dissolve the firm:

Liabilities	₹	*Assets*	₹
Bank Loan (Secured on Building)	5,00,000	Land Buildings	5,00,000
Mrs X's Loan (Secured on Stock)	3,00,000	Stock	3,00,000
Creditors	2,00,000	Debtors	10,21,000
X's Loan	1,00,000	Cash at Bank	2,00,000
Y's Loan	50,000	Others Assets	31,29,000
X's Capital	18,00,000		
Y's Capital	9,00,000		
Z's Capital	3,00,000		
Reserves	10,00,000		
	51,50,000		51,50,000

Note: There was a bill for ₹ 10,000 due on 15th Aug. under discount.

The assets were realised as follows:

15th April	Stock	₹ 3,20,000	Expenses	₹ 10,000
15th May	Land & Building	₹ 4,10,000	Expenses	₹ 20,000
15th June	Debtors	₹ 2,00,000	Expenses	₹ 10,000
15th July	Debtors	₹ 9,00,000	Expenses	₹ 30,000
15th Aug.	Other Assets	₹ 34,00,000	Expenses	₹ 1,10,000

The Acceptor of the bill under discount met the bill on due date. Prepare a statement showing the distribution of cash.

SOLUTION

STATEMENT SHOWING THE DISTRIBUTION OF CASH TOWARDS FIRMS' THIRD PARTIES' DEBTS AND PARTNERS' LOANS

Particulars		*Total* ₹	*Bank Loan (secured on building)* ₹	*Mrs X's Loan (Secured on stock*	*Creditors* ₹	*X's Loan* ₹	*Y's Loan* ₹
A.	Balance Due	11,50,000	5,00,000	3,00,000	2,00,000	1,00,000	50,000
B.	Amount Paid on 1st April	(2,00,000)	(1,00,000)	(60,000)	(40,000)	—	—
C.	Balance Due [A – B]	9,50,000	4,00,000	2,40,000	1,60,000	1,00,000	50,000
D.	Amount paid on 15th April						
	First ₹ 2,40,000	(2,40,000)	—	(2,40,000)	—	—	—
	Balance ₹ 70,000	(70,000)	(50,000)	—	(20,000)	—	—
E.	Balance Due [C – D]	6,40,000	3,50,000	—	1,40,000	1,00,000	50,000
F.	Amount paid on 15th May						
	First ₹ 3,50,000	(3,50,000)	(3,50,000)	—	—	—	—
	Balance ₹ 40,000	(40,000)	—	—	(40,000)	—	—

G. Balance Due [E – F]	2,50,000	—	—	1,00,000	1,00,000	50,000
H. Amount paid on 15th June						
First ₹ 1,00,000	(1,00,000)	—	—	1,00,000	—	—
Balance ₹ 90,000	(90,000)	—	—	—	(60,000)	(30,000)
I. Balance Due [G – H]	60,000	—	—	—	40,000	20,000
J. Amount paid on 15th July	—	—	—	—	40,000	20,000
K. Balance Due [I – J]	Nil	Nil	Nil	Nil	Nil	Nil

STATEMENT SHOWING THE DISTRIBUTION OF CASH AMONG THE PARTNERS

Particulars	*Total (₹)*	*X (₹)*	*Y (₹)*	*Z (₹)*
A. Balance Due [including partners]	40,00,000	20,00,000	12,00,000	8,00,000
B. *Less:* Maximum Loss (₹ 40,00,000 — ₹ 8,00,000)	32,00,000	(6,40,000)	(9,60,000)	(16,00,000)
		13,60,000	2,40,000	(8,00,000)
C. Deficiency of Z Charged to X and Y in 20:12		(5,00,000)	(3,00,000)	8,00,000
		8,60,000	(60,000)	—
D. Deficiency of Y charged to X		(60,000)	60,000	—
E. Cash paid on 15th July	8,00,000	8,00,000	—	—
F. Balance Due (A–D)	32,00,000	12,00,000	12,00,000	8,00,000
G. *Add:* Profit on Realisation				
[₹ 34,00,000 – ₹ 1,10,000 + ₹ 10,000 – ₹ 32,00,000]	1,00,000	20,000	30,000	50,000
H. Cash paid	33,00,000	12,20,000	12,30,000	8,50,000
I. Balance Due	Nil	Nil	Nil	Nil

ILLUSTRATION 19

The following is the Balance Sheet of A, B and C, who were sharing in the ratio of 5 : 3 : 2, on 31st December, 2015 when they decided to dissolve the partnership.

Liabilities	₹	*Assets*	₹
A's Capital	50,000	Cash	20,000
B's Capital	34,500	Machinery	2,00,000
C's Capital	29,500	Other assets	11,04,000
B's Loan	2,00,000	Miscellaneous Expenditure	10,000
General Reserve	20,000		
Creditors	8,00,000		
Bank loan (secured on machinery)	2,00,000		
	13,34,000		13,34,000

Note: There was a bill for ₹ 4,000 due on 1.4.2014 under discount.

Assets realised as under: 1st Jan.: Other assets ₹ 6,85,000, on 20th Jan. machineries ₹ 1,00,000, 1st Feb. Other assets: ₹ 4,00,000; 1st March: ₹ 8,000; 1st April: ₹ 5,000; 1st May: ₹ 10,000. The expenses of realisation were expected to be ₹ 5,000, but ultimately amounted to ₹ 4,000 only and were paid on 1st May. The acceptor of the bill under discount met the bill on the due date.

Required: Prepare a statement showing the monthly distribution of cash according to Maximum Loss Method.

SOLUTION

STATEMENT SHOWING THE DISTRIBUTION OF CASH TOWARDS FIRM'S OUTSIDE DEBTS AND PARTNER'S LOAN

Particulars	*Bank Loan* ₹	*Creditors* ₹	*B's Loan* ₹
A. Amount Due	2,00,000	8,00,000	2,00,000
B. Amount paid on 1st Jan. (₹ 20,000 + ₹ 6,85,000 – ₹ 5,000)	(1,40,000)	(5,60,000)	—
C. Balance Due (A – B)	60,000	2,40,000	2,00,000
D. Amount paid on 20th Jan.	(60,000)	(40,000)	—
E. Balance Due (C – D)	—	2,00,000	2,00,000
F. Amount paid on 1st Feb.	—	(2,00,000)	(2,00,000)

DISTRIBUTION OF CASH AMONG PARTNERS (ACCORDING TO MAXIMUM LOSS METHOD)

Particulars	*Total (₹)*	*A (₹)*	*B (₹)*	*C (₹)*
(i) *Distribution of ₹ 4,000*				
A. Amount due (including Reserves but excluding Misc. Exp.) as on 1st March	1,24,000	55,000	37,500	31,500
Less: Max. Possible Loss if the remaining assets fetch nothing (₹ 1,24,000 – ₹ 4,000) in the ratio of 5 : 3 : 2	1,20,000	60,000	36,000	24,000
Note: *Cash available = ₹ 8,000 – ₹ 4,000 (Reserved for discounted B/R) = ₹ 4,000*	4,000	(5,000)	1,500	7,500
Adjustment of A's Deficiency between B and C in their Capital ratio i.e. 375 : 315		5,000	(2,717)	(2,283)
		(1,217)	5,217	
Adjustment of B's Deficiency (charged to C)		—	1,217	(1,217)
B. Cash paid as on 1st March	4,000	—	—	4,000
(ii) *Distribution of ₹ 9,000 (including Amount kept reserved for B/R no longer required)*				
C. Balance due (A – B)	1,20,000	55,000	37,500	27,500
Less: Max. Possible Loss (₹ 1,20,000 – ₹ 9,000)	1,11,000	55,500	33,300	22,200
Note: *Cash available = ₹ 5,000 + ₹ 4,000 = ₹ 9,000*		(500)	4,200	5,300
Adjustment of A's Deficiency between B and C in their Capital ratio i.e. 375 : 315		500	(272)	(228)
D. Cash paid as on 1.4.96	9,000	—	3,928	5,072
(iii) *Distribution of ₹ 11,000*				
E. Balance due (C – D)	1,11,000	55,000	33,572	22,428
Less: Max. Possible Loss (₹ 1,11,000 – ₹ 11,000)	1,00,000	50,000	30,000	20,000
F. Cash paid as on 1st May	11,000	5,000	3,572	2,428
G. Unpaid Balance (E – F)	1,00,000	50,000	30,000	20,000

WHEN A PARTNER DESIRES TO TAKE OVER A PARTICULAR ASSET OF THE FIRM

Assuming that the remaining assets will realise nothing, the following steps are suggested to deal with this situation:

PRACTICAL STEPS WHEN A PARTNER DESIRES TO TAKE A PARTICULAR ASSET

Step 1: *Calculate maximum loss after taking into consideration the agreed value of the asset at which a partner is taking over that asset.*

Step 2: *Calculate the balance payable to each partner after distributing the maximum loss.*

Step 3: *If the agreed value of the asset taken over by a partner is equal to or less than the balance payable to this partner (after distributing maximum loss) then hand over the asset to the concerned partner and pay the balance (if any) in cash, or If the agreed value of the asset taken over by a partner is more than the balance payable to this partner (after distributing maximum loss) them ask that partner to bring in cash equal to the excess of agreed value of the asset over balance payable to this partner.*

Step 4: *Hand over the asset to the concerned partner and Distribute the cash available among other partners according to their entitlements as per Step 2.*

ILLUSTRATION 20

Sharad, Adesh, Rama and Ajay were partners in a firm. The capital of the firm consisted of ₹ 40,000 contributed originally in the proportion of 4 : 3 : 2 : 1. The profits and losses were shared in the same proportion. The firm was dissolved on 31st March, 2016. The Balance Sheet as on that date was as under:

Liabilities	₹	*Assets*	₹
Capitals:		Cash	6,000
Sharad	20,000	Debtors	50,000
Adesh	14,000	Stock	19,000
Rama	10,500		
Ajay	2,500		
Loans:			
Sharad	5,000		
Rama	8,000		
Creditors	15,000		
	75,000		75,000

It was decided on 15th April that the net realisations should be distributed on the first of each month in the appropriate order. The realisation and expenses at the end of each month were as under:

Particulars	*Debtors (₹)*	*Stock (₹)*	*Expenses (₹)*
April	15,000	7,000	500
May	8,500	5,000	1,000
June	11,000	Nil	250
July	5,500	4,000	150
August	7,000	2,500	100

The stock was completely disposed off. It was further agreed that Adesh should take over the remaining debts for ₹ 2,500.

Required: Show how the cash was distributed according to Maximum Loss Method.

SOLUTION

STATEMENT SHOWING THE DISTRIBUTION OF CASH (ACCORDING TO MAXIMUM LOSS METHOD)

	Particulars	*Creditors* ₹	*S's Loan* ₹	*R's Loan* ₹	*Sharad* ₹	*Adesh* ₹	*Rama* ₹	*Ajay* ₹
A.	Balances Due	15,000	5,000	8,000	20,000	14,000	10,500	2,500
B.	Cash balance ₹ 6,000 paid to creditors	6,000	—	—	—	—	—	—
C.	Balances Due [A – B]	9,000	5,000	8,000	20,000	14,000	10,500	2,500
D.	Paid to Creditors & S & R on 1st May	9,000	4,808	7,692	—	—	—	—
E.	Balances unpaid [C – D]		192	308	20,000	14,000	10,500	2,500
F.	First ₹ 500 out of Net Collection to B & R on 1st June		192	308	—	—	—	—
G.	Balance Unpaid				20,000	14,000	10,500	2,500
	Max Loss distributed [₹ 47,000 – ₹ 12,000]				(14,000)	(10,500)	(7,000)	(3,500)
					6,000	3,500	3,500	(1,000)
	Ajay's deficiency charged to other Partners				(450)	(315)	(235)	1,000
H.	Amount paid on 1st June				5,550	3,185	3,265	Nil
I.	Balance unpaid [G – H]				14,450	10,815	7,235	2,500
	Max Loss distributed [₹ 35,000 – ₹ 10,750]				(9,700)	(7,275)	(4,850)	(2,425)
J.	Amount paid on 1st July				4,750	3,540	2,385	75
K.	Balance Unpaid [I – J]				9,700	7,275	4,850	2,425
	Max. Loss distributed [₹ 24,250 – ₹ 9,350]				(5,960)	(4,470)	(2,980)	(1,490)
L.	Amount paid on 1st Aug.				3,740	2,805	1,870	935
M.	Balances unpaid [J – K]				5,960	4,470	2,980	1,490
N.	Max Loss distributed [₹ 14,900 – ₹ 9,400 – ₹ 2,500]				(1,200)	(900)	(600)	(300)
O.	Balances payable				4,760	3,570	2,380	1,190
P.	Cash paid on 1st Sept.				(4,760)	(1,070)	(2,380)	(1,190)
Q.	Book debts taken over on 1st Sept.				—	(2,500)	—	—
R.	Balances unpaid being loss on realisation				1,200	900	600	300

ILLUSTRATION 21

P, Q and R were partners in a firm, sharing profits and losses in the ratio of 3 : 2 : 1, respectively. Due to extreme competition, it was decided to dissolve the partnership on 31st December, 2015. The Balance Sheet on that date was as follows:

Liabilities		₹	*Assets*	₹
Capital Accounts:			Machinery	1,54,000
P	1,13,100		Furniture	25,800
Q	35,400		Investments	5,400

R	31,500	1,80,000	Stock	97,700
Current Accounts:			Debtors	56,400
P	26,400		Bank	29,700
R	6,000	32,400	Current Account: Q	18,000
Reserves		1,08,000		
Loan Account: R		15,000		
Creditors		51,600		
		3,87,000		3,87,000

The realisation of assets is spread over the next few months as follows:

February, Debtors, ₹ 51,900; March, Machinery, ₹ 1,39,500; April, Furniture, ₹ 18,000; May, R agreed to take over Investments at ₹ 6,300; June, Stock, ₹ 96,000.

Dissolution expenses, originally provided, were ₹ 13,500, but actually amounted to ₹ 9,600 and were paid on 30th April. The partners decided that after creditors were settled for ₹ 50,400, all cash received should be distributed at the end of each month in the most equitable manner.

Required: Prepare a statement of actual cash distribution as is received following "Maximum Loss basis".

SOLUTION

STATEMENT SHOWING THE DISTRIBUTION OF CASH (ACCORDING TO MAXIMUM LOSS METHOD)

	Particulars	Creditors	R's Loan	Capital Accounts			
				P	Q	R	Total
		₹	₹	₹	₹	₹	₹
A.	Balance due	51,600	15,000	1,93,500	53,400	55,500	3,02,400
B.	Paid to Creditors out of Bank (₹ 29,200 – ₹ 13,500)	(16,200)	—	—	—	—	—
	Paid to creditors & R on 28th Feb.	(34,200)	(15,000)				
C.	Balance due (A – B)			1,93,500	53,400	55,500	3,02,400
	Max. Possible Loss if remaining assets fetch nothing (₹3,02,400 – ₹2,700) in the ratio of 3:2:1			1,49,850	99,900	49,950	2,99,700
				43,650	– 46,500	5,550	
	Adjustment of Q 's Deficiency between P & R in the ratio of their fixed capitals i.e. 1,13,100 : 31,500			– 36,370	+46,500	–10,130	
	Balance			7,280	—	– 4,580	
	Adjustment of R 's Deficiency (charged to P)			– 4,580		+4,580	
D.	Cash paid to P on 29th Feb.			2,700	—	—	2,700
E.	Balance due (C – D)			1,90,800	53,400	55,500	2,99,700
	Possible Max. Loss (₹ 2,99,700 – ₹ 1,39,500)			80,100	53,400	26,700	1,60,200
F.	Cash paid on 31st Mar.			1,10,700	–	28,800	1,39,500
G.	Balance Due (E – F)			80,100	53,400	26,700	1,60,200
	Possible Max. Loss (₹ 1,60,200 – ₹ 21,900)			69,150	46,100	23,050	1,38,300
H.	Cash paid on 30th April			10,950	7,300	3,650	21,900
I.	Balance Due (G – H)			69,150	46,100	23,050	1,38,300
J.	Maximum Loss (₹ 1,38,300 – ₹ 6,300)			66,000	44,000	22,000	1,32,000

				3,150	2,100	1,050	6,300
K.	Cash brought in by R [6,300 – 1050]			—	—	5,250	5,250
L.	Cash Paid to P&Q			(3,150)	(2,100)		(5,250)
M.	Investment given to R			—	—	(6,300)	6,300
N.	Balance Due (I + K – L – M)			66,000	44,000	22,000	1,32,000
	Possible Max. Loss (₹ 1,32,000 – ₹ 96,000)			18,000	12,000	6,000	36,000
O.	Cash paid on 30th June			48,000	32,000	16,000	96,000
P.	Unpaid Balance (N – O)			18,000	12,000	6,000	36,000

Working Note:

STATEMENT SHOWING THE CALCULATION OF CASH AVAILABLE FOR DISTRIBUTION

	Particulars	*February* ₹	*March* ₹	*April* ₹	*May* ₹	*June* ₹
A.	Opening Balance	29,700	—	—	—	—
B.	*Add:* Net Amount realised	51,900	1,39,500	18,000	—	96,000
C.	*Less:* Provision for Expenses	13,500	—	—	—	—
D.	*Add:* Provision no longer required	—	—	3,900	—	—
E.	Cash available for distribution (A + B – C + D)	68,100	1,39,500	21,900	—	96,000

PROPORTIONATE CAPITAL METHOD

The basic presumption of this method is that a partner who has contributed more than his proportionate share of capital, should be paid first to the extent of his excess capital over and above the proportionate capital. The practical steps to be followed in determining to whom and to what extent the payment should be made are given below:

PRACTICAL STEPS IN CASE OF PROPORTIONATE CAPITAL METHOD

Step 1: *Calculate the actual capitals of all partners (after making adjustments for accumulated profits/reserves/losses and transfer of balances of current accounts etc.).*

Step 2: *Divide the Actual Capitals of the partners by their profit sharing ratio respectively and treat the smallest quotient as Base Capital.*

Step 3: *Calculate the Proportionate Capitals by multiplying Base Capital and profit sharing ratio.*

Step 4: *Calculate the Surplus Capital by deducting Proportionate Capital (as per Step 3) from the Actual Capital (as per Step 1).*

Step 5: *If there is only partner having Surplus Capital, make payment of such partner first. If there are two or more partners and their Surplus Capitals are in their profit sharing ratio, distribute the cash among such partners in the ratio of their Surplus Capitals till such Surplus Capitals are paid off.*

OR

If the Surplus Capitals of the partners are not in their profit sharing ratio, go to Step 6.

Step 6: *Divide the Surplus Capital (as per Step 4) by profit sharing ratio and treat the smallest quotient as Revised Base Capital.*

Step 7: *Calculate the Revised Proportionate Capitals by multiplying Revised Base Capital (as per Step 6) and profit sharing ratio.*

Step 8: *Calculate the Revised Surplus Capital by deducting Revised proportionate Capital (as per Step 7) from the Surplus Capital (as per Step 6).*

Step 9: *Go to Step 5 i.e., Repeat this process until the number of partners (having excess capital) reduces to one.*

TUTORIAL NOTES

(i) As adequate amount should be kept in reserve for estimated realisation expenses. When it becomes certain that such reserve is no longer required, the amount so kept as a reserve but not utilized, should be utilized for distribution.

(ii) An adequate amount should be kept in reserve for liabilities that may arise in future (e.g., for Bills Receivable already discounted) before any payment is made to partners.

(iii) In case an asset of the firm is purchased by any partner, an agreed value of such asset should be distributed among all partners (including the partner who has purchased the asset).

(iv) In case the profit sharing ratio is different from the loss sharing ratio (e.g., where a minor has been admitted as a partner) Maximum Loss Method should be used.

(v) In case, the capitals are in profit sharing ratio, distribute the cash among the partners in their profit sharing ratio.

(vi) The amounts finally left unpaid (i.e., the loss to be borne by the partners) should be in the profit sharing ratio and should be same under Maximum Loss Method and Proportionate Capital Method.

ILLUSTRATION 22

Taking the same information as given in Illustration 12 prepare a Statement showing the Distribution of Cash according to proportionate Capital Method.

SOLUTION

STATEMENT SHOWING THE DISTRIBUTION OF CASH AMONG PARTNERS (ACCORDING TO PROPORTIONATE CAPITAL METHOD)

Particulars	*Total* ₹	*A* ₹	*B* ₹	*C* ₹
A. Amount due	1,24,000	55,000	37,500	31,500
B. Amount distributed as on 1st March	(4,000)	—	—	(4,000)
C. Balance due (A – B)	1,20,000	55,000	37,500	27,500
D. Amount distributed as on 1st April				
First ₹ 2,500	(2,500)	—	—	(2,500)
Balance ₹ 6,500 (between B & C in ratio of 3 : 2)	(6,500)	—	(3,900)	(2,600)
E. Balance Due (C – D)	1,11,000	55,000	33,600	22,400
F. Amount distributed as on 1st May				
First ₹ 1,000 (between B & C in the ratio of 3 : 2)	(1,000)	—	(600)	(400)
Balance ₹ 10,000, (amount A, B and C in the ratio of 5 : 3 : 2)	(10,000	(5,000)	(3,000)	(2,000)
G. Unpaid Balance (E – F)	1,00,000	50,000	30,000	20,000

Working Note:

STATEMENT SHOWING THE CALCULATION OF HIGHEST RELATIVE CAPITALS

Particulars	A ₹	B ₹	C ₹
A. Actual Capitals	55,000	37,500	31,500
B. Profit Sharing Ratio	5	3	2
C. Actual Capital/Profit Sharing Ratio	11,000	12,500	15,750
D. Proportionate Capitals Taking A's Capital as Base Capital	55,000	33,000	22,000
E. Excess of Actual Capitals over proportionate Capitals (A – D)	—	4,500	9,500
F. Profit Sharing Ratio	—	3	2
G. Surplus Capital/Profit Sharing Ratio	—	1,500	4,750
H. Revised Proportionate Capitals taking B's Surplus Capital as Base Capital	—	4,500	3,000
I. Excess of Surplus Capitals over Revised Proportionate Capitals (E – H)	—	—	6,500

Scheme of Distribution of available cash: First instalment upto ₹ 6,500 will be paid to C. Next instalment upto ₹ 7,500 shall be paid to B and C in the ratio 3 : 2. Balance installments will be paid to A, B and C in the ratio of 5 : 3 : 2.

ILLUSTRATION 23

A partnership firm was dissolved on 30th June, 2016. Its Balance Sheet on the date of dissolution was as follows:

Liabilities	₹	Assets	₹
Capitals:		Cash	5,400
Ram	38,000	Sundry Assets	94,600
Shyam	24,000		
Mohan	18,000		
Loan A/c—Shyam	5,000		
Sundry Creditors	15,000		
	1,00,000		1,00,000

The assets were realised in instalments and the payments were made on the proportionate capital basis. Creditors were paid ₹ 14,500 in full settlement of their account. Expenses of realisation were estimated to be ₹ 2,700 but actual amount spent on this account was ₹ 2,000. This amount was paid on 15th September. Draw up a Memorandum of distribution of Cash, which was realised as follows:

On 5th July	₹ 12,600
On 30th August	₹ 30,000
On 15th September	₹ 40,000

The partners shared profits and losses in the ratio of 2 : 2 : 1. Give working notes.

SOLUTION

STATEMENT SHOWING THE DISTRIBUTION OF CASH (ACCORDING TO PROPORTIONATE CAPITAL METHOD)

Particulars	Creditors ₹	Shyam Loan ₹	Ram ₹	Shyam ₹	Mohan ₹
A. Balance Due	15,000	5,000	38,000	24,000	18,000
B. Cash paid (₹ 5,400 – ₹ 2,700)	2,700	—	—	—	—
C. Balances unpaid	12,300	5,000	38,000	24,000	18,000
D. 1st Instalment of ₹ 12,600	11,800	800	—	—	—
E. Balance unpaid [C – D]	500	4,200	38,000	24,000	18,000
F. *Less:* written-off	500				
G. 2nd instalment of ₹ 30,000		4,200	16,320	2,320	7,160
H. Balances unpaid (E – F – G)			21,680	21,680	10,840
I. 3rd Instalment (₹ 40,000 + ₹ 700)			16,280	16,280	8,140
J. Unpaid Balance (H – I)			5,400	5,400	2,700

Working Notes:

(I) STATEMENT SHOWING THE CALCULATION OF HIGHEST RELATIVE CAPITALS

Particulars	Ram ₹	Shyam ₹	Mohan ₹
A. Actual Capitals	38,000	24,000	18,000
B. Profit-sharing ratio	2	2	1
C. Actual Capitals/Profit Sharing Ratio	19,000	12,000	18,000
D. Proportionate Capitals taking Shyam's capital as the Base Capital	24,000	24,000	12,000
E. Surplus Capital [A – D]	14,000	Nil	6,000
F. Surplus Capital/Profit Sharing Ratio	7,000	—	6,000
G. Proportionate capitals taking Mohan's Capital as the basis	12,000	—	6,000
H. Revised Surplus Capital (E – G)	2,000	—	—
I. Distribution sequence:			
First ₹ 2,000 (2 : 0 : 0)	2,000	—	
Next ₹ 18,000 (2 : 0 : 1)	12,000		6,000
Balance ₹ 20,000 (2 : 2 : 1)			

(II) DISTRIBUTION OF SECOND INSTALMENT OF ₹ 30,000

Particulars		Ratio	Shyam's Loan	Ram	Shyam	Mohan
First	₹ 4,200		4,200	—	—	—
Next	₹ 2,000	(2 : 0 : 0)		2,000	—	—
Next	₹ 18,000	(2 : 0 : 1)		12,000	—	6,000
Balance	₹ 5,800	(2 : 2 : 1)		2,320	2,320	1,160
Total	₹ 30,000		4,200	16,320	2,320	7,160

ILLUSTRATION 24

The firm of Richpersons presented you with the following Balance Sheet drawn as on 31st March 2016:

Liabilities		₹	*Assets*		₹
Sundry creditors		37,000	Cash in hand		3,000
Capital Accounts:			Sundry debtors		34,000
A	40,000		Stock in trade		39,000
B	30,000		Plant and Machinery		51,000
C	27,000	97,000	Current Accounts:		
			B	4,000	
			C	3,000	7,000
		1,34,000			1,34,000

Partners shared profits and losses in the ratio of 4 : 3 : 3. Due to differences among the partners, it was decided to wind up the firm, realise the assets and distribute cash among the partners at the end of each month.

The following realisations were made:

(i) May — ₹ 15,000 from debtors and ₹ 20,000 by sale of stock. Expenses on realisation were ₹ 500.

(ii) June — Balance of debtors realised ₹ 10,000. Balance of stock fetched ₹ 24,000.

(iii) August — Part of machinery was sold for ₹ 18,000. Expenses incidental to sale were ₹ 600.

(iv) September — Part of machinery valued in the books at ₹ 5,000 was taken by B, in part discharge at an agreed value of ₹ 10,000. Balance of machinery was sold for ₹ 30,000 (net).

Partners decided to keep a minimum cash balance of ₹ 2,000 in the first 3 months and ₹ 1,000 thereafter.

Required: Show how the amounts due to partners will be settled.

SOLUTION

(I) STATEMENT SHOWING THE DISTRIBUTION OF PROCEEDS OF REALISATION (ACCORDING TO PROPORTIONATE CAPITAL METHOD)

Particulars	*Creditors*	*Capitals*		
	₹	*A (₹)*	*B (₹)*	*C (₹)*
A. Amount due	37,000	40,000	26,000	24,000
B. Amount distributed as on 31st May	35,500	—	—	—
C. Balance Due (A – B)	1,500	40,000	26,000	24,000
D. Amount Distributed as on 30th June				
First ₹ 1,500	1,500			
Next ₹ 5,333	—	5,333	—	—
Next ₹ 4,667	—	2,667	2,000	—
Balance ₹ 22,500	—	9,000	6,750	6,750
E. Balance due (C – D)		23,000	17,250	17,250
F. Amount Distributed as on 31st Aug.		7,360	5,520	5,520

G. Balance Due (E – F)		15,640	11,730	11,730
H. *Add:* Profit on realisation (₹ 41,000 – ₹ 39,100)		760	570	570
I. Amount Distributed (including Machinery taken by B) as on 30th Sept.		16,400	12,300*	12,300
*Includes value of Machinery ₹ 10,000 & Cash ₹ 2,300.				

Working Notes:

(i) *Assumption:* As the firm is dissolved due to differences among the partners, all partners are presumed to be solvent and the problem has been worked out on the basis of the highest relative capital.

(II) STATEMENT SHOWING THE CALCULATION OF HIGHEST RELATIVE CAPITALS

Particulars	*A*	*B*	*C*
A. Actual Capitals	40,000	26,000	24,000
B. Profit sharing ratio	4	3	3
C. Actual Capitals / Profit sharing ratio	10,000	8,667	8,000
D. Proportionate Capitals taking C's Capital as Base Capital	32,000	24,000	24,000
E. Surplus Capital of A and B (A – D)	8,000	2,000	—
F. Revised Proportionate Capital of A and B	2,667	2,000	—
G. Revised Surplus Capital of A (E – F)	5,333	—	—

While distributing surplus among partners, 1st instalment up to ₹ 5,333 will be paid to A, next instalment up to ₹ 4,667 will be distributed between A and B in the ratio of 4 : 3 and the Balance among A, B and C in the ratio of 4 : 3 : 3.

(III) STATEMENT SHOWING THE CALCULATION OF CASH AVAILABLE EACH MONTH

Particulars	*May* ₹	*June* ₹	*August* ₹	*September* ₹
A. Opening Balance	3,000	2,000	2,000	1,000
B. *Add:* Amount realised *less* Expenses	34,500	34,000	17,400	30,000
C. *Less:* Closing balance	2,000	2,000	1,000	—
D. Total Cash available for Distribution (A + B – C)	35,500	34,000	18,400	31,000

Dr. **(IV) REALISATION ACCOUNT** *Cr.*

Particulars	₹	*Particulars*	₹
To Sundry Debtors	34,000	By Sundry Creditors	37,000
To Stock in trade	39,000	By Cash/Bank	1,17,000
To Plant and Machinery	51,000	By A (Assets taken over)	10,000
To Cash/Bank:			
Creditors	37,000		
Expenses	1,100		
To Profit transferred to Capital A/c	1,900		
	1,64,000		1,64,000

ILLUSTRATION 25

Following is the Balance Sheet of X, Y and Z who were sharing in the ratio of 2:3:5 as at 31st March 2016, when they decided to dissolve the firm:

Liabilities	₹	*Assets*	₹
X's Capital	18,00,000	Cash at Bank	60,000
Y's Capital	9,00,000	Sundry Assets	39,40,000
Z's Capital	3,00,000		
Reserves	10,00,000		
	40,00,000		40,00,000

Note: There was a bill for ₹ 10,000 due on 15th Aug. under discount.

The sundry assets were realised as follows:

1st April	₹ 7,70,000	Expenses	₹ 10,000
1st June	₹ 12,35,000	Expenses	₹ 40,000
1st July	₹ 7,80,000	Expenses	₹ 20,000
1st July	Z decided to take some sundry assets having book value of ₹ 1,00,000 at ₹ 4,40,000.		
15th Aug.	₹ 9,05,000	Expenses	₹ 20,000

Partners decided to keep a minimum cash balance of ₹ 10,000 in the first two months and ₹ 5,000 thereafter. The acceptor of the bill under discount met the bill on the due date.

Required: Prepare the Statement showing the distribution of cash among the partners according to (a) Maximum Loss Method (b) Proportionate Capital Method.

SOLUTION

(A) STATEMENT SHOWING THE DISTRIBUTION OF CASH AMONG PARTNERS (ACCORDING TO MAXIMUM LOSS METHOD)

Particulars	*Total*	*X (₹)*	*Y (₹)*	*Z (₹)*
A. Capital as on 31st Mar. (including Reserves)	40,00,000	20,00,000	12,00,000	8,00,000
Maximum Loss (₹ 40,00,000 – ₹ 8,00,000)	32,00,000	6,40,000	9,60,000	16,00,000
		13,60,000	2,40,000	(8,00,000)
Deficiency of Z Charged to X, Y in 20:12		(5,00,000)	(3,00,000)	8,00,000
		8,60,000	(60,000)	—
Deficiency of Y charged to X		(60,000)	60,000	—
B. Cash paid on 1st April	8,00,000	8,00,000	—	—
C. Balance Due (A–B)	32,00,000	12,00,000	12,00,000	8,00,000
Maximum Loss (₹ 32,00,000 – ₹ 12,00,000)	20,00,000	4,00,000	6,00,000	10,00,000
		8,00,000	6,00,000	(2,00,000)
Deficiency of Z charged to X and Y (20:12)		(1,25,000)	(75,000)	2,00,000
D. Cash paid on 1st June	12,00,000	6,75,000	5,25,000	—
E. Balance Due (C–D)	20,00,000	5,25,000	6,75,000	8,00,000
Maximum Loss (₹ 20,00,000 – ₹ 7,60,000 – ₹ 4,40,000)	8,00,000	1,60,000	2,40,000	4,00,000
F. Balance Due	12,00,000	3,65,000	4,35,000	4,00,000

G.	Cash brought in by Z (₹ 4,40,000 – ₹ 4,00,000)	40,000			40,000
H.	Cash Paid to X and Y and Asset to Z	(12,40,000)	3,65,000	4,35,000	4,40,000
I.	Balance due	8,00,000	1,60,000	2,40,000	4,00,000
J.	*Add:* Profit on Realisation [₹ 9,05,000 + ₹ 5,000 (cash) – ₹ 10,000 (Exp.) – ₹ 8,00,000]	1,00,000	20,000	30,000	50,000
K.	Cash Paid	9,00,000	1,80,000	2,70,000	4,50,000
L.	Balance Due	Nil	Nil	Nil	Nil

(B) STATEMENT SHOWING THE DISTRIBUTION OF CASH (ACCORDING TO PROPORTIONAL CAPITAL METHOD)

	Particulars	*X*	*Y*	*Z*
A.	Capitals (including Reserves)	20,00,000	12,00,000	8,00,000
B.	Amount distributed as on 1st April	(8,00,000)	—	—
C.	Balance Due	12,00,000	12,00,000	8,00,000
D.	Amount Distributed as on 1st June			
	First ₹ 4,00,000	(4,00,000)	—	—
	Next ₹ 8,00,000	(3,20,000)	(4,80,000)	—
E.	Balance Due	4,80,000	7,20,000	8,00,000
F.	Amount Distributed as on 1st July			
	1st ₹ 4,00,000	(1,60,000)	(2,40,000)	—
	Cash brought in by Z	—	—	40,000
	Balance ₹ 4,00,000 in 2:3	(1,60,000)	(2,40,000)	—
	Asset taken over by Z	—	—	(4,40,000)
G.	Balance Due	1,60,000	2,40,000	4,00,000
H.	*Add:* Profit on Realisation [₹ 9,05,000 + ₹ 5,000 (cash) – ₹ 10,000 (Exp.) – ₹ 8,00,000]	20,000	30,000	50,000
I.	Cash Paid	1,80,000	2,70,000	4,50,000
J.	Balance Due	Nil	Nil	Nil

Working Notes:

(I) STATEMENT SHOWING THE CALCULATION OF HIGHEST RELATIVE CAPITALS

	Particulars	*X*	*Y*	*Z*
A.	Capitals (including Reserves)	20,00,000	12,00,000	8,00,000
B.	Profit Sharing Ratio (PSR)	2	3	5
C.	Actual Capital / PSR	10,00,000	4,00,000	1,60,000
D.	Proportionate Capitals taking Z's capital as base capital	3,20,000	4,80,000	8,00,000
E.	Surplus Capitals (A – D)	16,80,000	7,20,000	—
F.	Profit Sharing Ratio (PSR)	2	3	—
G.	Surplus Capitals / PSR	8,40,000	2,40,000	—
H.	Revised Proportionate Capital Taking Y's capital base capital	4,80,000	7,20,000	—
I.	Revised Surplus Capital (E–H)	12,00,000	—	—

(ii) Scheme of Distribution of Cash: 1st instalment up to ₹ 12,00,000 will be paid to X, next instalment upto ₹ 12,00,000 will be distributed between X and Y in the ratio of 2:3 and the balance among X, Y and Z in the ratio of 2:3:5.

(III) STATEMENT SHOWING THE CALCULATION OF CASH AVAILABLE EACH MONTH

	Particulars	*April (₹)*	*June (₹)*	*July (₹)*	*Aug (₹)*
A.	Opening Balance	60,000	10,000	5,000	5,000
B.	*Add:* Amount realised *less* expenses	7,60,000	11,95,000	7,60,000	8,85,000
C.	*Less:* Amount reserved for discounted B/R	(10,000)	—	—	—
D.	*Less:* Closing Minimum Balance	(10,000)	(5,000)	(5,000)	—
E.	*Add:* Reserved amount released	—	—	—	10,000
F.	Total Cash available for distribution	8,00,000	12,00,000	7,60,000	9,00,000

7.0 SALE OF A FIRM TO A COMPANY

MEANING SALE OF A FIRM TO A COMPANY

When a partnership firm is sold to a Company, it is nothing but dissolution of a firm resulting on account of sale to a Company. Thus, the same accounting procedure is followed for closing the books of the firm as followed for simple dissolution of a firm. The worth noting points are given below:

WORTHNOTING POINTS IN CASE OF SALE OF A FIRM TO A COMPANY

1. All assets and outside liabilities (whether *or* not taken over by the Purchasing Company) should be transferred to the Realisation Account at their respective book values. However, ₹Cash and Bank Account' should not be transferred to the Realisation Account if it is given that the purchasing company is not taking over the ₹Cash and Bank Balances'.
2. On making due the purchase consideration, the Purchasing Company's Account should be debited and Realisation Account should be credited.

   Note: *Practically speaking, the purchase consideration in case of sale of a firm to a company means the aggregate of the shares and other securities issued and the cash payment made by the purchasing Company to the partners of the vendor firm. In examination problems, purchase consideration is calculated as follows:*

Case	*Calculation of Purchase Consideration*
I. When the lump sum figure of purchase consideration is specified	Purchase Consideration = Lump sum figure
II. Where the lump sum figure of purchase consideration is not specified	
(i) *If all the modes of discharging purchase consideration along with their individual figures are specifically given*	(i) Purchase Consideration = Cash + Issue Price of Equity Shares issued (if any) + Issue Price of Preference Shares issued (if any)
(ii) *In other cases*	(ii) Purchase Consideration = Agreed values of acquired assets *less* agreed amounts of undertaken liabilities.

3. On receipt of purchase consideration, Cash Account/Equity Shares in Purchasing Company/ Preference Shares in Purchasing Company, should be debited at their issue prices and the Purchasing Company's Account should be credited.

Note: *A share being an indivisible unit, should be issued in whole number and not in fraction. Unless otherwise stated, the fractional portion of a shares should be valued at market price and should be discharged in cash.*

4. Where the issue price and the current market price of the shares do not coincide, the difference should be transferred to the partners' capital accounts in their profit sharing ratio.
5. In the absence of an agreement as to the division of shares (received from the Purchasing Company) among the partners, such shares should be distributed among the partners in the ratio of their final claims (i.e., in the ratio of capitals standing after making all adjustments like transfer of profit/loss on realisation, accumulated profits/reserves/losses) in accordance with the provisions of Sec. 48 (b) (ii) of The Indian Partnership Act 1932.

Notes:

(i) For the purpose of payment to partners, the shares should be treated as cash equivalent and should be distributed like cash in an ordinary case of dissolution.

(ii) A share being an indivisible unit, should be given in nearest whole number and not in fraction. The necessary adjustment should be made in cash.

ILLUSTRATION 26

X, Y and Z were carrying on business in partnership, sharing profits & losses in the ratio of 2:3:5 respectively. They sold the business to XYZ Ltd. The following is the Balance Sheet of the firm as at 31st March, 2016:

Liabilities	₹	*Assets*	₹
Capital Accounts: X	45,612	Sundry Assets	1,00,000
Y	21,168		
Z	3,780		
Sundry Creditors	29,440		
	1,00,000		1,00,000

The Company took over the firm's business for a total consideration of ₹ 1,05,000. The purchase consideration was to be discharged by a cash payment of ₹ 44,100, the allotment of 2,100 15% Preference Shares of ₹ 10 each (Issued at ₹ 9 each) and the balance by allotment of 2,100 Equity Shares of ₹ 10 each. Realisation Expenses ₹ 10,500, Equity Shares are taken over by the partners at an agreed market value of ₹ 52,500. Prepare Realisation Account, Partners' Capital Accounts, Cash Account, XYZ Ltd's Account, Pref. Shares in XYZ Ltd. Account and Equity Shares in XYZ Ltd. Account in the books of a firm.

SOLUTION

Dr. **1. REALISATION ACCOUNT** *Cr.*

Particulars	₹	*Particulars*	₹
To Sundry Assets	1,00,000	By Sundry Creditors	29,440
To Cash A/c (Realisation Exp.)	10,500	By Equity Shares in XYZ Ltd.	10,500
To Profit on Realisation t/f to:		(52,500 – 42,000)	
X's Capital A/c	6,888	By XYZ Ltd.	1,05,000
Y's Capital A/c	10,332	(Purchase Consideration)	
Z's Capital A/c	17,220		
	1,44,940		1,44,940

Dr. **2. CAPITAL ACCOUNTS OF PARTNERS** Cr.

Particulars	X ₹	Y ₹	Z ₹	Particulars	X ₹	Y ₹	Z ₹
To Balance c/d	52,500	31,500	21,000	By Balance b/d	45,612	21,168	3,780
				By Realisation A/c	6,888	10,332	17,220
	52,500	31,500	21,000		52,500	31,500	21,000
To Equity Shares	26,250	15,750	10,500	By Balance b/d	52,500	31,500	21,000
To 15% Pref. Shares	9,450	5,670	3,780				
To Cash	16,800	10,080	6,720				
	52,500	31,500	21,000		52,500	31,500	21,000

Note: *Unless otherwise agreed, Shares and Cash are distributed in the ratio of final claims [i.e. 52,500 : 31,500 : 21,000 or 5 : 3 : 2].*

Dr. **3. CASH ACCOUNT** Cr.

Particulars	₹	Particulars	₹
To XYZ Ltd.	44,100	By Realisation A/c (Expenses)	10,500
		By X's Capital A/c	16,800
		By Y's Capital A/c	10,080
		By Z's Capital A/c	6,720
	44,100		44,100

Dr. **4. XYZ LTD. ACCOUNT** Cr.

Particulars	₹	Particulars	₹
To Realisation A/c	1,05,000	By Cash A/c	44,100
		By Pref. Shares in XYZ Ltd.	18,900
		By Equity Shares in XYZ Ltd.	42,000
	1,05,000		1,05,000

Dr. **5. PREF. SHARES IN XYZ LTD. ACCOUNT** Cr.

Particulars	₹	Particulars	₹
To XYZ Ltd.	18,900	By X's Capital A/c	9,450
		By Y's Capital A/c	5,670
		By Z's Capital A/c	3,780
	18,900		18,900

Dr. **6. EQUITY SHARES IN XYZ LTD. ACCOUNT** Cr.

Particulars	₹	Particulars	₹
To XYZ Ltd.	42,000	By X's Capital A/c	26,250
To Realisation A/c	10,500	By Y's Capital A/c	15,750
		By Z's Capital A/c	10,500
	52,500		52,500

ILLUSTRATION 27

A and B were partners on 31st March, 2016, their Balance Sheet was as follows:

Liabilities	₹	*Assets*		₹
A's Capital	75,000	Fixed Asset	1,40,000	
B's Capital	35,000	*Less:* Provision for Dep.	45,000	95,000
A's Loan	10,000	Joint Life Policy		6,300
Sundry Creditors	26,800	Stock		27,000
		Debtors		15,000
		Cash		3,500
	1,46,800			1,46,800

On that date, the partners dissolved the firm. Fixed assets were sold to Jupiter Co. Ltd., for ₹ 1,00,000 payable in the form of 10,000 shares of ₹ 10 each. A took over joint life policy at an agreed valuation of ₹ 5,000. Stock and debtors realised ₹ 23,700.

Expenses came to ₹ 300. A and B agreed to distribute shares in Jupiter Co. Ltd., between themselves in the ratio of their final claims. Sundry creditors were paid at book value.

Required: Show the necessary ledger accounts.

SOLUTION

Dr. **REALISATION ACCOUNT** *Cr.*

Particulars	₹	Particulars	₹
To Fixed Assets	1,40,000	By Provision for Depreciation	45,000
To Joint Life Policy	6,300	By Sundry Creditors	26,800
To Stock	27,000	By Jupiter Co. Ltd.	1,00,000
To Debtors	15,000	By A's Capital A/c	
To Cash A/c		(Joint Life Policy)	5,000
(Payment of creditors)	26,800	By Cash A/c	
To Cash A/c (Expenses)	300	(Stock and Debtors)	23,700
		By Loss on Realisation t/f to:	
		A's Capital A/c	7,450
		B's Capital A/c	7,450
	2,15,400		2,15,400

Dr. **JUPITER CO. LTD.** *Cr.*

Particulars	₹	Particulars	₹
To Realisation A/c (Purchase price)	1,00,000	By Shares in Jupiter Co. Ltd.	1,00,000
	1,00,000		1,00,000

Dr. **A'S LOAN ACCOUNT** *Cr.*

Particulars	₹	Particulars	₹
To Cash A/c	100	By Balance b/d	10,000

To Shares in Jupiter Co. Ltd.	9,900		
	10,000		10,000

Dr. **PARTNERS' CAPITAL ACCOUNTS** Cr.

Particulars	*A* ₹	*B* ₹	*Particulars*	*A* ₹	*B* ₹
To Realisation A/c (J.L.P.)	5,000	–	By Balance b/d	75,000	35,000
To Realisation A/c (loss)	7,450	7,450			
To Shares in Jupiter Co. Ltd.	62,550	27,550			
	75,000	35,000		75,000	35,000

Dr. **CASH ACCOUNT** Cr.

Particulars	₹	*Particulars*	₹
To Balance b/d	3,500	By Realisation A/c (Payment of creditors)	26,800
To Realisation A/c (Sale of Current Assets)	23,700	By Realisation A/c (Expenses)	300
		By A's Loan A/c	100
	27,200		27,200

Dr. **SHARES IN JUPITER CO.LTD** Cr.

Particulars	₹	*Particulars*	₹
To Jupiter Co. Ltd.	1,00,000	By A's Loan A/c	9,900
		By A's Capital A/c	62,550
		By B's Capital A/c	27,550
	1,00,000		1,00,000

Notes:

(i) As enough cash is not available, for the balance of A's loan account, shares in Jupiter Co. Ltd. are given.

(ii) There is no need to establish the ratio of final claim, as the only assets available for closing the capital accounts are 'Shares in the Jupiter Co. Ltd.'

ILLUSTRATION 28

Anu and Sonu were in partnership sharing profit and losses in the ratio of 2 : 1. Their summarised Balance Sheet as on 31st March, 2016 was as under:

Liabilities		₹	*Assets*	₹
Capital Accounts:			Fixed Assets (incl. two motor cars for ₹ 28,000)	1,40,000
Anu	1,00,000			
Sonu	80,000	1,80,000	Stock	70,000
Current Accounts:			Debtors	1,00,000
Anu	40,000		Bills Receivable	25,000
Less: Sonu	23,000	17,000	Bank	20,000

Loan from Sonu	63,000	Advertisement Suspense Account	15,000
Creditors for Goods	1,10,000		
	3,70,000		3,70,000

They decided to dissolve the business and accepted the offer of Nanak and Co. Ltd. to acquire stocks and fixed assets excluding two motor cars at a total price of ₹ 3,35,000. The debtors realised ₹ 97,000, and bills receivable, ₹ 24,000. Creditors for goods allowed a discount of 5%. The purchase consideration was to be discharged by a cash payment of ₹ 83,000, the allotment by the company to the partners of 8,000 preference shares of ₹ 10 each (valued at ₹ 9 each) and the balance by the allotment of 9,000 ordinary shares of ₹ 10 each. The partners agreed that following should be the basis of distribution on dissolution of the firm.

(a) Anu to take over one Motor car at a value of ₹ 25,000, and Sonu, the other car at ₹ 15,000.

(b) Sonu to accept preference shares for her loan to the firm, the remainder to be taken over by Anu.

(c) The ordinary shares to be taken over by Anu and Sonu in proportion of their fixed capitals.

(d) The balance to be settled in cash.

Required: Prepare the necessary accounts to close the books of the firm:

SOLUTION

Dr. **REALISATION ACCOUNT** *Cr.*

Particulars		₹	*Particulars*	₹
To Fixed Assets		1,40,000	By Creditors for goods	1,10,000
To Stock		70,000	By Nanak & Co.	3,35,000
To Debtors		1,00,000	By Bank A/c (Debtors)	97,000
To Bills Receivable		25,000	By Bank A/c (B/R)	24,000
To Bank A/c (Creditors)		1,04,500	By Anu's Capital A/c	25,000
To Profit on Realisation t/f to:			By Sonu's Capital A/c	15,000
Anu's Capital A/c	1,11,000			
Sonu's Capital A/c	55,500	1,66,500		
		6,06,000		6,06,000

Dr. **PARTNERS' CAPITAL ACCOUNTS** *Cr.*

Particulars	*Anu* ₹	*Sonu* ₹	*Particulars*	*Anu* ₹	*Sonu* ₹
To Realisation A/c	25,000	15,000	By Balance b/d	1,00,000	80,000
To Equity Shares in Nanak & Co.	1,00,000	80,000	By Current A/c	1,41,000	27,500
To Pref. Shares in Nanak & Co.	9,000	—			
To Bank A/c	1,07,000	12,500			
	2,41,000	1,07,500		2,41,000	1,07,500

Dr. **PARTNERS' CURRENT ACCOUNTS** Cr.

Particulars	Anu ₹	Sonu ₹	Particulars	Anu ₹	Sonu ₹
To Balance b/d	–	23,000	By Balance b/d	40,000	–
To Advt. Suspense A/c	10,000	5,000	By Realisation A/c	1,11,000	55,500
To Capital A/c	1,41,000	27,500			
	1,51,000	55,500		1,51,000	55,500

Dr. **SONU'S LOAN ACCOUNT** Cr.

Particulars	₹	Particulars	₹
To Pref. Shares in Nanak & Co.	63,000	By Balance b/d	63,000
	63,000		63,000

Dr. **BANK ACCOUNT** Cr.

Particulars	₹	Particulars	₹
To Balance b/d	20,000	By Realisation A/c	1,04,500
To Realisation A/c	97,000	By Anu's Capital A/c	1,07,000
To Realisation A/c	24,000	By Sonu's Capital A/c	12,500
To Nanak & Co.	83,000		
	2,24,000		2,24,000

Dr. **NANAK & CO.** Cr.

Particulars	₹	Particulars	₹
To Realisation A/c	3,35,000	By Bank A/c	83,000
		By Pref. Shares in Nanak & Co.	72,000
		By Equity Shares in Nanak & Co.	1,80,000
	3,35,000		3,35,000

Dr. **PREF. SHARES IN NANAK & CO.** Cr.

Particulars	₹	Particulars	₹
To Nanak & Co.	72,000	By Sonu's Loan A/c	63,000
		By Anu's Capital A/c	9,000
	72,000		72,000

Dr. **EQUITY SHARES IN NANAK & CO.** Cr.

Particulars	₹	Particulars	₹
To Nanak & Co.	1,80,000	By Anu's Capital A/c	1,00,000
		By Sonu's Capital A/c	80,000
	1,80,000		1,80,000

ILLUSTRATION 29

The following is the balance sheet as at 31st March, 2016 of Antony, Birdy and Costello carrying on business in partnership sharing profits and losses as 2 : 2 : 1.

Liabilities	₹	*Assets*	₹
Antony's Capital	40,000	Fixed Assets	70,000
Birdy's Capital	25,000	Sundry Debtors	30,000
Mortgage Loan	40,000	Stock	10,000
Reserve	6,000	Cash	5,000
Sundry Creditors	10,000	Costello's Capital A/c	6,000
	1,21,000		1,21,000

They decided to dissolve the partnership and the following arrangements were agreed upon:

(a) Fixed assets included:

(i) Motor car ₹ 5,500 taken over by Birdy at an agreed value of ₹ 9,000 after necessary repairing cost amounting to ₹ 2,000 to be borne by the firm.

(ii) Land and building—₹ 50,000 subject to mortgage loan, taken over by Antony at an agreed value of ₹ 60,000 subject to mortgage loan to be taken over at ₹ 40,000.

(b) Other assets (excluding cash) and creditors are taken over by Eureka Limited in consideration of issue of 5,000 equity shares of ₹ 10 each fully paid. **These shares are taken over at a total agreed value of ₹ 48,000 equally by Antony and Birdy.**

(c) A creditor for ₹ 2,500 not provided for in the books had to be paid.

Required: Prepare the following accounts assuming that the final settlement was made by the partners bringing in the amounts due from, them:

Realisation account, Partners' capital accounts, and Cash account.

SOLUTION

Dr. **REALISATION ACCOUNT** *Cr.*

Particulars	₹	*Particulars*	₹
To Fixed Assets	70,000	By Mortgage Loan	40,000
To Sundry Debtors	30,000	By Sundry Creditors	10,000
To Stock	10,000	By Eureka Ltd	50,000
To Cash A/c (Repairs)	2,000	By Birdy's Capital A/c (Motor car)	9,000
To Antony's Capitals A/c (Loan)	40,000	By Antony's Capital A/c	
To Cash A/c (Sundry creditors)	2,500	(Land and buildings)	60,000
To Shares in Eureka Ltd (Loss)	2,000		
To Profit on Realisation t/f to:			
Antony's Capital A/c	5,000		
Birdy's Capital A/c	5,000		
Costello's Capital A/c	2,500		
	1,69,000		1,69,000

Dr. **PARTNERS' CAPITAL ACCOUNTS** Cr.

Particulars	Antony ₹	Birdy ₹	Costello ₹	Particulars	Antony ₹	Birdy ₹	Costello ₹
To Balance b/d	—	—	6,000	By Balance b/d	40,000	25,000	—
To Realisation A/c	—	9,000	—	By Reserve	2,400	2,400	1,200
To Realisation A/c	60,000	—	—	By Realisation A/c	40,000	—	—
To Shares in				By Realisation A/c	5,000	5,000	2,500
Eureka Ltd. A/c	24,000	24,000	—	By Cash A/c	—	600	2,300
To Cash A/c	3,400	—	—				
	87,400	33,000	6,000		87,400	33,000	6,000

Dr. **CASH ACCOUNT** Cr.

Particulars	₹	Particulars	₹
To Balance b/d	5,000	By Realisation A/c (Repairs)	2,000
To Birdy's Capital A/c	600	By Realisation A/c (Sundry creditors)	2,500
To Costello's Capital A/c	2,300	By Antony's Capital A/c	3,400
	7,900		7,900

Working Notes:

(i) The assets (14,500 + 30,000 + 10,000) and liabilities (₹ 10,000) have been transferred to Eureka Ltd for a purchase consideration of ₹ 50,000 discharged in the form of 5,000 shares of ₹ 10 each. These shares have been taken over by the partners at an agreed value of ₹ 48,000 resulting in a loss of ₹ 2,000. The same is transferred to the Realisation Account. The following accounts will show the accounting treatment.

Dr. **(II) EUREKA LTD ACCOUNT** Cr.

Particulars	₹	Particulars	₹
To Realisation A/c (Purchase price)	50,000	By Shares in Eureka Ltd	50,000
	50,000		50,000

Dr. **(III) SHARES IN EUREKA LTD. ACCOUNT** Cr.

Particulars	₹	Particulars	₹
To Eureka Ltd A/c	50,000	By Antony's Capital A/c	24,000
		By Birdy's Capital A/c	24,000
		By Realisation A/c—Loss	2,000
	50,000		50,000

ILLUSTRATION 30

A, B and C share profits and losses of a business as to 1/2, 1/3 and 1/6 respectively. Their balance sheet as at 31st March, 2016 was as follows:

Liabilities	₹	Assets	₹
Capital Accounts:		Goodwill	10,000
A	70,000	Land	20,000
B	80,000	Buildings	1,10,000

C	10,000	Machinery		50,000
General Reserve	18,000	Motor Car		28,000
Investment Fluctuation Fund	4,000	Furniture		12,000
C's loan	33,000	Investments		18,000
Mrs A's loan	15,000	Loose tools		7,000
Creditors (trade)	76,000	Stock		18,000
Creditors (expenses)	20,000	Bills receivable		20,000
Bills Payable	14,000	Debtors:	40,000	
Bank overdraft	60,000	*Less:* Provision	2,000	38,000
		Cash		1,000
		C's current A/c		56,000
		Profit and loss A/c		12,000
	4,00,000			4,00,000

The partners decide to convert their firm into a Joint Stock Company. For this purpose ABC Ltd. was formed with an authorised captial of ₹ 10,00,000 divided into ₹ 100 equity shares. The business of the firm was sold to the company as at the date of balance sheet given above on the following terms:

(i) Motor car, furniture, investments, loose tools, debtors & cash are not to be taken over by the co.

(ii) Liabilities for bills payable and bank overdraft are to be taken over by the company.

(iii) The purchase price is settled at ₹ 1,95,500 payable as to ₹ 75,500 in cash and the balance in company's fully paid shares of ₹ 100 each.

The remaining assets & liabilities of the firm are directly disposed of by the firm as per details given below:

Investments are taken over by A for ₹ 13,000; debtors realise in all ₹ 20,000; Motor car, furniture and loose tools fetch ₹ 24,000, ₹ 4,000, and ₹ 1,000 respectively. A agrees to pay his wife's loan and the creditors were paid ₹ 74,000 in final settlement of their claims. Creditors for expenses are paid in full. The realisation expenses amount to ₹ 500. The equity shares received from the vendor company are to be divided among the partners in profit-sharing ratio.

Required: Show the necessary ledger accounts.

SOLUTION

Dr. **REALISATION ACCOUNT** *Cr.*

Particulars	₹	*Particulars*		₹
To Goodwill	10,000	By Provision for Doubtful Debts		2,000
To Land	20,000	By Trade creditors		76,000
To Buildings	1,10,000	By Creditors (expenses)		20,000
To Machinery	50,000	By Bills Payable		14,000
To Motor car	28,000	By Bank overdraft		60,000
To Furniture	12,000	By Mrs A's loan		15,000
To Investments	18,000	By ABC Ltd. (Purchase price)		1,95,500
To Loose tools	7,000	By A's Capital A/c (Investments)		13,000
To Stock	18,000	By Cash A/c:		
To Bills receivable	20,000	Debtors	20,000	

To Debtors		40,000	Motor car	24,000	
To A's Capital A/c (Mrs A's loan)		15,000	Furniture	4,000	
To Cash A/c:			Loose tools	1,000	49,000
Creditors	74,000				
C's expenses	20,000				
Realisation Exp.	500	94,500			
To Profit on Realisation t/f to:					
A's Capital A/c	1,000				
B's Capital A/c	667				
C's Capital A/c	333	2,000			
		4,44,500			4,44,500

Dr. **ABC LTD ACCOUNT** Cr.

Particulars	₹	Particulars	₹
To Realisation A/c	1,95,500	By Cash A/c	75,500
		By Shares in ABC Ltd.	1,20,000
	1,95,500		1,95,500

Dr. **PARTNERS' CAPITAL ACCOUNTS** Cr.

Particulars	A (₹)	B (₹)	C (₹)	Particulars	A (₹)	B (₹)	C (₹)
To P & L A/c	6,000	4,000	2,000	By Balance b/d	70,000	80,000	10,000
To Realisation A/c	13,000	—	—	By C's Loan A/c	—	—	33,000
To C's Current A/c	—	—	56,000	By General reserve	9,000	6,000	3,000
To Shares in ABC Ltd.	60,000	40,000	20,000	By Investment Fluctuation Fund	2,000	1,333	667
To Cash A/c	18,000	44,000	—	By Realisation A/c	1,000	667	333
				By Mrs A's loan A/c	15,000	—	—
				By Cash A/c	—	—	31,000
	97,000	88,000	78,000		97,000	88,000	78,000

Dr. **C'S CURRENT ACCOUNT** Cr.

Particulars	₹	Particulars	₹
To Balance b/d	56,000	By C's Capital A/c—transfer	56,000
	56,000		56,000

Dr. **SHARES IN ABC LTD. ACCOUNT** Cr.

Particulars	₹	Particulars	₹
To ABC Ltd Account	1,20,000	By A's Captial A/c	60,000
		By B's Capital A/c	40,000
		By C's Capital A/c	20,000
	1,20,000		1,20,000

Dr. **CASH ACCOUNT** Cr.

Particulars	₹	*Particulars*	₹
To Balance b/d	1,000	By Realisation A/c	
To ABC Ltd.	75,500	(Liabilities and expenses)	94,500
To Realisation A/c (sale of assets)	49,000	By A's Capital A/c	18,000
To C's Capital A/c	31,000	By B's Capital A/c	44,000
	1,56,500		1,56,500

Note: *Investment Fluctuation Fund Account may be transferred to Realisation Account.*

ILLUSTRATION 31

XYZ & Co. is a partnership firm consisting of Mr. X, Mr. Y and Mr. Z who share profits and losses in the ratio of 2:2:1 and ABC Ltd. is a company doing similar business.

Following is the Balance Sheet of the firm and that of the company as at 31.3.2016:

Liabilities	*XYZ & Co.* ₹	*ABC Ltd.* ₹	*Assets*	*XYZ & Co.* ₹	*ABC Ltd.* ₹
Equity Shares of		20,00,000	Plant & Machinery	5,00,000	16,00,000
₹ 10 each			Furniture & Fixture	50,000	2,25,000
Partners Capitals:			Stock in trade	2,00,000	8,50,000
X	2,00,000		Sundry Debtors	2,00,000	8,25,000
Y	3,00,000		Cash in hand	40,000	1,00,000
Z	1,00,000		Cash at bank	10,000	4,00,000
General Reserve	1,00,000	7,00,000			
Sundry Creditors	3,00,000	13,00,000		—	—
	10,00,000	40,00,000		10,00,000	40,00,000

It was decided that the firm XYZ & Co. be dissolved and all the assets (except cash in hand and cash at bank) and all the liabilities of the firm be taken over by ABC Ltd. by issuing 50,000 shares of ₹ 10 each at a premium of ₹ 2 per share.

Partners of XYZ & Co. agreed to divide the shares issued by ABC Ltd. in the profit sharing ratio and bring necessary cash for settlement of their capital.

The creditors of XYZ & Co. includes ₹ 1,00,000 payable to ABC Ltd. An unrecorded liability of ₹ 25,000 of XYZ & Co. must also be taken over by ABC Ltd.

Required:

(i) Prepare Realisation Account, Partners' Capital Accounts and Cash in hand/Bank account in the books of XYZ & Co.

(ii) Pass journal entries in the books of ABC Ltd. for acquisition of XYZ & Co. and draw the Balance Sheet after the takeover.

SOLUTION

Dr. **REALISATION ACCOUNT OF XYZ & CO.** Cr.

Particulars	₹	*Particulars*	₹
To Plant & Machinery	5,00,000	By Sundry Creditors	3,00,000

	₹		₹
To Furniture & Fixture	50,000	By ABC Ltd.	6,00,000
To Stock in trade	2,00,000	By Partners' Capital Accounts (loss):	
To Sundry Debtors	2,00,000	X's Capital A/c	20,000
		Y's Capital A/c	20,000
		Z's Capital A/c	10,000
	9,50,000		9,50,000

Dr. **PARTNERS' CAPITAL ACCOUNTS** Cr.

Particulars	X ₹	Y ₹	Z ₹	Particulars	X ₹	Y ₹	Z ₹
To Realisation A/c	20,000	20,000	10,000	By Balance b/d	2,00,000	3,00,000	1,00,000
To Shares in ABC Ltd.	2,40,000	2,40,000	1,20,000	By General Reserve	40,000	40,000	20,000
To Cash A/c	—	80,000	—	By Cash A/c	20,000	—	10,000
	2,60,000	3,40,000	1,30,000		2,60,000	3,40,000	1,30,000

Dr. **CASH AND BANK ACCOUNT** Cr.

Particulars	₹	₹	Particulars	₹	₹
To Balance b/d	40,000	10,000	By Cash A/c (Contra)*	—	10,000
To Bank A/c (Contra)*	10,000		By Y	80,000	—
To X	20,000				
To Z	10,000				
	80,000	10,000		80,000	10,000

JOURNAL OF ABC LTD.

Date	Particulars		L.F.	Dr. (₹)	Cr. (₹)
1.	Business Purchase A/c	Dr.		6,00,000	
	To XYZ & Co.				6,00,000
	(Being business of XYZ & Co. purchased & payment due)				
2.	Plant and Machinery A/c	Dr.		5,00,000	
	Furniture and Fixture A/c	Dr.		50,000	
	Stock in Trade A/c	Dr.		2,00,000	
	Sundry Debtors A/c	Dr.		2,00,000	
	To Sundry Creditors A/c				3,00,000
	To Unrecorded Liability A/c				25,000
	To Business Purchase A/c				6,00,000
	To Capital Reserve A/c (Bal. Fig.)				25,000
	(Being take over of all assets and liabilities)				
3.	XYZ & Co.	Dr.		6,00,000	
	To Equity Share Capital A/c				5,00,000
	To Securities Premium A/c				1,00,000
	(Being purchase consideration discharged in the form of shares of ₹, 10 each issued at a premium of ₹ 2 each)				

4.	Sundry Creditors A/c	Dr.	1,00,000	
	To Sundry Debtors A/c			1,00,000
	(Being mutual owings eliminated)			

BALANCE SHEET OF ABC LTD. AS AT 31.3.2016

	Particulars	*Note No*	*₹ (lacs)*
I.	**Equity and Liabilities**		
	(1) Shareholders' Funds		
	(a) Share Capital	1	25,00,000
	(b) Reserves and Surplus	2	8,25,000
	(2) Non-Current Liabilities		
	(a) Long-term Borrowings		
	(3) Current Liabilities		
	(a) Trade Payables [Creditors] [3,00,000 + 13,00,000 – 1,00,000]		15,00,000
	(b) Short-term Provisions [Unrecorded Liability]		25,000
	Total		48,50,000
II.	**Assets**		
	(1) Non-Current Assets		
	(a) Fixed Assets		
	Tangible Assets	3	23,75,000
	(2) Current Assets		
	(a) Inventories [2,00,000 + 8,50,000]		10,50,000
	(b) Trade Receivables [2,00,000 + 8,25,000 – 1,00,000]		9,25,000
	(c) Cash and Cash Equivalents [4,00,000 + 1,00,000]		5,00,000
	Total		48,50,000

Notes To Accounts:

	Particulars	*₹ (lacs)*
1.	**Share Capital**	
	2,50,000 Equity Shares of ₹ 10 each	25,00,000
	(Of the above 50,000 Shares were issued for consideration otherwise than cash)	
2.	**Reserves and Surplus**	
	General Reserve	7,00,000
	Capital Reserve	25,000
	Securities Premium	1,00,000
	Total	8,25,000
3.	**Tangible Assets**	
	Plant & Machinery [5,00,000 + 16,00,000]	21,00,000
	Furniture & Fixtures [50,000 + 2,25,000]	2,75,000
	Total	23,75,000

Working Note:

(i) Purchase Consideration = 5000 × ₹ 12 = ₹ 6,00,000

Equity shares distributed among partners:

Partner X [20,000 shares @ ₹ 12]	₹ 2,40,000
Partner Y [20,000 shares @ ₹ 12]	₹ 2,40,000
Partner Z [10,000 shares @ ₹ 12]	₹ 1,20,000
	₹ 6,00,000

(ii) It is assumed that cash at bank has been withdrawn to pay ₹ 80,000 to partner Y. However payment to Y of ₹ 80,000 can also be made by cash ₹ 70,000 & by cheque ₹ 10,000.

ILLUSTRATION 32

X and Y carrying on business in partnership sharing Profit and Losses equally, wished to dissolve the firm and sell the business to 'X' Limited Company on 31.3.2016, when the firm's position was as follows:

Liabilities	₹	*Assets*	₹
X's Capital	1,50,000	Land and Building	1,00,000
Y's Capital	1,00,000	Furniture	40,0n00
Sundry Creditors	60,000	Stock	1,00,000
		Debtors	66,000
		Cash	4,000
	3,10,000		3,10,000

The arrangement with X Limited Company was as follows:

(i) Land and Building was purchased at 20% more than the book value.

(ii) Fumiture and stock were purchased at book values *less* 15%,

(iii) The goodwill of the firm was valued at ₹ 40,000.

(iv) The firm's debtors, cash and creditors were not to be taken over, but the company agreed to collect the book debts of the firm and discharge the creditors of the firm as an agent, for which services, the company was to be paid 5% on all collections from the firm's debtors and 3% on cash paid to firm's creditors.

(v) The purchase price was to be discharged by the company in fully paid equity shares of ₹ 10 each at a premium of ₹ 2 per share.

The company collected all the amounts from debtors. The creditors were paid off *less* by ₹ 1,000 allowed by them as discount. The company paid the balance due to the vendors in cash.

Required: Prepare the Realisation account, the Capital accounts of the partners and the Cash account in the books of partnership firm.

SOLUTION

Dr. **REALISATION ACCOUNT** *Cr.*

Particulars	₹	*Particulars*	₹
To Land & Building	1,00,000	By Sundry Creditors	60,000
To Furniture	40,000	By X Ltd. Co. (Purchase Cons.)	2,79,000
To Stock	1,00,000	By X Ltd. Company	

To Debtors	66,000	Sundry Debtors	66,000	
To X Ltd. Co. (Sundry Creditors)	59,000	*Less:* Commission @ 5% on	3,300	62,700
To X Ltd. Co. (Comm. @ 3% on ₹ 59,000)	1,770			
To Profits transferred to:				
A's Capital A/c	17,465			
B's Capital A/c	17,465			
	4,01,700			4,01,700

Dr. **CAPITAL ACCOUNTS OF PARTNERS** *Cr.*

Particulars	₹	₹	Particulars	₹	₹
To Shares in X Ltd. Co.	1,63,980	1,15,020	By Balance b/d	1,50,000	1,00,000
To Cash (Final Payment)	3,485	2,445	By Realisation A/c (Profit)	17,465	17,465
	1,67,465	1,17,465		1,67,465	1,17,465

Dr. **CASH ACCOUNT** *Cr.*

Particulars	₹	Particulars	₹
To Balance b/d	4,000	By A's Capital A/c (Final Payment)	3,485
To X Ltd. Co. (Amount realized from Debtors *less* amt. paid to creditors)	1,930	By B's Capital A/c (Final Payment)	2,445
	5,930		5,930

Working Notes:

(I) CALCULATION OF PURCHASE CONSIDERATION

Particulars	₹
Land & Building	1,20,000
Furniture	34,000
Stock	85,000
Goodwill	40,000
	2,79,000

(ii) The shares received from the company have been distributed between the two partners A & B in the ratio of their final claims i.e., 1,67,465: 1,17,465*.

No. of shares received from the company = 2,79,000/12 = 23,250

A gets $\frac{23,250 \times 1,67,465}{2,84,930}$ = 13,665 shares valued at 13,665 × 12 = ₹ 1,63,980.

B gets the 2,84,930 remaining 9,585 shares, valued at ₹ 1,15,020 (9,585 × 12)

(iii) *Calculation of net amount received from X Ltd on account of amount realized from debtors less amount paid to creditors.*

	Particulars	₹
A.	Amount realized from Debtors	66,000
B.	*Less:* Commission for realization from debtors (5% on 66,000)	3,300

C.	*Less:* Amount paid to creditors	59,000
D.	*Less:* Commission for cash paid to creditors (3% on 59,000)	1,770
E.	Net amount received	1,930

(iv) In the above situation, shares received from X Ltd. Company have been distributed between two partners A and B in the ratio of their final claims. Alternatively, shares received from X Ltd, can be distributed among the partners in their profit sharing ratio i.e. ₹ 2,79,000 × 1/2 = ₹ 1,39,500 each. In that case, firm will pay cash amounting ₹ 27,965 to A and will receive cash ₹ 22,035 from B.

ILLUSTRATION 33

A and B are carrying on business as equal partners. The firm's Balance Sheet as on 31st March, 2016 was as follows:

Liabilities	₹	*Assets*	₹
Capital Accounts:		Fixed Assets:	2,80,000
A	1,38,000	Current Assets:	
B	1,52,000	Stock	60,000
Bank Loan	40,000	Book Debts	68,000
		Cash at Bank	2,000
Current Liabilities:			
Sundry Creditors	70,000		
Bills Payable	10,000		
	4,10,000		4,10,000

The business was carried on till 30th Sept., 2016. The partners withdrew in equal amounts half the amount of profits made during the period of six months (from April to Sept. 2016) after charging depreciation on Fixed Assets at 10% per annum:

Meanwhile Sundry Creditors were reduced by ₹ 15,000, Bills Payable by ₹ 2,500 and Bank Loan by ₹ 20,000.

On 30th Sept. Stock was valued at ₹ 70,000, Book Debts were ₹ 75,000 and Cash at Bank was 2,500.

On 30th Sept., the firm sold the business to a Tulsian Ltd. for ₹ 4,00,000 payable in Equity Shares of ₹ 10 each.

The partners decided to take shares in the profit-sharing ratio, any difference to be settled in cash.

You are required to prepare:

(a) Statement of Net Assets as on 30th Sept., 2016.

(b) Statement of profit earned during the period six months ended on 30th Sept. 2016.

(c) Realisation Account.

(d) Capital Account of the partners.

SOLUTION

STATEMENT OF NET ASSETS AS ON 30TH SEPT. 2016

	Particulars		₹
A	Total Assets		
	Fixed Assets:	2,80,000	

	Less: Depreciation	14,000	2,66,000
	Current Assets:		
	Stock		70,000
	Book Debts		75,000
	Cash at Bank		2,500
			4,13,500
B	*Less:* Total Outsiders Liabilities		
	Bank Loan	20,000	
	Sundry Creditors	55,000	
	Bills Payable	7,500	82,500
C	Net assets [A – B]		3,31,000

STATEMENT OF PROFIT
FOR THE PERIOD FROM 1ST APRIL, 2013 TO 30TH SEPT., 2016

	Particulars		₹
A	Closing Net Assets as on 30th Sept.		3,31,000
B	Closing Net Assets as on 1st January		
	Capital—A	1,38,000	
	Capital—B	1,52,000	2,90,000
C	Increase in Net Assets after drawings [A – B]		41,000
D	*Add:* Profit withdrawn by partners		41,000
E	Net Profit earned during the period [C + D]		82,000

Dr. **REALISATION ACCOUNT** *Cr.*

Particulars	₹	*Particulars*	₹
To Fixed Assets	2,80,000	By Bank Loan	20,000
To Stock	70,000	By Sundry Creditors	55,000
To Sundry Debtors	75,000	By Bills Payable	7,500
To Cash at Bank	2,500	By Tulsian Ltd.	4,00,000
To Profit on Realisation t/f to:		(Purchase Consideration)	
A's Capital A/c	34,500		
B's Capital A/c	34,500		
	4,82,500		4,82,500

*It has been assumed that depreciation when charged is credited to the Asset Account.

Dr. **PARTNERS' CAPITAL ACCOUNTS** *Cr.*

Particulars	*A* ₹	*B* ₹	*Particulars*	*A* ₹	*B* ₹
To Drawings	20,500	20,500	By Balance b/d	1,38,000	1,52,000
To Equity Shares in			By Net Profit	41,000	41,000
Tulsian Ltd.	2,00,000	2,00,000	By Realisation A/c	34,500	34,500

To Bank A/c	—	7,000	By Bank A/c	7,000	—
	2,20,500	2,27,500		2,20,500	2,27,500

ILLUSTRATION 34

Mr. M and Mr. D were carrying on business as equal partners. The firm's Balance Sheet as on 31st March, 2016 was as follows:

Liabilities	₹	*Assets*	₹
Sundry Creditors	65,500	Stock	54,000
Bank Overdraft	30,000	Plant and Machinery	1,82,000
Bills Payable	12,500	Office Furniture	15,000
Capital Accounts:		Book Debts	73,000
M	1,50,000	Joint Life Policy	9,500
D	1,48,000	Leasehold Premises	34,500
		Profit and Loss A/c (Debit balance)	26,000
		Drawing Accounts:	
		M	9,000
		D	3,000
	4,06,000		4,06,000

The business was carried on till 30th Sept., 2016. The partners withdrew, in equal amounts, half the amount of profits made during the period of six months (From April-Sept.) after depreciation @10% p.a. had been written-off leasehold premises, 10% p.a. off plant and machinery and 5% p.a. off office furniture. Meanwhile sundry creditors were reduced by ₹ 10,000. On 30th Sept., Stock was valued at ₹ 63,400. Bills Payable were reduced by ₹ 2,300 and Bank Overdraft by ₹ 15,000. Book Debts were valued at ₹ 65,000, the Joint Life Policy was realised for ₹ 9,500 and the amount was utilised to reduce the Bank Overdraft. Other items remained the same as on 31st March.

On 30th Sept., the firm sold the business to a Tulsian Ltd. The value of the goodwill was estimated at ₹ 1,08,000 and the rest of the assets were valued on the basis of the balance as on 30th Sept. The Company paid the purchase consideration in fully paid equity shares of ₹ 10 each, at 150 % premium.

The partners decided to take shares in Profit Sharing ratio, any difference is to be settled in Cash.

Required: **Prepare a Realisation Account and Capital Accounts of the partners as on 30th Sept., 2016.**

SOLUTION

Dr. **REALISATION ACCOUNT** *Cr.*

Particulars	₹	*Particulars*	₹
To Leasehold Premises	32,775	By Sundry Creditors	55,500
To Plant and Machinery	1,72,900	By Bank Overdraft	5,500
To Office Furniture	14,625	By Bills Payable	10,200
To Stock	63,400	By Tulsian Ltd., (Purchase	
To Book Debts	65,000	Consideration)	3,85,500
To Profit on Realisation t/f to:			
M's Capital A/c	54,000		

D's Capital A/c	54,000		
	4,56,700		4,56,700

Dr. **PARTNERS' CAPITAL ACCOUNTS** *Cr.*

Particulars	*M* ₹	*D* ₹	*Particulars*	*M* ₹	*D* ₹
To Profit & Loss A/c	13,000	13,000	By Balance b/d	1,50,000	1,48,000
To Drawings	9,000	3,000	By Profit and Loss A/c	17,500	17,500
To Drawings	8,750	8,750	By Realisation A/c	54,000	54,000
To Shares in Co.	1,92,750	1,92,750	By Bank A/c	2,000	—
To Bank A/c	—	2,000			
	2,23,500	2,19,500		2,23,500	2,19,500

Working Notes:

(i) Net Assets as on 30th Sept.

= Leasehold Premises (After depreciation) + Plant and Machinery (after depreciation) + Furniture (after depreciation) + Stock + Book Debts – Sundry Creditors – Overdraft – Bills Payable.

= (34,500 – 1,725) + (1,82,000 – 9,100) + (15,000 – 375) + 63,400 + 65,000 – 55,500 – (15,000 – 9,500) – 10,200 = ₹ 2,77,500.

(ii) Net Assets as on 31st Mar

= M's Capital + D's Capital – Profit and Loss A/c (Dr. Balance) – Drawings.

= ₹ 1,50,000 + ₹ 1,48,000 – ₹ 26,000 – ₹ 12,000 = ₹ 2,60,000.

(iii) Profit earned and retained

(i.e., notwithdrawn) = ₹ 2,77,500 – ₹ 2,60,000 = ₹ 17,500.

(iv) Profit earned = Profit retained + Profit withdrawn = ₹ 17,500 + ₹ 17,500 = ₹ 35,000.

(v) Purchase Consideration = Net Assets (excluding goodwill) on 30th Sept. + Goodwill = 2,77,500 + ₹ 1,08,000 = ₹ 3,85,500.

SOLVED PROBLEMS

PROBLEM 1

Following is the Balance Sheet of A,B,C and D who were sharing in the ratio of 3: 3: 2: 2 as at 31st March, 2016, when they decided to dissolve the firm:

Liabilities	₹	*Assets*		₹
Trade Creditors	60,000	Cash at Bank		27,500
Bank Overdraft (Secured on Stock)	15,000	Sundry Debtors	50,000	
A's Loan	30,000	*Less:* Provision	(8,500)	41,500
Mrs. B's Loan	3,000	Stock		25,000
A's Capital	60,000	Prepaid Insurance		3,000
B's Capital	49,000	Goodwill		5,000
General Reserve	20,000	Tangible Fixed Assets		80,000

Employee's Provident Fund	5,000	B's Drawings	4,000
Machinery Replacement Reserve	20,000	C's Capital	48,000
		D's Capital	18,000
		Profit & Loss A/c	10,000
	2,62,000		2,62,000

(a) After preparing the Balance Sheet as at 31st March, it was discovered that purchases amounting to ₹ 10,000 in March, were not recorded in books, though the goods were received during March.

(b) Half the Trade Creditors accepted the Net Tangible Fixed Assets at ₹ 24,000 [being 20% less than the book value] and cash in full settlement of their claims after allowing a discount of ₹ 2,000; Remaining Trade Creditors were paid ₹ 31,000 in final settlement including an investment worth ₹ 2,000 unrecorded in the books.

(c) Remaining Net Tangible Fixed Assets realised at a loss of 100% on net collection.

(d) 60% of Sundry Debtors realized 34% less; B is to take over 40% of the balance of Sundry Debtors at 70%. Further, he is to be allowed ₹ 800 to cover future losses and the remaining debtors (if any) were sold to a debt collecting agency at 70%.

(e) Stock was taken over by the banker, and it realised 80% of cost. Bank paid back ₹ 4,000 after recovering its overdraft and interest due thereon.

(f) There was a joint life policy for a sum assured of ₹ 90,000. The Joint Life Policy was surrendered to the insurance company. The company paid a sum of ₹ 4,000 after deducting an amount of ₹ 6,500 towards loan and interest thereon by B against the policy.

(g) A Debtor whose debt of ₹ 5,000 was written off as bad in the previous year paid 40% in full settlement.

(h) There was one unrecorded asset estimated at ₹ 40,000, half of which was handed over at an agreed valuation of 60% to an unrecorded liability of ₹ 26,000 in settlement of claim of ₹ 13,000 and remaining half was taken over by B at an agreed valuation of 42%.

(i) There was a bill for ₹ 21,000 under discount. The bill was received from Z. Z proved insolvent and a first and final dividend of 60% was received from his estate.

(j) B was appointed to realise the assets and to pay off the liabilities. He was entitled to receive 5% commission on the amount finally paid to other partners as capital. He was to bear the expenses of realisation. Expenses of realisation amounted to ₹ 1,600 which were met by B out of his private funds. Such commission is to be borne by the concerned partner.

(k) C could bring in ₹ 11,100 only.

Required: Prepare Realisation A/c, Partners' Capital A/cs and Bank A/c according to Garner vs. Murray Rule. (Ignore Commission while determining Realisation Loss).

SOLUTION

Dr. **REALISATION ACCOUNT** *Cr.*

Particulars	₹	*Particulars*	₹
To Assets Transferred:		By Provision for Doubtful Debts	8,500
Stock	25,000	By Trade Creditors (60,000 + 10,000)	70,000
Debtors	50,000	By Bank Overdraft	15,000
Prepaid Insurance	3,000	By Mrs. B's Loan	3,000
Goodwill	5,000	By Employee's Provident Fund	5,000

Tangible Fixed Assets	80,000	By Machinery Replacement Reserve	20,000
To Bank A/c (Trade Creditors)	38,000	By Bank A/c:	
(9,000 + 29,000)		Tangible Fixed Assets	
To Bank A/c (Mrs B's Loan)	3,000	[30,000 – (100/200 × 30,000)]	15,000
To Bank A/c (EPF)	5,000	Debtors (₹ 50,000 × 60% × 66%)	19,800
To Bank A/c (Unrecored Liability)	13,000	Debtors (₹ 20,000 × 60% × 70%)	8,400
To Bank A/c (Discounted B/R)	21,000	Stock	4,000
		Joint Life Policy	4,000
		Bad Debts recovered	2,000
		from Z	12,600
		By B's Capital A/c (Debtors) [(20,000 × 40% × 70%) – 800]	4,800
		By B's Capital A/c (JLP)	6,500
		By B's Capital A/c (Unrecored Asset)(₹ 20,000 × 42%)	8,400
		By Loss on Realisation t/f to:	
		A's Capital A/c	10,800
		B's Capital A/c	10,800
		C's Capital A/c	7,200
		D's Capital A/c	7,200
	2,43,000		2,43,000

Dr. **PARTNERS' CAPITAL ACCOUNTS** Cr.

Particulars	*A*	*B*	*C*	*D*	*Particulars*	*A*	*B*	*C*	*D*
To Balance b/d	—	—	48,000	18,000	By Balance b/d	60,000	49,000	—	—
To Drawings	—	4,000	—	—	By General Reserve	6,000	6,000	4,000	4,000
To P&L A/c (Goods)	3,000	3,000	2,000	2,000	By Bank A/c	10,800	10,800	11,100	25,200
To P&L A/c (Loss)	3,000	3,000	2,000	2,000	By A's Capital A/c	—	—	25,200	—
To Realisation A/c	—	6,500	—	—	By B's Capital A/c	—	—	18,900	—
To Realisation A/c	—	4,800	—	—	By A's Capital A/c	—	1,143	—	—
To Realisation A/c	—	8,400	—						
To Realisation A/c	10,800	10,800	7,200	7,200					
To C's Capital A/c	25,200	18,900	—	—					
To B's Capital A/c	1,143	—	—	—					
To Bank A/c	33,657	7,543	—	—					
	76,800	66,943	59,200	29,200		76,800	66,943	59,200	29,200

Dr. **BANK ACCOUNT** Cr.

Particulars	₹	*Particulars*	₹
To Balance b/d	27,500.	By Realisation A/c (Trade Creditors)	38,000
To Realisation A/c (Assets)	65,800	By Realisation A/c (EPF)	5,000
To A's Capital A/c	10,800	By Realisation A/c (Mrs B's Loan)	3,000

To B's Capital A/c	10,800	By Realisation A/c (Dish. B/R)	21,000
To C's Capital A/c	11,100	By Realisation A/c (Unrecorded Liability)	13,000
To D's Capital A/c (Including Share of Loss on Realisation)	25,200	By A's Loan A/c	30,000
		By A's Capital A/c	33,657
		By B's Capital A/c	7,543
	1,51,200		1,51,200

Working Notes:

1. Total Trade Creditors = 60,000 + 10,000 (Ommited Purchases) = 70,000
2. Book Value of Net Tangible Fixed Assets = Tangible Fixed Assets – Machinery Replacement Reserve = 80,000 – 20,000 = 60,000
3. Book Value of Net Tangible Fixed Assets taken over by Trade Creditors = 24,000 /80% = 30,000
4. Book Value of Net Tangible Fixed Assets sold = 60,000 – 30,000 = 30,000

5. CALCULATION OF CAPITAL RATIO

Particulars	A ₹	B ₹
Capital	60,000	49,000
Less: B's Drawings	–	(4,000)
Less: Share of Debit Balance of Profit & Loss A/c [10,000 + 10,000 (Ommited Purchases)]	(6,000)	(6,000)
Add: Share of General Reserve	6,000	6,000
	60,000	45,000

C's Deficiency is to be borne by A and B in the ratio of 60,000 : 45,000 *or* 4 : 3.

A's Capital A/c [₹ 44,100 × 4/7]	Dr.	₹ 25,200	
B's Capital A/c [₹ 44,100 × 3/7]	Dr.	₹ 11,100	
To C's Capital A/c [₹55,200 – ₹ 11,100]			₹ 44,100

6. D will not bear nay portion of the loss due to C's insolvency since he had a debit balance in his capital account at the time of Insolvency.
7. The amount due to A, before B's commission is ₹ 24,000, ignoring the amount brought in by him on account of his share of the loss on realisation. Thus, B's commission = ₹ 24,000 × 5/105 = ₹ 1,143.

PROBLEM 2

A, B, C and D are sharing profits and losses in the ratio 5 : 5 : 4 : 2. Frauds committed by C during the year were found out and it was decided to dissolve the partnership on 31si March, 2016 when their Balance Sheet was as under:

Liabilities	₹	*Assets*	₹
Capitals:		Building	1,20,000
A	90,000	Stock	85,500
B	90,000	Investments	29,000

C	—	Debtors	42,000
D	35,000	Cash	14,500
General reserve	24,000	C's Current Account	15,000
Trade creditors	47,000		
Bills payable	20,000		
	3,06,000		3,06,000

Following information is given to you:

(i) A cheque for ₹ 4,300 received from debtor was not recorded in the books and was misappropriated by C.

(ii) Investments costing ₹ 5,400 were sold by C at ₹ 7,900 and the funds transferred to his personal account. This sale was omitted from the firm's books.

(iii) A creditor agreed to take overinvestments of the book value of ₹ 5,400 at ₹ 8,400. The rest of the creditors were paid off at a discount of 2%.

(iv) The other assets realized as follows:

Building	105% of book value
Stock	₹ 78,000
Investments	The rest of investments were sold at a profit of ₹ 4,800
Debtors	The rest of the debtors were realized at a discount of 12%

(v) The bills payable were settled at a discount of ₹ 400.

(vi) The expenses of dissolution amounted to ₹ 4,900

(vii) It was found out that realization from C's private assets would only be ₹ 4,000.

Required: Prepare the necessary Ledger Accounts.

SOLUTION

Dr. **REALISATION ACCOUNT** *Cr.*

Particulars	₹	*Particulars*		₹
To Building	1,20,000	By Trade Creditors		47,000
To Stock	85,500	By Bills Payable		20,000
To Investment	29,000	By Cash:		
To Debtors	42,000	Building	1,26,000	
To Cash (creditors paid) [98% (47,000 – 8,400)]	37,828	Stock	78,000	
		Investments	23,000	
To Cash (expenses)	4,900	Debtors	33,176	2,60,176
To Cash (bills payable) (20,000 – 400)	19,600	[88% (42,000 – 4,300)]		
		By C's Capital A/c [Debtors (unrecorded)]		4,300
		By C's Capital A/c		
To Profit on Realisation t/f to		[Investments (unrecorded)]		7,900
Partners' Capital A/cs:				
A	171			

B	171		
C	137		
D	69		
	3,39,376		3,39,376

Dr. **CASH ACCOUNT** Cr.

Particulars		₹	*Particulars*	₹
To Balance b/d		14,500	By Realisation (creditors paid)	37,828
To Realisation (assets) realised			By Realisation (Bills Payable)	19,600
Building	1,26,000		By Realisation (expenses)	4,900
Stock	78,000		By A's Capital A/c	90,528
Investments	23,000		By B's Capital A/c	90,528
Debtors	33,176	2,60,176	By D's Capital A/c	35,292
To C's capital A/c		4,000		
		2,78,676		2,78,676

Dr. **PARTNERS' CAPITAL ACCOUNTS** Cr.

Particulars	*A* ₹	*B* ₹	*C* ₹	*D* ₹	*Particulars*	*A* ₹	*B* ₹	*C* ₹	*D* ₹
To Balance b/d	—	—	15,000	—	By Balance b/d	90,000	90,000	–	35,000
To Realisation A/c	—		4,300		By General Reserve	7,500	7,500	6,000	3,000
[Debtors]					By Realisation A/c	171	171	137	69
To Realisation A/c	—		7,900	—	(Profit)				
[Investment]					By Cash A/c	—	—	4,000	—
To C's capital A/c	7,143	7,143	—	2,777	By A's capital A/c	—	—	7,143	—
To Cash A/c	90,528	90,528	—	35,292	By B's capital A/c	—	—	7,143	—
					By D's capital A/c	—	—	2,777	—
	97,671	**97,671**	**27,200**	**38,069**		**97,671**	**97,671**	**27,200**	**38,069**

Working Notes:

(I) AMOUNT RECEIVED FROM SALE OF INVESTMENTS

Book value	29,000
Less: Misappropriated by C	(5,400)
	23,600
Less: Taken over by a creditor	(5,400)
	18,200
Add: Profit on sale of investments	4,800
	23,000

(II) DEFICIENCY OF C

Balance of capital as on 31st March, 2012	15,000
Debtors-misappropriation	4,300

Investment-misappropriation	7,900
	27,200
Less: Realisation Profit	(137)
General Reserve	(6,000)
Contribution from private assets	(4.000)
Net Deficiency of Capital	17,063

This deficiency of ₹ 17,063 in C's capital account will be shared by other partners A, B and D in their capital ratio of 90: 90 : 35

Accordingly,

A's Share of deficiency = [17,063 × (90/215)] = ₹ 7,143

B's Share of deficiency = [17,063 × (90/215)] = ₹ 7,143

D's Share of deficiency = [17,063 × (35/215)] = ₹ 2,777

PROBLEM 3

X, Y and Z are partners sharing profits and losses in the ratio of 2 : 1 : 1. Their Balance Sheet as on 31st March, 2016 is as below:

Liabilities	₹	*Assets*	₹
Partners' Capitals:		Goodwill	15,000
X	90,000	Machineries	75,000
Y	60,000	Investments	5,000
Z	10,000	Current Assets:	
Bills Payable	30,000	Cash at Bank	5,000
Sundry Creditors	50,000	Debtors	80,000
		Stock	60,000
	2,40,000		2,40,000

Repairs ₹ 20,000 incurred three years ago was treated as capital expenditure and debited to Machinery account. Stock was overvalued by ₹ 10,000. Depreciation at 10% p.a. was charged on machinery on diminishing balance. ₹ 10,000 collected from debtors was not received in books but taken by Z. The accounts are rectified and then XY Ltd. is formed to take over the business. Y is to take the investments at ₹ 3,000 X will pay the creditors. Bills payable would be paid by X and Y in their profit sharing ratio. Goodwill and Stocks are valued at ₹ 12,000 and ₹ 42,580 respectively. Debtors are taken at 10% below book value, whereas other assets except cash at bank to be considered at their book values. XY Ltd. is to pay the firm by issue of equity shares of ₹ 10 each, Z is insolvent. Y agreed to take 6,000 shares and balance taken over by X.

Required: Show Profit and Loss Adjustment Account, Realisation Account and Partners' Capital Accounts in the books of the firm.

SOLUTION

Dr. **PROFIT AND LOSS ADJUSTMENT ACCOUNT** *Cr.*

Particulars	₹	*Particulars*	₹
To Machinery	14,580	By Loss transfererd to:	
[₹ 20,000 × 90% × 90% × 90%]		X's Capital A/c	12,290

To Stock	10,000	Y's Capital A/c	6,145
		Z's Capital A/c	6,145
	24,580		24,580

Dr. **REALISATION ACCOUNT** Cr.

Particulars	₹	Particulars	₹
To Goodwill	15,000	By Bills Payable	30,000
To Machinery	60,420	By Sundry Creditors	50,000
To Investments	5,000	By Y's Capital A/s (Investments)	3,000
To Debtors	70,000	By XY Ltd. (Purchase consideration)	1,78,000
To Stock	50,000	By Loss on Realisation tif to:	
To X's Capital A/c (Creditors)	50,000	X's Capital A/c	9,710
To Y's Capital A/c (B/P)	20,000	Y's Capital A/c	4,855
To Z's Capital A/c (B/P)	10,000	Z's Capital A/c	4,855
	2,80,420		2,80,420

Dr. **PARTNERS' CAPITAL ACCOUNTS** Cr.

Particulars	X ₹	Y ₹	Z ₹	Particulars	X ₹	Y ₹	Z ₹
To P & L Adj. A/c	12,290	6,145	6,145	By Balance b/d	90,000	60,000	10,000
To Realisation A/c	9,710	4,855	4,855	By Realisation A/c (Cr.)	50,000	—	—
To Debtors	—	—	10,000	By Realisation A/c (B/P)	20,000	10,000	—
To Realisation A/c	—	3,000	—	By X's Capital A/c	—	—	6,497
To Z's Capital A/c	6,497	4,503	—	By Y's Capital A/c	—	—	4,503
To Equity Shares	1,18,000	60,000	—	By Bank A/c	—	8,503	—
To Bank A/c	13,503	—	—				
	1,60,000	78,503	21,000		1,60,000	78,503	21,000

Workign Note:

Calculation of Purchase Consideration:

= Goodwill + Stock + Debtors + Machinery

= ₹ 12,000 + ₹ 42,580 + 90% of (₹ 80,000 – ₹ 10,000) + ₹ 60,420 = ₹ 1,78,000

PROBLEM 4

Ananth Associates is a reputed firm. On account of certain misunderstandings between the partners, it was decided to dissolve the firm on 31st March, 2016. Their Balance Sheet as on 31st March, 2016, was as follows:

Liabilities	₹	Assets	₹
Capitals:		Land and Buildings	7,00,000
A	3,00,000	Other Fixed Assets	3,00,000
B	2,00.000	Stock in trade	2,00,000
C (Minor)	1,00,000	Debtors	4,00,000

Mortgage loans	3,00,000	Bills Receivable	1,50,000
Bank Overdraft	3,00,000	Goodwill	30,000
Other Loans	2,00,000	Cash	20,000
Creditors	2,00,000		
Loans from C	2,00,000		
	18,00,000		18,00,000

It was decided that Mr. A shall be in charge of realisation. He shall set apart ₹ 10,000 towards expenses, he shall be paid a remuneration of 5% on the amounts distributed to partners towards their contribution other than loans. Assets realised as under:

1st April. Debtors 87.5%, 15th April. Fixed Assets ₹ 4,00,000, 1st May. Debtors Balance, 15th May, Bills Receivable ₹ 1,40,000, 1st June Fixed Assets ₹ 50,000, 15th June Land & Building ₹ 8,00,000.

Required: Prepare a statement showing how the amounts received on various dates will be distributed assuming:

(a) The actual expenses of realisation amounted to ₹ 20,005 on 15th June.

(b) The firm is solvent.

(c) The profit and loss sharing ratio was under:

Particulars	*Profit*	*Loss*
A	2	1
B	2	1
C	1	Nil

(d) The final distribution is made on 15th June.

SOLUTION

STATEMENT SHOWING THE PIECEMEAL DISTRIBUTION OF CASH

	Particular	Total	Mortagage Loan ₹	Bank Overdraft ₹	Other Loans ₹	Creditors ₹	C's Loan ₹	Capitals A ₹	Capitals B ₹	Capitals C ₹
April 1	A Amount Due		3,00,000	3,00,000	2,00,000	2,00,000	2,00,000	3,00,000	2,00,000	1,00,000
	B Cash paid (20,000 + 3,50,000 – 10,000) (Distributed pro rata among outsiders)		1,08,000	1,08,000	72,000	72,000				
	C Balance Due [A – B]		1,92,000	1,92,000	1,28,000	1,28,000	2,00,000	3,00,000	2,00,000	1,00,000
April 15	D Amount paid first	₹1,92,000	1,92,000							
	Balance Distributed among creditors pro rata	2,08,000	—	89,143	59,429	59,428				
	E Balance due [C – D]			1,02,857	68,571	68,572	2,00,000	3,00,000	2,00,000	1,00,000
May 2	F Amount Distributed among creditors pro rata	50,000		21,429	14,285	14,286				
	G Balance Due [E – F]			81,428	54,286	54,286	2,00,000	3,00,000	2,00,000	1,00,000
May 15	H Amount Distributed pro rata	1,40,000		60,000	40,000	40,000				
	I Balance Due [G – H]			21,428	14,286	14,286				
June 3	J Amount distributed	50,000		21,428	14,286	14,286				
	K Balance Due [I – J]						2,00,000	3,00,000	2,00,000	1,00,000
June 15	Land and Buildings	8,00,000								
	Less: Balance of expenses	10,005								
		7,89,995								
	C's Loan	2,00,000					2,00,000	—	—	—
		5,89,995								
	Commission to A 5/105 × 5,89,995 = 28,095									
	Payment to C since he is not to bear any loss Amount available 5,89,995 – (28,095 + 1,00,000) = 4,61,900									1,00,000
	Maximum Possible Loss = 5,00,000 – 4,61,900 = 38,100						– 19,050	– 19,050		
							2,80,950	1,80,950		

Note: When the piecemeal distribution of cash is made on the basis of Maximum Possible Loss Method, it is assumed at every stage of realisation that remaining assets will realise nothing. In that case even the secured creditors are treated as unsecured except when the assets on which they are secured is realised.

2A PARTNERSHIP—AMALGAMATION AND CONVERSION

LEARNING OBJECTIVES

After studying this chapter, you should be able to understand:

- ◇ Amalgamation of Firms
- ◇ Conversion of a Firm To a Company

1.0 AMALGAMATION OF FIRMS

MEANING OF AMALGAMATION

Under 'Amalgamation', two *or* more firms transfer their businesses to a new firm which is formed to take over such businesses.

REVALUATION ON AMALGAMATION

Usually all the assets and liabilities are revalued in order to ascertain the true position as on the date of amalgamation.

HOW TO CLOSE THE BOOKS OF AMALGAMATING FIRMS

PRACTICAL STEPS TO CLOSE THE BOOKS OF AMALGAMATING FIRMS

Step 1: *Prepare Revaluation Account to ascertain the Profit/Loss on Revaluation of all Assets and Liabilities, and transfer such Profit/Loss to the Partners' Capital Accounts in the profit sharing ratio.*

Step 2: *On raising Goodwill of the firm, Goodwill should be debited and partners' capital accounts should be credited in their profit sharing ratio.*

Step 3: *Realise those assets which have not been taken over by the new firm and transfer such unsold assets (if any) to the Capital accounts of all the partners in the ratio of their Capitals.*

Step 4: *Discharge those liabilities which have not been taken over by the new firm and transfer such undischarged liabilities (if any) to the Capital Accounts of all the Partners in the ratio of their Capitals.*

Step 5: *Transfer all Accumulated Reserves/Profits/Losses to the Capital Accounts of all the Partners in the ratio of their Capitals.*

Step 6: *Close the accounts of liabilities taken over and the Accounts of Assets taken over by passing the following journal entry:*

New Firm's Account	Dr.	[With excess of Agreed Values of Assets taken over the Agreed Amount of Liabilities taken over]
Liabilities taken over (Individually)	Dr.	[With Agreed Amount of Liabilities taken over]

To Assets taken over (Individually)		[With Agreed Values of Assets taken over]

Step 7: *Close the Partners' Capital Accounts and the New Firm's Account by passing the following Journal entry:*

Partners' Capital Accounts (Individually)	Dr.	[With Individual Capital of Partners]
To New Firm's Account		[With Total]

HOW TO OPEN THE BOOKS OF THE NEW FIRM

JOURNAL ENTRY TO OPEN THE BOOKS OF NEW FIRM

Assets taken over (Individually)	Dr.	[With Agreed Values of Assets taken over]
To Liabilities taken over (individually)		[With Agreed Amount of Liabilities taken over]
To Partners' Capital Accounts (Individually)		[With Individual Capital of Partners]

ILLUSTRATION 1

Two partnership firms, carrying on business under the styles of Black & Co., and White & Co. respectively, decide to amalgamate into Grey & Co. with effect from 1st April, 2013. The respective Balance Sheets as on 31st March, 2016 are:

BALANCE SHEET OF BLACK & CO. AS AT 31st MARCH 2016

Liabilities	₹	*Assets*	₹
Mr B 's Capital Account	19,000	Plant and Machinery	10,000
Sundry Creditors	10,000	Stock in trade	20,000
Bank Overdraft	15,000	Sundry Debtors	10,000
		Mr A's Capital Account	4,000
	44,000		44,000

A and B share profits and losses in the proportion of 1 : 2.

BALANCE SHEET OF WHITE & CO. AS AT 31st MARCH 2016

Liabilities	₹	*Assets*	₹
Mr X's Capital Account	10,000	Goodwill	10,000
Mr Y's Capital Account	2,000	Stock in trade	5,000
Sundry Creditors	28,000	Sundry debtors	10,000
		Cash in hand	6,000
		Cash at bank	9,000
	40,000		40,000

X and Y share profits and losses equally. The following further information is given:

All fixed assets are to be devalued by 20%. All Stock in trade is to be appreciated by 50%. Black & Co., owes ₹ 5,000 to White & Co., as on 31st March. This debt is settled at ₹ 2,000. Goodwill is to be ignored for the purpose of the amalgamation. The fixed capital accounts in the new firm are to be — Mr. A ₹ 2,000, Mr. B ₹ 3,000, Mr. X ₹ 1,000, Mr. Y ₹ 4,000. Mr B takes over the bank overdraft of

Black & Co. and gifts to Mr. A the amount of money to be brought in by Mr. A to make up his capital contribution. Mr X is paid off in cash from White & Co., and Mr. Y brings in sufficient cash to make up his required capital contribution. Pass the journal entries to close the books of both the firms as on 31st March, 2016.

SOLUTION

JOURNAL OF BLACK & CO.

Particulars		*L.F*	*Dr. (₹)*	*Cr.(₹)*
Revaluation A/c	Dr.		2,000	
To Plant and Machinery				2,000
(For Plant and Machinery devalued by 20%)				
Stock in trade A/c	Dr.		10,000	
Sundry Creditors A/c	Dr.		3,000	
To Revaluation A/c				13,000
(For appreciation of stock in trade and debt owing to White & Co., settled for ₹ 2,000 instead of ₹ 5,000)				
Bank overdraft	Dr.		15,000	
To B's Capital A/c				15,000
(For Bank Overdraft taken over by B)				
Revaluation A/c	Dr.		11,000	
To A's Capital A/c				3,667
To B's Capital A/c				7,333
(For profit on revaluation transferred to Capital Accounts in the profit sharing ratio)				
B's Capital A/c	Dr.		2,333	
To A's Capital A/c				2,333
(Being the gift by B to A)				
B 's Capital A/c	Dr.		36,000	
To B 's Loan A/c				36,000
(Being b 's excess capital treated as loan)				
Grey & Co.	Dr.		5,000	
B 's Loan A/c	Dr.		36,000	
Sundry Creditors A/c	Dr.		7,000	
To Plant and Machinery				8,000
To Stock-in-trade				30,000
To Sundry Debtors				10,000
(For assets and liabilities transferred to Grey & Co. for closing the books of the firm)				
A's Capital A/c	Dr.		2,000	
B's Capital A/c	Dr.		3,000	
To Grey & Co.				5,000
(For Capital accounts of the partners closed by t/f to Grey & Co.)				

Note: The Accounting entries show that B's Capital Account has a credit balance of ₹ 39,000 which is in excess by ₹ 36,000 of his required capital contribution. Since there are no liquid assets in Black & Co., from which B can be repaid, the excess amount will be taken in Grey & Co. as a loan from B.

JOURNAL OF WHITE & CO.

Particulars		*L.F*	*Dr. (₹)*	*Cr.(₹)*
Stock in Trade	Dr.		2,500	
To Revaluation A/c				2,500
(For Stock in trade appreciated by 50%)				
Revaluation A/c	Dr.		13,000	
To Sundry Debtors				3,000
To Goodwill				10,000
(For debt due from Black & Co. settled at a concession of ₹ 3,000; goodwill written off)				
X's Capital A/c	Dr.		5,250	
Y's Capital A/c	Dr.		5,250	
To Revaluation A/c				10,500
(for loss on Revaluation debited to partners' capital A/cs)				
Cash A/c	Dr.		7,250	
To Y's Capital A/c				7,250
(For cash introduced by Y to make up his capital to ₹ 4,000)				
X's Capital A/c	Dr.		3,750	
To Cash A/c				3,750
(For excess capital refunded to X to reduce his capital to ₹ 1,000)				
Grey & Co.	Dr.		5,000	
Sundry Creditors	Dr.		28,000	
To Stock in trade				7,500
To Sundry Debtors				7,000
To Cash in Hand				9,500
To Cash at Bank				9,000
(For Sundry Assets and Liabilities t/f to Grey & Co. to close the Books)				
X's Capital A/c	Dr.		1,000	
Y's Capital A/c	Dr.		4,000	
To Grey & Co.				5,000
(For Capital accounts of partners closed by transfer to Grey Co.)				

ILLUSTRATION 2

X and Y are partners of X and Co., sharing profits and losses in the ratio of 3 : 1 and Y and Z are partners of Y & Co., sharing profits and losses in the ratio of 2 : 1. On 31st March, 2016, they decide to amalgamate and form a new firm M/s XYZ & Co., wherein X, Y and Z would be partners sharing profits and losses in the ratio of 3 : 2 : 1. The Balance Sheets of two firms on the above date are as under:

Liabilities	*X & Co.* ₹	*Y & Co.* ₹	*Assets*	*X & Co.* ₹	*Y & Co.* ₹
X' s Capital	4,80,000	—	Building	1,00,000	—
Y' s Capital	3,20,000	4,00,000	Machinery	3,00,000	3,20,000
Z' s Capital	—	2,00,000	Furniture	40,000	12,000
Reserves	1,00,000	3,00,000	Current Assets:		
Creditors	2,40,000	2,32,000	Stock	2,40,000	2,80,000
Due to X & Co.	—	2,00,000	Debtors	3,20,000	4,00,000
Bank Loan	1,60,000	—	Cash at Bank	60,000	1,80,000
			Cash in hand	40,000	20,000
			Due from Y & Co.,	2,00,000	—
			Advances	—	1,20,000
	13,00,000	13,32,000		13,00,000	13,32,000

The amalgamated firm took over the business on the following terms:

(a) Building of X & Co., was valued at ₹ 2,00,000. (b) Machinery of X & Co., was valued at ₹ 4,50,000 and that of Y & Co. at ₹ 4,00,000. (c) Goodwill valued X and Co. ₹ 1,00,000 and Y & Co., ₹ 82,000 but the same will not appear in the books of XYZ & Co., (d) Partners of the new firm will bring the necessary cash to pay other partners to adjust their capitals according to the profit sharing ratio.

Required: Show journal entries in the books of M/s XYZ & Co. and Prepare the Balance Sheet as at 31.3.2016.

SOLUTION

JOURNAL OF XYZ & CO.

Particulars		*L.F*	*Dr. (₹)*	*Cr.(₹)*
Goodwill A/c	Dr.		1,00,000	
Building A/c	Dr.		2,00,000	
Machinery A/c	Dr.		4,50,000	
Furniture A/c	Dr.		40,000	
Stock A/c	Dr.		2,40,000	
Debtors A/c	Dr.		3,20,000	
Cash at Bank A/c	Dr.		60,000	
Cash in hand A/c	Dr.		40,000	
Due from Y & Co. A/c	Dr.		2,00,000	
To Creditors A/c				2,40,000
To Bank Loan A/c				1,60,000
To X's Capital A/c				8,17,500
To Y's Capital A/c				4,32,500
(Being the Assets and Liabilities of X & Co. taken over)				
Goodwill A/c	Dr.		82,000	
Machinery A/c	Dr.		4,00,000	
Furniture A/c	Dr.		12,000	

Stock A/c	Dr.	2,80,000	
Debtors A/c	Dr.	4,00,000	
Cash at Bank A/c	Dr.	1,80,000	
Cash in hand A/c	Dr.	20,000	
Advances A/c	Dr.	1,20,000	
To Creditors A/c			2,32,000
To Due to X & Co. A/c			2,00,000
To Y's Capital A/c			7,08,000
To Z's Capital A/c			3,54,000
(Being the Assets and Liabilities of Y & Co. taken over)			
X's Capital A/c	Dr.	91,000	
Y's Capital A/c	Dr.	60,667	
Z's Capital A/c	Dr.	30,333	
To Goodwill A/c			1,82,000
(Being Goodwill written off)			
Bank A/c	Dr.	3,69,833	
To X's Capital A/c			3,38,500
To Z's Capital A/c			31,333
(Being the Cash brought in by X and Z to make capitals proportionate)			
Y's Capital A/c	Dr.	3,69,833	
To Bank A/c			3,69,833
(Being the excess capital withdrawn by Y)			
Due to X & Co. A/c	Dr.	2,00,000	
To Due from Y & Co., A/c			2,00,000
(Being the elimination of mutual indebtedness of the merged firms X & Co., and Y & Co.,)			

BALANCE SHEET OF M/S XYZ & CO. AS AT 31st MARCH, 2016

Liabilities	₹	*Assets*	₹
Capitals:		Building	2,00,000
X	10,65,000	Machinery	8,50,000
Y	7,10,000	Furniture	52,000
Z	3,55,000	Stock	5,20,000
Creditors	4,72,000	Debtors	7,20,000
Bank Loan	1,60,000	Advances	1,20,000
		Cash at Bank	2,40,000
		Cash in hand	60,000
	27,62,000		27,62,000

Working Notes:

(I) STATEMENT SHOWING THE COMPUTATION OF PURCHASE CONSIDERATION

	Particulars	*X & Co.* ₹	*Y & Co.* ₹
A.	Assets:		
	Goodwill	1,00,000	82,000
	Building	2,00,000	–
	Machinery	4,50,000	4,00,000
	Furniture	40,000	12,000
	Stock	2,40,000	2,80,000
	Debtors	3,20,000	4,00,000
	Cash at Bank	60,000	1,80,000
	Cash in Hand	40,000	20,000
	Due from Y & Co.,	2,00,000	—
	Advances	—	1,20,000
		16,50,000	14,94,000
B.	Liabilities:		
	Creditors	2,40,000	2,32,000
	Due to X & Co.	—	2,00,000
	Bank Loan	1,60,000	—
		4,00,000	4,32,000
C.	Purchase Consideration (A – B)	12,50,000	10,62,000

(II) STATEMENT SHOWING THE COMPUTATION OF PROPORTIONATE CAPITALS

	Particulars	₹
A.	M/s XYZ & Co. (₹ 12,50,000 + ₹ 10,62,000)	23,12,000
B.	*Less:* Goodwill Adjustment	1,82,000
C.	Total Capital of new Firm	21,30,000
D.	X's proportionate Capital (₹ 21,30,000 × 3/6)	10,65,000
E.	Y's proportionate Capital (₹ 21,30,000 × 2/6)	7,10,000
F.	Z's Proportionate Capital (₹ 21,30,000 ×1/6)	3,55,000
		21,30,000

(III) STATEMENT SHOWING THE COMPUTATION OF CAPITAL ADJUSTMENTS

Particulars	*X* ₹	*Y* ₹	*Z* ₹	*Total* ₹
Balance transferred from X and Co.	8,17,500	4,32,500	—	12,50,000
Balance transferred from Y and Co.	—	7,08,000	3,54,000	10,62,000
	8,17,500	11,40,500	3,54,000	23,12,000
Less: Goodwill written off in the ratio of (3 : 2 : 1)	91,000	60,667	30,333	1,82,000

(a) Existing Capital	7,26,500	10,79,833	3,23,667	21,30,000
(b) Proportionate Capital	10,65,000	7,10,000	3,55,000	21,30,000
(c) Amount to be brought in (paid off) [(a) – (b)]	3,38,500	(3,69,833)	31,333	—

Dr. **(IV) CAPITAL ACCOUNTS (IN THE BOOKS OF X & CO.)** *Cr.*

Particulars	*X* ₹	*Y* ₹	*Particulars*	*X* ₹	*Y* ₹
To Capital A/c – M/s XYZ & Co. (Transfer)	8,17,500	4,32,500	By Balance b/d	4,80,000	3,20,000
			By Reserve (3 : 1)	75,000	25,000
			By Goodwill (3 : 1)	75,000	25,000
			By Realisation A/c* – Profit (3 : 1)	1,87,500	62,500
	8,17,500	4,32,500		8,17,500	4,32,500

*For Building ₹ 1,00,000 and Machinery ₹ 1,50,000.

Dr. **(V) CAPITAL ACCOUNTS (IN THE BOOKS OF Y & CO.)** *Cr.*

Particulars	*X* ₹	*Y* ₹	*Particulars*	*X* ₹	*Y* ₹
XYZ & Co. (Transfer)	7,08,000	3,54,000	By Balance b/d	4,00,000	2,00,000
			By Reserve (2 : 1)	2,00,000	1,00,000
			By Goodwill (2 : 1)	54,667	27,333
			By Realisation A/c* – Profit (2 : 1)	53,333	26,667
	7,08,000	3,54,000		7,08,000	3,54,000

*For Machinery ₹ 80,000.

ILLUSTRATION 3

P and Q have been carrying on same business independently. Due to competition in the market, they decided to amalgamate and form a new company called PQ Ltd.

Following is the Balance Sheet of P and Q as at 31.3.2016:

Liabilities	*P* ₹	*Q* ₹	*Assets*	*P* ₹	*Q* ₹
Capital	7,75,000	8,55,000	Plant & Machinery	4,85,000	6,14,000
Current liabilities	6,23,500	5,57,600	Building	7,50,000	6,40,000
			Current Assets	1,63,500	1,58,600
	13,98,500	14,12,600		13,98,500	14,12,600

Following are the additional information:

(i) The authorised capital of the new company will be ₹.25,00,000 divided into 1,00,000 equity shares of ₹ 25 each.

(ii) Liabilities of P includes ₹ 50 000 due to Q for the purchases made. Q made a profit of 20% on sale to P

(iii) P has goods purchased from Q, cost to him ₹ 10, 000. This is included in the Current asset of P as at 31st March, 2016.

(iv) The assets of P and Q are to be revalued as under:

Particulars	*P*	*Q*
Plant and Machinery	₹ 5,25,000	₹ 6,75,000
Building	₹ 7,75,000	₹ 6,48,000

(v) The purchase consideration is to be discharged as under:

(a) Issue 24,000 equity shares of ₹ 25 each fully paid up in the proportion of their profitability in the preceding 2 years.

(b) Profits for the preceding 2 years are given below:

Particulars	*P (₹)*	*Q (₹)*
Ist year	2,62,800	2,75,125
IInd Year	2,12,200	2,49,875
	4,75,000	5,25,000

(c) Issue 12% Preference Shares of ₹ 10 each fully paid up at par to provide income equivalent to 8% return on capital employed in the business as on 31.3.2016 after revaluation of assets of P and Q respectively.

You are required to:

(i) Compute the amount of equity and preference shares issued to P and Q.

(ii) Prepare the Balance Sheet of PQ Ltd. immediately after amalgamation.

SOLUTION

(I) CALCULATION OF NO. OF EQUITY SHARES ISSUED TO P AND Q

Profit	*P (₹)*	*Q (₹)*
Ist year	2,62,800	2,75,125
IInd year	2,12,200	2,49,875
Total	4,75,000	5,25,000

No. of shares to be issued:

P : 24000 × 475/1000 = 11,400 Equity Shares, Q : 24000 × 525/1000 = 12,600 Equity Shares.

CALCULATION OF AMOUNT OF 12% PREFERENCE SHARES ISSUED TO P AND Q

Particulars	*P*	*Q*
Capital Employed	₹ 8,40,000	₹ 9,24,000
8% Return on Capital Employed	₹ 67,200	₹ 73,920
12% Pref. Shares to be issued (67,200 × 100/12)		₹ 5,60,000
(73,920 × 100/12)		₹ 6,16,000

TOTAL PURCHASE CONSIDERATION

Particulars	*P*	*Q*
Equity Shares @ ₹ 25	₹ 2,85,000	₹ 3,15,000

12% Preference Shares @ ₹ 10	₹ 5,60,000	₹ 6,16,000
Total	₹ 8,45,000	₹ 9,31,000

(II) BALANCE SHEET OF PQ LTD. AS AT 31.3.2016

Particulars	Note No	₹ (lacs)
I. Equity and Liabilities		
(1) Shareholders' Funds		
(a) Share Capital	1	17,76,000
(b) Reserves and Surplus		—
(2) Non-Current Liabilities		—
(3) Current Liabilities		11,31,100
Total		29,07,100
II. Assets		
(1) Non-Current Assets		
(a) Fixed Assets		
Tangible Assets	2	26,23,000
Intangible Assets [Goodwill]		14,000
(2) Current Assets		2,70,100
Total		29,07,100

Notes To Accounts:

Particulars	₹ (lacs)
1. Share Capital	
24,000 Equity Shares of ₹ 25 each	6,00,000
1,17,600, 12% Pref. Shares of ₹ 10 each	11,76,000
(Of the above all Shares were issued for consideration otherwise than cash)	
	17,76,000
2. Tangible Assets	
Land & Building	14,23,000
Plant & Machinery	26,23,000
Total	26,23,000

Working Notes:

(I) GOODWILL

Particulars	P (₹)	Q (₹)
Plant and machinery	5,25,000	6,75,000
Building	7,75,000	6,48,000
Current assets	1,63,500	1,58,600
	14,63,500	14,81,600
Less: Current Liabilities	6,23,500	5,57,600
Net Assets taken (Capital Employed)	8,40,000	9,24,000

Less: Purchase Consideration	8,45,000	9,31,000
Goodwill	5,000	7,000
Total Purchased Goodwill		12,000
Add: Unrealised Profit of ₹.10,000 @ 20% ₹ 2,000 is adjusted from current assets and from goodwill (since P & L A/c is not given)	2,000	
Total Goodwill		14,000

(II) CURRENT ASSETS

Particulars	*P (₹)*	*Q (₹)*
Balances before amalgamation	1,63,500	1,58,600
Less: Liabilities of P due to Q	—	50,000
Less: Unrealised Profit on Stock (i.e. ₹ 10,000 × 20%)	2,000	—
Total	1,61,500	1,08,600
Grand Total		2,70,100

(III) CURRENT LIABILITIES

Particulars	*P (₹)*	*Q (₹)*
Balances before amalgamation	6,23,500	5,57,600
Less: Liabilities of P due to Q	50,000	—
Total	5,73,500	5,57,600
Grand Total		11,31,100

ILLUSTRATION 4

P and Q are partners of P & Co. sharing Profit and losses in the ratio of 3 : 1 and Q and R are partners of R & Co., sharing profits and losses in the ratio of 2 : 1. On 31st March, 2016, they decide to amalgamate and form a new firm M/s PQR & Co., wherein P, Q and R would be partners sharing profits and losses in the ratio of 3 : 2 : 1. The Balance Sheets of two firms on the above date are as under:

Liabilities	*P & Co.* ₹	*R & Co.* ₹	*Assets*	*P & Co.* ₹	*R & Co.* ₹
Capitals:			Fixed Assets:		
P	2,40,000	----	Building	50,000	60,000
Q	1,60,000	2,00,000	Plant & machinery	1,50,000	1,60,000
R	—	1,00,000	Office Equipment	20,000	6,000
Reserves	50,000	1,50,000	Current Assets:		
Sundry Creditors	1,20,000	1,16,000	Stock-in-trade	1,20,000	140,000
Due to P & Co.	....	1,00,000	Sundry Debtors	1,60,000	2,00,000
Bank overdraft	80,000	----	Bank Balance	30,000	90,000
			Cash in hand	20,000	10,000
	—	—	Due from R & Co.	1,00,000	—
	6,50,000	6,66,000		6,50,000	6,66,000

The amalgamated firm took over the business on the following terms:

(a) Building of P & Co. was valued at ₹ 1, 00, 000.

(b) Plant and machinery of P & Co. was valued at ₹ 2,50,000 and that of R & Co. at ₹ 2,00,000.

(c) All stock in trade is to be appreciated by 20%.

(d) Goodwill valued of P & Co. at ₹ 1,20,000 and R & Co. at ₹ 60,000, but the same will not appear in the books of PQR & Co.

(e) Partners of new firm wiil bring the necessary cash to pay other partners to adjust their capitals according to the profit sharing ratio.

(f) Provisions for doubtful debts has to be carried forward at ₹ 12,000 in respect of debtors of P & Co. and ₹ 26,000 in respect of debtors of R & Co.

You are required to prepare the Balance Sheet of new firm and capital accounts of the partners in the books of old firms.

SOLUTION

BALANCE SHEET OF M/S PQR & CO. AS AT 31ST MARCH, 2016

Liabilities	₹	*Assets*	₹
Capitals:		Building (₹.1, 00,000 + ₹.60,000)	1,60,000
P	5,52,000	Plant & Machinery	
Q	3,68,000	(₹ 2,50,000 + ₹ 2,00,000)	4,50,000
R	1,84,000	Office Equipment	
Sundry Creditors		(₹ 20,000 + ₹ 6,000)	26,000
(₹ 1,20,000 + 1,16,000)	2,36,000	Stock-in-trade	
Bank Overdraft	80,000	(₹.1, 44 ,000 + ₹.1, 68,000)	3,12,000
		Sundry Debtors 3,60,000	
		(₹ 1, 60,000 + ₹ .2,00,000)	
		Less: Provision (38,000)	
		(₹ 12,000 + ₹ 26,000)	3,22,000
		Bank Balance (₹ 30,000 + ₹ 90,000)	1,20,000
		Cash in hand	30,000
	14,20,000		14,20,000

Dr. **PARTNERS' CAPITAL ACCOUNTS IN THE BOOKS OF P & CO.** *Cr.*

Particulars	*P (₹)*	*Q (₹)*	*Particulars*	*P (₹)*	*Q (₹)*
To M/s PQR & Co.	4,89,000	2,43,000	By Balance b/d	2,40,000	1,60,000
			By Reserve (3 : 1)	37,500	12,500
			By Realisation A/c (Profit)	2,11,500	70,500
	4,89,000	2,43,000		4,89,000	2,43,000

Dr. **PARTNERS' CAPITAL ACCOUNTS IN THE BOOKS OF R & CO.** *Cr.*

Particulars	*P (₹)*	*Q (₹)*	*Particulars*	*P (₹)*	*Q (₹)*
To M/s PQR & Co	3,68,000	1,84,000	By Balance b/d	2,00,000	1,00,000

			By Reserve (2 : 1)	1,00,000	50,000
			By Realisation A/c (Profit)	68,000	34,000
	3,68,000	1,84,000		3,68,000	1,84,000

Working Notes:

(I) COMPUTATION OF PURCHASE CONSIDERATION

Particulars	*P & Co.* ₹	*R & Co.* ₹
Assets:		
Goodwill	1,20,000	60,000
Building	1,00,000	60,000
Plant & machinery	2,50,000	2,00,000
Office equipment	20,000	6,000
Stock-in-trade	1,44,000	1,68,000
Sundry Debtors	1,60,000	2,00,000
Bank balance	30,000	90,000
Cash in hand	20,000	10,000
Due from R & Co.	1,00,000	—
(A)	9,44,000	7,94,000
Less: Liabilities:		
Creditors	1,20,000	1,16,000
Provision for doubtful debts	12,000	26,000
Due to P & Co.	—	1,00,000
Bank overdraft	80,000	—
(B)	2,12,000	2,42,000
Purchase Consideration (A – B)	7,32,000	5,52,000

(II) COMPUTATION OF PROPORTIONATE CAPITAL

M/s PQR & Co. (Purchase Consideration) (₹ 7,32,000 + ₹ 5,52,000)	12,84,000
Less: Goodwill Adjustment	(1,80,000)
Total Capital of new firm (Distributed in ratio 3 : 2 : 1)	11,04,000
P's Proportionate Capital	5,52,000
Q's Proportionate Capital	3,68,000
R's proportionate capital	1,84,000

(III) COMPUTATION OF CAPITAL ADJUSTMENTS

Particulars	*P* ₹	*Q* ₹	*R* ₹	*Total* ₹
Balance transferred from P & Co.	4,89,000	2,43,000		7,32,000
Balance transferred from R & Co.	—	3,68,000	1,84,000	5,52,000
	4,89,000	6,11,000	1,84,000	12,84,000

Less: Goodwill written off in the ratio of 3 : 2 : 1	(90,000)	(60,000)	(30,000)	(1,80,000)
Existing capital	3,99,000	5,51,000	1,54,000	11,04,000
Proportionate capital	5,52,000	3,68,000	1,84,000	11,04,000
Amount to be brought in (paid off)	1,53,000	(1,83,000)	30,000	

Dr. **REALISATION ACCOUNT IN THE BOOKS OF P & CO.** *Cr.*

Particulars		₹	*Particulars*	₹
To Building		50,000	By Creditors	1,20,000
To Plant & Machinery		1,50,000	By Bank overdraft	80,000
To Office Equipment		20,000	By M/s PQR & Co.	7,32,000
To Stock-in-trade		1,20,000	(purchase consideration)	
To Sundry debtors		1,60,000		
To Bank balance		30,000		
To Cash in hand		20,000		
To Due from R & Co.		1,00,000		
To Profit on Realisation t/f to:				
P's Capital A/c	2,11,500			
Q's Capital A/c	70,500	2,82,000		
		9,32,000		9,32,000

Dr. **REALISATION ACCOUNT IN THE BOOKS OF R & CO.** *Cr.*

Particulars		₹	*Particulars*	₹
To Building		60,000	By Creditors	1,16,000
To Plant & machinery		1,60,000	By Due to P & Co.	1,00,000
To Office equipment		6,000	By M/s PQR & Co.	5,52,000
To Stock-in-trade		1,40,000	(purchase consideration)	
To Sundry debtors		2,00,000		
To Bank balance		90,000		
To Cash in hand		10,000		
To Profit on Realisation t/f to:				
Q's Capital A/c	68,000			
R's Capital A/c	34,000	1,02,000		
		7,68,000		7,68,000

ILLUSTRATION 5

Firm X & Co. conlsists of partners A and B sharing Profits and Losses in the rato of 3:2. The firm Y & Co. consists of partners B and C sharing Profits and Losses in the ratio of 5:3.

On 31st March, 2016 it was decided to amalgamate both the firms and form a new firm XY & Co., wherein A, B and C would be partners sharing Profits and Losses in the ratio of 4:5:1.

BALANCE SHEET AS AT 31.3.2016

Liabilities	*X & Co.* ₹	*Y & Co.* ₹	*Assets*	*X & Co.* ₹	*Y & Co.* ₹
Capitals: A	1,50,000		Cash in hand & Bank	40,000	30,000
B	1,00,000	75,000	Debtors	60,000	80,000
C	—	50,000	Stock	50,000	20,000
Reserve	50,000	40,000	Vehicles	—	90,000
Creditors	1,20,000	55,000	Machinery	1,20,000	—
			Building	1,50,000	—
	4,20,000	2,20,000		4,20,000	2,20,000

The following were the terms of amalgamation:

(i) Goodwill of X & Co., was valued at ₹ 75,000. Goodwill of Y & Co. was valued at ₹ 40,000. Goodwill account not to be opened in the books of the new firm but adjusted through the Capital accounts of the partners.

(ii) Building, Machinery and Vehicles are to be taken over at ₹ 2,00,000, ₹ 1,00,000 and ₹ 74,000 respectively.

(iii) Provision for doubtful debts at ₹ 5,000 in respect of X & Co. and ₹ 4,000 in respect of Y & Co, are to be provided.

You are required to:

(i) Show, how the Goodwill value is adjusted amongst the partners.

(ii) Propare the Balance Sheet of XY & Co. as at 31.3.2016 by keeping partners' capitals in their profit sharing ratio by taking capital of B as the basis. The excess *or* deficiency to be kept in the respective Partners' Current accounts.

SOLUTION

ADJUSTMENT FOR RAISING AND WRITING OFF OF GOODWILL

Raised in Old Profit Sharing Ratio			*Total Written off in new ratio 4 : 5 : 1*	*Difference*
X & Co. (3 : 2) ₹	*Y & Co. (5 : 3)* ₹	₹	₹	₹
45,000	—	45,000 Cr.	46,000 Dr.	1,000 Dr.
30,000	25,000	55,000 Cr.	57,500 Dr.	2,500 Dr.
—	15,000	15,000 Cr.	11,500 Dr.	3,500 Cr.
75,000	40,000	1,15,000	1,15,000	Nil

BALANCE SHEET OF X Y & CO. (NEW FIRM) AS AT 31.3.2016

Liabilities	₹	*Assets*	₹
Capital Accounts:		Vehicle	74,000
A	1,72,000	Machinery	1,00,000
B	2,15,000	Building	2,00,000
C	43,000	Stock	70,000
Current Accounts:		Debtors	1,31,000

A	22,000	Cash & Bank	70,000
C	18,000		
Creditors	1,75,000		
	6,45,000		6,45,000

Working Notes:

(I) BALANCE OF CAPITAL ACCOUNTS AT THE TIME OF AMALGAMATION OF FIRMS

Particulars	*X & Co. (3:2)*		*Y & Co. (5:3)*	
	A's Capital ₹	*B's Capital* ₹	*B's Capital* ₹	*A's Capital* ₹
Balance as per Balance Sheet	1,50,000	1,00,000	75,000	50,000
Add: Reserves	30,000	20,000	25,000	15,000
Revaluation Profit (Building)	30,000	20,000	—	—
Less: Revaluation Loss (Machinery)	(12,000)	(8,000)	(10,000)	(6,000)
Provision for doubtful debt	(3,000)	(2,000)	(2,500)	(1,500)
	1,95,000	1,30,000	87,500	57,500

(II) BALANCE OF CAPITAL ACCOUNTS IN THE BALANCE SHEET OF THE NEW FIRM

Particulars	*A* ₹	*B* ₹	*C* ₹
Balance b/d: X & Co.	1,95,000	1,30,000	
Y & Co.		87,500	57,500
	1,95,000	2,17,500	57,500
Adjustment for goodwill	(1,000)	(2,500)	3,500
	1,94,000	2,15,000	61,000
Total Capital ₹ 4,30,000 (B's Capital i.e. ₹ 2,15,000 × 2) to be contributed in 4:5:1 ratio.	1,72,000	2,15,000	43,000
Transfer to Current Account	22,000	—	18,000

ILLUSTRATION 6

A and B are partners of AB & Co. sharing profits and losses in the ratio of 2: 1 and C and D are partners of CD & Co. sharing profits and losses in the ratio of 3:2. On 1st April 2016, they decided to amalgamate and form a new firm M/S. AD & Co. wherein all the partners of both the firm would be partners sharing profits and losses in the ratio of 2:1:3:2 respectively to A, B, C and D.

Their balance sheets on that date were as under:

Liabilities	*AB & Co.* ₹	*CD & Co.* ₹	*Assets*	*AB & Co.* ₹	*CD & Co.* ₹
Capitals					
A	1,50,000		Building	75,000	90,000
B	1,00,000		Machinery	1,20,000	1,00,000
C		1,20,000	Furniture	15,000	12,000
D		80,000	Stock	24,000	36,000

Reserve	66,000	54,000	Debtors	65,000	78,000
Creditors	52,000	35,000	Due from CD& Co.	47,000	
Due to AB & Co.		47,000	Cash at Bank	18,000	15,000
			Cash in hand	4,000	5,000
	3,68,000	3,36,000		3,68,000	3,36,000

The amalgamated firm took over the business on the following terms:

(a) Building was taken over at ₹ 1,00,000 and ₹ 1,25,000 of AB & Co. and CD & Co. respectively. And machinery was taken over at ₹ 1,25,000 and ₹ 1,10,000 of AB & Co. and CD & Co. respectively.

(b) Goodwill of AB & Co. was worth ₹ 75,000 and that of CD & Co. was worth ₹ 50,000. Goodwill account was not to be opened in the books of the new firm, the adjustments being recorded through capital accounts of the partners.

(c) Provision for doubtful debts has to be carried forward at ₹ 5,000 in respect of debtors of AB & Co. and ₹ 8,000 in respect of CD & Co.

You are required:

(i) Compute the adjustments necessary for goodwill.

(ii) Pass the Journal Entries in the books of AD & Co. assuming that excess/deficit capital (taking D's capital as base) with reference to share in profits are to be transferred to current accounts.

SOLUTION

(I) ADJUSTMENT FOR RAISING & WRITING OFF OF GOODWILL

	Goodwill raised in old profit sharing ratio			*Goodwill written off in new ratio*	*Difference*
	AB&Co.	*CD&Co.*	*Total*	*AD&Co.*	
	₹	₹	₹	₹	₹
A	50,000		50,000 Cr.	31,250 Dr.	18,750 Cr.
B	25,000		25,000 Cr.	15,625 Dr.	9,375 Cr.
C		30,000	30,000 Cr.	46,875 Dr.	16,875 Dr.
D		20,000	20,000 Cr.	31,250 Dr.	11, 250 Dr.
	75,000	50,000	1,25,000	1,25,000	

(II) IN THE BOOKS OF AD&CO.

JOURNAL

Date	Particulars		L.F.	Dr. (₹)	Cr. (₹)
01.04.2016	Building A/c	Dr.		1,00,000	
	Machinery A/c	Dr.		1,25,000	
	Furniture A/c	Dr.		15,000	
	Stock A/c	Dr.		24,000	
	Debtors A/c	Dr.		65,000	
	CD & Co. A/c	Dr.		47,000	
	Cash at bank A/c	Dr.		18,000	

	Cash in hand A/c Dr.		4,000	
	To Provision for doubtful debts A/c			5,000
	To Creditors A/c			52,000
	To A's capital A/c			2,10,667
	To B's capital A/c			1,30,333
	(Being the sundry assets and liabilities of AB & Co. taken over at the values stated as per the agreement)			
	Building A/c Dr.		1,25,000	
	Machinery A/c Dr.		1,10,000	
	Furniture A/c Dr.		12,000	
	Stock A/c Dr.		36,000	
	Debtors A/c Dr.		78,000	
	Cash at bank A/c Dr.		15,000	
	Cash in hand A/c Dr.		5,000	
	To Provision for doubtful debts A/c			8,000
	To Creditors A/c			35,000
	To AB & Co. A/c			47,000
	To C's capital A/c			1,74,600
	To D's capital A/c			1,16,400
	(Being the sundry assets and liabilities of CD & Co. taken over at the values stated as per the agreement)			
	C's capital A/c Dr.		16,875	
	D's capital A/c Dr.		11,250	
	To A's capital A/c			18,750
	To B's capital A/c			9,375
	(Being adjustment in capital accounts of the partners on account of goodwill)			
	AB & Co. A/c Dr.		47,000	
	To CD & Co. A/c			47,000
	(Being mutual indebtedness of AB & Co. and CD&Co. cancelled)			
	A's Capital A/c Dr.		1,24,267	
	To A's Current A/c			1,24,267
	(Being excess amount in A's capital A/c transferred to A's current A/c)			
	B's Capital A/c Dr.		87,133	
	To B's Current A/c			87,133
	(Being excess amount in B's capital A/c transferred to B's current A/c)			

Working Notes:

(I) PROFIT ON REVALUATION

Particulars	*AB & Co.* ₹	*CD & Co.* ₹
Building (1,00,000 – 75,000)	25,000	
(1,25,000 – 90,000)		35,000
Machinery (1,25,000 – 1,20,000)	5,000	
(1,10,000 – 1,00,000)		10,000
	30,000	45,000
Less: Provision for doubtful debts	(5,000)	(8,000)
	25,000	37,000

(II) BALANCE OF CAPITAL ACCOUNTS OF PARTNERS

Particulars	*A's Capital* ₹	*B's Capital* ₹	*C's Capital* ₹	*D's Capital* ₹
Balance as per the B/S	1,50,000	1,00,000	1,20,000	80,000
Reserves	44,000	22,000	32,400	21,600
Profit on revaluation	16,667	8,333	22,200	14,800
	2,10,667	1,30,333	1,74,600	1,16,400

(III) CALCULATION OF CAPITAL OF EACH PARTNER IN THE NEW FIRM

Particulars	*A* ₹	*B* ₹	*C* ₹	*D* ₹
Balance	2,10,667	1,30,333	1,74,600	1,16,400
Adjustment for goodwill	18,750	9,375	(16,875)	(11,250)
	2,29,417	1,39,708	1,57,725	1,05,150
Total Capital ₹ 4,20,600* in the new ratio of 2 : 1 : 3 : 2	(1,05,150)	(52,575)	(1,57,725)	(1,05,150)
Transfer to Current Account	1,24,267	87,133		

* Taking D's capital as the base which is 2/8th of total capital; total capital will be 1,05,150 × 8/2 i.e ₹ 4,20,600.

2.0 CONVERSION OF A FIRM INTO A COMPANY

In case of conversion of a firm into a company if it is specifically given that the partners agree to preserve the same rights as regards the interest on capital and the sharing profits and losses as they had in the partnership, the question of equity shares and preference shares to be issued to partners may be dealt with in any one of the following two ways:

Method	*Manner of Issuing Shares*
I. If it is desired to receive the same amount of Interest on Fixed Capital	(a) Issue Preference Shares in the ratio of Fixed Capitals. (b) Issue Equity Shares for the balance in the profit sharing ratio.

II. If it is desired to compensate those partners who contribute Capital in excess of what is required as per profit sharing ratio.	(a) Issue Equity Shares in the ratio of Proportionate Capitals (taking the capital of a partner who contributed the least, base) (b) Issue Preference Shares for the Surplus Capitals.

Important Note for Examination: *In case of Conversion of a firm into a compnay, if the question is silent about the manner of issue of Equity Shares and Preference Shares, Second Method seems to be more appropriate and hence is recommended.*

ILLUSTRATION 7

X, Y and Z were carrying on business in partnership, sharing profits & losses in the ratio of 2:3:5 respectively after allowing Interest on Capitals @ 15% p.a. They decided to convert therir firm into a company and formed Jalan Private Limited. The following is the Balance Sheet of the firm as at 31st March, 2016:

Liabilities	₹	*Assets*	₹
Capital Accounts:		Sundry Assets	1,00,000
X	9,450		
Y	5,670		
Z	3,780		
Current Accounts:			
X	36,162		
Y	15,498		
Sundry Creditors	29,440		
	1,00,000		1,00,000

The Company took over the firm's business for a total consideration of ₹ 1,05,000. The purchase consideration was to be discharged by a cash payment of ₹ 44,100, the allotment of 1,890 15%. Non-cumulative Preference Shares of ₹ 10 each and the balance by allotment of 2,100 Equity Shares of ₹ 10 each.

Required: Prepare Realisation Account and Partners' Capital Accounts in the books of a firm in each of the following alternative cases:

Case (a) If it is desired to receive the same amount of Interest on Fixed Capital and the same % of Profits.

Case (b) If it is desired to compensate those partners who contribute Capital in excess of what is required as per profit sharing ratio and to receive the same % of Profits.

Case (c) If shares in the company are to be issued to the partners in such numbers and in such classes as will give the partners by reason of their shareholdings alone, the same rights as regards interest on capitals and the sharing of profits and losses as they had in the partnership.

SOLUTION

Case (a) Issue Preference Shares in the ratio of Fixed Capitals. Issue Equity Shares for the balance in the profit sharing ratio.

Dr. **REALISATION ACCOUNT** Cr.

Particulars	₹	Particulars	₹
To Sundry Assets	1,00,000	By Sundry Creditors	29,440
To Profit on Realisation t/f to:		By Jalan Private Limited	1,05,000
X 's Capital A/c	6,888	(Purchase Consideration)	
Y 's Capital A/c	10,332		
Z 's Capital A/c	17,220		
	1,34,440		1,34,440

Dr. **CAPITAL ACCOUNTS OF PARTNERS** Cr.

Particulars	X ₹	Y ₹	Z ₹	Particulars	X ₹	Y ₹	Z ₹
To Balance c/d	52,500	31,500	21,000	By Balance b/d	9,450	5,670	3,780
				By Realisation A/c	6,888	10,332	17,220
				By Current A/c	36,162	15,498	—
	52,500	31,500	21,000		52,500	31,500	21,000
To Equity Shares	8,400	12,600	21,000	By Balance b/d	52,500	31,500	21,000
To 15% Pref. Shares	9,450	5,670	3,780	By Cash A/c	—	—	3,780
To Cash A/c	34,650	13,230	—				
	52,500	31,500	24,780		52,500	31,500	24,780

Note: *In this case Z is required to bring in ₹ 3,780 cash.*

Case (b) Issue Equity Shares in the ratio of Proportionate Capitals (taking the capital of a partner who contributed the least, base) and Issue Preference Shares for the Surplus Capitals.

STEP 1: CALCULATION OF SURPLUS CAPITALS TO ISSUE PREF. SHARES

	Particulars	X	Y	Z
A.	Actual Capitals	52,500	31,500	21,000
B.	Profit Sharing Ratio	2	3	5
C.	Actual Capitals/Profit Sharing Ratio	26,250	10,500	4,200
D.	Proportionate Capitals taking Z 's Capital as Bank Capital	8,400	12,600	21,000
E.	Surplus Capital [A – D]	44,100	18,900	—

15% Preference Shares and Cash have been distributed in the ratio of Surplus Capitals (i.e. 44,100 : 18,900 *or* 441 : 189).

Step 2: Calculation of Value of Equity Shares to be issued in Profit Sharing Ratio

= 1,05,000 (Purchase Consideration) – 44,100 (Cash) – 18,900 (Pef. Shares) = 42,000 (Equity Shares)

Realisation Account and the first part of Capital accounts of partners will be same as appear in case (a) but the second part of Capital Accounts of partners will appear as under:

Dr. **CAPITAL ACCOUNTS OF PARTNERS** *Cr.*

Particulars	*X* ₹	*Y* ₹	*Z* ₹	*Particulars*	*X* ₹	*Y* ₹	*Z* ₹
To Equity Shares	8,400	12,600	21,000	By Balance b/d	52,500	31,500	21,000
To 15% Pref. Shares	13,230	5,670	—				
To Cash	30,870	13,230	—				
	52,500	31,500	21,000		52,500	31,500	21,000

Case (c) The question of equity and preference shares to be issued to partners should be dealt with as per Method II and hence the solution will be the same as appearing in case (b).

ILLUSTRATION 8

P, Q and R were carrying on business in partnership, sharing profits and losses in the ratio of 5 : 4 : 3 respectively. The trial balance of the firm as on 31st March, 2016 was the following:

Particulars		*Debit (₹)*	*Credit (₹)*
Plant and Machinery		85,000	—
Stock		64,200	—
Sundry Debtors		66,500	—
Sundry Creditors		—	84,700
Capital Accounts:	P	—	63,000
	Q	—	42,000
	R		21,000
Drawings Accounts:	P	20,000	—
	Q	20,000	—
	R	15,000	—
Depreciation on Plant and Machinery		—	25,000
Trading profit for the year		—	1,23,300
cash at Bank		88,300	—
		3,59,000	3,59,000

Interest on Capital accounts @ 5% p.a. on the amount standing to the credit of partner's Capital Account at the beginning of the year was not provided before preparing the above Trial Balance. On 31st March, they formed a Private Limited Co. with an authorised share capital of ₹ 2,00,000 in shares of ₹ 10 each to be divided in different classes to take over the business of partnership.

You are informed as under:

(a) Plant and Machinery is to be transferred at ₹ 66,000.

(b) Shares in the company are to be issued to the partners, in such numbers and such classes as will give the partners, by reason of their share holdings alone, the same rights as regards interest on capitals and the sharing of profit and losses as they had in the partnership.

(c) Before transferring the business, the partners wish to draw from the partnership their profit to such an extent that the Bank balance is reduced to ₹ 50,000. For this purpose, sufficient profits of the year are to be retained in profit sharing ratio.

(d) All assets and liabilities except plant and machinery and the bank balance are to be transferred at their values in the books of the partnership as on 31st March.

You are required to prepare:

(i) Profit and Loss Account for the year ending on 31.3.2016.

(ii) Capital Accounts showing all the adjustments required to dissolve the partnership.

(iii) A statement showing the number of shares of each class to be issued by the company to each of the partners and details of rights attaching to those shares.

(iv) The Balance Sheet of the company immediately after acquiring the partnership and issuing of shares.

SOLUTION

(I) PROFIT AND LOSS ACCOUNT

for the year ending on 31st March, 2016

Dr. *Cr.*

Particulars		₹	Particulars	₹
To Interest on Capitals:			By Trading Profit	123,300
P	3,150			
Q	2,100			
R	1,050	6,300		
To Profit transferred to Capital A/cs:				
P	48,750			
Q	39,000			
R	29,250	1,17,000		
		1,23,300		1,23,300

Dr. **(II) CAPITAL ACCOUNTS OF PARTNERS** *Cr.*

Particulars	*P* ₹	*Q* ₹	*R* ₹	*Particulars*	*P* ₹	*Q* ₹	*R* ₹
To Drawings	20,000	20,000	15,000	By Balance b/d	63,000	42,000	21,000
To Bank (drawings)	19,400	11,100	7,800	By Interest on Capital	3,150	2,100	1,050
To 5% Preference Shares	28,000	14,000	—	By P & L A/c	48,750	39,000	29,250
To Equity Shares	50,000	40,000	30,000	By Plant & Machinery (Profit on transfer)	2,500	2,000	1,500
	1,17,400	85,100	52,800		1,17,400	85,100	52,800

The question of preference and equity shares to be issued to P, Q and R can be dealt with in the following manner:

Particulars	*P* ₹	*Q* ₹	*R* ₹
A. Total amount due as capital	78,000	54,000	30,000
B. Proportionate Capitals taking R's Capital as the Base Capital (for which Equity Shares should be issued)	50,000	40,000	30,000
C. Surplus Capital (A – B) (for which 5% Non-Cum Pref. Shares should be issued)	28,000	14,000	Nil

The above treatment is based on the principle that the function of interest in case of partnership is to compensate those partners who contribute capital in excess of what is required as per profit sharing ratio.

BALANCE SHEET OF LTD AS AT 1st APRIL, 2016

Particulars	Note No.	₹
I. EQUITY AND LIABILITIES		
(1) Shareholders' Funds		
(a) Share Capital	1	1,62,000
(2) Non-Current Liabilities		
(3) Current Liabilities		
Trade Payables		84,700
Total		2,46,700
II. ASSETS		
(1) Non-Current Assets		
(a) Fixed Assets		
(i) Tangible Assets (Plant & Machinery)		66,000
(2) Current Assets		
Inventories		64,200
Trade Receivables		66,500
Cash and Cash Equivalents		50,000
Total		2,46,700

Notes to Accounts:

NOTE 1: SHARE CAPITAL

Authorised Capital	
0,000 Shares of ₹ 10 each	2,00,000
Issued & Subscribed Capital	
12,000 Equity Shares of ₹ 10 each	1,20,000
4,200, 5% Pref. Shares of ₹ 10 each	42,000
(Of the above all Shares were issued for consideration otherwise than cash)	
	1,62,000

Working Notes:

(I) CALCULATION OF ADDITIONAL DRAWINGS

Drawings (already made: ₹ 55,000, *plus* those to be made ₹ 38,300, (i.e. ₹ 88,300 – 50,000), are ₹ 93,300. Of these, ₹ 6,300 is for interest. The remaining ₹ 87,000 is to be drawn by the partners in the ratio of 5 : 4 : 3.

STATEMENT SHOWING THE CALCULATION OF ADDITIONAL DRAWINGS

Particulars	P ₹	Q ₹	R ₹
A. Total Drawings (excluding interest) (Ratio 5 : 4 : 3)	36,250	29,000	21,750
B. *Add:* Interest on Capital	3,150	2,100	1,050
	39,400	31,100	22,800

C. *Less:* Amount already drawn	20,000	20,000	15,000
D. Additional Drawings to be made (A + B – C)	19,400	11,100	7,800

(ii) Purchase Consideration = Agreed Value of Assets taken over – Agreed amt. of Liabilities taken over

= ₹ 66,000 + ₹ 64,200 + ₹ 66,500 + ₹ 50,000 – ₹ 84,700 = ₹ 1,62,000.

ILLUSTRATION 9

P, Q and R are partners sharing profits and losses in the ratio 3 : 2 : 1 after allowing interest on capital @ 9% p.a. Their balance Sheet as at 31st March, 2012 are as follows:

Liabilities	(₹)	*Assets*	(₹)
Capital Accounts:		Plant & Machinery	1,08,000
P	50,000	Fixtures	20,000
Q	30,000	Stock	50,000
R	20,000	Sundry Debtors	30,000
Reserve Fund	60,000		
Creditors	48,000		
	2,08,000		2,08,000

They applied for conversion of the firm into a Private Limited Company named PQR Pvt. Ltd. and the certificate was received on 01-04-2012. They decided to maintain same profit sharing ratio and the preserve the priority in regard to repayment of capital as far as possible. For that purpose they decided to insert a clause of issuance of Preference shares in Memorandum of Association in addition to issuance of Equity Shares of ₹ 10 each. On 01.04.2012, the value of goodwill is to be determined on the basis of 2 years' purchase of the average profit from the business of the last 5 years. The particulars of profits are as under:

Particulars		₹
Year ended 31.03.2008	Profit	10,000
Year ended 31.03.2009	Loss	5,000
Year ended 31.03.2010	Profit	18,000
Year ended 31.03.2011	Profit	27,000
Year ended 31.03.2012	Profit	30,000

The loss for the year ended 31-03-2009 was on account of loss by strike to the extent of ₹ 10,000. It was agreed that rest of the assets are valued on the basis of the Balance Sheet as at 31-03-2012 except Plant & machinery which is valued at ₹ 1,02,000.

You are required to prepare (a) the Balance Sheet of the Company as at 01.04.2012, (b) Partners' Capital Accounts and (c) Statement showing the final settlement between the partners taking Q's capital as basis.

SOLUTION

(A) **BALANCE SHEET OF THE PQR PVT LTD. AS AT 1.4.2012**

Particulars	*Note No.*	(₹)
I. EQUITY AND LIABILITIES		
(1) Shareholders' Funds		
(a) Share Capital	1	1,90,000

(2) Non-Current Liabilities		
(3) Current Liabilities		
(a) Trade Payables		48,000
Total		2,38,000
II. ASSETS		
(1) Non-Current Assets		
(a) Fixed Assets		
(i) Tangible Assets	2	1,22,000
(ii) Intangible Assets	3	36,000
(2) Current Assets		
(a) Inventories		50,000
(b) Trade Receivables		30,000
Total		2,38,000

Notes To Accounts:

1. Share Capital	
Authorised Capital	
18,000 Equity Shares of ₹ 10 each	1,80,000
9% Pref. Shares of ₹ 100 each	10,000
	1,90,000
Issued & Subscribed Capital	
18,000 Equity Shares of ₹ 10 each	1,80,000
9% Pref. Shares of ₹ 100 each	10,000
(All the shares have been issued for consideration other than cash)	
	1,90,000
2. Tangible Assets	
Plant and Machinery	1,02,000
Fixtures	20,000
	1,22,000
3. Intangible Asset	
Goodwill	36,000

Dr. **(B) CAPITAL ACCOUNTS OF PARTNERS** Cr.

Particulars	*P* ₹	*Q* ₹	*R* ₹	*Particulars*	*P* ₹	*Q* ₹	*R* ₹
To P & M A/c	3,000	2,000	1,000	By Balance b/d	50,000	30,000	20,000
To 9% Pref. Shares	5,000	–	5,000	By Reserve fund	30,000	20,000	10,000
To Equity Shares	90,000	60,000	30,000	By Realization A/c (Profit on Sale of Business)	18,000	12,000	6,000
	98,000	62,000	36,000		98,000	62,000	36,000

The question of preference and equity shares to be issued to P, Q and R can be dealt with in the following manner:

Particulars	P ₹	Q ₹	R ₹
A. Total amount due as capital	95,000	60,000	35,000
B. Proportionate Capitals taking Q's Capital as the Base Capital (for which Equity Shares should be issued)	90,000	60,000	30,000
C. Surplus Capital (A – B) (for which 9% Non-Cum Pref. Shares should be issued)	5,000	–	5,000

The above treatment is based on the principle that the function of interest in case of partnership is to compensate those partners who contribute capital in excess of what is required as per profit sharing ratio.

Working Notes:

1. CALCULATION OF GOODWILL

Particulars	2007-2008 ₹	2008-2009 ₹	2009-2010 ₹	2010-2011 ₹	2011-2012 ₹
Profits	10,000	(5,000)	18,000	27,000	30,000
Adjustment for abnormal loss in 2008-2009	–	10,000	–	–	–
	10,000	5,000	18,000	27,000	30,000

Particulars	₹
Total Profit from 2007-08 to 2011-12	90,000
Average Profit (90,000/5)	18,000
Goodwill equal to 2 years' Purchase	36,000

2. COMPUTATION OF PURCHASE CONSIDERATION

Particulars	₹
Assets	
Goodwill	36,000
Plant and Machinery	1,02,000
Fixtures	20,000
Stock	50,000
Sundry Debtors	30,000
	2,38,000
Less: Liabilities	
Creditors	48,000
Purchase Consideration	1,90,000

ILLUSTRATION 10

The following is the Balance Sheet of M/s P and Q as on 31st March, 2012:

Liabilities	₹	*Assets*	₹
P's Capital	50,000	Machinery	54,000
Q's Capital	30,000	Furniture	5,000
Q's Loan	15,000	Investments	50,000
General Reserve	20,000	Stock	20,000
Creditors	40,000	Debtors	21,000
		Cash	5,000
	1,55,000		1,55,000

It was agreed that Mr. R is to be admitted for a fourth share in the future profits from 1st April, 2012. He is required to contribute cash towards goodwill and ₹ 15,000 towards capital. The following further information is furnished:

(a) P and Q share the profits in the ratio of 3 : 2.

(b) Mr P was receiving a salary of ₹ 750 p.m from the very inception of the firm in 2005 in addition to share of profit.

(c) The future profit sharing ratio between P, Q and R will be 2 : 1 : 1. Mr P will not get any salary after the admission of Mr R.

(d) The goodwill of the firm shall be determined on the basis of 3 years' purchase of the average profits from business of the last 5 years. The particulars of the profits are as under:

2007-2008 Profit ₹ 25,000, 2008-2009 Profit ₹ 12,500, 2009-2010 Loss ₹ 2,500, 2010-2011 Profit ₹ 35,000, 2011-2012 Profit ₹ 30,000.

The above profits and losses are after charging the salary of Mr P. The profit for the year ended. 31st March 2008 included an extraneous profits of ₹ 40,000 and the loss of the year ended 31st March 2010 was on account of loss by strike to the extent of ₹ 20,000. It was agreed that the value of the goodwill of the firm shall appear in the book of the firm.

(e) The cash trading profit for the year ended 31st March, 2013 was ₹ 50,000 before depreciation.

(f) Each partner withdrew ₹ 1,000 p.m. as drawings.

(g) The value of the other assets and liabilities as on 31st March, 2013 were Machinery (before depreciation) ₹ 60,000, Furniture (before depreciation) ₹ 10,000, Investments ₹ 50,000, Stock ₹ 15,000, Debtors ₹ 30,000, Creditors ₹ 20,000.

(h) Provide depreciation @ 10% on Machinery and @ 5% on furnitures on the closing balance and interest @ 6% on Q's loan. The loan along with interest would be repaid within next 12 months.

(i) Investments are held from inception of the firm and interest is received @ 10% p.a.

(j) The partners applied for conversion of the firm into a Private Limited Company. Certificate was received on 1st April, 2013. They decided to convert Capital A/cs of the partners into share capital in the ratio of 2 : 1 : 1 on the basis of total Capital as on 31st March, 2013. If necessary, partners have to subscribe to fresh capital *or* withdraw.

Required: Prepare the profit and loss Account for the year ended 31st March, 2013 and the Balance Sheet as at 1st April 2013.

SOLUTION

PROFIT AND LOSS ACCOUNT

Dr. *for the year ending on 31st March, 2013* *Cr.*

Particulars		₹	Particulars	₹
To Depreciation on Machinery		6,000	By Trading Profit	50,000
To Depreciation on furniture		500	By Interest on Investment	5,000
To Interest on Q's loan		900		
To Net Profit to:				
P's Capital A/c	23,800			
Q's Capital A/c	11,900			
R's Capital A/c	11,900	47,600		
		55,000		55,000

BALANCE SHEET OF THE PQR PVT LTD. AS AT 1.4.2013

Particulars	Note No.	(₹)
I. EQUITY AND LIABILITIES		
(1) Shareholders' Funds [Share Capital]		1,41,600
(2) Current Liabilities		
(a) Short Term borrowings	1	15,900
(b) Trade Payables		20,000
Total		1,77,500
II. ASSETS		
(1) Non-Current Assets		
(a) Fixed Assets		
(i) Tangible Assets	2	63,500
(ii) Non-current investments		50,000
(2) Current Assets		
(a) Inventories		15,000
(b) Trade Receivables		30,000
(c) Cash and cash equivalents		19,000
Total		2,38,000

Notes To Accounts:

Particulars	₹
1. Short term borrowings	
Loan from Q	15,900
2. Tangible assets	
Machinery	54,000
Furniture	9,500
	63,500

Working Notes:

1. CALCULATION OF GOODWILL

Particulars	*2007-08* ₹	*2008-09* ₹	*2009-10* ₹	*2010-11* ₹	*2011-12* ₹
Profits/(Loss)	25,000	12,500	(2,500)	35,000	30,000
Adjustment for Abnormal Profit & Loss	(40,000)	—	20,000	—	—
Add: Salary of partner (750 × 12)	9,000	9,000	9,000	9,000	9,000
Less: Interest on Non-Trading Investments	(5,000)	(5,000)	(5,000)	(5,000)	(5,000)
	(11,000)	16,500	21,500	39,000	34,000

Particulars	₹
Total Profit for five years	1,00,000
Average Profit (₹ 1,00,000/5)	20,000
Goodwill equal to 3 years' Purchase	60,000
New partner's share of goodwill for 1/4 share	15,000

2. Sacrificing Ratio: P's sacrifice = 3/5 – 1/2 = 1/10, Q's sacrifice = 2/5 – 1/4 = 3/20.
3. As per AS 26 "Intangible Assets", only purchased goodwill should appear in the books. Therefore, goodwill though required to be shown in the books as per the requirement of the question, has been adjusted through capital accounts of the partenrs in line with the provisions of AS 26.

Dr. **4. CAPITAL ACCOUNTS OF PARTNERS** *Cr.*

Particulars	*P* ₹	*Q* ₹	*R* ₹	*Particulars*	*P* ₹	*Q* ₹	*R* ₹
To Drawings A/c	12,000	12,000	12,000	By Balance b/d	50,000	30,000	—
To P	—	—	6,000	By General Reserve	12,000	8,000	—
To Q	—	—	9,000	By R	6,000	9,000	—
To Balance c/d	79,800	46,900	14,900	By Bank A/c	—	—	30,000
				By P & L A/c	23,800	11,900	11,900
	91,800	58,900	41,900		91,800	58,900	41,900

5. BALANCE SHEET OF M/S XYZ & CO. AS AT 31st MARCH, 2013

Liabilities		₹	*Assets*		₹
P's Capital	79,800		Machinery	60,000	
Q's Capital	46,900		Less : Depreciation	(6,000)	54,000
R's Capital	14,900	1,41,600	Furniture	10,000	
			Less : Depreciation	(500)	9,500
Q's Loan	15,000		Investments		50,000
Add : Interest due	900	15,900	Stock-in-trade		15,000

Creditors	20,000	Debtors	30,000
		Cash	19,000
	1,77,500		1,77,500

6. CALCULATION OF CLOSING CASH BALANCE

Particulars	₹
Opening cash balance	5,000
Add: Cash brought in by R	30,000
Less: Drawings (12,000 + 12,000 + 12,000)	36,000
Less: Additions to Machine (60,000 – 54,000)	6,000
Less: Addition to Furniture (10,000 – 5,000)	5,000
Cash Trading Profit	50,000
Add: Investment Interest	5,000
Add: Decrease in Stock Balance	5,000
Less: Increase in Debtors	9,000
Less: Decrease in Creditors	20,000
Closing Cash Balance	19,000

7. ADJUSTMENT OF CAPITALS

Particulars	*P*	*Q*	*R*
A. Adjusted Capitals	79,800	46,900	14,900
B. Distribution of Shares in the ratio of 2:1:1	70,800	35,400	35,400
C. Surplus to be withdrawn (Shortage to be brought in)	9,000	11,500	(20,500)

3 ACCOUNTING FOR EMPLOYEE STOCK OPTION PLAN

LEARNING OBJECTIVES

After studying this chapter, you should be able to understand:

- ◇ What is Included in the term 'Employee' for the purpose of Employee Share-based Payments
- ◇ What are the various forms of Employee Share-based Payments?
- ◇ What is Objective and Importance of Employee Share-based Payments?
- ◇ What are the various Transfers that are Treated as Employee Share-based Payments?
- ◇ Which Transactions are not treated as Employee share-based Payments?
- ◇ Accounting Treatment of Employee Share - Based Plans in Financial Statements of an Enterprise
- ◇ Fair Value Method
- ◇ Intrinsic Value Method

1.0 WHAT IS INCLUDED IN THE TERM 'EMPLOYEE' FOR THE PURPOSE OF EMPLOYEE SHARE-BASED PAYMENTS

The term 'employee' includes a director of the enterprise, whether whole time *or* not for the purpose of Employee Share - based Payments

2.0 WHAT ARE THE VARIOUS FORMS OF EMPLOYEE SHARE - BASED PAYMENTS?

Employee share-based payments generally take the following three forms:

1. Employee Stock Option Plan [ESOP]	It is a plan under which the enterprise grants employee stock option. Employee Stock Option is a contract that gives the employees of the enterprise the right, but not the obligation, for a specified period of time to purchase *or* subscribe to the shares of the enterprise at a fixed *or* determinable price.
2. Employee Stock Purchase Plan [ESPP]	It is a plan under which the enterprise grants rights to its employees to purchase its shares at a stated price at the time of public issue *or* otherwise.
3. Stock Appreciation Rights [SARs]	It is a right that entitles the employees to receive cash *or* shares for an amount equivalent to any excess of the market value of a stated number of enterprise's shares over a stated price. The form of payment may be specified when the rights are granted *or* may be determined when they are exercised. However, in some plans, the employee may choose the form of payment.

3.0 WHAT IS OBJECTIVE AND IMPORTANCE OF EMPLOYEE SHARE - BASED PAYMENTS?

1. Objective	The objective of Employee Share-based payments is to encourage employees to have a higher participation in the company.
2. Importance	1. Stock options provide an opportunity to employees to share in the growth of the company. 2. Stock options create long-term wealth in the hands of the employees. 3. Stock options create a common sense of ownership between the company and its employees paving the way for a unified approach to the common objective of enhancing overall shareholder value. 4. Stock options are important means to attract, retain and motivate the best available talent for the company.

4.0 LEGAL POSITION [SECTION 62 (1)(B)]

Where at any time, a company having a share capital proposes to increase its subscribed capital by the issue of further shares, such shares shall be offered to employees under a scheme of employees' stock option, subject to special resolution passed by company and subject to such conditions as may be prescribed.

Explanation: For the purposes of section 62 (1)(b) and this rule "Employee" means.

(a) a permanent employee of the company who has been working in India *or* outside India*; or*

(b) a director of the company, whether a whole time director *or* not but excluding an independent director*; or*

(c) an employee as defined in clauses (a) *or* (b) of a subsidiary, in India *or* outside India, *or* of a holding company of the company *or* of an associate company but does not include-

(i) an employee who is a promoter *or* a person belonging to the promoter group*; or*

(ii) a director who either himself *or* through his relative *or* through any body corporate, directly *or* indirectly, holds more than 10% of the outstanding equity shares of the company.

5.0 TERMS USED WITH REFERENCE TO ESOS

1. Grant	Grant means the issue of option to the employee under ESOS.
2. Grant Date	Grant Date is the date at which the enterprise grants rights to its employees to receive cash *or* shares of the enterprise, on satisfaction of specified vesting conditions under an employee share-based payment plan.
3. Vesting	Vesting means the proce4ss by which the employee is given the right to apply for the shares of the company against the option granted to him under the ESOS.
4. Vesting Period	Vesting Period is the period between the grant date and the date on which all the specified vesting conditions of an employee share-based payment plan are to be satisfied.
5. Minimum Gap	There must be a minimum period of one year between the date of grant of option and the date of vesting of the optiion.
6. Exercise	Exercise means making of an application by an employee to the company for issue of shares against option vested in him under the ESOS.
7. Exercise Period	Exercise Period means the time period after vesting within which an employeee should exercise his right to apply for the shares vested in him under the ESOS.

8. Vesting Conditions	Vesting Conditions are the conditions that must be satisfied for the employee to become entitled to receive cash, *or* shares of the enterprise, pursuant to an employee share-based payment plan. Vesting conditions include service conditions, which require the employee to complete a specified period of service, and performance conditions, which require specified performance targets to be met (such as a specified increase in the enterprise's share price over a specified period of time).

6.0 WHAT ARE THE VARIOUS TRANSFERS THAT ARE TREATED AS EMPLOYEE SHARE-BASED PAYMENTS?

The following transfers are treated as employee share - based payments:

1. A transfer of shares *or* stock options of an enterprise by its shareholders to its employees, unless the transfer is clearly for a purpose other than payment for services rendered to the enterprise.
2. A transfer of shares *or* stock options of the parent of the enterprise.
3. A transfer of shares *or* stock options of another enterprise in the same group as the enterprise, to the employees of the enterprise.

   Note: A 'Group' is a parent and all its subsidiaries

7.0 WHICH TRANSACTIONS ARE NOT TREATED AS EMPLOYEE SHARE - BASED PAYMENTS?

The following transactions are not treated as employee share - based payments:

TRANSACTION IN THE CAPACITY OF SHAREHOLDER

A transaction with an employee in his/her capacity as a holder of shares of the enterprise. ***For Example***, if an enterprise grants all holders of a particular class of its shares the right to acquire additional shares *or* stock options of the enterprise at a price that is *less* than the fair value of those shares *or* stock options, and an employee receives such a right because he/she is a holder of shares *or* stock options of that particular class, the granting *or* exercise of that right is not an employee share - based payment.

RIGHT TO ACQUIRE SHARES ON THE SAME TERMS AS APPLICABLE TO INVESTORS

A grant of shares to the employees at the time of public issue if the price and other terms at which the shares are offered to employees are the same *or* similar to those at which the shares have been offered to general investors. ***For Example***, in a public issue an enterprise grants shares to its employees as a preferential allotment while the price and other terms remain the same as those to other investors.

8.0 ACCOUNTING TREATMENT OF EMPLOYEE SHARE - BASED PLANS IN FINANCIAL STATEMENTS OF AN ENTERPRISE

WHAT ARE THE VARIOUS CATEGORIES OF EMPLOYEE SHARE - BASED PLAN FOR THE PURPOSE OF THE REPORTING IN THE FINANCIAL STATEMENTS OF AN ENTERPRISE?

The various categories of employee share - based plan for the purpose of the reporting in the financial statements of an enterprise are as follows:

1. Equity-settled plans	Under these plans, the employees receive shares.
2. Cash-settled plans	Under these plans, the employees receive cash based on the price (or value) of the enterprise's shares.

3. Equity/cash-settled plans	Under these plans, either the enterprise *or* the employee has a choice of whether the enterprise settles the payment in cash *or* by issue of shares.

HOW SHOULD THESE CATEGORIES BE ACCOUNTED FOR IN THE FINANCIAL STATEMENTS OF THE ENTERPRISE?

These categories may be accounted for in the financial statements of the enterprise by any of the following two methods:

1. Fair Value Method	A fair value is the amount for which stock option granted *or* a share offered for purchase could be exchanged between knowledgeable, willing parties in an arm's length transaction.
2. Intrinsic Value Method	An Intrinsic Value is the amount by which the quoted market price of the underlying share in case of a listed enterprise *or* the value of the underlying share determined by an independent valuer in case of an unlisted enterprise exceeds the exercise price of an option. This method may be followed as alternative but with fair value disclosure.

9.0 FAIR VALUE METHOD

TOTAL FAIR VALUE OF OPTIONS

Total No. of Options expected to vest at the end of the Vesting Period × Fair value of each Option

HOW TO MEASURE FAIR VALUE

(a) If Market Prices are available	On the basis of market prices as on grant date and the terms and conditions upon which those shares *or* stock options were granted.
(b) If Market Prices are not available	The enterprise should estimate the fair value of the instruments granted using a valuation technique to estimate what the price of those instruments would have been on the grant date in an arm's length transaction between knowledgeable, willing parties. The valuation technique should be consistent with generally accepted valuation methodologies for pricing financial instruments (e.g., use of an option pricing model for valuing stock options) and should incorporate all factors and assumptions that knowledgeable, willing market participants would consider in setting the price.

SHOULD MARKET CONDITIONS BE TAKEN INTO ACCOUNT WHILE ESTIMATING THE FAIR VALUE OF SHARES OR STOCK OPTIONS?

Yes, market conditions should be taken into account while estimating the fair value of shares *or* stock options.

Note: Market Condition is a condition that is related to the market price of the shares of the enterprise, upon which the exercise price, vesting *or* exercise ability of a share *or* a stock option depends, such as attaining a specified share price *or* a specified amount of intrinsic value of a stock option, *or* achieving a specified target that is based on the market price of the shares of the enterprise relative to an index of market prices of shares of other enterprises.

SHOULD VESTING CONDITIONS OTHER THAN MARKET CONDITIONS BE TAKEN INTO ACCOUNT WHILE ESTIMATING THE FAIR VALUE OF SHARES OR STOCK OPTIONS?

No, vesting conditions other than market conditions should not be taken into account when estimating the fair value of the shares *or* stock options at the grant date.

WHAT ARE THE FACTORS TO BE TAKEN INTO ACCOUNT WHILE ESTIMATING THE FAIR VALUE OF THE SHARES?

The fair value of the shares granted are measured at the market price of the share at the grant date *or* an estimated value by an independent valuer. However, the following factors are to be considered while estimating the fair value of the shares:

1. Dividend	If the employee is not entitled to receive dividends during the vesting period then the present value of such dividend should be deducted from fair value of the shares. However, if employee is entitled to receive dividends during the vesting period then no adjustment is required.
2. Restriction on transfer	If the shares are subject to restrictions on transfer after vesting date, that factor should be taken into account, but only to the extent that the post-vesting restrictions affect the price that a knowledgeable, willing market participant would pay for that share. ***For Example***, if the shares are actively traded in a deep and liquid market, post-vesting transfer restrictions may have little, if any, effect on the price that a knowledgeable, willing market participant would pay for those shares. Restrictions on transfer *or* other restrictions that exist during the vesting period should not be taken into account while estimating the fair value of the shares granted at grant date, because those restrictions stem from the existence of vesting conditions.

WHAT ARE THE FACTORS TO BE TAKEN INTO ACCOUNT WHILE ESTIMATING THE FAIR VALUE OF THE STOCK OPTION?

In many cases of stock option granted to employees market prices are not available, because the options granted are subject to terms and conditions that do not apply to traded options. If traded options with similar terms and conditions do not exist, the fair value of the options granted should be estimated by applying an option pricing model. An Option Pricing Model, as a minimum, should consider the following factors:

(a) **Exercise Price of the Option:** It is the price payable by the employee for exercising the option granted to him in pursuance of the Employee Stock Option Plan.

(b) **Expected Life of the Option:** It is the period of time from grant date to the date on which an option is expected to be exercised.

(c) Current price of the underlying shares

(d) **Expected Volatility of the Share Price:** It is a measure of the amount by which a price has fluctuated (historical volatility) *or* is expected to fluctuate (expected volatility) during a period. The volatility of a share price is the standard deviation of the continuously compounded rates of return on the share over a specified period.

(e) Dividends expected on the shares (if appropriate)

(f) Risk-free interest rate for the life of the option

(g) Other factors that knowledgeable, willing market participants would consider in setting the price should also be taken into account

Note: There is difference between exercise period and expected life of the option. Exercise period means the time period after vesting period within which the employee should exercise his right to apply for shares against the option vested in him in pursuance of the Employee Stock Option Plan whereas the expected life of the option is the total period of time from grant date to the date on which an option is expected to be exercised.

HOW SHOULD EXPECTED NUMBER OF SHARES OR STOCK OPTIONS EXPECTED TO VEST BE MEASURED?

The enterprise should estimate the expected number of shares *or* stock options expected to vest during the vesting period based on the best available estimate and should revise that estimate, if necessary, if subsequent information indicates that the number of shares *or* stock options expected to vest differs from previous estimates on vesting date, the enterprise should revise the estimate to equal the number of shares *or* stock options that ultimately vest.

Note: In case of grants of shares *or* stock options with market conditions, the enterprise should recognize the services received from an employee who satisfies all other vesting conditions other than market condition (e.g., services received from an employee who remains in service for the specified period of service), irrespective of the fact whether that market condition is satisfied *or* not since market conditions are incorporated into measurement of fair value.

ILLUSTRATION 1

Determine the total fair value of options expected to vest from the information given below:

No. of Employees	2500
No. of Options to be granted to each employee	500
Vesting period	3 years
Expected Annual Forfeitures	10%
Fair Value per option	₹ 5

SOLUTION

A. Total No. of Options expected to vest at the end of the period
= 2500 × 500 × 0.90 × 0.90 × 0.90 = 9,11,250.

B. Fair Value of Options expected to vest = 9,11,250 × ₹ 5 = ₹ 45,56,250.

ILLUSTRATION 2

Determine the Total Fair Value of Options expected to vest from the information given below:

No. of employees	2500
No. of options to be granted to each employee	500
Vesting period	3 years
No. of employees not expected to fulfill the vesting conditions other than market conditions	
1st year	20%
2nd year	15%
3rd year	10%
Fair Value per Option	₹ 5

SOLUTION

A.	No. of Employees expected to exercise options [2500 × 80% × 85% × 90%]	1530
B.	No. of Options to be granted to each employee	500
C.	Fair value of each option	₹ 5
D.	Total Fair Value of Options expected to vest [A × B × C]	38,25,000

HOW SHOULD AN ENTERPRISE RECOGNIZE THE LIABILITY IN RESPECT OF EQUITY SETTLED SHARE -BASED PAYMENT TO EMPLOYEES?

(a) In Case of Shares or Stock Options that vest immediately	An enterprise should immediately recognize as an expense (except where service received qualifies to be included as a part of the cost of an asset) the services received in full with a corresponding credit to an appropriate equity account, i.e. 'Stock Options Outstanding Account'.
(b) In case of Shares or Stock Options that do not vest immediately	The enterprise should account for those services as they are rendered by the employee during the vesting period on time proportion basis with a corresponding credit to the Equity Account. If the shares *or* stock options granted do not vest until the employee completes a specified period of service, the enterprise should presume that the services to be rendered by the employee as consideration for those instruments will be received in the future, during the vesting period.

Notes:

(i) A grant of shares *or* stock options to an employee is typically conditional on the employee remaining in the employment of the enterprise for a specified period of time. Thus, if an employee is granted stock options conditional upon completing three years' service, then the enterprise should presume that the services to be rendered by the employee as consideration for the stock options will be received in the future, over that three-year vesting period.

(ii) There might be performance conditions that must be satisfied, such as the enterprise achieving a specified growth in profit *or* a specified increase in the share price of the enterprise. Thus, if an employee is granted stock options conditional upon the achievement of a performance condition and remaining in the employment of the enterprise until that performance condition is satisfied, and the length of the vesting period varies depending on when that performance condition is satisfied, the enterprise should presume that the services to be rendered by the employee as consideration for the stock options will be received in the future, over the expected vesting period. The enterprise should estimate the length of the expected vesting period at grant date, based on the most likely outcome of the performance condition.

(iii) If the performance condition is a market condition, the estimate of the length of the expected vesting period should be consistent with the assumptions used in estimating the fair value of the options granted, and should not be subsequently revised since fair market value which has been calculated has already taken into consideration the market conditions.

(iv) If the performance condition is not a market condition, the enterprise should revise its estimate of the length of the vesting period, if necessary, if subsequent information indicates that the length of the vesting period differs from previous estimates.

EXPENSE TO BE RECOGNIZED

$$= [\text{Total Fair Value of Options expected to vest estimated at the end of each accounting period} \times \frac{\text{Vesting Period Expired}}{\text{Total Vesting Period}}] - [\text{Expense already recognized during previous years.}]$$

STATEMENT SHOWING THE EXPENSE TO BE RECOGNISED IN EACH YEAR

Particulars	*Year 1*	*Year 2*	*Year 3*
A. No.of Employees entitled to Option			
B. No.of Options per Employee			
C. Fair Value of Option per Share			

D. Total Fair Value of Option [A*B*C]				
E. Expense to be recognized [Total Fair Value* No. of years expired/ Vesting Period] – [Expenses already recognized during previous years]				

ILLUSTRATION 3

Determine the amount of Fair Value of Options expected to vest to be recognized as an expense during each accounting year in respect of employees stock option plan:

No. of employees	2500
No. of options to be granted to each employee	500
Vesting period	4 years
No. of employees not expected to fulfill the vesting conditions other than market conditions	
1st year	20%
2nd year	15%
3rd year	10%
4th year	10%
Fair value of the option	₹ 5

SOLUTION

STATEMENT SHOWING THE EXPENSE TO BE RECOGNISED IN EACH YEAR

	Particulars	*Year 1*	*Year 2*	*Year 3*	*Year 4*
A.	No.of Employees entitled to Option	1,377	1,377	1,377	1,377
B.	No.of Options per Employee	500	500	500	500
C.	Fair Value of Option per Share	5	5	5	5
D.	Total Fair Value of Option [A*B*C]	34,42,500	34,42,500	34,42,500	34,42,500
E.	Expense to be recognized [Total Fair Value* No. of years expired/ Vesting Period] – [Expenses already recognized during previous years]	= 34,42,500/4 = 8,60,625	= (34,42,500 × 2/4) – 8,60,625 = 8,60,625	= (34,42,500 × 3/4) – 8,60,625 – 8,60,625 = 8,60,625	= 34,42,500 – 8,60,625 – 8,60,625 – 8,60,625 = 8,60,625

ILLUSTRATION 4

Determine the amount of Fair Value of Options expected to vest to be recognized as an expense during each accounting year in respect of employees stock option plan:

No. of employees	2500
No. of options to be granted to each employee	500
Vesting period	4 years
No. of employees not expected to fulfill the vesting conditions other than market conditions	
1st year	20%
2nd year	15%

3rd year	10%
4th year	10%
Fair value of the option	₹ 5

At the end of third year it has been re-estimated that all vesting conditions have been fulfilled and no other further conditions are required for options to vest.

SOLUTION

STATEMENT SHOWING THE EXPENSE TO BE RECOGNISED IN EACH YEAR

	Particulars	Year 1	Year 2	Year 3	Year 4
A.	No.of Employees entitled to Option	1,377	1,377	1,530	—
B.	No.of Options per Employee	500	500	500	
C.	Fair Value of Option per Share	5	5	5	
D.	Total Fair Value of Option [A*B*C]	34,42,500	34,42,500	38,25,000	
E.	Expense to be recognized [Total Fair Value* No. of years expired/ Vesting Period] – [Expenses already recognized during previous years]	= 34,42,500/4 = 8,60,625	= (34,42,500 × 2/4) – 8,60,625 = 8,60,625	= 38,25,000 – 8,60,625 – 8,60,625 = 21,03,750	

Since vesting period has been revised in 3rd year all the remaining liabilities in respect of employees stock option plan has been recognized at the end of 3rd year and data for the 4th year has been ignored.

WHAT SHOULD BE THE CONSIDERATION FOR SHARES ISSUED BY THE ENTERPRISE ON EXERCISE OF THE RIGHT TO OBTAIN SHARES *or* STOCK OPTIONS?

The shares issued by the enterprise on exercise of the right to obtain shares *or* stock options should be considered to have been issued at the consideration comprising the Exercise Price and the corresponding amount standing to the credit of the relevant equity account (i.e. Employee Stock Options Outstanding Account)

Note: Where the right to obtain shares *or* stock option expires unexercised, the balance standing to the credit of the relevant equity account should be transferred to General Reserve.

ACCOUNTING TREATMENT

The following journal entries are required to be passed to account for Employee Share Based Payments:

1. ***To recognize an appropriate proportion of the Total Fair Value of Options/Shares expected to vest as an expense at the end of each accounting period during the vesting period.***

Employees Compensation Expense A/c	Dr.
To Employee Stock Option Outstanding A/c	
(Being expense in respect of ESOP recognized during the year)	

Note: Expense to be recognized:

$$= \left[\text{Total Fair Value of Options expected to vest estimated at the end of each accounting period} \times \frac{\text{Vesting Period Expired}}{\text{Total Vesting Period}}\right]$$

$$- [\text{Expense already recognized during previous years.}]$$

2. ***To transfer Employees Compensation Expense Account to Profit & Loss Account at the end of each accounting period during the vesting period.***

Profit & Loss A/c	Dr.
To Employees Compensation Expense A/c	
(Being the transfer of Employees Compensation Expense A/c. to P&L A/c.)	

3. ***To record the issue of shares when the options are exercised during exercise period.***

Bank A/c	Dr.	[No. of options × Exercise Price]
Employee Stock Option Outstanding A/c	Dr.	[No. of options × Fair Value of option]
To Share Capital A/c		[No. of options × Face Value]
To Securities Premium A/c (Being ...... options exercised during ..... period)		[No. of options × (Exercise Price + Fair Value of option – Face Value)]

4. ***To cancel Fair Value of options lapsed***

Employee Stock Option Outstanding A/c To General Reserve	Dr.	[No. of options lapsed × Fair Value of each option]
(Being the fair value of options lapsed transferred to General Reserve)		

Disclosure: Stock Options Outstanding Account will continue to appear on the liabilities side of the Balance Sheet under the head **'Reserves & Surplus'** until all the options are exercised/lapsed.

ILLUSTRATION 5

Prarthna Ltd. having 500 employees grants 2 options to each employees on 1.4.2012 at ₹ 60. The vesting period is two and a half years. The maximum period is one year. Market price on that date is ₹ 90. 450 employees exercised their options on 30.9.2015.

Journalize, If the face value of equity share is ₹ 10 per share.

SOLUTION

JOURNAL OF PRARTHNA LTD.

Date	*Particulars*		*Dr. (₹)*	*Cr. (₹)*
31.3.2013	Employees Compensation Expense A/c	Dr.	12,000	
	To Employees Stock Option Outstanding A/c			12,000
	(Being compensation expense recognized in respect of 1,000 options granted to employees at discount of ₹ 30 each, amortized on straight line basis over 2½ years)			
	Profit and Loss A/c	Dr.	12,000	
	To Employees Compensation Expense A/c			12,000
	(Being employees compensation expense of the year transferred to P&L A/c)			
31.3.2014	Employees Compensation Expense A/c	Dr.	12,000	
	To Employees Stock Option Outstanding A/c			12,000
	(Being compensation expense recognized in respect of 1,000 options granted to employees at discount of ₹ 30 each, amortized on straight line basis over 2½ years)			

	Profit and Loss A/c	Dr.	12,000	
	To Employees Compensation Expense Account			12,000
	(Being employees compensation expense of the year transferred to P&L A/c)			
31.3.2015	Employees Compensation Expense A/c	Dr.	6,000	
	To Employees Stock Option Outstanding A/c			6,000
	(Being balance of compensation expense amortized ₹ 30,000 *less* ₹ 24,000)			
	Profit and Loss A/c	Dr.	6,000	
	To Employees Compensation Expense A/c			6,000
	(Being employees' compensation expense of the year transferred to P&L A/c)			
30.09.2015	Bank A/c (₹ 60 × 900)	Dr.	54,000	
	Employees Stock Option Outstanding A/c (₹ 30 × 900)	Dr.	27,000	
	To Equity Share Capital A/c (900 × ₹ 10)			9,000
	To Securities Premium A/c (900 × ₹ 80)			72,000
	(Being exercise of 900 options at an exercise price of ₹ 60 each and an accounting value of ₹.30 each)			
30.09.2015	Employees Stock Option Outstanding A/c (100 × ₹ 30)	Dr.	3,000	
	To General Reserve A/c			3,000
	(Being the fair value of options lapsed t/f to General Reserve)			

Working Notes:

(i) Total Employees Compensation Expense = 500 × 2 (₹ 90 – ₹ 60) = ₹ 30,000

(ii) Employees Compensation Expense has been written off during 2½ years on straight line basis as under:

I year = ₹ 30,000 × 1/2.5 = ₹ 12,000

II year = (₹ 30,000 × 2/2.5) – ₹ 12,000 = ₹ 12,000

III year = (₹ 30,000 – ₹ 24,000) = ₹ 6,000

ILLUSTRATION 6

Tulsian [ESOP] Ltd. provides you the following information

No. of employees	2500
No. of options to be granted to each employee	500
Vesting period	4 years
No. of employees not expected to fulfill the vesting conditions other than market conditions	
1st year	20%
2nd year	15%
3rd year	10%
4th year	10%
No. of employees not expected to fulfill the vesting conditions based on market conditions	
1st year	5%

2nd year	7%
3rd year	10%
4th year	12%
Fair value of the option	₹ 5
Exercise price	₹ 50
Exercise period	3 years
Face value of each share	₹ 10

At the end of third year it has been re-estimated that all vesting conditions have been fulfilled and no other further conditions are required for options to vest and 600 employees exercise their option at the end of 4th year, 800 employees exercise their option at the end of 5th year and 100 employees exercise their option at the end of 6th year. Rights of 30 employees expire unexercised at the end of 6th year.

Required: Pass necessary journal entries.

SOLUTION

JOURNAL

Date	*Particulars*	*L.F.*	*Dr. (₹)*	*Cr. (₹)*
At the end of Year 1	Employees Compensation Expense A/c Dr.		8,60,625	
	To Employee Stock Options Outstanding A/c			8,60,625
	(Being expense in respect of ESOP recognized for the year 1)			
	Profit and Loss A/c Dr.		8,60,625	
	To Employees Compensation Expense A/c			8,60,625
	(Being the t/f of Employees Compensation Expense to P&L A/c)			
At the end of Year 2	Employees Compensation Expense A/c Dr.		8,60,625	
	To Employee Stock Options Outstanding A/c			8,60,625
	(Being expense in respect of ESOP recognized for the year 2)			
	Profit and Loss A/c Dr.		8,60,625	
	To Employees Compensation Expense A/c			8,60,625
	(Being the t/f of Employees Compensation Expense to P&L A/c)			
At the end of Year 3	Employees Compensation Expense A/c Dr.		21,03,750	
	To Employee Stock Options Outstanding A/c			21,03,750
	(Being expense in respect of ESOP recognized for the year 3)			
	Profit and Loss A/c Dr.		21,03,750	
	To Employees Compensation Expense A/c			21,03,750
	(Being the t/f of Employees Compensation Expense to P&L A/c)			

At the end of Year 4	Bank A/c (600 × 500 × ₹ 50) Dr. Employee Stock Options Outstanding A/c Dr. (600 × 500 × ₹ 5) To Share Capital A/c (600 × 500 × ₹ 10) To Securities Premium A/c (600 × 500 × ₹ 45) (Being 3,00,000 options exercised at the end of 4th year)		1,50,00.000 15,00,000	 30,00,000 1,35,00,000
At the end of Year 5	Bank A/c (800 × 500 × ₹ 50) Dr. Employee Stock Option Outstanding A/c Dr. (800 × 500 × ₹ 5) To Share Capital A/c (800 × 500 × ₹ 10 To Securities Premium A/c (800 × 500 × ₹ 45) (Being 4,00,000 options exercised at the end of 5th year)		2,00,00, 000 20,00,000	 40,00,000 1,80,00,000
At the end of Year 6	Bank A/c (100 × 500 × ₹ 50) Dr. Employee Stock Option Outstanding A/c Dr. (100 × 500 × ₹ 5) To Share Capital A/c (100 × 500 × ₹ 10) To Securities Premium A/c (100 × 500 × ₹ 45) (Being 50,000 options exercised at the end of 6th year)		25,00,000 2,50,000	 5,00,000 22,50,000
At the end of Year 6	Employee Stock Options Outstanding A/c Dr. (30 × 500 × ₹.5) To General Reserve (Being the fair value of options lapsed t/f to Gen. Reserve)		75,000	 75,000

Working Note:

STATEMENT SHOWING THE EXPENSE TO BE RECOGNISED IN EACH YEAR

	Particulars	*Year 1*	*Year 2*	*Year 3*	*Year 4*
A.	No.of Employees entitled to Option	1,377	1,377	1,530	—
B.	No.of Options per Employee	500	500	500	
C.	Fair Value of Option per Share	5	5	5	
D.	Total Fair Value of Option [A*B*C]	34,42,500	34,42,500	38,25,000	
E.	Expense to be recognized [Total Fair Value* No. of years expired/ Vesting Period] – [Expenses already recognized during previous years]	= 34,42,500/4 = 8,60,625	= (34,42,500 × 2/4) – 8,60,625 = 8,60,625	= 38,25,000 – 8,60,625 – 8,60,625 = 21,03,750	

Since vesting period has been revised in 3rd year all the remaining liabilities in respect of employees stock option plan has been recognized at the end of 3rd year and data for the 4th year has been ignored.

Note: No adjustment is required for no. of employees not expected to fulfill vesting conditions based on market conditions since they are already adjusted in calculating fair value of the option.

10.0 INTRINSIC VALUE METHOD

Intrinsic Value (in case of a Listed Enterprise) is the difference between Quoted Market Price on Grant Date and Exercise Price of an option. Intrinsic Value (in case of an Unlisted Enterprise) is the difference between Value determined by an Independent Valuer on Grant Date and Exercise Price of an option . Under Intrinsic Value Method Employee Share-Based Payment Plans are accounted for in the same manner as under Fair Value Method with the following differences:

1. Intrinsic Value is used in place of Fair Value.
2. Securities Premium is = Market Price on Grant Date – Nominal Value.

ILLUSTRATION 7

Tulsian (ESOP) Ltd provides you the following particulars in respect of stock options granted:

Grant Date	April 1,2011
Number of Employees covered	1050
Number of Options granted per Employee	50
Vesting Condition: Continuous employment for 3 years	
Nominal Value per share (₹)	100
Exercise Price per share (₹)	125
Market Price per share on Grant Date (₹)	149
Vesting Date	March 31, 2014
Exercise Date	March 31, 2015
Fair Value of Option per share on Grant Date (₹)	30

Position on	*31.03.2012*	*31.03.2013*	*31.03.2014*
Estimated Annual Rate of Departure	2%	3%	
Number of Employees left	30	20	16
Number of employees entitled to exercise option			984

On 31st March, 2015 ,960 Employees exercised the option and 24 Employees did not exercise the option.

Required: Compute Expenses to be recognised in each year by (i) Fair Value Method (ii) Intrinsic Value Method and Prepare Employees Compensation Expense Account and ESOP Outstanding Account in books of the company by both of the Methods.

SOLUTION

(i) Fair Value Method

EXPENSE TO BE RECOGNISED IN EACH YEAR

	Particulars	*2011-2012*	*2012-2013*	*2013-2014*
A.	No.of Employees entitled to Option	=1050*0.98*0.98*0.98	=1020*0.97*0.97	984
B.	No.of Options per Employee	50	50	50
C.	Fair Value of Option per Share	30	30	30
D.	Total Fair Value of Option [A*B*C]	14,82,000	14,39,580	14,76,000
E.	Expense to be recognized [Total Fair Value* No. of years expired/ Vesting	= 14,82,000/3 = 4,94,000	= [14,39,580*2/3] – [4,94,000]	= 14,76,000 – 4,94,000 –

Period] – [Expenses already recognized during previous years]		=4,65,720	4,65,720 =5,16,280

Value of Options Forfeited = [(984 – 960) × 50 × ₹ 30] = ₹ 36,000

Dr. **EMPLOYEES' COMPENSATION EXPENSE ACCOUNT** *Cr.*

Year	*Particulars*	₹	*Year*	*Particulars*	₹
31.03.2012	To ESOP Outstanding A/c	4,94,000	31.03.2012	By Profit & Loss A/c	4,94,000
31.03.2013	To ESOP Outstanding A/c	4,65,720	31.03.2013	By Profit & Loss A/c	4,65,720
31.03.2014	To ESOP Outstanding A/c	5,16,280	31.03.2014	By Profit & Loss A/c	5,16,280

Dr. **ESOP OUTSTANDING ACCOUNT** *Cr.*

Year	*Particulars*	₹	*Year*	*Particulars*	₹
31.03.2012	To Balance c/d	4,94,000	31.03.2012	By Employees' Compensation Exp. A/c	4,94,000
		4,94,000			4,94,000
31.03.2013	To Balance c/d	9,59,720	31.03.2013	By Balance b/d	4,94,000
				By Employees' Compensation Exp. A/c	4,65,720
		9,59,720			9,59,720
31.03.2014	To Balance c/d	14,76,000	31.03.2014	By Balance b/d	9,59,720
				By Employees' Compensation Exp. A/c	5,16,280
		14,76,000			14,76,000
31.03.2015	To General Reserve (1,200 × 30)	36,000	31.03.2015	By Balance b/d (49,200 × 30)	14,76,000
	To Share Capital (48,000 × 100)	48,00,000		By Bank (48,000 × 125)	60,00,000
	To Securities Premium (48,000 × 55)	26,40,000			
		74,76,000			74,76,000

Note: Securities Premium = (Exercise Price + Fair Value) – Nominal Value = (125 + 30) – 100 = 55

(ii) Intrinsic Value Method

EXPENSE TO BE RECOGNISED IN EACH YEAR

	Particulars	*2011-2012*	*2012-2013*	*2013-2014*
A.	No.of Employees entitled to Option	=1050*0.98*0.98*0.98	= 1020*0.97*0.97	984
B.	No.of Options per Employee	50	50	50
C.	Intrinsic Value of Option per Share	24	24	24
D.	Total Intrinsic Value of Option [A*B*C]	11,85,600	11,51,664	11,80,800
E.	Expense to be recognized [Total Intrinsic Value * No. of years expired/ Vesting Period] – [Expenses already recognized during previous years]	=11,85,600/3 = 3,95,200	=[11,51,664*2/3] – [3,95,200] = 3,72,576	= 11,80,800 – 3,95,200 – 3,72,576 = 4,13,024

Value of Options Forfeited = [(984 – 960) × 50 × ₹ 24] = ₹.28,800

Dr. **EMPLOYEES' COMPENSATION EXPENSE ACCOUNT** *Cr.*

Year	*Particulars*	₹	*Year*	*Particulars*	₹
31.03.2012	To ESOP Outstanding A/c	3,95,200	31.03.2012	By Profit & Loss A/c	3,95,200
31.03.2013	To ESOP Outstanding A/c	3,72,576	31.03.2013	By Profit & Loss A/c	3,72,576
31.03.2014	To ESOP Outstanding A/c	4,13,024	31.03.2014	By Profit & Loss A/c	4,13,024

Dr. **ESOP OUTSTANDING ACCOUNT** *Cr.*

Year	*Particulars*	₹	*Year*	*Particulars*	₹
31.03.2012	To Balance c/d	3,95,200	31.03.2012	By Employees' Compensation Exp. A/c	3,95,200
		3,95,200			3,95,200
31.03.2013	To Balance c/d	7,67,776	31.03.2013	By Balance b/d	3,95,200
				By Employees' Compensation Exp. A/c	3,72,576
		7,67,776			7,67,776
31.03.2014	To Balance c/d	11,80,800	31.03.2014	By Balance b/d	7,67,776
				By Employees' Compensation Exp. A/c	4,13,024
		11,80,800			11,80,800
31.03.2015	To General Reserve (1,200 × 24)	28,800	31.03.2015	By Balance b/d (49,200 × 24)	11,80,800
	To Share Capital (48,000 × 100)	48,00,000		By Bank A/c (48,000 × 125)	60,00,000
	To Securities Premium (48,000 × 49)	23,52,000			
		71,80,800			71,80,800

Working Note: *Calculation of Intrinsic Value and Securities Premium*

A. Intrinsic Value=Market Price on Grant Date – Exercise Price = ₹ 149 – ₹ 125 = 24

B. Securities Premium = Market Price on Grant Date – Nominal Value = ₹ 149 – ₹ 100 = ₹ 49

11.0 ACCOUNTING TREATMENT OF EMPLOYEES' STOCK PURCHASE PLANS (ESPP)

Meaning	Under Employees' Stock Purchase Plans (ESPP), employees are given an option to subscribe to shares of employer in a public issue *or* otherwise. The exercise price is set at a specified rate of discount on the issue price/ market price on the date of exercise. ***For Example***, a company may offer specified number of shares to its employees at 25% discount on market price on grant date. Note: ESPP with option features is treated as ESOP. ***For Example***, If employees have the option to pay either 75% of market price of shares on grant date *or* on date of purchase, the plan is treated as ESOP rather than ESPP.

Accounting	**Step 1:** *Compute the Total Fair Value of ESPP as follows:* *= No. of Shares issued × (Fair Value of a Share – Issue Price)* **Step 2:** *Recognise Expense over the vesting period in the same way as ESOP.* **Note:** *The Fair Value of ESPP can be less than the discount due to post-vesting restrictions on transfers and similar other factors.*
Journal Entry to Record the Issue of Shares	Bank A/c [No. of Shares issued × Issue Price] Dr. Employees' Compensation Exp. A/c [No. of Shares issued × (Fair Value of Share – Issue Price] Dr. To Share Capital A/c [No. of Shares issued × Nominal Value] To Securities Premium A/c [No. of Shares issued × (Fair Value of Share – Nominal Value]

ILLUSTRATION 8

On April 1, 2015, Tulsian [ESPP] Ltd. offered 100 shares to each of its 500 employees at 20% discount on marke price on grant date. The employees are given a month to decide whether *or* not to accept the offer. The shares issued under the plan shall be subject to lock-in on transfers for three years from grant date. The market price of shares of the company on the grant date is ₹ 250 per share. Due to post-vesting restrictions on transfer, the fair value of shares issued under the plan is estimated at ₹ 240 per share.

On April 30, 2015, 400 employees accepted the offer and paid ₹ 200 per share purchased. Nominal value of each share is ₹ 10.

Required: Record the issue of shares in book of the company under the aforesaid plan.

SOLUTION

Fair value of ESPP = (400 × 100) × (₹ 240 – ₹ 200) = ₹ 16,00,000

Vesting period = One month, Expense recognised in 2015-2016 = ₹ 16,00,000

Date	*Particulars*	*L.F.*	*Dr. (₹)*	*Cr. (₹)*
30.04.2015	Bank A/c [40,000 × ₹ 200] Dr.		80,00,000	
	Employees' Compensation Exp. A/c [40,000 × ₹ 40] Dr.		16,00,000	
	To Share Capital A/c [40,000 × ₹ 10]			4,00,000
	To Securities Premium A/c [40,000 × ₹ 230]			92,00,000

PROFESSIONAL EXAMINATION PROBLEMS

PROBLEM 1

On 1st April 2015, a company offered 100 shares to each of its 500 employees at ₹ 50 per share. The employees are given a month to decide whether *or* not to accept the offer. The shares issued under the plan (ESPP) shall be subject to lock in one transfers for three years from grant date. The market price of shares of the company on the grant date is ₹ 60 per share. Due to post-vesting restrictions on transfer, the fair value of shares issued under the plan is estimated at ₹ 56 per share.

On 30th April, 2015, 400 employees accepted the offer and paid ₹ 50 per share purchased. Nominal value of each share is ₹ 10.

Required: Record the issue of shares in the books of the company under the aforesaid plan.

SOLUTION

Fair value of an ESPP = ₹ 56 – ₹ 50 = ₹ 6

Number of shares issued = 400 employees × 100 shares per employee = 40,000 shares

Fair value of ESPP with be recognized as expenses in the year 2015-2016

= 40,000 shares × ₹ 6 = ₹ 2,40,000.

Vesting period = 1 month

Expenses recognized in 31.03.2014 = ₹ 2,40,000

JOURNAL

Date	*Particulars*		*L.F.*	*Dr. (₹)*	*Cr. (₹)*
30.04.2015	Bank [40,000 shares × ₹ 50]	Dr.		20,00,000	
	Employees' Compensation Expenses A/c	Dr.		2,40,000	
	To Share Capital A/c (40,000 shares × ₹ 10)				4,00,000
	To Securities Premium A/c (40,000 shares × ₹ 46)				18,40,000
	(Being shares issued under ESPP @ ₹ 50)				

PROBLEM 2

S Ltd. grants 1,000 options to its employees on 1.4.2012 at ₹ 60. The vesting period is two and a half years. The maximum period is one year. Market price on that date is ₹ 90. All the options were exercised on 31.7.2015. Journalize, if the face value of equity share is ₹ 10 per share.

SOLUTION

JOURNAL OF S LTD.

Date	*Particulars*		*Dr. (₹)*	*Cr. (₹)*
31.3.2013	Employees Compensation Expense A/c	Dr.	12,000	
	To Employees Stock Option Outstanding A/c			12,000
	(Being compensation expense recognized in respect of 1,000 options granted to employees at discount of ₹ 30 each, amortized on straight line basis over 2½ years)			
	Profit and Loss A/c	Dr.	12,000	
	To Employees Compensation Expense A/c			12,000
	(Being employees compensation expense of the year transferred to P&L A/c)			
31.3.2014	Employees Compensation Expense A/c	Dr.	12,000	
	To Employees Stock Option Outstanding A/c			12,000
	(Being compensation expense recognized in respect of 1,000 options granted to employees at discount of ₹ 30 each, amortized on straight line basis over 2½ years)			
	Profit and Loss A/c	Dr.	12,000	
	To Employees Compensation Expense Account			12,000
	(Being employees compensation expense of the year transferred to P&L A/c)			

31.3.2015	Employees Compensation Expense A/c Dr.	6,000	
	To Employees Stock Option Outstanding A/c		6,000
	(Being balance of compensation expense amortized ₹ 30,000 less ₹ 24,000)		
	Profit and Loss A/c Dr.	6,000	
	To Employees Compensation Expense A/c		6,000
	(Being employees compensation expense of the year transferred to P&L A/c)		
31.7.2015	Bank A/c (₹ 60 × 1,000) Dr.	60,000	
	Employees Stock Option Outstanding A/c (₹ 30 × 1,000) Dr.	30,000	
	To Equity Share Capital A/c		10,000
	To Securities Premium A/c		80,000
	(Being exercise of 1,000 options at an exercise price of ₹ 60 each and an accounting value of ₹.30 each)		

Working Notes:

(i) Total Employees Compensation Expense = 1,000 × (₹ 90 – ₹ 60) = ₹ 30,000

(ii) Employees Compensation Expense has been written off during 2½ years on straight line basis as under:

I year = ₹ 12,000 (for full year)

II year = ₹ 12,000 (for full year)

III year = ₹ 6,000 (for half year)

PROBLEM 3

X Co Ltd has its share capital divided into equity shares of ₹ 10 each, On 1.10.2014 it granted 20,000 employees' stock option at ₹ 50 per share, when the market price was ₹ 120 per share. The options were to be exercised between 10th December, 2010 and 31st March, 2015. The employees exercised their options for 16,000 shares only and the remaining options lapsed. The company closes its books on 31st March every year.

Show Journal entries (with narration) as would appear in the books of the company upto 31st March, 2015.

SOLUTION

JOURNAL

Date	Particulars	Dr. (₹)	Cr. (₹)
1.10.2014	Employee Compensation Expense A/c Dr.	14,00,000	
	To Employee Stock Option Outstanding A/c		14,00,000
	(Being the grant of 20,000 stock options to employees at ₹ 50 when market price is ₹ 120)		
10.12.2014	Bank A/c Dr.	8,00,000	
to	Employee Stock Option Outstanding A/c Dr.	11,20,000	
31.3.2015	To Equity Share Capital A/c		1,60,000

	To Securities Premium A/c (Being the shares issued to the employees against the options vested to them in pursuance of Employee Stock Option Plan)		17,60,000
31.3.2015	Employee Stock Option Outstanding A/c Dr. To Employee Compensation Expense A/c (Being the reverse entry passed for lapse of 4,000 stock options)	2,80,000	2,80,000
31.3.2015	Profit and Loss A/c Dr. To Employee Compensation Expense A/c (Being the transfer of employee compensation transferred to Profit and Loss Account)	11,20,000	11,20,000

PROBLEM 4

CAJI Ltd. granted 500 options to each of its 2,500 employees in 2010 at an exercise price of ₹.50 when the market price was the same. The contractual life (vesting and exercise period) of the options granted is 6 years with the vesting period and exercise period being 3 years each. The expected life is 5 years and the expected annual forfeitures are estimated at 3 per cent. The fair value per option is arrived at ₹ 15. Actual forfeitures in 2010 were 5 per cent. However at the end of 2010 the management of CAJI Ltd. still expects that the actual forfeitures would average only 3 per cent over the entire vesting period. During 2011 the management revises its estimated forfeiture rate to 10% p.a. Of the 2,500 employees, 1,900 employees have completed the 3 year vesting period. 1,000 employees exercise their right to obtain shares vested in them in pursuance of ESOP at the end of 2014 and 500 employees exercise their right at the end of 2015. The rights of the remaining employees expire unexercised at the end of 2015. The face value per share is ₹ 10. Show the necessary journal entries with suitable narrations.

SOLUTION

JOURNAL

Particulars		*Dr. (₹)*	*Cr. (₹)*
Year 2010			
Employee Compensation Expense A/c	Dr.	57,04,205	
To Employee Stock Options Outstanding A/c			57,04,205
(Being the compensation exp. recognized in respect of the ESOP)			
Profit and Loss A/c	Dr.	57,04,205	
To Employee Compensation Expense A/c			57,04,205
(Being the expenses of the year transferred to P & L A/c)			
Year 2011			
Employee Compensation Expense A/c	Dr.	34,08,295	
To Employee Stock Options Outstanding A/c			34,08,295
(Being the compensation exp. recognized in respect of the ESOP)			
Profit and Loss A/c	Dr.	34,08,295	
To Employee Compensation Expense A/c			34,08,295
(Being expenses of the year transferred to P & L A/c)			

Year 2012			
Employee Compensation Expense A/c	Dr.	51,37,500	
To Employee Stock Options Outstanding A/c			51,37,500
(Being the compensation exp. recognized in respect of the ESOP)			
Profit and Loss A/c	Dr.	51,37,500	
To Employee Compensation Expense A/c			51,37,500
(Being expenses of the year transferred to P & L A/c)			
Year 2014			
Bank A/c [1000 × 500 × ₹ 50]	Dr.	2,50,00,000	
Employee Stock Options Outstanding A/c [1000 × 500 × ₹ 15]	Dr.	75,00,000	
To Share Capital A/c [1000 × 500 × ₹ 10]			50,00,000
To Securities Premium [1000 × 500 × ₹ 55]			2,75,00,000
(Being shares issued to employees against options vested in them in pursuance of the ESOP)			
Year 2015			
BankA/c [500 × 500 × ₹ 50]	Dr.	1,25,00,000	
Employee Stock Options Outstanding A/c [500 × 500 × ₹ 15]	Dr.	37,50,000	
To Share Capital A/c [500 × 500 × ₹ 10]			25,00,000
To Securities Premium A/c [500 × 500 × ₹ 55]			1,37,50,000
(Being shares issued to employees against options vested in them in pursuance of the ESOP)			
Employee Stock Options Outstanding A/c	Dr.	30,00,000	
To General Reserve A/c			30,00,000
(Being the balance standing to the credit of stock options outstanding account, in respect of vested options expired unexercised, transferred to general reserve account)			

Working Notes:

(i) Fair Value of Options recognized as Expense

Year 2010

Number of options expected to vest = 500 × 2,500 × .97 × .97 × .97 = 11,40,841 options

Fair value of options expected to vest = 11,40,841 × ₹.15 = ₹.171,12,615

One third of fair value recognized as expense = ₹.171,12,615/3 = ₹ 57,04,205

Year 2011

Fair Value of options revised in the year = 500 × 2500 × 0.90 × 0.90 × 0.90 × ₹.15

= ₹ 136,68,750

Revised cumulative expenses in year 2011 (136,68,750 × 2/3)	91,12,500
Less: Already recognized in year 2010	(57,04,205)
Expenses to be recognized in year 2011	34,08,295
Year 2012	
Number of options actually vested (1900 × 500 = 9,50,000)	

Fair Value of options actually vested (9,50,000 × 15)	1,42,50,000
Less: Expense recognized till year 2011	(91,12,500)
Balance amount to be recognized	51,37,500

(II) AMOUNT RECORDED IN SHARE CAPITAL ACCOUNT AND SECURITIES PREMIUM ACCOUNT UPON ISSUE OF SHARES

Particulars	*Years 2014*	*Year 2015*
Number of employees exercising option	1,000	500
Number of shares issued upon exercise of option @ 500 per employee	5,00,000	2,50,000
Exercise price received @ ₹.50 per share	2,50,00,000	1,25,00,000
Corresponding amount recognized in the 'Employee Stock Options Outstanding A/c' @ ₹.15 per option	75,00,000	37,50,000
Total Consideration	3,25,00,000	1,62,50,000
Amount to be recorded in 'Share Capital A/c' @ ₹.10 per share	50,00,000	25,00,000
Amount to be recorded in 'Securities Premium A/c' @ ₹.55 (i.e. 65 – 10) per share	2,75,00,000	1,37,50,000
	3,25,00,000	1,62,50,000

PROBLEM 5

At the beginning of year 1, an enterprise grants 10,000 stock options to a senior executive, conditional upon the executive remaining in the employment of the enterprise until the end of year 3. The exercise price is ₹40. However, the exercise price drops to ₹ 30 if the earnings of the enterprise increase by at least an average of 10 per cent per year over the three-year period.

On the grant date, the enterprise estimates that the fair value of the stock options, with an exercise price of ₹ 30, is ₹ 15 per option. If the exercise price is ₹ 40, the enterprise estimates that the stock options have a fair value of ₹ 11 per option. During year 1, the earnings of the enterprise is 12 per cent, and the enterprise expects that earnings will continue to increase at this rate over the next two years. The enterprise, therefore, expects that the earnings target will be achieved, and hence the stock options will have an exercise price of ₹ 30. During year 2, the earnings of the enterprise is 13 per cent, and the enterprise continues to expect that the earnings target will be achieved.

During year 3, the earnings of the enterprise is only 3 per cent, and therefore the earnings target was not achieved. The executive completes three years' service, and therefore satisfies the service condition.

Because the earnings target was not achieved, 10,000 vested stock options have an exercise price of ₹ 40.

Calculate the amount to be charged to Profit and Loss Account every year on account of compensation expenses.

SOLUTION

Since the exercise price varies depending on the outcome of a performance condition which is not a market condition the effect of that performance condition (i.e. the possibility that the exercise price might be ₹ 40 and the possibility that the exercise price might be ₹ 30) is not taken into account while estimating the fair value of the stock options at the grant date. Instead, the enterprise estimates the fair value of the stock options at the grant date under each scenario and revises the transaction amount to reflect the outcome of that performance condition at the end of every year based on the information available at the point of time.

CALCULATION OF COMPENSATION EXPENSES TO BE CHARGE EVERY YEAR

Year	*Calculation*	*Compensation expenses for the period (₹)*	*Cumulative compensation expenses (₹)*
1	(10,000 options × ₹ 15 × 1/3)	50,000	50,000
2	(10,000 options × ₹ 15 × 2/3) – ₹ 50,000	50,000	1,00,000
3	(10,000 options × ₹ 11 × 3/3) – ₹ 1,00,000	10,000	1,10,000

PROBLEM 6

At the beginning of year 1, the enterprise grants 100 stock options to each of its 500 employees, conditional upon the employees remaining in the employment of the enterprise during the vesting period. The options will vest at the end of year 1 if the earnings of the enterprise is 20%, at the end of year 2 if the earnings of the enterprise is an average of 16% per year over the two year period; and at the end of year 3 if the earnings of the enterprise is an average of 12% per year over the three year period. The fair value of the options, calculated at the grant date using an option pricing model, is ₹ 60 per option. No dividends are expected to be paid over the three-year period.

By the end of year 1, the earnings of the enterprise was 15%, and 30 employees had left. The enterprise expected that earnings will continue at a similar rate in year 2, and therefore expected that the options will vest at the end of year 2. The enterprise expected on the basis of a weighted average probability, that a further 30 employees will leave during the year 2, and therefore, assumed that options will vest in 440 employees at the end of year 2.

By the end of year 2, the earnings of the enterprise was only 13%. 28 employees have left during the year. The enterprise expected that a further 25 employees will leave during year 3, and that the earnings of the enterprise will be at least 6 per cent, thereby achieving the average of 10% per year.

By the end of the year 3, 23 employees had left and the earnings of the enterprise had been 10%. You are required to determine the compensation expense to be recognised each year.

SOLUTION

In the given case, the length of the vesting period varies, depending on when the performance condition is satisfied. In such a situation, the enterprise estimates the length of the expected vesting period, based on the most likely outcome of the performance condition and revises that estimate, if necessary, if subsequent information indicates that the length of the vesting period is likely to differ from previous estimates.

STATEMENT SHOWING DETERMINATION OF THE COMPENSATION EXPENSE TO BE RECOGNISED EACH YEAR

Particulars	*Year 1*	*Year 2*	*Year 3*
Vesting condition (earnings)	20%	16 (avg.)	12% (avg.)
Actual earnings	15%	14% (avg.)	12.67% (avg.)
Length of the expected vesting period		[(15 + 13)/2]	[(15 + 13 + 10)/3]
(at the end of the year)	2 years	3 years	3 years
A. No. of Employees expected to meet vesting conditions	440	417	419
B. No. of Options per employee	100	100	100
C. Fair Value of An option	₹ 60	₹ 60	₹ 60
D. Total Fair Value of Option [A × B × C]	26,40,000	25,02,000	25,14,000

E. Expense accrued at the end of year (₹)	13,20,000 (D/2)	16,68,000 (D × 2/3)	25,14,000 (D × 3/3)
F. Expense recognised till the end of previous year (₹)	Nil	13,20,000	16,68,000
G. Exp. to be recognized for the year (₹) [E – F]	13,20,000	3,48,000	8,46,000

PROBLEM 7

Virtual Limited granted on 1st April 2011, 1,00,000 Employees Stock Option at ₹ 40, when the Market Price was ₹ 60. These options will vest at the end of Year 1, if the earning of Virtual Limited is more than 15% *or* it will vest at the end of the year 2, if the average earnings of two years is more than 12% *or* lastly it will vest at the end of third year, if the average earnings of 3 years will be 9% *or* more. 6000 unvested options lapsed on 31st March 2012. 5,500 unvested options lapsed on 31st March 2013 and finally 3,000 unvested options lapsed on 31st March 2014.

The earnings of Virtual Limited was as follows:

Year ended on	*Earnings in %*
31.3.2012	13%
31.3.2013	9%
31.3.2014	7%

Employees exercised for 85,000 Stock Options which vested in them at the first opportunity and the balance options were lapsed. Pass necessary journal entries and show the necessary working.

SOLUTION

JOURNAL OF VIRTUAL LTD

Date	*Particulars*		*Dr. (₹)*	*Cr. (₹)*
31.3.2012	Employees Compensation Expenses A/c	Dr.	9,40,000	
	To ESOS Outstanding A/c			9,40,000
	(Being Compensation Expenses recognized in respect of Employee Stock Option, i.e. 94,000 options at a discount of ₹ 20 each)			
	P & L A/c	Dr.	9,40,000	
	To Employees Compensation Expense A/c			9,40,000
	(Being the t/f of ECE A/c)			
31.3.2013	Employees Compensation Expenses A/c	Dr.	2,40,000	
	To ESOS Outstanding A/c			2,40,000
	(Being Compensation Expenses recognized in ESOP A/c)			
	P & L A/c	Dr.	2,40,000	
	To Employees Compensation Expense A/c			2,40,000
	(Being the t/f of ECE A/c)			
31.3.2014	Employees Compensation Expenses A/c	Dr.	5,30,000	
	To ESOS Outstanding A/c			5,30,000
	(Being Compensation Expenses recognized in ESOP)			

	P & L A/c	Dr.	5,30,000	
	To Employees Compensation Expense A/c			5,30,000
	(Being the t/f of ECE A/c)			
31.12.2014	Bank A/c [85,000 × ₹ 20]	Dr.	34,00,000	
	ESOS Outstanding A/c	Dr.	17,00,000	
	To Equity Share Capital A/c [85,000 × ₹ 10]			8,50,000
	To Securities Premium A/c [85,000 × ₹ 50]			42,50,000
	(Being 85,000 Options exercised)			
During FY 31.12.2015	ESOS Outstanding A/c [500 × ₹ 20]	Dr.	10,000	
	To General Reserve A/c			10,000
	(Being ESOP outstanding A/c on lapse of 500 options transferred to General Reserve)			

Working Notes:

EXPENSE TO BE RECOGNISED EACH YEAR

Particulars	*Year 1*	*Year 2*	*Year 3*
Length of the expected vesting period (at the end of the year)	2 years	3 years	3 years
A. No. of Options expected to vest	94,000	88,500	85,500
B. Fair Value of An option	₹ 20	₹ 20	₹ 20
C. Total Fair Value of Option [A × B]	18,80,000	17,70,000	17,10,000
D. Total Expense accrued at the end of year (₹)	9,40,000 (D/2)	11,80,000 (D × 2/3)	17,10,000 (D × 3/3)
E. Expense recognised till the end of previous year (₹)	Nil	9,40,000	11,80,000
F. Expense to be recognized for the year (₹) [D – E]	9,40,000	2,40,000	5,30,000

4 ACCOUNTING FOR BUY-BACK OF SHARES

LEARNING OBJECTIVES

After studying this chapter, you should be able to understand:

- ◇ Meaning of Buy-back of Shares
- ◇ Three Sources of Funds for Buy-back
- ◇ Conditions for Buy-Back
- ◇ Accounting Entries for Buy-Back

1.0 MEANING OF BUY-BACK OF SHARES

The term buy-back of shares implies the act of purchasing its own shares by a company.

2.0 THREE SOURCES OF FUNDS FOR BUY-BACK [SEC. 68(1)]

A company may purchase its own shares *or* other specified securities out of —

(i) its Free Reserves; or

(ii) the Securities Premium Account; or

(iii) the proceeds of any shares *or* other specified securities;

Provided that no buy-back of any kind of shares *or* other specified securities shall be made out of the proceeds of an earlier issue of the same kind of shares *or* same kind of other specified securities.

3.0 CONDITIONS FOR BUY-BACK [SEC 68]

PROCEDURAL CONDITIONS

1. **Authorised by Articles**—The buy-back must be authorized by the Articles
2. **Special Resolution/Board's Resolution**—The **special resolution** must be passed in the General Meeting of shareholders.

   OR

   The Board must pass a resolution at its meeting where the buy-back does not exceed 10% of the total equity paid up capital and free reserves of the company.
3. **Fully Paid Shares**—All the shares for buy-back must be fully paid-up.
4. **Time Limit**—The buy-back must be completed within 12 months from the date of passing the Special Resolution/Board's Resolution.
5. **From Whom**— The buy-back can be:

   (a) from the existing shareholders *or* security holders on a proportionate basis;

   (b) from the open market;

(c) by purchasing the securities issued to employees of the company pursuant to a scheme of stock option *or* sweat equity.

6. **Declaration of Solvency**—The company must file **Declaration of Solvency** with the Registrar and SEBI in the form of an affidavit signed by at least two directors of the company. The affidavit must state that the Board has made full inquiry into the affairs of the company as a result of which they have formed an option that the company is capable of meeting its liabilities and will not render insolvent within a period of one year from the date of declaration adopted by the Board.

7. **Destroy**— Company shall extinguish and physically destroy the shares *or* securities so bought back within 7 days of the last date of completion of buy-back.

8. **Restriction on further issue within 6 months**— Where a company completes a buy-back of its shares *or* other specified securities, it shall not make a further issue of the same king of shares *or* other secutiries including allotment of new shares *or* other specified securities within a period of 6 months except by way of:

(a) a bonus issue or

(b) in the discharge of subsisting obligations such as conversion of warrants, stock option schemes, sweat equaity *or* conversion of preference shares *or* debentures into equity shares.

9. **As per SEBI Guidelines**— In case of listed shares buy-back must be as per SEBI Guidelines and In case of unlisted shares buy-back must be as per Share Capital & Debentures Rules 2014.

SEBI's Regulations for listed shares:

(i) No offer of buy-back for at least 15% of the paid up capital and free reserves of the company shall be made from the open market.

(ii) A company shall not make any offer of buy-back within a period 1 year reckoned from the date of closure of the preceding offer of buy-back, if any.

(iii) The company shall ensure that at least 50% of the amount earmarked for buy-back is utilized for buying-back shares *or* other specified securities.

ACCOUNTING TREATMENT CONDITION [SEC 69(1)]

10. **Transfer of Certain Sums to Capital Redemption Reserve Account**—Where a company purchases its own shares out of free reserves *or* Secturities Premium, than a sum equal to the nominal value of the shares so purchased shall be transferred to the Capital Redemption Reserve (CRR) Account and details of such transfer must be disclosed in the Balance Sheet. The CRR can be utilized to issue fully paid bonus shares to members.

THREE TESTS CONDITIONS

11. **Maximum Limit of Amount of Equity Shares to be bought back**—The buy-back of the shares must **not exceed 25% of total paid-up capital and free reserves.**

12. **Maximum Limit of Number of Equity Shares to be bought back in any Financial Year**—The buy-back of equity shares in any financial year must not exceed **25% of its total paid up equity capital.**

13. **Maximum Debt-Equity Ratio**—The debt-equity ratio must **not be more than 2:1** after such buy-back. Here,

Debt (after buy-back) = Secured + Unsecured Debt,

Equity (after buy-back) = Capital + Free Reserves

Note: For the purposes of Section 68, Free Reserves mean Free Reserves available for free distribution as dividend and include the Balance of Securities Premium A/c.

4.0 HOW TO CALCULATE THE MAXIMUM NO. OF SHARES THAT CAN BE BOUGHT BACK

Step 1: *Calculate the Maximum No. of Equity Shares that can be bought back as per following 3 tests.*

Test	Max. No. of shares that can be bought back
1.Outstanding Share Test	= 25% of Total Outstanding Equity Shares
2.Resources Test	$= \frac{\text{25\% of (Paid up Capital + Free Reserves)}}{\text{Buy back Price per share}}$
3.Debt – Equity Ratio Test	$= \frac{\text{[(Paid up Capital (after buy-back) + Free Reserves (after buy-back)) – Minimum Equity Funds (i.e. Debt Funds/2)]}}{\text{Buy back Price per Share}}$

Step 2: *Max. No. of Equity Shares that can be bought back = Least in above 3 Tests*

5.0 ACCOUNTING ENTRIES

The various journal entries to be passed on buy back are given as follows:

1. To make partly paid Equity Shares Fully paid up		
(a) ***On making final call***		
Equity Share Final Call A/c	Dr.	
To Equity Share Capital A/c		
(b) ***On Receipt of Final Call***		
Bank A/c	Dr.	
To Equity Share Final Call A/c		
2. To realize Investments to provide Cash for buy back		
Bank A/c	Dr.	*[With Sale Proceeds]*
Profit & Loss A/c	Dr.	*[With Loss]*
To Investments A/c		*[With Book value]*
To Profit & Loss A/c		*[With Profit]*
3. To issue fresh other kind of Shares *or* Securities (say Preference Shares/Debentures)		
(a) ***On receipt of Application Money***		
Bank A/c	Dr.	
To Pref. Share Application & Allotment A/c		
(b) ***On Allotment***		
(i) *If at par*		
Pref-share Application & Allotment A/c	Dr.	
To Pref. Share Capital A/c		
(ii) *If at Premium*		
Pref. Share Application & Allotment A/c	Dr.	
To Pref. Share Capital A/c		
To Securities Premium A/c		

	(iii) *If at Discount*		
	Pref. Share Application & Allotment A/c	Dr.	
	Discount on Issue of Shares A/c	Dr.	
	To Pref. Share Capital A/c		
4.	**To make payment on buy-back of Equity Shares**		
	Equity Shares Buy Back A/c	Dr.	*[With Amount paid]*
	To Bank A/c		
5.	**To Cancel the Shares Bought back**		
	Equity Share Capital A/c	Dr.	[With Nominal Value]
	Securities Premium A/c	Dr.	[With Premium]
	General Reserve A/c	Dr.	[With Balancing Figure]
	To Equity Shares Buy Back A/c		[With Total]
6.	**To transfer Free Reserves to Capital Redemption Reserve Account equal to the Nominal Value of Equity Shares bought back out of Free Reserves**		
	Revenue Reserve	Dr.	
	Profit & Loss A/c	Dr.	
	To Capital Redemption Reserve A/c		
	Tutorial Note: Capital Redemption Reserve can be utilized only for issuing fully paid bonus shares to members.		

ILLUSTRATION 1 [Calculation of Max. No. of Equity Shares that can be Bought]

Tulsian Ltd. provides you the following information as on 31.03.2013: *₹ in Crores*

(a) Equity Shares of ₹ 10 each fully paid	330
(b) 10% Red Pref. Shares of ₹ 100 each fully paid	70
(c) Securities Premium	90
(d) General Reserve	240
(e) Profit and Loss A/c	20
(f) Infrastructure Development Reserve (Statutory Reserve)	100
(g) Capital Redemption Reserve	50
(h) Plant Revaluation Reserve	30
(i) Secured Loans	1000
(j) Current Liabilities	200

The company has offered buy back price of ₹ 30 per equity share.

Required: Calculate the Maximum permissible number of Equity Shares that can be bought back if the company also has Unsecured Loans of (a) ₹ 800 crores; (b) 200 crores (c) ₹ 500 crores.

SOLUTION

Step 1: Application of 3 Tests

(a) Shares Outstanding Test:

Max. No. of Shares that can be bought back = 25% of 33 = 8.25 crores

(b) Resources Test:

Max. Number of shares that can be bought back

= [25% of (Paid up Capital + Free Reserves)/Buy Back Price per Share]

= [25%(₹ 400 + 350)]/₹ 30 = 6.25 crores

(C) DEBT EQUITY RATIO TEST

*Particulars**	*Situation 1*	*Situation 2*	*Situation 3*
(a) Loan Funds (₹ in crores)	1,800	1,200	1,500
(b) Minimum Equity to be maintained after buy back in the ratio of 2 : 1 (₹ in crores)	900	600	750
(c) Present Equity Shareholders Funds (₹ in crores)	750	750	750
(d) Future Equity Shareholder's Funds	N.A.	712.50 [750–37.5]	N.A.
(e) Maximum permitted buy back of Equity (₹ in crores) [(b) – (c)]	Nil	112.50	Nil
(f) Maximum number of shares that can be bought back @ ₹ 30 per share (shares in crores) [(e)/₹ 30]	Nil	3.75	Nil

Step 2: Max No of Equity Shares that can be bought back

= Least of 8.25 or 6.25 or 3.75

= Max. 3.75 crores Shares can be bought back

Notes:

(i) *Infrastructure Development Reserve, Capital Redemption Reserve and Plant Revaluation Reserve are not free reserves.*

(ii) *For Debt-Equity Ratio, both Secured and Unsecured Loans are considered.*

(iii) Let X = Amount to be t/f to CRR; Y = Maximum permitted buyback of Equity

Y = 750 – X – 600 ...Eq. I

X = (Y/30) × 10 = Y/3 ...Eq. II

by Solving both the Equations

X = ₹ 37.5 crores, Y = ₹ 150 – ₹ 37.5 = ₹ 112.50 crores

ILLUSTRATION 2 [Buy-Back of Shares at Premium out of Free Reserves]

Bharat Ltd. provides you the following information:

1. Issued Capital :	2,00,000 Equity Shares of ₹ 10 each	
2. Reserves & Surplus :	Capital Reserve	₹ 10,00,000
	Securities Premium	₹ 18,00,000
	Revenue Reserve	₹ 30,00,000
	Profit & Loss A/c	₹ 40,00,000

3. Resolution passed to buy back: 25% of its Equity Shares @ ₹ 50 per share.

Required: Pass journal entries to record the above transactions assuming that the company achieved the target of buy-back.

SOLUTION

JOURNAL

Date	Particulars		L.F.	Dr. (₹)	Cr. (₹)
1.	Equity Shares Buy Back A/c	Dr.		25,00,000	
	To Bank A/c				25,00,000
	(Being the payment made on buy-back of 50,000 shares @₹ 50)				
2.	Equity Share Capital A/c	Dr.		5,00,000	
	Securities Premium A/c	Dr.		18,00,000	
	Revenue Reserve A/c	Dr.		2,00,000	
	To Equity Share Buyback A/c				25,00,000
	(Being the cancellation of equity shares bought back)				
3.	Revenue Reserve A/c	Dr.		5,00,000	
	To Capital Redemption Reserve A/c				5,00,000
	(Being the amount equal to nominal value of equity shares bought back out of free reserves t/f to CRR)				

ILLUSTRATION 3 [Buy-Back of Shares Partly out of Proceeds and Partly out of Free Reserves]

Tushar Ltd. provides you the following information:

1. **Issued Capital**	:	2,00,000 Equity Shares of ₹ 10 each	
		2,000, 10% Pref. Shares of ₹ 100 each (Issued two months back for the purpose of buy-back)	
2. **Reserves & Surplus**	:	Capital Reserve	₹ 10,00,000
		Securities Premium	₹ 18,00,000
		Revenue Reserve	₹ 30,00,000
		Profit & Loss A/c	₹ 40,00,000

3. **Resolution passed to buy back:** 25% of its Equity Shares @ ₹ 50 per share.

Required: Pass journal entries to record the above transactions assuming that the company achieved the target of buy-back.

SOLUTION

JOURNAL

Date	Particulars		L.F.	Dr. (₹)	Cr. (₹)
1.	Equity Shares Buy Back A/c	Dr.		25,00,000	
	To Bank A/c				25,00,000
	(Being the payment made on buy-back of 50,000 shares @₹ 50)				
2.	Equity Share Capital A/c	Dr.		5,00,000	
	Securities Premium A/c	Dr.		18,00,000	
	Revenue Reserve A/c	Dr.		2,00,000	

	To Equity Share Buyback A/c			25,00,000
	(Being the cancellation of equity shares bought back)			
3.	Revenue Reserve A/c	Dr.	3,00,000	
	To Capital Redemption Reserve A/c			3,00,000
	(Being the amount equal to nominal value of equity shares bought back out of free reserves t/f to CRR)			

ILLUSTRATION 4

From the following information calculate the maximum number of shares that can be bought back and pass the necessary journal entries in the books of BHARAT TUSHAR Ltd.:

(a) 10% Redeemable Pref. shares of ₹ 10 each fully paid up	₹ 100 lacs
(b) Equity Shares of ₹ 10 each fully paid up	₹ 300 lacs
(c) Securities Premium	₹ 50 lacs
(d) General Reserve	₹ 250 lacs
(e) Profit & Loss Account	₹ 300 lacs
(f) Capital Redemption Reserve	₹ 20 lacs
(g) Plant Revaluation Reserve	₹ 500 lacs
(h) Capital Reserve	₹ 600 lacs
(i) Export Reserve (Statutory Reserve)	₹ 700 lacs
(j) Secured Loans	₹ 1000 lacs
(k) Unsecured Loans	₹ 640 lacs
(l) Current Liabilities	₹ 100 lacs
(m) Market Price per share ₹ 40	
(n) Buy Back Price offer 25% over the Market Price.	
(o) Investments [Face Value ₹ 200 lacs]	₹ 400 lacs
Sufficient Investments were realized at market price which was 125% of the face value.	
(p) Later the company issued one fully paid up Equity Share of ₹ 10 each by way of bonus shares for every four equity shares held.	

SOLUTION

1. **Outstanding Shares Test:** Max. No. of shares than can be bought back

   = 25% of O/s shares = 25% of 30 lacs = 7.5 lacs

2. **Resources Test:** Max. No. of shares that can be bought back

   = (25% of Paid up Share Capital + Free Reserves)/Buy back price per share

   = 25% (₹ 400 + ₹ 50 + ₹ 250 + ₹ 300)/ (40 + 25%) = 5 lacs

3. **Debt-Equity Test:**

Note: Let X = Amount to be t/f to CRR; Y = Maximum permitted buyback of Equity

Minimum Equity to be maintained = Debt/2 = 1640/2 = 820

Max. Loss on Sale of Suficient Investments = Y × 150/250

X = (Y/50) × 10 = Y/5 ...Eq. I

Y = 1,000 – 820 – X – Y × 150/250 ...Eq. II

Putting Equation I in Equation II

Y = 180 – Y/5 – 3/5 Y

Y = 180 – 4Y/5

Y + 4Y/5 = 180

Y = 900/9 = ₹ 100 lacs

X = ₹ 100/5 = ₹ 20 lacs

Max. No of shares that can be bought back = ₹ 100/₹ 50 = 2 lacs

Hence, 2 lacs shares being the least in 3 tests can at the most be bought back.

JOURNAL OF TULSIAN LTD. *[₹ in lacs]*

Data	Particulars		Dr. (₹)	Cr. (₹)
1	Bank A/c [₹ 80 lakh × 125%]	Dr.	100	
	Profit & Loss A/c	Dr.	60	
	To Investments A/c			160
	(Being the Investments (Face Value of 80 Lacs) of Book value of ₹ 160 lacs sold at 125% of face value)			
	Book value = ₹ 400 × ₹ 80/₹ 200 = ₹ 160 lacs			
	Sale Proceeds = ₹ 80 lacs × 125% = ₹ 100 lacs			
2	Equity Shares Buy Back A/c	Dr.	100	
	To Bank A/c			100
	(Being the payment made on buy-back)			
3	Equity Share Capital A/c	Dr.	20	
	Securities Premium A/c	Dr.	50	
	General Reserve	Dr.	30	
	To Equity Shares Buy Back A/c			100
	(Being the cancellation of shares bought back)			
4	General Reserve	Dr.	20	
	To Capital Redemption Reserve A/c			20
	(Being the amount equal to nominal value of Equity Shares bought back out of free reserves t/f to CRR)			
5	Capital Redemption Reserve A/c	Dr.	40	
	General Reserve A/c	Dr.	30	
	To Bonus to Equity Share holders A/c			70
	(Being the utilization CRR and GR to issue 1 bonus share for every 4 shares held)			
6.	Bonus to Equity Shareholders A/c	Dr.	70	
	To Equity Shares Capital A/c			70
	(Being the issue of one bonus share for every 4 equity share hold)			

SOLVED PROBLEMS

PROBLEM 1

ACS Limited furnishes the extracts of the Balance Sheet as at 31 March 2015:

Particulars	*₹ (in crores)*
13% Preference Shares of ₹ 100 each fully paid	75
Equity Shares of ₹ 10 each fully paid	50
Capital Reserve	50
Revenue Reserve	250
Current Liabilities	140
	565
Fixed Assets	150
Investments	120
Current Assets	295
	565

The company purchased its own 100 lakh equity shares of ₹ 10 each at ₹ 25 per share on 1 April 2015 out of free reserves. The company also redeemed preference shares on same date. The payments for the above were made out of bank account which forms part of current assets.

Required: Pass necessary journal entries and prepare the Balance Sheet.

SOLUTION

JOURNAL *(₹ in Crores)*

Date	*Particulars*		*L.F.*	*Dr. (₹)*	*Cr. (₹)*
1.	Equity Shares Buy Back A/c	Dr.		25	
	To Bank A/c				25
	(Being the payment made on buy back)				
2.	Equity Share Capital A/c	Dr.		10	
	Revenue Reserve A/c			15	
	To Equity Shares Buy Back A/c				25
	(Being the cancellation of shares bought back)				
3.	Revenue Reserve A/c	Dr.		85	
	To Capital Redemption Reserve A/c				85
	(Being the transfer of Revenue Reserve to CRR)				
4.	13% Preference Share Capital A/c	Dr.		75	
	To Preference Shareholders A/c				75
	(Being the amount due to preference shareholders on redemption of preference shares)				
5.	Preference Shareholders' A/c	Dr.		75	
	To Bank A/c				75
	(Being the payment made to preference shareholders)				

BALANCE SHEET OF ACS LTD. AS AT 01.04.2015

Particulars	*Note No*	*₹ (lacs)*
I. Equity and Liabilities		
(1) Shareholders'Funds		
(a) Share Capital (₹ 10 each) [50 – 10]		40
(b) Reserves and Surplus	1	285
(2) Non-Current Liabilities		
(3) Current Liabilities		140
Total		465
II. Assets		
(1) Non-Current Assets		
(a) Fixed Assets		150
(b) Non-Current Investments		120
(2) Current Assets [295 – 100]		195
Total		465

Notes To Accounts:

Particulars	*₹ (lacs)*
1. Reserves and Surplus	
Revenue Reserve [250 – 15 – 85]	150
Capital Reserve	50
Capital Redemption Reserve	85
Total	285

PROBLEM 2

Given below are the extracts from the Balance Sheet of FCS Limited as at 31th March 2015:

Particulars	*(₹ in lakhs)*
Equity Share Capital (Fully paid up shares of ₹ 10 each)	2,400
Securities Premium	350
General Reserve	930
Profit and Loss Account	340
Sundry Creditors	2,250
Sundry Provisions	490
Machinery	3,600
Furniture	452
Investments [Face Value ` 200 lacs]	148
Stock	1,200
Debtors	520
Cash at Bank	740

On 1 April 2015 the company announced the buy-back of 25% of its equity shares @ 15 per share. For this purpose, it sold all of its investments @ 75% and issued 2,00,000, 14% preferences shares of ₹ 100 each at par, the entire amount being payable with application.

The issue was fully subscribed. The company achieved the target of buy-back. Later the company issued one fully paid up equity share of ₹ 10 by way of bonus shares for every four equity shares held by the equity shareholders.

Required: Pass journal entries for all transactions including cash transactions.

SOLUTION

JOURNAL *(₹ in Lakhs)*

Date	*Particulars*		*L.F.*	*Dr. (₹)*	*Cr. (₹)*
1.	Bank A/c	Dr.		150	
	To Investments A/c				150
	(Being the sale of investments)				
2.	Investments A/c	Dr.		2	
	To Profit and Loss A/c				2
	(Being the t/f of Profit on sale of Investments)				
3.	Bank A/c	Dr.		200	
	To 14% Preference Share Application & Allotment A/c				200
	(Being the Application money received)				
4.	14% Preference Share Application & Allotment A/c	Dr.		200	
	To 14% Preference Share Capital A/c				200
	(Being the Allotment of Shares)				
5.	Equity Shares Buy Back A/c	Dr.		900	
	To Bank A/c				900
	(Being the payment made to equity shareholders on buy-back)				
6.	Equity Share Capital A/c	Dr.		600	
	Securities Premium A/c	Dr.		300	
	To Equity Shares Buy Back A/c				900
	(Being the cancellation of share bought back)				
7.	General Reserve A/c	Dr.		400	
	To Capital Redemption Reserve A/c				400
	(Being the Buy-back out of general reserves to the extent not covered by fresh issue of share capital)				
8.	Capital Redemption Reserve A/c	Dr.		400	
	Securities Premium A/c	Dr.		50	
	To Bonus Issue A/c				450
	(Being the utilisation of capital redemption reserve and securities premium to issue one bonus share for every four shares held)				

9.	Bonus Issue A/c	Dr.	450	
	To Equity Share Capital a/c			450
	(Being the Issue of one bonus share for every four equity shares)			

Note: Amount of Bonus Issue = 25% of (2400 – 25% of 2400) = 450 lakhs.

PROBLEM 3

Given below are the extracts from the Balance Sheet of CANH Ltd. as on 31.3.2015:

Particulars	*(₹ in '000)*
Equity Shares of ₹ 10 each	800
Securities Premium	100
General Reserve	780
Profit and Loss Account	120
Creditors	2,320
Fixed Assets	2,700
Non-trade Investments	300
Stock	600
Sundry Debtors	360
Cash and Bank	160

CANH Ltd. buy back 16,000 shares of ₹ 20 per share. For this purpose, the Company sold its all non-trade investments for ₹ 3,20,000. Pass Journal Entries with full narrations effecting the buy back.

SOLUTION

JOURNAL OF CANH LTD.

Data	*Particulars*		*Dr. (₹)*	*Cr. (₹)*
1.	Bank A/c	Dr.	3,20,000	
	To Non-trade Investments			3,00,000
	To Profit & Loss A/c			20,000
	(Being the entry for sale of Non-trade Investments)			
2.	Equity Shares Buy back A/c (16,000 × ₹ 20)	Dr.	3,20,000	
	To Bank A/c			3,20,000
	(Being purchase of 16,000 shares @ ₹.20 per share)			
3.	Equity Share Capital A/c (16,000 × ₹.10)	Dr.	1,60,000	
	Securities Premium A/c	Dr.	1,00,000	
	General Reserve	Dr.	60,000	
	To Equity Shares Buy-back A/c			3,20,000
	(Being cancellation of shares bought back)			
4.	General Reserve	Dr.	1,60,000	
	To Capital Redemption Reserve A/c			1,60,000
	(Being the entry for t/f of General Reserve to Capital Redemption Reserve to the extent of face value of equity shares bought back)			

PROBLEM 4

CAS Ltd. furnishes you with the extracts of Balance Sheet as at 31st March, 2015

(₹ in crores)

12% Redeemable Preference Shares of ₹ 100 each fully paid		75
Equity shares of ₹ 10 each fully paid		25
Capital reserve		15
Securities premium		25
Revenue reserves		260
Current liabilities		40
		440
Funds employed in:		
Fixed assets: Cost	100	
Less: Provision for depreciation	100	nil
Investment at cost (market value ₹ 400 Cr.)		100
Current assets		340
		440

The company redeemed preference shares on 1st April, 2015. It also bought back 50 lakh equity shares of ₹ 10 each at ₹ 50 per share. The payments for the above were made out of the huge bank balances, which appeared as part of current assets.

You are asked to:

(i) Pass journal entries to record the above.

(ii) Prepare Balance Sfreet. (iii) Value equity share on net asset basis.

SOLUTION

JOURNAL OF CAS LTD. *(₹ in lakhs)*

Particulars	*Dr. (₹)*	*Cr. (₹)*
Redeemable Preference Share Capital A/c Dr.	75	
To Red. Pref. Shareholders A/c		75
(Being redemption of 12% preference shares pursuant to capital re-organisation)		
Red. Rref. Shareholders A/c Dr.	75	
To Bank A/c		75
(Being the payment made to Red. Pref. Share holders)		
Revenue Reserves A/c Dr.	75	
To Capital Redemption Reserve A/c		75
(Being amount equal to par value of preference shares redeemed out of profits, transferred to capital redemption reserve)		
Equity Shares Buy Back A/c Dr.	25	
To Bank A/c		25
(Being buyback of 50 lakh equity shares of ₹ 10 each from the members at a price of ₹ 50 per share, premium paid out of revenue reserves)		

Particulars		Dr.	Cr.
Equity Share Capital A/c	Dr.	5	
Revenue Reserves A/c	Dr.	20	
To Equity Share Buy Back A/c			25
(Being the concellation of Equity Share Buy Back A/c)			
Revenue Reserves A/c	Dr.	5	
To Capital Redemption Reserve A/c			5
(Being transfer to capital redemption reserve, as required by Section 77AA, on buyback out of reserves)			

BALANCE SHEET OF CAS LTD. AS AT 01.04.2015

Particulars	Note No	₹ (lacs)
I. Equity and Liabilities		
(1) Shareholders' Funds		
(a) Share Capital (₹ 10 each) [25 – 5]		20
(b) Reserves and Surplus	1	280
(2) Non-Current Liabilities [Debentures]		
(3) Current Liabilities		40
Total		340
II. Assets		
(1) Non-Current Assets		
(a) Fixed Assets [100 – 100]		0
(b) Non-Current Investments [Market Value ₹ 400 crores]		100
(2) Current Assets [340 – 75 – 25]		240
Total		340

Notes To Accounts:

Particulars	₹ (lacs)
1. Reserves and Surplus	
Revenue Reserve [260 – 80 – 20]	160
Capital Reserve	15
Capital Redemption Reserve	80
Securities Premium	25
Total	280

NET ASSET VALUE OF AN EQUITY SHARE *(₹ in crores)*

Particulars	₹ in crores
Investments (at market value)	400
Net current assets	200
Net assets available to equity shareholders	600
No. of equity shares = 2 crores	
Value of an equity share = 600 crores/2crores = ₹ 300 crores	

PROBLEM 5

CAMJ Ltd. has the following Capital Strucuture as on 31.03.2015:

Particulars	(₹ in crores)	
(1) Equity Share Capital (Shares of ₹ 10 each fully paid)	—	330
(2) Reserves and Surphus		
General Reserve	240	—
Securities Premium Account	90	—
Profit & Loss Account	90	—
Infrastructure Development Reserve	180	600
(3) Loan Funds		1,800

The Share holders CAMJ Ltd., on the recommendation of their Board of Directors, have approved on 12.09.2015 a proposal to buy back the maximum permissible number of Equity shares considering the large surplus funds available a: the disposal of the company.

The prevailing market value of the company's shares is ₹ 25 per share and in order to induce the existing shareholders to offer their shares for buy back, ft was decided to offer a price of 20% over market

You are also informed that the Infrastructure Reserve is created to comply with Income-tax Act requirements.

You are required to compute the maximum number of shares that can be bought back in the light of the above information and also under a situation where the loan funds of the company were either ₹ 1,200 crores *or* ₹ 1,500 crores.

Assuming that the entire back is compteted by 09.12.2015, Show the accounting entries in the company's books in each situation. Narrations should form part of your answer.

SOLUTION

(A) STATEMENT DETERMINING THE MAX. NUMBER OF SHARES TO BE BOUGHT BACK

*Particulars**	*Situation 1 (Loan 1800)*	*Situation 2 (Loan 1200)*	*Situation 3 (Loan 1500)*
Shares Outstanding Test	8.25	8.25	8.25
Resources Test	6.25	6.25	6.25
Debt Equity Ratio Test	Nil	3.75	Nil
Maximum number of share that can be			
bought back [least of above]	Nil	3.75	Nil

JOURNAL ENTRIES FOR BUY BACK (APPLICABLE ONLY FOR SITUATION 2) ₹ *in crores*

Data	Particulars		*Dr. (₹)*	*Cr. (₹)*
1	Equity Share Buy Back A/c	Dr.	112.50	
	To Bank A/c			112.50
	(Being buy back of 3.75 crores equity shares of ₹ 10 each @ ₹ 30 per share)			
2	Equity Share Capital A/c	Dr.	37.50	
	Securities Premium A/c	Dr.	75.00	

	To Equity Share Buy Back A/c (Being cancellation of shares bought back)			112.50
3	General Reserve A/c	Dr.	37.50	
	To Capital Redemption Reserve A/c (Being transfer of free reserves to capital redemption reserve to the extent of nominal value of capital redeemed through free reserves)			37.50

Note: Under Situations 1 & 3 the company does not qualify for buy back of shares as per the provisions of Section 68 of The Companies Act, 2013.

Working Notes:

(i) Shares Outstanding Test:

Max. No. of Shares that can be bought back = 25% of 33 = 8.25 crores

(ii) Resources Test:

Max. Number of shares that can be bought back

= [25% of (Paid up Capitals + Free Reserves)/Buy Back Price per share

= [25%(₹ 330 + 420)]/₹ 30 = 6.25 crores

Particulars*	Situation 1	Situation 2	Situation 3
(a) Loan Funds (₹ in crores)	1,800	1,200	1,500
(b) Minimum Equity to be maintained after buy back in the ratio of 2 : 1 (₹ in crores)	900	600	750
(c) Present Equity Shareholders Funds (₹ in crores)	750	750	750
(d) Future Equity Shareholder's Funds	N.A.	712.50 [750–37.5]	N.A.
(e) Maximum permitted buy back of Equity (₹ in crores) [(b) – (c)]	Nil	112.50	Nil
(f) Maximum number of shares that can be bought back @ ₹ 30 per share (shares in crores) [(d)/₹ 30]	Nil	3.75	Nil

Note: *Infrastructure Development Reserve and Capital Redemption Reserve are not free reserves.*

Step 2: Max No of Equity Shares that can be bought back

= Least of 8.25 or 6.25 or 3.75

= Max. 3.75 crores Shares can be bought back

Notes: Let X = Amount to be t/f to CRR; Y = Maximum permitted buyback of Equity

Y = 750 – X – 600 ...Eq. I

X = (Y/30) × 10 = Y/3 ...Eq. II

by Solving both the Equations

X = ₹ 37.5 crores, Y = ₹ 150 – ₹ 37.5 = ₹ 112.50 crores.

5 UNDERWRITING OF SHARES AND DEBENTURES

LEARNING OBJECTIVES

After studying this chapter, you should be able to understand:

- Meaning of Underwriting Agreement and Underwriting Commission
- Purpose for which Underwriting Commission may be paid
- Conditions for Payment of Underwriting Commission
- Can Commission be paid to any person on Shares or Debentures which are not offered to public for Subscription?
- Brokerage
- Distinction Between Brokerage and Underwriting Commission
- Penalty for Default
- Terms Used in Underwriting
- Practical Steps Involved in the Calculation of Net and Total Liability
- How to Prepare Statement Showing the Net and Total Liability of Underwriters?
- How to Prepare Statement Showing the Net Amount Due To/From Underwriters
- Accounting Entries

1.0 MEANING OF UNDERWRITING AGREEMENT AND UNDERWRITING COMMISSION

An underwriting agreement is an agreement between the company and certain party *(known as underwriter)* under which the latter agrees to take up the whole *or* part of the securities which may not be subscribed by the public for an agreed consideration *(known as underwriting commission)*. It is in the nature of an assurance against the risk involved in placing the securities before the public.

Note: An underwriting agreement is enforceable against the executors of deceased underwriter.

[Wasner Engineering Co. v. Benan (1913) 307 L.R. 191]

2.0 PURPOSE FOR WHICH UNDERWRITING COMMISSION MAY BE PAID

A company may pay a commission to any person in consideration of the number of securities underwritten *or* subscribed by underwriter whether absolutely *or* conditiionally.

[Rule 13 of Companies (Prospectus and Allotment of Securities) Rules, 2014]

3.0 CONDITIONS FOR PAYMENT OF UNDERWRITING COMMISSION [RULE 13]

A company may pay underwriting commission if the following conditions are fulfilled, namely:

1. **Authorised by Articles** — The payment of the commission must be authorised by the articles.
2. **Source** — The commission may be paid out of proceeds of issue *or* Profits of the Company.

3. **Maximum Rate of Commission** — The commission paid *or* agreed to be paid must not exceed in the case of shares, 5% of the price at which the shares are issued *or* the amount *or* rate authorised by the articles, whichever is *less* and in the case of debentures, 2½% of the price at which the debenturs are issued *or* the amount *or* rate authorised by the articles, whichever is less.

4(i). **Disclosure of Amount and Rate** — The amount and rate per cent of the commission paid *or* agreed to be paid must be disclosed in the prospectus *or* in the statement in lieu of prospectus *or* in a statement in the prescribed form signed in a like manner as a statement in lieu of prospectus and filed before the payment of the commission with the Registrar.

4(ii). **Disclosure of No. of Securities Underwritten** — The number of shares *or* debentures underwritten by each of the underwriters must be disclosed in the prospectus *or* statement in lieu of prospectus.

5. **No Commission** — No commission shall be paid to any underwriter on securities which are not offered to the public for subscription.

6. **Delivery of the Contract** — A copy of the contract for the payment of the commission must be delivered to the Register at the time of delivery of the prospectus for registration.

4.0 DISTINCTION BETWEEN BROKERAGE AND UNDERWRITING COMMISSION

Brokerage is paid to brokers for procuring other persons who will take shares *or* debentures where underwriter commission is paid to the underwriters for agreeing to take up the whole *or* part of shares *or* debentures which may not be subscribed by the public.

If broker fails to place any share, he is not personally liable to take them *nor* he is entitled to any brokerage. On the other hand, the underwriter is bound to take up the shares which have not been subscribed by public.

5.0 TERMS USED IN UNDERWRITING

MARKED APPLICATIONS

(a) The application forms bearing the stamp of the underwriter are termed as "Marked Application forms.

(b) The benefit of marked applications is given to the concerned underwriters in whose favour application forms have been marked.

UNMARKED APPLICATIONS

(a) The application forms which do not bear the stamp of the underwriter are termed as 'Unmarked Application forms'.

(b) The benefit of unmarked applications is given first to the company to the extent of issue not underwritten by underwriters (in case any part of the issue is not underwritten).

(c) In case there is surplus, the benefit of surplus unmarked applications will be given to the underwriters in the ratio of their gross liability.

FULL UNDERWRITING

(a) When the entire issue is underwritten such underwriting is termed as 'full underwriting'. For example, X Ltd. decided to make a public issue of 1,00,000 Equity Shares of ₹ 10 each which is entirely underwritten by A, B, C and D in the ratio of 2 : 2 : 1 : 1.

(b) In such a case the benefit of unmarked applications is given to the underwriter in the ratio of their gross liability i.e., 2 : 2 : 1 : 1.

PARTIAL UNDERWRITING

(a) When only a part of issue is underwritten, such underwriting is termed as 'Partial Underwriting.' For example, X Ltd. decided to make a public issue of 1,00,000 Equity Shares of ₹ 10 each out of which 90,000 shares are underwritten by A, B, C and D in the ratio of 2 : 2 : 1 : 1. It means 10,000 shares are underwritten by the company itself.

(b) In such a case, the benefit of unmarked applications will first be given to the company.

(c) In case there is surplus, such surplus will be distributed among other underwriters in the ratio of their gross liability.

SOLE UNDERWRITING

(a) When the issue is underwritten only by one underwriter, such underwriting is termed as 'Sole Underwriting'. For example, if an issue of 1,00,000 shares of ₹ 10 each of X Ltd. is underwritten by A, it is a case of sole underwriting.

(b) In such a case, the distinction between marked and unmarked applications is not of such significance.

JOINT UNDERWRITING

(a) When the issue is underwritten by two *or* more underwriters, such underwriting is termed as 'Joint Underwriting'. For example, if an issue of 1,00,000 shares of ₹ 10 each of X Ltd. is underwritten by A, B, C and D in the ratio of 2 : 2 : 1 : 1, it is a case of joint underwriting.

(b) In such a case the benefit of unmarked applications is given to the underwriters in the ratio of their gross liability.

(c) The benefit of marked applications is given to the concerned underwriters in whose favour applications have been marked.

FIRM UNDERWRITING

(a) **Meaning** Firm underwriting refers to a definite commitment by the underwriter to take up a specified number of securities irrespective of the number of securities subscribed by the public.

For example, the entire issue of X Ltd. is underwritten as follows:

A. 1,60,000 shares (firm underwriting 3,600 shares)

B. 1,60,000 shares (firm underwriting 2,000 shares)

C. 80,000 shares (firm underwriting 1,200 shares)

D. 80,000 shares (firm underwriting 10,000 shares)

In this case only 4,63,200 shares (i.e., 4,80,000 shares — firm underwriting of 16,800 shares) will be offered to public and 16,800 shares will be taken up by the underwriters even if the issue is oversubscribed.

(b) **Treatment** The benefit of firm underwriting may be given either:

(i) to an individual underwriter on the basis of his individual firm underwriting,or

(ii) to all the underwriters in the ratio of their gross liability

In otherwords, firm underwriting shares may be treated at par with *either* 'Marked Applications' *or* 'Unmarked Applications'.

6.0 PRACTICAL STEPS INVOLVED IN THE CALCULATION OF NET AND TOTAL LIABILITY

Step 1: *Calculate Gross Liability of each underwriter by dividing the number of securities underwritten in the ratio of shares underwritten by underwriters.*

Step 2: *Give credit for Marked Application on actual basis.*

Step 3: *Give credit for 'Unmarked application' in the ratio of their gross liability.*

Note: *In case of partial Underwriting, the credit of unmarked applications will first be given to the company to the extent of securities not underwritten and then to the underwriters.*

Step 4: *Give credit for 'Firm Underwriting' applications either in the ratio of individual firm underwriting applications or in the ratio of gross liability.*

Step 5: *Calculate the balance (i.e., Step 1 – Step 2 – Step 3 – Step 4).*

Step 6: *Give the credit for total negative balance to the underwriter(s) having positive balance(s) in the ratio of their gross liability.*

At the same time, eliminate the negative balance(s) of underwriter(s) of adding an equivalent number.

Step 7: *Calculate the Balance.*

Step 8: *If Balance of any underwriter is still negative, go to Step 6, otherwise go to Step 9.*

Note: *Net Positive Balance represents Net Liability.*

Step 9: *Add liability for firm underwriting to individual underwriter on actual basis.*

Step 10: *Calculate total liability by adding Step 8 and Step 9.*

7.0 HOW TO PREPARE STATEMENT SHOWING THE NET AND TOTAL LIABILITY OF UNDERWRITERS

STATEMENT SHOWING THE NET AND TOTAL LIABILITY OF UNDERWRITERS (NO. OF SHARES)

	Particulars	Basis	A	B	C	Total
A.	Gross Liability (No. of Shares)	Ratio of shares underwritten	...	...	...	...
B.	*Less:* Marked Applications	Actual	(...)	(...)	(...)	(...)
C.	Balance (A – B)		...	...	...	...
D.	*Less:* Unmarked Applications [Total Applications – Marked Applications]	Ratio of Gross Liability	(...)	(...)	(...)	(...)
E.	Balance (C – D)		...	...	...	...
F.	*Less:* Firm Underwriting	Actual Ratio/Ratio of Gross Liability	(...)	(...)	(...)	(...)
G.	Net Liability (if no balance is negative) [E – F]		...	...	...	...
H.	*Add:* Liability for firm underwriting	Actual	...	...	...	...
I.	Total Liability [G + H]		...	...	...	...

8.0 HOW TO PREPARE STATEMENT SHOWING THE NET AMOUNT DUE TO/FROM UNDERWRITERS

STATEMENT SHOWING THE NET AMOUNT DUE TO/FROM UNDERWRITERS

	Particulars	A	B	C
A	Total Liability (including firm underwriting) (No. of Shares)	...	...	...
B	Amount Due on Total Liability	...	...	...

C	*Less:* Amount already paid on Firm Applications	(...)	(...)	(...)
D	Amount Due on Net Liability	...	...	...
E	*Less:* Underwriting Commission	(...)	(...)	(...)
F	Net Amount Due to Underwriters (if D < E)			
	or			
	Net Amount Due from Underwriters (if D > E)			

ILLUSTRATION 1

Tulsian Ltd. made a public issue of 4,80,000 equity shares of ₹ 10 each, ₹ 5 payable on application and the balance on allotment. The entire issue was underwritten by A, B, C and D in the proportion of 2:2:1:1 and respectively at the maximum rate of commission permissible as per SEBI Guidelines. The total subscription received were for 4,20,000 shares.

Required: Prepare the statement showing the liability of the individual underwriter in each of the following alternative cases:

Case (a) If no other information is given:

Case (b) If marked applications received were as under:

A 60,000, C 68,000, B 1,12,000, D 1,20,000

The credit for unmarked applications is to be given to underwirter, in proportion to their gross liability.

Case (c) If marked applications received were as under:

A 60,000, C 68,000, B, 1,12,000, D 1,20,000

The credit for unmarked applications is to be given in the ratio of liability after giving credit for marked applications.

Case (d) If marked applications received were A, 60,000, C 68,000, B 1,12,000, D 1,20,000

A, B, C, and D also agreed on firm underwriting of 3,600, 2,000, 1,200 and 10,000 shares respectively. The benefit of firm underwriting is to be given to individual underwriter.

Case (e) If marked applications received were A 60,000, C 68,000, B 1,12,000, D 1,20,000.

A, B, C and D also agreed on firm underwriting of 3,600, 2,000, 1,200 and 10,000 shares respectively. The benefit of firm underwriting is not to be given on individual basis.

SOLUTION

CASE (A) STATEMENT SHOWING THE LIABILITY OF UNDERWRITERS FOR SUBSCRIPTION OF SHARES NOT YET SUBSCRIBED FOR

	Particulars	*Basis*	*A*	*B*	*C*	*D*	*Total*
A	Gross Liability	2 : 2 : 1 : 1	1,60,000	1,60,000	80,000	80,000	4,80,000
B	*Less:* Credit for Application received	2 : 2 : 1 : 1	(1,40,000)	(1,40,000)	(70,000)	(70,000)	(4,20,000)
C	Net Liability [A – B]		20,000	20,000	10,000	10,000	60,000

Note: *In the absence of any information regarding marked/unmarked applications, it has been assumed that the applications have been received in the proportion of the total number of the shares underwritten and hence the total applications received have been divided in the ratio of gross liability of underwriters.*

CASE: (B) STATEMENT SHOWING THE LIABILITY OF UNDERWRITERS FOR SUBSCRIPTION OF SHARES NOT YET SUBSCRIBED FOR

	Particulars	*Basis*	*A*	*B*	*C*	*D*	*Total*
A	Gross Liability	2 : 2 : 1 : 1	1,60,000	1,60,000	80,000	80,000	4,80,000
B	*Less:* Marked Applications	Actual	(60,000)	(1,12,000)	(68,000)	(1,20,000)	(3,60,000)
C	Balance (A – B)		1,00,000	48,000	12,000	–40,000	1,20,000
D	*Less:* Unmarked Applications [4,20,000 – 3,60,000]	2:2:1:1	(20,000)	(20,000)	(10,000)	(10,000)	(60,000)
E	Balance (C – D)		80,000	28,000	2,000	– 50,000	60,000
F	Credit for D 's oversubscription	2:2:1	(20,000)	(20,000)	(10,000)	50,000	—
G	Balance [E – F]		60,000	8,000	– 8,000	—	60,000
H	Credit for C 's oversubscription	2:2	(4,000)	(4,000)	8,000		
I	Net Liability [G – H]		56,000	4,000	—	—	60,000

CASE: (C) STATEMENT SHOWING THE LIABILITY OF UNDERWRITERS FOR SUBSCRIPTION OF SHARES NOT YET SUBSCRIBED FOR

	Particulars	*Basis*	*A*	*B*	*C*	*D*	*Total*
A	Gross Liability	2 : 2 : 1 : 1	1,60,000	1,60,000	80,000	80,000	4,80,000
B	*Less:* Marked App.	Actual	(60,000)	(1,12,000)	(68,000)	(1,20,000)	(3,60,000)
C	Balance (A – B)		1,00,000	48,000	12,000	(40,000)	1,20,000
D	*Less:* Unmarked App. [4,20,000 – 3,60,000]	100 : 48 : 12	(37,500)	(18,000)	(4,500)	—	(60,000)
E	Balance (C – D)		62,500	30,000	7,500	(40,000)	60,000
F	Credit for D 's oversubscription	100 : 48 : 12	(25,000)	(12,000)	(3,000)	40,000	—
G	Net Liability (E – F)		37,500	18,000	4,500	—	60,000

CASE: (D) STATEMENT SHOWING THE LIABILITY OF UNDERWRITERS FOR SUBSCRIPTION OF SHARES NOT YET SUBSCRIBED FOR

	Particulars	*Basis*	*A*	*B*	*C*	*D*	*Total*
A	Gross Liability	2 : 2 : 1 : 1	1,60,000	1,60,000	80,000	80,000	4,80,000
B	*Less:* Marked App.	Actual	(60,000)	(1,12,000)	(68,000)	(1,20,000)	(3,60,000)
C	Balance (A – B)		1,00,000	48,000	12,000	(40,000)	1,20,000
D	*Less:* Unmarked App. [4,20,000 – 3,60,000]	2 : 2 : 1 : 1	(20,000)	(20,000)	(10,000)	(10,000)	(60,000)
E	Balance (C – D)		80,000	28,000	2,000	(50,000)	60,000
F	*Less:* Firm Underwriting	Actual	(3,600)	(2,000)	(1,200)	(10,000)	(16,800)

G	Balance (E – F)		76,400	26,000	800	(60,000)	43,200
H	Credit for D's oversubscription	2 : 2 : 1	(24,000)	(24,000)	(12,000)	60,000	—
I	Balance (G – H)		52,400	2,000	(11,200)	—	43,200
J	Credit for C's oversubscription	2 : 2	(5,600)	(5,600)	11,200	—	—
K	Balance (I – J)		46,800	(3,600)	—	—	43,200
L	Credit for B's subscription		(3,600)	3,600	—	—	
M	Net Liability excluding firm oversubscription		43,200	—	—	—	43,200
N	*Add:* Firm underwriting	Actual	3,600	2,000	1,200	10,000	16,800
O	Total Liability including firm underwriting		46,800	2,000	1,200	10,000	60,000

CASE: (E) STATEMENT SHOWING THE LIABILITY OF UNDERWRITERS FOR SUBSCRIPTION OF SHARES NOT YET SUBSCRIBED FOR

	Particulars	*Basis*	*A*	*B*	*C*	*D*	*Total*
A	Gross Liability	2 : 2 : 1 : 1	1,60,000	1,60,000	80,000	80,000	4,80,000
B	*Less:* Marked App.	Actual	(60,000)	(1,12,000)	(68,000)	(1,20,000)	(3,60,000)
C	Balance (A – B)		1,00,000	48,000	12,000	(40,000)	1,20,000
D	*Less:* Unmarked App. [4,20,000 – 3,60,000]	2 : 2 : 1 : 1	(20,000)	(20,000)	(10,000)	(10,000)	(60,000)
E	Balance (C – D)		80,000	28,000	2,000	(50,000)	60,000
F	*Less:* Firm Underwriting	2 : 2 : 1 : 1	(5,600)	(5,600)	(2,800)	(2,800)	(16,800)
G	Balance (E – F)		74,400	22,400	(800)	(52,800)	43,200
H	Credit for C' & D's oversubscription	2 : 2	(26,800)	(26,800)	800	52,800	—
I	Balance (G – H)		47,600	(4,400)	—	—	43,200
J	Credit for B's oversubscription		(4,400)	4,400	—	—	—
K	Net Liability excluding firm underwriting		43,200	—	—	—	43,200
L	*Add:* Firm underwriting	Actual	3,600	2,000	1,200	10,000	16,800
M	Total Liability including firm underwriting		46,800	2,000	1,200	10,000	60,000

9.0 ACCOUNTING ENTRIES

1. **On receipt of Application Money from general public and from underwriters (for shares underwritten firm)**

   Bank A/c Dr.

   To Share Application A/c

2. **On Adjustment of Application Money**

   Share Application A/c Dr.

   To Share Capital A/c

   To Securities Premium A/c *(if any payable on Application)*

3. **On Making Allotment Money due from general public and from Underwriters (for shares underwritten firm)**

   Share Allotment A/c Dr. [with Allotment money due from Public]

   Underwriter's A/c Dr. [with Allotment money due on firm underwriting]

   To Share Capital A/c

   To Securities Premium A/c

4. **On Making Application & Allotment Money due on Net liability (i.e. excluding firm underwriting) devolved on underwriters**

   Underwriters' A/c Dr. [With App. & Allotment Money Due on Net Liability]

   To Share Capital A/c

   To Securities Premium A/c

5. **On Receipt of Allotment Money from General Public**

   Bank A/c Dr.

   To Share Allotment A/c

6. **On Making Underwriting Commission due**

   Underwriting Commission A/c Dr. [With Total]

   To Underwriters' A/c [Individually]

7. **On Receipt of amount from Underwriter on final settlement**

   Bank A/c

   To Concerned Underwriter's A/c

8. **On Payment of amount to Underwriter on final settlement**

   Concerned Underwriter's A/c Dr.

   To Bank A/c

Tutorial Note: Subject to agreement, Underwriting Commission may be adjusted against the money due on allotment/call.

ILLUSTRATION 2

CAMHE Ltd. comes out with a public issue of share capital on 1st Jan. of 10,00,000 equity shares of ₹ 10 each at a premium of 5%. ₹ 2.50 is payable on application (on *or* before 31st Jan. and ₹ 3.00 (including premium) on allotment (31st March).

The issue is underwritten by two underwriters-A and B equally, the maximum commission as per Sec 76. Each of the underwriters underwrites 20,000 shares firm.

Subscriptions totalled (including firm underwriting) 9,60,000 shares, the distribution of forms being:

A: 5,20,000, B: 3,60,000 and unmarked forms: 80,000.

One of the allottees (using forms marked with the name of A) for 2,000 shares, fails to pay the amount due to allotment, all other money due being received in all including any due from the shares developing upon the underwriters. The shares of defaulter were forfeited and reissued @ ₹ 4 per share on June 30.

Required: Pass journal entries to record the above transactions (including cash).

SOLUTION

JOURNAL

Date	Particulars		L.F.	Dr. (₹)	Cr. (₹)
Jan. 31	Bank A/c	Dr.		24,00,000	
	To Equity Share Application A/c				24,00,000
	(Being application money received @ ₹ 2.50 per share)				
Mar. 31	Equity Share Application A/c	Dr.		24,00,000	
	To Equity Share Capital A/c				24,00,000
	(Being the transfer of application money to share capital on 9,60,000 shares vide Board's Resolution)				
Mar. 31	Equity Share Allotment A/c	Dr.		27,60,000	
	A	Dr.		60,000	
	B	Dr.		60,000	
	To Equity Share Capital A/c				24,00,000
	To Securities premium A/c				4,80,000
	(Being allotment money due on 9,20,000 allotted to public, on 20,000 shares allotted to A, 20,000 shares allotted to B under firm underwriting)				
	B	Dr.		2,20,000	
	To Equity Share Capital A/c				2,00,000
	To Securities Premium A/c				20,000
	(Being the application and allotment money due on net liability of underwriter)				
Mar. 31	Bank A/c	Dr.		27,54,000	
	To Equity Share Allotment A/c				27,54,000
	(Being the receipt of money due on allotment except from the allottee for 2,000 shares including premium on 9,18,000 shares)				
Mar. 31	Underwriting Commission A/c	Dr.		5,25,000	
	To A				2,62,500
	To B				2,62,500
	(Being commission @ 5% on issue price of ₹ 10.50 for 10 lakhs shares payable to underwriters)				

	A	Dr.	2,02,500	
	To Bank A/c			2,02,500
	(Being amount paid to A in final settlement)			
	Bank A/c	Dr.	17,500	
	To B			17,500
	(Being amount received from B in final settlement)			
June 30	Equity Share Capital A/c	Dr.	10,000	
	Securities Premium A/c	Dr.	1,000	
	To Share Allotment A/c			6,000
	To Forfeited Shares A/c			5,000
	(Being 2,000 shares forfeited vide Board's Resolution)			
June 30	Bank A/c (2000 × ₹ 4)	Dr.	8,000	
	Forfeited Shares A/c	Dr.	2,000	
	To Equity Share Capital A/c (2000 × ₹ 5)			10,000
	(Being the reissue of 2,000 shares @ ₹4 as ₹5 paid up)			
	Forfeited Shares A/c	Dr.	3,000	
	To Capital Reserve A/c			3,000
	(Being the transfer of profit on reissue)			

Working Notes:

(I) STATEMENT SHOWING THE NET AND TOTAL LIABILITY OF UNDERWRITERS

Particulars	*Basis*	*A*	*B*
A. Gross Liability [No. of shares]	1 : 1	5,00,000	5,00,000
B. *Less:* Marked Applications [Net of firm underwriting]		(5,00,000)	(3,40,000)
C. Balance [A – B]		0	1,60,000
D. *Less:* Unmarked Applications	1 : 1	(40,000)	(40,000)
E. Balance [C – D]		(40,000)	1,20,000
F. *Less:* Firm Underwriting		(20,000)	(20,000)
G. Balance		(60,000)	1,00,000
H. Credit for A's Oversubscription		60,000	(60,000)
I. Net Liability		0	40,000
J. *Add:* Firm Underwriting		20,000	20,000
K. Total Liability [No. of Shares]		20,000	60,000

(II) STATEMENT SHOWING NET AMOUNT DUE TO/FROM UNDERWRITERS

Particulars	*A*	*B*
A. Total Liability [including firm underwriting]	20,000	60,000
B. Amount due on total liability [Amount payable @₹ 5.50 per share]	1,10,000	3,30,000
C. *Less:* Amount paid already on Firm Applications @2.50 per share	(50,000)	(50,000)
D. Amount on Net Liability [B – C]	60,000	2,80,000

E.	*Less:* Underwriting Commission @5%	(2,62,500)	(2,62,500)
F.	Net Amount Due to A	2,02,500	
G.	Net Amount Due from B		17,500

SOLVED PROBLEMS

PROBLEM 1

CAS Limited issued a prospectus inviting applications for 40,000 equity shares of ₹ 10 each. The whole issue was fully underwritten by A, B and C as follows:

A 20,000 Shares, B 12,000 Shares, C 8,000 Shares

Applications were received for 32,000 shares, of which marked applications were as follows:

A 16,000 Shares, B 5,700 Shares, C 8,300 Shares

Required: Find out the liabilities of individual underwriters.

SOLUTION

STATEMENT OF NET LIABILITY OF UNDERWRITERS (NUMBER OF SHARES)

	Gross Liability	*Marked applications*	*Unmarked applications in the ratio of gross liability*	*Total (2) + (3)*	*Credit for C's Surplus (10 : 6)*	*Total (4) + (5)*	*Net liability (1) – (6)*
	(1)	*(2)*	*(3)*	*(4)*	*(5)*	*(6)*	*(7)*
A	20,000	16,000	1,000	17,000	438	17,438	2,562
B	12,000	5,700	600	6,300	262	6,562	5,438
C	8,000	8,300	400	8,700	(700)	8,000	—
	40,000	30,000	2,000	32,000	—	32,000	8,000

Note: *The applications are for 32,000 shares out of which those for 30,000 are marked. Hence unmarked applications are for 2,000 shares.*

PROBLEM 2

CANHF Ltd. issued 10,000 shares of ₹ 100 each at a premium of ₹ 15 each. Ninety per cent of the issue was underwritten by A at a commission of 1% on the nominal face value. Applications were received for 8,000 shares and allotment was fully made. All the moneys due from allottees was received in one instalment. The accounts with A were settled.

Required: Show the Journal entries to record the transactions.

SOLUTION

JOURNAL

Date	*Particulars*	*L.F.*	*Dr. (₹)*	*Cr. (₹)*
	Bank A/c Dr.		9,20,000	
	To Share Application and Allotment A/c			9,20,000
	(Moneys received in respect of 8,000 shares at ₹ 115 per share)			

	Share Application and Allotment A/c Dr.		9,20,000	
	To Share Capital A/c			8,00,000
	To Securities Premium A/c			1,20,000
	(Transfer of moneys received on 8,000 Shares to Capital Account and Securities Premium A/c @ ₹ 100 and ₹ 15 respectively vide Board's Resolution....)			
	A Dr.		2,07,000	
	To Share Capital A/c			1,80,000
	To Securities Premium A/c			27,000
	(Being the amount due on 1,800 shares taken up in terms of underwriting agreement by A)			
	Underwriting Commission A/c Dr.		9,000	
	To A			9,000
	(Commission at 1% on 9,000 shares at ₹ 100 each nominal value)			
	Bank A/c Dr.		1,98,000	
	To A			1,98,000
	(Moneys received from the broker in settlement of the account)			

Working Notes:

(i) It has been assumed that the remaining 10% of the shares are underwritten by the company itself.

In the absence of details of 'marked' application, 'net liability' is worked out on the basis of gross liability as follows:

Particulars	*A* ₹	*CANHF Ltd.* ₹
Gross Liability (Number of shares)	9,000	1,000
Less: Applications received allotted in the ratio of 9 : 1	7,200	800
	1,800	200

PROBLEM 3

CAMHD Ltd. came up with an issue of 20,00,000 equity shares of ₹ 10 each at par. 5,00,000 shares were issued to the promoters and the balance offered to the public was underwritten by three underwriters — A, B and C — equally with firm underwriting of 50,000 shares each. Subscriptions totalled 12,97,000 shares including the marked forms which were:-

A 4,25,000 shares, B 4,50,000 shares, C 3,50,000 shares

The underwriters had applied for the number of shares covered by firm underwriting. The amounts payable on application and allotment were ₹ 2.50 and ₹ 2 respectively. The agreed commission was 5%.

Required: Pass summary journal entries for:

(a) the allotment of shares to the underwriters;

(b) the commission due to each of them; and

(c) the net cash paid and/or received.

Note: *Unmarked applications are to be credited to the underwriters equally.*

SOLUTION

JOURNAL

Date	Particulars	L.F.	Dr. (₹)	Cr. (₹)
	Bank A/c Dr. To Equity Share Application A/c (Application money received on firm applications for, 1,50,000 shares @ ₹ 2.50 per share from underwriters)		3,75,000	3,75,000
	Equity Share Application A/c Dr. To Equity Share Capital A/c (Being the transfer of share Application money to Share Capital A/c)		3,75,000	3,75,000
	A Dr. B Dr. C Dr. To Equity Share Capital A/c (Allotment of shares to underwriters — 50,000 to A; 50,000 to B and 1,03,000 to C; application money due on 53,000 shares and allotment money due on 2,03,000 shares)		1,00,000 1,00,000 3,38,500	5,38,500
	Underwriting Commission A/c Dr. To A To B To C (Amount of underwriting commission payable to underwriters 5% on the amount of shares underwritten)		7,50,000	2,50,000 2,50,000 2,50,000
	A Dr. B Dr. To Bank A/c (Amount paid to A & B in final settlement of underwriting commission due *less* amount payable on shares allotted)		1,50,000 1,50,000	3,00,000
	Bank A/c Dr. To C (Amount received from C on shares allotted *less* underwriting commission payable to him)		88,500	88,500

Working Notes:

(I) CALCULATION OF THE NET AND TOTAL LIABILITY OF UNDERWRITERS:

	Particulars	A ₹	B ₹	C ₹
A	Gross liability (No. of shares)	5,00,000	5,00,000	5,00,000
B	*Less:* Marked Applications	(4,25,000)	(4,50,000)	(3,50,000)

C	*Less:* Unmarked Applications (equally)	(36,000)	—	(36,000)
D	*Less:* Firm Underwriting	(50,000)	(50,000)	(50,000)
E	Balance	(11,000)	—	64,000
F	Adjustment of A's surplus	11,000	—	(11,000)
G	Net liability (excluding firm underwriting)	—	—	53,000
H	*Add:* Firm underwriting	50,000	50,000	50,000
I	Total liability	50,000	50,000	1,03,000

Note: Since B's firm underwriting (i.e. 50,000 shares) is equal to his gross liability *less* marked applications, no credit for unmarked applications has been given.

(II) CALCULATION OF AMOUNTS PAYABLE BY UNDERWRITERS:

Liability (No. of shares)	*50,000* ₹	*50,000* ₹	*1,03,000* ₹
Amount payable @ ₹ 4.50 per share	2,25,000	2,25,000	4,63,500
Less: Amount paid on Firm Application for 50,000 each @ ₹ 2.50	(1,25,000)	(1,25,000)	(1,25,000)
Balance payable	1,00,000	1,00,000	3,38,500
Underwriting Commission Receivable	(2,50,000)	(2,50,000)	(2,50,000)
Amount Paid	1,50,000	1,50,000	—
Amount Received by the Co.	—	—	88,500

*Benefit of unmarked applications has not been given to B as his surplus would have ultimately been credited for A & C.

PROBLEM 4

CANHG Ltd. made a public issue of 1,25,000 equity shares of ₹ 100 each, ₹ 50 payable on application. The entire issue was underwritten by four parties—A, B, C and D in the proportion of 30%, 25%, 25% and 20% respectively. Under the terms agreed upon, a commission of 2% was payable on the amounts underwritten.

A, B, C and D had also agreed on "firm" underwriting of 4,000, 6,000, Nil and 15,000 shares respectively.

The total subscriptions, excluding firm underwriting, including marked applications were for 90,000 shares. Marked applications received were as under:

A 24,000 C 12,000 B 20,000 D 24,000

Required: Ascertain the liability of the individual underwriters.

SOLUTION

Approach I—*If benefit of firm underwriting is given to individual underwriters*

(I) TOTAL MARKED APPLICATIONS

A	B	C	D
24,000	+20,000	+12,000	+24,000 = 80,000

(II) SHARES SUBSCRIBED EXCLUDING FIRM UNDERWRITING BUT

including marked applications	90,000 shares
Less: Marked	80,000 shares
Unmarked	10,000

(III) STATEMENT SHOWING THE NET AND TOTAL LIABILITY OF UNDERWRITERS

Particulars	*A*	*B*	*C*	*D*	*Total*
Gross liability (30 : 25 : 25 : 20)	37,500	31,250	31,250	25,000	1,25,000
Less: Marked applications	(24,000)	(20,000)	(12,000)	(24,000)	(80,000)
Balance	13,500	11,250	19,250	1,000	45,000
Less: Unmarked (In Gross Ratio)	(3,000)	(2,500)	(2,500)	(2,000)	(10,000)
Balance	10,500	8,750	16,750	(1,000)	35,000
Less: Firm Underwriting	(4,000)	(6,000)	—	(15,000)	(25,000)
Balance	6,500	2,750	16,750	(16,000)	10,000
Surplus of D allocated to A B & C 30 : 25 : 25	(6,000)	(5,000)	(5,000)	16,000	—
Balance	500	(2,250)	11,750	—	10,000
Surplus of 'B' allocated	(500)	2,250	(1,750)	—	—
Net liability	—	—	10,000	—	10,000
Add: Firm underwriting	4,000	6,000	—	15,000	25,000
Total Liability	4,000	6,000	10,000	15,000	35,000

(IV) STATEMENT SHOWING THE AMOUNT DUE FROM UNDERWRITERS

Particulars		*A*	*B*	*C*	*D*	*Total*
Shares to be subscribed		4,000	6,000	10,000	15,000	35,000
Amount due @ ₹ 50 per share	(₹)	2,00,000	3,00,000	5,00,000	7,50,000	17,50,000
Less: Commission due @2% on nominal value of share under written	(₹)	(75,000)	(62,500)	(62,500)	(50,000)	(2,50,000)
	(₹)	1,25,000	2,37,500	4,37,500	7,00,000	15,00,000

Approach II—*If the benefit of firm underwriting is not given to individual underwriter*

(i) Total marked applications = 80,000

(II) SHARE SUBSCRIBED EXCLUDING 'FIRM' UNDERWRITING BUT

including marked application	90,000 shares
Firm underwriting	25,000 shares
Total subscription	1,15,000 shares
Less: Marked application	80,000 shares
Balance being unmarked	35,000 shares

(III) STATEMENT SHOWING THE LIABILITY OF UNDERWRITERS

	Particulars	*A*	*B*	*C*	*D*	*Total*
A	Gross liability	37,500	31,250	31,250	25,000	1,25,000
B	*Less:* Marked applications	(24,000)	(20,000)	(12,000)	(24,000)	(80,000)
C	*Less:* Unmarked Applications	(3,000)	(2,500)	(2,500)	(2,000)	(10,000)
D	*Less:* Firm underwriting (in the ratio of 30:25:25:20)	(7,500)	(6,250)	(6,250)	(5,000)	(25,000)
E	Balance	3,000	2,500	10,500	(6,000)	10,000
F	Surplus of D transferred to others in the ratio of 30 : 25 : 25	(2,250)	(1,875)	(1,875)	6,000	—
G	Net Liability	750	625	8,625	—	10,000
H	*Add:* Firm underwriring	4,000	6,000	Nil	15,000	25,000
I	Total Liability	750	625	8,625	—	10,000
		4,750	6,625	8,625	15,000	35,000

(V) STATEMENT SHOWING THE AMOUNT DUE FROM UNDERWRITERS

Particulars	*A*	*B*	*C*	*D*	*Total*
Shares to be subscribed	4,750	6,625	8,625	15,000	35,000
Amount due @ ₹ 50 shares (₹)	2,37,500	3,31,250	4,31,250	7,50,000	17,50,000
Less: Commission due at 2% on nominalvalue of shares underwritten (₹)	(75,000)	(62,500)	(62,500)	(50,000)	(2,50,000)
(₹)	1,62,500	2,68,750	3,68,750	7,00,000	15,00,000

(VI) VERIFICATION

(a) Taken by public-unmarked application	10,000 shares
(b) Public through underwriters—marked	80,000 shares
(c) By underwriters—under agreement	35,000 shares
	1,25,000 shares

PROBLEM 5

CAMIJ Limited issued to public 1,50,000 equity shares of ₹ 100 each at par. ₹ 60 per shares was payable along with application and the balance on allotment. The issue was underwritten equally by A, B, and C for a commission of 5 per cent. Applications for 1,40,000 shares were received as per details below:

Underwriter	*Firm Applications*	*Marked Applications*	*Total*
A	5,000	40,000	45,000
B	5,000	46,000	51,000
C	3,000	34,000	37,000
Unmarked Applications			7,000
Total			1,40,000

It was agreed to credit the unmarked applications equally to A and C. CAMIJ Ltd. accordingly made the allotment and received the amounts due from the public. The underwriters settled their accounts.

You are required to:

(i) Prepare a statement showing the liability of the underwriters, and

(ii) Journalise the above transactions (including cash) in the books of CAMIJ Ltd.

SOLUTION

CAMIJ LIMITED

(a) If the benefit of firm underwriting is given to individual underwriters.

(I) STATEMENT SHOWING THE NET AND TOTAL LIABILITY OF UNDERWRITERS

Particulars	*A*	*B*	*C*	*Total*
Gross Liability	50,000	50,000	50,000	1,50,000
Less: Marked Applications	(40,000)	(46,000)	(34,000)	(1,20,000)
Balance	10,000	4,000	16,000	30,000
Less: Unmarked Applications	(3,500)	—	(3,500)	(7,000)
Balance	6,500	4,000	12,500	23,000
Less: Firm Underwriting	(5,000)	(5,000)	(3,000)	(13,000)
Balance	1,500	(1,000)	9,500	10,000
Credit for B 's oversubscription to A and C in the ratio 1 : 1	(500)	1,000	(500)	—
Net Liability	1,000	—	9,000	10,000
Add: Firm Underwriting	5,000	5,000	3,000	13,000
Total Liability	6,000	5,000	12,000	23,000

(II) STATEMENT SHOWING THE NET AMOUNT DUE FROM UNDERWRITERS

Particulars	*A*	*B*	*C*	*Total*
Shares to be subscribed	6,000	5,000	12,000	23,000
Amount due @ ₹ 60 per share (₹)	3,60,000	3,00,000	7,20,000	13,80,000
Less: Commission due @ 5% on nominal value of shares underwritten (₹)	(2,50,000)	(2,50,000)	(2,50,000)	(7,50,000)
(₹)	1,10,000	50,000	4,70,000	6,30,000

(B) IF THE BENEFIT OF FIRM UNDERWRITING IS NOT GIVEN TO INDIVIDUAL UNDERWRITERS

(i) Total subscription	1,40,000 Shares
Less: Marked Applications	1,20,000 Shares
Firm and Unmarked Applications	20,000 Shares

(II) STATEMENT SHOWING THE NET AND TOTAL LIABILITY OF UNDERWRITERS

Particulars	*A*	*B*	*C*	*Total*
Gross Liability	50,000	50,000	50,000	1,50,000
Less: Firm and Unmarked applications	(10,000)	—	(10,000)	(20,000)
Balance	40,000	50,000	40,000	1,30,000

Less: Marked applications	(40,000)	(46,000)	(34,000)	(1,20,000)
Net liability	—	4,000	6,000	10,000
Firm underwriting	5,000	5,000	3,000	13,000
	5,000	9,000	9,000	23,000

(III) STATEMENT SHOWING THE AMOUNT DUE FROM UNDERWRITERS

Particulars	*A*	*B*	*C*	*Total*
Shares to be subscribed	5,000	9,000	9,000	23,000
	₹	₹	₹	₹
Amount due @ ₹ 60 per share	3,00,000	5,40,000	5,40,000	13,80,000
Less: Commission due @ 5% on nominal value of shares underwritten	(2,50,000)	(2,50,000)	(2,50,000)	(7,50,000)
	50,000	2,90,000	2,90,000	6,30,000

JOURNAL

Date	*Particulars*		*L.F.*	*Dr. (₹)*	*Cr. (₹)*
	Bank A/c	Dr.		82,50,000	
	Underwriting Commission A/c	Dr.		7,50,000	
	To Equity Share Capital A/c				90,00,000
	(Being amount received @ ₹ 60/- per share on issue of 1,50,000 equity shares and underwriting commission paid @ 5% on nominal value of shares underwritten vide Directors' resolution No...........dated..........)				
	Bank A/c	Dr.		60,00,000	
	To Share Capital A/c				60,00,000
	(Amount of allotment money received on 1,50,000 shares @ ₹ 40 per share credited to share capital vide resolution dated.........)				

PROBLEM 6

CAMID Limited planned to set up a unit for manufacture of bulk drugs. For the purpose of financing the unit the Board of Directors have issued 15,00,000 equity shares of ₹ 10 each. 30% of the issue was reserved for promoters and the balance was offered to the public. A, B and C have come forward to underwrite the public issue in the ratio of 3:1:1 and also agreed for firm undertaking of 30,000; 20,000 and 10,000 shares, respectively. The underwriting commission was fixed at 4%. The amount payable on application was ₹ 2.50 per share. The details of subscriptions (excluding firm underwriting) are:

Marked forms of A	5,50,000 Shares
Marked forms of B	2,00,000 Shares
Marked forms of C	1,50,000 Shares
Unmarked forms	50,000 Shares

(a) You are required to show the allocation of liability among underwriters with workings.

(b) Pass journal entries in the books of CAMID Limited:

(i) For underwriters' net liability and the receipt *or* payment of cash to *or* from underwriters.

(ii) Determining the liability towards the payment of commission to the underwriters.

SOLUTION

(A) STATEMENT SHOWING THE NET AND TOTAL LIABILITY OF UNDERWRITERS

	Particulars	*A (No. of Shares)*	*B (No. of Shares)*	*C (No. of Shares)*	*Total (No. of Shares)*
A	Gross Liability	6,30,000	2,10,000	2,10,000	10,50,000
B	*Less:* Marked Applications	(5,50,000)	(2,00,000)	(1,50,000)	(9,00,000)
C	*Less:* Unmarked Applications (in the ratio of 3 : 1 : 1)	(30,000)	(10,000)	(10,000)	(50,000)
D	*Less:* Firm underwriting	(30,000)	(20,000)	(10,000)	(60,000)
E	Balance	20,000	(20,000)	40,000	40,000
F	Surplus of B distributed between A and C in the ratio of 3 : 1	(15,000)	20,000	(5,000)	—
G	Net liability	5,000	—	35,000	40,000
H	*Add:* Firm underwriting	30,000	20,000	10,000	60,000
I	Total Liability	35,000	20,000	45,000	1,00,000

JOURNAL

Date	*Particulars*		*L.F.*	*Dr. (₹)*	*Cr. (₹)*
	A	Dr.		12,500	
	C	Dr.		87,500	
	To Equity Share Capital A/c				1,00,000
	(Allotment of shares to underwriters: 5,000 shares to A and 35,000 shares to C)				
	Underwriting Commission A/c	Dr.		4,20,000	
	To A				2,52,000
	To B				84,000
	To C				84,000
	(Underwriting commission payable @ 4% on the amount of shares underwritten)				
	A	Dr.		2,39,500	
	B	Dr.		84,000	
	To Bank A/c				3,23,500
	(Amount paid to A and B in final settlement)				
	Bank A/c	Dr.		3,500	
	To C				3,500
	(Amount received from C on shares allotted *less* underwriting commission)				

Working Notes:

(I) CALCULATION OF AMOUNTS PAYABLE TO/BY UNDERWRITERS

Particulars	*A*	*B*	*C*
Liability (No. of shares)	35,000	20,000	45,000
Less: Firm underwriting (No. of shares)	30,000	20,000	10,000
Net Liability (No. of shares)	5,000	—	35,000

Particulars	₹	₹	₹
Amount payable on application @ ₹ 2.50 per share	12,500	—	87,500
Less: Underwriting commission receivable by underwriters @ 4%	(2,52,000)	(84,000)	(84,000)
Amount payable to underwriters	2,39,500	84,000	—
Amount receivable from underwriters	—	—	3,500

(ii) No Journal entry is shown for firm underwritings by the underwriters on the assumption that the amounts have been already paid by the underwriters at the opening days of the issue. Alternatively, the students may pass entries for firm underwriting on the ground that the allotment of shares will be made by the company at a time.

PROBLEM 7

CAS Ltd. made a public issue of 8,00,000 Equity Shares of ₹ 10 each ₹ 2 payable on application. The entire issue was underwritten by five underwriters as follows: A: 25% B: 25%; C: 25% D: 10% and E: 15%. Under the underwritten terms a commission of 2% was payable on the amounts underwritten. Further, the underwriter was at liberty to apply, during the tenure of public issue, for any number of shares in which case he was entitled to a brokerage equal to 1/2% of the par value of shares so applied for.

Applications received were to be analysed on the basis of Rubber Stamp of the underwriter, who was to be given credit for the number of applications received bearing his rubber stamp. Applications received which did not bear any Rubber Stamp were considered as "Direct applications" to be credited to all the underwriters in the ratio of their respective underwriting commitment. If, on such credits being given, a "surplus" result in respect of any underwriter, as compared to his commitment, such surplus was to be distributed amongst the remaining underwriters in the ratio of their respective underwriting commitments.

As a result of the issue the following applications were received;

Bearing rubber stamp of:

A	2,04,000 shares
B	1,90,000 shares
C	1,20,000 shares
D	64,000 shares
E	1,02,000 shares
Not bearing any stamp	20,000 shares
	7,00,000 shares

Included in the number of applications mentioned against D in the above table was an application made by D himself for 20,000 shares. The underwriters were informed of the amounts due to *or* from them and the amounts were duly received *or* paid.

Required: Show, with the aid of necessary workings, the entries to record the amounts so received *or* paid.

SOLUTION

JOURNAL

Date	*Particulars*		*L.F.*	*Dr. (₹)*	*Cr. (₹)*
	B	Dr.		4,000	
	C	Dr.		1,44,000	
	D	Dr.		25,600	
	E	Dr.		26,400	
	To Equity Share Capital A/c				2,00,000
	(Being the amount due from underwriters on Net Liability)				
	Underwriting Commission A/c	Dr.		1,60,000	
	To A				40,000
	To B				40,000
	To C				40,000
	To D				16,000
	To E				24,000
	(Being the underwriting commission due)				
	Brokerage A/c	Dr.		1,000	
	To D				1,000
	(Being the brokerage due to D)				
	Bank A/c	Dr.		1,15,000	
	To C				1,04,000
	To D				8,600
	To E				2,400
	(Being the net amount received from C, D and E)				
	A	Dr.		40,000	
	B	Dr.		36,000	
	To Bank A/c				76,000
	(Being the net amount paid to A and B)				

Workings:

Name	*Commitment No. of Shares*	*Market Applications*	*Additional Propertionate No. of direct Applications*	*Total (2) + (3) of*	*Allocation of Surplus*	*Total (4) + (5)*	*Final Deficit (1) – (6)*	*Amount Receivable @ ₹ 2/- per share* ₹	*Underwriting commission due @ on nominal value* ₹	*Brokerage Due @ %* ₹	*Due from Underwriters* ₹	*Due to Underwriters* ₹
	(1)	(2)	(3)	(4)	(5)	(6)	(7)	(8)	(9)	(10)	(11)	(12)
A	2,00,000	2,04,000	5,000	2,09,000	– 9,000	2,00,000	—	—	40,000	—	—	40,000
B	2,00,000	1,90,000	5,000	1,95,000	3,000	1,98,000	2,000	4,000	40,000			36,000
C	2,00,000	1,20,000	5,000	1,25,000	3,000	1,28,000	72,000	1,44,000	40,000		1,04,000	
D	80,000	64,000	2,000	66,000	1,200	67,200	12,800	25,600	16,000	1,000	8,600	
E	1,20,000	1,02,000	3,000	1,05,000	1,800	1,06,800	13,200	26,400	24,000		2,400	
	8,00,000	6,80,000	20,000	7,00,000	—	7,00,000	1,00,000	2,00,000	1,60,000	1,000	1,15,000	76,000

PROBLEM 8

ABC Ltd. came up with public issue of 3,00,000 Equity Shares of ₹ 10 each ₹ 15 per share. P, Q and R took underwriting of the issue in ratio of 3 : 2 : 1 with the provisions of firm underwriting of 20,000, 14,000 and 10,000 shares respectively.

Applications were received for 2,40,000 shares excluding firm underwriting. The marked applications from public were received as under:

P-60,000; Q-50,000; R-60,000

Compute the liability of each underwriter as regards the number of shares to be taken up assuming that the benefit of firm underwriting is not given to individual underwriters.

SOLUTION

CALCULATION OF LIABILITY OF EACH UNDERWRITER (IN NO. OF SHARES)

Particulars	*P*	*Q*	*R*	*Total*
Gross Liability	1,50,000	1,00,000	50,000	3,00,000
Less: Marked Applications (excluding firm underwriting)	(60,000)	(50,000)	(60,000)	(1,70,000)
Balance	90,000	50,000	(10,000)	1,30,000
Less: Surplus of R allocated to P and Q in the ratio of 3.2	(6,000)	(4,000)	10,000	
Balance	84,000	46,000	–	1,30,000
Less: Unmarked applications including firm underwriting (Refer W.N.)	(57,000)	(38,000)	(19,000)	(1,14,000)
Net Liability	27,000	8,000	(19,000)	16,000
Less: Surplus of R allocated to P and Q in the ratio of 3 : 2	(11,400)	(7,600)	19,000	
	15,600	400	–	16,000
Add: Firm underwriting	20,000	14,000	10,000	44,000
Total Liability	35,600	14,400	10,000	60,000

Working Note:

A.	Applications received from public	2,40,000
B.	*Add:* Shares underwritten firm (20,000 + 14,000 + 10,000)	44,000
C.	Total Applciations [A + B]	2,84,000
D.	*Less:* Marked applications (60,000 + 50,000 + 60,000)	(1,70,000)
E.	Unmarked applications including firm underwriting [C – D]	1,14,000

PROBLEM 9

A company issued 1,50,000 shares of ₹ 10 each at a premium of ₹ 10. The entire issue was underwritten as follows:

X – 90,000 shares (Firm underwriting 12,000 shares)

Y – 37,500 shares (Firm underwriting 4,500 shares)

Z – 22,500 shares (Firm underwriting 15,000 shares)

Total applications received by the company (excluding firm underwriting and marked applications) were 22,500 shares.

The marked applications (excluding firm underwriting) were as follows:

X- 15,000 shares; Y- 30,000 shares: Z- 7,500 shares.

Commission payable to underwriters is at 5% of the issue price. The underwriting contract provides that credit for unmarked applications be given to the underwriters in proportion to the shares underwritten and benefit of firm underwiriting is to be given to individual underwriters.

(i) Determine the liability of each underwriter (number of shares)

(ii) Compute the amount payable *or* due to underwriters; and

(iii) Pass necessary journal entries in the books of co. relating to underwriting.

SOLUTION

COMPUTATION OF UNDERWRITERS' LIABILITY (NUMBER OF SHARES)

	Particulars	*X*	*Y*	*Z*
A	Gross Liability	90,000	37,500	22,500
B	*Less:* Marked applications	(15,000)	(30,000)	(7,500)
C	*Less:* Unmarked applications in ratio of 12:5:3	(13,500)	(5,625)	3,375
D	*Less:* Firm Underwriting	(12,000)	(4,500)	(15,000)
E	Balance	49,500	(2,625)	(3,375)
F	*Less:* Surplus of Y & Z distributed to X	(6,000)	2,625	3,375
G	Net Liability (excluding firm underwriting)	43,500	Nil	Nil
H	*Add:* Firm Underwriting	12,000	4,500	15,000
I	Total Liability (number of shares)	55,500	4,500	15,000

(B) COMPUTATION OF AMOUNTS PAYABLE BY UNDERWRITERS

Particulars	₹	₹	₹
Liability towards shares to be subscribed @ 20 per share	11,10,000	90,000	3,00,000
Less: Commission @ 5% on 1,50,000 shares @ ₹ 20	(90,000)	(37,500)	(22,500)
Net Amount to be paid by Underwriters	10,20,000	52,500	2,77,500

(C) JOURNAL OF THE COMPANY

Date	*Particulars*		*L.F.*	*Dr. (₹)*	*Cr. (₹)*
	X	Dr.		11,10,000	
	Y	Dr.		90,000	
	Z	Dr.		3,00,000	
	To Share Capital A/c				7,50,000
	To Securities Premium A/c				7,50,000
	(Being shares including firm underwritten shares allotted to underwriters)				
	Underwriting Commission A/c	Dr.		1,50,000	
	To X				90,000

	To Y			37,500
	To Z			22,500
	(Being underwriting commission on the shares underwritten)			
	Bank A/c Dr.		13,50,000	
	To X			10,20,000
	To Y			52,500
	To Z			2,77,500
	(Being the amount received from underwritters)			

6 REDEMPTION OF DEBENTURES

LEARNING OBJECTIVES

After studying this chapter, you should be able to understand:

- Meaning of Redemption of Debentures
- Methods of Redemption of Debentures
- Sources of Redemption of Debentures
- Redemption out of Capital
- Redemption out of Profits
- Redemption by Conversion
- Financing of Redemption of Debentures
- Sinking Fund Method or Debentures Redemption Fund Method
- Redemption by Purchase in the Open Market

1.0 MEANING OF REDEMPTION OF DEBENTURES

Redemption of debentures means discharge of liability on account of Debentures by making repayment to the Debentureholders.

2.0 METHODS OF REDEMPTION OF DEBENTURES

The various methods of redemption of Debentures are as follows:

1. BY PAYMENT IN LUMPSUM

Under this method, the payment of entire Debenture debt is made in one lot at the expiry of a specified period (i.e., at maturity) *or* even before the expiry of the specified period after passing the necessary resolution at the meeting of the debenture-holders. ***For Example***, Reliance Petroleum has made the payment of TOCD (i.e., Triple Option Convertible Debentures) before the expiry of the specified period.

2. BY PAYMENT IN INSTALMENTS

Under this method, the payment of specified portion of Debentures debt is made in instalments at specified dates. ***For Example***, a Debenture of ₹ 100 may be discharged as given below:

20% or ₹ 20 on 1.1.2011, 20% or ₹ 20 on 1.1.2013, 30% or ₹ 30 on 1.1.2015, 30% or ₹ 30 on 1.1.2017

3. REDEMPTION BY PURCHASE IN THE OPEN MARKET

When a company purchases its own debentures in the open market for the purposes of cancellation, such an act of purchasing and cancelling the debentures constitutes redemption by purchase in the open market.

3.0 SOURCES OF REDEMPTION OF DEBENTURES

The various sources out of which the Debentures may be redeemed are as follows:

1. Redemption out of Capital
2. Redemption out of Profits
3. Redemption by Conversion

4.0 REDEMPTION OUT OF CAPITAL

MEANING OF REDEMPTION OUT OF CAPITAL

When adequate profits are not transferred from Profit & Loss Appropriation Account to the Debenture Redemption Reserve Account before the redemption of debentures, such redemption is said to be out of capital.

Note: ***The Companies Act has indirectly placed restrictions on this method of redemption by requiring every company to create a Debenture Redemption Reserve equivalent to at least 25% of the amount of debentures outstanding before the commencement of redemption.***

JOURNAL ENTRIES

Date	*Particulars*	*L.F.*	*Dr. (₹)*	*Dr. (₹)*
	1. For the Amount due to Debentureholders on redemption (a) ***If the Debentures are to be redeemed at par*** Debentures A/c [With Nominal Value] Dr. To Debenture-holders' A/c (Being the Amount due on redemption)			
	(b) ***If the Debentures are to be redeemed at a premium*** Debentures A/c [With Nominal Value] Dr. Premium on Redemption of Debentures A/c Dr. *[With Premium]* To Debenture-holders' A/c [With Total] (Being the Amount due on redemption)			
	2. For Payment to Debentureholders Debenture-holders' A/c (With Payment) Dr. To Bank A/c (Being the Payment made to Debentureholders)			

5.0 REDEMPTION OUT OF PROFITS

MEANING OF REDEMPTION OUT OF PROFITS

When adequate profits are transferred from Profit & Loss Appropriation Account to the Debenture Redemption Reserve Account before the redemption of debentures, such redemption is said to be out of profits.

DEBENTURE REDEMPTION RESERVE [DRR] [RULE 18(7)]

Meaning	DRR is a reserve created out of profits for the purpose of redemption of debentures.
Creation	As per Rule 18(7) of The Companies Act, 2013, a company is red- requi to transfer **adequate amounts out of its profits every year** to Debenture Redemption Reserve until such debentures are redeemed.
When to Create	Debenture Redemption Reserve must be created **before the redemption starts.**
Amount	Debenture Redemption Reserve Account must have a credit balance of **at least an amount equal to 25%* of the value of Debentures issued** at the time of redemption of debentures. * As per MCA Circular no. 04/2013 dated 11.02.2013. ***For Example**: X Ltd issued Debentures of ₹ 2 crores with the condition to start redemption in the third year. In such a case, before the debenture redemption begins in 3rd year, the Debenture Redemption Reserve Account must have a balance of at least equal to 2 crores × 25% = 0.50 crore.*
Applicability	DRR is required to be created only in case of **Non-convertible Debentures (NCD) and Non-convertible portion of Partly Convertible Debentures (PCD).**
Utilisation	The amounts credited to the Debenture Redemption Reserve must be utilised **for the purpose of redemption of debentures.**
Disclosure	Debenture Redemption Reserve Account appears under the head **"Shareholders' Funds"** and Sub-head **'Reserves & Surplus'** in the Balance Sheet. On the completion of **redemption of all the debentures,** DRR account is closed by transferring it to General Reserve.
Not Mandatory as per Rule 18 (7)	**Creation of Debenture Redemption Reserve is not mandatory–** 1. For Fully Convertible Debentures 2. For Debentures issued by All India Financial Institutions regulated by RBI. 3. For Debentures issued by Banking Companies 4. For Debentures issued by NBFCs registered with RBI on private palcement basis.
Not Mandatory as per SEBI	**Creation of Debenture Redemption Reserve is not mandatory–** 1. For Debentures with a maturity period of 18 months *or* less. 2. For Infrastructure Companies (i.e., companies engaged in the business of developing, maintaining and operating infrastrucure facilities)

MINIMUM DEBENTURE REDEMPTION RESERVE INVESTMENTS [RULE 18(7)(C)]

Every company required to create/maintain DRR shall **before the 30th day of April** of each year, deposit *or* invest (as the case may be) **at least 15% of the amount of its debentures maturing during the year** ending on the 31st day of March next following in any one *or* more of the following methods, namely:

(a) In Deposits with any Scheduled Bank, free from charge *or* lien;

(b) In Unencumbered Securities of the Central Government *or* of any State Government;

(c) In Unencumbered Securities mentioned under Section 20 (a) to (d) and (ee) of the Indian Trusts Act, 1882;

(d) In Unencumbered Bonds issued by any other company which is notified under Section 20 (f) of the Indian Trusts Act, 1882;

JOURNAL ENTRIES

Date	*Particulars*		*L.F.*	*Dr. (₹)*	*Cr.(₹)*
1.	**For Creation of Debenture Redemption Reserve**				
	Profit & Loss Appropriation A/c *[With DRR created]*	Dr.			
	To Debentures Redemption Reserve A/c				
	(Being the DRR created as per Rule 18 (7))				
2.	**For the Purchase of DRR Investments**				
	Debenture Redemption Reserve Investments A/c	Dr.			
	To Bank A/c				
	(Being the DRR Investments made equal to 15% of Debentures Maturing)				
3.	**For the Sale of DRR Investments**				
	Bank A/c	Dr.			
	To Debenture Redemption Reserve Investments A/c				
	(Being the DRR Investments realised)				
4.	**For the Amt. due to Debentureholders on redemption**				
	(a) ***If the Debentures are to be redeemed at par***				
	Debentures A/c *[With Nominal Value]*	Dr.			
	To Debenture-holders' A/c				
	(Being the Amount due on redemption)				
	(b) ***If the Debentures are to be redeemed at a premium***				
	Debentures A/c *[With Nominal Value]*	Dr.			
	Premium on Redemption of Debentures A/c *[With Premium]*	Dr.			
	To Debenture-holders' A/c [With Total]				
	(Being the Amount due on redemption)				
5.	**For Payment to Debentureholders**				
	Debentureholders' A/c *[With Payment]*	Dr.			
	To Bank A/c				
	(Being the Payment made to Debentureholders)				
6.	**For Closure of DRR after redemption of all Debentures**				
	Debentures Redemption Reserve A/c *[With DRR T/F]*	Dr.			
	To General Reserve				
	(Being the t/f of balance of DRR to General Reserve)				

ILLUSTRATION 1

X Ltd. issued 10,000 10% Debentures of ₹ 100 each at a premium of 8% on 1st April, 2014 redeemable on 31st Aug. 2015. How much amount of Debenture Redemption Reserve is to be created before redemption of debentures?

SOLUTION

As per SEBI Guidelines, No Debenture Redemption Reserve is required to be created since maturity period of debentures does not exceed 18 months but as per Rule 18(7) of The Companies Act, 2013, atleast ₹ 2,50,000 (i.e., 25% of ₹ 10,00,000) must be transferred to Debenture Redemption Reserve.

ILLUSTRATION 2

On 01.04.2015, Y Ltd. issued 2,000, 15% Convertible Debentures of ₹ 100 each at a discount of 5% redeemable at par after 4 years by converting their holdings into equity shares of ₹ 100 each at a premium of 25%. How much amount of Debenture Redemption Reserve is to be created before redemption of debentures?

SOLUTION

No Debenture Redemption Reserve is required to be created in a case of Fully Convertible Debentures.

ILLUSTRATION 3

Gurgaon Toll Bridge Corporation Ltd. (An infrastructure Company) has outstanding 10,000, 12% Debentures of ₹ 100 each issued on 1st Oct., 2013 due for redemption on 31st March, 2015 at 10% Premium. (a) How much minimum amount of Debenture Redemption Reserve should be created as per MCA clarification? (b) State the amount required to be deposited/invested in the year of redemption. (c) Pass the Journal Entries during the years of issue and redemption of Debentures without providing for the Interest and Loss on issue of Debentures.

SOLUTION

As per SEBI Guidelines, infrastructure companies are exempted from creating Debenture Redemption Reserve (DRR). However, (a) As per Rule 18(7), the minimum amount to be transferred to Debenture Redemption Reserve will be ₹ 2,50,000 (i.e. 25% of ₹10,00,000). (b) As per Rule 18(7), the minimum amount to be invested will be ₹ 1,50,000 (i.e. 15% of ₹10,00,000).

JOURNAL

Date	Particulars		L.F.	Dr. (₹)	Cr.(₹)
01.10.2014	Bank A/c	Dr.		10,00,000	
	To Debentures Application & Allotment A/c				10,00,000
	(Being the receipt of application money)				
	Debentures Application & Allotment A/c	Dr.		10,00,000	
	Loss on Issue of Debentures A/c	Dr.		1,00,000	
	To 12% Debentures A/c				10,00,000
	To Premium on Redemption of Debentures A/c				1,00,000
	(Being the issue of Debentures)				
31.03.2015	Profit & Loss Appropriation A/c	Dr.		2,50,000	
	To Debenture Redemption Reserve A/c				2,50,000
	[Being the creation of DRR as per Rule 18 (7)]				
29.04.2015	Debenture Redemption Reserve Investments A/c	Dr.		1,50,000	
	To Bank A/c				1,50,000
	(Being the DRR Investments made equal to 15%)				

31.03.2015	Bank A/c Dr. To Deben. Redemption Reserve Investments A/c (Being the DRR Investments realised)		1,50,000	1,50,000
31.03.2015	12% Debentures A/c Dr. Premium on Redemption of Debentures A/c Dr. To Debentureholders' A/c (Being the amount due on redemption)		10,00,000 1,00,000	11,00,000
	Debentureholders' A/c Dr. To Bank A/c (Being the payment made to Debentureholders)		11,00,000	11,00,000
	Debenture Redemption Reserve A/c Dr. To General Reserve (Being the transfer of DRR to General Reserve)		2,50,000	2,50,000

ILLUSTRATION 4

On 1st April, 2012, PQR Ltd. issued ₹ 40,00,000, 12% Debentures of ₹ 100 each at par and redeemable at a premium of 10%. 60% of Debentures are to be redeemed at the end of 2 years and the balance at the end of 3 years. The Board of Directors decided to transfer the minimum required amount to Debenture Redemption Reserve at the end of first year. Pass the necessary journal entries during the years of Issue and Redemption of Debentures without providing for the Interest and Loss on issue of Debentures.

SOLUTION

JOURNAL

Date	*Particulars*	*L.F.*	*Dr. (₹)*	*Cr.(₹)*
01.04.2012	Bank A/c Dr. To Debentures Application & Allotment A/c (Being the receipt of application money)		40,00,000	40,00,000
	Debentures Application & Allotment A/c Dr. Loss on Issue of Debentures A/c Dr. To 12% Debentures A/c To Premium on Redemption of Debentures A/c (Being the issue of Debentures)		40,00,000 4,00,000	40,00,000 4,00,000
31.03.2013	Profit & Loss Appropriation A/c Dr. To Debenture Redemption Reserve A/c [Being the creation of Min. DRR as per Rule 18 (7)]		10,00,000	10,00,000
29.04.2013	Debenture Redemption Reserve Investments A/cDr. To Bank A/c (Being the DRR Investments made equal to 15%)		3,60,000	3,60,000
31.03.2014	Bank A/c Dr. To Deben. Redemption Reserve Investments A/c (Being the DRR Investments realised)		3,60,000	3,60,000

31.03.2014	12% Debentures A/c Dr. Premium on Redemption of Debentures A/c Dr. To Debenture holders' A/c (Being the amount due on redemption)		24,00,000 2,40,000	 26,40,000
	Debentureholders' A/c Dr. To Bank A/c (Being the payment made to Debenture holders)		26,40,000	 26,40,000
29.04.2014	Debenture Redemption Reserve Investments A/c Dr. To Bank A/c (Being the DRR Investments made equal to 15%)		2,40,000	 2,40,000
31.03.2015	Bank A/c Dr. To Deben. Redemption Reserve Investments A/c (Being the DRR Investments realised)		2,40,000	 2,40,000
31.03.2015	12% Debentures A/c Dr. Premium on Redemption of Debentures A/c Dr. To Debenture holders' A/c (Being the amount due on redemption)		16,00,000 1,60,000	 17,60,000
	Debentureholders' A/c Dr. To Bank A/c (Being the payment made to Debenture holders)		17,60,000	 17,60,000
	Debenture Redemption Reserve A/c Dr. To General Reserve (Being the transfer of DRR to General Reserve)		10,00,000	 10,00,000

ILLUSTRATION 5

On 1st April, 2012, XYZ Ltd. issued ₹ 40,00,000, 12% Debentures of ₹ 100 each at a premium of 5% and redeemable at a premium of 10%. 60% of Debentures are to be redeemed at the end of 2 years and the balance at the end of 3 years fully out of Profits. Pass the necessary journal entries during the years of Issue and Redemption of Debentures without providing for the Interest and Loss on issue of Debentures.

SOLUTION

JOURNAL

Date	*Particulars*	*L.F.*	*Dr. (₹)*	*Cr.(₹)*
01.04.2012	Bank A/c Dr. To Debentures Application & Allotment A/c (Being the receipt of application money)		42,00,000	 42,00,000
	Debentures Application & Allotment A/c Dr. Loss on Issue of Debentures A/c Dr. To 12% Debentures A/c		42,00,000 4,00,000	 40,00,000

	To Premium on Redemption of Debentures A/c			4,00,000
	To Securities Premium A/c			2,00,000
	(Being the issue of Debentures)			
31.03.2013	Profit & Loss Appropriation A/c	Dr.	24,00,000	
	To Debenture Redemption Reserve A/c			24,00,000
	[Being the creation of DRR as per Rule 18 (7) *or* as per terms whichever is higher]			
29.04.2013	Debenture Redemption Reserve Investments A/c	Dr.	3,60,000	
	To Bank A/c			3,60,000
	(Being the DRR Investments made equal to 15%)			
31.03.2014	Bank A/c	Dr.	3,60,000	
	To Deben. Redemption Reserve Investments A/c			3,60,000
	(Being the DRR Investments realised)			
31.03.2015	12% Debentures A/c	Dr.	24,00,000	
	Premium on Redemption of Debentures A/c	Dr.	2,40,000	
	To Debentureholders' A/c			26,40,000
	(Being the amount due on redemption)			
	Debentureholders' A/c	Dr.	26,40,000	
	To Bank A/c			26,40,000
	(Being the payment made to Debenture holders)			
31.03.2014	Profit & Loss Appropriation A/c	Dr.	16,00,000	
	To Debenture Redemption Reserve A/c			16,00,000
	[Being the creation of DRR as per Rule 18 (7) *or* as per terms whichever is higher]			
29.04.2014	Debenture Redemption Reserve Investments A/c	Dr.	2,40,000	
	To Bank A/c			2,40,000
	(Being the DRR Investments made equal to 15%)			
31.03.2015	Bank A/c	Dr.	2,40,000	
	To Deben. Redemption Reserve Investments A/c			2,40,000
	(Being the DRR Investments realised)			
31.03.2015	12% Debentures A/c	Dr.	16,00,000	
	Premium on Redemption of Debentures A/c	Dr.	1,60,000	
	To Debenture holders' A/c			17,60,000
	(Being the amount due on redemption)			
	Debentureholders' A/c	Dr.	17,60,000	
	To Bank A/c			17,60,000
	(Being the payment made to Debenture holders)			
	Debenture Redemption Reserve A/c	Dr.	40,00,000	
	To General Reserve			40,00,000
	(Being the transfer of DRR to General Reserve)			

ILLUSTRATION 6

X Ltd. has a balance of ₹ 42,00,000 in the Profit and Loss Account. The company decided to forego the payment of dividend and instead utilise the profits to repay ₹ 30,00,000, 12% Debentures (issued on 1st April, 2011) fully out of profits on 30th June, 2015 at a premium of 10%. Debentures interest is payable annually on 31st December every year when the accounts are closed. The company also has a balance of ₹ 20,00,000 in the Debenture Redemption Reserve. Journalise the transactions during the year of Redemption of Debentures.

SOLUTION

JOURNAL

Date	*Particulars*	*L.F.*	*Dr. (₹)*	*Cr.(₹)*
29.04.2015	Profit & Loss Appropriation A/c Dr.		10,00,000	
	To Debenture Redemption Reserve A/c			10,00,000
	[Being the creation of DRR as per Rule 18 (7) *or* as per terms whichever is higher]			
29.04.2015	Debenture Redemption Reserve Investments A/c Dr.		4,50,000	
	To Bank A/c			4,50,000
	(Being the DRR Investments made equal to 15%)			
30.06.2015	Bank A/c Dr.		4,50,000	
	To Deben. Redemption Reserve Investments A/c			4,50,000
	(Being the DRR Investments realised)			
30.06.2015	Interest on Debentures A/c [30,00,000 × 6/12 × 12%] Dr.		1,80,000	
	To Debentureholders' A/c			1,80,000
	(Being the interest on debentures made due)			
30.06.2015	12% Debentures A/c Dr.		30,00,000	
	Premium on Redemption of Debentures A/c Dr.		3,00,000	
	To Debentureholders' A/c			33,00,000
	(Being the amount due on redemption)			
30.06.2015	Debentureholders' A/c Dr.		34,80,000	
	To Bank A/c [₹33,00,000 + ₹1,80,000]			34,80,000
	(Being the payment made to Debentureholders)			
	Debenture Redemption Reserve A/c Dr.		30,00,000	
	To General Reserve			30,00,000
	(Being the transfer of DRR to General Reserve)			
	Profit & Loss A/c Dr.		1,80,000	
	To Interest on Debentures A/c			1,80,000
	[Being the transfer of Interest on Debentures A/c to P&L A/c]			

Notes:

1. *Accrued Interest for 6 months upto 30th June, 2015 has been paid on redemption.*
2. *₹ 10,00,000 has been transferred to DRR so as to redeem the Debentures fully out of profits.*

ILLUSTRATION 7 [REDMPTION OF DEBENTURES IN INSTALMENTS BY DRAW OF LOTS]

On 1st April, 2013, Tulsian Ltd. issued ₹ 40,00,000, 12% Debentures of ₹ 100 each at a premium of 5% and redeemable at a premium of 10% in equal annual drawings by draw of lots in 2 years. Pass the necessary journal entries during the years of Issue and Redemption of Debentures without providing for the Interest and Loss on issue of Debentures.

SOLUTION

JOURNAL

Date	*Particulars*		*L.F.*	*Dr. (₹)*	*Cr.(₹)*
01.04.2013	Bank A/c	Dr.		42,00,000	
	To Debentures Application & Allotment A/c				42,00,000
	(Being the receipt of application money)				
	Debentures Application & Allotment A/c	Dr.		42,00,000	
	Loss on Issue of Debentures A/c	Dr.		4,00,000	
	To 12% Debentures A/c				40,00,000
	To Premium on Redemption of Debentures A/c				4,00,000
	To Securities Premium A/c				2,00,000
	(Being the issue of Debentures)				
29.04.2013	Profit & Loss Appropriation A/c	Dr.		10,00,000	
	To Debenture Redemption Reserve A/c				10,00,000
	[Being the creation of DRR as per Rule 18 (7)]				
29.04.2013	Debenture Redemption Reserve Investments A/c	Dr.		3,00,000	
	To Bank A/c				3,00,000
	(Being the DRR Investments made equal to 15%)				
31.03.2014	Bank A/c	Dr.		3,00,000	
	To Deben. Redemption Reserve Investments A/c				3,00,000
	(Being the DRR Investments realised)				
31.03.2014	12% Debentures A/c	Dr.		20,00,000	
	Premium on Redemption of Debentures A/c	Dr.		2,00,000	
	To Debentureholders' A/c				22,00,000
	(Being the amount due on redemption)				
31.03.2014	Debentureholders' A/c	Dr.		22,00,000	
	To Bank A/c				22,00,000
	(Being the payment made to Debentureholders)				
29.04.2014	Debenture Redemption Reserve Investments A/c	Dr.		3,00,000	
	To Bank A/c				3,00,000
	(Being the DRR Investments made equal to 15%)				
31.03.2015	Bank A/c	Dr.		3,00,000	
	To Deben. Redemption Reserve Investments A/c				3,00,000
	(Being the DRR Investments realised)				

31.03.2015	12% Debentures A/c Dr.		20,00,000	
	Premium on Redemption of Debentures A/c Dr.		2,00,000	
	To Debentureholders' A/c			22,00,000
	(Being the amount due on redemption)			
31.03.2015	Debentureholders' A/c Dr.		22,00,000	
	To Bank A/c			22,00,000
	(Being the payment made to Debentureholders)			
31.03.2015	Debenture Redemption Reserve A/c Dr.		10,00,000	
	To General Reserve			10,00,000
	(Being the transfer of DRR to GR)			

6.0 REDEMPTION BY CONVERSION

MEANING OF REDEMPTION BY CONVERSION

Redemption by conversion means redeeming the debentures by converting them into new class of debentures *or* shares. However, the debenture-holders would exercise their right of conversion only when they find it beneficial from their viewpoint *or* as agreed as per terms of issue.The new shares *or* debentures can be issued at par, premium *or* discount. There is no requirement of creating Debenture Redemption Reserve in case of redemption of debentures by conversion.

CONVERSION OF DEBENTURES WHICH WERE ORIGINALLY ISSUED AT PAR OR PREMIUM

JOURNAL ENTRY FOR AMOUNT DUE ON REDEMPTION

Date	*Particulars*	*L.F.*	*Dr. (₹)*	*Cr.(₹)*
	Debentures A/c [with Nominal Value] Dr.			
	Premium on Redemption of Debentures A/c Dr.			
	[with Premium, if any payable on redemption]			
	To Debenture-holders' A/c [with Amount Due]			
	(Being the amount due to Debenture-holders on red.)			

JOURNAL ENTRY FOR CONVERSION

Date	*Particulars*	*L.F.*	*Dr. (₹)*	*Cr.(₹)*
(i)	**If New Shares/Debentures are issued at par**			
	Debenture-holders' A/c *[with Amount Due]* Dr.			
	To Share Capital A/c/New Debentures A/c			
	[with Nominal Value]			
	(Being the issue of .... shares/debentures of ₹ .... each at par)			
(ii)	**If New Shares/Debentures are issued at a Premium**			
	Debenture-holders' A/c *[with Amount Due]* Dr.			
	To Share Capital/New Debentures A/c			
	[with Nominal Value]			
	To Securities Premium A/c *[with Premium on Issue]*			

	(Being the issue of ... Shares/Debentures of the ... each at a premium of ...)			
(iii)	**If New Debentures are issued at a discount** Debenture-holders' A/c [with Amount Due] Dr. Discount on Issue of Debentures A/c Dr. *[with Discount on Issue]* To New Debentures A/c [with Nominal Value] (Being the issue of ... debentures of ₹ .... each at a discount of ...)			

TUTORIAL NOTES

1. *At the time of conversion of convertible debentures into new shares or debentures, no transfer is required to be made from Profit and Loss Appropriation Account to Debenture Redemption Reserve.*
2. *The debenture-holders* ***can not demand the conversion of the unpaid interest*** *into shares unless such right is given expressly.*
3. *An issue of Shares at discount is void as per Sec 53 of The Companies Act, 2013.*

CONVERSION OF DEBENTURES ISSUED AT PAR AND REDEEMABLE AT PAR

ILLUSTRATION 8

950, 14% Debentures of ₹ 100 each issued at par and redeemable at par were converted into Equity Shares of ₹ 10 each issued at par. Journalise the issue and redemption of debentures.

SOLUTION

JOURNAL

Date	*Particulars*	*L.F.*	*Dr. (₹)*	*Cr.(₹)*
	On Issue Bank A/c Dr. To Debentures Application & Allotment A/c (Being the receipt of application money)		95,000	95,000
	Debentures Application & Allotment A/c Dr. To 14% Debentures A/c (Being the issue of Debentures)		95,000	95,000
	On Redemption 14% Debentures A/c Dr. To Debenture-holders' A/c (Being the amount due on redemption)		95,000	95,000
	Debenture-holders' A/c Dr. To Equity Share Capital A/c (Being the issue of 9,500 equity shares of ₹ 10 each at par on conversion of 950 Debentures)		95,000	95,000

Note: *No. of Shares to be issued* = *₹ 95,000/₹ 10 = 9,500*

ILLUSTRATION 9

₹ 95,000, 14% Debentures of ₹ 100 each issued at par and redeemable at par were converted into Equity Shares of ₹ 10 each issued at a premium of 25%. Journalise the issue and redemption of debentures.

SOLUTION

JOURNAL

Date	*Particulars*		*L.F.*	*Dr. (₹)*	*Cr.(₹)*
	On Issue				
	Bank A/c	Dr.		95,000	
	To Debentures Application & Allotment A/c				95,000
	(Being the receipt of application money)				
	Debentures Application & Allotment A/c	Dr.		95,000	
	To 14% Debentures A/c				95,000
	(Being the issue of Debentures)				
	On Redemption				
	14% Debentures A/c	Dr.		95,000	
	To Debenture-holders' A/c				95,000
	(Being the amount due on redemption)				
	Debenture-holders' A/c	Dr.		95,000	
	To Equity Share Capital A/c				76,000
	To Securities Premium A/c				19,000
	(Being the issue of 7,600 equity shares of ₹ 10 each at 25% premium on conversion of 950 Debentures)				

Note: *No. of Shares to be issued* = *₹ 95,000/₹ 12.50 = 7,600*

ILLUSTRATION 10

₹ 95,000, 14% Debentures of ₹ 100 each issued at par and redeemable at par were converted into Equity Shares of ₹ 10 each issued at ₹ 9.50 paid up. Journalise the issue and redemption of debentures.

SOLUTION

JOURNAL

Date	*Particulars*		*L.F.*	*Dr. (₹)*	*Cr.(₹)*
	On Issue				
	Bank A/c	Dr.		95,000	
	To Debentures Application & Allotment A/c				95,000
	(Being the receipt of application money)				

	Debentures Application & Allotment A/c Dr. To 14% Debentures A/c (Being the issue of Debentures)		95,000	95,000
	On Redemption 14% Debentures A/c Dr. To Debenture-holders' A/c (Being the amount due on redemption)		95,000	95,000
	Debenture-holders' A/c Dr. To Equity Share Capital A/c (Being the issue of 10,000 equity shares of ₹ 10 each as ₹ 9.50 paid up on conversion of 950 Debentures)		95,000	95,000

Note: *No. of Shares to be issued = ₹ 95,000/₹ 9.50 = 10,000*

CONVERSION OF DEBENTURES ISSUED AT PAR AND REDEEMABLE AT PREMIUM

ILLUSTRATION 11

950, 14% Debentures of ₹ 100 each issued at par and redeemable at 10% premium were converted into Equity Shares of ₹ 10 each issued at par. Journalise the issue and redemption of debentures.

SOLUTION

JOURNAL

Date	*Particulars*	*L.F.*	*Dr. (₹)*	*Cr.(₹)*
	On Issue Bank A/c Dr. To Debentures Application & Allotment A/c (Being the receipt of application money)		95,000	95,000
	Debentures Application & Allotment A/c Dr. Loss on Issue of Debentures A/c Dr. To 14% Debentures A/c To Premium on Redemption of Debentures A/c (Being the issue of Debentures)		95,000 9,500	95,000 9,500
	On Redemption 14% Debentures A/c Dr. Premium on Redemption of Debentures A/c Dr. To Debenture-holders' A/c (Being the amount due on redemption)		95,000 9,500	1,04,500
	Debenture-holders' A/c Dr. To Equity Share Capital A/c (Being the issue of 10,450 equity shares of ₹ 10 each at par on conversion of 950 Debentures)		1,04,500	1,04,500

Note: *No. of Shares to be issued = ₹ 1,04,500/₹ 10 = 10,450*

ILLUSTRATION 12

₹ 95,000, 14% Debentures of ₹ 100 each issued at par and redeemable at 10% premium were converted into Equity Shares of ₹ 10 each issued at a premium of 25%. Journalise the issue and redemption of debentures.

SOLUTION

JOURNAL

Date	Particulars	L.F.	Dr. (₹)	Cr.(₹)
	On Issue			
	Bank A/c Dr.		95,000	
	To Debentures Application & Allotment A/c			95,000
	(Being the receipt of application money)			
	Debentures Application & Allotment A/c Dr.		95,000	
	Loss on Issue of Debentures A/c Dr.		9,500	
	To 14% Debentures A/c			95,000
	To Premium on Redemption of Debentures A/c			9,500
	(Being the issue of Debentures)			
	On Redemption			
	14% Debentures A/c Dr.		95,000	
	Premium on Redemption of Debentures A/c Dr.		9,500	
	To Debenture-holders' A/c			1,04,500
	(Being the amount due on redemption)			
	Debenture-holders' A/c Dr.		1,04,500	
	To Equity Share Capital A/c			83,600
	To Securities Premium A/c			20,900
	(Being the issue of 8,360 equity shares of ₹ 10 each at 25% premium on conversion of 950 Debentures)			

Note: *No. of Shares to be issued = ₹ 1,04,500/₹ 12.50 = 8,360*

ILLUSTRATION 13

₹ 95,000, 14% Debentures of ₹ 100 each issued at par and redeemable at 10% premium were converted into Equity Shares of ₹ 10 each issued at ₹ 9.50 paid-up. Journalise the issue and redemption of debentures.

SOLUTION

JOURNAL

Date	Particulars	L.F.	Dr. (₹)	Cr.(₹)
	On Issue			
	Bank A/c Dr.		95,000	
	To Debentures Application & Allotment A/c			95,000
	(Being the receipt of application money)			

	Debentures Application & Allotment A/c Dr. Loss on Issue of Debentures A/c Dr. To 14% Debentures A/c To Premium on Redemption of Debentures A/c (Being the issue of Debentures)		95,000 9,500	 95,000 9,500
	On Redemption 14% Debentures A/c Dr. Premium on Redemption of Debentures A/c Dr. To Debenture-holders' A/c (Being the amount due on redemption)		 95,000 9,500	 1,04,500
	Debenture-holders' A/c Dr. To Equity Share Capital A/c (Being the issue of 11,000 equity shares of ₹ 10 each as ₹ 9.50 paid up on conversion of 950 Debentures)		1,04,500	 1,04,500

Note: *No. of Shares to be issued = ₹ 1,04,500/₹ 9.50 = 11,000*

CONVERSION OF DEBENTURES ISSUED AT PREMIUM AND REDEEMABLE AT PREMIUM

ILLUSTRATION 14

950, 14% Debentures of ₹ 100 each issued at 5% premium and redeemable at 10% premium were converted into Equity Shares of ₹ 10 each issued at par. Journalise the issue and redemption of debentures.

SOLUTION

JOURNAL

Date	*Particulars*	*L.F.*	*Dr. (₹)*	*Cr.(₹)*
	On Issue Bank A/c Dr. To Debentures Application & Allotment A/c (Being the receipt of application money)		 99,750	 99,750
	Debentures Application & Allotment A/c Dr. Loss on Issue of Debentures A/c Dr. To 14% Debentures A/c To Securities Premium A/c To Premium on Redemption of Debentures A/c (Being the issue of Debentures)		99,750 9,500	 95,000 4,750 9,500
	On Redemption 14% Debentures A/c Dr. Premium on Redemption of Debentures A/c Dr. To Debenture-holders' A/c (Being the amount due on redemption)		 95,000 9,500	 1,04,500

	Debenture-holders' A/c Dr.		1,04,500	
	To Equity Share Capital A/c			1,04,500
	(Being the issue of 10,450 equity shares of ₹ 10 each at par on conversion of 950 Debentures)			

Note: *No. of Shares to be issued = ₹ 1,04,500/₹ 10 = 10,450*

ILLUSTRATION 15

₹ 95,000, 14% Debentures of ₹ 100 each issued at 5% premium and redeemable at 10% premium were converted into Equity Shares of ₹ 10 each issued at a premium of 25%. Journalise the issue and redemption of debentures.

SOLUTION

JOURNAL

Date	*Particulars*	*L.F.*	*Dr. (₹)*	*Cr.(₹)*
	On Issue			
	Bank A/c Dr.		99,750	
	To Debentures Application & Allotment A/c			99,750
	(Being the receipt of application money)			
	Debentures Application & Allotment A/c Dr.		99,750	
	Loss on Issue of Debentures A/c Dr.		9,500	
	To 14% Debentures A/c			95,000
	To Securities Premium A/c			4,750
	To Premium on Redemption of Debentures A/c			9,500
	(Being the issue of Debentures)			
	On Redemption			
	14% Debentures A/c Dr.		95,000	
	Premium on Redemption of Debentures A/c Dr.		9,500	
	To Debenture-holders' A/c			1,04,500
	(Being the amount due on redemption)			
	Debenture-holders' A/c Dr.		1,04,500	
	To Equity Share Capital A/c			83,600
	To Securities Premium A/c			20,900
	(Being the issue of 8,360 equity shares of ₹ 10 each at 25% premium on conversion of 950 Debentures)			

Note: *No. of Shares to be issued = ₹ 1,04,500/₹ 12.50 = 8,360*

ILLUSTRATION 16

₹ 95,000, 14% Debentures of ₹ 100 each issued at 5% premium and redeemable at 10% premium were converted into Equity Shares of ₹ 10 each issued at ₹ 9.50 paid-up. Journalise the issue and redemption of debentures.

SOLUTION

JOURNAL

Date	Particulars		L.F.	Dr. (₹)	Cr.(₹)
	On Issue				
	Bank A/c	Dr.		99,750	
	To Debentures Application & Allotment A/c				99,750
	(Being the receipt of application money)				
	Debentures Application & Allotment A/c	Dr.		99,750	
	Loss on Issue of Debentures A/c	Dr.		9,500	
	To 14% Debentures A/c				95,000
	To Securities Premium A/c				4,750
	To Premium on Redemption of Debentures A/c				9,500
	(Being the issue of Debentures)				
	On Redemption				
	14% Debentures A/c	Dr.		95,000	
	Premium on Redemption of Debentures A/c	Dr.		9,500	
	To Debenture-holders' A/c				1,04,500
	(Being the amount due on redemption)				
	Debenture-holders' A/c	Dr.		1,04,500	
	To Equity Share Capital A/c				1,04,500
	(Being the issue of 11,000 equity shares of ₹ 10 each as ₹ 9.50 paid up on conversion of 950 Deb)				

Note: *No. of Shares to be issued = ₹ 1,04,500/₹ 9.50 = 11,000*

7.0 CONVERSION OF DEBENTURES WHICH WERE ORIGINALLY ISSUED AT A DISCOUNT, INTO NEW DEBENTURES

In case of **Conversion of Debentures (which were originally issued at a discount) into New Debentures,** the **'Discount on Issue of Debentures Account' need not be credited** because there is no violation of Section 53 of The Companies Act, 1956.

JOURNAL ENTRY FOR AMOUNT DUE ON REDEMPTION

Date	Particulars		L.F.	Dr. (₹)	Cr.(₹)
	Debentures A/c *[with Nominal Value]*	Dr.			
	Premium on Redemption of Debentures A/c *[with Premium, if any payable on redemption]*	Dr.			
	To Debenture-holders' A/c [with Amount Due]				
	(Being the Amount due to Debenture-holders on redemption)				

JOURNAL ENTRY FOR CONVERSION

Date	*Particulars*	*L.F.*	*Dr. (₹)*	*Cr.(₹)*
(i)	**If New Debentures are issued at par** Debenture-holders' A/c *[with Amount Due]* Dr. To New Debentures A/c *[with Nominal Value]* (Being the issue of ....Debentures of ₹ .... each at par)			
(ii)	**If New Debentures are issued at a Premium** Debenture-holders' A/c *[with Amount Due]* Dr. To New Debentures A/c *[with Nominal Value]* To Securities Premium A/c *[with Premium on Issue]* (Being the issue of ... Debentures of the ... each at a premium of ...)			
(iii)	**If New Debentures are issued at a discount** Debenture-holders' A/c *[with Amount Due]* Dr. Discount on Issue of Debentures A/c Dr. *[with Discount on Issue]* To New Debentures A/c *[with Nominal Value]* (Being the issue of ... Debentures of ₹ ... each at a discount of ...)			

Note: *An issue of Debentures at discount is not void as per The Companies Act, 2013.*

ILLUSTRATION 17

1000, 14% Debentures of ₹ 100 each issued at a discount of 5% and redeemable at 10% premium after 4 years were converted into 15% Debentures of ₹ 100 each issued at par before maturity. Journalise the issue and redemption of debentures.

SOLUTION

JOURNAL

Date	*Particulars*	*L.F.*	*Dr. (₹)*	*Cr.(₹)*
	On Issue Bank A/c Dr. To Debentures Application & Allotment A/c (Being the receipt of application money)		 95,000	 95,000
	Debentures Application & Allotment A/c Dr. Loss on Issue of Debentures A/c Dr. To 14% Debentures A/c To Premium on Redemption of Debentures A/c (Being the issue of Debentures)		95,000 15,000	 1,00,000 10,000
	On Redemption 14% Debentures A/c Dr. Premium on Redemption of Debentures A/c Dr.		 1,00,000 10,000	

	To Debenture-holders' A/c (Being the amount due on redemption)			1,10,000
	Debenture-holders' A/c Dr. To 15% Debentures A/c (Being the issue of 1100 Debentures of ₹ 100 each at par on conversion of 1,000 Debentures)		1,10,000	1,10,000

Notes:

1. *No. of Debentures to be issued = ₹ 1,10,000/₹ 100 = 1100*
2. *In case of Conversion of debentures (which were originally issued at a discount) into new debentures, the 'Discount on Issue of Debentures Account' need not be credited because there is no violation of sec 79 of The Companies Act, 1956.*

ILLUSTRATION 18

₹ 1,00,000, 14% Debentures of ₹ 100 each issued at a discount of 5% and redeemable at 10% premium after 4 years were converted into 15% Debentures of ₹ 100 each issued at a premium of 25% before maturity. Journalise the issue and redemption of debentures.

SOLUTION

JOURNAL

Date	*Particulars*	*L.F.*	*Dr. (₹)*	*Cr.(₹)*
	On Issue Bank A/c Dr. To Debentures Application & Allotment A/c (Being the receipt of application money)		95,000	95,000
	Debentures Application & Allotment A/c Dr. Loss on Issue of Debentures A/c Dr. To 14% Debentures A/c To Premium on Redemption of Debentures A/c (Being the issue of Debentures)		95,000 15,000	1,00,000 10,000
	On Redemption 14% Debentures A/c Dr. Premium on Redemption of Debentures A/c Dr. To Debenture-holders' A/c (Being the amount due on redemption)		1,00,000 10,000	1,10,000
	Debenture-holders' A/c Dr. To 15% Debentures A/c To Securities Premium A/c (Being the issue of 880 Debentures of ₹ 100 each at 25% Premium on conversion of 1,000 Debentures)		1,10,000	88,000 22,000

Notes:

1. *No. of Debentures to be issued = ₹ 1,10,000/₹ 125 = 880*

2. *In case of Conversion of debentures (which were originally issued at a discount) into new debentures, the 'Discount on Issue of Debentures Account' need not be credited because there is no violation of sec 79 of The Companies Act, 1956.*

ILLUSTRATION 19

₹ 1,00,000, 14% Debentures of ₹ 100 each issued at a discount of 5% and redeemable at 10% premium after 4 years were converted into 15% Debentures of ₹ 100 each issued at ₹ 80 paid-up before maturity. Journalise the issue and redemption of debentures.

SOLUTION

JOURNAL

Date	Particulars	L.F.	Dr. (₹)	Cr.(₹)
	On Issue			
	Bank A/c Dr.		95,000	
	To Debentures Application & Allotment A/c			95,000
	(Being the receipt of application money)			
	Debentures Application & Allotment A/c Dr.		95,000	
	Loss on Issue of Debentures A/c Dr.		15,000	
	To 14% Debentures A/c			1,00,000
	To Premium on Redemption of Debentures A/c			10,000
	(Being the issue of Debentures)			
	On Redemption			
	14% Debentures A/c Dr.		1,00,000	
	Premium on Redemption of Debentures A/c Dr.		10,000	
	To Debenture-holders' A/c			1,10,000
	(Being the amount due on redemption)			
	Debenture-holders' A/c Dr.		1,10,000	
	To 15% Debentures A/c			1,37,500
	(Being the issue of 1375 Debentures of ₹ 100 each at ₹ 80 paid up on conversion of 1,000 Debentures)			

Notes:

1. *No. of Debentures to be issued = ₹ 1,10,000/₹ 80 = 1375*
2. *In case of Conversion of Debentures (which were originally issued at a discount) into New Debentures, the 'Discount on Issue of Debentures Account' need not be credited because there is no violation of Sec 79 of The Companies Act, 1956.*

8.0 CONVERSION OF DEBENTURES WHICH WERE ORIGINALLY ISSUED AT A DISCOUNT INTO SHARES

(A) CONVERSION BEFORE MATURITY

In case of conversion of Debentures (which were originally Issued at a discount) into shares, the actual amount realised (i.e., net of discount) from debentures at the time of issue, should be used as the basis for determining the number of shares to be issued otherwise it would amount to an issue of shares at discount which is void as per Sec. 53 of the Companies Act, 2013. Thus, at the time of making due the amount payable to debenture-holders in such a case, **Discount on issue of Debentures Account (Loss on issue of Debentures Account in case of Redemption at Premium)** should be credited with the amount of Discount/Loss which has not yet been written off and Profit & Loss Account should be credited with the amount of Discount/Loss which has already been written off.

(B) CONVERSION AT MATURITY

In case of conversion at maturity the debentures may be converted into the shares on the basis of the nominal value of the debentures and the provisions of Section 53 cannot be regarded as being violated.

JOURNAL ENTRY FOR AMOUNT DUE ON REDEMPTION AT PAR

Date	*Particulars*	*L.F.*	*Dr. (₹)*	*Cr.(₹)*
	Debentures A/c *[with Nominal Value]* Dr. To Discount on Issue of Debentures A/c *[with Discount not yet w/o]* To Profit & Loss A/c *[with Discount already w/o]* To Debenture-holders' A/c *[with Net Amount Due]* (Being the amount due to debenture-holders on redemption)			

JOURNAL ENTRY FOR AMOUNT DUE ON REDEMPTION AT PREMIUM

Date	*Particulars*	*L.F.*	*Dr. (₹)*	*Cr.(₹)*
	Debentures A/c *[with Nominal Value]* Dr. Premium on Redemption of Debentures A/c Dr. *[with Premium Payable]* To Loss on Issue of Debentures A/c *[with Loss on Issue not yet w/o]* To Profit & Loss A/c [with Loss on Issue already w/o] To Debentures-holders' A/c *[with Net Amount Due]* (Being the amount due to debenture-holders on redemption)			

JOURNAL ENTRY FOR CONVERSION

Date	*Particulars*	*L.F.*	*Dr. (₹)*	*Cr.(₹)*
(i)	**If New Shares are issued at Par** Debenture-holders' A/c *[with Amount Due]* Dr. To Share Capital A/c *[with Nominal Value]* (Being the issue of .... Shares of ₹ .... each at par)			

(ii)	**If New Shares are issued at a Premium** Debenture-holders' A/c *[with Amount Due]* Dr. To Share Capital A/c *[with Nominal Value]* To Securities Premium A/c *[with Premium on Issue]* (Being the issue of ...Shares of the ... each at a premium of ...)			

TUTORIAL NOTES

1. *An issue of Shares at discount is void as per Sec 53 of The Companies Act, 2013.*
2. *At the time of conversion of Convertible Debentures into new shares or debentures, no transfer is required to be made from Profit and Loss Appropriation Account to Debenture Redemption Reserve.*
3. *The Debenture-holders can not demand the conversion of the unpaid interest into shares unless such right is given expressly.*
4. *In case of Conversion of debentures (which were originally issued at a discount) into New Shares,*
   (a) if the information about the original period of redemption and actual period of conversion before maturity is given, 'Discount' on issue of Debentures Account' should be credited with the amount of discount which has not yet been written off and Profit & Loss Account should be credited with the amount of discount which has already been written off.
   (b) if the information about the original period of redemption and actual period of conversion before maturity is not given'Discount on Issue of Debentures Account' should be credited with the amount of discount originally allowed by giving a following Note:
   "It has been assumed no portion of 'Discount on Issue of debentures has yet been written off."

ILLUSTRATION 20

1000, 14% Debentures of ₹ 100 each issued at a discount of 5% and redeemable at par after 4 years were converted into Equity Shares of ₹ 10 each issued at par before maturity. Journalise the issue and redemption of debentures.

SOLUTION

JOURNAL

Date	Particulars	L.F.	Dr. (₹)	Cr.(₹)
	On Issue			
	Bank A/c Dr.		95,000	
	To Debentures Application & Allotment A/c			95,000
	(Being the receipt of application money)			
	Debentures Application & Allotment A/c Dr.		95,000	
	Discount on Issue of Debentures A/c Dr.		5,000	
	To 14% Debentures A/c			1,00,000
	(Being the issue of Debentures)			
	On Redemption			
	14% Debentures A/c Dr.		1,00,000	

	To Discount on Issue of Debentures A/c			5,000
	To Debenture-holders' A/c			95,000
	(Being the amount due to debenture-holders on conversion of 1,000,14% Debentures)			
	Debenture-holders' A/c Dr.		95,000	
	To Equity Share Capital A/c			95,000
	(Being the issue of 9,500, Equity Shares of ₹ 10 each at par on conversion of 1,000, 14% Debentures)			

Notes:

1. *No. of Shares to be issued = ₹ 95,000/₹ 10 = 9,500*
2. *It has been assumed that no portion of 'Discount on Issue of Debentures' has yet been written off.*

ILLUSTRATION 21

₹ 1,00,000, 14% Debentures of ₹ 100 each issued at a discount of 5% and redeemable at par after 4 years were converted into Equity Shares of ₹ 10 each issued at a premium of 25% before maturity. Journalise the issue and redemption of debentures.

SOLUTION

JOURNAL

Date	*Particulars*	*L.F.*	*Dr. (₹)*	*Cr.(₹)*
	On Issue			
	Bank A/c Dr.		95,000	
	To Debentures Application & Allotment A/c			95,000
	(Being the receipt of application money)			
	Debentures Application & Allotment A/c Dr.		95,000	
	Discount on Issue of Debentures A/c Dr.		5,000	
	To 14% Debentures A/c			1,00,000
	(Being the issue of Debentures)			
	On Redemption			
	14% Debentures A/c Dr.		1,00,000	
	To Discount on Issue of Debentures A/c			5,000
	To Debenture-holders' A/c			95,000
	(Being the amount due to debenture-holders on conversion of 1,000,14% Debentures)			
	Debenture-holders' A/c Dr.		95,000	
	To Equity Share Capital A/c			76,000
	To Securities Premium A/c			19,000
	(Being the issue of 7,600 Equity Shares of ₹ 10 each at a premium of 25% on conversion of 1,000, 14% Debentures)			

Notes:

1. *No. of Shares to be issued = ₹ 95,000/₹ 12.50 = 7,600*
2. *It has been assumed that no portion of 'Discount on Issue of Debentures has yet been written off.*

ILLUSTRATION 22

₹ 1,00,000, 14% Debentures of ₹ 100 each issued at a discount of 5% and redeemable at par after 4 years were converted into Equity Shares of ₹ 10 each issued at ₹ 9.50 paid up before maturity. Journalise the issue and redemption of debentures.

SOLUTION

JOURNAL

Date	*Particulars*	*L.F.*	*Dr. (₹)*	*Cr.(₹)*
	On Issue			
	Bank A/c Dr.		95,000	
	To Debentures Application & Allotment A/c			95,000
	(Being the receipt of application money)			
	Debentures Application & Allotment A/c Dr.		95,000	
	Discount on Issue of Debentures A/c Dr.		5,000	
	To 14% Debentures A/c			1,00,000
	(Being the issue of Debentures)			
	On Redemption			
	14% Debentures A/c Dr.		1,00,000	
	To Discount on Issue of Debentures A/c			5,000
	To Debenture-holders' A/c			95,000
	(Being the amount due to debenture-holders on conversion of 1,000,14% Debentures)			
	Debenture-holders' A/c Dr.		95,000	
	To Equity Share Capital A/c			95,000
	(Being the issue of 10,000 Equity Shares of ₹ 10 each ₹ 9.50 paid up on conversion of 1,000, 14% Debentures)			

Notes:

1. *No. of Shares to be issued = ₹ 95,000/₹ 9.50 = 10,000*
2. *It has been assumed that no portion of 'Discount on Issue of Debentures has yet been written off.*

ILLUSTRATION 23

1000, 14% Debentures of ₹ 100 each issued at a discount of 5% and redeemable at 10% premium after 4 years were converted into Equity Shares of ₹ 10 each issued at par before maturity. Journalise the issue and redemption of debentures.

SOLUTION

JOURNAL

Date	Particulars		L.F.	Dr. (₹)	Cr.(₹)
	On Issue				
	Bank A/c	Dr.		95,000	
	To Debentures Application & Allotment A/c				95,000
	(Being the receipt of application money)				
	Debentures Application & Allotment A/c	Dr.		95,000	
	Loss on Issue of Debentures A/c	Dr.		15,000	
	To 14% Debentures A/c				1,00,000
	To Premium on Redemption of Debentures A/c				10,000
	(Being the issue of Debentures)				
	On Redemption				
	14% Debentures A/c	Dr.		1,00,000	
	Debentures Redemption Premium A/c	Dr.		10,000	
	To Loss on Issue of Debentures A/c				15,000
	To Debenture-holders' A/c				95,000
	(Being the amount due to debenture-holders on conversion of 1,000,14% Debentures)				
	Debenture-holders' A/c	Dr.		95,000	
	To Equity Share Capital A/c				95,000
	(Being the issue of 9,500, Equity Shares of ₹ 10 each at par on conversion of 1,000,14% Debentures)				

Notes:

1. *No. of Shares to be issued = ₹ 95,000/₹ 10 = 9,500*
2. *It has been assumed that no portion of 'Loss on Issue of Debentures has yet been written off.*

ILLUSTRATION 24

₹ 1,00,000, 14% Debentures of ₹ 100 each issued at a discount of 5% and redeemable at 10% premium after 4 years were converted into Equity Shares of ₹ 10 each issued at a premium 25% before maturity. Journalise the issue and redemption of debentures.

SOLUTION

JOURNAL

Date	Particulars		L.F.	Dr. (₹)	Cr.(₹)
	On Issue				
	Bank A/c	Dr.		95,000	
	To Debentures Application & Allotment A/c				95,000
	(Being the receipt of application money)				

	Debentures Application & Allotment A/c Dr.		95,000	
	Loss on Issue of Debentures A/c Dr.		15,000	
	To 14% Debentures A/c			1,00,000
	To Premium on Redemption of Debentures A/c			10,000
	(Being the issue of Debentures)			
	On Redemption			
	14% Debentures A/c Dr.		1,00,000	
	Debentures Redemption Premium A/c Dr.		10,000	
	To Loss on Issue of Debentures A/c			15,000
	To Debenture-holders' A/c			95,000
	(Being the amount due to debenture-holders on conversion of 1,000,14% Debentures)			
	Debenture-holders' A/c Dr.		95,000	
	To Equity Share Capital A/c			76,000
	To Securities Premium A/c			19,000
	(Being the issue of 7,600 Equity Shares of ₹ 10 each at a premium of 25% on conversion of 1,000, 14% Debentures)			

Notes:

1. *No. of Shares to be issued = ₹ 95,000/₹ 12.50 = 7,600*
2. *It has been assumed that no portion of 'Loss on Issue of Debentures has yet been written off.*

ILLUSTRATION 25

₹ 1,00,000, 14% Debentures of ₹ 100 each issued at a discount of 5% and redeemable at 10% premium after 4 years were converted into Equity Shares of ₹ 10 each issued at ₹ 9.50 paid-up before maturity. Journalise the issue and redemption of debentures.

SOLUTION

JOURNAL

Date	*Particulars*	*L.F.*	*Dr. (₹)*	*Cr.(₹)*
	On Issue			
	Bank A/c Dr.		95,000	
	To Debentures Application & Allotment A/c			95,000
	(Being the receipt of application money)			
	Debentures Application & Allotment A/c Dr.		95,000	
	Loss on Issue of Debentures A/c Dr.		15,000	
	To 14% Debentures A/c			1,00,000
	To Premium on Redemption of Debentures A/c			10,000
	(Being the issue of Debentures)			
	On Redemption			
	14% Debentures A/c Dr.		1,00,000	

	Debentures Redemption Premium A/c Dr.		10,000	
	To Loss on Issue of Debentures A/c			15,000
	To Debenture-holders' A/c			95,000
	(Being the amount due to debenture-holders on conversion of 1,000,14% Debentures)			
	Debenture-holders' A/c Dr.		95,000	
	To Equity Share Capital A/c			95,000
	(Being the issue of 10,000 Equity Shares of ₹ 10 each ₹ 9.50 paid up on conversion of 1,000, 14% Debentures)			

Notes:

1. *No. of Shares to be issued = ₹ 95,000/₹ 9.50 = 10,000*
2. *It has been assumed that no portion of 'Loss on Issue of Debentures has yet been written off.*

ILLUSTRATION 26

On 1st April, 2013, a company issued 1,000, 12% debentures of ₹ 500 each at ₹ 450 each. Debenture-holders were given an option to get their debentures converted into equity shares of ₹ 100 each at a premium of ₹ 50 per share. On 31st March, 2015, one year's interest had accrued on these debentures which was not paid. A holder of 100 debentures informed that he wanted to exercise the option for conversion of debentures into equity shares. The company, therefore, accepted his request and redeemed these 100 debentures by issuing him equity shares. The interest, however, on these 100 debentures was paid to the debentureholder. Pass the necessary journal entries.

SOLUTION

JOURNAL

Date	Particulars	L.F.	Dr. (₹)	Cr.(₹)
01.04.12	Bank A/c Dr.		4,50,000	
	To Debentures Application & Allotment A/c Dr.		4,50,000	
	(Being the receipt of application money)			
01.04.12	Debentures Application & Allotment A/c Dr.		4,50,000	
	Discount on Issue of Debentures A/c Dr.		50,000	
	To 12% Debentures A/c			5,00,000
	(Being the Debentures issued at 10% discount)			
31.03.15	Interest on Debentures A/c Dr.		60,000	
	To Interest on debentures accrued & due A/c			60,000
	(Being the Interest due on debentures)			
31.03.15	12% Debentures A/c Dr.		50,000	
	To Discount on issue of Debentures A/c			5,000
	To Debentureholders' A/c			45,000
	(Being the amount due to debenture-holders)			
	Debentureholders' A/c Dr.		45,000	
	To Equity Share Capital A/c			30,000
	To Securities Premium A/c			15,000

	(Being the issue of 300 Equity Shares of ₹ 100 each at a premium of 50%)			
	Interest on Debentures accrued & due A/c Dr.		6,000	
	To Bank A/c			6,000
	(Being the Interest paid to a holder of 100 Debentures)			

Notes:

1. *No. of Shares to be issued = ₹ 45,000/₹ 150 = 300*
2. *It has been assumed that no portion of 'Discount on Issue of Debentures has yet been written off.*

MISCELLANEOUS

ILLUSTRATION 27

BHARAT Ltd. issued 2000, 14% Debentures of ₹ 100 each at a discount of 5% and redeemable at 10% premium after 4 years. It redeemed 50% Debentures by converting into equity shares of ₹ 10 each issued at par and the balance by converting into 15% Debentures of ₹ 50 each at a premium of ₹ 12.50 per Debenture before maturity. Journalise the issue and redemption of debentures.

SOLUTION

JOURNAL

Date	*Particulars*	*L.F.*	*Dr. (₹)*	*Cr.(₹)*
	On Issue			
	Bank A/c Dr.		1,90,000	
	To Debentures Application & Allotment A/c			1,90,000
	(Being the receipt of application money)			
	Debentures Application & Allotment A/c Dr.		1,90,000	
	Loss on Issue of Debentures A/c Dr.		30,000	
	To 14% Debentures A/c			2,00,000
	To Premium on Redemption of Debentures A/c			20,000
	(Being the issue of Debentures at 5% Discount and redeemable at 10% Premium)			
	On Redemption			
	14% Debentures A/c Dr.		1,00,000	
	Premium on Redemption of Debentures A/c Dr.		10,000	
	To Loss on Issue of Debentures A/c			15,000
	To Debenture-holders' A/c			95,000
	(Being the amount due to debenture-holders on conversion of 1,000,14% Debentures)			
	Debenture-holders' A/c Dr.		95,000	
	To Equity Share Capital A/c			95,000
	(Being the issue of 9,500 Equity Shares of ₹ 10 each at par on conversion of 1,000, 14% Debentures)			

	14% Debentures A/c Dr.		1,00,000	
	Premium on Redemption of Debentures A/c Dr.		10,000	
	To Debenture-holders' A/c			1,10,000
	(Being the amount due on redemption)			
	Debenture-holders' A/c Dr.		1,10,000	
	To 15% Debentures A/c			88,000
	To Securities Premium A/c			22,000
	(Being the issue of 1760 Debentures of ₹ 50 each at 25% Premium on conversion of 1,000 Debentures)			

Notes:

1. *No. of Shares to be issued = ₹ 95,000/₹ 10 = 9,500*
2. *No. of Debentures to be issued = ₹ 1,10,000/₹ 62.50 = 1760*
3. *It has been assumed that no portion of 'Loss on Issue of Debentures' has yet been written off.*
4. *In case of Conversion of debentures (which were originally issued at a discount) into new debentures, the 'Discount on Issue of Debentures Account' need not be credited because there is no violation of Sec 53 of The Companies Act, 2013.*

ILLUSTRATION 28

Tulsian Ltd. has to redeem its outstanding ₹ 5,00,000, 12% Debentures of ₹ 100 seach. It redeemed 40% Debentures in cash and the balance at a premium of 20% by converting into 15% Debentures of ₹ 50 each at a Discount of ₹ 2 per Debenture.

Required: Pass the necessary journal entries at the time of redemption of debentures.

SOLUTION

JOURNAL

Date	Particulars	L.F.	Dr. (₹)	Cr.(₹)
	12% Debentures A/c Dr.		5,00,000	
	Premium on Redemption of Debentures A/c Dr.		60,000	
	[₹ 3,00,000 × 20%]			
	To Debentureholders' A/c			5,60,000
	(Being the amount due on redemption)			
	Debentureholders' A/c Dr.		3,60,000	
	Discount on Issue of Debentures A/c Dr.		15,000	
	To 15% Debentures A/c			3,75,000
	(Being the issue of 7500 Debentures of ₹ 50 each at discount of ₹ 2)			
	Profit & Loss Appropriation A/c Dr.		50,000	
	To Debenture Redemption Reserve A/c			50,000
	(Being the transfer of profit equal to 25% of Nominal Value of Deb. Redeemed in cash to DRR as per Rule 18(7))			

	Debenture Redemption Reserve Investments A/c Dr. To Bank A/c (Being the DRR Investments made equal to 15%)		30,000	30,000
	Bank A/c Dr. To Debenture Redemption Reserve Investments A/c (Being the DRR Investments realised)		30,000 30,000	
	Debentureholders' A/c Dr. To Bank A/c (Being the payment made to Debenture-holders)		2,00,000	2,00,000
	Debenture Redemption Reserve A/c Dr. To General Reserve (Being the transfer of DRR to General Reserve)		50,000	50,000

Notes:

1. *No. of 15% Debentures to be issued = [(3000 × ₹ 100) + (₹ 3,00,000 × 20%)]/₹ 48 = 7500*
2. *Cash paid on Redemption = [(2000 × ₹ 100)] = ₹ 2,00,000*

ILLUSTRATION 29

Tulsian Ltd. served notice of its intention to redeem its outstanding ₹ 3,00,000, 15% Debentures of ₹ 100 each at 110 and offered the holders the following options:

(a) To convert their holdings into 12% Cumulative Preference Shares of ₹ 20 each at 110%.

(b) To convert their holdings into 15% Debentures at 96%.

(c) To have their holdings redeemed in cash unless otherwise opted.

Holders of 1,800 Debentures opted for (a) and Holders of 480 Debentures opted for (b).

Required: Pass the necessary journal entries.

SOLUTION

JOURNAL

Date	*Particulars*	*L.F.*	*Dr. (₹)*	*Cr.(₹)*
	15% Debentures A/c Dr. Premium on Redemption of Debentures A/c Dr. To Debentureholders' A/c (Being the amount due on redemption)		3,00,000 30,000	3,30,000
	Option (i) (a): Debentureholders' A/c Dr. To 12% Cumulative Preference Share Capital A/c To Securities Premium A/c (Being the issue of 9,000 Cum Pref Shares at 10% premium)		1,98,000	1,80,000 18,000
	Option (i) (b): Debentureholders' A/c Dr.		52,800	

	Discount on Issue of Debentures A/c Dr.		2,200	
	To 15% Debentures A/c			55,000
	(Being the issue of 550 Debentures at 4% discount)]			
	Option (ii):			
	Profit & Loss Appropriation A/c Dr.		18,000	
	To Debenture Redemption Reserve A/c			18,000
	(Being the transfer of profit equal to 25% of Nominal Value of Deb. Redeemed in cash to Debenture Redemption Reserve A/c as per Rule 18(7))			
	Debenture Redemption Reserve Investments A/c Dr.		10,800	
	To Bank A/c			10,800
	(Being the DRR Investments made equal to 15%)			
	Bank A/c Dr.		10,800	
	To Debenture Redemption Reserve Investments A/c			10,800
	(Being the DRR Investments realised)			
	Debentureholders' A/c Dr.		79,200	
	To Bank A/c			79,200
	(Being the payment made to Debenture-holders)			
	Debenture Redemption Reserve A/c Dr.		18,000	
	To General Reserve			18,000
	(Being the transfer of DRR to General Reserve)			

Notes:

1. *No. of Preference Shares to be issued = [(1800 × ₹ 100) + (₹ 1,80,000 × 10%)]/₹ 22 = 9,000*
2. *No. of 15% Debentures to be issued = [(480 × ₹ 100) + (₹ 48,000 × 10%)]/₹ 96 = 550*
3. *Cash paid on Redemption = [(720 × ₹ 100) + (₹ 72,000 × 10%)] = ₹ 79,200*
4. *No portion of discount on issue of new debentures has been written off in the absence of any information regarding the period of issue & redemption.*
5. *It has been assumed that the balance in P & L Appropriation Account is sufficient to carry out the aforesaid adjustments.*

ILLUSTRATION 30

Suresh Ltd. took over the Assets of ₹ 6,00,000 and Creditors of ₹ 70,000 of P & Co. for an agreed amount of ₹ 5,50,000 by the issue of fully paid 12% Debentures of ₹ 100 each at a premium of 10%. These Debentures are redeemable at a premium of 5% after 3 years. Pass the necessary journal entries both at the time of Issue and Redemption of Debentures without providing for the Interest and Loss on issue of Debentures.

SOLUTION

JOURNAL OF SURESH LTD.

Date	*Particulars*	*L.F.*	*Dr. (₹)*	*Cr.(₹)*
1.	Sundry Assets A/c Dr.		6,00,000	
	Goodwill [Balancing Figure] Dr.		**20,000**	

	To Sundry Creditors		70,000
	To P & Co.		5,50,000
	(Being the purchase of Business from P & Co.)		
2.	P & Co. Dr.	5,50,000	
	Loss on Issue of Debentures A/c Dr.	25,000	
	To 12% Debentures A/c		5,00,000
	To Securities Premium A/c		50,000
	To Premium on Redemption of Debentures A/c		25,000
	(Being the issue of 5000, 12% Debentures at a premium of 10% and repayable at a premium of 5%)		
	Profit & Loss Appropriation A/c Dr.	1,25,000	
	To Debenture Redemption Reserve A/c		1,25,000
	[Being the creation of DRR as per Rule 18(7)]		
	Debenture Redemption Reserve Investments A/c Dr.	75,000	
	To Bank A/c		75,000
	(Being the DRR Investments made equal to 15%)		
	Bank A/c Dr.	75,000	
	To Debenture Redemption Reserve Investments A/c	75,000	
	(Being the DRR Investments realised)		
	12% Debentures A/c Dr.	5,00,000	
	Premium on Redemption of Debentures A/c Dr.	25,000	
	To Debentureholders' A/c		5,25,000
	(Being the amount due on redemption)		
	Debentureholders' A/c Dr.	5,25,000	
	To Bank A/c		5,25,000
	(Being the payment made to Debentureholders)		
	Debenture Redemption Reserve A/c Dr.	1,25,000	
	To General Reserve		1,25,000
	(Being the transfer of DRR to General Reserve)		

Note: *No. of Debentures to be issued = ₹ 5,50,000/₹ 110 = 5,000*

ILLUSTRATION 31

X Ltd. took over the Assets of ₹ 7,00,000 and Creditors of ₹ 80,000 of Y Ltd. for a sum of ₹ 6,00,000 payable 10% by a cheque and the balance by the issue of fully paid 15% Debentures of ₹ 100 each at a discount of 10%.These Debentures are redeemable at a premium of 5% after 3 years.

Required: Pass the necessary journal entries both at the time of Issue and Redemption of Debentures without providing for the Interest and Loss on issue of Debentures.

SOLUTION

JOURNAL OF X LTD.

Date	*Particulars*	*L.F.*	*Dr. (₹)*	*Cr.(₹)*
1.	Sundry Assets A/c Dr.		7,00,000	
	To Sundry Creditors			80,000
	To Y Ltd.			6,00,000
	To **Capital Reserve A/c** (Balancing Figure)			**20,000**
	(Being the purchase of Business from Y Ltd.)			
2.	Y Ltd. Dr.		60,000	
	To Bank A/c			60,000
	(Being the payment made to Vendor by a cheque)			
3.	Y Ltd. Dr.		5,40,000	
	Loss on Issue of Shares A/c [₹ 60,000 + ₹ 30,000] Dr.		90,000	
	To 15% Debentures A/c			6,00,000
	To Premium on Redemption of Debentures A/c			30,000
	(Being the issue of 6000, 15% Debentures at a discount of 10% and repayable at a premium of 5%)			
4.	Profit & Loss Appropriation A/c Dr.		1,50,000	
	To Debenture Redemption Reserve A/c			1,50,000
	[Being the creation of DRR as per Rule 18(7)]			
5.	Debenture Redemption Reserve Investments A/c Dr.		90,000	
	To Bank A/c			90,000
	(Being the DRR Investments made equal to 15%)			
6.	Bank A/c Dr.		90,000	
	To Debenture Redemption Reserve Investments A/c		90,000	
	(Being the DRR Investments realised)			
7.	15% Debentures A/c Dr.		6,00,000	
	Premium on Redemption of Debentures A/c Dr.		30,000	
	To Debentureholders' A/c			6,30,000
	(Being the amount due on redemption)			
8.	Debentureholders' A/c Dr.		6,30,000	
	To Bank A/c			6,30,000
	(Being the payment made to Debentureholders)			
9.	Debenture Redemption Reserve A/c Dr.		1,50,000	
	To General Reserve			1,50,000
	(Being the transfer of DRR to General Reserve)			

Note: *No. of Debentures to be issued = ₹ 5,40,000/₹ 90 = 6,000*

ILLUSTRATION 32 [COMPREHENSIVE REVISIONAL ILLUSTRATION]

Bharat Tushar Ltd. took over the Assets of ₹ 7,00,000 and Creditors of ₹ 80,000 of Y Ltd. for a sum of ₹ 6,00,000 payable 10% by a cheque and the balance by the issue of fully paid 15% Debentures of ₹ 100 each at a discount of 10% and redeemable at a premium of 5%. 25% of these Debentures were redeemed by converting into Equity Shares of ₹ 10 each issued at a premium of 25% and 25% of these Debentures were redeemed by converting into 16% Debentures of ₹ 50 each at a discount of ₹ 5 per Debenture before maturity and the balance redeemed for Cash.

Required: Pass the necessary journal entries both at the time of Issue and Redemption of Debentures without providing for the Interest and Loss on issue of Debentures.

SOLUTION

JOURNAL OF BHARAT TUSHAR LTD.

Date	*Particulars*		*L.F.*	*Dr. (₹)*	*Cr.(₹)*
1.	Sundry Assets A/c	Dr.		7,00,000	
	To Sundry Creditors				80,000
	To Y Ltd.				6,00,000
	To **Capital Reserve A/c** [Balancing figure)				**20,000**
	(Being the purchase of Business from Y Ltd.)				
2.	Y Ltd.	Dr.		60,000	
	To Bank A/c				60,000
	(Being the payment made to Vendor by a cheque)				
3.	Y Ltd.	Dr.		5,40,000	
	Loss on Issue of Shares A/c	Dr.		90,000	
	To 15% Debentures A/c				6,00,000
	To Premium on Redemption of Debentures A/c				30,000
	(Being the issue of 6000, 15% Debentures at a discount of 10% and repayable at a premium of 5%)				
4.	Profit & Loss Appropriation A/c	Dr.		75,000	
	To Debenture Redemption Reserve A/c				75,000
	[Being the creation of DRR as per Rule 18(7)]				
5.	Debenture Redemption Reserve Investments A/c	Dr.		45,000	
	To Bank A/c				45,000
	(Being the DRR Investments made equal to 15%)				
6.	Bank A/c	Dr.		45,000	
	To Debenture Redemption Reserve Investments A/c				45,000
	(Being the DRR Investments realised)				
7.	15% Debentures A/c	Dr.		3,00,000	
	Premium on Redemption of Debentures A/c	Dr.		15,000	
	To Debentureholders' A/c				3,15,000
	(Being the amount due on redemption)				

8.	Debentureholders' A/c	Dr.	3,15,000	
	To Bank A/c			3,15,000
	(Being the payment made to Debentureholders)			
9.	Debenture Redemption Reserve A/c	Dr.	75,000	
	To General Reserve			75,000
	(Being the transfer of DRR to General Reserve)			
10.	15% Debentures A/c	Dr.	1,50,000	
	Premium on Redemption of Debentures A/c	Dr.	7,500	
	To Loss on Issue of Debentures A/c			22,500
	To Debenture-holders' A/c			1,35,000
	(Being the amount due to debenture-holders on conversion of 1,500,15% Debentures)			
11.	Debenture-holders' A/c	Dr.	1,35,000	
	To Equity Share Capital A/c			1,08,000
	To Securities Premium A/c			27,000
	(Being the issue of 10,800 Equity Shares of ₹ 10 each at 25% Premium on conversion of 1,500, 15% Debentures)			
12.	15% Debentures A/c	Dr.	1,50,000	
	Premium on Redemption of Debentures A/c	Dr.	7,500	
	To Debenture-holders' A/c			1,57,500
	(Being the amount due on redemption of 1,500, 15% Debentures)			
13.	Debenture-holders' A/c	Dr.	1,57,500	
	Discount on Issue of Debentures A/c	Dr.	17,500	
	To 16% Debentures A/c			1,75,000
	(Being the issue of 3500 Debentures of ₹ 50 each at at a discount of ₹ 5 per Debenture on conversion of 1,500 Debentures)			

Notes:

1. *No. of 15% Debentures to be issued = ₹ 5,40,000/₹ 90 = 6,000*
2. *No. of Shares to be issued on redemption = ₹ 1,35,000/₹ 12.50 = 10,800*
3. *No. of 16% Debentures to be issued on redemption = ₹ 1,57,500/₹ 45 = 3500*
4. *It has been assumed that no portion of 'Loss on Issue of Debentures has yet been written off.*
5. *In case of Conversion of debentures (which were originally issued at a discount) into new debentures, the 'Discount on Issue of Debentures Account' need not be credited because there is no violation of any of provision of Sec 53 of The Companies Act, 2013.*

ILLUSTRATION 33

What will be change in the Solution of Previous Illustration 32 if the balance redeemed fully out of profits ?

SOLUTION

Entry No. 4 & 9 (regarding DRR) will be with the amount of ₹ 3,00,000 (i.e., 100% of Nominal Value of Debentures redeemed fully out of profits).

9.0 FINANCING OF REDEMPTION OF DEBENTURES

To ensure the availability of sufficient cash to redeem the debentures at the end of specified period, a part of divisible profits is set aside and is invested outside the business. For investing the funds outside the business, the company may adopt any one of the following methods:

(a) Sinking Fund Method *or* Debenture Redemption Fund Method

(b) Insurance Policy Method

10.0 SINKING FUND METHOD OR DEBENTURE REDEMPTION FUND METHOD

PRACTICAL STEPS INVOLVED IN THE WORKING OF DEBENTURE REDEMPTION FUND METHOD

Step 1: Calculate the amount of profit to be set aside with the help of Sinking Fund Table

Step 2: Set aside the amount of profit at the end of each year

Step 3: Purchase the Investments at the end of each year (except last year)

Step 4: Receive the interest on investments at the end of each year

Step 5: Repeat Step 2 for each year, Repeat Step 3 for each year except last year, Repeat Step 4 for each year

Step 6: Realise the investments in the year of redemption

Step 7: Transfer profit/loss on sale of Investment to Debenture Redemption Fund Account.

Step 8: Make due the amount payable to Debenture-holders

Step 9: Make payment to Debenture-holders

Step 10: Transfer unwritten off amount of Loss on Issue of Debentures equivalent to Premium payable on redemption of Debentures, (if any), to the debit of Debenture Redemption Reserve Account.

Step 11: Transfer the balance left in Debenture Redemption Reserve Account to General Reserve after all the debentures have been redeemed

JOURNAL ENTRIES

I. At the end of First Year

1. ***For the transfer of profit to DRR***

   Profit & Loss Appropriation A/c Dr. *(With the amount of profit set aside)*

   To Debenture Redemption Reserve A/c

   [Refer to Para 7.3]

2. ***For Purchase of Investments***

   Debenture Redemption Fund Investment A/c Dr. *(With the amount of investment made)*

   To Bank A/c

   [Refer to Para 7.4]

II. At the end of Second year and subsequent years other than the last year

3. ***For Receiving the Interest on Investments***

Bank A/c Dr. *(With the amount of interest received)*
To Interest on Debenture Redemption Fund Investment A/c
[Refer to Para 7.5]

4. ***For the transfer of Interest on Deb. Red. Fund Investment to DRF A/c***

Interest on Deb. Red. Fund Investment A/c Dr.
To Debenture Redemption Reserve A/c

5. ***For transfer of profit to DRR***

Profit and Loss Appropriation A/c Dr. *(With the amount of profit set aside)*
To Debenture Redemption Reserve A/c

6. ***For Purchase of Investments***

Debenture Redemption Fund Investment A/c Dr. *(With the amount of investments made)*
To Bank A/c

III. At the end of last year

7. ***For Receiving the Interest on Investments made***

Bank A/c Dr. (With the amount of interest received)
To Interest on Debenture Redemption Fund Investment A/c

8. ***For the transfer of Interest on Deb. Red. Fund Investment to DRF A/c***

Interest on Deb. Red. Fund Investment A/c Dr.
To Debenture Redemption Reserve A/c

9. ***For the transfer of profit to DRR***

Profit and Loss Appropriation A/c Dr. (With the amount of profit set aside)
To Debenture Redemption Reserve A/c

10. ***For Sale of Investments***

Bank A/c Dr. (With the sale proceeds)
To Debenture Redemption Fund Investment A/c

11. ***For the t/f of profit/loss on realisation of Debenture Redemption Fund Investments***

(a) ***In case of Profit***

Debenture Redemption Fund Investment A/c Dr. (With the amount of profit)
To Debenture Redemption Reserve A/c

(b) ***In case of Loss reverse of the above entry is passed.***

12. ***For Making due the amount payable to Debenture holders***

(a) ***If the Debentures are to be redeemed at par***

Debentures A/c Dr. *(With the amount due)*
To Debenture-holders' A/c

(b) ***If the Debentures are to be redeemed at a premium***

Debentures A/c Dr. *(With Nominal value)*
Debentures Redemption Premium A/c Dr. *(With Premium payable)*
To Debenture-holders' A/c *(With Total)*

13. ***For Redemption***

Debenture-holders' A/c Dr. *(With the amount paid)*

To Bank A/c

14. ***For the transfer of Unwritten off amount of Loss on Issue of Debentures equivalent to the Premium payable on Redemption of Debentures (if any)***

Debenture Redemption Reserve A/c Dr. *(With the amount of*

To Loss on Issue of Debentures A/c *Premium on redemption)*

15. ***For the closure of the Debenture Redemption Reserve Account after all the debentures have been redeemed***

Debenture Redemption Reserve A/c Dr. *[With total]*

To Capital Reserve *[With Profit on Sale of DRRI]*

To General Reserve *[With Balance]*

TUTORIAL NOTES

1. ***Disclosure of Debenture Redemption Reserve Account*** — *Debenture Redemption Reserve A/c shall appear under the head **'Reserves and Surplus'** on the liabilities side of the Balance Sheet till the redemption of the debentures.*
2. ***Disclosure of Debenture Redemption Fund Investment Account*** — *Debenture Redemption Fund Investment A/c shall appear under the head **'Non-Current Investments'** on the assets side of the Balance Sheet till the realisation of the investments.*
3. *In case of redemption of debentures by draw of lots, withdrawal from Debenture Redemption Reserve can be made after Redemption of 10% of the debentures.*

HOW TO CALCULATE THE AMOUNT OF PROFIT TO BE SET ASIDE

The amount of profit to be set aside is to be calculated as follows:

(a) ***If the debentures are to be redeemed at par***

Amount of Profit to be set aside

= Nominal value of Debentures to be redeemed × Present value of ₹ 1 for given number of years at a given rate of interest i.e. $\left[\frac{r}{(1+r)^n - 1}\right]$

or = $\dfrac{\text{Nominal value of Debentures to be redeemed}}{\text{Present value of ₹1 for given number of years at a given rate of interest i.e. } \frac{r}{(1+r)^n - 1}}$

Example: The 4,420, 15% Debentures of ₹ 100 each issued at par are to be redeemed at par after 4 years. Investments are expected to realise 10% p.a. The table shows that ₹ 0.215470803 invested at the end of each year at 10% compound interest will amount to ₹ 1 at the end of 4 years and ₹ 1 p.a. at 10% interest amounts to ₹ 4.641 in 4 years.

SOLUTION

Amount of Profit to set aside = ₹ 4,42,000 × 0.215470803 = ₹ 95,238.09

or, Amount of Profit to be set aside = ₹ 4,42,000/4.641 = ₹ 95,238.09

(b) ***If the debentures are to be redeemed at a premium***

Amount of Profit

= Nominal value of Debentures *plus* Premium on redemption × Present value of ₹ 1 at a given rate of interest

Example: If the aforesaid debentures are to be redeemed at a premium of 5%, then the amount of profits to be set aside will be calculated as follows:

Amount of profit to be set aside

= (₹ 4,42,000 + ₹ 22,100) × (0.215470803) = ₹ 1,00,000

or = (₹ 4,42,000 + ₹ 22,100)/4.641 = ₹ 1,00,000

HOW TO CALCULATE THE AMOUNT OF INVESTMENTS TO BE MADE

The amount of investments to be made may be calculated as follows:

(a) In case the Investments are to be made in multiples of some specific denomination (say ₹ 10, ₹ 20) only, then only that amount which is fully divisible by the given denomination should be invested, e.g., if the amount available for investment is ₹ 95,238.09 and the investments are to be made in the multiple of ₹ 100 only, then only ₹ 95,200 will be invested and the balance of ₹ 38.09 will be kept separately in Debenture Redemption Fund Cash A/c which shall be considered at the time of making the investments during the next period.

(b) In other cases where no specific direction has been given, the amount of profit set aside **(in case of Non-cumulative Debenture Redemption Reserve)** *or* the amount of profit set aside together with the amount of interest received on DRF investments **(in case of Cumulative Debenture Redemption Reserve)** should be invested fully.

Debenture Redemption Fund may be *either* **cumulative or non-cumulative.**

(i) In case of ***Cumulative Debenture Redemption Reserve***, Interest on Debenture Redemption Fund Investments is credited to Debenture Redemption Reserve A/c and interest is reinvested.

(ii) In case of ***Non-cumulative Debenture Redemption Reserve***, Interest on Debenture Redemption Fund Investments is credited to P & L A/c and interest is not reinvested.

Tutorial Note: *No investment should be made in the last year since there is no logic behind first making investments in the last year and then immediately realising the same.*

HOW TO CALCULATE THE AMOUNT OF INTEREST ON DEBENTURE REDEMPTION FUND INVESTMENTS

In general, the amount of interest on Debenture Redemption Fund Investments is calculated on the Opening Balance of Debenture Redemption Fund Investment Account. Following tables may be helpful for this purpose:

Table I showing the Calculation of the Amount of Investments to be made and Interest to be received [when Investments are to be made equal to the Entire Profits set aside]

[*For Example,* Interest Rate = 10%, Profits to be set aside = ₹ 1,00,000, Year of Realisation of Investments — 4th year]

Year	*Opening Balance*	*Interest*	*Savings or Profits set aside*	*Investments*	*Closing Balance*
A	*B*	*C = B × 10/100*	*D*	*E = C + D*	*F = B + E*
20X1-X2	—	—	1,00,000	1,00,000	1,00,000
20X2-X3	1,00,000	10,000	1,00,000	1,10,000	2,10,000
20X3-X4	2,10,000	21,000	1,00,000	1,21,000	3,31,000
20X4-X5	3,31,000	33,100	1,00,000	—	—

Table II showing the Calculation of the Amount of Investments to be made and Interest to be received [when Investments are to be made equal to the nearest multiple of particular denomination say ₹ 10, ₹ 100 etc.]

[*For Example*, Interest Rate = 10%, Profits to be set aside = ₹ 23,701.79, Investments to be made in the nearest multiple of ₹ 100, Year of Realisation of Investments — 4th year]

Year	*Opening Balance*	*Interest*	*Savings or Profits set aside*	*Investments*	*Closing Balance*
A	*B*	*C = B x 10/100*	*D*	*E = C + D*	*F = B + E*
20X1	—	—	23,701.79	23,700	23,700
20X2	23,700	2,370	23,701.79	26,100	49,800
20X3	49,800	4,980	23,701.79	28,700	78,500
20X4	78,500	7,850	23,701.79	—	—

ILLUSTRATION 34

On 1st April 20X1 Tulsian Ltd. issued 4,420, 12% Debentures of ₹ 100 each at a discount of 10% redeemable at a premium of 5% after 4 years. It was decided to institute a Sinking Fund for the purposes of accumulating sufficient funds to redeem the Debentures and to invest in some readily convertible securities yielding 10% interest p.a. Reference to the table shows that ₹ 1.00 p.a. at 10% compound interest amounts to ₹ 4.641 in 4 years. Investments are to be made in the Bonds of ₹ 100 each available at par.

On 31st March 20X5, the investments realised ₹ 3,40,000 and debentures were redeemed. The bank balance as on that date was ₹ 1,00,000.

Required: Give the necessary journal entries and prepare Debenture Redemption Reserve Account and Debentures Redemption Fund Investments Account for 4 years. [Ignore Interest on Debentures and writing off of Discount on Issue of Debentures]

SOLUTION

JOURNAL OF TULSIAN LTD.

Date	*Particulars*	*L.F.*	*Dr. (₹)*	*Cr.(₹)*
01.04.X1	Bank A/c Dr.		3,97,800	
	To Debentures Application A/c			3,97,800
	(Being the receipt of application money)			
	Debenture Application A/c Dr.		3,97,800	
	Loss on Issue of Debentures A/c Dr.		66,300	
	To 12% Debentures A/c			4,42,000
	To Debentures Redemption Premium A/c			22,100
	(Being the issue of 4,420, 12% Debentures of ₹ 100 each at 10% Discount & redeemable at 5% premium)			
31.03.X2	Profit & Loss Appropriation A/c Dr.		1,00,000	
	To Debenture Redemption Reserve A/c			1,00,000
	(Being the transfer of profit to DRR A/c to provide for redemption of debentures)			
	Debenture Redemption Fund Investment A/c Dr.		1,00,000	
	To Bank A/c			1,00,000
	(Being the investments made in the multiples of ₹ 100)			

31.03.X3	Bank A/c	Dr.	10,000	
	To Interest on DRFI A/c			10,000
	(Being the receipt of interest on investments)			
	Interest on DRFI A/c	Dr.	10,000	
	To Debenture Redemption Reserve A/c			10,000
	(Being the transfer of Interest on DRFI to DRR A/c)			
	Profit & Loss Appropriation A/c	Dr.	1,00,000	
	To Debenture Redemption Reserve A/c			1,00,000
	(Being the transfer to profit to DRR A/c to provide for redemption of debentures)			
	Debenture Redemption Fund Investment A/c	Dr.		1,10,000
	To Bank A/c			1,10,000
	(Being the Investment made in the multiples of ₹ 100)			
31.03.X4	Bank A/c	Dr.	21,000	
	To Interest on DRFI A/c			21,000
	(Being the receipt of interest on DRFI)			
	Interest on DRFI A/c	Dr.	21,000	
	To Debenture Redemption Reserve A/c			21,000
	(Being the transfer of Interest on DRFI to DRR A/c)			
	Profit & Loss Appropriation A/c	Dr.	1,00,000	
	To Debenture Redemption Reserve A/c			1,00,000
	(Being the transfer of profit to DRR A/c to provide for the redemption of debentures)			
	Debenture Redemption Fund Investment A/c	Dr.	1,21,000	
	To Bank A/c			1,21,000
	(Being the investments made in the multiples of ₹ 100)			
31.03.X5	Bank A/c	Dr.	33,100	
	To Interest on DRFI A/c			33,100
	(Being the receipt of interest on DRFI)			
	Interest on DRFI A/c	Dr.	33,100	
	To Debenture Redemption Reserve A/c			33,100
	(Being the transfer of Interest on DRFI to DRR A/c)			
	Profit & Loss Appropriation A/c	Dr.	1,00,000	
	To Debenture Redemption Reserve A/c			1,00,000
	(Being the transfer of profit to DRR A/c to provide for the redemption of debentures)			
	Bank A/c	Dr.	3,40,000	
	To Debenture Redemption Fund Investment A/c			3,40,000
	(Being the realisation of Investments)			

	Debenture Redemption Fund Investment A/c To Debenture Redemption Reserve A/c (Being the transfer of profit on sale of Investment)	Dr.	9,000	 9,000
	15% Debentures A/c Debentures Redemption Premium A/c To Debenture-holders' A/c (Being the amount due on redemption)	Dr. Dr.	4,42,000 22,100	 4,64,100
	Debenture-holders' A/c To Bank A/c (Being the payment made to Debenture-holders)	Dr.	4,64,100	 4,64,100
	Debenture Redemption Reserve A/c To Loss on Issue of Debentures A/c (Being the transfer of loss on issue of debentures equal to the amount of premium payable on redemption)	Dr.	22,100	 22,100
	Debenture Redemption Reserve A/c To Capital Reserve A/c To General Reserve A/c (Being the transfer of the Profit to CR and balance in DRR A/c to General Reserve)	Dr.	4,51,000	 9,000 4,42,000

Dr. **DEBENTURES REDEMPTION RESERVE ACCOUNT** *Cr.*

Date	*Particulars*	₹	*Date*	*Particulars*	₹
31.03.X2	To Balance c/d	1,00,000	31.03.X2	By P & L App. A/c	1,00,000
31.03.X3	To Balance c/d	2,10,000	01.04.X2 31.03.X3	By Balance b/d By Interest on DRFI A/c By P & L App. A/c	1,00,000 10,000 1,00,000
		2,10,000			2,10,000
31.03.X4	To Balance c/d	3,31,000	31.04.X3 31.03.X4	By Balance b/d By Interest on DRFI A/c By P & L App. A/c	2,10,000 21,000 1,00,000
		3,31,000			3,31,000
31.03.X5	To Loss on Issue of Debentures A/c (premium) To Capital Reserve A/c To General Reserve A/c	22,100 9,000 4,42,000	01.04.X4 31.04.X5	By Balance b/d By Interest on DRFI A/c By P & L App. A/c By Debenture Red. Fund Investment A/c (Profit)	3,31,000 33,100 1,00,000 9,000
		4,73,100			4,73,100

Dr. **DEBENTURES REDEMPTION FUND INVESTMENT (DRFI) ACCOUNT** Cr.

Date	Particulars	₹	Date	Particulars	₹
31.03.X2	To Bank A/c	1,00,000	31.03.X2	By Balance c/d	1,00,000
01.04.X2	To Balance b/d	1,00,000	31.03.X3	By Balance c/d	2,10,000
31.03.X3	To Bank A/c	1,10,000			
		2,10,000			2,10,000
01.04.X3	To Balance b/d	2,10,000	31.03.X4	By Balance c/d	3,31,000
31.03.X4	To Bank A/c	1,21,000			
		3,31,000			3,31,000
01.04.X4	To Balance b/d	3,31,000	31.03.X5	By Bank A/c (Sales)	3,40,000
31.03.X5	To Debenture Redem. Reserve A/c (Profit)	9,000			
		3,40,000			3,40,000

Working Notes:

(I) CALCULATION OF THE AMOUNT OF PROFIT SET ASIDE

	Particulars	₹
A	Face Value of Debentures	4,42,000
B	Premium Payable on Redemption	22,100
C	Total Amount to be redeemed (A + B)	4,64,100
D	Value of annuity per Re 1	4.641
E	Annual amount of Profits to be set aside (C/D)	1,00,000

(II) CALCULATION OF THE AMOUNT OF INVESTMENTS AND INTEREST

Year A	Opening Balance B	Interest C = B × 10/100	Savings D	Investments E = C + D	Closing Balance F = B + E
20X1-X2	—	—	1,00,000	1,00,000	1,00,000
20X2-X3	1,00,000	10,000	1,00,000	1,10,000	2,10,000
20X3-X4	2,10,000	21,000	1,00,000	1,21,000	3,31,000
20X4-X5	3,31,000	33,100	1,00,000	—	—

ILLUSTRATION 35

Calculate the Profit *or* Loss on sale of Debenture Redemption Reserve Investments in each of the following alternative cases:

Case (a)	Debenture Redemption Reserve	₹ 1,80,000
	(represented by ₹ 2,00,000, 10% Govt. Stock)	
	Investments were sold at 83%	
Case (b)	Debenture Redemption Reserve	₹ 1,80,000
	(represented by ₹ 2,00,000, 10% Govt. Stock)	
	Investment were sold at 95%	

Case (c) Debenture Redemption Reserve	₹ 1,80,000
(represented by ₹ 1,50,000, 10% Govt. Stock purchased at 80% and ₹ 50,000, 10% Govt. Paper)	
Investments were sold as follows:	
10% Govt. Stock at 90%	
10% Govt. Paper at 110%	
Case (d) Debenture Redemption Reserve	₹ 1,80,000
(represented by ₹ 1,50,000 own Debentures purchased at 80% and ₹ 50,000, 10% Govt. Paper)	
10% Govt. Paper realised 110%	
Case (e) Debenture Redemption Reserve	₹ 1,80,000
(represented by ₹ 2,00,000, 10% Govt. Stock)	
₹ 1,50,000, 10% Govt. Stock realised 83% for redemption of a part of debentures.	

SOLUTION

CALCULATION OF PROFIT OR LOSS ON SALE OF DRR INVESTMENTS

A *Case*	*B* *Face Value*	*C* *Cost/Book Value*	*D* *Sale Proceeds*	*E = D – C* *Profit (Loss)*
(a)	2,00,000	1,80,000	1,66,000	(14,000)
(b)	2,00,000	1,80,000	1,90,000	10,000
(c) (i)	1,50,000	1,20,000	1,35,000	15,000
(c) (ii)	50,000	60,000 [₹ 1,80,000 – ₹ 1,20,000]	55,000	(5,000)
(d) (i)	1,50,000	1,20,000	1,50,000	30,000
(d) (ii)	50,000	60,000 [₹ 1,80,000 – ₹ 1,20,000]	55,000	(5,000)
(e)	1,50,000	1,35,000 [1,50,000/2,00,000 × 1,80,000]	1,24,500	(10,500)

ILLUSTRATION 36A [WHEN ALL THE DEBENTURES ARE REDEEMED]

The following balances appeared in the books of X Ltd. as on 1st Jan. 20X5.

9% Debentures	₹ 2,50,000
10% Debentures Redemption Reserve (represented by ₹ 2,00,000, 10% Govt Stock)	₹ 1,80,000

The annual contribution to the Debenture Redemption Reserve was ₹ 50,000 made on 31st Dec. each year. On 31st Dec. 20X5, Balance at Bank before the receipt of interest was ₹ 70,000. On the date all the investments were sold at 95% and the debentures were duly redeemed.

Required: (a) Pass the Journal entries for the year ending 31st Dec. 20X5 (b) Prepare (i) Debentures Redemption Reserve A/c, (ii) Debenture Redemption Reserve Investment A/c (iii) 9% Debentures A/c (iv) Debentureholders' A/c and (v) Bank A/c.

SOLUTION

(A) JOURNAL

Date	Particulars		L.F.	Dr. (₹)	Cr.(₹)
31.12.X5	Bank A/c	Dr.		20,000	
	To Interest on DRRI A/c				20,000
	(Being the receipt of interest on DRRI)				
	Interest on DRRI A/c	Dr.		20,000	
	To Debenture Redemption Reserve A/c				20,000
	(Being the transfer of Interest on DRRI to DRR A/c)				
	Profit & Loss Appropriation A/c	Dr.		50,000	
	To Debenture Redemption Reserve A/c				50,000
	(Being the transfer of profit to DRR A/c to provide for the redemption of debentures)				
	Bank A/c	Dr.		1,90,000	
	To Debenture Redemption Reserve Investment A/c				1,90,000
	(Being the realisation of Investments)				
	Debenture Redemption Reserve Investment A/c	Dr.		10,000	
	To Debenture Redemption Reserve A/c				10,000
	(Being the transfer of profit on sale of Investments)				
	9% Debentures A/c	Dr.		2,50,000	
	To Debenture-holders' A/c				2,50,000
	(Being the amount due on redemption)				
	Debenture-holders' A/c	Dr.		2,50,000	
	To Bank A/c				2,50,000
	(Being the payment made to Debenture-holders)				
	Debenture Redemption Reserve A/c	Dr.		2,60,000	
	To Capital Reserve A/c				10,000
	To General Reserve A/c				2,50,000
	(Being the transfer of Profit to CR A/c & the balance in DRR A/c to General Reserve)				

Ledger Accounts:

Dr. **DEBENTURES REDEMPTION RESERVE ACCOUNT** *Cr.*

Date	Particulars	₹	Date	Particulars	₹
31.12.X5	To Capital Reserve A/c	10,000	01.01.X5	By Balance b/d	1,80,000
	To General Reserve A/c	2,50,000	31.12.X5	By Interest on DRRI A/c (Int. @ 10% on ₹2,00,000)	20,000
			31.12.X5	By P&L Appropriation A/c	50,000
				By DRRI A/c (Profit)	10,000
		2,60,000			2,60,000

Dr. **DEBENTURE REDEMPTION RESERVE INVESTMENT ACCOUNT** Cr.

Date	Particulars	₹	Date	Particulars	₹
01.01.X5	To Balance b/d (Face value ₹2,00,000)	1,80,000	31.12.X5	By Bank A/c (95% of ₹ 2,00,000)	1,90,000
31.12.X5	To DRR A/c (Profit)	10,000			
		1,90,000			1,90,000

Dr. **9% DEBENTURES ACCOUNT** Cr.

Date	Particulars	₹	Date	Particulars	₹
31.12.X5	To Debentureholders' A/c	2,50,000	01.01.X5	By Balance b/d	2,50,000
		2,50,000			2,50,000

Dr. **DEBENTURE-HOLDERS' ACCOUNT** Cr.

Date	Particulars	₹	Date	Particulars	₹
31.12.X5	To Bank A/c	2,50,000	31.12.X5	By 12% Debentures A/c	2,50,000

Dr. **BANK ACCOUNT** Cr.

Date	Particulars	₹	Date	Particulars	₹
31.12.X5	To Balance b/d	70,000	31.12.X5	By Debentures-holders' A/c	2,50,000
31.12.X5	To Interest on DRRI A/c	20,000		By Balance c/d	30,000
31.12.X5	To Debenture Redemption Reserve Investment A/c	1,90,000			
		2,80,000			2,80,000

ILLUSTRATION 36B

Prepare Bank Account in Illustration 36A if the balance at Bank after the receipt of interest was ₹ 70,000.

SOLUTION

Dr. **BANK ACCOUNT** Cr.

Date	Particulars	₹	Date	Particulars	₹
31.12.X5	To Balance b/d	70,000	31.12.X5	By Debentures-holders' A/c	2,50,000
31.12.X5	To Interest on DRRI A/c	—		By Balance c/d	10,000
31.12.X5	To Debenture Redemption Reserve Investment A/c	1,90,000			
		2,60,000			2,60,000

ILLUSTRATION 37 [WHEN A PART OF DEBENTURES IS REDEEMED]

On 1.1.20X5 the Debentures Redemption Reserve of a company showed a balance of ₹ 1,80,000 represented by ₹ 2,00,000, 10% Govt. Stock. On that date the outstanding 9% debentures of the company were ₹ 2,50,000. The annual contribution to Debenture Redemption Reserve was ₹ 50,000.

On 31st Dec. 20X5, the company decided to redeem Debentures of ₹ 1,20,000. For this purpose ₹ 1,50,000 10% Govt. Stock was sold at 83% and debentures were duly redeemed. On 31st Dec. the bank balance before the receipt of interest on investments was ₹ 70,000.

Required: (a) Debentures Redemption Reserve A/c, (b) Debentures Redemption Reserve Investment A/c, (c) Debentures A/c, (d) Debentureholders' A/c and (e) Bank Account.

SOLUTION

Dr. **DEBENTURES REDEMPTION RESERVE ACCOUNT** Cr.

Date	*Particulars*	₹	*Date*	*Particulars*	₹
31.12.X5	To Debenture Redem. Reserve Investment A/c (Loss on sale)	10,500	01.01.X5	By Balance b/d	1,80,000
			31.12.X5	By Interest on DRRI A/c (Int. @ 10% on ₹ 2,00,000)	20,000
	To Balance c/d	2,39,500	31.12.X5	By P&L Appropriation A/c	50,000
		2,50,000			2,50,000

Dr. **DEBENTURE REDEMPTION RESERVE INVESTMENT ACCOUNT** Cr.

Date	*Particulars*	₹	*Date*	*Particulars*	₹
01.01.X5	To Balance b/d (Face value 2,00,000)	1,80,000	31.12.X5	By Bank A/c (83% of ₹ 1,50,000)	1,24,500
			31.12.X5	By Debenture Redemption Reserve A/c	10,500
				By Balance c/d	45,000
		1,80,000			1,80,000

Dr. **9% DEBENTURES ACCOUNT** Cr.

Date	*Particulars*	₹	*Date*	*Particulars*	₹
31.12.X5	To Debentureholders' A/c	1,20,000	01.01.X5	By Balance b/d	2,50,000
	To Balance c/d	1,30,000			
		2,50,000			2,50,000

Dr. **DEBENTURE-HOLDERS' ACCOUNT** Cr.

Date	*Particulars*	₹	*Date*	*Particulars*	₹
31.12.X5	To Bank A/c	1,20,000	31.12.X5	By 12% Debentures A/c	1,20,000

Dr. **BANK ACCOUNT** Cr.

Date	Particulars	₹	Date	Particulars	₹
31.12.X5	To Balance b/d	70,000	31.12.X5	By Debentures-holders' A/c	1,20,000
31.12.X5	To Interest on DRRI A/c	20,000		By Balance c/d	94,500
31.12.X5	To Debenture Redemption Reserve Investment A/c	1,24,500			
		2,14,500			2,14,500

ILLUSTRATION 38

A company had 16,000, 12% debentures of 100 each outstanding as on 1st April, 2014, redeemable on 31st March, 2015. On that day, Sinking fund was ₹ 14,98,000 represented by 2,000 own debentures purchased at the average price of ₹ 99 and 9% stocks face value of ₹ 13,20,000. The annual instalment was ₹ 56,800.

On 31st March, 2015 the investments were realized at ₹ 98 and the debentures were redeemed. You are required to write up the following accounts for the year ending 31si March 2015:

(a) 12% Debentures Account

(b) Debenture Redemption Sinking Fund Account.

SOLUTION

Dr. **(I) 12% DEBENTURES ACCOUNT** Cr.

Particulars	₹	Particulars	₹
To Own Debentures A/c	2,00,000	By Balance b/d	16,00,000
To Bank A/c	14,00,000		
	16,00,000		**16,00,000**

Dr. **(II) DEBENTURE REDEMPTION SINKING FUND ACCOUNT** Cr.

Particulars	₹	Particulars	₹
To 9% Stock A/c (loss)	6,400	By Balance b/d	14,98,000
To General Reserve A/c (b.f.)	16,93,200	By Profit and loss A/c	56,800
		By Interest on Sinking Fund A/c	1,42,800
		By Own Debentures A/c	2,000
	16,99,600		**16,99,600**

Working Notes:

(I) AMOUNT OF STOCK AS ON 1st APRIL, 2015

Sinking Fund Balance as on 1st April, 2010	₹ 14,98,000
Less: Own debentures	₹ (1,98,000)
	₹ 13,00,000

(ii) Sales Value of 9% Stock = (₹ 13,20,000/ ₹ 100) × ₹ 98 = ₹ 12, 93,600

(iii) Interest credited to Sinking Fund = (₹ 13,20,000 × 9%) + (₹ 2,00,000 × 12%)= ₹ 1,42,800

Dr. **(IV) OWN DEBENTURES ACCOUNT** Cr.

Particulars	₹	Particulars	₹
To Balance b/d	1,98,000	By 12% Debentures A/c	2,00,000
To Sinking Fund A/c	2,000		
	2,00,000		**2,00,000**

Dr. **(V) 9% STOCK ACCOUNT** Cr.

Particulars	₹	Particulars	₹
To Balance (Face value 13,20,000)	13,00,000	By Bank A/c	12,93,600
		By Sinking Fund A/c (loss on sales)	6,400
	13,00,000		**13,00,000**

11.0 INSURANCE POLICY METHOD

Under this Method, A Part of Divisible Profits is Set Aside and is Utilized for paying Premium on an Insurance Policy

PRACTICAL STEPS INVOLVED IN THE WORKING OF INSURANCE POLICY METHOD

Step 1: *Make Payment of Insurance Premium in the beginning of each year*

Step 2: *Set aside the amount of profits at the end of each year*

Step 3: *Repeat Step I and Step 2 each year*

Step 4: *Realize the amount of the policy in the year of redemption*

Step 5: *Transfer profit on realisation of policy to Debenture Redemption Fund Account*

Step 6: *Make due the amount payable to Debenture-holders*

Step 7: *Make payment to Debenture-holders*

Step 8: *Transfer unwritten off amount of Loss on Issue of Debentures equivalent to Premium payable on redemption of Debentures (if any), to the debit of Debenture Redemption Fund Account.*

Step 9: *Transfer the balance in Debenture Redemption Fund Account to General Reserve*

JOURNAL ENTRIES

I. During all the years (including last year) till the maturity of the Policy

1. ***For payment of premium at the beginning of the year***

   Debenture Redemption Fund Policy A/c Dr. *(With the amount of annual premium)*

   To Bank A/c

2. ***For setting aside the amount of profit at the end of the year***

   Profit & Loss Appropriation A/c Dr. *(With the amount of profit set aside)*

   To Debentures Redemption Fund A/c

II. During the last year in addition to the above two entries

3. ***For realising the policy amount from the insurance policy***

   Bank A/c Dr. *(With the sum realised)*

   To Debenture Redemption Fund Policy A/c

4. ***For the transfer of the profit/loss on the realisation of the policy***

(a) ***In case of profit***

Debenture Redemption Fund Policy A/c Dr. *(With the profit)*
 To Debenture Redemption Fund A/c

(b) ***In case of loss-reverse of the above entry Is passed.***

5. ***For making due the amount payable to debenture holders***

(a) ***If the Debentures are to be redeemed at par***

Debentures A/c Dr. *(With the amount due)*
 To Debenture-holders' A/c

(b) ***If the Debentures are to be redeemed at a premium***

Debentures A/c Dr. *(With Nominal value)*
Premium on Redemption of Debentures A/c Dr. *(With Premium payable)*
 To Debenture-holders' A/c *(With Total)*

6. ***For Payment to Debenture holders***

Debenture-holders' A/c Dr. *(With the amount paid)*
 To Bank A/c

7. ***For the transfer of unwritten off amount of Loss on Issue of Debentures equivalent to the Premium payable on Redemption of Debentures (If any)***

Debenture Redemption Fund A/c Dr. *(With Premium payable on redemption)*
 To Loss on Issue of Debentures A/c

8. ***For the transfer of the balance In DRF A/c to General Reserve***

Debenture Redemption Fund A/c Dr. *(With the balance left in Debenture Redemption Fund A/c)*
 To General Reserve A/c

TUTORIAL NOTES

1. ***Disclosure of Debenture Redemption Fund Account***

 *Debenture Redemption Fund A/c shall appear under the head **'Reserves and Surplus'** on the liabilities side of the Balance Sheet till the redemption of the debentures.*

2. ***Disclosure of Debenture Redemption Fund Policy Account***

 *Debenture Redemption Fund Policy A/c shall appear under the head **'Non-Current Investments'** on the assets side of the Balance Sheet till the realisation of the policy amount.*

DISTINCTION BETWEEN SINKING FUND METHOD AND INSURANCE POLICY METHOD

The Sinking Fund Method and the Insurance Policy Method can be distinguished as under:

Basis of Distinction	Sinking Fund Method	Insurance Policy Method
1. Timing of Investment	Investments are made **at the end** of the period.	Premium is paid **at the beginning** of the period.
2. Investment during last year	**No** investment is made during the last year.	Premium is paid **even during the last year.**
3. Certainity about the amount to be received	There **does not exist** such certainity because of market fluctuations.	There **exists** certainity about the receipt of a fixed sum at maturity.

4. Immediate liquidity	Funds can be obtained at **any time** by selling the securities in the market.	Funds are available only **at the expiry of the specified period unless the management is ready to accept the surrender value before the date of maturity.**
5. Periodic Income	Periodic income by way interest is **received.**	Periodic income by way of interest is **not received.**

ILLUSTRATION 39

On 01.01.20X1, PCT Ltd. issued 1,500, 15% Debentures of ₹ 100 each at a discount of 10%, redeemable at a premium of 10% after 4 years. It was decided to take out an Insurance Policy (Sum Assured ₹ 1,65,000) to provide the necessary funds for the redemption of the debentures. The annual premium for the policy, payable on 1st January every year, was ₹ 39,000. Give the necessary journal entries. *[Ignore Debenture Interest and wrriting off of Discount on Issue of Debentures]*

SOLUTION

JOURNAL OF PCT LTD.

Date	*Particulars*		*L.F.*	*Dr. (₹)*	*Cr. (₹)*
01.01.X1	Bank A/c	Dr.		1,35,000	
	Loss on Issue of Debentures A/c	Dr.		30,000	
	To 15% Debentures A/c				1,50,000
	To Premium on Redemption of Debentures A/c				15,000
	(Being the issue of debentures at a discount of 10% and redeemable at 10% premium)				
	Debenture Redemption Fund Policy A/c	Dr.		39,000	
	To Bank A/c				39,000
	(Being the payment of annual premium)				
31.12.X1	Profit & Loss Appropriation A/c	Dr.		39,000	
	To Debenture Redemption Fund A/c				39,000
	(Being the transfer of profit to DRF A/c)				
01.01.X2	Debenture Redemption Fund Policy A/c	Dr.		39,000	
	To Bank A/c				39,000
	(Being the payment of annual premium)				
31.12.X2	Profit & Loss Appropriation A/c	Dr.		39,000	
	To Debenture Redemption Fund A/c				39,000
	(Being the transfer of profit to DRF A/c)				
01.01.X3	Debenture Redemption Fund Policy A/c	Dr.		39,000	
	To Bank A/c				39,000
	(Being the payment of annual premium)				
31.12.X3	Profit & Loss Appropriation A/c	Dr.		39,000	
	To Debenture Redemption Fund A/c				39,000
	(Being the transfer of profit to DRF A/c)				

01.01.X4	Debenture Redemption Fund Policy A/c To Bank A/c (Being the payment of annual premium)	Dr.	39,000	 39,000
31.12.X4	Profit & Loss Appropriation A/c To Debenture Redemption Fund A/c (Being the transfer of profit to DRF A/c)	Dr.	39,000	 39,000
	Bank A/c To Debenture Redemption Fund Policy A/c (Being the receipt of policy amount on maturity)	Dr.	1,65,000	 1,65,000
	Debenture Redemption Fund Policy A/c To Debenture Redemption Fund A/c (Being the transfer of profit on the policy toDRF A/c)	Dr.	9,000	 9,000
	15% Debentures A/c Premium on Redemption of Debentures A/c To Debentureholders' A/c (Being the amount due on redemption)	Dr. Dr.	1,50,000 15,000	 165,000
	Debentureholders' A/c To Bank A/c (Being the payment made to Debentureholders)	Dr.	1,65,000	 165,000
	Debenture Redemption Fund A/c To Loss on Issue of Debentures A/c (Being the transfer of loss on Issue of debentures equal to the amount of premium payable on redemption)	Dr.	15,000	 15,000
	Debenture Redemption Fund A/c To General Reserve A/c (Being the transfer of balance in DRF. A/c to General Reserve)	Dr.	1,50,000	 1,50,000

12.0 REDEMPTION OUT OF PROCEEDS OF FRESH ISSUE OF SHARES/DEBEN-TURES

To keep the long term capital and working capital intact, the debentures may be redeemed out of proceeds of fresh issue of shares/debentures.

The following journal entries are required in this case:

1. **On Receipt of Application Money on issue of New Shares/Debentures**

   Bank A/c Dr.

   To Share Application & Allotment A/c

   To Debentures Application & Allotment A/c

2. **On Allotment of New Shares/Debentures**

   Share Application & Allotment A/c Dr.

   Debenture Application & Allotment A/c Dr.

   Discount on Issue of Shares/Debentures A/c Dr. (if any)

To Share Capital A/c		
To Debentures A/c		
To Securities Premium A/c		(if any)
3. **On Making Due on Redemption**		
Debentures A/c	Dr.	
Premium on Redemption of Debentures A/c	Dr.	(if any)
To Debentureholders' A/c		
4. **On Payment on Redemption**		
Debenturreholders' A/c	Dr.	
To Bank A/c		
5. **On writing off Premium on Redemption (if not recorded at the time of issue)**		
Securities premium A/c	Dr.	
Profit & Loss A/c	Dr.	
To Premium on Redemption A/c		

ILLUSTRATION 40

The following is the balance sheet of Tulsian Ltd. as on 1 April 2016:

Particulars	*₹ (lacs)*
50,0000 Equity Shares of ₹ 10 each	5.00
Profit and Loss Account	2.00
General Reserve	1.00
5,000, 12% Debentures of ₹ 100 each	5.00
Sundry creditors	3.00
Fixed Assets	10.00
Current Assets	5.90
Preliminary expenses	.10

The debenture trust deed provides that the company may redeem the debentures at a premium of 6% at any time before maturity. The directiors decided to exercise this option and issued 28,000 shares of ₹ 10 each at ₹ 12.50 per share and 2,000, 14% debentures of ₹ 100 each at ₹ 90 per share for the purpose of redemption. Show the journal entries and post-redemption balance sheet in the prescribed form.

SOLUTION

JOURNAL *[₹ in lacs]*

Date	*Particulars*		*L.F.*	*Dr. (₹)*	*Cr. (₹)*
01.04.2016	Bank A/c	Dr.		3.50	
	To Equity Share Application and Allotment A/c				3.50
	(Being the Receipt of application money on 28.000 shares of ₹ 10 each at ₹ 12.50 per share)				
	Equity Share Application and Allotment A/c	Dr.		3.50	
	To Equity Share Capital A/c				2.80

	To Securities Premium A/c (Being the Allotment of 28,000 shares of ₹ 10 each at ₹ 12.50)			.70
	Bank A/c Dr. To Debenture Application and Allotment A/c (Being the Receipt of debenture application money on 2,000 debentures of ₹ 100 each @ ₹ 90)		1.80	1.80
	Debenture Application and Allotment Account Dr. Discount on Issue of Debentures A/c Dr. To 14% Debentures A/c Being the Allotment of 14% debentures of ₹ 100 each)		1.80 .20	2.00
	12% Debentures A/c Dr. Premium on Redemption of Debentures A/c Dr. To Debentureholders A/c (Being the Amount due on redemption of debentures)		5.00 .30	5.30
	Debentureholders Account Dr. To Bank A/c (Being the Payment to Debentureholders)		5.30	5.30
	Securities Premium A/c Dr. To Premium on Redemption of Debentures A/c To Preliminary Expenses Account To Discount on Issue of Deb. A/c (Being the Writing off the premium on redemption and preliminary expenses & Discount against Securities Premium Account)		.60	.30 .10 .20

BALANCE SHEET OF TULSIAN LTD. AS AT 01.04.2016

	Particulars	*Note No*	*₹ (lacs)*
I.	**Equity and Liabilities**		
	(1) Shareholders'Funds		
	(a) Share Capital (₹ 10 each) [50000 + 28000]		7.80
	(b) Reserves and Surplus	1	3.10
	(2) Non-Current Liabilities[2000,12% Debentures]		2.00
	(3) Current Liabilities		3.00
	Total		15.90
II.	**Assets**		
	(1) Non-Current Assets		
	(a) Fixed Assets		10.00
	(2) Current Assets [5.90 + 3.50 + 1.80 – 5.30]		5.90
	Total		15.90

Notes To Accounts:

Particulars	₹ (lacs)
1. Reserves and Surplus	
General Reserve	1.00
Profit & Loss Account	2.00
Securities Premium	0.10
Total	3.10

13.0 REDEMPTION OF DEBENTURES BY PURCHASE IN THE OPEN MARKET

MEANING OF REDEMPTION OF DEBENTURES BY PURCHASE IN THE OPEN MARKET

When a company purchases its own debentures in the open market for the purposes of cancellation, such an act of purchasing and cancelling the debentures constitutes redemption by purchase in the open market.

The company may purchase its debentures in the open market with the objects of (i) immediate cancellation, *or* (ii) keeping them as Investments. Further these debenture may be purchased (i) on due date of interest, *or* (ii) on any date other than due date of interest. For the purpose of accounting entries, the various cases may be as follows:

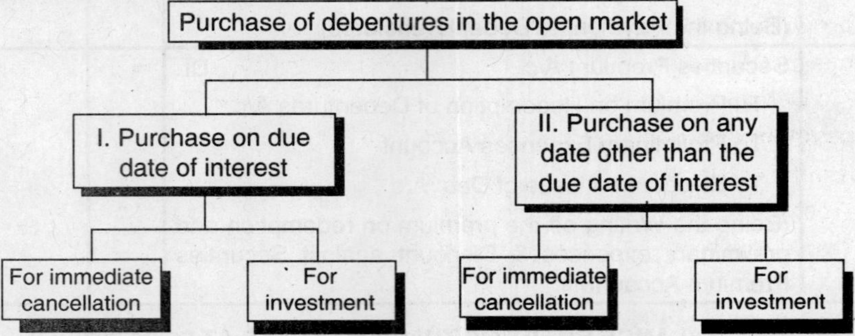

ADVANTAGES OF REDEMPTION OF DEBENTURES BY PURCHASE IN THE OPEN MARKET

This method of redemption is advantageous for several reasons as follows:

1. **Saving equal to the amount of discount** — Purchasing the debentures in the openmarket when they are available at a discount, would enable the company to save money equal to the amount of discount which would have been required to be paid by it in case the debentures are redeemed in the ordinary course.
2. **Reduction in interest burden** — Purchasing the debentures in the open market would also enable the company to reduce the interest burden on debentures purchased in the market and cancelled.
3. **Saving equal to premium payable on redemption** — Purchasing the debentures in the open market would also enable the company to save money equal to the premium which otherwise would have been payable on regular redemption in case of debentures redeemable at premium.

CREATION OF DEBENTURE REDEMPTION RESERVE

Before initiating the purchase of debentures for cancellation, the company must ensure that it has a credit balance of Debenture Redemption Reserve at least equal to 25% of the debenture issue. Unless otherwise stated in the question, it may be assumed that the company has already sufficient amount in the Debenture Redemption Reserve before initiating the purchase of debentures for cancellation by giving a suitable note to that effect.

14.0 ACCOUNTING TREATMENT WHEN DEBENTURES ARE PURCHASED IN THE OPEN MARKET FOR IMMEDIATE CANCELLATION ON DUE DATE OF INTEREST

The accounting entries in such a case will be as follows:

JOURNAL ENTRIES

1. **On purchase of own debentures for immediate cancellation**
   Own Debentures A/c Dr. *[With Purchase Price including Brokerage (if any)]*
   To Bank A/c
2. **On cancellation of Own Debentures**
   Debentures A/c Dr. *[With Nominal Value]*
   To Own Debentures A/c *[With Cost of Own Debentures]*
   To Gain on cancellation of Debentures A/c *[With Gain on Cancellation]*
3. **On transfer of Gain on cancellation**
   Gain on cancellation of Debentures A/c Dr. *[With gain on cancellation]*
   To Capital Reserve A/c
4. **On providing for Interest on Remaining Debentures**
   Interest on Debentures A/c Dr.
   To Debentureholders' A/c
5. **On payment of Interest on Debentures**
   Debentureholders' A/c Dr.
   To Bank A/c
6. **On Transfer of Interest on Debentures**
   Profit & Loss A/c Dr.
   To Interest on Debentures A/c

Tutorial Note: *Unless otherwise stated in the question, it may be assumed that the company has already sufficient amount in the Debenture Redemption Reserve before initiating the purchase of debentures for cancellation by giving a suitable note to that effect.*

ILLUSTRATION 41

On 1st April, 2014, Tulsian Ltd. had 1,000, 12% Debentures of ₹ 100 each. On 1st Oct. 2014, the company purchased 300 Own Debentures at ₹ 93 for immediate cancellation. Interest on debentures is payable half yearly on 30th Sept. and on 31st March.

Pass the necessary journal entries on 1st Oct. and 31st March.

SOLUTION

JOURNAL

Date	Particulars	L.F.	Dr. (₹)	Cr. (₹)
01.10.2014	Own Debentures A/c Dr.		27,900	
	To Bank A/c			27,900
	(Being the purchase of 300 own debentures @ ₹ 93)			

	12% Debentures A/c Dr.		30,000	
	To Own Debentures A/c			27,900
	To Gain on cancellation of Debentures A/c			2,100
	(Being the cancellation of 300 own Debentures)			
	Gain on cancellation of Debentures A/c Dr.		2,100	
	To Capital Reserve A/c			2,100
	(Being the transfer of gain on cancellation of debentures to Capital Reserve)			
31.03.2015	Interest on Debentures A/c Dr.		4,200	
	To Debentureholders' A/c			4,200
	(Being the interest due on debentures)			
	Debentureholders' A/c Dr.		4,200	
	To Bank A/c			4,200
	(Being the interest paid)			
31.03.2015	Profit & Loss A/c Dr.		10,200	
	To Interest on Debentures A/c			10,200
	(Being the transfer of debenture interest to P&L A/c)			

Note: *It is assumed that the company has sufficient amount in the Debenture Redemption Reserve, hence no further entry has been passed in this regard.*

15.0 ACCOUNTING TREATMENT WHEN DEBENTURES ARE PURCHASED IN THE OPEN MARKET FOR INVESTMENT PURPOSE ON DUE DATE OF INTEREST

The accounting entries in such a case will be as follows:

JOURNAL ENTRIES

1. **On purchase of own debentures**

   Investment in Own Debentures A/c Dr. *[With Purchase Price including Brokerage (if any)]*

   To Bank A/c

2. **On Sale of Own Debentures**

   Bank A/c Dr. *[With Net Sale Proceeds]*

   Loss on sale of Investment A/c Dr. *[Loss on Sale of Investments]*

   To Investment in Own Debentures A/c *[With Cost of Own Debentures]*

   To Gain on Sale of Investments A/c *[With Gain on Sale]*

3. **On transfer of Gain on Sale of Investments**

   Gain on Sale of Investments A/c Dr. *[With Gain on Sale]*

   To Profit & Loss A/c

4. **On cancellation of own debentures later on**

   Debentures A/c Dr. *[With Nominal Value]*

   To Investment in Own Debentures A/c *[With Cost]*

   To Gain on Cancellation of Debentures A/c *[With Gain on Cancellation]*

5. **On transfer of Gain on Cancellation**
Gain on Cancellation of Debentures A/c Dr. *[With Gain on Cancellation]*
To Capital Reserve A/c

Tutorial Note: *Unless otherwise stated in the question, it may be assumed that the company has already sufficient amount in the Debenture Redemption Reserve before initiating the purchase of debentures for cancellation by giving a suitable note to that effect.*

ILLUSTRATION 42

On 1st April. 2014, Tulsian Ltd. had 1,000, 12% Debentures of ₹ 100 each. On 1st Oct. 2014, the company purchased 300 Own Debentures at ₹ 93 for the investment purpose and sold the same @ ₹ 99 after few months. Interest on Debentures is payable half yearly on 30th Sept. and on 31st March.

Required: Record the necessary journal entries on date of purchase and sale.

SOLUTION

JOURNAL

Date	*Particulars*		*L.F.*	*Dr. (₹)*	*Cr. (₹)*
01.10.2015	Investment in Own Debentures A/c	Dr.		27,900	
	To Bank A/c				27,900
	(Being the purchase of 300 Own Debentures @ ₹ 93 as investments)				
After few months	Bank A/c	Dr.		29,700	
	To Investment in Own Debentures A/c				27,900
	To Gain on Sale of Investments A/c				1,800
	(Being the sale of investments in Own Debentures @ ₹ 99)				
	Gain on Sale of Investments A/c	Dr.		1,800	
	To Profit & Loss A/c				1,800
	(Being the transfer of gain on sale of Investments)				

16.0 ACCOUNTING TREATMENT WHEN DEBENTURES ARE PURCHASED IN THE OPEN MARKET FOR IMMEDIATE CANCELLATION ON A DATE OTHER THAN THE DUE DATE OF INTEREST

DIVISION OF TOTAL AMOUNT INTO PRINCIPLE AND INTEREST

Total amount to be paid on such debentures is required to be bifurcated as follows:

(a) **Capital Portion (Real Price)** i.e. the payment made towards principal.

(b) **Revenue Portion (Interest)** i.e. the payment made towards interest accrued from the last due date of interest to the date of purchase.

CUM INTEREST PRICE AND EX-INTEREST PRICE

There are two ways of expressing the price quotations:

(a) **Cum Interest Price** — If the interest accrued from the last due date of interest to the date of transaction is **included** in the price quoted, it is called Cum-Interest price which is the total amount paid for the purchase of debentures. Thus,

Cum-Interest Price = Payment towards Capital Portion + Payment towards Interest accrued from the last due date of interest to the date of transaction.

(b) **Ex-Interest Price** — If the interest accrued from the last due date of interest to the date of transaction is not included in the price quoted, it is called Ex-interest price.

Ex-Interest Price = Payment towards Capital Portion

The payment towards capital portion, payment towards interest and total amount paid for the purchase of debenture may be calculated with the help of following table:

Price Quotation A	*Payment towards Interest* B	*Payment towards Capital Portion (i.e. Real Price)* C	*Total Amount Paid* D = B + C
I. Cum-Interest	I = [Nominal Value × Rate/100 × Period/12]	C = Cum-Interest Price — Interest	Cum-Interest Price
II. Ex-Interest	I = [Nominal Value × Rate/100 × Period/12]	C = Ex-Interest Price	Ex-Interest Price + Interest

JOURNAL ENTRIES

1. **On Purchase of own debentures**		
Own Debentures A/c	Dr.	*[Ex-interest price or Real price]*
Interest on Debentures A/c	Dr.	*[Interest accrued]*
To Bank A/c		*[Total Amount paid]*
2. **On cancellation of debentures**		
X% Debentures A/c	Dr.	*[Nominal value of debentures)*
To Own Debentures A/c		*[Ex-interest price]*
To Gain on cancellation of Debentures A/c		*[Nominal value – Ex-Interest Price]*
3. **On Transfer of Gain on cancellation of Debentures**		
Gain on cancellation of Debentures A/c	Dr.	
To Capital Reserve A/c		
4. **On providing for Interest on Remaining Debentures**		
Interest on Debentures A/c	Dr.	
To Debentureholders' A/c		
5. **On payment of Interest on Debentures**		
Debentureholders' A/c	Dr.	
To Bank A/c		
6. **On Transfer of Interest on Debentures**		
Profit & Loss A/c	Dr.	
To Interest on Debentures A/c		

TUTORIAL NOTES

1. *Brokerage (if any payable) is always calculated with reference to the quotation price (whether cum-interest or ex-interest) of the transaction.*
2. *Interest is always calculated with reference to the face value (or nominal value) of the debentures.*

3. *Unless otherwise stated, the price quotation will be treated as 'Cum-interest' quotation in case of debentures issued by companies.*
4. *Unless otherwise stated in the question, it may be assumed that the company has already sufficient amount in the Debenture Redemption Reserve before initiating the purchase of debentures for cancellation by giving a suitable note to that effect.*

ILLUSTRATION 43 [IN CASE OF EX-INTEREST QUOTATION]

Calculate the Total amount paid for the purchase of debentures in each of the following alternative cases:

Case (a) On 1st Jan, X Ltd. purchased 300, 12% Debentures of ₹ 100 each at ₹ 93 ex-interest. The interest is payable half yearly on 30th June and 31st December.

Case (b) On 1st May, X Ltd. purchased 300, 12% Debentures of ₹ 100 each at ₹ 93 ex-interest. The interest is payable half yearly on 30th June and 31st December.

Case (c) On 30th June, X Ltd. purchased 300, 12% Debentures of ₹ 100 each at ₹ 93 ex-interest. The interest is payable half yearly on 30th June and 31st December.

SOLUTION

TABLE SHOWING THE TOTAL AMOUNT PAID

Case A	*Interest Accrued from last due date to the date of purchase* B	*Ex-Interest Amount or Real Price* C	*Total Amount Paid* D = B + C
(a)	₹ 30,000 × 12/100 × 0/12 = 0	300 × ₹ 93 = 27,900	₹ 27,900 + 0 = ₹ 27,900
(b)	₹ 30,000 × 12/100 × 4/12 = ₹ 1,200	300 × ₹ 93 = 27,900	27,900 + 1,200 = ₹ 29,100
(c)	₹ 30,000 × 12/100 × 6/12 = ₹ 1,800	300 × ₹ 93 = 27,900	27,900 + 1,800 = ₹ 29,700

ILLUSTRATION 44 [IN CASE OF CUM-INTEREST QUOTATION]

Calculate the Real Price paid for the purchase of debentures in each of the following alternative cases:

Case (a) On 1st Jan, X Ltd. purchased 300, 12% Debentures of ₹ 100 each at ₹ 93 Cum-interest. The interest is payable half yearly on 30th June and 31st December.

Case (b) On 1st May, X Ltd. purchased 300, 12% Debentures of ₹ 100 each at ₹ 93 Cum-interest. The interest is payable half yearly on 30th June and 31st December.

Case (c) On 30th June, X Ltd. purchased 300, 12% Debentures of ₹ 100 each at ₹ 93 Cum-interest. The interest is payable half yearly on 30th June and 31st December.

SOLUTION

TABLE SHOWING THE REAL PRICE PAID

Case A	*Interest Accrued from last due date to the date of purchase* B	*Cum-Interest Amount or Total Amount Paid* C	*Real Price or Ex-Interest Amount* D = C – B
(a)	₹ 30,000 ×12/100 × 0/12 = 0	300 × ₹ 93 = 27,900	₹ 27,900 – 0 = ₹ 27,900
(b)	₹ 30,000 × 12/100 × 4/12 = ₹ 1,200	300 × ₹ 93 = 27,900	27,900 – 1,200 = ₹ 26,700
(c)	₹ 30,000 × 12/100 × 6/12 = ₹ 1,800	300 × ₹ 93 = 27,900	27,900 – 1,800 = ₹ 26,100

ILLUSTRATION 45

On 1st Jan. 2014, Tulsian Ltd. had 1,000, 12% Debentures of ₹ 100 each. Interest on debentures is payable half yearly on 30th June and on 31st December. On 1st May 2014, the company purchased 300 Own Debentures at ₹ 93 ex-interest for immediate cancellation.

Required: Record the necessary journal entries on May 1 and June 30, 2014.

SOLUTION

JOURNAL OF TULSIAN LTD.

Date	Particulars		L.F.	Dr. (₹)	Cr. (₹)
01.05.14	Own Debentures A/c	Dr.		27,900	
	Interest on Debentures A/c	Dr.		1,200	
	To Bank A/c				29,100
	(Being the purchase of 300 Own Debentures @ ₹ 93 Ex-Interest)				
	12% Debentures A/c	Dr.		30,000	
	To Own Debentures A/c				27,900
	To Gain on cancellation of Debentures A/c				2,100
	(Being the cancellation of 300 own Debentures)				
	Gain on cancellation of Debentures A/c	Dr.		2,100	
	To Capital Reserve A/c				2,100
	(Being the transfer of gain on cancellation of debentures to Capital Reserve)				
30.06.14	Interest on Debentures A/c	Dr.		4,200	
	To Debentureholders' A/c				4,200
	(Being the interest due on debentures)				
	Debentureholders' A/c	Dr.		4,200	
	To Bank A/c				4,200
	(Being the interest paid)				

Working Notes:

1. Interest accrued on debentures purchased from the last due date to the date of purchase
   = ₹ 30,000 × 12/100 × 4/12 = 1,200
2. Total amount paid = Ex-interest Amount + Interest Accrued
   = (300 × ₹ 93) + ₹ 1,200 = ₹ 29,100
3. Gain on Cancellation = Nominal Value – Ex-Interest Amount
   = ₹ 30,000 – ₹ 27,900 = ₹ 2,100
4. It is assumed that the company has sufficient amount in the Debenture Redemption Reserve, hence no further entry has been passed in this regard.

ILLUSTRATION 46

On 1st Jan. 2014, Tulsian Ltd. had 1,000, 12% Debentures of ₹ 100 each. Interest on debentures is payable half yearly on 30th June and on 31st December. On 1st May 2014, the company purchased 300 Own Debentures at ₹ 97 Cum-interest for immediate cancellation.

Required: Record the necessary journal entries on May 1 and June 30, 2014.

SOLUTION

JOURNAL OF TULSIAN LTD.

Date	*Particulars*		*L.F.*	*Dr. (₹)*	*Cr. (₹)*
01.05.14	Own Debentures A/c	Dr.		27,900	
	Interest on Debentures A/c	Dr.		1,200	
	To Bank A/c				29,100
	(Being the purchase of 300 Own Debentures @ ₹ 97 Cum-Interest)				
	12% Debentures A/c	Dr.		30,000	
	To Own Debentures A/c				27,900
	To Gain on cancellation of Debentures A/c				2,100
	(Being the cancellation of 300 own Debentures)				
	Gain on cancellation of Debentures A/c	Dr.		2,100	
	To Capital Reserve A/c				2,100
	(Being the transfer of gain on cancellation of debentures)				
30.06.14	Interest on Debentures A/c	Dr.		4,200	
	To Debentureholders' A/c				4,200
	(Being the interest due on debentures)				
	Debentureholders' A/c	Dr.		4,200	
	To Bank A/c				4,200
	(Being the interest paid)				

Working Notes:

1. Interest accrued on debentures purchased from the last due date to the date of purchase
   = ₹ 30,000 × 12/100 × 4/12 = ₹ 1,200
2. Total Amount paid = Cum-interest Amount = 300 × ₹ 97 = ₹ 29,100
3. Ex-interest Amount paid = Cum-interest Amount – Interest Accrued
   = ₹ 29,100 – ₹ 1,200 = ₹ 27,900
4. Gain on Cancellation = Nominal Value – Ex-Interest Amount = ₹ 30,000 – ₹ 27,900 = ₹ 2,100
5. It is assumed that the company has sufficient amount in the Debenture Redemption Reserve, hence no further entry has been passed in this regard.

17.0 ACCOUNTING TREATMENT WHEN DEBENTURES ARE PURCHASED IN THE OPEN MARKET FOR INVESTMENT PURPOSE ON A DATE OTHER THE THAN DUE DATE OF INTEREST

TREATMENT OF 'INTEREST ON DEBENTURES' ON DUE DATE OF INTEREST

Interest	*Debited to*	*Credited to*
(a) Interest on Own Debentures held by the company	Interest on Debentures A/c	Interest on Own Debentures A/c
(b) Interest on Debentures held by outsiders	Interest on Debentures A/c	Debentureholders' A/c

CLOSURE OF INTEREST ON OWN DEBENTURES ACCOUNT

At the end of accounting, period, 'Interest on Own Debentures Account' is closed by transferring it to the credit side of profit & loss account.

CLOSURE OF INTEREST ON DEBENTURES ACCOUNT

'Interest on Debentures Account' is closed by transferring it to the debit side of Profit & Loss Account

JOURNAL ENTRIES

1. **On Purchase of Own Debentures**

   Own Debentures A/c Dr. *[Ex-Interest Price or Real Price]*

   Interest on Debentures A/c Dr. *[Interest Accrued]*

   To Bank A/c *[Total Amount paid]*

2. **Providing Interest on debentures:**

   Interest on Debentures A/c Dr. *[Total interest on debentures held by outsiders as well as by company itself]*

   To Debentureholders' A/c *[Interest on the debentures held by outsiders]*

   To Interest on Own Debentures A/c *[Interest on Debentures held by Co.]*

3. **On payment of Interest on Debentures**

   Debentureholders' A/c Dr. *[Amount of interest paid to outsiders]*

   To Bank A/c

4. **On transfer of Interest on Debentures to P&L A/c**

   Profit & Loss A/c Dr.

   To Interest on Debentures A/c

5. **On transfer of Interest on Own Debentures to Profit & Loss Account**

   Interest on Own Debentures A/c Dr.

   To Profit & Loss A/c

ILLUSTRATION 47

On 1st Jan. 2014, Tulsian Ltd. had 1,000, 12% Debentures of ₹ 100 each. Interest on debentures is payable half yearly on 30th June and on 31st December. On 1st May 2014, the company purchased 300 Own Debentures at ₹ 93 Ex-interest for the investment purpose and sold the same @ ₹ 99 cum-interest after six months.

Required: Record the necessary journal entries upto date of sale.

SOLUTION

JOURNAL

Date	*Particulars*		*L.F.*	*Dr. (₹)*	*Cr. (₹)*
01.05.14	Own Debentures A/c	Dr.		27,900	
	Interest on Debentures A/c	Dr.		1,200	
	To Bank A/c				29,100
	(Being the purchase of 300 Own Debentures @ ₹ 93 ex-interest as investments)				

30.06.14	Interest on Debentures A/c Dr.		4,800	
	To Debentureholders' A/c			4,200
	To Interest on Own Debentures A/c			600
	(Being the interest due on debentures)			
	Debentureholders' A/c Dr.		4,200	
	To Bank A/c			4,200
	(Being the interest paid on debentures held by outsiders)			
01.11.14	Bank A/c Dr.		29,700	
	To Own Debentures A/c			27,900
	To Interest on Own Debentures A/c			1,200
	To Gain on Sale of Investments A/c			600
	(Being the sale of investments in Own Debentures @ ₹ 99 cum-interest)			
	Gain on Sale of Investments A/c Dr.		600	
	To Profit & Loss A/c			600
	(Being the transfer of gain on sale of Investments)			

Working Notes:

1. Interest accrued on debentures purchased from the last due date to the date of purchase
   = ₹ 30,000 × 12/100 × 4/12 = ₹ 1,200
2. Total amount paid = Ex-interest Amount = Interest Accrued
   = (300 × ₹ 93) + ₹ 1,200 = ₹ 29,100
3. Interest accrued on debentures sold from the last due date to the date of purchase
4. Total Amount received = Cum-interest Amount = 300 × ₹ 99 = ₹ 29,700
   = ₹ 30,000 × 12/100 × 4/12 = ₹ 1,200
5. Ex-interest Amount received = Cum-interest Amount × Interest Accrued
   = ₹ 29,700 – ₹ 1,200 = ₹ 28,500
6. Gain on Sale of Investment = Ex-interest Amt. received – Book Value of Investments sold
   = ₹ 28,500 – ₹ 27,900 = ₹ 600

ILLUSTRATION 48

On 1.1.2014, X Ltd had 1,000 12% Debentures of ₹ 100 each and Debentures Redemption Reserve ₹ 45,000. In accordance with the powers in the deed, the following debentures were purchased in the open market during the year ended 31st Dec. 2014.

1st May 300 Debentures @ ₹ 97 cum-Interest

1st Aug. ₹ 20,000 nominal purchased for ₹ 19,350 Ex-Interest

Interest on debentures is payable half-yearly on 30th June and on 31st Dec.

Required: Give the necessary journal entries assuming that the own debentures purchased by the company (a) were cancelled immediately and (b) were cancelled on 31st Dec. 2014.

SOLUTION

(a) *If Own Debentures were cancelled immediately on date of purchase*

JOURNAL OF X LTD.

Date	*Particulars*		*L.F.*	*Dr. (₹)*	*Cr. (₹)*
01.05.14	Profit & Loss Appropriation A/c	Dr.		5,000	
	To Debenture Redemption Reserve A/c				5,000
	(Being the transfer of profits to DRR so as to have balance in DRR A/c equal to at least 50% of debentures issue)				
01.05.14	Own Debentures A/c	Dr.		27,900	
	Interest on Debentures A/c	Dr.		1,200	
	To Bank A/c				29,100
	(Being the purchase of 300 debentures @ ₹ 97 cum-interest for cancellation)				
01.05.14	12% Debentures A/c	Dr.		30,000	
	To Own Debentures A/c				27,900
	To Gain on cancellation of Debentures A/c				2,100
	(Being 300 Own Debentures cancelled by purchase @ ₹ 97 cum-interest)				
01.05.14	Gain on cancellation of Debentures A/c	Dr.		2,100	
	To Capital Reserve A/c				2,100
	(Being the transfer of gain on cancellation of debentures)				
30.06.14	Interest on Debentures A/c	Dr.		4,200	
	To Debentureholders' A/c				4,200
	(Being the interest due on ₹ 70,000 @ 12% p.a. for 6 months)				
	Debentureholders' A/c	Dr.		4,200	
	To Bank A/c				4,200
	(Being the interest paid on Debentures)				
2014	Own Debentures A/c	Dr.		19,350	
Aug. 1	Interest on Debentures A/c	Dr.		200	
	To Bank A/c				19,550
	(Being the purchase of 200 debentures for ₹ 19,350 Ex-interest for cancellation)				
Aug. 1	12% Debentures A/c	Dr.		20,000	
	To Own Debentures A/c				19,350
	To Gain on Cancellation of Debentures A/c				650
	(Being the 200 debentures cancelled by purchase @ ₹ 19,350 Ex-interest)				

Dec. 31	Gain on cancellation of Debentures A/c Dr.		650	
	To Capital Reserve A/c			650
	(Being the t/f of gain on cancellation of debentures)			
Dec. 31	Interest on Debentures A/c Dr.		3,000	
	To Debentureholders' A/c			3,000
	(Being the interest due on ₹ 50,000 @ 12% p.a. for 6 months)			
	Debentureholders' A/c Dr.		3,000	
	To Bank A/c			3,000
	(Being the interest paid on Debentures)			
Dec. 31	Profit & Loss A/c Dr.		8,600	
	To Interest on Debentures A/c			8,600
	(Being the transfer of debenture interest to P&L A/c)			

(b) *If Own Debentures were cancelled on 31st December.*

JOURNAL OF X LTD.

Date	*Particulars*	*L.F.*	*Dr. (₹)*	*Cr. (₹)*
2014 May 1	Own Debentures A/c Dr.		27,900	
	Interest on Debentures A/c Dr.		1,200	
	To Bank A/c			29,100
	(Being the purchase of 300 debentures @ ₹ 97 cum-interest)			
June 30	Interest on Debentures A/c Dr.		4,800	
	To Debentureholders' A/c			4,200
	To Interest on Own Debentures A/c			600
	(Being the interest due on ₹ 70,000 for 6 months & on ₹ 30,000 for 2 months)			
	Debentureholders' A/c Dr.		4,200	
	To Bank A/c			4,200
	(Being the interest paid on Debentures)			
Aug. 01	Own Debentures A/c Dr.		19350	
	Interest on Debentures A/c Dr.		200	
	To Bank A/c			19,550
	(Being the purchase of 200 debentures for ₹ 19,350)			
Dec 31	Interest on Debentures A/c Dr.		5,800	
	To Debentureholders' A/c			3,000
	To Interest on own Debentures A/c			2,800
	(Being the interest due on ₹ 30,000 for 6 months)			
	Debentureholders' A/c Dr.		3,000	
	To Bank A/c			3,000
	(Being the interest paid on Debentures)			

Dec. 31	Profit & Loss A/c	Dr.	12,000	
	To Interest on Debentures A/c			12,000
	(Being the tranmsfer of debenture interest to P & L A/c)			
Dec. 31	Interest on Own Debentures A/c	Dr.	3,400	
	To Profit & Loss A/c			3,400
	(Being the transfer of interest on Own Debentures to P & L A/c)			
Dec. 31	Profit & Loss Appropriation A/c	Dr.	5,000	
	To Debenture Redemption Reserve A/c			5,000
	(Being the transfer of profits to DRR so as to have balance in DRR A/c equal to at least 50% of debentures issue)			
Dec. 31	12% Debentures A/c	Dr.	50,000	
	To Own Debentures A/c			47,250
	To Gain on Cancellation of Debentures A/c			2,750
	(Being the cancellation of 500 own debentures)			
Dec. 31	Gain on Cancellation of Debentures A/c	Dr.	2,750	
	To Capital Reserve A/c			2,750
	(Being the transfer of gain on cancellation of Debentures)			

ILLUSTRATION 49

NSC Ltd. has an authorised capital of ₹ 300 crores divided into equity shares of ₹ 10 each and its Balance Sheet as at March 31, 2014 was as follows:

Particulars	*[₹ in lakhs]*
Share Capital Issued and fully paid-up	100
General Reserve	20
8% Debentures	40
Sundry Creditors	20
Fixed Assets	120
Current Assets	30
Own Debentures (nominal value (₹ 10 lakhs)	9
Cash at Bank	21

The company decided:

1. To redeem the 8% debentures due for redemption on September 30, 2014 and also to cancel its Own Debentures. [Due Date of Interest: 30th Sept. & 31st Mar.]
2. To pay interest to debentureholders being due on the date of redemption.

Required: Record necessary entries to give effect to the above transactions.

SOLUTION

JOURNAL OF NSC LTD.

[₹ in lakhs]

Date	*Particulars*		*L.F.*	*Dr. (₹)*	*Cr. (₹)*
30.9.14	Interest on Debentures A/c	Dr.		1.60	
	To Debentureholders A/c [30 × 8% × 6/12]				1.20
	To Interest on Own Debentures A/c [10 × 8% × 6/12]				0.40
	(Being the interest due on debenture outstanding including own debentureholders as investments)				
	Debentureholders' A/c	Dr.		1.20	
	To Bank A/c				1.20
	(Being the payment of interest to debentureholders)				
	General Reserve A/c	Dr.		20	
	To Debenture Redemption Reserve A/c				20
	(Being the transfer of General Reserve to DRR to have 50% of the debenture issue)				
30.9.14	8% Debentures A/c [40 – 10]	Dr.		30	
	To Debentureholders' A/c				30
	(Being the amount due on redemption)				
	Debentureholders' A/c	Dr.		30	
	To Bank A/c				30
	(Being the payment made to debentureholders)				
	8% Debentures A/c	Dr.		10	
	To Own Debentures A/c				9
	To Gain on cancellation of Debentures A/c				1
	(Being the cancellation of own debentures)				
	Gain on Cancellation of Debentures A/c [10 – 9]	Dr.		1	
	To Capital Reserve A/c				1
	(Being the Gain on cancellation of debentures transferred to capital reserve)				
31.3.15	Interest on own Debentures A/c	Dr.		0.4	
	To Profit and Loss A/c				0.4
	(Being the transfer of interest on own debentures to Profit and Loss Account)				
31.3.15	Profit and Loss A/c	Dr.		1.60	
	To Interest on Debentures A/c				1.60
	(Being the transfer of debenture interest to Profit and loss account)				

ILLUSTRATION 50

Arjun Ltd. issued 10,000 (Nos.) of 12% Debentures *or* ₹.100 each in April, 2010. Interest is payable on 30th September and 31st March every year. The company purchased 2,000 debentures at ₹ 104 per debenture on cum-interest basis on 1.7.2011. The own debentures were cancelled on 30.9.2012. Show Journal entries that are required to be passed for purchase of own debentures, interest on own debentures and for cancellation of those debentures.

SOLUTION

JOURNAL

Date	*Particulars*	*L.F.*	*Dr. (₹)*	*Cr. (₹)*
1.7.2011	12% Own Debentures A/c Dr.		2,02,000	
	Interest on Own Debentures A/c Dr.		6,000	
	To Bank A/c			2,08,000
	(Being purchase of 12% own debenture on cum interest basis)			
30.9.2011	12% Debenture Interest A/c Dr.		60,000	
	To Bank A/c			48,000
	To Interest on Own Debentures A/c			12,000
	(Being interest on Debentures including own debentures upto 30th Sept.)			
31.3.2011	1 2% Debenture Interest A/c Dr.		60,000	
	To Bank A/c			48,000
	To Interest on Own Debentures A/c			12,000
	(Being interest on Debentures including own debentures upto 31st Mar.)			
30.9.2012	1 2% Debenture Interest A/c Dr.		60,000	
	To Bank A/c			48,000
	To Interest on Own Debentures A/c			12,000
	(Being interest on Debentures including own debentures upto 30th Sept.)			
30.9.2012	12% Debentures A/c Dr.		2,00,000	
	Loss on cancellation of 12% Debentures A/c Dr.		2,000	
	To 12% Own Debentures A/c			2,02,000
	(Being cancellation of 2,000 own debentures)			
30.9.2012	Profit and Loss A/c Dr.		2,000	
	To Loss on cancellation of 12% Debentures A/c			2,000
	(Being loss on cancellation transferred)			

ILLUSTRATION 51

Rama Limited issued 8% Debentures of ₹ 3,00,000 in earlier year on which interest is payable half yearly on 31st March and 30th September. The company has power to purchase its own debentures in the open market for cancellation there of. The following purchases were made during the financial year 2011-12 and cancellation made on 31st March, 2012:

(a) On 1st April, ₹ 50,000 nominal value debentures purchased for ₹ 49,450, ex-interest.

(b) On 1sl September, ₹ 30,000 nominal value debentures purchased for ₹ 30,250 cum interest.

Show the Journal Entries (without narrations) for the transactions held in the year 2011-2012.

SOLUTION

JOURNAL OF RAMA LIMITED

Date	Particulars		L.F.	Dr. (₹)	Cr. (₹)
01.04.11	Own Debentures A/c	Dr.		49,450	
	To Bank A/c				49,450
01.09.11	Own Debentures A/c	Dr.		29,250	
	Interest on Debentures A/c [30,000 × 8% × 5/12]	Dr.		1,000	
	To Bank A/c				30,250
30.09.11	Interest on Debentures A/c	Dr.		11,000	
	To Bank A/c				8,800
	To Interest on Own Debentures A/c				2,200
31.03.10	Interest on Debentures A/c	Dr.		12,000	
	To Bank A/c				8,800
	To Interest on own debentures A/c				3,200
31.03.12	8% Debentures A/c	Dr.		80,000	
	To Own Debentures A/c				78,700
	To Profit on cancellation of Debentures A/c				1,300
	Interest on Own Debentures A/c	Dr.		5,400	
	To Profit and Loss A/c (3,200 + 3,200 – 1,000)				5,400
	Profit and Loss A/c (1,000 + 12,000)	Dr.		24,000	
	To Interest on Debentures A/c				24,000
	Profit on cancellation of Debentures A/c	Dr.		1,300	
	To Capital Reserve A/c				1,300

ILLUSTRATION 52

Himalayas Ltd. had ₹ 10,00,000, 8% Debentures of ₹ 100 each as on 31st March, 2012. The company purchased in the open market following debentures for immediate cancellation:

On 01-07-2012-1,000 Debentures @ ₹ 97 (cum interest), On 29-02-2013-1,800 Debentures @ ₹ 99 (ex interest), Debenture interest due date is 30th September and 31st March.

Give Journal Entries in the books of the company for the year ended 31st March, 2013.

SOLUTION

JOURNAL

Date	Particulars		L.F.	Dr. (₹)	Cr. (₹)
01.07.12	Own Debentures A/c	Dr.		95,000	
	Debenture Interest A/c [1,000 × 100 × 8% × (3/12)]	Dr.		2,000	
	To Bank A/c				97,000
	(Being 1,000 Debentures purchased @ ₹ 97 cum interest for immediate cancellation)				

01.07.12	8% Debentures A/c	Dr.	1,00,000	
	To Own Debentures A/c			95,000
	To Capital Reserve A/c			5,000
	(Being profit on cancellation of own Debentures t/f)			
30.09.12	Debenture Interest A/c [9,000 × 100 × 8% × (1/2)]	Dr.	36,000	
	To Debenture holders A/c			36,000
	(Being interest accrued on 9,000 Debentures)			
	Debentureholders A/c	Dr.	36,000	
	To Bank A/c			36,000
	(Being interest amount paid)			
29.02.13	Own Debentures A/c	Dr.	1,78,200	
	Debenture Interest A/c [1,800 × 100 × 8% × (5/12)]	Dr.	6,000	
	To Bank A/c			1,84,200
	(Being the Purchase of 1,800 Debentures @ ₹ 99 ex interest for immediate cancellation)			
29.02.13	8% Debentures A/c	Dr.	1,80,000	
	To Own Debentures A/c			1,78,200
	To Capital Reserve A/c			1,800
	(Being the Profit on cancellation of own Debentures t/f)			
31.03.13	Debentures Interest A/c [7,200 × 100 × 8% × (1/2)]	Dr.	28,800	
	To Debentureholders A/c			28,800
	(Being interest accrued on 7,200 Debentures)			
31.3.13	Profit and Loss A/c	Dr.	72,800	
	To Debentures Interest A/c			72,800
	(Being interest on debentures for the year transferred)			

18.0 ACCOUNTING ENTRIES WHEN SINKING FUND EXISTS AND OWN DEBENTURES ARE PURCHASED FOR IMMEDIATE CANCELLATION

1. **On Sale of Debentures Redemption Fund Investments**

Bank A/c	Dr.	*[Total Amount Received]*
To Debenture Redemption fund Investment A/c		*[Ex-Interest Amount]*
To Interest on Debenture Red. Fund Investment A/c		*[Accrued Interest]*

2. **On Transfer of Profit on sale of DRFI (other than own Deb.)**

Deb Red. Fund Investment A/c	Dr.	*[With Profit]*
To Debenture Redemption Fund A/c		

3. **On Purchase of Own Debentures for immediate cancellation**

Debentures A/c	Dr.	*[Nominal value]*
Interest on Debentures A/c	Dr.	*[Interest accrued]*
To Bank A/c		*[Total Amount paid]*
To Profit on cancellation of Debentures A/c		*[Nominal value – Ex-Interest Price]*

4.	**On Transfer of Profit on cancellation of Debentures**		
	Profit on cancellation of Debentures A/c	Dr.	
	To Capital Reserve A/c		
5.	**On Providing for Interest on Remaining Debentures**		
	Interest on Debentures A/c	Dr.	
	To Debentureholders' A/c		
6.	**On Payment of interest on Debentures**		
	Debentureholders' A/c	Dr.	
	To Bank A/c		
7.	**On Transfer of Interest on Debentures**		
	Profit & Loss A/c	Dr.	
	To Interest on Debentures A/c		
8.	**On Receipt of Interest on DRFI (other than own Debentures)**		
	Bank A/c	Dr.	
	To Interest on DRFI		
9.	**On Transfer of Interest on DRFI**		
	Interest on DRFI A/c	Dr.	
	To Debenture Redemption fund A/c		

Note: *Before initiating the cancellation of debentures, it must be ensured that the Debenture Redemption Reserve Account has a credit balance at least equal to 50% of the debenture issue.*

19.0 ACCOUNTING ENTRIES WHEN SINKING FUND EXISTS AND OWN DEBENTURES ARE PURCHASED FOR INVESTMENT PURPOSES.

1.	**On Sale of Debentures Redemption fund investments**		
	Bank A/c	Dr.	*[Total Amount Received]*
	To Debenture Redemption fund Investment A/c		*[Ex-Interest Amount]*
	To Interest on Debenture Red. Fund Investment A/c		*[Accrued Interest]*
2.	**On Transfer of Profit on sale of DRFI (other than own Deb.)**		
	Deb Red. Fund Investment A/c	Dr.	*[With Profit]*
	To Debenture Redemption Fund A/c		
3.	**On Purchase of Own Debentures as Investments**		
	DRFI (Own Debentures) A/c	Dr.	*[Ex-Interest Price of Real Price]*
	Interest on Debentures A/c	Dr.	*[Interest Accrued]*
	To Bank A/c		*[Total Amount paid]*
4.	**Providing Interest on debentures:**		
	Debentures Interest A/c	Dr.	*[Total interest on debentures held by outsiders as well as by co. itself]*
	To Debentureholders' A/c	Dr.	*[Interest on the debentures held by outsiders]*
	To Interest on Own Debenture A/c		*[Interest on Debentures held by company itself]*

5. **On payment of Interest on Debentures**

Debentureholders' A/c Dr. *[Amt. of interest paid to outsiders]*

To Bank A/c

6. **On transfer of Interest on Debentures to P&L A/c**

Profit & Loss A/c Dr.

To Interest on Debentures A/c

7. **On transfer of Interest on Own Debentures to DRF Account**

Interest on Own Debentures A/c Dr.

To Debenture Redemption Fund A/c

8. **On Receipt of Interest on DRFI (other than own Debentures)**

Bank A/c Dr.

To Interest on DRFI

9. **On Transfer of Interest on DRFI**

Interest on DRFI A/c Dr.

To Debenture Redemption fund A/c

10. **On Cancellation of DRFI (Own Debentures) Later on**

Debentures A/c Dr.

Interest on Debentures A/c Dr.

To DRFI (own Debentures) A/c

To Profit on cancellation of Debentures A/c

11. **On Transfer of Profit on cancellation of Debentures**

Profit on cancellation of Debentures A/c Dr.

To Capital Reserve A/c

Note: *Before initiating the cancellation of debentures, it must be ensured that the Debenture Redemption Reserve Account has a credit balance at least equal to 50% of the debenture issue.*

ILLUSTRATION 53 PROFIT/LOSS ON SALE OF DEBENTURE REDEMPTION FUND INVESTMENTS

The following balances appeared in the books X Ltd. as on 1st Jan. 2012

1. 6% Debentures (Face value ₹ 100 each) ₹ 2,00,000
2. Debenture Redemption Fund Account ₹ 1,00,000
3. Debenture Redemption Fund Investment represented by ₹ 50,000 own debentures purchased, @ ₹ 90 and the remaining amount by ₹ 60,000, 6% Govt. Securities.

On 1.5.2012, the company sold the Govt. Securities of the face value ₹ 20,000 @ ₹ 95 Ex-Interest and applied the proceeds realised in purchasing 200 own debentures.

Required: Journalise the sale and purchase transactions in each of the following alternative cases:

Case (a) The Interest on Debentures is payable on 30th June and 31st December & Interest on 6% Govt. Securities is receivable in the same dates.

Case (b) The Interest on Debentures is payable on 30th June and 31st Dec. & the interest on Govt. Securities is receivable on 31st March & 30 September.

SOLUTION

Case (a)

JOURNAL OF X LTD.

Date	*Particulars*	*L.F.*	*Dr. (₹)*	*Cr. (₹)*
2012				
May 1	Bank A/c Dr.		19,400	
	To Debenture Red. Fund Invsts. A/c (Govt. Security)			19,000
	To Interest on DRFI A/c			400
	(Being Sale of Govt. Securities ₹ 20,000 @ ₹ 95 ex. Interest)			
	Debenture Redemption Fund Investment A/c Dr.		667	
	To Debenture Redemption Fund A/c			667
	(Being the transfer of Profit on Sale of Govt. Securities)			
	DRFI (own Debentures) A/c Dr.		19,000	
	Debenture Interest A/c Dr.		400	
	To Bank A/c			19,400
	(Being Purchase of own Deb. ₹ 20,000 @ ₹ 97 cum interest)			

Working Notes:

1. CALCULATION OF THE BOOK VALUE OF GOVT. SECURITIES SOLD

	Particulars	₹
A	Book Value of Total Investments	1,00,000
B	*Less:* Book Value of Own Debentures (₹ 50,000 × 90/100)	45,000
C	Book Value of Total Govt. Securities (Face Value ₹ 60,000)	55,000
D	Book Value of Govt. Securities Sold (₹ 55,000 × ₹ 20,000/₹ 60,000)	18,333

2. CALCULATION OF TOTAL SALES PROCEEDS OF SALE OF GOVT. SECURITY

	Particulars	₹
A	Ex-Sale Proceeds (₹ 20,000 × 95/100)	19,000
B	*Add:* Interest Accrued on ₹ 20,000 for 4 months (₹ 20,000 × 4/12 × 6/100)	400
C	Cum-Sale Proceeds (A + B)	19,400

3. CALCULATION OF PROFIT ON SALE OF GOVT SECURITIES

	Particulars	₹
A	Ex-Sale Proceeds	19,000
B	*Less:* Book Value of Govt. Securities Sold	18,333
C	Profit on Sale (A – B)	667

4. CALCULATION OF ACTUAL COST OF OWN DEBENTURES PURCHASED ON 1ST MAY

	Particulars	₹
A	Cum-Purchase Price Paid for 200 own Debentures	19,400
B	*Less:* Interest Accrued on ₹ 20,000 own Debentures for 4 months (₹ 20,000 × 4/12 × 6/100)	400
C	Actual Cost Price of Debentures Purchased (A – B)	19,000

Case (b)

JOURNAL OF X LTD.

Date	*Particulars*	*L.F.*	*Dr. (₹)*	*Cr. (₹)*
2012				
May 01	Bank A/c Dr.		19,100	
	To Debenture Red. Fund Invsts. (Govt. securities) A/c			19,000
	To Interest on DRFI A/c			100
	(Being the sale of Govt. Securities of ₹ 20,000 @ ₹ 95 Ex-Interest)			
	Debenture Redemption Fund Investment A/c Dr.		667	
	To Debentures Redemption Fund A/c			667
	(Being the transfer of profit in sale of Govt. Securities)			
	Debenture Redumption Fund Investments (own Debentures) A/c Dr.		18,700	
	Debenture Interest A/c Dr.		400	
	To Bank A/c			19,100
	(Being the purchase of 200 own Debentures @ ₹ 95.5 cum-interest)			

Working Notes:

1. CALCULATION OF THE BOOK VALUE OF GOVT. SECURITIES SOLD

	Particulars	₹
A	Book Value of Total Investments	1,00,000
B	*Less:* Book Value of own Debenture (₹ 50,000 × 90/100)	45,000
C	Book Value of Total Govt. Securities (Fact Value ₹ 60,000)	55,000
D	Book Value of Govt. Securities Sold (₹ 55,000 × ₹ 20,000/₹ 60,000)	18,333

2. CALCULATION OF TOTAL SALE PROCEEDS OR SALE OF GOVT. SECURITIES

	Particulars	₹
A	Ex-Sale Proceeds on a/c of Cost (₹ 20,000 × 95/100)	19,000
B	*Add:* Interest Accrued on ₹ 20,000 for 1 month (₹ 20,000 × 1/2 × 6/100)	100
C	Cum-Sale Proceeds (A + B)	19,100

3. CALCULATION OF PROFIT ON SALE OF GOVT-SECURITIES

	Particulars	₹
A	Ex-Sale Proceeds	19,000
B	*Less:* Book Value of Govt Securities Sold	18,333
C	Profit on Sale (A — B)	667

4. CALCULATION OF ACTUAL COST OF OWN DEBENTURES PURCHASED ON 1ST MAY

	Particulars	₹
A	Cum Purchase Price Paid for 200 Debentures	19,100
B	*Less:* Interest Accrued on ₹ 20,000 Own Debentures Purchased for 4 months (₹ 20,000 × 4/12 × 6/100)	400
C	Actual Cost Price of Debentures purchased (A — B)	18,700

ILLUSTRATION 54

The following balances appeared in the books of CSS Ltd. as on 1.1.2012

12% Debentures (face Value ₹ 100)	₹ 1,00,000
Debenture Redemption Fund	₹ 37,500
Debenture Redemption Fund Investment A/c (represents 8% Govt. Securities of the face value of ₹ 45,000)	₹ 37,500

On 1.3.2012, this Company purchased 125 debentures in the market @ ₹ 93 Ex. out of funds raised by selling 8% Govt. Securities of the face value of ₹ 13,500. On 31.12.2012, ₹ 10,400 was appropriated for the Sinking Fund which together with the interest received on Sinking fund during the year was invested in 8% Govt. securities of the face value of ₹ 14,000. The Interest on debenture was payable on 30th June and 31st December and interest on 8% Govt. Securities was receivable on the same dates

Required: Give the necessary journal Entries & ledger accounts assuming that the own debentures purchased in the market (a) were cancelled immediately & (b) were retained as investments.

SOLUTION

(a) *If Debentures were cancelled immediately on date of purchase*

JOURNAL

Date	*Particulars*	*L.F.*	*Dr. (₹)*	*Cr. (₹)*
2012				
Mar. 01	Bank A/c Dr.		11,875	
	To Debenture Redemption Fund Investment A/c			11,695
	To Interest on Deb. Red. Fund Investment A/c			180
	(Being DRF Investments realised for ₹ 11,875 cum interest)			
	Debenture Redemption Fund Investment A/c Dr.		445	
	To Debenture Redemption Fund A/c			445
	(Being the transfer of Profit on Sale of DRF Investments to DRF A/c)			

	12% Debentures A/c Dr.		12,500	
	Debenture Interest A/c Dr.		250	
	To Bank A/c			11,875
	To Capital Reserve A/c			875
	(Being 125 Debentures cancelled)			
June 30	Debenture Interest A/c Dr.		5,250	
	To Bank A/c			5,250
	(Being Interest Paid on ₹ 87,500 @ 12% for 6 months)			
	Bank A/c Dr.		1,260	
	To Interest on DRFI A/c			1,260
	(Being interest on ₹ 31,500 @ 8% p.a for 6 month)			
Dec. 31	Debenture Interest Dr.		5,250	
	To Bank A/c			5,250
	(Being Interest Paid on ₹ 87,500 @ 12% for 6 months)			
	Bank A/c Dr.		1,260	
	To Interest on DRFI A/c			1,260
	(Being interest on ₹ 31,500 @ 8% p.a for 6 months)			
	Profit & Loss A/c Dr.		10,750	
	To Debenture Interest A/c			10,750
	(Being the transfer of Deb. Interest to P & L A/c)			
	Inerest on DRFI A/c Dr.		2,700	
	To DRF A/c			2,700
	(Being the transfer of Interest on DRFI to DRF A/c)			
	P & L Appropriation A/c Dr.		10,400	
	To DRF A/c			10,400
	(Being the transfer of annual profit to DRF A/c)			
	DRF Investments A/c Dr.		13,100	
	To Bank A/c			13,100
	(Being investments made)			

Ledger Accounts:

Dr. **12% DEBENTURES ACCOUNT** *Cr.*

Date	*Particulars*	₹	*Date*	*Particulars*	₹
2012			2012		
Mar. 01	To Bank A/c	11,625	Jan 01	By Balance b/d	1,00,000
	To Capital Reserve A/c	875			
Dec. 31	By Balance c/d	87,500			
		1,00,000			1,00,000

Dr. **DEBENTURE REDEMPTION FUND ACCOUNT** Cr.

Date	Particulars	₹	Date	Particulars	₹
2012			2012		
Dec 31	To Balance c/d	51,045	Jan. 01	By Balance b/d	37,500
			Mar. 01	By DRFI A/c	445
			Dec. 31	By Interest on DRFI A/c	2,700
				By P & L Appr. A/c	10,400
		51,045			51,045

Dr. **DEBENTURE REDEMPTION FUND INVESTMENTS ACCOUNT** Cr.

Date	Particulars	₹	Date	Particulars	₹
2012			2012		
Jan. 01	To Balance b/d	37,500	Mar. 01	By Bank A/c	11,695
	(Face Value ₹ 45,000)			(Face Value ₹ 13,500)	
Mar. 01	To DRF A/c	445	Dec. 31	By balance c/d	39,350
Dec. 31	To Bank A/c	13,100		(Face Value ₹ 40,500)	
	(Face Value ₹ 14,000)				
		51,045			51,045

Dr. **DEBENTURE INTEREST ACCOUNT** Cr.

Date	Particulars	₹	Date	Particulars	₹
2012			2012		
Mar. 01	To Bank A/c	250	Dec. 31	By P & L A/c	10,750
June 30	To Bank A/c	5,250			
Dec. 31	To Bank A/c	5,250			
		10,750			10,750

Working Notes:

1. CALCULATION OF TOTAL PAYMENT MADE FOR THE PURCHASE OF 125 DEBENTURES

	Particulars	₹
A	Cost of 125 debentures @ ₹ 93	11,625
B	Interest on ₹ 12,500 @ 12% for 2 months	250
C	Total Payment made (A + B)	11,875

2. CALCULATION OF THE PROFIT ON SALE OF 8% GOVT. SECURITIES

	Particulars	₹
A	Total proceeds Received	11,875
B	*Less:* Interest on ₹ 13,500 @ 8% for 2 months	180
C	Net proceeds of Investments (A – B)	11,695
D	Book value of 8% Govt. Securities sold (₹ 37,500 × ₹ 13,500/₹ 45,000)	11,250
E	Profit on Sale of Investment (C – D)	445

Note: *Unless otherwise stated, price equation is assumed to cum-interest as in case of Sale of Govt. Securities.*

(b) *If Debentures were retained as Investments*

JOURNAL OF X LTD.

Date	Particulars		L.F.	Dr. (₹)	Cr. (₹)
2012					
Mar. 01	Bank A/c	Dr.		11,875	
	To Debenture Redemption Fund Investment A/c				11,695
	To Interest on Deb. Red. Fund Investment A/c				180
	(Being DRF Investments realised for ₹ 11,875 cum interest)				
	Debenture Redemption Fund Investment A/c	Dr.		445	
	To DRF A/c				445
	(Being the transfer of Profit on Sale of DRF Investments to DRF A/c)				
	DRF Investments (own Deb.) A/c	Dr.		11,625	
	Debenture Interest A/c	Dr.		250	
	To Bank A/c				11,875
	(Being purchase of 125 deb. @ ₹ 93 ex-Interest)				
June 30	Debenture Interest A/c	Dr.		5,750	
	To Debenture Redemption Fund A/c				500
	To Bank A/c				5,250
	(Bank Interest due on ₹ 87,500 for 6 months & on ₹ 12,500 for 4 months @ 12% p.a.)				
	Bank A/c	Dr.		1,260	
	To Interest on DRF Investment A/c				1,260
	(Being Interest received on ₹ 31,500 @8% for 6 months)				
Dec. 31	Debentures Interest	Dr.		6,000	
	To Debenture Redemption Fund A/c				750
	To Bank A/c				5,250
	(Being Interest paid on 875 Debentures held by outsiders & credited on 125 Debentures held as DRF Investment to DRF A/c)				
	Bank A/c	Dr.		1,260	
	To Interest on DRF Investment A/c				1,260
	(Being Interest received on ₹ 31,500 @ 8% for 6 months)				
	Profit & Loss A/c	Dr.		12,000	
	To Debenture Interest A/c				12,000
	(Being the transfer of of Deb. Interest to P & L A/c)				

	Interest on DRFI A/c	Dr.	2,700	
	To DRF A/c			2,700
	(Being the transfer of Interest on DRFI to DRF A/c)			
	P&L Appropriation A/c	Dr.	10,400	
	To Debenture Redemption Fund A/c			10,400
	(Being the transfer of annual profit to DRF A/c)			
	Debenture Redemption Fund Investments A/c	Dr.	14,350	
	To Bank A/c			14,350
	(Being the investments made)			

Dr. **12% DEBENTURES ACCOUNT** *Cr.*

Date	Particulars	₹	Date	Particulars	₹
2012			2012		
Dec. 31	To Balance c/d	1,00,000	Jan. 01	By Balance b/d	1,00,000
		1,00,000			1,00,000

Dr. **DEBENTURE REDEMPTION FUND ACCOUNT** *Cr.*

Date	Particulars	₹	Date	Particulars	₹
2012			2012		
Dec. 31	To Balance c/d	52,295	Jan. 01	By Balance b/d	37,500
			Mar. 01	By DRFI A/c	445
			June 30	By Debenture Interest	500
			Dec. 31	By Deben. Interest A/c	750
			Dec. 31	By Interest on DRFI A/c	2,700
			Dec. 31	By P&L App.	10,400
		52,295			52,295

Dr. **DEBENTURE REDEMPTION FUND INVESTMENTS ACCOUNT (GOVT. SECURITIES)** *Cr.*

Date	Particulars	₹	Date	Particulars	₹
2012			2012		
Jan. 01	To Balance b/d (face value ₹ 45,000)	37,500	Mar. 01	By Bank A/c (face value ₹ 13,500)	11,695
Mar. 01	To DRF A/c	445	Dec. 31	By Balance c/d (face value 40,500)	40,600
Dec. 31	To Bank A/c (face value 14,000)	14,350			
		52,295			52,295

Dr. **DEBENTURE REDEMPTION FUND INVESTMENTS (OWN DEBENTURE) ACCOUNT** *Cr.*

Date	Particulars	₹	Date	Particulars	₹
2012			2012		
Mar. 01	To Bank A/c		Dec. 31	By Balance	11,625

	(face value 12,500)	11,625			
		11,625			11,625

Dr. **DEBENTURE INTEREST ACCOUNT** Cr.

Date	Particulars	₹	Date	Particulars	₹
2012			2012		
Mar. 01	To Bank A/c	250	Dec. 31	By P & L A/c	12,000
June 30	To Debenture Red.				
	Fund A/c	500			
June 30	To Bank A/c	5,250			
Dec. 31	To Debenture Red.				
	Fund A/c	750			
Dec. 31	To Bank A/c	5,250			
		12,000			12,000

ILLUSTRATION 55

CAS Ltd., issued 50,000 6% Debentures of ₹ 100 each on Ist January, 2009. The Debentures are redeemable by the creation of a Sinking Fund. The company had the right to call upon the Trustee to apply the Sinking Fund monies in purchasing own Debentures, if available below par. The following information is given:

(a) The annual appropriation is ₹ 50,000.

(b) Sinking Fund Balance as on 1st January, 2012 was ₹ 1,31,942 represented by 6% State Loan at cost of ₹ 74,262 (face value ₹ 80,000) and Sinking Fund cash ₹ 7,680. This cash balance together with the annual appropriation of ₹ 50,000 was invested in 6% State Loan. The loan bond, purchased cum interest, had a face value of Rupees 60,000.

(c) 1st September, 2012 sold the State Loan of the face value ₹ 40,000 out of loan held on 1st January 2012 for ₹ 38,000 (ex-interest) and the proceeds were applied in purchasing own debentures (face value ₹ 45,000 cum-interest).

(d) The debentures purchased are cancelled on 31st December.

(e) Interest on State Loan is received 31st March and 30th September.

(f) Interest on Debentures is paid on 30th June and 31st December.

(g) Debentures outstanding as on 1st January, 2012 were ₹ 4,67,000.

Required: Make ledger entries in the books of the company to give effect to the above.

SOLUTION

Dr. **SINKING FUND ACCOUNT** Cr.

Date	Particulars	₹	Date	Particulars	₹
2012			2012		
Dec. 31	To General Reserve t/f	45,000	Jan. 01	By Balance b/d	1,31,942
Dec. 31	To Balance c/d	1,52,761	Sept. 01	By Sinking Fund	
				Investment A/c,	
				(profit on sale)	869

			Dec. 31	By Own Debentures, (profit on concellation)	6,450
			Dec. 31	By Interest on S.F. Investments A/c	8,500
			Dec. 31	By Profit & Loss A/c	50,000
		1,97,761			1,97,761

Dr. **SINKING FUND INVESTMENT ACCOUNT 6% STATE LOAN** Cr.

Date	Particulars	Face Value ₹	Cost ₹	Date	Particulars	Face Value ₹	Cost ₹
2012				2012			
Jan. 01	To Balance b/d	80,000	74,262	Sept. 01	By S. Fund Cash	40,000	38,000
Jan. 01	To S. Fund Cash	60,000	56,780	Dec. 31	By Balance c/d	1,00,000	93,911
Sept. 01	To Sinking Fund A/c, profit on sale (assumed, FIFO basis)		869				
		1,40,000	1,31,911			1,40,000	1,31,911

Dr. **OWN DEBENTURES (S.F.) ACCOUNT** Cr.

Date	Particulars	Face Value ₹	Cost ₹	Date	Particulars	Face Value ₹	Cost ₹
2012				2012			
Sept. 01	To S. Fund (Cash)	45,000	38,550	Dec. 31	By Debentures A/c (cancellation)	45,000	45,000
	To Sinking Fund A/c (profit)		6,450				
		45,000	45,000			45,000	45,000

Dr. **INTEREST ON S.F. INVESTMENT ACCOUNT** Cr.

Date	Particulars	₹	Date	Particulars	₹
2012			2012		
Jan. 01	To Balance b/d (Accrued Intt. on ₹ 80,000 for 3 months)	1,200	Mar. 31	By S. Fund Cash A/c (on ₹ 1,40,000 for 6 months)	4,200
Jan. 01	To S. Fund Cash A/c (on ₹ 60,000 for 3 months)	900	Sept. 01	By S. Fund Cash A/c (Interest on ₹ 40,000 for 5 months)	1,000
Dec. 31	To Sinking Fund A/c, (transfer)	8,500	Sept. 30	By S. Fund Cash A/c (Interest on ₹1,00,000 for 6 months)	3,000
			Dec. 31	By Deb. Interest (on ₹ 45,000 for 4 months)	900

			Date	Particulars	₹
			Dec. 31	By Balance c/d (Accrued Interest on ₹1,00,000 for 3 mon.	1,500
		10,600			10,600

Dr. **DEBENTURE INTEREST ACCOUNT** Cr.

Date	Particulars	₹	Date	Particulars	₹
2012			2012		
June 30	To Bank A/c	14,010	Dec. 31	By P&L A/c (transfer)	28,020
Sept. 01	To S. Fund Cash A/c (Interest on ₹ 45,000 Deben. for 2 months)	450			
Dec. 31	By Bank A/c	12,660			
	By Interest on S.F. Investments A/c (on ₹ 45,000 for 4 months)	900			
		28,020			28,020

Dr. **SINKING FUND CASH ACCOUNT** Cr.

Date	Particulars	₹	Date	Particulars	₹
2012			2012		
Jan. 01	To Balance b/d	7,680	Jan. 01	By Interest on S.F. Investment A/c (on ₹ 60,000 for 3 months @ 6% p.a.)	900
	To Bank, A/c	50,000		By S.F. Investment A/c (6% State Loan)	56,780
Mar. 31	To Interest on S.F. Investments A/c	4,200	Sept. 01	By Debenture Interest A/c	450
Sept. 01	To S.F. Investment A/c (6% State Loan)	38,000	Sept. 01	By Own Debentures (S.F.) A/c	38,550
Sept. 01	To Interest on S.F. Investments	1,000	Dec. 31	By Balance c/d	7,200
Sept. 30	To Interest on S.F. Investments A/c	3,000			
		1,03,880			1,03,880

Dr. **6% DEBENTURES ACCOUNT** Cr.

Date	Particulars	₹	Date	Particulars	₹
2012			2012		
Dec. 31	To Own Debentures (S.F.) A/c	45,000	Jan. 01	By Balance b/d	4,67,000

	To Balance c/d	4,22,000			
		4,67,000			4,67,000

Working Notes:

1. The amount to be invested on Jan. 1, 2012 is ₹ 57,680; ₹ 60,000 6% State Loan has been purchased. Interest till date on this loan is ₹ 900; this has been debited to the Interest of S.F. Investments Account and the balance; ₹ 56,780, debited to the S.F. Investments Account.
2. The total amount realised by sale ₹ 40,000 State loan on Sept. 1, 2012 is ₹ 39,000 i.e. ₹ 38,000 *plus* ₹ 1,000 interest for 5 months on ₹ 40,000.
3. ₹ 39,000 is utilized for purchase of ₹ 45,000 own debentures the interest till date is ₹ 450 debited to Debenture Interest Account- the balance ₹ 38,550 is debited to Own Debentures (S.F) A/c.

SOLVED PROBLEMS

PROBLEM 1

On January 2012, CAS Ltd., had outstanding in its books 500 Debentures of ₹ 100 each interest at 6% per annum. In accordance with the powers in the deed, the directors acquired in the open market Debentures for immediate cancellation as follows:

March 1 ₹ 5,000 @ ₹ 98.00 (cum interest)

Aug. 1 ₹ 10,000 @ ₹ 100.25 (cum interest)

Dec. 15 ₹ 2,500 @ ₹ 98.50 (ex-interest)

Debenture interest is payable half-yearly, on 30th June and 31st December.

Reqiored: Show ledger account of Debentures, Debenture Interest and Profit *or* Loss on cancellation, ignoring income-tax.

SOLUTION

1st Half Year

Dr. **6% DEBENTURES ACCOUNT** *Cr.*

Date	*Particulars*	₹	*Date*	*Particulars*	₹
2012			2012		
Mar. 01	To Bank A/c		Jan. 01	By Balance b/d	50,000
	Deb. Purchased 4,850				
	P&L on cancellation of				
	Debentures A/c 150	5,000			
June 30	To Balance c/d	45,000			
		50,000			50,000

Dr. **PROFIT & LOSS ON CANCELLATION OF DEBENTURES ACCOUNT** *Cr.*

Date	*Particulars*	₹	*Date*	*Particulars*	₹
2012			2012		
June 30	To Capital Reserve A/c	150	Mar. 01	By 6% Debentures A/c	150

Dr. **DEBENTURE INTEREST ACCOUNT** *Cr.*

Date	Particulars	₹	Date	Particulars	₹
2012			2012		
Mar. 01	To Bank A/c (Interest for 2 months on ₹ 5,000 Debentures)	50	June 30	By P & L A/c	1,400
June 30	To Debenture-holders A/c (Interest)	1,350			
		1,400			1,400

Dr. **DEBENTURE-HOLDERS' (INTEREST) ACCOUNT** *Cr.*

Date	Particulars	₹	Date	Particulars	₹
2012			2012		
June 30	To Bank A/c	1,350	June 30	By Deb. Interest A/c (Int. on ₹ 45,000 @ 6% upto 30th June)	1,350
		1,350			1,350

2nd Half Year

Dr. **6% DEBENTURES ACCOUNT** *Cr.*

Date	Particulars	₹	Date	Particulars	₹
2012			2012		
Aug. 01	To Bank, (Debentures Purchased) 9,975 P&L on Cancellation 25	10,000	July 01	By Balance b/d	45,000
Dec. 15	To Bank A/c Debentures Purchased 2,462.50 P&L on Cancellation of Debentures 37.50	2,500			
Dec. 31	To Balance c/d	32,500			
		45,000			45,000

Dr. **PROFIT & LOSS CANCELLATION OF DEBENTURES ACCOUNT** *Cr.*

Date	Particulars	₹	Date	Particulars	₹
2012			2012		
Dec. 31	To Capital Reserve	62.50	Aug. 01	By Debenture A/c	25.00
			Dec. 15	By Debenture A/c	37.50
		62.50			62.50

Dr. **DEBENTURE INTEREST ACCOUNT** Cr.

Date	Particulars	₹	Date	Particulars	₹
2012			2012		
Aug. 01	To Bank A/c (Interest for one month on ₹ 10,000)	50.00	Dec. 31	By Profit & Loss A/c	1,093.75
Dec. 15	To Bank A/c	68.75			
Dec. 31	To Deben. holders' A/c	975.00			
		1,093.75			1,093.75

Dr. **DEBENTURE HOLDERS' (INTEREST) ACCOUNT** Cr.

Date	Particulars	₹	Date	Particulars	₹
2012			2012		
Dec. 31	To Bank A/c	975.00	Dec. 31	By Debenture Interest A/c (on ₹ 32,500 @ 6% for 6 months)	975.00
		975.00			975.00

PROBLEM 2

CAS Limited issued ₹ 1,50,000, 5 per cent Debentures on which interest is payable half yearly on 31st March and 30th September. The company has power to purchase debentures in the open market for cancellation thereof. The following purchases were made during the year ended 31st December 2012 and the cancellation were made on the following 31st March·

1st March ₹ 25,000 nominal purchased for ₹ 24,725 ex-interest.

1st September ₹ 20,000 nominal purchased for ₹ 20,125 cum-interest.

You are required to draw up the following accounts up to the date of cancellation:

(i) Debenture Account;

(ii) Own Debenture Investment Account; and

(iii) Debenture Interest Account.

Ignore taxation and make calculations to the nearest rupee.

SOLUTION

CAS LIMITED

Dr. **5% DEBENTURES ACCOUNT** Cr.

Date	Particulars	₹	Date	Particulars	₹
2012			2012		
Dec. 31	To Balance c/d	1,50,000	Jan. 01	By Balance b/d	1,50,000
2013			2013		
Mar. 31	To Own Debentures A/c	45,000	Jan. 01	By Balance b/d	1,50,000
	To Balance c/d	1,05,000			
		1,50,000			1,50,000

Dr. **DEBENTURE INTEREST ACCOUNT** Cr.

Date	Particulars		₹	Date	Particulars	₹
2012				2012		
Mar. 31	To Bank A/c (on ₹ 1,25,000 for 6 months)		3,125	Jan. 01	By Accrued Interest (on ₹ 1,50,000 @ 5% for 3 months)	1,875
	To Interest on Own Debentures		625		By Profit & Loss A/c	7,500
Sept. 30	To Bank A/c (₹ 1,05,000 @ 5% for 6 months)		2,625	Dec. 31		
	To Interest on Own Debentures A/c		1,125			
Dec. 31	To Interest Accrued A/c (on ₹ 105,000 for 3 months)	1,312				
	Own Debentures of (on ₹ 45,000 for 3 months)	563	1,875			
			9,375			9,375
2013				2013		
March 31	To Bank A/c (on ₹ 1,05,000 for 6 months)		2,625	Jan. 01	By Interest Accrued	1,875
	To Interest on Own Debenture A/c (on ₹ 45,000 for 6 months)		1,125	Mar. 31	By Profit and Loss A/c	1,875
			3,750			3,750

Dr. **OWN DEBENTURE INVESTMENT ACCOUNT** Cr.

Date	Particulars	Nominal ₹	Interest ₹	Cost ₹	Date	Particulars	Nominal ₹	Interest ₹	Cost ₹
2012					2012				
Mar. 01	To Bank A/c	25,000	521	24,725	Mar. 31	By Debenture Interest A/c	—	625	—
Sep. 01	To Bank A/c	20,000	417	19,708	Sept. 30	By Debenture Interest A/c	—	1,125	—
Dec. 31	To P&L A/c		1,375		Dec. 31	By Balance c/d	45,000	563	44,433
		45,000	2,313	44,433			45,000	2,313	44,433
2013					2013				
Jan. 01	To Balance b/d	45,000	563	44,433	Mar. 31	By Debenture Interest	—	1,125	—
Mar. 31	To Capital Reserve					By 5% Debentures A/c	45,000	—	45,000
	(Profit on cancellation)	—	—	567					
	To Profit and Loss A/c		562						
		45,000	1,125	45,000			45,000	1,125	45,000

PROBLEM 3

(i) Swati Associates Ltd. has issued 10,000 12% Debentures of ₹ 100 each on 1.1.2011. These Debentures are redeemable after 3 years at a premium of ₹ 5 per Debenture. Interest is payable annually.

(ii) On October 1, 2012 it buys 1,500 debentures from the market @ ₹ 98 per Debenture. These are sold away on June 30, 2013 at ₹ 105 per Debenture.

(iii) On January 1, 2013, it buys 1,000 debentures @ ₹ 104 per debenture from the open market. These are cancelled on April 1, 2013.

(iv) On October 1, 2013 it buys 2,000 debentures @ ₹ 106 per debenture from the open market. These debentures along with other debentures are redeemed on 31st December 2013.

Required: Prepare the relevant Ledger Account showing the above transactions. Workings should from part of your answer (Assume all transactions are ex-interest).

SOLUTION

Dr. **12% OWN DEBENTURES ACCOUNT** *Cr.*

Date	*Particulars*	*Interest* ₹	*Amount* ₹	*Date*	*Particulars*	*Interest* ₹	*Amount* ₹
2012				2012			
Oct. 01	To Bank (₹ 1,50,000)	13,500	1,47,000	Dec. 31	By Debenture Int. A/c	18,000	
	To P&L A/c	4,500			By Balance c/d		1,47,000
		18,000	1,47,000			18,000	1,47,000
2013				2013			
Jan. 01	To Balance b/d		1,47,000	Apr. 01	By Debenture Int. A/c	3,000	
Jan. 01	To Bank A/c		1,04,000		By 12% Deb A/c		1,00,000
Apr. 01	To P&L A/c	3,000			By P&L A/c		4,000
June 30	To P&L A/c	9,000	10,500	Jun 30	By Bank A/c	9,000	1,57,500
Oct. 01	To Bank A/c (₹ 2,00,000)	18,000	2,12,000	Dec. 31	By Deb. Int. A/c	24,000	
Dec. 31	To P&L A/c	6,000			By 12% Deb. A/c (cancelled)		2,00,000
					By P&L A/c		12,000
		36,000	4,73,500			36,000	4,73,500

Note: *The amount of such Interest has been calculated from the previous 1st January to the date of transaction since the Interest is payable annually.*

Dr. **DEBENTURE INTEREST ACCOUNT** *Cr.*

Date	*Particulars*	₹	*Date*	*Particulars*	₹
2011			2011		
Dec. 31	To Bank A/c	1,20,000	Dec. 31	By Profit & Loss A/c	1,20,000
		1,20,000			1,20,000
2012			2012		
Dec. 31	To Bank A/c	1,02,000	Dec. 31	By Profit & Loss A/c	1,20,000
	To Int. on Own Deb.	18,000			
		1,20,000			1,20,000

2013			2013		
April	To Int. on Own Debentures A/c	3,000	Dec. 31	By Profit & Loss A/c	1,11,000
Dec. 31	To Int. on Own Debentures A/c	24,000			
	To Bank A/c (on ₹ 7,00,000)	84,000			
		1,11,000			1,11,000

Dr. **AN EXTRACT OF PROFIT & LOSS ACCOUNT** Cr.

Date	*Particulars*	₹	*Date*	*Particulars*	₹
2011	To Deb. Int. A/c	1,20,000	2012	By Int. on Own Deb. A/c (18,000 – 13,500)	4,500
2012	To Deb. Interest A/c	1,20,000			
2013	To Debenture Interest A/c	1,11,000	2013	By Own Deb. A/c (Profit on cancellation)	10,500
	To Own Deb. A/c (Loss on cancellation (4,000 + 12,000)	16,000	2013	By Int. on Own Deb. A/c (36,000 — 18,000)	18,000
	To Premium on Redemption of Debentures (5% on ₹ 7,00,000)	35,000			

Dr. **PREMIUM ON REDEMPTION OF DEBENTURES ACCOUNT** Cr.

Date	*Particulars*	₹	*Date*	*Particulars*	₹
2013			2013		
Dec. 31	To Bank A/c	35,000	Dec. 31	By Profit & Loss A/c	35,000

Dr. **12% DEBENTURES ACCOUNT** Cr.

Date	*Particulars*	₹	*Date*	*Particulars*	₹
2011			2011		
Dec. 31	To Balance c/d	10,00,000	Jan. 01	By Bank A/c	10,00,000
2012			2012		
Dec. 31	To Balance c/d	10,00,000	Jan. 01	By Balance b/d	10,00,000
2013			2013		
Apr. 01	To Own Deb A/c	1,00,000	Jan. 01	By Balance b/d	10,00,000
Dec. 31	To Own Deb. A/c	2,00,000			
	To Bank A/c	7,00,000			
		10,00,000			10,00,000

Working Notes:

1. INTEREST PAID ON PURCHASE OF OWN DEBENTURES

Date		*Nominal Amount* ₹	*Period*	*Rate* ₹	*Interest*
2012	Oct. 01	1,50,000	9 months	12%	13,500
2013	Oct. 01	2,00,000	9 months	12%	18,000

2. INTEREST CREDITED TO INTEREST ON OWN DEBENTURES A/C

Date		*Nominal Amount* ₹	*Period*	*Rate* ₹	*Interest*
2012	Dec. 31	1,50,000	12 months	12%	18,000
2013	April 01	1,00,000	3 months	12%	3,000
	June 30	1,50,000	6 months	12%	9,000
	Dec. 31	2,00,000	12 months	12%	24,000

3. **Profit/Loss on cancellation/sales is difference between cost and nominal value/Sales price.**

PROBLEM 4

On 1st January, 2011 CANHB Ltd. made an issue of 10,000 12% Debentures of ₹ 100 each @ ₹ 98 per debenture. The terms of issue provided for the redemption of ₹ 50,000 debentures every year commencing from 2012 *either* by purchase *or* by drawing lots, at par, at the company's option. Profit, if any, on the redemption of debentures is to be transferred to capital reserve account. The company's accounting year ends on 31st December. Interest is payable on 30th June and 31st December.

During 2011, the company wrote-off ₹ 5,000 from debenture discount account.

During 2012, the company purchased for cancellation debentures of the face value of:-

(i) ₹ 20,000 at ₹ 97 per debenture on 30th June, and

(ii) ₹ 30,000 at ₹ 96 per debenture on 31st December.

Required: Show how these items will appear in the financial statements for the year ended 31st December, 2012. Also show the corresponding figures for the previous year.

SOLUTION

AN EXTRACT OF BALANCE SHEET OF TULSIAN LTD. AS AT ....

Particulars	*Note No*	*₹ (lacs)*
I. Equity and Liabilities		
(1) Shareholders' Funds		
(a) Share Capital		
(b) Reserves and Surplus[Capital Reserve]		1800
(2) Non-Current Liabilities [9500, 12% Debentures]		9,50,000
(3) Current Liabilities		
Total		

II. Assets		
(1) **Non-Current Assets**		
(a) Other Non-Current Assets [Discount on Issue of Debentures]		15,000
(2) **Current Assets**		
Total		

STATEMENT OF PROFIT & LOSS FOR THE YEAR ENDING 31ST DEECEMBER, 2012

2011	*Particulars*	₹
1,20,000	Interest on Debentures A/c	1,18,800
5,000	Discount on Issue of Debentures W/o	–

Working Notes:

1. DEBENTURE INTEREST

Particulars	₹
on 30.6.2012 on ₹ 10,00,000 for 6 months @ 12%	60,000
on 31.12.2012 on ₹ 9,80,000 for 6 months @ 12%	58,800
	1,18,800

2. *Profit on cancellation*

on ₹ 20,000 @ 3% = 600

on ₹ 30,000 @ 4% = 1,200

PROBLEM 5

CANHA Ltd., issued 10% Debentures at par for ₹ 8 lakh on 1st January, 2009. Interest was payable half yearly on 30th June and 31st December every year. Under the terms of the trust deed, the debentures are redeemable at par (after three years of issue) by the company purchasing them in the open market and cancelling them with a minimum redemption of ₹ 80,000 every year. In case, there was a short fall in redemption by the company by open market operations, the shortfall would be made good by the company by payment on the last day of the accounting year to the trustees who would draw lots and redeem the debentures.

The company purchased its own debentures for cancellation as under:-

(a) 30th September 2010 ₹ 1,00,000 at ₹ 98 cum-interest

(b) 31st May 2011 ₹ 60,000 at ₹ 95 ex-interest

(c) 31st July 2012 ₹ 90,000 at ₹ 96 cum-interest.

The company carried out its obligations under the deed.

Required: Prepare the following ledger accounts for calender years 2010, 2011 and 2012:

(i) Debentures account, (ii) Debenture Redemption account, and (iii) Debenture Interest account. Ignore taxation.

SOLUTION

Dr. **10% DEBENTURES ACCOUNT** *Cr.*

Date	Particulars	₹	Date	Particulars	₹
2010			2010		
Sept. 30	To Debentures Redemption A/c	1,00,000	Jan. 01	By Balance b/d	8,00,000
Dec. 31	To Balance c/d	7,00,000			
		8,00,000			8,00,000
2011			2011		
May 31	To Debenture Redemption A/c	60,000	Jan. 01	By Balance b/d	7,00,000
Dec. 31	To Debenture Redemption A/c	20,000			
Dec. 31	To Balance c/d	6,20,000			
		7,00,000			7,00,000
2012			2012		
July 31	To Debenture Redemption A/c	90,000	Jan. 01	By Balance b/d	6,20,000
Dec. 31	To Balance c/d	5,30,000			
		6,20,000			6,20,000

Dr. **DEBENTURES REDEMPTION ACCOUNT** *Cr.*

Date	Particulars	₹	Date	Particulars	₹
2010			2010		
Sept. 30	To Bank A/c	95,500	Sept. 30	By 10% Debentures A/c	1,00,000
Sept. 30	To Capital Reserve A/c (Profit on Cancellation)	4,500			
		1,00,000			1,00,000
2011			2011		
May 31	To Bank A/c	57,000	May 31	By 10% Debentures A/c	60,000
	To Capital Reserve A/c	3,000	Dec. 31	By 10% Debentures A/c	20,000
Dec. 31	To Bank A/c	20,000			
		80,000			80,000
2012			2012		
July 31	To Bank A/c	85,650	July 31	By 10% Debentures A/c	90,000
	To Capital Reserve A/c	4,350			
		90,000			90,000

Dr. **DEBENTURE INTEREST ACCOUNT** *Cr.*

Date	*Particulars*	₹	*Date*	*Particulars*	₹
2010			2010		
June 30	To Bank A/c	40,000	Dec. 31	By P & L A/c (transfer)	77,500
Sept. 30	To Bank A/c	2,500			
Dec. 31	To Bank A/c	35,000			
		77,500			77,500
2011			2011		
May 31	To Bank A/c	2,500	Dec. 31	By P & L A/c (transfer)	66,500
June 30	To Bank A/c	32,000			
Dec. 31	To Bank A/c	32,000			
		66,500			66,500
2012			2012		
June 30	To Bank A/c	31,000	Dec. 31	By P & L A/c (transfer)	58,250
July 31	To Bank A/c	750			
Dec. 31	To Bank A/c	26,500			
		58,250			58,520

Working Notes: *Calculation of Interest paid on Debentures @ 10% p.a.*

Date	*Amount of Debentures* ₹	*Period*	*Amount of Interest* ₹
2010			
June 30	8,00,000	6 months	40,000
Sept. 30	1,00,000	3 months	2,500
Dec. 31	7,00,000	6 months	35,000
2011			
May 31	60,000	5 months	2,500
June 30	6,40,000	6 months	32,000
Dec. 31	6,40,000	6 months	32,000
2012			
June 30	6,20,000	6 months	31,000
July 31	90,000	1 months	750
Dec. 31	5,30,000	6 months	26,500

PROBLEM 6

A Company had issued 20,000, 13% Convertible debentures of ₹ 100 each on 1st April, 2010. The debentures are due for redemption on 1st July, 2012. The terms of issue of debentures provided that they were redeemable at a premium of 5% and also conferred option to the debentureholders to convert 20% of their holding into equity shares (Nominal value ₹ 10) at a price of ₹ 15 per share. Debentureholders holding 2,500 debentures did not exercise the option. Calculate the number of equity shares to be allotted to the Debentureholders exercising the option to the maximum.

SOLUTION

(I) CALCULATION OF NUMBER OF EQUITY SHARES TO BE ALLOTTED

Total number of debentures	20,000
Less: Debenture holders not opted for conversion	(2,500)
Debenture holders opted for conversion	17,500
Option for conversion	20%
Number of Debentures to be converted (20% of 17,500)	3,500
Redemption Value of 3,500 debentures at a premium of 5% [3, 500 × (100 + 5)]	₹ 3,67,500
Equity Shares of ₹.10 each issued on conversion [₹ 3,67,500/ ₹.15]	24,500 shares

PROBLEM 7

Balance Sheet of Dee Limited on 31st March, 2012 was as follows:

Particulars	₹
Authorised Capital 50,000, Equity Shares of ₹ 10 each	5,00,000
Issued and Subscribed Capital 25,000 Equity shares of ₹ 10 each fully paid up	2,50,000
General Reserve	2,75,000
Profit and Loss A/c	1,00,000
Debenture Redemption Reserve	2,50,000
12% Convertible Debentures (5,000 Debentures of ₹.100 each)	5,00,000
Other Secured loans	2,50,000
Current Liabilities and Provisions	6,00,000
Proposed Dividend	25,000
Fixed Assets (at cost *less* depreciation)	8,00,000
Debenture Redemption Fund Investment	2,00,000
Cash balance	2,50,000
Other Current Assets	10,00,000

At the General Meeting it was resolved to:

1. Pay proposed dividend of 10% in cash.
2. Give existing shareholders the option to purchase one share of ₹.10 each at ₹.15 for every five shares held. This option was taken up by all the shareholders.
3. Redeem the debentures at a premium of 5% and also confer option to the debentureholders to convert 50% of their holding into equity shares at a predetermined price of ₹ 15 per share and balance payment to be made in cash.

Holders of 3,000 debentures opted to get their debentures redeemed in cash only while the rest opted for getting the same converted into equity shares as per the terms of issue. Debenture redemption fund investment realized ₹ 1,80,000 on sales.

Required: Redraft the Balance Sheet after giving effects to the right issue and redemption of debentures. Also show the calculations in respect of number of equity shares issued and cash payment.

SOLUTION

BALANCE SHEET OF DEE LTD. AS AT 31.3.2012

Particulars	*Note No*	₹ *(lacs)*
I. Equity and Liabilities		
(1) Shareholders' Funds		
(a) Share Capital (₹ 10 each)		3,70,000
(b) Reserves and Surplus	1	6,40,000
(2) Non-Current Liabilities[Secured Loans]		2,50,000
(3) Current Liabilities		6,00,000
Total		18,60,000
II. Assets		
(1) Non-Current Assets		
(a) Fixed Assets		
Tangible Assets		8,00,000
(2) Current Assets		
(a) Cash and Cash Equivalents		60,000
(b) Other Current Assets		10,00,000
Total		18,60,000

Notes To Accounts:

Particulars	₹ *(lacs)*
1. Reserves and Surplus	
General Reserve	4,80,000
Profit & Loss Account	1,00,000
Securities Premium	60,000
Total	6,40,000

CALCULATION OF NUMBER OF EQUITY SHARES ISSUED

I.	Number of equity shares issued as right issue (25,000 Shares/5)	5,000 shares
II.	Debentureholders who opted for the scheme of conversion into equity shares 2,000 debentureholders opted for the scheme	
	Total value (2,000 debentures × ₹.100)	₹ 2,00,000
	Premium on redemption @ 5%	₹ 10,000
		2,10,000
	50% of their holding converted into equity shares	₹ 1,05,000
	Number of equity shares to be issued to debentureholders (₹ 1,05,000/₹ 15) = [₹ 1,05,000/₹ 15]	7,000 shares
	Total number of equity shares issued = (5,000 + 7,000) shares	12,000 shares

CASH PAYMENT TO DEBENTUREHOLDERS

	Particulars		₹
I.	3,000 Debentureholders preferred cash		
	Total cash paid to them	3,00,000	
	Premium on redemption @ 5%	15,000	3,15,000
II.	2,000 Debentureholders opted for the scheme		
	Total Value	2,00,000	
	Add: Premium on redemption @ 5%	10,000	
		2,10,000	
	50% of their value converted into equity shares	1,05,000	
	Balance paid to debentureholders in cash		1,05,000
	Total cash paid to debentureholders		4,20,000

Working Notes:

Dr. **(I) DEBENTURE REDEMPTION RESERVE ACCOUNT** *Cr.*

Particulars	₹	*Particulars*	₹
To Premium on redemption of debentures (15,000 + 10,000)	25,000	By Balance b/d	2,50,000
To Loss on sale of Debenture Redemption Reserve Investment	20,000		
To General Reserve	2,05,000		
	2,50,000		2,50,000

Dr. **(II) GENERAL RESERVE ACCOUNT** *Cr.*

Particulars	₹	*Particulars*	₹
To Balance c/d	4,80,000	By Balance b/d	2,75,000
		By Debenture Redemption Reserve	2,05,000
	4,80,000		4,80,000

(iii) Total of Securities Premium = 12000 shares × ₹ 5 = ₹ 60,000

Dr. **(IV) CASH ACCOUNT** *Cr.*

Particulars	₹	*Particulars*	₹
To Balance b/d	2,50,000	By Proposed Dividend	25,000
To Equity Shareholders (5,000 × 15)	75,000	By Debentureholders (₹ 1,05,000 + ₹ 3,15,000)	4,20,000
To Sale of Debenture Redemption Reserve Investment	1,80,000	By Balance c/d	60,000
	5,05,000		5,05,000

PROBLEM 8

M Ltd. furnishes the followinh summarized Balance Sheet as at 31st March, 2013:

Particulars	*₹' 000*
Authorised Issued and Subscribed 3,00,000, Equity Shares of ₹ 10 each	3,000
20,000, 9% Preference Shares of ₹ 100 each fully paid up Issued two months back for buy back purposes)	2,000
Capital Reserve	10
Revenue Reserve	4,000
Securities Premium	500
Profit and Loss A/c	1,800
10% Convertible Debentures	400
Current Liabilities	40
Fixed Assets (at cost *less* depreciation)	2,750
Non-Current Investments	5,000
Current Assets	4,000

(1) **The company passed a resolution to buy back 20% of its equity capital @ ₹ 15 per share. For this purpose, it sold its investments of ₹ 30 lakhs for ₹ 25 lakhs.**

(2) **The company redeemed the preference shares at a premium of 10% on 1st April, 2013.**

(3) **Included in its investments were 'Investments in own debentures' costing ₹ 3 lakhs (face value ₹ 3.30 lakhs). These debentures were cancelled on 1st April, 2013.**

You are required to pass necessary Journal entries and prepare the Balance Sheet on 01.04.2013.

SOLUTION

JOURNAL *(₹ in '000)*

Date	*Particulars*		*L.F.*	*Dr. (₹)*	*Cr. (₹)*
	Bank A/c	Dr.		2,500	
	Profit and Loss A/c	Dr.		500	
	To Investments A/c	Dr.			3,000
	(Being the investments sold for Buy back)				
	9% Redeemable Preference Share Capital A/c	Dr.		2,000	
	Premium on redemption of Preference Shares A/c	Dr.		200	
	To Preference Sheraholders A/c				2,200
	(Being the amount due to Preference Shareholders)				
	Preference Shareholders A/c	Dr.		2,200	
	To Bank A/c				2,200
	(Being the payment made to Preference Shareholders)				
	Revenue Reserve A/c	Dr.		2,000	
	To Capital Redemption Reserve A/c				2,000
	(Being the creation of Capital Redemption Reserve to the extent of the face value of preference shares redeemed & equity shares bought back as per the law)				

	Particulars		Dr.	Cr.
	Equity Share Capital A/c	Dr.	600	
	Securities Premium A/c	Dr.	300	
	To Equity Shares buy back A/c			900
	(Being cancellation of shares bought back)			
	Equity Shares buy Back A/c	Dr.	90.00	
	To Bank A/c			90.00
	(Being the payment made for shares bought back)			
	10% Debentures A/c	Dr.	330	
	To Investments (Own Debentures) A/c			300
	To Capital Reserve A/c			30
	(Being cancellation of own debentures and T/F of profit on cancellation of debentures)			
	Securities Premium A/c	Dr.	200	
	To Premium on Redemption of Pref. Shares A/c			200
	(Being premium on redemption of preference shares adjusted through securities premium)			

BALANCE SHEET OF M LTD. AS AT 01.04.2013

	Particulars	Note No	₹ ('000)
I.	**Equity and Liabilities**		
	(1) Shareholders' Funds		
	(a) Share Capital	1	2,400
	(b) Reserves and Surplus	2	5,340
	(2) Non-Current Liabilities[10% Debentures] [400 – 330]		70
	(3) Current Liabilities [70 – 5]		40
	Total		7,850
II.	**Assets**		
	(1) Non-Current Assets		
	(a) Fixed Assets		2,750
	(b) Non-Current Investments [5,000 – 3,000 – 300]		1,700
	(2) Current Assets [4,000 + 2,500 – 2,200 – 900]		3,400
	Total		7,850

Notes To Accounts:

Particulars	₹ ('000)
1. Share Capital	
Authorised Capital	
2,40,000 Equity Shares of ₹ 10 each	2,400
Issued & Subscribed Capital	
2,40,000 Equity Shares of ₹ 10 each (60,000 Equity Shares bought back)	2,400

2.	**Reserves and Surplus**	
	Revenue Reserve [4,000 – 2,000]	2,000
	Capital Reserve [10 + 30]	40
	Capital Redemption Reserve	2,000
	Securities Premium [500 – 200 – 300]	0
	Surplus (P & L A/c) [1800 – 500]	1,300
	Total	5,340

PROBLEM 9

Extra Ltd. furnishes you with the following Balance Sheet as on 31st March, 2012:

Particulars	*[₹ in lakhs]*
Equity Shares of ₹ 10 each fully paid A	100
9% Redeemable Preference Shares of ₹ 100 each fully paid	20
Capital Reserves	8
Revenue Reserves	50
Securities Premium	60
10% Debentures	4
Current liabilities	70
Fixed Assets Less Depreciation	50
Investments at cost	120
Current Assets	142

(i) The company redeemed the preference shares at a premium of 10% on 1st April, 2012.

(ii) It also bought back 3 lakhs equity shares of ₹ 10 each at ₹ 30 per share.

The payment for the above were made out of huge bank balances, which appeared as a part of the current assets.

(iii) Included in its investment were “investments in own debentures” costing ₹ 2 lakhs (face value ₹ 2.20 lakhs). These debentures were cancelled on 1st April, 2012.

(iv) The company had 1,00,000 equity stock options outstanding on the above mentioned date, to the employees at ₹ 20 when the market price was ₹ 30. (This was included under current liabilities). On 1.04.2012 employees exercised their options for 50,000 shares.

(v) Pass the journal entries to record the above & Prepare Balance Sheet as at 01.04.2012.

SOLUTION

JOURNAL *(₹ in lakhs)*

Date	*Particulars*	*L.F.*	*Dr. (₹)*	*Cr. (₹)*
1.	9% Redeemable Preference Share Capital A/c Dr.		20.00	
	Premium on redemption of Preference Shares A/c Dr.		2.00	
	To Preference Sheraholders A/c			22.00
	(Being preference Share Capital Transferred to shareholders account)			

2.	Preference Shareholders A/c Dr.		22.00	
	To Bank A/c			22.00
	(Being payment made to shareholders)			
3.	Equity Shares buy Back A/c Dr.		90.00	
	To Bank A/c			90.00
	(Being 3 lakhs equity shares of 10 each bought back @ 30 per share)			
4.	Equity Share Capital A/c Dr.		30.00	
	Securities Premium A/c Dr.		60.00	
	To Equity Shares buy back A/c			90.00
	(Being cancellation of shares bought back)			
5.	Revenue Reserve A/c (20 + 30) Dr.		50.00	
	To Capital Redemption Reserve A/c			50.00
	(Being creation of capital redemption reserve account to the extent of the face value of preference shares redeemed & equity shares bought back as per the law)			
6.	10% Debentures A/c Dr.		2.20	
	To Investments (Own Debentures) A/c			2.00
	To Profit on cancellation of Own Debentures A/c			0.20
	(Being cancellation of own debentures costing ₹ 2 lakhs, face value being ₹ 2.20 lakhs and the balance being profit on cancellation of debentures)			
7.	Profit on cancellation of Debentures A/c Dr.		0.20	
	To Capital Reserve A/c			0.20
	(Being profit on cancellation of debentures transferred to capital reserve account)			
8.	Bank A/c Dr.		10.00	
	Employees Stock Option Outstanding (Current liabilities) A/c Dr.		5.00	
	To Equity Share Capital A/c			5.00
	To Securities Premium A/c			10.00
	(Being the allotment to employees, of 50,000 shares of ₹ 10 each at a premium of ₹ 20 per share in exercise of stock options by employees)			
9.	Securities Premium A/c Dr.		2.00	
	To Premium on Redemption of Pref. Shares A/c			2.00
	(Being premium on redemption of preference shares adjusted through securities premium)			

BALANCE SHEET OF EXTRA LTD. AS AT 01.04.2012

Particulars	Note No	₹ (lacs)
I. Equity and Liabilities		
(1) Shareholders' Funds		
(a) Share Capital (₹ 10 each) [100 + 5 – 30]		75.00
(b) Reserves and Surplus	1	66.20
(2) Non-Current Liabilities [10% Debentures] [4.00 – 2.20]		1.80
(3) Current Liabilities [70 – 5]		65.00
Total		208.00
II. Assets		
(1) Non-Current Assets		
(a) Fixed Assets		
Tangible Assets		50.00
(b) Non-Current Investments [120 – 2]		118.00
(2) Current Assets [142 + 10 – 22 – 90]		40.00
Total		208.00

Notes To Accounts:

Particulars	₹ (lacs)
1. Reserves and Surplus	
Revenue Reserve [50 – 50]	0
Capital Reserve [8.00 + 0.20]	8.20
Capital Redemption Reserve	50.00
Securities Premium [60 + 10 – 60 – 2]	8.00
Total	66.20

7 AMALGAMATION OF COMPANIES

LEARNING OBJECTIVES

After studying this chapter, you should be able to understand:

- General Meaning
- Legal Meaning of Amalgamation
- Provisions of Accounting Standard (AS) 14 Issued By ICAI
- Amalgamation in the Nature of Merger
- Amalgamation in the Nature of Purchase
- Distinction between Amalgamation in the Nature of Purchase and Amalgamation in the Nature of Merger
- Purchase Consideration
- Accounting Treatment in the Books of Transferor Company or VSendor Company
- Treatment of Difference between the Purchase Consideration and the Net Assets of the Transferor Company arising on Amalgamation in the Nature of Purchase
- Accounting Treatment in the Books of Transferee Company or Purchasing Company in case of Purchase
- Treatment of Reserves arising on Amalgamation in the Nature of Merger
- Accounting Treatment in the Books of Transferee Company or Purchasing Company In case of Merger

1.0 GENERAL MEANING

Amalgamation	Usually, the term 'Amalgamation' is used when two *or* more existing companies go into liquidation and a new company is formed to take over their business. ***For Example***, *if a new company XY Ltd. is formed to take over the businesses of two existing companies, X Ltd. and Y Ltd., it is a case of Amalgamation.*
Absorption	The term 'Absorption' is used when one *or* more existing company(s) goes into liquidation and some existing company takes over its business. ***For Example***, *if the business of an existing company X Ltd. is taken over by another existing company Y Ltd., it is a case of absorption.*
External Reconstruction	The term 'External Reconstruction' is used when one existing company goes into liquidation and a new company is formed to take-over its business. ***For Example***, *if a new company X (New) Ltd. is formed to take over the business of an existing company X Ltd., it is a case of 'External Reconstruction'.*

2.0 PROVISIONS OF ACCOUNTING STANDARD (AS) 14 ISSUED BY ICAI

Effective date	Accounting Standard (AS) 14 on 'Accounting for Amalgamations' came into effect in respect of accounting periods commencing on *or* after 1.4.1995.
Mandatory	AS 14 is mandatory in nature.
Meaning of Amalgamation	Amalgamation means an amalgamation pursuant to the provisions of the Companies Act, 1956 *or* any other statute which may be applicable to companies.
Types of Amalgamations	An amalgamation may be either (a) an amalgamation in the nature of merger *or* (b) and amalgamation in the nature of purchase.

3.0 AMALGAMATION IN THE NATURE OF MERGER

MEANING OF AMALGAMATION IN THE NATURE OF MERGER

Amalgamation in the nature of merger is an amalgamation which satisfies all the following **five** conditions:

1. Transfer of All Assets & Liabilities	All the assets and liabilities of the transferor company (i.e., the company which is amalgamated into another company) become, after amalgamation, the assets and liabilities of the transferee company (i.e., the company into which a transferor company is amalgamated).
2. Same Equity Shareholders Holding 90%	Shareholders holding at least 90% of the face value of the equity shares of the transferor company (other than the equity shares already held therein, immediately before the amalgamation, by the transferee company *or* its subsidiaries *or* their nominees) become equity shareholders of the transferee company by virtue of the amalgamation.
3. Purchase Consideration in Equity Shares	The consideration for the amalgamation receivable by those equity shareholders of the transferor company who agree to become equity shareholders of the transferee company is discharged by the transferee company wholly by the issue of equity shares in the transferee company, except that cash may be paid in respect of any fractional shares.
4. Same Business	The business of the transferor company is intended to be carried on, after the amalgamation, by the transferee company.
5. Recording of Assets & Liabilities at Book Values	No adjustment is intended to be made to the book values of the assets and liabilities of the transferor company when they are incorporated in the financial statements of the transferee company expect to ensure uniformity of accounting policies.

METHOD OF ACCOUNTING FOR AMALGAMATION IN THE NATURE OF MERGER

The **'Pooling of Interests Method'** should be used in accounting for amalgamation in the nature of merger. The salient features of this method are as follows:

Recording of Assets and Liabilities	In preparing the transferee company's financial statements, the assets and liabilities of the transferor company should be recorded at their existing carrying amounts and in the same form as at the date of amalgamation.

Recording of Reserves (whether capital or revenue or arising on revaluation)	The reserves should be recorded at their existing carrying amounts and in the same form as at the date of the amalgamation.
Recording of Balance of Profit and Loss A/c	The balance of the Profit and Loss Account of the transferor company should be aggregated with the corresponding balance of the transferee company *or* transferred to the General Reserve, if any.
Difference between the purchase consideration and the amount of share capital of the transferor company	The difference between the amount recorded as share capital issued *plus* any additional consideration in the form of cash *or* other assets and the amount of share capital of the transferor company should be adjusted in reserves.
Uniform Set of Accounting Policies	If, at the time of the amalgamation, the transferor and the transferee companies have conflicting accountant policies, a uniform set of accounting policies should be adopted following the amalgamation. The effects on the financial statements of any changes in a accounting policies should be reported in accordance with Accounting Standard (AS) 5, 'Prior Period and Extraordinary items and changes in Accounting Policies'.

4.0 AMALGAMATION IN THE NATURE OF PURCHASE

MEANING OF AMALGAMATION IN THE NATURE OF PURCHASE

Amalgamation in the nature of purchase is an amalgamation which does not satisfy anyone *or* more of the conditions specified for Amalgamation in the nature of merger.

METHOD OF ACCOUNTING FOR AMALGAMATION IN THE NATURE OF PURCHASE

The **'Purchase Method'** should be used in accounting for amalgamation in the nature of purchase. The salient features of this method are as follows:

Recording of Assets and Liabilities	In preparing the transferee company's financial statements, the assets and liabilities of the transferor company should be incorporated **at their existing carrying amounts or, alternatively,** the consideration should be allocated to individual identifiable assets and liabilities on the basis of their **fair values** at the date of amalgamation.
Recording of Statutory Reserves	Where the requirements of the relevant statute for recording the statutory reserves in the books of the transferee company are complied with, statutory reserves of the transferor company should be recorded in the financial statements of the transferee company. The corresponding debit should be given to a suitable account head (e.g., 'Amalgamation Adjustment Account') which should be disclosed as a part of "Miscellaneous Expenditure" *or* other similar category in the Balance Sheet. When the identity of the statutory reserves is no longer required to be maintained, both the reserves and the aforesaid account should be reversed.
Recording of Reserves other than Statutory Reserves	The reserves (whether capital *or* revenue *or* arising on revaluation) of the transferor company, other than the statutory reserves, should *not be included* in the financial statements of the transferee company.

Balance of Profit and Loss A/c	The balance of the Profit and Loss Account of the transferor company whether debit *or* credit *loses its identity.*
Difference between the Purchase Consideration and the Net Assets of the transferor company	Any **excess of** the amount of the **consideration over the value of the net assets** of the transferor company acquired by the transferee company should be recognised in the transferee company's financial statements **as goodwill** arising on amalgamation. If the amount of the consideration is lower than the value of the net assets acquired, the difference should be treated as **Capital Reserve.** The goodwill arising on amalgamation should be amortised to income on a systematic basis over its useful life. The amortisation period should not exceed 5 years unless a somewhat longer period can be justified.

5.0 DISTINCTION BETWEEN AMALGAMATION IN THE NATURE OF PURCHASE AND AMALGAMATION IN THE NATURE OF MERGER

Basis of Distinction	*Amalgamation in nature of Merger*	*Amalgamation in nature of Purchase*
1. Method of Accounting	Pooling of Interest Method	Purchase Method
2. T/f of Assets & Liabilities	There is transfer of all assets & liabilities.	There need not be transfer of all assets & liabilities.
3. Equity Shareholders holding 90%	Equity shareholders holding 90% equity shares in transferer company **become shareholders of transferee company.**	Equity shareholders, need **not become shareholders of transferee company.**
4. Purchase Consideration	Purchase consideration is discharged **wholly by issue of equity shares** (except cash for fractional shares)	Purchase consideration **need not** be discharged wholly by issue of equity shares.
5. Same Business	The **same business** of the transferor company is intended to be carried on by the transferee company.	The business of the transferor company **need not** be intended to be carried on by the transferee company.
6. Recording of Assets & Liabilities	The assets & liabilities taken over are recorded **at their existing carrying amounts** except where adjustment is required to ensure uniformity of accounting policies.	The assets & liabilities taken over are recorded at their existing carrying amounts *or* the basis of their **fair values.**
7. Recording of Reserves of Transferor Co.	**All reserves** are recorded at their **existing carrying amounts** and in the same form.	(a) **only statutory reserves** are recorded at their existing carrying amounts as follows: Amalagamation Adjustment A/c Dr. To Statutory Reserve A/c (b) Other reserves are not recorded at all.

8. Reording of Balance of Profit & Loss A/c of Transferor Co.	The balance of P&L A/c should be **aggregated** with the corresponding balance of the transferee co. *or* transferred to the General Reserve.	The balance of P&L A/c losses its identify and is **not recorded** at all.
9. Difference between the Purchase Consideration and Share Capital/Net Assets of transfer co.	The excess of the purchase consideration over the share capital of transferor company is **debited to Reserves** and the excess of share capital over purchase consideration is **creditted to reserves.**	The excess of purchase consideration over the net assets is treated as **Goodwill** and the excess of net assets over purchase consideration is treated as **Capital Reserve.**

6.0 PURCHASE CONSIDERATION

MEANING OF PURCHASE CONSIDERATION

Consideration for the amalgamation means the aggregate of the shares and other securities issued and the payment made in the form of cash *or* other assets by the transferee company to the shareholders of the transferor company.

The analysis of the aforesaid definition of 'Purchase Consideration' makes it clear that the payments made by the transferee company to discharge the debentureholders and other outside liabilities and the cost of winding up of transferor company shall not be considered as part of purchase consideration.

METHODS OF CALCULATING PURCHASE CONSIDERATION

(a) Depending upon the availability of information, the purchase consideration may be calculated on 'Net Assets taken over basis', *or* 'Net Payments to shareholders basis'.

(b) The following criteria may be adopted to select the basis of purchase consideration:

Case	*Basis of Purchase Consideration*
I. If all the modes of discharging the Purchase Consideration (e.g. Pref. Shares, Equity Shares or Cash payable to shareholders of transferor company) are given alongwith their individual amount	'Net Payment to Shareholders basis' should be used.
II. In other cases	'Net Assets taken over basis' should be used.

COMPUTATION OF PURCHASE CONSIDERATION (NET ASSETS BASIS)

	Particulars	₹
A.	Total Assets taken over at their agreed values	xxx
B.	*Less:* Total Liabilities taken over at their agreed amounts	xxx
C.	Net Assets taken over at their agreed values *or* Total Purchase Consideration [A – B]	xxx

$$\text{No. of Shares to be issued by Purchasing Co.} = \frac{\text{Amount to be discharged by issue of shares}}{\text{Issue Price of a share}}$$

COMPUTATION OF PURCHASE CONSIDERATION (ON NET PAYMENT BASIS)

Mode of Discharging Purchase Consideration	No. of Shares	Issue Price	₹
A. Preference Shares	xxx	xxx	xxx
B. Cash for Preference Shareholders	—	—	xxx
C. Equity Shares	xxx	xxx	xxx
D. Cash for Equity Shareholders	—	—	xxx
E. Total Purchase Consideration (A + B + C + D)			xxx

Note:

1. *The payment made by the transferee Company to discharge the debentureholders and other outside liabilities and the cost of winding up of transferor company* ***shall not be considered as part of purchase consideration.***
2. *The shares shall be issued in whole number and not in fraction.* ***For Example,*** *if no. of shares to be issued comes to 28454.55, only 28454 shares will be issued.*
3. *The fraction share shall be valued at market value and shall be paid in cash.* ***For Example,*** *if the market price of a share is ₹ 100 and the fractional share is 0.55, ₹ 55 (i.e., 0.55 × ₹ 100) will be paid in cash.*
4. *When it is decided to make entries relating to issue of shares at par value only, the number of shares to be issued by the purchasing company are calculated in the usual manner but thereafter are multiplied by par value only for the purposes of computing the purchase consideration.*

ILLUSTRATION 1

Given below are the extracts from the Balance Sheet of V Ltd. as at 31st March, 2016:

Particulars	₹
Equity Share Capital of ₹ 10 each	2,00,000
8% Pref. Share Capital of ₹ 100 each	50,000
Reserves & Surplus	41,100
10% Debentures	50,000
Current Liabilities	1,40,000
Tangible Fixed Assets	1,50,000
Current Assets	3,31,100

The business of V Ltd. is taken over by P Ltd. as on that date on the following terms:

(a) The issue of such an amount of fully paid 14% Debentures in P Ltd at 96 per cent as is sufficient to discharge 10% Debentures in V Ltd. at a premium of 20 per cent.

(b) The issue of such an amount of fully paid 10% Pref. Shares in P Ltd. at 125% as is sufficient to discharge 9% Pref. Shares in V Ltd. at a premium of 20%.

(c) One Equity Share of ₹ 10 each, ₹ 8 paid up valued at ₹ 15 per share and Cash ₹ 1.86 for every two Equity Shares held in V Ltd. The market value of an equity share of P Ltd. at present is ₹ 100.

(d) Expenses of liquidation of V Ltd. are to be reimbursed by P Ltd. to the extent of ₹ 10,000. Actual Expenses amounted to ₹ 12,000.

Show the calculation and discharge of Purchase Consideration.

SOLUTION

CALCULATION AND DISCHARGE OF PURCHASE CONSIDERATION

A. 10,000, Equity Shares to be issued [(20,000 × 1/2) × ₹ 15]	1,50,000
B. 480, 9% Pref. Shares to be issued [(50,000 × 120%)/125] × 125	60,000
C. Cash to Equity Shareholders [(20,000 × 1/2) × ₹ 1.86]	18,600
D. Total Purchase Consideration (A + B + C)	2,28,600

Note: *According to AS-14, the amount paid by purchasing Company to discharge the debentures holders and the liquidation expenses of Vendor Company are not considered as part of purchase consideration.*

ILLUSTRATION 2

Given below are the extracts from the Balance Sheets of B Ltd. as at 31.03.2016:

Particulars	(₹ *in lacs)*
Equity Share Capital of ₹ 100 each	75
12% Pref. Share Capital of ₹ 100 each	20
Reserves & Surplus	33
10% Debentures of ₹ 100 each	3
Current Liabilities	19
Tangible Fixed Assets	70
Current Assets	80

A Ltd. absorbs B Ltd.as on that date on the following terms:

(a) 10% Debentures of the transferor company are to be discharged by transferee company by issuing such number of its 15% Debentures of ₹ 100 each so as to maintain the same amount of interest.

(b) 12% Preference Shares of the transferor company are to be discharged by transferee company by issuing equivalent numbers of 15% preference Shares of ₹ 100 each at ₹ 150 each.

(c) The transferee company shall issue 4 equity shares of ₹ 10 each at ₹ 30 each for each equity share in the transferor company.

(d) The transferee company shall pay the cost of absorption which amounts to ₹ 1,00,000

Show the calculation and discharge of Purchase Consideration.

SOLUTION

CALCULATION OF PURCHASE CONSIDERATION

20,000,12% Preference Shares [(20,00,000/100) × ₹ 150]	30,00,000
3,00,000 Equity Shares [{(75,00,000/100) × 4} × ₹ 30]	90,00,000
	120,00,000

Note: *According to AS-14, the amount paid by purchasing Company to discharge the debentures holders and the liquidation expenses of Vendor Company are not considered as part of purchase consideration.*

ILLUSTRATION 3

Given below are the extracts from the Balance Sheets of Y Ltd. as at 31st March 2016:

Particulars	*(₹ in lacs)*
Equity Share Capital of ₹ 10 each	10.00
8% Pref. Share Capital of ₹ 100 each	2.00
Reserves & Surplus	3.00
12% Debentures of ₹ 100 each	1.00
Current Liabilities	2.20
Non-Current Assets	12.80
Current Assets	5.40

X Ltd. absorbs Y Ltd.as on that date on the following terms:

(a) 12% Debentures of Y Ltd. are to be discharged by X Ltd. by issuing such number of its 15% Debentures of ₹ 100 each so as to maintain the same amount of interest.

(b) The issue of such an amount of fully paid 9% Pref. Shares in X Ltd. at 125% as is sufficient to discharge 8% Pref. Shares in Y Ltd. at a premium of 20%.

(c) The Equity Shareholders of Y Ltd. will receive the requisite number of Equity Shares of X Ltd. The Equity Shares of X Ltd are to be of a nominal value of ₹ 10 each credited as ₹ 8 paid up and valued at ₹ 15 per share.

(d) The transferee company shall pay the cost of absorption which amounts to ₹ 1,00,000

Show the calculation and discharge of Purchase Consideration.

SOLUTION

CALCULATION OF PURCHASE CONSIDERATION

1920,9% Pref. Shares [(2,00,000 + 20%)/125) × ₹ 125]	2,40,000
1,00,000 Equity Shares [1,00,000 × 15]	15,00,000
	17,40,000

Note: *According to AS-14, the amount paid by purchasing Company to discharge the debentures holders and the liquidation expenses of Vendor Company are not considered as part of purchase consideration.*

ILLUSTRATION 4

Given below are the extracts from the Balance Sheet of V Ltd. as at 31st March, 2016:

Particulars	₹
Equity Share Capital of ₹ 10 each	2,00,000
8% Pref. Share Capital of ₹ 100 each	50,000
General Reserve	20,000
Profit & Loss A/c	16,100
Statutory Reserves	5,000
10% Debentures	50,000
Trade Payables	1,40,000
Tangible Assets	1,50,000

Goodwill	1,19,500
Inventories	55,000
Trade Receivables	65,000
Cash at Bank	91,600

The business of V Ltd. is taken over by P Ltd. as on that date on the following terms:

(a) 50% of Tangible Fixed Assets are taken over at 100% more than the book value and the remaining Tangible Fixed Assets are taken over at $16\frac{2}{3}\%$ less than the book value.

(b) Goodwill of V Ltd. is to be valued at ₹ 50,000.

(c) Inventories are taken over at book value less 10% and Trade Receivables are taken over at book value subject to an allowance of 10% to cover doubtful debts.

(d) Trade Payables are to be taken over subject to a discount of 5% and Unrecorded Loan Liability of ₹ 38,500 to be discharged by P Ltd. at book value.

(e) The purchase consideration payable by P Ltd. was agreed as follows:

(i) The issue of such an amount of fully paid 14% Debentures in P Ltd at 96 per cent as is sufficient to discharge 10% Debentures in V Ltd. at a premium of 20 per cent.

(ii) The issue of such an amount of fully paid 10% Pref. Shares in P Ltd. at 125% as is sufficient to discharge 9% Pref. Shares in V Ltd. at a premium of 20%.

(iii) One Equity Share of ₹ 10 each, ₹ 8 paid up valued at ₹ 15 per share for every two Equity Shares held in V Ltd. and the balance in cash. The market value of an equity share of P Ltd. at present is ₹ 100.

(iv) Expenses of liquidation of V Ltd. are to be reimbursed by P Ltd. to the extent of ₹ 10,000. Actual Expenses amounted to ₹ 12,000.

Show the calculation and discharge of Purchase Consideration.

SOLUTION

1. CALCULATION OF PURCHASE CONSIDERATION

	Particulars	₹
A	Assets taken over at agreed values	
	Tangible Fixed Assets [(₹ 1,50,000 × 50%) + 100%]	1,50,000
	Tangible Fixed Assets [(₹ 1,50,000 × 50%) – $16\frac{2}{3}\%$]	62,500
	Inventories [₹ 55,000 – ₹ 5,500]	49,500
	Trade Receivables [₹ 65,000 – ₹ 6,500]	58,500
	Cash at Bank [91,600 – 2,000(Expenses)]	89,600
	Goodwill	50,000
		4,60,100
B	*Less:* Liabilities taken over:	
	Trade Payables [₹ 1,40,000 – 5%]	1,33,000
	10% Debentures [₹ 50,000 + 20%]	60,000
	Unrecorded Loan	38,500
		2,31,500
C	Net Assets taken over (A – B)	2,28,600

2. DISCHARGE OF PURCHASE CONSIDERATION

A. 10,000, Equity Shares to be issued [(20,000 × 1/2) × ₹ 15]	1,50,000
B. 480, 9% Pref. Shares to be issued [(500 × 120%)]	60,000
C. Cash to Equity Shareholders [Balancing figure]	**18,600**
D. Total Purchase Consideration (A + B + C)	2,28,600

Note: *According to AS-14, the amount paid by purchasing Company to discharge the debentures holders and the liquidation expenses of Vendor Company are not considered as part of purchase consideration.*

ILLUSTRATION 5

Given below are the extracts from the Balance Sheet of V Ltd. as at 31st March, 2016:

Particulars	₹
Equity Share Capital of ₹ 10 each	2,00,000
8% Pref. Share Capital of ₹ 100 each	50,000
General Reserve	20,000
Profit & Loss A/c	16,100
Statutory Reserves	5,000
10% Debentures	50,000
Trade Payables	1,40,000
Tangible Assets	1,50,000
Goodwill	1,19,500
Inventories	55,000
Trade Receivables	65,000
Cash at Bank	91,600

The business of V Ltd. is taken over by P Ltd. as on that date on the following terms:

(a) 50% of Tangible Fixed Assets are taken over at 100% more than the book value and the remaining Tangible Fixed Assets are taken over at $16\frac{2}{3}\%$ less than the book value.

(b) Goodwill of V Ltd. is to be valued at ₹ 50,000.

(c) Inventories are taken over at book value less 10% and Trade Receivables are taken over at book value subject to an allowance of 10% to cover doubtful debts.

(d) Trade Payables are to be taken over subject to a discount of 5% and Unrecorded Loan Liability of ₹ 36,500 to be discharged by P Ltd. at book value.

(e) The purchase consideration payable by P Ltd. was agreed as follows:

- (i) The purchase consideration is to be discharged to the extent of 20% in cash.
- (ii) The issue of such an amount of fully paid 14% Debentures in P Ltd at 96 per cent as is sufficient to discharge 10% Debentures in V Ltd. at a premium of 20 per cent.
- (iii) The issue of such an amount of fully paid 10% Pref. Shares in P Ltd. at 125% as is sufficient to discharge 9% Pref. Shares in V Ltd. at a premium of 20%.
- (iv) The balance in the form of equity shares of ₹ 10 each, ₹ 8 paid up at a premium of ₹ 7 per share. The market value of an equity share of P Ltd. at present is ₹ 100.
- (v) Expenses of liquidation of V Ltd. are to be reimbursed by P Ltd. to the extent of ₹ 10,000. Actual Expenses amounted to ₹ 12,000.

Show the calculation and discharge of Purchase Consideration.

SOLUTION

1. CALCULATION OF PURCHASE CONSIDERATION

	Particulars	₹
A	Assets taken over at agreed values	
	Tangible Fixed Assets [(₹ 1,50,000 × 50%) + 100%]	1,50,000
	Tangible Fixed Assets [(₹ 1,50,000 × 50%) – $16\frac{2}{3}$%]	62,500
	Inventories [₹ 55,000 – ₹ 5,500]	49,500
	Trade Receivables [₹ 65,000 – ₹ 6,500]	58,500
	Cash at Bank [91,600 – 2,000(Expenses)]	89,600
	Goodwill	50,000
		4,60,100
B	*Less:* Liabilities taken over:	
	Trade Payables [₹ 1,40,000 – 5%]	1,33,000
	10% Debentures [₹ 50,000 + 20%]	60,000
	Unrecorded Loan	38,500
		2,31,500
C	Net Assets taken over (A – B)	2,28,600

2. DISCHARGE OF PURCHASE CONSIDERATION

A. Cash to Equity Shareholders [2,28,600 × 20%]	45,720
B. 480, 9% Pref. Shares to be issued [(500 × 120%)]	60,000
C. 8,192, Equity Shares to be issued [(2,28,600 – 45,720 – 60,000)/ ₹ 15] × ₹ 15	**1,22,880**
D. Total Purchase Consideration (A + B + C)	2,28,600

Note: *According to AS-14, the amount paid by purchasing Company to discharge the debentures holders and the liquidation expenses of Vendor Company are not considered as part of purchase consideration.*

ILLUSTRATION 6

Given below are the extracts from the Balance Sheet of V Ltd. as at 31st March, 2016:

Particulars	₹
Equity Share Capital of ₹ 10 each	2,00,000
8% Pref. Share Capital of ₹ 100 each	50,000
General Reserve	20,000
Profit & Loss A/c	16,100
Statutory Reserves	5,000
10% Debentures	50,000
Trade Payables	1,40,000
Tangible Assets	1,50,000
Goodwill	1,19,500

Inventories	55,000
Trade Receivables	65,000
Cash at Bank	91,600

Prior to absorption, V Ltd. decides to declare and pay equity dividend @ 5%.(Ignore Dividend Distribution Tax). The business of V Ltd. is taken over by P Ltd. as on that date on the following terms:

(a) 50% of Tangible Fixed Assets are taken over at 100% more than the book value and the remaining Tangible Fixed Assets are taken over at $16\frac{2}{3}\%$ less than the book value.

(b) Goodwill of V Ltd. is to be valued at ₹ 50,000.

(c) Inventories are taken over at book value less 10% and Trade Receivables are taken over at book value subject to an allowance of 10% to cover doubtful debts.

(d) Trade Payables are to be taken over subject to a discount of 5% and Unrecorded Loan Liability of ₹ 38,500 to be discharged by P Ltd. at book value.

(e) The purchase consideration payable by P Ltd. was agreed as follows:

(i) The issue of such an amount of fully paid 14% Debentures in P Ltd at 96 per cent as is sufficient to discharge 10% Debentures in V Ltd. at a premium of 20 per cent.

(ii) The issue of such an amount of fully paid 10% Pref. Shares in P Ltd. at 125% as is sufficient to discharge 9% Pref. Shares in V Ltd. at a premium of 20%.

(iii) One Equity Share of ₹ 10 each, ₹ 8 paid up valued at ₹ 15 per share for every two Equity Shares held in V Ltd. and the balance in cash. The market value of an equity share of P Ltd. at present is ₹ 100.

(iv) Expenses of liquidation of V Ltd. are to be reimbursed by P Ltd. to the extent of ₹ 10,000. Actual Expenses amounted to ₹ 14,100.

Show the calculation and discharge of Purchase Consideration.

SOLUTION

1. CALCULATION OF PURCHASE CONSIDERATION

	Particulars	₹
A	Assets taken over at agreed values	
	Tangible Fixed Assets [(₹ 1,50,000 × 50%) + 100%]	1,50,000
	Tangible Fixed Assets [(₹ 1,50,000 × 50%) – $16\frac{2}{3}\%$]	62,500
	Inventories [₹ 55,000 – ₹ 5,500]	49,500
	Trade Receivables [₹ 65,000 – ₹ 6,500]	58,500
	Cash at Bank [91,600 – 10,000(ED) – 4,000(PD) – 4,100(Exp.)]	73,500
	Goodwill	50,000
		4,44,000
B	*Less:* Liabilities taken over:	
	Trade Payables [₹ 1,40,000 – 5%]	1,33,000
	10% Debentures [₹ 50,000 + 20%]	60,000
	Unrecorded Loan	38,500
		2,31,500
C	Net Assets taken over (A – B)	2,12,500

2. DISCHARGE OF PURCHASE CONSIDERATION

A. 10,000, Equity Shares to be issued [(20,000 × 1/2) × ₹ 15]	1,50,000
B. 480, 9% Pref. Shares to be issued [(500 × 120%)]	60,000
C. Cash to Equity Shareholders [Balancing figure]	**2,500**
D. Total Purchase Consideration (A + B + C)	2,12,500

Note: *According to AS-14, the amount paid by purchasing Company to discharge the debentures holders and the liquidation expenses of Vendor Company are not considered as part of purchase consideration.*

ILLUSTRATION 7

X Ltd. takes over Y Ltd. Given below are the extracts from the Balance Sheets of these companies at 31.03.2016:

Particulars	*X Ltd. (₹)*	*Y Ltd. (₹)*
Equity Share Capital of ₹ 10 each	30,00,000	12,00,000
Reserves & Surplus		10,00,000
15% Debentures	—	8,00,000
Current Liabilities	3,00,000	1,00,000
Tangible Block	24,00,000	18,00,000
Goodwill	—	1,50,000
Non-Current Investments (₹ 1,00,000, 6% tax free G.P. Notes)	1,00,000	—
Inventories	1,90,000	2,20,000
Other Current Assets	6,10,000	9,30,000

Additional Information:

	X Ltd.	*Y Ltd.*
Tangible Block	Valued at 25% more than the book value	Valued at $16\frac{2}{3}$% less than the book value
Goodwill	₹ 17,90,000	₹ 70,000
Inventories	Undervalued by ₹10,000	Overvalued by ₹ 20,000

X Ltd. to issue shares to share-holders of Y Ltd., on the basis of the intrinsic value of shares on the date of take-over. Calculate Purchase Consideration and show the discharge thereof.

SOLUTION

CALCULATION OF PURCHASE CONSIDERATION

Particulars	*X Ltd.* ₹	*Y Ltd.* ₹
Tangible Block	24,00,000	18,00,000
Add: Undervaluation (24,00,000 × 25%)	6,00,000	
Less: Overvaluation (18,00,000 × $16\frac{2}{3}$%]		(3,00,000)
Net Tangible Block at Revalued figure	30,00,000	15,00,000

Goodwill	17,90,000	70,000
Non-Current Investments (₹ 1,00,000, 6% tax free G.P. Notes)	1,00,000	—
Inventories	1,90,000	2,20,000
Add: Undervaluation of Cl. Inventory	10,000	
Less: Overvaluation of Cl. Inventory		(20,000)
Other Current Assets	6,10,000	9,30,000
	57,00,000	27,00,000
Less: 15% Debentures	—	(8,00,000)
Less: Current Liabilities	(3,00,000)	(1,00,000)
Net Assets	54,00,000	18,00,000
No. of Shares	3,00,000	1,20,000
Intrinsic Value	18	15
No. of Equity Shares to be issued (1,20,000 × 15/18)		1,00,000
Share Capital [1,00,000 × ₹ 10]		10,00,000
Securities Premium [1,00,000 × ₹ 8]		8,00,000
Purchase Consideration		18,00,000

ILLUSTRATION 8

X Ltd. takes over Y Ltd. Given below are the extracts from the Balance Sheets of these companies at 31.03.2016:

Particulars	*X Ltd. (₹)*	*Y Ltd. (₹)*
Equity Share Capital of ₹ 10 each	30,00,000	12,00,000
Reserves & Surplus		10,00,000
15% Debentures	—	8,00,000
Current Liabilities	3,00,000	1,00,000
Tangible Block	24,00,000	18,00,000
Goodwill	—	1,50,000
Non-Current Investments (₹ 1,00,000, 6% tax free G.P. Notes)	1,00,000	—
Inventories	1,90,000	2,20,000
Other Current Assets	6,10,000	9,30,000

Additional Information:

	X Ltd.	*Y Ltd.*
Tangible Block	Understated by 20%	Overstated by 20%
Goodwill	17,90,000	70,000
Inventories	Understated by 5%	Overstated by 10%

X Ltd. to issue shares to share-holders of Y Ltd.at a price of ₹1 above the intrinsic value of its shares on the date of take-over.The market value of an equity share of X Ltd. at present is ₹ 100. The scheme of amalgamation was not supported by 100 shareholders of Y Ltd., and had to be paid ₹ 10 per share above their intrinsic value as consideration. The amount of the dissenting shareholders was borne by X Ltd.,Calculate Purchase Consideration and show the discharge thereof.

SOLUTION

CALCULATION OF PURCHASE CONSIDERATION

Particulars	*X Ltd.* ₹	*Y Ltd.* ₹
Tangible Block	24,00,000	18,00,000
Add: Undervaluation (24,00,000 × 20/80)	6,00,000	
Less: Overvaluation (18,00,000 × 20/120)		(3,00,000)
Net Tangible Block at Revalued figure	30,00,000	15,00,000
Goodwill	17,90,000	70,000
Non-Current Investments (₹ 1,00,000, 6% tax free G.P. Notes)	1,00,000	—
Inventories	1,90,000	2,20,000
Add: Undervaluation of Cl. Inventory (1,90,000 × 5/95)	10,000	
Less: Overvaluation of Cl. Inventory (2,20,000 × 10/110)		(20,000)
Other Current Assets	6,10,000	9,30,000
	57,00,000	27,00,000
Less: 15% Debentures	—	(8,00,000)
Less: Current Liabilities	(3,00,000)	(1,00,000)
Net Assets	54,00,000	18,00,000
No. of Shares	3,00,000	1,20,000
Intrinsic Value	18	15
Issue Price [₹18 + ₹1]	19	
No. of Equity Shares to be issued [(1,20,000 – 100) × 15/19]		94,657.89
Share Capital [94,657 × ₹ 10]		9,46,570
Securities Premium [94,657 × ₹ 9]		8,51,913
Cash for fraction [0.89 × ₹ 100]		89
Payment to dissenting shareholders[100 × (₹15 + ₹ 10)]		2,500
Purchase Consideration		18,01,072

ILLUSTRATION 8A

IN THE PREVIOUS ILLUSTRATION Calculate Purchase Consideration and show the discharge thereof if it is also decided to make the entries relating to the issue of shares at par value only.

SOLUTION

No. of Equity Shares to be issued [(1,20,000 – 100) × 15/19]	94,657.89
Share Capital [94,657 × ₹ 10]	9,46,570
Cash for fraction [0.89 × ₹ 100]	89
Payment to dissenting shareholders [100 × (₹15 + ₹ 10)]	2,500
Purchase Consideration	9,49,159

ILLUSTRATION 9

Given below are the extracts from the Balance Sheets of A Ltd. and B Ltd. on at 31st March 2016:

Particulars	₹
80,000 Equity shares of ₹ 10 each fully paid up	8,00,000
Reserves & Surplus	1,00,000
Current Liabilities	1,00,000
Non-Current Assets	7,00,000
Current Assets	3,00,000

The consideration was agreed to be paid as follows:

(a) A payment in cash of ₹ 5 per share in B Ltd., and

(b) The issue of shares of ₹ 10 each in A Ltd. on the basis of 2 equity shares (valued at ₹ 15) and one 10% Cumulative Preference shares (valued at ₹ 10) for every five shares held in B Ltd.

The whole of the share capital consists of shareholdings in exact multiple of five except the followings holdings:

A	116
B	76
C	72
D	28
Other individual	8 (each member holding one share each)
	300

It was agreed that A Ltd. will pay in cash for fractional shares equivalent at agreed value of shares in B Ltd.

Required: Prepare a Statement showing the purchase consideration receivable in shares and cash.

SOLUTION

STATEMENT SHOWING THE COMPUTATION OF PURCHASE CONSIDERATION

Particulars	₹
31,994 Equity Shares @ ₹ 15 each	4,79,910
15,997 Preference Shares @ ₹ 10 each	1,59,970
Cash [(80,000 – 15) × ₹ 5]	3,99,925
	10,39,805
Add: Cash for fractional shares [15 × ₹ 13]	195
	10,40,000

Working Notes:

(I) SCHEDULE SHOWING FRACTIONAL SHARES

Share holder	*Holding of Shares*	*Exchangeable in multiple of five*	*Non Exchangeable Shares*
A	116	115	1
B	76	75	1

C	72	70	2
D	28	25	3
Others	8	–	8
	300	285	15

(ii) Equity Shares to be issued by A Ltd. = [(80,000 – 15) × 2/5] = 31,994

(iii) Preference Shares to be issued by A Ltd. = [(80,000 – 15) × 1/5] = 15,997

(IV) VALUATION OF FRACTIONAL SHARES

Cash for 5 equity shares [5 × ₹5]	₹ 25
2 equity shares for 5 equity shares [2 × ₹15]	₹ 30
1 Pref. share for 5 equity shares [1 × ₹ 10]	₹ 10
Total	₹ 65
Value for 1 equity share [₹65/5]	₹13
No. of fractional shares	15
Cash for fractional shares [15 × ₹ 13]	195

7.0 ACCOUNTING TREATMENT IN THE BOOKS OF TRANSFEROR COMPANY OR VENDOR COMPANY

Step 1: Open a Realisation Account and transfer all the recorded assets [including intangible assets like goodwill at their respective book values (i.e., the values at which they are appearing in the books of vendor company) irrespective of the fact whether the purchasing company has taken over *or* not. However, Cash and Bank Balances are transferred to Realisation Account only to the extent it is taken over by the purchasing company.

JOURNAL ENTRY

Realisation A/c	Dr.	*(with the total)*
To Sundry Assets (individually)		*(with their individual book values)*

Note:

(i) An asset against which a provision or reserve has been created should be transferred at its gross figure and not at its net figure e.g., debtors.

(ii) Provision/Reserve against a liability is a separate account and thus, it should be transferred to Realisation Account separately like other assets e.g., reserve for discount on creditors.

(iii) The cash and bank balances should not be transferred to Realisation account if these are not taken over by the purchasing company.

Step 2: Transfer all third parties liabilities which are taken over by the purchasing company, at their respective book figures.

JOURNAL ENTRY

Sundry Assets (individually)	Dr.	*(with their individual book values)*
To Realisation A/c		*(with the total)*

Note:

(i) A liability against which a provision or reserve has been created should be transferred at its gross figure and not at its net figure, e.g., creditors.

(ii) *Items in the nature of 'Provisions' (e.g., Provision for taxation, Employees Provident Fund, Pension Fund, Provision for Doubtful Debt, Provision for Depreciation) should be transferred to Realisation Account.*

(iii) *Items in the nature of "Reserve" (e.g., credit balance of Profit and Loss Account, General Reserve, Dividend Equalisation Fund, Workmen Compensation Fund) should not be transferred to Realisation Account but that portion of any reserve/fund which represents a liability expected to arise in future should be transferred to Realisation Account (e.g., Estimated Workmen Compensation Claim out of Workmen Compensation Reserve).*

Step 3: Make due the Purchase Consideration from the Purchasing Company.

JOURNAL ENTRY

Purchasing Company's A/c	Dr.	*(with the Purchase Consideration Due)*
To Realisation A/c		

Step 4: Receive the Purchase Consideration from the Purchasing Company.

Cash/Bank A/c	Dr.	*(with Cash Received)*
Preference Shares in Purchasing Company	Dr.	*(with Issue Price of Pref. Shares)*
Equity Shares in Purchasing Company	Dr.	*(with Issue Price of Equity Shares)*
To Purchasing Company		*(With the total)*

Step 5: Do the Treatment of Liquidation/Realisation expenses.

Case	**JOURNAL ENTRY**	
(a) If these expenses are to be borne and paid by the Vendor Company	Realisation A/c To Bank A/c	
(b) If these expenses are to be reimbursed by the purchasing company		
(i) *On Payment by Vendor Company*	Purchasing Company *(with agreed amount)*	Dr.
	Realisation A/c *(with excess)*	Dr.
	To Bank A/c (with the total)	
(ii) *On reimbursement*	Bank A/c To Purchasing Company	

Step 6: Realise those assets which have not been taken over by the purchasing company.

JOURNAL ENTRY

Bank A/c	Dr.	*(with the amount realised)*
To Realisation A/c		

Step 7: Discharge the Claims of Preference Shareholders and transfer the difference between the amount actually payable and the book figure to the Realisation Account.

(A) JOURNAL ENTRY ON MAKING DUE

Preference Share Capital A/c	Dr.	*(with book figure)*
Realisation A/c	Dr.	*(with the loss)*

To Preference Shareholders' A/c's (with the amount actually payable)
To Realisation A/c (with the profit)

(B) JOURNAL ENTRY ON MAKING PAYMENT

Preference Shareholders' A/cs	Dr.
To Bank A/c	
To Preference Shares in purchasing Co.	

Step 8: Ascertain the Profit *or* Loss on Realisation and transfer the same to the Equity Shareholders' A/c.

(a) In case of Profit on Realisation	Realisation A/c	Dr.
	To Equity Shareholders' A/c	
(b) In case of Loss on Realisation	Equity Shareholders' A/c	Dr.
	To Realisation A/c	

Step 9: Transfer the Equity Share Capital A/c, Accumulated Profits, Reserve and losses to the Equity Shareholders' A/cs.

(a) For Transfer of Equity Share Capital, Accumulated Profits and Reserves [after making adjustment for Dividend, Dividend Tax etc.]	Equity Share Capital A/c	Dr.
	Profit and Loss A/c	Dr.
	General Reserve A/c	Dr.
	Dividend Equalisation Reserve	Dr.
	Workmen Compensation reserve	Dr.
	Capital Reserve A/c	Dr.
	Securities Premium A/c	Dr.
	Debenture redemption Reserve	Dr.
	Capital Redemption Reserve	Dr.
	Statutory Reserves	Dr.
	To Equity Shareholders' A/c	
(b) For Transfer of Accumulated Losses	Equity Shareholders' A/c	Dr.
	To Profit and Loss A/c (Dr. Balance)	
	To Preliminary Expenses	
	To Underwriting Commission	
	To Discount on Issue of Shares/Debentures	
	To Deferred Advertisement Expenditure	

Step 10: Make Final Payment to Equity Shareholders:

Equity Shareholders' A/c	Dr. *(with the total)*
To Equity Shares in Purchasing Co.	
To Cash/Bank A/c	

Note: *The net amount payable to the equity shareholders must be equal to the amount of shares in Purchasing Co. and Cash and Bank Balance left after the discharge of all outsiders' liabilities and claims of Preference Shareholders.*

8.0 TREATMENT OF DIFFERENCE BETWEEN THE PURCHASE CONSIDERATION AND THE NET ASSETS OF THE TRANSFEROR COMPANY ARISING ON AMALGAMATION IN THE NATURE OF PURCHASE

Case	Accounting Treatment
If Purchase Consideration > Net Assets	The excess of Purchase Consideration over the value of Net Assets acquired should be Treated as **Goodwill arising on amalgamation.** Such goodwill should be amortised on a systematic basis over a period not exceeding 5 years unless longer period can be justified.
If Net Assets > Purchase Consideration	The excess of net assets acquired over the Purchase Consideration should be treated as **Capital Reserve arising on Amalgamation.**

ILLUSTRATION 10 [Treatment of Reserves arising on Amalgamation in the nature of Purchase]

(₹ in lacs)

Particulars	*Case I* ₹	*Case II* ₹	*Case III* ₹
Share Capital issued by Transferee Co.	9.50	9.50	9.50
Cash for fractional Share paid by Transferee Co.	.50	.50	.50
Assets acquired by Transferee Co.	11.20	11.00	10.80
Liabilities undertaken by Transferee Co.	1.00	1.00	1.00

SOLUTION

CALCULATION OF CAPITAL RESERVE/GOODWILL

Particulars	*Case I* ₹	*Case II* ₹	*Case III* ₹
A. Purchase Consideration (9.50 + 0.50)	10.00	10.00	10.00
B. Net Assets acquired (Assets – Liabilities)	10.20	10.00	9.80
C. Goodwill	—	—	.20
or			
Capital Reserve	0.20	—	—

9.0 ACCOUNTING TREATMENT IN THE BOOKS OF TRANSFEREE COMPANY OR PURCHASING COMPANY IN CASE OF PURCHASE

Step 1: Record the Acquisition of business from the Vendor Company.

JOURNAL ENTRY

Business Purchase A/c	Dr.	*(with purchase consideration)*
To Liquidator of the Vendor Co.		

Step 2A: In case of Amalgamation in the nature of Purchase.

"Record the Assets and Liabilities taken over at their respective agreed values (i.e., not their book values) and debit the Goodwill Account with the excess of Purchase Consideration over the Net Assets taken over (if any) *or* credit the Capital Reserve Account with the excess of Net Assets over the Purchase Consideration (if any)".

JOURNAL ENTRY

Assets (Individually)	Dr.	*(with their respective agreed values of the assets taken over)*
Goodwill A/c	Dr.	*(with excess of Purchase Consideration over the Net Assets)*
To Liabilities (Individually)		*(with the respective agreed amount of the liabilities taken over)*
To Business Purchase A/c		*(with the Purchase consideration)*
To Capital Reserve A/c		*(with excess of Net Assets over the Purchase Consideration)*

Step 2B: In case of Amalgamation in the nature of Purchase.

"Record the Statutory Reserves of the Transferor Company"

JOURNAL ENTRY

Amalgamation Adjustment A/c	Dr.	*(with the total)*
To Statutory Reserves A/c (Individually)		*(with their respective book balances)*

Note: *Amalgamation Adjustment should be disclosed under the head 'Other Non-current Assets' on the Assets side of the Balance Sheet.*

Step 3: Make Payment to Vendor Company.

JOURNAL ENTRY

Liquidator of Vendor Co.'s A/c	Dr.	*(with the total)*
Discount on Issue of Shares A/c	Dr.	*(with the Discount allowed on shares)*
To Equity Share Capital A/c		*(with the paid up value of Equity Shares issued)*
To Preference Share Capital A/c		*(with the paid up value of Pref. Shares issued)*
To Securities Premium A/c		*(with the Securities Premium)*
To Cash A/c/Bank A/c		*(with the Cash Payment)*

Note: *The Shares issued by way of purchase consideration must be recorded at their paid up values (i.e., not at their issued prices) after giving due credit to Securities Premium Account (in case the shares have been issued at premium) or after giving due debit to "Discount on issue of Shares A/c' (in case the shares have been issued at discount).*

Step 4: Record the Issue of Debentures (if any) to discharge the existing Debentureholders of vendor company.

JOURNAL ENTRY

Debentures in Vendor Company	Dr.	*(with the amount of debentures)*
Discount on Issue of Debentures in Purchasing Company	Dr.	*(with the Debentures Discount)*
To Debentures in Purchasing Company		*(with the Nominal Value)*
To Securities Premium A/c		*(with the Debenture Premium)*

Step 5: Record the Reimbursement of the Liquidation Expenses of the Vendor Company.

JOURNAL ENTRY

Goodwill A/c (in case of Purchase)	Dr.
To Bank A/c	

Step 6: Eliminate the unrealised profit included in the unsold stock.

(a) Where the Unsold Inventories of the purchasing company includes the goods purchased from the vendor company

Goodwill A/c (in case of Purchase)	Dr.
To Inventories A/c	

(b) Where the Unsold Inventories of the vendor company includes goods purchased from the purchasing company, only the amount of stock is reduced to its cost while passing the entries on acquisition. (i.e., Entry in Step 2).

Note: *In case of sale of goods at loss, no adjustment is required*

Step 7: Eliminate the Inter Company Owings

(a) To eliminate the Debts owed by Vendor Company	Trade Payables of Vendor Co To Trade Receivables	Dr.
(b) To eliminate the Debts owed by Purchasing Company	Trade Payables To Trade Receivables of Vendor Co.	Dr.
(c) To eliminate the Bills drawn and retained by Vendor Co. upon Purchasing Company	Bills Payable A/c To Bills Receivable of Vendor Co.	Dr.
(d) To eliminate the Bills drawn and retained by Purchasing Company upon Vendor Co.	Bills Payable of Vendor Co. To Bills Receivable A/c	Dr.
(e) To eliminate the Debentures held by Vendor Co. in Purchasing Co.	Debentures A/c Goodwill A/c To Investment in Debentures A/c (Vendor Co.) To Capital Reserve A/c	Dr. [Face value] Dr. [If FV < BV] [Book Value] [If FV > BV]
(f) To eliminate the Debentures held by Purchasing Co. in Vendor Co.	Debentures in Vendor Co. Goodwill A/c To Investment in Debentures A/c To Capital Reserve A/c	Dr. [Face Value] Dr. [If FV < BV] Dr. [Book value] [If FV > BV]

Note:

(i) *Bills drawn by one company upon the other company and discounted with the bank should not be eliminated because these bills represent owing between the bank and the company and not the inter-company owings.*

(ii) *Where the debtors of a company include a sum due from another company but the creditors of another company include a lesser sum due to the former company. The difference should be treated as Cash-in-transit.*

(iii) *The entry (f) in Step 7 should be merged with entry in Step 4 so that the new debentures will be issued to discharge those debentures of vendor company which are held by outsiders (i.e., holders other than the purchasing company).*

(iv) *In case of entries (e) and (f), the loss should be debited to Goodwill A/c (in case of purchase) and the profit should be credited to Capital Reserve A/c.*

Step 8: Set off Goodwill against Capital Reserve

JOURNAL ENTRY

Capital Reserve A/c	Dr.	
To Goodwill A/c		

Note: *The objective of passing the aforesaid journal entry is to disclose only one item (i.e., out of Capital Reserve and Goodwill) which is net of other item.*

ILLUSTRATION 11

Given below are the extracts from the Balance Sheet of V Ltd. as at 31st March, 2016:

Particulars	₹
Equity Share Capital of ₹ 10 each	2,00,000
8% Pref. Share Capital of ₹ 100 each	50,000
General Reserve	20,000
Profit & Loss A/c	16,100
Statutory Reserves	5,000
10% Debentures	50,000
Trade Payables	1,40,000
Tangible Assets	1,50,000
Goodwill	1,19,500
Inventories	55,000
Trade Receivables	65,000
Cash at Bank	91,600

The business of V Ltd. is taken over by P Ltd. as on that date on the following terms:

(a) 50% of Tangible Fixed Assets are taken over at 100% more than the book value and the remaining Tangible Fixed Assets are taken over at $16\frac{2}{3}\%$ less than the book value.

(b) Goodwill of V Ltd. is to be valued at ₹ 50,000.

(c) Inventories are taken over at book value less 10% and Trade Receivables are taken over at book value subject to an allowance of 10% to cover doubtful debts.

(d) Trade Payables are to be taken over subject to a discount of 5% and Unrecorded Loan Liability of ₹ 38,500 to be discharged by P Ltd. at book value.

(e) The purchase consideration payable by P Ltd. was agreed as follows:

(i) The issue of such an amount of fully paid 14% Debentures in P Ltd at 96 per cent as is sufficient to discharge 10% Debentures in V Ltd. at a premium of 20 per cent.

(ii) The issue of such an amount of fully paid 10% Pref. Shares in P Ltd. at 125% as is sufficient to discharge 9% Pref. Shares in V Ltd. at a premium of 20%.

(iii) One Equity Share of ₹ 10 each, ₹ 8 paid up valued at ₹ 15 per share for every two Equity Shares held in V Ltd. and the balance in cash. The market value of an equity share of P Ltd. at present is ₹ 100.

(iv) Expenses of liquidation of V Ltd. are to be reimbursed by P Ltd. to the extent of ₹ 10,000. Actual Expenses amounted to ₹ 12,000.

(f) Statutory Reserves are to be maintained for 2 more years.

Required: *Pass Journal Entries in the books of V Ltd and P Ltd.*

SOLUTION

JOURNAL OF V LTD.

Date	Particulars		L.F.	Dr. (₹)	Cr. (₹)
1	Realisation A/c	Dr.		4,79,100	
	To Goodwill				1,19,500
	To Tangible Fixed Assets				1,50,000
	To Inventories				55,000
	To Trade Receivables				65,000
	To Cash at Bank [91,600 – 2,000 Exp.]				89,600
	(Being the transfer of various assets to Realisation A/c)				
2	10% Debentures	Dr.		50,000	
	Trade Payables	Dr.		1,40,000	
	To Realisation A/c				1,90,000
	(Being the transfer of various liabilities to Realisation A/c)				
3	P Ltd	Dr.		2,28,600	
	To Realisation A/c				2,28,600
	(Being the purchase consideration due)				
4	Equity Shares in P Ltd.	Dr.		1,50,000	
	9% Pref. Shares in P Ltd.	Dr.		60,000	
	Cash at Bank	Dr.		18,600	
	To P Ltd.				2,28,600
	(Being the receipt of purchase consideration)				
5	P Ltd.	Dr.		10,000	
	Realiasation A/c	Dr.		2,000	
	To Bank A/c				12,000
	(Being liquidation expenses paid out of which ₹ 10,000 are to be reimbursed by purchasing company)				
6	Bank A/c	Dr.		10,000	
	To P Ltd.				10,000
	(Being liquidation expenses reimbursed by purchasing company)				
7	8% Pref. Share Capital A/c	Dr.		50,000	
	Realiasation A/c	Dr.		10,000	
	To Pref. Shareholders' A/c				60,000
	(Being the transfer of Pref. Share Capital to Pref. shareholders' A/c & loss on discharge to Realiasation A/c)				
8	Pref. Shareholders' A/c	Dr.		60,000	
	To 9% Pref. Shares in P Ltd.				60,000

	(Being the claims of Pref. share holders discharged)			
9	Equity Shareholders' A/c Dr.		72,500	
	To Realisation A/c			72,500
	(Being the transfer of loss on Realisation)			
10	Equity Share Capital A/c Dr.		2,00,000	
	General Reserve Dr.		20,000	
	Profit & Loss A/c Dr.		16,100	
	Statutory Reserves A/c Dr.		5,000	
	To Equity Shareholders'A/c			2,41,100
	(Being the transfer of Share Capital & balance of P&L A/c & Reserves to Equity Shareholders' Account)			
11	Equity Shareholders' A/c Dr.		1,68,600	
	To Equity Shares in P Ltd.			1,50,000
	To Bank A/c			18,600
	(Being the claims of Equity Shareholders discharged)			

JOURNAL OF P LTD.

Date	Particulars	L.F.	Dr. (₹)	Cr. (₹)
1	Business Purchase A/c Dr.		2,28,600	
	To Liquidators of V Ltd.			2,28,600
	(Being the purchase of the business)			
2	Goodwill Dr.		50,000	
	Tangible Fixed Assets[₹ 1,50,000 + ₹ 62,500] Dr.		2,12,500	
	Inventories Dr.		49,500	
	Trade Receivables Dr.		65,000	
	Bank Dr.		89,600	
	Reserve for Discount on Trade Payables [5% of ₹ 1,40 000] Dr.		7,000	
	To Provision for Doubtful Debts [10% of ₹ 65,000]			6,500
	To Trade Payables			1,40,000
	To 10% Debentures [₹ 50,000 + 20%]			60,000
	To Unrecorded Loan			38,500
	To Business Purchase A/c			2,28,600
	(Being the Assets and Liabilities taken over)			
3	Liquidators of V Ltd. Dr.		2,28,600	
	To Equity Share Capital A/c [10,000 × ₹ 8]			80,000
	To 9% Pref. Share Capital A/c [480 × ₹ 100]			48,000
	To Securities Premium A/c [(10,000 × ₹ 7) + (480 × ₹ 25)]			82,000
	To Bank A/c			18,600
	(Being the purchase consideration discharged)			

4	Goodwill A/c	Dr.	10,000	
	To Bank A/c			10,000
	(Being the payment of Liquidation Expenses of Vendor co.)			
5	10% Debentures of V Ltd.	Dr.	60,000	
	Discount on Issue of 14% Debentures A/c	Dr.	2,500	
	To 14% Debentures A/c			62,500
	(Being 10% Debentures of Vendor co. redeemed by issue of 625, 14% Debentures of ₹ 100 each at a discount of 4%)			
	[Face Value of Debentures = ₹ 60,000/96% = ₹ 62,500]			
6	Unrecorded Loan A/c	Dr.	38,500	
	To Bank A/c			38,500
	(Being the liabilities of Vendor co. discharged)			
7	Amalgamation Adjustment A/c	Dr.	5,000	
	To Statutory Reserves			5,000
	(Being the identity of Statutory Reserves retained)			

Working Notes:

1. CALCULATION OF PURCHASE CONSIDERATION

	Particulars	₹
A	Assets taken over at agreed values	
	Tangible Fixed Assets [(₹ 1,50,000 × 50%) + 100%]	1,50,000
	Tangible Fixed Assets [(₹ 1,50,000 × 50%) – $16\frac{2}{3}$%]	62,500
	Inventories [₹ 55,000 – ₹ 5,500]	49,500
	Trade Receivables [₹ 65,000 – ₹ 6,500]	58,500
	Cash at Bank [91,600 – 2,000 (Expenses)]	89,600
	Goodwill	50,000
		4,60,100
B	*Less:* Liabilities taken over:	
	Trade Payables [₹ 1,40,000 – 5%]	1,33,000
	10% Debentures [₹ 50,000 + 20%]	60,000
	Unrecorded Loan	38,500
		2,31,500
C	Net Assets taken over (A – B)	2,28,600

2. DISCHARGE OF PURCHASE CONSIDERATION

A. 10,000, Equity Shares to be issued [(20,000 × 1/2) × ₹ 15]	1,50,000
B. 480, 9% Pref. Shares to be issued [(500 × 120%)]	60,000
C. Cash to Equity Shareholders [Balancing figure]	18,600
D. Total Purchase Consideration (A + B + C)	2,28,600

Note: *According to AS-14, the amount paid by purchasing Company to discharge the debentures holders and the liquidation expenses of Vendor Company are not considered as part of purchase consideration.*

ILLUSTRATION 12

What shall be the change in the solution of Previous Illustration 11 if the following information is also provided:

"V Ltd. owed P Ltd. ₹ 60,000 for the purchases of stock from P Ltd. which made a profit of 20% on cost. Four fifth of such stock were sold till 31.3.2016."

SOLUTION

1. There will be no change in the Journal Entries of V Ltd.

JOURNAL OF P LTD.

Date	Particulars		L.F.	Dr. (₹)	Cr. (₹)
1	Business Purchase A/c	Dr.		2,28,600	
	To Liquidators of V Ltd.				2,28,600
	(Being the purchase of the business)				
2	**Goodwill (Balancing figure)**	**Dr.**		**53,000**	
	Tangible Fixed Assets	Dr.		2,12,500	
	Inventories	Dr.		49,500	
	Trade Receivables	Dr.		65,000	
	Bank	Dr.		89,600	
	Reserve for Discount on Trade Payables [5% of ₹(1,40 000 – 60,000)]	**Dr.**		**4,000**	
	To Provision for Doubtful Debts [10% of ₹ 65,000]				6,500
	To Trade Payables				1,40,000
	To 10% Debentures [₹ 50,000 + 20%]				60,000
	To Unrecorded Loan				38,500
	To Business Purchase A/c				2,28,600
	(Being the Assets and Liabilities taken over)				
3	Liquidators of V Ltd.	Dr.		2,28,600	
	To Equity Share Capital A/c [10,000 × ₹ 8]				80,000
	To 9% Pref. Share Capital A/c [480 × ₹ 100]				48,000
	To Securities Premium A/c [(10,000 × ₹ 7) + (480 × ₹ 25)]				82,000
	To Bank A/c				18,600
	(Being the purchase consideration discharged)				
4	Goodwill A/c	Dr.		10,000	
	To Bank A/c				10,000
	(Being the payment of Liquidation Expenses of Vendor co.)				

5	10% Debentures of V Ltd. Dr.		60,000	
	Discount on Issue of 14% Debentures A/c Dr.		2,500	
	To 14% Debentures A/c			62,500
	(Being 10% Debentures of Vendor co. redeemed by issue of 625, 14% Debentures of ₹ 100 each at a discount of 4%) [Face Value of Debentures = ₹ 60,000/96% = ₹ 62,500]			
6	Unrecorded Loan A/c Dr.		38,500	
	To Bank A/c			38,500
	(Being the liabilities of Vendor co. discharged)			
7	Amalgamation Adjustment A/c Dr.		5,000	
	To Statutory Reserves			5,000
	(Being the identity of statutory Reserves retained)			
8	**Goodwill A/c Dr.**		**800**	
	To Inventories			**800**
	(Being the elimination of unrealized profit included in goods purchased by V Ltd.)[(20% of ₹ 60,000 × 1/6) – (10% of ₹ 12,000)]			
9	**Trade Payables (V Ltd.) A/c Dr.**		**60,000**	
	To Trade Receivables A/c			**60,000**
	(Being the cancellation of Inter Co. Owing)			

ILLUSTRATION 13

What shall be the change in the solution of Illustration 11 if the following information is also provided: "Prior to 31st March 2016 V Ltd. sold goods costing ₹ 30,000 to P Ltd. for ₹ 40,000. ₹ 25,000 worth of goods were still in stock of P Ltd.Trade Receivables include ₹ 20,000 still due from P Ltd."

SOLUTION

1. There will be no change in the Journal Entries of V Ltd.

JOURNAL OF P LTD.

Date	*Particulars*	*L.F.*	*Dr. (₹)*	*Cr. (₹)*
1	Business Purchase A/c Dr.		2,28,600	
	To Liquidators of V Ltd.			2,28,600
	(Being the purchase of the business)			
2	**Goodwill (balancing figure) Dr.**		**48,000**	
	Tangible Fixed Assets Dr.		2,12,500	
	Inventories Dr.		49,500	
	Trade Receivables Dr.		65,000	
	Bank Dr.		89,600	
	Reserve for Discount on Trade Payables [5% of ₹ 1,40 000] Dr.		7,000	
	To Pro. for Doubtful Debts [10% of ₹ (65,000 – 20,000)]			**4,500**

	To Trade Payables			1,40,000
	To 10% Debentures [₹ 50,000 + 20%]			60,000
	To Unrecorded Loan			38,500
	To Business Purchase A/c			2,28,600
	(Being the Assets and Liabilities taken over)			
3	Liquidators of V Ltd.	Dr.	2,28,600	
	To Equity Share Capital A/c [10,000 × ₹ 8]			80,000
	To 9% Pref. Share Capital A/c [480 × ₹ 100]			48,000
	To Securities Premium A/c [(10,000 × ₹ 7) + (480 × ₹ 25)]			82,000
	To Bank A/c			18,600
	(Being the purchase consideration discharged)			
4	Goodwill A/c	Dr.	10,000	
	To Bank A/c			10,000
	(Being the payment of Liquidation Expenses of Vendor co.)			
5	10% Debentures of V Ltd.	Dr.	60,000	
	Discount on Issue of 14% Debentures A/c	Dr.	2,500	
	To 14% Debentures A/c			62,500
	(Being 10% Debentures of Vendor co. redeemed by issue of 625, 14% Debentures of ₹ 100 each at a discount of 4%)			
	[Face Value of Debentures = ₹ 60,000/96% = ₹ 62,500]			
6	Unrecorded Loan A/c	Dr.	38,500	
	To Bank A/c			38,500
	(Being the liabilities of Vendor co. discharged)			
7	Amalgamation Adjustment A/c	Dr.	5,000	
	To Statutory Reserves			5,000
	(Being the identity of statutory Reserves retained)			
8	**Goodwill**	**Dr.**	**6,250**	
	To Inventories A/c			**6,250**
	(Being the Elimination of unrealized profit on unsold goods worth ₹ 25,000 bought from V Ltd. still unsold (25,000 × 10,000/40,000)			
9	**Trade Payables A/c**	**Dr.**	**20,000**	
	To Trade Receivables (V Ltd.) A/c			**20,000**
	(Being Elimination of the amount owed by us to V Ltd.)			

ILLUSTRATION 14

Given below are the extracts from the Balance Sheet of **PRARTHANA** Ltd. as at 31st March, 2016:

Particulars	₹
Share Capital [Equity Shares of ₹ 10 fully paid]	6,00,000
Statutory Reserves	1,70,000

General Reserve	10,000
Profit & Loss A/c	1,00,000
12% Debentures	1,00,000
Trade Payables	20,000
Tangible Assets	6,00,000
Intangible Assets [Goodwill]	1,00,000
Inventories	2,08,000
Trade Receivables	36,000
Cash at Bank	56,000

PIYUSH Ltd. agreed to absorb the business of PRARTHANA Ltd. with effect from 1st Apr. 2016. The purchase consideration payable by Piyush Ltd. was agreed as follows:

(a) A cash payment equivalent to ₹ 2.50 for every ₹ 10 share in PRARTHANA Ltd.

(b) The issue of 90,000 Equity Shares of ₹ 10 each fully paid in PIYUSH Ltd. having an agreed value of ₹ 15 per share.

(c) The issue of such an amount of fully paid 14% Debentures in PIYUSH Ltd. at 96 per cent as is sufficient to discharge 12% Debentures in PRARTHANA Ltd. at a premium of 20 per cent.

While computing purchase consideration, PIYUSH Ltd. valued Tangible Fixed Assets at 100% more than the book value, Inventories at ₹ 1,42,000 and Trade Receivables at their face value subject to a provision of 5 per cent for doubtful debts. The actual cost of liquidation of PRARTHANA Ltd. was ₹ 15,000. Liquidation cost of PRARTHANA Ltd. is to be reimbursed by PIYUSH Ltd. to the extent of ₹ 10,000. Statutory Reserves are to be maintained for 2 more years.

Required: (i) Close the books of PRARTHANA Ltd. by preparing Realisation Account, Piyush Ltd Account, Shareholders' Account and Debentures Account; and

(ii) Pass Journal Entries in the books of PIYUSH Ltd. regarding acquisition of business.

SOLUTION

BOOKS OF PRARTHANA LTD.

REALISATION ACCOUNT

Dr. *Cr.*

Particulars	₹	*Particulars*	₹
To Goodwill	1,00,000	By Trade Payables	20,000
To Tangible Fixed Assets	6,00,000	By PIYUSH Ltd.	15,00,000
To Inventories	2,08,000	By 12% Debentures	1,00,000
To Trade Receivables	36,000		
To Cash & Bank [₹ 56,000 – ₹ 5,000]	51,000		
To Cash & Bank (Expenses)	5,000		
To Profit on Realisation	6,20,000		
	16,20,000		16,20,000

PIYUSH LTD. ACCOUNT

Dr. *Cr.*

Particulars	₹	*Particulars*	₹
To Realisation A/c	15,00,000	By Bank A/c	1,50,000
To Bank A/c	10,000	By Equity Shares in PIYUSH Ltd.	13,50,000

		By Bank A/c	10,000
	15,10,000		15,10,000

Dr. **EQUITY SHAREHOLDERS' ACCOUNT** Cr.

Particulars	₹	Particulars	₹
To Cash A/c	1,50,000	By Share Capital	6,00,000
To Equity Shares in PIYUSH Ltd.	13,50,000	By Statutory Reserves	1,70,000
		By General Reserve	10,000
		By Profit & Loss A/c	1,00,000
		By Realisation A/c	6,20,000
	15,00,000		15,00,000

Dr. **12% DEBENTURES ACCOUNT** Cr.

Particulars	₹	Particulars	₹
To Realisation A/c	1,00,000	By Balance b/d	1,00,000

Dr. **CASH & BANK ACCOUNT** Cr.

Particulars	₹	Particulars	₹
To Balance b/d	56,000	By Realisation A/c (transfer)	51,000
To PIYUSH Ltd.	1,50,000	By Realisation A/c (Expenses)	5,000
To PIYUSH Ltd.	10,000	By PIYUSH Ltd.	10,000
		By Equity Shareholders' A/c	1,50,000
	2,16,000		2,16,000

JOURNAL OF PIYUSH LTD.

Particulars		L.F.	Dr. (₹)	Cr. (₹)
Business Purchase A/c	Dr.		15,00,000	
To Liquidators of PRARTHANA Ltd.				15,00,000
(Being the Purchase of the business of PRARTHANA Ltd. as per agreement dated ...)				
Goodwill A/c (Balancing Figure)	Dr.		2,12,800	
Tangible Fixed Assets	Dr.		12,00,000	
Inventories	Dr.		1,42,000	
Trade Receivables	Dr.		36,000	
Cash & Bank	Dr.		51,000	
To Trade Payables				20,000
To 12% Debentures in PRARTHANA Ltd.				1,20,000
To Provision for Doubtful Debts A/c				1,800
To Business Purchase A/c				15,00,000
(Being the assets & liabilities taken over recorded, Goodwill being the balancing figure)				

Liquidators of PRARTHANA Ltd.	Dr.	15,00,000	
To Equity Share Capital A/c			9,00,000
To Securities Premium A/c			4,50,000
To Bank A/c			1,50,000
(Being the purchase consideration discharged)			
12% Debentures in PRARTHANA Ltd. A/c	Dr.	1,20,000	
Discount on Issue of Debentures A/c	Dr.	5,000	
To 14% Debentures A/c			1,25,000
(Being the Issue of 14% Debentures to 12% Debenture holders of PRARTHANA Ltd. at a discount of 4%) [Face Value of Debentures ₹ 1,20,000/. 96 = ₹ 1,25,000]			
Amalgamation Adjustment A/c	Dr.	1,70,000	
To Statutory Reserves A/c			1,70,000
(Being the identity of Statutory Reserves retained)			
Goodwill A/c	Dr.	10,000	
To Bank A/c			10,000
(Being the payment of Liquidation Exp. of Vendor Co.)			

Working Notes:

(I) CALCULATION OF PURCHASE CONSIDERATION

Particulars	₹
Cash [₹ 2.50 × 60,000]	1,50,000
Equity Shares [90,000 × 15]	13,50,000
	15,00,000

(ii) It is assumed that PRARTHANA Ltd. will retain the required cash for expenses.

ILLUSTRATION 15

Ajanta Limited agreed to acquire the business of Elora Limited as on 31st March 2016. Given below are the extracts from the Balance Sheet of Elora Ltd. as at 31st March, 2016:

Particulars	₹
20,000 Equity Shares of ₹ 10 each	2,00,000
10,000, 12% Pref. Shares of ₹ 10 each	1,00,000
Statutory Reserves	13,000
General Reserve	2,000
Profit & Loss A/c	30,000
12% Debentures	1,00,000
Trade Payables	1,50,000
Tangible Assets	2,50,000
Inventories	2,50,000
Trade Receivables	50,000
Cash at Bank	45,000

The consideration payable by Ajanta Limited was agreed as under:

(a) The Preference Shareholders of Elora Limited were to be allotted 8% Preference Shares of ₹ 1,10,000.

(b) Equity Shareholders to be allotted six Equity Shares of ₹ 10 each issued at a premium of 10% and ₹ 3 cash against every five shares held.

(c) 12% Debenture holders of Elora Limited to be paid @ 8% premium by issue of 14% Debentures at 10% discount.

While arriving at the agreed consideration, the directors of Ajanta Limited valued Tangible Fixed Assets at 40% more than the book value. Inventories at 12% less than book value, and Trade Receivables at their book value subject to an allowance of 5% to cover doubtful debts. Trade Receivables of Elora Limited included ₹ 10,000 due from Ajanta Limited. It was agreed that before acquisition, Elora Limited will pay dividend at 10% on Equity Shares. Actual Liquidation expenses are ₹ 15,000. Liquidation Expenses are to be reimbursed by Ajanta Ltd. to the extent of ₹ 10,000. Ignore Corporate Dividend Tax.

Required: Pass Journal entries necessary to close the books of Elora Limited and to record acquisition in the books of Ajanta Limited.

SOLUTION

JOURNAL OF ELORA LTD.

Particulars		*L.F.*	*Dr. (₹)*	*Cr. (₹)*
Profit & Loss A/c	Dr.		30,000	
Reserve A/c	Dr.		2,000	
To Dividend Payable A/c				32,000
(Being the Dividend @ 10% on equity shares & @ 12% as Pref. shares declared)				
Dividend Payable A/c	Dr.		32,000	
To Bank A/c				32,000
(Being the payment of Divided)				
Realisation A/c	Dr.		5,58,000	
To Tangible Fixed Assets				2,50,000
To Inventories				2,50,000
To Trade Receivables				50,000
To Cash At Bank [₹ 45,000 – ₹ 32,000 (Div)– ₹ 5,000(Exp)]				8,000
(Being the transfer of Sundry assets to realisation account)				
12% Debentures A/c	Dr.		1,00,000	
Trade Payables A/c	Dr.		1,50,000	
To Realisation A/c				2,50,000
(Being the transfer of various liabilities taken over)				
Ajanta Limited A/c	Dr.		3,86,000	
To Realisation A/c				3,86,000
(Being the purchase consideration due from purchasing company)				
8% Preference Shares in Ajanta Ltd. A/c	Dr.		1,10,000	
Equity Shares in Ajanta Limited A/c	Dr.		2,64,000	

Bank A/c	Dr.		12,000	
To Ajanta Limited				3,86,000
(Being the receipt of purchase consideration)				
Realisation A/c	Dr.		5,000	
Ajanta Ltd.	Dr.		10,000	
To Bank A/c				15,000
(Being the payment of realisation expenses)				
Bank A/c	Dr.		10,000	
To Ajanta Ltd.				10,000
(Being the receipt of reimbursement of Exp.)				
12% Preference Share Capital A/c	Dr.		1,00,000	
Realisation A/c	Dr.		10,000	
To Preference Shareholders' A/c				1,10,000
(Being the transfer of Pref. share capital to Pref. shareholders' A/c and provision made for redemption of shareholders)				
Realisation A/c	Dr.		63,000	
To Equity Shareholders' A/c				63,000
(Being the transfer of Profit on realisation)				
Preference Shareholders' A/c	Dr.		1,10,000	
To 8% Preference Shares in Ajanta Ltd.				1,10,000
(Being the payment made to pref. shareholders)				
Equity Share Capital A/c	Dr.		2,00,000	
Statutory Reserves A/c	Dr.		13,000	
To Equity Shareholders' A/c				2,13,000
(Being the transfer of equity share capital and Reserve)				
Equity Shareholders' A/c	Dr.		2,76,000	
To Equity Shares in Ajanta Ltd.				2,64,000
To Bank A/c				12,000
(Being the final Payment made to equity shareholders)				

JOURNAL OF AJANTA LIMITED

Particulars		*L.F.*	*Dr. (₹)*	*Cr. (₹)*
Business Purchase A/c	Dr.		3,86,000	
To Liquidators of Elora Limited				3,86,000
(Being the purchase of business as per agreement dated...)				
Goodwill A/c (Balancing figure)	Dr.		18,000	
Tangible Fixed Assets	Dr.		3,50,000	
Inventories A/c	Dr.		2,20,000	
Trade Receivables A/c	Dr.		50,000	
Cash at Bank A/c	Dr.		8,000	

To Trade Payables A/c			1,50,000
To 12% Debentures in Elora Ltd.			1,08,000
To Provision for Doubtful Debts A/c [5% of ₹ (50,000 – 10,000)]			2,000
To Business Purchase A/c			3,86,000
(Being the assets & liabilities taken over recorded)			
Liquidators of Elora Ltd.	Dr.	3,86,000	
To 8% Preference Share Capital A/c			1,10,000
To Equity Share Capital A/c			2,40,000
To Securities Premium A/c			24,000
To Bank A/c			12,000
(Being the purchase consideration discharged)			
12% Debentures in Elora Ltd. A/c	Dr.	1,08,000	
Discount on Issue of Debentures A/c	Dr.	12,000	
To 14% Debentures A/c			1,20,000
(Being the Issue of 14% Debentures of Debentureholders of Elora Ltd.) [face value of Debentures = ₹ 1,08,000 / .90 = ₹ 1,20,000]			
Ajanta Ltd.'s Trade Payables A/c	Dr.	10,000	
To Elora Ltd.'s Trade Receivables A/c			10,000
(Being the inter-company's debt's cancelled)			
Amalgamation Adjustment A/c	Dr.	13,000	
To Statutory Reserves A/c			13,000
(Being the identity of Statutory Reserves retained)			
Goodwill A/c	Dr.	10,000	
To Bank A/c			10,000
(Being the liquidation expenses reimbursed)			

Working Notes:

(I) CALCULATION OF PURCHASE CONSIDERATION

Particulars	₹	₹
8% Preference Shares		1,10,000
Equity Shares (20,000 × × ₹ 10)	2,40,000	
Securities Premium	24,000	2,64,000
Cash (3/5 × 20,000)		12,000
		3,86,000

(II) It has been assured that Elora Ltd. will retain the adequate cash for liquidation expenses.

ILLUSTRATION 16

Given below are the extracts from the Balance Sheets of P Ltd. and V Ltd. as at 31st March, 2016:

Particulars	P Ltd. (₹)	V Ltd. (₹)
Equity Share Capital of ₹ 10 each	6,00,000	2,00,000

General Reserve	1,50,000	20,000
Profit & Loss A/c	1,77,000	10,000
Statutory Reserves	—	5,000
10% Debentures of ₹ 100 each	—	50,000
Trade Payables	37,500	1,40,000
Goodwill	—	1,19,500
Tangible Assets	4,75,000	1,50,000
Non-Current Investments (including 100 Debentures of V Ltd. purchased @ of ₹ 90)	1,09,000	—
Inventories	95,000	55,000
Trade Receivables	1,40,000	65,000
Cash at Bank	1,45,500	35,500

The business of V Ltd. is taken over by P Ltd. as on that date on the following terms:

(a) Prior to absorption, V Ltd and P Ltd decide to declare and pay equity dividend @ 5%.(Ignore Dividend Distribution Tax)

(b) 50% of Tangible Fixed Assets are taken over at 100% more than the book value and the remaining Tangible Fixed Assets are taken over at $16\frac{2}{3}\%$ less than the book value.

(c) Goodwill of V Ltd. is to be valued at ₹ 50,000.

(d) Inventories are taken over at book value less 10% and Trade Receivables are taken over at book value subject to an allowance of 10% to cover doubtful debts.

(e) Trade Payables are to be taken over subject to a discount of 5% and Unrecorded Loan Liability of ₹ 38,500 to be discharged by P Ltd. at book value.

(f) The purchase consideration is to be discharged to the extent of 20% in cash and the balance in the form of equity shares of ₹ 10 each, ₹ 8 paid up at a premium of ₹ 7 per share, The market value of an equity share of P Ltd. at present is ₹ 100.

(g) The issue of such an amount of fully paid 14% Debentures in P Ltd at 96 per cent as is sufficient to discharge 10% Debentures in V Ltd. at a premium of 20 per cent.

(h) Expenses of liquidation of V Ltd. are to be reimbursed by P Ltd. to the extent of ₹ 10,000. Actual Expenses amounted to ₹ 12,000.

(i) Statutory Reserves are to be maintained for 2 more years.

Prior to 31st March 2016 V Ltd. sold goods costing ₹ 30,000 to P Ltd. for ₹ 40,000. ₹ 25,000 worth of goods were still in stock of P Ltd.Trade Receivables include ₹ 20,000 still due from P Ltd. On the date of absorption, V Ltd. owed P Ltd. ₹ 60,000 for the purchases of stock from P Ltd. which made a profit of 20% on cost. Four fifth of such stock were sold till 31.3.2016. Investments of P Ltd. include ₹ 9,000 representing the cost of 10% Debentures of V Ltd.

Required: *(a) Prepare Realisation Account, Bank Account, Equity Shareholders Account and Shares in P Ltd. Account in the books of V Ltd. (b) Pass Journal Entries in the books of P Ltd. and prepare Balance Sheet.*

SOLUTION

IN THE BOOKS OF V LTD.

REALISATION ACCOUNT

Dr. *Cr.*

Particulars	₹	*Particulars*	₹
To Goodwill	1,19,500	By 10% Debentures	50,000

To Tangible Fixed Assets	1,50,000	By Trade Payables	1,40,000
To Inventories	55,000	By P Ltd. (Purchase Consideration)	1,62,557
To Trade Receivables	65,000	By Equity Shareholders' A/c (Loss)	62,443
To Bank [35,500 – 10,000 (Div.) – 2,000 (Exp.)]	23,500		
To Bank A/c (Expenses)	2,000		
	4,15,000		4,15,000

Dr. **BANK ACCOUNT** *Cr.*

Particulars	₹	*Particulars*	₹
To Balance b/d	35,500	By Dividend Payable A/c	10,000
To P Ltd. (Expenses)	10,000	By Realisation A/c (Takeover)	23,500
To P Ltd. (Consideration)	32,567	By Realisation A/c (Expenses)	2,000
		By P Ltd. (Expenses)	10,000
		By Equity Shareholders A/c	32,567
	78,067		78,067

Dr. **EQUITY SHAREHOLDERS' ACCOUNT** *Cr.*

Particulars	₹	*Particulars*	₹
To Realisation A/c (Loss)	62,443	By Share Capital	2,00,000
To Bank A/c	32,567	By General Reserve	20,000
To Shares in P Ltd.	1,29,990	By Statutory Reserves	5,000
	2,25,000		2,25,000

Dr. **SHARES IN P LTD. ACCOUNT** *Cr.*

Particulars	₹	*Particulars*	₹
To P Ltd.	1,29,990	By Sundry Shareholders (transfer)	1,29,990

JOURNAL OF P LTD.

Particulars		*L.F.*	*Dr.* (₹)	*Cr.* (₹)
Profit & Loss A/c	Dr.		30,000	
To Dividend Payable a/c				30,000
(Being the Dividend declared @ 5%)				
Dividend Payable A/c	Dr.		30,000	
To Bank A/c				30,000
(Being the Dividend paid)				
Business Purchase A/c	Dr.		1,62,557	
To Liquidators of V Ltd.				1,62,557
(Being the purchase price agreed to be paid for the business of V Ltd.)				

Goodwill (Balancing figure)	Dr.	51,057	
Tangible Fixed Assets	Dr.	2,12,500	
Inventories	Dr.	49,500	
Trade Receivables	Dr.	65,000	
Bank	Dr.	23,500	
Reserve for Discount on Trade Payables [5% of ₹(1,40 000 – 60,000)]	Dr.	4,000	
To Provision for Doubtful Debts [10% of ₹ (65,000 – 20,000)]			4,500
To Trade Payables			1,40,000
To 10% Debentures [₹ 50,000 + 20%]			60,000
To Unrecorded Loan			38,500
To Business Purchase A/c			1,62,557
(Being the assets and liabilities taken over from V Ltd.)			
Liquidators of V Ltd.	Dr.	1,62,557	
To Bank A/c			32,567
To Equity Share Capital A/c			69,328
To Securities Premium A/c			60,662
(Being the issue of Shares and payment in cash in satisfaction of purchase consideration)			
Goodwill A/c	Dr.	10,000	
To Bank A/c			10,000
(Being the payment of Realization Expenses of V Ltd.)			
Goodwill	Dr.	6,250	
To Inventories A/c			6,250
(Being the Elimination of unrealized profit on unsold goods worth ₹ 25,000 bought from V Ltd. still unsold (25,000 × 10,000/40,000)			
Trade Payables A/c	Dr.	20,000	
To Trade Receivables (V Ltd.) A/c			20,000
(Being Elimination of the amount owed by us to V Ltd.)			
Goodwill A/c	Dr.	800	
To Inventories			800
(Being the elimination of unrealized profit included in goods purchased by V Ltd.)[(20% of ₹ 60,000 x1/6) –(10% of ₹ 12,000)]			
Trade Payables (V Ltd.) A/c	Dr.	60,000	
To Trade Receivables A/c			60,000
(Being the cancellation of Inter Co. Owing)			
10% Debentures of V Ltd.	Dr.	60,000	
Discount on Issue of 14% Debentures A/c	Dr.	2,000	
To Investments in 10% Debentures of V Ltd.			9,000
To 14% Debentures A/c			50,000
To Capital Reserve A/c			3,000

(Being the Investment in 10% Debentures of V Ltd. cancelled and the remaining debentures redeemed by issue of 500, 14% Debentures of ₹ 100 each at a discount of 4%) [Face Value of Debentures= ₹ 48,000/96% = ₹ 50,000]			
Unrecorded Loan A/c Dr. To Bank A/c (Being the liabilities of V Ltd. discharged)		38,500	38,500
Amalgamation Adjustment A/c Dr. To Statutory Reserves (Being the identity of statutory Reserves retained)		5,000	5,000
Capital Reserve A/c Dr. To Goodwill A/c (Being the goodwill adjusted against Capital Reserve)		3,000	3,000

BALANCE SHEET OF P LTD. AS AT 31.03.2016

Particulars	*Note No*	X Ltd. (₹)
I. Equity and Liabilities		
(1) Shareholders'Funds		
(a) Share Capital	1	6,69,328
(b) Reserves and Surplus	2	3,60,662
(2) Non–Current Liabilities		
(a) Long–term Borrowings (14% Debentures)		50,000
(3) Current Liabilities		
(a) Trade Payables [(37,500 – 20,000) + (1,40,000 – 4,000 – 60,000)]		93,500
Total		11,73,490
II. Assets		
(1) Non–Current Assets		
(a) Fixed Assets		
Tangible Assets [4,75,000 + 2,12,500]		6,87,500
Intangible Assets [Goodwill] [51,057 + 10,000 + 6,250 + 800 – 3,000]		65,107
(b) Non–Current Investments[1,09,000 –9,000]		1,00,000
(c) Other Non–Current Assets[Amalgamation Adjustment A/c]		5,000
(2) Current Assets		
(a) Inventories [(95,000 – 6,250)+(49,500 – 800)]		1,37,450
(b) Trade Receivables [(1,40,000 – 60,000)+(65,000 – 4,500 – 20,000)]		1,20,500
(c) Cash and Cash Equivalents [Cash at Bank] [(1,45,500 –30,000 – 10,000 – 32,567 – 38,500) + (23,500)]		57,933
Total		11,73,490

Notes To Accounts:

	Particulars	X Ltd. (₹)
1.	**Share Capital**	
	Equity Shares of ₹ 10 each	6,00,000
	Equity Shares of ₹ 10 each,₹ 8 paid up	69,328
		6,69,328
2.	**Reserves and Surplus**	
	General Reserve	1,50,000
	Profit & Loss A/c[1,77,000 – 30,000]	1,47,000
	Statutory Reserves	5,000
	Securities Premium	60,662
	Less: Discount on Issue of 14% Debentures A/c	(2,000)
		3,60,662

Working Notes:

1. CALCULATION OF PURCHASE CONSIDERATION

	Particulars		₹
A	Assets taken over at agreed values		
	Tangible Fixed Assets [(₹ 1,50,000 × 50%) + 100%]		1,50,000
	Tangible Fixed Assets [(₹ 1,50,000 × 50%) – $16\frac{2}{3}$%]		62,500
	Inventories [₹ 55,000 – ₹ 5,500]		49,500
	Trade Receivables [₹ 65,000 – ₹ 6,500]		58,500
	Cash at Bank [35,500 – 10,000 – 2,000]		23,500
	Goodwill		50,000
			3,94,000
B	*Less:* Liabilities taken over:		
	Trade Payables	1,40,000	
	Less: Reserve for Discount @ 5%	7,000	1,33,000
	10% Debentures[₹ 50,000 + 20%]		60,000
	Unrecorded Loan		38,500
			2,31,500
C	Net Assets taken over (A – B)		1,62,500

(II) DISCHARGE OF PURCHASE CONSIDERATION

Particulars	₹
Payable in Cash(20% of ₹ 1,62,500)	32,500
In shares—[(80% of ₹ 1,62,500)/₹15]	
8,666 shares of ₹ 10 each, ₹ 8 paid up valued at ₹ 15 per share	1,29,990
Cash for Fractional Share(.67 × ₹ 100)	67
	1,62,557

ILLUSTRATION 17

Given below are the extracts from the Balance Sheet of V Ltd. as at 31st March, 2016:

Particulars	P Ltd ₹	V Ltd ₹
Equity Share Capital of ₹ 10 each	6,00,000	2,00,000
12% Pref. Share Capital of ₹ 100 each	1,00,000	50,000
General Reserve	1,50,000	20,000
Profit & Loss A/c	1,75,200	14,000
Statutory Reserves	—	5,000
10% Debentures	—	50,000
Trade Payables	37,500	1,40,000
Tangible Assets	4,75,000	1,50,000
Goodwill	—	1,19,500
Non-Current Investments (including 100 Debentures of V Ltd. purchased @ of ₹ 90)	1,09,000	—
Inventories	95,000	55,000
Trade Receivables	1,40,000	65,000
Cash at Bank	2,43,700	89,500

Prior to absorption, both the companies decide to declare and pay equity dividend @ 5%.(Ignore Dividend Distribution Tax). The business of V Ltd. is taken over by P Ltd. as on that date on the following terms:

(a) 50% of Tangible Fixed Assets are taken over at 100% more than the book value and the remaining Tangible Fixed Assets are taken over at $16\frac{2}{3}\%$ less than the book value.

(b) Goodwill of V Ltd. is to be valued at ₹ 50,000.

(c) Inventories are taken over at book value less 10% and Trade Receivables are taken over at book value subject to an allowance of 10% to cover doubtful debts.

(d) Trade Payables are to be taken over subject to a discount of 5% and Unrecorded Loan Liability of ₹ 38,500 to be discharged by P Ltd. at book value.

(e) The purchase consideration payable by P Ltd. was agreed as follows:

   (i) The purchase consideration is to be discharged to the extent of 20% in cash.

   (ii) The issue of such an amount of fully paid 14% Debentures in P Ltd at 96 per cent as is sufficient to discharge 10% Debentures in V Ltd. at a premium of 20 per cent.

   (iii) The issue of such an amount of fully paid 10% Pref. Shares in P Ltd. at 125% as is sufficient to discharge 9% Pref. Shares in V Ltd. at a premium of 20%.

   (iv) The balance in the form of equity shares of ₹ 10 each, ₹ 8 paid up at a premium of ₹ 7 per share. The market value of an equity share of P Ltd. at present is ₹ 100.

   (v) Expenses of liquidation of V Ltd. are to be reimbursed by P Ltd. to the extent of ₹ 10,000. Actual Expenses amounted to ₹ 12,000.

Show the calculation & discharge of Purchase Consideration & prepare the Balance Sheet of P Ltd.

SOLUTION

1. CALCULATION OF PURCHASE CONSIDERATION

	Particulars	₹
A	Assets taken over at agreed values	
	Tangible Fixed Assets [(₹ 1,50,000 × 50%) + 100%]	1,50,000
	Tangible Fixed Assets [(₹ 1,50,000 × 50%) – $16\frac{2}{3}$%]	62,500
	Inventories [₹ 55,000 – ₹ 5,500]	49,500
	Trade Receivables [₹ 65,000 – ₹ 6,500]	58,500
	Cash at Bank [89,500 – 10,000(ED) – 4,000(PD) – 2,000(Exp.)]	73,500
	Goodwill	50,000
		4,44,000
B	*Less:* Liabilities taken over:	
	Trade Payables [₹ 1,40,000 – 5%]	1,33,000
	10% Debentures [₹ 50,000 + 20%]	60,000
	Unrecorded Loan	38,500
		2,31,500
C	Net Assets taken over (A – B)	2,12,500

2. DISCHARGE OF PURCHASE CONSIDERATION

A. Cash to Equity Shareholders [2,12,500 × 20%]	42,500
B. 480, 9% Pref. Shares to be issued [(500 × 120%)]	60,000
C. 7,333, Equity Shares to be issued [(2,12,500 – 42,500 – 60,000)/ ₹ 15]	1,09,995
D. Cash for Fractional Share(.33 × ₹ 100)	33
E. Total Purchase Consideration (A + B + C + D)	2,12,528

Note: *According to AS-14, the amount paid by purchasing Company to discharge the debentures holders and the liquidation expenses of Vendor Company are not considered as part of purchase consideration.*

BALANCE SHEET OF P LTD. AS AT 31.03.2016

Particulars	*Note No*	X Ltd. (₹)
I. Equity and Liabilities		
(1) Shareholders'Funds		
(a) Share Capital	1	8,06,664
(b) Reserves and Surplus	2	3,49,531
(2) Non–Current Liabilities		
(a) Long–term Borrowings (14% Debentures)		50,000
(3) Current Liabilities		
(a) Trade Payables [(37,500 – 20,000) + (1,40,000 – 4,000 – 60,000)]		93,500
Total		12,99,695

II. Assets		
(1) Non–Current Assets		
(a) Fixed Assets		
Tangible Assets [4,75,000 + 2,12,500]		6,87,500
Intangible Assets [Goodwill] [51,028 + 10,000 + 6,250 + 800 – 3,000]		65,078
(b) Non–Current Investments[1,09,000 – 9,000]		1,00,000
(c) Other Non–Current Assets [Amalgamation Adjustment A/c]		5,000
(2) Current Assets		
(a) Inventories [(95,000 – 6,250) + (49,500 – 800)]		1,37,450
(b) Trade Receivables [(1,40,000 – 60,000) + (65,000 – 4,500 – 20,000)]		1,20,500
(c) Cash and Cash Equivalents [Cash at Bank] [(2,43,700 – 30,000 – 12,000 – 10,000 – 42,533 – 38,500) + (73,500)]		1,84,167
Total		12,99,695

Notes To Accounts:

Particulars	₹
1. Share Capital	
60,000, Equity Shares of ₹ 10 each	6,00,000
7,333, Equity Shares of ₹ 10 each,₹ 8 paid up	58,664
1,000, 8% Pref. Shares of ₹ 100 each	1,00,000
480, 9% Pref. Shares of ₹ 100 each	48,000
	8,06,664
2. Reserves and Surplus	
General Reserve	1,50,000
Profit & Loss A/c [1,75,200 – 30,000 – 12,000]	1,33,200
Statutory Reserves	5,000
Securities Premium [51,331 + 12,000]	63,331
Less: Discount on Issue of 14% Debentures A/c	(2,000)
	3,49,531

ILLUSTRATION 18 [Take-over on a date other than Balance Sheet Date]

Given below are the extracts from the Balance Sheets of CANHA Ltd. and Krishna Ltd., as at 31st March, 2016:

Particulars	*CAHANA Ltd.* ₹	*Krishna Ltd.* ₹
Equity Share Capital of ₹ 10 each	6,00,000	4,00,000
General Reserve	1,40,000	42,500
Statutory Reserves	—	60,000

Profit & Loss A/c	69,000	56,000
Trade Payables	37,500	30,000
Tangible Fixed Assets	5,00,000	3,50,000
Inventories	95,000	82,500
Trade Receivables	1,40,000	1,00,000
Cash at Bank	1,11,500	56,000

CANHA Ltd., took over and absorbed Krishna Ltd., as on 1st Oct. 2016. No Balance Sheet of Krishna Ltd. was prepared on the date of take-over. But the following information is made available to you:

(a) For the six months ended 30th Sept. 2016, CANHA Ltd and Krishna Ltd., made net profits of ₹ 1,51,000 and ₹ 64,000 after providing for depreciation at 10% per annum on fixed assets;

(b) .Both the companies had distributed dividends @ 10% on 1st July 2016.

(c) Goodwill of Krishna Ltd. on the date of take-over was estimated at ₹ 25,000 and it was agreed that the Inventories of Krishna Ltd., subject to an abnormal item of ₹ 7,500 to be fully written off, would be appreciated by 20% for the purpose of take-over:

(d) CANHA Ltd. to issue shares to share-holders of Krishna Ltd., on the basis of the intrinsic value of shares on the date of take-over.

Required: Draft the Balance Sheet of CANHA Ltd., after absorption. (Ignore Corporate Dividend Tax Rate).

SOLUTION

BALANCE SHEET OF CANHA LTD. AS AT 1.10.2016

Particulars	*Note No*	*₹ (lacs)*
I. Equity and Liabilities		
(1) Shareholders' Funds		
(a) Share Capital	1	10.100
(b) Reserves and Surplus	2	5.650
(2) Non-Current Liabilities		
(3) Current Liabilities Trade Payables [0.375 + 0.30]		0.675
Total		16.425
II. Assets		
(1) Non-Current Assets		
(a) Fixed Assets		
Tangible Assets [5 + 3.325 – 0.25]		8.075
Intangible Assets		0.250
(b) Other Non-Current Assets	3	0.600
(2) Current Assets		
(a) Inventories [0.95 + (82,500 – 7,500) + 20%]		1.850
(b) Trade Receivables [1.40 + 1.00]		2.400
(c) Cash and Cash Equivalents	(i)	3.250
Total		16.425

Notes To Accounts:

	Particulars	₹ (lacs)
1.	**Share Capital**	
	101,000 Equity Shares of ₹ 10 each	10.10
	(Of the above 41,000 Shares were issued for consideration otherwise than cash)	
2.	**Reserves and Surplus**	
	Securities Premium [41,000 x ₹ 5]	2.05
	General Reserve	1.40
	Statutory Reserves	0.60
	Profit & Loss Account [0.69 + 1.51 – 0.60]*	1.60
		5.65
3.	**Other Non-Current Assets** [Amalgamation Adjustment A/c]	0.60

Working Notes:

(I) CALCULATION OF CLOSING CASH & BANK BALANCE

	Particulars	*CAHANA Ltd.* ₹	*Krishna Ltd.* ₹
A	Opening Balance	1,11,500	56,000
B	Add Net Profit	1,51,000	64,000
C	*Add:* Depreciation	25,000	17,500
		2,87,500	1,37,500
D	*Less:* Dividend	60,000	40,000
E	Closing Cash & Bank Balance (A + B + C – D)	2,27,500	97,500

(II) CALCULATION OF INTRINSIC VALUE OF SHARES

	Particulars	*CAHANA Ltd.* ₹	*Krishna Ltd.* ₹
A	Total Assets at current values		
	Goodwill	—	25,000
	Fixed Assets	4,75,000	3,32,500
	Trade Receivables	1,40,000	1,00,000
	Inventories *[(82,500 -7,500) + 20%]	95,000	90,000*
	Cash & Bank [Refer to Working Note (i)]	2,27,500	97,500
		9,37,500	6,45,000
B	*Less:* Liabilities	(37,500)	(30,000)
C	Net Assets at current values [A – B]	9,00,000	6,15,000
D	No. of shares	60,000	40,000
E	Intrinsic value per share {C/D}	15	15.375

(III) CALCULATION OF NO. OF SHARES TO BE ISSUED BY PURCHASING COMPANY

A	Net assets of vendor company take over	6,15,000

B	Intrinsic value of an equity share of Purchasing company	15
C	No of shares to be issued by Purchasing company (A/B)	41,000

Note: *In the absence of information about changes in other assets, it is assumed that the profit has resulted in cash only.*

10.0 TREATMENT OF RESERVES ARISING ON AMALGAMATION IN THE NATURE OF MERGER

1. **Provision as per AS-14 [Paragraph 35]**

   The difference betwen the amount recorded as share capital issued (*plus any additional consideration in the form of cash and other assets*) and the amount of the share capital of the transferor company should be adjusted in reserves.

2. **Opinion of the Expert Advisory Committee of ICAI [Published in 22nd Volume]**

   (a) The difference between the share capital of the transferor companies and share capital issued by company on amalgamation should be treated as **Capital Reserve** for the purpose of paragraph 35 of AS-14.

   (b) Reserve created on amalgamation is not available for the purpose of distribution to shareholders as dividend and/or bonus shares.

3. **Author's Opinion**

   (a) The excess of share capital of the transferor company over the purchase consideration should be treated as **Capital Reserve** which shall not be available for distribution as dividend *or* bonus.

   (b) The excess of purchase consideration over the share capital of the transferor company should be treated as Capital loss and should be adjusted:

      (i) first against the Capital Reserves

      (ii) then against the Revenue Reserves (if capital reserves are insufficient)

Note: *If Revenue Reserves are also insuficient, the necessary required amount should be transferred to Revenue Reserves by debting Profit & Loss Account. After such transfer if Profit & Loss Account shows debit balance it will be shown as a negative item under Reserves and Surplus.*

ILLUSTRATION 19 [Treatment of Reserves arising on Amalgamation in the nature of Merger]

X Ltd. took over all the assets & liabilities of Y Ltd. and discharged the consideration by issue of equity shares and cash for fractional shares. Calculate the balances of Reserves and Profit & Loss Account which are to appear in the Balance Sheet of X Ltd. in each of the following cases:

(₹ *in lacs*)

Particulars	*Case I* ₹	*Case II* ₹	*Case III* ₹	*Case IV* ₹	*Case V* ₹
Share Capital issued by X Ltd.	9.50	9.50	9.50	9.50	9.50
Cash for Fractional Shares paid by X Ltd.	.50	.50	.50	.50	.50
Share Capital of Y Ltd.	9.65	9.45	9.15	9.00	8.80
Capital Reserves of Y Ltd.	.40	.40	.40	.40	.40
Revenue Reserves of Y Ltd.	.30	.30	.30	.30	.30
Statutory Reserves of Y Ltd.	.20	.20	.20	.20	.20
Profit & Loss A/c of Y Ltd.	.10	.10	.10	.10	.10
Capital Reserve of X Ltd.	.10	.10	.10	.10	.10

Revenue Reserve of X Ltd.	.20	.20	.20	.20	.20
Profit & Loss Account of X Ltd.	.05	.05	.05	.05	.05

SOLUTION

CALCULATION OF BALANCES OF RESERVES AND PROFIT & LOSS ACCOUNT *[₹ in lacs]*

Particulars	₹	₹	₹	₹	₹
A. Purchase Consideration					
Share Capital Issued:	9.50	9.50	9.50	9.50	9.50
Cash for Fractional Shares paid	.50	.50	.50	.50	.50
	10.00	10.00	10.00	10.00	10.00
B. *Less:* Share Capital of Transferor Co.	9.65	9.45	9.15	9.00	8.80
C. Difference to be adjusted (A–B)	0.35	0.55	0.85	1.00	1.20
D. Debited to:					
Capital Reserves (of Both Co.)	0.35	.50	.50	.50	.50
Revenue Reserves (of Both Co.)	—	.05	.35	.50	.50
Profit & Loss A/c (of Both Co.)	—	—	—	—	.20
	.35	.55	.85	1.00	1.20
Balances of Reserves & P&L A/c:					
Capital Reserves	.15	—	—	—	—
Revenue Reserves	.50	.45	.15	—	—
Statutory Reserves	.20	.20	.20	.20	.20
Profit & Loss A/c (Credit)	.15	.15	.15	.15	—
Profit & Loss A/c (Debit)	—	—	—	—	0.05

11.0 ACCOUNTING TREATMENT IN THE BOOKS OF TRANSFEREE COMPANY OR PURCHASING COMPANY IN CASE OF MERGER

Step 1: Record the Acquisition of business from the vendor company.

JOURNAL ENTRY

Business Merger A/c	Dr.	*(with Purchase Consideration)*
To Liquidator of the Vendor Co.		

Step 2: In case of Amalgamation in the nature of Merger

"Record the Assets, Liabilities and Reserves (whether Statutory Reserves *or* not) at their respective book values".

JOURNAL ENTRY

Assets (Individually)	Dr.	*[with their respective book values]*
To Liabilities (Individually)		*[with their respective book values]*
To Provision for Doubtful Debts		*[with the book balance]*

To Provision for Depreciation etc.	*[with the book balance]*
To Reserves (other than Revenue Reserves)	*[with their respective book balances]*
To General Reserve	*[Balancing figure]*
To Business Merger A/c	*[with Purchase Consideration]*

Step 3: Make Payment to Vendor Company.

JOURNAL ENTRY

Liquidator of Vendor Co.'s A/c	Dr.	*(with the total)*
Discount on Issue of Shares A/c	Dr.	*(with the Discount allowed on shares)*
To Equity Share Capital A/c		*(with the paid up value of Equity Shares issued)*
To Preference Share Capital A/c		*(with the paid up value of Pref. Shares issued)*
To Securities Premium A/c		*(with the Securities Premium)*
To Cash A/c Bank A/c		*(with the Cash Payment)*

Note: *The Shares issued by way of purchase consideration must be recorded at their paid up values (i.e., not at their issued prices) after giving due credit to Securities Premium Account (in case the shares have been issued at premium) or after giving due debit to "Discount on issue of Shares A/c' (in case the shares have been issued at discount).*

Step 4: Record the Issue of Debentures (if any) to discharge the existing debentureholders of Vendor Company.

JOURNAL ENTRY

Debentures in Vendor Company	Dr.	*(with the amount of debentures)*
Discount on Issue of Debentures in Purchasing Company	Dr.	*(with the debentures discount)*
To Debentures in Purchasing Company		*(with the nominal value)*
To Securities Premium A/c		*(with the debenture premium)*

Step 5: Record the Reimbursement of the Liquidation Expenses of the vendor company.

JOURNAL ENTRY

Profit & Loss A/c (in case of Merger)	Dr.
To Bank A/c	

Step 6: Eliminate the Unrealised Profit included in the Unsold Inventories.

(a) ***Where the Unsold Inventories of the purchasing company includes the goods purchased from the vendor company***

P&L A/c (in Case of Merger)	Dr.
To Inventories A/c	

(b) ***Where the Unsold Inventories of the vendor company includes goods purchased from the purchasing company, only the amount of stock is reduced to its cost while passing the entries on acquisition. (i.e., Entry in Step 2).***

Note: *In case of sale of goods at loss, no adjustment is required.*

Step 7: Eliminate the Inter Company Owings

(a) To eliminate the Debts owed by Vendor Company	Trade Payables of Vendor Co Dr. To Trade Receivables
(b) To eliminate the Debts owed by Purchasing Company	Trade Payables Dr. To Trade Receivables of Vendor Co.
(c) To eliminate the Bills drawn and retained by Vendor Co. upon Purchasing Company	Bills Payable A/c Dr. To Bills Receivable of Vendor Co.
(d) To eliminate the Bills drawn and retained by Purchasing Company upon Vendor Co.	Bills Payable of Vendor Co. Dr. To Bills Receivable A/c
(e) To eliminate the Debentures held by Vendor Co. in Purchasing Co.	Debentures A/c Dr. [Face value] Profit & Loss A/c Dr. [If FV < BV] To Investment in Debentures A/c (*Vendor Co.*) [Book Value] To Capital Reserve A/c [If FV > BV]
(f) To eliminate the Debentures held by Purchasing Co. in Vendor Co.	Debentures in Vendor Co. Dr. [Face Value] Profit & Loss A/c Dr. [If FV < BV] To Investment in Debentures A/c Dr. [Book value] To Capital Reserve A/c [If FV > BV]

Note:

(i) Bills drawn by one company upon the other company and discounted with the bank should not be eliminated because these bills represent owing between the bank and the company and not the inter-company owings.

(ii) Where the debtors of a company include a sum due from another company but the creditors of another company include a lesser sum due to the former company. The difference should be treated as cash-in-transit.

*(iii) The entry (f) in **Step 7** should be merged with entry in **Step 4** so that the new debentures will be issued to discharge those debentures of vendor company which are held by outsiders (i.e., holders other than the purchasing company).*

(iv) In case of entries (e) and (f), the loss should be debited to P & L A/c (in case of merger) and the profit should be credited to Capital Reserve A/c.

ILLUSTRATION 20

V Ltd has Equity Share Capital of ₹ 95,00,000, Tangible Fixed Assets of ₹ 65,00,000 and Current Assets of ₹ 85,00,000, Statutory Reserves of ₹ 5,00,000 and General Reserve of ₹ 28,00,000, Current Liabilities of ₹ 19,00,000, Non-Current Liabilities of ₹ 3,00,000 as at 31.3.2016. Statutory Reserves are to be maintained for 2 more years. The business of V Ltd. is taken over by P Ltd. by issue of 1,00,000 equity shares of ₹ 100 each at 20% premium. Journalise in the books of P Ltd.

SOLUTION

JOURNAL OF P LTD.

Date	Particulars	L.F.	Dr. (₹)	Cr. (₹)
	Business Merger A/c. Dr.		120,00,000	
	To Liquidator of V Ltd. A/c.			120,00,000
	(Being the Business taken over)			

	Tangible Fixed Assets	Dr.	65,00,000	
	Current Assets	Dr.	85,00,000	
	To Non-Current Liabilities			3,00,000
	To Current Liabilities			19,00,000
	To Business Merger A/c			120,00,000
	To General Reserve *(balancing figure)*			**3,00,000**
	To Statutory Reserves			5,00,000
	(Being the assets, liabilities and reserves taken over recorded)			
	Liquidator of V Ltd.	Dr.	120,00,000	
	To Equity Share Capital A/c.			100,00,000
	To Securities Premium A/c.			20,00,000
	(Being the purchase consideration discharged)			

Note: Closing Balance of General Reserve = Given Balance of General Reserve – Difference between purchase consideration and the amount of Share capital of the transferor company

= ₹28,00,000 – (₹120,00,000 – ₹ 95,00,000)

= ₹ 3,00,000

ILLUSTRATION 21

Given below are the extracts from the Balance Sheets of A Ltd. and B Ltd. as at 31.03.2016:

Particulars	*A Ltd. (₹ in lacs)*	*B Ltd. (₹ in lacs)*
Equity Share Capital of ₹ 100 each	80	75
12% Pref. Share Capital of ₹ 100 each	30	20
Capital Reserve	1	1
Capital Redemption Reserve	3	3
Statutory Reserves	5	5
General Reserve	31	22
Profit & Loss A/c	2	2
10% Debentures of ₹ 100 each	6	3
Current Liabilities	42	19
Tangible Fixed Assets	90	65
Non-Current Investments	15	5
Current Assets	95	80

Additional Information:

(a) 10% Debentures of the transferor company are to be discharged by transferee company by issuing such number of its 15% Debentures of ₹ 100 each so as to maintain the same amount of interest.

(b) 12% Preference shares of the transferor company are to be discharged by transferee company by issuing equivalent numbers of 15% preference Shares of ₹ 100 each at ₹ 150 each.

(c) The transferee company shall issue 4 equity shares of ₹ 10 each at ₹ 30 each for each equity share in the transferor company.

(d) The Statutory Reserves are to be maintained for 2 more years.

(e) The transferee company shall pay the cost of absorption which amount to ₹ 1,00,000

Required: (a) Prepare Journal of transferor company (b) Prepare the Journal and Balance Sheet of Transferee Company in each of the following alternative cases:

Case I If A Ltd. absorbs B Ltd. and the amalgamation is in the nature of a purchase.

Case II If A Ltd. absorbs B Ltd., and the amalgamation is in the nature of a merger.

SOLUTION

JOURNAL OF B LTD. *(₹ in lacs)*

Particulars		*L.F.*	*Dr. (₹)*	*Cr. (₹)*
Realisation A/c	Dr.		150	
To Tangible Fixed Assets				65
To Investments				5
To Current Assets				80
(Being the transfer of various assets)				
10% Debentures A/c	Dr.		3	
Current Liabilities	Dr.		19	
To Realisation A/c				22
(Being the t/f of various liabilities taken over by the Purchasing Co.)				
A Ltd.	Dr.		120	
To Realisation A/c				120
(Being the purchase Consideration due from A Ltd.)				
15% Pref. Shares in A Ltd.	Dr.		30	
Equity Shares in A Ltd.	Dr.		90	
To A Ltd.				120
(Being the receipt of purchase consideration)				
12% Preference Share Capital A/c	Dr.		20	
Realisation A/c	Dr.		10	
To 12% Preference Shareholders' A/c				30
(Being the amount due to 12% Pref. shareholders)				
12% Preference Shareholders' A/c	Dr.		30	
To 15% Pref. Shares in A Ltd.				30
(Being the payment made to pref. shareholders)				
Equity Shareholders' A/c	Dr.		18	
To Realisation A/c				18
(Being the transfer of loss on realisation)				

Equity Share Capital A/c Dr.		75	
Capital Reserve Dr.		1	
Capital Redemption Reserve Dr.		3	
Statutory Reserves Dr.		5	
General Reserve Dr.		22	
Profit & Loss A/c Dr.		2	
To Equity Shareholders' A/cs			108
(Being the transfer of Equity Share capital, Reserves and accumulated profits)			
Equity Shareholders' A/cs Dr.		90	
To Equity Shares in A Ltd.			90
(Being the final payment made to Equity shareholders)			

CASE I: IF THE AMALGAMATION IN THE NATURE OF PURCHASE

JOURNAL OF A LTD.

[₹ in lacs]

Particulars	*L.F.*	*Dr. (₹)*	*Cr. (₹)*
Business Purchase A/c Dr.		120	
To Liquidator of B Ltd.			120
(Being the purchase of business as per agreement dated...)			
Tangible Fixed Assets Dr.		65	
Investments Dr.		5	
Current Assets Dr.		80	
To 10% Debentures A/c			2
To Current Liabilities			19
To Business Purchase A/c			120
To Capital Reserve A/c			9
(Being the assets & liabilities taken over recorded)			
Amalgamation Adjustment A/c Dr.		5	
To Statutory Reserves A/c			5
(Being the identity of statutory Reserves retained)			
Liquidator of B Ltd. Dr.		120	
To Equity Share Capital A/c			30
To 15% Pref. Share Capital A/c			20
To Securities Premium A/c [60 + 10]			70
(Being the purchase consideration discharged)			
Goodwill A/c Dr.		1	
To Bank A/c			1
(Being the cost of absorption of B Ltd. paid)			

10% Debentures A/c	Dr.	2	
To 15% Debentures A/c			2
(Being the issue of 15% Debentures to 10% Debentureholders of B Ltd.) [No. of 15% Debentures = ₹ 30,000/15 = 2,000]			
Capital Reserve A/c	Dr.	1	
To Goodwill A/c			1
(Being the goodwill adjusted against Capital Reserve)			

BALANCE SHEET OF A LTD. AS AT 31.3.2016

	Particulars	Note No	₹ (lacs)
I.	**Equity and Liabilities**		
	(1) Shareholders' Funds		
	(a) Share Capital	1	160
	(b) Reserves and Surplus	2	125
	(2) Non-Current Liabilities		
	(a) Long-term Borrowings	3	8
	(3) Current Liabilities [42 + 19]		61
	Total		354
II.	**Assets**		
	(1) Non-Current Assets		
	(a) Fixed Assets		
	Tangible Assets [90 + 65]		155
	(b) Non-Current Investments [15 + 5]		20
	(c) Other Non-Current Assets [Amalgamation Adjustment A/c]		5
	(2) Current Assets [95 + 80 – 1]		174
	Total		354

Notes To Accounts:

	Particulars	₹ (lacs)
1.	**Share Capital**	
	80,000 Equity Shares of ₹ 100 each	80
	3,00,000 Equity Shares of ₹ 10 each	30
	30,000 Pref. Shares of ₹ 100 each	30
	20,000, 15% Pref. Shares of ₹ 100 each	20
	(Of the above 3 lacs equity Shares were issued for consideration otherwise than cash)	
		160
2.	**Reserves and Surplus**	
	Securities Premium [60 + 10]	70
	General Reserve	31
	Profit & Loss Account	2
	Capital Reserve	1

Capital Reserve on Amalgamation	8
Capital Redemption Reserve	3
Statutory Reserves	10
	125
3. Long-term Borrowings	
10% Debentures of ₹ 100 each	6
15% Debentures of ₹ 100 each	2
	8

Working Notes:

(I) CALCULATION OF PURCHASE CONSIDERATION

for preference Shareholders [(20,00,000/100) × ₹ 150]	30,00,000
for Equity Shareholders [{(75,00,000/100) × 4} × ₹ 150]	90,00,000
	120,00,000

(II) CALCULATION OF NET ASSETS TAKEN OVER AT THEIR AGREED VALUES

A	Total Assets taken over at their agreed values	
	Fixed Assets	65,00,000
	Investments	5,00,000
	Current Assets	80,00,000
		150,00,000
B	*Less:* Liabilities taken over at their agreed amounts	
	10% Debentures	2,00,000
	Current Liabilities	19,00,000
		21,00,000
C	Net Assets taken over (A – B)	129,00,000

(III) *Calculation of Capital Reserve on amalgamation*

Capital Reserve = Net Assets taken over at their agreed values – Purchase consideration

= ₹ 129,00,000 – ₹ 120,00,000 = ₹ 9,00,000

CASE II: IF AMALGAMATION IS IN THE NATURE OF MERGER JOURNAL OF A LTD.

(₹ *in lacs*)

Particulars		*L.F.*	*Dr. (₹)*	*Cr. (₹)*
Business Merger A/c	Dr.		120	
To Liquidator of B Ltd.				120
(Being the purchase of business as per agreement dated....)				
Tangible Fixed Assets	Dr.		65	
Investments	Dr.		5	
Current Assets	Dr.		80	
To 10% Debentures A/c				3
To Current Liabilities				19

To Business Merger A/c			120
To Capital Redemption Reserve			3
To Statutory Reserves			5
(Being the assets, liabilities and reserves taken over recorded)			
Liquidator of B Ltd.	Dr.	120	
To Equity Share Capital A/c			30
To 15% Preference Share Capital A/c			20
To Securities Premium A/c (60 + 10)			70
(Being the purchase consideration discharged)			
Profit & Loss A/c	Dr.	1	
To Bank A/c			1
(Being the cost of absorption of B Ltd. paid)			
10% Debentures A/c	Dr.	3	
To 15% Debentures, A/c			2
To Capital Reserve A/c			1
(Being the issue of 15% Debentures to 10% Debentureholders of B Ltd.) No. of 15% Debenturers = ₹ 30,000/.15 = 20,000]			

BALANCE SHEET OF A LTD. AS AT 31.3.2016

Particulars	*Note No*	*₹ (lacs)*
I. Equity and Liabilities		
(1) Shareholders' Funds		
(a) Share Capital	1	160
(b) Reserves and Surplus	2	120
(2) Non-Current Liabilities [Long-term Borrowings]	3	8
(3) Current Liabilities [42 + 19]		61
Total		349
II. Assets		
(1) Non-Current Assets		
(a) Fixed Assets		
Tangible Assets [90 + 65]		155
(b) Non-Current Investments [15 + 5]		20
(2) Current Assets [95 + 80 – 1]		174
Total		349

Notes To Accounts:

Particulars	*₹ (lacs)*
1. Share Capital	
80,000 Equity share of ₹ 100 each	80
3,00,000 Equity Shares of ₹ 10 each	30
30,000 Pref. Shares of ₹ 100 each	30

	20,000, 15% Pref. Sahres of ₹ 100 each	20
(Of the above 3 lacs equity Shares were issued for consideration otherwise than cash)		
		160
2.	**Reserves and Surplus**	
	Securities Premium [60 + 10]	70
	General Reserve[Refer to WN]	31
	Profit & Loss Account [2 + 2 – 1]	3
	Capital Redemption Reserve	6
	Statutory Reserves	10
		120
3.	**Long-term Borrowings**	
	10% Debentures of ₹ 100 each	6
	15% Debenture of ₹ 100 each	2
		8

Working Note:

(I) CALCULATION OF PURCHASE CONSIDERATION

Particulars	*No. of Shares*	*Issue Price*	*Total*
For Preference Shareholders	20,000	₹ 150	30,00,000
For Equity Shareholders (75000 × 4)	3,00,000	₹ 30	90,00,000
			120,00,000

(II) *Calculation of the difference between purchase consideration and the amount of share capital of the transferor company*

Difference = ₹ 120,00,000 – ₹ 95,00,000 (Equity + Pref.) = ₹ 25,00,000

(III) *Calculation of the difference between the amount of Debentures of transferor company taken over and the amount of Debentures of the transferee company issued in exchange*

Difference = ₹ 3,00,000 – ₹ 2,00,000 = ₹, 1,00,000 (Profit)

(IV) ADJUSTMENT OF DIFFERENCE AGAINST THE RESERVES AND ACCUMULATED PROFITS OF TRANSFEROR CO.

A	Difference between Purchase Consideration & Share Capital	25.00
B	*Less:* Capital Reserves of both Co. (1+1 + 1)	(3.00)
C	Balance to be adjusted against Revenue Reserve	22.00
D	General Reserves of both Co. (31 + 22)	53.00
E	Closing Balance of General Reserves [D–C]	31.00

AMALGAMATION OF TWO OR MORE COMPANIES IN THE NATURE OF PURCHASE WHEN A NEW COMPANY IS FORMED

ILLUSTRATION 22

Sun Ltd. and Moon Ltd. were amalgamated on and from 1st April, 2016. A new company Star Ltd. was formed to take over the business of the existing companies. Given below are the extracts from the Balance Sheets of Sun Ltd. and Moon Ltd. as at 31st March, 2016 :

(₹ in lakhs)

Particulars	*Sun Ltd.*	*Moon Ltd.*
Equity Shares of ₹ 100 each	400	375
12% Preference Shares of ₹100 each	150	100
Reserves & Surplus	210	165
10% Debentures (₹100 each)	30	15
Current Liabilities	210	95
Tangible Fixed Assets	450	275
Non-Current Investments	75	25
Current Assets	575	450

Additional Information:

(a) Star Ltd. will issue 5 equity shares for each equity share of Sun Ltd. and 4 equity shares for each equity share of Moon Ltd. The shares are to be issued @ ₹ 30 each, having a face value of ₹ 10 per share.

(b) Preference shareholders of the two companies are issued equivalent number of 15% preference shares of Star Ltd. at a price of ₹ 150 per share (face value ₹ 100).

(c) 10% Debentureholders of Sun Ltd. and Moon Ltd. are discharged by Star Ltd., issuing such number of its 15% Debentures of ₹100 each so as to maintain the same amount of interest.

(d) Investment allowance reserve is to be maintained for 4 more years.

(e) Liquidation expenses are: Sun Ltd. ₹2,00,000 Moon Ltd. ₹ 1,00,000. It was decided that these expenses would be borne by Star Ltd.

(f) All the assets and liabilities of Sun Ltd. and Moon Ltd. are taken over at book value.

Required: Calculate Purchase Consideration and show the discharge thereof.

SOLUTION

CALCULATION OF PURCHASE CONSIDERATION

Particulars	*X Ltd.*	*Y Ltd.*	*Total*
A. No of Equity Shares	4,00,000	3,75,000	
B. Exchange Ratio	5:1	4:1	
C. No of Equity Shares to be issued by [A × B]	20,00,000	15,00,000	35,00,000
Equity Share Capital @ ₹ 20	400,00,000	300,00,000	700,00,000
Securities Premium @ ₹ 10	200,00,000	150,00,000	350,00,000
D. No of 15% Pref.Shares to be issued	1,50,000	1,00,000	2,50,000
15% Pref. Share Capital @ ₹ 100	150,00,000	100,00,000	250,00,000

Securities Premium@ ₹ 50	75,00,000	50,00,000	125,00,000
Total Purchase Consideration	825,00,000	600,00,000	1425,00,000

Note: *According to AS-14, the amount paid by purchasing Company to discharge the debentures holders and the liquidation expenses of Vendor Company are not considered as part of purchase consideration.*

ILLUSTRATION 23

Given below are the extracts from the Balance Sheets of X Ltd and Y Ltd. as at 31st March 2016:

Particulars	*X Ltd. (₹ in lacs)*	*Y Ltd. (₹ in lacs)*
Equity Share Capital of ₹ 10 each	5.00	10.00
8% Pref. Share Capital of ₹ 100 each	1.00	2.00
Reserves & Surplus	21.71	3.00
12% Debentures of ₹ 100 each	2.00	1.00
Current Liabilities	1.00	2.20
Net Tangible Assets	19.00	7.60
Non-Current Investments	3.45	5.20
Current Assets	8.26	5.40

The two companies agree to amalgamate as on Ist April, 2016 and form a new company XY Ltd.

Additional Information:

(a) Goodwill of X Ltd. and Y Ltd. on the date of take-over was valued at ₹ 48,000 and ₹ 38,000 respectively and Net Tangible Blocks of X Ltd. and Y Ltd were valued at 10% above their book values on the date of take-over.Investments of X Ltd. and Y Ltd. are considered worth ₹ 4,16,000 and ₹ 6,26,000 respectively.

(b) 12% Debentures of X Ltd. and Y Ltd. are discharged by XY Ltd. by issuing such number of its 15% Debentures of ₹ 100 each so as to maintain the same amount of interest.

(c) The issue of such an amount of fully paid 10% Pref. Shares in X Y Ltd. at 125% as is sufficient to discharge 9% Pref. Shares in X Ltd. & Y Ltd. at a premium of 20%.

(d) The Equity Shares of XY Ltd are to be of a nominal value of ₹ 10 each credited as ₹ 8 paid up and valued at ₹ 15 per share.

(e) Liquidation expenses are: X Ltd. ₹ 2,000 ,Y Ltd. ₹ 1,000. It was decided that these expenses would be borne by XY Ltd.Expenses on incorporation of XY Ltd. were ₹ 1,000.

Required: Calculate Purchase Consideration and show the discharge thereof.

SOLUTION

(I) COMPUTATION OF VALUE OF NET ASSETS FOR EQUITY SHAREHOLDERS ₹ (LAKHS)

	Particulars	*X Ltd.*	*Y Ltd.*
A.	Total Assets at their Current Values:		
	Goodwill	0.48	0.38
	Net Tangible Block	20.90	8.36
	Non-Current Investments	4.16	6.26
	Current Assets	8.26	5.40

	33.80	**20.40**
B. *Less:* Liabilities at their Current Amounts:		
12% Debentures [Interest/15%]	1.60	0.80
Current Liabilities	1.00	2.20
8% Pref. Share Capital	1.20	2.40
	3.80	**5.40**
C. Net Assets for Equity Shareholders [A – B]	**30.00**	**15.00**

(II) CALCULATION OF NO. OF EQUITY SHARES TO BE ISSUED BY PURCHASING COMPANY

Particulars	*X Ltd.*	*Y Ltd.*	*Total*
A. Total Value (as calculated above)	30,00,000	15,00,000	45,00,000
B. Issue Price of an Equity Share	15	15	15
C. No of Equity Shares to be issued by [A/B]	2,00,000	1,00,000	3,00,000
Equity Share Capital @ ₹ 8	16,00,000	8,00,000	24,00,000
Securities Premium@ ₹ 7	14,00,000	7,00,000	21,00,000

(III) CALCULATION OF PURCHASING CONSIDERATION

Particulars	*X Ltd.*	*Y Ltd.*	*Total*
Equity Shares @ ₹ 15	30,00,000	15,00,000	45,00,000
9% Pref. Shares @ ₹ 125	1,20,000	2,40,000	3,60,000
Total	31,20,000	17,40,000	48,60,000

Note: *According to AS-14, the amount paid by purchasing Company to discharge the debentures holders and the liquidation expenses of Vendor Company are not considered as part of purchase consideration.*

ILLUSTRATION 24

P Ltd. and Q Ltd. were carrying on the business of manufacturing of auto components. both the companies decided to amalgamare and a new company PQ Ltd. is to be formed with an Authorized Capital of ₹ 10,00,000 divided into 1,00,000 equity shares of ₹ 10 each. The Balance Sheet of the companies as on 31.03.2016 were as under:

Particulars	*P (₹)*	*Q (₹)*
I. Equity and Liabilities		
1. Shareholder's Fund		
(a) Share Capital	1,40,000	2,50,000
(b) Reserves & Surplus (Profit & Loss A/c)	30,000	1,55,000
2. Non Current Liabilities (8 % Secured Debentures)	1,10,000	—
3. Current Liabilities (Trade Payables)	54,000	1,40,000
Total	3,34,000	5,45,000
II. Assets		
1. Non-current Assets		
(a) Tangible Fixed Assets	1,25,000	2,95,000

2. Current Assets		
(a) Inventories	1,35,000	50,000
(b) Trade Receivables	44,000	1,42,000
(c) Cash at bank	30,000	58,000
Total	3,34,000	5,45,000

The assets and liabilities of the existing companies are to be transferred at book value with the exception of some items detailed below:

(i) Goodwill of P Ltd. was worth ₹ 50,000 and of Q Ltd. was worth ₹ 1,50,000,.

(ii) Tangible Fixed Assets of Q Ltd. was valued at ₹ 3,05,000.

(iii) The Trade Receivables of P Ltd. are realized fully and bank balance of P Ltd. are to be retained by the liquidator and the Trade Payables are to be paid of the proceeds thereof.

(iv) The debentures of P Ltd. are to be dischareged by issue of 8% debentures of PQ Ltd. at a premium of 10%.

You are required to:

(i) Compute the basis on which shares in PQ Ltd. will be issued at par to the shareholders of the existing companies.

(ii) Draw up a Balance Sheet of PQ Ltd. as at 1st April, 2016, the date of completiion of amalgamatiion.

(iii) Write up Journal entires including bank entries for closing the books of P Ltd.

SOLUTION

CALCULATION OF PURCHASE CONSIDERATION

Particulars	*P Ltd. (₹)*	*Q Ltd. (₹)*
Assets taken over:		
Goodwill	50,000	1,50,000
Tangible Fixed Assets	1,20,000	3,05,000
Inventories	1,35,000	50,000
Trade Receivables	–	1,42,000
Cash at Bank	–	58,000
	3,10,000	7,05,000
Less: Liabilities taken over:		
8% Debentures	(1,21,000)	–
Trade Payables	–	(1,40,000)
Net Assets taken over	1,89,000	5,65,000
To be satisfied by issue of shares of PQ Ltd. of ₹ 10 each at par	18,900	56,500

BALANCE SHEET OF PQ LIMITED AS AT 1ST APRIL, 2016

Particulars	*Note No.*	*(₹)*
I. Equity and Liabilities		
(1) Shareholder's Funds		
(a) Share Capital	1	7,54,000
(b) Reserve & Surplus [Securities Premium]		11,000

(2) Non-Current Liabilities		
(a) Long term borrowings [8% Debentures]		1,10,000
(3) Current Liabilities		
(a) Trade Payables		1,40,000
Total		10,15,000
II. Assets		
(1) Non-Current Assets		
(a) Fixed Assets		
Tangible [₹ 1,25,000 + ₹ 3,05,000]		4,30,000
Intangible [₹ 50,000 + ₹ 1,50,000]		2,00,000
(2) Current Assets		
(a) Inventories		1,85,000
(b) Trade Receivables		1,42,000
(c) Cash at Bank		58,000
Total		10,15,000

Notes to Accounts:

Particulars	₹
1.Share Capital	
Authorized	
1,00,000 shares of ₹ 10 eac	10,00,000
Issued, Subscribed and Paid up	
75,400 shares of ₹ 10 each (All the above shares are allotted as fully paid up pursuant to scheme of amalgamation withut payments being received in cash)	7,54,000

JOURNAL OF P LTD.

Date	*Particulars*		*L.F.*	*Dr. (₹)*	*Cr. (₹)*
1	Realization A/c	Dr.		3,04,000	
	To Tangible Fixed Assets				1,25,000
	To Inventories				1,35,000
	To Trade Receivables				44,000
	(Being all assets except cash t/f to Realization A/c)				
2	8% Debentures A/c	Dr.		1,10,000	
	Trade Payables	Dr.		54,000	
	To Realization A/c				1,64,000
	(Being all liabilities transferred to Realization Account)				
3	Equity Share Capital A/c	Dr.		1,40,000	
	Profit & Loss A/c	Dr.		30,000	
	To Equity Shareholder's A/c				1,70,000
	(Being Equity transferred to Equity Shareholder's A/c)				

4	PQ Ltd. Dr.		1,89,000	
	To Realization A/c			1,89,000
	(Being Purchase consideration due)			
5	Bank A/c Dr.		44,000	
	To Realization A/c			44,000
	(Being cash received from trade receivables in full)			
6	Realization A/c Dr.		54,000	
	To Bank A/c			54,000
	(Being payment made to Trade Payables)			
7	Share in PQ Ltd. Dr.		1,89,000	
	To PQ Ltd.			1,89,000
	(Being purchase consideration received in the form of Equity Shares of PQ Ltd.)			
8	Realization A/c (balancing figure) Dr.		39,000	
	To Equity Shareholder's A/c			39,000
	(Being profit on realization transferred to Equity Shareholder's A/c)			
9	Equity Shareholder's A/c Dr.		2,09,000	
	To Shares in PQ Ltd.			1,89,000
	To Bank A/c			20,000
	(Being final payment made to shareholders)			

ILLUSTRATION 25

Given below are the extracts of Balance Sheets of M Ltd. and N Ltd. as at 31st March, 2016:

(₹ in lakhs)

Particulars	*M Ltd.*	*N Ltd.*
Equity Shares of ₹10 each	3,600	900
10% Preference Shares of ₹ 10 each	1,200	–
Capital Reserve	600	–
General Reserve	2,100	–
Profit and Loss Account	780	(39)
8% Redeemable Debentures of ₹ 1,000 each		300
Trade Payables	3,291	462
Tangible Fixed Assets	6,615	702
Inventories	2,370	444
Trade Receivables	1,044	237
Cash at Bank	1,542	240

A new Company MN Ltd. was incorporated with an authorised capital of ₹ 15,000 lakhs divided into shares of ₹ 10 each. For the purpose of amalgamation in the nature of merger, M Ltd. and N Ltd. were merged into MN Ltd. on the following terms:

(i) Purchase consideration for M Ltd.'s business is to be discharged by issue of 120 lakhs fully paid 11% preference shares and 720 lakhs fully paid equity shares of MN Ltd. to the preference and equity shareholders of M Ltd. in full satisfaction of their claims.

(ii) To discharge purchase consideration for N Ltd. 's business, MN Ltd. to allot 90 lakhs fully paid up equity shares to shareholders of N Ltd. in full satisfaction of their claims.

(iii) Expenses on the liquidation of M Ltd. and N Ltd. amounting to ₹ 6 lakhs are to be borne by MN Ltd.

(iv) 8% Redeemable Debentures of N Ltd. to be converted into 8.5% redeemable debentures of MN Ltd.

(v) Expenses on incorporation of MN Ltd. were ₹15 lakhs.

You are requested to:

(a) Pass necessary Journal Entries in the books of MN Ltd. to record above transactions, and

(b) Prepare Balance Sheet of MN Ltd. after merger.

SOLUTION

JOURNAL OF MN LTD. *(₹ in lakhs)*

Date	*Particulars*		*L.F.*	*Dr. (₹)*	*Cr. (₹)*
	Business Purchase A/c	Dr.		9,300	
	To Liquidator of M Ltd.				8,400
	To Liquidator of N Ltd.				900
	(Being consideration payable to liquidators of the two companies taken over)				
	Tangible Fixed Assets (6,615 + 702)	Dr.		7,317	
	Inventories A/c (2,370 + 444)	Dr.		2,814	
	Trade Receivables A/c (1,044 + 237)	Dr.		1,281	
	Cash at Bank A/c (1,542 + 240)	Dr.		1,782	
	Profit and Loss A/c (Refer W.N.)	Dr.		120	
	To 8% Redeemable Debentures of N Ltd. A/c				300
	To Trade Payables A/c (3,291 + 462)				3,753
	To Business Purchase A/c				9,300
	(Being incorporation of all the assets and liabilities and the excess of consideration over the share capital being adjusted against reserves and surplus)				
	Liquidator of M Ltd, A/c	Dr.		8,400	
	Liquidator of N Ltd. A/c	Dr.		900	
	To Equity Share Capital A/c (7,200 + 900)				8,100
	To 11% Preference Share Capital A/c				1,200
	(Being allotment of fully paid shares in discharge of purchase consideration)				
	Profit and Loss A/c	Dr.		6	
	To Bank A/c				6
	(Being payment of liquidation expenses of M Ltd, and N Ltd.)				

	Preliminary Expenses A/c Dr.		15	
	To Bank A/c			15
	(Being expenses on incorporation of MN Ltd.)			
	8% Redeemable Debentures of N Ltd. A/c Dr.		300	
	To 8.5% Redeemable Debentures A/c			300
	(Being conversion of 8% Debentures of N Ltd. into 8.5% Debentures)			
	Profit & Loss A/c Dr.		15	
	To Preliminary Expenses A/c			15
	(Being the Preliminary Exp. and Discount w/o as per Para 56 of AS 26)			

BALANCE SHEET OF MN LTD AS AT 1ST APRIL, 2016

Particulars	*Note No.*	*₹ (in lacs)*
I. EQUITY AND LIABILITIES		
(1) Shareholders' Funds		
(a) Share Capital	1	9,300
(b) Reserves and Surplus [120 + 6 + 48 + 6]		(180)
(2) Non-Current Liabilities		
Long-term Borrowings [Debentures]		300
(3) Current Liabilities		
Trade Payables [₹ 3,291 + ₹ 462]		3,753
Total		13,173
II. ASSETS		
(1) Non-Current Assets		
(a) Fixed Assets		
(i) Tangible Assets [₹ 6,615 + ₹ 702]		7,317
(2) Current Assets		
Inventories [₹ 2,370 + ₹ 444]		2,814
Trade Receivables [₹ 1,044 + ₹ 237]		1,281
Cash and Cash Equivalents [₹ 1,542 + ₹ 240 – 21]		1,761
Total		13,173

Notes To Accounts:

Particulars	₹
1. Share Capital	
810 lakhs Equity Shares of ₹ 10 each	8,100
120 lakhs Pref. Shares of ₹ 10 each	1,200
(Of the above all Shares were issued for consideration otherwise than cash)	9,300

Working Note:

BALANCE OF PROFIT LOSS ACCOUNT *(₹ in lakhs)*

Total Consideration = ₹ (8,400 + 900) lakhs		9,300
Less: Share Capital of Companies taken over [₹(3,600 + 1,200 + 900) lacs]		5,700
		3,600
Amount to be adjusted:		
Capital Reserve	600	
General Reserve	2,100	
Profit & Loss A/c	780	3,480
Debit balance of Profit & Loss Account		120

ILLUSTRATION 26

Sun Ltd. and Moon Ltd. were amalgamated on and from 1st April, 2016. A new company Star Ltd. was formed to take over the business of the existing companies. The Balance Sheets of Sun Ltd. and Moon Ltd. as at 31st March, 2016 are given below:

(₹ in lakhs)

Particulars	*Sun Ltd.*	*Moon Ltd.*
Equity Shares of ₹ 100 each	400	375
12% Preference Shares of ₹100 each	150	100
Revaluation Reserve	75	50
General Reserve	85	75
Investment Allowance Reserve	25	25
Profit and Loss Account	25	15
10% Debentures (₹100 each)	30	15
Trade Payables	210	95
Tangible Fixed Assets	450	275
Investments	75	25
Inventories	175	125
Trade Receivables	150	175
Cash and Bank balances	250	150

Additional Information:

(a) Star Ltd. will issue 5 equity shares for each equity share of Sun Ltd. and 4 equity shares for each equity share of Moon Ltd. The shares are to be issued @ ₹ 30 each, having a face value of ₹ 10 per share.

(b) Preference shareholders of the two companies are issued equivalent number of 15% preference shares of Star Ltd. at a price of ₹ 150 per share (face value ₹ 100).

(c) 10% Debentureholders of Sun Ltd. and Moon Ltd. are discharged by Star Ltd., issuing such number of its 15% Debentures of ₹100 each so as to maintain the same amount of interest.

(d) Investment allowance reserve is to be maintained for 4 more years.

(e) Liquidation expenses are: Sun Ltd. ₹2,00,000 Moon Ltd. ₹ 1,00,000. It was decided that these expenses would be borne by Star Ltd.

(f) All the assets and liabilities of Sun Ltd. and Moon Ltd. are taken over at book value.

(g) Authorised equity share capital of Star Ltd. is ₹ 5,00,00,000, divided into equity shares of ₹ 10 each. After issuing required number of shares to the Liquidators of Sun Ltd. and Moon Ltd., Star Ltd. issued balance shares to Public. The issue was fully subscribed.

Required: Prepare the Balance Sheet of Star Ltd. as at 1st April, 2016 after amalgamation has been carried out on the basis of Amalgamation in the nature of purchase.

SOLUTION

BALANCE SHEET OF STAR LTD AS AT 1ST APRIL, 2016

Particulars	*Note No.*	*₹ (in lacs)*
I. EQUITY AND LIABILITIES		
(1) Shareholders' Funds		
(a) Share Capital	1	750
(b) Reserves and Surplus	2	875
(2) Non-Current Liabilities		
Long-term Borrowings [Debentures] [20 + 10]		30
(3) Current Liabilities		
Trade Payables (210 + 95)		305
Total		1,960
II. ASSETS		
(1) Non-Current Assets		
(a) Fixed Assets		
(i) Tangible Assets [450 + 325]		775
(ii) Intangible Assets [Goodwill] [10 + 2 + 1]		13
(b) Non-Current Investments [75 + 25]		100
(c) Other Non-Current Assets [Amalgamation Adjustment A/c]		50
(2) Current Assets		
Inventories [175 + 125]		300
Trade Receivables [150 + 175]		325
Cash and Cash Equivalents [250 + 150 – 3]		397
Total		1,960

Notes To Accounts:

Particulars	₹
1. Share Capital	
50 lakhs Equity Shares of ₹ 10 each	500
2.5 lakhs Pref. Shares of ₹ 10 each	250
(Of the above all Shares were issued for consideration otherwise than cash)	750
2.Reserves and Surplus	
Securities Premium [75 + 50 + 400 + 300]	825
Investment Allowance Reserve [25 + 25]	50
	875

Working Notes:

1. CALCULATION OF PURCHASE CONSIDERATION

Particulars	X Ltd.	Y Ltd.	Total
A. No of Equity Shares	4,00,000	3,75,000	
B. Exchange Ratio	5:1	4:1	
C. No of Equity Shares to be issued by [A × B]	20,00,000	15,00,000	35,00,000
Equity Share Capital @ ₹ 20	400,00,000	300,00,000	700,00,000
Securities Premium@ ₹ 10	200,00,000	150,00,000	350,00,000
D. No of 15% Pref.Shares to be issued	1,50,000	1,00,000	2,50,000
15% Pref. Share Capital @ ₹ 100	150,00,000	100,00,000	250,00,000
Securities Premium@ ₹ 50	75,00,000	50,00,000	125,00,000
Total Purchase Consideration	825,00,000	600,00,000	1425,00,000

2. CALCULATION OF NUMBER OF DEBENTURES ISSUED (₹ in lakhs)

Particulars	Sun Ltd.	Moon Ltd.
10% Debentures of ₹100 each	30	15
15% Debentures to be issued to maintain same amount of interest:		
Interest = ₹30,00,000 × 10% = ₹3,00,000		
Number of 15% Debentures = (₹ 3,00,000/15) × 100	20	
Interest = ₹15,00,000 × 10%		
Number of 15% Debentures = (₹ 1,15,000/15) × 100		10

3. NET ASSETS TAKEN OVER (₹ in lakhs)

Particulars	Sun Ltd.	Moon Ltd.
A. Assets taken over		
Tangible Fixed Assets	450	325
Investments	75	25
Inventories	175	125
Trade Receivable	150	175
Cash and bank	150	100
	1,000	750
B. Less: Liabilities taken over		
Debentures	20	10
Trade Payable	210	95
	230	105
C. Net assets taken over	770	645
D. Purchase consideration	825	600
E. (Goodwill)/Capital Reserve	(55)	45
F. Net Goodwill		(10)

4. Liquidation expenses of Sun Ltd. and Moon Ltd., ₹ 2 lakhs and ₹ 1 lakhs respectively will be debited to Goodwill account in the books of Star Ltd.

ILLUSTRATION 27

Given below are the extracts from the Balance Sheets of X Ltd and Y Ltd. as at 31st March 2016:

Particulars	*X Ltd. (₹ in lacs)*	*Y Ltd. (₹ in lacs)*
Equity Share Capital of ₹ 10 each	5.00	10.00
8% Pref. Share Capital of ₹ 100 each	1.00	2.00
Reserve	15.46	0.70
Statutory Reserve	2.00	1.00
Profit & Loss A/c	4.25	1.30
12% Debentures of ₹ 100 each	2.00	1.00
Current Liabilities	1.00	2.20
Net Tangible Assets	19.00	7.60
Non-Current Investments	3.45	5.20
Current Assets	8.26	5.40

The two companies agree to amalgamate as on Ist April, 2016 and form a new company XY Ltd.

Additional Information:

(a) Goodwill of X Ltd. and Y Ltd. on the date of take-over was valued at ₹ 48,000 and ₹ 38,000 respectively and Net Tangible Blocks of X Ltd. and Y Ltd were valued at 10% above their book values on the date of take-over.Investments of X Ltd. and Y Ltd. are considered worth ₹ 4,16,000 and ₹ 6,26,000 respectively.

(b) 12% Debentures of X Ltd. and Y Ltd. are discharged by XY Ltd. by issuing such number of its 15% Debentures of ₹ 100 each so as to maintain the same amount of interest.

(c) The issue of such an amount of fully paid 10% Pref. Shares in X Y Ltd. at 125% as is sufficient to discharge 9% Pref. Shares in X Ltd. & Y Ltd. at a premium of 20%.

(d) The Equity Shares of XY Ltd are to be of a nominal value of ₹ 10 each credited as ₹ 8 paid up and valued at ₹ 15 per share.

(e) Statutory Reserve is to be maintained for 3 years more for Income Tax purposes.

(f) Liquidation expenses are: X Ltd. ₹ 2,000 ,Y Ltd. ₹ 1,000. It was decided that these expenses would be borne by XY Ltd.Expenses on incorporation of XY Ltd. were ₹ 1,000.

Required: Draft the Balance Sheet of XY Ltd. after amalgamation.

SOLUTION

BALANCE SHEET OF XY LTD. AS AT 31.3.2016

Particulars	*Note No*	*₹ (lacs)*
I. Equity and Liabilities		
(1) Shareholders'Funds		
(a) Share Capital	1	26.88
(b) Reserves and Surplus	2	24.72
(2) Non-Current Liabilities[Long-term Borrowings]	3	2.40

(3) Current Liabilities	3.20
Total	57.20
II. Assets	
(1) Non-Current Assets	
(a) Fixed Assets	
Tangible Assets (20.90 + 8.36)	29.26
Intangible Assets (Goodwill) (0.48 + 0.38 + 0.02+.01+.01)	0.90
(b) Non-Current Investments	10.42
(c) Other Non-Current Assets [Amalgamation Adjustment A/c]	3.00
(2) Current Assets [8.26+5.40-.02-.01-.01]	**13.62**
Total	57.20

Notes To Accounts:

Particulars	*₹ (lacs)*
1. Share Capital	
3,00,000 Equity Shares of ₹ 10 each, ₹ 8 paid up	24.00
2,880, 9% Pref. Shares of ₹ 100 each	2.88
(Of the above all Shares were issued for consideration otherwise than cash)	
	26.88
2. Reserves and Surplus	
Securities Premium [(3,00,000 × ₹ 7) + (2,880 × ₹ 25)]	21.72
Statutory Reserve	3.00
	24.72
3. Long-term Borrowings	
15% Debentures (1.60 + 0.80]	2.40

Working Notes:

(I) COMPUTATION OF VALUE OF NET ASSETS FOR EQUITY SHAREHOLDERS ₹ (LAKHS)

Particulars	*X Ltd.*	*Y Ltd.*
A. Total Assets at their Current Values:		
Goodwill	0.48	0.38
Net Tangible Block	20.90	8.36
Non-Current Investments	4.16	6.26
Current Assets	8.26	5.40
	33.80	**20.40**
B. *Less:* Liabilities at their Current Amounts:		
12% Debentures [Interest/15%]	1.60	0.80
Current Liabilities	1.00	2.20
8% Pref. Share Capital	1.20	2.40
	3.80	**5.40**
C. Net Assets for Equity Shareholders [A – B]	**30.00**	**15.00**

(II) CALCULATION OF NO. OF EQUITY SHARES TO BE ISSUED BY PURCHASING COMPANY

	Particulars	*X Ltd.*	*Y Ltd.*	*Total*
A.	Total Value (as calculated above)	30,00,000	15,00,000	45,00,000
B.	Issue Price of an Equity Share	15	15	15
C.	No of Equity Shares to be issued by [A/B]	2,00,000	1,00,000	3,00,000
	Equity Share Capital @ ₹ 8	16,00,000	8,00,000	24,00,000
	Securities Premium@ ₹ 7	14,00,000	7,00,000	21,00,000

(III) CALCULATION OF PURCHASE CONSIDERATION

Particulars	*X Ltd.*	*Y Ltd.*	*Total*
Equity Shares @ ₹ 15	30,00,000	15,00,000	45,00,000
9% Pref. Shares @ ₹ 125	1,20,000	2,40,000	3,60,000
Total	31,20,000	17,40,000	48,60,000

8 INTERNAL RECONSTRUCTION

LEARNING OBJECTIVES

After studying this chapter, you should be able to understand:

- Meaning of Internal Reconstruction
- Alteration of Share capital
- Reduction of Share Capital
- Variation of Shareholders' Rights
- Scheme of Compromise and Arrangement
- How to deal with Surrender of Shares?
- Accounting Entries

1.0 MEANING OF INTERNAL RECONSTRUCTION

In case of internal reconstruction, the company's existing financial structure is reorganised without dissolving the existing Company and without forming a new Company. Taking a wider meaning of the term 'Internal Reconstruction'. It includes:

1. Alteration of Share Capital u/s 61.
2. Reduction of Share Capital u/s 66.
3. Variation of Shareholders' Rights u/s 48.
4. Scheme of Compromise/Arrangement u/s 230 and 231.

2.0 DISTINCTION BETWEEN INTERNAL RECONSTRUCTION AND EXTERNAL RECONSTRUCTION

Basis of Distinction	Internal Reconstruction	External Reconstruction
1. Liquidation of Existing Company	Existing company does not go into liquidation.	Existing company goes into liquidation.
2. Formation of New Company	No new company is formed.	A new company is formed to take over the business of the existing company.
3. Reduction of Share Capital	It involves the reduction of share capital.	It may *or* may not involve reduction of share capital.

3.0 ALTERATION OF SHARE CAPITAL [SECTIONS 61]

LEGAL REQUIREMENTS

The main legal requirements in connection with the alteration of Share Capital are summarized as under:

Authorized by Articles	A Company may alter the Capital Clause of its memorandum only if it is authorised by its articles of association to do so.
Manner	A Company may alter the Capital Clause in the following manner: (i) by increasing its share capital by issue of new shares; [e.g. from 1 crore to 5 crores]. (ii) by consolidating the existing shares into shares of larger amount than its existing shares: [e.g. Conversion of Shares of ₹ 10 each into shares of ₹ 100 each]. (iii) by sub-diving the existing shares into shares of smaller amount than its existing shares; [e.g. Conversion of shares of ₹ 100 each into each into shares of ₹ 10 each]. (iv) by converting fully paid shares into stock *or* vice-versa. (v) by cancelling its unissued shares.
Ordinary Resolution	An ordinary resolution must be passed at a general meeting.
Notice	A notice specifying alteration made must be given to the Registrar within 30 days of alteration.

JOURNAL ENTRIES

The accounting entries in each case of alteration of share capital will be as under:

Particulars		*Dr. (₹)*	*Cr. (₹)*
(a) **For increase in Share Capital:**			
Example *X Ltd. issued 10,000 Equity Shares of ₹ 10 each at par.*			
(i) Bank A/c	Dr.	1,00,000	
To Equity Share Application and Allotment A/c			1,00,000
(Being the application money received)			
(ii) Equity Share Application and Allotment A/c	Dr.	1,00,000	
To Equity Share Capital A/c			1,00,000
(Being 10,000 Equity shares of ₹ 10 each allotted at par)			
(b) **For Consolidation of Shares:**			
Example *X Ltd. having 10,000 Equity Shares of ₹ 10 each decides to convert the Share Capital into Equity Shares of ₹ 100 each.*			
Equity Share Capital (₹ 10) A/c	Dr.	1,00,000	
To Equity Share Capital (₹ 100) A/c			1,00,000
(Being 10,000 Equity Shares of ₹ 10 each converted into 1,000 shares of ₹ 100 each)			
(c) **For Sub-division of Shares:**			
Example *X Ltd. having 1,000 Equity Shares of ₹ 100 each decides to convert the Share Capital into Equity Shares of ₹ 10 each.*			
Equity Share Capital (₹ 100) A/c	Dr.	1,00,000	
To Equity Share Capital (₹ 10) A/c			1,00,000
(Being 1,000 Equity Shares of ₹ 100 each converted into 10,000 Shares of ₹ 10 each)			

(d) **For Conversion of Shares into Stock:**		
Example *X Ltd. having 10,000 Equity Shares of ₹ 10 each decides to convert the Share Capital into Equity Stock*		
Equity Share Capital (₹ 10) A/c Dr.	1,00,000	
To Equity Stock A/c		1,00,000
(Being 1,000 Equity Shares of ₹ 10 each converted into equity stock)		
(e) **For Conversion of Stock into Shares:**		
Example *X Ltd. having Equity Stock of ₹ 1,00,000 decides to convert the Equity Stock into Equity Share Capital of ₹ 10 each*		
Equity Stock A/c Dr.	1,00,000	
To Equity Share Capital (₹ 10) A/c		1,00,000
(Being Equity Stock of ₹ 1,00,000 converted into 10,000 Equity Shares of ₹ 10 each)		
(f) **For Cancelling Unissued Shares:**		
No accounting entry is required to be passed. The Authorised Share Capital gets reduced by the amount of unissued shares now cancelled.		

4.0 REDUCTION OF SHARE CAPITAL [SECTION 66]

LEGAL REQUIREMENTS

The main legal requirements for reduction of Share Capital are summarised as follows:

Authorised by Articles	A company limited by shares *or* a company limited by guarantee having a Share Capital may reduce its Share Capital only if it is authorised by its articles of association to do so.
Ways	A company may reduce its Share Capital in any of the following ways: (i) by extinguishing/reducing the liability on any of its shares in respect of uncalled amount on shares; (ii) by cancelling the paid up Share Capital which is lost *or* is not represented by available assets; (iii) by paying off any paid up Share Capital which is in excess of the requirements of the Company.
Special Resolution	A Special Resolution must be passed at a general meeting.
Auditor's Certificate	Audtitor's Certificate to the affect that the proposed accounting treatment is as per prescribed Accounting Standard, must be filed with the Tribunal.
Tribunal's Order	A Tribunal's order confirming the reduction must be obtained.
Filing with ROC	A certified copy of Tribunal's order and Minutes approved by the Tribunal must be filed with the Registrar.
Notice	A Company must publish notice of registration in such manner as the Tribunal may direct.
Effective Date	A resolution for reducing Capital as confirmed by the order of the Tribunal shall take effect on its registration by the Registrar.

JOURNAL ENTRIES

The Accounting entries in each case of reduction of share capital will be as follows:

Particulars		Dr. (₹)	Cr. (₹)
(a) **For Reducing the liability in respect of Uncalled Amount**			
Example *X Ltd. having 1,000 Equity Shares of ₹ 100 each ₹ 60 paid up, decides to cancel the liability of member to the extent of ₹ 20 per share and make shares as of ₹ 80 each. ₹ 60 paid up.*			
Equity. Share Capital (₹ 100) A/c	Dr.	60,000	
To Equity Share Capital (₹ 80)			60,000
(Being Shares of ₹ 100 each converted into shares of ₹ 80 each)			
Note: *The Paid up Share Capital of the company will remain unchanged.*			
(b) **For Paying off the surplus paid up Capital**			
Example *A Ltd. having 1,000 Equity Shares of ₹ 100 each fully paid decides to repay to its members ₹ 20 per share and make shares as of ₹ 80 each fully paid up.*			
(i) Equity Share Capital (₹ 100) A/c	Dr.	1,00,000	
To Equity Share Capital (₹ 80) A/c			80,000
To Sundry Members A/c			20,000
(Being shares of ₹ 100 each converted into shares of ₹ 80 each and make ₹ 20 per share due to members)			
(ii) Sundry Members A/c	Dr.	20,000	
To Bank A/c			20,000
(Being the payment made to members)			
(c) **For Writing off the lost paid up Capital**			
Example *Look at the following Balance Sheet of Bad Luck Ltd.:*			

Liabilities	₹	*Assets*	₹
1,000 Shares of ₹ 100 each	*1,00,000*	*Intangible Assets*	*25,000*
Sundry Creditors.	*1,00,000*	*Other Fixed Assets*	*1,00,000*
		Current Assets	*25,000*
		P&L A/c	*50,000*
	2,00,000		*2,00,000*

Assets	*Present Worth (₹)*
Intangible	*Nil*
Other Fixed Assets	*1,05,000*
Current Assets	*15,000*
Thus, the Company has lost ₹ 80,000 if its paid up Capital as under:	
Intangible Assets	*₹ 25,000*
Current Assets	*₹ 10,000*
P&L A/c	*₹ 50,000*

	₹ 85,000
Less: Appreciation in Fixed Assets	*5,000*
	₹ 80,000

This reduction can be effected in any of the following two ways:

JOURNAL

Particulars		*Dr. (₹)*	*Cr. (₹)*
(i) By reducing the paid-up value (not Nominal Value) of existing shares			
Share Capital (₹ 100) A/c	Dr.	80,000	
To Capital Reduction A/c			80,000
(Being the paid-up value of a share reduced from ₹ 100 to ₹ 20)			
(ii) By reducing both the Nominal values and paid up values of Shares			
Share Capital (₹ 100) A/c	Dr.	1,00,000	
To Share. Capital (₹ 20) A/c			20,000
To Capital Reduction A/c			80,000
(Being the shares reduced to ₹ 20 per share)			

Note: The Shareholders will not ordinarily be willing for the first alternative since it puts additional burden on them.

5.0 VARIATION OF SHAREHOLDERS' RIGHTS [SECTION 48]

LEGAL REQUIREMENTS

The main legal requirements for variation of shareholders' rights are summarised as under:

Separate Meeting	If the rights attached to the shares of any particulars class of shareholders are to be varied, a separate meeting of that particular class of shareholders must be held.
Consent of atleast 3/4th	The consent of the holder of at least 3/4th of the shares of the class concerned (or a higher proportion if so required by the articles/yemorandum) must be obtained.
Right to Apply to the Tribunal	The holders of at least 10% of the issued shares of the class concerned whose rights are being varied, may apply to the Tribunal to have the variation cancelled within 21 days after the consent is obtained *or* the resolution is passed.
Tribunal's Confirmation	If such appeal is made, the variation will not have effect unless it is confirmed by the Tribunal whose decision is final.
Notice	Notice of the variation must be filed with the Registrar within 30 days of the Tribunal's order.

EXAMPLE 1

X Ltd. has 1,000, 10% Cum Pref. shares of ₹ 100 each. At a class meeting of Cum Pref. Shareholders, it was decided that the rate of dividend be reduced to 9%. In such a case following Journal Entry will be passed.

Particulars		*Dr. (₹)*	*Cr. (₹)*
10% Cum Pref. Share Capital A/c	Dr.	1,00,000	
To 9% Cum Pref. Share Capital A/c			1,00,000

EXAMPLE 2

Y Ltd. has 1,000, 10% Cumulative Pref. Shares of ₹ 100 each. At a meeting of Cum Pref. Shareholders, it was decided that the existing Cumulative-Pref-Shares be converted into Non-Cumulative-Pref. Shares.

Particulars		*Dr. (₹)*	*Cr. (₹)*
10% Cum Pref. Share Capital A/c	Dr.	1,00,000	
To 9% Cum Pref. Share Capital A/c			1,00,000

6.0 SCHEME OF COMPROMISE AND ARRANGEMENT [SECTIONS 230 TO 2310]

MEANING OF COMPROMISE

Compromise refers to an amicable settlement of differences by mutual concessions by parties to dispute. It may be noted that the compromise presupposes the existence of some dispute because there can be no compromise unless there is some dispute. The need for compromise may arise for the settlement of some dispute between the company and its creditors/members.

MEANING OF ARRANGEMENT

The term 'Arrangement' carries a wider sense than the term 'Compromise'. It implies re-arrangement of rights and/or liabilities of a member/a class of them/a creditor/a class of them without the existence of any dispute. According to Explanation to Section 230(1), of the Companies Act, 2013 the term 'Arrangement' includes re-organisation of the share capital of the company by the consolidation of shares of different classes *or* by the division of the shares into shares of different classes *or* by both these methods. An arrangement may involve anyone *or* more of the following:

(a) Debenture-holders foregoing their claims in whole *or* in part;

(b) Debentures exchanging their debentures for new debentures/shares;

(c) Creditors foregoing their claims in whole *or* in part;

(d) Creditor agreeing to receive shares/debentures in whole/in part payment of the claims;

(e) Preference shareholders forgoing their claims for arrears of dividend;

(f) Preference shareholders agreeing to accept a reduced rate of dividend in future;

(g) Fresh issue of shares to raise additional working capital;

(h) Writing off lost Paid-up Capital.

Example In the Balance Sheet 10% Debentures 14,70,000, Sundry Creditors 4,50,000

The debenture holders agree to reduce their claims to ₹ 5,00,000 in consideration of their getting 50,000 Equity Shares of ₹ 10 each. Sundry Creditors agree to reduce their claims to 20% and half the balance to be satisfied by the issue of Equity Shares of ₹ 10 each. The following Journal Entries shall be passed to record the aforesaid arrangement:

Particulars		Dr. (₹)	Cr. (₹)
(i) 10% Debentureholders' A/c	Dr.	9,70,000	
To Equity Shares Capital A/c (₹ 10)			5,00,000
To Reconstruction A/c			4,70,000
(ii) Sundry Creditors A/c	Dr.	4,05,000	
To Equity Share Capital A/c (₹ 10)			45,000
To Reconstruction A/c			3,60,000

7.0 HOW TO DEAL WITH SURRENDER OF SHARES?

Under a scheme of reconstruction, the shareholders may be required to surrender a part of their share-holdings. Such surrendered shares may be re-issued to other parties in whole/in part satisfaction of their claims *or* cancelled. The following Journal Entries may be required to be passed in such connection:

(a) On Surrender of Shares	Share Capital A/c To Shares Surrendered A/c	Dr.
(b) On Re-issue of Surrendered Shares	Shares Surrendered A/c To Share Capital A/c	Dr.
(c) On Cancellation of Surrendered Shares	Shares Surrendered A/c To Reconstruction A/c	Dr.

8.0 ACCOUNTING ENTRIES UNDER INTERNAL RECONSTRUCTION

Date	Particulars		Dr. (₹)	Cr. (₹)
1.	**To Reduce Both the Nominal Value and Paid up Value of Shares**			
	Share Capital A/c (₹ 100 each)	Dr.	100	
	To Share Capital A/c (₹ 80 each)			80
	To Reconstruction A/c/Capital Reduction A/c			20
2.	**To Reduce only the Paid up Value of Shares**			
	Share Capital A/c	Dr.	20	
	To Reconstruction A/c/Capital Reduction A/c			20
3.	**(a) To Pay the Arrears of Preference Dividend**			
	Reconstruction A/c	Dr.		
	To Bank A/c/Share Capital A/c			
	(b) To Cancel the Arrears of Preference Dividend			
	No Journal Entry is required to cancel a Contingent Liability.			
4.	**To Reduce the Claims of Debentureholders**			
	Debentures A/c	Dr.		
	Interest on Debentures A/c	Dr.		
	To New Debentures A/c/Share Capital A/c/Bank A/c			
	To Reconstruction A/c			

5.	**To Reduce the claims of Trade Creditors**			
	Trade Creditors A/c	Dr.		
	To Share Capital A/c/Bank A/c			
	To Reconstruction A/c			
6.	**To Settle the Tax Liability**			
	Provision for Tax A/c	Dr.		
	To Bank A/c			
	To Reconstruction A/c			
7.	**To Pay Reconstruction Expenses**			
	Reconstruction A/c	Dr.		
	To Bank A/c			
8.	**To Pay for Cancellation of Capital Commitments etc.**			
	Reconstruction A/c	Dr.		
	To Bank A/c			
9.	**To Record the Bad Debts and Doubtful Debts**			
	Reconstruction A/c	Dr. [With total]		
	To Debtors A/c	[With Bad Debts]		
	To Provision for Doubtful Debts A/c	[With Doubtful Debts]		
10.	**To Record the Appreciation in Value of Assets**			
	Investments A/c/Land and Building A/c	Dr.		
	To Reconstruction A/c			
11.	**To Transfer Capital Reserve for Reconstruction Purpose**			
	Capital Reserve A/c	Dr.		
	To Reconstruction A/c			
12.	**To write off the Accumulated Losses, Fictitious Assets and the over valuation of Over Valued Assets**			
	Capital Reduction A/c/Reconstruction A/c	Dr.		
	To Profit and Loss A/c			
	To Preliminary Expenses A/c			
	To Underwriting Commission A/c			
	To Discount on Issue of Shares/Debentures A/c			
	To Goodwill A/c (To the extent of over valuation)			
	To Patents A/c (To the extent of over valuation)			
	To Trade Marks A/c (To the extent of over valuation)			
	To Copy Right A/c (To the extent of over valuation)			
	To Other Overvalued Assets (individually)			
13.	**To Transfer the Credit Balance of Reconstruction A/c/**			
	Capital Reduction A/c			
	Capital Reduction A/c/Reconstruction A/c	Dr.		
	To Capital Reserve A/c			

Tutorial Notes:

(i) *The author recommends the use of 'Reconstruction Account' particularly when the scheme of compromise/arrangement is carried out under the provisions of Sections 391 to 393. The use of 'Capital Reduction Account' is purely justified when the capital reduction scheme is carried out without invoking the provisions of Sections 230 to 231.*

(ii) *Even if the question is silent as to writing off, the debit balance of Profit & Loss Account and Unamortized Expense Items (like Preliminary Expenses, Underwriting Comm., Discount on Issue of Shares/Debentures) should be written off to the extent of credit balance available in Reconstruction/Capital Reduction Account.*

(iii) *So far as Fixed Assets are concerned, the amount written off under a scheme of reconstruction must be shown in each Balance Sheet for five years.*

ILLUSTRATION 1

Pass journal entries for the following transactions:

(i) Conversion of 2 lakh fully paid equity shares of ₹ 10 each into stock of ₹ 1,00,000 and balance has 12% fully convertible Debenture.

(ii) Consolidation of 40 lakh fully paid equity shares of ₹2.50 each into 10 lakh fully paid equity share of ₹10 each.

(iii) Sub-division of 10 lakh fully paid 11% preference shares of ₹ 50 each into 50 lakh fully paid 11% preference shares of ₹ 10 each.

(iv) Conversion of 12% preference shares of ₹ 5,00,000 into 14% preference shares ₹ 3,00,000 and remaining balance as 12% Non-cumulative preference shares.

SOLUTION

JOURNAL

Date	*Particulars*		*Dr. (₹)*	*Cr. (₹)*
(i)	Equity share Capital A/c	Dr.	20,00,000	
	To Equity Stock			1,00,000
	To 12% Fully Convertible Debentures			19,00,000
	(Being conversion of 2 lakh equity shares of ₹ 10 each into stock of ₹ 1,00,000 and balance as fully convertible debentures as per resolution)			
(ii)	Equity Share Capital A/c (₹ 2.50)	Dr.	100,00,000	
	To Equity Share Capital A/c (₹ 10)			100,00,000
	(Being consolidation of 40 lakh shares of ₹ 2.50 each into 10 lakh shares of ₹ 10 each as per resolution)			
(iii)	11% Preference Shares Capital A/c (₹ 50)	Dr.	500,00,000	
	To 11% Preference Share Capital A/c (₹10)			500,00,000
	(Being subdivision of 10 lakh preference shares of ₹ 50 each into 50 lakh shares of ₹ 10 each as per resolution)			
(iv)	12% Preference Share Capital A/c	Dr.	5,00,000	
	To 14% Preference Share Capital			3,00,000

	To 12% Non-cumulative Pref. Share Capital (Being conversion of preference shares as per resolution)			2,00,000

ILLUSTRATION 2

V Ltd has Equity Share Capital (of ₹ 10 each) of ₹ 500 lacs. All the equity shares be converted into the same number of equity shares of ₹ 5 each, ₹ 2.50 paid up. Journalise

SOLUTION

JOURNAL

[₹ in Lacs]

Date	*Particulars*	*L.F.*	*Dr. (₹)*	*Cr. (₹)*
	Equity Share Capital (₹ 10 each) A/c Dr.		500	
	To Equity Share Capital (₹ 5 each) A/c			125
	To Reconstruction A/c			375
	(Being the conversion of all the equity shares into the same number of equity shares of ₹ 5 each, ₹ 2.50 paid up as per scheme of reconstruction)			

ILLUSTRATION 3

V Ltd has 6%Cum-Pref.Shares (of ₹ 100 each) of ₹ 100 lacs. The preference shares are converted from 6% to 15% but revalued in a manner in which the total return on them remains unaffected. Journalise

SOLUTION

JOURNAL

[₹ in Lacs]

Date	*Particulars*	*L.F.*	*Dr. (₹)*	*Cr. (₹)*
	6% Cum-Preference Share Capital (₹ 100) A/c Dr.		100	
	To 15% Cum-Pref. Share Capital (₹ 100) A/c			40
	To Reconstruction A/c			60
	(Being 40000 15% cum Pref. share of ₹ 100 each issued so as to maintain the same amount of dividend (i.e. ₹ 6 lacs) vide scheme of reconstruction dated.....)			

ILLUSTRATION 4

V Ltd has 6%Cum-Pref.Shares (of ₹100 each) of ₹ 100 lacs. Dividend on Preference Shares are in arrears for three years. Four equity shares of ₹ 5 each, ₹ 2.50 paid up to be issued for each ₹100 of arrears of preference dividend.Journalise

SOLUTION

JOURNAL

[₹ in Lacs]

Date	*Particulars*	*L.F.*	*Dr. (₹)*	*Cr. (₹)*
	Reconstruction A/c Dr.		1.8	
	To Equity Share Capital (₹. 5 each, ₹ 2.50 paid up) A/c			1.8
	(Being 72000 equity shares of ₹ 5 each, ₹ 2.50 paid up issued to Pref. Shareholders for dividend arrears vide scheme of Reconstruction dated.....)			

ILLUSTRATION 5

V Ltd has 10% first debentures for ₹ 60 lacs, 10% second debentures for ₹ 100 lacs and Interest on Debentures Outstanding ₹ 16 lacs. Mr. A holds 10% first debentures for ₹ 40 lacs and 10% second debentures for ₹ 60 lacs. He is also a creditor for ₹ 10 lacs. Mr. 'A' is to cancel ₹ 60 lacs of his total debt and to pay ₹ 10 lacs to the company and to receive new 12% Debentures for the balance amount.Journalise

SOLUTION

JOURNAL

[₹ in Lacs]

Date	*Particulars*	*L.F.*	*Dr. (₹)*	*Cr. (₹)*
	10% First Debentures A/c Dr.		40	
	10% Second Debentures A/c Dr.		60	
	Trade Creditors A/c Dr.		10	
	Interest on Debentures Outstanding A/c Dr. [16 x 100/160]		10	
	To Mr. A			120
	(Being the total amount due to A t/f to his A/c)			
	Bank A/c Dr.		10	
	To Mr. A			10
	(Being the amount received from Mr. A under the Reconstruc- tion Scheme)			
	Mr. A A/c Dr.		130	
	To 12% New Debentures A/c			70
	To Reconstruction A/c			60
	(Being ₹ 60 lacs due to A (Including creditors) cancelled and 12% new debentures allotted for balance amount as per scheme of reconstruction)			

ILLUSTRATION 6

V Ltd has 10% first debentures for ₹ 60 lacs, 10% second debentures for ₹ 100 lacs and Interest on Debentures Outstanding ₹ 16 lacs. Mr. B holds 10% first debentures for ₹ 20 lacs and 10% second debentures for ₹ 40 lacs and is also a creditor for ₹ 5 lacs. Mr. 'B' is to cancel ₹ 30 lacs of his total debt and to accept new 12% Debentures for the balance amount.Journalise

SOLUTION

JOURNAL

[₹ in Lacs]

Date	*Particulars*		*L.F.*	*Dr. (₹)*	*Cr. (₹)*
	10% First Debentures A/c	Dr.		20	
	10% Second Debentures A/c	Dr.		40	
	Trade Creditors A/c	Dr.		5	
	Interest on Debentures Outstanding A/c	Dr.		6	
	To Mr. B				71
	(Being the total amount due to Mr. B t/f to his A/c)				
	Mr. B			71	
	To 12% New Debentures A/c				41
	To Reconstruction A/c				30
	(Being ₹ 30 lacs due to B (including creditors) cancelled and 12% new debentures allotted for balance amount as per scheme of reconstruction)				

ILLUSTRATION 7

V Ltd has Trade Creditors for ₹ 165 lacs. Mr. A and Mr. B are creditors for ₹ 10 lacs and ₹ 5 lacs respectively. Trade Creditors (other than A and B) are given the option of either to accept equity shares of ₹ 5, ₹ 2.50 paid up each, for the amount due to them *or* to accept 80% of the amount due in cash. 40% Creditors accepted equity shares whereas the balance accepted cash in full settlement. Journalise

SOLUTION

JOURNAL

[₹ in Lacs]

Date	*Particulars*		*L.F.*	*Dr. (₹)*	*Cr. (₹)*
	Trade Creditors A/c	Dr.		150	
	To Equity Share Capital (₹ 5 each, ₹ 2.50 paid up) A/c				60
	To Bank A/c				72
	To Reconstruction a/c				18
	(Being the Trade creditors for ₹ 60 lakhs accepted 24 lakhs shares of ₹ 5 each, ₹ 2.50 paid up for full amount and those for ₹.90 lakhs accepted cash equal to 80% of claim in full settlement)				

ILLUSTRATION 8

There were capital commitments totalling ₹ 300 lacs. These contracts are to be cancelled on payment of 5% of the contract price as a penalty. The Directors refund ₹ 11 lacs of the fees previously received by them. A dissentient shareholder transferred his 100 shares to a director. Journalise

SOLUTION

JOURNAL

[₹ in Lacs]

Date	Particulars	L.F.	Dr. (₹)	Cr. (₹)
	Reconstruction A/c Dr. To Bank A/c (Being payment made for cancellation of capital commitments)		15	 15
	Bank A/c Dr. To Reconstruction A/c (Being refund of fees by directors credited to Reconstruction A/c)		11	 11

Note: *The transfer of 100 Shares by a dissentient shareholder to the director concerned need not be accounted for.*

ILLUSTRATION 9

V Ltd has Provision for Tax for ₹10 lacs. The taxation liability of the company is settled at ₹ 8.88 lacs and the same is paid immediately. Journalise.

SOLUTION

JOURNAL

[₹ in Lacs]

Date	Particulars	L.F.	Dr. (₹)	Cr. (₹)
	Provision for Tax A/c Dr. To Bank A/c To Reconstruction A/c (Being payment of tax liability in full settlement)		10	 8.88 1.12

ILLUSTRATION 10

Following items appear in the Balance Sheet of V Ltd:

Workmen's Compensation Fund:		
	Pune	₹1 lac
	Bombay	₹ 2 lacs
10% Government Loan Earmarked Against Workmen's Compensation Fund		₹ 3 lacs

Workmen's Compensation Fund (Bombay) disclosed the fact that actually there was a liability of ₹ 20,000 only. As a result the relevant fund amount balance was to be brought down to the required amount. Investments were realised at 10% above the book value. Journalise.

SOLUTION

JOURNAL

[₹ in Lacs]

Date	Particulars		L.F.	Dr. (₹)	Cr. (₹)
	Bank A/c	Dr.		0.88	
	To Investment in 10% Government Loan A/c				0.80
	To Workmen's Compensation Fund (Bombay) A/c				0.08
	(Being the Sale of Investments for Workmen's Compensation Fund (Bombay) and the profit on the sale of same transferred to Workmen Compensation Fund (Bombay) Account)				
	Workmen's Compensation Fund (Bombay) A/c	Dr.		0.88	
	To Reconstruction A/c				0.88
	(Being the Surplus in Workmen Compensation Fund at Bombay transferred to Reconstruction Account)				

ILLUSTRATION 11

V Ltd has Investments in Shares in Q Ltd. ₹ 32.4 lacs V Ltd. holds 21,600 shares in Q Ltd. This represents 15% of the share capital of that company. Q Ltd. is not a quoted company. The average net profit (after tax) of the company is ₹ 25 lacs. The shares would be valued based on 12% capitalization rate. Journalise.

SOLUTION

JOURNAL

[₹ in Lacs]

Date	Particulars		L.F.	Dr. (₹)	Cr. (₹)
	Reconstruction A/c	Dr.		1.15	
	To Investments in Shares in Q Ltd. A/c				1.15
	(Being reduction in the value of Investments)				

Working Notes:

(i) Valuation of Investments in Shares of Q Ltd.= (₹ 25 lacs/.12) × 15% = ₹ 31.25 lacs

(ii) Reduction in the Value of Investment in Shares of Q Ltd. = ₹ 32.40 lacs – ₹ 31.25 = ₹ 1.15 lacs

ILLUSTRATION 12

Following items appear in the Balance Sheet of V Ltd:

Capital Reserve	₹ 6 lacs
Profit and Loss Account	(₹ 15 lacs)
Goodwill	₹ 10 lacs
Patents & Copy Rights	₹ 5 lacs

Plant & Machinery	₹ 719.6 lacs
Land & Building	₹ 60 lacs
Debtors	₹ 10 lacs
Cash at Bank	₹ 104 lacs
Discount on issue of Debentures	₹ 1 lac

Goodwill is considered worthless. Land & Building is to be valued at 114% of book value. 80% of Debtors are considered as Bad and 20% of the balance Debtors are considered as Doubtful. Any surplus after writing off the various losses should be utilized in writing down the value of plant & machinery. The credit Balance available in Reconstruction A/c is ₹ 538.05 lacs. Journalise.

SOLUTION

JOURNAL

[₹ in Lacs]

Date	Particulars		L.F.	Dr. (₹)	Cr. (₹)
	Capital Reserve A/c	Dr.		6	
	To Reconstruction A/c				6
	(Being the transfer of Capital Reserve for purpose of reconstruction)				
	Land & Building A/c	Dr.		8.40	
	To Reconstruction A/c				8.40
	(Being the Land & Building revalued)				
	Reconstruction A/c	Dr.		8.40	
	To Debtors				8.00
	To Provision for Doubtful Debts.				0.40
	(Being the Debtors revalued)				
	Reconstruction A/c	Dr.		544.05	
	To Goodwill A/c				10
	To Profit and Loss A/c				15
	To Discount on issue of Debentures A/c				1
	To Plant & Machinery (balancing figure)				**518.05**
	(Being writing off of losses and reduction in the value of assets as per scheme of reconstruction)				

ILLUSTRATION 13

The ledger balances of X Ltd. as on 31st March, 2015 are:

Fixed Assets ₹ 7,00,000, Investments ₹ 10,000, Stock ₹ 3,90,000 Debtors ₹ 4,60,000, Preliminary Expenses ₹ 20,000, Equity Share Capital (60% paid) ₹ 6,00,000, 10% First Debentures ₹ 2,00,000, 12% Second Debentures ₹ 5,00,000, Bank overdraft ₹ 50,000, Trade Creditors (including Y for ₹ 8,50,000) ₹ 11,50,000, Outstanding interest for one year on both types of debentures.

Due to heavy losses, the following scheme of re-construction is agreed:

(a) To make the existing ₹ 100 equity shares fully paid up and then to reduce them to ₹ 20 each.

(b) To settle the claims of first debenture-holders by issuing 2,000, 13.5% debentures of ₹ 100 each,

(c) To discharge the claims of the second debenture-holders by issuing 15% 4,000 debentures of ₹ 100 each,

(d) To pay ₹ 3,00,000 to Mr. Y in full settlement of his account,

(e) To allot 15,000 fresh equity shares of ₹ 20 each to discharge the remaining trade creditors,

(f) Market value of investments is ₹ 20,000, and

(g) To write off the fictitious assets and to reduce the fixed assets.

Required: Pass journal Entries and prepare the post-reconstruction Balance-Sheet.

STEP 1: BALANCE SHEET OF X LTD. (BEFORE RECONSTRUCTION) AS AT 31st MARCH, 2015

Liabilities	₹	*Assets*	₹
Equity Share Capital (60% Paid-up)	6,00,000	Fixed Assets	7,00,000
10% First Debentures	2,00,000	Trade Debtors	4,60,000
12% Second Debentures	5,00,000	Stock	3,90,000
Outstanding Interest on Debentures for one year	80,000	Investments (Market value ₹ 20,000)	10,000
Bank Overdraft	50,000	Preliminary Expenses	20,000
Trade Creditors (including Y for ₹ 8,50,000)	11,50,000	Profit and Loss Account (Balancing figure)	10,00,000
	25,80,000		25,80,000

JOURNAL

Particulars		*L.F.*	*Dr. (₹)*	*Cr. (₹)*
Share Final Call A/c	Dr.		4,00,000	
To Equity Share Capital A/c				4,00,000
(Final call made for the balance on equity share)				
Bank A/c	Dr.		4,00,000	
To Equity Share Final Call A/c				4,00,000
(Receipt of Final Call money)				
Equity Share Capital (₹ 100 Shares) A/c	Dr.		10,00,000	
To Equity Shares (₹ 20 Shares) A/c				2,00,000
To Reconstruction A/c				8,00,000
(Reduction of ₹ 100 share capital to ₹ 20 each)				
10% First Debentures A/c	Dr.		2,00,000	
Debenture Interest (outstanding) A/c	Dr.		20,000	
To 13.5% Debentures A/c				2,00,000
To Reconstruction A/c				20,000
(Redemption of First Debentures)				
12% Second Debentures A/c	Dr.		5,00,000	
Debenture Interest (outstanding) A/c	Dr.		60,000	

Particulars			Dr. (₹)	Cr. (₹)
To 15% Debentures A/c				4,00,000
To Reconstruction A/c				60,000
(Redemption of Second Debentures)				
Sundry Creditors A/c	Dr.		11,50,000	
To Bank A/c				3,00,000
To Equity Share Capital A/c				3,00,000
To Reconstruction A/c				5,50,000
(Settlement of creditors' account)				
Reconstruction A/c	Dr.		15,30,000	
To Profit and Loss A/c				10,00,000
To Preliminary Expenses A/c				20,000
To Fixed Assets A/c				5,10,000
(Utilisation of reconstruction account for writing of past losses and fixed assets)				

BALANCE SHEET OF CONTINENTAL CONSTRUCTION LTD. (AND REDUCED) AS AT 31.3.2015

Particulars	Note No	₹
I. Equity and Liabilities		
(1) Shareholders' Funds		
(a) Share Capital (₹ 20 each)		5,00,000
(2) Non-Current Liabilities		
(a) Long-term Borrowings	1	6,00,000
(3) Current Liabilities		
Total		11,00,000
II. Assets		
(1) Non-Current Assets		
(a) Fixed Assets		
Tangible Assets [7,00,000 – 5,10,000 (Amt. w/o)]		1,90,000
(b) Non-Current Investments [Market Value ₹ 20,000]		10,000
(2) Current Assets		
(a) Inventories		3,90,000
(b) Trade Receivables [Debtors]		4,60,000
(c) Cash and Cash Equivalents		50,000
Total		11,00,000

Notes To Accounts:

1. Long-term Borrowings		
13.5% Debentures	2,00,000	
15% Debentures	4,00,000	6,00,000

ILLUSTRATION 14

Given below are the extracts from the Balance Sheet of Road Block Ltd. as at March 31, 2014:

Particulars		*(₹ in lakhs)*
Equity Shares of ₹ 10 each		500
6%Cum-Pref.Shares of ₹ 100 each		100
Capital Reserve		6
Workmen's Compensation Fund:		
Pune	2	
Bombay	1	3
10% First Debentures		60
10% Second Debentures		100
Debentures Interest outstanding		16
Trade Creditors		165
Provision for Tax		10
Goodwill		10
Patents & Copy Rights		5
Plant & Machinery		719.6
10% Government Loan Earmarked Against Workmen's Compensation Fund		3
Investments in Shares in Q Ltd.		32.4
Stock		60
Debtors		10
Cash at Bank		104
Discount on issue of Debentures		1
Profit and Loss Account		15

Note: *Dividend on Preference Shares are in arrears for three years.*

The following scheme of internal reconstruction was approved by the Court and implemented:

(a) All the equity shares be converted into the same number of equity shares of ₹ 5 each, ₹ 2.50 paid up.

(b) The preference shares are converted from 6% to 15% but revalued in a manner in which the total return on them remains unaffected. Four equity shares of ₹ 5 each, ₹ 2.50 paid up to be issued for each ₹ 100 of arrears of preference dividend.

(c) Mr. A holds 10% first debentures for ₹ 40 lacs and 10% second debentures for ₹ 60 lacs. He is also a creditor for ₹ 10 lacs. Mr. 'A' is to cancel ₹ 60 lacs of his total debt and to pay ₹ 10 lacs to the company and to receive new 12% Debentures for the balance amount.

(d) Mr. B holds 10% first debentures for ₹ 20 lacs and 10% second debentures for ₹ 40 lacs and is also a creditor for ₹ 5 lacs. Mr. 'B' is to cancel ₹ 30 lacs of his total debt and to accept new 12% Debentures for the balance amount

(e) Trade Creditors (other than A and B) are given the option of either to accept equity shares of ₹ 5, ₹ 2.50 paid up each, for the amount due to them *or* to accept 80% of the amount due in cash. 40% Creditors accepted equity shares whereas the balance accepted cash in full settlement.

(f) There were capital commitments totalling ₹ 300 lacs. These contracts are to be cancelled on payment of 5% of the contract price as a penalty.

(g) The Directors refund ₹ 11 lacs of the fees previously received by them.

(h) Workmen's Compensation Fund (Bombay) disclosed the fact that actually there was a liability of ₹ 20,000 only. As a result the relevant fund amount balance was to be brought down to the required amount. Investments were realised at 10% above the book value.

(i) The taxation liability of the company is settled at ₹ 8.88 lacs and the same is paid immediately.

(j) Road Block Ltd. holds 21,600 shares in Q Ltd. This represents 15% of the share capital of that company. Q Ltd. is not a quoted company. The average net profit (after tax) of the company is ₹ 25 lacs. The shares would be valued based on 12% capitalization rate.

(k) A dissentient shareholder transferred his 100 shares to a director.

(l) Stock is to be valued at 114% of book value. 80% of Debtors are considered as Bad and 20% of the balance Debtors are considered as Doubtful. Any surplus after writing off the various losses should be utilized in writing down the value of plant & machinery.

(m) All equity shareholders paid the balance to make the shares fully paid up and then all equity shares were consolidated into the shares of ₹ 10 each.

Required: Pass the Journal Entries and prepare the Reconstruction Account, Bank Account and Balance Sheet after Reconstructon assuming that the Authorised Capital was incresed to 500 lacs by compling with the necessary formalaties.

SOLUTION

JOURNAL *[₹ in Lacs]*

Date	Particulars		L.F.	Dr. (₹)	Cr. (₹)
(a)	Equity Share Capital (₹ 10 each) A/c	Dr.		500	
	To Equity Share Capital (₹ 5 each) A/c				125
	To Reconstruction A/c				375
	(Being the conversion of all the equity shares into the same number of equity shares of ₹ 5 each, ₹ 2.50 paid up as per scheme of reconstruction)				
(b)(i)	6% Cum-Preference Share Capital (₹ 100) A/c	Dr.		100	
	To 15% Cum-Pref. Share Capital (₹ 100) A/c				40
	To Reconstruction A/c				60
	(Being 40000 15% cum Pref. share of ₹ 100 each issued so as to maintain the same amount of dividend (i.e. ₹ 6 lacs) vide scheme of reconstruction dated.....)				
(b)(ii)	Reconstruction A/c	Dr.		1.8	
	To Equity Share Capital (₹ 5 each, ₹ 2.50 paid up) A/c				1.8
	(Being 72000 equity shares of ₹ 5 each, ₹ 2.50 paid up issued to pref. Shareholders for dividend arrears vide scheme of Reconstruction dated.....)				
(c)(i)	10% First Debentures A/c	Dr.		40	
	10% Second Debentures A/c	Dr.		60	
	Trade Creditors A/c	Dr.		10	
	Interest on Debentures Outstanding A/c	Dr.		10	
	To Mr. A				120
	(Being the total amount due to A t/f to his A/c)				

(c)(ii)	Bank A/c	Dr.	10	
	To Mr. A			10
	(Being the amount received from Mr. A under the Reconstruction Scheme)			
(c)(iii)	Mr. A A/c	Dr.	130	
	To 12% New Debentures A/c			70
	To Reconstruction A/c			60
	(Being ₹ 60 lacs due to A (Including creditors) cancelled and 12% new debentures allotted for balance amount as per scheme of reconstruction)			
(d)(i)	10% First Debentures A/c	Dr.	20	
	10% Second Debentures A/c	Dr.	40	
	Trade Creditors A/c	Dr.	5	
	Interest on Debentures Outstanding A/c	Dr.	6	
	To Mr. B			71
	(Being the total amount due to Mr. B t/f to his A/c)			
d(ii)	Mr. B		71	
	To 12% New Debentures A/c			41
	To Reconstruction A/c			30
	(Being ₹ 30 lacs due to B (including creditors) cancelled and 12% new debentures allotted for balance amount as per scheme of reconstruction)			
(e)	Trade Creditors A/c	Dr.	150	
	To Equity Share Capital (₹ 5 each, ₹ 2.50 paid up) A/c			60
	To Bank A/c			72
	To Reconstruction a/c			18
	(Being the Trade creditors for ₹ 60 lakhs accepted 24 lakhs shares of ₹ 5 each, ₹ 2.50 paid up for full amount and those for ₹.90 lakhs accepted cash equal to 80% of claim in full settlement)			
(f)	Reconstruction A/c	Dr.	15	
	To Bank A/c			15
	(Being payment made for cancellation of capital commts.)			
(g)	Bank A/c	Dr.	11	
	To Reconstruction A/c			11
	(Being refund of fees by directors credited to Reconstruction A/c)			
(h)(i)	Bank A/c	Dr.	0.88	
	To Investment in 10% Government Loan A/c			0.80
	To Workmen's Compensation Fund (Bombay) A/c			0.08
	(Being the Sale of Investments for Workmen's Compensation Fund (Bombay) and the profit on the sale of same transferred to Workmen Compensation Fund (Bombay) Account)			

(h)(ii)	Workmen's Compensation Fund (Bombay) A/c To Reconstruction A/c (Being the Surplus in Workmen Compensation Fund at Bombay transferred to Reconstruction Account)	Dr.		0.88	 0.88
(i)	Provision for Tax A/c To Bank A/c To Reconstruction A/c (Being payment of tax liability in full settlement)	Dr.		10	 8.88 1.12
(j)	Reconstruction A/c To Investments in Shares in Q Ltd. A/c (Being reduction in the value of Investments)	Dr.		1.15	 1.15
(k)	No Journal Equity is to be passed				
(l)(i)	Capital Reserve A/c To Reconstruction A/c (Being the transfer of Capital Reserve for purpose of reconstruction)	Dr.		6	 6
(l)(ii)	Stock A/c To Reconstruction A/c (Being the Stock revalued)	Dr.		8.40	 8.40
(l)(iii)	Reconstruction A/c To Debtors To Provision for Doubtful Debts. (Being the Debtors revalued)	Dr.		8.40	 8.00 0.40
(l)(iv)	Reconstruction A/c To Goodwill A/c To Profit and Loss A/c To Discount on issue of Debentures A/c To Plant & Machinery (balancing figure) (Being writing off of losses and reduction in the value of assets as per scheme of reconstruction)	Dr.		544.05	 10 15 1 518.05
(m)(i)	Equity Share First & Final Call A/c To Equity Share Capital A/c (Being the first & final call due on 74.72 lakhs Share @ ₹ 2.50)	Dr.		186.80	 186.80
(m)(ii)	Bank A/c To Equity Share First & Final Call A/c (Being the First & Final Call received)	Dr.		186.80	 186.80
(m)(iii)	Equity Share Capital (₹ 5 each) A/c To Equity Share Capital (₹ 10 each) A/c (Being the consolidation of 74.72 lakhs equity shares of ₹ 5 each into 37.36 lakhs equity shares of ₹ 10 each)	Dr.		373.60	 373.60

Working Notes:

(i) Valuation of Investments in Shares of Q Ltd.= (₹ 25 lacs/.12) × 15% = ₹ 31.25 lacs

(ii) Reduction in the Value of Investment in Shares of Q Ltd.
= ₹ 32.40 lacs – ₹.31.25 = ₹.1.15 lacs

(iii) *The transfer of 100 Shares by a dissentient shareholder to the director concerned and waiver of the right to arrears of pref., dividend need not be accounted for.*

Dr. **RECONSTRUCTION ACCOUNT** Cr.

Particulars	*₹ (lacs)*	*Particulars*	*₹ (lacs)*
To Equity Share Capital A/c (₹ 5 each)	1.80	By Equity Share Capital (₹ 10 each)	375.00
To Bank A/c	15.00	By 6% Cum. Pref. Share Capital	60.00
To Investment in Shares in Q Ltd.	1.15	By Mr. A (Sundries)	60.00
To Debtors	8.00	By Mr. B (Sundries)	30.00
To Provision for Doubtful Debts	0.40	By Trade Creditors	18.00
To Goodwill A/c	10.00	By Bank A/c	11.00
To Profit & Loss A/c	15.00	By Workmen's Compensation	
To Discount on Issue of		Fund (Bombay) A/c	0.88
Debentures A/c	1.00	By Provision for Tax A/c	1.12
To Plant & Machinery A/c	518.05	By Capital Reserve A/c	6.00
		By Stock A/c	8.40
	570.40		570.40

Dr. **BANK ACCOUNT** Cr.

Particulars	*₹ (lacs)*	*Particulars*	*₹ (lacs)*
To Balance b/d	104.00	By Trade Creditors	72.00
To Mr. A	10.00	By Reconstruction A/c	15.00
To Reconstruction A/c	11.00	By Provision for Tax	8.88
To Investment in Govt. Loan A/c	0.88	By Balance c/d	216.80
To Equity Share Capital A/c (₹ 5 each)	186.80		
	312.68		312.68

BALANCE SHEET OF ROAD BLOCK LTD. (AND REDUCED) AS AT 31.3.2014

Particulars	*Note No*	*₹ (lacs)*
I. Equity and Liabilities		
(1) Shareholders' Funds		
(a) Share Capital	1	413.60
(b) Reserves and Surplus [Workmen's Compensation Fund] [2.00 + 0.20]		2.20
(2) Non-Current Liabilities [12% Debentures]		111.00
(3) Current Liabilities		
Total		526.80

II. Assets		
(1) Non-Current Assets		
(a) Fixed Assets		
Tangible Assets [719.60 – 518.05 (Amt. w/o)]		201.55
Intangible Assets [Patents & Copy Rights]		5.00
(b) Non-Current Investments	2	33.45
(2) Current Assets		
(a) Inventories		68.40
(b) Trade Receivables [Debtors][2.00 – 0.40]		1.60
(c) Cash and Cash Equivalents		216.80
Total		526.80

Notes To Accounts:

Particulars	₹ *(lacs)*
1. Share Capital	
37.36 lacs Equity Shares of ₹ 10 each	373.60
40,000,15% Pref. Shares of ₹ 100 each	40.00
	413.60
2. Non-Current Investments	
10% Govt. Loan earmarked against Workmen's Compensation Fund	2.20
Investments in Shares of Q Ltd.	31.25
	33.45

ILLUSTRATION 15

Given below are the extracts from the Balance Sheet of Unfortunate Bad Luck Ltd. as at 31.3.2014:

Particulars	₹
6% Cum-Pref. Shares of ₹ 100 each	1,00,000
Equity Shares of ₹ 100 each	8,00,000
Securities Premium	70,000
Capital Reserve	10,000
10% Debentures	14,00,000
Accrued Interest on Debentures	70,000
Sundry Creditors	4,50,000
Provision for Tax	10,000
Goodwill	1,00,000
Plant & Machinery	10,00,000
Other Fixed Assets	4,30,000
Investments	15,000
Stock	1,00,000
Sundry Debtors	40,000

Cash at Bank	25,000
Other Current Assets	80,000
P & L A/c	10,60,000
Preliminary Expenses	30,000
Underwriting Commission	20,000
Discount on Issue of Shares & Debentures	10,000

Notes: (i) *Dividend on Preference shares are in arrears for three years.*

(ii) *There is a Bill receivable for ₹ 10,000 under discount. The bill was received from Z.*

The following scheme of reconstruction is sanctioned:

(a) Equity Shares to be sub-divided into shares of ₹ 10 each.

(b) Equity Shareholders to surrender 90% of their holdings.

(c) The preference shares are converted from 6% to 15% but revalued in a manner in which the total return on them remains unaffected.

(d) Five equity shares out of those surrendered to be issued for each ₹ 100 of arrears of preference dividend.

(e) The debentureholders agree to reduce their total claims to ₹ 5,00,000 in consideration of their getting equity shares of ₹ 5,00,000 out of the surrendered equity shares.

(f) Sundry Creditors agree to reduce their claims to 20% and 80% of the balance shall be satisfied by issue of equity shares out of those surrendered.

(g) the taxation liability was settled (but not discharged) at ₹ 15,000.

(h) Expenses of re-organization amounted to ₹ 10,000

(i) Z proved insolvent and a dividend of 10% was received from his estate.

(j) Shares surrendered and not re-issued to be cancelled.

(k) The balance in Securities Premium a/c and Capital Reserve A/c to be utilized.

(l) Goodwill is considered worthless.

(m) The company expected to earn profit @ ₹ 45,000 p.a. from the current year which would be utilized entirely for reducing the debit balance of profit & loss account for the next three consecutive years. The remaining balance of the said account would be written off at the time of Capital Reduction process.

(n) Plant & Machinery to be written down by 40%.

(o) Other fixed assets to be written down to ₹ 4,10,000.

(p) Stock to the extent of rs. 10,000 considered to be obsolete.

(q) Debtors to the extent of ₹ 11,000 considered irrecoverable.

(r) Other current assets to be revalued at 75,000.

(s) Any surplus after writing off the various losses & reducing the value of over-valued assets, should be utilized in writing down value of plant & machinery further.

(t) A dissentient shareholder transferred his 100 shares to a director.

Required: Pass the necessary journal entries and prepare the Balance-Sheet reconstruction.

SOLUTION

JOURNAL OF UNFORTUNATE BAD LUCK LTD.

Date	Particulars		Dr. (₹)	Cr. (₹)
(a)	Equity Share Capital (₹ 100) A/c	Dr.	8,00,000	
	To Equity Share Capital (₹ 10) A/c			8,00,000
	(Being equity of ₹ 100 each converted into equity shares of ₹ 10 each vide scheme of reconstruction dated......)			
(b)	Equity Share Capital (₹ 10) A/c	Dr.	7,20,000	
	To Shares Surrendered A/c			7,20,000
	(Being 90% of equity shares surrendered vide scheme of reconstruction dated.....)			
(c)	6% Cum-preference Shares Capital (₹ 100) A/c	Dr.	1,00,000	
	To 15% Cum-Pref. Share capital (₹ 100) A/c			40,000
	To Reconstruction A/c			60,000
	(Being 400 15% cum Pref. share of ₹ 100 each issued so as to maintain the same amount of dividend (i.e. ₹ 6,000) vide scheme of reconstruction dated.....)			
(d)	Shares Surrendered A/c	Dr.	9,000	
	To Equity Share Capital (₹ 10) A/c			9,000
	(Being 900 equity shares out of those surrendered issued to pref. Shareholders on their surrendering a claim for arrears vide scheme of Reconstruction dated.....)			
(e)(i)	10% Debentures A/c	Dr.	9,00,000	
	Accrued Interest on Debentures A/c	Dr.	70,000	
	To Reconstruction A/c			9,70,000
	(Being the amount sacrificed by debentureholders as per reconstruction scheme dated......)			
(e)(ii)	Shares surrendered A/c	Dr.	5,00,000	
	To Equity shares capital (₹ 10) A/c			5,00,000
	(Being 50,000 equity shares out of those surrendered issued to debentureholders on their surrendering a claim of 9,70,000)			
(f)(i)	Shares Surrendered A/c	Dr.	72,000	
	To Equity Share Capital (₹ 10) A/c			72,000
	(Being 7,200 Equity shares out of those surrendered issued to creditors in part satisfaction of their balance claim)			
(f)(ii)	Sundry Creditors A/c	Dr.	4,32,000	
	To Reconstruction A/c			4,32,000
	(Being total reduction in the claim of sundry creditors from 4,50,000 to ₹ 18,000)			
(g)(i)	Reconstruction A/c	Dr.	5,000	
	To Provision for Tax A/c			5,000
	(Being the writing up the provision for tax as per Reconstruction scheme dated.......)			

(g)(ii)	Provision for Tax A/c	Dr.	15,000	
	To Tax Payable A/c			15,000
	(Being the conversion of provision into settled liability)			
(h)	Reconstruction A/c	Dr.	10,000	
	To Bank A/c			10,000
	(Being the reconstruction expenses paid)			
(i)(i)	Z	Dr.	10,000	
	To Bank A/c			10,000
	(Being the discounted B/R dishonourd)			
(i)(ii)	Bank A/c	Dr.	1,000	
	Reconstruction A/c	Dr.	9,000	
	To Z A/c			10,000
	(Being the ₹ 1,000 received from Z in respect of Discounted B/R met)			
(j)	Shares Surrendered A/c	Dr.	1,39,000	
	To Reconstruction A/c			1,39,000
	(Being shares surrendered but not re-issued cancelled)			
(k)	Capital Reserve A/c	Dr.	10,000	
	Securities Premium A/c	Dr.	70,000	
	To Reconstruction A/c			80,000
	(Being the transfer of balances of Capital Reserve A/c and Share Premium A/c vide Scheme of reconstruction dated......)			
(l to s)	Reconstruction A/c	Dr.	16,57,000	
	To Goodwill A/c			1,00,000
	To P & L A/c			9,25,000
	To Preliminary Expenses A/c			30,000
	To Underwriting Commission A/c			20,000
	To Discount on Issue of Shares/Deb. A/c			10,000
	To Other fixed assets			20,000
	To Stock			10,000
	To Debtors			11,000
	To Other Current Assets			5,000
	To Plant & Machinery			5,26,000
	(Being the balance of Reconstruction A/c utilized to written off various losses & to reduce the value of various overvalued assets vide Reconstruction scheme dated.....)			

BALANCE SHEET OF UNFOTUNATE BAD LUCK LTD. (AND REDUCED) AS AT 31.3.2014

Particulars	Note No	₹
I. Equity and Liabilities		
(1) Shareholders' Funds		
(a) Share Capital	1	7,01,000

(b) Reserves and Surplus [Profit & Loss A/c (Dr.)]		(1,35,000)
(2) Non-Current Liabilities [10%Debentures]		5,00,000
(3) Current Liabilities		
(a) Trade Payables[Creditors]		18,000
(b) Short-term Provisions [Provision for Tax]		15,000
Total		10,99,000
II. Assets		
(1) Non-Current Assets		
(a) Fixed Assets		
Tangible Assets	2	8,84,000
Intangible Assets [Goodwill] [1,00,000 -1,00,000(Amt. w/o)]		0
(b) Non-Current Investments		15,000
(2) Current Assets		
(a) Inventories		90,000
(b) Trade Receivables [Debtors]		29,000
(c) Cash and Cash Equivalents		6,000
(d) Other Current Assets		75,000
Total		10,99,000

Notes To Accounts:

Particulars		₹
1. Share Capital		
66100 Equity Shares of ₹ 10 each,₹ paid		6,61,000
400,15% Pref. Shares of ₹ 100 each, ₹ paid		40,000
	7,01,000	
2. Tangible Assets		
Plant & Machinery	10,00,000	
Less: Amt. w/o under Reconstruction Scheme	5,26,000	4,74,000
Other Fixed Assets	4,30,000	
Less: Amt. w/o under Reconstruction Scheme	20,000	4,10,000
Total		8,84,000

Note: *The transfer of 100 Shares by a dissentient shareholder to the director concerned and waiver of the right to arrears of pref., dividend need not be accounted for.*

Working Notes:

(i) *Calculation of the amount of Shares Surrendered to be transferred to Reconstruction Account.*

Dr. **SHARES SURRENDERED ACCOUNT** *Cr.*

Particulars	₹	*Particulars*	₹
To Equity Shares Capital A/c (Issued to Debentureholders)	5,00,000	By Equity Share Capital A/c (₹ 10)	7,20,000
To Equity Shares Capital A/c (Issued to sundry Creditors)	72,000		

To Equity Share Capital A/c (Issued to Pref. Shareholders)	9,000		
To Reconstruction A/c (b.f.)	1,39,000		
	7,20,000		7,20,000

(ii) *Calculation of Debit Balance of P & L A/c to be written off now*

= ₹ 10,60,000 – (₹ 45,000 × 3) = ₹ 9,25,000.

(iii) *Calculation of the amount by which the value of Plant & Machinery is to be written down*

Dr. **RECONSTRUCTION ACCOUNT** Cr.

Particulars	₹	*Particulars*	₹
To To Provision for tax	5,000	By 6% Cum Pref. Share Capital A/c	60,000
To Bank A/c (Expenses)	10,000	By 10% Debentures A/c	9,00,000
To Bank A/c (Discounted B/R)	9,000	By Accrued Interest	70,000
To Goodwill A/c	1,00,000	By Sundry Creditors	4,32,000
To P & L A/c	9,25,000	By Share Surrendered A/c	1,39,000
To Preliminary Expenses	30,000	By Capital Reserve A/c	10,000
To Underwriting Commission	20,000	By Securities Premium A/c	70,000
To Discount on Issue of Shares/ Deb. A/c	10,000		
To Other Fixed Assets	20,000		
To Stock	10,000		
To Debtors	11,000		
To Other Current Assets	5,000		
To Plant & Machinery (b.f.)	5,26,000		
	16,81,000		16,81,000

SOLVED PROBLEMS

PROBLEM 1

The following is the balance sheet of CSJHB Ltd. as at 31st March, 2014:

Particulars	₹
Share Capital:	
Authorised:	
30,000 Equity Shares of ₹ 10 each	3,00,000
30,000, 13% Pref. Shares of ₹ 10 each	3,00,000
	6,00,000
Subscribed, Issued and Paid-up:	
20,000 Equity Shares of ₹ 10 each fully paid	2,00,000
18,000 13% Pref. Shares of ₹ 10 fully paid	1,80,000

Reserves & Surplus:		
Workmen's compensation fund:		
Pune	20,000	
Bombay	10,000	30,000
Secured loans:		
12% 'A' Debentures secured on Pune Property	30,000	
12% 'B' Debentures secured on Bombay Property	35,000	65,000
Current Liabilities & Provisions:		
(A) Current Liabilities:		
Sundry Creditors		25,000
(B) Provisions:		
Fixed Assets:		
Pune Property		1,60,000
Bombay Property		1,20,000
Plant and Machinery		1,50,000
Investments:		
10% Government loan earmarked against Workmen's compensation Fund		30,000
Miscellaneous expenditure and losses:		
Profit and Loss Account		40,000

The following scheme of reconstruction was duly approved:

(a) Equity shares were to be reduced to ₹ 1 each.

(b) Preference shares were to be reduced by ₹ 2 per share.

(c) Debentureholders were to forgo their unpaid interest ₹ 5,200 which is included in sundry creditors.

(d) 'B' Debentureholders agreed to take over the Bombay property at ₹ 50,000 and paid the balance amount due from them in cash.

(e) Workmen's compensation fund (Bombay) disclosed the fact that actually there was a liability of ₹ 2,000 only. As a result the relevant fund amount balance was to be brought down to the required amount. Investments were realised at 10% above the book value.

(f) The Plant and machinery were to be written down by ₹ 90,000.

(g) Any balance remaining was to be applied as to 75% in writing down Pune property and 25% transferred to capital reserve.

Required: Pass the necessary journal entries and prepare the Balance Sheet after reconstruction.

SOLUTION

JOURNAL

Particulars		*L.F.*	*Dr. (₹)*	*Cr. (₹)*
Equity Share Capital (Old) A/c	Dr.		2,00,000	
Preference Share Capital A/c	Dr.		36,000	
To Equity Share Capital (New) A/c				20,000
To Reconstruction A/c				2,16,000

(Being the reduction of 20,000 equity shares of ₹ 10 each to ₹ 1 and 18,000 13% preference shares by ₹ 2 per share vide special Resolution No..... dated .... confirmed by court vide order dated......)			
Sundry Creditors A/c Dr.		5,200	
To Reconstruction A/c			5,200
(Being the Cancellation of debenture interest)			
12% 'B' Debentures A/c Dr.		35,000	
To 'B' Debentureholders A/c			35,000
(Being Transfer of 'B' Debentures to debentureholders)			
₹B' Debentureholders A/c Dr.		35,000	
Bank A/c Dr.		15,000	
To Bombay Property			50,000
(Being the Payment to 'B' debentureholders by transfer of Bombay Property, the balance received from them in cash)			
Bank A/c Dr.		8,800	
To Investment in 10% Government Loan A/c			8,000
To Workmen's Compensation Fund (Bombay) A/c			800
[Being the Sale of investments for workmen's compensation fund (Bombay) and the profit on the sale of same transferred to workmen compensation fund (Bombay) account]			
Workmen's Compensation Fund (Bombay) A/c Dr.		8,800	
To Reconstruction A/c			8,800
(Being the Surplus in workmen compensation fund at Bombay transferred to reconstruction account)			
Reconstruction A/c Dr.		2,30,000	
To Profit and Loss A/c			40,000
To Plant and Machinery A/c			90,000
To Bombay Property			70,000
To Pune Property			22,500
To Capital Reserve A/c			7,500
(Being the utilisation of the amount available in the reconstruction account to write off the debit balance in the profit and loss account and to write down the value of various assets as per scheme of reconstruction)			

BALANCE SHEET OF CSJHB LTD. (AND REDUCED) AS AT 31.03.2014

Particulars	*Note No*	₹
I. Equity and Liabilities		
(1) Shareholders' Funds		
(a) Share Capital (₹ 10 each)	1	1,64,000
(b) Reserves and Surplus	2	29,500
(2) Non-Current Liabilities [10%Debentures]		30,000

(3) Current Liabilities		
(a) Trade Payables[Creditors]		19,800
Total		2,43,300
II. Assets		
(1) Non-Current Assets		
(a) Fixed Assets		
Tangible Assets	3	1,97,500
(b) Non-Current Investments[10% Govt. Loan]		22,000
(2) Current Assets		
(a) Cash and Cash Equivalents		23,800
Total		2,43,300

Notes To Accounts:

Particulars		₹
1. Share Capital		
20000 Equity Shares of ₹ 1 each		20,000
18000,15% Pref. Shares of ₹ 10 each, ₹ 8 paid		1,44,000
		1,64,000
2. Reserves and Surplus		
Capital Reserve		7,500
[Workmen's Compensation Fund] [20,000 + 2,000]		22,000
Total		29,500
3. Tangible Assets		
Pune Property	1,60,000	
Less: Amt. w/o under Reconstruction Scheme	22,500	1,37,500
Plant & Machinery	1,50,000	
Less: Amt. w/o under Reconstruction Scheme	90,000	60,000
Total		1,97,500

PROBLEM 2

Green Limited had decided to reconstruct the Balance Sheet since it has accumulated huge losses. The following is the Balance Sheet of the Company on 31.3.2014 before reconstruction:

BALANCE SHEET OF GREEN LIMITED AS AT 31.3.2014

Particulars	₹
Share Capital:	
Authorised:	
1,50,000 Equity Shares of ₹ 50 each	75,00,000
Subscribed 50,000 Equity Shares of ₹ 50 each	25,00,000
1,00,000 Equity Shares of ₹ 50 each, ₹ 40 per share paid up	40,00,000
Secured Loans:	

12% First Debentures	5,00,000
12% Second Debentures	10,00,000
Current Liabilities:	
Sundry Creditors	5,00,000
Fixed Assets:	
Goodwill	20,00,000
Building	10,00,000
Plant	10,00,000
Computers	25,00,000
Investments	Nil
Current Assets	Nil
Profit and Loss A/c (Loss)	20,00,000

The Following is the interest of Mr. X and Mr. Y in Green Limited:

Particulars	*Mr. X* ₹	*Mr. Y* ₹
12% First Debentures	3,00,000	2,00,000
12% Second Debentures	7,00,000	3,00,000
Sundry Creditors	2,00,000	1,00,000
	12,00,000	6,00,000
Fully paid up ₹ 50 shares	3,00,000	2,00,000
Parly paid shares (₹ 40 paid up)	5,00,000	5,00,000

The following Scheme of Reconstruction is approved by all parties interested and also by the Court:

(a) Uncalled capital is to be called up in full and such shares and the other fully paid up shares be converted into equity shares of ₹ 20 each.

(b) Mr. X is to cancel ₹ 7,00,000 of his total debt (other than share amount) and to pay ₹ 2 lakhs to the company and to receive new 14% First Debentures for the balance amount.

(c) Mr. Y is to cancel ₹ 3,00,000 of his total debt (other than equity shares) and to accept new 14% First Debentures for the balance.

(d) The amount thus rendered available by the scheme shall be utilised in writing off of Goodwill, Profit and Loss A/c Loss and the balance to write off the value of computers.

Required: Pass the Journal Entires and prepare the Balance Sheet of the reconstructed company.

SOLUTION

JOURNAL

Particulars		*L.F.*	*Dr. (₹)*	*Cr. (₹)*
Bank A/c	Dr.		10,00,000	
To Equity Share Capital A/c				10,00,000
(Being the balance of ₹ 10 per share on 1,00,000 equity shares called up as per reconstruction scheme)				
Equity Share Capital A/c (₹ 50)	Dr.		75,00,000	
To Equity Share Capital A/c (₹ 20)				30,00,000

Particulars		Dr. (₹)	Cr. (₹)
To Capital Reduction A/c			45,00,000
(Being the reduction of equity shares of ₹ 50 each to shares of ₹ 20 each as per reconstruction scheme)			
12% First Debentures A/c	Dr.	3,00,000	
12% Second Debentures A/c	Dr.	7,00,000	
Sundry Creditors A/c	Dr.	2,00,000	
To X			12,00,000
(Being the total amount due to X, transferred to his account)			
Bank A/c	Dr.	2,00,000	
To X			2,00,000
(Being the amount paid by X under the reconstruction scheme)			
12% First Debentures A/c	Dr.	2,00,000	
12% Second Debentures A/c	Dr.	3,00,000	
Sundry Creditors A/c	Dr.	1,00,000	
To Y			6,00,000
(Being the total amount due to Y, transferred to his account)			
X	Dr.	14,00,000	
To 14% First Debentures A/c			7,00,000
To Capital Reduction A/c			7,00,000
(Being the cancellation of ₹ 7,00,000 out of total debt of Mr. X and issue of 14% first debentures for the balance amount as per reconstruction scheme)			
Y	Dr.	6,00,000	
To 14% First Debentures A/c			3,00,000
To Capital Reduction A/c			3,00,000
(Being the cancellation of ₹ 3,00,000 out of total debt of Mr. Y and issue of 14% first debentures for the balance amount as per reconstruction scheme)			
Capital Reduction A/c	Dr.	55,00,000	
To Goodwill A/c			20,00,000
To Profit and Loss A/c			20,00,000
To Computers A/c (balancing figure)			15,00,000
(Being the balance amount of capital reduction account utilised in writing off goodwill, profit and loss account, and computers)			

BALANCE SHEET OF GREEN LTD. (AND REDUCED) AS AT 31.03.2014

Particulars	*Note No*	₹
I. Equity and Liabilities		
(1) Shareholders' Funds		
(a) Share Capital (₹ 10 each)		30,00,000
(2) Non-Current Liabilities[14% Debentures]		10,00,000

(3) Current Liabilities		
(a) Trade Payables[Creditors]		2,00,000
Total		42,00,000
II. Assets		
(1) Non-Current Assets		
(a) Fixed Assets		
Tangible Assets	3	30,00,000
(2) Current Assets		
(a) Cash and Cash Equivalents		12,00,000
Total		42,00,000

Notes To Accounts:

1. Tangible Assets	
Land & Building	10,00,000
Plant & Machinery	10,00,000
Computers	10,00,000
Total	30,00,000

Working Note:

Dr. **CAPITAL REDUCTION ACCOUNT** *Cr.*

Particulars	₹	*Particulars*	₹
To Goodwill A/c	20,00,000	By Equity Share Capital A/c	45,00,000
To P & L A/c	20,00,000	By X	7,00,000
To Computers (Bal. Fig.)	15,00,000	By Y	3,00,000
	55,00,000		55,00,000

PROBLEM 3

The following is the Balance Sheet of Rocky Ltd. as at March 31, 2014:

Particulars	*₹ in lacs*
Fully paid Equity Shares of ₹ 10 each	500
Capital Reserve	6
12% Debentures	400
Debenture Interest Outstanding	48
Trade Creditors	165
Director's Remuneration Outstanding	10
Other Outstanding Expenses	11
Provisions	33
Goodwill	15
Land and Building	184
Plant and Machinery	286

Furniture and Fixtures	41
Stock	142
Debtors	80
Cash at Bank	27
Discount on Issue of Debentures	8
Profits and Loss Account	390

The following scheme of internal reconstruction was framed, approved by the Court, all the concerned parties and implemented:

(i) All the equity shares be converted into the same number of fully-paid equity shares of ₹ 2.50 each.

(ii) Directors agree to forego their outstanding remuneration.

(iii) The debentureholders also agree to forego outstanding interest in return of their 12% debentures being converted into 13% debentures.

(iv) The existing shareholders agree to subscribe for cash, fully paid equity shares of ₹ 2.50 each for ₹ 125 lacs.

(v) Trade creditors are given the option of either to accept fully-paid equity shares of ₹ 2.50 each for the amount due to them *or* to accept 80% of the amount due in cash. Creditors for ₹ 65 lacs accept equity shares whereas those for ₹ 100 lacs accept ₹ 80 lacs in cash in full settlement.

(vi) The Assets are revalued as under:

Particulars	*₹ in lacs*
Land and building	230
Plant and Machinery	220
Stock	120
Debtors	76

Required: Pass Journal Entries and prepare Balance Sheet after reconstruction.

SOLUTION

JOURNAL *[₹ in lacs]*

Particulars		*L.F.*	*Dr. (₹)*	*Cr. (₹)*
Equity Share Capital (₹ 10 each) A/c	Dr.		500	
To Equity Share Capital (₹ 2.50 each) A/c				125
To Reconstruction A/c				375
(Being the conversion of all the equity shares into the same number of fully paid equity shares of ₹ 2.50 each as per scheme of reconstruction)				
Director's Remuneration Outstanding A/c	Dr.		10	
To Reconstruction A/c				10
(Being the outstanding remuneration foregone by the directors as per scheme of reconstruction)				
12% Debentures A/c	Dr.		400	
Debenture Interest Outstanding A/c	Dr.		48	

To 13% Debentures A/c			400
To Reconstruction A/c			48
(Being the conversion of 12% debentures into 13% debentures, Debentureholders forgoing outstanding debenture interest)			
Bank	Dr.	125	
To Equity Share Application and Allotment A/c			125
(Being the application money received for equity shares)			
Equity Share Application and Allotment A/c	Dr.	125	
To Equity Share Capital (₹ 2.50 each) A/c			125
(Being the application money transferred to share capital)			
Trade Creditors A/c	Dr.	165	
To Equity Share Capital (₹ 2.50 each) A/c			65
To Bank A/c			80
To Reconstruction A/c			20
(Being the Trade creditors for ₹ 65 lakhs accepting shares for full amount and those for ₹ 100 lakhs accepting cash equal to 80% of claim in full settlement)			
Capital Reserve A/c	Dr.	6	
To Reconstruction A/c			6
(Being the Capital Reserve being used for purpose of reconstruction)			
Land and Building	Dr.	46	
To Reconstruction A/c			46
(Being the appreciation made in the value of land and building as per scheme of reconstruction)			
Reconstruction A/c	Dr.	505	
To Goodwill			15
To Plant and Machinery			66
To Stock			22
To Debtors			4
To Discount on issue of Debentures			8
To Profit and Loss A/c			390
(Being the writing off losses and reduction in the values of assets as per scheme of reconstruction)			

BALANCE SHEET OF ROCKY LTD. (AND REDUCED) AS AT 31.03.2014

Particulars	*Note No*	₹
I. Equity and Liabilities		
(1) Shareholders' Funds		
(a) Share Capital (₹ 10 each)		315
(b) Reserves and Surplus		
(2) Non-Current Liabilities [13% Debentures]		400

	(3) Current Liabilities		
	(a) Trade Payables[Creditors]		
	(b) Short-term Provisions		33
	(c) Other Current Liabilities[O/S Expenses]		11
	Total		759
II.	**Assets**		
	(1) Non-Current Assets		
	(a) Fixed Assets		
	Tangible Assets	2	491
	Intangible Assets [Goodwill] [15 – 15]		0
	(2) Current Assets		
	(a) Inventories		120
	(b) Trade Receivables [Debtors – Prov] [80 – 4]		76
	(c) Cash and Cash Equivalents		72
	Total		759

Notes To Accounts:

	Particulars		₹
1.	**Share Capital**		
	126000 Equity Shares of ₹ 2.50 each		315
	(Of the above 26000 Shares were issued for consideration otherwise than cash)		
2.	**Tangible Assets**		
	Land & Building	184	
	Add: Amt. increased under Reconstruction Scheme	46	230
	Plant & Machinery	286	
	Less: Amt. w/o under Reconstruction Scheme	66	220
	Furniture& Fixtures		41
	Total		491

Working Notes:

Dr. **(I) REDUCTION ACCOUNT** *(₹ in lacs) Cr.*

Particulars	₹	*Particulars*	₹
To Goodwill	15	By Equity Share Capital A/c	375
To Plant and Machinery	66	By Director's Remuneration	
To Stock	22	By Outstanding A/c	10
To Debtors	4	By Deben. Interest Outstanding A/c	48
To Discount on issue of Debentures	8	By Trade Creditors	20
To Profit and Loss A/c	390	By Capital Reserve	6
		By Land and Building	46
	505		505

(ii) Equity share capital (after reconstruction)	₹
Equity Share Capital (₹ 2.50 each)	125
Add: Fresh issue	125
Add: Equity share issued to creditors	65
	315
(iii) Cash at bank (after reconstruction)	
Cash at bank (before reconstruction)	27
Add: Proceeds from issue of equity shares	125
	152
Less: Payment made to creditors	80
	72

PROBLEM 4

Following are the extracts of Balance Sheets as at March 31, 2013:

(₹ '000)

Particulars	*K Ltd.*	*W Ltd.*
Share capital:		
Equity Shares of ₹ 100 each	2,000	1,500
9% Preference Shares of ₹ 100 each	700	400
General Reserve	240	170
Profit & Loss A/c	—	15
12% Debentures of ₹ 100 each	600	200
Sundry Creditors	560	315
Goodwill	20	—
Other Fixed Assets	2,400	1,150
Debtors	625	615
Stock	412	680
Cash at bank	38	155
Own debentures [Nominal value ₹ 2,00,000]	192	—
Discount on issue of debentures	2	—
Profit & Loss A/c	411	—

On 1.4.2013, K Ltd. adopted the following scheme of reconstruction:

(a) Each equity share shall be sub-divided into 10 equity shares of ₹ 10 each fully paid up. 50% of the equity share capital would be surrendered to the company.

(b) Preference dividends are in arrear for 3 years. Preference shareholders agreed to waive 80% of the dividend claim and accept payment for the balance.

(c) Own debentures of ₹ 80,000 were sold at ₹ 98 own-interest and remaining own debentures were cancelled.

(d) Debentureholders of ₹ 3,00,000 agreed to accept one machinery of book value of ₹ 3,20,000 in full settlement.

(e) Creditors, Debtors and Stocks were valued at ₹ 5,00,000, ₹ 6,00,000 and ₹ 4,00,000 respectively. The goodwill, discount on issue of Debentures & Profit and Loss (Dr.) are to be written off.

(f) The Company paid ₹ 20,000 as penalty to avoid capital commitments of ₹ 4,00,000.

On 2.4.2013 a scheme of absorption was adopted. K Ltd. would take over W Ltd. The purchase consideration was fixed as below:

(i) Equity shareholders of W Ltd. will be given 50 equity shares of ₹ 10 each fully paid up, in exchange for every 5 shares held in W Ltd.

(ii) Issue of 10% Preference Shares of ₹ 100 each in the ratio of 4 Preference Shares of K Ltd. for every 5 Preference Shares held in W Ltd.

(iii) Issue of one 12% Debentures of ₹ 100 each of K Ltd. for every 12% Debentures in W Ltd.

Required: Give journal entries in the books of K Ltd. and draw the resultant Balance Sheet as at 2nd April, 2013.

SOLUTION

JOURNAL

Date	*Particulars*		*L.F.*	*Dr. (₹)*	*Cr. (₹)*
01.04.13	Equity Share Capital A/c	Dr.		20,00,000	
	To Equity Share Capital A/c				20,00,000
	(Being the sub-division of one share of ₹ 100 each into 10 shares of ₹ 10 each)				
	Equity Share Capital A/c	Dr.		10,00,000	
	To Reconstruction A/c				10,00,000
	(Being the reduction of capital by 50%)				
	Reconstruction A/c	Dr.		42,000	
	To Bank A/c				42,000
	(Being the payment in cash for 20% of arrears of preference dividend)				
	Bank A/c	Dr.		78,400	
	To Own Debentures A/c [(1,92,000/2,00,000) × 80,000]			76,800	
	To Reconstruction A/c				1,600
	(Being the T/f of profit on sale of own Debentures)				
	12% Debentures A/c	Dr.		1,20,000	
	To Own debentures A/c [(1,92,000/2,00,000) × 1,20,000]			1,15,200	
	To Reconstruction A/c				4,800
	(Being the T/f of profit on cancellation of own Debentures)				
	12.% Debentures A/c	Dr.		3,00,000	
	Reconstruction A/c	Dr.		20,000	
	To Machinery A/c				3,20,000
	(Being the machinery taken up by debentureholders)				

	Reconstruction A/c To Debtors A/c To Stock A/c (Being the Assets revalued)	Dr.	37,000	 25,000 12,000
	Creditors A/c To Reconstruction A/c (Being the liabilities revalued)	Dr.	60,000	 60,000
	Reconstruction A/c To Goodwill A/c To Discount on debentures A/c To Profit and Loss A/c (Being the losses w/o)	Dr.	4,33,000	 20,000 2,000 4,11,000
	Reconstruction A/c To Bank A/c (Being the penalty paid for avoidance of capital commitments)	Dr.	20,000	 20,000
	Reconstruction A/c To Capital Reserve A/c (Being the transfer of Balance to Capital Reserve)	Dr.	5,14,400	 5,14,400
02.04.13	Business Purchase A/c To Liquidators of W Ltd. (Being the purchase of business)	Dr.	18,20,000	 18,20,000
	Fixed assets A/c Stock A/c Debtors A/c Cash at bank A/c To Sundry Ceditors A/c To 12% Debentures A/c of W Ltd. To Profit and loss A/c To General Reserve A/c ₹ (1,70,000 + 80,000*) To Business Purchase A/c (Being the recording over of all assets and liabilities taken over)	Dr. Dr. Dr. Dr.	11,50,000 6,80,000 6,15,000 1,55,000	 3,15,000 2,00,000 15,000 2,50,000 18,20,000
	Liquidators of W Ltd. A/c To Equity share capital A/c To 10% Preference share capital A/c (Being the purchase consideration discharged)	Dr.	18,20,000	 15,00,000 3,20,000
	12% Debentures of W Ltd. A/c To 12% Debentures A/c (Being the issue of 12% Debentures against Debentures of W Ltd.)	Dr.	2,00,000	 2,00,000

**₹ 80,000 is the balancing figure adjusted to General Reserve Account as per AS 14 "Accounting for Amalgamation".

BALANCE SHEET OF K LTD. AS AT 02.04.2013

Particulars	*Note No*	₹
I. Equity and Liabilities		
(1) Shareholders'Funds		
(a) Share Capital	1	35,20,000
(b) Reserves and Surplus	2	10,19,400
(2) Non-Current Liabilities [12%Debentures]	3	3,80,000
(3) Current Liabilities		
(a) Trade Payables [Creditors]	4	8,15,000
Total		57,34,400
II. Assets		
(1) Non-Current Assets		
(a) Fixed Assets		
Tangible Assets	5	32,30,000
(2) Current Assets		
(a) Inventories	6	10,80,000
(b) Trade Receivables [Debtors]	7	12,15,000
(c) Cash and Cash Equivalents	8	2,09,400
Total		57,34,400

Notes To Accounts:

Particulars	₹
1. Share Capital	
2,50,000 Equity Shares of ₹ 10 each	25,00,000
10,200,9% Pref. Shares of ₹ 100 each	10,20,000
(Of the above 1,50,000 Equity Shares & 3200,9% Pref. Shares were issued for consideration otherwise than cash)	
Total	35,20,000
2. Reserves and Surplus	
General Reserve (2,40,000 + 2,50,000)	4,90,000
Profit & Loss Account	15,000
Capital Reserve	5,14,400
Total	10,19,400
3. Long-term Borrowings	
12% Debentures	6,00,000
Less: Settled in consideration of machinery	(3,00,000)
Less: Cancelled debentures	(1,20,000)
Add: 12% Debentures issue to W Ltd.	2,00,000
Total	3,80,000

4. Trade Payables	
of K Ltd.	5,60,000
Less: Reduction due to revaluation	(60,000)
Add: Trade Payables of W Ltd.	3,15,000
Total	8,15,000
5. Tangible assets	
Balance of Other Fixed Assets	24,00,000
Less: Machinery taken up by debenture holders	(3,20,000)
Add: Other Fixed Assets of W Ltd.	11,50,000
Total	32,30,000
6. Inventories	
of K Ltd.	4,12,000
Less: Reduction due to revaluation	(12,000)
Add: Inventories of W Ltd.	6,80,000
Total	10,80,000
7. Trade Receivables	
of K Ltd.	6,25,000
Less: Reduction due to revaluation	(25,000)
Add: Trade Receivables of W Ltd.	6,15,000
Total	12,15,000
8. Cash and Cash Equivalents	
of K Ltd.	38,000
Less: Payment of Arrear of Preference dividend	(42,000)
Add: Profit on Sale of own Debentures	78,400
Less: Penalty Paid	(20,000)
Add: Cash and Cash Equivalents of W Ltd.	1,55,000
Total	2,09,400

Working Notes:

(i) Purchase Consideration:	₹
Equity share capital [(15,000 × 50/5) × ₹ 10]	15,00,000
9% Preference share capital [(4,000 × 4/5) × ₹ 100]	3,20,000
	18,20,000
(ii) General Reserve:	₹
Share capital of W Ltd. (Equity + Preference)	19,00,000
Less: Share capital issued by K Ltd.	18,20,000
General reserve (resulted due to absorption)	80,000

PROBLEM 5

The summarized Balance Sheet of Bad Luck Ltd. as on 31st March, 2013 was as follows:

Particulars	Note No	₹ (lacs)
I. Equity and Liabilities		
(1) Shareholders' Funds		
(a) Share Capital	1	7.50
(b) Reserves and Surplus	2	(10.00)
(2) Non-Current Liabilities (Long-term Borrowings)	3	5.00
(3) Current Liabilities		
(a) Short-term Borrowings	4	5.00
(b) Trade Payables [Creditors]		2.50
Total		10.00
II. Assets		
(1) Non-Current Assets		
(a) Fixed Assets		
Tangible Assets	5	5.50
Intangible Assets [Goodwill]	6	1.50
(2) Current Assets		
(a) Inventories		1.50
(b) Trade Receivables		1.25
(c) Deferred revenue expenditure		0.25
Total		10.00

Notes To Accounts:

Particulars	₹ (lacs)
1. Share Capital	
5000 Equity Shares of ₹ 100 each	5.00
2500, 8% Pref. Shares of ₹ 100 each	2.50
	7.50
2. Reserves and Surplus (Profit and Loss A/c)	(10.00)
3. Long-term Borrowings (8% Debentures)	5.00
4. Short-term Borrowings	
Loan from Directors	3.00
Bank Overdraft	2.00
	5.00
5. Tangible Assets	
Freehold Property	4.00
Plant & Machinery	1.50
Total	5.50

6. Intangible Assets	
Goodwill	1.00
Trademark	0.50
	1.50

The followig scheme of internal reconstruction was framed, approved by the Court, all the concerned parties and implemented:

(i) The preference shares to be written down to ₹ 25 each and the equity shares to ₹ 20 each. Each class of shares then to be conveted into shares of ₹ 100 each.

(ii) The debenture holders to take over freehold property (book value ₹ 2,00,000) at a valuation of ₹ 2,50,000 in part repayment of their holdings. Remaining freehold property to be revalued at ₹ 6,00,000.

(iii) Loan from directors to be waived off in full.

(iv) Stock of ₹ 50,000 to be written off, ₹ 12,500 to be provided for bad debts.

(v) Profit and Loss account balance, Trademark, Goodwill and Deferred Revenue Expenditure to be written off.

Pass Journal Entries for all the above mentioned transactions. Also, Prepare Capital Reducation account and company's Balance Sheet immediately after reconstruction.

SOLUTION

JOURNAL OF BAD LUCK LTD.

Date	*Particulars*		*Dr. (₹)*	*Cr. (₹)*
(i)	8% Preference Share Capital A/c (₹ 100)	Dr.	2,50,000	
	To 8% Preference Share Capital A/c (₹ 25)			62,500
	To Capital Reduction A/c			1,87,500
	(Being preference shares of ₹100 each reduced to ₹ 25 each as per the scheme)			
(ii)	Equity Share Capital A/c (₹ 100)	Dr.	5,00,000	
	To Equity Share Capital A/c (₹ 20)			1,00,000
	To Capital Reduction A/c			4,00,000
	(Being equity shares of ₹ 100 each reduced to ₹ 20 each as per the scheme)			
(iii)	8% Preference Share Capital A/c (₹ 25)	Dr.	62,500	
	To 8% Preference Share Capital A/c (₹ 100)			62,500
	(Being the conversion of 2,500 shares of ₹ 25 each into 625 shares of ₹ 100 each as per the scheme)			
(iv)	Equity Share Capital A/c (₹ 20)	Dr.	1,00,000	
	To Equity Share Capital A/c (₹ 100)			1,00,000
	(Being the conversion of 5,000 shares of ₹ 20 each in to 1,000 shares of ₹ 100 each as per the scheme)			
(v)	Freehold Property A/c	Dr.	50,000	
	To Capital Reduction A/c			50,000
	(Being appreciation in the value of property)			

(vi)	8% Debentures A/c	Dr.	2,50,000	
	To Freehold Property A/c			2,50,000
	(Being claim of debentureholders settled in part by transfer of freehold property as per the scheme)			
(vii)	Freehold Property A/c	Dr.	4,00,000	
	To Capital Reduction A/c			4,00,000
	(Being appreciation in the value of remaining property)			
(viii)	Director's Loan A/c	Dr.	3,00,000	
	To Capital Reduction A/c			3,00,000
	(Being Director's loan waived in full)			
(ix)	Capital Reduction A/c	Dr.	13,37,500	
	To Profit and Loss A/c			10,00,000
	To Deferred Revenue Expenditure A/c			25,000
	To Inventories A/c			50,000
	To Provision for Doubtful Debts A/c			12,500
	To Goodwill A/c			1,00,000
	To Trademark			50,000
	To Capital Reserve A/c			1,00,000
	(Being the various assets written off as per the scheme)			

Dr. **CAPITAL REDUCTION ACCOUNT** *Cr.*

Particulars	₹	*Particulars*	₹
To Provision for Doubtful Debts A/c	12,500	By Preference Share Capital A/c	1,87,500
To Inventories A/c	50,000	By Freehold Property A/c	4,50,000
To Trademark A/c	50,000	By Equity Share Capital A/c	4,00,000
To Deferred Revenue Exp. A/c	60,000	By Director's loan A/c	3,00,000
To Goodwill A/c	1,00,000		
To Profit and loss A/c	10,00,000		
To Capital reserve A/c	1,00,000		
	13,37,500		13,37,500

BALANCE SHEET OF BAD LUCK LTD. (AND REDUCED) AS AT 31.03.2013

Particulars	*Note No*	₹
I. Equity and Liabilities		
(1) Shareholders' Funds		
(a) Share Capital	1	1,62,500
(b) Reserves and Surplus[Capital Reserve]		1,00,000
(2) Non-Current Liabilities		
Long-term Borrowings [8% Debentures]		2,50,000
(3) Current Liabilities		
(a) Short-term Borrowings [Bank Overdraft]		2,00,000

	(b) Trade Payables [Creditors]		2,50,000
	Total		9,62,500
II.	**Assets**		
	(1) Non-Current Assets		
	(a) Fixed Assets		
	Tangible Assets	2	7,50,000
	(2) Current Assets		
	(a) Inventories		1,00,000
	(b) Trade Receivables [1,50,000 – 12,500]		1,12,500
	Total		9,62,500

Notes To Accounts:

	Particulars	₹
1.	**Share Capital**	
	1,000 Equity Shares of ₹ 100 each	1,00,000
	625,8% Pref. Shares of ₹ 100 each	62,500
		1,62,500
2.	**Tangible Assets**	
	Frehold Property	6,00,000
	Plant & Machinery	1,50,000
	Total	7,50,000

PROBLEM 6

Given below are the extracts from the Balance Sheet of CANIC Limited as at 31st March, 2015:

Particulars	₹
2,00,000 Equity Shares of ₹ 10 each, ₹ 5 paid	10,00,000
6,000 8% Preference Shares of ₹ 100 each	6,00,000
Profit & Loss Account (Dr.)	(4,08,000)
9% Debentures	6,00,000
Interest accrued on debentures	1,08,000
Bank overdraft	1,50,000
Interest accrued on Bank overdraft	15,000
Creditors	69,000
Fixed Assets	11,40,000
Patents and Copyrights	80,000
Investments at cost (Market value ₹ 55,000)	65,000
Inventories	4,00,000
Debtors	4,39,000
Bank	10,000

Preference dividend is in arrear for one year:

(a) Preference shareholders to give up their claims, inclusive of dividends, to the extent of 30% and desire to be paid off, (b) Debenture-holders agree to give up their claims to interest in consideration of their interest being enhanced to 12%, (c) Bank agrees to give up 50% of its interest outstanding in consideration of its being paid off at once, (d) Creditors would like to grant a discount of 5% if they are paid immediately, (e) Balance of Profit & Loss Account, Patents and Copyright and Debtors of ₹ 30,000 to be written off, (f) Fixed Assets to be written down by ₹ 34,000, (g) Investments are to reflect their market value, (h) To the extent not specifically stated, equity shareholders suffer on reduction of their rights. Cost of reconstruction is ₹ 3,350.

Required: Pass journal entries assuming that the scheme has been put through fully with the equity shareholders bringing in necessary cash to pay off the parties and to leave a Balance of ₹ 30,000 and prepare the Balance Sheet after reconstruction.

SOLUTION

JOURNAL

Particulars		*L.F.*	*Dr. (₹)*	*Cr. (₹)*
8% Preference Share Capital A/c	Dr.		6,00,000	
To Preference Shareholders' A/c				4,20,000
To Reconstruction A/c				1,80,000
(Being 30% of claim given up by preference shareholders as per reconstruction scheme dated....)				
Reconstruction A/c	Dr.		33,600	
To Preference Shareholders A/c				33,600
(Being 70% of arrears preference dividend payable to preference shareholders as per reconstruction scheme)				
9% Debentures A/c	Dr.		6,00,000	
Interest accrued on debentures A/c	Dr.		1,08,000	
To 12% Debentures A/c				6,00,000
To Reconstruction A/c				1,08,000
(Being 9% debentures converted into equivalent number of 12% debentures and the accrued debenture interest sacrificed as per Reconstruction scheme)				
Equity Share Capital A/c	Dr.		3,00,000	
To Reconstruction A/c				3,00,000
(Being equity shareholders rights reduced to a share of ₹ 3.50 vide Board's Resolution No....dated....., the amount of sacrifice credited to Reconstruction Account) (Working Notes i)				
Bank A/c	Dr.		7,00,000	
To Equity Share Capital A/c				7,00,000
(Being the amount received on 2,00,000 equity shares @₹ 3.50 per share as per reconstruction scheme) (Working Notes ii)				
Bank of India A/c	Dr.		1,50,000	
Interest Accrued on Bank overdraft A/c	Dr.		15,000	
To Bank A/c				1,57,500

To Reconstruction A/c			7,500
(Being the Bank overdraft paid off including 50% of accrued interest as per reconstruction scheme, the interest sacrificed credited to Reconstruction A/c)			
Creditors A/c Dr.		69,000	
To Bank A/c			65,550
To Reconstruction A/c			3,450
(Being the Creditors claim discharged to the extent of 95% as per reconstruction scheme, the balance of the claim sacrificed)			
Reconstruction A/c Dr.		3,350	
To Bank A/c			3,350
(Being the Reconstruction expenses paid)			
Preference shareholders' A/c Dr.		4,53,600	
To Bank A/c			4,53,600
(Being the Amount due to preference shareholders discharged)			
Reconstruction A/c Dr.		5,62,000	
To Profit and Loss A/c			4,08,000
To Patents & copyright A/c			80,000
To Debtors A/c			30,000
To Investment A/c			10,000
To Fixed Assets A/c			34,000
(Being the debit balance of profit and loss account, patents & copy rights writing off and the value of debtors, investments and fixed assets written down as per reconstruction scheme)			

BALANCE SHEET OF CANIC LTD. (AND REDUCED) AS AT 31.03.2015

Particulars	*Note No*	₹
I. Equity and Liabilities		
(1) Shareholders' Funds		
(a) Share Capital (₹ 10 each, ₹ 7 paidup)		14,00,000
(b) Reserves and Surplus		
(2) Non-Current Liabilities [12%Debentures]		6,00,000
(3) Current Liabilities		
Total		20,00,000
II. Assets		
(1) Non-Current Assets		
(a) Fixed Assets		
Tangible Assets [11,40,000 – 34,000 (Amt. w/o)]		11,06,000
(b) Non-Current Investments [65,000 – 10,000 (Amt. w/o)]		55,000
(2) Current Assets		
(a) Inventories		4,00,000

(b) Trade Receivables [Debtors – Prov][80 – 4]		4,09,000
(c) Cash and Cash Equivalents		30,000
Total		20,00,000

Working Notes:

(I) STATEMENT SHOWING LIABILITIES AND EQUITY SACRIFICED AND THEIR USES AS PER SCHEME

Liabilities & Equity Sacrified	₹	*Uses*	₹
Preference shareholders:		Writing off:	
30% of ₹ 6,00,000	1,80,000	Reconstruction expenses	3,350
Debenture holders:		Profit and Loss account balance	4,08,000
Interest on Debentures	1,08,000	Patents and copyrights	80,000
Bank of India:		Pref. dividend Arrears (70% of	33,600
Interest on bank overdraft (50%)	7,500	₹ 48,000)	
Creditors:		Writing down:	
5% of ₹ 69,000	3,450	Debtors	30,000
Equity Shareholders:		Investment	10,000
Sacrifice @ ₹ 1.50 per share (Balancing figure)	3,00,000	Fixed Assets	34,000
	5,98,950		5,98,950

(II) CASH TO BE BROUGHT IN BY EQUITY SHAREHOLDERS:

Payments to: Preference shareholders (including arrears of preference dividend)	₹
70% of ₹ 6,48,000	4,53,600
Bank of India (including interest on bank overdraft) ₹ [1,50,000 + ₹ 7,500]	1,57,500
Creditors 95% of ₹ 69,000	65,550
Reconstruction expenses	3,350
Additional cash for working capital [₹ 30,000 – ₹ 10,000]	20,000
	7,00,000

Therefore, Contribution per Equity Share = ₹ 7,00,000/2,00,000 = ₹ 3.50

PROBLEM 7

Given below are the extracts from the Balance Sheet of Sickness Ltd. as at 31st March, 2015:

Particulars	₹
Share Capital:	
8,000 equity shares of ₹ 100 each, ₹ 50 per share paid up	4,00,000
4,000 11% Cumulative Preference shares of ₹ 100 each, fully paid up	4,00,000
Securities Premium A/c	40,000
General Reserve	60,000
Current Liabilities	3,10,000

Contingent liability not provided:	
Preference dividends are in arrears for three years including the year ended 31st March, 2014	—
Fixed Assets	
Tangible Fixed Assets	8,50,000
Less: Depreciation	(2,70,000)
Goodwill at cost	40,000
Investments	25,000
Inventories	2,10,000
Trade Debtors	2,55,000
Cash and Bank Balances	1,00,000

The funds of the Company are sufficient to discharge its liabilities including Preference Dividends in arrears. However, the company does not want to deplete its resources. It would also like to reflect the values of some of its assets in a realistic manner. The Board of Directors of the Company decided and proposed the following scheme of rehabilitation/reconstruction to be effective from 1st April, 2015.

(a) The cumulative preference shareholders are to be issued, in exchange of their holdings, 13% Debentures of the face value of ₹ 100 each at a premium of 10% Fractional holdings are to be paid off in cash.

(b) Arrears in preference dividends to be converted into equity shares of ₹ 100, ₹ 50 per share paid up.

(c) After the issue of the equity shares mentioned in (ii) above, the paid up value of all the equity shares is to be reduced to ₹ 25 each.

(d) The face value of all the equity shares to be reduced to ₹ 50 each and the balance of the unpaid portion is to be called up fully.

(e) Goodwill has lost its value and has to be written off. Market value of Tangible Fixed Assets is determined, as at 31st March, 2015 at ₹ 5,00,000.

(f) Investments have no market value and have to be written off.

(g) Inventories is to be valued at 110% of its book value and Trade Debtors are to be discounted by 5%.

The scheme, as approved by the Directors, is duly accepted by all authorities and put into effect.

During the working for the half year ended 30th September, 2015, it is noticed that the trading for the period has resulted in an increase of bank balances by ₹ 55,100, Sundry Debtors by ₹ 40,000, Trade Creditors by ₹ 26,000 and a decrease in stock by ₹ 8,000. Depreciation for the half year on fixed assets at 10% per annum is to be provided. The increase in the bank balances was prior to the company paying the half yearly interest on the debentures and redeeming one half of the debentures on 30th September, 2015.

Required: Prepare Journal, and the Balance Sheet of Sickness Ltd. as at 30th September, 2015.

SOLUTION

JOURNAL

Particulars		*L.F.*	*Dr. (₹)*	*Cr. (₹)*
11% Cumulative Preference Share Capital A/c	Dr.		4,00,000	
To 13% Debentures A/c				3,63,600
To Securities Premium A/c				36,360

Particulars		Dr. (₹)	Cr. (₹)
To Cash and Bank A/c (Being the issue of 3,636 13% debentures of ₹ 100 each at a premium of ₹ 10 to cancel 4,000 11% cumulative preference shares of ₹ 100 each, fraction ₹ 40 was paid in cash)			40
Capital Reduction A/c To Equity Share Capital A/c (Being the Issue of 2,640 equity shares of ₹ 100 each ₹ 50 paid-up for arrears preference dividend)	Dr.	1,32,000	1,32,000
Equity Share Capital A/c To Capital Reduction A/c (Being the Reduction of paid up value of 10,640 equity shares of ₹ 100 each, ₹ 50 paid up to shares of ₹ 50 each, ₹ 25 paid up)	Dr.	2,66,000	2,66,000
Equity Share Capital (₹ 100 each) A/c To Equity Share Capital (₹ 50 each) A/c (Being the face value of ₹ 100 reduced to ₹ 50 each as per scheme of reconstruction)	Dr.	2,66,000	2,66,000
Cash and Bank A/c To Equity Share Capital A/c (Being the Call money on 10,640 equity shares @ ₹ 25 to make the equity shares fully paid up)	Dr.	2,66,000	2,66,000
Capital Reduction A/c To Goodwill A/c To Investment A/c To Fixed Assets A/c (₹ 8,50,000 – ₹ 2,70,000) – ₹ 5,00,000 To Sundry Debtors A/c (Being the Value of Sundry assets written down)	Dr.	1,57,750	 40,000 25,000 80,000 12,750
Stock A/c To Capital Reduction A/c (Beig the Value of Stock written up	Dr.	21,000	21,000
General Reserve A/c To Capital Reduction A/c (Being the Transfer from General Reserve)	Dr.	2,750	2,750

BALANCE SHEET OF SICKNESS LTD. (AND REDUCED) AS AT 30.09.2015

Particulars	Note No	₹
I. Equity and Liabilities		
(1) Shareholders' Funds		
(a) Share Capital [₹ 50 each]		5,32,000
(b) Reserves and Surplus	1	1,46,076
(2) Non-Current Liabilities [13%Debentures]		1,81,800
(3) Current Liabilities		3,36,000
Total		11,95,876

II.	**Assets**		
	(1) Non-Current Assets		
	(a) Fixed Assets.		
	Tangible Assets [5,80,000 – 80,000 (Amt. w/o) – 25,000]		4,75,000
	Intangible Assets [Goodwill] [40,000 – 40,000(Amt. w/o)]		0
	(b) Non-Current Investments[25,000 – 25,000(Amt. w/o)]		0
	(2) Current Assets		
	(a) Inventories		2,23,000
	(b) Trade Receivables [Debtors]		2,82,250
	(c) Cash and Cash Equivalents		2,15,626
	Total		11,95,876

Notes To Accounts:

1. Reserves and Surplus	
General Reserve	57,250
Profit & Loss Account	12,466
Securities Premium	76,360
Total	1,46,076

Working Notes:

Dr. **(I) CAPITAL REDUCTION ACCOUNT** *Cr.*

Particulars	₹	*Particulars*	₹
To Equity Share Capital A/c	1,32,000	By Equity Share Capital A/c	2,66,000
To Sundries	1,57,750	By Stock	21,000
		By General Reserve	2,750
	2,89,750		2,89,750

Dr. **(II) CASH AND BANK ACCOUNT** *Cr.*

Particulars	₹	*Particulars*	₹
To Balance b/d	1,00,000	By 11% Cumulative Preference Shares A/c	40
To Equity Share Capital A/c	2,66,000	By Balance c/d	3,65,960
	3,66,000		3,66,000

(III) BALANCE SHEET (AFTER INTERNAL RECONSTRUCTION)

Liabilities	₹	*Assets*		₹
Share Capital:		Fixed Assets:		
10,640 Equity Shares of ₹ 50 each fully paid	5,32,000	Goodwill	40,000	
Reserves and Surplus:		*Less:* Amt w/o under Reconstruction		—
Securities Premium A/c	76,360	Scheme	40,000	
General Reserve	57,250	Other Fixed Assets	5,80,000	

Secured Loans:		*Less:* Amt w/o under Reconstruction	5,00,000	
13% Debentures	3,63,600	Scheme	80,000	
Current Liabilities:	3,10,000	Investments	25,000	
		Less: Amt w/o under		
		Reconstruction Scheme	25,000	—
		Current Assets:		
		Stock in Trade		2,31,000
		Sundry Debtors		2,42,250
		Cash and Bank		3,65,960
	13,39,210			13,39,210

Working Notes:

(I) CALCULATION OF HALF-YEARLY PROFIT

Particulars	₹	₹
Increase in bank balances	55,100	
Increase in sundry debtors	40,000	95,100
Less: Decrease in stock	8,000	
Less: Increase in trade creditors	26,000	34,000
Trading Profit before interest and depreciation		61,100
Less: Interest for 1/2 year @ 13% on ₹ 3,63,600	23,634	
Less: Depr. for 1/2 year on ₹ 5,00,000 @ 10% p.a	25,000	48,634
Net Profit		12,466

(II) CALCULATION OF CASH AND BANK BALANCE AS ON 30.9.2015

Particulars	₹	₹
Balance as on 31.3.2015		3,65,960
Add: Increase		55,100
Less: Interest	23,634	
Less: Redemption of 1/2 of 13% debentures	1,81,800	2,05,434
		2,15,626

PROBLEM 8

Given below are the extracts from the Balance Sheet of Munna Ltd. on 31st March, 2015:

Particulars	₹
20,000, Equity shares of ₹ 100 each	20,00,000
10,000, 7% preference shares of ₹ 100 each	10,00,000
Profit & Loss Account (Dr.)	(7,00,000)
Sundry Creditors	7,00,000
Bank overdraft	3,00,000
Goodwill	2,00,000

Plant and Machinery	18,00,000
Stock	3,00,000
Debtors	7,50,000
Cash	1,50,000
Preliminary Expenses	1,00,000

Two years' preference dividend are in arrears. The company had been bad time during the last two years and hopes for better business in future, earning profit and paying dividend provided the capital base is reduced.

An internal reconstruction scheme as follows was agreed to by all concerned:

(i) Creditors agreed to forego 50% of the claim.

(ii) Preference shareholders withdrew arrears dividend claim. They also agreed to lower their capital claim by 20% by reducing nominal value in consideration of 9% dividend effective after reorganisation in case equity shareholders' loss exceeded 50% on the application of the scheme.

(iii) Bank agreed to convert overdraft into term loan to the extent required for making current ratio equal to 2 : 1.

(iv) Revalued figure for plant and machinery was accepted as ₹ 15,00,000.

(v) Debtors to the extent of ₹ 4,00,000 were considered good.

(vi) Equity shares shall be exchanged for the same number of equity shares at a revised denomination as required after the reorganisation.

Required:

(a) Total loss to be borne by the equity and preference shareholders for the reorganisation;

(b) Shares of loss to the individual classes of shareholders;

(c) New structure of share capital after reorganisation;

(d) Working capital of the reorganised Co.; and

(e) A proforma balance sheet after reorganisation.

SOLUTION

(A) LOSS TO BE BORNE BY EQUITY AND PREFERENCE SHAREHOLDERS

Particulars	₹
Profit and Loss A/c (debit balance)	7,00,000
Preliminary Expenses	1,00,000
Goodwill	2,00,000
Plant and Machinery (₹ 18,00,000 – ₹ 15,00,000)	3,00,000
Debtors	3,50,000
Amount to be written off	16,50,000
Less: 50% of Sundry Creditors	3,50,000
Loss to be borne by equity and preference shareholders	13,00,000

Note: *Since preference dividend for 2 years which is in arrears is sacrificed by preference shareholders, the same may be ignored in the above calculation or alternatively may be included in the amount to be written off and then reduced therefrom as preference shareholders' sacrifice.*

(B) SHARES OF LOSS TO PREFERENCE SHAREHOLDERS AND EQUITY SHAREHOLDERS

Total loss being more than 50% of equity share capital:	
Preference shareholders' share of loss = 20% of ₹ 10,00,000	₹ 2,00,000
Equity shareholders' share of loss (₹ 13,00,000 – ₹ 2,00,000)	₹ 11,00,000
Total	₹ 13,00,000

(C) NEW STRUCTURE OF CAPITAL

Equity Shares	₹
20,000 shares of ₹ 45 each fully paid	9,00,000
Preference Shares	
10,000, 9% shares of ₹ 80 each fully paid	8,00,000
	17,00,000

(D) WORKING CAPITAL OF THE REORGANISED COMPANY

Current Assets	₹	₹
Stock		3,00,000
Debtors		4,00,000
Cash		1,50,000
		8,50,000
Less: Current Liabilities		
Creditors	3,50,000	
Bank overdraft (see Note)	75,000	4,25,000
Working Capital		4,25,000

Note: *Current ratio shall be 2: 1, i.e., total current liabilities shall be 50% of ₹ 8,50,000 = ₹ 4,25,000. Therefore, Bank overdraft = ₹ 4,25,000 – ₹ 3,50,000 = ₹ 75,000.*

BALANCE SHEET OF MUNNA LTD. (AND REDUCED) AS AT 31.3.2015

Particulars	Note No	₹
I. Equity and Liabilities		
(1) Shareholders' Funds		
(a) Share Capital	1	17,00,000
(b) Reserves and Surplus		
(2) Non-Current Liabilities [Term Loan with Bank]		2,25,000
(3) Current Liabilities		
(a) Trade Payables [Creditors]		3,50,000
(b) Other Current Liabilities [Bank overdraft]		75,000
Total		23,50,000
II. Assets		
(1) Non-Current Assets		
(a) Fixed Assets		
Tangible Assets [18,00,000 – 3,00,000(Amt. w/o)]		15,00,000

Intangible Assets [Goodwill] [2,00,000 – 2,00,000(Amt. w/o)]		0
(2) Current Assets		
(a) Inventories		3,00,000
(b) Trade Receivables [Debtors]		4,00,000
(c) Cash and Cash Equivalents		1,50,000
Total		23,50,000

Notes To Accounts:

Particulars	₹
1. Share Capital	
20000 Equity Shares of ₹ 45 each	9,00,000
10000,9% Pref. Shares of ₹ 80 each	8,00,000
	17,00,000

PROBLEM 9

Given below are the extracts from the Balance Sheet of X Ltd. as at March 31st, 2015.

Particulars	*(₹ in lakhs)*
Equity Shares of ₹ 100 each	600
14% Preference Shares of ₹ 100 each	200
Profit and Loss Account (Dr.)	(525)
13% Debentures	200
Debenture Interest accrued	26
Loan from bank	74
Trade creditors	340
Land and Building	200
Plant and Machinery	300
Furniture and Fixtures	50
Inventory	150
Sundry Debtors	70
Cash at bank	130
Preliminary expenses	10
Cost of issue of debentures	5

The company did not perform well and has suffered sizable losses during the last few years. However, it is that the company could be nursed back to health by proper financial restructuring. Consequently the following scheme of reconstruction has been drawn up.

(a) Equity shares are to be reduced to ₹ 25 per share, fully paid up;

(b) Preference shares are to be reduced (with coupon rate of 10%) to equal number of shares of ₹ 50 each, fully paid up

(c) Debenture holders have agreed to forgo the accrued interest due to them. In the future, the rate of interest on debentures is to be reduced to 9 percent.

(d) Trade creditors will forego 25% of the amount due to them.

(e) The company issued 6 lakh of equity shares at ₹ 25 each and the entire sum was to be paid on application. The entire amount was fully subscribed by promoters.

(f) Land and Building was to be revalued at ₹ 450 lakhs, Plant and Machinery was to be written down by ₹ 120 lakhs and a provision of ₹ 15 lakhs had to be made for doubtful debts.

Required:

(i) Show the impact of financial restructuring on the company's activities.

(ii) Prepare the fresh balance sheet after the reconstructions is completed on the basis of the above proposals.

SOLUTION

(A) IMPACT OF FINANCIAL RESTRUCTURING

(i) Benefits of X Ltd.	
A. Reduction of Liabilities payable	₹ in lakhs
Reduction in equity share capital (6 lakh shares × ₹ 75 per share)	450
Reduction in preference share capital (2 lakh shares × ₹ 50 per share)	100
Waiver of outstanding debenture Interest	26
Waiver from trade creditors (₹ 340 lakhs × 0.25)	85
	661
B. Revaluation of Assets	
Appreciation of Land and Building (₹ 450 lakhs – ₹ 200 lakhs)	250
	911
(ii) Amount of ₹ 911 lakhs utilized to write off losses, fictitious assets and over-valued assets.	
Writing of Profit and Loss Account	525
Cost of Issue of Debentures	5
Preliminary Expenses	10
Provision for Doubtful Debts	15
Revaluation of Plant and Machinery (₹ 300 lakhs – ₹ 104 lakhs)	120
	675
C. Capital Reserve [A – B]	236

(III) BALANCE SHEET OF X LTD. (AFTER RECONSTRUCTION) AS AT 31.3.2015

Particulars	*Note No*	*₹ (lacs)*
I. Equity and Liabilities		
(1) Shareholders' Funds		
(a) Share Capital	1	400
(b) Reserves and Surplus (Capital Reserve)		236
(2) Non-Current Liabilities [9% Debentures + Loan from Bank [200 + 74]		274
(3) Current Liabilities		
(a) Trade Payables [Creditors]		255

Total		1,165
II. Assets		
(1) Non-Current Assets		
(a) Fixed Assets		
Tangible Assets	2	680
(2) Current Assets		
(a) Inventories		150
(b) Trade Receivables [Debtors – Prov] [70 – 15]		55
(c) Cash and Cash Equivalents [balancing figure]		280
Total		1,165

Notes To Accounts:

Particulars		₹ *(lacs)*
1. Share Capital		
12 lacs Equity Shares of ₹ 25 each		300
2 lacs, 10% Pref. Shares of ₹ 50		100
		400
2. Tangible Assets		
Land & Building	200	
Add: Amt. increased under Reconstruction scheme	250	450
Plant & Machinery	300	
Less: Amt. w/o under Reconstruction scheme	(120)	180
Furniture & Fixtures		50
Total		680

PROBLEM 10

The Shareholders of Sunrise Ltd decided on a corporate restructuring exercise necessitated due to economic recession and a slump in business. From the audited prepare:

(i) Balance Sheet after the completion of the restructuring exercise,

(ii) The Capital Reduction Amount,

(iii) The Cash Account of the entity.

BALANCE SHEET OF SUNRISE LTD AS ON 31-03-2015

Particulars	₹
Share Capital	
30,000 Equity Shares (₹ 10 each)	3,00,000
40,000 8% Cumulative Preference Shares (₹ 10 each)	4,00,000
Reserves and Surplus	
Securities Premium Account	10,000
Profit & Loss Account	(1,38,400)
Non-Current Liabilities (Debentures)	1,25,400

Current Liabilities		
Creditors		1,20,000
Deferred Vat Payable		50,000
Temporary Bank Overdraft		2,23,100
Fixed Assets		
Trade Marks and Patents		1,10,000
Goodwill at cost		36,100
Freehold Land		1,20,000
Freehold Premises		2,44,000
Plant and Equipment		3,20,000
Investment (Market to Market)		64,000
Current Assets		
Inventories:		
Raw materials and packing		
Materials	60,000	
Finished goods	16,000	76,000
Trade receivable		1,20,000

Note: Preference Dividends are in arrears for 4 years.

The scheme of reconstruction that received the permission of the Court was on the following lines:

(1) The Authorized capital of the Company to be re-fixed at ₹ 10 Lakhs (Preference Capital ₹ 3 Lakhs and Equity Capital ₹ 7 Lakhs both ₹ 10/- shared each).

(2) The Preference shares are to be reduced to ₹ 5 each and equity share reduced by ₹ 3 per share. Post reduction, both classes of shares to be e-consolidated into ₹ 10 shares.

(3) Trade Investments are to be liquidation in open market

(4) One fresh equity share of ₹ 10 to issued for every ₹ 40 of preference dividends in arrears (ignore taxation).

(5) The Securities premium is to be fully utilized to meet the reconstruction programme.

(6) The debenture holder took over freehold land at ₹ 2,10,000 and settled the balance after adjusting their dues.

(7) Unprovided contingent Liabilities were settled at ₹ 54,000 and a pending insurance claim receivable settled at ₹ 12,500 on condition that claim will be immediately settled.

(8) The Intangible assets were all the written off along with ₹ 10,000 worth obsolete packing material and 10% of the Receivables.

(9) Reconstruction expenses amounted to ₹ 10,000.

(10) Remaining cash available as a result of the above transactions is to be utilised to pay off the bank overdraft to that extent.

(11) The equity shareholder agree that they who bring in cash to liquidate the balance outstanding on the overdraft account and also agree the sufficient funds will be brought in to bring up the net working capital, after completing the re-structuring exercise, to ₹ 2 lakhs. The Equity Shares will be issued at par for this purpose.

SOLUTION

(I) BALANCE SHEET OF SUNRISE LTD. (AND REDUCED) AS AT 31.03.2015

Particulars	*Note No*	₹
I. Equity and Liabilities		
(1) Shareholders' Funds		
(a) Share Capital	1	7,64,000
(b) Reserves and Surplus		—
(2) Non-Current Liabilities		
(3) Current Liabilities		
(a) Trade Payables [Creditors]		1,20,000
(b) Other Current Liabilities [Deferred VAT Payable]		50,000
Total		9,34,000
II. Assets		
(1) Non-Current Assets		
(a) Fixed Assets		
Tangible Assets	2	5,64,000
(2) Current Assets		
(a) Inventories [50,000 + 16,000]		66,000
(b) Trade Receivables [Debtors]		1,08,000
(c) Cash and Equivalents		1,96,000
Total		9,34,000

Notes to Accounts:

Particulars	₹
1. Share Capital	
56,400 Equity Shares of ₹ 10 each	5,64,000
20,000, 8% Pref. Shares of ₹ 10 each, ₹ 10 paid	2,00,000
(of the above 3,200 Equity Shares were issued for consideration otherwise than case)	
	7,64,000
2. Tangible Assets	
Free hold Premises	2,44,000
	3,20,000
	5,64,000

Dr. **(II) CAPITAL REDUCTION ACCOUNT** *Cr.*

Particulars	₹	*Particulars*	₹
To Equity Share Capital A/c [(4,00,000 × 8% × 4)/₹ 40] × ₹ 10	32,000	By 8% Cumulative Preference Share Capital A/c [40,000 × ₹ 5]	2,00,000
To Trademarks & Patents w/o To Goodwill w/o	1,10,000 36,100	By Equity Share Capital [30,000 × ₹ 3]	90,000

To Bank A/c (Contingent Liability)	54,000	By Securities Premium A/c	10,000
To Bank A/c (Expenses paid)	10,000	By Bank A/c (Insurance Claim)	12,500
To Trade Receivables (1,20,000 × 10%)	12,000	By Freehold Land (Profit on Transfer) [2,10,000 – 1,20,000]	90,000
To P&L A/c (Debit Bal. w/o)	1,38,400		
	4,02,500		4,02,500

Dr. **(III) CASH ACCOUNT** *Cr.*

Particulars	₹	*Particulars*	₹
To Investments A/c	64,000	By Capital Reduction A/c (Expenses)	10,000
To Capital Reduction (Insurance Claim)	12,500	By Capital Reduction A/c (Unrecorded Liability)	54,000
To Debentures Holders A/c [2,10,000 – 1,25,400]	84,600	By Bank Overdraft A/c (Settlement) (Balancing Figure)	97,100
	1,61,100		1,61,100

Working Notes:

(i) **Shortage of Working Capital** = ₹ 2,00,000 – Existing Working Capital

= ₹ 2,00,000 – [(60,000 – 10,000) + 16,000 + 1,08,000 – (1,20,000 + 50,000)]

= ₹ 1,96,000 (to be maintained by Bank Balance)

(ii) **Additional Equity Share Capital to be issued to have desired Bank Balance of ₹ 1,96,000**

Dr. **BANK ACCOUNT** *Cr.*

Particulars	₹	*Particulars*	₹
To Cash A/c	97,100	By Balance b/d (given)	2,23,100
To Equity Share Capital (b/f)	3,22,000	By Balance c/d (Desired Balance)	1,96,000
	4,19,100		4,19,100

(III) NO. OF SHARES AFTER RECONSTRUCTION

A. No. of Equity Shares After Consolidation into Shares of ₹ 10 Each = [2,10,000/10]	21,000
B. *Add:* Issued for Arrears of Dividend	3,200
C. *Add:* Issued for Cash Consideration [3,22,000/10]	32,200
D. No. of Shares After Reconstruction	56,400

9 LIQUIDATION OF COMPANIES

LEARNING OBJECTIVES

After studying this chapter, you should be able to understand:

- ◇ Meaning of Liquidation
- ◇ Different modes of winding up
- ◇ When is the winding up deemed to commence?
- ◇ Who appoints a liquidator?
- ◇ Statement of Affairs
- ◇ Deficiency Account
- ◇ Worth noting poins while preparing the statement of affairs
- ◇ Overriding Preferential Payments [Section 529A]
- ◇ Preferential creditors [section 530]
- ◇ Liquidator's final statement of account
- ◇ Worth noting points while preparing liquidator's final statement of account
- ◇ Steps involved in adjustment of rights of contributories of different classes
- ◇ Receiver for mortgagee (e.g., debentureholders having floating charge)
- ◇ Conributories

1.0 MEANING OF LIQUIDATION

According to Prof. Gower, "liquidation *or* winding up a company is the process where by its life is ended and its property is administered for the benefit of its creditors and members.

An administrator called liquidator, is appointed and he takes control of the company, collects its assets, pays its debts and finally distributes any surplus among the members in accordance with their rights.

2.0 DIFFERENT MODES OF WINDING UP

The three different modes of winding up are as under:

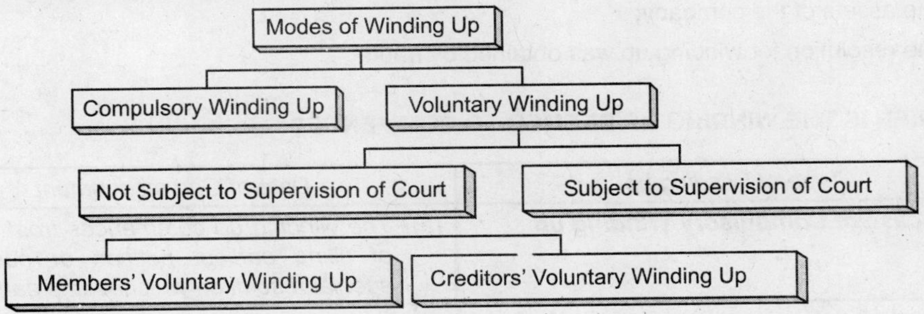

COMPULSORY WINDING UP U/S 433 TO 465

According to Section 433 of The Companies Act, the Tribunal may order for the compulsory winding up of a company in the following circumstances:

(a) if the company has by a **special resolution** resolved that it shall be wound up by the court;

(b) if default is made in delivering the statutory report to the Registrar *or* in holding the statutory meeting;

(c) if the company does **not commence** its **business within 1 year** from its incorporation *or* suspends its business for a whole year;

(d) if the number of **members** if reduced below 7 in case of a public cmpany *or* below 2 in case of a private company;

(e) if the company is **unable to pay** its debts;

(f) if the Tribunal is of opinion that it is **just and equitable** to wind up the company.

(g) if the company has made a default in filing with the registrar its Balance Sheet and Profit and Loss Account *or* annual return for any five consecutive financial years.

(h) if the company has acted against the interest of the sovereignty and integrity of India, the security of the state, friendly relations with foreign States, public order, decency *or* morality.

(i) if the tribunal is of the opinion that the company should be wound up under the circumstances specified in section 424(g).

VOLUNTARY WINDING UP U/S 484 TO 521

According to Section 484 of The Companies Act, a company may be wound up voluntarily:

(a) By passing an **ordinary resolution** in the general meeting.

  (i) When the period for the duration for which the company was formed, has expired; or

  (ii) When the event on the happening of which the termination of the existence of the Company was depended, has occured.

(b) By passing **special resolution** to wind up voluntarily.

There may be two kinds of Voluntary Winding up:

1. Members' Voluntary Winding up	1. When the directors are in position to make a Statutory Declaration of Sovency u/s 488
2. Creditors' Voluntary Winding up	2. When the directors are not in position to make a Statutory Declaration of Solvency u/s 488

VOLUNTARY WINDING UP SUBJECT TO THE SUPERVISION OF COURT U/S 522 TO 527

According to Section 522 of The Companies Act, the Court may on the application of any creditors *or* contributory *or* liquidator of the company itself, order for the winding up under its supervision under any of the following circumstances:

(a) the liquidator under voluntary winding up is prejudiced *or* is negligent in collecting the assets of the company;

(b) the resolution for winding up was obtained by fraud.

3.0 WHEN IS THE WINDING UP DEEMED TO COMMENCE?

Type of Winding up	*Date of Commencement*
(a) In case of Compulsory Winding up	*(a) The winding up commences from the date of filling earliest petition or passing of special resolution whichever is earliest.*

(b) In case of Voluntary Winding up	*(b) The winding up commences from the date of passing the resolution.*

4.0 WHO APPOINTS A LIQUIDATOR?

Type of Winding up	*Appointment of Liquidator*
(a) In case of Compulsory Winding up	(a) The Official Liquidator attached to High Court is appointed by the Central Government
(b) In case of Members' Voluntary Winding up	(b) Person(other than body corporate) is appointed by the Company in its general meeting.
(c) In case of Creditors' Voluntary Winding up	(c) Person (other than body corporate) is appointed by the Creditors in their meeting.

5.0 STATEMENT OF AFFAIRS

MEANING OF THE STATEMENT OF AFFAIRS

Statement of Affairs shows

(a) With regard to Assets:

(i) Estimated Realisable Value of Assets not specifically pledged (as per list A).

(ii) Estimated Surplus from Assets specifically pledged (as per list B)

(iii) Estimated Total Assets available for creditors and contributories.

(b) With regard to Liabilities:

(i) Secured Creditors (as per List B).

(ii) Preferential Creditors (as per List C).

(iii) Debenture holders secured by floating charge (as per List D).

(iv) Unsecured Creditors (as per List E).

(c) With regard to Share Capital:

(i) Paid up Preference Share Capital (as per List F).

(ii) Paid up Equity Share Capital (as per List G).

(d) Estimated deficiency/surplus as regards contributories (as per list H).

WHO ARE REQUIRED TO SUBMIT?

The directors, secretary, manager *or* chief officer of the Company are required to make out and submit a statement as to the affairs of the Company.

TIME LIMIT WITHIN WHICH THE STATEMENT IS REQUIRED TO BE SUBMITTED?

Such statement is required to be submitted within 21 days from the date of appointment of provisional liquidator *or* the date of winding up order as the case may be. The Official Liquidator *or* the Court may extend this time upto 3 months.

VERIFICATION AND SIGNATURE OF STATEMENT

Such statement must be duly verified by an affidavit and signed by a director and the manager, secretary *or* other Chief Officer of the Company *or* by such other person as the Official Liquidator subject to the direction of the Court, may require.

TO WHOM SUCH STATEMENT BE SUBMITTED?

Type of Winding up	*Statement is required to be submitted...*
(a) In case of Compulsory Winding up	(a) To the Official Liquidator.
(b) In case of Voluntary Winding up	(b) To the Liquidator.

PRESCRIBED FORM OF STATEMENT OF AFFAIRS

According to Rule 127 of the Companies (Court) Rules 1959, the Statement of Affairs is to be made in the Form No. 57, the specimen of which has been given below:

STATEMENT OF AFFAIRS AND LISTS TO BE ANNEXED

Statement as to affairs of .... Ltd., on the .... day of .... 20 .... being date of the winding up order (or order appointing Provisional Liquidator *or* the date directed by the Oficial Liquidator, as the case may be) showing assets estimated realisable values and liabilities expected to rank:

Assets not specifically pledged (as per list 'A')				*Estimated realisable value (₹)*
Balance at bank	...	...	...	...
Cash in hand	...	...	...	...
Marketable securities	...	...	...	...
Bills receivable	...	...	...	...
Trade Debtors	...	...	...	...
Loans and Advances	...	...	...	...
Unpaid calls ...	...	...	...	...
Stock-in-trade	...	...	...	...
Work-in-progress	...	...	...	...
....	...	...	...	...
....	...	...	...	...
Freehold property, Land and Building	...	...	...	...
Leasehold Property				...
Plant and Machinery		...	...	...
Furniture, Fittings, Utensils, etc.				...
Investments other than marketable securities Livestock	...	...	...	...
Other Property, etc.		...	...	...
....	...	...	...	...
....	...	...	...	...

Assets specifically pledged (as per list 'B')	*(a) Estimated realisable values ₹*	*(b) Due to secured creditors ₹*	*(c) Deficiency ranking as unsecured ₹*	*(d) Surplus carried to last column ₹*
Freehold property:	...	...	...	...

....				
....	...	...	...	...
Estimated surplus from assets specifically pledged				...
Estimated total assets available for preferential creditors, debenture-holders secured by a floating charge, and unsecured creditors* (carried forward)				...
Summary of gross assets				(d)
Gross realisable value of assets specifically pledged	...	...	...	₹ ....
Other Assets	...	...	...	₹ ....
Gross Assets				₹ ....
Estimated total assets available for preferential creditors, debentursholders secured by a floating charge, and unsecured creditors (brought forward)				

*All assets specifically mortgaged, pledged *or* otherwise given as security should be included under this head. In the case of goods given as security, those in possession of the company and those not in possession should be separately set out.

(e) Gross Liabilities	*Liabilities (to be deducted from surplus or added to deficiency as the case may be)*	₹
	Secured Creditors (as per list 'B') to the extent to which clams are estimated to be covered by assets specifically pledged [item (a) *or* (b) on preceeding page, whichever, is less] (insert in 'Gross Liabilities' column only)	
	Preferential creditors (as per list 'C')	...
	Estimated balance of assets available for Debenture holders secured by a floating charge and unsecued creditors*	...
	Debenture holders secured by a floating charge (as per list 'D')	...
	Estimated surplus/deficiency as regards debenture holders	...
	Unsecured creditors (as per list 'E')	...
	Estimated unsecured balance of claims of creditors partly secured on specific assets, brought from preceding pages (c)	
	Trade Account	
	Bills payable	
	Outstanding expenses	
	....	
	Contingent liabilities (state nature)	...
	....	
	Estimated surplus/deficiency as regard creditors [being difference between Gross assets brought from preceding page (d) and Gross liabilities as per column (e)]	
	Issued and Called-up capital:	

	.... Preference share of .... each ₹ .... called-up (as pr list 'F') ...	
	... Equity Shares of .... each ₹ .... called-up (as per list 'G') ...	
	Estimated surplus/deficiency as regards ₹ Members (as per list 'H') ₹	

*The figures must be read subject to the following notes:

1. (f) there is no unpaid capital liable to be called up, or
   (g) the nominal amount of unpaid capital liable to be called up is ₹ ... estimated to produce s ... which is/is not charged in favour of Debenture holders [Strike out (f) (g)].
2. The estimates are subject to cost of the winding up and to any surplus *or* deficiency on rading pending realisation of the assets.

6.0 DEFICIENCY ACCOUNT

Meaning	Deficiency Account explains how the deficiency stated in the Statement of Affairs has taken place. It is divided into two parts: (a) Items Contributing to Deficiency which start with the deficit on a given date and contains every item that increases deficiency. (b) Items reducing Deficiency which start with the surplus on a given date and contain every item that reduces deficiency.
Balance	The excess of first part over the second part is deficiency and the excess of second part over the first part is surplus. The amount of such deficiency/surplus must be the same as shown by the Statement of Affairs.
Period	Deficiency Account must be prepared for such period being not *less* than 3 years as may be directed by the Official Liquidator *(in case of Compulsory Winding Up)* *or* Liquidator *(in case of Voluntary Winding up)*.
Format	Deficiency Account is prepared in prescribed form (i.e., List H).

LIST H–DEFICIENCY *or* SURPLUS ACCOUNT

	Particulars	₹
	Items contributing to Deficiency (or reducing surplus):	
1.	Excess (if any) of capital and liabilities over assets on the ... 20 ... as shown by Balance Sheet (copy annexed)*	(...)
2.	Net dividends and bonuses declared during the period from ... 20 ... to the date of the statement.	(...)
3.	Net trading losses (after charging items shown in note below) for the same period.	(...)
4.	Losses other than trading losses written off *or* for which provision has been made in the books during the same period (given particulars *or* annex schedule).	(...)
5.	Estimated losses now written off for which provision has been made for the purposes of preparing the statement (given particulars *or* annex schedule).	(...)
6.	Other items contributing to deficiency *or* reducing surplus	(...)
	Items reducing Deficiency (or contributing to surplus):	
7.	Excess (if any) of assets over capital and liabilities on the 20 ... as shown in the Balance Sheet *(copy annexed).	...
8.	Net Trading Profit (after charging items shown in note below) for the period from the ... 20 ... to the date of statement.	...

9. Profits and income other than trading profits during the same period (give particulars *or* annex schedule).	...
10. Other items educing deficiency *or* contributing to surplus:	
Deficiency/Surplus (as shown by the statement of affairs)	...
*Only one item will appear.	

Note as to Net Trading Profits an Losses:

Particulars are to be inserted here (so far as applicable) of the items mentioned below, which are to be taken into account in arriving at the amount of net trading pofits *or* losses shown in this account:

1. Provisions for depreciation, renewals *or* diminution in value of fixed assets.	
2. Charges for Indian income-tax and other Indian taxation on profits.	
3. Interest on debentures and other fixed loans,	
4. Payments to directors made by the company and required by law to be disclosed in the accounts.	
5. Exceptional *or* non-recurring expenditure:	
....	
6. *Less:* Exceptional *or* non-recurring receipts:	...
....	
7. Balance, being other than trading profit *or* loss.	
8. Net trading profit *or* loss as shown in Deficiency *or* Surplus a/c above	...
Signature:	Dated... 20 ...

7.0 WORTH NOTING POINS WHILE PREPARING THE STATEMENT OF AFFAIRS

Name of the List	*Contents*	*Remarks*
1. List A	Assets not specifically pledged (i.e., Assets not having fixed charge)	(a) Include assets at value expected to realise (b) Include calls in arrears expected to realise (c) Do not include Uncalled Capital
2. List B	Assets Specifically pledged (i.e., Assets having fixed charge)	(a) Surplus from such assets to be included in the Statement. (b) Deficiency to be added to Unsecured Creditors in List E.
3. List C	Preferencial Creditors	(a) Include Over-riding Preferential Payments as per Section 529 A (b) Include Preferential payments as per Section 530 (c) Include Contingent Liability in respect of Preferential Payments which is expected to be paid
4. List D	Debenture holders Secured by a floating charge	Unless otherwise stated, the debentures should be assumed to have a floating charge.
5. List E	Unsecured Creditors	(a) Include Bills Payables unless secured otherwise (b) Include Contingent liability which is expected to be paid e.g. in respect of Bills Discounted

6. List F	Preference Share holders	(c) Include Unclaimed dividends
7. List G	Equity Share holders	Class-wise paid up Capital
8. List H	Reasons for the Surplus/ deficiency as shown by the Statement of Affairs	Class-wise paid up Capital

PREPARATION OF STATEMENT OF AFFAIRS

ILLUSTRATION 1

Shri Chopra is appointed liquidator of CAMGE Limited, in voluntary liquidation, on 1st July 2013. Following balances are extracted from the books on that date:

Particulars	₹
24,000 shares of ₹ 5 each	1,20,000
Provision for Doubtful Debts	15,000
Debentures	75,000
Bank Overdraft	27,000
Liabilities for purchases	30,000
Machinery	45,000
Leasehold properties	60,000
Stock-in-Trade	1,500
Book Debts	90,000
Investments	9,000
Calls-in-Arrear	7,500
Cash in hand	1,500
Profit and Loss Account	52,500

You are required to prepare a Statement of Affairs to be submitted to the meeting of the creditors. The following assets are valued as under;

Machinery ₹ 90,000, Leasehold Properties ₹ 1,09,000, Investments ₹ 6,000, Stock-in-trade ₹ 3,000.

Bad Debts are ₹ 3,000 and the doubtful debts are ₹ 6,000 which are estimated to realise ₹ 3,000. The bank overdraft is secured by deposit of title deeds of leasehold properties. Preferential creditors are ₹ 1,500. Telephone rent outstanding is ₹ 120.

SOLUTION

STATEMENT OF AFFAIRS OF CAMGE LTD.
as on 1st July, 2013

Assets not specifically pledged as per list A:	*Estimated Realisable Value* ₹
Cash in hand	1,500
Marketable Securities	6,000
Calls in arrear	7,500
Trade Debtors	84,000

Stock in trade		3,000
Machinery		90,000
		1,92,000

Assets specifically pledged as per list B:

Particulars	*Estimated Realisable Value* ₹	*Due to secured creditors* ₹	*Deficiency ranking as unsecured* ₹	*Surplus carried to last column* ₹
Leasehold Properties	1,09,000	27,000	—	82,000

Estimated surplus from assets specifically pledged		82,000
Estimated total assets available for preferential creditors, debentureholders having a floating charge & unsecured creditors c/fd.		2,74,000
Summary of Gross Assets:	₹	
Gross receivable value of assets specifically pledged	1,09,000	
Other assets	1,92,000	
	3,01,000	
Estimated total assets available for preferential creditors, debenture-holders having a floating charge and unsecured creditors, brought forward		2,74,000

Gross Liabilities ₹	*Liabilities*		
27,000	Secured creditors as per list B to the extent to which claims are estimated to be covered by assets specifically pledged.		
1,500	Preferential Creditors as per list C		1,500
	Estimated balance of assets available for debentureholders secured by a floating charge and unsecured creditors*	2,72,500	
75,000	Debentureholders secured by a floating charge as per list D		75,000
	Estimated surplus as regards debentureholders		1,97,500
30,120	Unsecured Creditors (as per list E)		
	Liability for purchases	30,000	
	Outstanding Expenses—telephone rent	120	30,120
1,33,620			
	Estimated surplus as regards creditors being the difference between Gross Assets & Gross Liabilities		1,67,380
	Issued & Called up Capital:		
	24,000 Equity Shares of ₹ 5 each, fully paid as list G		1,20,000
	Surplus as regards contributories		47,380

*These figures must be read subject to the following notes:

(1) There is no unpaid capital liable to be called up.

(2) The estimates are subject to costs of the winding-up and to any surplus *or* deficiency on trading pending realisation of the assets.

ILLUSTRATION 2

CAMHG Ltd. is to be liquidated. Their summarised Balances Sheet as at 30th September, 2013 appears as under:

Particulars	₹
2,50,000 equity shares of ₹.10 each	25,00,000
Secured debentures (on land and buildings)	10,00,000
Unsecured loans	20,00,000
Trade creditors	35,00,000
Land and Buildings	5,00,000
Other fixed assets	20,00,000
Current assets	45,00,000
Profit and Loss A/c	20,00,000

Contingent liabilities are:

For Bills discounted	1,00,000
For excise duty demands	1,50,000

On investigation, it is found that the contingent liabilities are certain to devolve and that the assets are likely to be realised as follows:

Particulars	₹
Land and Buildings	11,00,000
Other fixed assets	18,00,000
Current assets	35,00,000

Required: Taking the above into account, prepare the Statement of Affairs.

SOLUTION

STATEMENT OF AFFAIRS OF CAMHG LTD.

as at 30th Sept., 2013

Assets not specifically pledged as per list A:	*Estimated Realisable Value* ₹
Other fixed assets	18,00,000
Current assets	35,00,000
	53,00,000

Assets specifically pledged as per list B:

Particulars	*Estimated Realisable Value* ₹	*Due to secured creditors* ₹	*Deficiency ranking as unsecured* ₹	*Surplus carried to last column* ₹	
Land & Buildings	11,00,000	10,00,000	—	1,00,000	1,00,000

Estimated Total Assets available to unsecured creditors		54,00,000
Summary of Gross Assets	₹	
Gross realisable value of assets specifically pledged	11,00,000	

Other Assets	53,00,000	
Gross Assets	64,00,000	

Gross Liabilities ₹	*Liabilities*	₹
10,00,000	Secured Creditors (as per list B) to the extent to which claims are estimated to be covered by assets specifically pledged	—
1,50,000	Preferential creditors (as per list C)	1,50,000
		52,50,000
	Unsecured Creditors (as per list E)	
20,00,000	Unsecured Loans	20,00,000
35,00,000	Trade Creditors	35,00,000
1,00,000	Contingent Liability on Bills Discounted	1,00,000
67,50,000	Estimated deficiency as regards creditors (67,50,000 – 64,00,000).	3,50,000
	2,50,000 Equity shares of ₹ 10 each: as per (list G)	25,00,000
	Estimated deficiency as regards members	28,50,000

ILLUSTRATION 3

CAMIA Ltd. went into voluntary liquidation on 1st March, 2013. The following balances are extracted from its books on that date:

Particulars		₹
50,000 equity shares of ₹ 10 each		5,00,000
Debentures (secured by a floating charge)		2,00,000
Bank overdraft		30,000
Creditors		40,000
Buildings		1,50,000
Plant and Machinery		2,10,000
Stock in Trade		95,000
Book Debts	75,000	
Less: Provision	10,000	65,000
Calls in arrears		1,00,000
Cash on hand		10,000
Profit and Loss account		1,40,000

Plant and Machinery and Buildings are valued at ₹ 1,50,000 and ₹ 1,20,000 respectively; On realisation, losses of ₹ 15,000 are expected on Stock. Book Debts will realise ₹ 70,000. Calls in arrears are expected to realise 90%. Bank Overdraft is secured against Buildings. Preferential Creditors for taxes and wages are ₹ 6,000 and Miscellaneous Expenses outstanding ₹ 2,000.

Required: Prepare a Statement of Affairs to be submitted to the meeting of creditors.

SOLUTION

STATEMENT OF AFFAIRS OF CAMIA LTD. AS AT 1ST MARCH, 2013

Assets not specifically pledged as per list A:	*Estimated Realisable Value* ₹
Cash on hand	10,000
Book Debts	70,000
Unpaid calls (Calls in arrear)	90,000
Stock in trade	80,000
Plant & Machinery	1,50,000
	4,00,000

Assets specifically pledged as per list B:

Particulars	*Estimated Realisable Value* ₹	*Due to secured creditors* ₹	*Deficiency ranking as unsecured* ₹	*Surplus carried to last column* ₹
Buildings	1,20,000	30,000	—	90,000

Estimated surplus from assets specifically pledged		90,000
Estimated total assets available for preferential creditors, Debentureholders and unsecured creditors		4,90,000
Summary of Gross Assets		
Gross realisable value of assets specifically pledged:	1,20,000	
Other assets	4,00,000	
	5,20,000	

Gross Liabilities ₹	*Liabilities*	₹
	(To be deducted from surplus *or* added to deficiency as the case may be)	
30,000	Secured creditors (as per list B) to the extent to which claims are estimated to be covered by assets specifically pledged	—
	Preference creditors (List C)	
6,000	Creditors for taxes and wages	6,000
	Estimated balance of assets available for debentureholders and unsecured creditors	4,84,000
2,00,000	Debentureholders secured by first floating charge (list D)	2,00,000
	Estimated surplus as regards debenture holders	2,84,000
34,000	Unsecured creditors (List E)	34,000
2,70,000	Estimated surplus as regards = creditors	2,50,000
	Issued and paid up capital:	
	Preference shares (List F)	NIL

	50,000 Equity Shares of ₹ 10 each fully paid (List G) [₹ 5,00,000 – ₹ 10,000]	4,90,000
	Estimated deficiency as regards contributories	2,40,000

8.0 OVERRIDING PREFERENTIAL PAYMENTS [SECTION 326]

Acoding to Section 326 following are the over-riding preferential payments

(a) Workmen's dues;

(b) So much of the debts due to the secured creditors as could not be realised by him because of pari-passu charge in favour of workmen, over the security held by him.

All such debts must be paid in full unless the assets are insufficient, in which case they shall abate in equal proportion.

As per Sec 325(3)(b) workmen's dues, in relation to a company, mean the aggregate of the following sums:

(a) **all wages or salary** including wages payable for time *or* piece work and salary earned wholly *or* in part by way of commission of any workman and any compensation payable to any workman under any of the provisions of the Industrial Disputes Act, 1947;

(b) **all accrued holiday remuneration** becoming payable to any workman *or* in the case of his death to any other person in his right, on the termination of his employment before, *or* by the effect of, the winding up order;

(c) all amounts due in respect of **any compensation** or liability for compensation under Workmen's Compensation Act, 1923, in respect of death *or* disablement of any workman of the company;

(d) all sums due to any workman from a **provident fund, a pension fund, a gratuity fund** or any other fund for the welfare of the workmen maintained by the company.

As per Sec 325(3)(a) "workmen" in relation to a company, means the employees of the Company, being workmen within the meaning of the Industrial Dispute Act, 1947.

ILLUSTRATION 4 [CALCULATION OF OVERRIDING PREFERENTIAL PAYMENTS 326A]

From the following, Calculate Over-riding Preferential Payments u/s 326A

Secured Creditors (on Land and Building)	₹ 4,00,000
Land and Building realised	₹ 3,00,000
Wages and Salary of a workmen for the last 5 months @ ₹ 2,000 p.m.	
Accrued Holiday Remuneration of workmen	₹ 2,000
Compensation due to workmen under the Workmen Compensation Act, 1923	₹ 8,000
Provident Fund, Pension Fund and Gratuity Fund due to workmen	₹ 80,000

(i) Total Workmen Due = (5 × ₹ 2,000) + ₹ 2,000 + ₹ 8,000 + ₹ 80,000 = ₹ 1,00,000

(ii) Share of Secured Creditors and Workmen's Due in the value of security realised:

A. Share of Secured Creditors (₹ 3,00,000 × 4/5)	₹ 2,40,000
B. Share of Workmen's dues (₹ 3,00,000 × 1/5)	₹ 60,000
	₹ 3,00,000
(iii) Over-riding Preferential Payments	
A. Secured Creditors to the extent of their security being used for workmen dues	₹ 60,000
B. Balance of Workmen's Dues (₹ 1,00,000 – ₹ 60,000)	₹ 40,000
	₹ 1,00,000

9.0 PREFERENTIAL CREDITORS [SECTION 327]

Section 327 provides that subject to the provisions of Section 326, following preferential creditors shall be paid in priority to unsecured creditors *or* creditor having a floating charge:

(a) All revenues, taxes, cesses and rates, becoming due and payable by the company **within 12 months** next before the commencement of the winding up.

(b) All wages *or* salaries (including wages payable for time *or* piece work and salary earned wholly *or* in part by way of commission) of any employee due for the period not **exceeding 4 months within 12 months** next before commencement of winding up provided the amount payable to one claimant will not exceed such amount as may be notified.

(c) All accrued **holiday remuneration** becoming payable to any employee on termination of employment before winding up order *or* dissolution of the company.

(d) Unless the company is being wound up voluntarily for the purpose of reconstruction, all contributions payable during the 12 months next under the Employees' State Insurance Act, 1948, *or* any other law for the time being in force.

(e) All sums due as **compensation** to employees under the Workmen's Compensation Act, 1923.

(f) All sums due to any employee from a **provident fund, pension fund, gratuity fund** or any other fund, for the welfare of the employees maintained by the company.

(g) The expenses of any investigation held under Section 213 *or* 216 in so far as they are payable by the company.

All the preferential debts rank equally among themselves and are to be paid in full unless the assets are insufficient, in which case they will abate in equal proportion.

After retaining sufficient sum for costs, charges and expenses of winding up, preferential debts must be paid forthwith so far as assets are sufficient to meet them.

ILLUSTRATION 5 [CALCULATION OF PREFERENTIAL PAYMENTS U/S 327]

From the following, Calculate Preferential Payments u/s 327 in case of X Ltd. which went into liquidation on 1.4.2014.

1. Owing to Government for Tax due and payable

   For the year 2012 - 2013 ₹ 22,000

   For the year 2013 - 2014 ₹ 21,000
2. Owing to Government for Telephone, Electricity and Water (₹ 20,000) due and payable on 31st March, 2014.
3. Wages and Salaries of a supervisor 'X' for 5 months @ ₹ 4,000 per month.
4. Wages and Salaries of a supervisor 'Y' for 4 months @ ₹ 6,000 per month.
5. Accrued Holiday Remuneration payable to a supervisor 'Z' ₹ 21,000.
6. Compensation due to a supervisor 'W' ₹ 21,000 under the Workmen Compensation Act, 1923.
7. Provident Fund, Pension fund and Gratuity Fund due to a supervisor 'P' ₹ 21,000.
8. Directors fees ₹ 21,000
9. Rent for Godown ₹ 21,000

SOLUTION

Particulars	₹
1. Owing to Govt. for Tax due and payable within 12 months	21,000
2. Wages and Salaries of 'X' for 4 months (4000 × 4)	16,000

3. Wages and Salaries of 'Y' for 4 months	24,000
4. Accrued Holiday Remuneration	21,000
5. Compensation due to 'W'	21,000
6. Provident fund etc., due to 'P'	21,000
Total Preferential Payments u/s 327	1,20,000

Note: Directors fees & Rent for Godown are not included in preferential creditors.

ILLUSTRATION 6

A company went into liquidation whose creditors are ₹ 36,000 includes ₹ 6,000 on account of wages of 15 men at ₹ 100 per month for 4 months immediately before the date of winding up; ₹ 9,000 being the salaries of 5 employees at ₹ 300 per month for the previous 6 months, Rent for godown for the last six months amounting to ₹ 3,000; Income-tax deducted out of salaries of employees ₹ 1,000 and Directors fees ₹ 500. In addition it is estimated that the company would have to pay ₹ 5,000 as compensation to an employee for injuries suffered by him, which was contingent liability not accepted by the company and not included in above said creditors figure.

Find the amount of Preferential Creditors.

SOLUTION

CALCULATION OF PREFERENTIAL CREDITORS

Particulars	₹
Tax deducted at source on salaries (Since payable within 12 months)	1,000
Wages (15 men for 4 months at ₹ 100 each)	6,000
Salaries (5 men for 4 months at ₹ 300 each)	6,000
Workmen's compensation	5,000
Total	18,000

Note:

(i) Salaries payable to any employee due for the period not exceeding 4 months within the twelve months next before commencement of winding up.

(ii) Directors fees, rent for godown are not included in preferential creditors.

10.0 LIQUIDATOR'S FINAL STATEMENT OF ACCOUNT

MEANING OF LIQUIDATOR'S FINAL STATEMENT OF ACCOUNT

Liquidator's Final Statement of Account is basically a summary of Cash Book for the period begining with the date of commencement of winding up and ending with the date of completion of winding up. This statement shows the various sources from where he obtained the funds and the various uses to which he applied those funds.

WHO IS TO PREPARE SUCH STATEMENT?

(a) In case of Compulsory Winding up	Official Liquidator has to prepare.
(b) In case of Voluntary Winding up	Liquidator has to prepare.

TO WHOM SUCH STATEMENT HAS TO BE SUBMITTED

(a) In case of Compulsory Winding up	To the Court
(b) In case of Voluntary Winding up	To the Company

WHO FIXES THE REMUNERATION OF LIQUIDATOR?

(a) In case of Compulsory Winding up	Remuneration is fixed by the Court and the amount is payable to the Court since the Official Liquidator is a salaried employee of the government
(b) In case of Members' Voluntary Winding up	Members in their meeting
(c) In case of Creditors' Voluntary Winding up	Creditors in their meeting

PRESCRIBED FORM OF LIQUIDATOR'S STATEMENT OF ACCOUNT

LIQUIDATOR'S STATEMENT OF ACCOUNT OF THE WINDING UP (MEMBERS/CREDITORS' VOLUNTARY WINDING UP) (PURSUANT TO SECTION 497/509)

1. Name of the company .... Ltd.
2. Nature of Proceeding*
3. Date of commencement of the winding up
4. Name and address of the Liquidator.

Receipts	*Estimated Value* ₹ *P*	*Value Realised* ₹ *P*	*Payments*	*Payment* ₹ *P*
Assets:			Legal charges	...
Cash at Bank	...		Liquidator's remuneration where applicable	...
Cash in Hand	...		% on ₹ ... realised ...	
Marketable securities	...		% on ₹ ... distributed ...	
Bills receivable	...		Total	...
Trade Debtos	...		(By whom fixed...)	
Loans and Advances	...		Auctioneers' and valuers' charges ...	
Stock-in-trade	...		Costs of possession and maintenance of estate ...	
Work-in-progress	...		Gazette and newspapers	
Freehold Property	...		Incidental outlay (establishment charges and other expenses of liquidiation) ...	
Leasehold Property	...		Total costs and charges	...
Plant and Machinery	...			
Furniture Fittings, Utensils, etc.	...			
Patens, trade marks etc	....			
Investments other than marketable securities	...			

Surplus from securities	...		(i) Debenture holders:	...
Unpaid calls at commencement of winding up			Payment of ₹ ... per ₹ ... debenture	
Amout received from calls on			(ii) Creditors: ... *Preferential	...
contributories made in the			... *Unsecured:	...
winding up			Dividend(s), ... P, in the	
Receipts per Trading A/c	...		rupees on ₹ ...	
Other property, viz.,			(The estimate of the	
....			amount expected to rank	
....	...		for dividend was ₹..)	
Total	...		(iii) Returns to conributories:	
Less:			... P. per rupee...	
Payment to redeem	...		**share...	...
Securities	...		... P. per rupee...	
Cost of execution	...		**share...	...
Payments per	...		P. per rupee...	...
Trading A/c			**share...	
Net realisations	...			
	...	...		...

*State the number. Preferential creditors need not be separately shown if all creditors have been paid in full.

**State nominal value and class of share.

11.0 WORTH NOTING POINTS WHILE PREPARING LIQUIDATOR'S FINAL STATEMENT OF ACCOUNT

1. (a) Though debenture holders have been shown before preferential creditors in the prescribed form of the Liquidator's Statement of Account, **Preferential Creditors** subject to Section 326 are paid in priority to debenture holders having a floating charge on the assets of the Company.

   (b) **Unsatisfied portion of the secured creditors** to the extent which could not be paid because of their security being used for workmen dues, is to be treated as overriding preferential payment u/s 326 and the remaining portion is to be treated as unsecured.

   (c) **Dividends** (both Equity and Preference) declared but not paid are to be paid as unsecured debt in priority to any repayment of share capial.

[Refer to Illustation 7,8,9]

2. **Debenture Interest**

(a) In case the Company is Solvent	Interest on Debentures is to be paid upto the date of payment
(b) In other cases	Interest on Debentures is to be paid upto the date of winding up

Note: A company is said to be solvent when it has sufficient amount to pay off the principal and interest on all debts upto the commencement of winding up.

[Refer to Illustation 10].

3. **If Liquidator's Commission is based on realisation of assets,** unless otherwise stated, Liquidator is —
   (a) not entitled to a commission on Cash-in-hand;
   (b) entitled to commission only on the amount of surplus realised from assets specifically pledged *or* mortgaged.
   (c) entitled to commission on full value realised from sale of assets specifically hypothecated.

[Refer to Illustration 10, 11, 12]

4. **If Liquidator's Commission is based on payment made to unsecured creditors**
   (a) Unless specifically excluded for this purpose, the unsecured creditors include preferential creditors.
   (b) Such Commission may be calculated as follows:

(a) In case of sufficient amount	Amount of such creditors × Rate of commission
(b) In case of insufficient amount	Amount available × $\frac{\text{Rate of Commission}}{100 + \text{Rate of Commission}} \times 100$

[Refer to Illustration 10, 11, 12]

5. **Liquidator's commission based on payment made to Equity shareholders** is calculated as follows:

(a) In case of insufficient amount	Amount available × $\frac{\text{Rate of Commission}}{100 + \text{Rate of Commission}} \times 100$
(b) In case of sufficient amount	(Equity Share Capital × Rate of commission) + [Surplus towards Equity Share holders and commission thereon × $\frac{\text{Rate of Commission}}{100 + \text{Rate of Commission}} \times 100$]

[Refer to Illustation 10].

6. **Arrears of Dividends on Cummulative Preference shares** for the period upto the date of Commencement of winding up

(i) If the Articles provides for the payment of arrears of dividend in priority to the equity share holders in the event of winding up.	Arrears are payable after the settlement of all claims of outsiders but before anything is paid to the equity share holders. Thus, if need be and possible, call, should be made on the equity share holders to pay dividend on cummulative preference shares.
(ii) In other cases	Arrears are payable after the repayment of Equity Share Capital.

[Refer to Illustration 13]

7. **Call from Contributories**

While calling upon the Contributories to pay, the following two points should be kept in mind:

(a) First the equity shareholders should be called upon to contribute **(not exceeding the amount of Uncalled Capital),** then the preference shareholders should be called upon to contribute (not exceeding the amount of Uncalled Capital).

(b) Among the shareholders (whether Equity *or* Preference), first those who have paid *less* as compared to others, should be called upon to conribute.

[Refer to Illustration 14,15,16,17].

8. **Distribution of Cash among Equity Share Holders**

While distributing the Cash among equity shareholders the following points should be kept in mind:

(a) In case of deficiency, the available cash should be distributed among the share holders in such a way that the loss suffered by each class of shareholders is proportionate to the nominal value of the shares held by respective class.

(b) In case of surplus, the available cash should be distributed among the shareholders in such a way that the surplus gained by each class of shareholder is propotionate to the nominal value of the shares held by respective class.

(c) Among the shareholders, first those who have paid more as compared to others, should be paid.

(d) Calls-in advance—The Calls in-advance received by the company will be paid in priority to any payment to the shareholders of that class. *[Refer to Illustrations 14, 15, 16, 17].*

9. Participating Preference Shareholders are entitled to participate in the surplus assets remaining after the repayment of Equity Share Capital.

ILLUSTRATION 7

Arrange the following in priority order for payment in case of a liquidating Company:

(a) Preference share holders.

(b) Arrears of Preference Dividend for which Articles are silent.

(c) Equity shareholders in accordance with their rights.

(d) Over-riding Preferential Payments u/s 326.

(e) Costs and Charges of Winding up (including the liquidator's remuneration).

(f) Preferential Payments u/s 327.

(g) Creditors Secured by floating Charges.

(h) Unsecured Creditors.

SOLUTION (e), (d), (f), (g), (h), (a), (c), (b).

ILLUSTRATION 8

The position of Bad Luck Ltd. on its liquidation is as under:

Particulars	₹
Secured Creditors (on Land and Building)	4,00,000
Workmen's dues	1,00,000
Land and Building realised	3,00,000
Salaries of an employee for services rendered for 6 months	27,000
Debentures having a floating charge on all assets	50,000
Owing to Government for Taxes for previous year	20,000
Owing to Government for Telephone, Electricity and Water	25,000
Dividend declared but not yet paid	5,000
Book Value of Other Assets	4,00,000
Costs of winding up	10,000

Required: Prepare the Liquidator's Final Statement of Account if Other Assets realised 40%.

SOLUTION

LIQUIDATOR'S FINAL STATEMENT OF ACCOUNT

Receipts	₹	*Payments*		₹
Other Assets	1,60,000	Costs of Winding up		10,000
[40% of ₹ 4,00,000]		Overriding Preferential Creditors:		
		Secured Creditors	60,000	
		Workmen's Dues	40,000	1,00,000
		Other Preferential Creditors:		
		Owing to Govt. for Taxes	20,000	
		Salaries [₹ 27,000 × 4/6]	18,000	38,000
		Debenture having Floating Charge		12,000
	1,60,000			1,60,000

Working Notes:

(i) Share of Secured Creditors and Workmen's dues in the value of security realised:

A. Share of Secured Creditors (₹ 3,00,000 × 4/5) = ₹ 2,40,000

B. Share of Workmen's Dues (₹ 3,00,000 × 1/5) = ₹ 60,000

(II) TOTAL OVER-RIDING PREFERENTIAL PAYMENTS

	Particulars	₹
A.	Secured Creditors to the extent of their security being used for workmen' dues	60,000
B.	Balance of Workmen's Dues (₹ 1,00,000 – ₹ 60,000)	40,000
	Total	1,00,000

(iii) *Preferential Creditors have priority over Debentures having floating charge.*

ILLUSTRATION 9 [PRIORITY ORDER OF PAYMENT OF CREDITORS]

The position of Bad Luck Ltd. on its liquidation is as under:

Particulars	₹
Secured Creditors (on Land and Building)	4,00,000
Workmen's dues	1,00,000
Land and Building realised	3,00,000
Debentures having a floating charge on all assets	50,000
Owing to Government for Taxes	25,000
Owing to Government for Telephone, Electricity and Water	20,000
Dividend declared but not yet paid	5,000
Book Value of other Assets	4,00,000

Required: Prepare the Liquidator's Final Statement of Account if other assets realised (a) 20%, (b) 30%, (c) 40% and (d) 50%.

SOLUTION

(a) If other assets realised 20%

LIQUIDATOR'S FINAL STATEMENT OF ACCOUNT

Receipts	₹	*Payments*		₹
Other Assets	80,000	Overriding Preferential Creditors:		
		Secured Creditors	48,000	
		Workmen's Dues	32,000	80,000
	80,000			80,000

Working Notes:

(i) Share of Secured Creditors and Workmen's dues in the value of security realised:

A. Share of Secured Creditors (₹ 3,00,000 × 4/5) = ₹ 2,40,000

B. Share of Workmen's Dues (₹ 3,00,000 × 1/5) = ₹ 60,000

(II) TOTAL OVER-RIDING PREFERENTIAL PAYMENTS

	Particulars	₹
A.	Secured Creditors to the extent of their security being used for workmen' dues	60,000
B.	Balance of Workmen's Dues (₹ 1,00,000 – ₹ 60,000)	40,000
	Total	1,00,000

(b) If other assets realised 30%

LIQUIDATOR'S FINAL STATEMENT OF ACCOUNT

Receipts	₹	*Payments*		₹
Other Assets	1,20,000	Overriding Preferential Creditors:		
		Securied Creditors	60,000	
		Workmen's Dues	40,000	
		Other Preferential Creditors:		
		Owing to Govt. for Taxes	20,000	1,20,000
	1,20,000			1,20,000

Working Notes:

(i) Share of Secured Creditors and Workmen's dues in the value of security realised:

A. Share of Secured Creditors (₹ 3,00,000 × 4/5) = ₹ 2,40,000

B. Share of Workmen's Dues (₹ 3,00,000 × 1/5) = ₹ 60,000

(II) TOTAL OVER-RIDING PREFERENTIAL PAYMENTS

	Particulars	₹
A.	Secured Creditors to the extent of their security being used for workmen' dues	60,000
B.	Balance of Workmen's Dues (₹ 1,00,000 – ₹ 60,000)	40,000
	Total	1,00,000

(c) If other assets realised 40%

LIQUIDATOR'S FINAL STATEMENT OF ACCOUNT

Receipts	₹	*Payments*		₹
Other Assets	1,60,000	Debenture holders having a floating charges		35,000
		Overriding Preferential Creditors:		
		Secured Creditors	60,000	
		Workmen's Dues	40,000	
		Other Preferential Creditors:		
		Owing to Govt. for Taxes	25,000	1,25,000
	1,60,000			1,60,000

Working Notes:

(i) Share of Secured Creditors andWorkmen's dues in the value of security realised:

A. Share of Secured Creditors (₹ 3,00,000 × 4/5) = ₹ 2,40,000

B. Share of Workmen's Dues (₹ 3,00,000 × 1/5) = ₹ 60,000

(II) TOTAL OVER-RIDING PREFERENTIAL PAYMENTS

	Particulars	₹
A.	Secured Creditors to the extent of their security being used for workmen' dues	60,000
B.	Balance of Workmen's Dues (₹ 1,00,000 – ₹ 60,000)	40,000
	Total	1,00,000

(d) If other assets realised 50%

LIQUIDATOR'S FINAL STATEMENT OF ACCOUNT

Receipts	₹	*Payments*		₹
Other Assets	2,00,000	Debenture holders having a floating charge.		50,000
		Overriding Preferential Creditors:		
		Secured Creditors	60,000	
		Workmen's Dues	40,000	
		Other Preferential Creditors:		
		Owing to Govt. for Taxes	25,000	1,25,000
		Unsecured Creditors:		
		(Unsatisfied Portion of Secured Creditors)	20,000	
		Owing to Govt. for Telephone etc.	4,000	
		Dividend	1,000	25,000
	2,00,000			2,00,000

Working Notes:

(i) Share of Secured Creditors andWorkmen's dues in the value of security realised:

A. Share of Secured Creditors (₹ 3,00,000 × 4/5) = ₹ 2,40,000

B. Share of Workmen's Dues (₹ 3,00,000 × 1/5) = ₹ 60,000

(II) OVER-RIDING PREFERENTIAL PAYMENTS

Particulars	₹
A. Secured Creditors to the extent of their security being used for workmen' dues	60,000
B. Balance of Workmen's Dues (₹ 1,00,000 – ₹ 60,000)	40,000
Total	1,00,000

ILLUSTRATION 10 [CALCULATION OF LIQUIDATOR'S COMMISSION]

X Ltd. went into liquidation on 31st March, 2013, when their Balance Sheet was as follows:

(Figure being in lakhs of ₹)

Particulars	₹
2,500 Equity Shares of ₹ 100	2.50
5% Debentures (having floating charges on all assets)	2.00
Interest Outstanding on Debentures	0.25
Loan from ICICI (Secured by mortgage of Land and Buidling)	2.00
Loan from IDBI Bank (Secured by Hypothecation of Stock)	2.00
Owing to Govt. for:	
Taxes	0.75
Telephone, Electicity and Water	0.50
Land and Building	2.00
Pland and Machinery	2.00
Stock	2.00
Cash-in-hand	0.10
Cash at Bank	0.90
Other Current Assets	3.00

Other Informtion:

1. Expenses of Liquidation ₹ 30,000.
2. Legal Charges ₹ 2,000.
3. Liquidator is entitled to a commission of 3% on assets realised except Cash and Bank and 2% on the amount distributed to unsecured creditors (other than preferential creditors).
4. All payments were made on 30th September, 2013.
5. The realised amounts of assets were: Land and Building 150%, Plant and Machinery 50%, Stock 50%.

Note: Commission may be rounded off in the multiple of ₹ 100.

Required: Prepare Liquidator's Final Statement of Account if other current assets realised. (a) 33 - 1/3%, (b) 66 - 2/3%, (c) ₹ 3,50,000.

SOLUTION

(a) If other assets realised 33 - 1/3%

LIQUIDATOR'S FINAL STATEMENT OF ACCOUNT

Receipts	₹	*Payments*		₹
Assets realised:		Legal Charges		2,000
—Cash-in-hand	10,000	Liquidator's Remuneration		13,100
—Cash-at-bank	90,000	Expenses of Liquidation		30,000
—Other Current Assets	1,00,000	Debentures		
—Plant and Machinery	1,00,000	—Principal	2,00,000	
Surplus from Securities	1,00,000	—Interest	25,000	2,25,000
[₹ 3,00,000 – ₹ 2,00,000]		**Unsecured Creditors:**		
		—Preferential Crs.	75,000	
		—Partly Satisfied Creditors	36,600	
		—Other Creditors	18,300	1,29,900
	4,00,000			4,00,000

Working Notes:

(i) *Calculation of Liquidator's Remuneration*

Assets realised = Surplus + Stock + Plant and Machinery + Other Current Assets

= ₹ 1,00,000 + ₹ 1,00,000 + ₹ 1,00,000 + ₹ 1,00,000 = ₹ 4,00,000.

A.	Commission @3% on ₹ 4,00,000	₹ 12,000
B.	Commission @2% on Payment to Unsecured Creditors [Cash available for unsecured creditors other than Preferential Creditors × 2/102] i.e. (₹ 56,000 × 2/102)	₹ 1,098
C.	Total Commission [A + B]	₹ 13,098
	Total Commission rounded off to	₹ 13,100

(ii) *Since the company is insolvent interest on Debentures has been paid upto the date of commencement of winding up i.e., 31st March, 2013.*

(b) If other assets realised

LIQUIDATOR'S FINAL STATEMENT OF ACCOUNT

Receipts	₹	*Payments*		₹
Assets realised:		Legal Charges		2,000
—Cash-in-hand	10,000	Liquidator's Remuneration		18,000
—Cash-at-bank	90,000	Expenses of Liquidation		30,000
—Other Current Assets	2,00,000	Debentures		
—Plant and Machinery	1,00,000	—Principal	2,00,000	
Surplus from Securities	1,00,000	—Interest	25,000	2,25,000
[₹ 3,00,000 – ₹ 2,00,000]		**Unsecured Creditors:**		
		—Preferential Crs.	75,000	
		—Partly Satisfied Creditors	1,00,000	
		—Other Creditors	50,000	2,25,000
	5,00,000			5,00,000

Working Notes:

(i) *Calculation of Liquidator's Remuneration*

Assets realised = Surplus + Stock + Plant and Machinery + Other Current Assets

= ₹ 1,00,000 + ₹ 1,00,000 + ₹ 1,00,000 + ₹ 2,00,000 = ₹ 5,00,000.

A. Commission @3% on ₹ 5,00,000	₹ 15,000
B. Commission on Payment to Unsecured Creditors [₹ 1,53,000 × 2/102]	₹ 3,000
C. Total Commission [A + B]	₹ 18,000

(ii) *Since the company is insolvent interest on Debentures has been paid upto the date of commencement of winding up i.e., 31st March, 2013.*

(c) If other Assets realised ₹ 3,50,000

LIQUIDATOR'S FINAL STATEMENT OF ACCOUNT

Receipts	₹	*Payments*		₹
Assets realised:		Legal Charges		2,000
—Cash-in-hand	10,000	Liquidator's Remuneration		22,500
—Cash-at-bank	90,000	Expenses of Liquidation		30,000
—Other Current Assets	3,50,000	Debentures		
—Plant and Machinery	1,00,000	—Principal	2,00,000	
Surplus from Securities	1,00,000	–Interest [₹ 25,000 + ₹ 5,000]	30,000	2,30,000
[₹ 3,00,000 – ₹ 2,00,000]		Unsecured Creditors:		
		—Preferential Crs.	75,000	
		—Partly Satisfied Creditors	1,00,000	
		—Other Creditors	50,000	2,25,000
		Return to contributories:		
		₹ 56.20 on 2,500 Equity Shares of ₹ 100 each		1,40,500
	6,50,000			6,50,000

Working Notes:

(i) *Calculation of Liquidator's Remuneration*

Assets realised = Surplus + Stock + Plant and Machinery + Other Curent Assets

= ₹ 1,00,000 + ₹ 1,00,000 + ₹ 1,00,000 + ₹ 3,50,000 = ₹ 6,50,000.

A. Commission @ 3% on ₹ 6,50,000	₹ 19,500
B. Commission @ 2% on ₹ 1,50,000 (Payment to Unsecured Creditors)	₹ 3,000
C. Total Commission [A + B]	₹ 22,500

(ii) *Since the company is solvent interest on Debenture has been paid upto the date of final payment i.e., 30th September, 2013.*

Amount of Interest = ₹ 2,00,000 × 5/100 × 6/12 = ₹ 5,000.

ILLUSTRATION 11

The liquidator of a company is entitled to a remuneration of 2% on assets realized and 3% on the amount distributed to unsecured creditors. The assets realized ₹ 10,00,000. Amount available for distribution to unsecured creditors before paying liquidator's remuneration is ₹ 4,12,000. calculate liquidator's remuneration if the surplus is insufficient to pay off unsecured creditors, in toto.

SOLUTION

Liquidator's remuneration on assets realised (₹ 10,00,000 × 2/100)	₹ 20,000
Liquidator's remuneration on payment to unsecured creditors [(₹ 4,12,000 – 20,000) × 3/103]	11,417
Total liquidator's remuneration	₹ 31,417

ILLUSTRATION 12

X Ltd which went into voluntary liquidation on 31.3.2013 provides you the following information:

1. 5% Debentures (having floating charge on all assets)	₹ 5,00,000
2. Interest outstanding on above Debentures	₹ 25,000
3. Loan from IDBI (on Mortgage of Land & Builing)	₹ 1,50,000
4. Loan from ICICI Bank (on Hypothecation of Stock)	₹ 90,000
5. Owing to Govt. for Taxes for Assessment year 2008-2009	₹ 60,000
6. Owing to Govt. for Taxes for Assessment year 2009-2010	₹ 75,000
7. Owing to Govt. for Telephone, Electricity & Water	₹ 25,000
8. Cash & Bank Balance	₹ 1,50,000
9. The assets were realised as under:	
Land & Building	₹ 6,00,000 (By lender)
Plant & Machinery	₹ 1,00,000 (By liquidator)
Stock	₹ 50,000 (By liquidator)
Other Current Assets	₹ 4,00,000 (By liquidator)
10. Liquidator is entitled to commission @ 3% an assets realised and 2% an amount distributed to unsecured creditors other than Preferential Creditors.	
11. Legal charges ₹ 12,000 and Liquidation Expenes	₹ 50,000
12. Trade Creditors	₹ 3,75,000
13. Interest accrued on Loan from ICICI Bank and IDBI upto the date of payment amounted to ₹ 10,000 and ₹ 20,000 respectively.	
14. All Payments were made on 30th Sept 2013.	

Required: Calculate Liquidator's Remuneration. Also Calculate the percentage of amount paid to unsecured creditors (other than Preferential Creditors) to the total unsecured creditors (other than Preferential Creditors).

SOLUTION

Assets realised:	
Surplus from Securities (₹ 6,00,000 – 1,50,000)	4,50,000
Plant & Machinery	1,00,000
Stock	50,000
Other Current Assets	4,00,000
	10,00,000

Liquidator's Remuneration on Asses realised = 3% of ₹ 10,00,000 = ₹ 30,000

Amount available for Unsecured Creditors & Remuneration based on Payment

A.	Total Amount available:	
	Cash & bank	1,50,000
	Assets realised (₹ 10,00,000 – ₹ 50,000)	9,50,000
		11,00,000
B.	*Less:* Payments other than Unsecured Crs. & Remuneratiion based on Payement	
	Legal Charges	12,000
	Liquidator's Remuneration on assets realised	30,000
	Liquidation Expenses	50,000
	Debenture having floating charge	5,25,000
	Preferential Creditors	75,000
		6,92,000
C.	Amount available [A – B]	4,08,000
D.	Liquidator's Remuneration @2% [4,08,000 × 2/102]	₹ 8,000
	Total Remmuneration = ₹ 30,000 + ₹ 8,000 = ₹ 38,000	
	Total Unsecured Creditors:	
	Partly satisfied secured Creditors (₹ 90,000 – ₹ 50,000)	₹ 40,000
	Trade Creditors	₹ 3,75,000
	Owing to Govt. for Taxes for AY 2008-2009	₹ 60,000
	Owing to Govt. for Telephone Electricity & Water	₹ 25,000
		₹ 5,00,000
	% of Amount paid to Unsecured Creditors = ₹4,00,000/₹ 5,00,000 × 100 = 80%	

Note: *Interest accrued on loan from ICICI Bank and IDBI upto date of payment has not been paid since the company is insolvent.*

ILLUSTRATION 13 [PAYMENT OF ARREARS OF PREF. DIVIDEND]

The position of Keyless Ltd. on its liquiation is as under:

1. 6,000, 10% Preference Shares of ₹ 100 each, ₹ 50 paid up.
2. 2,000, Equity shares of ₹ 75 each, ₹ 50 paid up.
3. Unsecured Creditors ₹ 99,000.
4. Liquidation Expenses ₹ 1,000.
5. Preference Dividends are in arrears for one year.

Required: Prepare Liquidator's Final Statement of Account in each of the following alternative cases:

Case (a): If the assets are realised for ₹ 4,30,000 and the Articles of Association provide for payment of preference dividend arrears in priority to return of equity capital.

Case (b): If the assets are realised for ₹ 5,10,000 and the Articles of Association provide for payment of preference dividend arrears in priority to return of equity capital.

Case (c): If the assets are realised for ₹ 5,10,000 and the Articles of Association are silent about the arrears of preference dividends.

SOLUTION

(A) LIQUIDATOR'S FINAL STATEMENT OF ACCOUNT

Receipts	₹	*Payments*	₹
Assets realised	4,30,000	Liquidation Expenses	1,000
		Unsecured Creditors	99,000
		Preference Share holders	3,00,000
		Arrears of Pref. Dividend	30,000
	4,30,000		4,30,000

(B) LIQUIDATOR'S FINAL STATEMENT OF ACCOUNT

Receipts	₹	*Payments*	₹
Assets realised	5,10,000	Liquidation Expenses	1,000
		Unsecured Creditors	99,000
		Preference Share holders	3,00,000
		Arrears of Pref. Dividend	30,000
		Payment to Contributories:	
		₹ 40 on 2,000 Equity Shares	80,000
	5,10,000		5,10,000

(C) LIQUIDATOR'S FINAL STATEMENT OF ACCOUNT

Receipts	₹	*Payments*	₹
Assets realised	5,10,000	Liquidation Expenses	1,000
		Unsecured Creditors	99,000
		Preference Share holders	3,00,000
		Payment to Contributories:	
		₹ 50 on 2,000 Equity Shares	1,00,000
		Arrears of Pref. Dividend	10,000
	5,10,000		5,10,000

ILLUSTRATION 14 [CALCULATION OF CALL FROM CONTRIBUTORIES]

The position of Luckless Ld. on its Liquidation is as under:

1. 5,000, 10% Preference Shares of ₹ 100 each ₹ 60 paid up
2. 2,000, Equity shares of ₹ 75 each, ₹ 50 paid up
3. Unsecured Creditors ₹ 99,000
4. Liquidation Expenses ₹ 1,000
5. Liquidator is entitled to a commission of 2% on the amount realised from calls made on contributories.

Required: Prepare Liquidator's Final Statement of Account if the assets realised (a) ₹ 3,80,400, (b) ₹ 3,50,500, (c) ₹ 41,200.

SOLUTION

(A) LIQUIDATOR'S FINAL STATEMENT OF ACCOUNT

Receipts	₹	*Payments*	₹
Assets realised	3,80,400	Liquidation Expenses	1,000
Call on contributories:		Liquidators' Remuneration	400
2,000 Equity Shares @₹ 10 per share	20,000	Unsecured Creditors	99,000
		Preference Share holders	3,00,000
	4,00,400		4,00,400

Working Notes:

(I) CALCULATION OF SHORTAGE OF FUNDS

Particulars	₹
A. Total Amount Available	3,80,400
B. *Less:* Liquidation Expenses	1,000
C. Balance	3,79,400
D. *Less:* Unsecured Creditors	99,000
E. Balance	2,80,400
F. *Less:* Pref. Shareholders	3,00,000
G. Shortage of Funds	19,600

(ii) Calculation of funds required to meet shortage and commission payable on Calls to be made

$$\text{Shortage of Funds} \times \frac{100}{100 - \text{Rate of Commission}} = ₹19{,}600 \times \frac{100}{98-2} = ₹19{,}600 \times \frac{100}{98} = ₹\ 20{,}000$$

(iii) Uncalled Capital @ ₹ 25 on 2,000 shares = ₹ 50,000.

(iv) Amount of Calls to be made (least of funds required and uncalled capital) i.e., ₹ 20,000

(v) Commission on Call = ₹ 20,000 × 2/100 = ₹ 400.

(B) LIQUIDATOR'S FINAL STATEMENT OF ACCOUNT

Receipts	₹	*Payments*	₹
Assets realised	3,50,500	Liquidation Expenses	1,000
Call on contributories:		Liquidator's Remuneration	1,000
2,000 Equity Shares	50,000	Unsecured Creditors	99,000
@ ₹ 25 per share		Preference Shareholders	2,99,500
	4,00,500		4,00,500

Working Notes:

(I) CALCULATION OF SHORTAGE OF FUNDS

Particulars	₹
A. Total Amount Available	3,50,500
B. *Less:* Liquidation Expenses	1,000
C. Balance	3,49,500

D. *Less:* Unsecured Creditors	99,000
E. Balance	2,50,500
F. *Less:* Pref. Shareholders	3,00,000
G. Shortage of Funds	49,500

(ii) Calculation of funds required to meet shortage and Commission payable on Calls to be made

$$\text{Shortage of Funds} \times \frac{100}{100 - \text{Rate of Commission}} = ₹49,500 \times \frac{100}{98} = ₹\ 50,510$$

(iii) Uncalled Capital @ ₹ 25 on 2,000 shares = ₹ 50,000

(iv) Amount of Calls to be made (least of funds required and Uncalled Capital) i.e., ₹ 50,000

(v) Commission on Calls = ₹ 50,000 × 2/100 = ₹ 1,000

(C) LIQUIDATOR'S FINAL STATEMENT OF ACCOUNT

Receipts	₹	*Payments*	₹
Assets realised	41,200	Liquidator's Remuneration	1,200
Call on conributories:		Liquidation Expenses	1,000
2,000 Equity Shares	50,000	Unsecured Creditors	99,000
@ ₹ 25 per share			
5,000 Preference Shares @ ₹ 2	10,000		
	1,01,200		1,01,200

Working Notes:

(I) CALCULATION OF SHORTAGE OF FUNDS

Particulars	₹
A. Total Amount Available	41,200
B. *Less:* Liquidation Expenses	1,000
C. Balance	40,200
D. *Less:* Unsecured Creditors	99,000
E. Shortage	58,800

(ii) Calculation of funds required to meet shotage and Commission payable on Calls to be made
Shortage of Funds × = ₹ 58,800 × = ₹ 60,000

(iii) Uncalled Capital

Particulars	₹
@ ₹ 25 on 2,000 Equity Shares	50,000
@ ₹ 60 on 5,000 Pref. Shares	3,00,000
	3,50,000

(iv) Amount of Calls to be made (Being least of the funds required and Uncalled Capital) i.e., ₹ 60,000

(v) First equity shareholders should be called upon to pay (not exceeding their uncalled capital) i.e., ₹ 50,000 should be raised from equity shareholders @ ₹ 25 per share.

Then, the preference share holders should be called upon to pay the balance of ₹ 10,000 @ ₹ 2 per share.

(vi) Commission on Calls = ₹ 60,000 × 2/100 = ₹ 1,200.

12.0 PRACTICAL STEPS INVOLVED IN ADJUSTMENT OF RIGHTS OF CONTRIBUTORIES OF DIFFERENT CLASSES

Step 1: *First check whether Cash Deficit is less / more than Total Uncalled Amount. If Cash Deficit is more than / equal to Total Uncalled Amount. the full Uncalled Amout should be called up. In other cases take the following 2 Steps if there are two or more classes of contributories.*

Step 2: *Calculate Deficiency as % of Nominal Share Capital*

A.	Total Paid up Share Capital	xxx
B.	*Less:* Cash Available [i.e. Total Receipts (including Calls-in arrears) minus Total Payments (including calls-in-advance)]	(xxx)
	OR	
	Add: Cash Deficit [i.e. Total Payments (including Calls-in-adv.) – Total Receipts (including Calls-in arrears)	
C.	Total Deficiency to be borne (A – B) *or* (A + B)	xxx
D.	Total Nominal Share Capital	xxx
E.	Deficiency as % of Nominal Share Capital (C/D × 100)	xxx

Step 3: *Calculation of Net amount returnable/receivable per share*

	Particulars	*'A' (₹)*	*'B' (₹)*	*'C' (₹)*
A.	Paid up Amount per Share	...	...	...
B.	*Less:* Deficiency to be borne @ ... % of Nominal Value	(...)	(...)	(...)
C.	Net Amount returnable/(receivable)	...	...	...

Note: Figure in brackets indicates call to be made on that class of shareholders.

Tutorial Note: In Case of Surplus (i.e.Excess of Cash Available over Total Paid up Share Capital), Surplus should be distributed as % of Nominal Share Capital.

ILLUSTRATION 15 [ADJUSTMENT OF RIGHTS OF CONTRIBUTORIES]

X Ltd. went into voluntary liquidation when its position was as under:

Issued Share Capital

6,000, 10% Preference Shares of ₹ 100 each ₹ 50 paid up

Class 'A' 500 Equity Shares of ₹ 100 each fully paid up

Class 'B' 2,000 Equity Shares of ₹ 75 each ₹ 50 paid up

Class 'C' 1,000 Equity Shares of ₹ 50 each ₹ 25 paid up

Unsecured Creditors: ₹ 99,000

Liquidator's Remuneration: ₹ 1,000

Required: Prepare Liquidator's Final Statement of Account in each of following alternative Cases:

Case (a) If the assets were realised for ₹ 10,000

Case (b) If the assets were realised for ₹ 3,10,000

Case (c) If the assets were realised for ₹ 3,95,000

Case (d) If the assets were realised for ₹ 4,00,000

Case (e) If the assets were realised for ₹ 4,25,000

Case (f) If the assets were realised for ₹ 7,25,000

SOLUTION

(A) LIQUIDATOR'S STATEMENT OF ACCOUNT

Receipts	₹	*Payments*	₹
Assets realised:	10,000	Liquidator's Remuneration	1,000
Call on Contributories:		Unsecured Creditors	99,000
On 2,000 Shares @ ₹ 25	50,000		
On 1,000 Shares @ ₹ 25	25,000		
On 6,000 Pref. Shares @ ₹ 2.50	15,000		
	1,00,000		1,00,000

(B) LIQUIDATOR'S STATEMENT OF ACCOUNT

Receipts	₹	*Payments*	₹
Assets realised:	3,10,000	Liquidator's Remuneration	1,000
Call on Contributories:		Unsecured Creditors	99,000
On 2,000 Shares @ ₹ 25	50,000	Preference Share holders on	2,85,000
On 1,000 Shares @ ₹ 25	25,000	6,000 Shares @ ₹ 47.50	
	3,85,000		3,85,000

(C) LIQUIDATOR'S STATEMENT OF ACCOUNT

Receipts	₹	*Payments*	₹
Assets realised:	3,95,000	Liquidator's Remuneration	1,000
Call on Contributories:		Unsecured Creditors	99,000
On 2,000 Shares @ ₹ 4	8,000	Preference Share holders	3,00,000
On 1,000 Shares @ ₹ 11	11,000	Equity Share holders on 500 Shares @ ₹ 28	14,000
	4,14,000		4,14,000

Working Notes:

(I) CALCULATION OF % OF DEFICIENCY

A. Total Paid up Share Capital	₹ 1,75,000
B. *Add:* Cash Deficit	₹ 5,000
C. Total Deficiency to be borne (A + B)	₹ 1,80,000
D. Total Nominal Share Capital	₹ 2,50,000
E. Deficiency as % of Nominal	72%

(II) CALCULATION OF NET AMOUNT RETURNABLE/RECEIVABLE PER SHARE

Class of Shares	*A* (₹)	*B* (₹)	*C* (₹)
A. Paid up Amount per share	100	50	25
B. *Less:* Deficiency to be borne @ 72% of Nominal Value	72	54	36
C. Net Amount returnable (receivable)	28	(4)	(11)

(D) LIQUIDATOR'S STATEMENT OF ACCOUNT

Receipts	₹	*Payments*	₹
Assets realised	4,00,000	Liquidator's Remuneration	1,000
Call on Contributories:		Unsecured Creditors	99,000
On 2,000 Shares @ ₹ 2.50	5,000	Preference Share Holders	3,00,000
On 1,000 Shares @ ₹ 10	10,000	Equity Share holders on 500 Shares @ 30	15,000
	4,15,000		4,15,000

Working Notes:

(I) CALCULATION OF PRECENTAGE OF DEFICIENCY

A. Total Paid up Share Capital	₹ 1,75,000
B. *Less:* Cash Available	Nil
C. Deficiency to be borne (A – B)	₹ 1,75,000
D. Total Nominal Share Capital	₹ 2,50,000
E. Deficiency as % of Nominal value (C/D × 100)	70%

(II) CALCULATION OF NET AMOUNT RETURNABLE/RECEIVABLE PER SHARE

Class of Shares	*A (₹)*	*B (₹)*	*C (₹)*
A. Paid up Amount per Share	100	50.00	25
B. *Less:* Deficiency to be borne @ 70% of Nominal Value	70	52.50	35
C. Net Amount returnable/(receivable)	30	(2.50)	(10)

Note: Figure in bracket indicates call to be made on that class of shareholders.

(E) LIQUIDATOR'S STATEMENT OF ACCOUNT

Receipts	₹	*Payments*	₹
Assets realised	4,25,000	Liquidator's Remuneration	1,000
Call on Contributories:		Unsecured Creditors	99,000
On 1,000 Shares @ ₹ 5	5,000	Preference Share holders	3,00,000
		Equity Share holders:	
		On 500 Shares @ ₹ 40	20,000
		On 2,000 Shares @ ₹ 5	10,000
	4,30,000		4,30,000

Working Notes:

(I) CALCULATION OF % OF DEFICIENCY

A. Total Paid up Share Capital	₹ 1,75,000
B. *Add:* Cash Available	₹ 25,000
C. Total Deficiency to be borne (A – B)	₹ 1,80,000
D. Total Nominal Share Capital	₹ 2,50,000
E. Deficiency as % of Nominal (C/D × 100)	60%

(II) CALCULATION OF NET AMOUNT RETURNABLE/RECEIVABLE PER SHARE

Class of Shares	A (₹)	B (₹)	C (₹)
A. Paid up Amount per Share	100	50	25
B. *Less:* Deficiency to be borne @ 60% of Nominal Value	60	45	30
C. Net Amount returnable/(receivable)	40	5	(5)

Note: Figure in brackets indicates call to be made on that class of share holders.

(F) LIQUIDATOR'S STATEMENT OF ACCOUNT

Receipts	₹	Payments	₹
Assets realised	7,25,000	Liquidator's Remuneration	1,000
		Unsecured Creditors	99,000
		Preference Share holders	3,00,000
		Equity Share holders	
		— On 500 Shares @ ₹ 160	80,000
		— On 2,000 Shares @ ₹ 95	1,90,000
		— On 1,000 Shares @ ₹ 55	55,000
	7,25,000		7,25,000

Working Notes:

(I) CALCULATION OF % OF SURPLUS

A. Total Paid up Share Capital	₹ 1,75,000
B. *Add:* Cash Available	₹ 25,000
C. Surplus	₹ 1,80,000
D. Total Nominal Share Capital	₹ 2,50,000
E. Deficiency as % of Nominal	60%

(II) CALCULATION OF NET AMOUNT RETURNABLE TO EACH CLASS OF SHAREHOLDERS

Class of Shares	A (₹)	B (₹)	C (₹)
A. Paid up Amount per Share	100	50	25
B. *Add:* Surplus to given @ 60% of Nominal Value	60	45	30
C. Net Amount returnable (A + B)	160	95	55

ILLUSTRATION 16 [ADJUSTMENT OF RIGHTS OF CONTRIBUTORIES WHEN THERE ARE CALLS-IN-ADVANCE AND CALLS-IN-ARREARS]

X Ltd. went into liquidation when its position was as given below:

1. POSITION OF SHARE CAPITAL

Name of Shareholder	*Number and Nature of Share held*	*Nominal Value per Share* ₹	*Called up Amount per Share* ₹	*Paid up Amount per Share* ₹
'A'	6,000, 10% Pref. Shares	100	50	50

'B'	500 Equity Shares	100	100	100
'C'	1,000 Equity Shares	75	50	50
'D'	600 Equity Shares	75	50	53
'E'	400 Equity Shares	75	50	47
'F'	1,000 Equity Shares	50	25	25

2. Unsecured Creditors ₹ 99,000
3. Liquidator's Remuneration ₹ 1,000

Required: Prepare Liquidator's Final Statement of Account in each of the following alternative cases:

Case (a) If the assets are realised for ₹ 4,00,600

Case (b) If the assets were realised for ₹ 4,25,600

SOLUTION

(A) LIQUIDATOR'S FINAL STATEMENT OF ACCOUNT

Receipts	₹	*Payments*	₹
Assets realised	4,00,600	Liquidator's Remuneration	1,000
Call on Conributories:		Unsecured Creditors	99,000
'C'—@ ₹ 2.50 on 1,000 Shares	2,500	Pref. Share holders	3,00,000
'E'—@ ₹ 5.50 on 400 Shares	2,200	Equity Share holders:	
'F'—@ ₹ 10 on 1,000 Shares	10,000	'B'—@ ₹ 30 on 500 Shares	15,000
		'D'—@ ₹ 0.50 on 600 Shares	300
	4,15,300		4,15,300

Working Notes:

(I) CALCULATION OF % OF DEFICIENCY

Particulars	₹
A. Total Paid up Equity Share Capital	1,75,600
B. *Less:* Cash Available	600
C. Deficiency to be borne (A – B)	1,75,000
D. Total Nominal Equity Share Capital	2,50,000
E. Deficiency as % of Nominal Capital	70%

(II) CALCULATION OF NET AMOUNT RETURNABLE/RECEIVABLE PER SHARE FROM THE CONTRIBUTION

Name of Share holder	*B* ₹	*C* ₹	*D* ₹	*E* ₹	*F* ₹
A. Paid up Amount/Share	100	50	53	47	25
B. *Less:* Deficiency to be borne @ 70% of Nominal Value	70	52.50	52.50	52.50	35
C. Net Amount Retunable (receivable)	30	(2.50)	0.50	(5.50)	(10)

(B) LIQUIDATOR'S FINAL STATEMENT OF ACCOUNT

Receipts	₹	Payments	₹
Assets realised	4,25,600	Liquidator's Remuneration	1,000
Call on Contributories:		Unsecured Creditors	99,000
'F'—@ ₹ 5 on 1,000 Shares	5,000	Pref. Share holders	3,00,000
		Equity Share holders	
		'B'—@ ₹ 40 on 500 shares	20,000
		'C'—@ ₹ 5 on 1,000 shares	5,000
		'D'—@ ₹ 8 on 600 shares	4,800
		'E'—@ ₹ 2 on 400 shares	800
	4,30,600		4,30,600

Working Notes:

(I) CALCULATION OF % OF DEFICIENCY

	Particulars	₹
A.	Total Paid up Equity Share Capital	1,75,600
B.	*Less:* Cash Available	25,600
C.	Deficiency to be borne (A – B)	1,50,000
D.	Total Nominal Equity Share Capital	2,50,000
E.	Deficiency as % of Nominal Capital	60%

(II) CALCULATION OF NET AMOUNT RETURNABLE/RECEIVABLE PER SHARE FROM THE CONTRIBUTORIES

Name of Share holder	B ₹	C ₹	D ₹	E ₹	F ₹
A. Paid up Amount/Share	100	50	53	47	25
B. *Less:* Deficiency to be borne @ 60% of Nominal Value	60	45	45	45	30
C. Net Amount Retunable (receivable)	40	5	8	2	(5)

ILLUSTRATION 17

The position of Valueless Ltd. on its liquidation is as under:

Issued and paid up Capital:

3,000 11% Preference Shares of ₹ 100 each fully paid.

3,000 Equity Shares of ₹ 100 each fully paid.

1,000 Equity Shares of ₹ 50 each, ₹ 30 per share paid.

Calls in Arrears are ₹ 10,000 and Calls received in Advance ₹ 8,500. Preference dividends are in arrears for one year. Amount left with the liquidator after discharging all liabilities is ₹ 4,13,000. Articles of Association of the company provide for payment of preference dividend arrears in priority to return of equity capital. You are required to prepare the Liquidators Final Statement of Account.

SOLUTION

LIQUIDATOR'S FINAL STATEMENT OF ACCOUNT

Receipts	₹	*Payments*	₹
Cash	4,13,000	Return to Contributors:	
Realisation from:		Preference Dividend	33,000
Calls in arrears	10,000	Preference Share holders	3,00,000
Final call of ₹ 5.5 per Equity	5,500	Calls in Advance	8,500
Share of ₹ 50 each		Equity Share holders of	87,000
(₹ 5.5 × 1,000)		₹ 100 each (3,000 × ₹ 29)	
	4,28,500		4,28,500

Working Note:

(I) CALCULATION OF DEFICIENCY

A. Total Paid-up Share Capital	₹.3,30,000
B. *Less:* Cash Available [₹ 4,13,000 + 10,000 (Arrears)] – [(3,33,000) (Pref) + 8,500 (Adv.)]	₹ (81,500)
C. Deficiency to be borne (A – B)	2,48,500
D. Total Nominal Share Capital	3,50,000
E. Deficiency as % of Nominal Capital (C/D × 100)	71%

(II) CALCULATION OF NET AMOUNT RETURNABLE FOR SHARES

Class of Shares	*A*	*B*
A. Paid-up Amount Per Share	100	30
B. *Less:* Deficiency to be borne @ 71% of Nominal value	(71)	(35.5)
C. Net Amount Returnable (A – B)	29	(5.5)

ILLUSTRATION 18

CPT Ltd. went into voluntary liquidation on 31st March, 2013 when their Balance Sheet was as under: (Figure being in lakhs of ₹)

Particulars	₹
10,000 7% Pref. Shares of ₹ 100 each	10.00
5,000 Equity shares of ₹ 100 each, ₹ 75 paid	3.75
30,000 Equity Shares of ₹ 50 each, ₹ 30 paid	9.00
5% Debentures (having floating charge on all assets)	5.00
Interest outstanding on Debentures	.25
Loan from Financial Institution.	1.50
Loan from Bank	0.90
Trade Creditors	3.75
Owing To Govt. for	
Taxes	.75

Telephone, Electricity & water	.25
Land & Buildings	4.90
Plant & Machinery	12.50
Stock	2.00
Cash in hand	.10
Cash at Bank	1.40
Other Current Assets	8.25
Misc. Expenditure	6.00

Other Information:

(a) The Loan from financial institution is secured by mortgage of Land & Buildings & the Loan from Bank is secured by the hypothecation of stock.

(b) The Preference Dividends were in arrears for 1 year which are payable on liquidation in priority to any payment to equity shareholders. Pref-shares are to be redeemed at a permium of ₹ 5 per share.

(c) The assets were realised as under:

Land & Buildings	6.20	(By lender himself)
Plant & Machinery	11.00	(By liquidator)
Stock	0.50	(By liquidator)
Other Current Assets except cash & bank	7.00	(By liquidator)

(d) The interest accrued on loan from bank and financial institution upto the date of payment amounted to ₹ 10,000 and ₹ 20,000 respectively.

(e)(i) The expenses of liquidation amounted to ₹ 50,000

(ii) Legal Charges were amounted to ₹ 7,900

(f) Commission of liquidator

–3% on assets realised except Cash & Bank

–2% on amounts distributed to unsecured creditors (other than preferential creditors) and Equity Shares holders.

(g) All payments were made on 30th Sept., 2013.

Required: Prepare Liquidator's Statement of Account.

SOLUTION

LIQUIDATOR'S STATEMENT OF ACCOUNT

Receipts	*Book Values*	₹	*Payments*		₹
Assets Realised			Legal Charges		.079
—Cash-in-hand	0.10	0.10	Liquidator's Remuneration		
—Cash-at Bank	1.40	1.40	3% as ₹ 23.00	.69	
—Other Current Assets	8.25	7.00	2% on ₹ 4.50	.09	
—Plant & Machinery	12.50	11.00	2% on ₹ 0.80	.016	.796
Surplus from Securities	–	4.50	Expenses of Liquidation		.500
[₹ 6.20 – ₹ 1.70]			Debentures		

			—Principal	5.000	
			— Interest [.25 + .125]	.375	5.375
			Unsecured Creditors:		
			—Preferential Creditors	.75	
			—Partly satisfied S. Crs. (.40 + .10)	.50	
			—Other Creditors	4.00	5.250
			Payments to Pref. Shareholders		
			Share Capital	10.50	
			Pref. Dividend	0.70	11.200
			Payments to equity Shareholders		
			—₹ 15.25 on 5,000 Shares.	.7625	
			—₹ 0.125 on 30,000 Shares.	.0375	.800
		24.00			24.00

Working Notes:

(i) Interest on Debentures has also been paid from 1st April to 30th Sept. since the company is solvent.

(II) CALCULATION OF DEFICIENCY

Particulars	₹
A. Total Paid-up Share Capital	12,75,000
B. *Less:* Cash Available	(80,000)
C. Deficiency to be borne (A–B)	11,95,000
D. Total Nominal Share Capital	20,00,000
E. Deficiency as % of Nominal Capital (C/D × 100)	59.75%

(III) CALCULATION OF NET AMOUNT RETURNABLE FOR SHARES

Class of Shares	A	B
A. Paid-up Amount Per Share	75.00	30.000
B. *Less:* Deficiency to be borne @ 59.75% of Nominal value	(59.75)	(29.875)
C. Net Amount Returnable (A–B)	15.25	0.125

ILLUSTRATION 19

CANIA Ltd. went into voluntary liquidation on 31.3.2013. The balances in its books on that date were:

Particulars	₹
5,000 6% Preference Shares of ₹ 100 each fully paid	5,00,000
2,500 Equity Shares of ₹ 100 each ₹ 75 paid up	1,87,500
7,500 Equity Shares of ₹ 100 each ₹ 60 paid up	4,50,000
5% Debentures (secured by a floating charge on all assets)	2,50,000
Interest due on Debentures	12,500
Bank Overdraft	1,00,000

Unsecured creditors	2,00,000
Taxes due to Government within 12 months	12,500
Salaries and wages due for 5 months for two workers	60,000
Land	50,000
Building	2,00,000
Plant and Machinery	6,25,000
Stock	1,37,500
Sundry Debtors	2,75,000
Cash at Bank	75,000
Profit and Loss A/c	4,10,000

The liquidator is entitled to a remuneration of 5% on all assets realised except cash and 1% on the amount distributed to Unsecured Creditors other than Preferential Creditors.

Bank Overdraft is secured by deposit of title deed of land and building which realised ₹ 3,00,000. Other assets realised the following sums:

Plant and Machinery ₹ 5,00,000, Stock ₹ 1,50,000, Sundry Debtors ₹ 2,00,000

Expenses of liquidation amounted to ₹ 37,800.

Required: Prepare liquidator's final statement of account. Liquidator realised all assets on 31.3.2013 and discharged his obligation on the same date. Dividend on preference shares were in arrears for two years which are to be paid in priority to equity share capital as per Articles.

SOLUTION

LIQUIDATORS FINAL STATEMENT OF ACCOUNT

Receipts	*Book Value* ₹	₹	*Payments*		₹
Bank		75,000	Liquidator's remuneration		54,700
Surplus from			Liquidation expenses		37,800
Secured Bank O/D		2,00,000	Debentures including interest		2,62,500
Plant and Machinery	6,25,000	5,00,000	Preferential Creditors		52,500
Stock	1,37,500	1,50,000	Unsecured Creditors		2,20,000
Sundry Debtors	2,75,000	2,00,000	Preference Shares	5,00,000	
Calls on 7,500 shares			Dividend for Two years	60,000	5,60,000
@ ₹ 10 per share		75,000	2,500 equity shares		
			@ ₹ 5 per share		12,500
		12,00,000			12,00,000

Working Notes:

Particulars	₹
(i) Liquidator's Remuneration:	
5% on ₹ 10,50,000	52,500
1% on ₹ 2,20,000	2,200
	54,700

(ii) Preferential creditors:	
Outstanding Taxes	12,500
Outstanding Salaries and Wages (4month's wages but not exceeding ₹.20,000 per worker)	40,000
	52,500
(iii) Surplus from Secured Creditors:	
Realised value of Land & Building	3,00,000
Less: Bank Overdraft	1,00,000
	2,00,000

(IV)CALCULATION OF % OF DEFICIENCY

	Particulars	₹
A.	Total Paid up Share Capital	6,37,500
B.	*Add:* Cash Deficit [₹11,25,000 – ₹11,87,500]	62,500
C.	Total Deficiency to be borne (A + B)	7,00,000
D.	Total Nominal Share Capital	10,00,000
E.	Deficiency as % of Nominal	70%

(V) CALCULATION OF NET AMOUNT RETURNABLE/RECEIVABLE PER SHARE

	Class of Shares	*A* (₹)	*B* (₹)
A.	Paid up Amount per share	75	60
B.	*Less:* Deficiency to be borne @ 70% of Nominal Value	(70)	(70)
C.	Net Amount returnable (receivable)	5	(10)

13.0 RECEIVER FOR MORTGAGEE (E.G., DEBENTUREHOLDERS HAVING FLOATING CHARGE)

WHO IS RECEIVER?

Receiver is a person who is appointed to take possession of certain property for protective purposes for receiving income from the property and for applying it as directed.

WHO CAN APOINT RECEIVER?

If the mortgagee has express power to appoint a receiver in certain circumstances (e.g., on failure of the Company to pay him his interest *or* the installment on due date), he may appoint the Receiver. If the mortgagee has not an express power to appoint a Receiver, he may apply to the Court for the appointment of the Receiver.

DUTY OF RECEIVER

(a) Receiver (if appointed) shall realise the assets specifically/generally charged in the favour of mortgagee and after meeting his expenses, remuneration, making payments to person entitled to get payment in priority to the mortgagee he will be make the payment to the mortgagee.

(b) The Receiver shall prepare a Receips and Payment Account and shall submit the same together with surplus if any left, to the Company (if going concern) *or* to the liquidator of the Company (if liquidating Concern)

ILLUSTRATION 20

The following is the Balance Sheet of CAMHH Ltd. as at 30th Sept. 2013:

Particulars		₹
11% Pref. Shares of ₹ 10 each		1,00,000
10,000 equity shares of ₹ 10 each, fully paid up		1,00,000
5,000 equity shares of ₹ 10 each ₹ 7.50 per share paid up		37,500
13% Debentures		1,50,000
Mortgage Loan		80,000
Bank Overdraft		30,000
Creditors for Trade		32,000
Income-tax arrears:		
(assessments concluded in July 2013)		
assessment year 2011 – 2012	21,000	
assessment year 2012 – 2013	5,000	26,000
Land and Buildings		1,20,000
Sundry Current Assets		3,95,000
Profit and Loss Account		38,500
Debenture Issue expenses		
not written off		2,000

Mortgage loan was secured against land and buildings. Debentures were secured by a floating charge on all the other assets. The company was unable to meet the payments and therefore the debentureholders appointed a Receiver and this was followed by a resolution for members' voluntary winding up. The Receiver for the Debenture holders brought the land and buildings to auction and realised ₹ 1,50,000. He also took charge of Sundry assets of the value of ₹ 2,40,000 and realised ₹ 2,00,000. The Liquidator realised ₹ 1,00,000 on the sale of the balance of sundry current assets. The bank Overdraft was secured by a personal guarantee of two of the Directors of the Company and on the Bank raising a demand the Directors paid off the dues from their personal resources. Costs incurred by the Receiver were ₹ 2,000 and by the Liquidator ₹ 2,800. The Receiver was not entitled to any remuneration but the liquidator was to receive 3% fee on the value of assets realised by him. Preference shareholders had not been paid dividend for period after 30th September, 2013 and interest for the last half-year was due to the debenture holders.

Required: Prepare the accounts to be submitted by the Receiver and the Liquidator.

SOLUTION

RECEIVER'S RECEIPTS & PAYMENTS ACCOUNT

Receipts		₹	*Payments*		₹
Sundry Assets realised			Costs of the Receiver		2,000
Surplus received from			Preferential payments		
mortgage		2,00,000	Creditors paid—Taxes		
Sale proceeds of land			raised within 12 months		26,000
and Building	1,50,000		Debentures holders		
Less: Applied to			Principal	1,50,000	

discharge of mortgage			Interest for half year	9,750	1,59,750
Loan	80,000	70,000	Surplus transferred to the liquidator		82,250
		2,70,000			2,70,000

LIQUIDATOR' FINAL STATEMENT OF ACCOUNTS

Receipts	₹	*Payments*		₹
Surplus received from Receiver	82,250	Cost of Liquidation		2,800
Assets Realised:	1,00,000	Remuneration to Liquidator		3,000
Calls on contributories:		Unsecured Creditors:		
On holder of 5,000 partly paid shares		Trade	32,000	
at the rate of ₹ 2.17 per share	10,850	Directors for Bank O/D		
		cleared	30,000	62,000
		Preference Shareholders:		
		Principal	1,00,000	
		Arrears of dividends	22,000	1,22,000
		Equity Shareholders:		
		Return of money to contributors		
		to holders of 10,000 shares		
		at 33 paise each		3,300
	1,93,100			1,93,100

Working Note:

(I) CALCULATION OF % OF DEFICIENCY

A.	Total Paid up Share Capital	₹ 1,37,500
B.	*Add:* Cash Deficit [₹1,82, 250 – ₹ 1,89,800]	₹ 7,550
C.	Total Deficiency to be borne (A + B)	₹ 1,45,050
D.	Total Nominal Share Capital	₹ 1,50,000
E.	Deficiency as % of Nominal [C/D × 100]	96.7%

(II) CALCULATION OF NET AMOUNT RETURNABLE/RECEIVABLE PER SHARE

Class of Shares	*A* (₹)	*B* (₹)
A. Paid up Amount per share	10	7.5
B. *Less:* Deficiency to be borne @ 96.7% of Nominal Value	(9.67)	(9.67)
C. Net Amount returnable (receivable)	0.33	(2.17)

14.0 CONRIBUTORIES

WHO IS A CONTRIBUTORY? [SECTION 2(26)]

According to Section 2(26) "Contributory" means a person liable to Contribute to the assets of the Company in the event of its being wound up, and includes a holder of fully paid up shares. In some of the specific cases, the contributories will be as under:

Case	*Who is Contributory*
(a) In case of Death of a member	Legal Representatives
(b) In case of Insolvent member	Assignees subject to their power of disclaimer
(c) In case of winding up of a body corporate which was a member	Liquidator subject to his power ofdisclaimer

WHAT IS THE NATURE OF THEIR LIABILITY? [SECTION]

After winding up, the liability of a conributory is ex-lege (legal) and not ex-contract (contractual). The liability of a contributory shall create a debt accruing due from him at the time when his liability commenced but payable only when the call is made on him by the liquidator.

WHAT ARE THE LISTS OF CONTRIBUTORIES?

On Winding up, the liquidator prepares the following two lists:

1. List 'A' is the list of persons who are the members on the date of commencement of winding up.
2. List 'B' is the list of those persons who were the members during the 12 months preceding the date of commencement of winding up.

WHAT IS THE NATURE OF LIABILITY OF LIST 'A' AND LIST 'B' CONTRIBUTORIES?

The liability of the List 'A' Contributories is primary and absolute where as the liability of List 'B' Contributories is secondary. In other words, List 'B' can be resorted to only when the List 'A' has been exhausted.

WHEN DOES THE LIABILITY OF LIST 'B' CONTRIBUTORIES ARISE?

The liability of List 'B' Contributories arises only when the following 3 conditions are satisfied:

(a) if he had ceased to be a member during the 12 months preceding the date of Commencement of Winding up;

(b) if the debt/liability incurred upto the date of membership is still outstanding.

(c) if the present members are unable to pay the contribution required to be made by them.

WHAT IS THE ACTUAL AMOUNT OF LIABILITY OF LIST 'B' CONTRIBUTORIES?

The actual amount of liability of List 'B' Contributories is the least of the following 2 amounts:

(a) Creditors outstanding on date of ceasing to be member.

(b) Unpaid up amount on share (i.e., No. of shares held × Unpaid up amount per share).

Note: If there are more than one List 'B' Contributories then such Contributories shall be liable to pay the concerned Creditors in proportion to their No. of shares held.

ILLUSTRATION 21

Unfortunate Limited went into voluntary liquidation and the proceedings commenced on 2nd July, 2013. Certain creditors could not receive payment out of the realisation of assets and out of the contributions from the contributories of the 'A' list. The following are the details of share transfers.

I *Name of the transferor*	*II* *No. of shares transferred*	*III* *Date of transfer*	*IV* *Creditors remaining unpaid and outstanding at the time of the transferor ceasing to be a member*
(i) A	20	Ist March, 2012	₹ 6,000

(ii) B	25	14th August, 2012	₹ 8,000
(iii) C	10	Ist Oct. 2012	₹ 10,750
(iv) D	40	Ist Dec. 2012	₹ 13,000
(v) E	5	Ist April, 2013	₹ 15,000

All the shares of ₹ 400 each, on which ₹ 150 per share had been paid up. Ignoring other details like liquidator's expenses etc; you are required to workout the liability of the individual contributories listed above.

SOLUTION

STATEMENT OF LIABILITY OF 'B ' LIST CONTRIBUTORIES

Date	*Creditors Outstanding*	*Incremental Amount*	B	C	D	E
			No. of shares held			
			25	*10*	*40*	*5*
	₹	₹	₹	₹	₹	₹
14th Aug. 2012	8,000		2,500	1,000	4,000	500
Ist Oct. 2012	10,750	2,750	—	500	2,000	250
Ist Dec. 2012	13,000	2,250	—	—	2,000	250
Ist April 2013	15,000	2,000	—	—	—	2,000
A Max. amount payable to creditors			2,500	1,500	8,000	3,000
B Max liabilities on shares held @ ₹ 250 per share			6,250	2,500	10,000	1,250
C Actual liability lower of (A) *or* (B)			2,500	1,500	8,000	1,250
Total amount paid to creditors ₹ 13,250						

Notes:

(i) Incremental creditors of ₹ 2,000 on Ist April 2013 will get only ₹ 250 from E. Since the maximum amount recoverable from E is ₹ 1,250 of which ₹ 1,000 will be absorbed by creditors outstanding on Ist Dec.

(ii) The various amounts outstanding on the date of transfer of shares have been apportioned on the basis of the number of shareholders by 'B' list contributories.

(iii) 'B' List of contributories is the list of those persons who ceased to be members during 12 months proceeding the date of commencement of winding up.

(iv) "B" List Contributories are liable to pay only least of the following two amounts:

(a) Creditors Outstanding on the date of t/f & not thereafter

(b) Amount remained unpaid on the shares.

ILLUSTRATION 22

In a winding up a CANIG Ltd. certain creditors remained unpaid. The following persons had transferred their holding sometime before winding up:

Name	Date of Transfer	No. of shares transferred	Amount due to creditors on the date of transfer
P	January 1, 2012	1,000	7,500
Q	February 15, 2012	400	12,500
S	March 15, 2012	700	18,000
T	March 31, 2012	900	21,000
U	April 5, 2012	1,000	30,000

The shares were of ₹ 100 each, ₹ 80 being called up and paid up on the date of transfers.

A member, R, who held 200 shares died on 28th February, 2012 when the amount due to creditors was ₹ 15,000. His shares were transmitted to his son X.

Z was the transferee of shares held by T. Z paid ₹ 20 per share as calls in advance immediately on becoming a member.

The liquidation of the company commenced on 1st February, 2013 when the liquidator made a call on the present and the past contributories to pay the amount.

You are asked to quantify the maximum liability of the transferors of shares mentioned in the above table, when the transferees:

(i) pay the amount due as "present" member contributories;

(ii) do not pay the amount due as "present" member contributories.

Also quantify the liability of X to whom shares were transmitted on the demise of his father R.

SOLUTION

(i) The transferors are P, Q, S, T and U. When the transferees pay the amount due as "present" member contributories, there will not be any liability on the transferors.

(ii) It is only when the transferees do not pay as "present" member contributories that the liability would arise in the case of "past" members as contributories.

STATEMENT OF LIABILITY OF 'B' LIST CONTRIBUTORIES

Creditors outstanding on the date of transfer (ceasing to be member)	Q 400 shares ₹	R/X 200 shares ₹	S 700 shares ₹	U 1,000 shares ₹	Amount to be paid to the creditors ₹
(i) 12,500	2,174	1,087	3,804	5,435	12,500
(ii) 2,500 (i.e. 15,000 – 12,500)		263	921	1,316	2,500
(iii) 3,000 (i.e. 18,000 – 15,000)		316	1,105	1,579	3,000
(iv) 12,000 (i.e. 30,000 – 18,000)		2,000	—	10,000	12,000
Total (a) 30,000	2,174	3,666	5,830	18,330	30,000
Maximum Liability at ₹ 20 per share on shares held (b)	8,000	4,000	14,000	20,000	
Lower of (a) and (b)	2,174	3,666	5,830	18,330	

(a) X to whom shares were transmitted on demise of his father R would be liable as an existing member contributory. He steps into the shoes of his deceased father under section 430. His maximum liability would be at ₹ 20 per share on 200 shares received on transmission i.e. for ₹ 4,000.

(b) P will not be liable to pay any amount as the winding up proceedings commenced after one year from the date of the transfer.

(c) T also will not be liable as the transferee Z has paid the balance ₹ 20 per share as call in advance.

(d) Q, R/X, S and U will be liable, as former members, to the maximum extent as indicated, provided the transferees do not pay the calls.

SOLVED PROBLEMS

PROBLEM 1

CANIB Ltd. went into voluntary liquidation on 1st April, 2013. The following balances are extracted from its books on that date:

Particulars	₹
Capital:	
24,000 equity shares of ₹ 10 each	2,40,000
Deben. (secured by floating charge)	1,50,000
Bank overdraft	54,000
Creditors	60,000
Machinery	90,000
Leasehold properties	1,20,000
Stock	3,000
Debtors	1,50,000
Investments	18,000
Cash in hand	3,000
Profit and Loss Account	1,20,000

The following assets are valued as under:

Machinery ₹ 1,80,000, Leasehold properties ₹ 2,18,000, Investments ₹ 12,000, Stock ₹ 6,000, Debtors ₹ 1,40,000.

The bank overdraft is secured by deposit of title deeds of leasehold properties. There were preferential creditors ₹ 3,000 which were not included in creditors ₹ 60,000.

Required: Prepare a Statement of Affairs to be submitted to the meeting of members/creditors.

SOLUTION

STATEMENT OF AFFAIRS OF CANIB LTD. AS ON THE 1ST APRIL, 2013

Assets not specifically pledged as per list A:	*Estimated Realisable Value* ₹
Cash in hand	3,000
Investment	12,000
Debtors	1,40,000
Stock	6,000
Machinery	1,80,000
	3,41,000

Assets specifically pledged as per list B:

Particulars	*(a) Estimated Realisable Value* ₹	*(b) Due to secured creditors* ₹	*(c) Deficiency ranking as unsecured* ₹	*(d) Surplus carried to last column* ₹
Leasehold property	2,18,000	54,000	—	1,64,000

Estimated surplus from assets specifically pledged	1,64,000
Estimated total assets available for preferential creditors, debentureholders secured by floating charge, and unsecured creditors	5,05,000

SUMMARY OF GROSS ASSETS

Particulars	₹
Gross realisable value of assets specifically pledged:	2,18,000
Other assets	3,41,000
Gross assets	5,59,000

(e) Gross Liabilities ₹	*Liabilities*	₹
	(To be deducted from surplus *or* added to deficiency as the case may be)	
54,000	Secured creditors (as per list B) to the extent to which claims are estimated to be covered by assets specifically pledged	—
3,000	Preference creditors (List C)	3,000
	Estimated balance of assets available for debentureholders secured by a floating charge and unsecured creditors	5,02,000
1,50,000	Debentures (List D)	1,50,000
	Estimated surplus as regard debenture holders	3,52,000
60,000	Creditors (List E)	60,000
2,67,000		2,92,000
	Estimated surplus as regards creditors [being difference between gross assets (d) and gross liabilities (e)]	
	Issued and called up capital:	
	24,000 equity shares of ₹ 10 each (List G)	2,40,000
	Estimated surplus as regard members	52,000

PROBLEM 2

A winding up order has been issued CAMGG Ltd. The following information is obtained with regard to the assets and liabilities as on 30th June, 2013:

Particulars	₹
Freehold premises (book value ₹ 4,50,000) valued at	3,75,000

First Mortgage of Freehold premises		3,00,000
Second Mortgage of Freehold premises		1,12,500
8% Debentures carrying a floating charge on the undertaking, interest due 1st September and 1st April, and paid on due dates		1,50,000
Managing Director's emoluments (6 months)		22,500
Staff Salary unpaid (one month)		16,050
Trade Debtors:	Good	31,500
	Doubtful (Estimated to realise 50%)	12,900
	Bad	72,750
Plant and Machinery (Book value ₹ 2,47,500) Estimated to realise		1,74,000
Bank overdraft Unsecured		58,125
Cash in hand		825
Stock (at cost ₹ 50,850) Estimated to realise		33,900
Issued Capital:		
Equity Shares of ₹ 10 each fully called up		1,50,000
Calls in arrear, ₹ 3,000, Estimated to realise		1,500
Unsecured Creditors		2,96,250
Contingent Liability in respect of a claim for damages ₹ 37,500-Estimated to be settled for		18,000
Income-tax Liability:		
For 30.6.2011		5,250
For 30.6.2012		1,275
For 30.6 2013		2,700

The Reserves of the Company on 1.7.2012 amounted to ₹ 7,500.

Required: Prepare (i) Statement of Affairs and (ii) Deficiency Account.

SOLUTION

(I) STATEMENT OF AFFAIRS OF CAMGG LTD. (IN LIQUIDATION) AS ON 30TH JUNE, 2013

Assets not specifically pledged as per list A:	*Estimated Realisable Value* ₹
Cash in hand	825
Trade debtors	37,950
Unpaid calls	1,500
Stock	33,900
Plant and Machinery	1,74,000

Assets specifically pledged as per list B:

Particulars	*Estimated Realisable Value* ₹	*Due to secured creditors* ₹	*Deficiency ranking as unsecured* ₹	*Surplus carried to last column* ₹
Freehold premises	3,75,000	3,00,000	—	75.000

Second mortgage on above	75.000	1,12,500	37,500	—

Estimated total assets available for Preferential creditors, Debentureholders secured by a floating charge and other creditors (carried forward)		2,48,175
Summary of Gross Assets	₹	
Assets specifically pledged	3,75,000	
Other assets	2,48,175	
	6,23,175	
Estimated total assets available for Preferential creditors, Debentureholders secured by a floating charge and unsecured creditors brought forward		2,48,175

Gross Liabilities ₹	*Liabilities*		
3,75,000	Secured creditors as per List B to the extent claims are covered by assets specifically pledged.		—
20,025	Preferential creditors as per List C		20,025
	Estimated balance of assets available for debentureholders having a floating charge and unsecured creditors**		2,28,150
1,53,000	Debentureholders secured by floating charge as per List D.		1,53,000
	Estimated surplus as regards debentureholders		75,150
		₹	
37,500	Estimated unsecured balance of claims of partly secured creditors	37,500	
2,96,250	Trade creditors	2,96,250	
27,750	Outstanding expenses and taxes	27,750	
58,125	Bank overdraft	58,125	
18,000	Contingent liability for claim for damages	18,000	
9,85,650			4,37,625
	Estimated deficiency as regards creditors, being the excess of gross liabilities over gross assets.		3,62,475
	Issued and called up capital:		
	15,000 equity shares of ₹ 10 each fully called up *less* calls in arrears, ₹ 1,500 (As per List G)		1,48,500
	Estimated deficiency as regards contributories		5,10,975

**The figures must be read subject to the following:

1. There is no unpaid capital liable to be called up.
2. The estimates are subject to cost of the winding up and to any surplus *or* deficiency on trading pending realisation of assets.

(II) LIST H—DEFICIENCY ACCOUNT

Particulars		₹
A Items contributing to Deficiency		
1. Excess of capital and liabilities over assets three year ago		—

2.	Dividend and bonuses declared		—
3.	Net trading losses after charging depreciation, taxation, interest on debentures, etc.		2,55,825
4.	Losses other than trading losses		—
5.	Estimated losses now written off:	₹	
	Freehold Premises	75,000	
	Trade debtors	79,200	
	Plant & Machinery	73,500	
	Stock	16,950	
	Claim for damages	18,000	2,62,650
6.	Any other item		
	Total (A)		5,18,475
B	*Items reducing Deficiency:*		
7.	Excess of assets over capital and liabilities three years ago		7,500
8.	Net trading profits		—
9.	Profits and incomes other than trading profits.		—
10.	Other items.		—
	Total (B)		7,500
C.	Deficiency as explained in the Statement of Affairs [(A) – (B)]		5,10,975

Working Notes:

(I) BALANCE SHEET AS AT 30.6.2013

Liabilities	₹	*Assets*	₹
Capital, net	1,47,000	Freehold premises	4,50,000
Reserves	7,500	Plant and Machinery	2,47,500
1st Mortgage	3,00,000	Sundry Debtors	1,17,150
2nd Mortgage	1,12,500	Stock	50,850
8% Debentures	1,50,000	Cash	825
Interest for 3 Months	3,000	Profit and Loss Account (b.f.)	2,55,825
Sundry creditors (includ. managerial remuneration and salaries)	3,34,800		
Bank overdraft	58,125		
Provision for taxation	9,225		
	11,22,150		11,22,150

(II) PREFERENTIAL CREDITORS

Income tax:	2011-2012	1,275
	2012-2013	2,700
Staff Salary		16,050
		20,025

PROBLEM 3

CAS Ltd. was ordered to be wound up on March 31st, 2013 on which date its Balance Sheet was as follows:

Particulars		
10,000 shares of ₹ 100 each		10,00,000
5% Debentures	1,60,000	
Interest accrued (Secured by floating charge on all assets)	4,000	1,64,000
Bank Overdraft (Secured by hypothecation of stock)		25,000
Sundry Creditors		36,000
Goodwill		1,00,000
Building		3,50,000
Plant		5,50,000
Fixtures		23,000
Stock		38,000
Debtors		25,000
Cash		500
P & L A/c		1,38,500

The amount estimated to be realised are; Goodwill ₹ 1,000; Buildings ₹ 3,00,000; Plant ₹ 5,25,000; Fixtures ₹ 10,000; Stock ₹ 31,000; Debtors ₹ 20,000.

Creditors included ₹ 6,000 an account of wages of 15 men at ₹ 100 per month for 4 months immediately before the date of winding up: ₹ 9,000 being the salaries of 5 employees at ₹ 300 per month for the previous 6 months; Rent for godown for the last six months amounting to ₹ 3,000; Income-tax deducted out of salaries of employees ₹ 1,000 and Directors Fees ₹ 500.

Three years ago the debit balance in the Profit and Loss Account was ₹ 77,925 and since that date the accounts of the company have shown the following figures:

Particulars	*Year 31.3.2011*	*Year 31.3.2012*	*Year 31.3.2013*
Gross Profit	65,000	45,000	40,000
Wages & Salaries	40,500	36,000	34,400
Electricity, Water & Tax	5,750	6,380	5,260
Debentures interest	8,000	8,000	8,000
Bad debts	8,540	7,600	6,700
Depreciation	6,700	—	—
Directors' Fees	1,000	1,000	1,000
Miscellaneous Expenses	10,500	7,265	7,980
Total	80,990	66,245	63,340

In addition, it is estimated the company would have to pay ₹ 5,000 as compensation to an employee for injuries suffered by him which was a contingent liability not accepted by the company. Prepare the Statement of Affairs and the Deficiency Account in Form 57 of Companies (Court) Rules 1959.

SOLUTION

STATEMENT OF AFFAIRS (IN LIQUIDATION) X LTD. ON 31st MARCH, 2013

Assets not specifically pledged as per list A:	*Estimated Realisable Value* ₹
Cash-in-hand	500
Debtors	20,000
Building	3,00,000
Plant	5,25,000
Fixtures	10,000
Goodwill	1,000
	8,56,500

Assets specifically pledged as per list B:

Particulars	*(a) Estimated Realisable Value* ₹	*(b) Due to secured creditors* ₹	*(c) Deficiency ranking as unsecured* ₹	*(d) Surplus carried to last column* ₹
Stock	31,000	25,000	—	6,000

Estimated surplus from assets specifically pledged		6,000
Estimated total assets available for preferential		
creditors. Debenture holders secured by a floating		8,62,500
charge and unsecured creditors (carried forward).		
Summary of Gross Assets	₹	
Gross realisable value of assets specifically pledged	31,000	
Other Assets	8,56,000	8,87,500
Estimated total assets available for preferential creditors, Debenture holders secured by a floating charge and unsecured creditors brought forward.		8,62,500

E Gross Liabilities ₹	*Liabilities*		
25,000	Secured creditors (as per List B) to the extent to which claims are estimated to be covered by assets specifically pledged.		
18,000	Preferential Creditors (as per list C)		18,000
	Estimated balance of assets available for Debenture holders secured by a floating charge and unsecured creditors.		8,44,500
1,64,000	Debenture holders secured by floating charge (as per list D).		1,64,000
	Estimated surplus as regards Debenture holders*		6,80,500
	Unsecured Creditors (as per list E).		
	Estimated unsecured balance of claims of creditors partly secured on specific assets brought forward (C).	nil	

	Creditors on Trade Accounts	16,500	
24,000	Outstanding Expenses	6,500	23,000
2,31,000	Estimated Surplus as regards creditors, being the difference between Gross Assets (D) and Gross Liabilities as per column (E)		6,57,500
	Issued and Called-up capital:		
	1,000 Equity Shares of ₹ 100 each fully called up (as per list G).		10,00,000
	Estimated Deficiency as regards contributories		3,42,500

*Note: This must be read subject to the following:

(1) There is no unpaid capital to the called-up.

(2) The estimates are subject to cost of the winding up and to any surplus *or* deficiency on trading pending realisation of assets.

LIST H—DEFICIENCY ACCOUNT

	Particulars		₹
A	*Items contributing to deficiency:*		
	(1) Excess of capital and liabilities over assets three years ago as shown by Balance Sheet.		77,925
	(2) Net dividends *or* bonuses declared during the period		Nil
	(3) Net Trading Losses (after charging items shown in note below for the same period.		60,575
	(4) Losses other than trading losses written off *or* for which provision has been made in the books during the same period.		
	(5) Estimated losses now written off *or* for which provision has been made for the purpose of preparing the statement:	₹	
	Bad Debts	5,000	
	Loss on:		
	Goodwill	99,000	
	Buildings	50,000	
	Plant	25,000	
	Fixtures	13,000	
	Stock	7,000	
	Workmen's compensation	5,000	2,04,000
	(6) Other items contributing to deficiency:		3,42,500
B	*Items reducing deficiency:*		Nil
C	Deficiency as shown by the Statement of Affairs		3,42,500

Notes as to Net Trading Profits and Losses:

Provision for depreciation for renewals, diminution in value of fixed assets	6,700
Charged for Income-tax	Nil
Interest on Debentures	24,000

Payments to directors made by the company and required by law to be disclosed in the accounts	3,000
Total	33,700

Particulars of Creditors for expenses	*Unsecured* ₹	*Preferential* ₹
Directors' Fees	500	
Income-tax on salaries	—	1,000
Rent (not distrained by landlord)	3,000	—
Wages (15 men for 4 months at ₹ 100 each)	—	6,000
Salaries (5 men for 6 months at ₹ 300 each) (₹ 9,000, but not exceeding ₹ 1,000 each),	3,000	6,000
Workmen's Compensation	—	5,000
	6,500	18,000

Creditors on trade accounts are ₹ 16,500 (i.e., ₹ 36,000 *less* the total of creditors mentioned above, excluding ₹ 5,000 for workmen's compensation).

PROBLEM 4

CAMHD Ltd. went into voluntary liquidation on 31st March, 2013 when their Balance Sheet read as follows:

Particulars	₹
Issued and subscribed Capital:	
5,000 10% cumulative preference shares of ₹ 100 each fully paid	5,00,000
2,500 equity shares of ₹ 100 each, ₹ 75 paid	1,87,500
7,500 equity shares of ₹ 100 each, ₹ 60 paid	4,50,000
15% Debentures secured by a floating charge	2,50,000
Interest outstanding on Debentures	37,500
Creditors	3,18,750
Land and Buildings	2,50,000
Machinery and Plant	6,25,000
Patents	1,00,000
Stock	1,37,500
Sundry debtors	2,75,000
Cash at bank	75,000
Profit and Loss A/c	2,81,250

Preference dividends were in arrears for 2 years and the creditors included preferential creditors of ₹ 38,000.

The assets realised as follows:

Land and buildings ₹ 3,00,000, Machinery and plant ₹ 5,00,000, Patents ₹ 75,000, Stock ₹ 1,50,000: Sundry debtors ₹ 2,00,000.

The expenses of liquidation amounted to ₹ 27,250. The liquidator is entitled to a commission of 3% on assets realised except cash.

Required: Assuming the final payments including those on debentures is made on 30th Sept., 2013, show the liquidator's Final Statement of Account.

SOLUTION

CAMHD LIMITED
LIQUIDATORS' FINAL STATEMENT OF ACCOUNT

Receipts		₹	*Payments*		₹
Assets Realised:			Liquidation expenses		27,250
Bank		75,000	Liquidator remuneration		36,750
Other assets—			Debentureholders:		
Land & Buildings	3,00,000		Debentures	2,50,000	
Machinery & Plant	5,00,000		Interest Outstanding	37,500	
Patents	75,000		Accrued Interest upto		
Stock	1,50,000		30th June	18,750	3,06,250
Sundry Debtors	2,00,000	12,25,000	Preferential Creditors		38,000
Call on equity shareholders			Unsecured Creditors		2,80,750
(7,500 × ₹ 2.65)		19,875	Preference shareholders:		
			Pref. Capital	5,00,000	
			Arrears of Dividends	1,00,000	6,00,000
			Equity Shareholders ₹ 12.35		
			each on 2,500 shares		30,875
		13,19,875			13,19,875

Working Notes:

(i) Liquidator's remuneration @ 3% on amount realised: = 12,25,000 × 3% = 36,750

(ii) As the company is solvent, interest on the debentures will have to be paid up to 30th Sept. 2,50,000 × 15/100 × 6/12 = 18,750

(III) CALCULATION OF DEFICIENCY

A.	Total Paid-up Share Capital	6,37,500
B.	*Less:* Cash Available [₹ 13,00,000 – 12,89,000]	(11,000)
C.	Deficiency to be borne (A – B)	6,26,500
D.	Total Nominal Share Capital	10,00,000
E.	Deficiency as % of Nominal Capital (C/D × 100)	62.65%

(IV) CALCULATION OF NET AMOUNT RETURNABLE FOR SHARES

Particulars	*Class of Shares*	
	A	*B*
A.Paid-up Amount Per Share	75	60
B.*Less:* Deficiency to be borne @ 62.65% of Nominal value	62.65	62.65
C.Net Amount Returnable (A–B)	12.35	(2.65)

PROBLEM 5

CAMHG Ltd. was placed in voluntary liquidation on 31st March, 2013, when is Balance Sheet was follows:

Particulars	₹
50,000 Equity Shares of ₹ 10 each fully paid *less* calls in arrear amounting to ₹.25,000	4,75,000
6,000 5% Cumulative Preference Shares of ₹ 100 each fully paid	6,00,000
Securities Premium Account	50,000
5% Debentures Account	1,00,000
Interest on Debentures	2,500
Bank Overdrafts	58,000
Creditors	1,15,000
Freehold Factory	5,80,000
Plant and Machinery	2,89,000
Motor Vehicles	57,500
Stock	1,86,000
Debtors	74,000
Profit and Loss Account	2,14,000

The Preference dividends are in arrears from 2009–10 onwards

The Company's articles provide that on liquidation, out of the surplus assets remaining after payment of liquidation costs and outside liabilities, there shall be paid firstly all arrears of Preference dividend, secondly the amount paid up on the Preference Shares together with a premium thereon of ₹ 10 per share, and thirdly the balance then remaining shall be paid to the equity shareholders.

The Bank Overdraft was guaranteed by the directors who were called upon by the Bank to discharge their liability under the guarantee. The directors paid the amount to the Bank.

The liquidator realised the assets as follows:

Freehold Factory ₹ 7,00,000, Plant and Machinery ₹ 2,40,000, Motor Vehicles ₹ 59,000, Stock ₹ 1,50,000, Debtors ₹ 60,000 Calls in Arrears ₹ 25,000.

Creditors were paid *less* discount of 5 percent. The debentures and accrued interest were repaid on 30th June, 2013. Liquidation costs were ₹ 3,820 and the liquidator's remuneration was 2 per cent on the amounts realised.

Required: Prepare the Liquidator's Statement of Account.

SOLUTION

LIQUIDATOR'S STATEMENT OF ACCOUNT

Receipts	₹	*Payments*		₹
Assets Realised:		Liquidator's Remuneration		
Debtors	60,000	@ 2% on ₹ 12,34,000		24,680
Calls in Arrears	25,000	Liquidation costs		3,820
Stock	1,50,000	Debenure holders having		
Freehold Property	7,00,000	a floating charge:		
Plant & Machinery	2,40,000	Principal	1,00,000	
Motor Vehicles	59,000	Interest upto		

		31st March	3,750	1,03,750
		Unsecured Creditors:		
		Directors	58,000	
		Others	1,09,250	1,67,250
		Preference Shareholders:		
		Share capital and premium	6,60,000	
		Arrears of Dividend	1,20,000	7,80,000
		Equity Shareholders		1,54,500
	12,34,000			12,34,000

Working Notes:

	Particulars	₹
(i)	Amount payable to Sundry Creditors	1,15,000
	Less: discount 5%	5,750
		1,09,250
(ii)	Amount payable to Debenture holders	
	Principal amount	1,00,000
	Interest upto 31st March,	3,750
		1,03,750

PROBLEM 6

The following is the Balance Sheet of CANID Limited as at 31st March, 2013:

Particulars	₹
Share Capital:	
2,000 Equity Shares of ₹ 100 each ₹ 75 per share paid up	1,50,000
6,000 equity shares of ₹ 100 each ₹ 60 per share paid up	3,60,000
2,000 10% Preference Share of ₹ 100 each fully paid up	2,00,000
Secured Loans:	
10% Debentures (having a floating charge on all assets)	2,00,000
Interest accrued on Debentures (also secured as above)	10,000
Current Liabilities:	
Sundry Creditors	4,90,000
Fixed Assets:	
Land & Buildings	4,00,000
Plant and Machineries	3,80,000
Current Assets:	
Stock at cost	1,10,000
Sundry Debtors	2,20,000
Cash at Bank	60,000
Profit and Loss A/c	2,40,000

On that date, the company went into Voluntary Liquidation. The dividends on preference shares were in arrears for the last two years. Sundry Creditors include a loan of ₹ 90,000 on mortgage of Land and Buildings. Liquidator realised the assets as under:

Land and Buildings ₹ 3,40,000, Plant & Machineries ₹ 3,60,000, Stock ₹ 1,20,000, Sundry Debtors ₹ 1,60,000.

Interest accrued on loan on mortgage of buildings upto the date of payment amounted to ₹ 10,000. The expenses of Liquidation amounted to ₹ 4,600. The Liquidator is entitled to a remuneration of 3% on all the assets realised (except cash at bank) and 2% on the amounts distributed among equity shareholders. Preferential creditors included in sundry creditors amount to ₹ 30,000. All payments were made on 30th June, 2013.

Required: Prepare the liquidator's final statement of account.

SOLUTION

LIQUIDATOR'S FINAL STATEMENT OF ACCOUNT

Receipts		₹	*Payments*		₹
Cash at Bank		60,000	Liquidation Expenses		4,600
Assets realised:			Liquidator's remuneration		30,400
Sundry Debtors	1,60,000		Debenture holders:		
Stock	1,20,000		10% Debentures	2,00,000	
Plant & Machinery	3,60,000	6,40,000	Interest accrued	15,000	2,15,000
Surplus from Land &			Preferential Creditors		30,000
Buildings:			Unsecured Creditors		3,70,000
Amount realised	3,40,000		Preference shareholders:		
Less: Secured			Capital	2,00,000	
Creditors	1,00,000	2,40,000	Arrear Dividend	40,000	2,40,000
			Equity Shareholders		
			₹ 17.50 per share		
			on 2,000 shares	35,000	
			₹ 2.50 per share		
			on 6,000 shares	15,000	50,000
		9,40,000			9,40,000

Working Notes:

Particulars	₹
(i) Liquidator's remuneration:	
3% on Assets realised (3% of ₹ 9,80,000)	29,400
2% of the amounts distributed among	
Equity Shareholders (₹ 51,000 × 2/102)	1,000
	30,400
(ii) Interest accrued on 10% debentures	
Interest accrued as on 31st March,	10,000
Interest accrued upto the date of payment (upto 30th June)	5,000

		15,000
(iii)	Amount payable to Equity Shareholders	
A	Equity Share Capital	5,10,000
B	*Less:* Surplus available for Equity Shareholders	50,000
C	Loss to be made borne by them	4,60,000
D	Loss per Equity Share (₹ 4,60,000/8,000)	57.50
	Amount payable to Equity shareholders:	
	Each Equity Share of ₹ 75 paid up	17.50
	Each Equity Share of ₹ 60 paid up	2.50

PROBLEM 7

The following was the Balance Sheet of CANIH Limited as on 31.3.2013:

Particulars	₹
Share Capital:	
14%, 4,000 preference shares of ₹ 100 each fully paid up	4,00,000
8,000 equity shares of ₹ 100 each, ₹ 60 per share paid up	4,80,000
Reserve and Surplus	Nil
Secured Loans:	
1. 14% debentures (Having a floating charge on all assets)	2,30,000
Interest accrued on above debentures (Also having a floating charge as above)	32,200
2. Loan on mortgage of Land and Building	1,50,000
Unsecured Loans:	Nil
Current Liabilities and Provisions:	
A. Current Liabilities	
Sundry Creditors	1,17,800
Fixed Assets:	
Land	40,000
Buildings	1,60,000
Plant and Machinery	5,40,000
Patents	40,000
Investments	Nil
Current assets, loans & advances:	
A. Current assets	
Stock at cost	1,00,000
Sundry Debtors	2,30,000
Cash at Bank	60,000
B. Loans and Advances:	Nil
Miscellaneous Expenditure:	Nil
Profit and Loss A/c	2,40,000

On 31.3.2013 the company went into voluntary liquidation. The dividend on 14% preference shares was in arrears for one year. Sundry Creditors include preferential creditors amounted to ₹ 30,000. The liquidator realised the assets as under:

Land ₹ 80,000; Buildings ₹ 2,00,000; Plant and Machinery ₹ 5,00,000; Patent ₹ 50,000; Stock ₹ 1,60,000; Sundry Debtors ₹ 2,00,000.

The expenses of liquidation amounted to ₹ 29,434. The liquidator is entitled to a commission of 2% on all assets realised (except cash at bank) and 2% on amounts distributed among unsecured creditors other than preferential creditors. All payments were made on 30th June, 2013. Interest on mortgage loan shall be ignored at the time of payment.

Required: Prepare the Liquidator's Final Statement of Account.

SOLUTION

CANIH LTD.
LIQUIDATOR'S FINAL STATEMENT OF ACCOUNT

Receipts	*Book Value* ₹	*Value Realised* ₹	*Payments*		₹
Assets Realised:			Liquidators Expenses		29,434
Cash at Bank	60,000	60,000	Liquidators Remuneration:		
Sundry Debtors	2,30,000	2,00,000	2% on Assets Realised		
Stock	1,00,000	1,60,000	(i.e., on 11,90,000)	23,800	
Patents	40,000	50,000	2% on Payments to		
Plant & Machinery	5,40,000	5,00,000	Unsecured Creditors		
Surplus from			(i.e., on 87,800)	1,756	25,556
secured loan on			14% Debentures	2,30,000	
Mortgage of Land			Interest due upto		
& Building after			30th June		
payment of loan		1,30,000	(32,200 + 8,050)	40,250	2,70,250
			Preferential Creditors		30,000
			Unsecured Creditors		87,800
			Preference Shareholders	4,00,000	
			Add: Dividend Arrears	56,000	4,56,000
			Equity Shareholders willget ₹ 25.12 per share		2,00,960
		11,00,000			11,00,000

Working Notes:

(I) CALCULATION OF LIQUIDATOR'S REMUNERATION

Particulars	₹
(i) 2% on all assets realised i.e. ₹ 11,90,000	
(80,000 + 2,00,000 + 5,00,000 + 50,000 + 1,60,000 + 2,00,000)	23,800
(ii) 2% on amounts distributed to unsecured creditors i.e. ₹ 87,800	1,756
Total	25,556

(ii) *Payment to Equity Shareholders:*

Equity Shareholders will get ₹ 2,00,960 for their 8,000 Equity Shares of ₹ 100 each, ₹ 60 per Share paid up i.e. ₹ 25.12 per Share

PROBLEM 8

In a liquidation which commenced on April 2, 2013 certain creditors could not receive payments out of the realisation of assets and out of the contributions from "A" list contributories. The following are the details of certain transfers which took place in 2012 and 2013.

Shareholders	*No. of shares transferred*	*Date of ceasing to be member*	*Creditors remaining unpaid & outstanding at the date of ceasing to be member*
X	1,500	Ist March 2012	4,000
A	1,000	Ist May 2012	6,000
B	1,500	Ist Nov. 2012	7,500
C	300	Ist Dec. 2012	8,000
D	200	Ist Feb. 2013	9,500

All the shares were ₹ 10 each, ₹ 6 paid up. Ignoring expenses, remuneration to liquidator, etc., show the amount to be realised from the various persons listed above.

SOLUTION

STATEMENT OF LIABILITY OF 'B' LIST CONTRIBUTORIES

Incremental Creditors Outstanding on the date of ceasing to be member	*A 1,000 shares* ₹	*B 1,500 shares* ₹	*C 300 shares* ₹	*D 200 shares* ₹	*Amount to be paid to the creditors* ₹
(1) 6,000	2,000	3,000	600	400	6,000
(2) 1,500 (i.e. 7,500 – 6,000)	—	1,125	225	150	1,500
(3) 500 (i.e. 8,000 – 7,500)	—	—	300	200	500
(4) 1,500 (i.e. 9,500 – 8,000)	—	—	—	1,500	50
Total (a)	2,000	4,125	1,125	2,250	
(b) Maximum liability on shares held	4,000	6,000	1,200	800	
(c) Amount paid (a) *or* (b) whichever is lower	2,000	4,125	1,125	800	

*(₹ 800 – ₹ 400 – ₹ 150 – ₹ 200)

PROBLEM 9

CAMHA Limited went into voluntary liquidation and the proceedings commenced on 2nd July, 2013. Certain creditors could not receive payment out of the realisation of assets and out of the contributions from the contributories of the 'A' list. The following details of share transfers are made available to you.

Shareholders	*No. of shares transferred*	*Date of ceasing to be member*	*Creditors remaining unpaid and outstanding at the date of ceasing to be member*
(i) A	1,000	Ist March, 2012	₹ 6,000

(ii) B	1,250	15th August, 2012	₹ 8,000
(iii) C	500	Ist October, 2012	₹ 10,750
(iv) D	2,000	Ist December, 2012	₹ 13,000
(v) E	250	Ist April, 2013	₹ 15,000

All the shares were of ₹ 10 each, on which ₹ 5 per share had been paid up. Ignoring other details like liquidator's expenses etc., you are required to workout of the liability of the individual contributories listed above.

SOLUTION

STATEMENT OF LIABILITY OF 'B ' LIST CONTRIBUTORIES

Date	*Creditors Outstanding*	*Incremental Amount*	*B*	*C*	*D*	*E*
			No. of shares held			
	₹	₹	*1,250* ₹	*500* ₹	*2,000* ₹	*250* ₹
15 Aug. 2012	8,000	8,000	2,500	1,000	4,000	500
Ist Oct. 2012	10,750	2,750	—	500	2,000	250
Ist Dec. 2012	13,000	2,250	—	—	2,000	250
Ist April, 2013	15,000	2,000	—	—	—	2,000
A. Max. amount payable to creditors			2,500	1,500	8,000	3,000
B. Amount of calls in arrear @ ₹ 5 per share			6,250	2,500	10,000	1,250
C. Actual liability lower of A *or* B			2,500	1,500	8,000	1,250
D. Total amount paid to Creditors 13,250						

Notes:

(i) Incremental creditors of ₹ 2,000 on Ist April, 2013 will get only ₹ 250 from E. Since the maximum amount recoverable from E is ₹ 1,250 of which ₹ 1,000 will be absorbed by creditors outstanding on Ist Dec.

(ii) The various amounts outstanding on the date of transfer of shares have been apportioned on the basis of the number of shares held by B list contributories.

10 FINANCIAL STATEMENTS OF BANKING COMPANIES

LEARNING OBJECTIVES

After studying this chapter, you should be able to understand:

- Meaning of Banking [Section 5(b) of The Banking Regulation Act, 1949]
- Meaning of Banking Company
- Licensing of Banking Companies [Section 22]
- Prohibition of Trading (Section 8)
- Time Limit for Disposal of Non-Banking Assets [Section 9]
- Minimum Paid up Capital and Reserve [Section 11]
- Minimum Subscribed and Paid up Capital [Section 12]
- Maximum Voting Right of any Single Shareholder
- Maximum Rate of Commission etc. of Shares [Section 13]
- Restriction on Creation of Charge on Unpaid Capital [Section 14]
- Restriction on Creation of Floating Charge on the Assets [Section 14A]
- Restriction as to Payment of Dividend [Sections 15 (1) and (2)]
- Minimum Transfer of Profits to Reserve Fund [Section 17]
- Maintenance of Cash Reserve [Section 18]
- Restriction on Acquisition of Shares in other Company [Section 19]
- Restriction on Loans and Advances [Section 20]
- Liquidity Norms (Section 24)
- Unclaimed Deposits
- Duty to Prepare Annual Accounts [Section 29]
- Annual Accounts to be Signed
- Annual Accounts to be Audited [Section 30]
- Duty to Submit three Copies of Annual Accounts with Auditor's Report
- Bank's Book-keeping System
- Main Characteristics of a Bank's Book-keeping System
- Books of Accounts
- Returns to be Filed by Banking Companies
- Balance Sheet and Profit and Loss Account [Section 29]
- Note containing guidelines of Reserve Bank of India for compilation of Financial Statement
- Disclosure of Accounting Policies
- Capital Adequacy Norms

- Non-Performing Assets (NPAs)
- Basis of Income Recognition
- Classification of Bank Advances for determining the amount of Provision
- How to make provision in respect of Advances covered by the Guarantees of I DICGC/ECGC
- Classification of Investments for the Purposes of Valuation
- Bills for Collection
- Rebate on Bills Discounted
- Acceptances and Endorsements
- Statutory Liquidity Ratio (SLR), Cash Reserve Ratio (CRR) and Incremental CRR) for Scheduled Commercial Banks

1.0 MEANING OF BANKING [SECTION 5(B) OF THE BANKING REGULATION ACT, 1949]

"Banking" means, the accepting, for the purpose of lending *or* investment, of deposits of money from the public, repayable on demand *or* otherwise, and withdrawal by Cheque, draft, order *or* otherwise.

2.0 MEANING OF BANKING COMPANY

Banking Company means any company which transacts the business of banking in India.

3.0 LICENSING OF BANKING COMPANIES [SECTION 22]

A banking company must hold a licence issued by the Reserve Bank of India to carry on banking business in India.

4.0 PROHIBITION OF TRADING [SECTION 8]

A banking company cannot directly *or* indirectly deal in the buying *or* selling *or* bartering of goods. However, it may buy, sell *or* barter in connection with the bills of exchange received for collection *or* negotiation.

5.0 TIME LIMIT FOR DISPOSAL OF NON-BANKING ASSETS [SECTION 9]

Non-banking assets must be disposed off within 7 years from the date of acquisition *or* period extended by RBI.

6.0 MINIMUM PAID UP CAPITAL AND RESERVE [SECTION 11]

Banking Company	*Minimum Aggregate Value of Paid up Capital and Reserve*
1. In case of a Banking Company incorporated outside India:	
(a) *having a place(s) of business in the city of Mumbai or Kolkata or both*	₹ 20 lacs
(b) *not having a place(s) of business in the city of Mumbai or Kolkata or both*	₹ 15 lacs

2. In case of a banking company incorporated in India:	
(a) *having place of business in more than one State including place(s) business in the city of Mumbai or Kolkata or both*	₹ 10 lacs
(b) *having all its places of business in one state and none of which is in the city of Mumbai or Kolkata*	₹ 1 lac + ₹ 10,000 for each of other places of business in the district in which it has its principal place of business + ₹ 25,000 for each place of business elsewhere in the state subject of maximum of ₹ 5 lacs

7.0 MINIMUM SUBSCRIBED AND PAID UP CAPITAL [SECTION 12]

The subscribed capital of a banking company must be at least 50% of the authorised capital and the paid up capital must be at least 50% of the subscribed capital.

8.0 MAXIMUM VOTING RIGHT OF ANY SINGLE SHAREHOLDER

The voting right of any single shareholder must not exceed 1 % of the total voting rights.

9.0 MAXIMUM RATE OF COMMISSION ETC. ON ISSUE OF SHARES [SECTION 13]

A banking company cannot pay directly *or* indirectly commission, brokerage, discount, *or* remuneration in respect of any shares issued by it, an amount exceeding 2½% of the paid up value of such shares.

10.0 RESTRICTION ON CREATION OF CHARGE ON UNPAID CAPITAL [SECTION 14]

A banking company can not create any charge upon any unpaid capital of the company.

11.0 RESTRICTION ON CREATION OF FLOATING CHARGE ON THE ASSETS [SECTION 14A]

A banking company can not create floating charge on the undertaking *or* any property *or* any part thereof unless the creation of such floating charge is certified in writing by the Reserve Bank as not being detrimental to the interest of the depositors of such company.

12.0 *RESTRICTION AS TO PAYMENT OF DIVIDEND [SECTIONS 15 (1) AND (2)]

Before paying any dividend, a banking company has to write off completely all its capitalised expenses including preliminary expenses, organisation expenses, share-selling commission, brokerage, and amounts of losses incurred by tangible assets. However, a banking company may pay dividend on its shares without writing off:

1. the depreciation in the value of its investment in approved securities in any case where such depreciation has not actually been capitalised *or* accounted for as a loss;
2. the depreciation in the value of its investment in shares, debentures *or* bonds (other than approved securities) in any case where adequate provision for such depreciation has been made to the satisfaction of the auditor of the banking company;
3. the bad debts in any case where adequate provision for such debts had been made to the satisfaction of the auditor of the banking company.

13.0 *MINIMUM TRANSFER OF PROFITS TO RESERVE FUND [SECTION 17]

Every banking company incorporated in India is required to transfer **at least 25%** of its profit to the reserve fund.

The profit of the year as per the profit and loss account prepared u/s 29 is to be taken as base for the purpose of such transfer and transfer to reserve fund should be made before declaration of any dividend.

If any banking company makes any appropriation from the reserve fund *or* securities premium account, it has to report to the Reserve Bank of India the reasons for such appropriation within 21 days.

14.0 MAINTENANCE OF CASH RESERVE [SECTION 18]

Every non-scheduled bank has to maintain a cash reserve atleast to the extent of **at % prescribed (by RBI) of its demand and time liabilities in India on the last Friday** of the second preceding fortnight.

Cash reserve can be maintained by way of balance in a current account with the Reserve Bank of India *or* by way of net balance in current accounts.

Every non-scheduled bank has to submit a return showing the amount so held for cash reserve along with the particulars of its demand and time liabilities in India on such Friday before 20th day of every month.

If any such Friday is a holiday under the Negotiable Instruments Act 1881, such return is to be sent at the close of business on the preceding working day.

Every Scheduled Commercial Bank has to maintain cash reserve as per direction of the RBI issued under Section 42 (IA) of the Reserve Bank of India Act, 1934.

15.0 RESTRICTION ON ACQUISITION OF SHARES IN OTHER COMPANY [SECTION 19]

A banking company cannot form any subsidiary except for one *or* more of the following purposes:

1. The undertaking of any business permissible for banking company to undertake.
2. Carrying on business of banking exclusively outside India with previous permission in writing of the Reserve Bank.
3. The undertaking of such other business which the Reserve Bank of India permit with prior approval of the Central Government.

Other than formation of such subsidiary companies as mentioned above, a banking company cannot hold shares in any company either as pledge, mortgage, *or* absolute owner of an amount exceeding 30% of the paid-up share capital of that company *or* 30% of its own paid-up share capital and reserves, whichever is less.

16.0 RESTRICTION ON LOANS AND ADVANCES [SECTION 20]

A banking company cannot grant any loans *or* advances on the security of its own shares.

It cannot enter into any commitment for granting any loan *or* advance to *or* on behalf of:

(a) Any of its directors.

(b) Any firm in which any of its directors is interested as partner, manager, employee *or* guarantor.

(c) Any company other than the subsidiary of the banking company, *or* a company registered under Section 25 of the Companies Act, *or* a Government of which any of the directors of the banking company is a director, manager, employee *or* guarantor *or* in which he holds substantial interest.

(d). Any individual in respect of whom any of its directors is a partner *or* a guarantor.

17.0 LIQUIDITY NORMS (SECTION 24)

Every banking company has to maintain in cash, gold *or* unencumbered approved securities, an amount **at % prescribed (by RBI) of its demand and time liabilities in India.**

However, this percentage is changed by the Reserve Bank of India from time to time considering the general economic conditions.

This is in addition to the average daily balance which a scheduled bank is required to maintain under Section 42 of the Reserve Bank of India Act, and in case of other banking companies, the cash reserve required to be maintained under Section 18 of the Banking Regulation Act.

18.0 UNCLAIMED DEPOSITS

Every banking company is required to submit a return in the prescribed form and manner to the Reserve Bank of India at the end of each calendar year of all accounts in India which could not be operated for 10 years.

This report is to be submitted within 30 days after the close of each calendar year.

In case of fixed deposit, such 10 years are to be reckoned from the date of expiry of the fixed period.

19.0 DUTY TO PREPARE ANNUAL ACCOUNTS [SECTION 29]

Every banking company must prepare a Balance Sheet and Profit and Loss Account in the forms given in Third Schedule at the end of each financial year.

20.0 ANNUAL ACCOUNTS TO BE SIGNED

The statement of accounts must be signed by the manager *or* principal officer and by at least 3 *or* all directors if there are not more than 3 directors in case of a banking company incorporated in India.

In case of a banking company incorporated outside India, the statement of accounts must be signed by the manager *or* agent of the principal office of the company in India.

21.0 ANNUAL ACCOUNTS TO BE AUDITED [SECTION 30]

The Balance Sheet and Profit and Loss Account prepared in accordance with Section 29 shall be audited by a person duly qualified under any law for the time being in force to be an auditor of companies.

Every company is required to take previous approval of the Reserve Bank of India before appointing, re-appointing *or* removing any auditor *or* auditors.

In addition, the Reserve Bank can order special audit of the banking companies accounts if it thinks fit in the public interest of the banking company *or* its depositors.

22.0 DUTY TO SUBMIT THREE COPIES OF ANNUAL ACCOUNTS WITH AUDITOR'S REPORT

Every Banking Company must submit three copies of Profit and Loss Account and Balance Sheet together with Auditor's Report with:

(a) the Reserve Bank of India, and

(b) the Registrar of Companies.

23.0 *BANK'S BOOK-KEEPING SYSTEM

Entering transactions in the ledger directly from vouchers Under bank's Book-keeping system, every transaction particularly concerning the customers is entered in the personal ledger directly from vouchers as soon as it takes place.

The objective of the system is

(a) to keep up-to-date detailed ledgers,

(b) to balance the trial balance every day,

(c) to keep all control accounts in agreement with the detailed ledgers.

24.0 MAIN CHARACTERISTICS OF A BANK'S BOOK-KEEPING SYSTEM

The main characteristics of a bank's system of book-keeping are as follows:

Voucher Posting	Entries in the personal ledger are made directly from vouchers instead of being posted from the books of prime entry.
Voucher Summary Sheets	The vouchers entered into different personal ledgers each day are summarised on summary sheets, totals of which are posted to the control accounts in the general ledger.
Daily Trial Balance	The general ledger trial balance is extracted and agreed everyday.
Continuous Checks	All entries in the detailed personal ledgers and summary sheets are checked by persons other than those who have made the entries. A considerable force of such check is employed, with the general result that most clerical mistakes are detected before another day begins.
Control Accounts	A trial balance of the detailed personal ledgers is prepared periodically, usually every two weeks, agreed with general ledger control accounts.
Double Voucher System	Two vouchers are prepared for every transaction not involving cash-one debit voucher and another credit voucher.
Slip System of Posting	Under this system entries in the personal ledgers are made directly from vouchers instead of being posted from the day book. Pay-in-slips (used by the customers for making deposits) and the cheques (used by the customers for withdrawl) as slips which form the basis of most of the transactions directly recorded in the accounts of customers. As the slips are mostly filled by the customers themselves, this system saves a lot of time and labour of the bank staff. The vouchers entered into different personal ledgers are summarised on summary sheets every day, total of which are posted to the different control accounts which are maintained in the General Ledger.

25.0 BOOK OF ACCOUNTS

PRINCIPAL BOOKS OF ACCOUNTS

1. General Ledger	The General Ledger contains: (a) Control Accounts of all personal ledgers. (b) Profit and Loss Account. (c) Assets' Accounts.

	(d) Contra Accounts. **Usefulness** It facilitates the preparation of Balance Sheet.
2. Profit and Loss Ledger	The Profit and Loss Ledger contains: (a) Detailed Accounts of Revenue items. (b) Detailed Account of Expense items. **Usefulness** It facilitates the preparation of Profit and Loss Account.

SUBSIDIARY BOOKS

1. Personal Ledgers	(a) Current Accounts Ledger. (b) Saving Bank Accounts Ledgers. (c) Fixed Deposit (often further classified by length of period of deposit) Ledgers. (d) Loan Ledger. (e) Overdraft Ledger. (f) Cash Credit Ledger. (g) Customers' Acceptances, Endorsements and Guarantee Ledgers.
2. Bill Registers	(a) Inward Bills for Collection. (b) Outward Bills for Collection. (c) Bills Discounted and Purchased Register.

Note: *Entries in these registers are made by reference to the original documents.*

SUBSIDIARY REGISTERS

1. Demand Drafts, Telegraphic Transfers and Mail Transfers issued on Branches and Agencies.
2. Demand Drafts, Telegraphic Transfers and Mail Transfers received from Branches and Agencies.
3. Letters of Credit.
4. Letters of Guarantee

MEMORANDA BOOKS

1. Departmental Journals	Maintain a record of all the transfer entries originated by each department
2. Cash Department's	(a) Receiving Cashiers' Cash Book (pay-in-slips are vouchers). (b) Paying Cashiers' Cash Book (Bearer Cheques/drafts etc. are vouchers). (c) Main Cash Book (by person other than cashier). (d) Cash Balance Book.
3. Clearing Department's	(a) Outward Clearing (for cheques received from customers): (i) Clearing Cheques Received Book. (ii) Bank wise List of above Cheques (one copy of which is sent to the clearing house together with cheques). (b) Inward Clearing (for cheques issued by customers received from other Banks).

4. Loans and Overdraft Departments'	(a) Registers for shares and other securities held on behalf of each customer. (b) Summary Books of Securities giving details of Government securities, shares of individual companies etc. (c) Godown registers maintained by the godown-keeper of the bank. (d) Price register giving the wholesale price of the commodities pledged with the bank. (e) Overdraft Sanction register. (f) Drawing Power book. (g) Delivery Order books. (h) Storage books.
5. Deposits Department	(a) Account Opening and Closing registers. (b) For Fixed Deposits, Rate register giving analysis of deposits according to rates. (c) Due Date Diary. (d) Specimen signature book.
6. Establishment department	(a) Salary and allied registers, such as attendance register, leave register, overtime register, etc. (b) Register of fixed assets, e.g. furnitures and fixtures, motor cars, vehicles, etc. (c) Stationery registers. (d) Old records register.
7. General	(a) Signature book of bank's officers. (b) Private Telegraphic Code and Cyphers.

26.0 RETURNS TO BE FILED BY BANKING COMPANIES WITH RBI

1 **Monthly Return of unsecured loans and advances** granted to companies is which any of the banking company's directors is interested as director, managing agent *or* guarantor.

2 **Monthly Return of assets** maintained in accordance with Section 24 and time and demand liabilities at the close of business on every Friday.

3 **Quarterly Return of assets and liabilities** at the close of business on the last Friday of every quarter.

4 **Annual return of unclaimed accounts** which have not been operated upon for 10 years *or* more.

5 **Monthly Return of assets and liabilities** at the close of business on the last Friday of every month.

6 **Annual Return of remuneration** paid to directors and the first ten highest paid officers.

7 **Quarterly Return of Officers** in India.

8 **Any other statement or information** as may be required by the Reserve Bank.

27.0 BALANCE SHEET AND PROFIT AND LOSS ACCOUNT [SECTION 29]

Every banking company is required to prepare its Balance Sheet in Form 'A' and Profit and Loss Account in Form 'B' given in Third Schedule.

Twelve Schedules (1 to 12) are required to be annexed to Balance Sheet and Six Schedules (13 to 18) are required to be Profit and Loss Account as follows:

Balance Sheet in Form 'A'	Profit and Loss Account in Form 'B'
Schedule 1—Capital	Schedule 13—Interest Earned
Schedule 2—Reserves and Surplus	Schedule 14—Other Income
Schedule 3—Deposits	Schedule 15—Interest Expended
Schedule 4—Borrowings	Schedule 16—Operating Expenses
Schedule 5—Other Liabilities and Provisions	Schedule 17—Notes on Accounts
Schedule 6—Cash and Balances with Reserve Bank of India	Schedule 18—Principal Accounting Policies
Schedule 7—Balances with Banks &Money at Call & Short Notice	
Schedule 8—Investments	
Schedule 9—Advances	
Schedule 10—Fixed Assets	
Schedule 11—Other Assets	
Schedule 12—Contingent Liabilities	

The prescribed formats of Balance Sheet and Profit and Loss Account as per Third Schedule are given under Para 43 and 44.

28.0 NON-PERFORMING ASSETS (NPA)

MEANING OF NON-PERFORMING ASSET (NPA)

An asset becomes NPA when income from it is not received by the bank within a certain period from the end of the quarter. According to the Master Circular of the RBI dated July 1, 2015 an asset, including a leased asset becomes non performing when it ceases to generate income for the bank.

WHEN IS AN ASSET TREATED AS NPA?

Asset	When is treated NPA?
1. **Term Loan**	If interest and/or instalment of principal remains over due for a period of **more than 90 days.**
2. **Cash Credit and Overdrafts**	If it remains out of order for a period of more than 90 days. An account is treated as 'out of order' (a) if the outstanding balance remains continuously for 90 days in excess of the sanctioned limit/drawing power, *or* (b) if the outstanding balance in the principal operating account is less than the sanctioned limit/drawing power, and there are either no credits continuously for 90 days as on the date of Balance Sheet *or* credits are not enough to cover the interest debited during the same period.
3. **Bills Purchased and Discounted**	If they remain overdue and unpaid for a period of **more than 90 days.**
4. **Agricultural Advances for short duration crops**	If interest and/or instalment of principal remains over due for two harvest seasons.
5. **Agricultural Advances for long duration crops**	If interest and/or instalment of principal remain over due for one crop season.

WHEN IS IDENTIFICATION OF NPA TO BE DONE?

The identification of NPA is to be done on the basis of the position as on the balance sheet date. If an account has been regularised before the balance sheet date by payment of overdue amount through genuine sources (and not by sanction of additional facilities *or* transfer of funds between accounts), the account need not be treated as NPA. The bank should, however, ensure that the account remains in order subsequently.

OTHER GUIDELINES AS TO NPAS

1. An account should not classified as NPA merely due to existence of temporary deficiencies such as balance outstanding exceeding limit for some time.
2. Net worth of borrower/guarantor and the availability and realizable value of security should not be taken into account for the purpose of determining whether an account is NPA *or* not.
3. **Determination of NPAs: Borrower-wise, Not Facility-wise** If any of the credit facilities granted to a borrower becomes non-performing, all facilities granted to the borrower will have to be treated as NPA without any regard to performing status of other facilities. Exception to above is in respect of credit facility granted under on-leading system, to Primary Agricultural credit Societies (PACSs) *or* Farmers service Societies (FSSs).

   In these cases:

   (a) Only that particular credit facility is to be treated as NPA which is in default for a period of:

   (i) two harvest reason not exceeding 2 half years in case of agricultural advances

   (ii) more than 180 days in the case of other advances.

   (b) Other credit facilities will not be treated as NPA.
4. No interest should be charged after the account becomes NPA.
5. Interest accrued and credited to Income Account in respect of an NPA account should be reversed as follows:

Before Closure of Books	After Closure of Books
Income A/c	Income A/c
To Borrower's A/c	To Unrealised Interest A/c

6. The amount of recovery in case of NPA account should first be appropriated towards principal and the balance towards interest.
7. **Project Finance** In the case of bank finance given for industrial projects *or* for agricultural plantations, etc. where moratorium is available for payment of interest, payment of interest becomes due after the moratorium *or* gestation period is over, and not on the date of debit of interest.
8. **Advances to staff** As in the case of project finance, in respect of housing loans *or* similar advances granted to staff members where interest is payable after recovery of principal, the overdue status (in respect of payment of interest) should be reckoned from the date when there is default in payment of interest on due date of payment.

ILLUSTRATION 1

From the following information, identify the non-performing assets (NP A) of a commercial bank for the year ending 31st March, 2015:

I. *Term Loans:* ₹ 100 lakhs on which interest remains past due for 3 quarters on 30 lakhs, for 2 quarters on ₹ 20 lakhs, for 1 month on ₹ 10 lakhs.

II. *Cash Credits and Overdrafts-*₹ 200 lakhs on which interest remained past due for 3 quarters on ₹ 60 lakhs, for 2 quarters on ₹ 40 lakhs, for 1 month on ₹ 20 lakhs.

III. *Bills Purchased and Discounted*—₹ 300 lakhs on which interest remained unpaid for 3 quarters for ₹ 90 lakhs, 2 quarters for ₹ 60 lakhs, for 1 month for ₹ 30 lakhs.

SOLUTION

STATEMENT SHOWING NON-PERFORMING ASSETS [NPA]

Particulars	*(₹ in lakhs)*
Term Loan [30 + 20]	50
Cash Credit and Overdraft (60 + 40)	100
Bills Purchased and Discounted [90 + 60]	150
	300

29.0 BASIS OF INCOME RECOGNITION

Asset	Basis of Income Recognition
1. On Performing Assets (PA)	1. Income on PA is recognised on Accrual Basis whether *or* not realised
2. On Non-Performing Assets (NPA)	2. Income on NPA is recognised on Cash basis

ILLUSTRATION 2

Given below is the detail of interest on advances of a commercial bank.

(₹ in lakhs)

Advances	*On Performing Assets*		*On Non-performing Assets*	
	Interest Earned	*Interest Received*	*Interest Earned*	*Interest Received*
Term Loan	100	80	50	20
Cash Credit & Closing A/c	200	120	100	60
Bills Purchased & Discounted	300	180	150	90

Calculate the interest income to be recognised for the year ending 31st March, 2015.

SOLUTION

Interest on performing assets is recognised on accrual basis but interest on NPA is recognised on Cash basis.

Advances	*On Performing Assets*	*On NPA*	*Total*
Interest on Term Loan	100	20	120
Interest on Cash Credit & Overdrafts	200	60	260
Bills Purchased & Discounted	300	90	390
			770

ILLUSTRATION 3

Calculate the interest income to be recognised for the year ending 31.3.2015 from the following information:

Interest	Total Earned	On NPA	
		Earned	Collected
Interest on Cash Credit	1,820	820	400
Interest on Overdraft	1,750	450	100
Interest on Term Loans	1,540	750	250

SOLUTION

Interest on Cash Credit (1,820 – 820 + 400)	1,400
Interest on Overdraft (750 – 450 + 100)	1,400
Interest a Term Loan (1,540 – 750 + 250)	1,040
	2,840

ILLUSTRATION 4

Calculate the interest income to be recognised for the year ending 31.3.2015 from the following information:

Interest	Total Interest collected	Earned but not collected	
		on PA	on NPA
Interest on Cash Credit	1,000	400	420
Interest on Overdraft	300	100	350
Interest on Term Loans	1,000	40	500

SOLUTION

Interest on Cash Credit (1,000 + 400)	1,400
Interest on Overdraft (300 + 100)	1,400
Interest on Term Loan (1,000 + 40)	1,040
	2,840

ILLUSTRATION 5

Calculate the interest income to be recognised for the year ending 31.3.2015 from the following information:

Interest earned on term loans	17.26
Interest earned on term loans classified as NPA	4.52
Interest received on term loans classified as NPA	2. 04
Interest on cash credits and overdrafts	38.54
Interest earned but not received on cash credit and overdraft treated as NPA	8.39

SOLUTION

Interest on term loans [17.26 – (4.52 – 2.04)]	14.78
Interest on cash credits and overdrafts (38.54 – 8.39)	30.15
	44.93

30.0 CLASSIFICATION OF BANK ADVANCES FOR DETERMINING THE AMOUNT OF PROVISION

Bank advances are classified into following 4 groups to determine the amount of provision:

Group	*Meaning*	*% of Provision*
1. Standard Assets	Standard Asset is one which does not disclose any problem and which does not carry more than normal riskattached to the business (whether secured *or* unsecured).	
	(a) Direct Advances to Agricultural and SME	0.25
	(b) Advances to Commercial Real Estate (CRE) Sector	1.00
	(c) Other Loan A/cs	0.40
2. Sub-Standard Asset	Sub-standard asset is one which has been classified as NPA for a period not exceeding 12 months	
	on Secured Loan A/cs	15
	on Unsecured Infrastructure Loan A/cs where certain safeguards such as Escrow accounts are available.	20
	on Unsecured Other Loan A/cs	25
3. Doubtful Asset	A doubtful asset is one which has remained NPA for a period exceeding 12 months	
	On Unsecured Portion	100
	On Secured portion if period for which the advance has been considered as doubtful	
	(a) Upto 1 year	25
	(b) Exceeding 1 year but not exceeding 3 years	40
	(c) Exceeding 3 years	100
4. Loss Asset	A loss asset is one where loss has been identified by the Bank *or* internal *or* external auditors *or* the RBI inspection but the amount has not been written off, wholly *or* partly	100

Note: The provisions on Standard Assets should not be reckoned for arriving as Net NPAs. The provisions towards Standard Assets need not be netted from Gross Advances but shown separately as 'Contingent Provisions against Standard Assets' under 'Other Liabilities and Provisions Other's in Schedule 5 to the Blanace Sheet.

IMPORTANT NOTE FOR EXAMINATION

1. CA Students are advised to consider the latest % of Provisions as notified by RBI upto 31st Oct for May Examination and upto 30th April for Nov Examination.
2. Unless otherwise stated, Sub-standard, Doubtful Assets are assumed to be secured since in general no Bank would like to grant loan without security.

ILLUSTRATION 6 [CLASSIFICATION OF ADVANCES]

From the following information, classify the advances into Standard, Sub-Standard, Doubtful and Loss Assets for the year ending 31st March, 2015. *Cumulative figures of Interest past due*

Particulars	*Total*	*for 4 quarters*	*for 5 quarters*	*for 12 quarters*	*for 16 quarters*
On Term Loans	1,000	200	250	300	350

On Cash Credit & Overdraft	5,000	2,000	2,500	2,500	4,000

It is understood that of the terms loans interest on which is past due for 16 quarters, ₹ 20 lakhs are totally unsecured and identified as loss assets by internal auditor

SOLUTION

Particulars	*Asset Classification (₹ in lakhs)*			
	Standard Assets	*Sub-Standard Assets*	*Doubtful*	*Loss Assets*
Term Loan	650	200	130	20
Cash Credit	1,000	2,000	2,000	—

ILLUSTRATION 7

From the following information, find out the amount of provision to be shown in the Profit & Loss Account of a Commercial Bank. *(₹ in lakhs)*

Standard Assets	
(a) Direct Advances to Agricultural and SME	1,000
(b) Advances to Commercial Real Estate (CRE) Sector	2,000
(c) Other Loan A/cs	5,000
Sub-Standard Assets	
(a) Infrastructure Loan A/cs (Secured)	1,000
(b) Infrastructure Loan A/cs (Unsecured) where Escrow A/cs are available	120
(c) Other Loan A/cs (Secured)	1,000
(d) Other Loan A/cs (Unsecured)	120
Doubtful Assets not covered by security	200
Doubtful Assets covered by security	
for 1 year	50
for 2 years	100
for 3 years	200
for 4 years	150
Loss Assets	200

SOLUTION

Particulars	*Amount ₹ (in lacs)*	*% of Provision*	*Provision ₹ (in lacs)*
Standard Assets			
(a) Direct Advances to Agricultural and SME	1,000	0.25	2.50
(b) Advances to Commercial Real Estate Sector	2,000	1.00	20.00
(c) Other Loan A/cs	5,000	0.40	20.00
Sub-Standard Assets			
(a) Infrastructure Loan A/cs (Secured)	1,000	15	150.00
(b) Infrastructure Loan A/cs (Unsecured)	120	20	24.00
(c) Other Loan A/cs (Secured)	1,000	15	150.00

(d) Other Loan A/cs (Unsecured)	120	25	30.00
Doubtful Assets not covered by security	200	100	200.00
Doubtful Assets covered by security			
for 1 year	50	25	12.50
for 2 years	100	40	40.00
for 3 years	200	40	80.00
for 4 years	150	100	150.00
Loss Assets	200	100	200.00
			1079.00

ILLUSTRATION 8

Performing Assets (realizable value of security ₹ 90 lacs) ₹ 100 lacs

Non-performing Assets for 12 months (secured) ₹ 200 lacs

Non-performing Assets for 12 months (unsecured) ₹ 300 lacs

Non-performing Assets for 24 months (unsecured) ₹ 400 lacs

Non-performing Assets for 24 months (secured) ₹ 500 lacs

Non-performing Assets for 36 months (secured) ₹ 600 lacs

Non-performing Assets for 37 months (secured) ₹ 700 lacs

Non-performing Assets for 50 months (secured) ₹ 800 lacs

Calculate the amount of provision to be made.

SOLUTION

Particulars	*Amount*	*% Provision*	*Provision*
Standard	100	0.40%	0.40
Sub-standard (Secured)	200	15%	30.00
Sub-standard (Unsecured)	300	25%	75.00
Doubtful upto 1 year (Unsecured)	400	100%	400.00
Doubtful upto 1 year (Secured)	500	25%	125.00
Doubtful (Exceeding 1 year but not exceeding 3 year (Secured)	600	40%	240.00
Doubtful (Exceeding 1 year but not exceeding 3 year (Secured)	700	40%	280.00
Doubtful (Exceeding 3 years)	800	100%	800.00
Total Provision required			1950.40

ILLUSTRATION 9

It is found from the books, that a loan of ₹ 12 lakhs was advanced on 30.9.2013, @ 10 per cent p.a. interest payable half yearly; but the loan was outstanding as on 30.3.2015, without any payment recorded in the meantime, either towards principal *or* towards interest. The security for the loan was 20,000 fully paid shares of ₹ 100 each (the market value was ₹ 96 as per the Stock Exchange information as on 30th September, 2014). But due to fluctuations, the price fell to ₹ 30 per share in January, 2015. On 31.3.2015, the price as per Stock Exchange rate was ₹ 82 per share.

(a) State how you would classify the loan as secured/unsecured in the Balance Sheet of the Company; (b) Also State whether any provision is required to be made?

SOLUTION

(a) For classifying loans as fully secured *or* otherwise, the value of the security as on the last date of the year is considered. The value of the security is ₹ 16.40 lakhs covering the loan and the interest due comfortably. Hence it is to be treated as good and fully secured.

(b) It is a doubtful asset upto 1 year, hence a provision of 25% of ₹ 12 lakhs i.e., ₹ 3 lakhs is required to be made.

31.0 HOW TO MAKE PROVISION IN RESPECT OF ADVANCES COVERED BY THE GUARANTEES OF DICGC/ECGC

In the case of advances guaranteed by Export Credit Guarantee Corporation (ECGC) *or* by Deposit Insurance and Credit Guarantee Corporation (DICGC), provision is required to be made only for the balance in excess of the amount guaranteed by these corporations.

In case the bank also holds a security in respect of an advance guaranteed by ECGC/DICGC, the realisable value of the security should be deducted from the outstanding balance before the ECGC/ DICGC guarantee is off-set.

Where there is an upper limit to which the ECGC/DICGC guarantee applies, this fact should be duly recognised in computing the amount of provision required.

STATEMENT SHOWING THE CALCULATION OF PROVISION

Particulars	₹
A. Amount Outstanding	xxx
B. *Less:* Realizable value of Security (if any held)	(xxx)
	xxx
C. *Less:* ECGC/DICGC cover (% limited to ...)	(xxx)
D. Unsecured Portion [A – B – C]	xxx
E. Provision required for unsecured portion of Doubtful Asset @ 100%	xxx
F. Provision required for secured portion of Doubtful Asset @ 25% / 40% / 100% (for Doubtful Asset upto 1 year/3years/Exceeding 3 years)	xxx
G. Total Provision required [E + F]	xxx

ILLUSTRATION 10

Packing credit outstanding from Food Processors ₹ 60 lakhs against which the bank holds securities of ₹ 20 lakhs (Realisable value 75%). 40% is covered by ECGC limited to ₹ 16 lakhs. The above advance has remained doubtful upto 3 years. Calculate the amount of provision required to be made.

SOLUTION

Particulars	*(₹ in lakhs)*
A. Amount Outstanding	60
B. *Less:* Realizable value of Security	(15)
	45
C. *Less:* ECGC cover (40% of ₹ 45 lakhs limited to ₹ 16 lakhs)	(16)

D. Unsecured Portion [A – B – C]	29
E. Provision required for unsecured portion @ 100%	29
F. Provision required for secured portion @ 40%	6
G. Total Provision required [E + F]	35

ILLUSTRATION 11

In X Bank Ltd., the doubtful assets (more than 3 years) as on 31.3.2015 is ₹ 1,000 lakhs. The value of security (including DICGC 100% cover of ₹ 100 lakhs) is ascertained at ₹ 500 lakhs. How much provision must be made in the books of the Bank towards doubtful assets?

SOLUTION

Particulars	*(₹ in lakhs)*
Doubtful Assets (more than 3 years')	1,000
Less: Value of security (excluding DICGC cover)	(400)
Less: DICGC cover	(100)
Unsecured portion	500
Provision for unsecured portion @100%	500
Provision for secured portion @ 100%	400
Total Provision to be made	900

ILLUSTRATION 12

A loan outstanding of ₹ 50,00,000 has DICGC cover. The loan guaranteed by DICGC is assigned a risk weight of 50%. What is the value of Risk-adjusted asset?

SOLUTION

Value of Risk Adjusted Asset = Loan × Guaranteed by DICGC × Risk weight

= ₹ 50,00,000 × 50% = ₹ 25,00,000

ILLUSTRATION 13

CAMJB Bank Ltd. had extended the following credit lines to a Small Scale Industry which had not paid any interest since 1st March, 2010

Particulars	*Term Loan*	*Export Credit*
Balance outstanding on 31.3.2015	₹ 70 lacs	₹ 60 lacs
DICGC/ECGC Cover	50%	40%
Securities held	₹ 30 lacs	₹ 25 lacs
Realisable value of securities	2/3rd	60%

Required: Compute the necessary provisions to be made for the year ended 31st March, 2015.

SOLUTION

Particulars	*Term loan* *₹ in lacs*	*Export Credit* *₹ in lacs*
A Balance Outstanding	70	60

B	*Less:* Realisable Value of Securities	(20)	(15)
		50	45
C	*Less:* DICGC cover @ 50% of ₹ 50 lacs	(25)	—
	Less: ECGC Cover @ 40% of ₹ 45 lacs	—	(18)
D	Unsecured Portion	25	27
E	Provision for Unsecured Portion @ 100%	25	27
F	Provision for Secured Portion: @ 100%	20	15
G	Total Provision	45	42

32.0 BILLS FOR COLLECTION

MEANING OF BILLS FOR COLLECTION

Bills for Collection refer to the Bills received by bank from customers for the purpose of collection.

ACCOUNTING TREATMENT OF BILLS FOR COLLECTION

(a) On receipt of Bills for Collection, the particulars of such bills are recorded in 'Bills for Collection Register'.

(b) On Collection, the following entry is passed:

Cash A/c	Dr.	[with Bill Amount]
To Commission A/c		[with Commission]
To Customer's A/c		[with Balance]

DISCLOSURE OF BILLS FOR COLLECTION

Bills held for Collection are to be shown by way of note to the Balance Sheet.

ILLUSTRATION 14

Bharat Bank Ltd. provides you the following information:

Particulars	*₹ (in lakhs)*
Bills for Collection (as on 1.4.2014)	14.00
During the year 2014-2015	
Bills received for Collection	129.00
Bills Collected	94.00
Bills dishonoured and returned	11.01

Required: Prepare Bills for Collection (Assets) A/c and Bills for Collection (Liabilities) A/c.

SOLUTION

Dr. **BILLS FOR COLLECTION (ASSETS) ACCOUNT** *Cr.*

Date	*Particulars*	₹	*Date*	*Particulars*	₹
01.04.2014	To Balance b/d	14.00	2014-2015	By Bills for Collection	94.00
	To Bills for Collection	129.00		(Liabilities) A/c	
	(Liabilities) A/c			By Bills for Collection	11.01

				(Liabilities) A/c	
			31.03.14	By Balance c/d	37.99
		143.00			143.00

Dr. **BILLS FOR COLLECTION (LIABILITIES) ACCOUNT** Cr.

Date	*Particulars*	₹	*Date*	*Particulars*	₹
2014-2015	To Bills for Collection (Assets) A/c	94.00	01.04.2014	By Balance b/d	14.00
	To Bills for Collection (Assets) A/c	11.01		By Bills for Collection (Assets) A/c	129.00
31.03.2015	To Balance c/d	37.99			
		143.00			143.00

33.0 PURCHASE OR DISCOUNTING OF BILLS

MEANING OF PURCHASING OR DISCOUNTING OF BILLS

An act of purchasing of a bill and making payment for it before its maturity is called discounting of bill.

ACCOUNTING TREATMENT OF DISCOUNTED BILLS

(a) On Discounting

Discounted Bills A/c	Dr.	[with Face value of Bill]
To Discount A/c		[with Discount]
To Customer's A/c		[with Net Proceeds]

(b) On Collection

Cash A/c	Dr.
To Discounted Bills A/c	

(c) On Dishonour

Customer's A/c	Dr.
To Discounted Bills A/c	

DISCLOSURE OF DISCOUNTED BILLS

Discounted Bills are **assets** which are shown under the head **'Advances' (Schedule 9)** on the assets side of the Balance Sheet.

34.0 REBATE ON BILLS DISCOUNTED

MEANING OF REBATE ON BILLS DISCOUNTED

Rebate on bills discounted refers to the discount for the unexpired term of the bill at the end of the accounting period. ***For Example,*** if total term of the bill is 100 days of which 60 days fall in the next accounting period. 60% of the discount earned on this bill should be treated as a rebate.

HOW TO CALCULATE REBATE ON BILLS DISCOUNTED?

$$\text{Rebate on Bills Discounted} = \text{Total Annual Discount} \times \frac{\text{No. of Days after the close of year}}{365}$$

ACCOUNTING TREATMENT OF REBATE ON BILLS DISCOUNTED

(a) At the end of current accounting period

Discount on Bills A/c Dr	
To Rebate on Bills Discounted A/c	[with Rebate]

(b) At the beginning of next accounting period

Rebate on Bills Discounted A/c Dr.	
To Discount on Bills A/c	

DISCLOSURE OF REBATE ON BILLS DISCOUNTED

Rebate on Bills Discounted A/c is a **liability** and is shown under the head **'Other Liabilities and 'Provisions (Schedule 5)'** on the liabilities side of the Balance Sheet.

ILLUSTRATION 15

A 3 month's bill of ₹ 5,00,000 dated 9.3.2015 was discounted @16% p.a. Give journal entries on 9.3.2015 and 31.3.2015.

SOLUTION

JOURNAL

Date	*Particulars*	*Dr. (₹)*	*Cr.(₹)*
09.03.2015	Discounted Bills A/c Dr.	5,00,000	
	To Discount A/c		20,000
	To Customer's A/c		4,80,000
	(Being bills discounted & purchased)		
31.03.2015	Discount A/c Dr.	16,000	
	To Rebate on bill discounted A/c (₹ 80,000 × 73/365)		16,000
	To Profit & Loss A/c		4,000
	(Being unexpired discount carried over to Next Year & Balance T/f to P & L A/c)		

ILLUSTRATION 16

TULSIAN BANK Ltd provides you the following information:

1. Rebate on Bills Discounted as on 1st April, 2014,. ₹ 11.10 crores
2. An analysis of the bills discounted during the year

Date of Bill	*Amount (₹ in Crores)*	*Term (Months)*	*Rate of Discount (% p.a)*
27.12.2014	3,400	3	15%
09.03.2015	600	3	12%

Required:

(i) Pass the necessary journal entries for the year ended on 31st March, 2015

(ii) Prepare Rebate on Bills Discounted A/c and Discount on Bills A/c

(iii) Show how the relevant items will appear in the Bank's Financial Statements.

SOLUTION

JOURNAL

(₹ *in crores)*

Date	*Particulars*	*Dr.*	*L.F.*	*(₹)*	*Cr. (₹)*
01.04.2014	Rebate on Bills Discounted A/c	Dr.		11.10	
	To Discount on bills A/c				11.10
	(Being the t/f of opening balance in Rebate on Bills Discounted A/c to Discount on Bills A/c)				
27.12.2014	Bills Purchased and Discounted A/c	Dr.		3,400	
	To Discount on Bills A/c [3,400 × 15% × 3/12]				127.50
	To Customers' A/c				3,272.50
	(Being the discounting of bills)				
30.03.2015	Cash/Bank A/c	Dr.		3,400.00	
	To Bills Purchased & Discounted A/c				3,400.00
	(Being the discounted Bills collected)				
09.03.2015	Bills Purchased and Discounted A/c	Dr.		600	
	To Discount on Bills A/c [600 × 12% × 3/12]				18
	To Customers' A/c				582
	(Being the discounting of bills)				
31.03.2015	Discount on Bills A/c [600 × 12% × 73/365]	Dr.		14.40	
	To Rebate on Bills Discounted A/c				14.40
	(Being the unexpired discount on discounted bills carried forward to next year)				
	Discount on Bills A/c	Dr.		145.50	
	To Profit and Loss A/c				145.50
	(Being the t/f of Income from Bills Discounting to Profit and Loss A/c)				

Ledger Accounts:

Dr. **1. DISCOUNT ON BILLS ACCOUNT** *Cr.*

Date	*Particulars*	₹	*Date*	*Particulars*	₹
31.03.2015	To Rebate on Bills Discounted A/c	14.40	01.04.2014	By Rebate on Bills Discounted A/c	11.10
31.03.2015	To Profit & Loss A/c	142.20	27.12.2014	By Bills Purchased and Discounted A/c	127.50
			09.03.2015	By Bills Purchased and Discounted A/c	18.00
		156.60			156.60

Dr. **2. REBATE ON BILLS DISCOUNTED ACCOUNT** *Cr.*

Date	*Particulars*	₹	*Date*	*Particulars*	₹
01.04.2014	To Discount on Bills A/c	11.10	01.04.2014	By Balance B/f	11.10
31.03.2015	To Balance c/f	14.40			
27.12.2014	By Discount on Bills A/c	14.40			
		25.50			25.50

AN EXTRACT OF PROFIT & LOSS ACCOUNT
for the period ending 3103.2015

Particulars	₹
Opening 'Rebate on Bills Discounted'	11.10
Add: Discount on Bills	145.50
Less: Closing Rebate on Bills Discounted'	(14.40)
	142.20

AN EXTRACT OF BALANCE SHEET AS AT 3103.2015

Particulars	₹
Other Liabilities & Provisions:	
Rebate on bills discounted	14.40

Working Notes:

1. *Calculation of Date of Maturity & No. of Days After 31st March*

Date of Bill	Term of Bill in Months	Date of Maturity(including 3 days of grace)	No. of Days After 31st March
27.12.2014	3	30.3.2014	0
09.03.2015	3	12.6.2014	73

2. Discount Received = Amount of Bill × Discount Rate × Term of Bill

   On Bills of ₹ 3,400 = 3,400 × 15% × 3/12 = ₹127.50

   On Bills of ₹ 600 = 600 × 12% × 3/12 = ₹18

3. Rebate on Bills Discounted = Amount of Bill × Discount Rate × No. of Days After 31st March/365

   = 600 × 12% × 73/365 = ₹14.40

ILLUSTRATION 17

The following balances are extracted from the Trial Balance as 31.3.2015:

Particulars	*Dr.* ₹	*Cr.* ₹
Interest and Discounts		1,96,00,000
Rebate on bills discounted (as on 1.4.2014)		40,000
Bills discounted and purchased	8,00,000	

It is ascertained that the proportionate discounts not yet earned for bills to mature in 2014-2015, amount to ₹ 28,000.

Required: Prepare Rebate on Bills Discounted A/c and Interest and Discount A/c.

SOLUTION

Dr. **REBATE ON BILLS DISCOUNTED ACCOUNT** *Cr.*

Date	*Particulars*	₹	*Date*	*Particulars*	₹
01.04.2014	To Interest and Discount A/c	40,000	01.04.2014	By Balance b/d	40,000
			31.03.2015	By Interest & Discount	28,000

31.03.2015	To Balance c/d	28,000			
		68,000			68,000

Dr. **INTEREST AND DISCOUNT ACCOUNT** Cr.

Date	Particulars	₹	Date	Particulars	₹
31.03.2015	To Rebate on Bill Discounted A/c	28,000	2014-2015	By Discounted & purchased	1,96,00,000
31.03.2015	To P & L A/c	1,96,12,000	01.04.2014	By Rebate on Bills discounted A/c	40,000
		1,96,40,000			1,96,40,000

ILLUSTRATION 18

During the two years, the following bills were discounted @ 16% p.a. by a bank:

Date of Bill	Customer	Amount (₹)	Term (Months)
27.12.2013	W	1,00,000	3
09.02.2014	X	1,50,000	4
11.05.2014	Y	3,00,000	3
09.02.2015	Z	4,50,000	4

Required: Give the necessary journal entries for the year ended on 31st March, 2014 and on 31st March, 2015.

SOLUTION

JOURNAL

Date	Particulars	L.F.	Dr. (₹)	Cr. (₹)
27.12.2013	Bills Discounted & Purchased A/c Dr.		1,00,000	
	To Customers' A/c			96,000
	To Discount A/c			4,000
	(Being bills of ₹ 1,00,000 discounted & purchased)			
09.02.2014	Bills Discounted & Purchased A/c Dr.		1,50,000	
	To Customers' A/c			1,42,000
	To Discount A/c			8,000
	(Being bills of ₹ 1,50,000 discounted & purchased)			
30.03.2014	Bank A/c Dr.		1,00,000	
	To Bill Discounted & Purchased A/c			1,00,000
	(Being the payment for the Bill received at date of maturity)			
31.03.2014	Discount A/c Dr.		12,000	
	To Rebate on Bills Discounted A/c			4,800
	To Profit & Loss A/c			7,200
	(Being unexpired discount of ₹ 4,800 carried over to Next Year & Balance T/f to P & L A/c)			

01.04.2014	Rebate on Bills Discounted A/c	Dr.	4,800	
	To Discount A/c			4,800
	(Being Rebate in the beginning t/f to discount A/c)			
11.05.2014	Bills Discounted & Purchased A/c	Dr.	3,00,000	
	To Customers' A/c			2,88,000
	To Discount A/c			12,000
	(Being bills of ₹ 3,00,000 discounted & purchased)			
12.06.2014	Bank A/c	Dr.	1,50,000	
	To Bills Purchased & Discounted A/c			1,50,000
	(Being the payment for X 's Bill received)			
14.08.2014	Bank A/c	Dr.	3,00,000	
	To Bills Purchased & Discounted A/c			3,00,000
	(Being the payment for Y 's Bill received)			
09.02.2015	Bills Discounted & Purchased A/c	Dr.	4,50,000	
	To Customers's A/c			4,26,000
	To Discount A/c			24,000
	(Being Bills of ₹ 4,50,000 discounted & purchased)			
31.03.2015	Discount A/c	Dr.	40,800	
	To Rebate on Bills Discounted A/c			14,400
	To Profit & Loss A/c			26,400
	(Being unexpired discount of ₹ 14,400 carried over to Next year & balance T/f to P & L A/c)			

Working Notes:

(I) CALCULATION OF DATE OF MATURITY

Date of Bill	*Term in Months*	*Date of Maturity*
27.12.2013	3	30.3.2014
09.02.2014	4	12.6.2014
11.05.2014	3	14.8.2014
09.02.2015	4	12.6.2015

(II) CALCULATION OF TOTAL DISCOUNT RECEIVED & UNEXPIRED DISCOUNT

Amount of Bill	*Total Annual Discount @ 16% p.a.*	*Total Discount received*	*No. of Days After 31st March*	*Unexpired Discount as on 31st March*
1,00,000	16,000	4,000	0	—
1,50,000	24,000	8,000	73 Days	4,800
3,00,000	48,000	12,000	0	—
4,50,000	72,000	24,000	73 Days	14,400

(III) UNEXPIRED DISCOUNT HAS BEEN CALCULATED AS UNDER

$$\text{Total Annual Discount} \times \frac{\text{No. of Days after the close of year}}{365}$$

For a bill of ₹ 1,50,000 = ₹ 24,000 × 73/365 = ₹ 4,800

For a bill of ₹ 4,50,000 = ₹ 72,000 × 73/365 = ₹ 14,400

ILLUSTRATION 19

Given below is an extract from the Trial Balance of Bharat Bank Ltd. as at 31st March, 2015.

Particulars	₹	₹
Bills Discounted & Purchased	50,00,000	
Rebate on Bills Discounted (at 1.4.2014)		16,685
Discount Received		2,00,000

An analysis of the bills discounted @ 16% p.a. and held on 31.3.2015 is as follows:-

Date of Bill	*Amount (₹)*	*Term (Months)*
Feb. 9, 2015	5,00,000	4
Feb. 17, 2015	6,00,000	3
March 6, 2015	4,00,000	4

Required:

(a) Calculate the amount to be credited to Profit & Loss Account in respect of Discount;

(b) Pass the necessary Journal Entries.

SOLUTION

(a) The amount of discount to be credited P & L A/c will be ₹ 1,70,000

(B) JOURNAL

Date	*Particulars*	*L.F.*	*Dr. (₹)*	*Cr. (₹)*
	Rebate on Bills Discounted A/c Dr.		16,685	
	To Discount A/c			16,685
	(Being the transfer of Opening Balance of Unexpired discount to Discount A/c)			
	Discount A/c Dr.		2,16,685	
	To Rebate on Bills Discounted A/c			46,685
	To Profit & Loss A/c			1,70,000
	(Being the unexpired discount of ₹ 46,685 carried over to the next year & balance transfered to P & L A/c)			

Working Notes:

(i) In the Profit & Loss Account, the discount on bills will not appear as a separate item but will be included in the heading 'Interest and Discount' on the credit side.

(II) CALCULATION OF REBATE ON BILLS DISCOUNTED

Total Annual Discount @ 6% p.a.	*Date of Maturity*	*No. of Days After 31st March*	*Unexpired Discount for days after 31st March*
80,000	June 12	73	16,000
96,000	May 20	50	13,151
64,000	July 9	100	17,534
			Total 46,685

(iii) Date of Maturity is after including three days for grace.

(iv) Unexpired Discount has been calculated by employing the following formula:-

$$= \text{Total Annual Discount p.a.} \times \frac{\text{No. of Days after the close of year}}{365}$$

ILLUSTRATION 20

As on 31st March, 2015 the books of the CANHE Ltd. Bank, include among others, the following balances:-

Particulars	₹
Rebate on bills discounted (1.4.2014)	3,20,000
Discount received	46,00,000
Bills discounted and purchased	3,15,47,000
Bills for collection	12,00,000

Throughout 2014-2015, the Bank's rate for discounting has been 18% and the rate of commission on bills for collection, 4%.

On investigation and analysis, the average due date for the bills discounted and purchased is calculated on 15th May, 2015 and that for bills for collection as 15th April 2015.

Required: Show the calculation of the amount to be credited to the Bank's Profit and Loss Account under discount earned for the year 2014-2015 Show also the journal entries required to adjust the above-mentioned accounts.

SOLUTION

Particulars	₹
Unexpired Discount:	
On Bills Discounted [3,15,47,000 × 18/100 × 45/365]	7,00,084
On Bills for Collection [12,00,000 × 4/100 × 15/365]	1,973
Discount to be credited to Profit & Loss A/c:	7,02,057
(A) Balance in Discount Received A/c	46,00,000
(B) *Add:* Opening Balance in Rebate on bills A/c	3,20,000
(C) *Less:* Closing Balance in Rebate on bills A/c	(7,02,057)
(D) Discount to be transferred to Profit & Loss A/c: [A + B – C]	42,17,943

JOURNAL

Date	Particulars	L.F.	Dr. (₹)	Cr. (₹)
	Rebate on Bills Discounted A/c Dr.		3,20,000	
	To Discount Received A/c			3,20,000
	(Being transfer of opening balance in the rebate A/c)			
	Discount Received A/c Dr.		7,02,057	
	To Rebate on Bills Discounted A/c			7,00,084
	To Rebate on Bills for Collection A/c			1,973
	(Being provision for unexpired discount at the end)			
	Discount Received A/c Dr.		42,17,943	
	To Profit and Loss A/c			42,17,943
	(Being transfer of discount net after adjustment)			

ILLUSTRATION 21

On 31st March, 2014, Uncertain Bank Ltd. has a balance of ₹ 9 crores in "rebate on bills discounted" account. During the year ended 31st March, 2015. Uncertain Bank Ltd. discounted bills of exchange of ₹ 4,000 crores charging interest at 18% per annum, the average period of discount being for 73 days. Of these, bills of exchange of ₹ 600 crores were due for realisation from the acceptors/customers after 31st March, 2015, the average period outstanding after 31st March, 2015 being 36.5 days.

Required: Pass journal entries and show the ledger accounts pertaining to:

(i) discounting of bills of exchage and

(ii) rebate on bills discounted.

SOLUTION

JOURNAL (₹ in Crores)

Date	Particulars	L.F.	Dr. (₹)	Cr. (₹)
	Rebate on bills discounted A/c Dr.		9.00	
	To Discount on bills A/c			9.00
	(Being the transfer of opening balance in rebate on bills discounted account to discount on bills account)			
	Bills purchased and discounted A/c Dr.		144.00	
	To Discount on bills A/c [4,000 × 18/100 × 73/365]			144.00
	To Customers' A/c			3,856.00
	(Being the discounting of bills of exchange during the year)			
	Cash A/c [4,000 – 600] Dr.		3,400.00	
	To Bills Purchased & Discounted A/c			3,400.00
	(Being the discounted Bills collected)			
	Discount on bills A/c [600 × 18/100 × 36.5/365] Dr.		10.80	
	To Rebate on bills discounted A/c			10.80
	(Being the unexpired portion of discount in respect of the discounted bills of exchange carried forward)			

	Discount on bills A/c Dr.		142.20	
	To Profit and Loss A/c			142.20
	(Being the amount of income for the year from discounting of bills of exchange transferred to Profit and Loss A/c)			

Ledger Accounts:

Dr. **DISCOUNT ON BILLS ACCOUNT** Cr.

Date	*Particulars*	₹	*Date*	*Particulars*	₹
2015			2014		
Mar. 31	To Rebate on bills discounted A/c	10.80	April 1	By Rebate on bills discounted A/c	9.00
	To Profit and Loss A/c	142.20	2014-2015	By Bills purchased and discounted A/c	144.00
		153.00			153.00

Dr. **(II) REBATE ON BILLS DISCOUNTED ACCOUNT** Cr.

Date	*Particulars*	₹	*Date*	*Particulars*	₹
2014 April 1	To Discount on bills A/c	9.00	2014 April 1	By Balance b/d	9.00
2015 March 31	To Balance c/d	10.80	2015 March 31	By Discount on bills A/c	10.80
		19.80			19.80

35.0 ACCEPTANCES AND ENDORSEMENTS

Meaning	When a bank accepts *or* endorses bills on behalf of its customers: (a) The bank undertakes a liability towards the party which agrees to receive such bill, and (b) The bank has a corresponding claim against the customer on whose behalf, it has accepted *or* endorsed the bill.
Disclosure	Such liabilities which are outstanding at the close of the year and the corresponding assets, are disclosed as contingent items.
Record	The particulars of such bills as well as of securities (if any) collected from customers are recorded in the Bills Accepted Register.
Treatment At Maturity	The bank makes the payment of such bills at maturity and collects the amount from the customer. If the customer does not pay on demand, the bank disposes off the security deposited by the customer.

ILLUSTRATION 22

Bharat Bank Ltd. provides you the following information:

Particulars	₹ *(in lakhs)*
Acceptances, Endorsement and Guarantees (as on 1.4.2014)	29

During the year 2014-2015	
Acceptances, Endorsement and Guarantees	88
Bank honoured acceptances	50
Client paid off against guaranteed liability	20
Clients failed to pay which Bank had to pay	2

Required: Prepare Acceptances, Endorsements and other Obligations A/c.

SOLUTION

Dr. **ACCEPTANCES, ENDORSEMENTS AND OTHER OBLIGATIONS ACCOUNT** *Cr.*

Date	*Particulars*	₹ *(in lakh)*	*Date*	*Particulars*	₹ *(in lakh)*
2014-2015	To Bank Constituents' Liability for Acceptance, Endorsement, etc.	50	01.04.2014	By Balance b/d	29
	To Constituents' Liability for Acceptance, Endorsement, etc.	20	2014-2015	By Constituents, Liabilities for Acceptances, Endorsement, etc.	88
	To Bank Constituents' Liability for Acceptance, Endorsements, etc. (amount paid on failure of clients)	2			
31.03.2015	To Balance c/d	45			
		117			117

ILLUSTRATION 23

From the following details prepare "Acceptances, Endorsements and other Obligation A/c" as would appear in the General Ledger.

On 1-4-2014 Acceptances not yet satisfied stood at ₹ 22,30,000. Out of which ₹ 20 lacs were subsequently paid off by clients and bank had to honour the rest. A scrutiny of the Acceptance Register revealed the following:

Client	*Acceptances/Guarantees* ₹	*Remarks*
A	10,00,000	Bank honoured on 10-6-2014
B	12,00,000	Party paid off on 30-9-2014
C	5,00,000	Party failed to pay and bank had to honour on 30-11-2014
D	8,00,000	Not satisfied upto 31-3-2015
E	5,00,000	do
F	2,70,000	do
Total	42,70,000	

SOLUTION

Dr. **ACCEPTANCES, ENDORSEMENTS AND OTHER OBLIGATIONS ACCOUNT** *Cr.*

Date	*Particulars*	₹	*Date*	*Particulars*		₹
2014			2014			
Apr. 1	To Constituents' Liabilities for acceptance etc	20,00,000	Apr. 1	By Balance b/f		22,30,000
	To Bank (honoured)	2,30,000		By Constituents liabilities for Acceptances etc.		
June 10	To Bank (honoured)	10,00,000		A	10,00,000	
Sept. 30	To Constituents' Liabilities for acceptance etc	12,00,000		B	12,00,000	
				C	5,00,000	
Nov. 11	To Bank (paid due to failure of client)	5,00,000				
2015						
Mar. 31	To Balance c/f	15,70,000		D	8,00,000	
				E	5,00,000	
				F	2,70,000	42,70,000
		65,00,000				65,00,000

36.0 STATUTORY LIQUIDITY RATIO (SLR) AND CASH RESERVE RATIO (CRR)

PRESCRIBED SLR AND CRR

All scheduled commercial banks (excluding regional rural banks) are required to maintain:

(a) SLR of 23% of net demand and time liabilities in the form of Cash in hand, Cash with other Banks (other than RBI), Money at call & short notice, Gold *or* unencumbered approved securities.

(b) CRR of 4% of net demand and time liabilities with RBI.

(c) Net demand and time liabilities = Fixed Deposits (including Recurring Deposits) + Saving Bank Deposit + Current Accounts (Cr.)

Note: *Current Accounts (Dr.) are not to be deducted.*

IMPORTANT NOTE FOR EXAMINATION

CA Students are advised to consider the latest SLR and CRR as notified by RBI upto 31st Oct for May Examination and upto 30th April for Nov Examination.

ILLUSTRATION 24

Fixed Deposits ₹ 50,000 lacs, Recurring Deposits ₹ 1,700 lacs, Saving Deposits ₹ 45,000 lacs, Current Accounts (Cr.) ₹ 52,012 lacs. Current Accounts (Dr) ₹ 1,000 lacs. Calculate Cash Reserve @ 4% and Liquidity Reserve @ 23 % to be maintained.

SOLUTION

Cash Reserve = 4% of Net Demand and Time Liabilities [i.e. FD + RD + SD + C A/c (Cr)]

= 4% [₹ 50,000 + ₹ 1,700 + ₹ 45,000 + ₹ 52,012] = ₹ 5948.48 lacs

Liquidity Reserve = 23% of Net Demand and Time Liabilities

= 23% [₹ 50,000 + ₹ 1,700 + ₹ 45,000 + ₹ 52,012] = ₹ 34,204

Note: Current A/c (Dr balance) is not adjusted.

ILLUSTRATION 25

Sikkim Bank a non scheduled bank provides you the following information

Particulars	*Dr.* (*₹ in lakhs*)	*Cr.* (*₹ in lakhs*)
Fixed Deposits		50,000
Recurring Deposits		1,700
Saving Deposits		45,000
Current Accounts	2,800	52,012
Cash in hand	16,015	
Cash with other banks	15,587	
Money at call	21,012	
Gold	5,523	
Government Securities	11,017	
Shares	1,000	
Cash with RBI	3,788	

You are *Required:*

(a) to calculate the cash reserve to be maintained (assume present rate 4%)

(b) to calculate the necessary amount required to be transferred to RBI to maintain required cash reserve.

(c) to calculate the amount of liquidity to be maintained and comment thereupon. (assumed present rate is 23%)

SOLUTION

1. Demand and Time Liabilities

   = Fixed Deposits + Recurring Deposits + Savings Deposits + Current Accounts (Cr.)

   = ₹ 50,000 + ₹ 1,700 + ₹ 45,000 + ₹ 52,012 = ₹ 1,48,712

2. Cash Reserve to be maintained @ 4% = ₹ 1,48,712 × 4/100 = ₹ 5,948.48
3. Present Balance with RBI = ₹ 3,788
4. Transfer needed (₹ 5,948.48 – ₹ 3,788) = ₹ 2160.48
5. Liquidity Reserve to be maintained @ 23% of ₹ 1,48,712 = ₹ 34,204
6. Present liquid Assets (after the transfer of ₹ 2160.48 to RBI to meet the cash Reserve requirement.

Cash in hand (₹ 16,015 – ₹ 2160.48)	13,854.52
Cash with other bank	15,587.00
Money at call	21,012.00
Gold	5,523.00
Govt. securities	11,017.00
	66,993.52

Comment: Excess Liquity (₹ 66,993.52 – ₹ 34,204) = ₹ 32,789.52

37.0 HOW TO CALCULATE THE AMOUNT OF INTEREST EARNED OTHER INCOME AND INTEREST EXPENDED

SCHEDULE 13—LNTEREST EARNED

	Particulars	*Year ended as on 31.3... (Current year)*	*Year ended as on 31.3... (Previous year)*
I.	Interest/Discount on Advances/Bills		
II.	Income on Investments		
III.	Interest on balances with Reserve Bank of India & other Inter-Bank Funds		
IV.	Others		
	Total:		

SCHEDULE 14—OTHER INCOME

	Particulars	*Year ended as on 31.3... (Current year)*	*Year ended as on 31.3... (Previous year)*
I.	Commission, exchange and brokerage		
II.	Profit on sale of Investments		
	Less: Loss on Sale of Investments		
III.	Profit on Revaluation of Investments		
	Less: Loss on Revaluation of Investments		
IV.	Profit on sale of Land, Buildings and other Assets		
	Less: Loss on sale of Land, Building & other Assets		
V.	Profit on Exchange Transactions		
	Less: Loss on Exchange Transactions		
VI.	Income earned by way of dividends etc. from subsidiaries/ companies &/or joint ventures abroad/in India		
VII.	Miscellaneous Income		
	Total:		

Note: Under items II to V loss figures may be shown in brackets.

SCHEDULE 15—INTEREST EXPENDED

	Particulars	*Year ended as on 31.3... (Current year)*	*Year ended as on 31.3... (Previous year)*
I.	Interest on Deposits		
II.	Interest on RBIndia/inter-bank borrowings		
III.	Others		
	Total:		

ILLUSTRATION 26

From the following ledger balances calculate interest earned and interest expended as per Schedule 13 and 15 respectively (Figure being in thousands of ₹)

Particulars	₹	*Particulars*	₹
Interest on Term Loans	1,540	Discount on Bills Discounted	200
Interest on Fixed Deposits	1,000	Interest and Dividend on Investments	840
Interest on Recurring Deposits	500	Interest accrued on Investments	40
Interest on Saving Bank Deposits	600	Interest on balances with RBI	100
Interest on Cash Credits	1,820	Interest on Money at call	50
Interest on Borrowings	620	Interest on overdrafts	750

Additional information:

(a) Interest on NPA is as follows:

Particulars	*Earned* ₹ '000	*Collected* ₹ '000
Term Loans	750	250
Cash Credits	820	400
Overdrafts	450	100

(b) Rebate on Bills Discounted: Opening Balance ₹ 75, Closing Balance ₹ 125

SOLUTION

SCHEDULE 13—INTEREST EARNED

Interest	₹ '000	₹ '000
Interest on Term Loan (1,540 – 500)	1,040	
Interest on Cash Credits (1,820 – 420)	1,400	
Interest on Overdraft (750 – 350)	400	
Discount on Bills discounted (200 + 75 – 125)	150	2,990
Income on investments		840
Interest on Balances with RBI		100
Interest on Money at call and at short notice		50
		3,980

Note: *Rebate on Bills Discounted A/c is a* ***liability*** *and is shown under the head* ***'Other Liabilities' and 'Provisions (Schedule 5)'*** *on the liabilities side of the Balance Sheet.*

SCHEDULE 15—INTEREST EXPENDED

Interest/Discount	₹ '000
Interest on Fixed Deposits	1,000
Interest on Recurring Deposits	500
Interest on Saving Bank Deposits	600
Interest on Borrowings	620
	2,720

Note: *Interest accrued on Investments has already been adjusted in the figure of ₹ 840 and hence no further adjustment has been made.*

ILLUSTRATION 27

From the following information. Calculate the amount of 'other Income' as per schedule 14 (the figures being in thousands)

Particulars	₹	*Particulars*	₹
Commission on remittances and transfer	75	Loss on Exchange Transaction	52
Commission on letter of credit	118	Interest on Investments	50
Commission on Govt. Business	82	Rent and other receipts	45
Profit on sale of investments	30	Dividend from Subsidiaries	10
Loss on sale of investments	3	Profit on revaluation of Investments	50
		Lockers' Rent	10

SOLUTION

SCHEDULE 14—OTHER INCOME

	Particulars	₹ *'000*	₹ *'000*
I	Commission, Exchange & Brokerage		
	Commission on remittances and transfer	75	
	Commission on letter of credit	118	
	Commission on Govt. Business	82	
	Locker Rent	10	285
II	Profit on sale of investments	30	
	Less: Loss on sale of investments	3	27
III	Profit on revaluation of investments		50
IV	Loss on Exchange transaction		(52)
V	Rent and other receipts		45
VI	Dividend from subsidiaries		10
			365

Note: Interest on Investments appears in Schedule 13-Interest Earned.

38.0 HOW TO CALCULATE OPERATING EXPENSES

SCHEDULE 16—OPERATING EXPENSES

	Particulars	*Year ended as on 31.3... (Current year)*	*Year ended as on 31.3... (Previous year)*
I.	Payments to and provisions for employees		
II.	Rent, Taxes and Lighting		
III.	Printing and Stationery		
IV.	Advertisement and Publicity		

V. Depreciation on Bank's Property		
VI. Director's Fees, Allowances and Expenses		
VII. Auditor's Fees & Expenses (including branch auditors)		
VIII. Law Charges		
IX. Postages, Telegrams, Telephones, etc.		
X. Repair and Maintenance		
XI. Insurance		
XII. Other Expenditure		
Total:		

ILLUSTRATION 28

From the following information, prepare Schedule 16, 'Operating Expenses' of CANIB Bank Ltd. as on 31st March, 2015

Particulars	*(₹ '000)*	*Particulars*	*(₹ '000)*
Interest and discount	30,45	Printing and stationery	1,80
Income from investments	1,15	Advertisement and publicity	95
Interest on balances with RBI	1,80	Depreciation	92
Commission, exchange & brokerage	8,20	Director's fees	2,20
Profit on sale of investments	1,10	Auditor's fees	1,20
Interest on deposits	12,25	Law charges	2,30
Interest to RBI	1,61	Postage, telegrams and telephone	70
Payment to and provision for employees	10,44	Insurance	50
		Repairs and maintenance	48
Rent, taxes and lighting	2,10	Bad Debts	6

SOLUTION

SCHEDULE 16—OPERATING EXPENSES

Particulars	*(₹ '000)*
1. Payments to and provision for employees	10,44
2. Rent, taxes and lighting	2,10
3. Printing and stationery	1,80
4. Advertisement and publicity	95
5. Depreciation on bank's property	92
6. Director's fees, allowances and expenses	2,20
7. Auditor's fee and expenses (including branch auditors)	1,20
8. Law charges	2,30
9. Postage, telegram, telephones, etc.	70
10. Repairs and maintenance	48
11. Insurance	50

12. Other expenditure	6
	23,65

39.0 HOW TO CALCULATE THE AMOUNT OF PROVISIONS AND CONTINGENCIES

Provisions and Contingencies = Provision for Bad & Doubtful Debts + Provisions for Diminution in the Value of Investments (other than Held to Maturity) + Transfers to Contingencies + Provision for Tax

Note: Provision for Tax = Tax Rate [Total Income – Total Expenditure (Including Provisions and Contingencies but excluding Provision for Tax)]

ILLUSTRATION 29

Interest and discount ₹ 8,850 lacs, Other Income ₹ 220 lacs, Income from investment ₹ 40 lacs, interest expended ₹ 2,720 lacs, Operating Expenses ₹ 2,662 lacs. Additional Information: Provision for NPA ₹ 1,060.50 lacs, Total Investments ₹ 800 of which 25% are held to maturity. The market value of Investment, is 80%. Tax to be provided @35%. Calculate the amount of Provision and Contingences.

SOLUTION

CALCULATION OF THE AMOUNT OF PROVISION AND CONTINGENCES

A. Provision for Diminution in Value of Investments (other than Held to Maturity) = (₹ 800 – 25% of ₹ 800) – (80% of ₹ 600)	₹ 120
B. Provision for NPA	₹ 1,060.50
C. Provision & Contingencies (excluding tax) [₹ 1,060.50 + ₹ 120]	₹ 1,180.50
D. Tax = 35% of [Total Income – Total Expenditure (excluding tax)] = 35% of [(8,890 + 220) – (2,720 + 2,662 + 1180.50)]	₹ 891.625

40.0 HOW TO PREPARE PROFIT AND LOSS ACCOUNT

FORM 'B'

('000 omitted)

FORM OF PROFIT AND LOSS ACCOUNT FOR THE YEAR ENDED 31ST MARCH ...

Particulars	*Schedule No.*	*Year ended as on 31.3... (Current year)*	*Year ended as on 31.3... (Previous year)*
I. Income			
Interest earned	13	....	....
Other Income	14	....	....
Total:		....	....
II. Expenditure			
Interest expended	15	....	....
Operating Expenses	16	....	....
Provisions and Contingencies		....	....

Total:		....	....
III. Profit/Loss			
Net Profits/Loss (–) for the year		....	....
Profit/Loss (–) brought forward		....	....
Total:		....	....
IV. Appropriations			
Transfer to Statutory Reserves @ 25%		....	....
Transfer to Other Reserves		....	....
Transfer to Government/Proposed Dividends		....	....
Balance carried over to Balance Sheet		....	....
Total:		....	....

Important Note for Examination: Transfer 25% of Profits To Statutory Reserves even if the Question is silent on this Issue.

41.0 GENERAL INSTRUCTIONS FOR COMPILATION OF FINANCIAL STATEMENTS

1. Formats of Balance Sheet and Profit and Loss Account cover all items likely to appear in the statements. **In case a bank does not have any particular item to report, it may be omitted from the formats.**
2. Corresponding comparative figures for the previous year are to be disclosed as indicated in the format. The words "current year" and "previous year" used in the format are only to indicate the order of presentation and may appear in the accounts.
3. **Figures should be rounded off to the nearest thousand rupees.**

42.0 RBI GUIDELINES FOR COMPILATION OF PROFIT AND LOSS ACCOUNT

SCHEDULE 13–INTEREST EARNED

I. Interest/discount on advances/bills	Includes interest and discount on all types of loans and advances like cash credit, demand loans, overdraft, export loans, term loans, domestic and foreign bills purchased and discounted (including those rediscounted), overdue, interest and also interest subsidy, if any, relating to such advances/bills.
II. Income on investments	Includes all income derived from the investment portfolio by way of interest and dividend.
III. Interest on balances with Reserve Bank of India and other Inter-bank funds	Includes interest on balances with Reserve Bank and other banks, call loans, money market placements, etc.
IV. Others	Includes any other interest/discount income not included in above heads.

SCHEDULE 14–OTHER INCOME

I. Commission, exchange and brokerage	Includes all remuneration on services such as commission on collections, commission/ exchange on remittances and transfers, commission on letter of credit, letting out of lockers and guarantees, commission on Government business commission on other permitted agency business including consultancy and other services, brokerage, etc. on securities. It does not include foreign exchange income.
II. Profit on sale of investments *Less:* **Loss on sale of investments etc.**	Includes profit/loss on sale of securities, furniture land and buildings, motor vehicle, gold, silver. Only the net position should be shown. If the net position is a loss, the amount should be deducted.
III. Profit on revaluation of investments	The net profit/loss on revaluation of assets may also be shown under this item.
IV. Profit on sale of land, building and other assets *Less:* **Loss on sale of land, buildings and other assets**	
V. Profit on exchange transactions *Less:* **Loss on exchange transactions**	Includes profit/loss on dealing in foreign exchange, all incomes earned by way of foreign exchange, commission and charges on foreign exchange transactions excluding interest which will be shown under interest. Only the net position should be shown. If the net position is a loss, it is to be shown as a deduction.
VI. Income earned by way of dividends etc. from subsidiaries companies, joint ventures abroad/in India	
VII. Miscellaneous Income	Includes recoveries from constituents for the godown rents, income from bank's properties, security charges, insurance etc. and any other miscellaneous income. In case any item under this head exceeds one percentage of the total income, particulars may be given in the notes.

SCHEDULE 15–INTEREST EXPENDED

I. Interest on deposits	Includes interest paid on all types of deposits including deposits from banks & others institutions.
II. Interest on Reserve Bank of India/ inter-bank borrowings	Includes discount/interest on all borrowings & refinance from Reserve Bank of India & other banks.
III. Others	Includes discount/interest on all borrowings refinance from financial institutions. All other payments like interest on participation certificates, penal interest paid, etc. may also be included here.

SCHEDULE 16–OPERATING EXPENSES

I. Payments to and Provisions for employees	Includes staff salaries/wages, allowances, bonus, other staff benefits like provident fund, pension, gratuity liveries to staff, leave fare concessions, staff welfare, medical allowance to staff, etc.
II. Rent, taxes and lighting	Includes rent paid by the banks on building and other municipal and other taxes paid (excluding income tax and interest tax) electricity and other similar charges and levies. House rent allowance and other similar payments to staff should appear under the head 'Payments to and provisions for employees'.
III. Printing and Stationery	Includes books and forms and stationery used by the bank and other printing charges which are not incurred by way of publicity expenditure.
IV. Advertisement and Publicity	Includes expenditure incurred by the bank for advertisement and publicity purposes including printing charges of publicity matter.
V. Depreciation on Bank's property	Includes depreciation on bank's own property; motor cars and other vehicles, furniture, electric fittings, vaults, lifts, leasehold properties, non-banking assets, etc.
VI. Directors' fees, allowances and expenses	Includes sitting fees and all other items of expenditure incurred on behalf of directors. The daily allowances, hotel charges, conveyance charges, etc. which though in the nature of reimbursement of expenses incurred may be included under this head. Similarly expenses of local Committee members may also be included under this head.
VII. Auditors' fees and expenses (including branch auditors' fees and expenses)	Includes fees paid to the statutory auditors and branch auditors for professional services rendered and all expenses for performing their duties, even though they may be in the nature of reimbursement of expenses. If external auditors have been appointed by banks themselves for internal inspections and audits and other services the expenses incurred in that context including fees may not be included under this head but shown under 'other expenditure'.
VIII. Law charges	All legal expenses and reimbursement of expenses incurred in connection with legal services are to be included here.
IX. Postage, telegrams telephones, etc.	Includes all postal charges like stamps, telegram, telephones, teleprinter, etc.
X. Repairs and maintenance	Includes repairs to banks' property, their maintenance charges, etc.
XI. Insurance	Includes insurance charges on bank's property, insurance premia paid to Deposit Insurance and Credit Guarantee Corporation, etc. to the extent they are not recovered from the concerned parties.

XII. Other expenditure	All expenses other than those not included in any of the other heads, like, licence fees, donations, subscriptions to papers, periodicals, entertainment expenses, travel expenses. etc. may be included under this head. In case any particular item under this head exceeds one percentage of the total income particulars may be given in the notes.

PROVISIONS AND CONTINGENCIES

Includes all provisions made for bad and doubtful debts, provisions for taxation, provisions for diminution in the value of investments, transfers to contingencies and other similar items.

ILLUSTRATION 30

State the number and name of the schedule and item head in the Schedule for the following items of Bharat BANK.

1. Rebate on Bills Discounted appearing outside the Trial Balance
2. Rebate on Bills Discounted appearing in the Trial Balance
3. Interest accrued on Investment appearing outside the trial balance
4. Interest accrued on Investment appearing in the trial balance
5. Dividend on Investments
6. Dividend from Subsidiaries
7. Interest on Current Accounts (Dr)
8. Interest on Current Accounts (Cr)
9. Lockers' Rent
10. Commission on Foreign Exchange
11. Profit on Sale of Land & Building held as investments ₹ 10 lacs, Loss on sale of Gold held as investments ₹ 2 lacs
12. Recoveries from customers for godown rents
13. Interest paid on money at call and short notice
14. Interest on borrowings from Banks
15. Printing charges of Publicity matter
16. Depreciation on Non-banking Assets
17. Daily allowances of local committee members
18. Fees and Reimbursement of Expenses to Statutory Auditors & Branch Auditors
19. Fees and Reimbursement of Expenses to External Auditors appointed by banks themselves
20. Insurance Premia paid to Deposit Insurance & Credit Guarantee Corporation ₹ 5 lac (out of which ₹ 1 lac is recoverable from the customers)
21. Entertainment expenses, Donations, License Fees, Subscription to papers & periodicals

22. (a) Provisions for Doubtful Debts	₹ 4 lacs
(b) Provision for Taxation	₹ 3 lacs
(c) Provision for Diminution in the value of investments	₹ 2 lacs
(d) Transfers to contingencies	₹ 1 lacs

SOLUTION

Item No	*Schedule*	*Items head in Schedule*
1	13–Interest Earned in P & L A/c	– Interest/Discount on advance/bills
	5– Other Liabilities & Provisions in B/S	– Others (including Provisions)
2	5–Other Liabilities & Provisions in B/S	Other (including Provisions)
3	13–Interest Earned in P & L A/c 11–Other Assets in B/S	– Income on Invesments – Interest accrued
4	11–Other Assets in B/S	Interest accrued
5	13–Interest Earned in P & L A/c	Income on investments
6	14–Other Income in P & L A/c	Income earned by way of dividends from subsidiaries
7	13–Interest Earned in P & L A/c	Interest/Discount on advance/bills
8	15–Interest expended in P & L A/c	Interest on deposits
9	14–Other Income in P & L A/c	Commission, Exchange and brokerage
10	14–Other income in P & L A/c	Profit on exchange transactions
11	14–Other income in P & L A/c	Profit on sale of Investments ₹ 8 lacs
12	14–Other Income in P & L A/c	Miscellaneous Income
13	15–Interest Expended in P & L A/c	Interest on Deposits
14	15–Interest Expended in P & L A/c	Interest on RBI/Inter Bank borrowings
15	16–Operating Expenses in P & L A/c	Advertisement and Publicity
16	16–Operating Expenses in P & L A/c	Depreciation on bank's property
17	16–Operating Expenses in P & L A/c	Directors' Fees, allowances and expenses
18	16–Operating Expenses in P & L A/c	Auditors' fees and expenses (including branch auditors fees and expenses)
19	16–Operating Expenses in P & L A/c	Other Expenditure
20	16–Operating Expenses in P & L A/c	Insurance ₹ 4 lacs
21	16–Operating Expenses in P & L A/c	Other Expenditure
22	—Provisions & Contingencies in P & L A/c	– ₹ 10 lacs
	5–Other Liabilities and Provisions in B/S	– Others (including Provisions) ₹ 10 lacs

ILLUSTRATION 31

From the following ledger balances, prepare Profit & Loss Account of a Tulsian Bank Ltd. for the year ending 31.3.2015. (The figures being in thousands)

Particulars	₹	*Particulars*	₹
Interest and Discount	8,880	Interest Expended	2,720
Other Income	220	Operating Expenses	2,662
Income from Investments	30		5,000

Additional Information:

(a) Rebate on bills discounted: on 31.3.2014 on 31.3.2015	₹ 15 ₹ 45

(b)	Interest accrued on Investments	₹ 10
(c)	Classification of Advances:	₹
	Standard Assets	₹ 5,000
	Sub-Standard Assets	₹ 1,120
	Doubtful Assets not covered by security	₹ 510
	Doubtful Assets covered by security	
	for 1 year	50
	for 2 years	100
	for 3 years	200
	for 4 years	150
	Loss Assets	80
(d)	Make Tax provision @ 35%	
(e)	Profit and Loss A/c (Cr.) on 31.3.2014 ₹ 80	
(f)	The Directors desire to recommend 5% Dividend.	
(g)	Total Investments ₹ 800 of which 25% are held to maturity. The market value of Investment, is 80%.	

SOLUTION

TULSIAN BANK LTD.
PROFIT & LOSS ACCOUNT
for the year ended 31st March, 2015

	Particulars	*Schedule No.*	*year ended 31.3.2015 (₹'000)*
I	Income:		
	Interest Earned	13	8,890
	Other Income	14	220
			9,110
II	Expenditure:		
	Interest Expended	15	2,720
	Operating Expenses	16	2,662
	Provisions & Contingencies (1180.50 + 891.625 W.Note)		2,072.125
			7,454.125
III	Profit/Loss:		
	Net Profit/Loss for the year		1,655.875
	Profit/Loss brought forward		80
			1,735.875
IV	Appropriations:		
	Transfer to Statutory Reserve @ 25% of 1,655.875		413.970
	Proposed Dividend		250.000

Balance carried over to Balance-Sheet		1071.905
		1,735.875

SCHEDULE 13—INTEREST EARNED

	Particulars	*₹ '000*
I	Interest & Discount [8,880 + 15 (Opening Rebate) – 45 (Closing Rebate)]	8,850
II	Income on Investments (30 + 10)	40
		8,890

Working Notes:

1. PROVISION FOR NPA

Particulars	*Amount (₹ '000)*	*% of Provision*	*Provision (₹ '000)*
Standard	5,000	0.40	20.0
Sub Standard Assets	1,120	15	168.0
Doubtful Assets not covered by security	510	100	510.0
Doubtful Assets covered by security			
for 1 year	50	25	12.5
for 2 years	100	40	40.0
for 3 years	200	40	80.0
for 4 years	150	100	150.0
Loss Assets	80	100	80.0
			1060.5

2. CALCULATION OF THE AMOUNT OF PROVISION AND CONTINGENCES

A. Provision for Diminution in Value of Investments (other than Held to Maturity) = (₹ 800 – 25% of ₹ 800) – (80% of ₹ 600)	₹ 120
B. Provision for NPA	₹ 1,060.50
C. Provision & Contingencies (excluding tax) [₹ 1,060.50 + ₹ 120]	₹ 1,180.50
D. Tax = 35% of [Total Income – Total Expenditure (excluding tax)] = 35% of [(8,890 + 220) – (2,720 + 2,662 + 1180.50)]	₹ 891.625

ILLUSTRATION 32

From the following ledger balances, prepare Profit and Loss account of CANIB Bank Ltd. as on 31st March, 2015:

Particulars	*(₹ '000)*	*Particulars*	*(₹ '000)*
Interest and discount	30,45	Printing and stationery	1,80
Income from investments	1,15	Advertisement and publicity	95
Interest on balances with RBI	1,80	Depreciation	92
Commission, exchange & brokerage	8,20	Director's fees	2,20

Profit on sale of investments	1,10	Auditor's fees	1,20
Interest on deposits	12,25	Law charges	2,30
Interest to RBI	1,60	Postage, telegrams and telephone	70
Payment to and provision for employees	10,44	Insurance	50
		Repairs and maintenance	48
Rent, taxes and lighting	2,10	Bad Debts	6

Other information:

(i) Interest and discount mentioned above is after adjustment for the following:

Particulars	(₹ '000)
Tax provision for the year	2,20
Provision during the year for doubtful debts	1,02
Loss on sale of investments	12
Rebate on bills discounted	58
(ii) 25% of profit is transferred to statutory reserves	
5% of profit is transferred to revenue reserve.	
Profit brought forward from last year	16

SOLUTION

CANIB BANK LTD.
PROFIT AND LOSS ACCOUNT FOR THE YEAR ENDED 31ST MARCH, 2015

Particulars	Schedule	('000 ₹)
1. Income:		
Interest Earned	13	36,74
Others Income	14	9,18
Total		45,92
2. Expenditure:		
Interest Expended	15	13,85
Operating Expenses	16	23,65
Provisions & Contingencies [₹ 220 + ₹ 102]		322
Total		40,72
3. Profit/Loss:		
Net Profit for the year		5,20
Profit brought forward		16
		5,36
4. Appropriations:		
Transfer to Statutory Reserve @ 25%		1,30
Transfer to Other Reserve @ 5%		26
Balance carried to balance sheet		3,80
		5,36

SCHEDULE 13—INTEREST EARNED

Particulars	('000 ₹)
1. Interest/Discount [3045 + 220 + 102 + 12]	33,79
2. Income on Investment	1,15
3. Interest on Balance with RBI and other inter-bank fund	1,80
4. Others	—
	36,74

SCHEDULE 14—OTHER INCOME

Particulars		('000 ₹)
1. Commission, Exchange and Brokerage		8,20
2. Profit on Sale of investments	1,10	
Less: Loss on sale of investments	12	98
		9,18

SCHEDULE 15—INTEREST EXPENDED

Particulars	('000 ₹)
1. Interest on Deposits	12,25
2. Interest on RBI/Inter bank borrowings	1,60
	13,85

SCHEDULE 16—OPERATING EXPENSES

Particulars	('000 ₹)
1. Payments to and provision for employees	10,44
2. Rent, taxes and lighting	2,10
3. Printing and stationery	1,80
4. Advertisement and publicity	95
5. Depreciation on bank's property	92
6. Director's fees, allowances and expenses	2,20
7. Auditor's fee and expenses (including branch auditors)	1,20
8. Law charges	2,30
9. Postage, telegram, telephones, etc.	70
10. Repairs and maintenance	48
11. Insurance	50
12. Other expenditure	6
	23,65

ILLUSTRATION 33

The following are the figures extracted from the books of KLM Bank Limited as on 31.3.2015:

Particulars	₹
Interest and discount received	38,00,160
Interest paid on deposits	22,95,360
Issued and Subscribed capital	10,00,000
Salaries and allowances	2,50,000
Directors fee and allowances	35,000
Rent and Taxes paid	1,00,000
Postage and Telegrams	65,340
Statutory Reserve Fund	8,00,000
Commission, Exchange and Brokerage	1,90,000
Rent received	72,000
Profit on sale of Investments	2,25,800
Depreciation on Bank's properties	40,000
Statutory Expenses	38,000
Preliminary Expenses	30,000
Auditor's Fees	12,000

The following further information is given:

(i) A customer to whom a sum of ₹ 10 lakhs has been advanced has become insolvent and it is expected only 55% can be recovered from his estate.

(ii) There were also other debts for which a provision of ₹ 2,00,000 was found necessary by the auditors.

(iii) Rebate on Bills discounted on 31.3.2014 was ₹ 15,000 and on 31.3.2015 was ₹ 20,000.

(iv) Provide ₹ 2,00,000 for Income-tax.

(v) The Directos desire to declare 5% dividend.

Required: Prepare the Profit and Loss account of KLM Bank Limited for the year ended 31.3.2015 and also show, how the Profit and Loss account will appear in the Balance Sheet, if the Profit and Loss account opening balance was Nil as on 31.3.2014.

SOLUTION

KLM BANK LIMITED
PROFIT AND LOSS ACCOUNT FOR THE YEAR ENDED 31ST MARCH, 2015

	Particulars	*Schedule*	*Year ended 31.03.2015*
I.	**Income:**		
	Interest earned	13	37,95,160
	Other income	14	4,87,800
	Total		42,82,960
II.	**Expenditure**		
	Interest expended	15	22,95,360

Operating expenses	16	5,70,340
Provisions and Contingencies (₹ 4,50,000 + 2,00,000 + 2,00,000)		8,50,000
Total		37,15,700
III. Profits / Losses		
Net Profit for the year		5,67,260
Profit brought forward		NIL
		5,67,260
IV. Appropriations		
Transfer to Statutory Reserve (25%)		1,41,815
Proposed Dividend		50,000
Balance carried over to Balance Sheet		3,75,445
		5,67,260

The Profit & Loss Account balance of ₹ 3,75,445 will appear in the Balance Sheet under the head 'Reserve and Surplus' in Schedule 2.

SCHEDULE 13 – INTEREST EARNED

Particulars	*Year ended 31.03.2015* ₹
I. Income:	
Interest earned	37,95,160

SCHEDULE 14 – OTHER INCOME

I. Commission, exchange and brokerage	1,90,000
II. Profit on sale of investments	2,25,800
III. Rent received	72,000
	4,87,800

SCHEDULE 15–INTEREST EXPENDED

I. Interests on Deposits	22,95,360

SCHEDULE 16 – OPERATING EXPENSES

I. Payment to and provisions for employees	2,50,000
II. Rent, taxes and lighting	1,00,000
III. Depreciation on Bank's property	40,000
IV. Director's fees, allowances and expenses	35,000
V. Auditor's fees	12,000
VI. Law (statutory) charges	38,000
VII. Postage and telegrams	65,340
VIII. Preliminary expenses*	30,000
	5,70,340

*As per AS 26 Preliminary Expenses have been fully written off.

Working Note:

Interest/discount (net of rebate on bills discounted) (W.N. 1)	38,00,160
Add: Opening Rebate on bills discounted	15,000
Less: Closing Rebate on bills discounted	(20,000)
	37,95,160

ILLUSTRATION 34

From the following information prepare the Profit & Loss Account of HETARTH Bank Limited for the year ended 31st March, 2015. Also give necessary Schedules.

Particulars	(₹ '000s)
Interest earned on term loans	17.26
Interest earned on term loans classified as NPA	4.52
Interest received on term loans classified as NPA	2. 04
Interest on cash credits and overdrafts	38.54
Interest earned but not received on cash credit and overdraft treated as NPA	8.39
Interest on deposits	27.20
Commission	1.97
Profit on sale of investments	11.76
Profit on revaluation of investments	2. 76
Income from investments	15.53
Salaries, bonus and allowances	18. 75
Rent, taxes and lighting	1. 70
Printing and stationary	0. 75
Director's fees, allowances expenses	1.33
Law charges	0.22
Repairs and maintenance	0. 18
Insurance	0.30
Other information:	
Make necessary provision on risk assets:	
(i) Sub-standard	15.00
(ii) Doubtful for one year	7.00
(iii) Doubtful for two years	2.40
(iv) Loss assets	0.65
Investments	3700

Bank should not keep more than 25% of its investments as 'held-for-maturity' investment. The market value of its best 75% investments is ₹ 9,00,000 as on 31st March, 2015.

SOLUTION

HETARTH BANK LIMITED
PROFIT & LOSS ACCOUNT FOR THE YEAR ENDED 31ST MARCH, 2015

Particulars	*Schedule*	*(₹ '000s)*
I. Income		
Interest earned	13	60.46
Other income	14	16.49
Total		76.95
II. Expenditure		
Interest expended	15	27.20
Operating expenses	16	23.23
Provisions & Contingencies (Refer W.N.)		1880.61
Total		1931.04
III. Profit/Loss		(1854.09)
IV. Appropriations		Nil

SCHEDULE 13 - INTEREST EARNED

Particulars	*(₹ '000s)*
Interest/discount on advances bills	
Interest on term loans [17.26 – (4.52 – 2.04)]	14.78
Interest on cash credits and overdrafts (38.54 – 8.39)	30.15
Income on investments	15.53
	60.46

Note: Interest on non-performing assets is recognized on receipt basis.

SCHEDULE 14 - OTHER INCOME

Particulars	*(₹ '000s)*
Commission, exchange and brokerage	1.97
Profit on sale of investments	11.76
Profit on revaluation of investments	2.76
	16.49

SCHEDULE 15 - INTEREST EXPENDED

Particulars	*(₹ '000s)*
Interest on deposits	27.20

SCHEDULE 16 - OPERATING EXPENSES

Particulars	*(₹ '000s)*
Payments to and provision for employees - salaries, bonus and allowances	18.75
Rent, taxes and lighting	1.70

Printing & stationery	0.75
Director's fee, allowances and expenses	1.33
Law charges	0.22
Repairs & maintenance	0.18
Insurance	0.30
	23.23

Working Note:

Provisions & Contingencies		*(₹ '000s)*
Provision for non-performing assets*		
Sub-standard (15 × 15%)		2.25
Doubtful for one year (7 × 25%)		1.75
Doubtful for two years (2. 40 x 40%)		0.96
Loss Assets (0.65 × 100%)		0.65
		5.61
Diminution in the value of current Investments:		
Cost 75% of ₹ 3,700 thousands**	27,75	
Less: Market value	(900)	1875.00
		1880.61

Notes: (i) It is assumed that all sub-standard and doubtful assets are fully secured. (ii) 75% investments (Other than 'held for maturity') have been marked to market as per RBI Guidelines.

43.0 HOW TO PREPARE BALANCE SHEET OF A BANK

THE THIRD SCHEDULE
(SEE SECTION 29)
FORM 'A'
FORM OF BALANCE SHEET
BALANCE SHEET OF ... (HERE ENTER NAME OF THE BANKING COMPANY) ...
BALANCE SHEET AS ON 31st MARCH (YEAR)

(000's omitted)

Particulars	*Schedule*	*As on 31.3.... (Current year)*	*As on 31.3... (Previous year)*
Capital and Liabilities:			
Capital	1		
Reserves and Surplus	2		
Deposits	3		
Borrowings	4		
Other Liabilities and Provisions	5		
Total:			
Assets:			
Cash and Balances with RBI	6		

Balances with Banks and			
Money at call and short notice	7		
Investments	8		
Advances	9		
Fixed Assets	10		
Other Assets	11		
Total:			
Contingent Liabilities	12		
Bills for collection			

SCHEDULE 1—CAPITAL

	Particulars	*As on 31.3.... (Current year)*	*As on 31.3... (Previous year)*
I.	**For Nationalised Banks**		
	Capital (Fully owned by Central Government)		
II.	**For Banks Incorporated Outside India**		
	Capital		
(i)	(The amount brought in by banks by way of start-up capital as prescribed by RBI should be shown under this head)		
(ii)	Amount of deposit kept with the RBI under Section 11(2) of the Banking Regulation Act, 1949		
	Total:		
III.	**For Other Banks**		
	Authorised Capital		
	(.......... Shares of ₹ .... each)		
	Issued Capital		
	(.......... Shares of ₹ .... each)		
	Subscribed Capital		
	(.......... Shares of ₹ .... each)		
	Called-up Capital		
	(.......... Shares of ₹ .... each)		
	Less: Calls unpaid		
	Add: Forfeited Shares		

SCHEDULE 2—RESERVES AND SURPLUS

	Particulars	*As on 31.3.... (Current year)*	*As on 31.3... (Previous year)*
I.	**Statutory Reserves**		
	Opening Balance		
	Additions during the year		

	Deductions during the year		
II.	**Capital Reserves**		
	Opening Balance		
	Additions during the year		
	Deductions during the year		
III.	**Share Premium**		
	Opening Balance		
	Additions during the year		
	Deductions during the year		
IV.	**Revenue and Other Reserves**		
	Opening Balance		
	Additions during the year		
	Deductions during the year		
V.	**Balances in Profit and Loss Account**		
	Total: (I, II, III, IV and V)		

SCHEDULE 3—DEPOSITS

		Particulars	*As on 31.3.... (Current year)*	*As on 31.3... (Previous year)*
A.	**I.**	**Demand Deposits**		
		(i) From Banks		
		(ii) From Others		
	II.	**Savings Bank Deposits**		
	III.	**Term Deposits**		
		(i) From Banks		
		(ii) From Others		
	Total: (I, II and III)			
B.	(i)	Deposits of branches in India		
	(ii)	Deposits of branches outside India		
	Total:			

SCHEDULE 4—BORROWINGS

	Particulars	*As on 31.3.... (Current year)*	*As on 31.3... (Previous year)*
I.	**Borrowings in India**		
	(i) Reserve Bank of India		
	(ii) Other Banks		
	(iii) Other Institutions and Agencies		
II.	**Borrowings outside India**		
	Total: (I and II)		
	Secured Borrowings in I and II above-₹		

SCHEDULE 5—OTHER LIABILITIES AND PROVISIONS

Particulars	As on 31.3.... (Current year)	As on 31.3... (Previous year)
I. Bills Payable		
II. Inter-office adjustments (net)		
III. Interest accrued		
IV. Other (including provisions)		
Total:		

SCHEDULE 6—CASH AND BALANCES WITH RESERVE BANK OF INDIA

Particulars	As on 31.3.... (Current year)	As on 31.3... (Previous year)
I. Cash in hand (including foreign currency notes)		
II. Balances with Reserve Bank of India		
(i) In Current Account		
(ii) In Other Accounts		
Total: (I and II)		

SCHEDULE 7—BALANCES WITH BANKS AND MONEY AT CALL AND SHORT NOTICE

Particulars	As on 31.3.... (Current year)	As on 31.3... (Previous year)
I. In India		
(i) Balances with Banks		
(a) In Current Accounts		
(b) In Other Deposit Accounts		
(ii) Money at Call and Short Notice		
(a) With Banks		
(b) With other Institutions		
Total (I and II)		
II. Outside India		
(i) In Current Accounts		
(ii) In other Deposits Accounts		
(iii) Money at Call and Short Notice		
Total: (I, II and III)		
Grand Total (I and II):		

SCHEDULE 8—INVESTMENTS

Particulars	As on 31.3.... (Current year)	As on 31.3... (Previous year)
I. Investments in India		
(i) Government Securities		
(ii) Other Approved Securities		

(iii) Shares		
(iv) Debentures and Bonds		
(v) Subsidiaries and/or Joint Ventures		
(vi) Others (to be specified)		
Total:		
II. Investments Outside India		
(i) Government securities (including local authorities)		
(ii) Subsidiaries and/or Joint Ventures Abroad		
(iii) Other Investments (to be specified)		
Total:		
Grand Total: (I and II)		

SCHEDULE 9—ADVANCES

Particulars	*As on 31.3.... (Current year)*	*As on 31.3... (Previous year)*
A. (i) Bills Purchased and Discounted		
(ii) Cash Credits, Overdrafts and Loans payable on Demand		
(iii) Term Loans		
Total:		
B. (i) Secured by Tangible Assets		
(ii) Covered by Bank/Government Guarantees		
(iii) Unsecured		
Total:		
C. I. Advances in India		
(i) Priority Sectors		
(ii) Public Sector		
(iii) Banks		
(iv) Others		
Total:		
C. II. Advances Outside India		
(i) Due from Banks		
(ii) Due from others		
(a) Bills Purchased and Discounted		
(b) Syndicated Loans		
(c) Others		
Total:		
Grand Total: (C. I and II)		

SCHEDULE 10—FIXED ASSETS

	Particulars	*As on 31.3....* *(Current year)*	*As on 31.3...* *(Previous year)*
I.	**Premises**		
	At cost as on 31st March of the preceding year		
	Additions during the year		
	Deductions during the year		
	Depreciation to date		
	Total:		
II.	**Other Fixed Assets (Incl. Furniture & Fixtures)**		
	At cost as on 31st March of the preceding year		
	Additions during the year		
	Deductions during the year		
	Depreciation to date		
	Total:		
	Grand Total: I and II		

SCHEDULE 11—OTHER ASSETS

	Particulars	*As on 31.3....* *(Current year)*	*As on 31.3...* *(Previous year)*
I.	Inter-Office Adjustments (net)		
II.	Interest Accrued		
III.	Tax paid in Advance/Tax deducted at source		
IV.	Stationery and Stamps		
V.	Non-banking assets acquired in satisfaction of claims		
VI.	Others		
	Total:		

@ In case there is any unadjusted balances of loss the same may be shown under this item with appropriate foot-note.

SCHEDULE 12—CONTINGENT LIABILITIES

	Particulars	*As on 31.3....* *(Current year)*	*As on 31.3...* *(Previous year)*
I.	Claims against the bank not acknowledged as debts		
II.	Liability for partially paid investments		
III.	Liability on account of outstanding forward exchange contracts		
IV.	Guarantees given on behalf of constituents		
	(a) In India		
	(b) Outside India		
V.	Acceptances, endorsements and other obligations		

VI. Other items for which the bank is contingently liable		
Total		

44.0 RBI GUIDELINES FOR COMPILATION OF BALANCE SHEET

Item	Schedule	Coverage	Notes and Instructions for Compliation
Capital	1	**Nationalised Bank** Capital (Fully Owned by Central Government) Banking companies incorporated outside India **Other Banks (Indian)** Authorised Capital (... Shares *or* ₹... each) Issued Capital (...Shares of ₹...each) subscribed Capital (... shares of ₹... each) Called up Capital (... Shares of ₹...each. *Less:* Calls unpaid... *Add:* Forfeited shares... Paid up to capital...	The capital owned by Central Government as on the date of the Balance Sheet including contribution from Government, if any, for participating in World Bank Projects should be shown. (i) The amount brought in by banks by way of start-up capital as prescribed by RBI should be shown under this head. (ii) The amount of deposit kept with RBI, under sub-section 2 of Section 11 of the Banking Regulation Act, 1949 should also be shown. Authorised, Issued, Subscribed, Called-up Capital should be given separately. Calls-in-arrears will be deducted from Called up capital while the paid-up value of the forfeited shares should be added thus arriving at the paid-up capital. Where necessary, items which can be combined should be shown under one head for instance 'Issued and Subscribed Capital'. **Notes-General** The changes in the above items, if any, during the years, say fresh contribution made by Government, fresh issue of capital, capitalisation of reserves, etc. may be explained in the notes.
Reserves and Surplus	2	**(i) Statutory Reserves**	Reserves created in terms of Section 17 *or* any other section of Banking Regulation Act must be separately disclosed.
		(ii) Capital Reserves	The expression 'Capital reserves' shall not include any amount regarded as free for contribution through the profit and loss account. Surplus on revaluation should be treated as Capital Reserve Surplus on translation of the final instalment of foreign branches (which includes fixed assets also) is not a revaluation reserve.
		(iii) Share Premium	Premium on issue of share capital may be shown separately under this head.

		(iv) Revenue and other Reserves	The expression 'Revenue Reserve'. called any reserve other than capital reserve created will include all reserves other than those separately classified. The expression Reserve shall not include any amount retained by way of providing renewals *or* diminution in value of assets *or* retained by way of providing fund for known liability.
		(v) Balance of Profit	Includes balance of profit after appropriations. In case of loss the balance may be shown as a deduction. **Notes-General** Movement in various categories of Reserves should be shown as indicated in the schedule.
Deposits	3	**A.(i) Demand Deposits** *(i) from banks* *(ii) from others*	Includes all bank deposit repayable on demand. Includes all demand deposits of the non-bank sectors. Credit balances in overdrafts, cash credit accounts, deposits payable at call, overdue deposits, inoperative current accounts, matured time deposits & cash certificates, certificates of deposits, etc. are to be included under this category.
		(II) Saving Bank Deposits	Includes all saving bank deposits (including inoperative saving bank accounts)
		(iii) Term Deposits *(i) from banks* *(ii) from others*	Includes all types of bank deposits repayable after a specified term. Includes all types of deposits of the non-bank sector repayable after a specified term. Fixed deposits, cumulative and recurring deposits, cash certificates, certificates of deposits, annuity deposits, deposits mobilised under various schemes, ordinary staff deposits, foreign currency non-resident deposits accounts, etc. are to be included under this category.

		B. *(i) Deposits of branches in India* *(ii) Deposits of branches outside India*	The total of these two items will agree with the total deposits. **Notes-General** (a) Interest payable on deposits which is accrued but not due should not be included but shown under other liabilities. (b) Matured time deposits and cash certificates, etc. should be treated as demand deposits. (c) Deposits under special schemes should be included under term deposits if they are not payable on demand. When each deposits have matured for payments they should be shown under demand deposits. (d) Deposits from banks will include deposits from the banking system in India, cooperative banks, foreign banks which mayor may not have a presence in India.
Borrowings	4	**(i) Borrowings in India**	
		(i) Reserve Banks of India	Includes borrowings/refinance obtained from Reserve Bank of India.
		(ii) Other Banks	Includes borrowings/refinance obtained from commercial banks (including cooperative banks).
		(iii) Other Institutions and agencies	Includes borrowings/refinance obtained from Industrial Development Bank of India, Export-Import Bank of India, National Bank for Agriculture and Rural Development and other institutions, agencies (including liability against participation certificates, if any).
		(ii) Borrowings outside India	Includes borrowings of India branches abroad as well as borrowings of foreign branches.

		Secured borrowings included above	This item will be shown separately. Includes secured borrowings/refinance in India and outside India. **Notes-General** (i) The total of I and II will agree with the total borrowings shown in the balance sheet. (ii) Inter-office transactions should not be shown as borrowings. (iii) Funds raised by foreign branches by way of certificates of deposits, notes, bonds, etc. should be classified depending upon documentation, as 'deposits', 'borrowings', etc. (iv) Refinance obtained by banks from reserve Bank of India and various institutions are being brought under the head 'Borrowings'. Hence, advances will be shown at the gross amount on the assets side.
Other Liabilities and Provisions	5	**I. Bills payable**	Includes drafts, telegraphic transfers, travellers' cheques, mail transfers payable payslips, bankers cheques and other miscellaneous items
		II. Inter-office adjustment (net)	The inter-office adjustments balance, if in credit, should be shown under this head. Only net position of inter-office accounts, inland as well as foreign should be shown here
		III. Interest accrued	ncludes interest accrued but not due on deposits and borrowings.
		IV. Other (including provisions)	Includes the net provisions for income tax and other taxes like interest tax (less advance payment tax deducted at source, etc.) surplus in aggregate in provisions for bad debts, provisions for depreciation in securities, contingency funds which are not disclosed as a reserve but are actually in the nature of reserves, proposed dividend/transfer to Government, other liabilities which are not disclosed under any of the major heads such as unclaimed dividend, provisions and fund kept for specific purposes, unexpired discount, outstanding charges like rent, conveyance, etc. Certain types of deposits like staff security deposits, margin deposits, etc.

			where the repayment is not free, should also be included under this head. **Notes-General** (i) For arriving at the net balance of inter-office adjustments all connected inter-office accounts should be aggregated and the net balance only will be shown, representing mostly items in transit and unadjusted items. (ii) The interest accruing on all deposits, whether the payment is due *or* not, should be treated as a liability. (iii) It is proposed to show only pure deposits under this head 'deposits' and hence all surplus provisions for bad and doubtful debts, contingency funds, secret reserves, etc. which are not netted off against the relative assets, should be brought under the head 'Others (including provisions)'.
Cash and Balances with the Reserve Bank of India	6	I. Cash in hand (including foreign currency notes) II. Balance with Reserve with Reserve Bank of India (i) in Current Account (ii) in other Accounts	Includes cash in hand including foreign currency notes and also of foreign branches in case of banks having such branches.
Balances with banks and money at call and short notice	7	**I. In India** (i) Balance with banks (a) in current accounts (b) in other Deposit account	Includes all balances with banks in India (including co-operative banks). Balances in s current accounts and deposits accounts should be shown separately.
		(ii) Money at call and short notice (a) with banks (b) with other institutions	Includes deposits repayable within 15 days *or* less than 15 days notice lent in the inter-bank call money market.
		II. Outside India (i) Current accounts (ii) Deposits accounts	Includes balances held by foreign branches and balances held by Indian branches of the banks outside India. Balance held with foreign branches by other branches of the bank should not be shown under this head but should be included in inter-branch accounts. The amount held in 'current accounts' and 'deposit accounts' should be shown separately.

		(iii) Money at call and short notice	Includes deposits usually classified in foreign countries as money at call and short notice.
Investments	8	**I. Investments in India**	
		(i) Government securities	Includes Central and State Government securities and Government treasury bills. These securities should be shown at the book value. However, the difference between the book value and market value should be given in the notes to the Balance Sheet.
		(ii) Other approved securities	Securities other than Government securities, which according to the Banking Regulation Act, 1949 are treated as approved securities, should be included here.
		(iii) Shares	Investments in shares of companies and corporations not included in item (ii) should be included here.
		(iv) Debentures and Bonds companies	Investments in debentures and bonds of and corporations not, included in item (ii) should be included here.
		(v) Investment in subsidiaries/joint ventures	Investment in subsidiaries/joint ventures (including RRBs) should be included here.
		(vi) Others	Includes residual investments, if any, like gold, commercial paper and other instruments in the nature of shares/ debentures/bonds.
		II. Investments outside India	
		(i) Government securities (including local authorities)	All foreign Government securities including securities issued by local authorities may be classified under this head.
		(ii) Subsidiaries and/ or joint ventures abroad	All investment made in the share capital of subsidiaries floated outside India and/or joint ventures abroad should be classified under this head.
		(iii) Others	All other investments outside India may be shown under this head.
Advances	9	A (i) Bills purchased and discounted (ii) Cash credits, over-drafts and loans repayable on demand	In classification under section 'A'. All outstandings in India as well as outside- less bad debt, will be classified under three heads as indicated and both secured and unsecured advances will be included under these heads.
		(iii) Term loans	Including overdue instalments.

		B (i) Secured by tangible assets	All advances *or* part of advances which are secured by tangible assets may be shown here. The item will include advances in India and outside India.
		(ii) Covered by Bank/ Government Guarantee	Advances in India and outside India to the extent they are covered by guarantees of Indian and foreign governments and Indian and foreign banks and DICGC and ECGC are to be included.
		(iii) Unsecured	All advances not classified under (i) and (ii) will be included here.
		C. I. Advances in India (i) Priority sectors (ii) Public sector (iii) Banks (iv) Others **C II. Advances outside India** (i) Due from banks (ii) Due from others (a) Bills purchased and discounted (b) Syndicate loans (c) Others	Total 'A' should tally with the total of 'B'. Advances should be broadly classified into 'Advances in India, and 'Advances outside India'. Advances in India will be further classified on the sectoral basis as indicated. Advances on sectors which for the time being are classified as priority sectors according to the instructions of the Reserve Bank are to be classified under the head 'Priority sector'. Such advances should be excluded from item (ii) i.e. advances to public sector. Advances to Central and State. Governments and other Government undertaking including Government companies and corporations which are, according to the status, to be treated as public sector companies are to be included in the category "Public Sector". All advances to the banking sector including co-operative banks will come under the head 'Banks'. All the remaining advances will be included under the head 'Others' and typically this category will include non-priority advances to the private, joint and co-operative sectors. **Notes-General** (i) The gross amount of advances including refinance and rediscounts but excluding provisions made to the satisfaction of auditors should be shown as advances. (ii) Term loans will be loans not repayable on demand. (iii) Consortium advances would be shown net of share from other participating banks/institutions.

Fixed Assets	10	**I. Premises** (i) At cost as on 31st March of the preceding year (ii) Additions during the year (iii) Deductions during the year there from (iv) Depreciation to date	Premises wholly *or* partly owned by the banking company for the purpose of business including residential premises should be shown against 'Premises'. In the case of premises and other fixed assets, the previous during the year as also the total depreciation written off should be shown. Where sums have been written off on reduction of capital *or* revaluation of assets, every balance sheet after the first balance sheet subsequent to the reduction *or* revaluation should show the revised figures for a period of five years with the date and amount of the revision made.
		II. Other fixed Assets (including furniture and fixtures) (i) At cost on 31st March of the preceding year (ii) Additions during the year (iii) Deductions during the year **III. Depreciation to date**	Motor vehicles and other fixed assets other than premises but including furniture should be shown under this head.
Other Assets	11	**I. Inter/office adjustment (net)**	The inter-office adjustments balance, if in debit, should be shown under this head. Only net position of inter-office accounts, inland as well as foreign, should be shown here. For arriving at the net balance of inter-office adjustment accounts, all connected inter-office accounts should be aggregated and the net balance, if in debit, only should be shown representing mostly items in transit and unadjusted items.
		II. Interest accrued	Interest accrued but not due on investments and advance and interest due but not collected on investments will be the main components of this item. As banks normally debit the borrowings' accounts with interest due on the Balance Sheet date, usually there may not be any amount of interest due on advances. Only such interest as can be realised in the ordinary course should be shown under this head.

		III. Tax paid in advance/tax deducted at source	The amount of tax deducted at source on securities, advance tax paid, etc. to the extent that these items are not set oft against relative tax provisions should be shown against this item.
		IV. Stationery and stamps	Only exceptional items of expenditure on stationery like bulk purchase of securities paper, loose leaf *or* other ledgers, etc. which are shown as quasi-asset to be written oft over a period of time should be shown here. The value should be on a realistic basis and cost escalation should not be taken into account, as these items are for internal use.
		V. Non-banking assets acquired in satisfaction of claims	Immovable properties/tangible assets acquired in satisfaction of claims are to be shown under this head.
		VI. Others	This will include items claims which have not been met, for instance, clearing items, debit items representing addition to asset *or* reduction in liabilities which have not been adjusted for technical reasons, want of particulars, etc. advances given to staff by a bank as employer and not as a banker, etc. Items which are in the nature of expenses which are pending adjustments should be provided for and the provision netted against this item so that only realisable value is shown under this head. Accrued income other than interest may also be included here.
Contingent Liabilities	12	**I. Claims against the bank not acknowledged is debts**	
		II. Liability тor partly paid investments	Liabilities on partly paid shares, debentures, etc. will be included under this head.
		III. Liability on account of outstanding forward exchange contracts	Outstanding forward exchange contracts may be included here.
		IV. Guarantees given on behalf of constituents (i) In India (ii) Outside India	Guarantees given for constituents in India and outside India may be shown separately.

		V. Acceptances, endorsements and other obligations	This item will include letters of credit and bills accepted by the bank on behalf of customers.
		VI. Other items for which the Bank is contingently liable	Arrears of cumulative dividends, bills rediscounted under underwriting contracts, estimated amounts of contracts remaining to be executed on capital account and not provided for, etc. are to be included here.
Bills for Collection			Bills and other items in the course of collection and not adjusted will be shown against this item in the summary version only. No separate schedule is proposed.

ILLUSTRATION 35

State the number and name of the Schedule and item head in the Schedule for the following items of Tushar Bank:

1. Reserves created u/s 17
2. Matured Time Deposits
3. Interest accrued and due on Matured Time Deposits
4. Current Accounts (including accounts overdrawn to the extent of ₹ 2,500) ₹ 97,000
5. Fixed Deposits for 5 years
6. Interest accrued and due on Fixed Deposits
7. Interest accrued but not due on Fixed Deposits
8. Interest accrued but not due on Borrowings
9. Branch Adjustments (Credit) ₹ 1,00,000, Branch Adjustments (Dr.) ₹ 10,000
10. Branch Adjustment (Debit) ₹ 1,00,000, Branch Adjustments (Cr.) ₹ 10,000
11. Staff Security Deposits
12. Provision for Income Tax ₹ 1,00,000, Advance Tax ₹ 10,000, Tax Deducted at Source (Dr) ₹ 5,000
13. Provisions for Doubtful Debts
14. Proposed Dividend
15. Unclaimed Dividend
16. Rebate on Bills Discounted
17. Outstanding Rent & Salaries
18. US Dollars and Pounds
19. Balances with State Bank of India
20. Deposit with SBI payable within 15 days
21. Government Treasury Bills
22. Gold, Silver and Commercial Paper
23. Bills Purchased and discounted
24. Cash Credits, Over-drafts and Loan payable on demand ₹ 10 lacs (including an advance of ₹ 8,000 which is considered doubtful)
25. Term Loans ₹ 50 lacs (including overdue Instalments of ₹ 5 lacs)

26. Land & Buildings
27. Furniture & Fixtures and Motor Vehicles
28. Interest accrued but not due on Investments and Advances
29. Provision for Income Tax ₹ 15,000, Advance Tax ₹ 95,000, Tax Deducted at Source (Dr) ₹ 5,000
30. Securities Papers and Loose Leaf Ledgers
31. Land & Building acquired in satisfaction of a claims
32. Liability for Partly Paid shares held as investments
33. Liability on account of outstanding forward exchange contracts
34. Guarantees given on behalf of bank customers
35. Acceptances, Endorsements and Other Obligations
36. Arrears of cumulative Preference Dividends
37. Estimated Amounts of contracts remaining to be executed on capital account and not provided for
38. Bills for collection

SOLUTION

Item No	*Schedule No*	*Schedule Name*	*Items head in Schedule*
1	2	Reserves and Surplus	Statutory Reserves
2	3	Deposits	Demand Deposits
3	3	Deposits	Demand Deposits
4	3	Deposits	Demand Deposits ₹ 99,500
	9	Advances	Cash Credits, Overdrafts and Loans payable on demand ₹ 2,500
5	3	Deposits	Term Deposits
6	3	Deposits	Term Deposits
7	5	Other Liabilities and Provisions	Interest Accrued
8	5	Other Liabilities and Provisions	Interest Accrued
9	5	Other Liabilities and Provisions	Inter-office Adjustment (Net) ₹ 90,000
10	11	Other Assets	Inter-Office Adjustment (Net) ₹ 90,000
11	5	Other Liabilities and Provisions	Others (including Provisions)
12	5	Other Liabilities and Provisions	Other (including Provisions) ₹ 85,000
13	5	Other Liabilities and Provisions	Other (including Provisions)
14	5	Other Liabilities and Provisions	Other (including Provisions)
15	5	Other Liabilities and Provisions	Other (including Provisions)
16	5	Other Liabilities and Provisions	Other (including Provisions)
17	5	Other Liabilities and Provisions	Other (including Provisions)
18	6	Cash and Balance with RBI	Cash in hand
19	7	Balances with Banks and money at call and short notice	Balances with Banks

20	7	Balances with Banks and money at call and short notice	Money at call and Short notice
21	8	Investments	Government Securities
22	8	Investments	Others
23	9	Advances	Bills Purchased and Discounted
24	9	Advances	Cash Credits, Overdrafts and Loans payable on demand ₹ 10 lacs
	5	Other Liabilities and Provisions	Other (including Provisions) ₹ 8,000
25	9	Advances	Term Loans
26	10	Fixed Assets	Premises
27	10	Fixed Assets	Other Fixed Assets
28	11	Other Assets	Interest Accrued
29	11	Other Assets	Advance Tax ₹ 85,000
30	11	Other Assets	Stationery and Stamps
31	11	Other Assets	Non-Banking Assets
32	12	Contingent Liabilities	Liability for Partly paid Investments
33	12	Contingent Liabilities	Liability on account of outstanding forward exchange contacts
34	12	Contingent Liabilities	Guarantees given on behalf of constituents
35	12	Contingent Liabilities	Acceptances, Endorsements and other obligations
36	12	Contingent Liabilities	Others Items
37	12	Contingent Liabilities	Others Items
38	—	Bills for Collection	Bills for collection

ILLUSTRATION 36

In the trial balance of Tulsian Bank Ltd as at 31st March, 2015, Interest & Discount and Income from Investments appear at ₹ 8,880 and ₹ 30 respectively.

Additional Information:

(a) Rebate on bills discounted:	on 31.3.2014	₹ 15
	on 31.3.2015	₹ 45
(b) Interest accrued on Investments		₹ 10

How will you disclose the relevant items in the final accounts for the year ended 31st March, 2015? (The figures being in thousands)

SOLUTION

SCHEDULE 13—INTEREST EARNED

Particulars	*₹ '000*
I Interest & Discount [8,880 + 15 (Opening Rebate) – 45 (Closing Rebate)]	8,850
II Income on Investments [30 + 10 (accrued)]	40
	8,890

SCHEDULE 5—OTHER LIABILITIES AND PROVISIONS

Particulars	₹ '000
I Rebate on Bills Discounted	45

SCHEDULE 11—OTHER ASSETS

Particulars	₹ '000
Interest accrued on Investments	10

ILLUSTRATION 37

How will you disclose the following ledger balances in the final accounts of Tulsian Bank Ltd for the year ended 31st March 2015: (The figures being in thousands)

Interest and Discount	8,850
Income on Investments	40
Rebate on Bills Discounted as (at 31.3.2015)	45
Interest accrued on Investments as (at 31.3.2015)	10

SOLUTION

SCHEDULE 13—INTEREST EARNED

Particulars	₹ '000
I Interest & Discount	8,850
II Income on Investments	40
	8,890

SCHEDULE 5—OTHER LIABILITIES AND PROVISIONS

Particulars	₹ '000
I Rebate on Bills Discounted	45

SCHEDULE 11—OTHER ASSETS

Particulars	₹ '000
Interest accrued on Investments	10

Note: No further adjustment has been in respect of Rebate on Bills Discounted (45) and Interest accrued on Investments since (10) since these items have already been adjusted in figure of Interest & Discount and Income on Investments repectively.

ILLUSTRATION 38

From the following information of XYZ Bank Ltd. calculate the amount of Interest Earned (as per Schedule 13), Other Income (as per Schedule 14), Other Liabilities and Provisions (as per Schedule 5) and Provisions and Contingencies.

Particulars	(₹' 000)
Interest and Discount	₹ 2,045
Income from Investments	₹ 1,12

Interest on Balances with RBI	₹ 1,77
Commission, Exchange & Brokerage	7,12
Profit on Sale of Investments	1,22
Interest on Deposits	8,22
Interest to RBI	1,47
The following items are already adjusted with interest and discount (Cr)	(₹ ' 000)
Tax Provision	1,48
Provision for Doubtful Debts	92
Loss on Sale of Investments	12
Rebate on Bills Discounted	55

SOLUTION

SCHEDULE 13—INTEREST EARNED

Particulars	*(₹ ' 000)*
I. Interest/Discount [2045 + 148 + 92 + 12]	2,297
II. Income on Investment	112
III. Interest on Balance with RBI	177
	2,586

SCHEDULE 14—OTHER INCOME

I. Commission, Exchange and Brokerage		712
II. Profit on Sale of Investments	122	
Less: Loss on Sale of Investments	12	1,10

PROVISIONS AND CONTINGENCIES

I. Provision for Tax	1,48
II. Provision for Doubtful Debts	92
	240

SCHEDULE 5—OTHER LIABILITIES & PROVISIONS

I. Provision for Tax	1,48
II. Provision for Doubtful Debts	92
III. Rebate on Bills Discounted	55
	295

ILLUSTRATION 39

How will you disclose the following ledger balances in the final accounts of ABC Bank Ltd.:

Current Accounts	₹ 900 lacs
Saving Accounts	₹ 800 lacs
Fixed Deposits	₹ 700 lacs

Cash Credits	₹ 600 lacs
Term Loans	₹ 1400 lacs
Bills discounted & purchased	₹ 400 lacs

Additional Information:

1. Included in the current accounts ledger are accounts overdrawn to the extent of ₹ 100 lacs
2. One of the cash credit Accounts ₹ 10 lacs (including interest ₹ 1 lac) is doubtful for more than 3 years.
3. 50% of term loans are secured by government guarantees, 10% of cash credits are unsecured, other portion is secured by tangible assets.

SOLUTION

SCHEDULE 3—DEPOSITS

A. Demand deposits (₹ 900 lacs + ₹ 100 lacs)	₹ 1,000 lacs
B. Saving Bank Deposits	₹ 800 lacs
C. Term Deposits	₹ 700 lacs
	₹ 2,500 lacs

SCHEDULE 9—ADVANCES

A. (i)	Bills Discounted and Purchased	₹ 400 lacs
(ii)	Cash credits	₹ 600 lacs
	Over drafts	₹ 100 lacs
	Term loans	₹ 1400 lacs
		₹ 2500 lacs
B. (i)	Secured by tangible assets	₹ 1740 lacs
(ii)	Secured by Bank /Govt. Guarantees	₹ 700 lacs
(iii)	Unsecured	₹ 60 lacs
		₹ 2500 lacs

SCHEDULE 5—OTHER LIABILITIES & PROVISIONS

Others (Provision for Doubtful Debt)	₹ 10 lacs

PROFIT & LOSS ACCOUNT

Less: Provisions & Contingencies (Provision for Doubtful Debt)	₹ 10 lacs

PREPARATION OF PROFIT & LOSS ACCOUNT AND BALANCE SHEET

ILLUSTRATION 40

From the following trial balance as on 31st March, 2015, prepare final accounts of CAMID Bank Limited:

[₹ in '000]

Particulars	Dr. (₹)	Particulars	Cr. (₹)
Cash balance	200	Interest on Advances	800
Balance with Other Banks	400	Interest from Investments	125
Cash with RBI	100	Commission, Exchange & Brokerage	200
Investments in Govt. Securities	300	Profit on sale of investments	20
Other Approved Securities	100	Other revenue receipts	80
Bills purchased and discounted	250	Share capital	2,000
Cash credits, overdrafts and		Statutory Reserves	900
Demand loans	1,425	Profit & Loss Account	650
Term loans	1,275	Fixed Deposits	275
Premises (Net)	1,375	Savings Deposts	325
Furniture	250	Current Accounts	125
Interest paid	120	Borrowings from other banks	300
Salary	75	Borrowings from RBI	100
Printing and Stationery	35	Bills Payable	25
Postage & Telegram	20	Interest accrued	75
Repairs	25		
Interest accrued	50		
	6,000		6,000
		Bills for collection	235

Additonal Information:

Advances made have been classified as under:

Particulars	Cash credits Overdrafts, etc.	Term Loans	Bills Purchased
Standard Assets	1,000	975	225
Sub-standard Assets	125	100	25
Doubtful—Upto one year	100	20	—
One to three years	120	50	—
More than three years	50	80	—
Loss Assets	30	50	—
	1,425	1,275	250

No provision has been made so far against these assets. Doubtful assets are secured to the extent of 50% of the dues.

SOLUTION

CAMID BANK LIMITED
BALANCE SHEET AS AT 31ST MARCH, 2015

Particulars	Schedule No.	As on 31st March 2015 (₹ '000)	As on 31st March 2014 (₹ '000)
Capital and Liabilities:			
Share Capital	1	2,000.00	

Reserves and Surplus	2	2,049.70	
Deposits		3	725.00
Borrowings		4	400.00
Other Liabilities and Provisions	5	550.30	
			5,725.00
Assets:			
Cash and balances with Reserve Bank			
of India (RBI)	6	300.00	
Balances with banks and Money at			
call and short notice	7	400.00	
Investments	8	400.00	
Advances		9	2,950.00
Fixed Assets	10	1,625.00	
Other Assets	11	50.00	
			5,725.00
Contingent Liabilities:	12	Nil	
Bills for collection		235.00	

PROFIT AND LOSS ACCOUNT
FOR THE YEAR ENDED 31ST MARCH, 2015

Particulars	*Schedule No.*	*Year ended 31st March 2015 (₹ '000)*	*Year ended 31st March 2014 (₹ '000)*
I. Income:			
Interest earned	13	925.00	
Other income	14	300.00	
		1,225.00	
II. Expenditure:			
Interest expended	15	120.00	
Operating expenses	16	155.00	
Provisions and contingencies		450.30	
		725.30	
III. Profit/Loss:			
Net Profit for the year		499.70	
Profit brought forward		650.00	
		1,149.70	
IV. Appropriations:			
Transfer to Statutory Reserves @ 25%		124.925	
Balance carried over to Balance Sheet		1,024.775	
		1,149.700	

Schedule to Accounts:

Particulars	*As on 31st March 2015 (₹ '000)*	*As on 31st March 2014 (₹ '000)*
Schedule 1—Capital		
Authorised Capital		
.......shares of ₹ each		
Issued Capital		
.......shares of ₹ each		
Subscribed Capital		
.......shares of ₹ each		
Paid up Capital	2,000	
.......shares of ₹ each	2,000	
Schedule 2—Reserves and Surplus		
Statutory Reserves:		
Opening balance	900.000	
Additions during the year	124.925	
Balance in Profit & Loss Account	1,024.775	
	2,049.700	
Schedule 3—Deposits		
Demand Deposits	125	
Savings Deposits	325	
Fixed Deposits	275	
	725	
Schedule 4—Borrowings		
Borrowings in India:		
(i) From RBI	100	
(ii) From other banks	300	
	400	
Schedule 5—Other liabilities and provisions		
Bills Payable	25	
Interest accrued	75	
Other provisions (W.N.1)	450.30	
	550.30	
Schedule 6—Cash and Balance with RBI		
Cash in hand	200	
Balance with RBI	100	
	300	
Schedule 7—Balances with banks and Money at call and short notice		

In India:		
Balance with other banks	400	
Schedule 8—Investments		
Investments in India in:		
Government Securities	300	
Other Approved Securities	100	
	400	
Schedule 9—Advances		
A. Bills purchased and discounted	250	
Cash credits, overdrafts & demand loans	1,425	
Term loans	1,275	
	2,950	
B. (i) Secured by tangible assets	—	
(ii) Secured by Bank/Govt. guarantees	—	
(iii) Unsecured (Details are not available)	—	
Schedule 10—Fixed Assets		
Premises (net)	1,375	
Other fixed articles:		
Furniture	250	
	1,625	
Schedule 11—Other Assets		
Interest accrued	50	
Schedule 12—Contingent Liabilities	NIL	
Schedule 13—Interest Earned		
Interest on advances	800	
Inrterest from Investments	125	
	925	
Schedule 14—Other Income		
Commission, Exchange & Brokerage	200	
Profit on sale of investments	20	
Miscellaneous Income	80	
	300	
Schedule 15—Interest Expended		
Interest on deposits	120	
Schedule 16—Operating Expenses		
Payments to and provisions for employees	75	
Printing and Stationery	35	
Postage and Telegrams	20	
Repairs	25	
	155	

Working Notes:

(I) CALCULATION OF PROVISION ON ADVANCES

Assets	*Amount (₹ in '000)*	*% of Provision*	*Provision (₹ in '000)*
Standard Assets	2,200	0.40	8.80
Sub-Standard Assets	250	15	37.50
Doubtful Assets—Unsecured (50%)	210	100	210.00
Secured (50%)—Doubtful upto one year	60	25	15.00
Doubtful one to three years	85	40	34.00
Doubtful more than three years	65	100	65.00
Loss Assets	80	100	80.00
	2,950		450.30

45.0 CAPITAL ADEQUACY NORMS

OBJECTIVES OF CAPITAL ADEQUACY NORMS

The fundamental objectives are:

(a) to strengthen the soundness and stability of the banking system,

(b) to achieve a high degree of consistency in its application to banks in different countries.

MINIMUM CAPITAL ADEQUACY RATIO

All India Scheduled commercial Banks (excluding Regional Rural Banks) as well as foreign banks operating in India are required to achieve 9% Capital Adequacy Ratio (i.e., Ratio of Capital Fund to Risk Weighted Assets and off Balance Sheet Items).

MEANING OF CAPITAL FUNDS

(a) The Basle Committee has defined capital in two tiers—Tier I and Tier II.

(b) **Tier I Capital (also known as Core Capital)** It comprises elements that are the most permanent and readily available support to a bank against unexpected losses. It is calculated as follows:

Particulars		₹
A. Paid up Capital		xxx
B. Statutory Reserves		xxx
C. Securities Premium		xxx
D. Capital Reserve (representing surplus on sale of assets and held in a separate account only)		xxx
E. Other disclosed free reserves		xxx
Total		xxx
Less: (a) Equity Investments in Subsidiaries	(xxx)	
(b) Intangible Assets	(xxx)	
(c) Current and brought forward losses	(xxx)	(xxx)
Tier I Capital		xxx

(c) Tier II Capital It comprises elements that are less permanent-in -nature *or* less readily available than those comprising Tier I capital. It is calculated as follows:

			₹
A.	Undisclosed Reserves and fully paid up Cumulative Perpetual		
	Preference Shares		xxx
B.	Revaluation Reserve	xxx	
	Less: Discount @ 55%	(xxx)	xxx
C.	General Provisions and Loss Reserves (Not exceeding 1.25% of Weighted Risk Assets)		xxx
D.	Hybrid Debt Capital Instruments		xxx
E.	Subordinated Debt (Having initial maturity period of at least 5 years and remaining maturity period of more than 1 year)		
	(Not exceeding 50% of Tier I Capital)		xxx
	Tier II Capital (not exceeding Tier I Capital)		xxx

RISK ADJUSTED VALUE OF ON BALANCE SHEET ITEMS

(a) Risk Adjusted Value of on Balance Sheet Item

= Book Value of on Balance Sheet Item × Risk Weight assigned by RBI to this item

(b) Risk Weight assigned to various on Balance Sheet Items

A. Funded Risk Assets	% of Risk Weight
1.0 Assets carrying 0% Risk	
1.1 Cash in hand (including foreign currency notes)	0
1.2 Balances with Reserve Bank	0
1.3 Money at call and short notice	0
1.4 Loans and advances (including bills purchased and discounted and other credit facilities) guaranteed by Central/ State Government **Note:** *Where State Governments continue to be in default for a period of more than 90 days, a risk weight of 100% should be assigned.*	0
1.5 Advances against terms deposits, life policies, NSCs, Indira Vikas Patras & Kisan Vikas Patras(where adequate margin is available).	0
1.6 Income-tax deducted at source (net of provision)	0
1.7 Advance tax paid (net of provision)	0
1.8 Interest due on government securities	0
1.9 Accrued interest on CRR balances & claims on RBI on account of govt. transactions (net of claims of government/RBI on the bank on account of such transactions)	0
1.10 SSI Advances Guaranteed by Credit Guarantee Fund Trust for Small Industries (CGTSI) up to the guaranteed portion.	0
1.11 Investments in **Government Securities**	0
1.12 Invest. in **Other Approved Securities** guaranteed by the Central Government *or* a State Government	0

1.13 Investment in **Other Securities** where payment of interest & repayment of principal **are guaranteed** by the Central/State Govt. **Note:** *In case of a default in interest/principal by the State Government concerned, the risk weight in respect of those Securities issued by the defaulting entities would be 100%.*	0
2.0 Assets carrying 20% risk	
2.1 Balances with Banks *(other than Reserve Bank of India)*	20
2.2 Claims on Banks *(other than Reserve Bank of India)*	20
2.3 Investment in other approved securities where payment of interest and repayment of principal are **not guaranteed** by Central/State Govt.	20
2.4 Investment in government guaranteed **Securities of Government Undertakings** which **do not form part** of the approved market borrowing programme	20
2.5 Investment in bonds issued by other banks/public financial institutions	20
2.6 Investment in securities which are guaranteed by banks as to payment of interest and repayment of principal	
2.7 **Loans & Advances to Bank Staff** which are fully covered by superannuation benefits and mortgage of flat/house. **Note:** *where loans to staff are not covered by superannuation benefits and mortgage of flat or house, a risk weight of100% should be assigned.*	20
2.8 Take-out finance	
* Unconditional take-out finance where the full credit risk is assumed by the taking over institution	20
* Unconditional take-out finance where only partial credit risk is assumed by the taking over institution	
2.9 Amount to be taken over	20
3.0 Assets carrying 50% Risk	
3.1 Advances guaranteed by DICGC/ECGC (limited to the amount guaranteed) **Note:** *Outstandings in excess of guaranteed amount will carry 100% risk weight.*	50
3.2 Loans up to ₹ 1 lakh against gold and silver ornaments	50
3.3 Housing loans upto ₹ 30 lakhs sanctioned to Individuals against the mortgage of residential housing properties having LTVF ratio equal to *or* less than 75%. **Note:** *If restructured, 75%*	50
3.4 Investment in Mortgage Backed Securities (MBS) of residential assets of Housing Finance Companies (HFCs) which are recognised and supervised by National Housing Bank.	50
3.5 Investment in Mortgage Backed Securities (MBS) which are backed by housing loan qualifying for 50% risk weight.	50
3.6 Insurance cover under Business Credit Shield, the product of New India Assurance Company Ltd. **Note:** *Outstandings in excess of guaranteed amount will carry 100% risk weight.*	50
4.0 Assets carrying 75% Risk	
4.1 Housing loans above ₹ 30 lakhs sanctioned to Individuals against the mortgage of residential housing properties having LTVF ratio equal to *or* less than 75%. **Note:** *If restructured, 100%.*	75

5.0 Assets carrying 100% Risk	
5.1 Premises, Furniture and Fixtures, Leased Assets	100
5.2 Educational Loans	100
5.3 Loans granted to public sector undertaking of Central Government/State Government	100
5.4 All Other Investments including securities issued by PFIs/SPVs/NBFC-ND-SI **Note:** *Equity Investments in subsidiaries, intangible assets and losses deducted from Tier I capital should be assigned zero weight.*	100
5.5 Investment in subordinated debt issued in the form of Tier II capital bonds by the other banks/public financial institutions	100
5.6 NPA purchased from other banks	100
5.7 Fund based exposures commercial real estate	100
5.8 Funded liquidity facility for securitisation of standard asset transactions	100
5.9 Loans & Advances NBFC-NO-SI (other than Asset Finance Companies)	100
5.10 All unrated claims on corporate, long term as well as short term, regardless of the amount of the claim	100
5.11 Amount not to be taken over	100
5.12 Conditional take-out finance	100
5.13 All Other assets *(i.e. for which Risk Weight has been not been specified)*	100
6.0 Assets carrying 125% Risk	
6.1 Housing loans of ₹ 75 lakhs and above sanctioned to Individuals	125
6.2 Consumer Credit including Personal Loans and Credit Cards	125
6.3 Direct Investment in Equity Shares, Convertible Bonds, Debentures and Units of Equity Oriented Mutual Funds	125
6.4 Advances against Shares to Individuals for investment in Equity Shares (including IPOs/ESOPs), Bonds & Debentures, Units of Equity Oriented Mutual Funds, etc.	125
6.5 Secured and Unsecured Advances to Stock Brokers	125
7.0 Assets carrying 150% Risk	
7.1 Investment in Mortgaged Backed Securities and other securitised exposures to Commercial Real Estate	150
7.2 Investments in Venture Capital Funds	150

RISK ADJUSTED VALUE OF OFF BALANCE SHEET ITEMS

(a) Risk Adjusted Value of off Balance Sheet Items

= Face Value of off Balance Sheet Items × Credit Conversion Factor assigned by RBI × Risk weight assigned by RBI

Notes

(i) *Credit conversion factor reflects the risk of loss inherent in the nature of off the Balance Sheet item.*

(ii) *Risk weight attributable to the relevant counter party recognises the degree of likelihood of the counter party making the default.*

(b) Credit conversion factor and Risk weight assigned to different off Balance Sheet Items

	Off Balance Sheet Item	*Credit Conversion factor (per cent)*	*Risk weight (per cent)*
1.0	Direct credit substitutes, e.g. general guarantees of indebtedness (including stand-by letters of credit serving as financial guarantees for loans & securities) and acceptances (including endorsements with the character of acceptances)		
	1.1 Guaranteed by Central Government/State Govt.	100	0
	1.2 Counter-guaranteed by other banks	100	20
	1.3 Others	100	100
2.0	Sale and repurchase agreements & assets sales with recourse, where the credit risk remains with the bank		
	2.1 Guaranteed by Central Government/State Govt.	100	0
	2.2 Counter-guaranteed by other banks	100	20
	2.3 Others	100	100
3.0	Forward asset purchases, forward deposits and partly shares & securities, which represent commitments with certain draw down	100	100
4.0	Unconditional take-out finance where the bank is the taking-over institution	100	100
5.0	Conditional take-out finance where the banks is the taking-over institution		
	5.1 Where the counter-party risk is guaranteed by the Governments	50	0
	5.2 Others	100	100
6.0	Certain transaction-related contingent items (e.g. performance bonds, bid bonds, warranties and stand by letters of credit related to. articular transactions)		
	6.1 Guaranteed by Central Government/State Govt.	50	0
	6.2 Counter-guaranteed by other banks	50	20
	6.3 Others	50	100
7.0	Note issuance facilities & revolving under-writing facilities	50	100
8.0	Short-term self-liquidating trade-related contingencies (such as documentary credits collateralised by the underlying shipments)		
	8.1 Guaranteed by Central Government/State Govt.	20	0
	8.2 Counter-guaranteed by other banks	20	20
	8.3 Others	20	100
9.0	Other commitments (e.g. formal stand by facilities and credit lines) with an original maturity of over one year	50	0
10.0	Aggregate outstanding foreign exchange contracts of original maturity:		
	10.1 up to one year	2	100
	10.2 for each additional year *or* part thereof	3	100

11.0 Similar commitments with an original maturity up to one year, *or* which can be unconditionally cancelled at any time	0	0
12.0 Non-Funded exposures to commercial real estate	150	
13.0 Guarantees issued on behalf of stock brokers and market markers	125	
14.0 Commitment to provide liquidity facility for securitisation of standard asset transactions	100	
15.0 Second loss credit enhancement for securitisation of standard asset transactions provided by third party	100	
16.0 Non-funded exposure to NBFC-ND-SI	125	
17.0 Foreign exchange open position.	100	
18.0 Open position in gold	100	

PRACTICAL STEPS INVOLVED IN THE CALCULATION OF CAPITAL ADE-QUACY RATIO/ RISK WEIGHTED ASSETS RATIO

Step 1: *Calculate Capital Funds as follows:*

Tier I Capital	xxx
Tier II Capital	xxx
	xxx

Step 2: *Calculate Risk Weighted Assets as follows:*

A. CALCULATION OF RISK WEIGHTED ASSETS (ON BALANCE SHEET ITEMS)

Item No.	*On Balance Sheet Items*	₹	*Percentage Weight*	*Weighted Amount*
	Total A			

B. CALCULATION OF RISK WEIGHTED ASSETS (OFF BALANCE SHEET ITEMS)

Item No.	*Off Balance Sheet Items* *(A)*	₹ *(B)*	*Credit Conversion Factor* *(C)*	*Equivalent value B × C* *(D)*	*Risk Weight* *(E)*	*Weighted Amount D × E* *(F)*
	Total B					

Total Risk Weighted Assets = Total A + Total B

Step 3: *Calculate Risk Weighted Assets Ratio as follows:*

$$\text{Risk Weighted Assets Ratio} = \frac{\text{Capital Funds}}{\text{Risk Weighted Assets}} \times 100$$

Step 4: *Compare the Calculated Ratio with the Expected Ratio to determine the scope of improvement.*

ILLUSTRATION 41

From the following information, compute Risk Weighted Assets Ratio

Particulars	₹ *(in crores)*
1. 4.75 crores Equity Shares of ₹ 10 each, ₹ 8 paid up	
2. Equity Investment in Subsidiaries	1
3. Goodwill	1
4. Deferred Advertisement Expenditure	1
5. Statutory Reserves	4
6. Securities Premium	5
7. Capital Reserve (of which ₹ 5 lacs due to revaluation of assets and balance due to sale of assets)	7
8. Contingency Reserve	4
9. Cumulative Perpetual Preference Shares (of which 60% is fully paid up)	25
10. General Provision and loss Reserves	3
11. Hybrid Debt Capital Instruments	18
12. Subordinated Debt	
— Issued for 4 years	1
— Issued for 6 years	26
— Issued for 8 years (of which 60% have remaining maturity period of 1 year only)	5
13. (a) Cash in hand (of which 60% US Dollars)	10
(b) Balance with RBI	10
(c) Balance with other Banks	20
14. Money at call and short notice	10
15. Investment in Govt. Securities	60
16. Investment in Govt. Securities where payment of interest and principal	
(a) is guaranteed by Govt.	60
(b) is not guaranteed by Govt.	20
17. Investment in bonds issued by other Banks and public financial institutions	20
18. Investment in subordinated Debt issued in the form of Tier II Capital Bonds, by other Banks	100
19. Investment in fully secured debentures of Top Blue Chip private sector companies (NIFTY Indexed Based)	80
20. Loan and Advances guaranteed by:	
(a) Central and State Govt.	10
(b) 100% by DICGC/ECGC	50
21. Loans to Staff fully covered by super annuation benefits	20
22. Claims on other Banks	20
23. Loans granted to Public Sector Undertaking of Central/State Government	100
24. Premises and Furniture (Net of Depreciation), Leased Assets	100
25. Other Assets:	
(a) Branch Adjustments	16
(b) Non-Banking Assets	19

(c) Advance Tax paid	30
26. Investment in Mortgage Backed Securities (MBS) of Residential Assets of Housing Finance Companies	100
27. Housing loans of ₹ 70 lakhs each sanctioned to Individuals against the mortgage of residential housing properties having LTV ratio less than 75%.	100
28. Educational Loans	100
29. NPA purchased from other banks	100
30. Housing loans of ₹ 75 lakhs each sanctioned to Individuals	100
31. Investment in Mortgaged Backed Securities and other securitised exposures to Commercial Real Estate	100
32. Investments in Venture Capital Funds Expected Capital Adequacy Ratio 9%	100
33. Acceptances, Endorsements and Letters of Credit guaranteed by:	
(a) Central and State Government	100
(b) Other Banks	100
(c) Others	50
34. Guarantees & Other Obligations	50

SOLUTION

STATEMENT SHOWING CAPITAL FUNDS, RISK WEIGHTED ASSETS AND RISK WEIGHTED ASSETS RATIO

		Particulars		*₹ (in crores)*
I.	**Capital Funds**			
	A.	Tier I Capital Elements		
	(a)	Paid up Equity Share Capital	38.00)	
		Less: (i) Equity Investment in Subsidiaries	(1.00)	
		Less: (ii) Goodwill	(1.00)	
		Less: (iii) Deferred Advertisement Expenditure	(1.00)	35.00
	(b)	Reserves and Surplus		
		1. Statutory Reserves	4.00	
		2. Securities Premium	5.00	
		3. Capital Reserve (due to sale of assets)	2.00	
		4. Contingency Reserve	4.00	15.00
	(c)	Tier I Capital [a + b]		50.00
	B.	Tier II Capital Elements		
	(a)	Fully paid up Cumulative Perpetual Preference Shares (60% of ₹ 25 crores)		15.00
	(b)	Capital Reserve due to revaluation of assets (₹ 5 crores – 55%)		2.25
	(c)	General Provision and Loss Reserves		3.00
	(d)	Hybrid Debt Capital Instruments		18.00
	(e)	Subordinated Debt		
		(i) Issued for 6 years	26.00	

	(ii) Issued for 8 years	2.00	
	(having remaining maturity period exceeding 1 year	28.00	
	Since Subordinated Debt can not exceed 50% of		
	Tier I Capital, (i.e., ₹ 50 lakhs), it will be taken at ₹ 25 lakhs		25.00
			63.25
	Since Tier II Capital can not exceed Tier I		
	Capital, it is to be restricted to ₹ 50 lakhs only		50.00
C.	Total Capital Funds [A + B]		100.00

II. A. RISK WEIGHTED ON BALANCE SHEET ITEMS

On-Balance Sheet Items	*Book Value* 2	*Risk weight %* 3	*Risk Adjusted value* 4 = 2 × 3
1. Cash in hand (including US Dollars)	10	0	0
2. Balance with RBI	10	0	0
3. Balance with other Banks	20	20	4
4. Money at call and Short Notice	10	0	0
5. Investments in Govt. Securities	60	0	0
6. Investments in other approved securities where payment of interest and principal			
(a) is guaranteed by Govt.	60	0	0
(b) is not guaranteed by Govt.	20	20	4
7. Investments in bonds issued by Banks and Public Financial Institutions	20	20	4
8. Investment in subordinated Debt issued in the form of Tier II Capital Bonds, by other Bank	100	100	100
9. Investment in Debentures of Top Blue Chip private sector Co.	80	125	100
10. Loans and Advances guaranteed by:			
(a) Central and State Govt.	10	0	0
(b) 100% by DICGC/ECGC	50	50	25
11. Loans to Staff fully covered by superannuation benefits	20	20	4
12. Claims on other Banks	20	20	4
13. Loans granted to Public Sector undertakings of Central/ State Govt.	100	100	100
14. Premises & Furniture (Net of Depreciation), Leased Assets	100	100	100
15. Other Assets:			
(a) Branch Adjustments	16	100	16
(b) Non-Banking Assets	19	100	19
(c) Advance Tax paid	30	0	0

16. Investment in Mortgage Backed Securities (MBS) of Residential Assets of Housing Finance Companies	100	50	50
17. Housing loans of ₹ 70 lakhs each sanctioned to Individuals against the mortgage of residential housing properties having LTV ratio less than 75%.	100	75	75
18. Educational Loans	100	100	100
19. NPA purchased from other banks	100	100	100
20. Housing loans of ₹ 75 lakhs each sanctioned to Individuals	100	125	125
21. Investment in Mortgaged Backed Securities and other securitised exposures to Commercial Real Estate	100	150	150
22. Investments in Venture Capital Funds	100	150	150
Total A			1230

B. RISK WEIGHTED OFF BALANCE SHEET ITEMS

Nature of Item	*Book Value 2*	*Conversion Factor % 3*	*Equivalent Value 4 = 2 × 3*	*Risk Weight 5*	*Risk Adjusted Value 6 = 4 × 5*
Acceptances, Endorsement and					
Letters of Credit Guaranteed by					
(a) Central/State Govt.	100	100	100	0	0
(b) Other Public Sector Banks	100	100	100	20	20
(c) Others	50	100	50	100	50
Guarantees & Other Obligations	50	100	50	100	50
Total B					120

C. Total Risk Weighted Assets (A + B) = 1230 + 120 = 1350

III. Risk Weighted Assets Ratio = $\frac{\text{Capital Funds}}{\text{Risk Weighted Assets}} \times 100$ = 100/1350 × 100 = 7.407%

Comment Since the expected ratio is 9%, the bank has yet to improve this ratio.

ILLUSTRATION 42

A commercial bank has the following capital funds and assets. Calculate risk weighted assets ratio:

Particulars	*(₹ in lakhs)*
Capital Funds:	
Equity Share Capital	9,60,00
Statutory Reserve	5,00,00
Securities Premium	60,00
Capital Reserve (of which ₹ 560 lakhs were due to revaluation of assets and the balance due to sale)	24,20
Assets:	
Cash Balance with RBI	9,60
Balances with other Banks	25,00

Claims on Commercial Banks	12,00
Other Investments	1,56,500
Loans and Advances:	
(i) Guaranteed by government	25,640
(ii) Guaranteed by public sector undertakings of Government of India	1,40,420
(iii) Granted to staff of Bank fully Covered by Superannuation benefits	2,500
(iv) Others	10,40,000
Premises, furniture and fixtures	36,400
Other Assets	40,000
Off-Balance Sheet Items:	
Acceptances, endorsements and letters of credit	7,00,000
Guarantees and other obligations	40,500

SOLUTION

(I) CAPITAL FUNDS—TIER I

Particulars	*₹ in lakhs*	*₹ in lakhs*
Equity Share Capital		96,000
Statutory Reserve		50,000
Securities Premium		6,000
Capital Reserve (arising out of sale of assets)		1,860
		1,53,860

(II) CAPITAL FUNDS—TIER II

Particulars	*₹ in lakhs*	*₹ in lakhs*
Capital Reserve (arising out of revaluation of assets)	560	
Less: Discount to the extent of 55%	(308)	252
Total Risk Adjusted Assets		1,54,112

Particulars	*₹ in lakhs*	*Percentage Weight*	*Amount ₹ in lakhs*
Funded Risk Assets			
Cash Balance with RBI	960	0	—
Balances with other Banks	2,500	20	500
Claims on Commercial Banks	12,00	20	240
Other Investments	1,56,500	100	1,56,500
Loans and Advances:			
(i) Guaranteed by Government	25,640	0	—
(ii) Guaranteed by public sector undertakings of Central Government	1,40,420	0	—
(iii) Granted to staff of Bank fully secured	2,500	20	500

(iv) Others	10,40,000	100	10,40,000
Premises, Furniture and Fixtures	36,400	100	36,400
Other Assets	40,000	100	40,000
			12,74,140
Off-Balance Sheet Item			
Acceptances, Endorsements and Letters of Credit	7,00,000	100	7,00,000
Guarantees and other obligations	40,000	100	40,000
			20,14,140

Risk Weighted Assets Ratio: $\frac{\text{Capital Funds}}{\text{Risk Weighted Assets}} \times 100$ = 1,54,112/20,14,140 × 100 = 7.652%

Comment Since the Expected ratio is 9%, the bank is required to improve the ratio.

46.0 CLASSIFICATION OF INVESTMENTS FOR VALUATION PURPOSES

Banks are required to cloassifuy their entire investment portfolio into the categories as follows:

HELD-TO-MATURITY SECURITIES

Meaning	These are the securities which are acquired by bank with the intention to hold them upto maturity.	
Maximum Limit	The amount of these investments must not exceed 25% of the total investments of the bank.	
Valuation	The guidelines for the valuation of such securities are as follows:	
	(a) **Where securities have been acquired at Cost equal to/less than face value**	These should be valued at Cost.
	(b) **Where securities have been acquired at Cost more than face value**	These should be valued at face value and the premium should be amortised over the remaining period to maturity
	(c) **Where there is any diminution in the Value of investments in subsidiaries/joint ventures**	The permanent diminution should be determined and provided for each investment individually [AS 13]

HELD FOR TRADING SECURITIES

Meaning	These are the securities which are acquired by bank with the intention to trade by taking advantage of short-term price/interest rate movements. These are to be sold within 90 days.	
Valuation	(a) **Monthly Valuation**	The individual scrips should be valued at **monthly** or at more frequent intervals
	(b) **Recognition of Appreciation/ Depreciation in P&L A/c**	Net appreciation/depreciation of scrips under each of the categories in which investments are presented in the Balance Sheet should be recognised in the Profit and Loss Account.

	(c) **Recording of Appreciation/ Depreciation in Individual Scrip Account**	The de preciation/appreciation in value of an individual scrips is recorded in Individual Scrip Account.
	(d) **Change in Book Value of Individual Scrips**	The book value of the individual scrips should be changed to reflect the market-to-market valuations.

AVAILABLE-FOR-SALE SECURITIES

Meaning	These are the securities which do not fall within the above two categories.	
Valuation	The guidelines for valuation of such securities are as follows:	
	(a) **Marked to Market Valuation at year end**	The individual scrips should be marked to market at **quarterly** or at more frequent intervals.
	(b) **Provide Depreciation in P & L A/c**	Net depreciation of scrips under each of the categories in which investments are presented in the Balance Sheet should be recognised and fully provided for in the Profit and Loss Account.
	(c) **Ignore Appreciation**	Net appreciation of scrips under any of the categories should be ignored.
	(d) **Recording of Appreciation/ Depreciation in separate A/c in Individual Scrip A/c**	The depreciation/appreciation in value of an individual scrip is not recorded in Individual scrip Account but is recorded in a separate account.
	(e) **No Changes in book value**	The book value of the individual scrips should not be changed to reflect the marked to market valuations.
	Note: *Offsetting of gains and losses is allowed within a particular category and is not allowed across different categories.*	

ILLUSTRATION 43

Bharat Bank Ltd. provides you the following information:

Code No.	*Face value*	*Acquisition Cost*	*Market value as on 31.3.2015*
101 Government Securities	10	10	12
102 Government Securities	20	19	18
103 Other Approved Securities	30	29	35
104 Other Approved Securities	40	40	31

Required: How will you deal with the above while preparing Balance Sheet and Profit and Loss Account of the Bank if the securities are:

(a) Held-to maturity Securities,

(b) Held-for trading Securities,

(c) Available for sale Securities.

SOLUTION

(a) Held-to maturity Securities

In this case, the securities acquired at cost equal to/less than face value are to be valued at cost. Hence, in Schedule 8, these securities will appear as follows:

SCHEDULE 8—INVESTMENTS

Govt. Securities:		
Code 101	₹ 10	
Code 102	₹ 19	₹ 29 lakhs
Other Approved Securities:		
Code 103	₹ 29	
Code 104	₹ 40	₹ 69 lakhs
Total Investments		₹ 98 lakhs

(b) Held-for-trading Securities

SCHEDULE 8—INVESTMENTS

Govt. Securities:		
Code 101	₹ 12 lakh	
Code 102	₹ 18 lakh	₹ 30 lakh
Other Approved Securities:		
Code 103	₹ 35 lakh	
Code 104	₹ 31 lakh	₹ 66 lakh
Total Investments		₹ 96 lakh

SCHEDULE 14—OTHER INCOME

Net Profit on Revaluation of Government Securities	₹ 1 lakh
Net Loss on Revaluation of other Approved Securities	₹ 3 lakh
	(₹ 2 1akh)

(c) Available-for-sale-Securities

SCHEDULE 8—INVESTMENTS

Govt. Securities:		
Code 101	₹ 10	
Code 102	₹ 19	₹ 29 lakh
Other Approved Securities:		
Code 103	₹ 29	
Code 104	₹ 40	₹ 69 lakh
Total Investments		₹ 98 lakh

SCHEDULE 14—OTHER INCOME

Net Loss on Revaluation of other Approved Securities	₹ 3 lakh

	₹ 3 lakh

Dr. **INVESTMENT FLUCTUATION RESERVE OF OTHER APPROVED SECURITIES** *Cr.*

Particulars	₹	*Particulars*	₹
To Profit on Revaluation of Code 103 Securities	6	By Loss on Revaluation of Code 104 Securities	9
To Balance c/d	3		
	9		9

SOLVED PROBLEMS

PROBLEM 1

Given below are details of interest on advances of CAS Ltd. a Commercial bank as on 31.3.2015

Assets	*Interest Earned ₹ in lakhs*	*Interest Received ₹ in lakhs*
Performing Assets:		
Term Loan	240	160
Cash credit and overdraft	1,500	1,240
Bills purchased and discounted	300	300
Non-performing Assets:		
Term Loan	150	10
Cash credit and overdraft	300	24
Bills purchased and discounted	200	40

Required: Find out the Income to be recognised for the year ended 31.3.2015.

SOLUTION

Interest on performing assets should be recognised on accrual basis but interest on non performing assets should be recognized as per directions given in various circulars issued by R.B.I.

Particulars	*₹ in lakhs*
Interest on Term loan (240 + 10)	250
Interest on cash credit and overdraft (1,500 + 24)	1,524
Income from bills purchased and discounted (300 + 40)	340
Income to be recognised	2,114

PROBLEM 2

The following is an extract from the Trial Balance of a CWDHI Bank Ltd. as at 31st March, 2015:

Particulars	*Dr. (₹)*	*Cr. (₹)*
Bills discounted	51,50,000	
Rebate on bills discounted not yet due, March 31,2014		30,501
Discount received		1,45,500

An analysis of the bills discounted as shown above shows the following:

Date of Bill	*Amount* ₹	*Period months*	*Rate of Discount % p.a.*
13.1.2015	7,50,000	4	12
17.2.2015	6,00,000	3	10
06.3.2015	4,00,000	4	11
16.3.2015	2,00,000	2	10

Required: Find out the amount of discount received to be credited to Profit and Loss Account and pass appropriate Journal Entries for the same. How the relevant items will appear in the Bank's Balance Sheet?

SOLUTION

CALCULATION OF UNEXPIRED DISCOUNT *or* REBATE ON BILLS DISCOUNTED

Date of Bill	*Date of Maturity*	*No. of days after 31.3.2015*	*Amount* ₹	*Rate of Discount % p.a.*	*Total Amount of Discount* ₹	*Proportionate Discount of days after 31.3.2015* ₹
13.1.2015	16.5.2015	46	7,50,000	12	90,000	90,000 × 46/365 = 11342
17.2.2015	20.5.2015	50	6,00,000	10	60,000	60,000 × 50/365 = 8219
06.3.2015	09.7.2015	100	4,00,000	11	44,000	44,000 × 100/365 = 12055
16.3.2015	19.5.2015	49	2,00,000	10	20,000	20,000 × 49/365 = 2685
			Unexpired Discounts on 31.3.2015			34,301

The amount to be credited to P & L Account is ascertained from the Discount Account as follows:

Dr. **DISCOUNT ACCOUNT** *Cr.*

Date	*Particulars*	₹	*Date*	*Particulars*	₹
31.3.2015	To Rebate on Bills Discounted	34,301	1.4.2014	By Rebate on Bills Discounted as on 1.4.2014	30,501
	To Profit & Loss A/c	1,41,700		By Sundries	1,45,500
		1,76,001			1,76,001

JOURNAL

Particulars		*L.F.*	*Dr. (₹)*	*Cr. (₹)*
Rebate on Bills Discounted A/c	Dr.		30,501	
To Discount A/c				30,501
(Unexpired discount brought forward)				
Discount A/c	Dr.		34,301	
To Rebate on Bills Discounted A/c				34,301
(Provision for unexpired discount)				

Discount A/c	Dr.	1,41,700	
To Profit & Loss A/c			1,41,700
(Discount earned for the year)			

PROBLEM 3

Some of the items in the Trial Balance of CANHC Bank Limited as on March 31, 2015 were as follows:

Particulars	₹	*Particulars*	₹
Loans and Advances	71,50,000	Printing and Stationery	5,000
Current Accounts (including overdrafts of ₹ 15,00,000)	66,00,000	Interest on Saving Bank Deposits	75,000
		Auditor's Fees	5,000
Bills Discounted and Purchased	19,20,000	Directors' Fees	3,000
Interest on Fixed Deposits	1,55,000	Interest on Overdrafts	95,000
Interest on Loans	2,25,000	Provision for Doubtful Debts, April, 1, 2014	42,000
Discount (subject to unexpired discount ₹ 30,000)	2,01,000	Bad Debts	21,000
Interest on Cash Credits	1,05,000	Provision for Income-tax, April 1, 2014	66,000
Commission earned	47,000		
Loss on Investment	34,000	Income-tax paid for 2014-2015	54,000
Salaries and Allowances	82,000		

Required: Prepare the Profit and Loss Account of the Bank maintaining the Provision for Income-tax at ₹ 84,000 and Provision for Doubtful Debts at ₹ 52,000 for the year ended March 31,2015.

SOLUTION

CANHC BANK LTD.
PROFIT & LOSS ACCOUNT FOR THE YEAR ENDED 31ST MARCH, 2015

Particulars	*Schedule No.*	*Year ended 31st March 2015 (₹ '000)*	*Year ended 31st March 2014 (₹ '000)*
I. Income:			
Interest earned	13	596	
Other income	14	13	
Total		609	
II. Expenditure:			
Interest expended	15	230	
Operating expenses	16	95	
Provisions & Contingenies [72 + 31]		103	
Total		428	
III. Profit/Loss:			
Net Profit for the year		181	

Profit/Loss brought forward			—
		181	
IV. Appropriations:			
Transfer to Statutory Reserve @ 25%		45.25	
Balance carried over to Balance Sheet		135.75	
Total		181.0	

Particulars	*As on 31st March 2015 (₹ '000)*	*As on 31st March 2014 (₹ '000)*
Schedule 13—Interest Earned		
I. Interest/Discount [6,26,000 – 30,000 (Rebate)]	596	
II. Interest on investment	—	
III. Interest on balances with RBI & other inter bank fund	—	
	596	
Schedule 14—Other Income		
I. Commission, Exchange and Brokerage	47	
II. Loss on sale of investments	(–) 34	
	13	
Schedule 15—Interest Expended		
I. Interest on Deposits [Fixed and Savings Deposits]	230	
II. Interest on RBI/inter bank borrowings	—	
	230	
Schedule 16—Operating Expenses		
I. Payments to and provision for employees	82	
II. Printing & Stationery	5	
III. Directors' fees, allowances and expenses	3	
IV. Auditors' fees	5	
	95	

Dr. **PROVISION FOR DOUBTFUL DEBTS ACCOUNT** *Cr.*

Particulars	*(₹ '000)*	*Particulars*	*(₹ '000)*
To Bad Debts	21	By Balance b/d	42
To Balance c/d	52	By Profit & Loss A/c	31
	73		73

Dr. **PROVISION FOR TAXATION ACCOUNT** *Cr.*

Particulars	*(₹ '000)*	*Particulars*	*(₹ '000)*
To Bank A/c	54	By Balance b/d	66
To Balance c/d	84	By Profit & Loss A/c	72
	138		138

PROBLEM 4

The following are the ledger balances (as Rupees thousands) extracted from the books of CANHD CAS Bank Limited as on March 31, 2015

Particulars	₹	*Particulars*	₹
Share Capital	1,90,000	Cash in hand	35,000
Current accounts control	97,000	Balance with Reserve Bank	40,000
Employees' security deposits	7,420	Savings accounts	15,000
Investments in Govt. of India Bonds	94,370	Fixed deposits	23,050
Gold bullion	15,130	Balances with other banks	46,350
Silver	2,000	Other investments (Shares)	55,630
Constituents liabilities for acceptances and endorsements	56,500	Interest accrued on investments	24,620
		Reserve Fund	1,40,000
Borrowing from banks	77,230	Profit & Loss A/c (Cr.)	6,500
Building	65,000	Bills for collection	43,500
Furniture	5,000	Interest (Cr.)	62,000
Money at call and short notice	26,000	Loans	1,81,000
Commission & brokerage (Cr.)	25,300	Bills discounted	12,500
Discount (Cr.)	42,000	Interest	7,950
Rent (Cr.)	600	Miscellaneous Income	3,900
Audit fees	5,000	Depreciation reserve (buildings)	800
Depreciation reserve (furniture)	200	Director's fees	1,000
Salaries	21,200	Postage	1,250
Rent, rates and taxes	12,000	Loss on sale of investments	20,000
		Branch Adjustments (Dr.)	20,000

The Bank's Profit and Loss account for the year ended and Balance sheet as at 31st March 2015 are required to be prepared in appropriate form. Further information available are: (in Rupees thousands)

(a) Rebates on bills discounted to be provided 4,000

(b) Depreciation for the year: Building 5,000, Furniture 500

(c) Included in the current accounts ledger are accounts overdrawn to the extent of 2,500.

SOLUTION

BALANCE SHEET OF CANHD BANK LTD. AS ON 31ST MARCH, 2015

Particulars	*Schedule No.*	*As on 31st March 2015 (₹ '000)*	*As on 31st March 2014 (₹ '000)*
Capital and liabilities:			
Capital	1	19,00,00	
Reserves & Surplus	2	20,24,00	
Deposits	3	13,75,50	
Borrowing	4	7,72,30	
Other liabilities and provisions	5	1,14,20	

Total		61,86,00	
Assets:			
Cash and balance with			
Reserve Bank of India	6	7,50,00	
Balance with bank and Money at			
Call and short notice	7	7,23,50	
Investments	8	16,71,30	
Advances	9	19,60,00	
Fixed Assets	10	6,35,00	
Other Assets	11	4,46,20	
Total		61,86,00	
Contingent liabilities	12	5,65,00	
Bills for collection		4,35,00	

CANHD BANK LTD.
PROFIT AND LOSS ACCOUNT FOR THE YEAR ENDED 31.3.2015

Particulars	*Schedule No.*	*As on 31st March 2015 (₹ '000)*	*As on 31st March 2014 (₹ '000)*
I. Income:			
Interest & Discount	13	10,00,00	
Other income	14	98,00	
		10,98,00	
II. Expenditure:			
Interest Expended	15	79,50	
Operating Expenses	16	4,59,50	
		5,39,000	
III. Profit/Loss:			
Net Profit for the year		5,59,00	
Profit b/f		65,00	
		6,24,00	
IV. Appropriations:			
Transfer to Statutory Reserve @ 25%		1,39,75	
Balances carried over to Balance Sheet		4,84,25	
		6,24,00	

Particulars	As on 31st March 2015 (₹ '000)	As on 31st March 2014 (₹ '000)
Schedule 1—Capital		
III. For Other Banks		
Authorised Capital: Shares of ₹...each	—	
Issued Capital: Shares of ₹...each	—	
Subscribed Capital: Shares of ₹...each	—	
Called up Capital: Shares of ₹...each	—	
	19,00,00	
Total	19,00,00	
Schedule 2—Reserves & Surplus		
I. Statutory Reserves		
Openning Balance	14,00,00	
Additions during the year	1,39,75	
	15,39,75	
V. Balance in Profit and Loss Account	4,84,25	
Total	20,24,00	
Schedule 3—Deposits		
A. I. Demand Deposits	9,95,00	
II. Saving Bank Deposits	1,50,00	
III. Term Deposits	2,30,50	
Total	13,75,50	
Schedule 4—Borrowings		
I. Borrowings in India		
II. Other banks	7,72,30	
Total	7,72,30	
Schedule 5—Other Liabilities and Provisions		
IV. Other liabilities including provisions:		
Rebate on bills discounted	40,00	
Employees Security Deposit	74,20	
Total	1,14,20	
Schedule 6—Cash and Balances with Reserve Bank of India		
I. Cash in hand (including foreign currency notes)	3,50,00	
II. Balances with Reserve Bank of India:	4,00,00	
Total	7,50,00	
Schedule 7—Balances with Banks & Money at Call & Short Notice		
I. India		

(i) Balances with banks	4,63,50	
(ii) Money at call at short notice	2,60,00	
Total	7,23,50	
Schedule 8—Investments		
1. Investments in India in		
(i) Government securities	9,43,70	
(ii) Shares (assumed)	5,56,30	
(iii) Gold	1,51,30	
(iv) Silver	20,00	
Total	16,71,30	
Schedule 9—Advances		
A. (i) Bills purchased and discounted	1,25,00	
(ii) Cash credits, overdrafts and loans repayable on demand (1,81,000 + 2,500)	18,35,00	
	19,60,00	
Schedule 10—Fixed Assets		
I. Premises		
At cost as on 31st March, 2012	6,50,00	
Depreciation to date [5000 + 800]	58,00	
	5,92,00	
II. Other fixed assets (including Furniture and Fixture)		
At cost as on 31st March, 2012	50,00	
Depreciation to date [500 + 200]	7,00	
	43,00	
Total (I & II)	6,35,00	
Schedule 11—Other Assets		
I. Inter-office adjustments (net)	2,00,00	
II. Interest accrued on Investments	2,46,20	
	4,46,20	
Schedule 12—Contingent Liabilities		
V. Acceptances, endorsements and other obligations	5,65,00	
Total	5,65,00	
Schedule 13—Interest Earned		
I. Interest/discount on advance, bills [62,000 + 42,000 – 24,620 (Accrued) – 40,00 (Rebate)]	7,53,80	
II. Income on Investments	2,46,20	
Total	10,00,00	
Schedule 14—Other Income		
I. Commission, Exchange and Brokerage	2,53,00	
II. Profit on sale of investments		

Less: Loss on sale on investments	(–) 2,00,00	
	53,00	
VII. Miscellaneous Income		
Rent and Other Receipts	45,00	
Total	98,00	
Schedule 15—Interest Expended		
I. Interest on Deposits	79,50	
Total	79,50	
Schedule 16—Operating Expenses		
I. Payments to and provisions in employees	2,12,00	
II. Rent, Taxes and Lighting	1,20,00	
V. Depreciation on Bank's property	55,00	
VI. Directors' fees, allowances and expenses	10,00	
VII. Auditors' fees and expenses	50,00	
IX. Postage, Telegrams, Telephones etc.	12,50	
Total	4,59,50	

11 FINANCIAL STATEMENTS OF LIFE INSURANCE COMPANIES

LEARNING OBJECTIVES

After studying this chapter, you should be able to understand:

- ◇ Meaning of Insurance and Assurance
- ◇ Terms used in Insurance
- ◇ Preparation of Financial Statements by Life Insurer
- ◇ Format of Revenue Account
- ◇ Format of Profit and Loss Account
- ◇ Format of Balance Sheet

1.0 MEANING OF INSURANCE AND ASSURANCE

In general, Insurance is an arragnement of sharing and pooling of risks under which a large number of people contribute to a fund out of which compensation is paid to the person suffering a particular type of loss. Insurance is basically of two types, namely, life insurance and general insurance.

The term 'Insurance' is used where the compensation is to be paid only on the happening of an event which may *or* may not happen. ***For Example***, a warehouse may *or* may not catch fire. Ship may *or* may not sink in the high seas. If there is no loss, the claim for compensation does not arise. This term is used in case of Fire, Marine and General Insurance. The term 'Assurance' is used where the certain sum is to be paid on the happening of an event which is certain to happen. i.e., the maturity of the policy *or* the death of the assured. ***For Example***, in a contract of life insurance, the payment of sum assured is bound to be made *either* on the maturity of the policy *or* the death of the assured.

2.0 TERMS USED IN INSURANCE

Insurance Contract	'Insurance contract' refers to a contract in which the insurance company undertakes to indemnify the insured on the happening of certain event in consideration of a specified amount.
Insurance Policy	The document which contains all the terms and conditions of insurance and risks covered under insurance is known as *'Insurance policy'*.
Insured	The person whose risk is insured is called 'Insured' *or* 'assured'.
Insurer	The person who insures is known as *'Insurer'* or *'assurer'*.
Insurance Premium	The consideration in return for which the issurer agrees to make good the loss is known as *'Insurance Premium'*. The premium may be paid monthly, quarterly, half yearly *or* annually.
Sum Insured/Sum Assured	The amount for which the insurance policy is taken is called *'Sum Insured'*. (in case of general insurance) *or* 'Sum Assured' (in case of life insurance).

Term of Policy	The period for which an insurance policy is taken is known as the *'Term of the policy'*.
Catastrophic Loss	A loss (or related losses) which is unbearable i.e. it causes severe consequences such as bankruptcy to a family, organization, *or* insurer.
Example	Mr. X gets his life insured for ₹ 3,00,000 with Life Insurance Company Ltd. by paying ₹ 10,000 for 25 years. In this case: Mr. X is known as **'Insured'.** Life Insurance Company Ltd. is known as **'Insurer'.** ₹ 3,00,000 is called **'Sum Assured'.** ₹ 10,000 is called **'Insurance Premium'.** Period of 25 years is called **'Term of Policy'.** The document containing the terms and conditions in writing is called **'Insurance Policy'.**

3.0 MAIN PRINCIPLES OF INSURANCE

1. Principle of Indemnity	Insurance is a contract of indemnity. The insurer is called idemnifier and the insured is the indemnified. In a contract of indemnity, only those who suffer loss are compensated to the extent of actual loss suffered by them. One cannot make profit by insuring his risks.
2. Insurable interest	All and sundry cannot enter into contracts of insurance. ***For Example***, A cannot insure the life of B who is a stranger. But if B, happens to be his wife *or* his debtor *or* business manager, A has insurable interest i.e. vested interest and therefore he can insure the life of B. For every type of policy insurable interest is insisted upon. In the absence of such interest the contract will amount to a wagering contract.
3. Principle of UBERRIMAE FIDEI	All contracts of insurance are contracts of uberrima fidei, i.e., contracts of utmost good faith. In a contract of insurance, however there is an implied condition that each party must disclose every material fact known to him. This is because the assessment of the risk and the determination of the premium by the insurer depend on the full and frank disclosure of all material facts is the proposal form.

4.0 REINSURANCE

MEANING OF REINSURANCE

Re-insurance is an arrangement under which one insurance Company (called Re-insurer *or* Re-insurance Co.) insures the whole *or* a part of the subject matters already insured by another insurance Company (called Re-insured *or* Ceding Company). Thus, Ceding Company agrees to pass on whole *or* a part of risk to reinsurance company which agrees to accept the transferred risk.

WHO PAYS PREMIUM, COMMISSION & CLAIMS TO WHOM UNDER RE-INSURANCE

(a) Re-insurer receives the premium from the Re-insured. Such premium is called 'Premium received on Re-insurance accepted' for the Re-insurer' and is called 'Premium paid on Reinsurance ceded' for the Re-insured.

(b) Re-insurer pays the commission to the Re-insured. Such commission is called 'Commission paid on Re-insurance accepted' for the Re-insurer and is called 'Commission received on Re-insurance ceded' for the Re-insured.

(c) Re-insurer pays the claim (when arise) to the Re-insured. Such claim is called 'Claim paid on Re-insurance accepted' for the Re-insurer and is called 'Claim received on Re-insurance ceded' for the Re-insured.

Insured → Pays Premium to → Re-insured; Insured ← Receives Claim from ← Re-insured; Re-insured ← Receives Commission & Claim from ← Re-insurer; Re-insured → Pays Premium to → Re-insurer

5.0 SURRENDER VALUE

The value of the policy surrendered by the insured before the expiry of the term of the policy on a date of surrender is known as surrender value.

6.0 BONUS

Policy holders of with profit policies are entitled to receive the bonus at the declared rate. Bonus is usually declared on sum assured and not on already accumulated bonus. ***For Example***, in case of LIC of India with profit policy holders are entitled to participate in 95% of profit (i.e., excess of Balance of Life Assurance Fund over Net Liability as per actuarial valuation). Such bonus may be paid.

(a) in cash (i.e. Bonus in cash),

(b) by reduction of future premiums (i.e., Bonus in reduction of premium),

(c) on maturity of the policy. (i.e., Reversionary Bonus).

7.0 INTERIM BONUS

It is a bonus declared between dates of two valuation Balance Sheets. It is for a period for which valuation is not complete.

8.0 CONSIDERATION FOR ANNUITIES GRANTED

It refers to the lump sum amount paid to the insurer as consideration for the payment of annuities. Consideration for annuities granted is a source of income of the life insurance business and as such it is shown on the credit side of its Revenue Account.

9.0 LIFE ASSURANCE FUND

It refers to the fund which is retained to meet the aggregate liability on all outstanding policies. Until the liability on all outstanding policies is computed, the amount of profit of the life business cannot be ascertained. A life business is said to have earned profit only if its Life Assurance Fund exceeds its net liability on all outstanding policies.

The computation of the net liability on all outstanding policies is a complicated mathematical process which can be done only by experts in the field called 'Actuaries'.

This Computation is carried out by LIC, every two years. As such, the life Insurance business cannot ascertain its profits every year.

10.0 MEANING OF LIFE ASSURANCE

MEANING

In a contract of life assurance, the insurer undertakes to pay a fixed amount on the death of the insured *or* on the expiry of the term of the policy which ever is earlier. Since a fixed amount is assured to be paid, life insurance is appropriately called 'Life Assurance'.

LIFE INSURANCE COMPANIES

Now, life insurance business is carried on not only by Life Insurance Corporation (LIC) but also by other companies in private sector life ICICI Prudential, OM Kotak Mahindra, Max New York.

11.0 TYPES OF LIFE INSURANCE POLICIES

There are various life insurance policies. The popular life insurance policies are discussed below:

1. **With Profit Policies** Holder is entitled to receive the bonus at the declared rate. Traditionally, bonus rate is expressed per thousand rupee of the sum assured. Bonus gets accumulated year after year but is paid at the time of maturity of the policy. Bonus is delcared on sum assured and not on already accumulated bonus. ***For Example***, Mr. X takes with profit life insurance policy for a sum assured of ₹ 1,00,000 for 5 years. If bonus is declared @ ₹ 70, ₹ 71, ₹ 72, ₹ 73 and ₹ 74 for each of these 5 years. The amount to be received bgy KMr. X at the time of maturity of the policy will be calculated as under:

A.	Sum assured		₹ 1,00,000
B.	*Add:* Bonus		
	1st year [₹ 70 × ₹ 1,00,000/1,000]	7,000	
	2nd year [₹ 71 × ₹ 1,00,000/1,000]	7,100	
	3rd year [₹ 72 × ₹ 1,00,000/1,000]	7,200	
	4th year [₹ 73 × ₹ 1,00,000/1,000]	7,300	
	5th year [₹ 74 × ₹ 1,00,000/1,000]	7,400	36,000
C.	Total Amount Receivable [A + B]		₹ 1,36,000

2. **Without Profit Policies** Holder of Policy is not entiteld to receive the bonus declared from time to time.
3. **With Accident Benefit Policies** On payment of some extra premium, the holder is entitled to claim the accidental benefit. Under life insurance policies with accidental benefit, on death of the insured due to accident *either* double *or* triple the sum assured is paid according to the type of policy taken.
4. **Without Accident Benefit Policies** *Neither* extra premium is charged *nor* extra sum assured is paid.

   Some of the popular life insurance policies are discussed below:

   (a) **Whole Life Policy** Under this policy, the sum assured alongwith the bonuses (in case of with profit policies) is payable on death of insured.

   (b) **Endowment Policy** Under this policy, the sum assured alongwith the bonuses (in case of with profit policies) is payable on the expiry of specified term of policy *or* death of insured whichever is earlier.

12.0 STATUTORY BOOKS AND OTHER BOOKS

STATUTORY BOOKS

The Insurance Act, 1938 makes is obligatory on the part of all insurance companies including the general insurance companies to maintain the following books:

(i) **The Register of Policies** This book should contain the following particulars in respect of each policy Issued:

  (a) The name and address of the policy holder.

  (b) The date when the policy was effected.

(c) A record of any assignment of the policy.

(ii) **The Register of Claims** This book should contain the following particulars in respect of each claim:

(a) The date of claim.

(b) The name and address of the claimant.

(c) The date on which the claim was discharged.

(d) In the case of a claim which is rejected, the date of rejection and the ground for rejection.

(iii) The Register of licensed insurance agents.

OTHER BOOKS

In addition to the statutory books, the following subsidiary books are usua
companies:

(i) Proposal Register

(ii) New Premiums Cash Book

(iii) Renewal premiums Cash Book

(iv) Agency and Branch Cash Book

(v) Petty Cash Book

(vi) Claims Cash Book

(vii) General Cash Book

(viii) Agency Credit Journal

(ix) Agency Debit Jou

(x) Lapsed and Cance

(xi) Chief Journal

(xii) Commission Book

(xiii) Agency Ledger

(xiv) Policy Loan Ledger

(xv) General Loan Ledger

(xvi) Investment Ledger

13.0 PRACTICAL STEPS INVOLVED IN ACCOUNTING TREATMENT OF SURP LIFE INSURANCE BUSINESS

Step 1: *Prepare Valuation Balance Sheet to ascertain surplus for inter valuation period as follo*

VALUATION BALANCE SHEET

Particulars	₹	*Particulars*	₹
Net Liability as per acturial valuation	xxx	Life Assurance Fund	xxx
Surplus (Balancing figure)	xxx		
	xxx		xxx

TUTORIAL NOTES

(i) *'Net Liability' is the excess of the expected future liability on all outstanding policies over the value of premiums payable by the insured in the future on those policies.*

(ii) *'Acturial Valuation' is a complicated mathematical process by which the net liability on all outstanding policies is ascertained and is carried out by the expert in the field known as 'Actuary'.*

Step 2: *Calculate Net Profit for the inter-valuation period as follows:* **STATEMENT SHOWING THE NET PROFIT FOR THE INTER-VALUATION PERIOD**

Particulars	₹	₹
A. Surplus as per Valuation Balance Sheet		xxx
B. Adjustments still to be made (for example)		

	₹	₹
(a) Add: Interim Bonus	xxx	
(b) *Less:* Loss on In[vestmen]t to [b]e written off	xxx	
(c) *Less:* Pro[vision for Tax]ation	xxx	xxx
C. Total surplus		xxx
D. *Less:* Su[rplus at the b]eginning of the Inter-valuation period		xxx
E. Net P[rofit for the Int]er-valuation period (C – D)		xxx

Step 3: [Allocate] '*Surplus*' as follows:

Ac[cording to section] 28 o[f] the Life Insurance Corporation Act 1956, 95% of the surplus disclosed [must] be allocated/reserved for the policy holders and the remaining (i.e., 5%) must [be utilised for such] purposes as the Government may determine. The profit allocated to the policy-[holders is distrib]uted as bonus on with profit policies.

STATEMENT SHOWING THE DISTRIBUTION OF SURPLUS

	Particulars	₹
[A.]	[Tota]l Surplus after Taxation	xxx
[B.]	[Le]ss: Surplus to be carried forward (e.g. t/f to General Reserve)	(xxx)
[C.]	Surplus Available for distribution (A – B)	xxx
[D.]	Share of Shareholders @ 5%	xxx
[E].	Share of Policy holders @ 95%	xxx
F.	*Less:* Interim Bonus already paid	(xxx)
G.	Amount Due to Policy holders (E – F)	xxx

Step 4: *Pass the following Journal Entries:*

1.	Life Assurance Fund A/c To Profit and Loss A/c	Dr.	[With transfer of total profit as per Valuation B/s]
2.	Profit and Loss A/c To investments/Investments Flucation Reserve A/c	Dr.	[With Loss on valuation of investments]
3.	Profit and Loss A/c To Provision for Tax A/c	Dr.	[With Tax]
4.	Profit and Loss A/c To General Reserve	Dr.	[With T/f to General Reserve]
5.	Profit and Loss A/c To Bonus payable in cash A/c	Dr.	[With Bonus payable in cash]
6.	Profit and Loss A/c To Life Assurance Fund A/c	Dr.	[With Reversionary Bonus]

ILLUSTRATION 1

The Life Fund of a Life Assurance Ltd. was ₹ 90,00,000 as on 31st March, 2015. The interim bonus paid during the intervaluation period was ₹ 4,00,000. The periodical actuarial valuation determined the net liability at ₹ 74,00,000. Surplus brought forward from the previous valuation was ₹ 5,00,000. The directors of the company proposed to carry forward ₹ 10,00,000.

Required: Show: (a) the Valuation Balance Sheet; (b) the Net Profit for the valuation period; and (c) the distribution of the surplus.

Profit and Loss A/c	Dr.	50,000	
To Investment Fluctuation Reserve A/c			50,000
(Being additional reserve created to make Investment Fluctuation Reserve equal to ₹ 1,80,000 being the difference between the book value and market value of investments)			
Profit and Loss A/c	Dr.	1,00,000	
To Provision for Taxation A/c			1,00,000
(Being the Provision for Taxation made)			
Profit and Loss A/c	Dr.	3,50,000	
To General Reserve A/c			3,50,000
(Being the transfer to General Reserve)			
Profit and Loss A/c	Dr.	1,80,000	
To Bonus payable in Cash A/c			1,80,000
(Being bonus in Cash payable @ ₹ 6 per ₹ 1,000 on policies of ₹ 3 crores)			
Profit and Loss A/c	Dr.	9,00,000	
To Life Assurance Fund A/c			9,00,000
(Being transfer of the reverisonary bonus to Life Assurance Fund @ ₹ 15 per ₹ 1,000 on policies of ₹ 6 crores)			

14.0 PREPARATION OF FINANCIAL STATEMENTS BY LIFE INSURER [IRDA REGULATION 3]

An insurer carrying on life insurance business, after the commencement of IRDA Regulation, must comply with the requirements of Schedule A. Schedule A, is divided into 5 Parts as given below:

Part I	Accounting Principles for preparation of Financial Statements
Part II	Disclosures forming part of Financial Statements
Part III	General Instructions for preparation of Financial Statements
Part IV	Contents of Management Report
Part V	Preparation of Financial Statements: 1. Revenue Account (Policyholders account) in Form A-RA 2. Profit and Loss Account (Shareholder's Account) in Form APL 3. Balance Sheet in Form A-B5 4. Receipts and Payments Account as per Direct Method prescribed in AS-3 Cash Flow Statement issued by ICAI

Part I of Schedule 'A' (See Regulation 3) Accounting principles for preparation of financial statements:

1. **Applicability of Accounting Standards** Every Balance Sheet, Revenue Account [Policyholders' Account], Receipts and Payments Account [Cash Flow Statement] and Profit and Loss Account [Shareholders' Account] of an insurer shall be in conformity with the Accounting Standards (AS) issued by the ICAI, to the extent applicable to insurers carrying on life insurance business, except that:
   (i) **Accounting Standard 3 (AS 3)** Cash Flow Statements—'Cash Flow Statement' shall be prepared only under the Direct Method.
   (ii) **Accounting Standard 17 (AS 17)** Segment Reporting—shall apply irrespective of whether the securities of the insurer are traded publicly *or* not.

2. **Premium** Premium shall be recognised as income when due. For linked business the due date for payment may be taken as the date when the associated units are created.
3. **Premium Deficiency** Premium deficiency shall be recognised if the sum of expected caim costs, related expenses and maintenance costs exceeds related unearned premiums.
4. **Acquisition Costs** Acquisition costs, if any, shall be expensed in the period in which they are incurred.

   Acquisition costs are those costs that vary with and are primarily related to the acquisition of new and renewal insurance contracts. The most essential test is the obligatory relationship between costs and the execution of insurance contracts (i.e., commencement of risk).
5. **Claims Cost** The ultimate cost of claims shall comprise the policy benefit amount and claims settlement costs, wherever applicable.
6. **Acturial Valuation** Liability for Life Policies in force—The estimation of liability against life policies in force shall be determined by the appointed actuary of the insurer pursuant to his annual investigation of the life insurance business. Actuarial assumptions are to be disclosed by way of notes to the account.

   The liability shall be so calculated that together with future premium payments and investment income, the insurer can meet all future claims (including bonus entitlements to policy holders) and expenses.
7. **Procedure to determine the value of investments** An insurer shall determine the values of investments in the following manner:

   (a) **Real Estate—Investment Property**

   (i) The value of investment property shall be determined at historical cost, subject to revaluation at least once in every three years.

   (ii) The change in the carrying amount of the investment property shall be taken to Revaluation Reserve.

   (iii) The insurer shall assess at each balance sheet date whether any impairment of the investment property has occurred.

   (iv) Gains/losses arising due to changes in the carrying amount of real estate shall be taken to equity under 'Revaluation Reserve'.

   (v) The 'Profit on sale of investment', as the case may, shall include accumulated changes in the carrying amount previously recognised in equity under the heading 'Revaluation Reserve' in respect of a particular property and being recycled to the relevant Revenue Account *or* Profit and Loss Account on sale of that property.

   (vi) The basis for revaluation shall be disclosed in the notes to accounts.

   (vii) The Authority may issue directions specifying the amount to be released from the revaluation reserve for declaring bonus to the policyholders.

   (viii) For the removal of doubt, it is clarified that except for the amount that is released to policyholders as per the Authority's direction, no other amount shall be distributed to shareholders out of Revaluation Reserve Account.

   (ix) An impairment loss shall be recognised as an expense in the Revenue/Profit and Loss Account immediately, unless the asset is carried at revalued amount.

   (x) Any impairment loss of a revalued asset shall be treated as a revaluation decrease of that asset and if the impairment loss exceeds the corresponding revaluation reserve, such excess shall be recognised as an expense in the Revenue/Profit and Loss Account.

   (b) **Debt Securities** Debt securities, including government securities and redeemable preference shares, shall be considered as "held to maturity" securities and shall be measured at historical cost subject to amortisation.

(c) **Equity Securities and Derivative Instruments that are traded in active markets**

(i) Listed equity securities and derivative instruments that are traded in active markets shall be measured at fair value on the balance sheet date.

(ii) For the purpose of calculation of fair value, the lowest of the last quoted closing price at the stock exchanges where the securities are listed shall be taken.

(iii) The insurer shall assess on each Balance Sheet date whether any impairment of listed equity security(ies)/derivative(s) instruments has occurred.

(iv) An active market shall mean a market, where the securities traded are homogeneous, availability of willing buyers and willing sellers is normal and the prices are publicly available.

(v) Unrealised gains/losses arising due to changes in the fair value of listed equity shares and derivative instruments shall be taken to equity under the head 'Fair Value Change Account'.

(vi) The 'Profit on sale of investments' *or* 'Loss on sale of investments', as the case may be, shall include accumulated changes in the fair value previously recognised in equity under the heading 'Fair Value Change Account' in respect of a particular security and being recycled to the relevant Revenue Account *or* profit and Loss Account on actual sale of that listed security.

(vii) The Authority may issue directions specifying the amount to be released from the Fair Value Change Account for declaring bonus to the policyholders.

(viii) For the removal of doubt, it is clarified that amount that is released to policyholders as per the Authority's prescription, no other amount shall be distributed to shareholders out of Fair Value Change Account.

(ix) Also, any debit balance in Fair Value Change Account shall be reduced from profit/ free reserve while declaring dividends.

(x) The insurer shall assess, on each balance sheet date, whether any impairment has occurred.

(xi) An impairment loss shall be recognised as an expense in Revenue/Profit and Loss Account to the extent of the difference between the remeasured fair value of the security/investment and its acquisition cost as reduced by any previous impairment loss recognised as expense in Revenue/Profit and Loss Account.

(xii) Any reversal of impairment loss, earlier recognised in Revenue/Profit and Loss Account shall be recognised in Revenue/Profit and Loss Account.

(d) **Unlisted and other than actively traded Equity Securities and Derivative Instruments**

(i) Unlisted equity securities and derivative instruments and listed equity securities and derivative instruments that are not regularly traded in active markets shall be measured at historical cost.

(ii) Provision shall be made for diminution in value of such investments.

(iii) The provision so made shall be reversed in subsequent periods of estimates based on external evidence show an increase in the value of the investment over its carrying amount.

(iv) The increased carrying amount of the investment due to the reversal of the provision shall not exceed the historical cost.

(v) For the purposes of this regulation, a security shall be considered as being not actively traded, if its trading volume does not exceed ten thousand units in any trading session during the last twelve months.

8. **Loans**

(i) Loans shall be measured at historical cost subject to impairment provisions.

(ii) The insurer shall assess the quality of its loan assets and shall provide for impairment, the impairment provision shall not be *less* than the aggregate amount of loans which are subject to defaults of the nature mentioned below:

(i) interest remaining unpaid for over a period of 6 months; and

(ii) instalment(s) of loan falling due and remaining unpaid during the last 6 months

9. **Linked Business**

(i) The accounting principles used for valuatioon of investments are to be consistent with principles enumerated above.

(ii) A separate set of financial statements, for each segregated fund of the linked businesses, shall be annexed.

(iii) Segregated funds represent funds maintained in accounts to meet specific investment objectives of policyholders who bear the investment risk.

(iv) Investment income/gains and losses generally accrue directly to the policyholders.

(v) The assets of each account are segregated and are not subject to claims that arise out of any other business of the insurer.

10. **Funds for Future Appropriation**

(i) The funds for future appropriation shall be presented separately.

(ii) The funds for futre appropriation represent all funds, the allocation of which, *either* to the policyholders *or* to the shareholders, has not been determined by the end of the financial year.

PART II OF SCHEDULE 'A'— NOTES AND ACCOUNTING POLICIES

A. The following shall be disclosed by way of notes to the Balance Sheet:

1. **Contingent Liabilities:**

   (a) Partly-paid up investments

   (b) Underwriting commitments outstanding

   (c) Claims, other than those under policies, not acknowledged as debts

   (d) Guarantees given by *or* on behalf of the company

   (e) Statutory demands/liabilities in dispute, not provided for

   (f) Reinsurance obligations

   (g) Others (to the specified).

2. Acturial assumptions for valuation of liabilities for life policies in force.
3. Encumbrances to assets of the company in and outside India.
4. Commitments made and outstanding for Loans, Investments and Fixed Assets.
5. Basis of amortisation of debt securities.
6. Claims settled and remaining outstanding for a period of more than six months on the Balance Sheet date.
7. Value of contracts in relation to investments, for

   (a) Purchases where deliveries are pending;

   (b) Sales where payments are overdue.

8. Operating expenses relating to insurance business: basis of allocation of expenditure to various segments of business.

9. Computation of managerial remuneration.
10. Historical costs of those investments valued on fair value basis.
11. Basis of revaluation investment property.

B. The following accounting policies shall form an integral part of the financial statements:

1. All significant accounting policies in terms of the accounting standards issued by the ICAI, and significant principles and policies given in Part I of Accounting Principles. Any other accounting policies, followed by the insuerer, shall be stated in the manner required under Accounting Standard AS I issued by ICAI.
2. Any departure from the accounting policies shall be separately disclosed with reasons for such departure.

C. The following informaton shall also be disclosed:

1. Investments made in accordance with any statutory requirement should be disclosed separately together with its amount, nature, security and any special rights in and outside India;
2. Segregation into performing/non-performing investments for purpose of income recognition as per the directions, if any, issued by the Authority;
3. Assets to the extent required to be deposited under local laws *or* otherwise encumbered in *or* outside India;
4. Percentage of business sector-wise;
5. A summary of financial statements for the last five years, in the manner as may be prescribed by the Authority;
6. Basis of allocation of all investment and income there on between Policyholders' Account and Shareholders' Account;
7. Accounting Ratios as may be prescribed by the Authority.

PART III OF SCHEDULE 'A' — GENERAL INSTRUCTIONS FOR PREPARATION OF FINANCIAL STATEMENTS

1. The corresponding amounts for the immediately preceding financial year for all items shown in the Balance Sheet, Revenue Account, Profit and Loss Account and Receipts and Payments Account shall be given.
2. The figures in the financial statements may be rounded off to the nearest thousands.
3. Interest, dividends and rentals receivable in connection with an investment should be stated at gross amount, the amount of income tax deducted at source should be included under 'advance taxes paid' and taxes deducted source.
4. I For the purposes of financial statements, unless the context otherwise requires:

   (a) the expression **'provision'** shall, subject to II below mean any amount written off *or* retained by way of providing for depreciation, renewals *or* diminution on value of assets, *or* retained by way of providing for any knonw liability *or* loss of which the amount cannot be determined with substantial accuracy;

   (b) the expression **'reserve'** shall not, subject to as aforesaid, include any amount written off *or* retained by way of providing for depreciation, renewals *or* diminution in value of assets *or* retained by way of providing for any known liability *or* loss;

   (c) the expression **'capital reserve'** shall not include any amount regarded as free for distribution through profit and loss account; and the expression 'revenue reserve' shall mean any reserve other than a capital reserve;

   (d) The expression **'liability'** shall include all liabilities in respect of expenditure contracted for and all disputed *or* contingent liabilities.

II Where

(a) any amount written off *or* retained by way of providing for depreciation, renewals *or* diminution in value of assets, *or*

(b) any amount retained by way of providing for any known liability *or* loss, is in excess of the amount which in the opinion of the directors is reasonably necessary for the purpose, the excess shall be treated as a reserve and not provision.

5. The company shall make provisions for damages under lawsuits where the management is of the opinion that the award may go against the insurer.
6. Risks assumed in excess of the statutory provisions, if any, shall be separately disclosed indicating the amount of premiums involved and the amount of risks covered.
7. Any debit balance of the Profit and Loss Account shall be shown as deduction from uncommitted reserves and the balance, if any, shall be shown separately.

PART IV OF SCHEDULE 'A' — CONTENTS OF MANAGEMENT REPORT

There shall be attached to the financial statements, a management report containing, *inter alia,* the following duly authenticated by the management:

1. Confirmation regarding the continued validity *or* the registration granted by the Authority;
2. Certification that all the dues payable to the statutory authorities have been duly paid;
3. Confirmation to the effect that the shareholding pattern and any transfer of shares during the year are in accordance with the statutory requirements;
4. Declaration that the management has not directly *or* indirectly invested outside India the funds of the holders of policies issued in India;
5. Confirmation that the required solvency margins have been maintained;
6. Certification to the effect that the values of all the assets have been reviewed on the date of the Balance Sheet and that in his (insurer's) belief the assets set forth in the Balance Sheets are shown in the aggregate at amounts not exceeding their realisable *or* market value under the several headings—"Loans", "Investments", "Agents balance", "Outstanding Premiums", "Interest, Dividends and Rents outstanding", "Interest, Dividends and Rents accruing but not due", "Amounts due from other persons *or* Bodies carrying on insurance business", "Sundry Debtors", "Bills Receivable", "Cash" and the several items specified under "Other Accounts";
7. Certification to the effect that no part of the life insurance fund has been directly *or* indirectly applied in contravention of the provisions of the Insurance Act, 1938 (4 of 1938) relating to the application and investment of the life insurance funds;
8. Disclosure with regard to the overall risk exposure and strategy adopted to mitigate the same;
9. Operations in other countries, if any, with a separate statement giving the management's estimate of country risk and exposure risk and the hedging strategy adopted;
10. Ageing of claims indicating the trends in average claim settlement time during the preceding five years;
11. Certification to the effect as to how the values, as shown in the balance sheet, of the investments and stocks and shares hae been arrived at, and how the market value there of has been ascertained for the purpose of comparision with the values so shown;
12. Review of asset quality and performance of investment in terms of portfolios, i.e., separately in terms of real estate, loans, investment, etc.
13. A responsibility statement indicating therein that:

    (a) in the preparation of financial statements, the applicable accounting standards, principles and policies have been followed along with proper explanations relating to material departures, if any;

(b) the management has adopted accounting policies and applied them consistently and made judgements and estimates that are reasonable and prudent so as to give a true and fair view of the state of affairs of the company at the end of the financial year and of the operating profit *or* loss and of the profit *or* loss of the company for the year;

(c) the management has taken proper and sufficient care for the maintenance of adequate accounting records in accounting records in accordance with the applicable provisions of the Insurance Act, 1938 (4 of 1938)/Companies Act, 1956 (1 of 1956), for safeguarding the assets of the company and for preventing and detecting fraud and other irregularities;

(d) the management has prepared the financial statements on a going concern basis;

(e) the management has ensured that an internal audit system commensurate with the size and nature of the business exists and is operating effectively.

PART V OF SCHEDULE 'A' — PREPARATION OF FINANCIAL STATEMENTS

1. An insurer shall prepare the Revenue Account [Policyholders' Account], Profit and Loss Account [Shareholders' Account] and the Balance Sheet in Form A-RA, Form A-PL and Form A-BS, as prescribed in this Part, *or* as near there to as the circumstances permit

   Provided that an insurer shall prepare Revenue Account for the undermentioned businesses separately and to the extent the applicable of AS 17 shall stand modified:

   (a) Participating policies and Non-participating policies;

   (b) Linked, Non-Linked, and Health Insurance;

   (c) Business within India and Business outside India.

2. An insurer shall prepare separate Receipts and Payments Account in accordance with the Direct Method prescribed in AS 3—"Cash Flow Statement" issued by the ICAI.

15.0 PRACTICAL STEPS INVOLVED IN THE CALCULATION AND DISCLOSURE OF PREMIUM EARNED (NET)

Step 1: Calculate Premium earned on Direct Business and Re-insurance accepted as follows:

Particulars	*Direct Business (₹ '000)*	*Re-Insurance Accepted (₹ '000)*
A. Received	xxx	xxx
B. *Add:* Receivable at the end of the year	xxx	xxx
C. *Less:* Receivable in the beginning of the year	(xxx)	(xxx)
D. Total (A + B – C)	xxx	xxx

Step 2: Calculate Premium incurred on Re-insurance business Ceded as follows:

Particulars	*Re-Insurance Ceded (₹ '000)*
A. Paid during the year	xxx
B. *Add:* Payable at the end of the year	xxx
C. *Less:* Payable in the beginning of the year	(xxx)
D. Total (A + B – C)	xxx

Step 3: Disclose the Premium items in Revenue Account and Schedule as follows:

REVENUE ACCOUNT FOR THE YEAR ENDED...

Particulars	*Schedule*	*Current Year* ₹	*Previous Year* ₹
Premium earned (net)	1		
Premium on direct business written		xxx	xxx
Add: Premium on Re-insurance accepted		xxx	xxx
Less: Premium on Re-insurance ceded		(xxx)	(xxx)
Net premium		xxx	xxx

SCHEDULE 1 PREMIUM EARNED (NET)

Particulars	*Current* ₹ '000	*Previous* ₹ '000
1. First year Premium	xxx	xxx
2. Renewal Premiums	xxx	xxx
3. Single Premium	xxx	xxx
Total Premium	xxx	xxx
Premium Income from business written:		
In India	xxx	xxx
Outside India	xxx	xxx
	xxx	xxx

ILLUSTRATION 3

PCT Life Insurance Co. Ltd. provides you the following information:

Particulars	*Direct Business* ₹	*Re-Insurance* ₹
Premium Received	23,00,000	3,60,000
Premium Receivable on 1.4.2014	1,24,000	14,000
Premium Receivable on 31.3.2015	1,68,000	17,000
Premium Paid	—	2,30,000
Premium Payable 1.4.2014	—	19,000
Premium payable on 31.3.2015		31,000

Required: How will you show the above items in the 'Revenue' Account for the year ended 31st March, 2015?

SOLUTION

REVENUE ACCOUNT FOR THE YEAR ENDED 31st MARCH, 2015

Particulars	*Schedule*	*Current Year* (₹ '000)	*Previous Year* (₹ '000)
Premium earned (net)			
(a) Premium on direct business		2,344	

(b) Re-insurance ceded		(242)	
(c) Re-insurance accepted		363	

Working Notes:

(I) PREMIUM EARNED ON DIRECT BUSINESS AND RE-INSURANCE ACCEPTED

Particulars	*Direct Business (₹ '000)*	*Re-Insurance Business accepted (₹ '000)*
A. Received	2300	360
B. *Add:* Receivable at the end of the year	168	17
C. *Less:* Receivable in the beginning of the year	(124)	(14)
D. Total (A + B – C)	2344	363

(II) RE-INSURANCE PREMIUM ON RE-INSURANCE BUSINESS CEDED FOR THE YEAR

Particulars	*(₹ '000)*
A. Paid during the year	230
B. *Add:* Payable at the end of the year	31
C. *Less:* Payable in the beginning of the year	(19)
D. Total (A + B – C)	242

16.0 PRACTICAL STEPS INVOLVED IN THE CALCULATION & DISCLOSURE OF COMMISSION

Step 1: Calculate Commission incurred on Direct Business and Re-insurance business accepted as follows:

Particulars	*Direct Business (₹'000)*	*Re-Insurance (₹'000)*
A. Paid	xxx	xxx
B. *Add:* Payable at the end	xxx	xxx
C. *Less:* Payable in the beginning	(xxx)	(xxx)
	xxx	xxx

Step 2: Calculate Commission earned on Re-insurance Business ceded as follows:

Particulars	*Re-Insurance (₹ '000)*
A. Received during the year	xxx
B. *Add:* Receivable at the end	xxx
C. *Less:* Receivable in the beginning	(xxx)
D. Total (A + B – C)	xxx

Step 3: Disclose the Commission items in Revenue Account and Schedule 2 as follows:

REVENUE ACCOUNT FOR THE YEAR ENDED....

Particulars	*Schedule*	*Current Year (₹ '000)*	*Previous Year (₹ '000)*
Commission	2	xxx	xxx

SCHEDULE-2 COMMISSION EXPENSES

Particulars	*Current Year (₹ '000)*	*Previous Year (₹ '000)*
Commission paid		
Direct — First year premium	xxx	xxx
— Renewal premiums	xxx	xxx
— Single premiums	xxx	xxx
Add: Commission on Re-insurance accepted	xxx	xxx
Less: Commission on Re-insurance Ceded	(xxx)	(xxx)
Net Commission	xxx	xxx

ILLUSTRATION 4

Tulsian Life Insurance Co.Ltd. provides you the followoing information:

Particulars	*Direct Business (₹'000)*	*Re-Insurance (₹'000)*
Commission Paid	1,11,000	10,000
Commission Payable on 1.4.2014	2,000	1,000
Commission Payable on 31.3.2015	1,000	3,000
Commission Received		14,000
Commission Receivable on 1.4.2014		1,000
Commission Receivable on 31.03.2015		3,000

Required: How will you show the various figures in respect of Commission on Re-Insurance ceded in the Revenue Account for the year ended 31st March, 2015.

SOLUTION

REVENUE ACCOUNT FOR THE YEAR ENDED 31st MARCH, 2015

Particulars	*Schedule*	*Current Year (₹ '000)*	*Previous Year (₹ '000)*
Commission	2	106	

SCHEDULE-2 COMMISSON EXPENSES

Particulars	*Current Year (₹ '000)*	*Previous Year (₹ '000)*
Commission paid		
Direct	110	

Add: Commission on Re-insurance accepted	12	
Less: Commission on Re-insurance Ceded	(16)	
Net Commission	106	

Notes:

(I) COMMISSION INCURRED ON INSURANCE ACCEPTED

Particulars	Direct Business (₹'000)	Re-Insurance (₹'000)
A. Paid	111	10
B. *Add:* Payable at the end	1	3
C. *Less:* Payable in the beginning	(2)	(1)
	110	12

(II) COMMISSION EARNED ON INSURANCE CEDED

Particulars	₹
A. Received during the year	14
B. *Add:* Receivable at the end	3
C. *Less:* Receivable in the beginning	(1)
D. Total (A + B – C)	16

17.0 HOW TO DISCLOSE OPERATING EXPENSES RELATED TO INSURANCE

Step 1: Prepare Schedule 3 as follows:

SCHEDULE 3—OPERATING EXPENSES RELATED TO INSURANCE BUSINESS

Particulars	Current Year (₹ '000)	Previous Year (₹ '000)
1. Employees' remuneration and welfare benefits		
2. Travel, Conveyance and Vehicle running expenses		
3. Rents, Rates and Taxes		
4. Repairs		
5. Printing and Stationary		
6. Communication Expenses		
7. Legal and Professional charges [excluding those related to settlement of claims]		
8. Medical Fees		
9. Auditors' Fees, Expenses etc.		
(a) as auditor		
(b) as advisor *or* in any other capacity, in respect of:		
(i) Taxation matters		
(ii) Insurance matters		

(iii) Managements services, and		
(c) in any other capacity		
10. Advertisement and Publicity		
11. Interest and Bank Charges		
12. Others (to be specified)		
13. Depreciation		
Total		

Notes:

(a) *Items of expenses in excess of one percent of the net premium or ₹ 5,00,000 whichever is higher, shall be shown as a separate line item.*

(b) *Under the sub-head "Others", "Operating Expenses (Insurance Business)". Shall include items like foreign exchange gains or losses and other items.*

Step 2: Disclose the Operating Expenses related to Insurance in Revenue Account as follows:

REVENUE ACCOUNT FOR THE YEAR ENDED........

Particulars	*Schedule*	*Current Year (₹ '000)*	*Previous Year (₹ '000)*
Operating Expenses related to insurance business	3	......	......

ILLUSTRATION 5

Tulsian a Life Insurance Company Ltd., provides you the following information:

Particulars	₹	*Particulars*	₹
Salaries	3,20,000	Rent Rates and Taxes	29,000
Communication Expenses	20,000	Printing and Stationary	20,000
Policy Stamps	3,000	Medical Fees	5,000
Profit on Sale of Motor Car	5,000	Advertisement & Publicity	15,000
Legal and Professional Charges (inclusive of ₹ 40,000 in connection with settlement of claims)	72,000	Rate of Depreciation on Furniture: 10 % on original cost	
		Travel, Convenyance and Vehicle running expenses	15,000
Repairs	5,000		
Auditors' Fees	10,000		
Interest and Bank Charges	5,000		
Furniture & Fixtures (cost ₹ 1,00,000)	58,000		

Required: How will you disclose the above items in the Revenue Account for the year ended 31st March, 2015?

SOLUTION

REVENUE ACCOUNT FOR THE YEAR ENDED 31st MARCH, 2015

Particulars	*Schedule*	*Current Year (₹ '000)*	*Previous Year (₹ '000)*
Operating Expenses related to insurance business	3	489	......

SCHEDULE-3 OPERATING EXPENSES RELATED TO INSURANCE BUSINESS

Particulars	Current Year (₹ '000)	Previous Year (₹ '000)
1. Employee's Remuneration and Welfare Benefits	320	
2. Travel, Conveyance and Vehicle running Expenses	15	
3. Rents, Rates and Taxes	29	
4. Repairs	5	
5. Printing and Stationery	20	
6. Communication Expenses	20	
7. Legal and Professional Charges	32	
8. Medical Fees	5	
9. Auditor's Fees	10	
10. Advertisement and Publicity	15	
11. Interest and Bank Charges	5	
12. Policy Stamps	3	
13. Depreciation	10	
Total	489	

18.0 PRACTICAL STEPS INVOLVED IN THE CALCULATION AND DISCLOSURE OF CLAIMS INCURRED (NET)

Step 1: *Calculate Claims incurred on Direct Business and Re-insurance Business accepted as follows:*

Particulars	Direct Business (₹'000)	Re-Insurance (₹'000)
A. Paid	xxx	xxx
B. *Add:* Outstanding at the end	xxx	xxx
C. *Add:* Expenses in connection with settlement of claim	xxx	xxx
D. *Less:* Outstanding at the beginning	(xxx)	(xxx)
E. Claims incurred [A + B + C – D]	xxx	xxx

Step 2: *Calculate Claims earned on Re-insurance Business ceded as follows:*

Particulars	₹ '000
A. Received	xxx
B. *Add:* Recoverable at the end	xxx
C. *Less:* Recoverable at the beginning	(xxx)
	xxx

Step 3: *Disclose the Claims items in Revenue Account and Schedule 4 as follows:*

REVENUE ACCOUNT FOR THE YEAR ENDED...

Particulars	Schedule	Current Year (₹ '000)	Previous Year (₹ '000)
Benefits Paid (Net)	4	xxx	xxxx

SCHEDULE-4 BENEFITS PAID [NET]

Particulars	Current Year (₹ '000)	Previous Year (₹ '000)
1. Insurance Claims		
(a) Claims by Death	xxx	xxx
(b) Claims by Maturity	xxx	xxx
(c) Annuities/Pensions in payment	xxx	xxx
(d) Other Benefits, specify	xxx	xxx
2. (Amount ceded in reinsurance)		
(a) Claims by Death	(xxx)	(xxx)
(b) Claims by Maturity	(xxx)	(xxx)
(c) Annuities/Pensions in payment	(xxx)	(xxx)
(d) Other Benefits, specify	(xxx)	(xxx)
3. Amount accepted in Reinsurance		
(a) Claims by Death	xxx	xxx
(b) Claims by Maturity	xxx	xxx
(c) Annuities/Pensions in payment	xxx	xxx
(d) Other Benefits, specify	xxx	xxx
Total	xxx	xxx
Benefits paid to Claimants:		
1. In India	xxx	xxx
2. Outside India	xxx	xxx
Total Benefits paid (Net)	xxx	xxx

Notes:

(a) *Claims include claims settlement costs, wherever applicable.*

(b) *The legal and other fees and expenses shall also form part of the claims cost, wherever applicable.*

ILLUSTRATION 6

Tulsian Life Insurance Company Ltd. provides you the following information:

Particulars	Direct Business ₹	Reinsurance Accepted ₹	Reinsurance Ceded ₹
Claims by Death Paid	10,80,000	5,40,000	
Claims Payable on 1.4.2014	1,00,000	50,000	
Claims Payable on 31.03.2015	2,00,000	1,00,000	
Claims Received	—		2,70,000
Claims Receivable on 1.4.2014	—		20,000
Claims Receivable on 31.3.2015	—		50,000

Expenses in Connection with			
Settlement of Claims			
— Surveyor's Charges	12,000	6,000	
— Legal Expenses	8,000	4,000	
Claim by Maturity	6,00,000	3,00,000	1,50,000
Annuities and Pensions	3,00,000	1,50,000	75,000
Total Claims in India	80%	80%	80%

Required: *How will you show the above item in the Revenue Account for the year ended 31st March, 2015?*

SOLUTION

REVENUE ACCOUNT FOR THE YEAR ENDED 31st MARCH, 2015

Particulars	*Schedule*	*Current Year (₹ '000)*	*Previous Year (₹ '000)*
Benefits Paid (Net)	4	2,625	

SCHEDULE-4 BENEFITS PAID [NET]

Particulars	*Current Year (₹ '000)*	*Previous Year (₹ '000)*
1. **Insurance Claims**		
(a) Claims by Death	1200	
(b) Claims by Maturity	600	
(c) Annuities/Pensions in payment	300	
	2100	
2. **Amount ceded in reinsurance**		
(a) Claims by Death	(300)	
(b) Claims by Maturity	(150)	
(c) Annuities/Pensions in payment	(75)	
Total	(525)	
3. **Amount accepted in Reinsurance**		
(a) Claims by Death	600	
(b) Claims by Maturity	300	
(c) Annuities/Pensions in payment	150	
Total	1050	
Benefits paid to Claimants:		
1. In India	2100	
2. Outside India	525	
Total Benefits Paid (Net)	2625	

Working Note:

CALCULATION OF CLAIMS BY DEATH

	Particulars	*Direct Business (₹ '000)*	*Reinsurance Accepted (₹ '000)*	*Reinsurance Ceded (₹ '000)*
A.	Paid / Received	1080	540	270
B.	*Add:* Outstanding at end	200	100	50
C.	*Add:* Expenses in connection with settlement	20	10	—
D.	*Less:* Outstanding at beg.	(100)	(50)	(20)
		1200	600	300

19.0 FORMAT OF REVENUE ACCOUNT

FORM A-RA

Name of the Insurer:	....
Registration No. and Date of Registration with the IRDA	....

REVENUE ACCOUNT FOR THE YEAR ENDED 31ST MARCH, 20______
POLICYHOLDERS' ACCOUNT (TECHNICAL ACCOUNT)

Particulars	*Schedule*	*Current Year (₹ '000)*	*Previous Year (₹ '000)*
Premiums earned—net	1		
(a) Premium		......	......
(b) Reinsurance ceded		(......)	(......)
(c) Reinsurance accepted:		......	......
Income from Investments			
(a) Interest, Dividends and Rent—Gross		......	......
(b) Profit on sale/redemption of investments		......	......
(c) (Loss on sale/redemption of investments)		......	......
(d) (Transfer/Gain on revaluation/change in fair value*)		......	......
Other Income (to be specified) [e.g. Profit on sale of Asset, Double Income Tax Refund]		......	......
Total (A)		......	......
Commission	2	......	......
Operating Expenses related to Insurance Business	3	......	......
Other Expenses (to be specified)			
Provisions (other than taxation)			
(a) For diminution in the value of investments (Net)		......	......
(b) Others (to be specified) [e.g. Bad Debts, Indian & Foreign Taxes]		......	......

Total (B)		......	......
Benefits Paid (net)	4	......	......
Interim Bonuses Paid		......	......
Change in valuation of liability against life policies in force		......	......
(a) Gross**			
(b) (Amount ceded in Reinsurance)		......	......
(c) Amount accepted in Reinsurance		......	......
Total (C)		......	......
Surplus/(Deficit) (D) = (A) – (B) – (C)		......	......
Appropriations:			
Transfer to Share holder's Account [i.e.5% of Surplus]		......	......
Transfer to Other Reserves (to be specified)		......	......
Transfer to Funds for Future Appropriations		......	......
Total (D)		......	......

Notes:

* Represents the deemed realised gain as per norms specified by the Authority.

** Represents Mathematical Reserves after allocation of bonus.

The total surplus shall be dislosed separately with the following details:

(a) Interim Bonuses Paid:

(b) Allocation of Bonus to policyholders:

(c) Surplus shown in the Revenue Account:

(d) Total Surplus: [(a) + (b) + (c)]:

SCHEDULES FORMING PART OF REVENUE ACCOUNT

SCHEDULE 1—PREMIUM

Particulars	*Current Year (₹ '000)*	*Previous Year (₹ '000)*
1. First year premiums	......	......
2. Renewal Premiums	......	......
3. Single Premiums	......	......
Total Premium	......	......
Premium Income from business written:		
1. In India	......	......
2. Outside India	......	......
Total Premium	......	......

Notes: *Reinsurance premums whether or business ceded or accepted are to be brought into account, before deducting commission, under the head of reinsurance premiums.*

SCHEDULE 2—COMMISSION EXPENSES

Particulars	*Current Year (₹ '000)*	*Previous Year (₹ '000)*
Commission paid		
Direct — First year premiums	......	......
— Renewal Premiums	......	......
— Single premiums	......	......
Add: Commission on Reinsurance accepted	......	......
Less: Commission on Reinsurance ceded	(......)	(......)
Net Commission	......	......

SCHEDULE 3—OPERATING EXPENSES RELATED TO INSURANCE BUSINESS

Particulars	*Current Year (₹ '000)*	*Previous Year (₹ '000)*
1. Employees' remuneration and welfare benefits	......	......
2. Travel, Conveyance and Vehicle running expenses	......	......
3. Rents, Rates and Taxes	......	......
4. Repairs	......	......
5. Printing and Stationary	......	......
6. Comminication Expenses	......	......
7. Legal and Professional charges	......	......
8. Medical Fees	......	......
9. Auditors' Fees, Expenses etc.	......	......
(a) as auditor		
(b) as adviser *or* in any other capacity, in respect of:		
(i) Taxation matters		
(ii) Insurance matters		
(iii) Managements services, and		
(c) in any other capacity		
10. Advertisement and Publicity	......	......
11. Interest and Bank Charges	......	......
12. Others (to be specified)	......	......
13. Depreciation	......	......
Total	......	......

Notes:

(a) *Items of expenses in excess of one percent of the net premium or ₹ 5,00,000 whiever is higher, shall be shown as a separate line item.*

(b) *Under the sub-head "Others", "Operating Expenses (Insurance Business)". Shall include items like foreign exchange gains or losses and other items.*

SCHEDULE 4—BENEFITS PAID [NET]

Particulars	*Current Year (₹ '000)*	*Previous Year (₹ '000)*
1. **Insurance Claims:**		
(a) Claims by Death,	.....	.....
(b) Claims by Maturity,	.....	.....
(c) Annuities/Pensions in payment,	.....	.....
(d) other benefits, specify,	.....	.....
2. **(Amount ceded in reinsurance):**		
(a) Claims by Death,	(.....)	(.....)
(b) Claims by Maturity,	(.....)	(.....)
(c) Annuities/Pensions in payment,	(.....)	(.....)
(d) Other Benefits, specify,	(.....)	(.....)
3. **Amount accepted in reinsurance:**		
(a) Claims by Death,	.....	.....
(b) Claims by Maturity,	.....	.....
(c) Annuities/Pensions in payment,	.....	.....
(d) Other Benefits, specify,	.....	.....
Total		.....
Benefits paid to claimants:		
1. In India		.....
2. Outside India	.....	.....
Total Benefits paid (net)	.....	.....

Notes:

(a) *Claims include claims settlement costs, wherever applicable.*

(b) *The legal and other fees and expenses shall also form part of the claims cost, whever applicable.*

ILLUSTRATION 7

From the following information, prepare Revenue Account of PCT Life Assurance Company Ltd. for the year ended 31st March, 2015:

Particulars	*Direct Business* ₹	*Reinsurance Ceded* ₹	*Reinsurance Accepted* ₹
1. (a) Premium	30,00,000	10,00,000	20,00,000
(b) Commission	3,00,000	1,00,000	2,00,000
(c) Total Claims			
(i) by Death	4,20,000	1,40,000	2,80,000
(ii) by Maturity	1,20,000	40,000	80,000
(iii) Annuities/Pensions in payment	60,000	20,000	40,000

	Claims in India	80%	80%	80%
2.	Expenses:			
	Employees' remuneration & Welfare Benefits	4,31,000		
	Travel, Conveyance & vehicle running exp.	59,000		
	Rents Rates and Taxes	30,000		
	Repairs	20,000		
	Printing and Stationery	10,000		
	Communication	5,000		
	Legal and Professional charges	6,000		
	Medical Fees	7,000		
	Auditors' Fees, Expenses etc.	8,000		
	Advertisement and Publicity	6,000		
	Interest and Bank Charges	5,000		
	Policy Stamps	3,000		
	Furniture & Fixtures (cost ₹ 1,00,000)	58,000		
	Indian and foreign Taxes	95,000		
	Interest, Dividend & Rent received	90,000		
	Income Tax deducted at Source thereon	10,000		
	Loss on Sale of Investments	20,000		
	Profit on Sale of Motor Car	5,000		
	Double Income tax Refund	15,000		
	Interim Bonus Paid	1,00,000		
	Rate of Depreciation on Furniture—10% on original cost Bad Debts	5,000		

REVENUE ACCOUNT FOR THE YEAR ENDED 31st MARCH, 2015

	Particulars	*Schedule*	*Current Year (₹ '000)*	*Previous Year (₹ '000)*
1.	**Premium earned (Net)**			
	(a) Premium		3000	
	(b) Reinsurance ceded		(1000)	
	(c) Reinsuance accepted		2000	
2.	**Income from Investments:**			
	(a) Interest, Dividends and Rent (Gross)		100	
	(b) Loss on Sale of Investments		(20)	
3.	**Other Incomes:**			
	Profit on Sale of Motor Car		5	
	Double Income Tax Refund		15	
	Total (A)		4100	

1. Commission	2	400
2. Operating Expenses related to Insurance Business	3	600
3. Other Expenses:		
Bad Debts		5
Indian and Foreign Taxes		95
Total (B)		1100
1. Benefits paid	4	800
2. Interim Bonuses paid		100
Total (C)		900
Surplus (D) = (A) – (B) – (C)		2100
Appropriations:		
Transfer to Shareholders' Accopunt		105
Transfer to Funds for future appropriations		1995
		2100

SCHEDULE-2 COMMISSION EXPENSES

Particulars	*Current Year (₹ '000)*	*Previous Year (₹ '000)*
Commission Paid		
Direct	300	
Add: Commission on Re-insurance accepted	200	
Less: Commission on Re-insurance ceded	(100)	
	400	

SCHEDULE-3 OPERATING EXPENSES RELATED TO INSURANCE BUSINESS

Particulars	*Current Year (₹ '000)*	*Previous Year (₹ '000)*
1. Employees' remuneration and welfare benefits	431	
2. Travel, Conveyance and Vehicle running expenses	59	
3. Rents, Rates and Taxes	30	
4. Repairs	20	
5. Printing and Stationary	10	
6. Communication Expenses	5	
7. Legal and Professional charges	6	
8. Medical Fees	7	
9. Auditors' Fees, Expenses etc.	8	
10. Advetisement and Publicity	6	
11. Interest and Bank Charges	5	

12. Policy Stamps	3	
13. Depreciation	10	
Total	600	

SCHEDULE-4 BENEFITS PAID [NET]

Particulars	*Current Year (₹ '000)*	*Previous Year (₹ '000)*
1. Insurance Claims		
(a) Claims by Death	420	
(b) Claim by Maturity	120	
(c) Annuities/Pension in payments	60	
	600	
2. (Amount ceded in Re-insurance)		
(a) Claim by Death	(140)	
(b) Claim by Maturity	(40)	
(c) Annuities/Pension in payments	(20)	
	(200)	
3. Amount accepted in Re-insurance		
(a) Claim by Death	280	
(b) Claim by Maturity	80	
(c) Annuities/Pension in payments	40	
	400	
Total (1 + 2 + 3)	800	
Benefits paid to claimants		
1. India	640	
2. Outside India	160	
Total Benefits paid (net)	800	

20.0 FORMAT OF PROFIT AND LOSS ACCOUNT

FORM A-PL

Name of the Insurer:	....
Registration No. and Date of Registration with the IRDA	....

PROFIT AND LOSS ACCOUNT FOR THE YEAR ENDED 31ST MARCH, 20____
SHAREHOLDERS' ACCOUNT (NON-TECHNICAL ACCOUNT)

Particulars	*Schedule*	*Current Year (₹ '000)*	*Previous Year (₹ '000)*
Balance brought forward from/transferred to the Policy holders Account (Technical Account)		. . .	. . .

Income from Investments		. . .	. . .
(a) Interest, Dividends and Rent—Gross			
(b) Profit on Sale/Redemption of Investments			
(c) (Loss on Sale/Redemption of Investments)			
Other Income (to be specified)[e.g. transfer fees]		. . .	. . .
Total (A)			
Expense other than those directly related to the insurance business [e.g. Past Time Directors Fees etc.]		. . .	. . .
Provisions (other than taxation)		. . .	. . .
(a) For diminution in the value of investments (Net)		. . .	. . .
(b) Others (to be specified)			
Total (B)			
Profit/(Loss) before tax [(A) – (B)]		. . .	. . .
Provision for Taxation		(. . .)	(. . .)
Profit after tax		. . .	. . .
***Less:* Appropriations:**			
(a) Interim dividends paid during the year			(. . .)
(b) Proposed final dividend		(. . .)	(. . .)
(c) Dividend distribution on tax		(. . .)	(. . .)
(d) Transfer to reserves/other accounts		(. . .)	(. . .)
(to be specified)		(. . .)	(. . .)
Profit carried forward to the Balance Sheet			

Notes:

(a) In case of premiums, *less* reinsurance in respect of any segment of insurance business of total premium earned, the same shall be disclosed separately.

(b) Premium income received from business concluded in and ouside India shall be separately disclosed.

(c) Reinsurance premiums whether on business ceded *or* accepted are to be brought into account gross (i.e., before deducting commissions) under the head reinsurance premiums.

(d) Claims incurred shall comprise claims paid, settlement costs wherever applicable and change in the outstanding provision for claims at the year-end.

(e) Items of expenses and income in excess of one percent of the total premiums (less reinsurance) *or* ₹ 5,00,000 whichever is higher, shall be shown as a separate line item.

(f) Fees and expenses connected with claims shall be included in claims.

(g) Under the sub-head "Others" shall be included items like foreign exchange gains *or* losses and other items.

(h) Interest, dividends and rentals receivable in connection with an investment should be stated as gross amount, the amount of income tax deducted at source being included under "advance taxes paid and taxes deducted at source."

(i) Income from rent shall include only the realised rent. It shall not include any notional rent.

ILLUSTRATION 8

From the following information, prepare Profit and Loss Account of PCT Life Assurance Ltd. for the year ended 31st March, 2015.

Particulars	₹
Balance brought forward from Revenue A/c	19,95,000
Transfer Fees	1,05,000
Miscelleaneous Income	1,00,000
Part Time Diectors" Fees	75,000
Travelling Expenses of Part Time Directors	25,000
Donations	90,000
Provision for diminution in Value of Investments	10,000
Provision for Tax	6,00,000
Profit and Loss A/c (as on 1.4.2014)	3,50,000
Interim Dividends paid	2,00,000
Proposed Final Dividend	3,00,000
Dividend Distribution Tax	50,000
Transfer to General Reserve	2,00,000

SOLUTION

PROFIT AND LOSS ACCOUNT FOR THE YEAR ENDED 31ST MARCH, 2015

Particulars	*Schedule*	*Current Year (₹ '000)*	*Previous Year (₹ '000)*
1. Balance brought forward from Revenue A/c		1995	
Other Income:			
Transfer Fees		105	
Miscelleneous Income		100	
Total (A)		2200	
Part Time Directors' Fees		75	
Travelling Expenses of Part Time Directors		25	
Donation		90	
Provision for diminution in the value of Investments		10	
Total (B)		200	
Profit before Tax [(A) – B)]		2,000	
Provision for Tax		(600)	
Profit after tax		1400	
P&L A/c (as on 1.4.2014)		350	
Appropriations			
Interim Dividends Paid		(200)	
Prospoosed Final Dividend		(300)	

Dividend Distribution Tax		(50)	
Transfer to General Reserve		(200)	
Profit carried forward to the Balance Sheet		1000	

21.0 FORMAT OF BALANCE SHEET

FORM A-BS

Name of the Insurer:	....
Registration No. and Date of Registration with the IRDA	....

BALANCE SHEET AS AT 31ST MARCH, 20____

Particulars	*Schedule*	*Current Year (₹ '000)*	*Previous Year (₹ '000)*
Sources of Funds:			
Share holders' funds:			
Share Capital	5	......	......
Reserves and Surplus	6	......	......
Credit/[Debit] Fair Value Change Account		......	......
Sub-Total		......	......
Borrowings	7	......	......
Policy holders' Funds:			
Credit/[Debit] Fair Value change Account		......	......
Policy Liabilities		......	......
Insurance Reserves		......	......
Provision for Linked Liabilities		......	......
Sub-Total		......	......
Funds for Future Appropriations		......	......
Total		......	......
Application of Funds:			
Investments:			
Share holders'	8	......	......
Policy holders'	8A	......	......
Assets held to Cover Linked Liabilities			
Loans	9	......	......
Fixed Assets	10	......	......
Current Assets			
Cash and Bank Balance	11	......	......
Advances and Other Assets	12	......	......
Sub-Total (A)		......	......
Current Liabilities	13	......	......

Provisions	14	......	......
Sub-Total (B)			......
Net Current Assets (C) = (A – B)			......
Miscellaneous Expenditure	15	......	......
(to the extent not written off *or* adjusted)		......	......
Debit Balance in Profit and Loss Account		......	......
(Share holders' Account)		......	......
Total			

CONTINGENT LIABILITIES

Particulars	*Schedule*	*Current Year (₹ '000)*	*Previous Year (₹ '000)*
1. Partly paid-up investments		......	......
2. Claims, other than against policies, not acknowledged as debts by the company		......	......
3. Underwriting commitments outstanding		......	......
4. Guarantees given by *or* on behalf of the company		......	......
5. Statutory demands/liabilities in dispute, not provided for		......	......
6. Reinsurance obligations		......	......
7. Others (to be specified)		......	......
Total		......	......

SCHEDULES FORMING PART OF BALANCE SHEET

SCHEDULE 5—SHARE CAPITAL

Particulars	*Current Year (₹ '000)*	*Previous Year (₹ '000)*
1. Authorised Capital		
Equity Shares of ₹ .... each	......	......
2. Issued Capita		
Equity Shares of ₹ .... each	......	......
3. Subscribed Capital		
Equity Shares of ₹ .... each	......	......
4. Called-up Capital		
Equity Shares of ₹ .... each	......	......
5. *Less:* Calls unpaid		
Add: Shares forfeited (Amount originally paid-up)	......	......
Less: Par value of Equity Shares bought back	(......)	(......)
Expenses including commission *or* brokerage on Underwriting *or* subscription of shares	......	......
Total	......	......

Notes:

(a) Particular of the different classes of capital should be separately stated..

(b) The amount capitalised on account of issue of bonus shares should be disclosed.

(c) In case any part of the capital is held by a holding company, the same should be separately disclosed.

SCHEDULE 5A—PATTERN OF SHAREHOLDING

[As certified by the Management]

Particulars	*Current Year*		*Previous Year*	
	Number of Shares	*% of Holding*	*Number of Shares*	*% of Holding*
Promoters	......	......	......	......
Indian	......	......	......	......
Foreign	......	......	......	......
Others	......	......	......	......
Total	......	......	......	......

SCHEDULE 6—RESERVES AND SURPLUS

Particulars	*Current Year (₹ '000)*	*Previous Year (₹ '000)*
1. Capital Reserve	......	......
2. Capital Redemption Reserve	......	......
3. Share Premium	......	......
4. Revaluatioin Reserve	......	......
5. General Reserves:	......	......
Less: Debit balance in profit and Loss Account, if any	(......)	(......)
Less: Amount utilised for Buy-back	(......)	(......)
6. Catastrophe reserve	......	......
7. Other Reserves (to be specified)	......	......
8. Balance of Profit in Profit and Loss Account	......	......
Total	......	......

Notes: *Additions to and deductions from the reserves should be disclosed under each of the specified heads.*

SCHEDULE 7—BORROWINGS

Particulars	*Current Year (₹ '000)*	*Previous Year (₹ '000)*
1. Debentures/Bonds	......	......
2. Fixed Deposits	......	......

3. Banks	......	......
4. Financial Institutions	......	......
5. Other entities carrying on insurance business	......	......
6. Other (to be specified)	......	......
Total	......	......

Notes:

(a) *The extent to which the borrowings are secured shall be separately disclosed stating the nature of the security under each sub-head.*

(b) *Amounts due within 12 months from the date of Balance Sheet should be shown separately.*

SCHEDULE 8—INVESTMENTS-SHAREHOLDERS

Particulars	*Current Year (₹ '000)*	*Previous Year (₹ '000)*
Long Term Investments:		
1. Government securities and Government guaranteed bonds including Treasury Bills		
2. Other Approved Securities	......	......
3. Other Investments	......	......
(a) Shares		
(i) Equity		
(ii) Preference		
(b) Mutual Funds		
(c) Derivative Instruments		
(d) Debentures/Bonds		
(e) Other Securities (to be specified)		
(f) Subsidiaries		
(g) Investment Properties-Real Estate		
Short Term Investments:		
1. Government Securities and Government guaranteed bonds including Treasury Bills	......	
2. Other Approved Securities	......	......
3. Other Investments:	......	......
(a) Shares		
(i) Equity		
(ii) Preference		
(b) Mutual Funds		
(c) Derivative Instruments		
(d) Debentures/Bonds		
(e) Other Securities (to be specified)		
(f) Subsidiaries		

(g) Investment Properties-Real Estate		
Total		
Investments:		
1. In India	......	......
2. Outside India	......	......
Total	......	......

Notes: *Refer notes under Schedule 8A.*

SCHEDULE 8A—INVESTMENTS-POLICYHOLDERS

Particulars	*Current Year (₹ '000)*	*Previous Year (₹ '000)*
Long Term Investments:		
1. Government securities and Government guaranteed bonds includeing Treasury Bills	......	......
2. Other Approved Securities	......	......
3. Other Investments	......	......
(a) Shares		
(i) Equity		
(ii) Preference		
(b) Mutual Funds		
(c) Derivative Instruments		
(d) Debentures/Bonds		
(e) Other Securities (to be specified)		
(f) Subsidiaries		
(g) Investment Properties-Real Estate		
4. Investments in Infrastructure and Social Sector	......	......
5. Other than Approved Investments	......	......
Short Term Investments:		
1. Government Securities & Government guaranted bonds including	......	......
2. Other Approved Securities	......	......
3. Other Investments:	......	......
(a) Shares		
(i) Equity		
(ii) Preference		
(b) Mutual Funds		
(c) Derivative Instruments		
(d) Debentures/Bonds		
(e) Other Securities (to be specified)		
(f) Subsidiaries		

(g) Investment Properties-Real Estate		
4. Investments in Infrastructure and Social Sector	......	......
5. Other than Approved Investments	......	......
Total	......	......
Investments:		
1. In India	......	......
2. Outside India	......	......
Total	......	......

Notes: *(applicable to Schedule 8 and 8A):*

(a) Investments in subsidiary/holding companies, joint ventures and associates shall be separately disclosed, at cost.

(i) Holding company and subsidiary shall be construed as defined in the Companies Act, 1956.

(ii) Joint Venture is a contractual arrangement where by two *or* more parties under take an economic activity, which is subject to joint control.

(iii) Joint control is the contractually agreed sharing of power to govern the financial and operating policies of an economic activity to obtain benefits from it.

(iv) Associate is an enterprise in which the company has significant in influence and which is neither a subsidiary *nor* a joint venture of the company.

(v) Significant in influence (for the purpose of this schedule) means participation in the financial and operating policy decisions of a company, but not in control of those policies. Significant in influence may be exercised in several ways, for example, by representation on the board of directors, participatioin in the policy making process, material inter-company transaction, interchange of managerial personnel *or* dependence on technical information. Significant in influence may be gained by share ownership, if an investor holds, directly *or* indirectly holds, directly *or* indirectly through subsidiaries, 20 percent *or* more of the voting power of the investee, it is presumed that the investor does have siginificant in influence, unless it can be clearly demonstrated that this is not the case. Conversely, if the investor holds, directly *or* indirectly through subsidiaries, *less* than 20 per cent of the voting power of the investee, it is presumed that the investor does not have significant influence, unless such influece is clearly demonstrated. A substantial *or* majority ownership by another investor does not necessarily preclude an investor from having significant influence.

(b) Aggregate amount of company's investments other than listed equity securities and derivative instruments and also the market value there of shall be disclosed.

(c) Investments made out of Catastrophe reserve should be shown separately.

(d) Debt securities will be considered as "held to maturity" securities and will be measured at historical costs subject to amortisation.

(e) Investment Property means a property [land *or* building *or* part of a building *or* both] held to earn rental income *or* for capital appreciation *or* for both, rather than for use in services *or* for administrative purposes.

SCHEDULE 9—LOANS

Particulars	*Current Year (₹ '000)*	*Previous Year (₹ '000)*

1. Security-wise Classification Secured		
(a) On mortgage of property	......	......
(i) In India		
(ii) Outside India		
(b) On Shares, Bonds, Govt. Securities, etc.	......	......
(c) Others (to be specified)	......	......
Unsecured		
(a) Loans against policies	......	......
(b) Others (to be specified)	......	......
Total	......	......
2. Borrower-wise Classification		
(a) Central and State Governments	......	......
(b) Banks and Financial Institutions	......	......
(c) Subsidiaries	......	......
(d) Companies	......	......
(e) Loans against policies	......	......
(f) Others (to be specified)	......	......
Total	......	......
3. Performance-wise Classification		
(a) Loans classified as standard	......	......
(i) In India	......	......
(ii) Outside India	......	......
(b) Non-standard Loans		
(i) In India	......	......
(ii) Outside India	......	......
Total	......	......
4. Maturity-wise Classification		
(a) Short Term	......	......
(b) Long term	......	......
Total	......	......

Notes:

(a) *Short-term loans shall include those, which are repayable within 12 months from the date of balance sheet. Long term loans shall be the loans other than short-term loans.*

(b) *Provisions against non-performing loans shall be shown separately.*

(c) *The nature of the security in case of all long term securied loans shall be specified in each case. Secured loans for the purposes of this schedule, means loans secured wholly or partly against an asset of the company.*

(d) *Loans considered doubtful and the amount of provision created against such loans shall be disclosed.*

SCHEDULE 10—FIXED ASSETS

Particulars	*Cost/Gross*	*Depreciation Block*			*Net Block*		
	Opening Additions Deductions	*Upto Last Year Closing*	*For the Year*	*On Sales Adjustments*	*To Date*	*As at Year end*	*Previous Year*
Goodwill	......	......	......	......	......	......	......
Intangibles (specify)	......	......	......	......	......	......	......
Land-Freehold	......	......	......	......	......	......	......
Leasehold	......	......	......	......	......	......	......
Property	......	......	......	......	......	......	......
Buildings	......	......	......	......	......	......	......
Furniture and Fittings	......	......	......	......	......	......	......
Information Technology	......	......	......	......	......	......	......
Equiptment	......	......	......	......	......	......	......
Vehicles	......	......	......	......	......	......	......
Office Equipment	......	......	......	......	......	......	......
Others (specify nature)	......	......	......	......	......	......	......
Total	......	......	......	......	......	......	......
Previous Year	......	......	......	......	......	......	......

Note: *Assets included in land, property and building above exclude Investment Properties as defined in note (e) to Schedule 8.*

SCHEDULE 11—CASH AND BANK BALANCES

Particulars	*Current Year (₹ '000)*	*Previous Year (₹ '000)*
1. Cash (including cheques, drafts and stamps)	......	......
2. Bank Balances	......	......
(a) Deposit Accounts	......	......
(i) Short-term (due within 12 months of the date of Balance Sheet)		
(ii) Others		
(b) Current Accounts	......	......
(c) Others (to be specified)	......	......
3. Money at Call and Short Notice	......	......
(a) With Banks	......	......
(b) With other Institutions	......	......
4. Others (to be specified)		......
Total	......	......
Balance with non-scheduled banks included in 2 and 3 above		
Cash and Bank Balances		
1. In India		

2. Outside India		
Total		

Note: *Bank Balance may include remittances in transit. If so, the nature and amount should be separately stated.*

SCHEDULE 12—ADVANCES AND OTHER ASSETS

Particulars	*Current Year (₹ '000)*	*Previous Year (₹ '000)*
Advances		
1. Reserve deposits with ceding companies	......	......
2. Advances to ceding companies	......	......
3. Application money for investments	......	......
4. Prepayments	......	......
5. Advances to Officers/Directors	......	......
6. Advance tax paid and taxes deducted at source	......	......
7. Others (to be specified)	......	......
Total (A)	......	......
Others Assets		
1. Income accrued on investments	......	......
2. Outstanding premiums	......	......
3. Agents' Balances	......	......
4. Foreign Agencies' Balances	......	......
5. Due from other entities carrying on insurance business	......	......
6. Due from subsidiaries/holding company	......	......
7. Resinsurance claims/balances receivable	......	......
8. Deposit with Reserve Bank of India [Pursuant to Section 7 of Insurance Act, 1938]	......	......
9. Others (to be specified)	......	......
Total (B)	......	......
Total (A + B)	......	......

Notes:

(a) *The items under the above heads shall not be shown net of provisions for doubtful amounts. The amount of provision against each head should be shown separately.*

(b) *The term 'officer' should confirm to the definition of the word 'officer' under the Companies Act, 1956.*

SCHEDULE 13—CURRENT LIABILITIES

Particulars	*Current Year (₹ '000)*	*Previous Year (₹ '000)*
1. Agents' Balances	......	......

2. Balances due to other insurance companies	......	......
3. Advances from Treaty Companies	......	......
4. Deposits held on re-insurance ceded	......	......
5. Premiums received in advance	......	......
6. Sundry creditors	......	......
7. Due to subsidiaries/holding company	......	......
8. Claims Outstanding	......	......
9. Annuities Due	......	......
10. Due to Officers/Directors	......	......
11. Others (to be specified)	......	......
Total	......	......

SCHEDULE 14—PROVISIONS

Particulars	*Current Year (₹ '000)*	*Previous Year (₹ '000)*
1. For taxation (less payments & taxes deducted at source)	......	......
2. For proposed dividends	......	......
3. For dividend distribution tax	......	......
4. Bonus payable to the Policy holders	......	......
5. Others (to be specified)	......	......
Total	......	......

SCHEDULE 15—MISCELLANEOUS EXPENDITURE

(To the extent not written off or adjusted)

Particulars	*Current Year (₹ '000)*	*Previous Year (₹ '000)*
1. Discount allowed on issue of Shares/Debentures	......	......
2. Others (to be specified)	......	......
Total	......	......

Notes:

(a) No item shall be included under the head "Miscellaneous Expenditure" and carried forward un*less:*

(i) *some benefit from the expenditure can reasonably be expected to be received in future, and*

(ii) *the amount of such benefit is reasonably determinable.*

ILLUSTRATION 9

From the following information, prepare the Balance Sheet of PCT Life Insurance Co. Ltd. as at 31st March, 2015:

Particulars	*₹ in Lakhs*
1. (a) Authorised Capital	200
(b) Share of ₹ 10 each, ₹ 5 called up and paid up	97

2.	(a)	Profit and Loss A/c Balance (Credit)	10
	(b)	General reserve	2
3.	(a)	Debentures	3
	(b)	Fixed Deposits	2
	(c)	Loans from Banks	5
	(d)	Policy Liabilities	9
4.	(a)	Investments—Share holders	
		Govt. Securities (Long-term)	5
		Mutual Funds (Short-term)	3
	(b)	Investments—Policy holders	
		Real Estate (Long-term)	6
		Derivative Instruments (Short-term)	4
5.	(a)	Loans to Companies (Non-Standard)	20
		(40% short-term)	
		[40% secured on Govt. Securities]	
	(b)	Loan to Banks (60% long-term) (Standard)	30
		[60% secured on mortgage of property]	
	(c)	Loans against policies (short-term) (non-Standard)	10
6.	(a)	Goodwill	5
	(b)	Land-Freehold	10
	(c)	Building	20
7.	(a)	Stamps	1
	(b)	Short-term Deposits with Bank	2
	(c)	Long-term Deposits with Bank	3
	(d)	Current Account Balance (credit)	4
	(e)	Money at call and short notice	5
8.	(a)	Application money for investments	2
	(b)	Prepaid Expenses	1
	(c)	Income accrued on Investments	1
	(d)	Outstanding Premium	2
	(e)	Agents Balance (Dr.)	3
	(f)	Due from other insurance companies	4
	(g)	Deposits with RBI	5
9.	(a)	Balances due to other insurance companies	2
	(b)	Premium received in advance	1
	(c)	Claim Outstanding	2
	(d)	Annuities Due	3
10.	(a)	Provision for Taxation	5
	(b)	Advance Tax	2
	(c)	Tax Deducted at Source (Dr.)	1

	(d) Proposed Dividend	3
	(e) Dividend Distribution Tax	0.50
	(f) Bonus Payable to Policy holders	5
11.	(a) Discount allowed on Issue of Shares and Debentures	1
	(b) Underwriting Commission on Issue of Shares and Debentures	0.50
12.	(a) There are nvestments in 5,00,000 shares of ₹ 10 each, ₹ 6 paid up	
	(b) Claims (other than against policies) not acknowledged as debts	3.00
13.	Rate of Depreciation on Building – 5%	

SOLUTION

BALANCE SHEET AS AT 31ST MARCH, 2015

Particulars	*Schedule*	*Current Year (₹ in lakhs)*	*Previous Year (₹ in lakhs)*
Sources of Funds:			
Shareholders' Funds:			
Share Capital	5		96.50
Reserve Surplus	6		12.00
Sub Total			108.50
Borrowings	7		10.0
Policies Liabilities			9.00
Total			127.50
Application of Funds:			
Investments:			
Share holders'	8		8
Policy holders'	8A		10
Loans:	9		60
Fixed Assets	10		34
Current Assets:			
Cash and Bank Balance	11	15.00	
Advances and Other Assets	12	18.00	
Sub Total (A)		33.00	
Current Liabilities:	13	8.00	
Provisions	14	10.50	
Sub Total (B)		18.50	
Net Current Assets (c) = A – B			14.50
Miscellaneous Expenditure	15		1.00
(To the extent not written off *or* adjusted)			
Total			127.50
Contingent Liabilities:			
Partly paid up investments			2.00

Claims (other than against policies) not acknowledged as debt			3.00
			5.00

SCHEDULE-5 SHARE CAPITAL

	Particulars	*Current Year (₹ in lakhs)*	*Previous Year (₹ in lakhs)*
1.	**Authorised Capital**		
	20,00,000 Shares of Ra 10 each	200	
2.	**Issued Capital**		
	19,40,000 shares of ₹ 10 each	194	
3.	**Subscribed Capital**		
	19,40,000 Shares of ₹ 10 each	194	
4.	**Called up Capital**		
	19,40,000 Shares of ₹ 10 each, ₹ 5 called up	97.0	
	Less: Underwriting Commission	0.5	
		96.5	

SCHEDULE-6 RESERVES AND SURPLUS

	Particulars	*Current Year (₹ in lakhs)*	*Previous Year (₹ in lakhs)*
1.	General Reserve	2	
2.	Balance of Profit in Profit and Loss A/c	10	
		12	

SCHEDULE-7 BORROWINGS

	Particulars	*Current Year (₹ in lakhs)*	*Previous Year (₹ in lakhs)*
1.	Debentures	3	
2.	Fixed Deposits	2	
3.	Loans from Banks	5	
		10	

SCHEDULE-8 INVESTMENTS-SHAREHOLDERS

	Particulars	*Current Year (₹ in lakhs)*	*Previous Year (₹ in lakhs)*
1.	**Long-term Investments**		
	Govt. Secuities	5	
2.	**Short-term Investments**		
	Mutual Funds	3	
		8	

SCHEDULE-8A INVESTMENTS-POLICYHOLDERS

Particulars	Current Year (₹ in lakhs)	Previous Year (₹ in lakhs)
1. Long-term Investments		
Real Estate	6	
2. Short-term Investments		
Derivative Instruments	4	
	10	

SCHEDULE-9 LOANS

Particulars	Current Year (₹ in lakhs)	Previous Year (₹ in lakhs)
1. Security-wise Classification		
Scured		
(a) On Mortage of Property [60% of 30]	18	
(b) On Govt. Securities [40% of 20]	8	
Unsecured		
(a) Loans against policies	10	
(b) Loans to Companies [60% of 20]	12	
(c) Loans to Banks [40% of 30]	12	
Total	60	
2. Borrower-wise Classifications		
(a) Loans to Banks	30	
(b) Loans to companies	20	
(c) Loans against policies	10	
	60	
3. Performance wise classification		
(a) Standard	30	
(b) Non-standard [20 + 10]	30	
Total	60	
4. Maturity-wise Classification		
(a) Short-term [8 + 12 + 10]	30	
(b) Long-term [12 + 18]	30	
Total	60	

SCHEDULE-10 FIXED ASSETS

Particulars	Gross Block [₹ in lakhs]	Depreciation [₹ in lakhs]	Net Block [₹ in lakhs]
1. Goodwill	5	—	5
2. Land	10	—	10

3. Building	20	1	19
			34

SCHEDULE-11 CASH AND BANK BALANCE

Particulars	*Current Year (₹ in lakhs)*	*Previous Year (₹ in lakhs)*
1. Cash (Stamps)	1	
2. Bank Balance		
(a) Deposit Acounts		
(i) Short-term	2	
(ii) Others	3	
(b) Current Accounts	4	
3. Money at call and Short Notice	5	
	15	

SCHEDULE-12 ADVANCES AND OTHER ASSETS

Particulars	*Current Year (₹ in lakhs)*	*Previous Year (₹ in lakhs)*
Advances:		
1. Application Money for Investments	2	
2. Prepaid Expenses	1	
Total (A)	3	
Other Assets:		
1. Income accrued on Investments	1	
2. Outstanding Pemium	2	
3. Agents' Balances (Dr.)	3	
4. Due from other Insurance Companies	4	
5. Deposis with RBI	5	
Total (B)	15	
Total [(A) + (B)]	18	

SCHEDULE-13 CURRENT LIABILITIES

Particulars	*Current Year (₹ in lakhs)*	*Previous Year (₹ in lakhs)*
1. Balances due to other Insurance Companies	2	
2. Premium received in advances	1	
3. Claims Outstanding	2	
4. Annuities Due	3	
	8	

SCHEDULE-14 PROVISIONS

Particulars	*Current Year (₹ in lakhs)*	*Previous Year (₹ in lakhs)*
1. Provision for Taxation (5-2-1)	2.00	
2. Proposed Dividend	3.00	
3. Dividend Distribution Tax	0.50	
4. Bonus Payable to Policy holders	5.00	
	10.50	

SCHEDULE-15 MISCELLANEOUS EXPENDITURE

Particulars	*Current Year (₹ in lakhs)*	*Previous Year (₹ in lakhs)*
Discount allowed on Issue of Shares and Debentures	1	
	1	

12 FINANCIAL STATEMENTS OF GENERAL INSURANCE COMPANIES

LEARNING OBJECTIVES

After studying this chapter, you should be able to understand:

- ◇ Meaning of General Insurance
- ◇ Fire Insurance
- ◇ Marine Insurance
- ◇ Preparation of Financial Statements By Gereral Insurer [IRDS Regulation 3]
- ◇ Format of Revenue Account
- ◇ Format of Profit & Loss Account
- ◇ Format of Balance Sheet
- ◇ Format of 15 Schedules forming part of financial statements.
- ◇ Provision for Unexpired Risks

1.0 MEANING OF GENERAL INSURANCE

General insurance means insurance other than life insurance. Section 2 (6B) of the Insurance Act defines 'General Insurance Business' as fire, marine *or* miscellaneous insurance business whether carried on singly *or* in combination with one *or* more of them.

Some common types of miscellaneous insurance in India are: exchange risk insurance, motor vehicle insurance, credit insurance, burglary insurance, workmen's compensation insurance, professional liability insurance, cash in transit insurance, fidelity insurance, etc.

An important feature of the general insurance policy is that the insured gets compensation only in case of loss sustained by him due to reasons specified in the policy.

Fire, marine and miscellaneous insurance business represents the type of contract under which, in return for premiums paid by the insured, the insurer undertakes to reimburse the insured for any loss *or* liability he may incur on the happening of an uncertain event. There are several types of policies issued for each class of business.

2.0 FIRE INSURANCE

MEANING OF FIRE INSURANCE

In a contract of fire insurance,the insurer undertakes to compensate the insured for the actual loss suffered due to the damage *or* destruction of property by fire subject to the maxmum limit of the sum insured. The insured is not allowed to make any profit out of this transaction.

AVERAGE CLAUSE UNDER FIRE INSURANCE

It may be noted that Fire Insurance Policies are always subject to Average Clause. Average clause is introduced to discourage under insurance. Average clause is applicable in case of under insurance (i.e., where the sum insured of policy is *less* than the value of the subject matter of the insurance). In such a case the actual claim is proportionately reduced as under:

ACTUAL CLAIM ACCODING TO AVERAGE CLAUSE IN CASE OF UNDER INSURANCE

$$\text{Claim} = \text{Actual loss} \times \frac{\text{Sum Insured}}{\text{Sum Insurable}}$$

The calculation of claim can be understood with the help of the following example:

Particulars	*Case I*	*Case II*	*Case III*	*Case IV*
A. Actual value of Property	1.00	1.00	1.00	1.00
B. Sum Insured	1.00	0.50	0.50	1.50
C. Actual Loss	0.50	0.60	0.40	1.00
D. Amount of Claim	0.50 [Being Actual Loss *or* Sum insured which-ever is lower]	.30 [60 × .50/1.00] **Note** Average Clause applies in case of under insurance	.20 [40 × .50/1.00] **Note** Average Clause applies in case of under insurance	1.00 **Note** Average Clause does not apply in case of over-insurance

CAN THE SAME PROPERTY BE GOT INSURED WITH DIFFERENT INSURERS?

Yes, the same property can be got insured with different insurers. In this case, all the insurers are jointly liable to bear the loss. But in no case, the total amount payable to the insured can exceed the amount of actual loss.

TYPES OF FIRE INSURANCE POLICIES

There are various types of fire insurance policies. The popular fire insurance policies are discussed as follows:

Types of Fire Insurance Policies	***Meaning***
1. Specific Policy	A policy in which the liability of the insurer is limited to a specified amount which is *less* than the value of the property insured.
2. Valued Policy	A policy in which the insuer agrees to pay a fixed amount in the event of loss irrespective of the actual loss suffered.
3. Floating Policy	A policy which is taken to insure the goods at different places and the quantity and value of which vary from time to time.
4. Replacement Policy	A policy in which an insurer has option to pay the loss in case *or* replace the property.
5. Loss of Profit Policy	A policy which protects the insured against loss of profit due to discloation of business because of fire.
6. Comprehensive Policy *or* Houeholders' Policy	A policy which provides a cover against risks of loss due to various causes such as fire, riots, strike, earthquake, flood, storm, burglary, electric fluctuations, urning and overflowing of water tanks *or* pipes.

DOUBLE INSURANCE

When more than one policy is taken to cover the same risk, it is called double insurance. Any person is free to insure her/his goods *or* property against fire *or* perils of the sea under more than one policy. But, in such cases, the insured cannot recover more than the insured value of peroperty from his insurers. All the insurers with whom she/he had insured will be liable to pay only a reteable proportion of the loss suffered by the insured.

Example A house worth ₹ 1,00,000 has been insued against fire under two policies, each for ₹ 1,00,000 and the house is destroyed by fire. The insured cannot claim ₹ 1,00,00 under each of the policies. Because, according to the principle of indemnity he cannot make a profit. If he is allowed a claim of ₹ 1,00,000 on each of the two policies, he will make a clear gain of ₹ 1,00,000. therefore, it is provided under law that in such case the insurer of each policy will pay him proportionately, e.g. the insured will receive ₹ 50,000 on one policy, and ₹ 50,000 on the other. In aggregate she/he gets ₹ 1,00,000 the amount of full compensation.

Note: The concept of double insurance explained above does not apply to life insurance. This is because of the unlimited extent of insuable interest in a human life.

3.0 MARINE INSURANCE

MEANING OF MARINE INSURANCE

In a contract of marine insurance, the insurer undertakes to compensate the insured in return for the premium for the actual loss suffered due to perils of the sea.

SUBJECT MATTER OF MARINE INSURANCE

Marine Insurance may be in respect of ship, cargo, feight *or* any other subject conectedwith a marine voyage. The three important types of marine insurance are:

1. **Ship Insurance** The ship owner takes the policy to cover the risk of loss *or* damage to the ship.
2. **Cargo Insurance** The cargo owner takes the policy to cover the risk of loss of *or* damage to the cargo.
3. **Freight Insurance** The transport company takes the policy to cover the risk of loss due to non-recovery of freight.

MARINE POLICY

The document which contains the terms and conditions, subject matters of insurance and the risks covered is called marine policy *or* sea policy.

UNDERWRITER

The insurer who agrees to insure is called underwriter.

TYPES OF MARINE INSURANCE POLICIES

There are various marine insurance policies. The popular marine insuance policies are discussed below:

Types of Marine Insurance Policies	*Meaning*
1. Voyage Policy	A policy which insures the subject matter for a specified voyage.
2. Time Policy	A policy which insures the subject matter for a specified period of time. (usually not exceeding a year)

3. Mixed Policy *or* Voyage cum Time Policy	A policy which insures the subject matter on a specified voyage for a specified period of time. For example, a ship may be insured for a yogage between Mumbai and U.S.A. for a period of 6 months.
4. Valued Policy	A policy in which the insurer agrees to pay a fixed amount agreed at the time of taking a policy, in the event of loss irrespective of the actual loss suffered.
5. Floating Poicy	A policy in which cargo owner gets the regular shipments of cargo automatically insured by making declaration about the value of cargo shipped. The total value of the policy goes on reducing by the amount of each declaration.
6. Fleet Policy	A policy which insures the ship when it is anchored in a port.
7. Port Policy	A policy which insures the ship when it is anchored in a port.

4.0 PREPARATION OF FINANCIAL STATEMENTS BY GENERAL INSURER [IRDA REGULATION 3]

An insurer carrying on general insurance business, after the commencement of IRDA Regulations, must comply with the requirements of Schedule B.

Provided that this sub-regulation shall apply, mutatis mutandis, to reinsures, until separate regulations are made.

SCHEDULE B IS DIVIDED INTO 5 PARTS AS FOLLOWS

Part I	Accounting Principles for preparation of financial statements
Part II	Disclosures forming part of Financial Statements
Part III	General Insruction for preparation of Financial Statements
Part IV	Contents of Management Report
Part V	Preparation of Financial Statements 1. Revenue Account in Form B-RA 2. Profit and Loss Account in Form B-PL 3. Balance Sheet in Form B-PL 4. Receipts and Payment Account as per Direct Method prescribed in AS 3-Cash Flow Statement issued by ICAI.

PART I OF SCHEDULE 'B'

Accounting principls for preparation of financial statements

1. **Applicability of Accounting Standards** Every Balance Sheet, Receipts and Payments Account [Cash Flow statement] and Profit and Loss Account [Shareholders' Account] of the insurer shall be in conformity with the Accounting Standards (AS) issued by the ICAI, to the extent applicable to the insurers carrying on general insurance business, except that:
   (i) Accounting Standard 3 (AS3)—Cash Flow Statements—Cash Flow Statement shall be prepared only under the direct Method.
   (ii) Accounting Standard 13 (AS13)—Accounting for Investments, shall not be applicable.
   (iii) Accounting Standard 17 (AS17)—Segment Reporting-shall apply irrespective of whether the securities of the insurer are traded publicly *or* not.
2. **Premium**
   (a) Premium shall be recognised as income over the contract period *or* the period of risk, whichever is appropriate.

(b) Unearned premium as well as pemium received in advance, both of which represent premium income not relating to the current accounting period, shall be disclosed separately in the financial statements.

(c) A reserve for Unearned Premium, may be created as the amount representing that part of the premium written which is attributable and to be allocated to the succeeding accounting periods.

(d) Premium Received in Advance, which represents premium received prior to the commencement of the risk, shall be shown separately under the head *'Current Liabilities'* in the financial statements.

(e) Unearned premium shall be shown separately under the head *'Current Liabilities'* and appropriate disclosures regarding management's basis of assessment shall be made in the financial statements.

(f) Premium received in advance shall not be included in the unearned pemium and shall be shown separately.

(g) Premium revenue recoginition is based on the pattern of risk to which the insuer is exposed.

(h) An insurer, based on past experience can eliably estimate the pattern of risk for a particular type of insuance business.

(i) Most insurers bring premium revenue to account on the basis of the passage of time. This is generally appropriate where the risk of events occurring that give rise to claims is more *or* less uniform throughout out the policy subject to any regulatory prescription in this regard.

(j) For some classes of insurance,it is usual for the premium to be adjusted as a result of events and information that becomes known during *or* after the policy period, e.g. marine cargo. Further, in some cases, risk pattern may not be evenly spread over the period of insurance because of the very nature of the risk covered e.g. some infrastructure projects involving varying degree of risk factors. A deposit premium is paid in such cases at the beginning of the policy period and subsequently adjusted.

(k) The basis of determination of pemium earned shall be adequately justified, preferably supported by external evidence such as by certification from an actuary and/or other technical experts. Adequate disclosure of such basis shall be made.

3. **Premium Deficiency:** Premium deficiency shall be recognised if the sum of expected claim costs, related expenses and maintenance costs exceeds related earned pemiums. For contracts exceeding four years, once a premium deficiency has occured, future changes to the liability shall be based on actuarial/technical evaluation.

4. **Acquisition Costs:** Acquisition costs, if any, shall be expensed in the period in which they are incurred.

   Acquisition costs are those costs that vary with, and are primarily related to, the acquisition of new and renewal insurance conracts. The most essential test is the obligatory relationship between costs and the execution of insurance contracts (i.e., commencement of risk).

5. **Claims**

(a) The components of the ultimate cost of claim to an insurer comprise the claims under policies and claims settlement costs. Claims under policies comprise the claims made for losses incurred, and those estimated *or* anticipated under the policies.

(b) A Liability for outstanding claims shall be brought to account in respect of both direct business and inward reinsurance business. The liability shall include:

   (i) Future payments in relation to unpaid reported claims;

   (ii) Claims Incurred But Not Reported (IBNR) including inadequate reserves (somtimes referred to as Claims Incurred But Not Enough Reported (IBNER)).

Which will result in future cash/asset out go for settling liabilities of those claims.

(c) Change in estimated liability represents the difference between the estimated liability for outstanding claims in respect of claims under policies whether due *or* intimated at the beginning and at the end of the financial period. The accounting estimate shall also include claims cost adjusted for estimated salvage value if there is sufficient degree of certainty of its realisation.

(d) **Actuarial Valuation of claim liability in some cases**

Estimate of claims made in respect of contracts exceeding four years shall be recognised on an actuarial basis, subject to regulations that may be prescribed by the Authority. In such cases, certificate from a recognised actuary as to the fairness of liability assessment must be obtained. Actuarial assumptions shall be suitably disclosed by way of notes to the account.

Necessary provision for unexpired risk shall be made subject to any minimum, statutorily required.

6. **Procedure to determine the value of investments** An insuer shall determine the values of invstments in the following manner:

(a) **Real Estate**—Investment Property—Investment Property shall be measured at historical cost *less* accumulated depreciation and impairment loss, residual value being considered zero and no revaluation being permissible.

The Insurer shall assess at each Balance Sheet date whether any impairment of the investment property has occurred.

An impairment loss shall be recognised as an expense in the Revenue/Profit and Loss Account immediaely.

Fair value as at the balance sheet date and the basis of its determination shall be disclosed in the financial statements as additional information.

(b) **Debt Securities**—Debt securities including government securities and redemable preference shares shall be considered as "held to maturity" securities and shall be measured at historical cost subject to amortisation.

(c) **Equity Securities and Derivative Instruments that are traded in active markets**—Listed equity securities and derivative instruments that are traded in active markets shall be measured at fair value as at the balance sheet date. For the purpose of calcultion of fair value, the lowest of the last quoted closing price of the stock exchanges where the securities are listed shall be taken.

The insurer shall assess on each balance sheet date whether any impairmnt of listed equity security(ies)/derivative(s) instrument has occurred.

An active market shall mean a market, where the securities traded are homogenous, availability of willing buyers and willing sellers is normal and the prices are publicly available.

Unrealised gains/losses arising due to changes in the fair value of listed equity shares and derivative instrumens shall be taken to equity under the head 'Fair Value Change Account' and on realisation reported in Profit and Loss Account. The 'Profit on sale of investments' *or* 'Loss on sale of investments', as the case may be, shall include accumulated changes in the fair value previously recognised in equity under the heading Fair Value Change Account in respect of a particular security and being recycled to Profit and Loss Account on actual sale of that listed security.

For the removal of doubt, it is clarified that balance *or* any part there of shall not be available for distribution as dividends. Also, any debit balance in the said Fair Value Change Account shall be reduced from the Profit/free reserves while declaring dividends.

The insurer shall assess, at each balance sheet date, whether any impairment has occurred. An impairment loss shall be recognised as an expense in Revenue/Profit and Loss Account to the extent of the difference between the remeasured fair value of the security/investment and its acquisition cost as reduced by any previous impairment loss recognised as expense in Revenue/Profit and Loss Account. Any reversal of impairment loss, earlier recognised in Revenue/Profit and Loss Account shall be recognised in Revenue/Profit and Loss Account.

(d) **Unlisted and other than actively traded Equity Securities and Derivative Insruments—** Unlisted equity securities and derivative instrumens and listed equity securities and derivative instruments that are not regularly traded in active market will be measured at historical costs. Provision shall be made for diminution in value of such invstments. The provision so made shall be reversed in subsequent period if estmates based on external evidence show an increase in the value of the invesment over its carrying amount. The increased carrying amount of the investment due to the reversal of the provision shall not exceed the histoical cost.

For the purposes of this regulation, a security shall be considered as being not actively trade, if its trading volume does not exceed 10,000 units in any trading session during the last twelve months.

7. **Loans** Loans shall be measured at historical cost subject to impairment provisions. the insurer shall assess the quality of its loan assets and shall provide for impairment. The impairment provision shall not be *less* than the aggregate amount of loans which are subject to defaults of the nature mentioned below:

   (i) interest remaining unpaid for over a period of 6 months; and

   (ii) instalment(s) of loan falling due and remaining unpaid during the last 6 months.

8. **Catastrophe Reserve** Catastrophe reserve shall be created in accordance with norms, if any, prescribed by the Authority. Investment of funds out of catastrophe reserve shall be made in accordance with prescription of the Authority.

   It is clarified that this reserve is towards meeting losses which might arise due to an entirely unexpected set of events and not for any specific known purpose. This reserve is in the nature of an amount set aside for the potential future liability against the insurance policies in force.

PART II OF SCHEDULE 'B': DISCLOSURES FORMING PART OF FINANCIAL STATEMENTS

A. The following shall be disclosed by way of notes to the Balance Sheet

1. **Contingent Liabilities**
   (a) Partly-paid up investments
   (b) Underwriting commitments outstanding
   (c) Claims, other than those under policies, not acknowledged as debts
   (d) Guarantees given by *or* on behalf of the company
   (e) Statutory demands/liabilitis in dispute not provided for
   (f) Reinsuance obligations
   (g) Others (to be specified).
2. Encumberances to assets of the company in and outside India.
3. Commitments made and outstanding for Loans, Investmens and Fixed Assets.
4. Claims, *less* reinsurance, paid to claimants in/outside India.
5. Actuarial assumptions for claim liabilities in he case of policies exceeding four years.
6. Ageing of claims distinguishing between claims outstanding for more than six months and other claims.

7. Premiums, *less* reinsurance, written from business in/outside India.
8. Exent of premium income ecognised, based on varying risk pattern, category wise, with basis and justification there for, including whether reliance has been placed on external evidence.
9. Value of contracts in relation to investments, for
   (a) Purchases where deliveries are pending;
   (b) Sales where payments are over due.
10. Operating expenses relating to insurance business: basis of allocation of expenditue to arious classes of businss.
11. Historical costs of those investments valued on fair value basis.
12. Computation of managerial remuneration.
13. Basis of amortisation of debt securities.
14. (a) Unrealised gain/losses arising dur to changes in the fair value of lised equity shares and derivative instrments are to be taken to equity under the head 'Fair Value Change Accont' and on realisation reported in Profit and Loss Account.
    (b) Pending realisation, the credit balance in the 'Fair Value Change Account' is not available for distribution.
15. Fair value of investmen property and the basis therefor.
16. Claims settled and remaining outstanding for a period of more than 6 months on he balance sheet date.

B. The following accounting policies shall form an integral part of the financial statements

1. All significant accounting policies in erms of the accounting standards issued by the ICAI, and significant principles and policies given in Part I of Accounting Principles. Any other accounting policies followed by the insurer shall be stated in the manner required under Accounting Standard AS 1 issued by ICAI.
2. Any departure from the accounting policies as aforesaid shall be separately disclosed with reasons for such departure.

C. The following information shall also be disclosed:

1. Investments made in accordance with any statutory requirement should be disclosed separately together with its amount, nature, security and any special rights in and outside India.
2. Segregation into performing/non performin instmens for purpose of income recognition as per the directions, if any, issued by the Authority.
3. Percentage of business sector-wise
4. A summary of financial statements for the last 5 years, in the manner as may be prescribed by the Authority.
5. Accounting Ration as may be prescribed by the Authority.
6. Basis of allocation of Interest, Dividends and Rent between Revenue Account and Profit and Loss Account.

PART III OF SCHEDULE 'B'

General Insructions for Preparation of Financial Statements

1. The corresponding amounts for the immediately preceding financial year for all items shown in the Balance Sheet, Revenue Account and Profit and Loss Account should be given.
2. The figures in the financial statements may be rounded off to the nearest thousands.

3. Interest, dividends and rentals receivable in connection with an investment should be stated as gross value, the amount of income tax deducted at source being included under 'advance taxes paid'.
4. Income from rent shall not include any notional rent.
5. I. For the purposes of financial statements, unless the context oherwise requires.
   (a) The expression **'provision'** shall, subject to note II below mean nay amount written off *or* retained by way of providing for depreciation, renewals *or* diminution in value of assets, *or* retained by was of providing for any known liability *or* loss of which the amount cannot be determined with substantial accuracy;
   (b) The expression **"reserve"** shall not, subject *or* as aforesaid, include any amount written off *or* retained by way of providing for depreciation, renewals *or* diminution in value of assets *or* retained by way of providing for any known liability;
   (c) The expression **'capital reserve'** shall not include any amount regarded as free for distribution through the Profit and Loss Account; and the expression "revenue reserve" shall mean any reserve other than a capital reserve;
   (d) The expression **"liability"** shall include all liability in respect of expenditure contracted for and all disputed *or* contingent liabilitis.

   II. Where:
   (a) any amount written off *or* retaind by way of providing for depreciation, enewals *or* diminution in value of assets, or
   (b) any amount retained by way of providing for any known liability is in excess of the amount which in the opinion of the directors is reasonably necessary for the purpose, the excess shall be treated for the purposes of these accouns as a reserve and not as a provision.
6. The company should make povisions for damages under lawsuits where the management is of the opinion that the award may go against the insurer.
7. Risks assumed in excess of the statutory provisions, if any, shall be separately disclosed indicating the amount of premiums involved and the amount of risks covered. The auditor shall, however, make an appropriate qualification in this regard in his repot.
8. Any debit balance of Profit and Loss account shall be shown as deduction from uncommitted eserves and the balance if any, shall be shown separately.

PART IV OF SCHEDULE 'B': CONTENS OF MANAGEMENT REPORT

There shall be attached to the financial statements, a management repot containing, *inter alia*, the following duly authenticated by the management

1. Confirmation regarding the continued validity fo the registration granted by the Authority;
2. Certification that all the dues payable to the statutory authoriies have been duly paid;
3. Confirmation to the effect that the shareholding pattern and any transferof shares duringthe year are in accordance with the statutory *or* regulatory requirements;
4. Declaration that the management has not directly *or* indirectly invested outside India the funs of the holders of policies sissued in India;
5. Confirmation that the required solency margins have beenmaintained;
6. Certification to the effect that the value of all the assets have been reviewed on the date of the Balance Sheet and that in his (insurer's) belief the assets set forth in the Balancesheets are shown in the aggregate at amounts not exceeding their realisable *or* market value under the several headings "Loans", "Investmens", "Agents balances", "Outstanding Premiums", "Interest, dividends and Rents outstanding", "Interest, Dividens and Rents accruing but not due", "Amount due from other persons *or* Bodies carryign on insurance business", "Sundry Debtors", "Blls Receivable", "Cash" and the several items specified under "Other Accounts".

7. Certification to the efect that no part of the lie insurance fund has been directly *or* indirectly applied in contravention of the provisions ofthe Insurance Act, 1938 (4 of 1938), relating to the application and investment of the life insurance funds;
8. Disclosue with regard to the overall risk exposure and strategy adopted to mitigate the same;
9. Operations in other countris, if any, with a separate statement giving the managemen's estimate of country risk and exposure risk and the hedging strategy adopted;
10. Ageing of claims indicating the trends in average claim settlement time during the preceding five years;
11. Certification to the effect as to how the value, as shown in the balance sheet, o the investments and stocks and shares have been arrived at, and how the market value there of has been ascertained for the purpose of comparision with the values so shown;
12. Review of asset quality and performance of investment in terms of portfolios, i.e., separately in terms of real estate, loans, investments, etc.
13. A Responsibility statement indicating there in that:
    (i) in thepreparation of fiancial statements, the applicable accounting standards, picniples and policies have beenfollowed along with proper explanations relatin to material departues, if any;
    (ii) the management has adopted accounting policies and applied them consistently and made judgements and estimates that reasnable and prodent so as to give a true and fair view of the state of affairs of the company at the end of the financial year ando the operating profit *or* loss of the company for theyear;
    (iii) the management has taken proper and suficient care the maintenance of adequate accounting records in accordance with the applicable provisions of the Insurance Act, 1938 (4 of 1938)/companies Act, 1956 (1 of 1956), for safeguarding the assets o the company and for preventing and detectin fraud and other irregularities;
    (iv) the management has prepared the financial statemens on a going concern basis;
    (v) the management has ensued that an internal audit system commensurate with the size and nature of the business exists and is operating effectively.

PART V OF SCHEDULE 'B': PREPARATION OF FINANCIAL STATEMENTS

1. An insurer shall prepare the Revenue Account, Profit and Loss Account [Shareholders' Account] and the Balance Sheet in Form B-RA, Form B-PL, and Form B-BS, *or* as near there to as the circumstances permit.

   Provided that an insuer shall prepare ?Revenue Account separately for fire, marine, and miscellaneous insuranc business.
2. An insurer shall prepare separate eceivpts an Payments Account in accordance with the Direct Method prescribed in AS 3-"Cash Fow Statement" issued by the ICAI.

5.0 PRACTICAL STEPS INVOLVED IN THE CALCULATION AND DISCLOSURE OF PREMIUM EARNED (NET)

Step 1: *Calculate Premium earned on Direct Business and Re-insurance accepted as follows:*

	Particulars	*Direct Business (₹ '000)*	*Re-Insurance accepted (₹ '000)*
A.	Received	xxx	xxx
B.	*Add:* Receivable at the end of the year	xxx	xxx

C. *Less:* Receivable in the beginning of the year	(xxx)	(xxx)
D. Total (A + B – C)	xxx	xxx

Step 2: *Calculate Premium incurred on Re-insurance business Ceded as follows:*

Particulars	*Re-Insurance Ceded (₹ '000)*
A. Paid during the year	xxx
B. *Add:* Payable at the end of the year	xxx
C. *Less:* Payable in the beginning of the year	(xxx)
D. Total (A + B – C)	xxx

Step 3: *Disclose the Premium items in Revenue Account and Schedule as follows:*

FIRE/MARINE/MISC. INSURANCE REVENUE ACCOUNT FOR THE YEAR ENDED...

Particulars	*Schedule*	*Current Year (₹ '000)*	*Previous Year (₹ '000)*
Premium earned (net)	1	xxx	xxx

SCHEDULE 1 PREMIUM EARNED (NET)

Particulars	*Current (₹ '000)*	*Previous (₹ '000)*
Premium on direct business written	xxx	xxx
Add: Premium on Re-insurance accepted	xxx	xxx
Less: Premium on Re-insurance ceded	(xxx)	(xxx)
Net Premium	xxx	xxx
Premium Income from business written:		
In India	xxx	xxx
Outside India	xxx	xxx
	xxx	xxx

ILLUSTRATION 1

From the following information of Tulsian Fire Insurance Company for the year ended 31st March 2015, Calculate the Net Premium earned and Reserve for Unexpired Risk which is to be maintained @ 40%. Additional Reserve is to be maintained @ 5%. The balance of Reserve for Unexpired Risk as on 01.04.2014 was ₹ 31,95,000 (including Additional Reserve ₹ 3,55,000)

Particulars	*Direct Business (₹)*	*Reinsurance (₹)*
Premium received	75,25,000	8,25,000
Premium Receivable as on 01.04.2014	3,25,000	2,00,000
Premium Receivable as on 31.03.2015	5,00,000	3,75,000
Premium Paid		4,90,000
Premium Payable as on 01.04.2014		1,00,000
Premium payable as on 31.03.2015		4,50,000

SOLUTION

SCHEDULE 1 – PREMUM EARNED (NET)

Particulars	*This Yr*
Premiums from Direct Business written (75,25,000 + 5,00,000 – 3,25,000)	77,00,000
Add: Premium on Re-Insurance accepted (8,25,000 + 3,75,000 – 2,00,000)	10,00,000
Less: Premium on Re-Insurance ceded (4,90,000 + 4,50,000 – 1,00,000)	(8,40,000)
Total Premium Earned (Net)	78,60,000
Less: Adjustment for change in Unexpired Risk Reserve (Note)	(3,42,000)
Total Premium Earned (Net)	75,18,000

Note: Adjustment for Changes in Reserve for Unexpired Risks is computed as under:

Particulars	*Reserve*
Closing balance required [(40% of 78,60,000) + (5% of 78,60,000)]	35,37,000
Less: Opening Balance available(28,40,000 + 3,55,000)	31,95,000
Amt to be transferred to Reserve for the year	3,42,000

6.0 PRACTICAL STEPS INVOLVED IN THE CALCULATION AND DISCLOSURE OF CLAIMS INCURRED (NET)

Step 1: *Calculate Claims incurred on Direct Business and Re-insurance Business accepted as follows:*

Particulars	*Direct Business (₹ '000)*	*Re-Insurance Business accepted (₹ '000)*
A. Paid	xxx	xxx
B. *Add:* Outstanding at the end	xxx	xxx
C. *Add:* Expenses in connection with settlement of claim	xxx	xxx
D. *Less:* Outstanding at the beginning	(xxx)	(xxx)
E. Claims incurred [A + B + C – D]	xxx	xxx

Step 2: *Calculate Claims earned on Re-insurance Business ceded as follows:*

Particulars	*Re-Insurance Ceded (₹ '000)*
A. Received	xxx
B. *Add:* Recoverable at the end	xxx
C. *Less:* Recoverable at the beginning	(xxx)
D. Claims earned [A + B – C]	xxx

Step 3: *Disclose the Claims Items In Revenue Account and Schedule 2 as follows:*

FIRE/MARINE/MISC. INSURANCE REVENUE ACCOUNT FOR THE YEAR ENDED....

Particulars	*Schedule*	*Current Year (₹ '000)*	*Previous Year (₹ '000)*
Claims Incurred (Net)	2	xxx	xxx

SCHEDULE 2 CLAIMS INCURRED (NET)

Particulars	*Current Year (₹ '000)*	*Previous Year (₹ '000)*
Claims on Direct Business	xxx	xxx
Add: Claims on Reinsurance accepted	xxx	xxx
Less: Claims on Reinsurance ceded	(xxx)	(xxx)
Total Claims incurred	xxx	xxx
Claims paid to claiments:		
In India	xxx	xxx
Outside India	xxx	xxx
	xxx	xxx

ILLUSTRATION 2

From the following information of Tulsian Fire Insurance Company for the year ended 31st March 2015, Calculate the Net Claims Incurred:

Particulars		*Direct Business (₹)*	*Reinsurance (₹)*
Claims Paid during the Year		49,70,000	5,10,000
Claims Payable:	1st April 2014	6,85,000	95,000
	31st March 2015	7,38,000	70,000
Claims Received		–	3,95,000
Claims Receivable:	1st April 2014	–	75,000
	31st March 2015	–	1,25,000
Surveyor's Fees		45,000	
Legal Expenses		55,000	

ANSWER:

SCHEDULE 2 – CLAIMS PAID (NET)

Particulars	This Yr
Claims Paid – Direct (49,70,000 + 7,38,000 – 6,85,000)	50,23,000
Add: Claims on Re-Insurance accepted (5,10,000 + 70,000 – 95,000)	4,85,000
Less: Claims on Re-Insurance Ceded (3,95,000 + 1,25,000 – 75,000)	(4,45,000)
Add: Surveyor's Fees	45,000
Add: Legal Expenses	55,000
Total claims Incurred	51,63,000

7.0 PRACTICAL STEPS INVOLVED IN THE CALCULATION & DISCLOSURE OF COMMISSION INCURRED (NET)

Step 1: *Calculate Commission incurred on Direct Business and Re-insurance business accepted as follows:*

Particulars	*Direct Business (₹ '000)*	*Re-Insurance (₹ '000)*
A. Paid	xxx	xxx
B. *Add:* Payable at the end	xxx	xxx
C. *Less:* Payable in the beginning	(xxx)	(xxx)
D. Total [A + B – C]	xxx	xxx

Step 2: *Calculate Commission learned on Re-insurance Business ceded as follows:*

Particulars	*Direct Business (₹ '000)*	*Re-Insurance Ceded (₹ '000)*
A. Received during the year	xxx	xxx
B. *Add:* Recoverable at the end	xxx	xxx
C. *Less:* Recoverable at the beginning	(xxx)	(xxx)
D. Total [A + B – C]	xxx	xxx

Step 3: *Disclose the Commission In Revenue Account and Schedule 3 as follows:*

FIRE/MARINE/MISC. INSURANCE REVENUE ACCOUNT FOR THE YEAR ENDED....

Particulars	*Schedule*	*Current Year (₹ '000)*	*Previous Year (₹ '000)*
Commission	3	xxx	xxx

SCHEDULE 3 COMMISSION

Particulars	*Current Year (₹ '000)*	*Previous Year (₹ '000)*
A. Commission on Direct Business	xxx	xxx
B. *Add:* Commission on Re-insurance Accepted	xxx	xxx
C. *Less:* Commission on Reinsurance ceded	(xxx)	(xxx)
D. Net Commission	xxx	xxx

ILLUSTRATION 3

From the following information of Tulsian Fire Insurance Company for the year ended 31st March 2015, Calculate the Net Commission earned:

Particulars		Direct Business (₹)	Reinsurance (₹)
Commission received on Insurance Accepted		1,60,000	15,000
Commission Receivable:	1st April 2014	10,000	5,000
	31st March 2015	30,000	15,000
Commission paid on Insurance Ceded		–	46,000
Commission Payable:	1st April 2014		3,000
	31st March 2015		5,000

SOLUTION

SCHEDULE 3 – COMMISSION

Particulars	*This Yr*
Commision paid: Direct [1,60,000 + 30,000 – 10,000]	1,80,000
Add: Commission on Re-Insurance accepted [15,000 + 15,000 – 5,000]	25,000
Less: Commission on Re-Insurance ceded [46,000 + 5,000 – 3,000]	(48,000)
Net Commission	1,57,000

8.0 PROVISION FOR UNEXPIRED RISKS

<table>
<tr><td rowspan="1">1. Meaning</td><td colspan="2">Provision for Unexpired Risks is a provision created to meet the claims which may arise in respect of the policies which remain unexpired at the end of the year.</td></tr>
<tr><td rowspan="4">2. Minimum Reserve to be kept</td><td>Types of General Insurance Business</td><td>% of Net Premium</td></tr>
<tr><td>I. Marine Hull Insurance</td><td>100%</td></tr>
<tr><td>II. Fire, Marine Cargo and Misc. Insurance</td><td>40%</td></tr>
<tr><td colspan="2">However, the income tax authorities allow 100% of the net premium in case of marine insurance and 50% of the net premium in case of other insurance.
Since there is no bar on creating such reserve at a percentage higher than those laid down by the Executive Committee, the Company may maintain such reserve at a higher percentage. The excess reserve over the minimum reserve is termed as 'Additional Reserve'.
Tutorial Note: Unless otherwise stated, the same % of additional reserve as at the beginning of the year, should be maintained at the close of the year.</td></tr>
<tr><td>3. Accounting Treatment</td><td colspan="2">1. The difference between the aggregate amount of minimum provision and additional provision in the beginning and aggregate amount there of at the end is disclosed as 'Adjustment for Change in Provision for Unexpired Risks' in Schedule 1: Premium Earned.
2. Balance of Minimum provision and additional provision of unexpired risks is shown on the liabilities side of Balance Sheet.</td></tr>
</table>

ILLUSTRATION 4

PCT General Insurance Co. Ltd. provides you the following information:

Particulars	*Fire (₹ '000)*	*Marine (₹ '000)*
Premium on Direct Business	30	60
Premium on Re-insurance ceded	10	20
Premium on Re-insurance accepted	20	40
Provision for unexpired Risks (as on 1.4.2014)	10	20
Additional Provision for Unexpired Risks (as on 1.4.2014)	1	—

Required: How will you show the above items in Revenue Account for the year ended 31st March 2015?

SOLUTION

FIRE INSURANCE REVENUE ACCOUNT FOR THE YEAR ENDED 31ST MARCH, 2015

Particulars	*Schedule*	*Current Year (₹ '000)*	*Previous Year (₹ '000)*
1. Premium earned (Net)	1	29	

SCHEDULE 1 PREMIUM EARNED (NET)

Particulars	*Current Year (₹ '000)*	*Previous Year (₹ '000)*
Premium for Direct Business	30	
Add: Premium on Re-insurance accepted	20	
Less: Premium on Re-insurance ceded	(10)	
	40	
Less: Adjustment for Change in Provision for Unexpired Risks	(11)	
	29	

Note: The solution with minimum provision @40 of net premium is also not incorrect. But it is appropriate to create provision @50% of net premium because every prudent company would like to take minimum tax advantage by creative the maximum provision (i.e., 50% of Net Premium) permissible under the Income Tax Act, 1961.

MARINE INSURANCE REVENUE ACCOUNT FOR THE YEAR ENDED 31ST MARCH, 2015

Particulars	*Schedule*	*Current Year (₹ '000)*	*Previous Year (₹ '000)*
1. Premium earned (Net)	1	20	

SCHEDULE 1 PREMIUM EARNED (NET)

Particulars	*Current Year (₹ '000)*	*Previous Year (₹ '000)*
Premium on Direct Business	60	
Add: Premium on Re-insurance accepted	40	
Less: Premium on Re-insurance ceded	(20)	
	80	
Less: Adjustment for Change in Provision for Unexpired Risks	(60)	
	20	

Working Note:

CHANGE IN PROVISION FOR UNEXPIRED RISKS

Particulars	*Fire (₹ '000)*	*Marine (₹ '000)*
A. Closing Provision for Unexpired Risks		

(i) Minimum Provision @50% of ₹ 40,00,00	20	80
(ii) Additional Provision @5% of ₹ 40,00,000	2	—
	22	80
B. *Less:* Opening Provision for Unexpired Risks		
(i) Minimum Provision	10	20
(ii) Additional Provision	1	—
	11	20
C. Change in Provision for Unexpired Risk [A – B]	11	60

9.0 FORMAT OF REVENUE ACCOUNT

FORM B-RA

Name of the Insurer: _ _ _ _ _ _ _ _ _.
Registration No. and Date of Registration with the IRDA _ _ _ _ _ _ _ _

REVENUE ACCOUNT FOR THE YEAR ENDED 31ST MARCH, 20____

(To be prepared separately for Fire, Marine, and Miscellaneous Insurance)

Particulars	*Schedule*	*Current Year (₹ '000)*	*Previous Year (₹ '000)*
1. Premiums earned (Net)	1		
2. Others (to be specified)			
3. Interest, Dividend and Rent-Gross			
Total (A)			
1. Claims Incurred (Net)	2		
2. Commission	3		
3. Operating Expenses related to Insurance Business	4		
4. Others-To be specified			
Total (B)			
Operating Profit/(Loss) from Fire/Marine/Miscellaneous Business (A–B)			

SCHEDULES FORMING PART OF REVENUE ACCOUNT

SCHEDULE - 1 PREMIUM EARNED [NET]

Particulars	*Current Year (₹ '000)*	*Previous Year (₹ '000)*
Premium from direct business written		
Add: Premium on reinsurance accepted		
Less: Premium on reinsurance ceded		

Net Premium		
Ajustment for changes in unearned Premium		
Adjustment for changes in premium received in advance		
Total Premium Earned (Net)		
Less: Adjustment for Change in Provision for Unexpired Risks		
Premium Income from business effected:		
In India		
Outside India		
Total Premium Earned (Net)		

Notes:

(a) *In case of premiums less reinsurance, in respect of any segment of insurance business exceeds 10 per cent of total premium earned, the same shall be disclosed separately.*

(b) *Reinsurance premiums whether on business ceded or accepted are to be brought into account, before deducting commission, under the head of reinsurance pemiums.*

SCHEDULE - 2 CLAIMS INCURRED [NET]

Particulars	*Current Year (₹ '000)*	*Previous Year (₹ '000)*
Claim paid		
Direct		
Add: Re-insurance accepted		
Less: Re-insurance Ceded		
Net Claims paid		
Total Claims Incurred		
Claims paid to claimants		
In India		
Outside India		
Total Claims Incurred		

Notes:

(a) Incurred But Not Reported (IBNR), Incurred but not enough reported [IBNER] claims should be included in the amount for claims.

(b) Claims include claims settlement costs.

(c) The surveyor fees, legal and other expenses shall also form part of claims cost.

(d) Claims cost should be adjusted for estimated salvage value if there is a sufficient certainty of its realisation.

SCHEDULE - 3 COMMISSION

Particulars	*Current Year (₹ '000)*	*Previous Year (₹ '000)*
Commission paid		
Direct		
Add: Re-insurance accepted		

Less: Commission on Re-Insurance Ceded		
Net Commission paid		

Note: *The profit/commission, if any, are to be combined with the Re-insuance accepted or Re-insurance ceded figures.*

SCHEDULE - 4 OPERATING EXPENSES RELATED TO INSURANCE BUSINESS

Particulars	*Current Year (₹ '000)*	*Previous Year (₹ '000)*
1. Employees' remuneration & welfare benefits		
2. Managerial Remuneration		
3. Travel, Conveyance & vehicle running expenses		
4. Rents, rates & taxes		
5. Repairs		
6. Printing & stationery		
7. Communication expenses		
8. Legal & professional charges		
9. Medical fees		
10. Auditors' fees, expenses etc.		
(a) as auditor		
(b) as adviser *or* in any other capacity, in respect of		
(i) Taxation matters		
(ii) Insurance matters		
(iii) Management services; and		
(c) in any other capacity		
11. Advertisement and publicity		
12. Interest & Bank Charges		
13. Others (to be specified)		
14. Depreciation		
Total		

Notes:

(a) *Items of expenes in excess of one percent of net premium or ₹ 5,00,000 whichever is higher, shall be shown as a separate line item.*

(b) *Under the sub-head "Others", 'Operating Expenses (Insurance Business)' shall include items like foreign exchange gains or losses and other items.*

ILLUSTRATION 5

Tulsian Fire Insurance Company submits the following information for the year ended 31st march 2015:

Particulars	*Direct Business (₹)*	*Reinsurance (₹)*
Premium received	77,00,000	10,00,000
Premium Paid		8,40,000

Claims Paid during the Year	50,23,000	4,85,000
Claims Received		4,45,000
Expenses of Management	2,90,000	–
Commission: On Insurance Accepted	1,60,000	15,000
On Insurance Ceded	–	18,000

The aollowing additional information are also available:

(i) Expenses of Management include ₹ 45,000 Surveyor's Fees and ₹ 55,000. Legal Expenses for settlement of claims.

(ii) Reserve for Unexpired Risk is to be maintained @ 40%. Additional Reserve is to be maintained @ 5%. The balance of Reserve for Unexpired Risk as on 01.04.2014 was ₹ 31,95,000 (including Additional Reserve ₹ 3,55,000)

(iii) Interest, Dividend & Rent Received (after TDS @ 10%) ₹ 34,200

You are required to make the Revenue Account for the year ended 31st March 2015.

SOLUTION

FROM–B–RA–REVENUE ACCOUNT OF TULSIAN FIRE INSURANCE CO. LTD

for the year ending 31st March 2015

Particulars	*Sch.*	*Current Yr*	*Previous Yr*
Premium Earned (Net)	1	75,18,000	
Interest, Dividend & Rent (Gross) (₹ 34,200 × 100/90)		38,000	
Total (A)		75,56,000	
1. Claims Incurred (Net)	2	51,63,000	
2. Commission	3	1,57,000	
3. Operating Expenses related to Insurance Business	4		
(2,90,000 – Legal Exps 55,000 – Surveyor Fees 45,000)		1,90,000	
Total (B)		55,10,000	
Operating Profit/(Loss) from Insurance Business (A – B)		20,46,000	
Appropriations		NIL	
Total (C)		20,46,000	

SCHEDULE 1 – PREMUM EARNED (NET)

Particulars	*This Yr*
Premiums from Direct Business written	77,00,000
Add: Premium on Re-Insurance accepted	10,00,000
Less: Premium on Re-Insurance ceded	(8,40,000)
Total Premium Earned (Net)	78,60,000
Less: Adjustment for change in Unexpired Risk Reserve (Note)	(3,42,000)
Total Premium Earned (Net)	75,18,000

Note: Adjustment for Changes in Reserve for Unexpired Risks is computed as under:

Particulars	Reserve
Closing balance required [(40% of 78,60,000) + (5% of 78,60,000)]	35,37,000
Less: Opening Balance available (28,40,000 + 3,55,000)	31,95,000
Amt to be transferred to Reserve for the year	3,42,000

SCHEDULE 2 – CLAIMS PAID (NET)

Particulars	This Yr
Claims Paid – Direct	50,23,000
Add: Claims on Re-Insurance accepted	4,85,000
Less: Claims on Re-Insurance Ceded	(4,45,000)
Add: Surveyor's Fees	45,000
Add: Legal Expenses	55,000
Total claims Incurred	51,63,000

SCHEDULE 3 – COMMISSION

Particulars	This Yr
Commision paid: Direct	1,60,000
Add: Commission on Re-Insurance accepted	15,000
Less: Commission on Re-Insurance ceded	(18,000)
Net Commission	1,57,000

ILLUSTRATION 6

Tulsian Fire Insurance Company submits the following information for the year ended 31st march 2015:

Particulars		*Direct Business (₹)*	*Reinsurance (₹)*
Premium received		75,25,000	8,25,000
Premium Receivable as on 01.04.2014		3,25,000	2,00,000
Premium Receivable as on 31.03.2015		5,00,000	3,75,000
Premium Paid			4,90,000
Premium Payable as on 01.04.2014			1,00,000
Premium payable as on 31.03.2015			4,50,000
Claims Paid during the Year		49,70,000	5,10,000
Claims Payable:	1st April 2014	6,85,000	95,000
	31st March 2015	7,38,000	70,000
Claims Received		–	3,95,000
Claims Receivable:	1st April 2014	–	75,000
	31st March 2015	–	1,25,000
Expenses of Management		2,90,000	–
Commission:	On Insurance Accepted	1,60,000	15,000
	On Insurance Ceded	–	18,000

The aollowing additional information are also available:

(i) Expenses of Management include ₹ 45,000 Surveyor's Fees and ₹ 55,000. Legal Expenses for settlement of claims.

(ii) Reserve for Unexpired Risk is to be maintained @ 40%. Additional Reserve is to be maintained @ 5%. The balance of Reserve for Unexpired Risk as on 01.04.2014 was ₹ 31,95,000 (including Additional Reserve ₹ 3,55,000)

(iii) Interest, Dividend & Rent Received (after TDS @ 10%) ₹ 34,200

You are required to make the Revenue Account for the year ended 31st March 2015.

SOLUTION

FROM–B–RA–REVENUE ACCOUNT OF TULSIAN FIRE INSURANCE CO. LTD

for the year ending 31st March 2015

Particulars	*Sch.*	*Current Yr*	*Previous Yr*
Premium Earned (Net)	1	75,18,000	
Interest, Dividend & Rent (Gross) (₹ 34,200 × 100/90)		38,000	
Total (A)		75,56,000	
1. Claims Incurred (Net)	2	51,63,000	
2. Commission	3	1,57,000	
3. Operating Expenses related to Insurance Business	4		
(2,90,000 – Legal Exps 55,000 – Surveyor Fees 45,000)		1,90,000	
Total (B)		55,10,000	
Operating Profit/(Loss) from Insurance Business (A – B)		20,46,000	
Appropriations		NIL	
Total (C)		20,46,000	

SCHEDULE 1 – PREMUM EARNED (NET)

Particulars	*This Yr*
Premiums from Direct Business written (75,25,000 + 5,00,000 – 3,25,000)	77,00,000
Add: Premium on Re-Insurance accepted (8,25,000 + 3,75,000 – 2,00,000)	10,00,000
Less: Premium on Re-Insurance ceded (4,90,000 + 4,50,000 – 1,00,000)	(8,40,000)
Total Premium Earned (Net)	78,60,000
Less: Adjustment for change in Unexpired Risk Reserve (Note)	(3,42,000)
Total Premium Earned (Net)	75,18,000

Note: Adjustment for Changes in Reserve for Unexpired Risks is computed as under:

Particulars	*Reserve*
Closing balance required [(40% of 78,60,000) + (5% of 78,60,000)]	35,37,000
Less: Opening Balance available(28,40,000 + 3,55,000)	31,95,000
Amt to be transferred to Reserve for the year	3,42,000

SCHEDULE 2 – CLAIMS PAID (NET)

Particulars	*This Yr*
Claims Paid – Direct (49,70,000 + 7,38,000 – 6,85,000)	50,23,000
Add: Claims on Re-Insurance accepted (5,10,000 + 70,000 – 95,000)	4,85,000
Less: Claims on Re-Insurance Ceded (3,95,000 + 1,25,000 – 75,000)	(4,45,000)
Add: Surveyor's Fees	45,000
Add: Legal Expenses	55,000
Total claims Incurred	51,63,000

SCHEDULE 3 – COMMISSION

Particulars	This Yr.
Commision paid: Direct	1,60,000
Add: Commission on Re-Insurance accepted	15,000
Less: Commission on Re-Insurance ceded	(18,000)
Net Commission	1,57,000

ILLUSTRATION 7

From the following information prepare the Revenue Account of PCT Fire Insurance Company Ltd. for the year ended 31st March, 2015.

1. PREMIUM, CLAIMS AND COMMISSION:

Particulars	*On Direct Business* ₹	*On Re-Insurance* ₹	*On Accepted Re-insured* ₹
(a) Total Premium	30,00,000	10,00,000	20,00,000
In India	80%	80%	80%
(b) Total Claims	6,00,000	2,00,000	4,00,000
Outside India	20%	20%	20%
(c) Commission	3,00,000	1,00,000	2,00,000

2. EXPENSES

Particulars	₹
1. Employees' remuneration and welfare benefits	2,31,000
2. Managerial Remuneration	2,00,000
3. Travel, conveyance and vehicle running expenses	59,000
4. Rents, rates and taxes	30,000
5. Repairs	20,000
6. Printing and Stationery	10,000
7. Communication expenses	5,000
8. Legal and Professional charges	6,000
9. Medical fees	7,000

10. Auditor's fees, expenses etc.	8,000
11. Advertisement and publicity	6,000
12. Interest and Bank Charges	5,000
13. Policy Stamps	3,000

3.OTHERS

Particulars	₹
Furniture and Fixture (Cost ₹ 1,00,000)	58,000
Rate of Depreciation on Furniture-10% an original cost	
Bad Debts	5,000
Indian and Foreign Taxes	95,000
Interest, Dividend and Rent Received	90,000
Income Tax deducted at source thereon	10,000
Profit and Sale of Motor Car	5,000
Double Income Tax Refund	15,000
Provision of Unexpired Risks (as on 1.4.2014)	10,00,000
Additional Provision for Risks (as on 1.4.2014)	1,00,000
Accounting Policy Regarding Additional Provision in Fire-5% of net prem. of the year	

SOLUTION

FIRE INSURANCE REVENUE ACCOUNT FOR THE YEAR ENDED 31st MARCH, 2015

Particulars	*Schedule*	*Current Year (₹ '000)*	*Previous Year (₹ '000)*
1. Premium earned (Net)	1	2900	
2. Other Incomes:			
(a) Profit on sale of Motor Car		5	
(b) Double Income Tax Refund		15	
3. Interest, Dividend and Rent (Gross)		100	
Total (A)		3020	
1. Claims Incurred (Net)	2	800	
2. Commission	3	400	
3. Operating expenses related to Insurance Business	4	600	
4. Other Expenses:			
Bad Debts		5	
Indian and Foreign Taxes		95	
Total (B)		1900	
Operating Profit from fire Insurance Business		1120	

SCHEDULE 1 PREMIUM EARNED (NET)

Particulars	*Current Year (₹ '000)*	*Previous Year (₹ '000)*
Premium for Direct Business written	3000	
Add: Premium on Re-insurance accepted	2000	
Less: Premium on Re-insurance ceded	(1000)	
Net Premium	4000	
Less: Adjustment for Change in Provision for Unexpired Risks		(1100)
	2900	
Premium Income from bueinss effected		
In India	3200	
Outside India	800	
	4000	

SCHEDULE 2 CLAIMS INCURRED (NET)

Particulars	*Current Year (₹ '000)*	*Previous Year (₹ '000)*
Claim		
Direct	600	
Add: Re-insurance accepted	4,00	
Less: Re-insurance ceded	(200)	
Total claim incurred	800	
Claim paid to claimaints:		
In India	640	
Outside India	160	
	800	

SCHEDULE 3 COMMISSION

Particulars	*Current Year (₹ '000)*	*Previous Year (₹ '000)*
Commission		
Direct	300	
Add: Commission on Re-insurance accepted	200	
Less: Commission on Re-insurance ceded	(100)	
Total	400	

SCHEDULE 4 OPERATING EXPENSES RELATED TO INSURANCE BUSINESS

Particulars	*Current Year (₹ '000)*	*Previous Year (₹ '000)*
1. Employees' remuneration and welfare benefits	231	
2. Managerial Remuneration	200	

3. Travel, conveyance and vehicle running expenses	59	
4. Rents, rates and taxes	30	
5. Repairs	20	
6. Printing and Stationery	10	
7. Communication expenses	5	
8. Legal and Professional charges	6	
9. Medical fees	7	
10. Auditors' fees, expenses etc.	8	
11. Advertisement and publicity	6	
12. Interest and Bank Charges	5	
13. PolicyStamps	3	
14. Depreciation (10% on ₹ 1,00,000)	10	
Total	600	

Working Note:

CHANGE IN PROVISION FOR UNEXPIRED RISKS

Particulars	*(₹ '000)*
A. Closing Provision for Unexpired Risks	
(i) Minimum Provision @50% of ₹ 40,00,00	2,000
(ii) Additional Provision @5% of ₹ 40,00,000	200
	2,200
B. *Less:* Opening Provision for Unexpired Risks	
(i) Minimum Provision	1,000
(ii) Additional Provision	100
	1,100
C. Change in Provision for Unexpired Risk [A – B]	1,100

10.0 FORMAT OF PROFIT & LOSS ACCOUNT

FORM B-PL

Name of the Insurer: ______
Registration No. and Date of Registration with the IRDA ______

PROFIT AND LOSS ACCOUNT FOR THE YEAR ENDED 31st MARCH, 20__

Particulars	*Current Year (₹ '000)*	*Previous Year (₹ '000)*
1. Operating Profit/(Loss)		
(a) Fie Insurance		
(b) Marine Insurance		
(c) Miscellaneous Insurance		
2. Income From Investments		
(a) Interest, Dividend & Rent Gross		

(b) Profit on sale of investments		
Less: Loss on sale of investments		
3. Other Income (to be specified)		
Total (A)		
4. Provisions (to be specified)		
(a) For diminution in the value of investments		
(b) Others (to be specified)		
5. Other Expenses		
(a) Exp. other than those related to Insurance Business		
(b) Others (to be specified)		
Total (B)		
Profit before Tax [(A) – (B)]		
Less: Provision for Taxation		
Profit After Tax		
Less: Catastrophe Reserve*		
Profit available for Appropriation		
Less: Appropriations:		
(a) Interim dividends paid during the year		
(b) Proposed final dividend		
(c) Dividend distribution tax		
(d) Transfer to any Reserves *or* Other A/cs (to be specified)		
Net Profit/Loss for the current year		
Balance of Profit/Loss brought forward from last yr.		
Balance Carried forward to Balance Sheet		

*Cumulative Shortfall in the Catastrophe appropriation ₹—pending surplus.

ILLUSTRATION 8

From the following infomation prepare Profit and Loss Account of PCT General Insurance Co. Ltd. for the year ended 31st March, 2015:

Particulars	(₹)
1. Operating Profit	
Fire	11,20,000
Marine	6,00,000
Miscelleneous	80,000
2. Interest, Dividend and Rent received	2,00,000
Tax reduced at source	15,000
3. Transfer Fees	1,05,000
4. Miscelleneous Income	1,00,000
5. Provision for Diminution in the value of Investments	10,000
6. Donation	1,90,000

7. Provision for Tax	6,00,000
8. Catastrophe Reserve	1,00,000
9. Interim Dividends Paid	2,00,000
10. Proposed Final Dividend	3,00,000
11. Dividend Distribution ax	50,000
12. Transfer to General Reserve	2,00,000
13. Profit and Loss A/c (as on 1.4.2014)	3,50,000
14. Loss on sale of Investments	20,000

SOLUTION

PROFIT AND LOSS ACCOUNT FOR THE YEAR ENDED 31st MARCH, 2015

Particulars	*Current Year (₹ '000)*	*Previous Year (₹ '000)*
1. Operating Profit		
(a) Fire Insurance	1120	
(b) Marine Insurance	600	
(c) Miscelleneous Insurance	80	
2. Income from Investments		
(a) Interest, Dividend & Rent (Gross)	215	
(b) Loss on Sale of Investments	(20)	
3. Other Income:		
Transfer fees	105	
Miscelleneous Income	100	
Total (A)	2200	
4. Provision for Diminution in the value of Investments	10	
5. Donation	190	
Total (B)	200	
Profit before Tax [(A) – (B)]	2000	
Provision for Tax	(600)	
	1400	
Less: Catastrophe Reserve	100	
Profit available for Appropriation	1300	
Less: Appropriations		
(a) Interim dividends Paid	(200)	
(b) Proposed Final dividend	(300)	
(c) Dividend Distribution Tax	(50)	
(d) Transfer to General Revenue	(200)	
Net Profit for Current Year	550	
Balance of Profit brought forward from last year	350	
Balance Carried forward to Balance Sheet	900	

11.0 FORMAT OF BALANCE SHEET

FORM B-BS

Name of the Insurer:	_ _ _ _ _ _ _
Registration No. and Date of Registration with the IRDA	_ _ _ _ _ _ _

BALANCE SHEET AS AT 31st MARCH, 20_ _ _

Particulars	*Schedule*	*Current Year (₹ '000)*	*Previous Year (₹ '000)*
Sources of Funds:			
Share Capital	5		
Reserves and Surplus	6		
Borrowings	7		
Fair Value Change Account			
Total			
Application of Funds:			
Investments	8		
Loans	9		
Fixed Assets	10		
Current Assets			
Cash and Bank Balances	11		
Advances and Other Assets	12		
Sub-Total (a)			
Current Liabilities	13		
Provisions	14		
Sub-Total (B)			
Net Current Assets (C) = (A – B)			
Miscellaneous Expenditure (to the extent not written off *or* adjusted)	15		
Debit Balance in Profit and Loss Account			
Total			

CONTINGENT LIABILITIES

Particulars	*Current Year (₹ '000)*	*Previous Year (₹ '000)*
1. Partly paid-up investments		
2. Claims, other than against policies, not acknowledged as debt		
3. Underwriting commitments outstanding		
4. Guarantees given by *or* on behalf of the Company		
5. Statutory demands/liabilities in dispute, not provided for		
6. Reinsurance obligations		

7. Others (to be specified)		
Total		

SCHEDULE FORMING PART OF BALANCE SHEET

SCHEDULE - 5 SHARE CAPITAL

Particulars	*Current Year (₹ '000)*	*Previous Year (₹ '000)*
1. **Authorised Capital**		
Equity Shares of ₹ ... each		
2. **Issued Capital**		
Equity Shares of ₹ ... each		
3. **Subscribed Capital**		
Equity shares of ₹ ... each		
4. **Called-up Capital**		
Equity Shares of ₹ ... each		
5. ***Less:* Calls unpaid**		
Add: Equity Shares forfeited (Amount originally paid up)		
Less: Preliminary Expenses		
Expenses including commission *or* brokerage on underwriting *or* subscription of shares		
Total		

Notes:

(a) *The amount capitalised on account of issue of bonus shares should be disclosed.*

(b) *In case any part of the capital is held by a holding co., the same should be separately disclosed.*

SCHEDULE - 5A SHARE CAPITAL
Pattern of Shareholding [As certified by the Management]

Particulars	*Current Year (₹.'000)*		*Previous Year (₹.'000)*	
	Number of Shares	*% of Holding*	*Number of Shares*	*% of Holding*
Promoters				
(a) Indian				
(b) Foreign				
Others				
Total				

SCHEDULE - 6 RESERVES AND SURPLUS

Particulars	*Current Year (₹ '000)*	*Previous Year (₹ '000)*
1. Capital Reserve		
2. Capital Redemption Reserve		

3. Share Premium		
4. General Reserves		
Less: Debit balance in Profit & Loss Account		
Less: Amount utilized for Buy-back		
5. Catastrophe Reserve		
6. Other Reserves (to be specified)		
7. Balance of Profit in Profit & Loss Account		
Total		

Note: *Additions to and deductions from the reserves should be disclosed under each of the specified heads.*

SCHEDULE - 7 BORROWINGS

Particulars	*Current Year (₹ '000)*	*Previous Year (₹ '000)*
1. Debentures/Bonds		
2. Fixed Deposits		
3. Banks		
4. Financial Institutions		
5. Other entities carrying on insurance business		
6. Others (to be specified)		
Total		

Notes:

(a) *The extent to which the borrowings are secured shall be separately disclosed stating the nature of the security under each sub-head.*

(b) *Amounts due within 12 months from the date of Balance Sheet should be shown separately.*

SCHEDULE - 8 INVESTMENTS

Particulars	*Current Year (₹ '000)*	*Previous Year (₹ '000)*
Long Term Investments:		
1. Government securities and Government guaranteed bonds including Treasury Bills		
2. Other Invstments		
(a) Shares		
(i) Equity		
(ii) Preference		
(b) Mutual Funds		
(c) Derivative Instruments		
(d) Debentures/ Bonds		
(e) Other Securities (to be specified)		
(f) Subsidiaries		
(g) Investment Properties-Real Estate		

Short Term Investments:		
1. Government securities and Government guaranteed bonds including Treasury Bills		
2. Other Approved Securities		
3. Other Investments		
(a) Shares		
(i) Equity		
(ii) Preference		
(b) Mutual Funds		
(c) Derivative Instruments		
(d) Debentures/ Bonds		
(e) Other Securities (to be specified)		
(f) Subsidiaries		
(g) Investment Properties-Real Estate		
Total		
Investments		
1. In India		
2. Outside India		
Total		

Notes:

(a) Investments in subsidiary/holding companies, joint ventures and associated shall be separately disclosed, at cost.

(i) Holding company and subsidiary shall be consrued as. Significant influence may be exercised in several ways, for example, by representation on the board of directors, participation in the policy making process, material inter company transactions, interchange of managerial defined in the Companies Act, 1956:

(ii) Joint Venture is a contractual arrangement where by two *or* more parties under take an economic activity, which is subject to joint control.

(iii) Joint control is the contractually agreed sharing of power to govern the financial and operating policies of an economic activity to obtain benefits from it.

(iv) Associate is an enterprise in which he company has significant influence and which is neither a subsidiary *nor* a joint venture of the company.

(v) significant influence (for the purpose of this schedule) means participation in the financial and operating policy decisions of a company, but not necessarily control of those policies personally dependence on technical information. Significant influence may be gained by share ownership, statute *or* agreement. As regards share ownership, if an investor holds, directly *or* indirectly through subsidiaries, 20 percent *or* more of the voting power of the investee, it is presumed that the investor does have significant influence, unless it can be clearly demonstrated that this is not the case. Conversely, if the investor holds, directly *or* indirectly through subsidiaries, *less* than 20 percent of the voting power of the investee, it is presumed that the investor does not have significant influence, unless such influence is clearly demonstrated. A substantial *or* majority ownership by another investor does not necessarily preclude an investor from having significant influence.

(b) Aggregate amount of company's investments other than listed equity securities and derivative instruments and also the market value there of shall be disclosed.

(c) Investments made out of Catasrophe Reserve should be shown separately.

(d) Debt securities will be considered as "held to maturity" securities and will be measured at historical cost subject to amortisation.

(e) Investment Property means a property [land *or* building *or* part of a building *or* both] held to earn rental income *or* for capital appreciation *or* for both, rather than for use in services *or* for administative purposes.

SCHEDULE - 9 LOANS

Particulars	*Current Year (₹ '000)*	*Previous Year (₹ '000)*
1. Security-Wise Classification:		
Secured:		
(a) On mortgage of property		
(i) In India		
(ii) Outside India		
(b) On Shares, Bonds, Govt. Securities		
(c) Others (to be specified)		
Unsecured:		
Total		
2. Borrower-Wise Classification:		
(a) Central and State Governments		
(b) Banks and Financial Institutions		
(c) Subsidiaries		
(d) Industrial Undertakings		
(e) Others (to be specified)		
Total		
3. Performance-wise Classification:		
(a) Loans classified as standard		
(i) In India		
(ii) Outside India		
(b) Non-performing loans *less* povisions		
(i) In India		
(ii) Outside India		
Total		
4. Maturity-Wise Classification		
(a) Short Term		
(b) Long Term		
Total		

Notes:

(a) *Short term loans shall include those, which are repayable within 12 months of the balance sheet date. Long term loans shall be the loans other than short term loans.*

(b) *Provision against non-performing loans shall be shown separately.*

(c) *The nature of the security in case of all long term securited loans shall be specified in each case. Secured loans for the purposes of this schedule, means loans secured wholly or partly against an asset of the company.*

(d) *Loans considered doubtful and the amount of provision created against such loans shall be disclosed.*

SCHEDULE - 10 FIXED ASSETS

Particulars	*Cost/Gross Block*				*Depreciation*				*Net Block*	
	Opening	*Additions*	*Deduction*	*Closing*	*Upto Last Yr.*	*For the Yr.*	*On Sales*	*To Date*	*As at Yr.*	*Prev. Yr.*
Goodwill										
Intangibles (specify)										
Land-Freehold										
Leasehold Property										
Buildings										
Furniture & Fittings										
Information										
Technology										
Equipment										
Vehicles										
Office Equipment										
Othrs (Specify nature)										
Total										
Previous Year										

Notes: Assets inclued in land, building and property above exclude Investment Properties as defined in note (e) to Schedule 8.

SCHEDULE-11 CASH AND BANK BALANCES

Particulars	*Current Year (₹ '000)*	*Previous Year (₹ '000)*
1. Cash (including cheques, drafts and stamps)		
2. Bank Balances		
(a) Deposit Accounts		
(i) Short-term (due within 12 months)		
(ii) Others		
(b) Current Accounts		
(c) Others (to be specified)		
3. Money at Call and Short Notice		
(a) With Banks		
(b) With other Institutions		
4. Others (to be specified)		
Total		
Balances with non-scheduled banks included in 2 and 3 above		

Cash & Bank Balances		
1. In India		
2. Outside India		
Total		

Notes: *Bank balance may include remittances in transit. If so, the nature and amount should be separately stated.*

SCHEDULE-12 ADVANCES AND OTHER ASSETS

Particulars	*Current Year (₹ '000)*	*Previous Year (₹ '000)*
Advances		
1. Reserve deposits with cedin companies		
2. Advances to ceding companies		
3. Application money for investments		
4. Prepayments		
5. Advances to Officers/Directors		
6. Advance tax paid & taxes deducted at source		
7. Others (to be specified)		
Total (A)		
Other Assets		
1. Income accrued on investments		
2. Oustanding Premiums		
3. Agents' Balances		
4. Foreign Agencies' balances		
5. Due from othe Insurance Entities		
6. Due from subsidiaries/holding		
7. Reinsurance clams/balances receivable		
8. Deposit with Reserve Bank of India [Pursuant to Section 7 of Insurance Act, 1938]		
9. Others (to be specified)		
Total (B)		
Total (A + B)		

Notes:

(a) *The item under the above heads shall not be shown net of provisions for doubtful amounts. The amount of provision against each head should be shown separately.*

(b) *The term 'officer' should conform to the definition of the word 'Officer' given under the Companies Act, 1956.*

SCHDULE-13 CURRENT LIABILITIES

Particulars	*Current Year (₹ '000)*	*Previous Year (₹ '000)*
1. Reserve for Unearned Premium		

2. Agents' balances		
3. Balances due to other insurance companies		
4. Advances from Treaty Companies		
5. Deposits held on re-insuance ceded		
6. Premiums received in advance		
7. Sundry creditors		
8. Due to subsidiaries/holding company		
9. Claims Outstanding		
10. Due to Officers/Directors		
11. Others (to be specified)		
Total		

SCHDULE-14 PROVISIONS

Particulars	*Current Year (₹ '000)*	*Previous Year (₹ '000)*
1. Reserve Unexpired risk		
2. For taxation (less: advance tax paid and taxes deducted at source)		
3. For proposed dividends		
4. For dividend distribution tax		
5. Others (to be specified)		
Total		

SCHEDULE-15 MISCELLANEOUS EXPENDITURE

(To the extent not written off or adjusted)

Particulars	*Current Year (₹ '000)*	*Previous Year (₹ '000)*
1. Discount Allowed in issue of shares/debentues		
2. Others (to be specified)		
Total		

Notes:

(a) *No item shall be included under the head* ***"Miscellaneous Expenditure"*** *and carried forward unless:*

1. *some benefit from the expenditue can reasonably be expected to be received in future, and*
2. *the amount of such benefit is reasonably determinable.*

(b) *The amount to be carried forwad in respect of any item included under the head "Miscellaneous Expenditure" shall not exceed the expected future revenue/other benefits related to the expenditure.*

ILLUSTRATION 9

From the following information, prepare the Balance Sheet of PCT General Insurance Co. Ltd. for the year ended 31st March, 2015:

		Particulars	*₹ in lakhs*
1.	(a)	Authorised Capital	200
	(b)	Shares of ₹ 10 each, ₹ 5 called up and paid up	97
2.	(a)	Profit and Loss A/c Balance (Credit)	10
	(b)	General Reserve	2
3.	(a)	Debentues	3
	(b)	Fixed Deposits	2
	(c)	Loans from Banks	5
4.		Investments	
		Govt. Securities (Long-term)	5
		Mutual Funds (Short-term)	3
5.	(a)	Loans to Companies (Non Standard)	20
		(40% short term)	
		[40% secured on Govt. Securities]	
	(b)	Loan to Banks (60% long-term) (Standard)	30
		[60% secured on mortgage of property]	
	(c)	Loans against policies (short-term) (non-Standard)	10
6.	(a)	Goodwill	5
	(b)	Land Freehold	10
	(c)	Building	20
7.	(a)	Stamps	1
	(b)	Short-term Deposit with Bank	2
	(c)	Long-term Deposits with Bank	3
	(d)	Current Account Balance (credit)	4
	(e)	Money at call and short notice	5
8.	(a)	Application money for investments	2
	(b)	Prepaid Expenses	1
	(c)	Income accrued on Investments	1
	(d)	Outstanding Premium	2
	(e)	Agents Balance (Dr.)	3
	(f)	Due from other insurance companies	4
	(g)	Deposit with RBI	5
9.	(a)	Balances due to other insurance companies	2
	(b)	Premium received in advance	1
	(c)	Claim Outstanding	2
10.	(a)	Provision for Taxation	5
	(b)	Advance Tax	2

(c) Tax Deducted at Source (Dr.)	1
(d) Proposed Dividend	3
(e) Dividend Disribution Tax	0.50
(f) Reverse for Unexpired Risk	7
(g) Provision for Depreciation on Building	1
11. (a) Discount allowed on Issue of Shares and Debentures	1
(b) Underwriting Commission on Issue of Shares and Debentures	0.50
12. (a) There are Investments in 50,000 shares of ₹ 10 each, ₹ 6 paid up	
(b) Claims (other than against policies) not acknowledged as debts	3.00

SOLUTION

BALANCE SHEET AS AT 31st MARCH, 2015

Particulars	*Schedule*	*Current Year (₹ in Lakhs)*	*Previous Year (₹ in Lakhs)*
Sources of Funds:			
Shareholders' funds:			
Share Capital	5	96.50	
Reserve Surplus	6	12.00	
Borrowings	7	10.0	
Total		118.50	
Application of Funds:			
Investments:	8	8.00	
Loans:	9	60,00	
Fixed Assets	10	34.00	
Current Assets:			
Cash and Bank Balance	11		15.00
Advances and Other Assets	12		18.00
Sub-Total (A)			33.00
Curent Liabilities	13		5.00
Provision	14		12.50
Sub Total (B)			17.50
Net Current Assets (c) = A – B		15.50	
Miscellaneous Expenditure (To the extent not written off *or* adjusted)	15	1.00	
Total		118.50	
Contingent Liabilities:			
Partly paid up investments		2.00	
Claims (other than against policies) not acknowledged as debts		3.00	
		5.00	

SCHEDULE 5 SHARE CAPITAL

Particulars	Current Year (₹ in Lakhs)	Previous Year (₹ in Lakhs)
1. **Authorised Capital**		
20,00,000 shares of ₹ 10 each	200	
2. **Issued Capital**		
19,40,000 shares of ₹ 10 each	194	
3. **Subscribed Capital**		
19,40,000 Shares of ₹ 10 each	194	
4. **Called up Capital**	97.0	
19,40,000 Shares of ₹ 10 each, ₹ 5 called up		
Less: Underwriting Commission	0.5	
	96.5	

SCHEDULE 6 RESERVES AND SURPLUS

Particulars	Current Year (₹ in Lakhs)	Previous Year (₹ in Lakhs)
1. General Reserve	2	
2. Balance of Profit and Loss A/c	10	
	12	

SCHEDULE 7 BORROWINGS

Particulars	Current Year (₹ in Lakhs)	Previous Year (₹ in Lakhs)
1. Debentures	3	
2. Fixed Debtors	2	
3. Loans from banks	5	
	10	

SCHEDULE 8 INVESTMENTS

Particulars	Current Year (₹ in Lakhs)	Previous Year (₹ in Lakhs)
1. Long-term Investments	5	
Govt. Securities		
2. Shot-term Investments	3	
Mutual Funds		
	8	

SCHEDULE 9 LOANS

Particulars	Current Year (₹ in Lakhs)	Previous Year (₹ in Lakhs)
1. **Security-wise Classification**		

Secured		
(a) On Mortagage of Property	18	
(b) On Govt. Securities	8	
Unsecured		
(a) Loans against policies	10	
(b) Loans to Companies	12	
(c) Loans to banks	12	
Total	60	
2. Borrower-wise Classifications		
(a) Loans to banks	30	
(b) Loans to Companies	20	
(c) Loans against policies	10	
	60	
3. Performance wise classificatiion		
(a) Standard	30	
(b) Non-standard	30	
Total	60	
4. Maturity-wise Classification		
(a) Short-term (8 + 12 + 10)	30	
(b) Long-term	30	
Total	60	

SCHEDULE 10 FIXED ASSETS

Particulars	*Gross Block*	*Depreciation (₹ in lakhs)*	*Net Block (₹ in lakhs)*
1. Goodwill	5	—	5
2. Land	10	—	10
3. Building	20	1	19
Total			34

SCHEDULE 11 CASH AND BANK BALANCES

Particulars	*Current Year (₹ in Lakhs)*	*Previous Year (₹ in Lakhs)*
1. Cash (Stamps)	1	
2. Bank Balances		
(a) Deposit accounts		
(i) Short-term	2	
(ii) Others	3	
(b) Current Accounts	4	
3. Money at call and Short notice	5	
Total	15	

SCHEDULE 12 ADVANCES AND OTHER ASSETS

Particulars	Current Year (₹ in Lakhs)	Previous Year (₹ in Lakhs)
Advances:		
1. Application Money for Investments	2	
2. Prepaid Expenses	1	
Total (a)	3	
Other Assets:		
1. Income accrued on Investments	1	
2. Outstanding Premium	2	
3. Agents' Balances (Dr.)	3	
4. Due from other Insurance Companies	4	
5. Deposits with RBI	5	
Total (B)	15	
Total [(A) + (B)]	18	

SCHEDULE 13 CURRENT LIABILITIES

Particulars	Current Year (₹ in Lakhs)	Previous Year (₹ in Lakhs)
1. Balance due to other Insurance Companies	2	
2. Premium received in advance	1	
3. Claims Outstading	2	
	5	

SCHEDULE 14 PROVISIONS

Particulars	Current Year (₹ in Lakhs)	Previous Year (₹ in Lakhs)
1. Reserve for Unexpired Risks	7.00	
2. Provision for Taxation (5-2-1)	2.00	
3. Proposed Dividend	3.00	
4. Dividend Distribution Tax	0.50	
	12.50	

SCHEDULE 15 MISCELLANEOUS EXPENDITURE

Particulars	Current Year (₹ in Lakhs)	Previous Year (₹ in Lakhs)
1. Discount allowed on Issue of Shares and Debentures	1	
	1	

SOLVED PROBLEMS

PROBLEM 1

CAMIH Insurance Co. Ltd. furnishes you with the following information:

(i) On 31.3.2014 it had reserve for unexpired risks to the tune of ₹ 40 crores. It comprised of ₹ 15 crores in respect of marine insurance business; ₹ 20 crores in respect of fire insurance business and ₹ 5 crores in respect of miscellaneous insurance business.

(ii) It is the practice of Indian Insurance Co. Ltd. to create reserves at 100% of net premium income in respect of marine insurance policies and at 50% of net premium income in respect of fire and miscellaneous income policies.

(iii) During 2014 – 2015, the following business was conducted:

Particulars	*Marine (₹ in crores)*	*Fire (₹ in crores)*	*Miscellaneous (₹ in crores)*
Premia collected from:			
(a) Insureds in respect of Policies issued	18	43	12
(b) Other insurance companies in respect of risks undertaken	7	5	4
Premia paid/payable to other insurance companies on business ceded	6.7	4.3	7

Indian Insurance Co. Ltd. asks you to:

(a) Pass journal entries relating to "Unexpired risks reserve".

(b) Show in columnar form "Unexpired risks reserve" Account for 2015.

SOLUTION

JOURNAL OF CAMHI INSURANCE CO. LTD. *[₹ in crores]*

Particulars		*L.F.*	*Dr. (₹)*	*Cr. (₹)*
Reserve for Unexpired Risk A/c	Dr.		15	
To Marine Revenue A/c				15
(Being the opening balance t/f to Revenue A/c)				
Reserve for Unexpired Risk A/c	Dr.		20	
To Fire Revenue A/c				20
(Being the opening Balance t/f to Revenue A/c)				
Reserve for Unexpired Risk A/c	Dr.		5	
To Miscellaneous Revenue A/c				5
(Being the opening balance t/f to Revenue A/c)				
Marine Revenue A/c	Dr.		18.30	
To Revenue for Unexpired Risk A/c				18.30
(Being the reserve for unexpired risk created @ 100% of net premium of ₹ 18.30 (i.e. 18+7–6.7) in respect of Marine insurance business)				
Fire Revenue A/c	Dr.		21.85	
To Reserve for Unexpired Risk A/c				21.85
(Being the reserve for unexpired risk created @ 50% of net premium of ₹ 43.70 (i.e. 43 + 5 – 4.3) in respect of fire Insurance Business)				

Miscellaneous Revenue A/c Dr.		4.50	
To Reserve for Unexpired Risk A/c			4.50
(Being the reserve for unexpired risk created @ 50% of net premium of ₹ 9 crores (i.e. 12 + 4 – 7) in respect of Misc. Insurance business)			

Dr. **RESERVE FOR UNEXPIRED RISKS ACCOUNT** *Cr.*

(₹ in crores)

Date	*Particulars*	*Marine* ₹	*Fire* ₹	*Miscellaneous* ₹	*Date*	*Particulars*	*Marine* ₹	*Fire* ₹	*Miscellaneous* ₹
1.4.14	To Revenue A/c	15.00	20.00	5.00	1.4.14	By Balance b/d	15.00	20.00	5.00
31.3.15	To Balance c/d	18.30	21.85	4.50	31.3.15	By Revenue A/c	18.30	21.85	4.50
		33.30	41.85	9.50			33.30	41.85	9.50

PROBLEM 2

From the following information as on 31st March, 2015, prepare the Revenue Account of Tulsian Co. Ltd. engaged in Marine Insurance Business:

Particulars	*Direct Business (₹)*	*Re-insurance (₹)*
I. Premium:		
Received	24,00,000	3,60,000
Receivable— 1st April, 2014	1,20,000	21,000
— 31st March, 2015	1,80,000	28,000
Premium paid	—	2,40,000
Payable — 1st April, 2014	—	20,000
— 31st March, 2015		42,000
II. Claims:		
Paid	16,50,000	1,25,000
Payable — 1st April, 2014	95,000	13,000
— 31st March, 2015	1,75,000	22,000
Received	—	1,00,000
Receivable— 1st April, 2014	—	9,000
— 31st March, 2015	—	12,000
III. Commission:		
On Insurance accepted	1,50,000	11,000
On Insurance ceded	—	14,000

Other Expenses and Income:

Salaries—₹ 2,60,000; Rent, Rates and Taxes—₹ 18,000; Printing and Stationery—₹ 23,000; Indian Income Tax paid—₹ 2,40,000; Interest, Dividend and Rent received (net)—₹ 91,500; Income Tax deducted at source—₹ 24,500; Legal Expenses (Inclusive of ₹ 20,000 in connection with the settlement of clams)—₹ 60,000; Bad Debts—₹ 5,000; Double Income Tax refund—₹ 12,000; Profit on Sale of Motor car—₹ 5,000, Indian and Foreign taxes ₹ 2,40,000.

Balance of Fund on 1st April, 2014, was ₹ 26,50,000 including Additional Reserve of ₹ 3,25,000. Additional Reserve has to be maintained at 5% of the net premium of the year.

SOLUTION

FORM B-RA (PRESCRIBED BY IRDA)
REVENE ACCOUNT FOR THE YEAR ENDED 31st MARCH, 2015
MARINE INSURANCE BUSINESS

Particulars	*Schedule*	*Current Year (₹ '000)*	*Previous Year (₹ '000)*
Premium earned (Net)	1	2522	
Interest, Dividends and Rent (Gross)		116	
Double Income Tax refund		12	
Profit on sale of motor car		5	
Total (A)		2655	
Claims incurred (Net)	2	1781	
Commission	3	147	
Operating exp. related to Insurance business	4	341	
Bad debts		5	
Indian and Foreign taxes		240	
Total (B)		2514	
Profit from Marine Insurance Business (A – B)		141	

Schedules forming part of Revenue Account

SCHEDULE 1 PREMIUM EARNED (NET)

Particulars	*Current Year (₹ '000)*	*Previous Year (₹ '000)*
Premiums from direct business	2460	
Premium Re-insurance accepted	367	
Less: Premium on reinsurance ceded	(262)	
Net Premium earned	2565	
Less: Adjustment for Change in Provision for Unexpired Risks	(43)	
	2522	

SCHEDULE 2 CLAIMS INCURRED (NET)

Particulars	*Current Year (₹ '000)*	*Previous Year (₹ '000)*
Direct (including Legal Expenses ₹ 20,000)	1750	
Add: Re-insurance accepted	134	
Less: Re-insurance ceded	(103)	
Net Claims Incurred	1781	

SCHEDULE 3 COMMISSION

Particulars	*Current Year (₹ '000)*	*Previous Year (₹ '000)*
Direct	150	
Add: Re-insurance accepted	11	
Less: Re-insurance ceded	(14)	
Net Commission	147	

SCHEDULE 4 OPERATING EXPENSES RELATED TO INSURANCE BUSINESS

Particulars	*Current Year (₹ '000)*	*Previous Year (₹ '000)*
Employees' remuneration and welfare benefits	260	
Rent, Rates and Taxes	18	
Printing and Stationery	23	
Legal and Professional charges	40	
	341	

Working Notes:

(I) PREMIUM EARNED ON DIRECT BUSINESS AND RE-INSURANCE ACCEPTED

Particulars	*Direct (₹ '000)*	*Re-insurance (₹ '000)*
A. Received	2400	360
B. *Add:* Receivable at end	180	28
C. *Less:* Receivable at beginning	(120)	(21)
D. Total [A + B – C]	2460	367

(II) PREMIUM PAID ON RE-INSURANCE CEDED

Particulars	*Re-insurance (₹ '000)*
A. Paid	240
B. *Add:* Payable at end	42
C. *Less:* Payable at beginning	(20)
D. Total [A + B – C]	262

(III) CLAIMS INCURRED

Particulars	*On Direct Business (₹ '000)*	*On Re-insurance Accepted (₹ '000)*	*On Re-insurance Ceded (₹ '000)*
A. Paid/Received	1650	125	100
B. *Add:* Outstanding at end	175	22	12
C. *Add:* Exp. in connection with Settlement of Claim	20		

D. *Less:* Outstanding at beginning	(95)	(13)	(9)
	1750	134	103

PROBLEM 3

From the following balances extracted from the books of Perfect General Insunace Company Limited as on 31.3.2015 you are requested to prepare Revenue Accounts in respect of Fire and Marine Insurance Business for the year ended 31.3.2015 and a Profit and Loss Account for the same period.

Particulars	₹	*Particulars*	₹
Director's Fees	80,000	Interest received	19,000
Dividend received	1,00,000	Fixed Assets (1.4.2014)	90,000
Provision for Taxation (as on 1.4.2014)	85,000	Income-Tax paid during the year	60,000

Particulars	*Fire*	*Marine*
Outstanding Claims on 1.4.2014	28,000	7,000
Claims paid	1,00,000	80,000
Reserve for Unexpired Risk on 1.4.2014	2,00,000	1,40,000
Premiums Received	4,50,000	3,30,000
Agents Commission	40,000	20,000
Expenses of Management	60,000	45,000
Re-insurance Premium (Dr.)	25,000	15,000

The following additional points are also to be taken into account:

(a) Depreciation on Fixed Assets to be provided at 10% p.a.

(b) Interest accrued on investments ₹.10,000.

(c) Closing provision for taxation on 31.3.2015 to be maintained at ₹ 1,24,138

(d) Claims outstanding on 31.3.2015 were Fire Insurance ₹.10,000; Marine Insurance ₹.15,000

(e) Premium Outstanding on 31.3.2015 were Fire Insurance ₹ 30,000; Marine Insurance ₹.20,000.

(f) Reserve for unexpired risk to be maintained at 50% and 100% of net premiums in respect of Fire and Marine insurance respectively.

(g) Expenses of management due on 31.3.2015 were ₹ 10,000 for Fire Insurance and ₹.5,000 in resepect of Marine Insurance.

SOLUTION

FORM B – RA (PRESCRIBED BY IRDA)
PERFECT GENERAL INSURANCE CO. LTD.
REVENUE ACCOUNT FOR THE YEAR ENDED 31st MARCH, 2015
FIRE AND MARINE INSURANCE BUSINESSES

Particulars	*Schedule*	*Fire Current Year (₹.'000)*	*Marine Current Year (₹.'000)*
Premiums earned (net)	1	427	140
Interest, Dividends and Rent – Gross	—	—	
Double Income Tax refund	—	—	

Profit on sale of motor car	—		
Total (A)		427	140
Claims incurrent (net)	2	82	88
Commission	3	40	20
Operating expenses related to insurance business	4	70	50
Bad debts		—	
Indian and Foreign taxes	—		
Total (B)		192	158
Profit (Loss) (A – B)		235	(18)

Schedules forming part of Revenue Account

SCHEDULE—1 PREMIUMS EARNED (NET)

Particulars	*Fire Current Year (₹.'000)*	*Marine Current Year (₹.'000)*
Premiums from direct business written	480	350
Less: Premiums on reinsurance ceded	(25)	(15)
Total Premium earned (net)	455	335
Less: Adjustment for Change in Provision for Unexpired Risks	(28)	(195)
	427	140
Schedule—2 Claims incurred (net)	82	88
Schedule—4 Operating exp. related to insurance business		
Expenses of Management	70	50

FORM B – RA (PRESCRIBED BY IRDA)
PERFECT GENERAL INSURANCE CO. LTD.
PROFIT & LOSS ACCOUNT FOR THE YEAR ENDED 31st MARCH, 2015
FIRE AND MARINE INSURANCE BUSINESSES

Particulars	*Schedule*	*Fire Current Year (₹.'000)*	*Marine Current Year (₹.'000)*
Operating Profit / (Loss)			
(a) Fire insurance		235	
(b) Marine Insurance		(18)	
(c) Miscellaneous Insurance			—
Income From Investments			
(a) Interest, Dividend and Rent-Gross		129	
(b) Profit on sale of investments			
Less: Loss on sale of investments			
Other Income (To be specified)			
Total (A)		346	
Provisions (Other than Taxation)		—	
Depreciation		9	

Other Expenses – Director's Fee		80	
Total (B)		89	
Profit Before Tax		257	
Provision for Taxation		99	
Profit after Tax		158	

Working Notes:

Particulars	Fire (₹.'000)	Marine (₹.'000)
(i) Claims under policies *less* reinsurance		
Claims paid during the year	100	80
Add: Outstanding at the end	10	15
Less: Outstanding at the beginning	28	7
	82	88
(ii) Expenses of management		
Expenses paid during the year	60	45
Add: Outstanding at the end	10	5
	70	50
(iii) Premiums *less* reinsurance		
Premiums received during the year	450	330
Add: Outstanding at the end	30	20
Less: Reinsurance premiums	25	15
	455	335

(iv) Reserve for unexpired risks is 50% of net premium for Fire Insurance and 100% of net premium for Marine Insurance.

Dr. **(V) PROVISION FOR TAXATION ACCOUNT** *Cr.*

Date	Particulars	₹.'000	Date	Particulars	₹.'000
2014-15	To Bank A/c (Taxes paid)	60	01.4.2014	By Balance b/d	85
31.3.2015	To Balance c/d	124	31.3.2015	By P & L A/c	99
		184			184

PROBLEM 4

The following are the Balances of Hercules Insurance Co. Ltd. as on 31st March 2015.

Particulars	(₹.'000)
Capital	320,00
Balances of Funds as on 1.4.2014	
Fire Insurance	800,00
Marine Insurance	950,00
Miscellaneous Insurance	218,65
Unclaimed Dividends	8,50
Amount Due to other Insurance Companies	34,50

Sundry Creditors	72,50
Deposit and Suspense Account (Cr.)	22,80
Profit and Loss Account (Cr.)	80,40
Agents Balances (Dr.)	135,00
Interest Accrued but not due (Dr.)	22,50
Due from other Insurance Companies	64,50
Cash in Hand	3,50
Balance in Current Account with Bank	74,80
Furniture and Fixtures WDV (Cost 100,00)	58,00
Stationery Stock	1,40
Expenses of Management:	
Fire Insurance	280,00
Marine Insurance	160,00
Miscellaneous Insurance	40,00
Others	30,00
Foreign Taxes — Marine	8,00
Outstanding premium	82,00
Donation Paid (No. 80G Benefit)	10,00
Transfer Fees	1,00
Provision for Bad Debts	11,70
Income Tax Paid	120,00
Mortgage Loan (Dr.)	975,00
Sundry Debtors	25,00
Government Securities (1020,00)	37,00
Debentures	1020,00
Equity Shares of Joint Stock Companies	465,50
Claims *less* Re-insurance:	225,00
Fire	450,00
Marine	358,90
Miscellaneous	68,00
Premium Less Re-insurance:	
Fire	1762,50
Marine	10,22,50
Miscellaneous	262,25
Interest and Dividends Received on Investments	46,80
Tax Deducted at Source	11,70
Commission:	
Fire	500,00
Marine	350,00
Miscellaneous	80,00

You are required to make the following provisions:

(a) Depreciation of Furniture — 10% of Original cost	
(b) Depreciation on investments of Joint stock companies shares	10,00
(c) Transfer to General Reserve	10,00
(d) Outstanding claims as on 31.3.2015	
Fire	200,00
Marine	50,00
Miscellaneous	32,50

Provision for tax @ 50%, Proposed Dividends @ 20%, Provision for the unexpired risk is to be made as follows:

(a) On Marine Policies @ 100% Premium *less* reinsurance.

(b) On other Policies @ 50% Premium *less* reinsurance.

You are required to prepare the Revenue and Profit and Loss Account for the year ended 31.3.2015.

SOLUTION

FORM B – RA (PRESCRIBED BY IRDA)
PERFECT GENERAL INSURANCE CO. LTD.
REVENUE ACCOUNT FOR THE YEAR ENDED 31st MARCH, 2015
FIRE AND MARINE INSURANCE BUSINESSES

Particulars	*Schedule*	*Fire Current Year (₹.'000)*	*Marine Current Year (₹.'000)*	*Misc. Current Year (₹.'000)*
Premiums earned (Net)	1	1681,25	950,00	349,77
Interest, Dividends and Rent – Gross	–	—	—	—
Double Income Tax refund		—	—	—
Profit on sale of motor car		—	—	—
Total (A)		1681,25	950,00	349,77
Claims incurred (net)	2	650,00	408,90	100,50
Commission	3	500,00	350,00	80,00
Operating Expenses related to				
Insurance business	4	280,00	160,00	40,00
Bad debts		—	—	—
Indian and Foreign Taxes		—	8,00	—
Total (B)		1430,00	926,90	220,50
Profit from Insurance business (A – B)		251,25	23,10	129.,27

SCHEDULES FORMING PART OF REVENUE ACCOUNT

SCHEDULE 1 PREMIUMS EARNED (NET)

Particulars	*Fire Current Year (₹.'000)*	*Marine Current Year (₹.'000)*	*Misc. Current Year (₹.'000)*
Premium *less* reinsruance (net)	1762,50	1022,50	26225
Less: Change in Provision for Unexpired Risk	(81,25)	(72,50)	87,52
	1681,25	950,00	349,77
Schedule — 2 Claims incurred (net)	650,00	408,90	100,50
Schedule — 3 Commission paid	50,000	350,00	80,00
Schedule — 4 Operating expenses related to insurance business			
Expenses of Management	280,00	160,00	40,00

FORM B – RA (PRESCRIBED BY IRDA)
PERFECT GENERAL INSURANCE CO. LTD.
PROFIT & LOSS ACCOUNT FOR THE YEAR ENDED 31st MARCH, 2015
FIRE AND MARINE INSURANCE BUSINESSES

Particulars	*Schedule*	*Current Year (₹ '000)*	*Previous Year (₹ '000)*
Operating Profit/(Loss)			
(a) Fire Insurance		251,25	
(b) Marine Insurance		23,10	
(c) Miscellaneous		129,27	
Income from Investments			
(a) Interest Dividends & Rent-Gross		58,50	
Other Income			
Transfer Fees		1,00	
Total (A)		463,12	
Provisions (Other then taxation)			
Depreciation of Furniture		10,00	
Depreciation of Investments		10,00	
Other Expenses:			
Expenses of Management		30,00	
Donation		10,00	
Total (B)		60,00	
Profit Before Tax		403,12	
Provision for Taxation		206,56	
Profit After Tax		196,56	
Less: Appropriations			
(a) Interim dividends paid during the year		—	

(b) Proposed final dividend		64,00	
(c) Dividend distribution tax		—	
(d) Transfer to General Reserve *or* Other Account (to be specified)		10,00	
Profit after Appropriations		122,56	
Balance of Profit/Loss brought forward from last year		80,40	
Balance carried forward to balance sheet		202,96	

Working Notes:

(i) Reserve for unexpired risk @ 50% of net premium for fire and miscellaneous and @ 100% of net premium for marine.

(II) PROVISION FOR TAXATION

Particulars	₹
Net Profit before tax	403,12
Add: Donation	10,00
Taxable Profit	413,12
Tax 50%	206,56

PROBLEM 5

Prepare the Fire Insurance Revenue A/c as per IRDA regulations for the year ended 31st March, 2015 from the following details:

Particulars	₹
Claims paid	5,00,000
Legal expenses regarding claims	10,000
Premiums received	12,50,000
Re-insurance premium paid	50,000
Commission	3,00,000
Expenses of Management	2,00,000
Provision against unexpired risk on 1st April, 2014	5,75,000
Claims unpaid on 1st April, 2014	50,000
Claims unpaid on 31st March, 2015	80,000

Provision against unexpired risk @ 50% *less* Re-insurance

SOLUTION

FORM B - RA

Name of the Insurer:

Registration No. and Date of Registration with the IRDA

FIRE INSURANCE REVENUE ACCOUNT
For the year ended 31st March, 2015

	Particulars	*Schedule*	*Amount*
1.	Premium earned	1	11,75,000
2.	Other income		—
3.	Interest, dividend and rent		—
	Total (A)		11,75,000
4.	Claims incurred	2	5,40,000
5.	Commission	3	3,00,000
6.	Operating expenses related to Insurance business	4	2,00,000
	Total (B)		10,40,000
	Operating Profit (A) – (B)		1,35,000

Particulars	₹
Schedule 1: Premium earned	
Premium received	12,50,000
Less: Re-insurance Premium	(50,000)
	12,00,000
Less: Adjustment for Change in provision for un-expired risk (Refer W.N.)	25,000
	11,75,000
Schedule 2: Claims Incurred	
Claims paid including legal expenses (5,10,000 + 10,000)	5,10,000
Add: Claims outstanding at the end of the year	80,000
Less: Claims outstanding at the beginnging of the year	(50,000)
Total claims incurred	5,40,000
Schedule 3: Commission	
Commission paid	3,00,000
Schedule 4: Operating Expenses	
Expenses of Management	2,00,000

Working Note:

CHANGE IN THE PROVISION FOR UNEXPIRED RISK

Particulars	₹
Closing Unexpired Risk Reserve [50% of ₹ 12,00,000]	6,00,000
Opening Unexpired Risk Reserve	(5,75,000)
	25,000

13 ACCOUNTING FOR DEPARTMENTS

LEARNING OBJECTIVES

After studying this chapter, you should be able to understand:

- ◇ Meaning and Objective of Departmental Accounts
- ◇ Distinction Between Branch Accounts and Departmental Accounts
- ◇ Basis of Allocation of Common Expenses
- ◇ Inter-Departmental Transfers

1.0 MEANING AND OBJECTIVE OF DEPARTMENTAL ACCOUNTS

Departmental Accounts are the accounts relating to the several departments *or* division of business and are prepared to ascertain the operating results of each department separately. Separate Trading and Profit and Loss Account are prepared for each department in order to measure the relative efficiency and profitability of each department. Departmental Accounts are of great help and assistance to the Management as an information for taking a decision to continue *or* expand *or* to shut down a department.

2.0 DISTINCTION BETWEEN BRANCH ACCOUNTS AND DEPARTMENTAL ACCOUNTS

Branch Accounts differ from Departmental Accounts in the following respects:

Basis of Distinction	Branch Accounts	Departmental Accounts
1. Place at which accounts may be maintained	Branch accounts may be maintained at Head office *or* Branch.	Departmental Accounts are maintained at one place.
2. Allocation of Common Expenditure	There is usually no problem in allocation of common allocation of common expenditure (except for H.O. expenditure) since the amount of expense in respect of each branch can be identified.	There is problem of allocation of common expenditure among different Departments.
3. Problem of Reconciliation	In case of an independent branch, reconciliation of Head Office and Branch accounts is necessary.	No such problem arises.
4. Problem of conversion of Foreign Branch Figures	In case of Foreign Branch, the problem of conversion of foreign branch figures arises.	No such problem arises.

3.0 BASIS OF ALLOCATION OF COMMON EXPENSES

While preparing Departmental Accounts the expenses should be allocated among the different departments on a rational basis. Some of the practical guidelines in this regard are as follows:

1. **Charging of Individually Identifiable Expenses:** The expenses which can be directly identified with a particular department, are charged directly thereto.
2. **Charging of Common Expenses:** The common expenses which have been incurred for various departments are charged to various departments proportionately on some equitable basis. Some bases of distribution of the common costs are given below:

Item	*Basis*
(a) Rent, Rates, Taxes, Repairs and Maintenance of Building	Floor Area of each Department
(b) Lighting	No. of light points in each Department *or* by Separate meters.
(c) Power	Consumption as per separate meter *or* horse power of Machines.
(d) Discount received/Carriage inwards	Purchases of each Department.
(e) Carriage outward, Discount allowed, Bad Debts, Salesman's Commission, Advertisement, Delivery Expenses	Sales of each Department
(f) Depreciation, Insurance, Maintenance of Capital Assets. Repairs and	Asset value of each Department
(g) Canteen Expenses and other Labour welfare expenses	No. of employees in each Department
(h) P.F. Contribution, ESI contribution	Wages and Salaries of each Department
(i) General Manger's Salary	Time devoted to each Department.

4.0 INTER-DEPARTMENTAL TRANSFERS

1. **Basis of Inter-Departmental Transfers:** The Goods *or* Services may be transferred by one department to another department on *either* of the following basis:
   (i) At Actual Cost (ii) At Cost *plus* agreed percentage of profit. (iii) At Ruling Market Price, The transfer by transferor department is treated as sales and as purchases by transferee department.
2. **Elimination of Unrealized Profit:** When the transfer price includes an element of profit, the unrealized profit included in the unsold stock at the end of the year is to be excluded so as to eliminate an anticipated profit included therein. Such unrealized profit is eliminated by creating a Stock Reserve.
3. **How to calculate Stock Reserve:** The amount of Stock Reserve is calculated as follows:

   Step 1: *Treat the Transfer of Goods as Sales of the Transferor Deptt and as Purchases of the Transferee Deptt.*

   Step 2: *Treat the Return of Goods as Purchase Returns of the Returning Deptt and as Sales Returns of the Receiving Deptt.*

   Step 3: *Show All Direct Expenses in the Individual Trading Account of each Deptt*

   Step 4: *Calculate the Gross Profit of each Deptt*

   Step 5: *Calculate the Net Sales (i.e. Sales + Internal Transfers – Sales Returns) of each Deptt*

   Step 6: *Calculate the Stock Reserve (i.e. Unrealised Profit included in Closing Stock of each Deptt)*

$$= \text{Transfer Price of Unsold Stock of Transferee Deptt.} \times \frac{\text{Gross Profit of Transferor Deptt.}}{\text{Net Sales of Transferor Deptt.}}$$

4. **Journal Entry:** The following Journal entry is passed in this regard:

   Profit and Loss A/c Dr.

   To Stock Reserve A/c

   (Being the provision made for unrealised profit included in closing stock)

5. **Disclosure In Balance Sheet:** The unsold closing stock acquired from another department will appear on the assets side of the Balance Sheet as under:

Liabilities	₹	*Assets*	₹
		Current Assets:	
		Closing Stock	xxx
		Less: Stock Reserve	xxx
			xxx

6. **Accounting in the Next Year:** In the beginning of the next year, the aforesaid journal entry is reversed as under:

   Stock Reserve A/c Dr.

   To Profit and Loss A/c

ILLUSTRATION 1

X Ltd. provides you the following information:

	Stock as on 1.4.2015	Purchases (for ₹ 1,00,000)	Sales
Department A	120 units	1000 Units	1020 units @ ₹ 20.00
Department B	80 units	2000 Units	1920 units @ ₹ 22.50
Department C	152 units	2400 Units	2496 Units @ ₹ 25.00

The rate of gross profit is the same in each case.

Required: Prepare Departmental Trading Account for the year 2015–2016.

SOLUTION

Dr. **DEPARTMENTAL TRADING ACCOUNT FOR THE YEAR ENDING ON MARCH 31, 2016** *Cr.*

Particulars	A Dept. ₹	B Dept. ₹	C Dept. ₹	Total ₹	Particulars	A Dept. ₹	B Dept. ₹	C Dept. ₹	Total ₹
To Op. Stock	1,920	1,440	3,040	6,400	By Sales	20,400	43,200	62,400	1,26,000
To Purchases	16,000	36,000	48,000	1,00,000	By Cl. Stock	1,600	2,880	1,120	5,600
To Gross profit	4,080	8,640	12,480	25,200					
	22.000	46,080	63,520	1,31,600		22,000	46,080	63,520	1,31,600

Working Notes:

1. Closing Stock of Deptt. A = Opening Stock + Purchases – Sales = 120 + 1,000 – 1,020 = 100
2. Closing Stock of Deptt. B = 80 + 2,000 – 1,920 = 160
3. Closing Stock of Deptt. C = 152 + 2,400 – 2,496 = 56
4. The rate of gross profit: Assuming all the purchases are sold,the sale proceeds would be:

Particulars	₹
A. 1,000 units @ ₹ 20.00	20,000
B. 2,000 units @ ₹ 22.50	45,000
C. 2,400 units @ ₹ 25.00	60,000
	1,25,000

5. Gross Profit = Sales – Cost = ₹ 1,25,000 – ₹ 1,00,000 = ₹ 25,000

$$\text{Gross Profit Ratio} = \frac{\text{Gross Profit}}{\text{Sales}} \times 100 = \frac{25,000}{1,25,000} \times 100 = 20\%$$

Profit and Cost for each article:

Particulars	Profit (₹)	Cost (₹)
A. 20% of ₹ 20.00	4.00	16.00
B. 20% of ₹ 22.50	4.50	18.00
C. 20% of ₹ 25.00	5.00	20.00

ILLUSTRATION 2

X Ltd. has three departments A, B and C. From the particulars given below compute:

(a) the values of stock as on 31st March 2016 and

(b) the departmental results

(i)

Particulars	*A* ₹	*B* ₹	*C* ₹
Opening Stock	24,000	36,000	12,000
Purchases	1,46,000	1,24,000	48,000
Actual Sales	1,72,500	1,59,400	74,600
Gross Profit on normal selling price	20%	25%	33.1/3%

(ii) During the year certain items were sold at discount and these discounts were reflected in the value of sales shown above. The items sold at discount were:

Particulars	*A* ₹	*B* ₹	*C* ₹
Sales at normal price	10,000	3,000	1,000
Sales at actual price	7,500	2,400	600

SOLUTION

1. CALCULATION OF DEPARTMENTAL RESULTS (ACTUAL GROSS PROFIT)

Particulars	*A (₹)*	*B (₹)*	*C (₹)*
Actual Sales	1,72,500	1,59,400	74,600
Add back: Discount (Normal Price – Actual Price)	2,500	600	400
Normal Sales	1,75,000	1,60,000	75,000
Gross Profit % on normal Sales	20%	25%	33.33%
Normal Gross Profit	35,000	40,000	25,000

Less: Discount	(2,500)	(600)	(400)
Actual Gross Profit	32,500	39,400	24,600

2. COMPUTATION OF VALUE OF STOCK AS ON 31ST MARCH 2016

Particulars	*A (₹)*	*B (₹)*	*C (₹)*
Opening Stock	24,000	36,000	12,000
Add: Purchases	1,46,000	1,24,000	48,000
	1,70,000	1,60,000	60,000
Add: Actual Gross Profit	32,500	39,400	24,600
	2,02,500	1,99,400	84,600
Less: Actual Sales	(1,72,500)	(1,59,400)	(74,600)
Closing Stock (bal Fig.)	30,000	40,000	10,000

Working Note:

COMPUTATION OF DISCOUNT ON SALES

Particulars	*A (₹)*	*B (₹)*	*C (₹)*
Sales at normal price	10,000	3,000	1,000
Less: Sales at actual price	(7,500)	(2,400)	(600)
	2,500	600	400

ILLUSTRATION 3

X Ltd., has two departments A and B. From the following particulars, prepare the Departmental Trading Account and Consolidated Trading & Profit & Loss Account for the year ending on 31st March, 2016:

Particulars	*A* ₹	*B* ₹
Opening Stock (at cost)	20,000	12,000
Purchases	92,000	68,000
Sales	1,40,000	1,12,000
Wages	12,000	8,000
Carriage	2,000	2,000
Closing Stock:		
(i) Purchased goods	4,500	6,000
(ii) Finished goods	24,000	14,000
Purchased goods transferred:		
by B to A	10,000	
by A to B		8,000
Finished goods transferred:		
by A to B	35,000	
by B to A		40,000

Return of finished goods:		
by A to B	10,000	
by B to A		7,000

You are informed that purchased goods have been transferred mutually at their respective departmental purchase cost and finished goods at departmental market price and that 20% of the finished stock (closing) at each department represented finished goods received from the other department.

SOLUTION

DEPARTMENTAL TRADING ACCOUNT
FOR THE YEAR ENDING ON 31ST MARCH, 2016

Dr. *Cr.*

Particulars	*Dept. A* ₹	*Dept. B* ₹	*Particulars*	*Dept. A* ₹	*Dept. B* ₹
To Stock	20,000	12,000	By Sales	1,40,000	1,12,000
To Purchases	92,000	68,000	By Purchased Goods		
To Wages	12,000	8,000	t/f to other Dept.	8,000	10,000
To Carriage	2,000	2,000	By Finished goods t/f		
To Purchased Goods			to other Dept	35,000	40,000
from other Dept.	10,000	8,000	By Return of finished		
To Finished Goods t/f			Goods to other Dept.	10,000	7,000
from other dept.	40,000	35,000	By Closing Stock:		
To Return of Finished			Purchased Goods	4,500	6,000
goods from other Dept.	7,000	10,000	Finished Goods out		
To Gross Profit	38,500	46,000	of t/f	4,800	2,800
			Balance	19,200	11,200
	2,21,500	1,89,000		2,21,500	1,89,000

CONSOLIDATED TRADING AND PROFIT & LOSS ACCOUNT
FOR THE YEAR ENDING ON 31ST MARCH, 2016

Dr. *Cr.*

Particulars		₹	*Particulars*	₹
To Opening Stock		32,000	By Sales	2,52,000
To Purchases		1,60,000	By Closing Stock:	
To Wages		20,000	Purchased Goods	10,500
To Carriage		4,000	Finished Goods	38,000
To Gross Profit c/d		84,500		
		3,00,500		3,00,500
To Stock Reserve		2,197	By Gross Profit b/d	84,500
To Net Profit		82,303		
		84,500		84,500

Working Notes:

(I) CALCULATION OF NET SALES (INCLUDING TRANSFERS)

Particulars	*Dept. A* ₹	*Dept. B* ₹
(a) Sales	1,40,000	1,12,000
(b) *Add:* Transfer	35,000	40,000
(c) *Less:* Returns	7,000	10,000
(d) Net Sales *plus* Transfer	1,68,000	1,42,000

(II) Unrealised Profit on Closing Stock: Dept. A 4,800 × 46,000/1,42,000 = ₹ 1,555

Dept. B 2,800 × 38,500/1,68,000 = ₹ 642

ILLUSTRATION 4

From the following, Prepare Departmental Trading Account, General Profit & Loss Account and the Balance Sheet as at 31st March, 2016:

Particulars	*Dr.* (₹)	*Cr.* (₹)
Capital		3,00,000
Fixed Assets	1,50,000	
Opening Stock:		
Department A	30,000	
Department B	40,000	
Purchases:		
Department A	10,00,000	
Department B	15,00,000	
Sales:		
Department A		20,00,000
Department B		32,00,000
General Expenses	13,06,750	
Debtors	10,00,000	
Bank	2,06,250	
Creditors		1,00,000
Drawings	2,80,000	
Discount Received	—	25,000
Discount Allowed	52,000	—
Rent & Rates	60,000	—
	56,25,000	56,25,000

Additional Information:

(a) Closing Stock of Department A is ₹ 1,30,000. It includes Stock of ₹ 40,000 which B Department has sent to A Department.

(b) Closing Stock of B Department ₹ 2,60,000. It includes Stock of ₹ 90,000 which A Department has sent to B Department.

(c) Sales of A Department include goods of ₹ 2,00,000 transferred to B Department. Sales of B Department, include goods of ₹ 3,00,000 transferred to A Department. Both of these transfers have been made at market price.

(d) Opening Stock of A Department includes goods of ₹ 10,000 taken from B Department and Opening Stock of B Department includes goods of ₹ 15,000 taken from A department.

(e) Depreciate Fixed Assets @ 10% p.a. The Area occupied by Deptt. A and Deptt. B is in the ratio of 3 : 2.

SOLUTION

DEPARTMENTAL TRADING ACCOUNT FOR THE YEAR ENDED 31ST MARCH, 2016

Dr. *Cr.*

Particulars	*A* ₹	*B* ₹	*Particulars*	*A* ₹	*B* ₹
To Opening Stock	30,000	40,000	By Sales	20,00,000	32,00,000
To Purchases	10,00,000	15,00,000	By Closing Stock	1,30,000	2,60,000
To Gross Profit c/d	11,00,000	19,20,000			
	21,30,000	34,60,000		21,30,000	34,60,000
To Discount Allowed	20,000	32,000	By Gross Profit b/d	11,00,000	19,20,000
To Rent & Rates	36,000	24,000	By Discount Received	10,000	15,000
To Net Profit	10,54,000	18,79,000			
	11,10,000	19,35,000		11,10,000	19,35,000

GENERAL P&L ACCOUNT FOR THE YEAR ENDED 31ST MARCH, 2016

Dr. *Cr.*

Particulars		₹	*Particulars*		₹
To General Expenses		13,06,750	By Net Profit b/d:		
To Depreciation:		15,000	A	10,54,000	
To Stock Reserve: (Closing Stock)			B	18,79,000	29,33,000
Dept. A	24,000		By Stock Reserve (Opening Stock)		
Dept.	B49,500	73,500	Dept A	6,000	
To Net Profit		15,52,000	Dept B	8,250	14,250
		29,47,250			29,47,250

BALANCE SHEET AS AT 31ST MARCH, 2016

Liabilities		₹	*Assets*		₹
Capital	3,00,000	—	Fixed Assets	1,50,000	
Add: Net Profit	15,52,000		*Less:* Depreciation	(15,000)	1,35,000
Less: Drawings	2,80,000	15,72,000	Bank		2,06,250
Creditors		1,00,000	Debtors		10,00,000
Stock Reserve (Net):			Closing Stock:		
Closing Stock	73,500		Deptt. A	1,30,000	
Opening Stock	(14,250)	59,250	Deptt. B	2,60,000	3,90,000
		17,31,250			17,31,250

Working Notes:

(i) Percentage of Profit: $A = \frac{11,00,000}{20,00,000} \times 100 = 55\%$, $B = \frac{19,20,000}{32,00,000} \times 100 = 60\%$

(ii) Opening Stock Reserve: $A = 10,000 \times \frac{60}{100} = ₹6,000$, $B = 15,000 \times \frac{55}{100} = ₹8,250$

(iii) Closing Stock Reserve: $A = 40,000 \times \frac{60}{100} = ₹24,000$, $B = 90,000 \times \frac{55}{100} = ₹49,500$

(iv) Stock Reserve is calculated on unsold stock of inter-department sales. Hence Stock of Department A is adjusted according to the profit rate applicable to B. Similarly stock of Department B is adjusted according to the profit rate applicable to A.

(v) Discount Received are divided in the ratio of purchase value i.e., 10 : 15

Rent and rates are divided in the ratio of area i.e., 3 : 2

Discount allowed are divided in the ratio of Sales i.e., 20 : 32

ILLUSTRATION 5

A firm has two departments, cloth and readymade cloths. The cloths were made by the firm itself out of cloth supplied by the cloth department at its usual selling price. From the following figure prepare Departmental Trading and Profit and Loss Account for the year 2015 – 2016:

Particulars	*Cloth Department* ₹	*Readymade Cloth department* ₹
Opening Stock	3,00,000	50,000
Purchases	20,00,000	15,000
Sales	22,00,000	4,50,000
Transfer to Readymade Cloths Dept.	3,00,000	—
Manufacturing Expenses	—	60,000
Selling, Rent & Warehousing Expenses	20,000	6,000
Closing Stock	2,00,000	60,000

The Stock of the readymade clothes department may be considered as consisting of 75% cloth and 25% other expenses. The cloth department earned gross profit at the rate of 15% in 2014 – 2015. General Expenses of the business as a whole came to ₹ 1,10,000.

SOLUTION

DEPARTMENTAL TRADING AND PROFIT AND LOSS ACCOUNT FOR THE YEAR ENDING 31ST MARCH, 2016

Dr. *Cr.*

Particulars	*Cloth* ₹	*Readymade* ₹	*Particulars*	*Cloth* ₹	*Readymade* ₹
To Opening Stock	3,00,000	50,000	By Sales	22,00,000	4,50,000
To Purchases	20,00,000	15,000	By Transfer to		
To T/f to Readymade			redymade from cloth	3,00,000	—
cloth deptt.	—	3,00,000	By Closing Stock	2,00,000	60,000
To Mfg. Expenses	—	60,000			
To Gross Profit C/d	4,00,000	85,000			
	27,00,000	5,10,000		27,00,000	5,10,000

To Selling Expenses	20,000	6,000	By Gross profit b/d	4,00,000	85,000
To Net Profit	3,80,000	79,000			
	4,00,000	85,000		4,00,000	85,000

GENERAL PROFIT AND LOSS ACCOUNT
FOR THE YEAR ENDING 31ST MARCH, 2016

Dr. Cr.

Particulars	₹	*Particulars*		₹
To General Expenses	1,10,000	By Net Profit:		
To Stock Reserve (closing stock)	7,200	Cloth	3,80,000	
To Net Profit	3,47,425	Readymade	79,000	4,59,000
		By Stock Reserve [Opening Stock]		5,625
	4,64,625			4,64,625

Working Notes:

(i) Rate of Gross Profit for Cloth Department for 2015 – 2016:

$$\text{Rate} = \frac{\text{G.P. of Cloth Dept.}}{\text{Sales of Cloth Dept.}} \times 100 = \frac{4,00,000}{22,00,000 + 3,00,000} \times 100. = 16\%$$

(ii) Stock Reserve on Opening Stock = 50,000 × 75% × 15% = ₹, 5,625

(Opening Stock of 2015 – 2016 is nothing but Closing Stock of 2011 – 2015. Therefore G.P. 15% of 2011-12 is taken).

(iii) Stock Reserve on Closing Stock = ₹ 60,000 × 75% × 16% = ₹ 7,200

ILLUSTRATION 6

Department X sells goods to Department Y at a profit of 25% on cost and to Department Z at 10% profit on cost. Department Y sells goods to X and Z at a profit of 15% and 20% on sales, respectively. Department Z charges 20% and 25% profit on cost to Department X and Y, respectively.

Department Managers are entitled to 10% commission on net profit after eliminating unrealised profit on departmental sales being eliminated. Departmental profits after charging Managers' commission, but before adjustment of unrealised profit are as under:

Department X	₹ 36,000
Department Y	₹ 27,000
Department Z	₹ 18,000

Stocks lying at different departments at the end of the year are as under:

Particulars	*Dept. X* ₹	*Dept. Y* ₹	*Dept. Z* ₹
Transfer from Department X	—	15,000	11,000
Transfer from Department Y	14,000	—	12,000
Transfer from Department Z	6,000	5,000	—

Required: Find out the correct departmental Profits after charging Managers' commission.

SOLUTION

UNREALISED PROFIT ON UNSOLD STOCK

Particulars	*Department X* ₹	*Department Y* ₹	*Department Z* ₹	*Total* ₹
Unrealised Profit of Department X	—	1/5 of 15,000 = 3,000	1/11 of 11,000 = 1,000	4,000
Unrealised Profit of Department Y	15% of 14,000 = 2,100	—	20% of 12,000 = 2,400	4,500
Unrealised Profit of Department Z	1/6 of 6,000 = 1,000	1/5 of 5,000 = 1,000	—	2,000

CALCULATION OF CORRECT DEPARTMENTAL PROFITS AFTER CHARGING DEPARTMENTAL MANAGER'S COMMISSION

Particulars	*Department X (₹)*	*Department Y (₹)*	*Department Z (₹)*
Profit after charging managers' commission	36,000	27,000	18,000
Add: Managers' commission (1/9)	4,000	3,000	2,000
Profit before commission & unrealised profit	40,000	30,000	20,000
Less: Unrealised profit on stock	4,000	(4,500)	(2,000)
Profit before Manager's Commission	36,000	25,500	18,000
Less: Commission of Departmental Managers @10%	3,600	(2,550)	(1,800)
Correct Departmental Profits	32,400	22,950	16,200

ILLUSTRATION 7

FGH Ltd. has three departments I.J.K. The following information provided for the year ended 31.3.2016.

Particulars	*I* ₹	*J* ₹	*K* ₹
Opening Stock	5,000	8,000	19,000
Opening Reserve for unrealised profit	—	2,000	3,000
Materials consumed	16,000	20,000	—
Direct labour	9,000	10,000	—
Closing stock	5,000	20,000	5,000
Sales	—	—	80,000
Area occupied (sq. mtr.)	2,500	1,500	1,000
No. of employees	30	20	10

Stocks of each department are valued at costs to the department concerned. Stocks of I are transferred to J at cost *plus* 20% and stocks of J are transferred to K at a gross profit of 20% on sales. Other common expenses are salaries and staff welfare ₹ 18,000, rent ₹ 6,000.

Prepare Departmental Trading, Profit and Loss Account for the year ending 31.3.2016.

SOLUTION

FGH LTD. DEPARTMENTAL TRADING AND PROFIT AND LOSS ACCOUNT FOR THE YEAR ENDED 31ST MARCH, 2016

Dr. *Cr.*

Particulars	*I* ₹	*J* ₹	*K* ₹	*Total* ₹	*Particulars*	*I* ₹	*J* ₹	*K* ₹	*Total* ₹
To Opening stock	5,000	8,000	19,000	32,000	By Sales			80,000	80,000
To Material consumed	16,000	20,000		36,000	By Interdepartmental transfer	30,000	60,000		90,000
To Direct labour	9,000	10,000		19,000	By Closing stock	5,000	20,000	5,000	30,000
To Inter-deptt. transfer		30,000	60,000	90,000					
To Gross profit	5,000	12,000	6,000	23,000					
	35,000	80,000	85,000	2,00,000		35,000	80,000	85,000	2,00,000
To Salaries and staff welfare	9,000	6,000	3,000	18,000	By Gross profit b/d	5,000	12,000	6,000	23,000
To Rent	3,000	1,800	1,200	6,000	By Net loss	7,000			7,000
To Net profit		4,200	1,800	6,000					
	12,000	12,000	6,000	30,000		12,000	12,000	6,000	30,000
To Net loss (I)				7,000	By Stock reserve b/d (J + K)				5,000
To Stock reserve (J + K) (Refer W.N.)				3,000	Net profit (J + K)				6,000
To Balance transferred to P&L a/c				1,000					
				11,000					11,000

Working Note:

CALCULATION OF UNREALIZED PROFIT ON CLOSING STOCK

Particulars	₹
Stock reserve of J department Cost	30,000
Transfer from I department	30,000
	60,000
Stock of J department	20,000

Proportion of stock of I department = ₹ 20,000 × (₹ 30,000/₹ 60,000) = ₹ 10,000

Stock reserve = ₹ 10,000 × (20/120) = ₹ 1667 (approx.)

Stock reserve of K department	₹
Stock transferred from J department	5,000
Less: Profit (stock reserve) 5,000 × 20%	1,000
Cost to J department	4,000

Proportion of stock of I department = ₹ 4,000 × (₹ 30,000/₹ 60,000) = ₹ 2,000

Stock reserve = ₹ 2,000 × (20/120) = ₹ 333 (approx.)

Total stock reserve = ₹ 1,000 + ₹ 333 = ₹ 1,333.

ILLUSTRATION 8

Complex Ltd., has 3 departments, A, B, C. The following information is provided:

Particulars	*A* ₹	*B* ₹	*C* ₹
Opening Stock	3,000	4,000	6,000
Consumption of direct materials	8,000	12,000	—
Wages	5,000	10,000	—
Closing Stock	4,000	14,000	8,000
Sales	—	—	34,000

Stock of each department is valued at cost to the department concerned. Stocks of A department are transferred to B at a margin of 50% above departmental cost. Stocks of B department are transferred to C department at a margin of 10% above departmental cost. Other expenses were: Salaries ₹ 2,000, Printing & Stationery ₹ 1,000, Rent ₹ 6,000, Interest paid ₹ 4,000, Depreciation ₹ 3,000, Allocate expenses in the ratio of departmental gross profit. Opening figures of reserves for unrealised profits on departmental stocks were; Department B ₹ 1,000; Department C ₹ 2,000.

Required: Prepare Departmental Trading and Profit & Loss Account for the year ending on March 31, 2016.

SOLUTION

DEPARTMENTAL TRADING AND PROFIT & LOSS ACCOUNT FOR THE YEAR ENDING ON 31ST MARCH, 2016

Dr. *Cr.*

Particulars	*A* ₹	*B* ₹	*C* ₹	*Total* ₹	*Particulars*	*A* ₹	*B* ₹	*C* ₹	*Total* ₹
To Opening Stock	3,000	4,000	6,000	13,000	By Internal t/f	18,000	33,000	—	51,000
To Direct material consumed	8,000	12,000	—	20,000	By Sales	—	—	34,000	34,000
To Wages	5,000	10,000	—	15,000	By Closing Stock	4,000	14,000	8,000	26,000
To Internal Transfer	—	18,000	33,000	51,000					
To Gross Profit c/d	6,000	3,000	3,000	12,000					
	22,000	47,000	42,000	1,11,000		22,000	47,000	42,000	1,11,000
To Salaries	1,000	500	500	2,000	By Gross Profit b/d	6,000	3,000	3,000	12,000
To Printing & Stationery	500	250	250	1,000	By Net Loss c/d	2,000	1,000	1,000	4,000
To Rent	3,000	1,500	1,500	6,000					
To Depreciation	1,500	750	750	3,000					
To Interest paid	2,000	1,000	1,000	4,000					
	8,000	4,000	4,000	16,000		8,000	4,000	4,000	16,000
To Net Loss b/d				4,000	By Provision for unrealised profit on opening stock				3,000
To Provision for unrealised profit on closing stock				3,918	By Balance t/f to profit & Loss A/c				4,918
				7,918					7,918

Working Notes:

(I) Fifo method for stock issue has been assumed. Alternatively this question could have been solved by assuming other methods for stock issue like LIFO Basis, Weighted Average basis, etc.

(II) CALCULATION OF UNREALISED PROFIT ON CLOSING STOCK OF DEPT. B

	Particulars	₹
A.	Current cost incurred by Dept. B (₹ 12,000 + ₹ 10,000 + ₹ 18,000)	40,000
B.	Profit included in Above (₹ 18,000 × 50/150)	6,000
C.	Profit included in closing stock of ₹ 14,000 (₹ 6,000 × ₹ 14,000/ ₹ 40,000)	2,100

(III) CALCULATION OF UNREALISED PROFIT ON CLOSING STOCK OF DEP. C

	Particulars	₹
A.	Current Cost incurred by Dept. C	33,000
B.	Profit of Dept. B included in above (₹ 33,000 × 10/110)	3,000
C.	Cost element of Dept. B included in current cost (₹ 33,000 – 3,000)	30,000
D.	Profit of Dept. A included in above cost (₹ 6,000 × ₹ 30,000/₹ 40,000)	4,500
E.	Total Profit included in current cost of Dept. C (₹ 3,000 + ₹ 4,500)	7,500
F.	Unrealised profit included in closing stock of ₹ 8,000 (₹ 7,500 × ₹ 8,000/₹ 33,000)	1,818
(IV)	Total unrealised profit (₹ 2,100 + ₹ 1,818)	3,918

SOLVED PROBLEMS

PROBLEM 1

Mixed goods were purchased for ₹ 1,00,000 and later they were assorted into three categories X, Y, Z as follows:

X 1,000—Selling Price ₹ 20 each

Y 2,000—Selling Price ₹ 22.50 each

Z 2,400—Selling Price ₹ 25 each

All categories yield the same rate of profit. Calculate the purchase price of each category.

SOLUTION

CALCULATION OF COST PURCHASE

Goods	*X*	*Y*	*Z*
Ratio of Quantity	1000 : *or* 5 :	2000 *or* 10:	2400 *or* 12:
Ratio of Sales price.	20:	22.50:	25:
composite Ratio	5 × 20 = 100	10 × 22.50 = 225	12 × 25 = 300

Total Purchase of ₹ 1,00,000 is divided into composite ratio i.e., 100:225:300

$X = \frac{1,00,000}{625} \times 100 =$ ₹16,000 Purchase Price per unit of X = 16,000/1,000 = ₹.16

$Y = \frac{1,00,000}{625} \times 225 =$ ₹36,000 Purchase Price per unit of Y = 36,000/2,000 = ₹.18

$Z = \frac{1,00,000}{625} \times 300 =$ ₹48,000. Purchase Price per unit of Z = 48,000/2,400 = ₹.20

PROBLEM 2

From the data prepare Departmental Trading Profit and Loss Account and thereafter the combined Income Account revealing the concern's true result for the year ended on 31st March, 2016:

Particulars	*Departments*	
	A (₹)	*B (₹)*
Stock (January)	40,000	—
Purchase from outside	2,00,000	20,000
Wages	10,000	1,000
Transfer of goods from Dept. A	—	50,000
Stock (March 31st) at cost to the Department	30,000	10,000
Sale to outside	2,00,000	71,000

B's entire stock represents goods from Department A which transfers them at 25% above its cost. Administrative and selling expenses amount to ₹ 15,000 which are to be allocated between departments A and B in the ratio 4:1 respectively.

SOLUTION

DEPARTMENTAL TRADING & PROFIT AND LOSS ACCOUNT FOR THE YEAR ENDING ON 31.03.2016

Dr. *Cr.*

Particulars	*A* ₹	*B* ₹	*Particulars*	*A* ₹	*B* ₹
To Opening Stock	40,000	—	By Sales	2,00,000	71,000
To Purchases	2,00,000	20,000	By Transfer of goods	50,000	—
To Wages	10,000	1,000	(A to B)		
To Transfer of goods			By Closing stock	30,000	10,000
(A to B)	—	50,000			
To Gross Profit C/d	30,000	10,000			
	2,80,000	81,000		2,80,000	81,000
To Adm. & Selling			By Gross Profit b/d	30,000	10,000
Exp., (4 : 1)	12,000	3,000			
To Profit	18,000	7,000			
	30,000	10,000		30,000	10,000

GENERAL PROFIT AND LOSS ACCOUNT

Dr. *Cr.*

Particulars	₹	*Particulars*		₹
To Stock Reserve		By Profit A		18,000
(Loading on unsold stock at		B	7,000	25,000
Dept. B] 10,000 × 1/5]	2,000			
To Net Profit	23,000			
	25,000			25,000

PROBLEM 3

From the following figures prepare accounts to disclose total profit and the profit of of the two departments A and B:

Particulars	₹	*Particulars*	₹
Opening Stock:		Advertising	8,100
A	15,200	Insurance	1,000
B	10,800	General Expenses	5,400
Purchases:		Discount Allowed	1,800
A	75,100	Accountancy Charges	500
B	69,800	Sales:	
Carriage inwards	2,860	A	1,00,000
Salaries:		B	80,000
A	9,000	Purchases Returns:	
B	8,500	A	1,100
General Salaries	11,600	B	800
Rent and Rates	6,000	Discount Received	1,430

The following further information is supplied:

(a) Goods transferred from department A to B were ₹ 5,000. This has not yet been recorded.

(b) General Salaries are to be allocated equally.

(c) The area occupied is in the ratio of 3:2

(d) Insurance premium is for a comprehensive policy, allocation being inconvenient.

(e) The closing stock of the two departments were:

A—₹ 17,800 and B—₹ 15,600

SOLUTION

DEPARTMENT TRADING AND PROFIT AND LOSS ACCOUNT FOR THE YEAR ENDING...

Particulars	A	B	*Particulars*	A	B
To Opening Stock	15,200	10,800	By Sales:	1,00,000	80,000
To Purcha. Less Returns			By Transfer [to B Deptt.]	5,000	—
[A = 75,100 – 1,100;			By Closing Stock	17,800	15,600
B = 69,800 – 800]	74, 000	69,000			
To Transfer [from A					
Department]	—	5,000			
To Carriage inwards	1,480	1,380			
To Gross Profit c/d	32,120	9,420			
	1,22,800	95,600		1,22,800	95,600
To Salaries	9,000	8,500	By Gross Profit b/d	32,120	9,420
To General Salaries	5,800	5,800	By Discount Recd.	740	690
To Rent and Taxes	3,600	2,400	By Net Loss (b/f)	—	13,390
To Advertising	4,500	3,600			

To General Expenses	3,000	2,400			
To Discount allowed	1,000	800			
To Net Profit (c/f)	5,960	—			
	32,860	23,500		32,860	23,500

Dr. **GENERAL PROFIT AND LOSS ACCOUNT FOR THE YEAR ENDED...** Cr.

Particulars	₹	*Particulars*	₹
To Net Loss:		By Net Profit:	
Department B	13,390	Department A	5,960
To Insurance	1,000	By Balance transferred to	
To Accounting charges	500	Balance Sheet (b/f)	8,930
	14,890		14,890

Working Notes:

(i) Carriage inward, Discount Received are divided in the ratio of purchase value i.e., 74:69

(ii) Rent and rates are divided in the ratio of area i.e., 3:2

(iii) Advertisement, General expenses, Discount allowed are divided in the ratio of Sales i.e., 5:4

(iv) Accounting charges are common, therefore shown in General Profit and Loss Account.

PROBLEM 4

A hotel proprietor has two departments viz., Apartment Department and meals Department. Following is the trial balance of his business:

Debit	₹	*Credit*	₹
Provisions	15,500	Income from apartment department	46,000
Stocks of provisions in the beginning	1,020	Income from meals department	32,000
Cash in hand and at bank	10,000	Capital	2,20,000
Customers' debit balance	800	Suppliers A/c	9,800
Building (1/10th used		Provision for depreciation on Building	24,000
for meals department)	2,10,000	Interest	1,130
Furniture and Equipment	60,000		
General Expenses	27,410		
Interest Accrued	200		
Life Insurance	1,600		
Income tax	400		
Wages	6,000		
	3,32,930		3,32,930

Additional Information:

(a) The Servants in the Apartment Dept. had occupied a room worth ₹ 120 and took meals worth ₹ 60. Similarly, servants in the Meals Dept. had occupied a room worth ₹ 150 and took meals worth ₹ 90.

(b) Wages are charged in the proportion of 1/2 to the Apartment Dept. 1/4th to the Provision dept. and remaining to the General P&L A/c.

(c) Increase provision for depreciation on building to ₹ 30,000.

(d) A sum of ₹ 800 representing accommodation ₹ 240 and meals ₹ 560 to be charged to proprietor of the hotel.

Required: Prepare Profit and Loss A/c and Balance Sheet as on 31.3.2016.

SOLUTION

DEPARTMENTAL TRADING ACCOUNT
Dr. **FOR THE YEAR ENDING ON 31ST MARCH, 2016** *Cr.*

Particulars	*Aprtt.* ₹	*Meals* ₹	*Particulars*	*Aprtt.* ₹	*Meals* ₹
To Stock	—	1,020	By Income	46,000	32,000
To Provisions	—	15,500	By Proprietor' A/c (drawing)	240	560
To Dep. on buildings	5, 400	600	By Inter-dept. adjustment	270	150
To Wages	3,000	1,500			
To Inter-dept. adjustment	180	240			
To Net Profit c/d	37,930	13,850			
	46,510	32,710		46,510	32,710

GENERAL P&L ACCOUNT
Dr. **FOR THE YEAR ENDING ON 31ST MARCH 2016** *Cr.*

Particulars	₹	*Particulars*	₹
To Wages	1,500	By Net Profit b/d:	
To General Expenses	27,410	Apartment	37,930
to Net Profit c/d	24,000	Meals	13,850
		By Interest	1,130
	52,910		52,910

BALANCE SHEET AS AT 31ST MARCH 2016

Liabilities		₹	*Assets*		₹
Capital	2,20,000		Buildings	2,10,000	
Less: Drawing:			*Less:* Provision for		
Income tax	400		Depreciation	30,000	1,80,000
Premium	1,600		Furniture and Equipment		60,000
Meals	560		Customer A/c		800
Apartment	240		Interest Accrued		200
Add: Net profit	24,000	2,41,200	Cash in hand at bank		10,000
Suppliers A/c		9,800			
		2,51,000			2,51,000

Working Notes:

Particulars	Apartment Dept.	Meals Dept.	Total expenses	
(i) Expenses pm Servants in Apartment dept.	120	60	180	(for Apartment dept.
(ii) Expenses on servants in Meals dept.	150	90	240	(for Meals dept.)
	270	150	420	

PROBLEM 5

Trading and Profit and Loss Account of Janaki Radio and Gramophone Equipment Co. for the six months end 31.3.2016 is presented to you in the following form:

Particulars	₹	Particulars	₹
Purchases:		Sales:	
Radios (A)	1,40,700	Radios (A)	1,50,000
Gramophones (B)	90,600	Gramophones (B)	1,00,000
Spare parts (C)	64,400	Spare parts (C)	25,000
Salaries and wages	48,000	Stock as on 31-3-2016	
Rent	10,800	Radios (A)	60,100
Sundry Expenses	11,000	Gramophones (A)	20,300
Profit	34,500	Spare Parts (C)	44,600
	4,00,000		4,00,000

Required: Prepare Departmental Accounts for each of the three departments A, B and C mentioned above after taking into account the following:

(i) Radios and Gramophones are sold at the show room and spare parts at work shop.

(ii) Salaries and wages comprise as follows:

Shop rooms 3/4 and work shop 1/4.

It was decided to allocate the show room salaries and wages in the ratio of 1 : 2 between the departments A and B.

(iii) The work shop rent is ₹ 500 per month. The rent of show room is to be divided equally between the departments A and B.

(iv) Sundry expenses are to be allocated on the basis of the turnover of each department.

SOLUTION

DEPARTMENTAL TRADING AND PROFIT AND LOSS ACCOUNT FOR THE SIX MONTHS ENDING 31.3.2016

Dr. *Cr.*

Particulars	A ₹	B ₹	C ₹	Particulars	A ₹	B ₹	C ₹
To Purchases	1,40,700	90,600	64,400	By Sales	1,50,000	1,00,000	25,000
To Gross Profit c/d	69,400	29,700	5,200	By Closing Stock	60,100	20,300	44,600
	2,10,100	1,20,300	69,600		2,10,100	1,20,300	69,600
To Salaries & Wages	12,000	24,000	12,000	By Gross Profit b/d	69,400	29,700	5,200

To Rent	3,900	3,900	3,000				
To Sundry exp. (6:4:1)	6,000	4,000	1,000	By Net Loss (Departmental)	—	2,200	10,800
To Net Profit (Departmental)	47,500						
	69,400	31,900	16,000		69,400	31,900	16,000

GENERAL PROFIT AND LOSS ACCOUNT
FOR THE SIX MONTHS ENDING 31.3.2016

Dr. *Cr.*

Particulars	₹	Particulars	₹
To P&L A/c (Dept. B)	2,200	By P&L A/c (Dept. A)	47,500
To P&L A/c (Dept. C)	10,800		
To Profit (to be t/f to Balance Sheet)	34,500		
	47,500		47,500

Working Notes

(i) Salaries and wages are to be allocated first between show room 3/4 i.e., ₹ 36,000; workshop 1/4 i.e., ₹ 12,000. Work shop salaries are to be charged to Dept. C.

(ii) Since Radio and Gramophones are sold at show room, salaries are to be allocated to Dept. 'A' and Dept. 'B' respectively in the ratio of 1 : 2

(iii) Rent of workshop at ₹ 500 p.m. for six months, ₹ 3,000 is to be charged to Dept. 'C' First and the balance ₹ 7,800 is to be divided equal between Dept. 'A' and 'B'.

(iv) Turnover Ratio = 1,50,000 : 1,00,000 : 25,000 = 6 : 4 : 1.

PROBLEM 6

Messers D, B and R carried on a business of Drapers and Tailors in Delhi; D was in charge of Department "A" dealing in cloth, B of Department "B" for selling garments and R of Department "C" the tailoring section. It had been agreed that each of the three partners would receive 75% of the profits disclosed by accounts of the department of which he was in charge and the balance of the profits would be shared in the proportion: D 1/2, B 1/4,and R 1/4. The following is the trading and profit and Loss Account of the firm for the six months ended 31st March, 2016.

TRADING AND PROFIT AND LOSS ACCOUNT

Dr. *Cr.*

Particulars	₹	Particulars	₹
To Opening Stock:		By Sales:	
Cloth (A)	37,890	Cloth (A)	1,80,000
Ready-made Garments (B)	24,000	Ready-made Garments (B)	1,30,000
Tailoring Jobs (C)	20,000	Tailoring Jobs (C)	90,000
To Purchases:		By Discount received	800
Cloth (A)	1,40,700	By Closing Stock:	
Ready-made Garments (B)	80,600	Cloth (A)	45,100
Tailoring Goods (C)	44,400	Ready-made Garments (B)	22,300
To Salaries and Wages	48,000	Tailoring Jobs (C)	
To Advertising	2,400	[including ₹ 5,700 for	
To Rent	10,800	goods transferred from	
To Discount Allowed	1,200	department (A)]	21,600

To Sundry Expenses	12,000		
To Depreciation on Furniture and Fittings	750		
To Net Profit	67,060		
	4,89,800		4,89,800

After consideration of the following, prepare Departmental Accounts and Profit and Loss Appropriation Account.

(i) Cloth of the value of ₹ 10,700 and other goods of the value of ₹ 600 were transferred at selling price by Departments A and B respectively to Department C. These transfers have not yet been adjusted in above Trading A/c.

(ii) Cloth and garments are sold in the show-room. Tailoring work is carried out in the workshop.

(iii) The details of salaries and wages were as follows:

(a) General Office 50%, show-room 25% and 25% for workshop 75% of which is for tailoring alone.

(b) Allocate General Office Expenses, in the proportion of 3:2:1 among the Departments A,B,C.

(c) Distribute show-room expenses in the proportion of 1:2 between Departments A and b.

(iv) The workshop rent is ₹ 1,000 per month. The rent of the General Office and Show-room is to be divided equally between Departments A and B.

(v) Depreciation charges are to be allocated equally amongst the three Departments.

(vi) All other expenses are to be allocated on the basis of turnover (excluding Internal Transfers).

(vii) Discounts received are to be credited to the three Departments as follows: A ₹ 400; B ₹ 250; C ₹ 150.

(viii) The opening stock of Department C does not include any goods transferred from Department A.

SOLUTION

DEPARTMENTAL TRADING AND PROFIT & LOSS ACCOUNT FOR THE SIX MONTHS ENDING ON 31ST MARCH, 2016

Dr. *Cr.*

Particulars	*A* ₹	*B* ₹	*C* ₹	*Total* ₹	*Particulars*	*A* ₹	*B* ₹	*C* ₹	*Total* ₹
To Opening Stock	37,890	24,000	20,000	81,890	By Sales	1,80,000	1,30,000	90,000	4,00,000
To Purchases	1,40,700	80,600	44,400	2,65,700	By Transfer	10,700	600	—	11,300
To Transfer	—	—	11,300	11,300	By Closing Stock	45,100	22,300	21,600	89,000
To Wages	—	—	9,000	9,000					
To Gross Profit c/d	57,210	48,300	26,900	1,32,410					
	2,35,800	1,52,900	1,11,600	5,00,300		2,35,800	1,52,900	1,11,600	5,00,300
To Salaries & Wages:					By Gross Profit b/d	57,210	48,300	26,900	1,32,410
General Office	12,000	8,000	4,000	24,000	By Discount Received	400	250	150	800
Showroom	4,000	8,000	—	12,000					
Workshop	—	—	3,000	3,000					
To Advertising	1,080	780	540	2,400					
To Rent	2,400	2,400	6,000	10,800					
To Discount Allowed	540	390	270	1,200					
To Sundry Expenses	5,400	3,900	2,700	12,000					
To Depreciation	250	250	250	750					

To Net Profit t/f to P & L Appropriation A/c	31,940	24,830	10,290	67,060					
	57,610	48,550	27,050	1,33,210		57,610	48,550	27,050	1,33,210

Note: Gross profit of Department A is 30% in Sales (including transfer to Dept C). There is some unrealised profit only on inter departmental stock. 30% of ₹ 5,700 is required as stock reserve. This will be debited to Profit and Loss Appropriation account.

Dr. **PROFIT & LOSS APPROPRIATION ACCOUNT** *Cr.*

Particulars		₹	*Particulars*	₹
To Stock Reserve (₹ 5,700 × 30/100)		1,710	By Net Profit from Profit & Loss A/c	67,060
To D: 75% of Profit of				
Dept. A	23,955			
50% of Common pool	7,527	31,482		
To B: 75% of profit of				
Dept B	18,623			
25% of Common pool	3,763	22,386		
To R: 75% of profit of				
Deptt. C	7,718			
25% of Common Pool	3,764	11,482		
		67,060		67,060

PROBLEM 7

Following is the Trial Balance of Mr. Rajan as on 31.03.2016:

Particulars		*Debit (₹)*	*Credit (₹)*
Capital Account			40,000
Drawing Account		1,500	
Opening Stock:	Department A	8,500	
	Department B	5,700	
	Department C	1,200	
Purchases:	Department A	22,000	
	Department B	17,000	
	Department C	8,000	
Sales:	Department A		54,000
	Department B		33,000
	Department C		21,000
Sales Returns:	Department A	4,000	
	Department B	3,000	
	Department C	1,000	
Freight and Carriage:	Department A	1,400	
	Department B	800	

	Department C	200	
Furnitures and Fixtures		4,600	
Plant and Machinery		20,000	
Bills Receivable		4,200	
Bills payable			8,000
Motor Vehicles		40,000	
Sundry Debtors		8,000	
Sundry Creditors			7,000
Salaries		4,500	
Power and water		1,200	
Telephone charges		2,100	
Bad debts		750	
Rent and taxes		6,000	
Insurance		1,500	
Wages:	Department A	800	
	Department B	550	
	Department C	150	
Printing and Stationaries		2,000	
Advertising		3,500	
Bank Overdraft			12,000
Cash in hand		850	
		1,75,000	1,75,000

Required: Prepare Department Trading, Profit and Loss Account and the Balance Sheet taking into account the following adjustments:

(a) Outstanding Wages: Department B – ₹ 150, Department C – ₹ 50,

(b) Salaries Payable ₹ 500

(c) Depreciate Plant and Machinery and Motor Vehicles at the rate of 10%.

(d) Create a Reserve of 5% for doubtful debts.

(e) Each Department shall share the expenses in proportion to their sales.

(f) Closing Stock: Department A – ₹ 3,500, Department B – ₹ 2,000, Department C – ₹ 1,500

SOLUTION

TRADING AND PROFIT AND LOSS ACCOUNT FOR THE YEAR ENDED ON 31ST MARCH 2016

Dr. *Cr.*

Particulars	*A* ₹	*B* ₹	*C* ₹	*Particulars*	*A* ₹	*B* ₹	*C* ₹
To Opening Stock	8,500	5,700	1,200	By Sales *less*			
To Purchases	22,000	17,000	8,000	Sales returns	50,000	30,000	20,000
To Freight & carriage	1,400	800	200	By Closing Stock	3,500	2,000	1,500
To Wages outstanding	800	700	200				
To Gross profit	20,800	7,800	11,900				
	53,500	32,000	21,500		53,500	32,000	21,500

To Salaries add o/s	2,500	1,500	1,000	By Gross Profit	20,800	7,800	11,900
To Power & Water	600	360	240	By Net Loss	—	735	—
To Telephone charges	1,050	630	420				
To Bad debts	375	225	150				
To rent & taxes	3,000	1,800	1,200				
To Insurance	750	450	300				
To Printing & stationery	1,000	600	400				
To Advertising	1,750	1,050	700				
To Depreciation (2,000 + 4,000)	3,000	1,800	1,200				
To Provision for doubtful debts	200	120	80				
To Net Profit	6,575	—	6,210				
	20,800	8,535	11,900		20,800	8,535	11,900

BALANCE SHEET AS AT 31.03.2016

Liabilities		₹	*Assets*		₹
Capital A/c	40,000		Furniture & Fixtures		4,600
Add: Net Profit			Plant & Machinery	20,000	
(₹ 6,575 + ₹ 6,210)	12,785		*Less:* Depreciation	2,000	18,000
	52,785		Motor Vehicles	40,000	
Less: Net loss in Dept B	735		*Less:* Depreciation	4,000	36,000
	52,050		Bills Receivable		4,200
Less: Drawings	1,500	50,550	Sundry Debtors	8,000	
Bills Payable		8,000	*Less:* Provision	400	7,600
Sundry Creditors		7000	Cash in hand		850
Bank Overdraft		12,000	Closing Stock		7,000
Wages outstanding		200			
Salary outstanding		500			
		78,250			78,250

SOLVED PROBLEMS II

PROBLEM 8

M/s Bright and Co, had four departments A B C and D. Each department being managed by a departmental manager whose commission was 10% of the respective departmental profit, subject to a minimum of ₹ 6,000 in each case. Interdepartmental transfers took place at a 'loaded' price as follows:

From Department A to Department B 10% above cost
From Department A to Department D 20% above cost
From Department C to Department D 20% above cost
From Department C to Department B 20% above cost

For the year ending on 31st March the firm had already prepared and closed the departmental Trading and profit and Loss Account. Subsequently, it was discovered that the closing stocks of departments had included interdepartmentally transferred goods at loaded price instead of cost price. From the following information, prepare a statement recomputing the departmental profit *or* loss:

Particulars	*Dept. A* ₹	*Dept. B* ₹	*Dept. C* ₹	*Dept. D* ₹
Final Profit (Loss)	(38,000)	50,400	72,000	1,08,000
Inter departmental transfers included at loaded price in the departmental stock		70,000	—	4,800
		(₹ 22,000 from Dept. A and ₹ 48,000 from Dept. C)		(₹ 3,600 from Dept. C and ₹ 1,200 from Dept.A)

SOLUTION

STATEMENT SHOWING THE RECOMPUTATION OF DEPARTMENTAL PROFIT OR LOSS

	Particulars	*A* ₹	*B* ₹	*C* ₹	*D* ₹
A.	Final Profit/(Loss) (Computed earlier)	(38,000)	50,400	72,000	1,08,000
B.	*Add:* Departmental Manager's Commission @ 10% of Deptt. Profit subject to a minimum of ₹ 6,000 [Working Note (i)]	6,000	6,000	8,000	12,000
C.	Profit before Deptt. Manager's Commission (A + B)	(32,000)	56,400	80,000	1,20,000
D.	*Less:* Profit earned through transfer of goods at loaded price remaining in stock at transfer department	(2,200)	—	(8,600)	—
E.	Correct Departmental profit (before manager's commission) (C – D)	(34,200)	56,400	71,400	1,20,000
F.	*Less:* Manager's commission @ 10% of profit subject to a minimum of ₹ 6,000	(6,000)	(6,000)	(7,140)	(12,000)
G.	Departmental profit after Manager's Commission (E – F)	(40,200)	50,400	64,260	1,08,000

Working Notes:

(I) MANAGER'S COMMISSION

	Dept. Profit/Loss	*Commission*	
A	(–)38,000	6,000	
B	50,400	6,000	i.e. (50,400*1/9 = ₹ 5,600 *less* than ₹ 6,000)
C	72,000	8,000	i.e. (72,000*1/9 = ₹ 8,000)
D	1,08,000	12,000	i.e. (1,08,000*1/9 = ₹ 12,000)

(II) UNREALISED PROFIT ON STOCK TRANSFER:

Dept A: ₹ 22,000 to Dept.B @110%, Profit thereon 22,000*10/110	= ₹ 2,000
₹ 1,200 to Dept. D @120%, Profit thereon 1,200*20/120	= ₹ 200
	₹ 2,200
Dept.C: ₹ 48,000 to Dept.B @ 120% Profit thereon 48,000*20/120	= ₹ 8,000
₹ 3,600 to Deptt.D @ 120% Profit thereon 3,600*20/120	= ₹ 600
	₹ 8,600

PROBLEM 9

X Limited is a retail organisation with several departments.Goods supplied to each department are debited to a Memorandum departmental stock account at cost, *plus* fixed percentage (mark-up) to give the normal selling price. The mark up is credited to a memorandum departmental "Mark-up account". any reduction in selling prices (mark-down) will require adjustment in the stock account and in mark-up account. The mark up for Department A for the last three years has been 40%. Figures relevant to Department A for the ended 31st March, 2016 were as follows:

Stock 1st April, 2015 at cost, ₹ 80,000, Purchases at cost ₹ 1,80,000, Sales ₹ 3,20,000

It is further ascertained that:

(a) Goods purchased in the period were marked down by ₹ 1,400 from a cost of ₹ 16,000. Marked-down stock costing ₹ 4,000 remained unsold on 31st March 2016.

(b) Stock shortages at the year end, which had cost ₹ 1,200 were to be written off.

(c) Stock at 1st April 2015 including goods costing ₹ 8,200 had been sold during the year and has been mark down in the selling price by ₹ 740. The remaining stock had been sold during the year.

(d) The departmental closing stock is to be valued at cost subject to adjustments for mark-up and mark-down.

Required: Prepare (i) A Departmental Trading Account (ii) A Memorandum Stock Account (iii) A Memorandum Mark-up Account for the year 2015 – 2016.

SOLUTION

(I) DEPARTMENTAL TRADING ACCOUNT FOR THE YEAR ENDING ON 31ST MARCH, 2016

Dr. Cr.

Particulars	₹	*Particulars*	₹
To Opening Stock	80,000	By Sales	3,20,000
To Purchases	1,80,000	By Shortage	1,200
To Gross Profit c/d	90,150	By Closing stock	28,950
		(₹ 40,180 – ₹ 11,230)	
	3,50,150		3,50,150

(II) MEMORANDUM DEPARTMENTAL STOCK ACCOUNT (AT SELLING PRICE)

Dr. Cr.

Particulars	₹	*Particulars*	₹
To Balance b/d		By profit & Loss A/c	1,200
(₹ 80,000 + ₹ 32,000)	1,12,000	(Cost of Shortage)	
To Purchases		By Memorandum Departmental	

(₹ 1,80,000 + ₹ 72,000)	2,52,000	Mark-up A/c (Load on Shortage)	480
		By Mark-up A/c (Mark Down in Current Purchases)	1,400
		By Debtors A/c (Sales)	3,20,000
		By Memorandum Departmental Mark-up A/c (Mark Down on Opening Stock)	740
		By balance c/d	40,180
	3,64,000		3,64,000

Dr. **(III) MEMORANDUM DEPARTMENTAL MARK UP ACCOUNT** *Cr.*

Particulars	₹	*Particulars*	₹
To Memorandum Departmental Stock A/c (₹ 1,200 × 40/100)	480	By Balance b/d (₹ 1,12,000 × 40/140)	32,000
To Memorandum Departmental Stock A/c	1400	By Memorandum Departmental Stock A/c (₹ 2,52,000 × 40/140)	72,000
To Memorandum Departmental Stock A/c	740		
To Gross Profit transferred to Profit & Loss A/c	90,150		
To Balance c/d [(₹ 40,180 + ₹ 350)* × 40/140 – (₹ 350)]	11,230		
*[₹.1,400 × 4000 / 16,000]	1,04,000		1,04,000

Working Notes:

(I) CALCULATION OF COST OF SALES

Particulars	₹
A. Sales as per Books	3,20,000
B. *Add:* Mark-down in opening stock (given)	740
C. *Add:* Mark-down in sales out of current Purchases (₹ 1,400 × 12,000/16,000)	1,050
D. Value of sales if there was no mark-down (A + B + C)	3,21,790
E. *Less:* Gross Profit (40/140 of ₹ 3,21,790) subject to Mark Down (₹ 740 + ₹ 1,050)	(91,940)
F. Cost of sales (D – E)	2,29,850

(II) CALCULATION OF CLOSING STOCK

Particulars	₹
A. Opening Stock	80,000
B. *Add:* Purchases	1,80,000
C. *Less:* Cost of Sales	2,29,850

D. *Less:* Shortage	1,200
E. Closing Stock (A + B – C – D)	28,950

PROBLEM 10

Southern Store Ltd. is a retail store operating two departments.The company maintains Memorandurm Stock account and Memorandum mark-up account for each of the departments. Supplies issued to the department are debited to the memorandum stock account of the department at cost *plus* the mark-up, and departmental sales are credited to this account. The mark-up on supplies issued to the departments is credited to the mark-up account for the department. When it is necessary to reduce the selling price below the normal selling price, i.e. cost *plus* mark-up, the reduction (mark down) is entered in the memorandum stock account and in the mark-up account. Department Y has a mark-up of 33-1/3% on cost, and Department Z 50% on cost. The following information has been extracted from the records of Southern Store Ltd. for the year ended 31st March,2016:

Particulars	*Department Y* ₹	*Department Z* ₹
Stock, 1st April, 2015 at cost	24,000	36,000
Purchases	1,62,000	1,90,000
Sales	2,10,000	2,85,000

(a) The stock of Department Y on 1st April, 2015 included goods on which the selling price has been marked down by ₹ 510. These goods were sold in April, 2015 at the reduced price.

(b) Certain goods purchased in 2015 – 2016 for ₹ 2,700 for department Y,were transferred during the year to department Z, and sold for ₹ 4,050. purchase and sale are recorded in the purchases of department Y and the sales of department Z respectively, but no entries in respect of the transfer have been made.

(c) Goods purchased in 2015 – 2016 were marked down as follows:

Particulars	*Department Y* ₹	*Department Z* ₹
Cost	8,000	21,000
Mark down	800	4,100

At the end of the year there were some items in the stock of department Z, which had been marked down to ₹ 2,300. With this exception all goods marked down in 2015 – 2016, were sold during the year at the reduced prices.

(d) During stock taking on 31st March 2016, goods which had cost ₹ 240 were found to be missing in department Y. It was determined that the loss should be regarded as irrecoverable.

(e) The closing stock in both departments are to be valued at cost for the purpose of the annual a/cs..

Required: Prepare for each department for the year ended 31st March 2016:

(i) a Trading Account, (ii) a Memorandum Stock Account, and (iii) a Memorandum Mark-up Account.

SOLUTION

SOUTHERN STORES LTD.

Dr. **TRADING ACCOUNT FOR THE YEAR ENDING ON 31ST MARCH, 2016** Cr.

Particulars	*Dept. Y* ₹	*Dept. Z* ₹	*Particulars*	*Dept. Y* ₹	*Dept. Z* ₹
To Opening Stock	24,000	36,000	By Sales	2,10,000	2,85,000

To Purchases	1,62,000	1,90,000	By Transfer to Dept. Z	2,700	—
To Transfer from Y Dept.	—	2,700	By Goods Lost	240	—
To Gross Profit c/d	51,518	92,496	By Cl. Stock (at cost)	24,578	36,196
	2,37,518	3,21,196		2,37,518	3,21,196

Dr. **MEMORANDUM STOCK ACCOUNT (AT SELLING PRICE)** Cr.

Particulars	*Dept. Y* ₹	*Dept. Z* ₹	*Particulars*	*Dept. Y* ₹	*Dept. Z* ₹
To Balance b/d (Cost + Mark-up)	32,000	54,000	By Balance b/d	510	
To Purchases (Cost)	1,62,000	1,90,000	By Sales	2,10,000	2,85,000
To Memorandum Mark-up A/c (on purchases)	54,000	95,000	By Transfer	2,700	
To Transfer		2,700	By Memorandum Mark-up A/c (on transfer)	900	—
To Memorandum Mark-up A/c (on t/f)		1,350	By Memorandum Mark-up A/c (Marked down on current purchasers)	800	4,100
To Memorandum Mark-up A/c (on Marked down goods still in Stock)		344	By P & L A/c (Cost of Shortage)	240	
			By Memorandum Mark-up A/c (on lost Stock)	80	
			By Balance c/d (Closing Stock)	32,770	54,294
	2,48,000	3,43,394		2,48,000	3,43,394

Dr. **MEMORANDUM MARK-UP ACCOUNT** Cr.

Particulars	*Dept. Y* ₹	*Dept. Z* ₹	*Particulars*	*Dept. Y* ₹	*Dept. Z* ₹
To Balance b/d	510		By Balance b/d	8,000	18,000
To Memorandum Stock A/c (Mark-up on Transfer)	900		By Memorandum Stock A/c (purchase)	54,000	95,000
To Memorandum Stock A/c (Mark down on Current Purchases)	800	4,100	By Memorandum Stock A/c (Mark-up on transfer)		1,350
To Memorandum Stock A/c (Mark down on goods lost)	80		By Memorandum Stock A/c (Marked down on goods still in Stock)		344

To Gross profit (b.f.)	51,518	92,496			
To Balance c/d	8,192	18,098			
	62,000	1,14,694		62,000	1,14,694

Working Notes:

(I) CALCULATION OF CLOSING STOCK AT COST

Particulars	Dept. Y (₹)	Dept. Z (₹)
A. Calculation of Cl. Stock at Invoice price	32,770	54,294
B. Calculation of Closing Stock at Cost	32,770 × 3/4 = ₹ 24,578	54,294 × 2/3 = 36,196

(II) *Calculation of Mark Down in unsold Stock of Z Dept*

$$\frac{\text{Mark Down} \times \text{Value of Stock}}{\text{Value after Mark Down}} = \frac{₹\,4,100 \times ₹\,2,300}{₹\,27,400} = ₹\,344$$

(III) VERIFICATION OF GROSS PROFIT

Particulars	Dept. Y (₹)	Dept. Z (₹)
A. Sales	2,10,000	2,85,000
B. *Add:* Reduction	510	—
C. *Add:* Mark down	800	3,756
	2,11,310	2,88,756
D. Gross Profit	(1/4) 52,828	(1/3) 96,252
E. *Less:* Mark down	(1,310)	(3,756)
F. Gross Profit as per Memorandum Mark up Account	51,518	92,496

PROBLEM 11

X Ltd, has a factory with two manufacturing Departments 'X'and 'Y'. Part of the output of Department X is transferred to department Y for further processing and the balance is directly transferred to selling department. The entire production of department Y is directly transferred to the selling department. inter departmental stock transfers are made as follows:

X Department to Y Department at 33-1/3% over Departmental Cost.

X Department to selling department at 50% over Departmental Cost.

Y Department to selling department at 25% over Departmental Cost.

The following information is given for the year ending on 31st march, 2016

Particulars	Dept. X		Dept. Y		Selling Dept.	
	Units	₹	Units	₹	Units	₹
Opening Stock of Finished Goods	60	60,000	20	40,000	50	1,28,000
Opening Stock of Raw Materials	—	—	—	—	—	—
Raw material Consumed	—	1,82,000	—	20,000	—	—
Labour Charges	—	70,000	—	32,000	—	—
Sales	—	—	—	—	120	4,80,000
Closing Stock of Finished Goods	40	—	50	—	60	—

Out of the total transfer by X department, 30 units were transferred to selling department, while the remaining to Department Y. The per unit material and labour consumption in X Department on production to be transferred directly to selling department is 300 per cent of the labour and material consumption on units transferred to Y Department. General Administration expenses ₹ 80,000.

Required: Prepare departmental Profit and Loss Account and General Profit and Loss Account for the year ending on 31.3.2016.

SOLUTION

DEPARTMENTAL PROFIT AND LOSS ACCOUNT
FOR THE YEAR ENDING ON 31ST MARCH, 2016

Dr. *Cr.*

Particulars	X Dept.		Y Dept.		Selling Dept.		Particulars	X Dept.		Y Dept.		Selling Dept.	
	Qty.	₹	Qty.	₹	Qty.	₹		Qty.	₹	Qty.	₹	Qty.	₹
To Opening stock	60	60,000	20	40,000	50	1,28,000	By Stock t/f	160	3,70,000	100	2,50,000	—	—
To Raw Material consumed		1,82,000	—	20,000	—	—	By Sales	—		—		120	4,80,000
To Units Produced	140	—	—	—	—		By Closing Stock	40	48,000	50	1,00,000	60	1,80,000
To Labour Charges		70,000	—	32,000	—	—							
To Stock Transferred From X Dept.			130	2,08,000	30	1,62,000							
To Stock Transferred From Y Dept.					100	2,50,000							
To Departmental Profit t/f to General P & L A/c		1,06,000	—	50,000	—	1,20,000							
	200	4,18,000	150	3,50,000	180	6,60,000		200	4,18,000	150	3,50,000	180	6,60,000

GENERAL PROFIT AND LOSS ACCOUNT
FOR THE YEAR ENDING ON 31ST MARCH, 2016

Dr. *Cr.*

Particulars	₹	Particulars	₹
To General Adm. Expenses	80,000	By Profit transferred from:	
To Stock Reserve for Closing		X Dept.	1,06,000
Stock:		Y Dept.	50,000
on Dept. Y	12,000	Selling Dept.	1,20,000
on selling Dept.	18,175		
To Net profit	1,65,825		
	2,76,000		2,76,000

Working Notes:

(A) SELLING DEPT.

Particulars	Units	Particulars	Units
Opening Stock	50	Sales	120
T/f from X Dept.	30	Closing Stock	60
T/f from Y Dept. (b.f.)	100		
	180		180

(B) Y DEPT.

Particulars	*Units*	*Particulars*	*Units*
Opening Stock	20	T/f to Selling Dept.	100
T/f from X Dept.	130	Closing Stock	50
	150		150

(C) X DEPT.

Particulars	*Units*	*Particulars*	*Units*
Opening Stock	60	T/f to Selling Dept.	30
Production (Balancing figure)	140	T/f to Y Dept.	130
		Closing Stock	40
	200		200

(D) Total Equivalent units produced in X Dept. in terms of those t/f to Y Dept.

= Equivalent units of those t/f to Sell Dept. + t/f to Y Dept.+ Closing Stock

= (30 × 300/100) + 130 + 40 = 260

(E) CALCULATION OF TRANSFER PRICES AND CLOSING STOCK

Particulars	*X Dept.* ₹	*Y Dept.* ₹	*Selling Dept.* ₹
A. Cost of Opening Stock	60,000	40,000	1,28,000
B. *Add:* Cost of Raw Materials consumed	1,82,000	20,000	—
C. *Add:* Labour charges	70,000	32,000	—
D. *Add:* T/f from X Dept.	—	2,08,000	1,62,000
E. *Add:* T/f from Y Dept.	—	—	2,50,000
F. Total Cost (A + B + C + D + E)	3,12,000	3,00,000	5,40,000
G. Equivalant Units	260	150	180
H. Average Cost per Equivalent Unit (F/G)	1,200	2,000	3,000
I. Transfer Price of 130 Units t/f to Dept. Y			
(a) Cost of 130 Units (130 × ₹ 1,200)	1,56,000		
(b) *Add:* Profit element @ 33-1/3%	52,000		
	2,08,000		
J. Transfer Price of Units t/f to Selling Dept.			
(a) Cost of Units t/f	1,08,000	2,00,000	
(b) *Add:* Profit element	54,000	50,000	—
	1,62,000	2,50,000	
K. Closing Stock	48,000 (40 × ₹ 1,200)	1,00,000 (50 × ₹ 2,000)	1,80,000 (60 × ₹ 3,000)

(F) *Unrealised Profit on Increase in Closing Stock of Y Dept.* (₹ 1,00,000 – ₹ 40,000)

A Current Cost incurred by Dept. Y

= ₹ 20,000 + ₹ 32,000 + ₹ 2,08,000 = ₹ 2,60,000

B Profit charged by Dept. X included in above (₹ 2,08,000 × 1/4) = ₹ 52,000

C Profit included in Increase in Closing Stock

= (₹ 52,000 × ₹ 60,000/₹ 2,60,000) = ₹ 12,000

(G) *Profit Included in output transferred by Y Deptt. to Selling Dept.*

A. Transfer Price = ₹ 2,50,000

B. Profit of Dept. Y included in Above (₹ 2,50,000 × 25/125) = ₹ 50,000

C. Cost Element of dept. X in Transfer Price (₹ 2,50,000 – ₹ 50,000) = ₹ 2,00,000

D. Profit of Dept. X included in above

(₹ 2,00,000 × ₹ 52,000/₹ 2,60,000) = ₹ 40,000

E. Total Profit Included in Transfer price (₹ 50,000 + ₹ 40,000) = ₹ 90,000

(H) Profit Included in output transferred by X Dept. to Selling dept.

= (₹ 1,62,000 × 50/150) = ₹ 54,000

(I) Total Profit included in output transferred to Selling Dept.

= ₹ 90,000 + ₹ 54,000 = ₹ 1,44,000

(J) Total Transfer Price for the Transfers made by X Dept. and Y Dept.

= ₹ 1,62,000 + ₹ 2,50,000 = ₹ 4,12,000

(K) Unrealised Profit included in increase in closing Stock of Sell Dept.

= ₹ 1,44,000 × ₹ 52,000/₹ 4,12,000 = ₹ 18,175

14A ACCOUNTING FOR BRANCHES

LEARNING OBJECTIVES

After studying this chapter, you should be able to understand:

- ◇ Meaning of a Branch
- ◇ Classification of Branches
- ◇ Accounting For Dependent Branches
- ◇ Debtors Method
- ◇ Accounting Treatment of Goods Returned and Cash Remitted by Branch Customers Directly to Head Office
- ◇ Accounting Treatment of Branch Manager's Commission
- ◇ When goods are sent to Branch at Cost plus Profit
- ◇ Stock and Debtors Method
- ◇ Journal Entries under Stock and Debtors Method
- ◇ Final Accounts Method
- ◇ Whole Sale Branch Method
- ◇ Accounting For Independent Branches
- ◇ Incorporation of Branch Results in the Books of Head Office

1.0 MEANING OF A BRANCH

A Branch is a subordinate division of an office. The concept of branch *presupposes* the existence of a head office. A branch is any establishment carrying on *either* the same *or substantially* the same activity as that carried on by the head office of the company. According to Sec. 2(14) of the Companies Act 2013 "branch office", in relation to a company, means any establishment described as such by the company;

2.0 CLASSIFICATION OF BRANCHES

From the accounting point of view, Branches may be classified as follows:

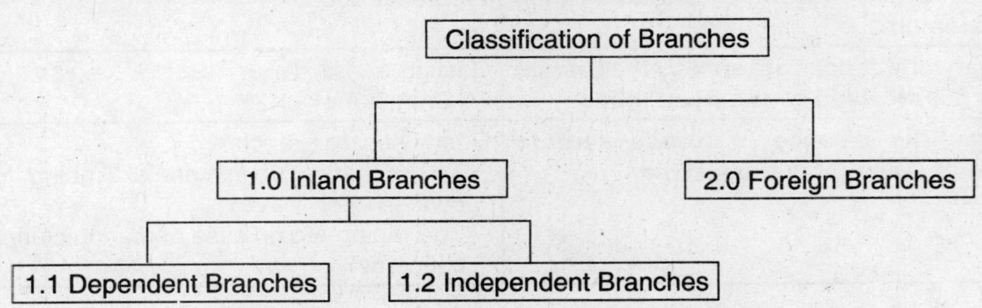

3.0 ACCOUNTING FOR DEPENDENT BRANCHES

The branch which does not maintain a complete record of its transactions is said to be dependent one. The head office may maintain the accounts of such branches according to any of the following methods:

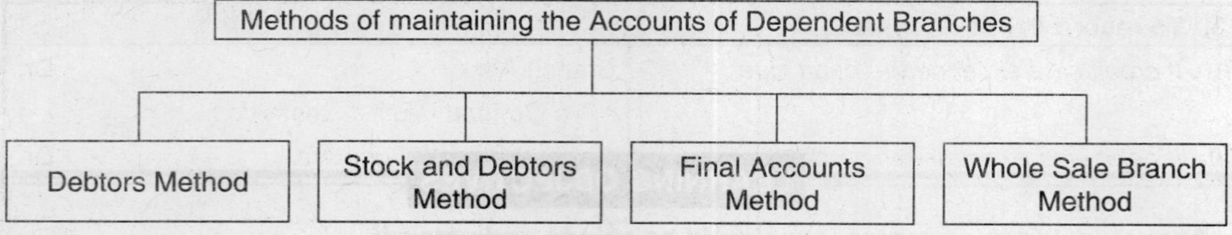

4.0 DEBTORS METHOD

MEANING OF DEBTORS METHOD

This method is usually adopted when the branch is of small size. Under this method, the head office maintains separate Branch Account for each branch. Its purpose is to ascertain profit *or* loss made by each branch.

JOURNAL ENTRIES UNDER DEBTORS METHOD

Transaction	Journal Entry
1. To record opening balances of Branch Assets	Branch A/c Dr. To Branch Assets (Individually)
2. To record opening balances of Branch Liabilities	Branch Liabilities (Individually) Dr. To Branch A/c
3. When goods are supplied by the Head office/another branch to Branch	Branch A/c Dr. To Goods sent to Branch A/c
4. When goods are returned by the branch/ branch customers directly to the Head Office	Goods Sent to Branch A/c Dr. To Branch A/c
5. When goods are supplied by the branch to another branch under instructions of Head office	Goods Sent to Branch A/c Dr. To Branch A/c
6. When goods are supplied by the Head office but not received by the Branch head	Goods-in Transit A/c Dr. To Branch A/c
7. When the Head office meets the branch expenses *or* sends cash to the branch for meeting its expenses	Branch A/c Dr. To Cash/Bank A/c
8. When remittances are received by the Head Office from the Branch/Branch Customers	Cash/Bank A/c Dr. To Branch A/c
9. When remittances are sent by the Branch but not received by the Head office	Cash in-transit A/c Dr. To Branch A/c
10. When the balance in Goods sent to Branch Account is transferred	Goods sent to Branch A/c Dr. To Purchases A/c (in case of Trading concerns) or, To Trading A/c (in case of manufacturing concerns)

11. To record the closing balances of Branch Assets	Branch Assets A/c (Individually) Dr. To Branch A/c
12. To record the closing balances of Branch Liabilities	Branch A/c Dr. To Branch Liabilities (Individually)
13. To record Profit *or* Loss	
(i) If credit side exceeds the debit side	Branch A/c Dr. To General Profit & Loss A/c
(ii) If debit side exceeds the credit side	General Profit & Loss A/c Dr. To Branch A/c

FORMAT OF BRANCH ACCOUNT

A format of Branch Account is given below:

Dr. **BRANCH ACCOUNT** *Cr.*

Particulars	₹	*Particulars*	₹
To Balance b/d:		By Balance b/d:	
Stock	xxx	Creditors	xxx
Debtors	xxx	Outstanding Expenses	xxx
Petty Cash	xxx	By Bank (remittances to H.O.):	
Fixed Assets	xxx	by Branch	xxx
Prepaid Expenses	xxx	by Branch Debtors directly to H.O.	xxx
To Goods sent to Branch A/c:		By Goods Sent to Branch A/c:	
Goods sent by H.O.	xxx	Returned by Branch	xxx
Goods sent by other Branches	xxx	Returned by Branch debtors	
To Bank (Remittances by H.O.)	xxx	directly to H.O.	xxx
		Sent to other Branches	xxx
To Balance c/d:			
Creditors	xxx	By Balance c/d:	
Outstanding Expenses	xxx	Stock-in-hand	xxx
		Stock-in-transit	xxx
		Cash in-transit	xxx
*To Net Profit t/f to General		Debtors	xxx
P & L A/c	xxx	Petty Cash	xxx
		Fixed Assets	xxx
		Prepaid Expenses	xxx
		*By Net Loss t/f to General P & L A/c	xxx
	xxx		xxx

*Only one figure shall appear.

Note:

(i) The following **transactions do not appear in the Branch Account:**

(a) Expenses met by Branch out of cash, since *either* reduced cash balance at the end is decreased *or* the liability at the end is increased.

(b) Purchase of Goods/Fixed Assets by Branch, since book value of Goods/Fixed assets at the end is increased and *either* the amount of remittances is reduced *or* the Creditors at the end are increased.

(c) Sale of Goods/Fixed Assets by Branch since book value of Goods/Fixed assets at the end is decreased and *either* the amount of remittances is increased *or* the Debtors at the end are increased.

(d) Bad debts, discount allowed, sales returns by customers to branch, cash received by Branch from Branch Debtors, etc., since the debtors at the end appear at the adjusted figure.

(e) Depreciation and Profit/Loss on sale of fixed assets since fixed assets at the end appear at the adjusted figure.

(f) Abnormal Losses since stock at the end appears at the adjusted figure.

(ii) When the branch is not authorised to keep any sum out of collections, expenses met by Branch out of petty cash maintained may be dealt with as under:

(a) In case the petty cash is maintained on Imprest System, the expenses met by the branch are to be shown in the same manner as the branch expenses met by the Head Office. In such a case, petty cash balance at the end appears at the same amount at which it appears in the beginning.

(b) In case the petty cash is not maintained on Imprest System, the expenses met by branch are automatically charged to the Branch Account since the petty cash at the end appears at the adjusted figure.

(iii) When goods are returned *either* by Branch Debtors to the H.O. directly *or* are sent by one branch to another branch, the entry is made in the same manner as in the case of goods returned by the Branch to the H.O.

(iv) In case any insurance claim is admitted and paid to the Branch, *either* the Bank balance at the end will increase *or* the remittances to H.O., will increase. In case, the insurance claim is admitted but not paid, the insurance company will appear as a debtor at the end.

(v) To ascertain any missing figure, relating to Stock and /or Debtors, Memorandum Branch Stock Account & Memorandum Branch Debtors Account may be prepared.

ILLUSTRATION 1 [WHEN ALL REQUIRED AMOUNTS ARE GIVEN]

From the following information, prepare Madras Branch Account in the books of head office for the year ending on 31st March 2016:

Particulars	₹	*Particulars*	₹
Opening Stock (at cost)	3,56,000	Closing Stock (at cost)	3,76,800
Opening Debtors	28,000	Closing Debtors	1,92,000
Opening Petty Cash	500	Closing Petty Cash	240
Furniture (in the beginning)	12,000	Furniture at the end	?
Opening Creditors	12,000	Closing Creditors	12,000
Goods sent to Branch (at cost)	10,44,000	Cheques sent to Branch for Exp.	99,740
Goods returned by Branch to H.O. (at Cost)	17,200	Cash received from Debtors	12,78,000
		Cash Sales	64,000
Goods returned by Customers to Branch	13,800		

Depreciate the furniture @ 10% p.a.

SOLUTION

Dr. **MADRAS BRANCH ACCOUNT IN THE BOOKS OF H.O** *Cr.*

Particulars	₹	*Particulars*		₹
To Balance b/d:		By Balance b/d: (Creditors)		12,000
Stock	3,56,000	By Bank A/c (remittance		
Debtors	28,000	from Branch)		
Petty Cash	500	Cash sales	64,000	
Furniture	12,000	Collection from Debtors	12,78,000	13,42,000
To Goods sent to Branch A/c	10,44,000	By Goods sent to Branch A/c		
To Bank A/c (Remittance to Branch)	99,740	(Returns)		17,200
To Balance c/d (Creditors)	12,000	By Balance c/d:		
To Net Profit t/f to General P&L A/c	3,98,800	Stock		3,76,800
		Debtors		1,92,000
		Petty Cash		240
		Furniture (₹ 12,000 – ₹ 1,200)		10,800
	19,51,040			19,51,040

ILLUSTRATION 2 [TREATMENT OF DIRECT PAYMENT BY H.O. FOR EXPENSES AND DIRECT PURCHASES BY BRANCH]

CAS Bros, Bombay have a branch at Nagpur. They send goods at cost to their branch at Nagpur. However, direct purchases are also made by the branch for which payments are made at head office. All the daily collections are transferred from the branch to the head office.

From the following prepare Nagpur branch account in the books of head office:

Particulars	₹	*Particulars*	₹
Opening Balances:		Bad Debts	1,000
Impress Cash	2,000	Discount to Customers	2,000
Sundry Debtors	25,000	Remittances to H.O. (recd. by H.O.)	1,65,000
Stock: Transferred from H.O.	24,000	Remittances to H.O.	
Direct Purchases	16,000	(not recd. by H.O. so far)	5,000
Cash Sales	45,000	Branch Exp. Directly paid by H.O.	30,000
Credit Sales	1,30,000	*Closing Balances:*	
Direct Purchases	45,000	Stock: Direct Purchases	10,000
Returns from Customers	3,000	Transfer from H.O.	15,000
Goods sent to branch from H.O.	60,000	Debtors	?
Transfer from H.O. for Petty			
Cash Expenses	4,000		
Imprest Cash	?		

SOLUTION

Dr. **NAGPUR BRANCH ACCOUNT IN THE BOOKS OF H.O.** *Cr.*

Particulars	₹	*Particulars*		₹
To Opening Balances		By Bank—Remittances		
Stock	40,000	rec. from the branch		
Debtors	25,000	Cash Sales	45,000	
Imprest Cash	2,000	Cash from Drs.	1,20,000	
To Goods sent to Branch A/c	60,000	Cash from Drs. in transit	5,000	1,70,000
To Creditors (Direct purchases)	45,000	By Closing Balances:		
To Bank (Sundry expenses)	30,000	By Stock: Transfer from H.O.		15,000
To Bank (Petty Cash expenses)	4,000	Direct purchases		10,000
To Net Profit transferred to		By Sundry Debtors		24,000
General Profit & Loss A/c	15,000	By Imprest Cash		2,000
	2,21,000			2,21,000

Working Notes:

(I) Collection from debtors = Total Remittances – Cash Sales
= (₹ 1,65,000 + ₹ 5,000) – ₹ 45,000 = ₹ 1,25,000

Dr. **(II) SUNDRY DEBTORS ACCOUNTS** *Cr.*

Particulars	₹	*Particulars*	₹
To Balance b/d	25,000	By Branch Stock (Return)	3,000
To Credit Sales	1,30,000	By Discount	2,000
		By Bad Debts	1,000
		By Collection	1,25,000
		By Balance c/d	24,000
	1,55,000		1,55,000

(III) It is assumed that petty cash expenses of the branch for the year were ₹ 4,000.

ILLUSTRATION 3 [WHEN CLOSING BALANCES OF BRANCH DEBTORS, BRANCH STOCK, BRANCH PETTY CASH AND REMITTANCE TO H.O. ARE NOT GIVEN]

From the following information, prepare Delhi Branch Account in the books of head office for the year ending on 31st March 2016:

Particulars	₹	*Particulars*	₹
Opening Stock (at cost)	1,78,000	Discount allowed to Customers	500
Opening Debtors	14,000	Bad Debts written off	1,000
Opening Petty Cash	250	Credit sales	7,29,400
Furniture (in the beginning)	6,000	Cash Sales	32,000
Opening Creditors	6,000	Petty Expenses paid by Branch	8,000
Goods sent to Branch (at Cost)	5,22,000	Cheques sent to Branch for exp.:	

Goods returned by Branch to H.O (at cost)	7,800	Salaries	30,000
Goods returned by Customers to Branch	5,700	Rent and Insurance	12,000
Cash received by Branch from its Customers	6,11,000	Petty Cash	7,870

Goods are sold to customers at cost *plus* 50%. Depreciate the furniture @ 10% p.a.

SOLUTION

Dr. **DELHI BRANCH ACCOUNT IN THE BOOKS OF H.O.** Cr.

Particulars	₹	*Particulars*	₹
To Balance b/d:		By Balance b/d: creditors	6,000
Stock	1,78,000	By Bank A/c (Remittan. from Branch)	6,43,000
Debtors	14,000	By Goods sent to Branch A/c	
Petty Cash	250	(return by branch)	7,800
Furniture	6,000	By Balance c/d:	
To Goods sent to Branch A/c	5,22,000	Stock	1,88,400
To Bank A/c (Remittance by H.O.)	49,870	Debtors	1,25,200
To Balance c/d (creditors)	6,000	Petty Cash	120
To Net Profit t/f to General P & L A/c	1,99,800	Furniture (₹ 6,000 – ₹ 600)	5,400
	9,75,920		9,75,920

Working Notes:

Dr. **(I) MEMORANDUM BRANCH DEBTORS ACCOUNT** Cr.

Particulars	₹	*Particulars*	₹
To Balance b/d	14,000	By Returns to Branch	5,700
To Credit Sales	7,29,400	By Discount allowed	500
		By Bad Debts	1,000
		By Cash received by Branch	6,11,000
		By Balance c/d	1,25,200
	7,43,400		7,43,400

Dr. **(II) MEMORANDUM BRANCH STOCK ACCOUNT** Cr.

Particulars	₹	*Particulars*	₹
To Balance b/d	1,78,000	By Goods sent to Branch A/c (Return)	7,800
To Goods sent to Branch A/c	5,22,000		
		By Cost of Net Goods sold [(32,000 + 7,29,400 – 5,700) × 100/150]	5,03,800
		By Balance c/d	1,88,400
	7,00,000		7,00,000

Dr. **(III) MEMORANDUM BRANCH PETTY CASH ACCOUNT** Cr.

Particulars	₹	Particulars	₹
To Balance b/d	250	By Petty Expenses A/c	8,000
To Remittance from H.O.	7,870	By Balance c/d	120
	8,120		8,120

Dr. **(IV) MEMORANDUM BRANCH CASH ACCOUNT** Cr.

Particulars	₹	Particulars	₹
To Cash Sales	32,000	By Salaries	30,000
To Remittance by H.O.	49,870	By Rent & Insurance	12,000
To Collection from Debtors	6,11,000	By Petty Cash	7,870
		By Remittance to HO	6,43,000
	6,92,870		6,92,870

ACCOUNTING TREATMENT OF GOODS RETURNED AND CASH REMITTED BY BRANCH CUSTOMERS DIRECTLY TO HEAD OFFICE

Item	Treatment in Branch A/c	Treatment in Memorandum Branch Debtors A/c
1. Goods returned by Branch customers directly to H.O.	Treat like goods returned by Branch to H.O. and thus, show the Cost/Invoice price (as the case may be) of these goods on credit side of Branch Account.	Show the selling price of these goods on credit side of Branch Debtors Account.
2. Cash remitted by Branch customers directly to H.O.	Treat like cash remitted by branch to H.O. and thus, show on the credit side of Branch Account.	Show on the credit side of Branch Debtors Account.

ILLUSTRATION 4 [TREATMENT OF GOODS RETURNED AND CASH REMITTED DIRECTLY BY BRANCH CUSTOMERS DIRECTLY TO H.O.]

Taking the same information as given in Illustration 3 along with the following information, prepare the Delhi Branch Account:

(i) Goods returned by Branch Customers directly to H.O. ₹ 1,200

(ii) Cash remitted by Branch Customers directly to H.O. ₹ 28,000

SOLUTION

Dr. **DELHI BRANCH ACCOUNT IN THE BOOKS OF H.O.** Cr.

Particulars	₹	Particulars	₹
To Balance b/d:		By Balance b/d: (creditors)	6,000
Stock	1,78,000	By Bank A/c (Remittan. from Branch)	
Debtors	14,000	Remittance by Branch	6,43,000
Petty cash	250	**Direct Remittance by Branch**	
Furniture	6,000	**customers**	28,000
To Goods sent to Branch A/c	5,22,000	By Goods sent to Branch A/c:	

To Bank A/c (Remittance by H.O.)	49,870	Return by Branch	7,800
To Balance c/d: (creditors)	6,000	**Direct Return by Branch**	
To Net Profit t/f to General P&L A/c	1,99,400	**customers [1200 × 100/150]**	800
		By Balance c/d:	
		Stock	1,88,400
		Debtors	96,000
		Petty Cash	120
		By Furniture (₹ 6,000 – ₹ 600)	5,400
	9,75,520		9,75,520

Working Notes:

Dr. **(I) MEMORANDUM BRANCH DEBTORS ACCOUNT** *Cr.*

Particulars	₹	*Particulars*	₹
To Balance c/d	14,000	By Returns to Branch	5,700
To Credit Sales	7,29,400	**By Returns to H.O**	1,200
		By Discount allowed	500
		By Bad Debts	1,000
		By Cash remitted to H.O.	28,000
		By Cash remitted to Branch	6,11,000
		By Balance c/d	96,000
	7,43,400		7,43,400

Dr. **(II) MEMORANDUM BRANCH STOCK ACCOUNT** *Cr.*

Particulars	₹	*Particulars*	₹
To Balance b/d	1,78,000	By Goods sent to Branch A/c:	
To Goods Sent to Branch A/c	5,22,000	— Return by Branch	7,800
		— Direct Return by Branch	
		Customers [₹ 1,200 × 100/150]	800
		By Cost of Net Goods Sold	5,03,000
		[(32,000 + 7,29,400 –	
		5,700 –1,200) × 100/150]	
		By Balance c/d	1,88,400
	7,00,000		7,00,000

(III) & (IV) Memorandum Branch Petty Cash Account and Memorandum Branch Cash Account – Refer to Working Note [(iii) & (iv) of Illustration 3].

ACCOUNTING TREATMENT OF GOODS SENT TO ANOTHER BRANCH AND GOODS RECEIVED FROM ANOTHER BRANCH

Item	*Treatment in Branch A/c*	*Treatment in Memorandum Branch Stock A/c*
1. Goods sent to another branch	Treat like goods returned to H.O. and thus, show on the credit side of Branch Account.	Treat like goods returned to H.O. and thus, show on the credit side of Branch Stock Account.

2. *Goods received from another branch.*	Treat like goods received from H.O. and thus, show on the debit side of Branch Account.	Treat like goods received from H.O. and thus, show on the debit side of Branch Stock Account.

ILLUSTRATION 5 [TREATMENT OF GOODS SENT TO ANOTHER BRANCH AND GOODS RECEIVED FROM ANOTHER BRANCH]

Taking the same information as given in Illustration 3 alongwith the following information, prepare the Delhi Branch Account.

(i) Goods transferred by Calcutta Branch to Delhi Branch under H.O. instructions (at cost) ₹ 34,000.

(ii) Goods sent by Delhi Branch to Bombay Branch under H.O. instructions (at cost) ₹ 4,000.

SOLUTION

Dr. **DELHI BRANCH ACCOUNT IN THE BOOKS OF H.O** *Cr.*

Particulars	₹	*Particulars*	₹
To Balance b/d		By Balance b/d (Creditors)	6,000
Stock	1,78,000	By Bank A/c (Remitta. from Branch)	6,43,000
Debtors	14,000	By Goods sent to Branch A/c:	
Petty Cash	250	— Returned by Branch	7,800
Furniture	6,000	**— Sent to Bombay Branch**	4,000
To Goods Sent to Branch A/c:		By Balance c/d:	
— Sent by H.O	5,22,000	Stock	2,18,400
— Sent by Calcutta Branch	34,000	Debtors	1,25,200
To Bank A/c (Remittance by H.O.)	49,870	Petty Cash	120
To Balance c/d (Creditors)	6,000	Furniture (₹ 6,000 – ₹ 600)	5,400
P & L A/c	1,99,800		
	10,09,920		10,09,920

Working Notes:

(I) Memorandum Branch Debtors A/c, Memorandum Petty Cash A/c, Memorandum Branch Cash A/c—Refer to working Notes (I), (III) & (IV) given in Illustration 2.

Dr. **(II) MEMORANDUM BRANCH STOCK ACCOUNT** *Cr.*

Particulars	₹	*Particulars*	₹
To Balance b/d	1,78,000	By Goods sent to Branch A/c	
To Goods Sent to Branch A/c:		—Returned by Branch	7,800
—sent by H.O.	5,22,000	**—Sent to Bombay Branch**	4,000
—sent by Calcutta Branch	34,000	By Cost of Net Goods sold [(₹ 32,000 + 7,29,400 – 5,700) × 100/150]	5,03,800
		By Balance c/d	2,18,400
	7,34,000		7,34,000

ACCOUNTING TREATMENT OF NORMAL LOSS, ABNORMAL LOSS, INSURANCE CLAIM AND AGREED ALLOWANCE/TRADE DISCOUNT

Item	*Treatment in Branch A/c*	*Treatment in Memorandum Branch Stock A/c*
1. *Normal loss*	Normal loss does not appear in the Branch Account since the Closing Stock appears at the adjusted figure.	Cost/Invoice price (as the case may be) of normal loss appears on the credit side of Branch Stock Account in order to reduce the figure of Closing Stock.
2. *Abnormal loss*	Abnormal loss does not appear in the Branch Account since the Closing Stock appears at the adjusted figure.	Cost/Invoice price (as the case may be) of abnormal loss appears on the credit side of Branch Stock Account in order to reduce the figure of Closing Stock.
3. *Insurance claim* (a) *Admitted and received*	Shown on the credit side of Branch Account by way of Increased Closing *either* Cash/Bank Balance *or* remittance to H.O.	No Treatment
(b) *Admitted but not yet received*	Shown Insurance Co. as a debtor at the end on the credit side of Branch Account.	No Treatment
4. *Agreed allowance/ Trade discount*	Agreed Allowance/Trade Discount does not appear in the Branch Account since the closing debtors appear at the adjusted figure.	Cost/Invoice Price (as the case may be) of Agreed Allowance/ Trade Discount appears on the credit side of Branch Stock A/c.

ILLUSTRATION 6 [TREATMENT OF NORMAL LOSS, ABNORMAL LOSS, INSURANCE CLAIM, AGREED ALLOWANCE/TRADE DISCOUNT]

Taking the same information as given in Illustration 3 along with the following information, prepare the Delhi Branch Account:

(i) Goods costing ₹ 2,500 were damaged in transit and a sum of ₹ 2,000 was recovered from the insurance company in full settlement of claim.

(ii) Loss-in-weight (Normal) (at cost) ₹ 2,900.

(iii) Agreed allowance to customers off selling price ₹ 1,000 (already taken into account while invoicing).

SOLUTION

Dr. **DELHI BRANCH ACCOUNT IN THE BOOKS OF H.O.** *Cr.*

Particulars	₹	*Particulars*	₹
To Balance b/d:		By Balance b/d: (Creditors)	6,000
Stock	1,78,000	By Bank A/c	
Debtors	14,000	(Remittance from Branch)	6,45,000
Petty Cash	250	By Goods sent to Branch A/c	
Furniture	6,000	(Returns)	7,800
To Goods sent to Branch A/c	5,22,000	By Balance c/d:	

To Bank A/c (remittance by H.O.)	49,870	Stock	1,82,333
To Balance c/d: (Creditors)	6,000	Debtors	1,25,200
To Net Profit t/f to General P & L A/c	1,95,733	Petty Cash	120
		Furniture (₹ 6,000 – ₹ 600)	5,400
	9,71,853		9,71,853

Working Notes:

(I) Memorandum Branch Debtors A/c, Memorandum Branch Petty Cash A/c Refer to working Notes (I), (III) is given in Illustration 2.

Dr. **(II) MEMORANDUM BRANCH STOCK ACCOUNT** Cr.

Particulars	₹	*Particulars*	₹
To Balance b/d	1,78,000	By Goods Sent to Branch A/c	
To Goods sent to Branch A/c	5,22,000	(Returns)	7,800
		By Cost of Net Goods sold [(32,000 + 7,29,400 + 1000 (agreed allowance) – 5,700) × 100/150]	5,04,467
		By Cost of Abnormal Loss	2,500
		By Cost of Normal Loss	2,900
		By Balance c/d	1,82,333
	7,00,000		7,00,000

Dr. **(III) MEMORANDUM BRANCH CASH ACCOUNT** Cr.

Particulars	₹	*Particulars*	₹
To Cash Sales	32,000	By Remittance to H.O.	6,45,000
To Remittance by H.O.	49,870	By Salaries	30,000
To Collection from Debtors	6,11,000	By Rent & Insurance	12,000
To Claim from Insurance Co.	2,000	By Petty Cash	7,870
	6,94,870		6,94,870

ACCOUNTING TREATMENT OF BRANCH MANAGER'S COMMISSION

(a) Calculation of Commission to Branch Manager

Commission may be allowed as percentage of Net Profit before charging such commission *or* after charging such commission.

(i) Commission as % of Net Profit before charging such Commission

$$= \text{Net Profit before Commission} \times \frac{\text{Rate of Commission}}{100}$$

(ii) Commission as % of Net profit after charging such Commission

$$= \text{Net Profit before Commission} \times \frac{\text{Rate of Commission}}{100 + \text{Rate of Commission}}$$

(b) Accounting Treatment of Branch Manager's Commission

Outstanding Branch Manager's Commission appears on the debit side of Branch Account.

ILLUSTRATION 7

The following information and particulars relate to New Delhi Branch for the year 2015-2016:

Particulars	Opening	Closing
Stock	₹ 50,000	₹ 75,000
Debtors	₹ 70,000	₹ 95,000
Petty Cash	₹ 250	₹ 120

Goods costing ₹ 5,50,000 were sold by the Branch @ 25% on cost. Cash sales amounted to ₹ 1,50,000 and the rest were credit sales. Branch spent ₹ 30,000 for Salaries, ₹ 12,000 for Rent and ₹ 8,000 for Petty expenses.

All expenses were remitted by H.O. Branch receives all goods from H.O. The Branch Manager is entitled to a commission of 5% of the profit of the Branch before charging such commission.

Required: Prepare New Delhi Branch Account.

SOLUTION

Dr. **NEW DELHI BRANCH ACCOUNT IN THE BOOKS OF H.O.** *Cr.*

Particulars	₹	Particulars	₹
To Balance b/d:		By Bank (Remittances by Branch)	6,62,500
Stock	50,000	By Balance c/d:	
Debtors	70,000	Stock	75,000
Petty Cash	250	Debtors	95,000
To Goods sent to Branch A/c	5,75,000	Petty Cash	120
To Bank (Remittances by H.O.):			
Salaries	30,000		
Rent	12,000		
Petty Expenses	7,870		
To Branch Manager's Commission	4,375		
[5% of ₹ 87,500]			
To Net Profit t/f to General P&L A/c	83,125		
	8,32,620		8,32,620

Working Notes:

(I) Total Sales = ₹ 5,50,000 + 25% of ₹ 5,50,000 = ₹ 6,87,500,

(II) Credit Sales = ₹ 6,87,500 – ₹ 1,50,000 = ₹ 5,37,500

Dr. **(III) MEMORANDUM BRANCH DEBTORS ACCOUNT** *Cr.*

Particulars	₹	Particulars	₹
To Balance b/d	70,000	By Cash A/c (b.f.)	5,12,500
To Credit Sales	5,37,500	By Balance c/d	95,000
	6,07,500		6,07,500

Dr. **(IV) MEMORANDUM BRANCH STOCK ACCOUNT** *Cr.*

Particulars	₹	Particulars	₹
To Balance b/d	50,000	By Expenses	5,50,000
To Goods Sent to Branch A/c (b.f)	5,75,000	By Balance c/d	75,000
	6,25,000		6,25,000

Dr. **(V) MEMORANDUM BRANCH PETTY CASH ACCOUNT** *Cr.*

Particulars	₹	Particulars	₹
To Balance b/d	250	By Petty Expenses	8,000
To H.O. A/c (b.f.)	7,870	By Balance c/d	120
	8,120		8,120

(vi) Remittance by Branch = Collection from Debtors + Cash Sales
= ₹ 5,12,500 + ₹ 1,50,000 = ₹ 6,62,500

ILLUSTRATION 8 [WHEN BRANCH MANAGER IS ENTITLED TO COMMISSION AS % OF PROFITS AFTER CHARGING SUCH COMMISSION]

From the following details relating to the Delhi Branch for the year ending on 31st March 2016, prepare the Branch Account in the books of the Head Office.

Particulars	₹	Particulars	₹
Opening Stock	25,000	Cash received from Debtors	65,000
Opening Debtors	10,000	Cash paid by Debtors directly to H.O.	5,000
Opening Furniture	6,000	Goods returned by Branch	2,000
Opening Petty Cash	1,000	Goods returned by Debtors	2,000
Pre-paid Insurance in the beginning	300	Cash sent to Branch for Expenses:	
Salaries outstanding in the beginning	4,000	Rent (₹ 800 p.m.)	9,600
Goods sent to Branch	2,00,000	Salary (₹ 4,000 p.m.)	48,000
Cash Sales during the year	2,70,000	Petty Cash	2,000
Total Sales	3,50,000	Insurance (upto June, 20XI)	1,200
Petty Cash Expenses	2,200		
Discount allowed to Debtors	500		

Goods costing ₹ 2,500 were damaged in transit and a sum of ₹ 2,000 was recovered from the insurance company in full settlement of the claim. Depreciate the Furniture @ 10% p.a. The Branch Manager is entitled to a commission of 5% of profit of Branch after charging such commission. Goods are sold by branch at cost *plus* 100%.

SOLUTION

Dr. **DELHI BRANCH ACCOUNT IN THE BOOKS OF H.O.** *Cr.*

Particulars	₹	Particulars	₹
To Balance b/d:		By Balance b/d (o/s Salary)	4,000
Stock	25,000	By Bank (Remittances):	
Debtors	10,000	—by branch	3,37,000

Petty Cash	1,000	—by Branch debtors	
Furniture	6,000	directly to H.O.	5,000
Prepaid Insurance	300	By Goods Sent to Branch A/c	
To Goods sent to Branch A/c	2,00,000	(returns by branch)	2,000
To Bank A/c (Remittances (by H.O.)	60,800	By Balance c/d:	
To Balance c/d (o/s salary)	4,000	Stock	46,500
To Branch Manager's Commission	5,305	Debtors	17,500
[₹ 1,11,400 × 5/105]		Petty Cash	800
To Net Profit t/f to General P & L A/c	1,06,095	Furniture	5,400
		Prepaid Insurance	300
	4,18,500		4,18,500

Working Notes:

Dr. **(I) MEMORANDUM BRANCH STOCK ACCOUNT** *Cr.*

Particulars	₹	*Particulars*	₹
To Balance b/d:	25,000	By Cost of Net Goods Sold	
To Goods sent to branch A/c	2,00,000	[3,50,000 – 2,000) × 100/200]	1,74,000
		By Goods sent to branch A/c	2,000
		(goods returned by branch)	
		By Abnormal Loss A/c	2,500
		By Balance c/d (balancing figure)	46,500
	2,25,000		2,25,000

Dr. **(II) MEMORANDUM BRANCH DEBTORS ACCOUNT** *Cr.*

Particulars	₹	*Particulars*	₹
To Balance b/d	10,000	By Cash A/c (collection by H.O.)	5,000
To Branch Stock A/c (Credit Sales)	80,000	By Branch Cash A/c (collection	
		by Branch)	65,000
		By Returns Inwards	2,000
		By Discount Allowed	500
		By Balance c/d (b.f.)	17,500
	90,000		90,000

Dr. **(III) MEMORANDUM BRANCH PETTY CASH ACCOUNT** *Cr.*

Particulars	₹	*Particulars*	₹
To Balance b/d	1,000	By Petty Expenses A/c	2,200
To Branch Cash A/c	2,000	By Balance c/d (b.f.)	800
	3,000		3,000

Dr. **(IV) MEMORANDUM BRANCH CASH ACCOUNT** Cr.

Particulars	₹	*Particulars*	₹
To Cash Sales	2,70,000	By Salaries for the previous year	4,000
To Collection from Debtors	65,000	By Rent A/c	9,600
To Remittance from H.O.	60,800	By Salaries for current year	44,000
To Claim from Insurance Co.	2,000	By Petty Cash A/c	2,000
		By Insurance	1,200
		By Remittance to H.O. (b.f.)	3,37,000
	3,97,800		3,97,800

WHEN GOODS ARE SENT TO BRANCH AT COST PLUS PROFIT

(a) Meaning of Invoice Price and Loading Sometimes, the Head Office does not want to reveal the cost of goods to the Branch and therefore, invoices goods at a price which is higher than the Cost Price (CP). Such price is known as 'Invoice Price' (IP) and the difference between the Invoice Price (IP) and the Cost price (CP) is called 'loading'.

(b) How to Eliminate/Remove Loading When goods are sent at invoice price, to ascertain correct profit/loss on consignment, the items recorded at invoice price should be brought down to Cost Price level. For this purpose, the loading included in various items (like Opening Stock, Goods Sent to Branch, Goods Returned by Branch, Closing Stock) should be eliminated by passing the following adjusting entries.

1. **To remove loading from the amount of Net Goods sent to Branch [i.e., Goods Sent to Branch *less* Returns by Branch (or Branch Customers) to H.O.]**

   Goods sent to Branch A/c Dr.

   To Branch A/c

2. **To remove loading from the amount of Closing Stock at Branch**

   Branch A/c Dr.

   To Branch Stock Reserve A/c

   The closing stock at the end of current accounting period becomes the opening stock of the next accounting period. The aforesaid entry will be reversed in the beginning of the next accounting period as follows:

   Branch Stock Reserve A/c Dr.

   To Branch A/c

(c) **How to Disclose relevant items after adjusting entries?** After passing the aforesaid adjusting entries, the relevant items will appear in the Branch Account as follows:

Dr. **AN EXTRACT OF BRANCH ACCOUNT** Cr.

Particulars	₹	*Particulars*	₹
To Opening Stock	xxx	By Stock Reserve Account	xxx
(at invoice price)		(Loading on Opening Stock)	
To Goods sent to Branch	xxx	By Goods sent to Branch A/c	xxx
(at invoice price)		(Returns at Invoice Price)	
To Stock Reserve A/c	xxx	By Goods Sent to Branch A/c	xxx
(loading on Closing Stock)		(Loading on net Goods sent to Br.)	

		By Closing Stock (at Invoice Price)	
	xxx		xxx

TUTORIAL NOTES

(i) Unless otherwise stated, goods sent to branch and branch stocks are deemed to be at invoice price

(ii) Stock at Branch (at cost to branch) *or* Stock at Branch at its cost means Stock at invoice price.

ILLUSTRATION 9 [CALCULATION OF INVOICE PRICE AND LOADING]

Calculate the invoice price of the Goods sent to branch and the profit included therein in each of the following alternative cases:

(a) Goods sent to branch (at cost) ₹ 1,20,000. Goods are invoiced to the Branch at cost *plus* 25%.

(b) Goods sent to branch (at cost) ₹ 2,40,000. Goods are invoiced to the Branch at 25% above the cost.

(c) Goods sent to branch (at cost) ₹ 4,80,000. Goods are invoiced to the Branch at 125% of the cost price of Head office.

(d) Goods sent to Branch (at cost) ₹ 1,20,000. Goods are invoiced to the branch to give a gross margin of 20% on sale price.

(e) Goods sent to Branch (at cost to Branch) ₹ 1,50,000. Goods are invoiced to the Branch at 25% above the cost.

(f) Goods received from H.O. ₹ 1,00,000. Goods in transit from H.O. ₹ 50,000. Goods are invoiced to the Branch at cost *plus* 25%.

SOLUTION

Case	*Invoice Price = Cost + Profit*	*Profit (loading) = Total Invoice Price × Profit / Invoice price*
(a)	₹ 1,20,000 + 25% of ₹ 1,20,000 = ₹ 1,50,000	₹ 1,50,000 × 25/125 = ₹ 30,000
(b)	₹ 2,40,000 + 25% of ₹ 2,40,000 = ₹ 3,00,000	₹ 3,00,000 × 25/125 = ₹ 60,000
(c)	₹ 4,80,000 + 25% of ₹ 4,80,000 = ₹ 6,00,000	₹ 6,00,000 × 25/125 = ₹ 1,20,000
(d)	If Sale Price = ₹ 100, Profit = ₹ 20 and Cost ₹ 80 Thus, ₹ 1,20,000 × 100/80 = ₹ 1,50,000	₹ 1,50,000 × 20/100 = ₹ 30,000
(e)	₹ 1,50,000 (at cost to branch means Invoice Price)	₹ 1,50,000 × 25/125 = ₹ 30,000
(f)	₹ 1,00,000 + ₹ 50,000 = ₹ 1,50,000	₹ 1,50,000 × 25/125 = ₹ 30,000

ILLUSTRATION 10 [WHEN THE GOODS ARE SENT AT INVOICE PRICE]

Delhi head office supplies goods to its branch at Kanpur at invoice price which is cost *plus* 50%. All cash received by branch is remitted to Delhi and all branch expenses are paid by the head office. From the following particulars related to Kanpur branch for the year 2015–2016, prepare Kanpur Branch Account.

Particulars	₹	*Particulars*	₹
Opening Stock at Branch	60,000	Discount allowed to Debtors	2,400
Opening Branch Debtors	12,000	Exp. (Cash paid by Head Office):	

Opening Petty Cash Balance	100	Rent	₹ 2,400	
Goods received from Head office	1,86,000	Salaries	₹ 24,000	
Goods returned to Head office	3,000	Petty Cash	₹ 1,000	27,400
Allowance to Customer off Selling Price		Cash Sales		1,04,000
		Closing Petty Cash Balance		100
(already adjusted while invoicing)	1,000	Closing Branch Debtors		3,600
Cash received from Debtors	90,000			

The Branch Manager is entitled to a commission of 5% of the profit of Branch after charging such commission.

SOLUTION

Dr. **KANPUR BRANCH ACCOUNT IN THE BOOKS OF H.O.** *Cr.*

Particulars	₹	*Particulars*	₹
To Balance b/d:		By Bank A/c (Remittances by Branch)	1,94,000
Stock	60,000	By Goods Sent to Branch A/c	3,000
Debtors	12,000	By Goods Sent to Branch A/c	
Petty Cash	100	(₹ 1,83,000 × 50/150)	61,000
To Goods sent to Branch A/c	1,86,000	By Stock Reserve A/c	
To Bank A/c (Remittance by H.O. for expenses)	27,400	(₹ 60,000 × 50/150)	20,000
To Stock Reserve A/c		By Balance c/d:	
(₹ 54,000 × 50/150)	18,000	Stock	54,000
To Branch Manager's Commission [₹ 32,200 × 5/105]	1,533	Debtors	3,600
		Petty Cash	100
To Net Profit t/f to General P & L A/c	30,667		
	3,35,700		3,35,700

Working Notes:

Dr. **(I) MEMORANDUM BRANCH DEBTORS ACCOUNT** *Cr.*

Particulars	₹	*Particulars*	₹
To Balance b/d	12,000	By Branch Cash A/c	90,000
To Credit Sales (b.f)	84,000	By Discount Allowed	2,400
		By Balance c/d	3,600
	96,000		96,000

Dr. **(II) MEMORANDUM BRANCH STOCK ACCOUNT** *Cr.*

Particulars	₹	*Particulars*	₹
To Balance b/d	60,000	By Goods sent to Branch A/c	3,000
To Goods sent to Branch A/c	1,86,000	By Branch Debtors A/c (Cr. Sales)	84,000
		By Branch Cash A/c (cash sales)	1,04,000

		By Agreed Allowance	1,000
		By Balance c/d (b.f.)	54,000
	2,46,000		2,46,000

Dr. **(III) MEMORANDUM BRANCH CASH ACCOUNT** Cr.

Particulars	₹	*Particulars*	₹
To H.O	27,400	By Rent	2,400
To Cash Sales	1,04,000	By Salaries	24,000
To Collection from Debtors	90,000	By Petty Cash A/c	1,000
		By H.O. A/c (Balancing figure)	1,94,000
	2,21,400		2,21,400

ILLUSTRATION 11 [WHEN GOODS SENT TO BRANCH AND CLOSING BALANCE OF BRANCH DEBTORS ARE NOT GIVEN]

M Ltd Mumbai has a branch in Kolkata. Goods are invoiced to the branch at selling price designed to produce a gross profit of 20% on sales. From the following data, prepare a Kolkata Branch Account for the year ending on 31 March, 2016:

Particulars	₹
Opening Balances as on 1 April:	
Branch Stock (at Cost to H.O.)	20,000
Branch Debtors	17,000
Branch Cash	4,000
Personal Computers	50,000
Transactions During the year:	
Credit Sales at Branch	1,75,000
Cash Sales at Branch	1,02,500
Goods returned to H.O. at selling price	12,500
Cash received from customers	1,57,300
Bills receivable received from debtors at Branch	10,000
Discounting of bills stated above	9,800
Cash sent to branch for expenses	36,000
Actual cash expenses at branch	35,900
Shortage of stock at branch at selling price	150
Cash discount allowed to branch customers	780
Sale of one personal Computer on 1st October	
(Book value on the date of sale ₹ 18,000)	12,000
Closing Balances as on 31st March:	
Branch Stock (at Cost to Branch)	59,850
Branch Debtors	?
Branch Cash	9,000
Depreciation at 20% p.a. is to be provided on Personal Computers.	

The Manager is entitled to commission of 10% of profit of branch after charging such commission.

SOLUTION

Dr. **KOLKATA BRANCH ACCOUNT** Cr.

Particulars	₹	Particulars	₹
To Balance b/d:		By Stock Reserve A/c	5,000
Stock (20,000 + 5,000)	25,000	(₹ 25,000 × 20/100]	
Debtors	17,000	By Goods sent to Branch A/c	62,500
Cash	4,000	[₹ 3,12,500 × 20/100]	—
Personal Computers	50,000	By Bank (Remittance) A/c	2,76,700
To Cash (expense) A/c	36,000	sent Branch A/c	12,500
To Goods sent to Branch A/c	3,25,000	By Balance c/d:	
To Stock Reserve A/c	11,970	Personal Computers	24,000
[₹ 59,850 × 20/100]		Stock	59,850
To Branch Manager's Commission	410	Cash	9,000
(₹ 4,500 × 10/110]		Debtors	23,920
To Net Profit t/f P & L A/c	4,090		
	4,73,470		4,73,470

Working Notes:

Dr. **(I) MEMORANDUM BRANCH STOCK ACCOUNT** Cr.

Particulars	₹	Particulars	₹
To Balance b/d	25,000	By Credit Sales	1,75,000
To Goods sent to Branch Ac (b.f.)		By Cash Sales	1,02,500
	3,25,000	By Goods sent to Branch A/c	12,500
		By Shortage	150
		By Balance c/d	59,850
	3,50,000		3,50,000

Dr. **(II) MEMORANDUM BRANCH DEBTORS ACCOUNT** Cr.

Particulars	₹	Particulars	₹
To Balance b/d	17,000	By Cash	1,57,300
To Credit Sales	1,75,000	By Bills Receivable	10,000
		By Discount	780
		By Balance c/d (b.f.)	23,920
	1,92,000		1,92,000

Dr. **(III) MEMORANDUM BRANCH CASH ACCOUNT** Cr.

Particulars	₹	Particulars	₹
To Balance b/d	4,000	By Expenses	35,900
To Cash Sales A/c	1,02,500	By Remittance	2,76,700

To Branch Debtors A/c	1,57,300	(Balancing Figure)	
To Bills Receivable A/c	9,800	By Balance c/d	9,000
To Cash (for Expenses) A/c	36,000		
To Personal Computers A/c	12,000		
	3,21,600		3,21,600

(IV) CALCULATION OF CLOSING BOOK VALUE OF THE COMPUTERS

	Particulars	₹
A.	Total book value on 1st April	50,000
B.	*Less:* Book value of the Computer sold on 1st Oct. [₹ 18,000 × 100/90]	20,000
C.	Book value of Remaining computers	30,000
D.	*Less:* Deprecation @ 20% for 1 year	6,000
E.	Closing Book value	24,000

ILLUSTRATION 12

CSFDIE Ltd. had a branch at Kolkata. Goods are invoiced to the branch at cost *plus* 25%. Branch is instructed to deposit cash every day in the head office account with the bank. All expenses are paid by cheques by the head office except petty cash expenses which are paid by branch manager. From the following particulars, prepare Branch Account in the books of head office:

Particulars	₹	Particulars	₹
Opening Stock	2,500	Cash remitted to the head office	15,000
Closing Stock	3,000	Furniture purchased by the branch manager	1,200
Opening Sundry debtors	1,400		
Closing Sundry debtors	1,800	Expenses paid by the head office	1,540
Cash sales for the year	10,700	Expenses paid by the branch	120
Credit sales for the year	7,000		
Cost of goods sent to Branch	14,560		

Branch Manager is entitled to a commission of 5% of profit of the branch after charging such commission.

SOLUTION

Dr. **KOLKATA BRANCH ACCOUNT** *Cr.*

Particulars	₹	Particulars	₹
To Balance b/d:		By Branch Stock Reserve A/c	500
Branch Stock A/c	2,500	[₹ 2,500 × 25/125]	
Branch Debtors A/c	1,400	By Goods Sent to Branch A/c	3,640
To Goods Sent to Branch A/c	18,200	[₹ 18,200 × 25/125]	
[₹ 14,560 + ₹ 3,640]		By Cash (remittance)	15,000
To Bank (expenses)	1,540	By Balance c/d:	
To Branch Stock Reserve A/c	600	Branch Stock A/c	3,000
[₹ 3,000 × 25/125]		Branch Debtors A/c	1,800

To Branch Manager's Commission		Branch Furniture A/c	1,200
[₹ 1,880 × 5/105]	90	Branch Cash A/c	980
To Net profit transfer to			
general Profit & Loss A/c	1,790		
	26,120		26,120

Working Notes:

Dr. **(I) MEMORANDUM BRANCH DEBTORS ACCOUNT** Cr.

Particulars	₹	Particulars	₹
To Balance b/d	1,400	By Cash (Balancing figure)	6,600
To sales (credit)	7,000	By Balance c/d	1,800
	8,400		8,400

Dr. **(II) MEMORANDUM BRANCH CASH ACCOUNT** Cr.

Particulars	₹	Particulars	₹
To Sales (cash)	10,700	By Cash Remitted	15,000
To Debtors	6,600	By Furniture	1,200
		By Petty Expenses	120
		By Balance c/d (Balancing figure)	980
	17,300		17,300

ILLUSTRATION 13 [WHEN NORMAL LOSS, TRADE DISCOUNT AND GOOD-IN-TRANSIT ARE GIVEN

CSFID Ltd. of Delhi has a branch at Bhiwani. Goods are invoiced to the branch at cost *plus* 25%. The branch does not maintain account books and all collections at the branch are remitted to head office. The expenses of the branch are reimbursed by the office. From the following particulars, prepare the branch account in the books of head office for the six months ending on 30th September, 2016.

Particulars	₹	Particulars	₹
Opening Stock		Bad debts	400
(at cost to head office)	55,000	Trade discount to customers	
Opening Debtors	15,000	(already taken into account	
Opening Furniture	12,000	while invoicing)	12,000
Opening Petty Cash	500	Goods sent to branch on 27th Sept.	
Transactions for six months:		received by branch on 5th Oct.	1,500
Goods received from head office		Cash sent to branch for expenses	10,500
(at cost to Branch)	2,25,000	Cash discount allowed to customers	800
Cash sales	1,95,000	Balances on 30th Sept.	
Credit sales	80,000	Stock in-hand	5,600
Goods returned to head office	12,750	Debtors	?
Normal loss	1,000	Petty cash	500
Sales returns by customers			

to branch	500		
Cash received from debtors	50,000		
Bills receivable received from customers at branch	15,000		

Depreciate Furniture @ 40% per annum. Branch manager is entitled to a commission of 5% of profit of branch after charging such commission.

SOLUTION

Dr. **BHIWANI BRANCH ACCOUNT** *Cr.*

Particulars	₹	*Particulars*		₹
To Opening Balances:		By Stock reserve		13,750
Stock (₹ 55,000 + ₹ 13,750)	68,750	By Bank (Remittance):		
Debtors	15,000	Cash sales	1,95,000	
Furniture	12,000	Cash from debtors	50,000	2,45,000
Petty Cash	500	By Goods sent to Branch (returns to HO)		12,750
To Goods sent to branch A/c (₹ 2,25,000 + ₹ 1,500)	2,26,500	By Goods sent to branch A/c [(₹ 2,26,500 – ₹ 12,750) × 25/125]		42,750
To Bank (expenses)	10,500	By Closing Balances:		
To Stock Reserve (1/5 of ₹ 7,100)	1,420	Debtors		28,300
To Branch Manager's Commission [₹ 40,080 × 5/105]	1,909	Stock (₹ 5,600 + ₹ 1,500)		7,100
To Net Profit transferred to Profit and Loss A/c	38,171	Bills receivable		15,000
		Furniture (₹ 12,000 – ₹ 2,400)		9,600
		Petty cash		500
	3,74,750			3,74,750

Working Note:

Dr. **MEMORANDUM BRANCH DEBTORS ACCOUNT** *Cr.*

Particulars	₹	*Particulars*	₹
To Balance b/d	15,000	By Sales returns	500
To Credit sales	80,000	By Bad debts	400
		By Bills receivable	15,000
		By Bank	50,000
		By Discount	800
		By Balance c/d (b.f.)	28,300
	95,000		95,000

ILLUSTRATION 14 [WHEN PURCHASES ARE MADE BY THE BRANCH WITH H.O. PERMISSION]

Raja (India) Ltd. have a head office and many retail branches which are supplied goods from the head office at 20% profit on sales price. Accounts are kept at head office where all expenses (except petty expenses) are paid. Such petty expenses are paid by the branches which are allowed to maintain petty cash balance of ₹ 300 on *imprest system*. From the following balances, as shown by the books, prepare Branch Account.

Particulars	₹	Particulars	₹
Balances on 1st April 2015:		Cash purchases by the branch (on permission from head office).	10,500
Petty cash in hand at branch	300	Credit purchases by the branch (with permission)	9,800
Stock at branch at its cost	20,000	*Payments made by the head office:*	
Sundry debtors at branches	5,000	Rent for one year (paid on 1.7.2015)	1,800
Sundry creditors at branches	1,200	Salaries	2,000
Furniture and fixtures at branch	8,000	Insurance paid for the year ending on 30th June, 2016	360
Rent prepaid (up to 30th June 2015)	300	*Payments made by the branch:*	
Transactions for the year:		Petty expenses	180
Goods sent to branch	1,04,000		
Cash sales at branch	64% of Total Sales		
Credit sales at branch	45,000	*Balances on 31st March, 2016:*	
Allowances to debtors	500	Stock at cost	30,000
Bad debts to be written off	200	Creditors at the end	3,000
Debtors at the end	9,300		

Write off 10% depreciation on furniture. The Branch manager is entitled to commission 5% of profit of branch after charging such commission.

SOLUTION

Dr. **BRANCH ACCOUNT IN THE BOOKS OF HEAD OFFICE** *Cr.*

Particulars	₹	Particulars	₹
To Balance b/d:		By Balance b/d: Creditors	1,200
Petty Cash	300	By Remittances	1,01,320
Stock	20,000	By Stock Reserve A/c (Op. Stock) (20,000 × 20%)	4,000
Debtors	5,000		
Furniture	8,000	By Goods sent to Branch (Loading) (1,04,000 × 20%)	20,800
Rent prepaid	300		
To Goods sent to Branch	1,04,000	By Balance c/d:	
To Bank (Remittance to Branch)	4,160	Stock [₹ 30,000 + ₹ 7,500]	37,500
To Stock Reserve	7,500	Debtors	9,300
To Balance c/d—creditors	3,000	Petty Cash	300
To Branch Manager's Commission [₹ 29,900 × 5/105]	1,424	Furniture [₹ 8,000 – ₹ 800]	7,200
		Rent Prepaid	450
To Net Profit transferred to P&L Ac	28,476	Insurance	90
	1,82,160		1,82,160

Working Notes:

Dr. **(I) MEMORANDUM BRANCH DEBTORS ACCOUNT** Cr.

Particulars	₹	Particulars	₹
To Balance b/d	5,000	By Allowances	500
To Sales (credit)	45,000	By bad debts	200
		By Cash received from debtors	40,000
		By Balance c/d (bal. fig.)	9,300
	50,000		50,000

Dr. **(II) MEMORANDUM BRANCH CREDITORS ACCOUNT** Cr.

Particulars	₹	Particulars	₹
To Cash A/c (Balancing figure)	8,000	By Balance b/d	1,200
To Balance c/d	3,000	By Purchases	9,800
	11,000		11,000

Dr. **(III) MEMORANDUM BRANCH CASH ACCOUNT** Cr.

Particulars	₹	Particulars	₹
To Cash Sales	80,000	By Purchases	10,500
To Remittances from H.O.	4,160	By Creditors	8,000
To Debtors	40,000	By Petty cash A/c	180
		By Rent	1,800
		By Salaries	2,000
		By Insurance	360
		By Cash remitted to H.O. (b.f.)	1,01,320
	1,24,160		1,24,160

Dr. **(IV) MEMORANDUM BRANCH PETTY CASH ACCOUNT** Cr.

Particulars	₹	Particulars	₹
To Balance c/d	300	By Petty expenses	180
To Cash A/c (b.f.)	180	By Balance c/d	300
	480		480

ILLUSTRATION 15 [WHEN CREDIT SALES ARE NOT GIVEN]

CANHF Ltd. Bombay started on 1st April, 2015 has one branch at Kanpur. All goods sold at the branch are received from the head office invoiced at cost *plus* 25%. All expenses relating to branch are paid by the head office. Each branch has its own Sales Ledger and sends weekly statement. All cash collections are remitted daily to head office by the branch. The following particulars relating to the year ending on 31st March, 2016 have been extracted from the weekly statements sent by the branches:

Particulars	₹	Particulars	₹
Cash Sales (40% of Net Sales)	78,600	Cost of Goods sent to Branch	1,93,200

Sales Returns	7,300	Branch Expenses	27,800
Sundry Debtors	34,500	Goods received from H.O.	2,31,500
Bad Debts	1,000		

The Branch manager is entitled to a commission of 5% of profit of branch after charging such commission.

Required: Prepare Kanpur Branch Account as it would appear in the books of the head office.

SOLUTION

Dr. **BRANCH ACCOUNT IN THE BOOKS OF HEAD OFFICE** *Cr.*

Particulars	₹	*Particulars*	₹
To Goods Sent to Branch A/c	2,41,500	By Bank A/c (Remittance):	
(₹ 1,93,200 + ₹ 48,300)		Cash Sales	78,600
To Bank A/c (Remittance):		Collection from Debtors	82,400
Branch Expenses	27,800	By Goods Sent to Branch A/c	
To Stock Reserve A/c		(₹ 2,41,500 × 25/125)	48,300
(₹ 45,000 × 25/125)	9,000	By Balance c/d:	
To Branch Manager's Commission		Debtors	34,500
[₹ 10,500 × 5/105]	500	Stock in hand	35,000
To Net Profit t/f to General P & L A/c	10,000	Stock in transit	10,000
		[₹ 2,41,500 – ₹ 2,31,500]	
	2,88,800		2,88,800

Working Note:

Dr. **(I) MEMORANDUM KANPUR BRANCH DEBTORS ACCOUNT** *Cr.*

Particulars	₹	*Particulars*	₹
To Credit Sales	1,25,200	By Sales Returns	7,300
[(₹ 78,600 × 60/40) + ₹ 7,300]		By Bad Debts	1,000
		By Bank A/c (Balancing figure)	82,400
		By Balance c/d	34,500
	1,25,200		1,25,200

Dr. **(II) MEMORANDUM KANPUR BRANCH STOCK ACCOUNT** *Cr.*

Particulars	₹	*Particulars*	₹
To Goods Sent to Branch A/c	2,41,500	By Branch Cash A/c (Cash Sales)	78,600
To Branch Debtors A/c	7,300	By Branch Debtors A/c (Credit Sales)	1,25,200
		By Balance c/d:	
		In hand	35,000
		transit (₹ 2,41,500 – ₹ 2, 31,500)	10,000
	2,48,800		2,48,800

ILLUSTRATION 16 [WHEN MONTHLY DETAILS ARE GIVEN]

CAM (HG) Ltd. carried on a retail business opened a branch X on 1st April, 2016 where all sales were on credit basis. All goods required by the branch were supplied from the head office and were invoiced to the branch at 10% above cost. The following were the transactions:

Particulars	*April* ₹	*May* ₹	*June* ₹
Goods sent to Branch (Cost to H.O)	40,000	50,000	60,000
Sales as shown by the branch monthly report	38,000	42,000	55,000
Cash received from Debtors and remitted to H.O.	20,000	51,000	35,000
Returns to H.O. (Cost to Branch)	1,200	600	2,400

The stock of goods held by the branch on June 30, amounted to ₹ 53,400 at invoice price to branch. Record these transactions in the Head Office books, showing balances as on 30th June, 2016 and the branch gross profit for the three months ended on that date.

SOLUTION

Dr. **X BRANCH ACCOUNT IN THE BOOKS OF HEAD OFFICE** *Cr.*

Particulars	₹	*Particulars*	₹
To Goods Sent to Branch A/c		By Bank A/c (remittance)	1,06,000
(₹ 1,50,000 × 110/100)	1,65,000	By Goods Sent to Branch A/c	4,200
To Stock Reserve A/c		By Goods Sent to Branch A/c	
(₹ 53,400 × 10/110)	4,855	[₹ 1,65,000 – ₹ 4,200) × 10/110]	14,618
To Net Profit t/f to General P & L A/c	37,363	By Balance c/d:	
		Debtors (₹ 1,35,000 – ₹ 1,06,000)	29,000
		Stock	53,400
	2,07,218		2,07,218

ILLUSTRATION 17 [CALCULATION OF THE COMMISSION DUE TO MANAGER]

Rani India Ltd. has a retail shop under the supervision of a manager. The ratio of gross profit to selling price is constant at 25 per cent throughout the year to 31st March, 2016.

Branch manager is entitled to a commission of 10 per cent of the profit earned by his branch, calculated before charging his commission but subject to a deduction from such commission equal to 25 per cent of any ascertained deficiency of branch stock. All goods were supplied to the branch by head office.

From the under mentioned figures, calculate the commission due to manager for the year to 31st March, 2016.

Particulars	₹	*Particulars*	₹
Opening Stock, (at cost)	37,368	Chargeable expenses	24,560
Goods sent to branch (at cost)	1,44,840	Closing Stock (Selling Price)	61,664
Sales	1,80,640		
Manager's commission paid on A/c	1,200		

SOLUTION

Step 1: *Calculation of Deficiency*

Dr. **BRANCH STOCK ACCOUNT (AT INVOICE PRICE)** *Cr.*

Particulars	₹	*Particulars*	₹
To Opening Stock		By Sales	1,80,640
[₹ 37,368 + 1/3 of ₹ 37,368)	49,824	By Closing Stock	61,664
To Goods sent to Branch A/c		By Deficiency at sale price (b.f.)	640
[₹ 1,44,840 + 1/3 of ₹ 1,44,840]	1,93,120		
	2,42,944		2,42,944

Step 2: *Calculation of Net Profit before Commission*

Dr. **BRANCH ACCOUNT** *Cr.*

Particulars	₹	*Particulars*	₹
To Opening Stock		By Sales	1,80,640
[₹ 37,368 + 1/3 of ₹ 37,368]	49,824	By Closing Stock	61,664
To Goods sent to Branch A/c		By Stock Reserve A/c	12,456
[₹ 1,44,840 + 1/3 of ₹ 1,44,840]	1,93,120	By Goods sent to Branch A/c	48,280
To Expenses	24,560		
To Stock Reserve A/c	15,416		
[₹ 61,664 × 25/100]			
To Net Profit—subject to			
manager's commission	20,120		
	3,03,040		3,03,040

STEP 3: CALCULATION OF COMMISSION STILL DUE TO MANAGER

	Particulars	₹
A.	Commission at 10% profit before charging his commission [₹ 20,120 × 10/100]	2,012
B.	*Less:* 25% of cost of deficiency in stock [25% of (75% of ₹ 640)]	(120)
C.	Commission for the year [A – B]	1,892
D.	*Less:* Paid on account	(1,200)
E.	Balance due [C – D]	692

ILLUSTRATION 18 [WHEN CASH SALES AT INVOICE PRICE & CREDIT SALES AT LIST PRICE]

Rank (India) Ltd., Delhi invoices goods to its Noida Branch at 20% *less* than the list price which is cost *plus* 100% with instructions that cash sales were to be made at invoice price and credit sales at list price. From the following particulars available from Noida Branch, prepare Noida Branch Account to reveal the profit for the period ending on 31.3.2016.

Particulars	₹	*Particulars*	₹
Opening Stock	18,000	Actual expenses at Branch	30,900
Opening Debtors	10,000	Shortage of Stock (at cost)	2,500

Personal Computer (P.C.)	50,000	Bad debts written off	400
Goods received from Head Office	1,80,000	Goods returned by customers direct to Head Office at list price	1,500
Cash Sales	82,000		
Credit Sales	1,20,000	Debtors at the end	8,100
Goods in transit on 31 March, 20XI	10,000	Depreciate Personal Computer by	20%
Cash sent to Branch for expenses	32,900		

Branch manager is entitled to a commission of 5% of profits after charging such commission.

SOLUTION

Dr. **NOIDA BRANCH ACCOUNT** *Cr.*

Particulars		₹	*Particulars*		₹
To Balance b/d:			By Cash remittance:		
Stock		18,000	Cash Sales	82,000	
Debtors		10,000	Cash from Debtors	1,20,000	2,02,000
Personal Computer		50,000	By Stock Reserve A/c		
To Goods sent to Branch A/c			[18,000 × 60/160]		6,750
Received	1,80,000		By Goods sent to Branch A/c		
In Transit	10,000	1,90,000	(Returns) [₹ 1,500 × 160/200]		1,200
To Cash (Expenses)		32,900	By Goods sent to Branch A/c		
To Stock Reserve A/c			[1,88,800 × 60/160]		70,800
[₹ 26,000 × 60/160]		9,750	By Balance c/d:		
To Manager's Commission			Stock-in-hand	16,000	
[₹ 46,200 × 5/105]		2,200	Stock-in-transit	10,000	26,000
To Net Profit t/f to			Debtors		8,100
General Profit and Loss A/c		44,000	Personal Computer		
			(₹ 50,000 – ₹ 10,000)		40,000
			Cash (₹ 32,900 – ₹ 30,900)		2,000
		3,56,850			3,56,850

Working Notes:

(I) CALCULATION OF COST PRICE RELATIONSHIPS

A. Cost	100
B. *Add:* Profit	60
C. Invoice Price	160
D. *Add:* Profit on Credit Sale	40
E. List Price	200

Dr. **(II) MEMORANDUM NOIDA BRANCH STOCK ACCOUNT (AT INVOICE PRICE)** *Cr.*

Particulars	₹	*Particulars*	₹
To Balance b/d	18,000	By Goods sent to Branch A/c	

To Goods sent to Branch A/c:			(₹ 1,500 × 160/200)	1,200
Goods received	1,80,000		By Sales:	
Goods in Transit	10,000	1,90,000	Cash Sales	82,000
To Surplus (Excess of selling			Credit Sales 1,20,000	
price over Invoice price)			*Less:* Returns 1,500	2,00,500
in case of credit sales		23,700	By Shortage	4,000
(₹ 1,18,500 × 40/200)			By balance c/d:	
			In Hand (bal. fig.) 16,000	
			In Transit 10,000	26,000
		2,31,700		2,31,700

Dr. **(III) MEMORANDUM NOIDA BRANCH DEBTORS ACCOUNT** Cr.

Particulars	₹	*Particulars*	₹
To Balance b/d	10,000	By Cash (Balancing figure)	1,20,000
To Credit Sales	1,20,000	By Bad debts	400
		By Returns	1,500
		By balance c/d	8,100
	1,30,000		1,30,000

5.0 STOCK AND DEBTORS METHOD

MEANING OF STOCK AND DEBTORS METHOD

Under Stock and Debtors Method, in order to exercise more control over the working of a branch, the head office usually maintains the following accounts:

Accounts	*Purpose*
1. Branch Stock Account at Invoice Price	To ascertain any shortage *or* surplus
2. Branch Debtors Account	To ascertain the closing debtors
3. Branch Expenses Account	To ascertain the total expenses incurred at the Branch
4. Branch Adjustment Account	To ascertain Gross Profit/Gross Loss
5. Branch Profit and Loss Account	To ascertain Net Profit/Net Loss
6. Goods Sent to Branch Account	To ascertain the net cost of goods sent to branch
7. Branch Cash Account	To record all cash transactions of the branch
8. Branch Fixed Assets Account	To record all transactions relating to branch fixed assets

JOURNAL ENTRIES UNDER STOCK AND DEBTORS METHOD

1. When goods are supplied by the H.O./ another branch	Branch Stock A/c Dr. To Goods sent to Branch A/c
2. When goods are returned by the Branch/ or when goods are supplied to another branch	Goods Sent to Branch A/c Dr. To Branch Stock A/c

3. When goods are returned by branch Customers directly to H.O.	Goods sent to Branch A/c Dr. To Debtors A/c
4. When goods are sold on credit	Branch Debtors A/c Dr. To Branch Stock A/c
5. When goods are sold for cash	Branch Cash A/c Dr. To Branch Stock A/c
6. When goods are returned by Branch Debtors to branch	Branch Stock A/c Dr. To Branch Debtors A/c
7. When cash is received by branch from its debtors	Branch Cash A/c Dr. To Branch Debtors A/c
8. To record bad debts, discount allowed etc.	Branch Expenses A/c Dr. To Branch Debtors A/c
9. To record branch Expenses paid by branch	Branch Expenses A/c Dr. To Branch Cash A/c
10. To record abnormal loss of Stock [Due to abnormal factors like fire, flood, theft etc.]	Branch Adjustment A/c Dr. [Loading] Branch Profit & Loss a/c Dr. [Cost] To Branch Stock A/c Dr. [Invoice Price]
11. To record normal loss of stock [Due to the inherent nature of the product]	Branch Adjustment A/c Dr. [Invoice Price] To Branch Stock A/c
12. To record surplus representing of selling price over invoice price excess	Branch Stock A/c Dr. [Invoice Price] To Branch Adjustment A/c
13. To remove loading from the net amount of goods sent to branch (i.e., goods sent *less* returns by branch)	Goods sent to Branch A/c Dr. [Loading] To Branch Adjustment A/c
14. To remove loading from the amount of closing stock	Branch Adjustment A/c Dr. [Loading] To Stock Reserve A/c
15. To remove loading from the amount of opening stock	Stock Reserve A/c Dr. [Loading] To Branch Adjustment A/c
16. To record gross profit made by branch	Branch Adjustment A/c Dr. To Branch Profit & Loss A/c *Note: The entry will be reversed in case of gross loss.*
17. To record the transfer of branch expenses	Branch Profit & Loss A/c Dr. To Branch Expenses A/c
18. To record net profit made by branch	Branch Profit & Loss A/c Dr. To General Profit & Loss A/c *Note: The entry will be reversed in case of net loss.*
19. To transfer the balance in Goods sent to Branch A/c	Goods Sent to Branch A/c Dr. To Trading A/c/Purchases A/c

FORMATS OF ACCOUNTS OPENED UNDER STOCK & DEBTORS METHOD

Dr. **1. BRANCH STOCK ACCOUNT** *Cr.*

Particulars	₹	*Particulars*	₹
To Balance b/d	xxx	By Branch Cash A/c (Cash Sales)	xxx

To Goods Sent to Branch A/c	xxx	By Branch Debtors A/c (Credit Sales)	xxx
To Branch Debtors A/c (Return by Customers to Branch)	xxx	By Goods Sent to Branch A/c (Returns to H.O.)	xxx
To Goods sent to Branch A/c (T/f of goods from other Branch)	xxx	By Goods Sent to Branch A/c (T/f of Goods to other Branch)	xxx
To Branch Adjustment A/c (Excess of Selling Price over Invoice Price) (i.e. surplus)	xxx	By Branch Adjustment A/c (Load on Abnormal Loss due to fire etc.)	xxx
		By Branch Profit & Loss A/c (Cost of Abnormal Loss due to fire etc.)	xxx
		By Branch Adjustment A/c (Normal Loss)	xxx
		By Balance c/d:	
		In hand	xxx
		In transit	xxx
	xxx		xxx

Dr. **2. BRANCH ADJUSTMENT ACCOUNT** Cr.

Particulars	₹	Particulars	₹
To Direct Expenses like wages etc.	xxx	By Stock Reserve A/c (Load on Opening Stock)	xxx
To Branch Stock A/c (Load on Abnormal Loss due to Fire, etc.)	xxx	By Goods Sent to Branch A/c (Load on Net Goods Sent)	xxx
To Branch Stock A/c (Normal Loss)	xxx	By Branch Stock A/c (Excess of Selling Price over Invoice Price) (Surplus)	xxx
To Stock Reserve A/c (Load on Closing Stock)	xxx		
To Gross Profit t/f to branch P&L A/c	xxx		
	xxx		xxx

Dr. **3. BRANCH EXPENSES ACCOUNT** Cr.

Particulars	₹	Particulars	₹
To Salaries	xxx	By Branch Profit and Loss A/c	xxx
To Rent	xxx		
To Petty Expenses	xxx		
To Bad Debts	xxx		
To Discount	xxx		
To Depreciation	xxx		
	xxx		xxx

Dr. **4. BRANCH PROFIT AND LOSS ACCOUNT** Cr.

Particulars	₹	Particulars	₹
To Branch Stock A/c (Cost of Abnormal Loss)	xxx	By Branch Adjustment A/c (Gross Profit b/d)	xxx
To Branch Expenses	xxx	By Branch Cash A/c (Insurance claim received)/Insurance Co. (claim admitted but not recei.)	xxx
*To Net Profit t/f to General P&L A/c	xxx	*By Net Loss t/f to General P&L A/c	xxx
	xxx		xxx

*Only one figure shall appear.

Dr. **5. BRANCH DEBTORS ACCOUNT** Cr.

Particulars	₹	Particulars	₹
To Balance b/d	xxx	By Branch Cash A/c (Cash paid to branch)	xxx
To Branch Stock A/c (Credit Sales)	xxx	By Bills Receivable A/c	xxx
To Bills Receivable A/c (B/R dishonoured)	xxx	By Cash A/c (Cash paid directly to H.O)	xxx
		By Branch Stock A/c (Returns to Branch)	xxx
		By Goods Sent to Branch A/c (Goods returned directly to H.O.)	xxx
		By Discount A/c	xxx
		By Bad Debts A/c	xxx
		By Balance c/d	xxx
	xxx		xxx

Dr. **6. GOODS SENT TO BRANCH ACCOUNT** Cr.

Particulars	₹	Particulars	₹
To Branch Stock A/c (Returns)	xxx	By Branch Stock A/c (goods sent)	xxx
To Branch Adjustment A/c [Load on net goods sent]	xxx		
To Purchases/Trading A/c	xxx		
	xxx		xxx

ILLUSTRATION 19

CAS Ltd. Madras has a branch at New Delhi to which goods are sent @ 20% above cost. The branch makes both cash and credit sales. Branch expenses are met partly from H.O. and partly by the branch. The statement of expenses incurred by the branch every month is sent to head office for recording. Following further details are given for the year ended 31st March 2016:

Particulars	₹
Cost of Goods sent to Branch at cost	2,00,000
Goods received by Branch till 31.12.2015 at invoice price	2,20,000
Credit Sales for the year at invoice price	1,65,000
Cash Sales for the year at invoice price	59,000
Cash Remitted to head office	2,22,500
Expenses paid by H.O.	12,000
Bad Debts written off	750

Particulars	*Opening Balances* ₹	*Closing Balances* ₹
Stock in hand	25,000 (Cost)	28,000 (invoice price)
Debtors	32,750	26,000
Cash in Hand	5,000	2,500

Required: Show necessary ledger accounts in the books of the head office and determine the Profit and Loss of the Branch for the year ended 31st March 2016 (a) under Debtors Method (b) Under Stock & Debtors Method.

SOLUTION

Dr. **(A) UNDER DEBTORS METHOD NEW DELHI BRANCH ACCOUNT** *Cr.*

Particulars	₹	*Particulars*		₹
To Balance b/d:		By Stock Reserve A/c		
Stock	30,000	[₹ 30,000 × 20/120]		5,000
Debtors	32,750	By Goods sent to Branch A/c		40,000
Cash	5,000	[₹ 2,40,000 × 20/120]		
To Goods Sent to Branch A/c	2,40,000	By Bank A/c (Remittance)		
To Bank A/c (Exp. paid by H.O.)	12,000	received from the Branch		
To Stock Reserve A/c		Cash Sales	59,000	
(on closing stock)	8,000	Drs. Collection	1,63,500	2,22,500
(₹ 48,000 × 20/120)		(Net of expenses)		
To Net Profit Transferred to		(₹ 2,22,500 – ₹ 59,000)		
Profit and Loss A/c	16,250	By Balance c/d:		
		Stock (including Transit)		48,000
		Debtors		26,000
		Cash		2,500
	3,44,000			3,44,000

Working Notes:

Dr. **(I) MEMORANDUM BRANCH STOCK ACCOUNT** *Cr.*

Particulars	₹	*Particulars*	₹
To Balance b/d	30,000	By Branch Debtors A/c	1,65,000

	₹		₹
To Goods Sent to Branch A/c	2,40,000	By Branch Cash A/c	59,000
To Surplus		By Balance c/d:	
(Excess of Selling Price over		Goods-in-transit	20,000
Invoice Price) (Balancing figure)	2,000	[₹ 2,40,000 – ₹ 2,20,000]	
		Stock at Branch	28,000
	2,72,000		2,72,000

Dr. **(II) MEMORANDUM BRANCH DEBTORS ACCOUNT** *Cr.*

Particulars	₹	*Particulars*	₹
To Balance b/d	32,750	By Bad Debts A/c	750
To Branch Stock A/c	1,65,000	By Branch Cash A/c (b.f.)	1,71,000
		By Balance c/d	26,000
	1,97,750		1,97,750

Dr. **(III) MEMORANDUM BRANCH CASH ACCOUNT** *Cr.*

Particulars	₹	*Particulars*	₹
To Balance b/d	5,000	By Bank (Remittance to H.O.)	2,22,500
To Branch Stock A/c	59,000	By Expenses	12,000
To Branch Debtors A/c	1,71,000	By Expense (paid by Branch) (b.f.)	10,000
To Bank A/c (Remittance from H.O.)	12,000	By Balance c/d	2,500
	2,47,000		2,47,000

(B) UNDER STOCK AND DEBTORS METHOD

Dr. **(A) BRANCH STOCK ACCOUNT** *Cr.*

Particulars	₹	*Particulars*	₹
To Balance b/d	30,000	By Branch Debtors A/c	1,65,000
To Goods Sent to Branch A/c	2,40,000	By Branch Bank A/c	59,000
To Branch Adjustment A/c		By Balance c/d	
(Excess of sales over		Goods in Transit	
invoice price) (b.f.)	2,000	(₹ 2,40,000 – ₹ 2,20,000)	20,000
		Stock at Branch	28,000
	2,72,000		2,72,000

Dr. **(B) BRANCH DEBTORS ACCOUNT** *Cr.*

Particulars	₹	*Particulars*	₹
To Balance b/d	32,750	By Bad Debts A/c	750
To Branch Stock A/c	1,65,000	By Branch Cash A/c (b.f.)	1,71,000
		By Balance c/d	26,000
	1,97,750		1,97,750

Dr. **(C) BRANCH CASH ACCOUNT** Cr.

Particulars	₹	*Particulars*	₹
To Balance b/d	5,000	By Bank Remittance to H.O.	2,22,500
To Branch Stock A/c	59,000	By Branch Profit & Loss A/c	12,000
To Bank A/c	12,000	(Exp. paid by H.O.)	
To Branch Debtors A/c	1,71,000	By Branch Profit & Loss A/c (b.f.)	
		(Exp. paid by Branch)	10,000
		By Balance c/d	2,500
	2,47,000		2,47,000

Dr. **(D) BRANCH ADJUSTMENT ACCOUNT** Cr.

Particulars	₹	*Particulars*	₹
To Stock Reserve A/c (on closing		By Stock Reserve A/c	
stock) (48,000 × 20/120)	8,000	[30,000 × 20/120]	5,000
To Gross Profit c/d	39,000	By Goods sent to Branch A/c	40,000
		By Branch Stock A/c	2,000
	47,000		47,000

Dr. **(E) BRANCH PROFIT AND LOSS ACCOUNT** Cr.

Particulars	₹	*Particulars*	₹
To Branch Expenses		By Gross Profit b/d	39,000
(paid by H.O. ₹ 12,000 and paid by Branch ₹ 10,000)	22,000		
To Branch Debtors (Bad debts)	750		
To Net Profit	16,250		
	39,000		39,000

Dr. **(F) GOODS SENT TO BRANCH ACCOUNT** Cr.

Particulars	₹	*Particulars*	₹
To Branch Adjustment A/c	40,000	By Branch to Stock A/c	2,40,000
To Purchase A/c (Transfer)	2,00,000		
	2,40,000		2,40,000

ILLUSTRATION 20 [WHEN THERE ARE GOODS-IN TRANSIT AND ABNORMAL LOSS]

Rocky (India), Khandwa, opened a Branch at Delhi. The goods were sent by the Head Office to the Branch and invoiced at selling price of the Branch which was 125% of the cost price of the head office.

The following are the particulars relating to the transactions of Delhi Branch:

Particulars		₹
Goods sent to branch (at cost to Head Office)		2,80,800

Sales:		
Cash		1,25,000
Credit		1,75,000
Cash collected from Debtors		1,56,000
Discounts allowed		4,000
Returns from Debtors		5,000
Cash sent to branch for:		
Wages	3,000	
Freight	11,000	
Other Expenses	6,000	20,000
Spoiled cloth in bales written off at invoice price		500
Closing Stock in hand		54,500
Goods received by Branch till date at invoice price		3,50,000

Required: Ascertain the profit *or* loss for the Delhi Branch for the year ended 31st March, 2016 after preparing Branch Stock Account and Branch Debtors Account.

SOLUTION

Dr. **DELHI BRANCH STOCK ACCOUNT** *Cr.*

Particulars	₹	*Particulars*	₹
To Goods Sent to Branch A/c	3,51,000	By Branch Debtors A/c (Credit Sales)	1,25,000
[₹ 2,80,800 + ₹ 70,200]		By Branch Cash A/c (Cash Sales)	1,75,000
To Branch Debtors A/c —Returns	5,000	By Branch Adjustment A/c	100
		[₹ 500 × 25/125]	
		By Branch Profit & Loss A/c	
		(Cost of spoiled cloth)	400
		By Balance c/d:	
		Stock-in-hand	54,500
		Stock-in-transit	1,000
		[₹ 3,51,000 – ₹ 3,50,000]	
	3,56,000		3,56,000

Dr. **DELHI BRANCH DEBTORS ACCOUNT** *Cr.*

Particulars	₹	*Particulars*	₹
To Branch Stock A/c (Cr. sales)	1,75,000	By Cash A/c	1,56,000
		By Discounts A/c	4,000
		By Branch Stock A/c (Returns)	5,000
		By Balance c/f	10,000
	1,75,000		1,75,000

Dr. **DELHI BRANCH ADJUSTMENT ACCOUNT** Cr.

Particulars	₹	Particulars	₹
To Branch Stock A/c—Loading	100	By Goods sent to branch A/c	70,200
To Wages (treated as Direct)	3,000	[₹ 3,51,000 × 25/125]	
To Freight (treated as Direct)	11,000		
To Stock Reserve A/c	11,100		
To Gross Profit transferred			
—to Branch P and L A/c	45,000		
	70,200		70,200

Dr. **DELHI BRANCH PROFIT & LOSS ACCOUNT** Cr.

Particulars	₹	Particulars	₹
To Expenses	6,000	By Branch Adjustment A/c	45,000
To Discounts	4,000	(Gross Profit)	
To Branch Stock A/c			
[Cost of Spoiled cloth]	400		
To P & L A/c (Net Profit)	34,600		
	45,000		45,000

ILLUSTRATION 21 [CALCULATION OF CREDIT SALES, NORMAL LOSS AND MANAGER'S COMMISSION]

Rosy (India) Ltd. of Delhi operates a retail branch at Madras. The head office makes all the purchases and the branch is charged at cost price *plus* 50%. All cash received by the Madras branch is remitted to Delhi. Branch expenses are paid by the branch out of an imprest account which is reimbursed by Delhi H.O. monthly.

The branch keeps a sales ledger and certain essential subsidiary books, but otherwise all branch transactions are recorded by H.O. Debtors' balances were ₹ 4,000. Branch stock ₹ 6,000.

During the year ended 31st March 2016, the following branch transactions were made.

Particulars	₹	Particulars	₹
Goods received from Delhi	15,000	Collections from debtors	4,800
Cash Sales	6,900	Debtors written off as irrecoverable	250
Goods returned to Delhi	300	Cash discounts allowed to debtors	100
Authorised reductions in selling		Closing Debtors	5,150
price of goods sold	150	Branch Debtors' cheques returned	
		dishonoured (not yet recorded)	5,000

A consignment of goods despatched to the branch on 28th March, with a selling price of ₹ 180 was not received until 5th April, and had not been included in stock figure, which at selling price was ₹ 7,290.

The expenses relating to the branch for the year ended 31st March 2016 amounted to ₹ 1,810.

Branch manager is entitled to a commission of 5% of profits after charging such commission.

Note: Any stock unaccounted for is to be regarded as normal wastage and pilferage.

Required: Write up the necessary ledger accounts according to stock and debtors system.

SOLUTION

Dr. **(A) MADRAS BRANCH STOCK ACCOUNT** Cr.

Particulars		₹	Particulars	₹
To Balance b/d		6,000	By Branch cash A/c (cash sales)	6,900
To Goods sent to Branch A/c			By Goods sent to Branch A/c	
Goods received from H.O.	15,000		(Return)	300
Goods from H.O. in transit	180	15,180	By Branch Debtors A/c (Cr. Sale)	6,300
			By Branch Adjustment A/c	
			(Reduction in S.P.)	150
			By Branch adjustment A/c (b.f.)	
			(Normal Loss)	60
			By Balance c/d:	
			In hand	7,290
			In transit	180
		21,180		21,180

Dr. **(B) MADRAS BRANCH DEBTORS ACCOUNT** Cr.

Particulars	₹	Particulars	₹
To Balance b/d	4,000	By Cash A/c	4,800
To Bank A/c (Dishonoured cheques)	5,000	By Bad debts	250
To Branch Stock A/c		By Discounts	100
(Credit sales) (b.f.)	6,300	By Balance c/d	10,150
	15,300		15,300

Dr. **(C) MADRAS BRANCH ADJUSTMENT ACCOUNT** Cr.

Particulars	₹	Particulars	₹
To Branch Stock A/c:		By Stock Reserve A/c [6,000 × 1/3]	2,000
(Reduction in Selling price)	150	By Goods sent to Branch A/c	
To Branch Stock A/c		[(₹ 15,000 + 180 – 300) × 1/3]	4,960
[Normal shortage]	60		
To Stock Reserve A/c			
[(₹ 7,290 + 180) × 1/3]	2,490		
To Gross profit t/f to Branch P&L A/c	4,260		
	6,960		6,960

Dr. **(D) MADRAS BRANCH PROFIT AND LOSS ACCOUNT** Cr.

Particulars		₹	Particulars	₹
To Branch expenses A/c:			By Branch Adjustment A/c	4,260
Expenses	1,810		(Gross Profit)	
Bad debts	250			

Discounts	100	2,160		
To Manager's Commission				
[₹ 2,100 × 5/105]		100		
To Net Profit t/f to General P&L A/c		2,000		
		4,260		4,260

ILLUSTRATION 22 [ADJUSTMENT OF ABNORMAL LOSS]

CANHI Ltd, sends goods to its Madras Branch at cost *plus* 25 per cent. The following particulars are available in respect of the Branch for the year ended 31st March, 2016.

Particulars	₹	*Particulars*	₹
Opening Stock at Branch		Closing stock at branch	
at cost to Branch	80,000	at cost to Branch	40,000
Loss-in-transit at invoice price	15,000	Expenses	60,000
Pilferage at invoice price	6,000	Sales	12,19,000
Recovered from Insurance			
Company against loss-in-transit	10,000		

Required: Prepare (a) Branch Stock Account (b) Branch Adjustment Account (c) Branch Profit and Loss Account (d) Goods sent to Branch Account.

SOLUTION

Dr. **(A) MADRAS BRANCH STOCK ACCOUNT** *Cr.*

Particulars	₹	*Particulars*	₹
To Balance b/d	80,000	By Branch Cash/Debtors A/c	12,19,000
To Goods Sent to Branch A/c (b.f)	12,00,000	By Branch Adjustment A/c	
		(₹ 15,000 × 25/125)	3,000
		By Branch P & L A/c	
		(Cost of Loss-in-transit)	12,000
		By Branch Adjustment A/c	
		(₹ 6,000 × 25/125)	1,200
		By Branch P & L A/c	
		(Cost of Pilferage)	4,800
		By Balance c/d	40,000
	12,80,000		12,80,000

Dr. **(B) MADRAS BRANCH ADJUSTMENT ACCOUNT** *Cr.*

Particulars	₹	*Particulars*	₹
To Branch Stock A/c		By Stock Reserve A/c	
(Load on Loss-in transit)	3,000	(₹ 80,000 × 25/125)	16,000
To Branch Stock A/c		By Goods Sent to Branch A/c	2,40,000
(Load on Pilferage)	1,200	(₹ 12,00,000 × 25/125)	

To Stock Reserve A/c			
(₹ 40,000 × 25/125)	8,000		
To Gross Profit t/f to General P&L A/c	2,43,800		
	2,56,000		2,56,000

Dr. **(C) MADRAS BRANCH PROFIT AND LOSS ACCOUNT** Cr.

Particulars	₹	*Particulars*	₹
To Branch Expenses	60,000	By Branch Adjustment A/c	
To Branch Stock A/c		(Gross Profit)	2,43,800
(Cost of Loss-in-transit)	12,000	By Branch Cash A/c	
To Branch Stock A/c		(Claim from Insurance Co.)	10,000
(Cost of Pilferage)	4,800		
To Net Profit t/f to General P&L A/c	1,77,000		
	2,53,800		2,53,800

Dr. **(D) GOODS SENT TO MADRAS BRANCH ACCOUNT** Cr.

Particulars	₹	*Particulars*	₹
To Branch Adjustment A/c	2,40,000	By Branch Stock A/c	12,00,000
(₹ 12,00,000 × 25/125)			
To Trading A/c/Purchases A/c	9,60,000		
	12,00,000		12,00,000

ILLUSTRATION 23 [ADJUSTMENT OF ABNORMAL LOSS]

Multichained Stores Ltd, Delhi has its branches at Lucknow and Madras. It charges goods to its branches at cost *plus* 25%. Following information is available about the transactions of the Lucknow branch for the year ended on 31st March, 2016.

Particulars	₹	*Particulars*	₹
Opening Stock	30,000	Insurance co. paid to H.O. for loss	
Opening Debtors	10,000	by fire at Lucknow	3,000
Opening Petty Cash	50	Cash sent for Petty Expenses	34,000
Goods sent to Lucknow Branch	3,25,000	Bad Debts at branch	500
Goods Returned to Head Office	10,000	Goods transferred to Madras Branch	
Cash Sales	1,00,000	under H.O. advice	15,000
Collection from Debtors	1,70,000	Insurance Charges paid by H.O.	500
Goods pilfered (Invoice Price)	2,000	Goods lost in fire (Invoice Price)	5,000
Closing Petty Cash	230	Goods Returned by Debtors	500
Closing Debtors	14,000		

Goods worth ₹ 15,000 (included above) sent by Lucknow Branch to Madras Branch was in transit on 31.3.2016. Show the following accounts in the books of Multichained Stores Ltd.

(a) Lucknow Branch Stock A/c (b) Lucknow Branch Adjustment A/c (c) Lucknow Branch Profit & Loss A/c (d) Lucknow Branch Debtors A/c (e) Goods Sent to Lucknow Branch A/c (f) Stock Reserve A/c.

SOLUTION

Dr. **(A) LUCKNOW BRANCH STOCK ACCOUNT** Cr.

Particulars	₹	Particulars	₹
To Balance b/d	30,000	By Branch Cash A/c (Cash Sales)	1,00,000
To Goods Sent to Branch A/c	3,25,000	By Branch Debtors A/c (Credit Sales)	1,75,000
To Branch Debtors A/c	500	By Goods Sent to Branch A/c	
(Return by customers to Branch)		(Returns to H.O.)	10,000
		By Goods Sent to Branch A/c	15,000
		(t/f of goods to other Branch)	
		By Branch Adjustment A/c	
		(₹ 5,000 × 20/100)	1,000
		By Branch P & L A/c	
		(Cost of Abnormal Loss)	4,000
		By Branch Adjustment A/c	
		(₹ 2,000 × 20/100)	400
		By Branch P & L A/c	
		(Cost of goods pilfered)	1,600
		By Balance c/d	48,500
	3,55,500		3,55,500

Dr. **(B) LUCKNOW BRANCH ADJUSTMENT ACCOUNT** Cr.

Particulars	₹	Particulars	₹
To Branch Stock A/c		By Stock Reserve A/c	
(Load on goods lost)	1,000	(₹ 30,000 × 25/125)	6,000
To Branch Stock A/c		By Goods Sent to Branch A/c	60,000
(Load on Goods pilfered)	400	[(₹ 3,25,000 – ₹ 10,000 – ₹ 15,000)	
To Stock Reserve A/c		× 25/125]	
(₹ 48,500 × 25/125)	9,700		
To Gross Profit t/f to Branch P&L A/c	54,900		
	66,000		66,000

Dr. **(C) LUCKNOW BRANCH PROFIT AND LOSS ACCOUNT** Cr.

Particulars	₹	Particulars	₹
To Insurance Charges	500	By Branch Adjustment A/c	
To Petty Expenses		(Gross Profit)	54,900
(₹ 50 + 34,000 – ₹ 230)	33,820	By Branch Cash A/c	
To Bad Debts	500	(Insurance claim received)	3,000
To Branch Stock A/c			
(Cost of Goods lost)	4,000		
To Branch Stock A/c			

(Cost of goods pilfered)	1,600		
To Net Profit t/f to General P&L A/c	17,480		
	57,900		57,900

Dr. **(D) LUCKNOW BRANCH DEBTORS ACCOUNT** Cr.

Particulars	₹	Particulars	₹
To Balance b/d	10,000	By Branch Cash A/c	1,70,000
To Branch Stock A/c (Credit Sales)	1,75,000	By Branch Stock A/c	
(Balancing figure)		(Returns to Branch)	500
		By Bad Debts	500
		By Balance c/d	14,000
	1,85,000		1,85,000

Dr. **(E) GOODS SENT TO LUCKNOW BRANCH ACCOUNT** Cr.

Particulars	₹	Particulars	₹
To Branch Stock A/c	10,000	By Branch Stock A/c	3,25,000
To Branch Stock A/c	15,000		
To Branch Adjustment A/c	60,000		
To General Trading A/c/ Purchases A/c	2,40,000		
	3,25,000		3,25,000

Dr. **(F) LUCKNOW BRANCH STOCK RESERVE ACCOUNT** Cr.

Particulars	₹	Particulars	₹
To Branch Adjustment A/c (t/f)	6,000	By Balance b/d	6,000
To Balance c/d	9,700	By Branch Adjustment A/c (t/f)	9,700
	15,700		15,700

ILLUSTRATION 24 [TREATMENT OF SURPLUS]

Maruti Ltd. has a Branch at Lucknow. Goods are invoiced from Head Office at cost *plus* 50%. Branch remits all cash received to Head office and all expenses are met by Head Office. Prepare the necessary accounts in the books of Maruti Ltd under Stock and Debtors system to show profit earned at the branch from the following:

Particulars	₹	Particulars	₹
Opening Stock (Invoice Price)	15,600	Closing Debtors	7,150
Opening Debtors	8,700	Goods returned by Debtors	1,500
Goods sent to Branch (at cost)	36,000	Surplus in Stock (invoice Price)	300
Cash Sales	35,000	Discount allowed to Debtors	350
Cash collected from Debtors	29,800	Expenses at Branch	6,700
Goods received by Branch till date at invoice price	51,000		

SOLUTION

Dr. **(A) LUCKNOW BRANCH STOCK ACCOUNT** Cr.

Particulars	₹	Particulars		₹
To Balance b/d	15,600	By Cash A/c (Cash Sales)		35,000
To Goods Sent to Branch A/c		By Branch Debtors A/c		
[₹ 36,000 + ₹ 18,000]	54,000	(Credit Sales)		30,100
To Branch Debtors A/c		By Balance c/d (b.f.)		
(Return by customers)	1,500	in hand (b.f.)	3,300	
To Branch Adjustment A/c (Surplus)	300	in transit	3,000	6,300
	71,400			71,400

Dr. **(B) LUCKNOW BRANCH ADJUSTMENT ACCOUNT** Cr.

Particulars	₹	Particulars	₹
To Stock Reserve A/c		By Stock Reserve A/c	
(₹ 6,300 × 50/150)	2,100	(₹ 15,600 × 50/150)	5,200
To Gross Profit t/f to Branch		By Goods sent to Branch A/c	
Profit and Loss A/c	21,400	(₹ 54,000 × 50/150)	18,000
		By Branch Stock A/c (Surplus)	300
	23,500		23,500

Dr. **(C) LUCKNOW BRANCH PROFIT AND LOSS ACCOUNT** Cr.

Particulars	₹	Particulars	₹
To Branch Expenses	6,700	By Branch Adjustment A/c	
To Discount Allowed	350	(Gross Profit)	21,400
To Net Profit t/f to General P&L A/c	14,350		
	21,400		21,400

Dr. **(D) LUCKNOW BRANCH DEBTORS ACCOUNT** Cr.

Particulars	₹	Particulars	₹
To Balance b/d	8,700	By Branch Cash A/c	29,800
To Branch Stock A/c (Credit Sales)	30,100	By Branch Stock A/c	1,500
(Balancing figure)		By Discount Allowed	350
		By Balance c/d	7,150
	38,800		38,800

ILLUSTRATION 25 [TREATMENT OF SURPLUS]

Hindustan Industries, Bombay has a branch in Cochin to which office goods are invoiced at cost *plus* 25%. The branch sells both for cash and on credit. Branch Expenses are paid direct from head office and the Branch has to remit all cash received into the Head Office Bank Account at Cochin. From the following details, prepare the accounts in the Head Office Ledger and ascertain the Branch Profit. Branch does not maintain any books of account, but sends weekly returns to the Head Office:

Particulars	₹	Particulars	₹
Goods received from Head Office	6,00,000	Cash received from Debtors	3,20,000
Returns to Head Office	12,000	Closing Stock at Branch	1,20,000
Opening Stock at Cochin	60,000	Discount allowed to Debtors	6,000
Cash Sales	2,00,000	Bad Debts	4,000
Closing Sundry Debtors	94,000	Sales returns at Cochin Branch	8,000
Opening Sundry Debtors at Cochin	72,000	Rent Rates, Taxes at Branch	18,000
Salaries, Wages, Bonus at Branch	60,000	Office Expenses	6,000

SOLUTION

Dr. **(A) COCHIN BRANCH STOCK ACCOUNT** Cr.

Particulars	₹	Particulars	₹
To Balance b/d	60,000	By Branch Cash A/c	
To Goods Sent to Branch A/c	6,00,000	(Cash Sales)	2,00,000
To Branch Debtors A/c		By Branch Debtors A/c	
(Return by Customers)	8,000	(Credit Sales)	3,60,000
To Branch Adjustment A/c		By Goods Sent to Branch A/c	
(Surplus) (b.f.)	24,000	(Returns to H.O.)	12,000
		By Balance c/d	1,20,000
	6,92,000		6,92,000

Dr. **(B) COCHIN BRANCH ADJUSTMENT ACCOUNT** Cr.

Particulars	₹	Particulars	₹
To Stock Reserve A/c		By Stock Reserve A/c	
(₹ 1,20,000 × 25/125)	24,000	(₹ 60,000 × 25/125)	12,000
To Gross Profit t/f to Branch P&L A/c	1,29,600	By Goods Sent to Branch A/c	1,17,600
		[₹ 6,00,000 – ₹ 12,000 × 25/125]	
		By Branch Stock A/c (Surplus)	24,000
	1,53,600		1,53,600

Dr. **(C) COCHIN BRANCH PROFIT AND LOSS ACCOUNT** Cr.

Particulars	₹	Particulars	₹
To Branch Expenses	84,000	By Branch Adjustment A/c	
To Discount Allowed	6,000	(Gross Profit)	1,29,600
To Bad Debts	4,000		
To Net Profit t/f to General P&L A/c	35,600		
	1,29,600		1,29,600

Dr. **(D) COCHIN BRANCH DEBTORS ACCOUNT** Cr.

Particulars	₹	Particulars	₹
To Balance b/d	72,000	By Branch Cash A/c (Collection)	3,20,000
To Branch Stock A/c (b.f.)	3,60,000	By Branch Stock A/c	
		(Returns to Branch)	8,000
		By Discount Allowed	6,000
		By Bad Debts	4,000
		By Balance c/d	94,000
	4,32,000		4,32,000

Dr. **(E) COCHIN BRANCH EXPENSES ACCOUNT** Cr.

Particulars	₹	Particulars	₹
To Bank A/c (Rent etc.)	18,000	By Branch P & L A/c	84,000
To Bank A/c (Salaries etc.)	60,000		
To Bank A/c (Office Expenses)	6,000		
	84,000		84,000

ILLUSTRATION 26 [TREATMENT OF NORMAL LOSS AND SURPLUS]

CAN (HJ) Ltd, invoices goods to its branch at cost *plus* 33-1/3%. From the following particulars, prepare the Branch Stock Account, Branch Stock Adjustment Account and Branch Profit and Loss Account as they would appear in the books of the Head Office.

Particulars	₹	Particulars	₹
Stock in hand at commencement at Branch	1,50,000	Return of goods to Head Office	50,000
Stock in hand at close at Branch	1,20,000	Credit Sales at Branch	3,80,000
Goods sent to branch (Including goods invoiced at ₹ 20,000 to branch on 31st March but not received by branch before close of the year).	10,00,000	Invoice value of goods pilfered	10,000
		Normal loss at Branch due to wastage and deterioration of Stock at invoice value	15,000
		Cash Sales at Branch	60% of Net sales

Madras Ltd closes its books on 31st March 2016.

SOLUTION

Dr. **BRANCH STOCK ACCOUNT** Cr.

Particulars	₹	Particulars	₹
To Balance b/d	1,50,000	By Bank A/c (Cash sales)	5,70,000
To Goods Sent to Branch A/c	10,00,000	[₹ 3,80,000 × 60/40]	
To Branch Adjustment A/c (Surplus)	15,000	By Branch Debtors A/c	
		(Credit Sales)	3,80,000
		By Goods Sent to Branch A/c	

	₹		₹
		(Return to H.O.)	50,000
		By Branch Adjustment A/c	
		(₹ 10,000 × 25/100)	2,500
		By Branch P & L A/c	
		(cost of Abnormal Loss)	7,500
		By Branch Adjustment A/c	15,000
		(Invoice Price of Normal Loss)	
		By Balance c/d:	
		In hand	1,20,000
		In transit	20,000
	11,65,000		11,65,000

Dr. **BRANCH ADJUSTMENT ACCOUNT** Cr.

Particulars	₹	Particulars	₹
To Branch Stock A/c		By Stock Reserve A/c	
(Load on Abnormal Loss)	2,500	(₹ 1,50,000 × 25/100)	37,500
To Branch Stock A/c (Normal Loss)	15,000	By Goods Sent to Branch A/c	2,37,500
To Stock Reserve A/c		[₹ 10,00,000 – ₹ 50,000 × 25/100]	
(₹ 1,40,000 × 25/100)	35,000	By Branch Stock A/c (Surplus)	15,000
To Gross Profit t/f to General P&L A/c	2,37,500		
	2,90,000		2,90,000

Dr. **BRANCH PROFIT AND LOSS ACCOUNT** Cr.

Particulars	₹	Particulars	₹
To Branch Stock A/c		By Branch Adjustment A/c	
[Cost of Abnormal Loss]	7,500	[Gross Profit]	2,37,500
To Net Profit t/f to General P&L A/c	2,30,000		
	2,37,500		2,37,500

ILLUSTRATION 27

Linken Ltd with a head office in Calcutta opened a branch at Kanpur where all sales were to be made on credit basis. All goods required by the branch were supplied by the company from Calcutta and invoiced to the branch at 20% above cost. During the year ended 31.03.2016, the following transactions took place:

Particulars	₹	Particulars	₹
Goods sent to Kanpur Branch		Cash received from debtors	
(at cost to H.O.)	22,000	and remitted to Calcutta	15,190
Returns to Calcutta Office		Debtor's balances at Branch	
(at cost to H.O.)	840	written off as bad	640
Sales as shown by Kanpur			
Branch report	19,670		

Loss of Goods at branch through pilferage is estimated at 1% of goods received. The Closing Stock of goods held by Branch on 31st march amounted to ₹ 5,820 at invoiced price. Record the entries in the appropriate accounts in the Head Office Ledger showing the balances as on 31st March 2016 and the Branch Gross Profit for the year ended on that date.

SOLUTION

Dr. **(I) KANPUR BRANCH STOCK ACCOUNT** *Cr.*

Particulars	₹	*Particulars*	₹
To Goods Sent to Branch A/c [₹ 22,000 + 20%]	26,400	By Branch Debtors A/c (Credit Sales)	19,670
To Branch Adjustment A/c (Surplus) (Excess of Selling Price over Invoice Price)	362	By Goods Sent to Branch A/c (Returns to H.O.) [₹ 840 + 20%]	1,008
		By branch Adjustment A/c (Invoice Value of Normal Pilferage Loss) [1% of ₹ 26,400]	264
		By Balance c/d	5,820
	26,762		26,762

Dr. **(II) KANPUR BRANCH ADJUSTMENT ACCOUNT** *Cr.*

Particulars	₹	*Particulars*	₹
To Branch Stock A/c (Pilferage Loss)	264	By Goods Sent to Branch A/c [(₹ 26,400 – ₹ 1,008) × 20/120]	4,232
To Stock reserve A/c (₹ 5,820 × 20/120)	970	By Branch Stock A/c (Surplus)	362
To Gross profit t/f to Branch P&L A/c	3,360		
	4,594		4,594

Dr. **(III) KANPUR BRANCH PROFIT AND LOSS ACCOUNT** *Cr.*

Particulars	₹	*Particulars*	₹
To Bad Debts	640	By Branch Adjustment A/c (Gross Profit b/d)	3,360
To Profit subject to Other Expenses	2,720		
	3,360		3,360

ILLUSTRATION 28 [CALCULATION OF CASH SALES]

CAN (GD) Ltd, Calutta, started a branch in Bombay to which goods were sent at 20% above cost. The branch makes both credit and cash sales. Branch expenses are met from branch cash and balance money remitted to H.O. The branch does not maintain double entry books of account and necessary accounts relating to branch are maintained in H.O. Following further details are given for year ending on 31st March 2016:

Particulars	₹	*Particulars*	₹
Cost of goods sent to Branch	50,000	Cash remitted to H.O.	43,000
Goods received by Branch till 31st March at invoice price	54,000	Closing Cash in hand at branch	2,000
		Cash remitted by H.O to Branch	3,000

Credit sales for the year	58,000	Closing Stock in hand at Branch	
Closing Debtors	20,800	at invoice price	6,000
Bad Debts and Discount written off	200	Expenses incurred at Branch	12,000

Required: Show the necessary ledger account according to Stock and Debtors system in the books of the Head office.

SOLUTION

Dr. **(I) BOMBAY BRANCH DEBTORS ACCOUNT** *Cr.*

Particulars	₹	*Particulars*	₹
To branch Stock A/c	58,000	By Branch Cash A/c (Collection) (b.f.)	37,000
		By Bad Debts and Discount	200
		By Balance c/d	20,800
	58,000		58,000

Dr. **(II) BOMBAY BRANCH CASH ACCOUNT** *Cr.*

Particulars	₹	*Particulars*	₹
To Bank A/c (Remittance from H.O.)	3,000	By Branch Expenses A/c	12,000
To Branch Debtors A/c	37,000	By Bank A/c (Remittances to H.O.)	43,000
To Branch stock A/c (Cash sales)		By Balance c/d	2,000
(Balancing Fig.)	17,000		
	57,000		57,000

Dr. **(III) BOMBAY BRANCH STOCK ACCOUNT** *Cr.*

Particulars	₹	*Particulars*	₹
To Goods sent to Branch A/c	60,000	By Branch Cash A/c (Cash Sales)	17,000
To Branch Adjustment A/c	27,000	By Branch Debtors A/c (Credit sales)	58,000
(Excess of Selling Price		By Balance c/d: In hand	6,000
over Invoice Price)		Stock-in-transit	6,000
	87,000		87,000

Dr. **(IV) GOODS SENT TO BOMBAY BRANCH ACCOUNT** *Cr.*

Particulars	₹	*Particulars*	₹
To Branch Adjustment A/c		By Branch Stock A/c	60,000
(₹ 60,000 × 20/120)	10,000		
To Purchases/Trading A/c	50,000		
	60,000		60,000

Dr. **(V) BOMBAY BRANCH ADJUSTMENT ACCOUNT** *Cr.*

Particulars	₹	*Particulars*	₹
To Stock Reserve A/c		By Goods Sent to Branch A/c	
(₹ 12,000 × 20/120)	2,000	(₹ 60,000 × 20/120)	10,000

To Branch P & L A/c (Gross Profit)	35,000	By Branch Stock A/c (Surplus)	27,000
	37,000		37,000

Dr. **(VI) BOMBAY BRANCH PROFIT AND LOSS ACCOUNT** Cr.

Particulars	₹	*Particulars*	₹
To Bad Debts & Discounts	200	By Branch Adjustment A/c	
To Branch Expenses	12,000	(Gross Profit)	35,000
To Branch P & L A/c	22,800		
	35,000		35,000

ILLUSTRATION 29 [TREATMENT OF ABNORMAL LOSS, GOODS-IN-TRANSIT, GOODS SENT TO ANOTHER BRANCH]

Tulsian & Co. has two retail sales branches, X and Y, selling goods supplied to them by the company's central warehouse. All such supply of goods are charged at fixed selling price of cost *plus* 50 per cent. Sales are mainly for cash but the Branch Managers authorised to give limited credit in appropriate cases. Statement of accounts are sent by the Head Office to credit customers at monthly intervals with the request there they remit direct to Head Office where entire accounting is centralised. On 31st March, 2016, summarised branch statements show the following particulars in respect of the transactions of the branch X:

Particulars	₹	*Particulars*	₹
Opening Stock at cost to Branch	2,67,000	Cash Sales	32,000
Opening Debtors	14,000	Goods returned by branch	
Cash remitted to H.O		to Head Office	11,700
by Branch credit customers	28,000	Goods returned by credit	
Goods returned by customers		customers to H.O.	1,200
to branch	5,700	Cost of Goods sent to branch	
Goods transferred by X branch		by H.O.	5,22,000
to Y branch	45,000	Cash remitted by customers	
Bad Debts written off	1,500	to Branch	6,11,000
		Goods received by Branch till date	
		at invoice price	7,80,000

The amount due by Branch credit customers as on 31st March, 2016 was ₹ 96,000 and apart from goods (of the sales value of ₹ 6,600) lost in transit from Head Office to branch, the actual stock in that date was in agreement with the book figures. A claim was made against the carrier in respect of lost stock and the sum of ₹ 6,400 was accepted in full settlement. The Branch manager is entitled to a commission of 5% of profit of the branch after charging such commission.

Required: Record the whole of the foregoing in ledger accounts in the Head Office books.

SOLUTION

Dr. **(A) X BRANCH STOCK ACCOUNT** Cr.

Particulars	₹	*Particulars*	₹
To Balance b/d	2,67,000	By Branch Cash A/c (Cash Sales)	32,000

	₹		₹
To Goods Sent to Branch A/c	7,83,000	By Branch Debtors A/c	
To Branch Debtors A/c		(Credit Sales)	7,29,400
(Return by Customers		By Goods sent to Branch A/c	
to Branch)	5,700	(Returns to H.O.)	11,700
		By Goods sent to Branch A/c	
		(Transfer to Y Branch)	45,000
		By Branch Adjustment A/c	
		(₹ 6,600 × 50/150)	
		(load on Abnormal loss)	2,200
		By Branch Profit & Loss A/c	4,400
		(Cost of Abnormal Loss)	
		By Balance c/d	
		In hand (b.f.) 2,28,000	
		In transit 3,000	2,31,000
		[₹ 7,83,000 – ₹ 7,80,000]	
	10,55,700		10,55,700

Dr. **(B) X BRANCH ADJUSTMENT ACCOUNT** Cr.

Particulars	₹	*Particulars*	₹
To Branch Stock a/c		By Stock Reserve A/c	
(Load on Abnormal Loss)	2,200	(₹ 2,67,000 × 50/150)	89,000
To Stock Reserve A/c		By Goods Sent to Branch A/c	2,41,700
(₹ 2,31,000 × 50/150)	77,000	(Load on Net Goods sent)	
To Gross Profit t/f to Branch		[(7,83,000 – 11,700 – 1,200	
P & L A/c	2,51,500	– 45,000) × 50/150)]	
	3,30,700		3,30,700

Dr. **(C) X BRANCH PROFIT AND LOSS ACCOUNT** Cr.

Particulars	₹	*Particulars*	₹
To Bad Debts	1,500	By Gross Profit b/d	2,51,500
To Loss-in-transit	4,400	By Branch Cash A/c (Claim)	6,400
To Branch Manager's Commission			
[₹ 2,52,000 × 5/105]	12,000		
To Net Profit c/d	2,40,000		
	2,57,900		2,57,900

Dr. **(D) X BRANCH DEBTORS ACCOUNT** Cr.

Particulars	₹	*Particulars*	₹
To Balance b/d	14,000	By Branch Cash A/c	6,11,000
To Credit Sales (b.f.)	7,29,400	By H.O. A/c (Remitted to H.O.)	28,000
		By Branch Stock A/c	5,700

		By Goods Sent to Branch A/c	
		(Returned to H.O.)	1,200
		By Bad Debts	1,500
		By Balance c/d	96,000
	7,43,400		7,43,400

Dr. **(E) GOODS SENT TO X BRANCH ACCOUNT** Cr.

Particulars	₹	Particulars	₹
To Branch Stock A/c	11,700	By Branch Stock A/c	7,83,000
To Branch Stock A/c	45,000		
To Branch Debtors A/c	1,200		
To Branch Adjustment A/c	2,41,700		
To Trading A/c/Purchases A/c	4,83,400		
	7,83,000		7,83,000

ILLUSTRATION 30

Tulsian Ltd has two branches, at Delhi and at Mumbai. Goods are invoiced to Branches at cost *plus* 50%. Goods are transferred by/to another branch at its cost. Following information is available of the transactions of Delhi Branch for the year ended on 31st March.

	Particulars	₹
1.	Opening Stock at its cost	2,67,000
2.	Goods sent to Branch (including goods invoiced at ₹ 15,000 to Branch on 31st March but not received by Branch before close of the financial year)	7,83,000
3.	Goods received from Mumbai Branch	6,000
4.	Goods transferred to Mumbai Branch	51,000
5.	Goods returned by Branch to H.O.	11,700
6.	Goods returned by Credit Customers to Branch	5,700
7.	Goods returned by credit Customers directly to H.O.	1,200
8.	Agreed allowance to Customers off the selling price (already taken into account while invoicing)	1,000
9.	Normal loss due to wastage and deterioration of stock (at cost)	1,000

10. Loss-in-transit (at invoice price) ₹ 6,600 against which a sum of ₹ 4,067 was recovered from the insurance company in full settlement of the claim.
11. Cash sales ₹ 32,000 and Credit Sales 7,29,400
12. Branch Expenses (including Insurance charges) 50,000
13. Bad Debts ₹ 1,000 and Discount allowed to Customers 500

The Branch Manager is entitled to a commission of 5% of profit of Branch after charging such commission.

Required: Prepare Branch Stock Account, Branch Adjustment Account and Branch Profit and Loss Account in each of the following alternative cases:

Case I If the Closing Stock at Branch at its cost as per physical verification amounted to ₹ 2,00,000.

Case II If the Closing Stock at Branch at its cost as per physical verification amounted to ₹ 2,27,000.

SOLUTION

Case I

Dr. **DELHI BRANCH STOCK ACCOUNT** *Cr.*

Particulars	₹	Particulars	₹
To Balance b/d	2,67,000	By Goods Sent to Branch A/c (Returns to H.O.)	11,700
To Goods Sent to Branch A/c	7,83,000	By Goods sent to Branch A/c (Transfer to Mumbai Branch)	51,000
To Branch Debtors A/c (Returns to Branch)	5,700	By Branch Cash A/c (Cash Sales)	32,000
To Goods Sent to Branch A/c (Transfer from Mumbai Branch)	6,000	By Branch Debtors A/c (Credit Sales)	7,29,400
		By Branch Adjustment A/c (Load on Loss-in-transit)	2,200
		By Branch Profit and Loss A/c (Cost of Loss-in-transit)	4,400
		By Branch Adjustment A/c (Normal Loss)	1,500
		By Branch Adjustment A/c (Agreed Allowance Allowed)	1,000
		By Branch Adjustment A/c (Load on Shortage) (b.f.)	4,500
		By Branch Profit and Loss A/c (cost of shortage) (b.f.)	9,000
		By Balance c/d:	
		In hand	2,00,000
		In transit	15,000
	10,61,700		10,61,700

Dr. **DELHI BRANCH ADJUSTMENT ACCOUNT** *Cr.*

Particulars	₹	Particulars	₹
To Branch Stock A/c [Load on loss-in-transit]	2,200	By Stock Reserve A/c (Load on Op. Stock)	89,000
To Branch Stock A/c [Normal loss]	1,500	By Goods Sent to Branch A/c (Load on Net Goods Sent) [(₹ 7,83,000 + 6,000 – 11,700 – ₹ 51,000 – 1,200) ´ 50/150]	2,41,700
To Branch Stock A/c [Agreed Allowance]	1,000		
To Branch Stock A/c [Load on Shortage]	4,500		
To Stock Reserve A/c (Load on Cl. Stock)	71,667		

To Gross Profit t/f to			
Branch P & L A/c	2,49,833		
	3,30,700		3,30,700

Dr. **DELHI BRANCH PROFIT AND LOSS ACCOUNT** Cr.

Particulars	₹	*Particulars*	₹
To Branch Expenses A/c	50,000	By Branch Adjustment A/c	2,49,833
To Branch Stock A/c		(Gross Profit)	
[Cost of loss-in-transit]	4,400	By Bank A/c (Claim)	4,067
To Branch Stock A/c			
[Cost of shortage]	9,000		
To bad debts	1,000		
To Discount allowed	500		
To Branch Manager's Commission			
[₹ 1,89,000 × 5/105]	9,000		
To Net Profit t/f to General P&L A/c	1,80,000		
	2,53,900		2,53,900

Note: *Unless otherwise specifically stated, shortage arising in Branch stock is presumed to have occurred due to abnormal factors like theft and thus, the load portion thereof is debited to Branch Adjustment Account and the cost portion thereof is debited to Branch Profit and Loss Account.*

Case II

Dr. **DELHI BRANCH STOCK ACCOUNT** Cr.

Particulars	₹	*Particulars*	₹
To Balance b/d	2,67,000	By Goods Sent to Branch	11,700
To Goods Sent to Branch A/c	7,83,000	(Return to H.O.)	
To Branch Debtors A/c	5,700	By Goods sent to Branch A/c	51,000
(Returns to Branch)		(Transfer to Bombay Branch)	
To Goods sent to Branch A/c	6,000	By Branch Cash A/c (Cash sales)	32,000
(Transfer from Bombay Branch)		By Branch Debtors A/c	7,29,400
To Branch Adjustment A/c	13,500	(Credit Sales)	
[Surplus being Excess of		By Branch Adjustment A/c	2,200
selling price over		(Load on Loss-in-transit)	
Invoice Price]		By Branch Profit and Loss A/c	4,400
[Balancing figure]		(cost of Loss-in-transit)	
		By Branch Adjustment A/c	
		(Normal Loss)	1,500
		By Branch Adjustment A/c	1,000
		(Agreed Allowance Allowed)	
		By Balance c/d:	
		In hand	2,27,000

		In transit	15,000
	10,75,200		10,75,200

DELHI BRANCH ADJUSTMENT ACCOUNT

Dr. *Cr.*

Particulars	₹	*Particulars*	₹
To Branch stock A/c (Load on loss-in-transit)	2,200	By Stock Reserve A/c (Load on Op. Stock)	89,000
To Branch Stock A/c (Normal Loss)	1,500	By Goods Sent to Branch A/c (Load on net Goods Sent) [(₹ 7,83,000 + 6,000 – 11,700 – ₹ 51,000 –1,200) × 50/150]	2,41,700
To Branch Stock A/c (Agreed Allowance)	1,000	By Branch Stock A/c (Surplus)	13,500
To Stock Reserve A/c (Load on Cl. Stock)	80,667		
To Gross Profit t/f to Branch P&L A/c	2,58,833		
	3,44,200		3,44,200

DELHI BRANCH PROFIT AND LOSS ACCOUNT

Dr. *Cr.*

Particulars	₹	*Particulars*	₹
To Branch Expenses A/c	50,000	By Branch Adjustment A/c (Gross Profit)	2,58,833
To Branch Stock A/c (Cost of loss-in-transit)	4,400	By Bank A/c (Claim)	4,067
To Bad Debts	1,000		
To Discount Allowed	500		
To Branch Manager's Commission [₹ 2,07,000 × 5/105]	9,857		
To Net Profit t/f to General P&L A/c	1,97,143		
	2,62,900		2,62,900

Note: *Unless otherwise specifically stated, surplus arising in Branch Stock is presumed to have occurred due to excess of selling price over invoice price and thus, the entire amount of surplus is credited to Branch Adjustment Account.*

ILLUSTRATION 31 [WHEN LOCAL PURCHASES ARE MADE BY BRANCH]

Hritik established a retail business in Delhi several years ago and has since opened branch shops at Mumbai, Kolkata and Chennai. All the purchasing and administration is done at the Head Office. Branches are also allowed to purchase locally in special circumstances. Branches sell both for cash and on credit terms, but all invoices for credit sales are invoiced from Delhi and payments from credit customers received there. The branches are expected to achieve a profit of 50% on cost price. The following information relates to the Mumbai Branch for the first six months ending 30th Sept. 2016.

Particulars	₹
Opening stock of goods at branch (cost price)	56,000
Opening debtors	18,000
Goods received by branch at selling price	3,60,000

Credit sales	1,20,000
Cash sales	2,04,000
Transfer from other branches to Mumbai branch at selling price	24,000
Transfer to other branches from Mumbai at selling price	42,000
Goods returned to H.O. at selling price	12,000
Cash from debtors received at H.O.	1,06,000
Bad debts written off	4,000
Goods returned by credit customers to branch	4,800
Goods returned by credit customers to H.O.	2,400
Goods purchased by Mumbai branch from local suppliers (cost)	30,000
Expenses at the branch	15,000
Closing stock in hand at branch	
From H.O. at selling price	90,000
Out of local purchases	6,000

Additional information:

(i) Goods amounting to ₹ 12,000 at cost to H.O. were in transit

(ii) Branch had on 1st April, 2016 furniture and other equipment at a book value of ₹ 15,000 Depreciation at 10% p.a. is to be provided on this item.

(iii) Goods purchased locally were sold at 25% profit on sale price.

Required: Prepare Branch Stock Account, Branch Debtors Account and Mumbai Branch Account.

SOLUTION

Dr. **(A) MUMBAI BRANCH STOCK ACCOUNT** *Cr.*

Particulars	₹	*Particulars*	₹
To Balance b/d		By Branch Cash A/c (Cash Sales)	2,04,000
(56,000 + 28,000)	84,000	By Branch Debtors A/c	1,20,000
To Goods Sent to Branch A/c		By Goods sent to Branch A/c	42,000
(3,60,000 + 18,000)	3,78,000	By Goods sent to Branch A/c	2,400
To Goods sent to Branch A/c	24,000	By Goods sent to Branch A/c	12,000
To Branch Debtors A/c	2,400	By Shortage (Balancing figure)	36,800
To Branch Cash A/c		By Balance c/d: From H.O.	90,000
(Local Purchases)	30,000	Local Purchases (6,000 + 2,000)	8,000
To Branch Adjustment A/c		In transit	18,000
(30,000 × 1/3)	10,000		
To Branch Debtors A/c	4,800		
	5,33,200		5,33,200

Dr. **(B) MUMBAI BRANCH DEBTORS ACCOUNT** *Cr.*

Particulars	₹	*Particulars*	₹
To Balance b/d	18,000	By Branch Stock A/c	4,800

To Branch Stock A/c	1,20,000	By Branch Stock A/c	2,400
		By Branch Cash A/c	1,06,000
		By Branch Profit and Loss A/c	4,000
		By Balance c/d	20,800
	1,38,000		1,38,000

Dr. **(C) MUMBAI BRANCH ACCOUNT** *Cr.*

Particulars	₹	*Particulars*		₹
To Balance b/d:		By Stock Reserve A/c		28,000
Stock	84,000	By Goods sent to Branch A/c		1,15,200
Debtors	18,000	By Bank (Remittances):		
Furniture and Equipment	15,000	Cash Sales	2,04,000	
To Goods sent to Branch A/c	3,78,000	From Debtors	1,06,000	3,10,000
To Goods sent to Branch A/c	24,000	By Goods sent to Branch A/c		42,000
To Branch Cash A/c		By Goods sent to Branch A/c		12,000
(Local Purchases)	30,000	By Goods sent to Branch A/c		2,400
To Branch Cash A/c (Expenses)	15,000	By Balance c/d:		
To Stock Reserve A/c	36,000	Stock from H.O.		90,000
(30,000 + 6,000)		Stock-Local Purchases		6,000
To Profit and Loss A/c	58,650	Stock-in-transit		18,000
		Debtors		20,800
		By Furniture and Equipment		14,250
	6,58,650			6,58,650

ILLUSTRATION 32

XY Limited with its head office in Calcutta invoiced goods to its branch at Mumbai at 20% *less* than the catalogue price which is cost *plus* 50% with instructions that cash sales were to be made at invoice price and credit sales at catalogue price *less* discount at 15% on prompt payments.

From the particulars available from the branch, prepare at the Branch Stock Account, Branch Adjustment Account and Branch Profit and Loss Account for the year ended 31 March 2016.

Particulars	₹
Opening Stock (Invoice Price)	12,000
Opening Debtors	10,000
Goods received from H.O. (Invoice Price)	1,32,000
Cash Sales	46,000
Credit Sales	1,00,000
Cash received from Debtors	85,635
Discount allowed to Debtors	13,365
Expenses at the Branch	6,000
Closing Stock on (invoice Price)	15,000

It was further reported that a part of the stock was lost by fire (not covered by insurance) during the year whose value is to be ascertained and a provision should be made for discount to be allowed to debtors as on 31 March 2016 on the basis of year's trend of prompt payments.

SOLUTION

COST-PRICE STRUCTURE

Particulars	₹
A. Cost Price	100
B. *Add:* Profit	20
C. Invoice Price (A + B)	120
D. *Add:* Extra Profit	30
E. Catalogue Price (C + D)	150

Dr. **MUMBAI BRANCH STOCK ACCOUNT** Cr.

Particulars	₹	*Particulars*	₹
To Balance b/d	12,000	By Branch Cash A/c (Cash Sales)	46,000
To Goods sent to Branch A/c	1,32,000	By Branch Debtors A/c	
To Branch Adjustment A/c		(Credit Sales)	1,00,000
[₹ 1,00,000 × 30/150]	20,000	By Branch Adjustment A/c (Load)	500
		By Branch Profit and Loss A/c	
		(Stock destroyed by fire) (b.f.)	2,500
		By Balance c/d	15,000
	1,64,000		1,64,000

Dr. **MUMBAI BRANCH ADJUSTMENT ACCOUNT** Cr.

Particulars	₹	*Particulars*	₹
To Stock Reserve A/c		By Stock Reserve A/c	
[₹ 15,000 × 20/120]	2,500	[₹ 12,000 × 20/120]	2,000
To Branch Stock A/c		By Goods sent to Branch A/c	22,000
(load on stock destroyed by fire)	500	By Branch Stock A/c	
To Branch Profit and Loss A/c		(Excess of catalogue price	
(Gross profit)	41,000	over invoice price)	20,000
	44,000		44,000

Dr. **MUMBAI BRANCH PROFIT AND LOSS ACCOUNT** Cr.

Particulars	₹	*Particulars*	₹
To Branch Expenses A/c		By Branch Adjustment A/c	
(6,000 + 13,365)	19,365	(Gross Profit)	41,000
To Branch Stock A/c			
(Cost of Loss by fire)	2,500		

To Provision for Discount A/c	1,485		
To General Profit and Loss A/c	17,650		
	41,000		44,000

Dr. **MUMBAI BRANCH DEBTORS ACCOUNT** Cr.

Particulars	₹	*Particulars*	₹
To Balance b/d	10,000	By Cash/Bank A/c	85,635
To Branch Stock A/c (Credit Sales)	1,00,000	By Discount Allowed A/c	13,365
		By Balance c/d (b.f.)	11,000
	1,10,000		1,10,000

Working Note: *Computation of Provision for discount*

(a) Prompt paying debtors who availed of discount = ₹ 13,365 × 100/15 = 89,100

(b) Total debtors who made payment during the year = ₹ 13,365 + 85,635 = ₹ 99,000

(c) Proportion of prompt payers to those who made payment = $\frac{89,100}{99,000} \times 100 = 90\%$

(d) Likely Prompt paying debtors included in closing Debtors = 90% of ₹ 11,000 = ₹ 9,900

(e) Provision for discount on the closing balance = 15% of ₹ 9,900 = ₹ 1,485

6.0 FINAL ACCOUNTS METHOD

MEANING FINAL ACCOUNTS METHOD

Under this method, the profit *or* loss of the branch is ascertained by preparing the Memorandum Branch Trading and Profit and Loss Account in place of Branch Account. Under this method, if Branch Account is prepared, that is of personal nature and not of nominal nature (as in case of debtors method).

HOW TO PREPARE FINAL ACCOUNTS

The Branch Trading and Profit and Loss Account is prepared exactly on the same basis as in case of other normal concerns. It is to be noted that Opening Stock. Goods Sent to Branch, Goods Returned by branch and Closing Stock are to be shown at Cost (i.e., excluding loading, if any, charged)

FORMAT

The format of Branch Trading and Profit and Loss Account is given below:

Dr. **BRANCH TRADING AND PROFIT AND LOSS ACCOUNT FOR THE YEAR ENDING ON...** *Cr.*

Particulars		₹	*Particulars*		₹
To Opening Stock (at Cost)		xxx	By Sales		
To Goods sent	xxx		Cash	xxx	
Less: Returns to H.O.	xxx		Credit	xxx	
To Direct Purchases		xxx	*Less:* Returns form		
To Direct Expenses		xxx	Branch Debtors	xxx	xxx
To Gross Profit c/d		xxx	By Abnormal Loss due to fire etc.		xxx
			By Closing Stock:		
			Direct Purchases	xxx	

		Supplied by H.O. xxx	
		In transit xxx	xxx
	xxx		xxx
To Branch Expenses	xxx	By Gross Profit b/d	xxx
To Abnormal Loss due to Fire etc.	xxx	By Bank A/c/Insurance Co.	
To Net Profit t/f to general P&L A/c	xxx	Insurance Claim)	xxx
	xxx		xxx

ILLUSTRATION 33

M/s Bright and Company with its H.O. in Madras invoiced goods to its branch at Bombay at 20% *less* than the catalogue price which is cost *plus* 50% with instructions that cash sales were to be made at invoice price and credit sales at catalogue price. Discount on credit sales at 15% on prompt payment will be allowed. From the following particulars available from the branch, prepare branch Trading and Profit and Loss Account for the year ended 31st March 2016, in the H.O. books.

Opening Stock (invoice price) ₹ 12,000; Goods received from H.O. (invoice price) ₹ 1,32,000; Opening Debtors ₹ 10,000; Sales—Cash ₹ 46,000; Sales—Credit ₹ 1,00,000; Cash realised from debtors ₹ 85,635; Discount allowed to debtors ₹ 13,365; Expenses at the branch ₹ 6,000; Remittances to H.O. ₹ 1,20,000; Closing Debtors ₹ 11,000; Closing Cash in hand ₹ 5,635; Closing Stock (Invoice price) ₹ 15,000.

It was reported that a part of the stock at the branch was lost by fire during the year whose value is to be ascertained; and a provision should be made for discount to be allowed to debtors as at 31st March 2016 on the basis of the year's trend of prompt payment.

SOLUTION

BOMBAY BRANCH TRADING AND PROFIT AND LOSS ACCOUNT

Dr. *for the year ended 31st March, 2016* Cr.

Particulars	₹	Particulars	₹
To Opening Stock [12,000 × 100/120]	10,000	By Sales—Cash	46,000
To Goods from H.O	1,10,000	—Credit	1,00,000
[1,32,000 × 100/120]		By Abnormal loss: [3,000 × 100/120]	2,500
To Gross Profit c/d	41,000	By Closing Stock	12,500
	1,61,000		1,61,000
To Branch expenses	6,000	By Gross Profit b/d	41,000
To Discount	13,365		
To Abnormal Loss	2,500		
To Provision for discount	1,337		
To Net Profit transferred to			
General Profit & Loss A/c	17,798		
	41,000		41,000

Working Notes:

(I) *Computation of invoice price*

Let Cost price be = ₹ 100

Thus, Catalogue price will be = ₹(100 + 50% of 100) = ₹ 150

Thus Invoice price being 20% *less* than Catalogue Price (150 × 80/100) = ₹ 120

Dr. **(II) BOMBAY BRANCH STOCK ACCOUNT (AT INVOICE PRICE)** *Cr.*

Particulars	₹	*Particulars*	₹
To Balance b/d	12,000	By Branch Cash A/c (Cash sales)	46,000
To Goods sent to Branch A/c	1,32,000	By Branch Debtors A/c (Cr. Sales)	
		[₹ 1,00,000 × 120/150]	80,000
		By Abnormal Loss (b.f)	3,000
		By Balance b/d	15,000
	1,44,000		1,44,000

(III) Computation of provision for discount:

(a) Prompt paying debtors who availed of discount = ₹ 13,365 × 100/15 = 89,100

(b) Total debtors during the year = O. Balance + Credit Sales = 10,000 + 1,00,000 = 1,10,000

(c) Proportion of prompt payers to total debtors = $\frac{89,100}{1,10,000}$ × 100 = 81%

(d) Likely Prompt paying debtors included in closing Debtors = 81% of ₹ 11,000 = ₹ 8,910

(e) Provision for discount on the closing balance = 15% of ₹ 8,910 = ₹ 1,337 App.

ILLUSTRATION 34

CANHI Ltd Bombay has two branches at Kanpur and lucknow. All goods sold at the branches are received from the Head Office invoiced at cost *plus* 25 percent. All expenses relating to Branches are paid by the Head Office. Each branch has its own Sales Ledger and sends weekly statement. All cash collections are remitted daily to Head Office by the branches. The following particulars relating to the year ended 31st March, 2016 have been extracted from the weekly statement sent by the branches:—

Particulars	*Kanpur* ₹	*Lucknow* ₹
Credit Sales	1,25,200	1,10,000
Cash Sales	78,600	85,200
Sales Returns	2,300	1,200
Sundry Debtors	34,500	23,600
Rent and Rates	3,200	4,500
Bad Debts	6,000	—
Salaries	16,000	18,000
General Expenses	2,600	1,500
Goods received from H.O.	1,50,000	1,25,000
Advertisement	7,500	5,200
Closing Stock	45,000	35,000

You are required to prepare the Branch Account as they would appear in the books of the Head Office, showing the Profit *or* Loss for the period and the Trading and Profit and Loss Account separately for each Branch.

SOLUTION

BRANCH TRADING AND PROFIT AND LOSS ACCOUNT

Dr. *for the year ending on 31st March, 2016* *Cr.*

Particulars	*Kanpur Branch* ₹	*Lucknow Branch* ₹	*Particulars*	*Kanpur Branch* ₹	*Lucknow Branch* ₹
To Goods received			By Sales Credit	1,25,200	1,10,000
from H.O.	1,20,000	1,00,000	*Less:* Sales Returns	(2,300)	(1,200)
To Gross Profit c/d	1,17,500	1,22,000	*Add:* Cash Sales	78,600	85,200
			By Closing Stock	36,000	28,000
	2,37,500	2,22,000		2,37,500	2,22,000
To Salaries	16,000	18,000	By Gross profit b/d	1,17,500	1,22,000
To General Expenses	2,600	1,500			
To Bad Debts	6,000	—			
To Rent and Rates	3,200	4,500			
To Advertisement	7,500	5,200			
To Net Profit	82,200	92,800			
	1,17,500	1,22,000		1,17,500	1,22,000

BRANCH ACCOUNT

Dr. *Cr.*

Particulars	*Kanpur Branch* ₹	*Lucknow Branch* ₹	*Particulars*	*Kanpur Branch* ₹	*Lucknow Branch* ₹
To Goods sent to			By Cash A/c		
Branch A/c	1,50,000	1,25,000	(Remittance to H.O.)		
To Cash Account			Cash Sales	78,600	85,200
(Expenses):			Received from Debtors	82,400	85,200
Rent and Rates	3,200	4,500	By Goods sent to		
Salaries	16,000	18,000	Branch A/c	30,000	25,000
General Expenses	2,600	1,500	(Load on Goods sent)		
Advertisement	7,500	5,200	By Branch Debtors	34,500	23,600
To Stock Reserve A/c			By Branch Stock	45,000	35,000
(Loading)	9,000	7,000			
To P & L A/c	82,200	92,800			
	2,70,500	2,54,000		2,70,500	2,54,000

Working Note:

MEMORANDUM BRANCH DEBTORS ACCOUNT

Dr. *Cr.*

Particulars	*Kanpur Branch* ₹	*Lucknow Branch* ₹	*Particulars*	*Kanpur Branch* ₹	*Lucknow Branch* ₹
To Sales	1,25,200	1,10,000	By Sales Returns	2,300	1,200

			By Bad Debts	6,000	—
			By Cash A/c (b.f.)	82,400	85,200
			By Balance c/d	34,500	23,600
	1,25,200	1,10,000		1,25,200	1,10,000

ILLUSTRATION 35

A Ltd. has its head office at New Delhi and two branches at Calicut and Mangalore. The branches purchase goods independently. The Calicut branch makes a profit of 33-1/3% on cost while the Mangalore branch makes a profit of 20% on sales. Goods are also supplied by one branch to another at the respective sales price. From the following particulars, prepare the Trading and Profit and Loss Account of each of the branches and find out the profit *or* loss made by each of them after taking into account the reserve for unrealised profits:

Particulars	*Calicut Branch* ₹	*Mangalore Branch* ₹
Opening Stock	80,000	60,000
Purchases (including Inter Branch Transfers)	4,00,000	5,00,000
Sales	5,60,000	5,91,250
Chargeable Expenses	30,000	55,000
Closing Stock	60,000	87,000
Office and Adm. Expenses	26,500	14,000
Selling and Distribution Expenses	30,000	20,000

Information:

(i) Opening stock at Calicut Branch includes goods of ₹ 20,000 taken from Mangalore Branch, (ii) Opening stock at Mangalore Branch includes goods of ₹ 34,000 taken from Calicut Branch at cost to receiving branch, (iii) The Calicut Branch sales include transfer of goods to Mangalore Branch at selling price ₹ 40,000 (iv) The sales at Mangalore Branch include transfer of goods to Calicut Branch at selling price ₹ 30,000. (v) Closing stock at Calicut Branch includes goods received from Mangalore Branch ₹ 10,000. (vi) Closing stock at Mangalore Branch includes goods of ₹ 8,000 received from Calicut Branch.

SOLUTION

CALICUT BRANCH TRADING AND PROFIT AND LOSS ACCOUNT

for the year ending on...

Dr. | *Cr.*

Particulars	₹	*Particulars*	₹
To Opening Stock (including ₹20,000 from M. Branch)	80,000	By Sales (including ₹ 40,000 to M. Branch)	5,60,000
To Purchases	4,00,000	By Closing Stock (including ₹10,000 from M. Branch)	60,000
To Chargeable Expenses	30,000		
To Gross Profit c/d (before making adjustment for unrealised profit)	1,10,000		
	6,20,000		6,20,000

To Stock Reserve (for unrealised profit in Closing Stock lying at Mangalore Branch) (₹ 8,000 × 25/100)	2,000	By Gross Profit b/d	1,10,000
To Office & Adm. Expenses	26,500	By Stock Reserve (for unrealised profit in Opening Stock lying at Mangalore Branch) (₹ 34,000 × 25/100)	8,500
To Selling & Distribution Expenses	30,000		
To Net Profit	60,000		
	1,18,500		1,18,500

MANGALORE BRANCH TRADING AND PROFIT AND LOSS ACCOUNT

Dr. *for the year ending on....* Cr.

Particulars	₹	*Particulars*	₹
To Opening Stock (including ₹ 34,000 from C. Branch)	60,000	By Sales (including ₹ 30,000 to C. Branch)	5,91,250
To purchases	5,00,000	By Closing Stock (including ₹ 8,000 from C. Branch)	87,000
To Chargeable Expenses	55,000		
To Gross Profit c/d (before making adjustment for unrealised profit)	63,250		
	6,78,250		6,78,250
		By Gross Profit b/d	63,250
To Stock Reserve (for unrealised Profit on Closing Stock lying at Calicut Branch) (₹ 10,000 × 20/100)	2,000	By Stock Reserve (for unrealised profit on Opening Stock at Calicut Branch) (₹ 20,000 × 20/100)	4,000
To Office & Adm. Expenses	14,000		
To Selling & Distribution Expenses	20,000		
To Net Profit	31,250		
	67,250		67,250

7.0 WHOLE SALE BRANCH METHOD

MEANING OF WHOLE SALE BRANCH METHOD

Under this method, the head office supplies goods to owned retail branches as well as to other retailers at wholesale price which is cost *plus* wholesale profit. The owned retail branches sell these goods to customers at list *or* catalogue price which is wholesale price *plus* retail profit.

• HOW TO ASCERTAIN PROFIT

In such a case the head office is interested in knowing the additional profit which has been earned by opening retail branch. For this purpose, Trading and Profit Loss Account of the branch should be prepared in the usual manner taking the opening stock, goods sent by H.O./returned to H.O. Closing Stock, Losses of Goods at wholesale price. However, while preparing Trading and P&L Account of H.O., Stock Reserve (i.e., Loading equal to difference between wholesale price and its cost to H.O.)

in respect of opening stock and in respect of closing stock at branch should be credited and debited respectively to Head Office Profit and Loss Account. In such type of problems, first the relationship between Cost, Wholesale Profit and Retail Profit should be ascertained as follows:

A. Cost	xxx
B. Wholesale Profit	xxx
C. Wholesale Price (A + B)	xxx
D. Retail Profit	xxx
E. Retail Price (C + D)	xxx

FORMATS

The formats of Branch Stock Account/Branch Trading Account, Branch Profit and Loss Account, Branch Stock Reserve A/c, H.O. Profit and Loss Account are given below:

Dr. **(A) BRANCH STOCK ACCOUNT (AT WHOLESALE PRICE)/ BRANCH TRADING ACCOUNT** *Cr.*

Particulars		₹	*Particulars*		₹
To Balance b/d (at Wholesale Price)		xxx	By Sales (at Retail Price/list		
To Goods sent to Branch		xxx	Price/Catalogue Price)		
(at wholesale price)			Cash	xxx	
Sent	xxx		Credit	xxx	
Less: Returns to H.O.	xxx	xxx	*Less:* Returns	xxx	xxx
To Gross Profit t/f to P&L A/c		xxx	By Abnormal Loss (at wholesale Price)		xxx
			By Balance c/d (at wholesale Price)		xxx
		xxx			xxx

Dr. **(B) BRANCH PROFIT AND LOSS ACCOUNT** *Cr.*

Particulars	₹	*Particulars*	₹
To Branch Expenses	xxx	By Gross Profit b/d	xxx
To Abnormal Loss		By Claim from Insurance Co. (if any)	xxx
(at Wholesale Price	xxx		
To Net Profit t/f to H.O. P&L A/c	xxx		
	xxx		xxx

Dr. **(C) BRANCH STOCK RESERVE ACCOUNT** *Cr.*

Particulars	₹	*Particulars*	₹
To H.O. P&L A/c	xxx	By Balance b/d	xxx
(T/f of Opening Stock reserve		[Wholesale Profit included	
To Balance c/d	xxx	in Opening Stock]	
[Wholesale profit included		By H.O. P&L A/c	xxx
in Closing Stock]		[Wholesale Profit included	
		in Closing stock]	
	xxx		xxx

Dr. **(D) AN EXTRACT OF H.O. PROFIT AND LOSS ACCOUNT** Cr.

Particulars	₹	*Particulars*	₹
To Stock Reserve A/c [Provision made for unrealised wholesale profit included in Closing Stock]	xxx	By Branch Profit and Loss A/c (Net Profit)	xxx
		By Stock Reserve A/c [Transfer of Provision for unrealised profit included in opening stock, now no longer required]	xxx
	xxx		xxx

ILLUSTRATION 36

Opening Stock at Branch ₹ 36,000, Goods sent to Branch ₹ 2,64,000, Sales at Branch ₹ 2,64,000. Calculate the value of closing stock at Branch in each of the following alternative cases:

Case (a) If Head Office invoices goods to its branch at 20% *less* than the list price which is cost *plus* 100%.

Case (b) If Head Office invoice goods to its branch at cost *plus* 25%. Goods are sold to customers at cost *plus* 100%.

Case (c) If Head Office sends goods at cost *plus* 20%. Branch sells goods at the list price which is wholesale price *plus* 10%.

SOLUTION

CALCULATION OF WHOLESALE PROFIT, WHOLESALE PRICE, RETAIL PROFIT AND RETAIL PRICE

Particulars	*Case (a)*	*Case (b)*	*Case (c)*
A. Cost Price (assumed)	100	100	100
B. *Add:* Wholesale Profit	60 (b.f.)	25	20
C. Wholesale Price (A + B)	160	125	120
D. *Add:* Retail Profit	40	75 (b.f.)	12
E. List Price/Catalogue Price/Retail Price [C + D]	200	200	132(b.f.)

Closing Stock at Branch = Opening Stock + Goods sent to Branch – Wholesale Price of Sales

Case (a) ₹ 36,000 + ₹ 2,64,000 – (₹ 2,64,000 × 160/200) = ₹ 88,800.

Case (b) ₹ 36,000 + ₹ 2,64,000 – (₹ 2,64,000 × 125/200) = ₹ 1,35,000.

Case (c) ₹ 36,000 + ₹ 2,64,000 – (₹ 2,64,000 × 120/132) = ₹ 60,000.

ILLUSTRATION 37

Opening Stock at H.O. ₹ 36,000, Purchases by H.O. ₹ 4,00,000, Goods sent to Branch ₹ 2,64,000, Sales at H.O. ₹ 2,64,000. Calculate the value of Closing Stock at Head Office in each of the following alternative cases:

Case (a) If head office invoices goods to its branch at 20% *less* than the list price which cost *plus* 100%.

Case (b) If head office invoices goods to its branch at cost *plus* 25%. Goods are sold to customers at cost *plus* 100%.

Case (c) If head office sends goods at cost *plus* 20%. Goods are sold to customers at the list price which is wholesale price *plus* 10%.

SOLUTION

Closing Stock at H.O. = Opening Stock + Purchases – Cost of Goods sent to Branch – Cost of Sales

Case (a): = ₹ 36,000 + ₹ 4,00,000 – (₹ 2,64,000 × 100/160) – (₹ 2,64,000 × 100/200) = ₹ 1,39,000

Case (b): = ₹ 36,000 + ₹ 4,00,000 – (₹ 2,64,000 × 100/125) – (₹ 2,64,000 × 100/200) = ₹ 92,800

Case (c): = ₹ 36,000 + ₹ 4,00,000 – (₹ 2,64,000 × 100/120) – (₹ 2,64,000 × 100/132) = ₹ 16,000

ILLUSTRATION 38

A Ltd. operates a number of retail shops to which goods are invoiced at wholesale price which is cost *plus* 25%. Shops sell the goods at the list price which is cost *plus* 100%. From the following particulars, prepare the necessary ledger accounts: Opening Stock at shops ₹ 200, Goods sent to shops ₹ 80,000, Goods returned by shops ₹ 800. Goods sold at the shops ₹ 52,000. Goods returned by customers at the shops ₹ 2,000, Goods destroyed by accident (retail value) ₹ 640, Expenses at the shop ₹ 10,150.

SOLUTION

Dr. **(I) BRANCH STOCK ACCOUNT (AT WHOLESALE PRICE)** *Cr.*

Particulars		₹	*Particulars*		₹
To Balance b/d		200	By Sales	52,000	
To Goods sent to Branch	80,000		*Less:* Returns	2,000	50,000
Less: Returns	800	79,200	By Abnormal Loss (₹ 640 × 125/200)		400
To Gross Profit t/f to Branch P&L A/c		18,750	By Balance c/d		47,750
(₹ 50,000 × 75/200)					
		98,150			98,150

Dr. **(II) BRANCH PROFIT & LOSS ACCOUNT** *Cr.*

Particulars	₹	*Particulars*	₹
To Branch Expenses	10,150	By Gross Profit b/d	18,750
To Abnormal Loss	400		
To Net Profit t/f to H.O. P & L A/c	8,200		
	18,750		18,750

Dr. **(III) BRANCH STOCK RESERVE ACCOUNT** *Cr.*

Particulars	₹	*Particulars*	₹
To H.O. P & L A/c		By Balance b/d (₹ 200 × 25/125)	40
(t/f of opening reserve)	40	By H.O. P & L A/c	9,550
To Balance c/d [₹ 47,750 × 25/125]	9,550		
	9,590		9,590

Dr. **(IV) AN EXTRACT OF H.O. PROFIT AND LOSS ACCOUNT** Cr.

Particulars	₹	*Particulars*	₹
To Stock Reserve A/c	9,550	By Branch Profit & Loss A/c	8,200
(Provision for unrealised		By Stock Reserve A/c	
profit on Branch closing stock)		(t/f of Provision for unrealised	
		profit on Branch opening stock)	40

Working Notes:

CALCULATION OF VARIOUS PRICES AND PROFIT

Particulars	₹
A. Cost Price	100
B. *Add:* Wholesale Profit	25
C. Wholesale Price (A – B)	125
D. *Add:* Retail Profit	75
E. List Price (C + D)	200

ILLUSTRATION 39

Tulsian (India) Ltd. with its head office at Madras has a branch at Kanpur. The company supplies goods to its branch at selling price *less* 20%. The Company as well as branch sell goods to consumers at a profit of 100% on cost. The Company also sell goods to their approved stockists at the same price at which they are sending to their branch at Kanpur. From the following particulars, prepare Trading and Profit and Loss Account of the head office and of the branch for the second year of their business and show the provisions for unrealised profits on stock at the branch supplied by the head office.

Particulars	*Head Office* ₹	*Branch* ₹
Stock in the beginning	36,000	1,600
Purchases during the year	2,50,000	
Goods sent to the branch	40,000	
Goods received from the head office		40,000
Goods sold to approved stockiest	60,000	
Goods sold to customers	1,20,000	36,000
Goods destroyed by Accident	1000 (Retail Value)	1,000
Expenses	8,500	400

SOLUTION

Dr. **HEAD OFFICE TRADING AND PROFIT & LOSS ACCOUNT** Cr.

Particulars	₹	*Particulars*	₹
To Opening Stock	36,000	By Goods sent to branch	40,000
To Purchases	2,50,000	By Goods sold to stockist	60,000
To Gross Profit c/d	97,500	By Goods sold to customers	1,20,000

		By Abnormal Loss (₹1000 × 100/200)	500
		By Closing Stock	1,63,000
	3,83,500		3,83,500
To Abnormal Loss	500	By Gross Profit b/d	97,500
To Expenses	8,500	By Stock Reserve A/c	
To Stock Reserve A/c		(₹ 1,600 × 60/160)	600
(₹ 12,000 × 60/160)	4,500	By Branch P&L A/c (Profit)	6,000
To Net Profit t/f to General P&LA/c	90,600		
	1,04,100		1,04,100

Dr. **BRANCH TRADING AND PROFIT & LOSS ACCOUNT** *Cr.*

Particulars	₹	*Particulars*	₹
To Opening Stock	1,600	By Sales to consumers	36,000
To Goods from head office	40,000	By Closing Stock	12,000
To Gross Profit c/d	7,200	By Abnormal Loss [₹1000 × 160/200]	800
	48,800		48,800
To Abnormal Loss	800	By Gross Profit b/d	7,200
To Expenses	400		
To Net Profit at branch t/f to General P&L A/c	6,000		
	7,200		7,200

Working Notes:

(I) CALCULATION OF CLOSING STOCK AT HEAD OFFICE

	Particulars		₹
A	Opening Stock of goods		36,000
B	*Add:* Purchases made during the year		2,50,000
C	*Less:* Cost of goods sent to branch [₹ 40,000 × 100/160]	25,000	
	Cost of goods sold to stockist [₹ 60,000 × 100/160]	37,500	
	Cost of goods sold to consumers [₹ 1,20,000 × 100/200]	60,000	
	Cost of Abnormal Loss (₹.1000 × 100/200)	500	1,23,000
D	Closing Stock at Head Office		1,63,000

(II) CALCULATION OF CLOSING STOCK OF BRANCH

	Particulars	₹
A	Opening Stock of Goods (at wholesale price)	1,600
B	*Add:* Received from the head office (at wholesale price)	40,000
C	*Less:* Wholesale price of goods sold to consumers [₹ 36,000 × 160/200]	28,800
	Less: Wholesale Price of Abnormal Loss (₹.1000 × 160/200)	800
D	Closing Stock (at wholesale price)	12,000

8.0 ACCOUNTING FOR INDEPENDENT BRANCHES

The branch which maintains a complete record of its transactions is said to be an independent one. In such a case the connection between branch and an head office is maintained through the medium of a Branch Account in the books of head office and Head Office Account in the books of branch. The transactions involving the remittance of fund by/to Branch and goods sent by/to Branch are passed in the usual manner as in case of other methods explained earlier. However, the treatment of the following transactions is worth noting:

I Accounting for Fixed Assets
II Accounting for Head Office Expenses to be charged to branch
III Accounting for Inter-Branch transactions
IV Accounting for Goods-in-transit and Cash-in-transit.

ACCOUNTING FOR FIXED ASSETS

The accounts of Branch Fixed Assets may be maintained *either* at the Head Office *or* at the branch.

Transaction	*If the accounts are maintained at H.O.*		*If the accounts are maintained at Branch*	
	Branch Books	*H.O. Books*	*Branch Books*	*H.O. Books*
(a) **On Purchase by Head Office**	No entry	Branch Assets A/c Dr. To Cash A/c	Assets A/c Dr. To H.O. A/c	Branch A/c Dr. To Cash A/c
(b) **On Purchase by Branch**	Head Office A/c Dr. To Cash A/c	Branch Assets A/c Dr. To Branch A/c	Assets A/c Dr. To Cash A/c	No Entry
(c) **On Providing Depreciation**	Depreciation A/c Dr. To H.O. A/c	Branch A/c Dr. To Branch Assets A/c	Depreciation A/c Dr. To Assets A/c	No Entry

Tutorial Notes:

(i) Branch Asset Account is always opened in the books of that party which is maintaining Branch Assets Accounts.

(ii) Depreciation on Branch Assets Account is always opened in the books of Branch only.

ILLUSTRATION 40

On 1st April 2015, a head office purchased a plant costing ₹ 66,000 for the branch. On 1st January 2016, the branch purchased furniture for ₹ 10,000. The rate of depreciation on plant is 33-1/3% p.a. and on furniture 10% p.a. The accounting year of the head office and branch is the financial year.

Required: Give the necessary journal entries in the books of H.O. and Branch if fixed assets accounts are maintained (a) at Head Office (b) at Branch.

SOLUTION

(a) If Fixed Assets Accounts are maintained at H.O.

(I) JOURNAL OF HEAD OFFICE

Date	*Particulars*	*L.F.*	*Dr. (₹)*	*Cr. (₹)*
01.04.2015	Branch plant A/c		66,000	
	To Cash A/c			66,000
	(Being the Plant purchased for Branch)			
01.01.2016	Branch Furniture A/c		10,000	
	To Branch A/c			10,000
	(Being the Furniture purchased by Branch)			

31.03.2016	Branch A/c To Branch Plant A/c To Branch Furniture A/c (Being the depreciation provided)		22,250	 22,000 250

(II) JOURNAL OF BRANCH

Date	*Particulars*	*L.F.*	*Dr. (₹)*	*Cr. (₹)*
01.04.2015	No entry			
01.01.2016	Head Office A/c To Cash A/c (Being Furniture Purchased)		10,000	 10,000
31.03.2016	Depreciation A/c To H.O. A/c (Being the depreciation provided)		22,250	 22,250

(b) If Fixed Assets Accounts are maintained at branch

(I) JOURNAL OF HEAD OFFICE

Date	*Particulars*	*L.F.*	*Dr. (₹)*	*Cr. (₹)*
01.04.2015	Branch A/c To Cash A/c (Being Plant purchased for Branch)		66,000	 66,000
01.01.2016	No Entry			
31.03.2016	No Entry			

(II) JOURNAL OF BRANCH

Date	*Particulars*	*L.F.*	*Dr. (₹)*	*Cr. (₹)*
01.04.2015	Plant A/c To H.O. A/c (Being Plant purchased by H.O.)		66,000	 66,000
01.01.2016	Furniture A/c To Cash A/c (Being Furniture Purchased)		10,000	 10,000
31.03.2016	Depreciation A/c To Plant A/c To Furniture A/c (Being the depreciation provided)		22,250	 22,000 250

ACCOUNTING FOR H.O. EXPENSES TO BE CHARGED TO BRANCH

When head office decides to raise a charge against the branch in respect of services rendered to the branch, the following journal entry shall be passed.

In the Books of Branch	*In the Books of H.O.*
H.O. Expenses A/c Dr.	Branch A/c Dr.
To H.O. A/c	To P&L A/c/Respective Expenses A/c

ILLUSTRATION 41

Journalise the following transactions in the books of the head office and Delhi Branch

(a) Head office charges ₹ 4,000 from Delhi Branch as Accounts Office Expenses (b) An analysis of Head Office and Adm, services shows that the share of branches therein is half of the share of Head Office. Among the branches the share of Delhi Branch is twice the share of Agra Branch. Total Head Office and Adm. Expenses paid ₹ 80,000, ₹ 10,000 being paid in advance and ₹ 20,000 being still outstanding.

SOLUTION

JOURNAL OF HEAD OFFICE

Date	*Particulars*	*L.F.*	*Dr. (₹)*	*Cr. (₹)*
(a)	Delhi Branch A/c Dr.		4,000	
	To Accounts Office Expenses A/c			4,000
	(Being the A/cs Office Exp. charged to Delhi Branch)			
(b)	Delhi Branch A/c			
	[(₹ 80,000 – ₹ 10,000 + ₹ 20,000 × 1/3 × 2/3] Dr.		20,000	
	Agra Branch A/c			
	[(₹ 80,000 – ₹ 10,000 + ₹ 20,000) × 1/3 × 1/3] Dr.		10,000	
	To H.O. Office & Adm. Expenses A/c			30,000
	(Being the share of Delhi Branch and Agra Branch in Office and Adm. Expenses charged)			

JOURNAL OF DELHI BRANCH

Date	*Particulars*	*L.F.*	*Dr. (₹)*	*Cr. (₹)*
(a)	Account Office Expenses A/c Dr.		4,000	
	To H.O. A/c			4,000
	(Being the Account Office Expenses charged by H.O.)			
(b)	H.O. Office and Adm. Expenses A/c Dr.		20,000	
	To H.O. A/c			20,000
	(Being the H.O. Office & Adm. Exp. charged by H.O.)			

ACCOUNTING FOR INTER-BRANCH TRANSACTIONS

(a) The transactions taking place among various branches of a head office are said to be inter-branch transactions.

(b) While recording the inter-branch transactions in the books of the head office, the receiving branch is debited and the supplying branch is credited.

(c) While recording the inter-branch transactions (i.e. Goods/Cash received from antoher branch *or* customer of another branch) in the books of Receiving Branch, Head Office Account is credited.

(d) While recording the inter-branch transactions (i.e. Goods/Cash sent to another branch) in the books of Giving Branch, Head Office Account is debited.

ILLUSTRATION 42

Journalise the following transactions in the books of Head Office, Delhi Branch and Agra Branch:

(a) Goods worth ₹ 5,000 are supplied by Delhi Branch to Agra Branch under the instructions of Head Office. (b) Delhi Branch draws a bill receivable for ₹ 4,000 on Agra Branch which sends its acceptance. (c) Delhi Branch received ₹ 1,000 from Agra Branch. (d) Goods worth ₹ 2,000 were returned by a customer of Agra Branch to Delhi Branch. (e) Agra Branch collected ₹ 2,000 from a customer of Delhi Branch.

SOLUTION

JOURNAL OF HEAD OFFICE

Date	*Particulars*	*L.F.*	*Dr. (₹)*	*Cr. (₹)*
(a)	Agra Branch A/c Dr.		5,000	
	To Delhi Branch A/c			5,000
	(Being the goods supplied by Delhi Branch to Agra Branch)			
(b)	Delhi Branch A/c Dr.		4,000	
	To Agra Branch A/c			4,000
	(Being a B/R drawn by Delhi upon Agra Branch)			
(c)	Delhi Branch A/c Dr.		1,000	
	To Agra Branch A/c			1,000
	(Being cash sent by Agra Branch to Delhi Branch)			
(d)	Delhi Branch A/c Dr.		2,000	
	To Agra Branch A/c			2,000
	(Being the goods returned by customer of Agra Branch to Delhi Branch)			
(e)	Agra Branch A/c Dr.		2,000	
	To Delhi Branch A/c			2,000
	(Being the cash collected by Agra Branch from a customer of Delhi Branch)			

JOURNAL OF DELHI BRANCH

Date	*Particulars*	*L.F.*	*Dr. (₹)*	*Cr. (₹)*
(a)	H.O. A/c Dr.		5,000	
	To Goods sent to Branch A/c			5,000
	(Being the goods supplied to Agra Branch)			
(b)	Bills Receivable A/c Dr.		4,000	
	To H.O. A/c			4,000
	(Being the acceptance of a B/R received from Agra Branch)			

(c)	Cash A/c Dr. To H.O. A/c (Being the cash received from Agra Branch)		1,000	1,000
(d)	Goods Sent to Branch A/c Dr. To H.O. A/c (Being the goods received from a customer of Agra Branch)		2,000	2,000
(e)	H.O. A/c Dr. To Debtors A/c (Being the cash collected by Agra Branch from our customer)		2,000	2,000

JOURNAL OF AGRA BRANCH

Date	*Particulars*	*L.F.*	*Dr. (₹)*	*Cr. (₹)*
(a)	Goods sent to Branch A/c Dr. To H.O. A/c (Being the goods received from Delhi Branch)		5,000	5,000
(b)	H.O. A/c Dr. To Bill Payable A/c (Being a B/P accepted for Delhi Branch)		4,000	4,000
(c)	H.O. A/c Dr. To Cash A/c (Being cash paid to Delhi Branch)		1,000	1,000
(d)	H.O. A/c Dr. To Debtors A/c (Being the goods returned by our customer to Delhi Branch)		2,000	2,000
(e)	Cash A/c Dr. To H.O. A/c (Being the cash received from a customer of Delhi Branch)		2,000	2,000

ILLUSTRATION 43

A Calcutta head office passes one entry at the end of each month to adjust the position arising out of inter-branch transactions during the month. From the following inter-branch transactions in April 2016, make the entry in the books of Calcutta head office:

(a) Delhi Branch:

(i) Received goods from Nagpur branch ₹ 9,000 and Ahmedabad branch ₹ 6,000.

(ii) Sent goods to Ahmedabad branch ₹ 15,000 and Nagpur branch ₹ 12,000.

(iii) Received B/R from Ahmedabad branch ₹ 9,000.

(iv) Sent acceptances to Nagpur branch ₹ 6,000 and Ahmedabad branch ₹ 3,000.

(b) Kanpur branch [apart from (a) above]:

(i) Received goods from Nagpur branch ₹ 15,000 and Delhi branch ₹ 6,000.

(ii) Cash sent to Nagpur branch ₹ 3,000 and Delhi branch ₹ 6,000.

(c) Nagpur Branch [apart from (a) and (b) above]:

(i) Sent goods to Ahmedabad branch ₹ 9,000.

(ii) Received B/R from Ahmedabad branch ₹ 9,000.

(iii) Received cash from Ahmedabad branch ₹ 5,000.

SOLUTION

JOURNAL OF HEAD OFFICE

Date	*Particulars*		*L.F.*	*Dr. (₹)*	*Cr. (₹)*
	Kanpur Branch A/c	Dr.		12,000	
	Nagpur Branch A/c	Dr.		2,000	
	To Delhi Branch A/c				12,000
	To Ahmedabad Branch A/c				2,000
	(Being the inter-branch transactions recorded based on the details in statement given below)				

STATEMENT OF INTER-BRANCH TRANSACTIONS

Item	*Delhi*		*Kanpur*		*Nagpur*		*Ahmedabad*	
	Dr.	*Cr.*	*Dr.*	*Cr.*	*Dr.*	*Cr.*	*Dr.*	*Cr.*
Goods	15,000	—	—	—	—	9,000	—	6,000
Goods	—	27,000	—	—	12,000	—	15,000	—
B/R	9,000	—	—	—	—	—	—	9,000
B/P	—	9,000	—	—	6,000	—	3,000	—
Goods	—	6,000	21,000	—	—	15,000	—	—
Cash	6,000	—	—	9,000	3,000	—	—	—
Goods	—	—	—	—	—	9,000	9,000	—
B/R	—	—	—	—	9,000	—	—	9,000
Cash	—	—	—	—	5,000	—	—	5,000
	30,000	42,000	21,000	9,000	35,000	33,000	27,000	29,000
Balance	12,000	—	—	12,000	—	2,000	2,000	—
	42,000	42,000	21,000	21,000	35,000	35,000	29,000	29,000

ACCOUNTING FOR GOODS IN TRANSIT AND CASH IN TRANSIT

If the balance of Branch Account in the head office books and that of Head Office Account in the branch books do not tally. These must be reconciled before the preparation of the final accounts of the concern as a whole. Practical steps for reconciliation are shown below:

PRACTICAL STEPS FOR RECONCILIATION

Step 1: Calculate the difference between the balance of Branch Account (Given in the trial balance of H.O.) and H.O. Account (given in the trial balance of branch). If one account shows the debit balance and the other account shows the credit balance.

OR

Calculate the aggregate of the balance of Branch Account and that of the H.O. Account if both these accounts show *either* the debit *or* credit balance.

Step 2: Calculate Goods-in-transit by comparing the 'Goods sent to Branch Account', with 'Goods Received by Branch Account' *or* 'Goods Returned by Branch Account' with 'Goods received by H.O. Account'.

Step 3: Calculate Cash-in-transit by comparing Cash Remitted Account.

Note: *It is to be noted if either Cash-in-transit or Goods-in-transit is not given, the same may be found out by subtracting the given item from the amount calculated as per Step 1. It is also to be noted that if the total of Cash-in-transit and Goods-in-transit is not equal to the amount as per Step ₹ 1' then the difference may be put to Suspense Account.*

Step 4: Pass the Adjusting Entry *either* in the books of Head office *or* Branch as under.

In the Books of Head Office		*In the Books of Branch*	
(a) Goods-in-transit A/c	Dr.	(a) Goods-in-transit A/c	Dr.
To Branch A/c		To Head Office A/c	
(b) Cash-in-transit A/c	Dr.	(b) Cash-in-transit A/c	Dr.
To Branch A/c		To Head Office A/c	

ILLUSTRATION 44

Journalise the following transactions in the books of the Head Office. The Head Office follows the financial year as its accounting year; (a) Goods returned by Agra Branch on 28th March, worth ₹ 1,000 to its Head Office not received by the head office upto 31st March (b) Goods worth ₹ 2,000 sent by the Head Office to its Delhi Branch on 29th March, were received on 3rd April following; (c) ₹ 5,000 remitted by Delhi Branch to Head Office on 28th March was received on 4th April.

SOLUTION

JOURNAL OF HEAD OFFICE

Date	*Particulars*	*L.F.*	*Dr. (₹)*	*Cr. (₹)*
(a)	Goods-in-transit A/c Dr.		1,000	
	To Agra Branch A/c			1,000
	(Being the goods returned by Agra Branch not yet received)			
(b)	Goods-in-transit A/c Dr.		2,000	
	To Delhi Branch A/c			2,000
	(Being the goods sent to Delhi Branch, not yet received by Branch)			
(c)	Cash-in-transit A/c Dr.		5,000	
	To Delhi Branch A/c			5,000
	(Being the Cash sent by Delhi Branch, not yet received)			

ILLUSTRATION 45

From the following particulars, reconcile the H.O. Account with Branch Account.

Particulars	H.O.		Branch	
	Dr. (₹)	Cr. (₹)	Dr. (₹)	Cr. (₹)
Goods sent to Branch	—	13,02,400	—	—
Goods received by Branch	—	—	12,80,400	—
Branch A/c	4,11,100	—	—	—
H.O. A/c	—	—	—	3,01,600

SOLUTION

A Net Difference = ₹ 4,11,100 – ₹ 3,01,600 = ₹ 1,09,500

B Goods sent by H.O. to Branch but not yet received by Branch
= ₹ 13,02,400 – ₹ 12,80,400 = ₹ 22,000

C Cash remitted by Branch to h.O. but not yet received by H.O.
= ₹ 1,09,500 – ₹ 22,000 = ₹ 87,500

D Journal Entry in the book of H.O. to reconcile both the Accounts:

Goods in transit A/c	Dr.	₹ 22,000	
Cash in transit A/c	Dr.	₹ 87,500	
To Branch A/c			₹ 1,09,500

Now,

Dr. **BRANCH ACCOUNT IN THE BOOKS OF H.O.** *Cr.*

Particulars	₹	Particulars	₹
To Balance b/d	4,11,100	By Goods in transit A/c	22,000
		By Cash in transit A/c	87,500
		By Balance c/d	3,01,600
	4,11,100		4,11,100

ILLUSTRATION 46

From the following particulars, reconcile the H.O. Account with Branch Account:

Particulars	H.O.		Branch	
	Dr. (₹)	Cr. (₹)	Dr. (₹)	Cr. (₹)
Goods sent to Branch	—	13,02,400	—	—
Goods received by Branch	—	—	12,80,400	—
Branch A/c	4,11,100		—	—
H.O. A/c	—	—	3,01,600	—

SOLUTION

A. Total Difference = ₹ 4,11,100 + ₹ 3,01,600 = ₹ 7,12,700

B. Goods not yet received by branch = ₹ 22,000

C. Cash not yet received by H.O. = ₹ 7,12,700 – ₹ 22,000 = ₹ 6,90,700

D. Journal Entry to reconcile in the books of H.O.:

Goods in transit A/c	Dr.	₹ 22,000	
Cash in transit A/c	Dr.	₹ 6,90,700	
To Branch A/c			₹ 7,12,700

Dr. **BRANCH ACCOUNT IN THE BOOKS OF H.O.** Cr.

Particulars	₹	*Particulars*	₹
To Balance b/d	4,11,100	By Goods in transit A/c	22,000
To Balance c/d	3,01,600	By Cash in transit A/c	6,90,700
	7,12,700		7,12,700

ILLUSTRATION 47

From the following particulars, reconcile the H.O. Account with Branch Account.

Particulars	*H.O.*		*Branch*	
	Dr. (₹)	*Cr. (₹)*	*Dr. (₹)*	*Cr. (₹)*
Goods sent to Branch	—	13,02,400	—	—
Goods received by Branch	—	—	12,80,400	—
Branch A/c	4,11,100	—	—	—
H.O. A/c	—	—	—	3,01,600

During the year cash remitted by Branch was ₹ 1,86,500 but cash received by head office was ₹ 1,00,000.

SOLUTION

A. Net Difference = ₹ 4,11,100 – ₹ 3,01,600 = ₹ 1,09,500

B. Goods in transit = ₹ 13,02,400 – ₹ 12,80,400 = ₹ 22,000

C. Cash in transit = ₹ 1,86,500 – ₹ 1,00,000 = ₹ 86,500

D. Difference due to any other error = ₹ 1,09,500 – ₹ 22,000 – ₹ 86,500
= ₹ 1,000 may be put to Suspense Account for want of details.

E. Journal Entry to reconcile in the books of H.O.:

Goods in transit A/c	Dr.	₹ 22,000	
Cash in transit A/c	Dr.	₹ 86,500	
Suspense A/c	Dr.	₹ 1,000	
To Branch A/c			₹ 1,09,500

Dr. **BRANCH ACCOUNT IN THE BOOKS OF H.O.** Cr.

Particulars	₹	*Particulars*	₹
To Balance b/d	4,11,100	By Goods-in-transit A/c	22,000
		By Cash-in-transit A/c	86,500
		By Suspense A/c	1,000

		By Balance c/d	3,01,600
	4,11,100		4,11,100

9.0 INCORPORATION OF BRANCH RESULTS IN THE BOOKS OF HEAD OFFICE

The Branch result may be incorporated in the books of head office by adopting any of the following three methods:

(i) Separate Final Accounts Method, (ii) Abridged Consolidated Method, (iii) Detailed Consolidated Method.

SEPARATE FINAL ACCOUNTS METHOD

The practical steps to be taken under this method are shown below:

PRACTICAL STEPS UNDER SEPARATE FINAL ACCOUNTS METHOD

Step 1: Prepare separate Trading and Profit and Loss Account and Balance Sheet of the Branch in the books of the respective Branch.

Step 2: Transfer only the amount of net profit/loss as shown by Branch Profit and loss Account to Head Office by passing the following journal entry.

Profit and Loss A/c Dr.

To Head Office A/c

Note: *A reverse entry is passed in case of Net Loss.*

Step 3: Incorporate only the net profit of the branch in the books of Head Office by passing the following journal entry:

Branch A/c Dr.

To General P&L A/c

Note: *A reverse entry is passed in case of Net Loss.*

Step 4: Prepare separate Trading and Profit and Loss Account and the Balance Sheet of the head office in its books.

Note: *The H.O. Account in the books of Branch will show the net balance due to/from head office and the Branch Account in the books of Head Office will show the net balance due to/from the branch.*

ILLUSTRATION 48

Following are the Trial balances of Tulsian & Sons as at 31.3.2016:

Particulars	*H.O.*		*Branch*	
	Dr. (₹)	*Cr. (₹)*	*Dr. (₹)*	*Cr. (₹)*
Goods sent to Branch	—	6,51,200	—	—
Goods received by Branch	—	—	6,40,200	—
Branch A/c	2,05,550	—	—	—
H.O. A/c	—	—	—	1,50,800
Purchases	19,93,350	—	—	—
Sales	—	14,20,000	—	6,40,000
Debtors	2,30,000	—	92,000	—
Creditors	—	5,83,350	—	2,400

Bank Balance	67,000	—	30,000	—
Capital	—	1,95,000	—	—
Direct Expenses	34,650	—	—	—
Office & Adm. Expenses	1,12,000	—	7,000	—
Selling & Distribution Expenses	1,12,000	—	20,000	—
Fixed Assets	95,000	—	4,000	—
	28,49,550	28,49,550	7,93,200	7,93,200

Information:

(a) Stock in hand at the end—Head Office ₹ 3,00,000, Branch Office ₹ 72,600 (b) Depreciate the fixed assets by 10% (c) Office Expenses of Branch still outstanding as on 31.3.2016 ₹ 1,000 (d) Selling Expenses of Branch paid in the advance as on 31.3.2016 ₹ 2,000.

Required:

(a) Pass Adjusting Entries and prepare the Trading and Profit and Loss Account and the Balance Sheet of Branch and H.O.'s Current Account in Branch's Books and

(b) Pass adjusting entries and prepare Trading and Profit & Loss Account of H.O. and Branch's Current Account in the books of H.O.

SOLUTION

BOOKS OF BRANCH
JOURNAL

Date	*Particulars*		*L.F.*	*Dr. (₹)*	*Cr. (₹)*
(a)	Depreciation A/c	Dr.		400	
	To Fixed Assets A/c				400
(b)	Office & Adm. Expenses A/c	Dr.		1,000	
	To Outstanding Office & Adm. Expenses A/c				1,000
(c)	Prepaid Selling & Distribution Expenses A/c	Dr.		2,000	
	To Selling & Distribution Expenses A/c				2,000
(d)	Closing Stock A/c	Dr.		72,600	
	To Trading A/c				72,600
(e)	Goods received from H.O. A/c	Dr.		11,000	
	To Trading A/c				11,000
(f)	Goods - in transit A/c	Dr.		11,000	
	To H.O. Current A/c				11,000
(g)	Profit & Loss A/c	Dr.		46,000	
	To H.O. Current A/c				46,000

TRADING AND PROFIT AND LOSS ACCOUNT OF BRANCH

Dr. *for the year ending on 31st March, 2016* *Cr.*

Particulars	₹	*Particulars*	₹
To Goods received from H.O.	6,51,200	By Sales	6,40,000
To Gross Profit c/d	72,400	By Closing Stock	

		In hand	72,600	
		In Transit	11,000	83,600
	7,23,600			7,23,600
To Off. & Adm. Expenses				
(₹ 7,000 + ₹ 1,000)	8,000	By Gross Profit b/d		72,400
To Selling & Dist. Expenses				
(₹ 20,000 – ₹ 2,000)	18,000			
To Depreciation on Fixed Assets	400			
To N.P. t/f to H.O. Current A/c	46,000			
	72,400			72,400

BALANCE SHEET OF BRANCH AS AT 31ST MARCH, 2016

Liabilities		₹	*Assets*		₹
H.O. Current A/c:			S. Debtors		92,000
Balance	1,61,800		Bank		30,000
Add: Profit	46,000	2,07,800	Stock		
Creditors		2,400	In hand	72,600	
Outstanding Office Expenses		1,000	In Transit	11,000	83,600
			Fixed Assets		3,600
			Prepaid Selling Expenses		2,000
		2,11,200			2,11,200

Dr. **H.O.'S CURRENT ACCOUNT** *Cr.*

Particulars	₹	*Particulars*	₹
To Balance c/d	2,07,800	By Balance b/d	1,50,800
		By Goods in Transit	11,000
		By Profit	46,000
	2,07,800		2,07,800

BOOKS OF H.O.
JOURNAL

Date	*Particulars*	*L.F.*	*Dr. (₹)*	*Cr. (₹)*
(a)	Branch's Current A/c Dr.		46,000	
	To P & L A/c			46,000
	(Being the Profit of Branch incorporated)			
(b)	Cash-in-transit A/c Dr.		43,750	
	To Branch's Current A/c			43,750
	(Being the transit item incorporated)			
(c)	Closing Stock A/c Dr.		3,00,000	
	To Trading A/c			3,00,000
	(Being the Closing Stock incorporated)			

(d)	Depreciation A/c	Dr.	9,500	
	To Fixed Assets A/c			9,500
	(Being the depreciation on fixed assets provided)			

TRADING AND PROFIT AND LOSS ACCOUNT OF H.O.

Dr. *for the period ending on 31st March, 2016* Cr.

Particulars	₹	*Particulars*	₹
To Purchases	19,93,350	By Sales	14,20,000
To Mfg. Expenses	34,650	By Goods sent to Branch	6,51,200
To Gross Profit c/d	3,43,200	By Closing Stock	3,00,000
	23,71,200		23,71,200
To Office and Adm. Expenses	1,12,000	By Gross Profit b/d	3,43,200
To Selling and Dist. Expenses	1,12,000	By Branch's Current A/c	46,000
To Depreciation on Fixed Assets	9,500	(Transfer of Branch Profit)	
To Net Profit	1,55,700		
	3,89,200		3,89,200

BALANCE SHEET OF H.O. AS AT 31ST MARCH, 2016

Liabilities		₹	*Assets*	₹
Capital	1,95,000		Sundry Debtors	2,30,000
Add: Profit	1,55,700	3,50,700	Stock-in-hand	3,00,000
Sundry Creditors		5,83,350	Bank A/c	67,000
			Remittance-in-Transit	43,750
			Fixed Assets (₹ 95,000 – ₹ 9,500)	85,500
			Branch Current A/c	2,07,800
		9,34,050		9,34,050

Dr. **BRANCH'S CURRENT ACCOUNT** Cr.

Particulars	₹	*Particulars*	₹
To Balance b/d	2,05,550	By Cash-in-transit	43,750
To Profit	46,000	By Balance c/d	2,07,800
	2,51,550		2,51,550

ABRIDGED CONSOLIDATED METHOD

The practical steps to be taken under this method are shown below:

PRACTICAL STEPS UNDER ABRIDGED CONSOLIDATED METHOD

Step 1: Prepare separate Trading and Profit and Loss Account of the Branch in the books of respective Branch.

Step 2: Transfer only the amount of net profit/loss, the assets and the liabilities of the branch to Head Office Account.

Step 3: Incorporate the net profit/loss, the assets and the liabilities of the branch in the books of Head office.

Step 4: Prepare Trading and Profit and Loss Account after incorporating Branch net profit/loss and Consolidated Balance Sheet in the books of Head Office.

JOURNAL ENTRIES

Under this method, the journal entries which are passed by the Branch to transfer its net profit/loss, assets and liabilities and by the head office to incorporate the net profit/loss, assets and liabilities of the branch are shown on next page:

JOURNAL ENTRIES IN THE BOOKS OF BRANCH AND H.O. UNDER ABRIDGED CONSOLIDATED METHOD

Item	*In the Books of Branch*	*In the Books of H.O.*
1. For Transfer of branch Net Profit	Profit and Loss A/c Dr. To Head Office A/c	Branch A/c Dr. To General P&L A/c
2. For Transfer of Branch Assets	Head Office A/c Dr. To Branch Assets A/c (Individually)	Branch Assets A/c Dr. To Branch A/c (Individually)
3. For Transfer of Branch Liabilities	Branch Liabilities A/c Dr. To Head Office A/c (Individually)	Branch A/c Dr. To Branch Liabilities A/c (Individually)

Note:

(i) In case of net loss, the entry no. 1 will be reversed.

(ii) As a result of these entries the H.O. A/c in the books of Branch and Branch A/c in the books of H.O. will be completely closed.

(iii) In the beginning of next year, the entry No. 2 and 3 will be reversed.

ILLUSTRATION 49

Taking the same information as given in Illustration 48, you are required:

(a) to give the necessary adjusting journal entries in the books of Branch and Head office:

(b) to prepare trading and Profit and Loss Account and H.O. Account in the books of Branch;

(c) to prepare trading and profit & loss Account, Branch Account and the Balance Sheet in the books of Head office.

Note: *The profit, assets and liabilities of the branch are to be transferred to the head office books.*

SOLUTION

BOOKS OF BRANCH
JOURNAL

Date	*Particulars*		*L.F.*	*Dr. (₹)*	*Cr. (₹)*
(a)	Depreciation A/c	Dr.		400	
	To Fixed Assets A/c				400
(b)	Office & Adm. Expenses A/c	Dr.		1,000	
	To Outstanding Office Expenses A/c				1,000
(c)	Prepaid Selling & Distribution Expenses A/c	Dr.		2,000	
	To Selling & Distribution Expenses A/c				2,000

(d)	Closing Stock A/c	Dr.	72,600	
	To Trading A/c			72,600
(e)	Goods received from H.O. A/c	Dr.	11,000	
	To Trading A/c			11,000
(f)	Goods - in transit A/c	Dr.	11,000	
	To H.O. A/c			11,000
(g)	Profit & Loss A/c	Dr.	46,000	
	To H.O. A/c			46,000
(h)	H.O. A/c	Dr.	2,11,200	
	To Debtors			92,000
	To Bank			30,000
	To Fixed Assets			3,600
	To Closing Stock			72,600
	To Goods-in-transit			11,000
	To Prepaid Selling Expenses			2,000
(i)	Creditors A/c	Dr.	2,400	
	Outstanding Office Expenses A/c	Dr.	1,000	
	To H.O. A/c			3,400

TRADING AND PROFIT AND LOSS ACCOUNT

Dr. *for the period ending on 31st March, 2016* Cr.

Particulars	₹	*Particulars*		₹
To Goods received from H.O.	6,51,200	By Sales		6,40,000
To Gross Profit c/d	72,400	By Closing Stock		
		In hand	72,600	
		In Transit	11,000	83,600
	7,23,600			7,23,600
To Office & Adm. Expenses	8,000	By Gross Profit b/d		72,400
To Selling & Dist. Expenses	18,000			
To Depreciation on Fixed Assets	400			
To Net Profit t/f to Capital A/c	46,000			
	72,400			72,400

Dr. **H.O.'S ACCOUNT IN THE BOOKS OF BRANCH** Cr.

Particulars	₹	*Particulars*	₹
To Debtors	92,000	By Balance b/d	1,50,800
To Bank	30,000	By Goods received from H.O. A/c	11,000
To Fixed Assets	3,600	By Profit & Loss A/c	46,000
To Prepaid Selling Expenses	2,000	By Creditors	2,400
To Closing Stock	72,600	By Outstanding Office Expenses	1,000

To Goods-in-transit	11,000		
	2,11,200		2,11,200

BOOKS OF HEAD OFFICE
JOURNAL OF HEAD OFFICE

Date	*Particulars*		*L.F.*	*Dr.* (₹)	*Cr.* (₹)
(a)	Branch A/c	Dr.		46,000	
	To General P & L A/c				46,000
	(Being Net Profit transferred to General P & L A/c)				
(b)	Branch Debtors	Dr.		92,000	
	Branch Bank	Dr.		30,000	
	Branch Stock	Dr.		72,600	
	Goods in transit A/c	Dr.		11,000	
	Branch Fixed Assets	Dr.		3,600	
	Branch Prepaid Selling & Distribution Expenses	Dr.		2,000	
	To Branch A/c				2,11,200
	(Being the Branch Assets incorporated)				
(c)	Branch A/c	Dr.		3,400	
	To Branch Creditors A/c				2,400
	To Outstanding Office & Adm. Expenses				1,000
	(Being the Branch liabilities incorporated)				
(d)	Cash in transit A/c	Dr.		43,750	
	To Branch A/c				43,750
	(Being the adjustment for items-in-transit)				
(e)	Closing Stock A/c	Dr.		3,00,000	
	To Trading A/c				3,00,000
	(Being the closing stock incorporated)				
(f)	Depreciation A/c	Dr.		95,000	
	To Fixed Assets A/c				95,000
	(Being the depreciation on fixed assets provided)				

TRADING AND PROFIT AND LOSS ACCOUNT
for the year ending on 31st March, 2016

Dr. Cr.

Particulars	₹	*Particulars*	₹
To Purchases	19,93,350	By Sales	14,20,000
To Mfg. Expenses	34,650	By Goods sent to Branch	6,51,200
To Gross Profit c/d	3,43,200	By Closing Stock	3,00,000
	23,71,200		23,71,200
To Office & Adm. Expenses	1,12,000	By Gross Profit b/d	3,43,200
To Selling & Dist. Expenses	1,12,000	By Branch's Current A/c	46,000
To Depreciation on Fixed Assets	9,500	(Transfer of Branch Profit)	

To net Profit	1,55,700		
	3,89,200		3,89,200

CONSOLIDATED BALANCE SHEET OF HEAD OFFICE AND ITS BRANCH

as at 31st March, 2016

Liabilities	*H.O.* ₹	*Branch* ₹	*Total* ₹	*Assets*	*H.O.* ₹	*Branch* ₹	*Total* ₹
Capital	1,95,000	—		Fixed Assets	95,000	4,000	99,000
Add: Net Profit	1,55,700			*Less:* Depreciation	(9,500)	(400)	(9,900)
	3,50,700	—	3,50,700		85,500	3,600	89,100
Creditors	5,83,350	2,400	5,85,750	Stock in hand	3,00,000	72,600	3,72,600
Outstanding Office Exp.	—	1,000	1,000	Stock in transit	—	11,000	11,000
H.O. A/c	—	2,07,800	—	Debtors	2,30,000	92,000	3,22,000
				Cash at Bank	67,000	30,000	97,000
				Cash-in-transit	43,750	—	43,750
				Prepaid selling Expenses	—	2,000	2,000
				Branch A/c	2,07,800	—	—
	9,34,050	2,11,200	9,37,450		9,34,050	2,11,200	9,37,450

Dr. **BRANCH ACCOUNT IN THE BOOKS OF H.O.** *Cr.*

Particulars	₹	*Particulars*	₹
To Balance b/d	2,05,550	By Branch Debtors	92,000
To Profit & Loss A/c	46,000	By Branch Bank	30,000
To Branch Creditors	2,400	By Branch Stock	72,600
To Outstanding Office & Adm.		By Goods in transit A/c	11,000
Expenses A/c	1,000	By Branch Fixed Assets	3,600
		By Branch Prepaid selling expenses	2,000
		By Cash-in-transit A/c	43,750
	2,54,950		2,54,950

ILLUSTRATION 50

The head office of a business and its branch keep their own books and each prepare Profit and Loss Account. The following are the balances appearing in the two sets of books as on 31st March, 2016, after ascertainment of profit and after making all adjustments except those referred to below:

Particulars	*H.O.*		*Branch*	
	Dr. (₹)	*Cr.* (₹)	*Dr.* (₹)	*Cr* (₹)
Capital		1,00,000		
Fixed Assets	36,000		16,000	
Stock	34,200		10,740	
Debtors and Creditors	7,820	3,960	4,840	1,920
Cash	10,740		1,420	
Profit and Loss Account		14,660		3,060

Branch Office Account	29,860			
Head Office Account				28,020
	1,18,620	1,18,620	33,000	33,000

Required: Set out the Balance Sheet of the business as on 31st March, 2016 and the Journal entries (in both set of books) to record the adjustment dealing with the following:

(a) On 31st March, the branch had sent a cheque for ₹ 1,000 to the head office, not received by head office *nor* credited to Branch Account till 3rd April,

(b) Goods valued at ₹ 840 had been forwarded by the head office to the branch and invoiced on 30th March, but were not received by the branch *nor* dealt with in branch's books till 11th April,

(c) The profit shown by the branch is to be transferred to the head office books.

(d) Branch assets and liabilities are to be recorded in the books of head office.

SOLUTION

JOURNAL OF HEAD OFFICE

Date	*Particulars*		*L.F.*	*Dr. (₹)*	*Cr. (₹)*
	Branch Fixed Assets	Dr.		16,000	
	Branch Stock	Dr.		10,740	
	Branch Debtors	Dr.		4,840	
	Branch Cash	Dr.		1,420	
	Goods-in-transit	Dr.		840	
	To Branch A/c				33,840
	(Being the Branch Assets incorporated for H.O. Books)				
	Branch A/c	Dr.		1,920	
	To Branch Creditors A/c				1,920
	(Being the Branch Liabilities incorporated in H.O. Books)				
	Cash-in-transit	Dr.		1,000	
	To Branch A/c				1,000
	(Being the goods and cash in transit incorporated in H.O. Books)				
	Branch A/c	Dr.		3,060	
	To Profit & Loss A/c				3,060
	(Being Branch profit transferred to P & L A/c)				

Dr. **BRANCH ACCOUNT** *Cr.*

Particulars	₹	*Particulars*	₹
To Balance b/d	29,860	By Branch Fixed Assets	16,000
To Branch Creditors	1,920	By Branch Stock	10,740
To P & L A/c	3,060	By Branch Debtors	4,840
		By Branch Cash	1,420
		By Goods-in-transit	840

		By Cash-in-transit	1,000
	34,840		34,840

CONSOLIDATED BALANCE SHEET OF H.O. AND ITS BRANCH

as at 31st March, 2016

Liabilities		₹	*Assets*		₹
Capital		1,00,000	Fixed Assets		
P & L A/c:			H.O.	36,000	
H.O.	14,660		Branch	16,000	52,000
Branch	3,060	17,720	Stock:		
Creditors:			H.O.	34,200	
H.O.	3,960		Branch	10,740	
Branch	1,920	5,880	In-transit	840	45,780
			Debtors:		
			H.O.	7,820	
			Branch	4,840	12,660
			Cash:		
			H.O.	10,740	
			Branch	1,420	
			In-transit	1,000	13,160
		1,23,600			1,23,600

JOURNAL OF BRANCH

Date	*Particulars*		*L.F.*	*Dr. (₹)*	*Cr. (₹)*
	Goods-in-transit	Dr.		840	
	To HO A/c				840
	(Being the Goods-in-Transit recorded)				
	H.O. A/c	Dr.		33,840	
	To Branch Fixed Assets				16,000
	To Branch Stock				10,740
	To Branch Debtors				4,840
	To Branch Cash				1,420
	To Goods-in-transit A/c				840
	(Being the Branch Assets transferred to H.O.)				
	Branch Creditors	Dr.		1,920	
	To H.O. A/c				1,920
	(Being the Branch Liabilities transferred to H.O.)				
	Profit & Loss A/c	Dr.		3,060	
	To H.O. A/c				3,060
	(Being the Profit transferred to H.O.)				

ILLUSTRATION 51

From the following trial balance as on 31st March, 2016, prepare the combined balance sheet and show the branch current account as it would appear in the head office books:

Particulars	*Head Office* ₹	*Branch* ₹
Capital	30,000	—
Profit and Loss Account 1st April	2,715	—
Current year profit	8,415	3,484
Creditors on open account	5,930	—
Creditors for expenses	390	—
Goods from head office	—	7,000
Cash received from branch	9,987	—
Head Office Current Account 1st April	—	17,298
Premises	8,000	4,000
Fixtures and Fittings	800	400
Stock-in-trade	9,000	1,800
Trade debtors	8,000	650
Branch Current Account 1st April	17,298	—
Goods sent to branch	7,200	—
Cash remitted to head office	—	10,287
Cash at bank	7,139	10,645

SOLUTION

Dr. **BRANCH CURRENT ACCOUNT** *Cr.*

Particulars	₹	*Particulars*		₹
To Balance b/d	17,298	By Cash A/c		9,987
To Goods sent to branch	7,200	By Goods-in-transit (7,200 – 7,000)		200
To Profit and loss A/c	3,484	By Cash-in-transit (10,287 – 9,987)		300
		By Branch Assets A/c		
		Premises	4,000	
		Fixtures	400	
		Stock	1,800	
		Debtors	650	
		Bank	10,645	17,495
	27,982			27,982

BALANCE SHEET AS AT 31ST MARCH, 2016

Liabilities	₹	*Assets*		₹
Capital	30,000	Premises:		
Profit and Loss Account:		Head office	8,000	

Last year	2,715		Branch	4,000	12,000
Current year	11,899	14,614	Fixtures:		
Trade creditors		5,930	Head office	800	
Creditors for expenses		390	Branch	400	1,200
			Stock:		
		—	Head office	9,000	
			Branch	1,800	
			In transit	200	11,000
			Debtors:		
			Head office	8,000	
			Branch	650	8,650
			Bank:		
			Head office	7,139	
			Branch	10,645	17,784
			Cash-in-transit		300
		50,934			50,934

DETAILED CONSOLIDATED METHOD

The practical steps under this method are shown below:

PRACTICAL STEPS UNDER CONSOLIDATED ACCOUNTS METHOD

Step 1: Transfer all revenue items, assets and liabilities of the Branch to Head Office Account in the books of Branch.

Step 2: Incorporate all the revenue items, assets and liabilities transferred by the Branch in the books of Head Office.

Step 3: Prepare Consolidated Trading and Profit and Loss Account and Consolidated Balance Sheet in the books of H.O.

JOURNAL ENTRIES

Under this method, the journal entries which are passed by the Branch to transfer its trial balance to H.O. and by the head office to incorporate the trial balance of Branch in its books are shown below:

JOURNAL ENTRIES IN THE BOOKS OF BRANCH AND H.O. UNDER CONSOLIDATED FINAL ACCOUNTS METHOD

Item of Trial Balance	*In the Books of Branch*	*In the Books of H.O.*
1. ***For items which are shown on the debit side of Trading A/c after (adjustments relating to outstanding and prepaid expenses)***	Head Office A/c Dr. To Opening Stock To Purchases To Goods received from H.O. To Direct expenses To Sales Returns	Branch Trading A/c Dr. To Branch A/c

2. ***For items which are shown on the credit side of Trading A/c (after adjustments relating to outstanding and prepaid expenses)***	Sales A/c Dr. Closing Stock Dr. Purchase Returns Dr. To Head Office A/c	Branch A/c Dr. To Branch Trading A/c
3. ***For transfer of Gross Profit***	No Entry	Branch Trading A/c Dr. To Branch P&L A/c
4. ***For items which are shown on the debit side of Profit and Loss A/c (after adjustments relating to outstanding and prepaid expenses)***	Head Office A/c Dr. To Office & Adm. Exp. A/c To Selling & Dist. Exp. A/c To Depreciation A/c etc.	Branch P&L A/c Dr. To Branch A/c
5. ***For items which are shown on the credit side of Profit and Loss A/c (after adjustments relating to outstanding and prepaid expenses)***	Interest Received Dr. Discount Received etc. Dr. To Head Office A/c	Branch A/c Dr. To Branch P&L A/c
6. ***For transfer of Net Profit***	No Entry	Branch P&L A/c Dr. To H.O. P&L A/c
7. ***For transfer of Branch Assets (after Adjustments)***	Head Office A/c Dr. To Branch Assets (Individually)	Branch Assets A/c Dr. (Individually) To Branch A/c
8. ***For Transfer of Branch Liabilities (after adjustments)***	Branch Liabilities Dr. (Individually) To Head Office A/c	Branch A/c Dr. To Branch Liabilities A/c (Individually)

Note:

(i) In case of gross loss, the entry no. 3 will be reversed.

(ii) In case of net loss, entry no. 6 will be reversed.

(iii) As a result of these entries the H.O. A/c in the books of Branch and Branch A/c in the books of H.O. will be completely closed.

(iv) In the beginning of next accounting year, the entry no. 7 and 8 will be reversed.

ILLUSTRATION 52

Taking the same information as given in Illustration 48, you are required:

(a) to give journal entries to close various accounts and to prepare H.O. Account in the books of Branch.

(b) to give journal entries to incorporate the trial balance of branch and to prepare Branch Account in the books of Head Office.

(c) to prepare Consolidated Trading and P & L A/c and Balance Sheet of both H.O. and Branch in the books of H.O.

SOLUTION

(A) BOOKS OF BRANCH
JOURNAL OF BRANCH

Date	Particulars		L.F.	Dr. (₹)	Cr. (₹)
(a)	Goods received from H.O. A/c	Dr.		11,000	
	To H.O. A/c				11,000
(b)	Depreciation A/c	Dr.		400	
	To Fixed Assets A/c				400
(c)	Office & Adm. Expenses A/c	Dr.		1,000	
	To Outstanding Office & Adm. Expenses A/c				1,000
(d)	Prepaid Selling & Distribution Expenses A/c	Dr.		2,000	
	To Selling & Distribution Expenses A/c				2,000
(e)	H.O. A/c	Dr.		6,51,200	
	To Goods Received from H.O. A/c				6,51,200
(f)	Sales A/c	Dr.		6,40,000	
	Closing Stock A/c	Dr.		72,600	
	Goods in transit			11,000	
	To H.O. A/c				7,23,600
(g)	H.O. A/c	Dr.		26,400	
	To Office & Adm. Expenses A/c				8,000
	To Selling & Dist. Expenses A/c				18,000
	To Depreciation A/c				400
(h)	H.O. A/c	Dr.		2,11,200	
	To Debtors				92,000
	To Bank				30,000
	To Fixed Assets				3,600
	To Closing Stock				72,600
	To Goods in transit				11,000
	To Prepaid Selling & Distribution Expenses				2,000
(i)	Creditors A/c	Dr.		2,400	
	Outstanding Office & Adm. Expenses A/c	Dr.		1,000	
	To H.O. A/c				3,400

Dr. **H.O.'S ACCOUNT IN THE BOOKS OF BRANCH** Cr.

Particulars	₹	Particulars	₹
To Goods Received A/c		By Balance b/d	1,50,800
(6,40,200 + 11,000)	6,51,200	By Sales	6,40,000
To Office & Adm. Expenses A/c	8,000	By Closing Stock	72,600
To Selling & Distribution Exp. A/c	18,000	By Creditors	2,400
To Depreciation A/c	400	By Outstanding Office &	

To Debtors	92,000	Adm. Expenses	1,000
To Bank	30,000	By Goods received H.O.	11,000
To Fixed Assets	3,600	By Goods-in-transit A/c	11,000
To Prepaid Selling & Dist. Exp.	2,000		
To Closing Stock	72,600		
To Goods-in-transit A/c	11,000		
	8,88,800		8,88,800

(B) BOOKS OF HEAD OFFICE
JOURNAL OF HEAD OFFICE

Date	Particulars		L.F.	Dr. (₹)	Cr. (₹)
(a)	Branch Trading A/c	Dr.		6,51,200	
	To Branch A/c				6,51,200
	(Being the items belonging to Dr. side of Branch Trading A/c incorporated)				
(b)	Branch A/c	Dr.		7,23,600	
	To Branch Trading A/c				7,23,600
	(Being the items belonging to Cr. side of Branch Trading A/c incorporated)				
(c)	Branch Trading A/c	Dr.		72,400	
	To Branch P & L A/c				72,400
	(Being the Gross Profit transferred to P & L A/c)				
(d)	Branch P & L A/c	Dr.		26,400	
	To Branch A/c				26,400
	(Being the item belonging to Dr. side of Branch P & L A/c incorporated)				
(e)	Branch P & L A/c	Dr.		46,000	
	To General P & L A/c				46,000
	(Being Net Profit transferred to General P & L A/c)				
(f)	Branch Debtors	Dr.		92,000	
	Branch Bank	Dr.		30,000	
	Branch Stock	Dr.		72,600	
	Goods-in-transit	Dr.		11,000	
	Branch Fixed Assets	Dr.		3,600	
	Branch Prepaid Selling & Distributiion Exp.	Dr.		2,000	
	To Branch A/c				2,11,200
	(Being the Branch Assets uncorporated)				
(g)	Branch A/c	Dr.		3,400	
	To Branch Creditors A/c				2,400
	To Outstanding Office & Adm. Expenses				1,000
	(Being the Branch Liabilities incorporated)				

(h)	Cash in transit A/c	Dr.	43,750	
	To Branch A/c			43,750
	(Being the adjustment for items-in-transit)			
(i)	Closing Stock A/c	Dr.	3,00,000	
	To Trading A/c			3,00,000
	(Being the closing stock incorporated)			
(j)	Depreciation A/c	Dr.	95,000	
	To Fixed Assets A/c			95,000
	(Being the depreciation on fixed assets provided)			

(C) CONSOLIDATED TRADING AND PROFIT AND LOSS ACCOUNT

Dr. *for the year ending on 31st March, 2016* *Cr.*

Particulars	*H.O.* ₹	*Branch* ₹	*Total* ₹	*Particulars*	*H.O.* ₹	*Branch* ₹	*Total* ₹
To Purchases	19,93,350	—	19,93,350	By Sales	14,20,000	6,40,000	20,60,000
To Mfg Expenses	34,650	—	34,650	By Goods sent to Branch	6,51,200	—	—
To Goods received from H.O.	—	6,51,200	—	By Closing Stock	3,00,000	72,600	3,72,600
To Gross Profit c/d	3,43,200	72,400	4,15,600	By Stock-in-transit	—	11,000	11,000
	23,71,200	7,23,600	24,43,600		23,71,200	7,23,600	24,43,600
To Office & Adm. Expenses	1,12,000	8,000	1,20,000	By Gross Profit b/d	3,43,200	72,400	4,15,600
To selling & Dist. Expenses	1,12,000	18,000	1,30,000				
To Depreciation on fixed Assets	9,500	400	9,900				
To Net Profit	1,09,700	46,000	1,55,700				
	3,43,200	72,400	4,15,600		3,43,200	72,400	4,15,600

CONSOLIDATED BALANCE SHEET OF HEAD OFFICE AND ITS BRANCH

Dr. *as at 31st March, 2016* *Cr.*

Particulars	*H.O.* ₹	*Branch* ₹	*Total* ₹	*Particulars*	*H.O.* ₹	*Branch* ₹	*Total* ₹
Capital	1,95,000	—		Fixed Assets	95,000	4,000	99,000
Add: Net Profit	1,55,700			*Less:* Depreciation	(9,500)	(400)	(9,900)
	3,50,700	—	3,50,700		85,500	3,600	89,100
Creditors	5,83,350	2,400	5,85,750	Stock in hand	3,00,000	72,600	3,72,600
Outstanding Office Expenses	—	1,000	1,000	Stock in transit	—	11,000	11,000
				Debtors	2,30,000	92,000	3,22,000
H.O. A/c	—	2,07,800	—	Cash at bank	67,000	30,000	97,000
				Cash-in-transit	43,750	—	43,750
				Prepaid Selling Exp.	—	2,000	2,000
				Branch A/c	2,07,800	—	—
	9,34,050	2,11,200	9,37,450		9,34,050	2,11,200	9,37,450

ILLUSTRATION 53

Particulars	Dr. (₹)	Cr. (₹)
Opening Stock	6,000	
Purchases	97,800	
Goods received from Head Office	19,000	
Sales		1,38,000
Goods supplied to Head Office		6,000
Salaries	4,500	
Debtors	3,700	
Creditors		1,850
Rent	1,960	
Sundry Office Expenses	1,470	
Cash at Bank	1,780	
Furniture	6,000	
Depreciation on Furniture	400	
H.O.	3,240	
	1,45,850	1,45,850

Stock at branch on 31st March, 2016 was valued at ₹ 7,700, Meerut Branch Account in the head office books on 31st March, 2016 stood at ₹ 460 (debit balance). On 28th March, the head office forwarded goods of the value of ₹ 3,700 to the branch where they were received on 3rd April,

(i) Prepare Trading and Profit & Loss Account of Meerut Branch for the year ending on 31st March 2016 and its Balance Sheet as on that date.

(ii) Pass journal entries in the books of head office to incorporate the above mentioned trial balance.

(iii) Show Meerut Branch Account as it would be closed in head office's ledger.

SOLUTION

(I) TRADING AND PROFIT AND LOSS ACCOUNT OF MEERUT BRANCH
for the year ending on 31st March, 2016

Dr. Cr.

Particulars	₹	Particulars	₹
To Opening Stock	6,000	By Sales	1,38,000
To Purchases	97,800	By Goods supplied to H.O.	6,000
To Goods from H.O.	22,700	By Closing Stock	7,700
To Gross Profit c/d	28,900	By Goods-in-transit	3,700
	1,55,400		1,55,400
To Salaries	4,500	By Gross Profit b/d	28,900
To Rent	1,960		
To Sundry Office Expenses	1,470		
To Depreciation on Furniture	400		
To Net Profit	20,570		
	28,900		28,900

BALANCE SHEET OF MEERUT BRANCH AS AT 31ST MARCH, 2016

Liabilities		₹	*Assets*	₹
Creditors		1,850	Debtors	3,700
H.O. Account:			Cash at Bank	1,780
Profit	20,570		Closing Stock	7,700
Less: Dr. Balance	3,240		Goods-in-transit	3,700
Add: Goods-in-transit	3,700	21,030	Furniture	6,000
		22,880		22,880

(II) JOURNAL OF HEAD OFFICE

Particulars		*L.F.*	*Dr. (₹)*	*Cr. (₹)*
Meerut Branch Trading A/c	Dr.		1,26,500	
To Meerut Branch A/c				1,26,500
(For incorporation of Op. Stock, Purchases & goods from H.O. in Branch Trading A/c)				
Meerut Branch A/c	Dr.		1,55,400	
To Meerut Branch Trading A/c				1,55,400
(For incorporation of Sales & Goods supplied by the H.O. & Cl. Stock in Branch Trading A/c)				
Meerut Branch Trading A/c	Dr.		28,900	
To Meerut Branch Profit & Loss A/c				28,900
(For the transfer of Gross Profit)				
Branch Profit & Loss A/c	Dr.		8,330	
To Meerut Branch A/c				8,330
(For incorporation of the various expenses incurred by the Branch in Branch P & L A/c)				
Meerut Branch Profit & Loss A/c	Dr.		20,570	
To General Profit & Loss A/c				20,570
(For the transfer of Net Profit of Branch)				
Meerut Branch Assets A/c	Dr.		19,180	
To Meerut Branch A/c				19,180
(For incorporation of various Branch Assets)				
Meerut Branch A/c	Dr.		1,850	
To Meerut Branch Creditors A/c				1,850
(For incorporation of Branch Creditors)				
Goods-in-Transit A/c	Dr.		3,700	
To Meerut Branch A/c				3,700
(Beiung goods in transit taken into account)				

Dr. **(III) MEERUT BRANCH ACCOUNT (IN H.O. BOOKS)** Cr.

Particulars		₹	Particulars		₹
To Balance b/d (as given)		460	By Branch Trading A/c:		
To Branch Trading A/c:			Opeining Stock	6,000	
Sales	1,38,000		Purchases	97,800	
Goods to H.O.	6,000		Goods from H.O.	19,000	
Closing Stock	7,700		Goods-in-transit	3,700	1,26,500
Goods-in-transit	3,700	1,55,400	By Branch P & L A/c:		
To Branch Creditors		1,850	Salaries	4,500	
			Rent	1,960	
			Office Expenses	1,470	
			Depreciation	400	8,330
			By Branch Assets:		
			Branch Debtors	3,700	
			Branch Bank	1,780	
			Branch Furniture	6,000	
			Closing Stock	7,700	
			Goods in Transit A/c	3,700	22,880
		1,57,710			1,57,710

ILLUSTRATION 54

Following are the Trial Balances of MG (India) Ltd and its Delhi Branch as on March 31, 2016:

Particulars	Head Office ₹	Delhi Branch ₹	Particulars	Head Office ₹	Delhi Branch ₹
Opening Stock	45,000	16,400	Creditors	20,300	5,400
Purchases	1,10,000	25,600	Goods sent to Branch	14,400	—
Wages	80,800	13,100	Sales	3,30,200	69,900
Manufacturing Exp.	35,400	6,800	Head Office Account	—	28,000
Machinery:			Capital in Shares of ₹ 10 each	2,00,000	—
H.O.	1,00,000	—	Discount earned	1,100	300
Branch	50,000	—	Purchase Returns	2,500	600
Furniture:					
H.O.	5,000	—			
Branch	2,000	—			
Rent	6,000	3,400			
Salaries	32,000	11,000			
Debtors	38,000	8,000			
General Expenses	18,000	4,000			
Goods Received from H.O.	—	14,400			
Cash in hand & bank	10,300	1,500			

Branch Account	36,000	—			
	5,68,500	1,04,200		5,68,500	1,04,200

Closing stock at head office was ₹ 38,700 and at Delhi, ₹ 28,700. Depreciation is to be allowed @ 10% p.a. on machinery and @ 15% p.a on furniture. Rent still payable in respect of 20XI-2016 is ₹ 300 (for Branch).

Required: Prepare the Trading and Profit and Loss Account in columnar form, and the Consolidated Balance Sheet. Also show the Branch Account.

SOLUTION

TRADING AND PROFIT AND LOSS ACCOUNT

Dr. *for the year ended 31 March, 2016* *Cr.*

Particulars	*Head Office* ₹	*Delhi Branch* ₹	*Particulars*	*Head Office* ₹	*Delhi Branch* ₹
To Opening Stock	45,000	16,400	By Goods sent to Branch	14,400	—
To Purchases (Net)	1,07,500	25,000	By Sales	3,30,200	69,900
To Goods sent to Branch	—	14,400	By Stock at the end	38,700	28,700
To Wages	80,800	13,100			
To Manufacturing Exp.	35,400	6,800			
To Gross Profit c/d	1,14,600	22,900			
	3,83,300	98,600		3,83,300	98,600
To Rent Paid and outstanding	6,000	3,700	By Gross Profit b/d	1,14,600	22,900
To Salaries	32,000	11,000	By Discount	1,100	300
To General Expenses	18,000	4,000	By Net Loss	—	800
To depreciation on:					
Machinery	10,000	5,000			
Furniture	750	300			
To Net Profit	48,950	—			
	1,15,700	24,000		1,15,700	24,000

(A) BALANCE SHEET OF THE MG (INDIA) LTD. AS AT 31ST MARCH, 2016

Particulars	*Note No.*	(₹)
I. EQUITY AND LIABILITIES		
(1) Shareholders' Funds		
(a) Share Capital		2,00,000
(b) Reserves and Surplus (48,950 – 800)		48,150
(2) Non-Current Liabilities		
(3) Current Liabilities		
(a) Trade Payables (20,300 + 5,400)		25,700
(b) Other Current Liabilities		300
Total		2,74,150

II. **ASSETS**		
(1) Non-Current Assets		
(a) Fixed Assets		
(i) Tangible Assets (94,250 + 46,700)	1	1,40,950
(2) Current Assets		
(a) Inventories (38,700 + 28,700)		67,400
(b) Trade Receivables (38,000 + 8,000)		46,000
(c) Cash and Cash Equivalents (10,300 + 1,500 + 8,000)		19,800
Total		2,74,150

Notes To Accounts:

Particulars	*Head Office*	*Branch*
1. Tangible Assets		
Plant and Machinery	1,00,000	50,000
Less: Depreciation	(10,000)	(5,000)
Total	90,000	45,000
Furnitures	5,000	2,000
Less: Depreciation	(750)	(300)
	4,250	1,700
Total	94,250	46,700

Dr. **DELHI BRANCH ACCOUNT** Cr.

Particulars	₹	*Particulars*	₹
To Balance b/d	36,000	By Delhi Branch Trading A/c Opening Stock, Purchases	75,700
To Delhi Branch Assets (Depreciation)	5,300	By Delhi Branch Profit and Loss A/c (Expenses)	24,000
To Delhi Branch Trading A/c— Sales and Stock	98,600	By Branch Sundry Assets A/c	46,200
To Delhi Branch P & L A/c (Discount)	300		
To Sundry Branch Liabilities	5,700		
	1,45,900		1,45,900

Note: *The difference of ₹ 8,000 in H.O. account (28,000 Cr.) and Branch Account (36,000 Dr.) is presumed to be on account of cash in transit.*

ILLUSTRATION 55

The Head Office of GM (India) Ltd and its branch keep their own books and prepare own Profit and Loss Account. The following are the balances appearing on the two sets of books as on 31 March 2016 after ascertainment of profits and after making all adjustments except those referred to below:

Particulars	*H.O.*		*Branch*	
	Dr. (₹)	*Cr. (₹)*	*Dr. (₹)*	*Cr. (₹)*
Capital	—	1,00,000	—	—

Fixed Assets	36,000	—	16,000	—
Stock	34,200	—	10,740	—
Debtors and Creditors	7,820	3,960	4,840	1,920
Cash	10,740	—	1,420	—
Profit and Loss Account	—	14,660	—	3,060
Branch Account	29,860	—	—	—
Head Office Account	—	—	—	28,020
	1,18,620	1,18,620	33,000	33,000

Set out the Balance Sheet of the business as on 31st March 2016 and the Journal Entries necessary (in both set of books) to record the adjustment dealing with the following:—

(a) On 31st March, the branch had sent a cheque for ₹ 1,000 to the Head Office, not received by them *nor* credited to the branch till next month.

(b) Goods valued at ₹ 440 had been forwarded by the Head Office to the branch and invoiced on 31st March, but were not received by the branch *nor* dealt with in their books till next month.

(c) It was agreed that the branch should be charged with ₹ 300 for administration service, rendered by the Head Office during the year.

(d) Stock stolen in transit from the Head office to the branch and charged to the branch by the Head Office but not credited to the Head Office in the branch books as the branch manager declined to admit any liabilities, ₹ 400 (not covered by insurance).

(e) Depreciation of branch assets, of which accounts are maintained by the Head Office, not provided for, ₹ 250.

(f) The balance of profit shown by the branch is to be transferred to Head Office books.

SOLUTION

JOURNAL OF HEAD OFFICE

Particulars		*L.F.*	*Dr. (₹)*	*Cr. (₹)*
Cash-in-Transit A/c	Dr.		1,000	
To Branch A/c				1,000
Branch A/c	Dr.		300	
To Profit and Loss A/c				300
Profit & Loss A/c	Dr.		400	
To Branch A/c				400
Branch A/c	Dr.		250	
To Branch Fixed Assets A/c				250
Branch Profit and Loss A/c	Dr.		2,510	
To General Profit & Loss A/c				2,510
Profit and Loss A/c	Dr.		14,560	
To General Profit and Loss A/c				14,560

JOURNAL OF BRANCH

Particulars		*L.F.*	*Dr. (₹)*	*Cr. (₹)*
Goods-in-Transit A/c	Dr.		440	

To Head Office A/c			440
Profit and Loss A/c	Dr.	300	
To Head Office A/c			300
(Head Office expenses & charges)			
Profit and Loss A/c	Dr.	250	
To Head Office A/c			250
(Depreciation on assets)			
Profit and Loss A/c	Dr.	2,510	
To Head Office A/c			2,510

Note: *The profit at Branch and at H.O. is calculated as follows:*

Dr. **H.O. PROFIT AND LOSS ACCOUNT** *Cr.*

Particulars	₹	*Particulars*	₹
To Branch A/c (stock stolen)	400	By Profit (as given)	14,660
To Profit transferred to General Profit and Loss A/c	14,560	By Administrative Expenses charged to Branch	300
	14,960		14,960

Dr. **BRANCH PROFIT AND LOSS ACCOUNT** *Cr.*

Particulars	₹	*Particulars*	₹
To Head Office Expenses	300	By Profit (as given)	3,060
To Depreciation	250		
To Profit t/f to General P&L A/c	2,510		
	3,060		3,060

BALANCE SHEET OF THE GM (INDIA) LTD. AS AT 31ST MARCH, 2016

Particulars	*Note No.*	(₹)
I. EQUITY AND LIABILITIES		
(1) Shareholders' Funds		
(a) Share Capital		1,00,000
(b) Reserves and Surplus (14,560 + 2,510)		17,070
(2) Non-Current Liabilities		
(3) Current Liabilities		
(a) Trade Payables (3,960 + 1,920)		5,880
Total		1,22,950
II. ASSETS		
(1) Non-Current Assets		
(a) Fixed Assets		
(i) Tangible Assets (36,000 + 15,750)	1	51,750
(2) Current Assets		
(a) Inventories (34,200 + 10,740 + 440)		45,380

(b) Trade Receivables (7,820 + 4,840)	12,660
(c) Cash and Cash Equivalents (10,740 + 1,420+ 1,000)	13,160
Total	1,22,950

ILLUSTRATION 56

Raj (India) & Sons a Bombay merchant opens a new branch in Delhi which trades independently of the Head office. The transactions of the branch for the year ended 31.3.2016 are as under:

Particulars	₹	₹
Goods supplied by head office		20,000
Purchases from outsiders:		
Credit	15,500	
Cash	3,000	18,500
Sales:		
Credit	25,000	
Cash	4,600	29,600
Cash received from customers		30,400
Cash paid to creditors		14,200
Expenses paid by branch		8,950
Furniture purchased by branch on credit		3,500
Cash received from head office initially		4,000
Remittances to Head Office		11,000

Prepare the Branch Trading and Profit and Loss Account and the Branch Account in the head office books and Head office Account in the books of Branch, after incorporation of the branch trial balance, taking the following into consideration:

(a) The accounts of the branch fixed assets are maintained in head office books.

(b) Write off depreciation on furniture @ 5% p.a.

(c) A remittance of ₹ 2,000 from the branch to the head office is in transit.

(d) The branch closing stock is valued at ₹ 12,000.

SOLUTION

Dr. **DELHI BRANCH ACCOUNT IN H.O. BOOKS** *Cr.*

Particulars	₹	*Particulars*	₹
To Bank A/c	4,000	By Branch furniture A/c	3,500
To Goods sent to Branch A/c	20,000	By Bank A/c—remittances	9,000
To Branch Furniture A/c — Dep.	175	By Balance c/d	11,675
	24,175		24,175
To Balance b/d	11,675	By Branch Trading A/c	38,500
To Branch Trading A/c	41,600	By Branch P & L A/c (Expenses)	9,125
		By Balance c/d	5,650
	53,275		53,275

BRANCH TRADING AND PROFIT AND LOSS ACCOUNT IN H.O. BOOKS
for the year ended 31st March, 2016

Dr. Cr.

Particulars		₹	Particulars		₹
To Branch Account:			By Branch Account:		
Goods supplied by head office		20,000	Credit sales	25,000	
Credit purchases		15,500	Cash sales	4,600	29,600
Cash purchases		3,000	By Closing stock		12,000
To Branch P & L A/c					
—Gross Profit c/d		3,100			
		41,600			41,600
To Branch Account:			By Branch Trading A/c		
Expenses	8,950		—Gross profit b/d		3,100
Depreciation on furniture	175	9,125	By General P & L A/c		
			—Net loss transferred		6,025
		9,125			9,125

IN THE BOOKS OF THE BRANCH
BOMBAY HEAD OFFICE ACCOUNT

Dr. Cr.

Particulars	₹	Particulars	₹
To Branch Trading A/c	38,500	By Branch Trading A/c	41,600
To Branch P & L A/c	9,125	By Bank A/c	4,000
To Bank A/c—remittances	11,000	By Goods received from head	
To Profit and loss A/c		office A/c	20,000
—Net loss	6,025	By Remittances in transit	2,000
To Supplier of furniture	3,500	By Depreciation A/c	175
To Balance c/d	5,650		
	67,775		67,775

ILLUSTRATION 57

M/s CAS & Sons of Hyderabad have a branch in Delhi. The Delhi branch deals not only in the goods from the head office but also buys some auxiliary goods and deals in them. They, however, do not prepare any profit and loss account but submit all the accounts to the head office at the end of the year and open them afresh on the basis of the advice from their head office. The fixed assets accounts are also maintained at the head office. The goods from the head office are invoiced at selling prices to give a profit of 20% on the sale price. The goods sent from the branch to the head office are at cost. From the following prepare the Branch Account, Branch Trading and Profit and Loss Account and Branch assets accounts in head office books.

TRIAL BALANCE OF DELHI BRANCH
as at 31.3.2016

Dr. Cr.

Particulars	₹	Particulars	₹
Head Office		Sales	1,00,000
(opening balance 1.4.2015)	15,000	Goods to head office	3,000

Goods from head office	50,000	Head office current account	15,000
Purchases	20,000	Sundry creditors	3,000
Opening stock			
(H.O. goods at invoice price)	4,000		
Opening stock of other goods	500		
Salaries	7,000		
Rent	3,000		
Office expenditure	2,000		
Cash on hand	500		
Cash at bank	4,000		
Sundry debtors	15,000		
	1,21,000		1,21,000

The Branch Opening Balances as on 1st April were as under:

Furniture ₹ 5,000; sundry debtors ₹ 9,500; Cash ₹ 1,000; Creditors ₹ 30,000; Stock (H.O. goods at invoice price) ₹ 4,000; Other goods ₹ 500. The Closing Stock at branch of the head office goods at invoice price is ₹ 3,000 and that of purchased goods at cost is ₹ 1,000. Depreciation is to be provided at 10 per cent on branch assets.

SOLUTION

BOOKS OF HEAD OFFICE
BRANCH TRADING AND PROFIT AND LOSS ACCOUNT
Dr. *for the year ending 31st March, 2016* *Cr.*

Particulars		₹	Particulars		₹
To Opening Stock:			By Sales		1,00,000
Head office goods	3,200		By Goods from Branch		3,000
Others	500	3,700	By Closing Stock:		
To Goods sent to Branch		40,000	Head Office goods	2,400	
To Purchases		20,000	Others	1,000	3,400
To Gross profit c/d		42,700			
		1,06,400			1,06,400
To Salaries		7,000	By Gross Profit b/d		42,700
To Rent		3,000			
To Office Expenses		2,000			
To Depreciation on furniture @ 10%		500			
To Net profit		30,200			
		42,700			42,700

Note:

(i) Stock and goods sent to branch are shown at cost as the account is prepared only on memorandum basis.

(ii) For the net profit ascertained on memorandum basis, the following entry will be made:

Branch A/c Dr. ₹ 30,200
To General Profit and Loss A/c ₹ 30,200

(iii) For depreciation on branch furniture the following entry will be made:

Branch A/c	Dr.	500	
To Branch Furniture A/c			₹ 500

Dr. **DELHI BRANCH ACCOUNT** Cr.

Particulars	₹	Particulars			₹
To Goods sent to Branch A/c	50,000	By Balance b/d:			
To Branch Assets A/c		Sundry Creditors		30,000	
(Depreciation)	500	*Less:* Assets:			
To General Profit and Loss A/c		Debtors	9,500		
(Net Profit)	30,200	Cash	1,000		
To Stock Reserve A/c		H.O. goods	4,000		
(on closing stock)	600	Other goods	500	15,000	15,000
		By Stock Reserve A/c			
		(on opening stock)			800
		By Goods sent to Branch A/c			10,000
		By Cash A/c			32,000
		By Goods sent to Branch A/c			3,000
		By Balance c/d:			
		Stock			
		—H.O. Goods		3,000	
		—Others		1,000	
		Debtors		15,000	
		Cash and Bank		4,500	
				23,500	
		Less: Creditors		3,000	20,500
	81,300				81,300

Dr. **DELHI BRANCH FURNITURE ACCOUNT** Cr.

Particulars	₹	Particulars	₹
To Balance b/d	5,000	By Delhi Branch A/c	500
		By Balance c/d	4,500
	5,000		5,000

Dr. **CASH AND BANK ACCOUNT** Cr.

Particulars	₹	Particulars	₹
To Balance b/d	1,000	By Salaries	7,000
To Collection from debtors	94,500	By Rent	3,000
		By Office expenses	2,000
		By Payment to creditors	47,000
		By Head Office remittance (b.f.)	32,000

		By Balance c/d:		
		Cash	500	
		Bank	4,000	4,500
	95,500			95,500

Dr. **DELHI BRANCH TOTAL DEBTORS ACCOUNT** Cr.

Particulars	₹	Particulars	₹
To Balance b/d	9,500	By Cash A/c (balancing figure)	94,500
To Sales	1,00,000	By Balance c/d	15,000
	1,09,500		1,09,500

Dr. **DELHI BRANCH TOTAL CREDITORS ACCOUNT** Cr.

Particulars	₹	Particulars	₹
To Cash A/c	47,000	By Balance b/d	30,000
To Balance c/d	3,000	By Purchases	20,000
	50,000		50,000

Note:

(i) All sales and all purchases are assumed to be on credit.

(ii) Since the head office account is ₹ 15,000 debit as shown in the branch trial balance, the branch balance must be ₹ 15,000 credit. This is also confirmed as the branch liabilities minus branch assets equal ₹ 15,000 credit.

(iii) Head office current account should not be confused with head office account. The current account is the result of current year's transactions between the head office and branch as shown below:

Dr. **HEAD OFFICE CURRENT ACCOUNT** Cr.

Particulars	₹	Particulars	₹
To Goods sent to Head office A/c	3,000	By Goods from Head Office A/c	50,000
To Bank A/c (remittance)	32,000		
To Balance c/d	15,000		
	50,000		50,000

As the items influencing the current account are adjusted in the branch account, the current account itself has been left out.

ILLUSTRATION 58

Ghalib (India) Ltd having Head Office in Bombay has Branch at Madras where a complete set of books is maintained. All purchses are made at Bombay and stock required by the Branch is invoiced to it by the Head office at selling price *less* 15 per cent. The Branch Manager is entitled to a commission equal to one-third of the net profit earned by the Branch on the basis of invoice price. The following are the respective Trial Balances of the Head Office and the Branch as on 31st March, 2016:

Particulars	H.O.		Branch	
	Dr. (₹)	Cr. (₹)	Dr. (₹)	Cr. (₹)
Capital		94,200		

Sundry Debtors and Sundry Creditors	89,700	24,600	7,550	6,150
Stock at the beginning of year at cost:				
Head Office	1,24,150			
Branch	32,150			
Stock at Branch at the beginning of year as invoiced		36,270	36,270	
Purchases	3,07,250			
Goods invoiced during the year		1,02,500	1,02,500	
Salaries	35,280		14,680	
Sundry Expenses	16,170		2,290	
Branch Account	23,230			
Head Office Account			5,800	
Cash on hand and at Bank	24,800		3,260	
Furniture	15,000		2,000	
Sales		4,10,160		1,68,200
	6,67,730	6,67,730	1,74,350	1,74,350

The cost price of goods invoiced to Madras was ₹ 81,900. The stock in hand at the end of the year at Bombay was valued at ₹ 45,270 at cost and at Madras ₹ 14,160 at cost and ₹ 17,660 at invoice price. The difference between the adjustment account is due to a remittance in transit from the Branch to the Head Office.

Required: Prepare the Trading and Profit and Loss Account for the year ending on 31st March, 2016 (in columnar form) and the consolidated Balance Sheet as at that date.

SOLUTION

TRADING AND PROFIT AND LOSS ACCOUNT

Dr. *for the year ending on 31st March, 2016* Cr.

Particulars	*H.O.* ₹	*Branch* ₹	*Particulars*	*H.O.* ₹	*Branch* ₹
To Opening Stock	1,24,150	32,150	By Sales	4,10,160	1,68,200
To Purchases	3,07,250	—	By Goods Sent to Branch	81,900	—
To Goods Received from Head Office	—	81,900	By Closing Stock	45,270	14,160
To Gross Profit c/d	1,05,930	68,310			
	5,37,330	1,82,360		5,37,330	1,82,360
To Salaries	35,280	14,680	By Gross Profit b/d	1,05,930	68,310
To Sundry Expenses	16,170	2,290			
To Branch Manager's Commission Outstanding	—	10,040			
To Net Profit	54,480	41,300			
	1,05,930	68,310		1,05,930	68,310

BALANCE SHEET OF THE GHALIB (INDIA) LTD. AS AT 31ST MARCH, 2016

Particulars	*Note No.*	*(₹)*
I. EQUITY AND LIABILITIES		
(1) Shareholders' Funds		
(a) Share Capital		94,200
(b) Reserves and Surplus (54,480 + 41,300)		95,780
(2) Non-Current Liabilities		
(3) Current Liabilities		
(a) Trade Payables (24,600 + 6,150)		30,750
(b) Other Current Liabilities		10,040
Total		2,30,770
II. ASSETS		
(1) Non-Current Assets		
(a) Fixed Assets		
(i) Tangible Assets (15,000 + 2,000)	1	17,000
(2) Current Assets		
(a) Inventories (45,270 + 14,160)		59,430
(b) Trade Receivables (89,700 + 7,550)		97,250
(c) Cash and Cash Equivalents (24,800 + 3,260 + 23,230 + 5,800)		57,090
Total		2,30,770

Working Note: *Calculation of Manager's Commission*

MEMORANDUM MADRAS BRANCH TRADING AND PROFIT AND LOSS ACCOUNT

(Invoice value)

Dr. *Cr.*

Particulars	₹	*Particulars*	₹
To Opening Stock	36,270	By Sales	1,68,200
To Goods Received from Head Office	1,02,500	By Closing Stock	17,660
To Gross Profit c/d	47,090		
	1,85,860		1,85,860
To Salaries	14,680	By Gross Profit b/d	47,090
To Sundry Expenses	2,290		
To Manager's Commission— 1/3 of ₹ 30,120 i.e. (₹ 47,090 – ₹ 14,680 – ₹ 2,290)	10,040		
To Net Profit	20,080		
	47,090		47,090

ILLUSTRATION 59

CAS Bros. of Calcutta has a branch at Delhi. Goods sold at Delhi are supplied from Calcutta but no charges is made in the books as between the branch and the Head Office. On 31st March, 2016 the Branch Balance Sheet, after closing the books, was as follows:—

Liabilities	₹	*Assets*	₹
Sundry Creditors	40,000	Sundry Debtors	2,00,000
Head Office Account	1,68,000	Building Extension A/c—	
		transferred to H.O. A/c	
		Cash at Bank	8,000
	2,08,000		2,08,000

For the six months ending with Sept., 2016, the following transactions took place at Delhi Branch:

Particulars	₹
Sales	12,30,000
Purchases	5,48,000
Wages paid	1,20,000
Salaries (inclusive of ₹ 2,000 paid in advance to a clerk)	1,44,000
General Expenses	8,600
Fire Insurance Premium paid for one year ending on 31st March, 2017	9,200
Manager's Salary for 7 months ending on 31st October, 2016	40,600
Cash collection from debtors	11,30,000
Discounts allowed	28,000
Discounts earned	11,200
Cash paid to creditors	5,50,000
Cash sent to Bank	80,000
Building Account (further payment to contractors)	1,04,000
Cash in Hand	1,600
Cash at Bank	21,600

Required: Give the closing journal entries, Head Office Account and Balance Sheet in the books of Branch as on 30th September 2016.

SOLUTION

JOURNAL OF DELHI BRANCH

Particulars		*L.F.*	*Dr. (₹)*	*Cr. (₹)*
Prepaid Salaries	Dr.		7,800	
To General Salaries				2,000
To Manager's Salary A/c				5,800
(Being the adjustment made for Prepaid Salaries)				
Prepaid Fire Insurance Premium	Dr.		4,600	
To Fire Insurance Premium A/c				4,600
(Being the adjustment made for prepaid insurance)				

Head Office A/c	Dr.	1,04,000	
To Building A/c			1,04,000
(The transfer of payment for construction of Building to Head Office.)			
Head Office A/c	Dr.	8,86,000	
To Purchases A/c			5,48,000
To Wages A/c			1,20,000
To Salaries A/c			1,42,000
To General Expenses A/c			8,600
To Fire Insurance Premium A/c			4,600
To Manager's Salary A/c			34,800
To Discount Allowed A/c			28,000
(The debit balance of revenue items transferred to Head Office A/c—prepaid salaries and insurance premium have not been t/f.)			
Sales A/c	Dr.	12,30,000	
Discount Earned A/c	Dr.	11,200	
To Head Office A/c			12,41,200
(The transfer of credit balances of revenue items to Head Office Account.)			
Bank A/c	Dr.	80,000	
To Cash A/c			80,000
(Being the cash deposited into Bank)			

Dr. **HEAD OFFICE ACCOUNT** *Cr.*

Particulars	₹	*Particulars*	₹
To Cash/Bank		By Balance b/d	1,68,000
(remittances as per cash book)	1,38,400	By Sales A/c	12,30,000
To Building A/c	1,04,000	By Discount Earned A/c	11,200
To Purchases A/c	5,48,000		
To Wages A/c	1,20,000		
To Salaries A/c	1,42,000		
To General Expenses A/c	8,600		
To Fire Insurance Premium A/c	4,600		
To Manager's Salary A/c	34,800		
To Discount Allowed A/c	28,000		
To Balance c/d	2,80,800		
	14,09,200		14,09,200

BALANCE SHEET OF DELHI BRANCH AS ON 30TH SEPTEMBER, 2016

Liabilities	₹	*Assets*	₹
Sundry Creditors	26,800	Sundry Debtors	2,72,000

Head Office	2,80,800	Prepaid Insurance		4,600
		Salaries paid in Advance—		
		Manager	5,800	
		General	2,000	7,800
		Cash at bank		21,600
		Cash in hand		1,600
	3,07,600			3,07,600

Working Notes:

Dr. **(I) CASH BOOK** *Cr.*

Particulars	₹	*Particulars*		₹
To Balance b/d	8,000	By Wages		1,20,000
To Sundry Debtors—		By Salaries		1,44,000
cash collected	11,30,000	By General Expenses		8,600
To Cash (C)	80,000	By Fire Insurance		9,200
		By Manager's Salary		40,600
		By Sundry Creditors		5,50,000
		By Bank (C)		80,000
		By Building A/c		1,04,000
		By Remittances to H.O. (b.f.)		1,38,400
		By Balance c/d:		
		In Hand	1,600	
		At Bank	21,600	23,200
	12,18,000			12,18,000

Dr. **(II) SUNDRY DEBTORS ACCOUNT** *Cr.*

Particulars	₹	*Particulars*	₹
To Balance b/d	2,00,000	By Cash	11,30,000
To Sales	12,30,000	By Discount Allowed	28,000
		By Balance c/d	2,72,000
	14,30,000		14,30,000

(III) SUNDRY CREDITORS ACCOUNTS

Particulars	₹	*Particulars*	₹
To Cash A/c	5,50,000	By Balance b/d	40,000
To Discounts Earned	11,200	By Purchases	5,48,000
To Balance c/d	26,800		
	5,88,000		5,88,000

SOLVED PROBLEMS

PROBLEM 1

TUSHAR Ltd. with its Head Office in Delhi invoices goods to its Branches at Mumbai and Kolkata at 20% *less* than the catalogue price which is cost *plus* 50% with instructions that cash sales are to be made at invoice price and credit sales at catalogue price *less* discount at 15% on prompt payments. Provision is to be made for discount to be allowed to debtors, at year end on the basis of year's trend of prompt payments. All branch expenses are paid by the Head Office and all branch collections are remitted daily to Head Office.

1. Opening Stock At Branch at its cost ₹ 12,000.
2. Opening Branch Debtors ₹ 10,000.
3. Goods Sent to branch (at cost to H.O.) ₹ 1,10,000.
4. Goods received by Branch till close of the year ₹ 1,27,000.
5. Transfer from Kolkata branch to Mumbai branch at catalogue price ₹ 75,000.
6. Transfer to Kolkata branch from Mumbai branch at catalogue price ₹ 30,000.
7. Goods purchased by Mumbai branch from local suppliers (cost) ₹ 30,000. Closing stock in hand at branch out of local purchases (cost) ₹ 6,000.
8. Cash Sales ₹ 74,800.
9. Credit Sales ₹ 1,45,000.
10. Goods returned by Credit Customers to branch ₹ 30,000.
11. Goods returned by Credit Customers directly to H.O. ₹ 15,000.
12. Goods returned by Branch to H.O. ₹ 24,000.
13. Cash remitted by Credit Customers directly to Branch ₹ 45,635.
14. Cash remitted by Credit Customers directly to H.O. ₹ 40,000.
15. Discount Allowed to Debtors ₹ 13,365.
16. Loss of Goods by fire (at invoice price) ₹ 3,000 against which 80% of cost was recovered from the insurance Company.
17. Loss of goods at Branch through normal pilferage (at catalogue price) ₹ 3,000.
18. Branch Expenses: Paid ₹ 9,000, Outstanding ₹ 741.
19. Branch Manager is entitled to a commission @ 6% of net profits after charging such commission.

Required: (a) Prepare Mumbai Branch Stock Account, Mumbai Branch adjustment A/c, Mumbai Branch Expenses A/c and Mumbai Branch Profit & Loss A/c and Mubmai Branch Debtors A/c under Stock & Debtors Method. (b) Prepare Mumbai Branch Account under Debtors Method.

SOLUTION(A)

COST PRICE STRUCTURE

Particulars	₹
A. Cost Price	100
B. *Add:* Profit	20
C. Invoice Price (A + B)	120
D. *Add:* Extra Profit	30
E. Catalogue Price (C + D)	150

Dr. **MUMBAI BRANCH STOCK ACCOUNT** Cr.

Particulars	₹	Particulars	₹
To Balance b/d	12,000	By Goods sent to Branch A/c [₹ 30,000 × 120/150]	24,000
To Goods sent to Branch A/c [₹ 1,10,000 + 20%]	1,32,000	By Branch Cash A/c (Cash Sales)	74,800
To Goods sent to Branch A/c [₹ 75,000 × 120/150]	60,000	By Branch Debtors A/c (Credit Sales)	1,45,000
To Branch Debtors A/c (Returns)	30,000	By Goods sent to Branch A/c (Returns)	24,000
To Branch Debtors A/c (Returns)	15,000	By Goods sent to Branch A/c (Returns) [₹ 15,000 × 120/150]	12,000
To Branch Cash A/c [local purchases]	30,000	By Branch Adjustment A/c (Load)	500
To Branch Adjustment A/c [Load on local purchases]	6,000	By Branch Profit and Loss A/c (Stock destroyed by fire)	2,500
To Branch Adjustment A/c (Excess of catalogue price of Net Credit Sales over invoice price) (₹ 1,45,000 – ₹ 30,000 – 15,000) × 30/150]	20,000	By Branch Adjustment A/c [Invoice Price of Normal Loss] [₹ 3,000 × 120/150]	2,400
		By Balance c/d:	7,200
		Stock out of local purchases Stock in transit from H.O. [₹1,32,000 – ₹1,27,000]	5,000
		Stock in hand from H.O.(B. f.)	7,600
	3,05,000		3,05,000

Dr. **MUMBAI BRANCH ADJUSTMENT ACCOUNT** *Cr.*

Particulars	₹	Particulars	₹
To Stock Reserve A/c [₹ 19,800 × 20/120]	3,300	By Stock Reserve A/c [₹ 12,000 × 20/120]	2,000
To Branch Stock A/c [load on abnormal Loss]	500	By Branch Stock A/c [Loading on local purchases]	6,000
To Branch Stock A/c [Invoice Price of Normal Loss]	2,400	By Branch Stock A/c (Excess of catalogue price of Net Credit Sales over invoice price)	20,000
To Branch Profit and Loss A/c (Gross profit)	43,800	By Goods sent to Branch A/c ; [Load on Net Goods sent] [₹ 1,32,000 + ₹ 60,000 – ₹ 24,000 – ₹24,000 – 12,000] [₹ 1,32,000 × 20/120]	22,000
	50,000		50,000

Dr. **MUMBAI BRANCH EXPENSES ACCOUNT** Cr.

Particulars	₹	Particulars	₹
To Branch Cash A/c	9,741	By Branch Profit & Loss A/c	23,106
To Discount Allowed A/c	13,365		
	23,106		23,106

Dr. **MUMBAI BRANCH PROFIT AND LOSS ACCOUNT** Cr.

Particulars	₹	Particulars	₹
To Branch Expenses A/c	23,106	By Branch Adjustment A/c (Gross Profit)	43,800
To Branch Stock A/c (Cost of Loss by fire)	2,500	By Insurance Claim	2000
To Provision for Discount A/c	1,485		
To Manager's Commission	1,059		
To General Profit and Loss A/c [₹ 18,709 × 6/106]	17,650		
	45,800		45,800

Dr. **MUMBAI BRANCH DEBTORS ACCOUNT** Cr.

Particulars	₹	Particulars	₹
To Balance b/d	10,000	By Branch Stock A/c	30,000
To Branch Stock A/c (Credit Sales)	1,45,000	By Goods sent to Branch A/c	15,000
		By Branch Cash/Bank A/c	45,635
		By Cash/Bank A/c	40,000
		By Discount Allowed A/c	13,365
		By Balance c/d (b.f.)	**11,000**
	1,55,000		1,55,000

Working Note: *Computation of Provision for discount*

(a) Prompt paying debtors who availed of discount = ₹ 13,365 × 100/15 = 89,100

(b) Total debtors who made payment during the year = ₹ 13,365 + 85,635 = ₹ 99,000

(c) Proportion of prompt payers to those who made payment = (89,100/99,000) × 100 = 90%

(d) Likely Prompt paying debtors included in closing Debtors = 90% of ₹ 11,000 = ₹ 9,900

(e) Provision for discount on the closing balance = 15% of ₹ 9,900 = ₹ 1,485

SOLUTION(B)

Dr. **MUMBAI BRANCH ACCOUNT UNDER DEBTORS METHOD** Cr.

Particulars	₹	Particulars	₹
To Balance b/d:		By Goods sent to Branch A/c [₹ 30,000 × 120/150]	24,000
Opening Stock	12,000		
Opening Debtors	10,000		

	₹		₹
To Goods sent to Branch A/c [₹ 1,10,000 + 20%]	1,32,000	By Cash/Bank A/c(Remmitance) [₹ 74,800 + ₹ 45,635 + ₹ 40,000 + ₹ 2,000 – ₹ 30,000]	1,32,435
To Goods sent to Branch A/c [₹ 75,000 × 120/150]	60,000	By Goods sent to Branch A/c (Returns)	24,000
To Stock Reserve A/c [₹ 19,800 × 20/120]	3,300	By Goods sent to Branch A/c (Returns) [₹ 15,000 × 120/150]	12,000
To Cash/Bank A/c(Remmitance)	9,000	By Stock Reserve A/c [₹ 12,000 × 20/120]	2,000
To Balance c/d:		By Goods sent to Branch A/c	22,000
Provision for Discount A/c	1,485	[Load on Net Goods sent]	
Manager's Commission [₹ 18,709 × 6/106]	1,059	[₹ 1,32,000 + ₹ 60,000 – ₹ 24,000 – ₹ 24,000 – 12,000] × 20/120	
Outstanding Expenses	741		
To General Profit and Loss A/c	17,650	By Balance c/d:	
		Stock out of local purchases	7,200
		Stock in transit from H.O. [₹ 1,32,000 – ₹ 1,27,000]	5,000
		Stock in hand from H.O.(B. f.)	7,600
		Debtors	11,000
	2,47,235		2,47,235

Working Notes:

1. COST PRICE STRUCTURE

Particulars	₹
A. Cost Price	100
B. *Add:* Profit	20
C. Invoice Price (A + B)	120
D. *Add:* Extra Profit	30
E. Catalogue Price (C + D)	150

Dr. **2. MUMBAI BRANCH STOCK ACCOUNT** **Cr.**

Particulars	₹	*Particulars*	₹
To Balance b/d	12,000	By Goods sent to Branch A/c [₹ 30,000 × 120/150]	24,000
To Goods sent to Branch A/c [₹ 1,10,000 + 20%]	1,32,000	By Branch Cash A/c (Cash Sales)	74,800
To Goods sent to Branch A/c [₹ 75,000 × 120/150]	60,000	By Branch Debtors A/c (Credit Sales)	1,45,000
To Branch Debtors A/c (Returns)	30,000	By Goods sent to Branch A/c (Returns)	24,000
To Branch Debtors A/c (Returns)	15,000	By Goods sent to Branch A/c (Returns) [₹ 15,000 × 120/150]	12,000
To Branch Cash A/c [local purchases]	30,000	By Branch Abnormal Loss A/c (Stock destroyed by fire)	3,000

To Load on local purchases	6,000	By Normal Loss	2,400
To Excess of catalogue price of Net Credit Sales over invoice price (₹ 1,45,000 – ₹ 30,000 – 15,000) × 30/150]	20,000	By Balance c/d: Stock out of local purchases	7,200
		Stock in transit from H.O. [₹1,32,000 – ₹1,27,000]	5,000
		Stock in hand from H.O.(B. f.)	7,600
	3,05,000		3,05,000

Dr. **3. MUMBAI BRANCH DEBTORS ACCOUNT** *Cr.*

Particulars	₹	*Particulars*	₹
To Balance b/d	10,000	By Branch Stock A/c	30,000
To Branch Stock A/c (Credit Sales)	1,45,000	By Goods sent to Branch A/c	15,000
		By Branch Cash/Bank A/c	45,635
		By Cash/Bank A/c	40,000
		By Discount Allowed A/c	13,365
		By Balance c/d (b.f.)	**11,000**
	1,55,000		1,55,000

4. COMPUTATION OF PROVISION FOR DISCOUNT

A. Prompt paying debtors who availed of discount [₹ 13,365 × 100/15]	₹ 89,100
B. Total debtors who made payment during the year [₹ 13,365 + 85,635]	₹ 99,000
C. Proportion of prompt payers to those who made payment [(89,100/99,000) × 100]	90%
D. Likely Prompt paying debtors included in closing Debtors [90% of ₹ 11,000]	₹ 9,900
E. Provision for discount on the closing balance [15% of ₹ 9,900]	₹ 1,485

PROBLEM 2

Journalise the following transactions in the books of Head Office & Branches of Tulsian Ltd.:

1. Head office purchased a furniture costing ₹ 20,000 for Delhi branch which also purchased furniture for ₹ 5,000. Depreciate furniture by 10%. Fixed assets accounts of Delhi branch are maintained by Head Office.
2. Head office purchased a furniture costing ₹ 10,000 for Agra branch which also purchased furniture for ₹ 2,500. Depreciate furniture by 10%. Fixed assets accounts are maintained by Agra Branch itself.
3. It was agreed that the Delhi Branch and Agra Branch should be charged with ₹ 300 & ₹ 200 respectively for administration service, rendered by the Head Office during the year.
4. Goods worth ₹ 5,000 are supplied by Delhi Branch to Agra Branch.
5. Delhi Branch draws a bill receivable for ₹ 4,000 on Agra Branch which sends its acceptance.
6. Delhi Branch received ₹ 1,000 from Agra Branch.
7. Goods worth ₹ 2,000 were returned by a customer of Agra Branch to Delhi Branch.
8. Agra Branch collected ₹ 2,000 from a customer of Delhi Branch.
9. On 31st March, Delhi branch had sent a cheque for ₹ 1,000 to the Head Office, not received by them *nor* credited to the branch till next month.

10. Goods valued at ₹ 440 had been forwarded by the H. O. to Delhi branch and invoiced on 31st March, but were not received by the branch *nor* dealt with in their books till April.
11. Stock stolen in transit from the Head office to the Delhi branch and charged to the branch by the Head Office but not credited to the Head Office in the branch books as the branch manager declined to admit any liabilities, ₹ 400 (not covered by insurance).
12. The profit(₹ 2,510) shown by Delhi branch is to be transferred to Head Office books.

SOLUTION

(I) JOURNAL OF HEAD OFFICE

Date	Particulars		L.F.	Dr. (₹)	Cr. (₹)
1(a)	Delhi Branch Furniture A/c	Dr.		20,000	
	To Cash A/c				20,000
	(Being the Furniture purchased for Branch)				
1(b)	Delhi Branch Furniture A/c	Dr.		5,000	
	To Delhi Branch A/c				5,000
	(Being the Furniture purchased by Branch)				
1(c)	Delhi Branch A/c	Dr.		2,500	
	To Delhi Branch Furniture A/c				2,500
	(Being the depreciation provided)				
2(a)	Agra Branch A/c	Dr.		10,000	
	To Cash A/c				10,000
	(Being Furniture purchased for Branch)				
3	Delhi Branch A/c	Dr.		300	
	Agra Branch A/c	Dr.		200	
	To H.O. Adm. Exp./Profit and Loss A/c				500
4	Agra Branch A/c	Dr.		5,000	
	To Delhi Branch A/c				5,000
	(Being the goods supplied by Delhi Branch to Agra Branch)				
5	Delhi Branch A/c	Dr.		4,000	
	To Agra Branch A/c				4,000
	(Being a B/R drawn by Delhi upon Agra Branch)				
6	Delhi Branch A/c	Dr.		1,000	
	To Agra Branch A/c				1,000
	(Being cash sent by Agra Branch to Delhi Branch)				
7	Delhi Branch A/c	Dr.		2,000	
	To Agra Branch A/c				2,000
	(Being the goods returned by customer of Agra Branch to Delhi Branch)				
8	Agra Branch A/c	Dr.		2,000	
	To Delhi Branch A/c				2,000

	(Being the cash collected by Agra Branch from a customer of Delhi Branch)			
9	Cash in Transit A/c Dr. To Delhi Branch A/c		1,000	 1,000
10	Profit & Loss A/c Dr. To Delhi Branch A/c		400	 400
11	Delhi Branch Profit and Loss A/c Dr. To General Profit & Loss A/c (Being the t/f of Delhi Branch Profit)		2,510	 2,510

(II) JOURNAL OF DELHI BRANCH

Date	*Particulars*	*L.F.*	*Dr. (₹)*	*Cr. (₹)*
1(b)	Head Office A/c Dr. To Cash A/c (Being Furniture Purchased)		5,000	 5,000
1(c)	Depreciation A/c Dr. To H.O. A/c (Being the depreciation provided)		2,500	 2,500
3	H.O. Adm. Exp./Profit and Loss A/c Dr. To Head Office A/c (Head Office expenses & charges)		300	 300
4	H.O. A/c Dr. To Goods sent to Branch A/c (Being the goods supplied to Agra Branch)		5,000	 5,000
5	Bills Receivable A/c Dr. To H.O. A/c (Being the acceptance of a B/R received from Agra Branch)		4,000	 4,000
6	Cash A/c Dr. To H.O. A/c (Being the cash received from Agra Branch)		1,000	 1,000
7	Goods Sent to Branch A/c Dr. To H.O. A/c (Being the goods received from a customer of Agra Branch)		2,000	 2,000
8	H.O. A/c Dr. To Debtors A/c (Being the cash collected by Agra Branch from our customer)		2,000	 2,000
10	Goods-in-Transit A/c Dr. To Head Office A/c		440	 440
12	Profit & Loss A/c Dr. To Head Office A/c (Being the t/f of Branch Profit)		2,510	 2,510

(III) JOURNAL OF AGRA BRANCH

Date	Particulars		L.F.	Dr. (₹)	Cr. (₹)
2(a)	Furniture A/c	Dr.		10,000	
	To H.O. A/c				10,000
	(Being Plant purchased by H.O.)				
2(b)	Furniture A/c	Dr.		2,500	
	To Cash A/c				2,500
	(Being Furniture Purchased)				
2(c)	Depreciation A/c	Dr.		1,250	
	To Furniture A/c				1,250
	(Being the depreciation provided)				
3	H.O. Adm. Exp./Profit & Loss A/c	Dr.		200	
	To Head Office A/c				200
	(Being the Head Office expenses & charges)				
4	Goods sent to Branch A/c	Dr.		5,000	
	To H.O. A/c				5,000
	(Being the goods received from Delhi Branch)				
5	H.O. A/c	Dr.		4,000	
	To Bill Payable A/c				4,000
	(Being a B/P accepted for Delhi Branch)				
6	H.O. A/c	Dr.		1,000	
	To Cash A/c				1,000
	(Being cash paid to Delhi Branch)				
7	H.O. A/c	Dr.		2,000	
	To Debtors A/c				2,000
	(Being the goods returned by our customer to Delhi Branch)				
8	Cash A/c	Dr.		2,000	
	To H.O. A/c				2,000
	(Being the cash received from a customer of Delhi Branch)				

PROBLEM 3

Give Journal Entries in the books of Branch A to rectify *or* adjust the following:

(i) Head Office expenses ₹ 1,35,000 allocated to the Branch, but not recorded in the Branch Books.

(ii) Depreciation of branch assests, whose accounts are kept by the Head Office not provided earlier for ₹ 1,15,000.

(iii) Branch paid ₹ 1,40,000 as salary to a H.O. Inspector, but the amount paid has been debited by the Branch to Salaries account.

(iv) H.O. collected ₹ 1,30,000 directly from a customer on behalf of the Branch, but no intimation to this effect has been received by the Branch.

(v) A remittance of ₹ 1,50,000 sent by the Branch has not yet been received by the Head Office.

(vi) Branch A incurred advertisement expenses of ₹ 30,000 on behalf of Branch of B.

(vii) Goods sent to Branch ₹ 12,000 stolen during transit. Branch manager refused to accept any liability.

(viii) On 28th March, 2015, the H.O. dispatched goods to the Branch invoiced at ₹ 25,000 which was not received by Branch till 31st March, 2015.

(ix) Head Office made payment of ₹ 25,000 for purchase of goods by Branch and wrongly debited its own Purchase Account.

SOLUTION

JOURNAL OF BRANCH A

Date	*Particulars*	*L.F.*	*Dr. (₹)*	*Cr. (₹)*
(i)	H.O. Expenses A/c Dr. To Head Office A/c (Being the allocated expenditure by the head office recorded in branch books)		1,35,000	 1,35,000
(ii)	Depreciation A/c Dr. To Head Office A/c (Being the depreciation provided)		1,15,000	 1,15,000
(iii)	Head Office A/c Dr. To Salaries A/c (Being the rectification of salary paid on behalf of H.O.)		1,40,000	 1,40,000
(iv)	Head Office A/c Dr. To Debtors A/c (Being the adjustment of collection from branch debtors)		1,30,000	 1,30,000
(v)	No entry in branch books but Cash-in-transit will be shown in H.O. Books			
(vi)	Head Office A/c Dr. To Cash A/c (Being the expenditure on account of Branch B, recorded in books)		30,000	 30,000
(vii)	Loss in transit A/c Dr. To Purchases A/c (Being the Goods lost on account of theft during transit)		12,000	 12,000
(viii)	No entry in the books of head office for goods sent to branch not received by branch till 31st March			
(ix)	Branch A/c Dr. To Purchases A/c (Being rectification of entry for payment for goods purchased by branch wrongly debited to Purchase A/c)		25,000	 25,000

PROBLEM 4

Head Office passes adjustment entry at the end of each month to adjust the position arising out of inter-branch transactions during the month. From the following inter-branch transactions in January, 2016 make the entry in the books of Head Office:

(a) Bombay Branch
   (1) Received Goods: ₹ 6,000 from Calcutta Branch, ₹ 4,000 from Patna Branch.
   (2) Sent Goods to: ₹ 10,000 to Patna, ₹ 8,000 to Calcutta.
   (3) Received B/R: ₹ 6,000 from Patna.
   (4) Sent Acceptance: ₹ 4,000 to Calcutta, ₹ 2,000 to Patna.

(b) Madras Branch (Apart from the above)
   (5) Received Goods: ₹ 10,000 from Calcutta, ₹ 4,000 from Bombay.
   (6) Cash Sent: ₹ 2,000 to Calcutta, ₹ 6,000 to Bombay.

(c) Calcutta Branch (Apart from the above)
   (7) Sent Goods to Patna: ₹ 6,000.
   (8) Paid B/P: ₹ 4,000 to Patna, ₹ 4,000 cash to Patna.

SOLUTION

IN THE BOOKS OF HEAD OFFICE
JOURNAL

Date	*Particulars*		*L.F.*	*Dr. (₹)*	*Cr. (₹)*
2016					
Jan. 31	Madras Branch A/c	Dr.		6,000	
	Patna Branch A/c	Dr.		16,000	
	To Bombay Branch A/c				6,000
	To Calcutta Branch A/c				16,000
	(Being adjustment entry passed by head office in respect of inter-branch transactions during the month.)				

Working Note:

Particulars	*Inter-branch transactions*			
	Bombay ₹	*Madras* ₹	*Calcutta* ₹	*Patna* ₹
(a) *Bombay Branch*				
(1) Received Goods	10,000 (Dr.)		6,000 (Cr.)	4,000 (Cr.)
(2) Sent Goods	18,000 (Cr.)		8,000 (Dr.)	10,000 (Dr.)
(3) Received B/R	6,000 (Dr.)			6,000 (Cr.)
(4) Sent Acceptance	6,000 (Cr.)		4,000 (Dr.)	2,000 (Dr.)
(b) *Madras Branch*				
(5) Received Goods	4,000 (Cr.)	14,000 (Dr.)	10,000 (Cr.)	
(6) Cash Sent	6,000 (Dr.)	8,000 (Cr.)	2,000 (Dr.)	
(c) *Calcutta Branch*				
(7) Sent Goods			6,000 (Cr.)	6,000 (Dr.)
(8) Paid B/P and Cash			8,000 (Cr.)	8,000 (Dr.)
	6,000 (Cr.)	6,000 (Dr.)	16,000 (Cr.)	16,000 (Dr.)

PROBLEM 5

A Limited has retail branch at Noida. Goods are sold to customers at cost *plus* 100%. The wholesale price is cost *plus* 80%. Goods are invoiced to Noida at wholesale price. From the following particulars, find out the profit made by the Head Office and Noida Branch for the year ended 31st March, 2016 using invoice method.

Particulars	Head Office ₹	Noida ₹
Stock on April I 2015	50,000	—
Purchases	3,00,000	—
Goods sent to branch (at invoice value)	1,08,000	—
Sales	3,06,000	1,00,000
Expenses	90,000	4,000

Sales at Head Office are made only on wholesale basis and sales at branch are made only to customers. Stock at branch is valued at invoice price.

SOLUTION

TRADING ACCOUNT FOR THE YEAR ENDED 31ST MARCH, 2016

Particulars	*HO* ₹	*Branch* ₹	*Particulars*	*HO* ₹	*Branch* ₹
To Opening Stock	50,000	—	By Sales	3,06,000	1,00,000
To Purchases	3,00,000	—	By Goods sent to Branch	1,08,000	—
To Goods received from Head Office	—	1,08,000	By Closing Stock	1,20,000	18,000
To Gross Profit	1,84,000	10,000			
	5,34,000	1,18,000		5,34,000	1,18,000

Dr. **PROFIT AND LOSS A/C FOR THE YEAR ENDED 31ST MARCH, 2016** *Cr.*

Particulars	₹	₹	*Particulars*	₹	₹
To Expenses	90,000	4,000	By Gross Profit	1,84,000	10,000
To Stock Reserve against Branch [18,000 × 80/180]	8 000	—			
To Net Profit	86,000	6,000			
	184,000	10,000		184,000	10,000

Working Note:

CALCULATION OF CLOSING STOCK

Particulars	*Head Office* ₹	*Noida Branch* ₹
Opening Stock	50,000	—
Goods purchased *or* Received from Head Office	3,00,000	1,08,000
Less: Cost of Goods sold *or* sent to Branch:		
Head Office [3,06,000 + 1,08,000) × 100/180]	(2,30,000)	
Branch 1,00,000 × 180/200]		(90,000)
Value of Closing Stock	1,20,000	18,000

14B ACCOUNTING FOR FOREIGN BRANCHES

LEARNING OBJECTIVES

After studying this chapter, you should be able to understand:

- ◇ Meaning of a Foreign Branch
- ◇ Integral Foreign Operations (IFO)
- ◇ Non-Integral Foreign Operations (NIFO)
- ◇ Treatment of Exchange Difference arising on Translation of Financial Statements
- ◇ Exchange Rate to be Used for Reporting at Balance Sheet Dates

1.0 MEANING OF FOREIGN BRANCH

A Branch outside the home country in which Head office is situated is known as a foreign branch. It may be noted that the accounting principles which apply to a home branch (i.e., Inland Branch), also apply to a foreign branch after converting the trial balance of the foreign branch in the home currency.

2.0 MEANING OF INTEGRAL FOREIGN OPERATIONS (IFO)

A foreign operation, the activities of which are an integral part of those of the reporting enterprise is known as Integral Foreign Operations (IFO). [e.g. Foreign Branch]

3.0 NON-INTEGRAL FOREIGN OPERATIONS (NIFO)

ANSWER: A foreign operation, that is not an integral part of the reporting enterprise. is known as Non-Integral Foreign Operations (NIFO). [e.g. Foreign Branch/Subsidiary]

4.0 TREATMENT OF EXCHANGE DIFFERENCE ARISING ON TRANSLATION OF FINANCIAL STATEMENTS

Integral Foreign Operations [IFO]	*Non-Integral Foreign Operations [NIFO]*
Recognised as Income *or* Expense in the period which they arise.	Accumulated in Foreign Currency Translation Reserve until the disposal of Net Investment

5.0 EXCHANGE RATE TO BE USED FOR REPORTING

Basis of Comparison	*Integral Foreign Operations [IFO]*	*Non-Integral Foreign Operations [NIFO]*
1. Monetary Items [e.g. Cash, Debtors, Creditors, Prepaid Exp., O/s Exp.	Closing Rate	Closing Rate

2. Opening Stock if carried at historical cost	Actual Exchange Rate as on the date of purchase of Stock **Note:** Use Opening Rate in the absence of Actual Exchange Rate.	Opening Rate
3. Closing Stock if carried at historical cost	Actual Exchange Rate as on the date of purchase of Stock **Note:** Use Closing Rate in the absence of Actual Exchange Rate.	Closing Rate
4. Non-Monetary Items (excluding Stocks) carried at Historical [e.g. Fixed Assets]	**Actual Exchange Rate as on the date of purchase of Assets**	**Closing Rate**
5. Depreciation if asset is carried at historicalcost	**Actual Exchange Rate as on the date of purchase of Assets**	**Closing Rate**
6. Other Revenue Items [e.g. Purchases, Sales, Interest, Expenses]	Actual Exchange Rate **Note:** Use Average Rate in the absence of Actual Exchange Rate.	Actual Exchange Rate **Note:** Use Average Rate in the absence of Actual Exchange Rate.
7. Goods received from HO/ Sent to HO	Taken at amounts recorded in H.O.Books	Taken at amounts recorded in H.O.Books
8. Balance in HO A/c in Branch Books	Taken at amounts recorded in H.O.Books	Taken at amounts recorded in H.O.Books
9. Remittances	Actual Exchange Rate	Actual Exchange Rate
10. Contingent Liability	Closing Rate	Closing Rate

Important Note for Examination: *Unless otherwise indicated, it is reasonable to assume that the Branch is an* ***Integral Foreign Operation [IFO]*** *of the head office.*

ILLUSTRATION 60

Tulsian Limited, an Indian company has a branch at New York (USA). The trial balance of the Branch as at 31st March, 2016 is as follows:

Particulars	*US $*	
	Dr.	*Cr.*
Fixed Assets	51,200	
Opening Stock	22,400	
Purchases/Sales	96,000	1,66,400
Goods Sent from HO	32,000	
Carriage Inward	400	
Branch Expenses	4,800	
Head Office Account	—	45,600
Sundry Debtors/Creditors	9,600	6,800
Cash and Bank	2,400	
	2,18,800	2,18,800

The following further information's are given:

(1) Expenses outstanding $ 400.

(2) Depreciate Fixed Assets @ 10% p.a. at written down value.

(3) The Head Office sent goods to Branch for ₹ 15,80,000

(4) The head Office shown an amount of ₹ 20,50,000 due from Branch.

(5) Closing Stock $ 21,500.

(6) There were no transit items *either* at the start *or* at the end of the year.

(7) On April 1,2014 when the fixed assets were purchased the rate of exchange was ₹ 43 to one $. On April, 1, 2015, the rate was ₹ 47 per $. On March 31, 2016 the rate was ₹ 50 per $. Average Rate during the year was ₹ 45 to one $.

Required: Assuming that the Branch is an Integral foreign operation of the Indian Company. Calculate the Difference in Exchange and show its Accounting Treatment as per AS 11.

SOLUTION

TRIAL BALANCE (IN RUPEES) OF NEW YORK (USA) BRANCH AS ON 31ST MARCH, 2016

Particulars	*Dr. US $*	*Cr. US $*	*Conversion Rate*	*Dr. ₹*	*Cr. ₹*
Fixed Assets	46,080		43	19,81,440	
Depreciation on Fixed Assets	5,120		43	2,20,160	
Opening Stock	22,400		47	10,52,800	
Purchases	96,000		45	43,20,000	
Sales		1,66,400	45		74,88,000
Goods sent from H.O.	32,000			15,80,000	
Carriage inward	400		45	18,000	
Branch Expenses (4,800 + 400)	5,200		45	2,34,000	
Outstanding Expenses		400	50		20,000
Head Office A/c		45,600			20,50,000
Trade debtors	9,600		50	4,80,000	
Trade creditors		6,800	50		3,40,000
Cash & bank	2,400		50	1,20,000	
Exchange gain (bal. fig.)					1,08,400
	2,19,200	2,19,200		1,00,06,400	1,00,06,400
Closing Stock	21,500		50	10,75,000	

Accounting Treatment of Difference in Exchange: Difference in Exchange [e.g. 1,08,400] will be credted to the Statement of Profit & Loss.

ILLUSTRATION 61

Assuming that the Branch in Previous QUESTION is a Non-Integral foreign operation of the Indian Company, Calculate the Difference in Exchange and show its Accounting Treatment as per AS 11.

SOLUTION

TRIAL BALANCE (IN RUPEES) OF NEW YORK (USA) BRANCH AS ON 31ST MARCH, 2016

Particulars	*Dr. US $*	*Cr. US $*	*Conversion Rate*	*Dr. ₹*	*Cr. ₹*
Fixed Assets	46,080		50	23,04,000	
Depreciation on Fixed Assets	5,120		50	2,56,000	
Opening Stock	22,400		47	10,52,800	
Purchases	96,000		45	43,20,000	
Sales		1,66,400	45		74,88,000
Goods sent from H.O.	32,000			15,80,000	
Carriage inward	400		45	18,000	
Branch Expenses (4,800 + 400)	5,200		45	2,34,000	
Outstanding Expenses		400	50		20,000
Head Office A/c		45,600			20,50,000
Trade debtors	9,600		50	4,80,000	
Trade creditors		6,800	50		3,40,000
Cash & bank	2,400		50	1,20,000	
Exchange gain (bal. fig.)					4,66,800
	2,19,200	2,19,200		1,03,64,800	1,03,64,800
Closing Stock	21,500		50	10,75,000	

Accounting Treatment of Difference in Exchange : Difference in Exchange [e.g. 4,66,800] will be credted to Foreign Currency Translation Reserve which will be shown in the balance Sheet.

ILLUSTRATION 62

The New York Branch of Fine Textiles Limited, Delhi sent the following Trial Balance (in Dollars) as on 31st March, 2016. The Branch is an integral foreign operation of the Indian Company.

Particulars	$	$
Fixed Assets	1,20,000	
Opening Stock	56,000	
Goods from H.O.	3,20,000	
Expenses	24,000	
Debtors and Creditors	24,000	16,000
Cash at Bank	6,000	
H.O. Account		1,14,000
Sales		4,20,000
	5,50,000	5,50,000

In the H.O. Books, the Branch Account stood as shown below:

NEW YORK BRANCH ACCOUNT

Particulars	₹	*Particulars*	₹
To Balance b/d	10,05,000	By Cash	26,08,000
To Goods sent to Branch	24,63,000	By Balance c/d	8,60,000
	34,68,000		34,68,000

(a) Goods are invoiced to the branch at cost *plus* 10% and the branch has instruction to sell at invoice price *plus* 25%.

(b) Fixed assets were acquired on 1st April, 2014 when $100 = ₹ 380.

(c) Rates of exchange were:

1st April, 2015 $ 100 = ₹ 760

31st March, 2016 $ 100 = ₹ 770

Average $ 100 = ₹ 750

(d) Fixed Assets are to be depreciated @ 10% p.a.

(e) The Branch Manager is entitled to commission of 5% on the profit of the branch (on invoice price basis) after charging such commission.

(f) Expenses outstanding – $ 2,000, Prepaid Expenses $ 1,000

You are required to;

(i) prepare Branch Trading and Profit & Loss Account and Branch balance Sheet in Dollars;

(ii) convert the Branch trial balance into rupees and prepare the Branch Trading & Profit & Loss Account and the Branch Account and Branch Balance Sheet in rupees;

SOLUTION

Note: It is assumed that rate of depreciation is at 10% on written down value basis and value of fixed assets in the Trial balance are at written down value on 1.4.2015.

(I) NEW YORK BRANCH TRADING & PROFIT & LOSS ACCOUNT (IN DOLLARS)

Dr. **FOR THE YEAR ENDING ON 31ST MARCH, 2016** *Cr.*

Particulars	$	*Particulars*	$
To Opening Stock	56,000	By Sales	4,20,000
To Goods from H.O.	3,20,000	By Closing Stock (b.f.)	40,000
To Gross Profit c/d			
(₹ 4,20,000 × 20/100)	84,000		
	4,60,000		4,60,000
To Expenses(24,000 + 2,000–1,000)	25,000	By Gross Profit b/d	84,000
To Depreciation	12,000		
To commission (47,000 × 5/105)	2,238		
To Profit	44,762		
	84,000		84,000

BALANCE SHEET AS AT 31ST MARCH, 2016 (IN DOLLARS)

Liabilities		$	*Assets*	$
Creditors		16,000	Fixed Assets	1,08,000
Outstanding Expenses		2,000	Closing Stock	40,000
Commission Payable		2,238	Debtors	24,000
H.O. Account:			Cash at Bank	6,000
Balance	1,14,000		Prepaid Expenses	1,000
Add: Profit	44,762	1,58,762		
		1,79,000		1,79,000

(II) NEW YORK BRANCH ADJUSTED TRIAL BALANCE

Particulars	*Rate*	*Dr. ($)*	*Cr. ($)*	*Dr. (₹)*	*Cr. (₹)*
Fixed Assets	380	1,08,000	—	4,10,400	—
Depreciation	380	12,000	—	45,600	—
Opening Stock	760	56,000	—	4,25,600	—
Goods from H.O.	—	3,20,000	—	24,63,000	—
Sales	750	—	4,20,000	—	31,50,000
Expenses (24,000 + 2,000 – 1000)	750	25,000	—	1,87,500	—
Debtors/Creditors	770	24,000	16,000	1,84,800	1,23,200
Outstanding Expenses	770	—	2,000	—	15,400
Prepaid Expenses	770	1,000	—	7,700	—
Cash at Bank	770	6,000	—	46,200	—
H.O. Account	—	—	1,14,000	—	8,60,000
Difference in exchange	—	—	—	3,77,800	—
Manager's Commission	770	2,238	—	17,233	—
O/s Manager's Commission	770	—	2,238	—	17,233
		5,54,238	5,54,238	41,65,833	41,65,833
Closing Stock	770	40,000		3,08,000	

(III) NEW YORK BRANCH TRADING AND PROFIT & LOSS ACCOUNT

Dr. *for the year ending on 31st March, 2016* Cr.

Particulars	₹	*Particulars*	₹
To Opening Stock	4,25,600	By Sales	31,50,000
To Goods from H.O.	24,63,000	By Closing Stock	3,08,000
To Gross Profit c/d	5,69,400		
	34,58,000		34,58,000
To Expenses	1,87,500	By Gross Profit b/d	5,69,400
To Depreciation	45,600	By Net Loss	58,733
To commission	17,233		
($ 2,238 @ $ 100 = 770)			

To Difference in Exchange	3,77,800		
	6,28,133		6,28,133

Dr. **NEW YORK BRANCH ACCOUNT** Cr.

Particulars	₹	Particulars	₹
To Balance b/d	8,60,000	By Net Loss	58,733
		By Balance c/d	8,01,267
	8,60,000		8,60,000

(IV) BALANCE SHEET AS AT 31ST MARCH, 2016 (AS PER TRIAL BALANCE IN ₹)

Liabilities		₹	Assets	₹
Creditors		1,23,200	Fixed Assets	4,10,400
Outstanding Expenses		15,400	Stock	3,08,000
Commission Payable		17,233	Debtors	1,84,800
H.O. A/c	8,60,000		Cash	46,200
Less: Loss	(58,733)	8,01,267	Prepaid Expenses	7,700
		9,57,100		9,57,100

ILLUSTRATION 63

CANII Ltd., Delhi has a branch at Washington. The Branch is an integral foreign operation of the Indian Company. Its Trial Balance as at 31st March, 2016 is as follows:

Particulars	Dr. US$	Cr. US$
Fixed Assets	1,28,000	—
Opening Stock	56,000	—
Purchases	2,40,000	—
Sales	—	4,16,000
Goods from Indian Co. (H.O.)	80,000	—
Wages	2,000	—
Carriage inward	1,000	—
Adm. & Selling Expenses	10,000	—
Head Office A/c	—	1,14,000
Trade debtors	24,000	—
Trade creditors	—	17,000
Cash at bank	6,000	—
	5,47,000	5,47,000

The following further information is given:

(a) Wages outstanding—$ 1,000

(b) Depreciate Fixed Assets @ 10 per cent pa.

(c) The Head Office sent goods to Branch for ₹ 39,40,000

(d) The Head Office shows an amount of ₹ 43,00,000 due from Branch.

(e) Closing Stock—$ 52,000

(f) There were no in transit items *either* at the start *or* at the end of the year

(g) On April 1, 2014, when the fixed assets were purchased, the rate of exchange was ₹ 38 to one $.

On April 1, 2015, the rate was ₹ 39 to one $.

On March 31, 2016, the rate was ₹ 41 to one $.

Average rate during the year was ₹ 40 to one $.

You are asked to prepare:

(a) Trial balance incorporating adjustments given under 1 to 4 above, converting dollars into rupees;

(b) Trading and Profit and Loss Account for the year ended 31st March, 2016 and Balance Sheet as on that date depicting the profitability and net position of the branch as would appear in India for the purpose of incorporating in the main Balance Sheet.

SOLUTION

(A) CONVERTED TRIAL BALANCE AS ON 31ST MARCH, 2016

Particulars	*Dr.* $	*Cr.* $	*Rate*	*Dr.* ₹	*Cr.* ₹
Fixed Assets	1,15,200		38	43,77,600	
Depreciation on above	12,800		38	4,86,400	
Opening Stock	56,000		39	21,84,000	
Purchases	2,40,000		40	96,00,000	
Sales		4,16,000	40		1,66,40,000
Goods from Indian Co.	80,000		Actual	39,40,000	
Wages (2,000 + 1,000)	3,000		40	1,20,000	
Outstanding wages		1,000	41		41,000
Carriage Inwards	1,000		40	40,000	
Adm. & Selling Expenses	10,000		40	4,00,000	
Head office A/c		1,14,000	Actual		43,00,000
Trade debtors	24,000		41	9,84,000	
Trade creditors		17,000	41		6,97,000
Cash at bank	6,000		41	2,46,000	
Difference in exchange					7,00,000
				2,23,78,000	2,23,78,000

Closing stock at ₹ 41 per dollar i.e. 52,000 × 41 = ₹ 21,32,000

Note: It is assumed that rate of depreciation is at 10% on written down value basis and value of fixed assets in the Trial balance are at written down value on 1.4.2015.

Part (b)

TRADING, PROFIT & LOSS ACCOUNT

Dr. *for the year ended 31st March, 2016* Cr.

Particulars	₹	*Particulars*	₹
To Opening stock	21,84,000	By Sales	1,66,40,000
To Purchases	96,00,000	By Closing stock	21,32,000
To Goods from H.O.	39,40,000		
To Wages	1,20,000		
To Carriage Inward	40,000		
To Gross profit c/d	28,88,000		
	1,87,72,000		1,87,72,000
To Adm. & Selling Exp.	4,00,000	By Gross Profit b/d	28,88,000
To Depreciation	4,86,400		
To Net Profit	20,01,600		
	28,88,000		28,88,000
To net profit to H.O.	27,01,600	By net profit	20,01,600
		By Difference in exchange	7,00,000
	27,01,600		27,01,600

BRANCH BALANCE SHEET AS AT 31ST MARCH, 2016

Liabilities	₹	*Assets*		₹
Head Office A/c	43,00,000	Fixed Assets	48,64,000	
Profit & Loss A/c	27,01,600	less: Depreciation	4,86,400	43,77,600
Creditors	6,97,000	Stock		21,32,000
Outstanding wages	41,000	Debtors		9,84,000
		Cash at Bank		2,46,000
	77,39,600			77,39,600

ILLUSTRATION 64

CAMII & Co. has head office at and branch at Mumbai (India). The Branch is an integral foreign operation of the New York (U.S.A.) Company. Mumbai branch furnishes you with its trial balance as on 31st March, 2016 and the additional information given thereafter:

Particulars	*Dr.* (₹ '000)	*Cr.* (₹ '000)
Opening Stock	300	—
Purchases and Sales	800	1,200
Sundry Debtors and Creditors	520	540
Wages and Salaries	560	—
Rent, Rates and Taxes	360	—

Sundry Charges	160	—
Computers	240	—
Bank Balance	420	—
New York Office A/c	—	1,620
	3,360	3,360

Additional Information:

(a) Computers were acquired from a remittance of US $ 6,000 received from New York head office and paid to the suppliers. Depreciate computers at 60% for the year.

(b) Unsold Closing Stock of Mumbai branch was worth ₹ 4,20,000.

(c) The rates of exchange may be taken as follows:

(i) on 1.4.2015 @ ₹ 40 per US $

(ii) on 31.3.2016 @ ₹ 42. per US $

(iii) average exchange rate for the year @ ₹ 41. per US $

(iv) conversion in $ shall be made up to two decimal accuracy.

You are asked to prepare in US dollars the Revenue Statement for the year ended 31st March, 2016 and the Balance Sheet as on that date of Mumbai branch as would appear in the books of New York head office of CAMII & Co. You are informed that Mumbai branch account showed a debit balance of US $ 39609.18 on 31.3.2016 in New York books and there were no items pending reconciliation.

SOLUTION

REVENUE STATEMENT OF MUMBAI BRANCH (IN DOLLARS)

Dr. *for the year ending 31st March, 2016* *Cr.*

Particulars	$	*Particulars*	$
To Opening Stock	7,500.00	By Sales	29,268.29
To Purchases	19,512.20	By Closing Stock	10,000.00
To Wages & Salaries	13,658.54	By Net loss	17,685.38
To Rent, Rates & Taxes	8,780.49		
To Sundry Charges	3,902.44		
To Depreciation on Computer	3,600.00		
	56,953.67		56,953.67

BALANCE SHEET AS AT 31ST MARCH, 2016

Liabilities	$	*Assets*	$
Creditors	12,857.15	Computer	6,000
H.O. A/c	39,609.18	*Less:* Depreciation	3,600
			2,400.00
		Debtors	12,380.95
		Bank Balance	10,000.00
		Closing Stock	10,000.00
		Net Loss at Mumbai Branch	17,685.38
	52,466.33		52,466.33

Working Notes:

MUMBAI BRANCH TRIAL BALANCE

Particulars	Rate	Dr. ₹ ('000)	Cr. ₹ ('000)	Dr. $	Cr. $
Opening Stock	40	300		7,500.00	
Purchase & Sales	41	800	1,200	19,512.20	29,268.29
Debtors/Creditors	42	520	540	12380.95	12,857.15
Wages & Salaries	41	560		13,658.54	
Rent, Rates and Taxes	41	360		8,780.49	
Sundry charges	41	160		3,902.44	
Computers	as given	240		6,000.00	
Bank balance	42	420		10,000.00	
New York Office A/c	as given		1,620		39,609.18
		3,360	3,360	81,734.62	81,734.62
Closing Stock	42	4,20		10,000	

ILLUSTRATION 65

CAMIE Ltd., Bombay, have a branch in Sydney, Australia. The Branch is an integral foreign operation of the Indian Company. At the end of 31st March, 2016, the following ledger balances have been extracted from the books of the Bombay Office and the Sydney office.

Particulars	Bombay (₹ thousands)		Sydney (Astr dollars thousands)	
	Debit	Credit	Debit	Credit
Share Capital	—	2,000	—	—
Reserve & Surplus	—	1,000	—	—
Land	500	—	—	—
Buildings (Cost)	1,000	—	—	—
Buildings Depreciation Reserve	—	200	—	—
Plant & Machinery (Cost)	2,500	—	200	—
Plant & Machinery Depreciation Reserve	—	600	—	130
Debtors/Creditors	280	200	60	30
Opening Stock	100	—	20	—
Branch Stock Reserve	—	4	—	—
Cash & Bank Balances	10	—	10	—
Purchases/Sales	240	520	20	123
Goods sent to Branch	—	100	5	—
Managing Director's salary	30	—	—	—
Salaries & Wages	75	—	45	—
Rent	—	—	12	—
Office Expenses	25	—	18	—
Commission Receipts	—	256	—	100

Branch/H.O. Current A/c	120	—	—	7
	4,880	4,880	390	390

Additional Information

(i) Closing Stock: Bombay ₹ 1,50,000, Sydney A$ 3,125, (ii) Head Office always sent goods to the Branch at cost *plus* 25%, (iii) Provision is to be made for doubtful debts at 5%, (iv) Depreciation is to be provided on buildings at 10% and on plant and machinery at 20% on written down values, (v) The Managing Director is entitled to 2% commission on net profits, (vi) Income-tax is to be provided at 47.5%

You are required:

(a) to convert the Branch Trial balance into rupees; (use the following rates of exchange) Opening rate A$ = ₹ 20, Closing rate A$ = ₹ 24, Average rate A$ = ₹ 22, For Fixed Assets A$ = ₹ 18

(b) to prepare the Trading and Profit & Loss Account for the year ending on 31st March, 2016, showing to the extent possible, H.O. results and Branch results separately. (Balance Sheet not required)

SOLUTION

CAMIE LTD.

(A) SYDNEY BRANCH TRIAL BALANCE (IN RUPEES) AS ON 31ST MARCH, 2016

Particulars	*Conversion rate per A $*	*(₹ '000) Dr.*	*(₹ '000) Cr.*
Plant & Machinery (cost)	₹ 18	36,00	
Plant & Machinery Depreciation			
Reserve	₹ 18		23,40
Debtors/Creditors	₹ 24	14,40	7,20
Opening Stock	₹ 20	4,00	
Cash & Bank Balances	₹ 24	2,40	
Purchases/Sales	₹ 22	4,40	27,06
Goods received from H.O.	—	1,00	
Salaries & Wages	₹ 22	9,90	
Rent	₹ 22	2,64	
Office expenses	₹ 22	3,96	
Commission Receipts	₹ 22		22,00
H.O. Current Account			1,20
Exchange loss (balancing figure)		78,70	80,86
		2,16	—
		80,86	80,86

(B) TRADING AND PROFIT & LOSS ACCOUNT
for the year ending on 31st March, 2016

Dr. *Cr.*

Particulars	*H.O. (₹ '000)*	*Branch (₹ '000)*	*Total (₹ '000)*	*Particulars*	*H.O. (₹ '000)*	*Branch (₹ '000)*	*Total (₹ '000)*
To Opening Stock	1,00	4,00	5,00	By Sales	5,20	27,06	32,26
To Purchases	2,40	4,40	6,80	By Goods sent to Branch	1,00	—	1,00
To Goods received	—	1,00	1,00	By Closing Stock	1,50	75	2,25
To Gross Profit	4,30	18,41	22,71				
	7,70	27,81	35,51		7,70	27,81	35,51
To Salaries & Wages	75	9,90	10,65	By Gross profit b/d	4,30	18,41	22,71
To Rent	—	2,64	2,64	By Commission receipts	2,56	22,00	24,56
To Office expenses	25	3,96	4,21				
To Provision for doubtful debts @ 5%	14	72	86				
To Depreciation	4,60	2,52	7,12				
To Balance c/d	1,12	20,67	21,79				
	6,86	40,41	47,27		6,86	40,41	47,27
To Exchange loss			2,16	By Balance b/d		21,79	
To Branch Stock Reserve [See W Note (ii)]	11		11				
To Managing Director's remuneration: Salary		30					
Commission [See w Note (iii)]		41	71				
To Provision for Income tax [see W.Note. (iv)]			8,93				
To Balance c/d			9,88				
		21,79				21,79	

Working Notes:

(I) CALCULATION OF DEPRECIATION

(₹ '000)

	Particulars	*H.O.*	*Branch*
A	Building-Cost	10,00	—
B	*Less:* Depreciation Reserve	2,00	—
C	Building at WDV	8,00	
D	Depreciation on Building @ 10%	80	
E	Plant & Machinery Cost	25,00	36,00
F	*Less:* Depreciation Reserve	6,00	23,40
G	Plant & Machinery at WDV	19,00	12,60
H	Depreciation on Plant & Machinery @ 20%	3,80	2,52
I	Total Depreciation (D + H)	4,60	2,52

(II) CALCULATION OF BRANCH STOCK RESERVE (₹ '000)

A	Reserve on closing stock (75 × 1/5)	15
B	*Less:* Branch Stock Reserve (as on 1.4.2015)	4
C	Additional Reserve required	11

(III) CALCULATION OF MANAGING DIRECTOR'S COMMISSION

A	Profit before adjustment		21,79
B	*Add:* Provision for doubtful debts		86
C	*Less:* Branch Stock Reserve	11	
	Exchange loss	2,16	(2,27)
D	Profit u/s 349 (A + B – C)		20,38
E	Managing Director's Commission (2% of ₹ 20,38)		41 (approx)

(IV) CALCULATION OF PROVISION FOR INCOME TAX

A	Profit u/s 349 as computed above		20,38
B	*Less:* Provision for doubtful debts	86	
	MD's remuneration (30 + 41)	71	(1,57)
C	Profit before tax (A – B)		18,81
D	Provision for tax @ 47.5% on ₹ 18,81	(approx.)	8,93

ILLUSTRATION 66

An Indian company Moon Star Limited has a branch at Virginia (USA). The Branch is a non-integral foreign operation of the Indian Company. The trial balance of the Branch as at 31st March, 2016 is as follows:

Particulars	US $	
	Dr.	*Cr.*
Office equipments	48,000	
Furniture and Furniture's	3,200	
Opening Stock	22,400	
Purchase	96,000	
Sales	—	1,66,400
Goods Sent from HO	32,000	
Salaries	3,200	
Carriage inward	400	
Rent, Rate & Taxes	800	
Insurance	400	
Trade Expenses	400	
Head Office Account	—	45,600
Sundry Debtors	9,600	
Sundry Creditors	—	6,800

Cash at Bank	2,000	
Cash in Hand	400	
	2,18,800	2,18,800

The following further information's are given:

(1) Salaries outstanding $400.

(2) Depreciate Office Equipment and Furniture & Fixtures @ 10% p.a. at written down value.

(3) The Head Office sent goods to Branch for ₹ 15,80,000

(4) The head Office shown an amount of ₹ 20,50,000 due from Branch.

(5) Closing Stock $21,500.

(6) There were no transit items *either* at the start *or* at the end of the year.

(7) On April 1,2014 when the fixed assets were purchased the rate of exchange was ₹ 43 to one $. On April, 1, 2015, the rate was ₹ 47 per $. On March 31, 2016 the rate was ₹ 50 per $. Average Rate during the year was ₹ 45 to one $.

Required: Prepare

(a) Trial Balance incorporating adjustment given converting dollars into rupees.

(b) Trading Profit and Loss Account for the year ended 31st March, 2016 and Balance Sheet as on date depicting the profitability and net position of the Branch as would appear in the books of Indian company for the purpose of incorporating in the main Balance Sheet.

SOLUTION

(A) TRIAL BALANCE (IN RUPEES) OF VIRGINIA (USA) BRANCH AS ON 31ST MARCH, 2016

Particulars	*Dr. US $*	*Cr. US $*	*Conversion rate*	*Dr. US $*	*Cr. US $*
Office Equipment	43,200		50	21,60,000	
Dep. on Office Equipment	4,800		50	2,40,000	
Furniture and Fixtures	2,880		50	1,44,000	
Dep. of furniture and fixtures	320		50	16,000	
Opening Stock	22,400		47	10,52,800	
Purchase	96,000		45	43,20,000	
Sales		1,66,400	45		74,88,000
Goods sent from H.O.	32,000			15,80,000	
Carriage inward	400		45	18,000	
Salaries (3,200 + 400)	3,600		45	1,62,000	
Outstanding salaries		400	50		20,000
Rent, rates and taxes	800		45	36,000	
Insurance	400		45	18,000	
Trade expenses	400		45	18,000	
Head Office A/c		45,600			20,50,000
Trade debtors	9,600		50	4,80,000	
Trade creditors		6,800	50		3,40,000
Cash at bank	2,000		50	1,00,000	

Cash in hand	400		50	20,000	
Exchange gain (bal. fig.)					4,66,800
	2,19,200	2,19,200		1,03,64,800	1,03,64,800

TRADING AND PROFIT AND LOSS ACCOUNT OF VIRGINIA BRANCH

Dr. *for the year ended 31st March, 2016* *Cr.*

Particulars	₹	*Particulars*	₹
To Opening Stock	10,52,800	By Sales	74,88,000
To Purchases	43,20,000	By Closing Stock	
To Goods from Head Office	15,80,000	(21,500 US $ × 50)	10,75,000
To Carriage inward	18,000		
To Gross profit c/d	15,92,200		
	85,63,000		85,63,000
To Salaries	1,62,000	By Gross profit b/d	15,92,200
To Rent, rates and taxes	36,000		
To Insurance	18,000		
To Trade expenses	18,000		
To Depreciation of office equipment	2,40,000		
To Dep. of furniture and fixtures	16,000		
To Net Profit c/d	11,02,200		
	15,92,200		15,92,200

BALANCE SHEET OF VIRGINIA BRANCH AS AT 31ST MARCH, 2016

Liabilities		₹	*Assess*		₹
Head Office A/c	20,50,000		Office Equipment	24,00,000	
Add: Net Profit	11,02,200	31,52,000	*Less:* Depreciation	(2,40,000)	21,60,000
Foreign Currency			Furniture and fixtures	1,60,000	
Translation Reserve		4,66,800	*Less:* Depreciation	(16,000)	1,44,000
Trade creditors		3,40,000	Closing stock		10,75,000
Outstanding salaries		20,000	Trade debtors		4,80,000
			Cash in hand		20,000
			Cash at bank		1,00,000
		39,79,000			39,79,000

PAPER–5: ADVANCED ACCOUNTING (GROUP II)

SECTION–B

ACCOUNTING STANDARDS

[CONCEPTUAL FRAMEWORK, AS 4, AS 5, AS 11, AS 12, AS 16, AS 19, AS 20, AS 26, AS 29]

1 CONCEPTUAL FRAMEWORK FOR PREPARATION & PRESENTATION OF FINANCIAL STATEMENTS

THEORETICAL BASE

QUESTION 1. State the meaning and purposes of the Framework.

ANSWER:

MEANING OF THE FRAMEWORK

Conceptual framework provides the fundamental basis for development of new standards as also for review of existing standards. In July 1989, The International Accounting Standards Committee (IASC) issued a Conceptual Framework to serve as a basis for the accounting standards. In July 2000 the Accounting Standards Board of the ICAI has issued a similar framework for the same purpose.

PURPOSES OF THE FRAMEWORK

1. To assist enterprises in preparation of their financial statements in compliance with the accounting standards and in dealing with the topics not yet covered by any accounting standard.
2. To assist ASB in its task of development and review of accounting standards.
3. To assist ASB in promoting harmonisation of regulations, accounting standards and procedures relating to the preparation and presentation of financial statements by providing a basis for reducing the number of alternative accounting treatments permitted by accounting standards.
4. To assist auditors in forming an opinion as to whether financial statements conform to the accounting standards.
5. To assist the users in interpretation of financial statements.

QUESTION 2. State the Status and Scope of the Framework.

ANSWER: The framework applies to general-purpose financial statements usually prepared annually for external users, by all commercial, industrial and business enterprises, whether in public or private sector. The special purpose financial reports, for example prospectuses and computations prepared for tax purposes are outside the scope of the framework. Nevertheless, the framework may be applied in preparation of such reports, to the extent not inconsistent with their requirements.

Nothing in the framework overrides any specific Accounting Standard. In case of conflict between an accounting standard and the framework, the requirements of the Accounting Standard will prevail over those of the framework.

QUESTION 3. State the Components of Financial Statements.

ANSWER:

1. Balance Sheet	Portrays value of economic resources controlled by an enterprise and the way they are financed.
2. Profit & Loss A/c	Presents the result of operations of an enterprise for an accounting period.
3. Cash Flow Statement	Shows the way an enterprise has generated cash and the way they have been used in an accounting period.
4. Notes and Schedules	Present supplementary information explaining different items of financial statements. They may include disclosures about the risks and uncertainties affecting the enterprise and such items as disclosure of accounting policies, segmental reports, report on operations in the process of discontinuation and do on.

QUESTION 4. State the Objectives of Financial Statements.

ANSWER:

1. The framework identifies seven broad groups of users of financial statements, namely, (a) Investors, (b) Employees, (c) Lenders, (d) Suppliers and other Trade Creditors, (e) Customers (f) Governments and their agencies (g) public.
2. Users of financial statements expect the statements to provide useful information needed to make economic decisions. The financial statements provide information to suit the common needs of most users. However, they cannot and do not intend to provide all information that may be needed, e.g. they do not provide non-financial data even if they may be relevant for making decisions. The financial statements also show the results of stewardship or accountability of the management in respect of resources entrusted to it.

QUESTION 5. State the Three Fundamental Accounting Assumptions.

ANSWER:

1. Going Concern	The financial statements are normally prepared on the assumption that an enterprise will continue in operation in the foreseeable future and neither there is intention, nor there is need to materially curtail the scale of operations.
2. Consistency	The principle of consistency refers to the practice of using same accounting policies for similar transactions in all accounting periods. The consistency improves comparability of financial statements through time. An accounting policy can be changed if the change is required (i) by a statute (ii) by an accounting standard (iii) for more appropriate presentation of financial statements.
3. Accrual	Under this basis of accounting, transactions are recognised as soon as they occur, whether or not cash or cash equivalent is actually received or paid.

Note: If nothing has been written about the fundamental accounting assumption in the financial statements then it is assumed that they have already been followed in their preparation of financial statements. However, if any of the above mentioned fundamental accounting assumption is not followed then this fact should be specifically disclosed.

QUESTION 6. Explain the Qualitative Characteristics.

ANSWER:

The qualitative characteristics are attributes that improve the usefulness of information provided in financial statements. The framework suggests that the financial statements should observe and maintain the following four qualitative characteristics as far as possible within limits of reasonable cost/benefit.

1. Understandability	The financial statements should present information in a manner as to be readily understandable by the users with reasonable knowledge of business and economic activities. It is not right to think that more one discloses better it is. A mass of irrelevant information creates confusion and can be even more harmful than non-disclosure. No relevant information can be however withheld on the grounds of complexity.
2. Relevance	The financial statements should contain relevant information only. Information, which is likely to influence the economic decisions by the users, is said to be relevant. Such information may help the users to evaluate past, present or future events or may help in confirming or correcting past evaluations. The relevance of a piece of information should be judged by its materiality. A piece of information is said to be material if its omission or misstatement can influence economic decisions of a user.

3. Reliability	To be useful, the information must be reliable; that is to say, they must be free from material error and bias. The information provided are not likely to be reliable unless: (a) Transactions and events reported are faithfully represented. (b) Transactions and events are reported in terms of their substance and economic reality not merely on the basis of their legal form. This principle is called the principle of 'substance over form'. (c) The reporting of transactions and events are neutral, i.e. free from bias. (d) Prudence is exercised in reporting uncertain outcome of transactions or events.
4. Comparability	Comparison of financial statements is one of the most frequently used and most effective tools of financial analysis. The financial statements should permit both inter-firm and intra-firm comparison. One essential requirement of comparability is disclosure of financial effect of change in accounting policies.
5. True and Fair View	Financial statements are required to show a true and fair view of the performance, financial position and cash flows of an enterprise. The conceptual framework does not deal directly with this concept of true and fair view, yet the application of the principal qualitative characteristics and of appropriate accounting standards normally results in financial statements portraying true and fair view of information about an enterprise.

QUESTION 7. Explain the Elements of Financial Statements.

ANSWER:

The framework classifies items of financial statements in five broad groups depending on their economic characteristics. These five financial elements are Assets, Liabilities, Equity, Income/Gains and Expenses/ Losses.

1. Assets	An asset is a resource cost or value that can be measured reliably (which may or not have a physical substance)controlled (need not be owned) by the enterprise as a result of past events from which future economic benefits are expected to flow to the enterprise beyond current accounting period. Note: When flow of economic benefit to the enterprise beyond the current accounting period is considered improbable, the expenditure incurred is recognised as expense rather than as asset.
2. Liabilities	A liability is a present obligation of the enterprise arising from past events, the settlement of which is expected to result in an outflow of a resource embodying economic benefits and the value of outflow can be reliably measured.
3. Equity	1. Equity is defined as residual interest in the assets of an enterprise after deducting all its liabilities. 2. Equity is the excess of aggregate assets of an enterprise over its aggregate liabilities. 3. In other words, equity represents owners' claim consisting of items like capitals and reserves, which are clearly distinct from liabilities, which are claims of parties other than owners. 4. The value of equity may change either through contribution from / distribution to equity participants or due to income earned /expenses incurred.

4. Income	1. Income is increase in economic benefits during the accounting period in the form of inflows or enhancement of assets or decreases of liabilities that result in increases in equity other than those relating to contributions from equity participants. 2. The definition of income encompasses revenue and gains. Revenue is an income that arises in the ordinary course of activities of the enterprise, e.g. sales by a trader. 3. Gains are income, which may or may not arise in the ordinary course of activity of the enterprise, e.g. profit on disposal of fixed assets. Gains are shown as a separate line item in the statement of income because knowledge of them is useful in assessing performance of the enterprise. 4. Income earned is always associated with either increase of asset or reduction of liability. This means, no income can be recognised unless the corresponding increase of asset or decrease of liability can be recognised by application of the recognition criteria stated in para 8.
5. Expense	1. Expense is decrease in economic benefits during the accounting period in the form of outflows or depletions of assets or incurrence of liabilities that result in decrease in equity other than those relating to distributions to equity participants. The definition of expenses encompasses expenses that arise in the ordinary course of activities of the enterprise, e.g. wages paid. The losses may or may not arise in the ordinary course of activity of the enterprise, e.g. loss on disposal of fixed assets. Losses are shown as a separate line item in the statement of income because knowledge of them is useful in assessing performance of the enterprise. 2. Expenses are always incurred simultaneously with either reduction of asset or increase of liability. Thus, expenses are recognised when the corresponding decrease of asset or increase of liability are recognised by application of the recognition criteria stated above. Expenses are recognised in Profit & Loss A/c by matching them with the revenue generated. However, application of matching concept should not result in recognition of an item as asset (or liability), which does not meet the definition of asset or liability as the case may be. 3. Where economic benefits are expected to arise over several accounting periods, expenses are recognised in the Profit & Loss A/c on the basis of systematic and rational allocation procedures. The obvious example is that of depreciation. 4. An expense is recognised immediately in the Profit & Loss A/c when it does not meet or ceases to meet the definition of asset or when no future economic benefit is expected. An expense is also recognised in the Profit & Loss A/c when a liability is incurred without recognition of an asset, as is the case when a liability under a product warranty arises.

QUESTION 8. When is an item of financial element, (Asset, Liability, Equity, Expense or Income) recognised in financial statements?

ANSWER:

1. An item of financial element, (Asset, Liability, Equity, expense or Income) is recognised in financial statements if both the following criteria are met:
   (a) It is probable that any future economic benefit associated with the item will flow to or from the enterprise. Concept of probability is used to ascertain the degree of uncertainty associated with the flow of economic benefits, and
   (b) It has a cost or value that can be measured reliably.

2. In assessing whether an item of financial element meets the recognition criteria regard should be given to the materiality consideration. An item is material if misstatement or omission of the item can influence economic decision of the user. For example, an expense even if small, should be recognised if it is not tax-deductible, because one of the users of the financial statements is the taxation authority.
3. The recognition criteria of financial elements are inter-related. For example recognition of an asset implies that corresponding liability, income or equity should also be recognised. In other words, recognition is possible only when both of the related financial elements satisfy the specified recognition criteria. For example, in case of credit sale, the income (i.e. Sales) and asset (i.e. Debtors) can be recognised if on the basis of evidence available on balance sheet date, it is probable that the customer shall not return the goods and cash shall actually be realised.
4. The failure to recognise an item of financial element that meets the above criteria, is not rectified by disclosure of accounting policies used nor by notes or explanatory material.

QUESTION 9. Explain the Measurement bases of Elements in Financial Statements.

ANSWER:

MEANING OF MEASUREMENT BASES OF ELEMENTS IN FINANCIAL STATEMENTS

Measurement is the process of determining money value at which an element can be recognised in the balance sheet or statement of profit and loss. The framework recognises four alternative measurement bases for the purpose. These bases relate explicitly to the valuation of assets and liabilities. The valuation of income or expenses, i.e. profit is implied, by the value of change in assets and liabilities.

FOUR MEASUREMENT BASES OF ELEMENTS IN FINANCIAL STATEMENTS

1. **Historical Cost:** Historical cost means acquisition price According to this base, assets are recorded at an amount of cash or cash equivalent paid or the fair value of the asset at the time of acquisition. Liabilities are recorded at the amount of proceeds received in exchange for the obligation. In some circumstances a liability is recorded at the amount of cash or cash equivalent expected to be paid to satisfy it in the normal course of business. For example, the businessman paid ₹ 1,00,000 to purchase the machine, its acquisition price including installation charges is ₹ 1,20,000. The historical cost of machine would be ₹ 1,20,000
2. **Current Cost:** According to this base, assets are recorded at the amount of cash or cash equivalent that would have to be paid if the same or an equivalent asset was acquired currently. Liabilities are carried at the undiscounted amount of cash or cash equivalents that would be required to settle the obligation currently. Take that Mr. X purchased a machine on 1st January, 2001 at ₹ 5,00,000. As on 1.1.2011, Mr. X found that it would cost ₹ 15,00,000 to purchase that machine.
3. **Realisable (Settlement) Value:** As per realisable value, assets are carried at the amount of cash or cash equivalents that could currently be obtained by selling the assets in an orderly disposal. Haphazard disposal may yield something less. Liabilities are carried at their settlement values; i.e. the undiscounted amount of cash or cash equivalents expressed to be paid to satisfy the liabilities in the normal course of business.
4. **Present Value:** As per present value, assets are carried at present value of future net cash flows generated by the concerned assets in the normal course of business. Liabilities under this convention are carried at present value of future net cash flows that are expected to be required to settle the liability in the normal course of business. Example Carrying amount of a machine is ₹ 4,00,000 (Historical Cost less Depreciation). The machine is expected to generate ₹ 1,00,000 net cash inflow. The net realisable value (or net selling price) of the machine on current date is ₹ 3,50,000. The enterprise's required earning rate is 10% per year. The enterprise can use the machine to earn ₹ 1,00,000 for 5 years. This is equivalent of receiving present value of ₹ 1,00,000 for 5 years at discounting rate 10% on current date. The value realised by use of the asset is called value in use. The value in use is

the value of asset by present value convention.

Value in use = ₹ 1,00,000 (0.909 + 0.826 + 0.751 + 0.683 + 0.621)
= ₹ 3,79,000
Net selling price = ₹ 3,50,000

The company should use the asset to realise ₹ 3,79,000 which is called its recoverable value. It is obviously not appropriate to carry any asset at a value higher than its recoverable value.

The asset is currently overstated by ₹ 21,000 (i.e. ₹ 4,00,000 – ₹ 3,79,000).

The overstatement of the asset is called impairment loss. The accounting entries to recognise the impairment loss and to bring down the asset to its recoverable value are suggested below:

Impairment Loss A/c	Dr.	₹21.000	
To Machinery			₹21.000
Profit & Loss A/c	Dr.	₹21.000	
To Impairment Loss A/c			₹21.000

QUESTION 10. Explain the Financial Capital Maintencance (a) At Historical Cost, (b) At Current Purchasing power and (c) At Currect Cost.

ANSWER: Capital refers to net assets of a business. The value of retained profit depends on the valuation of assets and liabilities. A business must ensure that retained profit (RP) is not negative, i.e. closing equity should not be less than capital to be maintained, which is sum of opening equity and capital introduced.

In order to check maintenance of capital, i.e. whether or not retained profit is negative, one can use any of the following three bases:

1. Financial Capital Maintenance at Historical Cost	Under this convention, opening and closing assets are stated at respective historical costs to ascertain opening and closing equity. If retained profit is greater than zero, the capital is said to be maintained at historical costs. This means the business will have enough funds to replace its assets at historical costs. This is quite right as long as prices do not rise.
2. Financial Capital Maintenance at Current Purchasing Power	Under this convention, opening and closing equity at historical costs are restated at closing prices using average price indices. For example, suppose opening equity at historical cost is 3,00,000 and opening price index is 100. The opening equity at closing prices is ₹ 3,60,000 if closing price index is 120. A positive retained profit by this method means the business has enough funds to replace its assets at average closing price. This may not serve the purpose because in reality prices of all assets do not change at average rate. For example, price of a machine can increase by 30% while the average increase is 20%.
3. Physical Capital Maintenance at Current Costs	Under this convention, the historical costs of opening and closing assets are restated at closing prices using specific price indices applicable to each asset. The liabilities are also restated at a value of economic resources to be sacrificed to settle the obligation at current, i.e. closing date. The opening and closing equity at closing current costs are obtained as excess of aggregate of current cost values of assets over aggregate of current cost values of liabilities. A positive retained profit by this method ensures retention of funds for replacement of each asset at respective closing prices.

PRACTICAL QUESTIONS FOR PRACTICE

QUESTION 1. A proprietor, Mr. X has reported a profit of ₹ 2,50,000 at the end of the financial year after taking into consideration the following amount:

(i) The cost of an asset of ₹ 50,000 has been taken as en expense.

(ii) Mr. X is anticipating a profit of ₹ 20,000 on the future sale of a car shown as an asset in his books.

(iii) Salary of ₹ 14,000 payable in the financial year has not been taken into account.

(iv) Mr. X purchased an asset for ₹1,50,000 but its fair value on the date of purchase was ₹1,70,000. Mr. X recorded the value of asset in his books by ₹ 1,70,000.

On the basis of the above facts answer the following questions from the given choices:

(i) What is the correct amount of profit to be reported in the books?
(a) ₹ 2,50,000, (b) ₹ 2,70,000,
(c) ₹ 3,00,000, (d) ₹ 2,66,000,

(ii) Which measurement base should be followed in the statement (iv)?
(a) Historical cost, (b) Current cost
(c) Replacement cost (d) Present value

(iii) Which concept should be followed in the statement (ii)?
(a) Conservatism, (b) Materiality,
(c) Historical cost, (d) Accrual,

(iv) Which concept should be followed in the statement (iii)?
(a) Materiality, (b) Historical cost,
(c) Current cost, (d) Accrual,

ANSWER:

(i) (d); (ii) (a); (iii) (a); (iv) (d).

QUESTION 2. Ram started a business on 1st April 2012 with ₹ 10,00,000 represented by 50,000 units of ₹ 20 each. During the financial year ending on 31st March, 2013, he sold the entire stock @ ₹ 30 each. In order to maintain the capital intact, calculate the maximum amount, which can be withdrawn by Ram in the year 2012-13 if Financial Capital is maintained at historical cost.

ANSWER:

Particulars	Financial capital maintenance at Historical cost (₹)
Closing Equity (₹ 30 × 50,000 units)	₹15,00,000 represented by cash
Opening Equity	50,000 units × ₹ 20 = ₹10,00,000
Permissible Drawings to keep Capital intact	₹ 5,00,000 (i.e.₹15,00,000 – ₹10,00,000)

2 APPLICABILITY OF ACCOUNTING STANDARDS

THEORETICAL BASE

QUESTION 1: What is the meaning of "small and medium sized company" as per the companies Accounting Standards) Rules, 2006?

ANSWER: As per the companies (Accounting Standards) Rules, 2006 "Small and Medium Sized Company" (SMC) means, a company which satisfies all the following 5 conditions at the end of relevant accounting period.

1. Non-Listed	Whose equity or debt securities are not listed or are not in the process of listing on any stock exchange, whether in India or outside India.
2. Non-Banking etc.	Which is not a bank, financial institution or an insurance company;
3. Turnover up to 50 Crores	Whose turnover (excluding other income) does not exceed ₹ 50
4. Borrowings up to 10 crore	crores crore in the immediately preceding accounting year; Whose total borrowings (including public deposits) does not exceed₹ 10 crore at any time during the immediately preceding accounting year; and
5. Neither Holding nor Subsidiary	Which is not a holding or subsidiary company of a company which is not small and medium-sized company.

QUESTION 2: XYZ, with a turnover of ₹ 35 lakhs and borrowing of ₹ 10 lakhs during any time in the previous year, wants to avail the exemptions available in adoption of Accounting Standard applicable to companies for the year ended 31.3.2015. Advise the management the exemptions that are available as per Companies (AS) Rules, 2006.

ANSWER:

(a) XYZ, is a small and medium sized enterprise (SME) company as per Companies (AS) Rules, 2006. Since its turnover does not exceed ₹ 50 crores and its borrowings do not exceed ₹ 10 crores. It is assumed that its shares are not listed and it is neither Banking Co. nor a financial institution nor an insurance Co. nor a holding Co. nor a subsidiary Co. of a company which is not SMC.

(b) The following relaxations and exemptions are available.

1. As 3 "Cash Flow Statements" is not mandatory.
2. As 17 "Segment Reporting" is not mandatory.
3. SMEs are exempt for some paragraphs of AS 19 "Leases".
4. SMEs are exempt for disclosures of diluted EPS (both including and excluding extraordinary items).
5. SMEs are allowed to measure the 'value in use' on the basis of reasonable estimate thereof instead of computing the value in use by present value technique under AS 28 "impairment of Assets".
6. SMEs are exempt from disclosure requirements of paragraphs 66 and 67of AS 29 "Provisions , Contingent Liabilities and Contingent Assets".
7. SMEs are exempt from certain requirements of AS 15 "Employee Benefits".

8. Accounting Standards 21, 23, 27 are not applicable to SMEs.

   If XYZ is not a company, it will be treated as a level III enterprise instead of level II enterprise; XYZ Ltd. will be exempt from requirements of AS 18 "Related Party Disclosures" and AS 24 "Discontinuing Operations".

QUESTION 3: Is XYZ Ltd, on Indian company (having Turnover & Borrowing each of ₹ 60 crores listed on NASDAQ only and having 51% Equity in S Ltd., an Indian Unlisted company with negligible Turnover and Borrowings required to prepare consolidated financial statements?

ANSWER: XYZ Ltd. is not required to prepare Consolidated Financial Statements even though it is non-SMC enterprise becouse SEBI requires only those Indian companies whose shares are listed on Indian Stock exchange, to prepare CFS.

QUESTION 4: X Ltd. an US company (having Turnover of 51 crores and Borrowings of ₹ 1 crore) is listed on NASDAQ only, has acquired 51% equity in S Ltd. an Indian unlisted company (having Turnover & Borrowings of ₹ 40 lakhs each). Is X Ltd. required to prepare Consolidated Financial Statement (CFS)? Is S Ltd. required to prepare Cash Flow Statement?

ANSWER:

(a) X Ltd is not required to prepare. CFS even though it is non SMC since its equity is not listed in India.

(b) S Ltd is not required to prepare Cash Flow Statement since it is a subsidiary of non-Indian holding company.

QUESTION 5: Y Ltd avail Sales Tax deferral benefit under which it is required to pay the Tax collected after 5 years to the Govt. Such Tax collected of ₹ 11 crores is shown as Unsecured Loan. Is Y Ltd a SMC or Non-SMC enterprise?

ANSWER: Y Ltd is a SMC since Tax deferral would not be considered as 'Borrowing' for the purposes of determine SMC or Non-SMC enterprise since the amount has not been actually borrowed.

QUESTION 6: Is Z Ltd. engaged only in insurance broking business a SMC on Non-SMC enterprise?

ANSWER: Z Ltd. is a SMC enterprise since Insurance broking business would not be considered as "Insurance Business' for the purpose of determining SMC or Non-SMC enterprise.

QUESTION 7: W Ltd., an unlisted and a Not-for-profit company registered u/s 25 of The Companies Act. provides micro finance to backward classes and its interest income is ₹ 40 crores. Is W Ltd. a SMC or non-SMC enterprise?

ANSWER: W Ltd. is a Non-SMC enterprise since it is engaged in commercial activities (i.e. providing loans & earning Interest therefrom). The objective of formation of enterprise is not relevant for the purpose of determining SMC or Non-SMC enterprises.

QUESTION 8: An organization whose objects are charitable or religious, holds that the Accounting Standards are not applicable to it since only a very small proportion of its activities are business in nature. Comment.

ANSWER: Accounting Standards apply in respect of any enterprise (whether organised in corporate, co-operative or other forms) engaged in commercial, industrial or business activities, whether or not profit oriented and even if established for charitable or religious purposes. Exclusion of an enterprise from the applicability of the Accounting Standards would be permissible only if no part of the activity of such enterprise is commercial, industrial or business in nature. Even if a very small proportion of the activities of an enterprise were considered to be commercial, industrial or business in nature, the Accounting Standards would apply to all its activities including those, which are not commercial, industrial or business in nature.

QUESTION 9: Comment whether the following Companies can be classified as a Small and Medium Sized Company (SMC) as per the Companies (Accounting standards) Rules, 2006:

(i) A Pvt. Ltd., a subsidiary of a multinational company listed on London Stock Exchange. It has a turnover of ₹.12 crores and borrowings of ₹ 5 crores.

(ii) B Pvt. Ltd. has a turnover of ₹ 45 crores, other income of ₹ 7 crores and bank borrowings of ₹ 9 crores.

(iii) C Ltd. Has appointed Merchant bankers to prepare a Red-herring prospectus for the purpose of filing the same with Securities and Exchange Board of India.

ANSWER:

(a) As per the Companies (Accounting Standards) Rules 2006, "Small and Medium Sized Company" (SMC) means, a company:

  (i) Whose equity or debt securities are not listed or are not in the process of listing on any stock exchange, whether in India or outside India;

  (ii) Which is not a bank, financial institution or an insurance company;

  (iii) Whose turnover (excluding other income) does not exceed rupee; fifty crore in the immediately preceding accounting year,

  (iv) Which does not have borrowings (including public deposits) in excess of rupees ten crore at any time during the immediately preceding accounting year; and

  (v) which is not a holding or subsidiary company of a company which is not a small and medium-sized company.

Explanation: For the purposes of clause (f) , a company shall qualify as a Small and Medium Sized Company, if the conditions mentioned. therein are satisfied as at the end of the relevant accounting period.

(a) As per the definition of SMC, point (v), a company will be a SMC if it is not a holding or subsidiary company of another company which is not a SMC. Since A Pvt. Ltd. is a subsidiary of another Company which is listed, on London Stock Exchange (and is therefore not a SMC), A Pvt. Ltd. cannot be a SMC. The turnover and borrowings are not relevant in this case.

(b) As per the definition of SMC, point (iii), a company will be a SMC if its turnover does not exceed ₹ 50 corers or borrowings do not exceed ₹ 10 crore. For calculating this turnover, other income is not to be included. Since B Pvt. Ltd. has a turnover of ₹ 45 corers and borrowing; of ₹ 9 corers, it will satisfy the definition and can be classified as SMC.

(c) As per the definition of SMC, point (i) a company will be a SMC if it is not listed or in the process of listing. Since C Pvt. Ltd. has appointed merchant bankers to prepare a Red Herring Prospectus for the purpose of filling the same with SEBI, it is in the process of listing on a Stock Exchange. Hence C Ltd. cannot be classified as a SMC.

3 AS 4 – CONTINGENCIES AND EVENTS OCCURING AFTER THE BALANCE SHEET DATE

THEORETICAL BASE

QUESTION 1: What is meant by Events occurring after the balance sheet date?

ANSWER: Events occurring after the balance sheet date are those significant events, both favourable and unfavourable, that occur between the balance sheet date and the date on which the financial statements are approved by the Board of Directors in the case of a company, and, by the corresponding approving authority in the case of any other entity.

QUESTION 2: State the Accounting Treatment of Events occurring after the Balance Sheet Date.

ANSWER:

Nature of Events occurring after the Balance Sheet Date	Accounting Treatment
1. Events that provide additional evidence to assist the estimation of amounts relating to conditions existing at the balance sheet date.	Assets and Liabilities should be adjusted.
2. Events that indicate that the fundamental accounting assumption of going concern (i.e., the continuance of existence or substratum of the enterprise) is not appropriate.	Assets and Liabilities should be adjusted.
3. Dividend proposed or declared by the enterprise after the Balance Sheet Date	Dividend should be adjusted.
4. Other events occurring after the Balance Sheet Date that represent material changes and commitments affecting the financial position of the enterprise.	Disclosure should be made in the report of Approving Authority.

QUESTION 3: State the Disclosure Requirements as to Events occurring after the Balance Sheet Date.

ANSWER:

1. Nature of the Event
2. An Estimate of the financial effect, or a statement that such an estimate cannot be made.

PRACTICAL QUESTIONS FOR PRACTICE

QUESTION 1: Which of the following events should be taken into account while finalizing (on 30th September, 2015) the annual accounts for the year ending March 31, 2015

(a) The wages of the employees are revised retrospectively from January 1, 2015 vide agreement with the trade union signed on August 1, 2015.

(b) In the Finance Act passed in May 2015, the surcharge on income tax applicable for the assessment year 2015–2016 is increased by 5%.

(c) A debtor against whom insolvency proceedings were instituted prior to March 31, 2015 is declared insolvent on July 21, 2015.

(d) A theft of cash of ₹ 1 crore by the Cashier in Jan. 2015 was detected on 17th May 2015.

(e) A major production plant destroyed by fire on August 28, 2015.

(f) The factory of the entrepreneur is permanently sealed under Supreme Court order since it was polluting industry on September 20, 2015.

(g) The board of directors at their meeting on September 30, 2015 have recommended a dividend of 20% to be paid to shareholders after it is approved at the annual general meeting.

(h) A major debtor died along with his family in Gujarat earthquake on May 13,2015.

(i) A fire occurred in the godown on April 1, 2015, damaging a huge quantity of stocks.

(j) During Aug. 2015 it was estimated that the total cost of project shall be inflated by ₹ 50 crores which would not be recoverable from contractee.

(k) One of the several factories destroyed by fire on July 28, 2015.

ANSWER:

ACCOUNTING TREATMENT OF VARIOUS EVENTS

Event	Accounting Treatment
(a)	Liability on account of arrears of wages for 3 months from January 1, 2015 should be provided. **Reason:** As per AS 4 Assets and liabilities should be adjusted for events occurring after the balance sheet date that provide additional evidence to assist the estimation of amounts relating to conditions existing at the balance sheet date.
(b)	Liability on account of increase in surcharge should be provided. **Reason:** As per AS 4 Assets and liabilities should be adjusted for events occurring after the balance sheet date that provide additional evidence to assist the estimation of amounts relating to conditions existing at the balance sheet date.
(c)	Debtors should be reduced by the amount of bad debts. **Reason:** As per AS 4 Assets and liabilities should be adjusted for events occurring after the balance sheet date that provide additional evidence to assist the estimation of amounts relating to conditions existing at the balance sheet date.
(d)	Loss due to theft should recognised. Reason: As per AS 4 Assets and liabilities should be adjusted for events occurring after the balance sheet date that provide additional evidence to assist the estimation of amounts relating to conditions existing at the balance sheet date.
(e)	The financial statements should be prepared by not following the fundamental assumption of going concern. **Reason:** As per AS – 4, assets and liabilities should be adjusted for events occurring after the balance sheet date that indicate that the fundamental accounting assumption of going concern (i.e., the continuance of existence or substratum of the enterprise) is not appropriate.
(f)	The financial statements should be prepared by not following the fundamental assumption of going concern. **Reason:** As per AS – 4, assets and liabilities should be adjusted for events occurring after the balance sheet date that indicate that the fundamental accounting assumption of going concern (i.e., the continuance of existence or substratum of the enterprise) is not appropriate.
(g)	Dividend should be adjusted. **Reason:** As per para 14 of AS 4, dividends in respect of period covered by the financial statements, which are proposed or declared by the enterprise after the Balance Sheet Date but before the approval of the financial statements should be adjusted in the financial statements. The Schedule III, classifies 'Proposed Dividend' as commitments'.Accounting Standards now have overriding impact over Schedule III. Therefore, unless Para 14 of AS 4 is changed, Proposed Dividend shall be adjusted.

(h)	Disclosure should be made in the report of the approving authority since the amount of loss is material. Such loss should not be recognised in the financial statements for the year 2014-2015 since such event does not relate to the conditions existing at the Balance Sheet Date.
(i)	Disclosure should be made in the report of the approving authority since the amount of loss is material. Such loss should not be recognised in the financial statements for the year 2014-2015 since such event does not relate to the conditions existing at the Balance Sheet Date.
(j)	Liability on account of increase in cost should be provided. **Reason:** As per AS 4 Assets and liabilities should be adjusted for events occurring after the balance sheet date that provide additional evidence to assist the estimation of amounts relating to conditions existing at the balance sheet date.
(k)	Disclosure should be made in the report of the approving authority if the amount of loss is considered material. Such loss should not be recognised in the financial statements for the year 2014-2015 since such event does not relate to the conditions existing at the Balance Sheet Date.

QUESTION 2: State the disclose requirement of Proposed Dividend while preparing Financial Statements on company.

ANSWER:

Schedule III	The Schedule III, classifies 'Proposed Dividend' as commitments'.
AS 4	Para 14 of AS 4 requires that "Dividends stated to be in respect of the period covered by the financial statements, which are proposed or declared by the enterprise after the Balance Sheet Date but before approval of the financial statements, should be adjusted." Accounting Standards now have overriding impact over Schedule III. Therefore, unless Para 14 of AS 4 is changed, Proposed Dividend shall be adjusted.
ICAI Guidance Note	The ICAI Guidance Note on the Schedule III has clarified that the 'Proposed Dividend' is a provision.

QUESTION 3: A Ltd. Company closed its accounting year on 31.3.2015 and the accounts for that period were considered and approved by the board of directors on 20th August, 2015. The company was engaged in laying pipe line for an oil company, deep beneath the earth. While doing the boring work on 1.9.2015, it had met a rocky surface for which it was estimated that there would be an extra cost to tune of ₹ 80 lakhs. You are required to state with reasons, how the event would be dealt with the financial statements for the year ended 31.3.2015.

ANSWER:

PROVISION OF AS 4

As per AS 4'events occurring after the balance sheet date' are those significant events, both favourable and unfavourable, that occur between the balance sheet date and the date on which financial statements are approved by the Board of Directors in the case of a company'.

Advice

The incidence, which was expected to push up cost, became evident after the date of approval of the accounts. Hence it is not an 'event occurring after the balance sheet date'.

QUESTION 4: A company deals in petroleum products. The sale price of petrol is fixed by the Government. After the balance sheet date, but before the finalization of the company's accounts, the Government unexpectedly increased the price retrospectively. Can the company account for additional revenue at the close of the year? Discuss.

ANSWER: The unexpected increase in petroleum product prices retrospectively by the Government before the finalization of the company accounts can be considered as an event occurring after the balance sheet date which requires an adjustment on the balance sheet date as per AS - 4 assuming that there were no circumstances of price increase persisting on the date of balance sheet.

QUESTION 5: A major fire has damaged the assets in a factory of a Limited Company on 5th April – five days after the year end and closure of accounts. The loss is estimated at ₹.10 crores out of which ₹.7 crores will be recoverable from the insurers. Explain briefly how the loss should be treated in the final accounts for the previous year.

ANSWER: The loss due to break out of fire is an example of event occurring after the balance sheet date. The event does not relate to conditions existing at the balance sheet date. It has not affected the financial position as on the date of balance sheet and therefore requires no specific adjustments in the financial statements. However, paragraph 8.6 of AS 4 states that disclosure is generally made of events occurring after balance sheet date i.e.in subsequent periods that represent unusual changes affecting the existence or substratum of the enterprise after the balance sheet date. In the given case, the amount of loss of assets in a factory is material and may be considered as an event affecting the substratum of the enterprise. Hence, as recommended in paragraph 15 of AS 4, disclosure of the event should be made in the report of the approving authority.

QUESTION 6: In Raj Co. Ltd., theft of cash of ₹ 2 lakhs by the cashier in January, 2015 was detected in May, 2015. The accounts of the company were not yet approved by the Board of Directors of the company. Whether the theft of cash has to be adjusted in the accounts of the company for the year ended 31.3.2015. Decide.

ANSWER:

PROVISION OF AS 4

As per AS 4(revised), assets and liabilities should be adjusted for events occurring after the balance sheet date that provide additional evidence to assist the estimation of amounts relating to conditions existing at the balance sheet date.

ADVICE

Since the theft of cash is an additional information materially affecting the determination of the cash amount relating to conditions existing at the balance sheet date, it is necessary to adjust theft of cash in the financial statements of the company for the year ended 31st March, 2015.

QUESTION 7: A Company follows April to March as its financial year. The Company recognizes cheques dated 31st March or before, received from customers after balance sheet date, but before approval of financial statement by debiting 'Cheques in hand account' and crediting 'Debtors account'. The 'cheques in hand' is shown in the Balance Sheet as an item of cash and cash equivalents. All cheques in hand are presented to bank in the month of April and are also realised in the same month in normal course after deposit in the bank. State with reasons, whether the collection of cheques bearing date 31st March or before, but received after Balance Sheet date is an adjusting event and how this fact is to be disclosed by the company?

ANSWER:

PROVISION OF AS 4

Since the cheques bearing the date 31st March or before, and received after 31st March do not represent any **condition existing on the balance sheet** date i.e. 31st March. The collection of cheques after balance sheet date is not an adjusting event. Cheques that are received after the Balance Sheet Date should be accounted for in the period in which they are received.

ADVICE

Since the collection of cheques after balance sheet date does not represent any **material change affecting financial position of the enterprise,** no disclosure in the Director's Report is **necessary.**

QUESTION 8: An earthquake destroyed a major warehouse of ACO Ltd. on 20.5.2015. The accounting year of the company ended on 31.3.2015. The accounts were approved on 30.6.2015. The loss from earthquake is estimated at ₹ 30 lakhs. State with reasons, whether the loss due to earthquake is an adjusting or non-adjusting event and how the fact of loss is to be disclosed by the company?

ANSWER:

PROVISION OF AS 4

As per AS 4 adjustments to assets and liabilities are not appropriate for events occurring after the balance sheet date, if such events do not relate to conditions existing at the balance sheet date.

ADVICE

(i) The destruction of warehouse due to earthquake did not exist on the balance sheet date i.e. 31.3.2015. Therefore, loss occurred due to earthquake is not to be recognised in the financial year 2014-2015.

(ii) Since the earthquake has caused major destruction; fundamental accounting assumption of going concern is called upon. Hence, the fact of earthquake together with an estimated loss of ₹ 30 lakhs should be disclosed in the Report of the Directors for the financial year 2014-2015.

QUESTION 9: A company entered into an agreement to sell its immovable property to another company for 35 lakhs. The property was shown in the Balance Sheet at ₹ 7 lakhs. The agreement to sell was concluded on 15th February, 2015 and sale deed was registered on 30th April, 2015. The financial statements for the year 2014-2015 were approved by the Board on 12th May, 2015. You are required to state, how this transaction would be dealt with in the financial statements for the year ended 31st March, 2015.

ANSWER:

PROVISION OF AS-4

As per AS 4 assets and liabilities should be adjusted for events occurring after the balance sheet date that provide additional evidence to assist the estimation of amounts relating to conditions existing at the balance sheet date.

ADVICE

Since agreement to sell before the balance sheet date and Registration of the sale deed after the balance sheet date provides additional information relating to the conditions existing at the balance sheet date, adjustment to assets for sale of immovable property is necessary in the financial statements for the year ended 31st March, 2015.

QUESTION 10: While preparing its final accounts for the year ended 31st March 2015, a company made a provision for bad debts @4% of its total debtors (as per trend follows from the previous years). In the first week of March 2015, a debtor for ₹ 3,00,000 had suffered heavy loss due to an earthquake; the loss was not covered by any insurance policy. In April, 2015 the debtor became a bankrupt. Can the company provide for the full loss arising out of insolvency of the debtor in the final accounts for the year ended 31st March, 2015.

ANSWER:

PROVISION OF AS 4

As per AS 4 adjustment to assets and liabilities are required for events occuring after the balance sheet date that provide additional information materially affecting the determination of the amounts relating to conditions existing at the Balance Sheet date.

ADVICE

A debtor for ₹ 3,00,000 suffered heavy loss due to earthquake in the first week of March, 2015 and he became bankrupt in April, 2015 (after the balance sheet date). The loss was also not covered by any insurance policy. Accordingly, full provision for bad debts amounting ₹ 3,00,000 should be made, to cover the loss arising due to the insolvency of a debtor, in the final accounts for the year ended 31st March 2015.

QUESTION 11:

(i) **The Company's sales tax assessment for assessment year 2012-2013 has been completed on 14th February, 2015 with a demand of ₹ 2.76 crore. The company paid the entire due under protest without prejudice to its right of appeal. The Company files its appeal before the appellate authority wherein the grounds of appeal cover tax on additions made in the assessment order for a sum of 2.10 crore. Advise.**

(ii) **The Company has entered into a wage agreement in May, 2015 whereby the labour union has accepted a revision in wage from June, 2011. The agreement provided that the hike till May, 2015 will not be paid to the employees but will be settled to them at the time of retirement. The company agrees to deposit the arrears in Government Bonds by September, 2015.**

ANSWER:

(i) Since the company is not appealing against the addition of ₹ 0.66 crore, the same should be provided for, in its accounts for the year ended on 31st March, 2015. The amount paid under protest can be kept under the sub-heading 'Short-term Loans & Advances' and disclosed along with the contingent liability of ₹ 2.10 crore.

(ii) The arrears for the period from June, 2011 to March, 2015 are required to be provided for in the accounts of the company for the year ended on 31st March, 2015:

QUESTION 12: The Company invested ₹ 560 lakhs in April, 2015 in the acquisition of another company doing similar business, the negotiations for which had started during the current financial year.

ANSWER:

PROVISION OF AS 4

As per AS 4 no adjustment to assets and liabilities is required if the event does not affect the determination and the condition of the amounts stated in the financial statements for the year ended 31st March, 2015: Disclosure should be made in the report of the approving authority of those events occurring after the balance sheet date that represent material changes and commitments affecting the financial position of the enterprise.

ADVICE

The investment of ₹ 560 lakhs in April, 2015 in the acquisition of another company should be disclosed in the report of the Board of Directors to enable users of financial statements to make proper evaluations and decisions.

QUESTION 13: On 15th April, 2015, due to destruction of the factory by fire, X, one of the company's debtors, declared himself insolvent. He owed ₹ 3,00,000 to Z Ltd. Advice the Z Ltd. about the treatment of the above in the final statement of accounts for the year ended 31st March, 2015.

ANSWER:

PROVISION OF AS 4

As per AS 4 Assets and liabilities should be adjusted for events occurring after the balance sheet date that provide additional evidence to assist the estimation of amounts relating to conditions existing at the balance sheet date.

ADVICE

The debtor became insolvent on 15th April, 2015 I.e. after the balance sheet date because of destruction of his factory by fire. In this case this event does not provide any information about the condition existing at balance sheet date. However, a disclosure is required to be made in director's report.

QUESTION 14: Bottom Ltd. entered into a sale deed for its immovable property before the end of the year. But registration was done with registrar subsequent to balance sheet date. But before finalization, is it possible to recognize the sale and the gain at the balance sheet date? Give your view with reasons.

Soluton:

PROVISION OF AS 4

As per AS 4 Assets and Liabilities should be adjusted for events occurring after the balance sheet date that provide additional evidence to assist the estimation of amounts relating to conditions existing at the balance sheet date.

ADVICE

Sale of immovable property was concluded before approval by the board. This is clearly an event occurring after the balance sheet date. Agreement to sell was entered into before the balance sheet date. Registration of the sale deed simply provides additional information relating to the conditions existing at the balance sheet date. So adjustments to assets are necessary as per AS - 4.

QUESTION 15: You are an accountant preparing accounts of A Ltd., as on 31.3.2015. After year end the following events have taken place in April, 2015:

(i) **A fire broke out in the premises damaging, uninsured stock worth ₹ 10 lakhs (Salvage value ₹ 2 lakhs).**

(ii) **Dividend proposed @ 20% on share capital of ₹ 100 lakhs.**

Describe, how above will be dealt with in the account of the company for the year ended on 31.3.2015.

ANSWER:

(i) Events occurring after the Balance Sheet date that represent material changes and commitments affecting the financial position of the enterprise must be disclosed as per AS-4 on Contingencies and Events occurring after the Balance Sheet date. Hence, fire accident and loss thereof must be disclosed by **way of Note in the Report of Directors.**

(iii) There are events which although take place after the balance sheet date, are sometimes reflected in the financial statements because of statutory requirements or because of their special nature. Such items include the amount of dividend proposed or declared by the enterprise after the balance sheet date in respect of the period covered by financial statements. Thus, dividends which are proposed or declared after the balance sheet date but before approval of the financial statements, **should be adjusted as per AS-4.**

QUESTION 16: One of the manufacturing unit of B Ltd. equal to 40% of the total assets was destroyed in a fire for which there was no insurance cover. The chief accountant of the company contends that the destruction of the unit took place only after the date of the Balance Sheet and therefore there was no need to make disclosure of loss in the annual accounts as at the Balance Sheet date. Comment.

ANSWER:

PROVISION OF AS 4

As per AS 4 Assets and liabilities should be adjusted for events occurring after the balance sheet date that provide additional evidence to assist the estimation of amounts relating to conditions existing at the balance sheet date or that indicate that the fundamental accounting assumption of going concern (i.e., the continuance of existence or substratum of the enterprise) is not appropriate.

ADVICE

Therefore, having regard to the quantum of loss, the auditor has to consider whether it is material enough to affect the very existence of the enterprise. In case destruction of 40% of total assets for which no insurance cover is available affects the existence of B Ltd. then annual accounts would have to be prepared by not following the fundamental accounting assumption of going concern despite the fact that the event has occurred after the balance sheet date. Alternatively, if due to loss the enterprise not ceased to be a going concern then the disclosure stating nature of event and estimate of the financial effect or a statement that such an estimate cannot be made will have to be made in the report of Board of Directors.

QUESTION 17: There was a government notification in June, 2015 increasing the limit of gratuity payment with effect from 24th September, 2015. The accounts were approved by the board of directors in July, 2015. The chief accountant is of the opinion that since the change took place after the balance sheet date, no effect should be given to it in the financial statements for the year ended 31st March, 2015. Comment.

ANSWER:

PROVISION OF AS 4

As per AS – 4, Assets and Liabilities should be adjusted for events occurring after the balance sheet date that provide additional evidence to assist the estimation of amounts relating to conditions existing at the balance sheet date.

ADVICE

In this instant case increasing the limit of gratuity by the government provide additional evidence in estimating the amount of gratuity payable by the company. Hence, the company must provide for increase in gratuity in the financial statements of the year 2014 – 2015.

QUESTION 18: Some companies are notified for air pollution in the vicinity of a historic building. It was certain that legislation will be brought shortly requiring close down of air pollution units. Court proceeding shows evidence that the Supreme Court will direct such units to close down. What is the treatment under AS – 4?

ANSWER:

PROVISION OF AS 4

As per AS 4 Assets and liabilities should be adjusted for events occurring after the balance sheet date that provide additional evidence to assist the estimation of amounts relating to conditions existing at the balance sheet date or that indicate that the fundamental accounting assumption of going concern (i.e., the continuance of existence or substratum of the enterprises) is not appropriate.

ADVICE

In this case, the fundamental accounting assumption of going concern (i.e., continuance of existence or substratum of the enterprise) is not appropriate and therefore assets and liabilities should be adjusted.

QUESTION 19: After the close of the accounting year 2014 – 2015 of ABC Co. Ltd., there was a severe earthquake. As a result of which, a portion of the building and the rolling mill was destroyed. The extent of the damage was beyond repair. The company's resources were inadequate to fund the replacement of the assets so destroyed, Comment.

ANSWER:

PROVISION OF AS 4

As per AS – 4, assets and liabilities should be adjusted for events occurring after the balance sheet date that indicate that the fundamental accounting assumption of going concern (i.e., the continuance of existence or substratum of the enterprise) is not appropriate

ADVICE

In this case it is evident that a company cannot continue further as a going concern hence, its assets and liabilities should be adjusted and financial statements for the year 2013 – 2014 should be prepared on liquidation basis

QUESTION 20: A company's financial year end on 31st March, 2015. Its accounts were considered and approved by the board of directors on 15th May, 2015. The company had taken a large - sized civil construction contract, for a public sector undertaking, valued at ₹ 10 crores. In the course of execution of the work on 29th May, 2015, the company found while raising the foundation work that it had met a rocky surface and costs of contract would go up by an extra ₹ 1 crore which would not be recoverable from the contractee. How this event would be dealt in the financial statements for the year ended 31st March, 2015.

ANSWER:

PROVISION OF AS 4

As per AS – 4, events occurring after the balance sheet date are those events, both favourable and unfavourable, that occur between the balance sheet date and the date on which financial statements are approved.

ADVICE

In this case the incidence, which was expected to push up cost, became evident after the date of approval of the balance sheet. So that was not any 'event occurring after the balance sheet date'. If the cost push up is believed to be material, this may be mentioned in the Director's report. (Even if the contract is profitable after taking into account the additional cost, it would be prudent to disclose the fact of increase in the cost of the contract in the director's report).

QUESTION 21: Pure Oil Ltd. closed the books of accounts on March 31, 2015 for which financial statements were finalized by the Board of Directors on September 04, 2015 During the month of December 2014, company under took the project of lying a pipeline across the country and during May 2015 engineers realized that due to unexpected heavy rain, the total cost of the project shall be inflated by ₹ 50 crores. How this should be provided for in the balance sheet of 2014 – 2015 in accordance with AS – 4.

ANSWER: The event occurred after March 31, 2015 but before September 04, 2015 hence it is event occurring after the balance sheet date. But this event is not affecting financial position on the date of balance sheet therefore it should be disclosed in the financial statement by the directors.

QUESTION 22: The Company invested ₹ 50 lakhs in April, 2015 in the acquisition of another company doing similar business, the negotiations for which had started during the current financial year. How will you deal with the financial statements for the year ended 31st March 2015?

ANSWER:

PROVISION OF AS 4

As per AS 4 no adjustment to assets and liabilities is required if the event does not affect the determination and the condition of the amounts stated in the financial statements for the year ended 31st March, 2015: Disclosure should be made in the report of the approving authority of those events occurring after the balance sheet date that represent material changes and commitments affecting the financial position of the enterprise.

ADVICE

The investment in April, 2015 in the acquisition of another company should be disclosed in the report of the Board of Directors to enable users of financial statements to make proper evaluations and decisions.

QUESTION 23: Cashier of A-One Limited embezzled cash amounting to ₹ 6,00,000 during March, 2015. However same comes to the notice of Company management during April, 2015 only. financial statements of the company are not approved by the Board of Directors of the company.

(a) With the help of provisions of AS 4 "contingencies and Event Occurring after the Balance Sheet Date" decide, whether the embezzlement of cash should be adjusted in the books of accounts for the ending March, 2015?

(b) What will be your replay, if embezzlement of cash comes to the notice of company management only after approval of financial statements by the Board Directors of the company?

ANSWER:

PROVISION OF AS 4

As per AS 4, Assets and Liabilities should be adjusted for events occurring after the balance sheet date that provide additional evidence to assist the estimation of amounts relating to conditions existing at the balance sheet date.

ADVICE

(a) Though the theft, by the cashier ₹ 6,00,000 was detected after the balance sheet date (before approval of financial statements) but it is an additional information materially affecting the determination of the cash amount relating to conditions existing at the balance sheet date. Therefore, it is necessary to make the necessary adjustments in the financial statements of the company for the ended 31st March, 2015 for recognition of the loss amounting ₹ 6,00,000.

(b) If embezzlement of cash comes to the notice of company management only after approval of financial statements by board of directors of the company, then the treatment will be done as per the provisions of AS 5. This being extra ordinary item should be disclosed in the Statement of Profit and Loss as a part of loss for the year ending March, 2015. The nature and the amount of prior period item should be separately disclosed on the Statement of Profit and Loss in a manner that its impact on current profit on loss can be perceived.

QUESTION 24: During the year 2014-2015, X Ltd. was used by a competitor for ₹ 50 lakhs for infringement of a trademark. Based on the advice of the company's legal counsel, the company provided for a sum of ₹ 30 lakhs in its financial statements for the year ended 31st March, 2015. On 20th May, 2015, the Court decided in favour of the party alleging infringement

of the trademark and ordered the company to pay the aggrieved party a sum of ₹ 45 lakhs. The financial statements were prepared by the company's management on 30th April, 2015, and approved by the Board on 31st May, 2015. Should the company adjust its financial statements for the year ended 31st March, 2015?

ANSWER:

PROVISION OF AS 4

As per para 8 of AS 4, "Adjustments" to Assets and Liabilities are required for events occurring after the Balance Sheet date that provide additional information materially affecting the determination of the amounts relating to conditions existing at the Balance Sheet date.

ADVICE

The decision of the Court for payment of the penalty will constitute as an adjusting event because it is an event occurred before approval of the financial statements. Therefore, the company should adjust the provision upward by ₹ 15 lakhs to reflect the amount decreed by the Court and to be paid by them to its competitor.

PROBLEM 25: During the course of audit of D Co. Ltd. you as an auditor have observed that inter Corporate deposit of ₹ 50 lakhs has been overdue. The D Co. Ltd. have disclosed this in the notes to Accounts Note No. 15 in schedule no. 21 stating that ₹ 50 lakhs is overdue from XYZ Co. Ltd. and the said company is the process of liquidation. The management is taking steps to appoint the liquidators. Comment

ANSWER:

PROVISION OF AS 4

As per AS-4 "Contingencies and Events occurring after the Balance Sheet Date", adjustments to assets and liabilities are required for events occurring after the balance sheet date that provide additional information materially affecting the determination of the amounts relating to conditions existing at the balance sheet date.

ADVICE

It appears from the note no 15 that the overdue to outstanding inter corporate deposit may not be realisable in full. The company is the process of liquidation, makes it clear that on the balance sheet date, the amount of deposit is not safe and is not likely to be realised.

Therefore as per AS 4 provision for the loss is required in the accounts. Hence the auditor should qualify the Audit Report.

QUESTION 26: AS-4 prescribes that adjustments to assets and liabilities are required for events occurring after the Balance Sheet date that provide additional information materially affecting the determination of the amount relating to conditions existing at the Balance sheet date-generally called adjusting events. "Proposed Dividend" is shown and adjusted in the Balance Sheet even if it is not an adjusting event as per AS-4 because it is proposed by the Board of Directors of the company after the Balance sheet date. Keeping this in view, is it not violation of AS-4 to show proposed dividends as current liabilities and provisions?

ANSWER:

PROVISION OF AS 4

As per para 8 of AS 4 "Contingencies arid Events occurring after the Balance sheet Date", adjustments to assets and liabilities are required for events occurring after the balance sheet date that provide additional information materially affecting the determination of the amounts relating to conditions existing at the balance sheet date. Accordingly, proposed dividend is not an adjusting event. However, para 14 of the Standard states that dividends stated to be in respect of the period covered by the financial statements, which are proposed or declared by the enterprise after the balance sheet date but before approval of the Financial statements, should be adjusted in the financial statements. Revised Schedule VI of the Companies Act 1956 prescribes that proposed dividend should be in the Notes to Accounts.

ADVICE

Proposed Dividends under the head **'Current Liabilities'** and Subhead, **'Short-term Provisions'** by adjusting it in the Balance Sheet is not in violation of AS 4.

QUESTION 27: Neel Limited has its corporate office in Mumbai and sells its products to stockists all over India. On 31st March, 2015, the company wants to recognize receipt of cheques bearing date 31st March, 2015 or before, as "Cheques in Hand" by reducing "Trade Receivables". The "Cheques in Hand" is shown in the Balance Sheet as an item of cash and cash equivalents. All cheques are presented to the bank in the month of April 2015 and are also realized in the same month in normal course after deposit in the bank. State with reasons, whether each of the following is an adjusting event and how this fact is to be disclosed by the company, with reference to the relevant accounting standard.

(i) Cheques collected by the marketing personnel of the company from the stockists on or before 31st March, 2015.

(ii) Cheques sent by the stockists through courier on or before 31st March, 2015.

ANSWER:

(i) 1. Collection of cheques by the marketing personnel is an adjusting event as per AS 4 'Contingencies and Events Occurring after the Balance Sheet Date'.

2. **Reason:** Handing over of cheques by the stockist to the marketing employees discharges the liability of the stockist. Therefore, cheques collected by the marketing personnel of the company on or before 31-3-2015 require adjustment from the Stockists' Accounts i.e. from 'Trade Receivables A/c' even though these cheques (dated on or before 31-3-2015) are presented in the bank in the month of April, 2015 in the normal course.

3. **Disclosure:** Such 'cheques in hand' will be shown in the Balance Sheet as 'Cash and Cash equivalents' with a disclosure in the Notes to accounts about the accounting policy followed by the company from such cheques.

(ii) 1. The collection of cheques after balance sheet date is not an adjusting event since Collection of cheques after 31-3-2015 does not represent any condition existing on the Balance Sheet date i.e. 31st March.

2. Cheques that are received after the balance sheet date should be accounted for in the period in which they are received even though the same may be dated 31st March or before as per AS 4.

3. The collection of cheques after Balance Sheet date does not represent any material change affecting financial position of the enterprise, hence no disclosure in the Director's Report is necessary.

4 AS 5 – NET PROFIT OR LOSS FOR THE PERIOD, PRIOR PERIOD ITEMS & CHANGES IN ACCOUNTING POLICIES

THEORETICAL BASE

QUESTION 1: State the Meaning and Disclosure Requirements of Ordinary Activities.

ANSWER:

Meaning	Ordinary activities are any activities which are undertaken by an enterprise as part of its business and such related activities in which the enterprise engages in furtherance of, incidental to, or arising from, these activities.
Disclosure Requirements	The nature and the amount of such items should be disclosed separately when items of income and expense within profit or loss from ordinary activities are of such size, nature or incidence that their disclosure is relevant to explain the performance of the enterprise for the period.
Circumstances under which separate Disclosure required	Circumstances which may give rise to separate disclosure of items of income and expense includes: 1. the write-down of inventories to net realizable value as well as the reversal of such write-downs; 2. a restructuring of the activities of an enterprise and the reversal of any provisions for the costs of restructuring; 3. disposals of items of fixed assets; 4. disposals of long-term investments; 5. legislative changes having retrospective application; 6. litigation settlements; and 7. other reversals of provisions.

QUESTION 2: State the Meaning, Examples and Disclosure Requirements of Extraordinary Items.

ANSWER:

Meaning	Extraordinary items are incomes or expenses that arise from events or transactions that are clearly distinct from the ordinary activities of the enterprise and, therefore, are not expected to recur frequently or regularly. **Example:** Attachment of property of the enterprise; or an Earthquake.
Examples	1. Loss due to earthquakes/fire/strike 2. Attachment of property of the enterprise by government
Disclosure Requirements	1. Extraordinary items should be disclosed in the statement of profit and loss as part of net profit or loss for the period. 2. The nature and the amount of each extraordinary item should be separately disclosed in the statement of profit and loss in a manner that its impact on current profit or loss can be perceived.

QUESTION 3: State the Meaning, Examples and Disclosure Requirements of Prior Period Items.

ANSWER:

Meaning	(i) Prior period items are incomes or expenses which arise in the current period as a result of errors or omissions in the preparation of the financial statements of one or more prior periods.
	(ii) The term 'prior period items', as defined refers only to incomes or expenses which arise in the current period as a result of errors or omissions in the preparation of the financial statements of one or more prior periods.
	(iii) The term does not include other adjustments necessitated by circumstances, which though related to prior periods, are determined in the current period, e.g., arrears payable to workers as a result of revision of wages with retrospective effect during the current period.
Examples	1. Applying incorrect Rate of Depreciation in one or more prior periods.
	2. Omission to account for Income or Expenditure in one or more prior periods.
	3. Omission to include Stock Sheets containing inventory costing ₹ 20 lacs while valuing closing stock of previous year.
	4. Omission to pass an entry for receipt of insurance claim received during previous year.
	5. Theft of stock during previous year but detected during current year
Disclosure Requirements	1. The nature and amount of prior period Requirements items should be separately disclosed in the statement of profit and loss in a manner that their impact on the current profit or loss can be perceived.
	2. Prior period items are normally included in the determination of net profit or loss for the current period (above line).
	3. An alternative approach is to show such items in the statement of profit and loss after the determination of current net profit or loss (below line).

QUESTION 4: State the Meaning, Examples, Accounting Treatment and Disclosure Requirements of Accounting Estimate.

ANSWER:

Meaning	As a result of the uncertainties inherent in business activities, many financial statement items cannot be measured with precision but can only be estimated.
Examples	1. Estimates of likely bad debts 2. Estimates of Inventory Obsolescence 3. Estimates of useful lives of depreciable assets. 4. Provision for Warranties, Restructuring Costs, Gratuity 5. Contingencies 6. Estimates of Insurance Reserves by insurance companies.
Accounting Treatment	1. The effect of a change in an accounting estimate should be included in the determination of net profit or loss in (a) The period of the change, if the change affects the period only; or (b) The period of the change and future periods, if the change affects both.
	2. The effect of a change in an accounting estimate should be classified using the same classification in the statement of profit and loss as was used previously for the estimate.

Disclosure Requirements	1. The nature and amount of a change in an accounting estimate which has a material effect in the current period, or which is expected to have a material effect in subsequent periods, should be disclosed. 2. If it is impracticable to quantify the amount, this fact should be disclosed.
Whether Restatement is required when there is Change in Accounting Estimate?	No

QUESTION 5: When is the Change in Accounting Policies recommended?

ANSWER: A change in the Accounting Policy should be made only if adoption of different Accounting Policy is required

1. by Statute or
2. For compliance with an Accounting Standard or
3. If it is considered that the change would result in more appropriate presentation of financial statements.

QUESTION 6: Give two examples of Change in Accounting Policy.

ANSWER:

1. Change of Depreciation method from WDV to SLM and vice-versa.
2. Change in Cost formula in measuring the cost of inventories.

QUESTION 7: State the Disclosure Requirements as to the Change in Accounting Policies .

ANSWER:

Case	***What is to be disclosed?***
(a) When the change has material effect in current period.	(i) The nature of change. (ii) Financial effect of change on Accounting Policies items to the extent ascertainable. (iii) Where the amount is not ascertainable in wholly or part then indicate this fact.
(b) When the change has material effect in later period(s).	(i) The nature of change. (ii) The fact that change in accounting policies has an effect in later period.

QUESTION 8: Whether Restatement is required when there is change in accounting policy?

ANSWER: Yes

PRACTICAL QUESTIONS FOR PRACTICE

QUESTION 1: Give two examples on each of the following items:

(i) Change in Accounting Policy

(ii) Change in Accounting Estimate

(iii) Extra Ordinary Items

(iv) Prior Period Items

ANSWER:

(i) Examples of Changes in Accounting Policy:

1. Change of Depreciation method from WDV to SLM and vice-versa.
2. Change in Cost formula in measuring the cost of inventories.

(ii) Examples of Changes in Accounting Estimates:

1. Change in estimate of provision for doubtful debts on sundry debtors.
2. Change in estimate of useful life of fixed assets.

(iii) Examples of Extraordinary items:

1. Loss due to earthquakes/fire/strike
2. Attachment of property of the enterprise by government

(iv) Examples of Prior period items:

1. Applying incorrect Rate of Depreciation in one or more prior periods.
2. Omission to account for Income or Expenditure in one or more prior periods.
3. Omission to include Stock Sheets containing inventory costing ₹ 20 lacs while valuing closing stock of previous year.
4. Omission to pass an entry for receipt of insurance claim received during previous year.
5. Theft of stock during previous year but detected during current year.

QUESTION 2: The surplus arising from a change in the basis of accounting was set off by X Ltd. against a non-recurring loss. Comment.

ANSWER:

PROVISION OF AS 5

As per AS-5 any change in any accounting policy which has a material effect should be disclosed. The impact of, and the adjustments resulting from such change, if material, should be shown in the financial statements of the period in which such changes is made, to reflect the effect of such change. Transactions which are of an abnormal or non-recurring nature may also be considered material, even though prima facie, they do not appear to be material. Materiality is an important and relevant consideration in determining whether or not such exclusion/non-disclosure will distort the true and fair view of the financial statements.

ADVICE

Thus, it would be important that users must know the quantum of non-recurring loss. **In off setting and aggregating items, care need to be taken to ensure that material items are not offset against each other.** Accordingly, it would not be prudent to set off the surplus emanating from a 'change in the basis of accounting' against a 'non-recurring loss'. Accordingly, it would be better to disclose the surplus on account of change in the basis of accounting and non-recurring loss separately.

QUESTION 3: A Limited Company finds that the stock sheets as on 31.3.2014 had included twice an item the cost of which was ₹ 20,000. You are asked to suggest, how the error would be dealt with in the accounts of the year ended 31.3.2015.

ANSWER:

PROVISION OF AS 5

As per AS-5 the nature and amount of prior period items should be separately disclosed in the statement of profit and loss in a manner that their impact on the current profit or loss can be perceived.

ADVICE

The error in the recording of closing stock of the year ended 31st March, 2014 must have also resulted in overstatement of profits of previous year, brought forward to the current year ended

31st March, 2015. Accordingly, ₹ 20,000 should be deducted from opening stock in the Profit and Loss Account and ₹ 20,000 should be charged as prior period adjustment in the Profit and Loss Account for the year ended 31st March 2015. The prior period item should be adjusted by passing the following entries.

Prior Period Expense A/c	Dr.	₹ 20,000	
To Opening Inventory			₹ 20,000
Profit and Loss A/c	Dr.	₹ 20,000	
To Prior Period Expense A/c			₹ 20,000

QUESTION 4: While finalizing the financial statements of the year ending 31/03/2015 the company finds that the stock sheets of 31/03/2014 did not include two pages containing details of inventory worth ₹ 25 lakhs. Comment.

ANSWER

PROVISION OF AS 5

As per AS-5 prior period items are incomes or expenses which arise in the current period as a result of errors or omissions in the preparation of the financial statements of one or more prior periods. The nature and amount of prior period items should be separately disclosed in the statement of profit and loss in a manner that their impact on the current profit or loss can be perceived.

ADVICE

In this case stock sheet of 31/03/2014 (prior year) did not include two pages containing details of inventory worth ₹ 25 lakhs which is the omission, and this omission was detected in current period i.e. 31/03/2015. Therefore, it is a prior item. It has resulted in under statement of profit of previous period. Entry to be passed is as under:

JOURNAL

₹ in Lakhs

Opening Inventory A/c	Dr.	25	
To Prior Period Income			25
Prior Period Income	Dr.	25	
To Profit and Loss A/c			25

QUESTION 5: Fuel surcharge is billed by the State Electricity Board at provisional rates. Final bill for fuel surcharge of ₹ 5.30 lakhs for the period October 2006 to September, 2013 has been received and paid in February, 2015. Comment.

ANSWER:

PROVISION OF AS 5

As per AS-5 the nature and amount of prior period items should be separately disclosed in the statement of profit and loss in a manner that their impact on the current profit or loss can be perceived.

ADVICE

The final bill having been paid in February, 2015 should have been accounted for in the annual accounts of the company for the years ending 31st March, 2007, 31st March, 2011, 31st March, 2012, 31st March, 2013 and 31st March, 2014. However it seems that as a result of error or omission in the preparation of the financial statements of prior period i.e., for the year 31st March, 2007, 31st March, 2011, 31st March, 2012, 31st March, 2013 and 31st March, 2014, this material charge has arisen in the current period i.e., year ends 31st March, 2015.

It may be mentioned that it is an expense arising from the **ordinary course of business**. Although abnormal in amount or infrequent in occurrence, such an expense **does not qualify as an extraordinary item as per AS-5.** For better understanding, the fact that power bill is accounted for at provisional rated billed by the State Electricity Board and final adjustment thereof is made as and when final bill is received may be mentioned as accounting policy.

QUESTION 6: During the course of the last three years, a company owning and operating Helicopters lost four Helicopters. The company directors felt that after the crash, the maintenance provision created in respect of the respective helicopters was no longer required, and proposed to write - back to the profit and loss account as prior period item. Is the company's proposed accounting treatment correct? Comment.

ANSWER: No, the company's accounting treatment is not correct. Because writing back the balance of the maintenance provision, no longer required due to crash of the helicopters, is not a prior period item as there is no error in the preparation of previous period financial statements. The amount so written - back (if material) should be disclosed separately as per AS - 5 in the profit and loss account.

QUESTION 7: A company created a provision of ₹ 75,000 for staff welfare while preparing the financial statements for the year 2014-2015. On 31st March, in a meeting with staff welfare association, it was decided to increase the amount of provision for staff welfare to ₹ 1,00,000. The accounts were approved by Board of Directors on 15th April, 2015. Explain the treatment of such revision in financial statements for the year ended 31st March, 2015.

ANSWER:

PROVISION OF AS 5

As per AS 5 normally, all items of income and expense which are recognised in a period are included in the determination of the net profit or loss for the period. This includes extraordinary items and the effects of changes in accounting estimates. However, the effect of such change in accounting estimate should be classified using the same classification in the statement of profit and loss, as was used previously, for the estimate.

ADVICE

As per AS 5 in the change in amount of staff welfare provision amounting ₹ 25,000 is neither a prior period item nor an extraordinary item. It is a change in estimate, which has occurred in the year 2014-2015.

QUESTION 8: Closing stock for the year ending on 31.3.2015 is ₹ 50,000 which includes stock damaged in a fire in 2013-2014. On 31.3.2014, the estimated net realisable value of the damaged stock was ₹ 12,000. The revised estimate of net realisable value of damaged goods amounting ₹ 4,000 has been included in closing stock of ₹ 50,000 as on 31.3.2015. Find the value of closing stock to be shown in Profit and Loss account for the year 2014-2015.

ANSWER:

PROVISION OF AS 5

As per AS 5 the effect of a change in accounting estimate should be classified using the same classification in the statement of profit and loss as was used previously for the estimate.

ADVICE

The fall in estimated net realisable value of damaged stock ₹ 8,000 is the effect of change in accounting estimate. Thus, the value of closing stock for the year 2014-2015 will be as follows:

Particualrs	₹
Closing Stock (including damaged goods)	50,000
Less: Revised value of damaged goods	(4,000)
Closing stock (excluding damaged goods)	46,000

QUESTION 9: Goods of ₹ 5,00,000 were destroyed due to flood in September, 2012. A claim was lodged with insurance company, but no entry was passed in the books for insurance claim. In March, 2015, the claim was passed and the company received a payment of ₹ 3,50,000 against the claim. Explain the treatment of such receipt in final accounts for the year ended 31st March, 2015.

ANSWER:

PROVISION OF AS 5

As per the provisions of AS 5 prior period items are income or expenses, which arise, in the current period as a result of error or omissions in the preparation of financial statements of one or more prior periods. Further, the nature and amount of prior period items should be separately disclosed in the statement of profit and loss in a manner that their impact on current profit or loss can be perceived.

ADVICE

It is clearly a case of error in preparation of financial statements for the year 2012-2013. Hence, claim received in the financial year 2013-2014 is a prior period item and should be separately disclosed in the Statement of Profit and Loss.

QUESTION 10: XY Ltd. was making provisions for non-moving stocks based on no issues for the last 12 months upto 31.03.2014. Based on technical evaluation the company wants to make provisions during the year 31.03.2015

Total value of stock — ₹ 150 lakhs.

Provisions required based on 12 months issue ₹ 4.0 lakhs.

Provisions required based on technical evaluation ₹ 3.20 lakhs.

Does this amount to change in accounting policy? Can the company change the method of provision?

ANSWER:

PROVISION OF AS 5

As per AS 5. The method of estimating the amount of provision may be changed, in case, a more prudent estimate can be made by adopting the changed method.

ADVICE

The decision of making provision for non-moving stocks on the basis of technical evaluation does not amount to change in accounting policy as per AS 5. In the given case, considering the total value of stocks, the change in the amount of required provision of non-moving stocks from ₹ 4.0 lakhs to ₹ 3.20 lakhs is also not material. The disclosure can be made for such change by way of notes to the accounts in the financial statements of XY Ltd. for the year ending on 31.03.2015, in the following manner:

"The company has provided for non-moving stocks on the basis of technical evaluation unlike preceding years. Had the same method been followed as in the previous year, the profit for the year and the corresponding effect on the year end, the net assets would have been higher by ₹ 0.80 lakhs".

QUESTION 11: There was a major theft of stores valued at ₹ 46 lakhs in the preceding year detected only during the current financial year.

ANSWER:

PROVISION OF AS 5

As per AS 5. The adjustments are required to be made in the current year as 'Prior Period Items'.

ADVICE

Due to major theft of stores in the preceding year which was detected only during the current financial year there was overstatement of closing stock of stores in the preceding year. This must have also resulted in the overstatement of profits of previous year, brought forward to the current year; Accordingly, the adjustments relating to both opening stock of the current year and profit brought forward from the previous year should be separately disclosed in the Statement of Profit and Loss together with their nature and amount in a manner that their impact on the current profit or loss can be perceived. The disclosure as to the theft and the resulting loss is required in the notes to the accounts for the current year.

QUESTION 12: M/s Dinesh & Company signed an agreement with workers tor increase in wages with retrospective effect. The out-flow on account of arrears was for 2011-2012—₹ 10.00 lakhs, for 2012–2013 ₹ 12.00 lakhs and for 2013-2014 ₹ 12.00 lakhs. This amount is payable in September, 2014. The accountant wants to charge ₹ 22.00 lakhs as prior period charges in financial statement for 2014-2015. Discuss.

ANSWER:

PROVISION OF AS 5

As per AS 5 the term prior period item refers only to income or expenses which arise in the current period as a result of errors or omission in the preparation of the financial statements of one or more prior periods. The term does not include other adjustments necessitated by circumstances, which though related to prior periods are determined in the current period.

ADVICE

The full amount of wage arrears paid to workers will be treated as an expense of current year and it will be charged to profit and loss account as current expenses and not as prior period expenses.

It may be mentioned that additional wages is an expense arising from the ordinary activities of the company. Although abnormal in amount, such an expense does not qualify as an extraordinary item. However, as per Para 12 of AS 5 (Revised), when items of income and expense within profit or loss from ordinary activities are of such size, nature or incidence that their disclosure is relevant to explain the performance of the enterprise for the period, the nature and amount of such items should be disclosed separately.

QUESTION 13: In the previous year "R" Ltd. has made a provision of 11% of the contract value on an ongoing project. The actual loss on completion of the contract in the subsequent year was 12%. The management adjusted the difference in the previous year's account. Comment.

ANSWER:

PROVISION OF AS 5

As per AS 5 on 'Net Profit of Loss for the Period, Prior Period Items and Changes in Accounting Policies', effect of a change in an accounting estimate should be included in determination of net profit or loss in the period of the change, if the change affects the period only.

ADVICE

The provision of loss of 11% of the contract value of R Ltd. in previous year is in the nature of accounting estimate since due to uncertainties inherent in any business activity; it is difficult to measure such item in a precise manner. Accordingly, adjusting the difference in the previous year's account is not correct. Thus, the management should adjust the difference in the current period only. If such treatment is not done the auditor should quality his report.

QUESTION 14: MRE Ltd. provided ₹ 25 lakhs for inventory obsolence in 2014-2015. In the subsequent years, it was determined the 50% of such stock was usable. The Board of Directors wants to adjust the same through prior period adjustment. Comment.

ANSWER:

PROVISION OF AS 5

As per AS 5 on "Net Profit or Loss for the Period, Prior Period Items and Changes in Accounting Policies", prior period items are income or expenses which arise in the current period as a result of errors or omissions in the preparation of the financial statements of one or more prior periods. The write-back of provision made in respect of inventories in the earlier year does not constitute prior period adjustment sine it *neither* constitutes error *nor* omission but it merely involves making estimates based on prevailing circumstance when financial statements were being prepared. It is a mere estimate process involving judgement based on the latest information available.

An estimate may have to be revised if changes occur regarding the circumstances on which the estimate was based, or as a result of new information, more experience or subsequent development. The revision of the estimate, by its nature, does not bring the adjustment with in the definitions of an extraordinary item or a prior period item.

ADVICE

MRE Ltd. provided ₹ 25 lakhs for inventory obsolescence in 2014-2015. In the subsequent year due to change in circumstances, it was determined at 50% of such stock was usable. Revision of such an estimate does not bring the resulting amount of ₹ 12.5 lakhs within the definition either of a prior period item or of an extraordinary item. The amount, however, involved is material and requires separate disclosure to understand the financial position and performance of an enterprise. Accordingly, adjustment in the value of the inventory through prior period item would not be proper.

QUESTION 15:

(i) The difference between actual expense or income and the estimated expense or income as accounted for in earlier year's accounts, does not necessarily constitute the item to be a "prior period" item. Comment.

(ii) When can an item qualify to be a prior period item ?

ANSWER:

(i) To statement given in the question is correct and is in accordance with the accounting standard AS-5.

The use of reasonable estimates is an essential party of the preparation of financial statements and does not undermine their reliability. An estimate may have to be revised if changes occur regarding the circumstances on which the estimate was based, or as a result of new information or subsequent developments. The revision of the estimate, by its nature, does not bring the adjustments within the definition of an extraordinary item or a prior period item.

(ii) Prior Period Item: When incomes or expenses arise in the current period as a result of errors or omissions in the preparation of the financial statements of one or more prior periods, the said incomes or expenses have to be classified as prior period items. The errors may occur as a result of mathematical mistakes, mistakes in applying accounting policies, misinterpretation of facts or oversight.

QUESTION 16: During the year 2014 - 2015, a company write down its inventories to net realizable value by ₹ 10,00,000. Is a disclosure in this behalf is necessary?

ANSWER:

PROVISION OF AS 5

As per AS-5 when item of income and expense within profit and loss from ordinary activities are of such size, nature or incidence that their disclosure is relevant to explain the performance of enterprise for the period, the nature and amount of such items should be disclosed separately.

ADVICE

Yes, it is necessary to make a separate disclosure in respect of writing down inventories to its net realizable value. Accordingly, the nature and amount of this item should be disclosed separately as per AS-5.

QUESTION 17: X Ltd. has been including interest in the valuation of closing stock. In 2014-2015, the management of the company decided to follow AS - 2 and accordingly interest has been excluded from the valuation of closing stock. This has resulted in a decrease in profits by ₹ 5,00,000. Is a disclosure necessary?

ANSWER:

PROVISION OF AS 5

As per AS-5, a change in accounting policy should be made only if adoption of different accounting policy is required by statute or for compliance with an accounting standard or if it is considered that the change would result in more appropriate presentation. As per AS - 5, whenever there is a change in accounting policy and the change have material effect in current period then the company must disclose the nature of change, financial affect of change on items to the extent ascertainable and where the amount is not ascertainable in wholly or part then indicate this fact.

ADVICE

Yes, disclosure is necessary since this is change in accounting policy. This change has been made for compliance with AS-2.

QUESTION 18: A suit for damages for ₹ 1 lakhs for breach of contract of sale (breach occurred in 2008) was decided in favour of May Ltd. in March 2015. The Company has included the amount in its turnover for the financial year 2014-2015.

ANSWER:

PROVISION OF AS 5

As per AS-5 The separate disclosure of such an item should be called for in case having regard to nature, size or incidence of the item concerned and that the separate disclosure is relevant to explain the performance of the enterprise for the period.

ADVICE

It is not a prior period item as the suit was decreed only during the current financial year. Securing damages for breach of contract cannot be treated as an extraordinary item also since it forms part of ordinary activities of the business. **Thus, having regard to the materially of the amount received it may be considered whether the same way be disclosed separately the profit and loss account. Alternatively, a separate disclosure may be made in the notes to financial statements.**

QUESTION 19: A Limited company estimated 1 % bad debt while preparing financial statements for the year ended 31.03.2014. Provision for doubtful debts was created accordingly. However, it appears in 2014-2015 that some receivables are still lying uncollected. The management

feels that an additional 40 % provision is necessary on such debts. Should such change in estimate be treated as extraordinary item? Is it prior period item? Discuss briefly.

ANSWER:

PROVISION OF AS 5

As per AS-5 a change in accounting estimate which has a material effect in the current period should be disclosed and quantified. Any change in an accounting estimate which is expected to have a material effect in later periods should also be disclosed.

ADVICE

The preparation of financial statements involve making estimates which are based on the circumstances existing at the time when the financial statements are prepared. It may be necessary to revise an estimate in a subsequent period if there is a change in the circumstances on which the estimate was based. As per AS - 5, revision of an estimate does not bring the resulting amount within the definition either of prior period item or of an extraordinary item.

In the given case, a limited company estimated 1 % debt at the end of the accounting year 2013-2014 and accordingly made a provision for doubtful debt. Subsequently in 2014-2015 they revised the estimates based on the changed circumstances and wants to create 40% provision. As per AS - 5, this change in estimate is neither a prior period item nor an extraordinary item.

QUESTION 20: A loss of ₹ 2 lakhs on account of embezzlement of cash was suffered by the company and it was debited to salary account. Comment.

ANSWER:

PROVISION OF AS 5

As per AS-5 when item of income and expense within profit and loss from ordinary activities are of such size, nature or incidence that their disclosure is relevant to explain the performance of enterprise for the period, the nature and amount of such items should be disclosed separately.

ADVICE

In this instant case the loss on account of embezzlement should be disclosed separately and not be merged with salary account

QUESTION 21: A company deals in petroleum products. The sale price of petrol is fixed by the Government. In the current year the Government unexpectedly increased the price of the petrol retrospectively. Can the revenue from unexpected increase relating to prior periods be treated as prior period item? Discuss.

ANSWER: The revenue relating to prior periods due to the unexpected increase in petroleum product prices retrospectively by the Government cannot be considered as prior period item as per AS - 5 because there was no error or omission in preparation of financial statements of previous year. Therefore, revenue due to unexpected increase in prices is to be recognized only in the year when the Government announced the price increase.

QUESTION 22: Some of the transport claims lodged in 2014-2015 has been settled by the carrier in February, 2015 by paying ₹ 2,00,000. These claims were not recorded in the books of the company so far. Comment.

ANSWER: As per AS - 9 where the ability to assess the ultimate collection with reasonable certainty is lacking at the time of raising any claim, revenue recognition is postponed the extent of uncertainty involved. As per AS - 9 when recognition of revenue is postponed due to the effect of uncertainties, it is also considered as revenue of the period in which it is reasonable certain that ultimate collection will be made. In this case, it may be assumed that collectability of claim was not certain in the earlier years. So this transaction cannot be taken as 'Prior - period item'. It will not be treated as extraordinary item as per AS-5. However, AS-5 states that when item of income and expense within profit and loss from ordinary activities are of such size, nature or incidence that their disclosure is relevant to explain the performance of enterprise for the period, the nature and amount of such items should be disclosed separately. Accordingly, the nature and amount of this item should be disclosed separately as per AS-5.

QUESTION 23: Finished Goods costing ₹ 10 Lakhs were damaged due to flood in July 2013. These goods were included in Closing Stock as on March 31, 2014 at an estimated realizable value of ₹ 4.00 Lakhs. These goods could be ultimately sold for ₹ 3 Lakhs only in August 2014. The difference of ₹ 1 Lakh was debited as Prior Period expenditure in financial year 2014-2015. As an auditor, please comment in the light of provisions of Accounting Standards.

ANSWER:

PROVISION OF AS 5

Prior Period Item: Write–back of provision made in respect of inventories in the earlier year does not constitute Prior Period Adjustment since it is not an error or omission relating to prior period Financial Statements. It merely involves making estimates based on prevailing circumstances when these Financial Statements were being prepared.

Revision of Estimate: An estimate may have to be revised – (a) if changes occur in the circumstances on which the estimate was based, (b) or as a result of new information, more experience or subsequent developments. The revision of the estimate, by its nature, does not bring the adjustment within the definitions of an Extra–Ordinary Item or a Prior Period Item.

ADVICE

There is no error or omission in the Prior Period. It is a case of change in accounting estimates as to the estimated NRV of damaged item, which have changed when the damaged goods have been finally sold.

The difference of ₹ 1 Lakh is not a Prior Period Item. Hence, debiting it to Prior Period Expenditure in the accounting year 2014–2015 is a **wrong accounting treatment.**

QUESTION 24: A Limited company created a provision for bad and doubtful debts at 5% on debtors in preparing the financial statements for the year 2014-2015. Subsequently on a review of the credit period allowed and financial capacity of the customers, the company decided to increase the provision to 10% on debtors as on 31-03-2015. The accounts are not approved by the Board of Directors till the date of decision. While applying the relevant accounting standard, can this revision be considered as an extraordinary item or prior period item?

ANSWER:

PROVISION OF AS 5

As per AS 5 'Net Profit or Loss for the Period, Prior Period Items and Changes in Accounting Policies', the preparation of financial statements involve making estimates which are based on the circumstances existing at the time when the financial statements are prepared. It may be necessary to revise an estimate in a subsequent period if there is a change in the circumstances on which the estimate was based. Revision of an estimate, by its nature, does not bring the adjustment within the definitions of a prior period item or an extra ordinary item.

ADVICE

The change in estimated provision for doubtful debts is neither a prior period item nor an extra ordinary item.

However, as per para 27 of the standard, a change in accounting estimate which has material effect in the current period should be disclosed and quantified. Any change in the accounting estimate which is expected to have a material effect in later periods should also be disclosed and quantified.

QUESTION 25: X Co. Ltd. signed an agreement with its employees union for revision of wages in June, 2015. The wage revision is with retrospective effect from 1.4.2011. The arrear wages upto 31.3.2015 amounts to ₹ 80 lakhs. Arrear wages for the period from 1.4.2015 to 30.6.2015 (being the date of agreement) amounts to ₹ 7 lakhs. Decide whether a separate disclosure of arrear wages is required.

ANSWER

PROVISION OF AS 5

As per AS 5, when items of income and expense within profit or loss from ordinary activities are of such size, nature or incidence that their disclosure is relevant to explain the performance of the enterprise for the period, the **nature and amount of such items should be disclosed separately.**

ADVICE

It is given that revision of wages took place in June, 2015 with retrospective effect from 1.4.2011. The arrear wages payable for the period from 1.4.2011 to 30.6.2015 cannot be taken as an error or omission in the preparation of financial statements and hence this expenditure **cannot be taken as a prior period item.**

Additional liability on account of wages amounting ₹ 87 lakhs (from 1.4.2011 to 30.6.2015) should be included in current year's wages.

It may be mentioned that additional wages is an expense arising from the ordinary activities of the company. Although abnormal in amount, such an expense does not qualify as an extraordinary item.

However, wages payable for the current year (from 1.4.2015 to 30.6.2015) amounting ₹ 7 lakhs is not a prior period item hence need not be disclosed separately. This may be shown as current year wages.

5 AS 11 – THE EFFECTS OF CHANGES IN FOREIGN EXCHANGE RATES

THEORETICAL BASE

QUESTION 1: State the areas to which AS 11 is not applicable.

ANSWER:

1. Accounting for Foreign Currency Derivatives to which AS-30 applies,
2. Hedge Accounting for foreign currency items,
3. Hedging of a Net Investment in a Foreign Operation.

QUESTION 2: Define Foreign Currency Transaction as per AS 11.

ANSWER: A foreign currency transaction is a transaction which is denominated in or requires settlement in a foreign currency, including transactions arising when an enterprise *either*.

(a) buys or sells goods or services whose price is denominated in a foreign currency; *or*

(b) borrows or lends funds when the amounts payable or receivable are denominated in a foreign currency; *or*

(c) otherwise acquires or disposes of assets, or incurs or settles liabilities, denominated in a foreign currency

QUESTION 3: Define Exchange Rate, Average Rate, Closing Rate, Monetary Items and Non-Monetary Items as per AS 11.

ANSWER:

1. Exchange Rate	Exchange Rate is the ratio for exchange of two currencies.
2. Average Rate	Average Rate is the mean of the exchange rates in force during a period. **Note:** Average Rate should not be used if exchange rates fluctuate significantly.
3. Closing Rate	Closing rate is the Exchange rate at the Balance Sheet Date
4. Monetary Items	Monetary items are money held and assets and liabilities to be received or paid in fixed or determinable amounts of money, *e.g.*, Cash, Receivables, Payables,Loans.
5. Non-Monetary Items	Non-monetary items are assets and liabilities other than the monetary items *e.g.* Fixed Assets, Inventories, Investments in equity shares.

QUESTION 4: Define Exchange Difference as per AS 11. When does Exchange Difference arise?

ANSWER:

Meaning	Exchange difference is the difference resulting from reporting the same number of units of a foreign currency in the reporting currency at different exchange rates.
When arises	An exchange difference results when there is a change in the exchange rate between the transaction date and the settlement date/reporting date of any foreign currency monetary items.

QUESTION 5: State the indications that a Foreign Operation is a Non-Integral Foreign Operation as per AS 11.

ANSWER:

1. Degree of Autonomy
2. Proportion of the Foreign Operation's Activities;
3. Proportion of Finance from the reporting enterprise.
4. Settlement of Foreign Operation's Sales, Purchases, Other Transactions

QUESTION 6: Distinguish between Integral and Non Integral Foreign Operations as per AS 11.

ANSWER:

Basis of Comparison	Integral Foreign Operations [IFO]	Non-Integral Foreign Operations [NIFO]
1. Meaning	A foreign operation, the activities of which are an integral part of those of the reporting enterprise [*e.g.* Foreign Branch]	A foreign operation that is not an integral foreign operation [*e.g.* Foreign Subsidiary]
2. Treatment of Exchange Difference arising on translation	Recognised as Income or Expense in the period which they arise.	Accumulated in Foreign Currency Translation Reserve until the disposal of Net Investment
3. Exchange Rate To Be Used For Reporting		
(a) Opening Stock if carried at historical cost	Actual Exchange Rate as on the date of purchase	Opening Rate
(b) Closing Stock if carried at historical cost	Actual Exchange Rate as on the date of purchase	Closing Rate
(c) Non-Monetary Items (excluding Stocks) carried at Historical [*e.g.* Fixed Assets]	Actual Exchange Rate as on the date of purchase	Closing Rate
(d) Depreciation if asset is carried at historicalcost	Actual Exchange Rate as on the date of purchase	Closing Rate

QUESTION 7: State the Items for which the same translation rate is used for Integral and Non Integral Foreign Operations as per AS 11.

ANSWER:

Basis of Comparison	Integral Foreign Operations [IFO]	Non-Integral Foreign Operations [NIFO]
(a) Monetary Items [e.g. Cash, Debtors, Creditors, Prepaid Exp., O/s Exp.,	Closing Rate	Closing Rate
(b) Contingent Liability	Closing Rate	Closing Rate
(c) Other Revenue Items [e.g. Purchases, Sales, Interest, Expenses]	Actual Exchange Rate	Actual Exchange Rate

(d) Remittances	Actual Exchange Rate	Actual Exchange Rate
(e) Goods received from HO/ Sent to HO	Taken at amounts recorded in H.O.Books	Taken at amounts recorded in H.O.Books
(f) Balance in HO A/c in Branch Books	Taken at amounts recorded in H.O.Books	Taken at amounts recorded in H.O.Books

QUESTION 8: State the Option available to Companies for Treatment of Exchange Difference as per Para 46A of The Companies (Accounting Standards) Rules, 2012.

ANSWER:

1. Long-term Foreign Currency Loans relating to Depreciable Assets	Exchange Difference should be debited(in case of Exchange Loss) or credited (in case of Exchange Profit) to **Respective Asset A/c.**
2. Long-term Foreign Currency Loans relating to Non-Depreciable Assets like land	1. Exchange Difference should be debited(in case of Exchange Loss) or credited (in case of Exchange Profit) to **Foreign Currency Monetary Items Translation Difference A/c.** 2. Such Exchange Difference should be transferred to Profit & Loss A/c in equal proportion over reporting periods ending on March 31,2020. **Note:** The Dr. or Cr. Balance of FCMITD A/c should be shown on the Equity & Liabilities side of the Balance Sheet under the head **'Reserves & Surplus'.**
Note: Once Option as per Para 46A is exercised,it is irrevocable. If Option as per Para 46A is not exercised, the Exchange Difference is transferred to Profit & Loss A/c.	

QUESTION 9: state the accounting treatment of a foreign currency transaction at date of transaction as per as 11.

ANSWER: At date of transaction a foreign currency transaction will be recorded at an Amount
= Foreign Currency Amount × Exchange Rate as on Date of Transaction

QUESTION 10: State the accounting treatment of a foreign currency transaction at Reporting Date as per as 11.

ANSWER:

1. At Reporting date a foreign currency transaction will be recorded at an Amount
   = Foreign Currency Amount × Exchange Rate as on Reporting Date
2. Exchange Difference will be recognised as Income/Expense in Profit and Loss A/c:
   = Foreign Currency Amount × (Exchange Rate as on Date of Transaction – Exchange Rate as on Date of Reporting)

QUESTION 11: State the accounting treatment of a foreign currency transaction at Settlement Date as per as 11.

ANSWER: At Settlement date Exchange Difference will be recognised as Income/Expense in Profit and Loss A/c for the period in which settlement takes place.

= Foreign Currency Amount × (Exchange Rate as on Date of Reporting – Exchange Rate as on Date of Settlement)

QUESTION 12: State the accounting treatment of Forward Exchange Contracts entered for trading or speculation purposes as per as 11.

ANSWER:

1. **Premium/Discount** on Forward Contract [i.e. the difference between the Spot Rate and the Forward Contract Rate] **will not be recorded in the books.**
2. Only **when** the Forward Contract is **sold** the **difference** between the Forward Contract rate and Sale Rate will be **recorded** in the Profit & Loss Account.

QUESTION 13: State the accounting treatment of Forward Exchange Contracts entered for hedging purposes.

ANSWER:

1. Premium/Discount on Forward Exchange contracts entered for hedging purposes.
   = Forward Contract Amount × (Forward Contract Rate – Spot Rate)
2. Premium/Discount pertaining to the period falling in current financial year will be recognised in the Profit and Loss A/c for the current financial year.
3. Premium/Discount pertaining to the period falling in next financial year will be recognised in the Profit and Loss A/c for the next financial year.

QUESTION 14: State the Disclosure Requirements as per AS 11.

ANSWER:

1. Exchange Differences transferred to Profit & Loss A/c.
2. Exchange Differences capitalized as per Para 46 of The Companies (Accounting Standards) Rules, 2012 alongwith benefits.
3. Net Exchange Differences accumulated in Foreign Currency Translation Reserve as a separate component of shareholders' funds, and a reconciliation of the amount of such exchange differences at the beginning and end of the period
4. Reason for & Impact of the Change in classification of Foreign Operation as IFO/NIFO on shareholders' funds; or on net profit or loss
5. Realistic Rate to be disclosed if Closing Rate is not used.

QUESTION 15: Explain "Monetary Item" as per Accounting Standard 11. How are foreign currency monetary items to be recognized at each Balance Sheet date? Classify the following as monetary or non-monetary item:

(i) Share Capital (ii) Trade Receivables (iii) Investments (iv) Fixed Assets

ANSWER:

1. As per AS 11 'The Effects of Changes in Foreign Exchange Rates', Monetary items are money held and assets and liabilities to be received or paid in fixed or determinable amounts of money.
2. Foreign currency monetary items should be reported **using the closing rate** at each balance sheet date. However, in certain circumstances, the closing rate may not reflect with reasonable accuracy the amount in reporting currency that is likely to be realised from, or required to disburse, a foreign currency monetary item at the balance sheet date. In such circumstances, the relevant monetary item should be reported in the reporting currency at the amount which is likely to be realised from or required to disburse, such item at the balance sheet date.

Share capital	Non-monetary
Trade receivables	Monetary
Investments	Non-monetary
Fixed assets	Non-monetary

PRACTICAL QUESTIONS FOR PRACTICE

QUESTION 1: On 31st March, 2015, the following ledger balances have been extracted from the books of Washington branch office:

Ledger Accounts	**$**
Building	**180**
Opening Stock	**26**
Cash and Bank Balances	**57**
Purchases	**96**
Sales	**110**
Commission receipts	**28**
Debtors	**46**
Creditors	**65**

You are required to convert above Ledger balances into Indian Rupees. Use the following rates of exchange:

	₹ per $
Opening rate	**46**
Closing rate	**50**
Average rate	**48**
For fixed assets	**42**

ANSWER:

CONVERSION OF LEDGER BALANCES (IN DOLLARS) INTO RUPEES

	$ Ruees	**Rate per $**	**Amount in**
Building	180	42	7,560
Opening Stock	26	46	1,196
Cash and bank balances	57	50	2,850
Purchases	96	48	4,608
Sales	110	48	5,280
Commission receipts	28	48	1,344
Debtors	46	50	2,300
Creditors	65	50	3,250

QUESTION 2: Goods purchased on 24.2.2015 of US $ 1,000 for which payment made on 05.06.2015. Exchange Rate on: 24.2.2015 ₹ 61.60 per US$, 31.3.2015 ₹ 62.00 per US $, 05.06.2015 ₹ 62.50 per US $. State the Accounting Treatment at the date of transaction, reporting date and settlement date as per AS 11.

ANSWER: Accounting Treatment at the Date of Transaction

As per para 9 of AS 11 on 'The Effects of Changes in Foreign Exchange Rates', a foreign currency transaction should be recorded, on initial recognition in the reporting currency, by applying to the foreign currency amount the exchange rate at the date of the transaction. Accordingly, Goods purchased and corresponding Creditors would be recorded at ₹ 61,600 [i.e. 1,000 × ₹ 61.60]

Accounting Treatment at the Reporting Date

As per para 11 of AS 11, at balance sheet date all monetary items should be reported using the Closing Rate.Accordingly,

1. Closing Creditors will be reported at ₹ 62,000 [i.e. 1,000 × ₹ 62.00]
2. Exchange Loss of ₹ 400 [i.e.₹ 62,000 – ₹ 61,600] should be debited in Profit and Loss Account for the year 2014-2015.

Accounting Treatment at the Settlement Date

Exchange Differences on settlement of monetary items should be transferred to Profit and Loss Account as gain or loss, Accordingly,Exchange Difference of ₹ 500 [i.e.₹ 62,500 – ₹ 62,000] should be debited in Profit and Loss Account for the year 2015-2016.

QUESTION 3: Sunshine Company Limited imported raw materials worth US Dollars 9,000 on 25th February, 2015, when the exchange rate was ₹ 44 per US Dollar. The transaction was recorded in the books at the above mentioned rate. The payment for the transaction was made on 10th April, 2015, when the exchange rate was ₹ 48 per US Dollar. At the year end 31st March, 2015, the rate of exchange was ₹ 49 per US Dollar.

The Chief Accountant of the company passed an entry on 31st March, 2015 adjusting the cost of raw material consumed for the difference between ₹ 48 and ₹ 44 per US Dollar. Discuss whether this treatment is justified as per the provisions of AS-11 (Revised).

ANSWER:

PROVISION OF AS-11

As per AS 11, 'The Effects of Changes in Foreign Exchange Rates', initial recognition of a foreign currency transaction is done in the reporting currency by applying the exchange rate at the date of the transaction.

ACCOUNTING TREATMENT

1. **At the Date of Transaction** the raw material purchased and its creditors will be recorded at US dollar 9,000 × ₹ 44 = ₹ 3,96,000.
2. **At Balance Sheet date** such transaction is reported at closing rate of exchange, hence it will be valued at the closing rate i.e. ₹ 49 per US dollar (USD 9,000 × ₹ 49 = ₹ 4,41,000)
3. The difference of ₹ 5 (i.e., 49 – 44) per US dollar i.e. ₹ 45,000 (USD 9,000 × ₹ 5) will be shown as an exchange loss in the profit and loss account for the year ended 31st March, 2015 and **will not be adjusted against the cost of raw materials.**
4. **At settlement date**, the company would recognize or provide in the Profit and Loss account an exchange gain of ₹ 1 per US dollar, i.e. the difference from balance sheet date to the date of settlement between ₹ 49 and ₹ 48 per US dollar i.e. ₹ 9,000.
5. Hence, the accounting treatment adopted by the Chief Accountant is not as per AS 11.

QUESTION 4: Mr. A bought a forward contract for three months of US $ 1,00,000 on 1st December at 1 US $ = ₹ 62.10 when exchange rate was US $ 1 = ₹ 62.02, On 31st December when he closed his books, exchange rate was US $ 1 = ₹ 62.15. On 31st January, he decided to sell the contract at ₹ 62.18 per dollar. Show how the profits from contract will be recognised in the books.

ANSWER:

PROVISION OF AS-11

As per AS 11 'Effect of Changes in Foreign Exchange Rates', in recording a forward exchange contract intended for trading or speculation purpose, the premium or discount on the contract is ignored and at each balance sheet date, the value of contract is marked to its current market value and the gain or loss on the contract is recognised.

TREATMENT OF PROFIT ON FORWARD CONTRACT FOR TRADING/SPECULATION PURPOSES

It is apparent from the facts given in the QUESTION that Mr. A entered into forward exchange contract for speculation purpose.Hence,

1. Premium on forward contract [i.e. the difference between the spot rate and the forward contract rate] will not be recorded in the books.
2. Only when the forward contract is sold the difference between the forward contract rate and sale rate will be recorded in the Profit & Loss Account.

   Profit on contract = Contract Amount × [Sale Rate – Contract Rate]

   = US$ 1,00,000 × (₹ 62.18 – ₹ 62.10)] = ₹ 8,000 will be recognized on 31st January.

DISCLOSURE

An enterprise should disclose the following:

(i) The amount of exchange differences included in the net profit or loss for the period.

(ii) Net exchange differences accumulated in foreign currency translation reserve as a separate component of shareholder's funds, and a reconciliation of the amount of such exchange differences at the beginning and end of the period.

Note: The answer has been given on the basis thai Mr. A is a small and mediumsized entity and AS 30 "Financial instruments: Recognition and Measurement" is not applicable to him.

QUESTION 5: Sterling Ltd. purchased a plant for US $20,000 on 31st December, 2014 payable after 4 months. The company entered into a forward contract for 4 months @ ₹ 48.85 per dollar. On 31st December, 2014, the exchange rate was ₹ 47.50 per dollar.How will you recognize the profit or loss on forward contract in the books of Sterling Limited for the year ended 31st March, 2015.

ANSWER:

TREATMENT OF PROFIT ON FORWARD CONTRACT FOR HEDGING PURPOSES

Particulars	₹
Premium on entering into forward contract = [$20,000 × (₹ 48.85 - ₹ 47.50)]	₹ 27,000
Loss for 3 months falling in the year 2014-2015 will be (₹ 27,000 × 3/4)	20,250
Balance Loss of ₹ 6,750 (i.e. ₹ 27,000 × 1/4) for the month of April, 2015 will be recognised in the financial year 2015-2016.	

QUESTION 6: X Ltd. borrowed US $ 3,78,000 on 31-12-2014 when the exchange rate was ₹ 60 per US Dollar. X Ltd. prepares its financial statements ending on 31-03-2015 when the exchange rate was ₹ 62 per US Dollar. Discuss Accounting treatment as per AS-11 (Revised) in each of the following cases:

(a) If Option as per Para 46A is not exercised

(b) If Option as per Para 46A is exercised and such Loan relates to purchase of a Machine

(c) If Option as per Para 46A is exercised and such Loan relates to purchase of Land

(d) If Borrower is a Partnership Firm and not a Company

ANSWER: Exchange Loss = $ 3,78,000 × (₹ 60 – ₹ 62) = (₹ 7,56,000)

If Option as per Para 46A is not exercised	Exchange Loss (₹ 7,56,000) should be debited to Profit & Loss A/c.
If Option as per Para 46A is exercised and such Loan relates to purchase of a Machine	Exchange Loss (₹ 7,56,000) should be debited to Machine A/c. Depreciation on the revised book value will be provided prospectively over the residual useful life of the asset.

If Option as per Para 46A is exercised and such Loan relates to purchase of Land	1. Exchange Loss (₹ 7,56,000) should be debited to Foreign Currency Monetary Items Translation Difference A/c. 2. Such Exchange Loss should be transferred to Profit & Loss A/c in equal proportion over reporting periods ending on March 31,2020. Hence ₹ 1,26,000 (i.e.₹ 7,56,000 /8) should be transferred to Profit & Loss A/c on 31.03.2015. **Note:** The Dr. Balance of FCMITD A/c (i.e. ₹ 6,30,000) should be shown on the Equity & Liabilities side of the Balance Sheet under the head 'Reserves & Surplus'.
If Borrower is a Partnership Firm and not a Company	Exchange Loss(₹7,56,000) should be debited to Profit & Loss A/c since Option as per Para 46A is available only to a Company.

QUESTION 7: X Ltd. purchased Fixed Assets costing ₹ 6,000 lakhs on 1.4.2014. This was financed by foreign currency loan (U.S. Dollars) payable in three annual equal instalments. Exchange rates were 1 Dollar = ₹ 57 and ₹ 62 as on 1.4.2014 and 31.3.2015 respectively. First instalment was paid on 31.3.2015. X Ltd. provides depreciation on Fixed Assets @20% on WDV basis.State, how these transactions would be accounted for?

ANSWER:

PROVISION OF AS-11

As per AS 11 (Revised) exchange differences arising on the settlement of monetary items or on reporting an enterprise's monetary items at rates different from those at which they were initially recorded during the period, or reported in previous financial statements, should be recognized as income or as an expense in the period in which they arise. Thus, exchange differences arising on repayment of liabilities incurred for the purpose of acquiring fixed assets are recognized as income or expenses.

Exchange Difference

Foreign Exchange Loan = ₹ 6000 lakhs/140 = US $150 lakhs

Exchange Difference = US $150 lakhs × (₹ 62 – ₹ 57) = ₹ 750 lakhs.

ACCOUNTING TREATMENT

1. Initially Fixed Assets should be recognised at ₹ 6,000 lakhs.
2. Exchange Loss of ₹ 750 lakhs should be charged to Profit and Loss Account for the year ended 31st March 2015,.
3. Depreciation of ₹ 1200 lakhs (i.e. 20% of ₹ 6,000 lakhs) should be provided in the Financial Statements for the year ended 31st March 2015.
4. Closing Balance of Fixed Assets will be ₹ 4,800 lakhs.

QUESTION 8: X Ltd. purchased Fixed Assets costing ₹ 6,000 lakhs on 1.4.2014. This was financed by foreign currency loan (U.S. Dollars) payable in three annual equal instalments. Exchange rates were 1 Dollar = ₹ 57 and ₹ 62 as on 1.4.2014 and 31.3.2015 respectively. First instalment was paid on 31.3.2015. X Ltd. provides depreciation on Fixed Assets @20% on WDV basis. The company excercises the Option as per Para 46A . State, how these transactions would be accounted for?

ANSWER:

PROVISION OF PARA 46A OF THE COMPANIES (ACCOUNTING STANDARDS) RULES, 2012.

As per Para 46A, in case of **Long-term Foreign Currency Loans relating to Depreciable Assets,** Exchange Difference should be debited(in case of Exchange Loss) or credited (in case of Exchange

Profit) to the Respective Asset A/c.

Exchange Difference

Foreign Exchange Loan = ₹ 6000 lakhs/140 = US $150 lakhs

Exchange Difference = US $150 lakhs × (₹ 62 – ₹ 57) = ₹ 750 lakhs.

ACCOUNTING TREATMENT

1. Initially Fixed Assets should be recognised at ₹ 6,000 lakhs.
2. Exchange Loss of ₹ 750 lakhs should be debited to Fixed Assets Account.
3. Depreciation of ₹ 1350 lakhs (i.e. 20% of ₹ 6,750 lakhs) should be provided in the Financial Statements for the year ended 31st March 2015.
4. Closing Balance of Fixed Assets will be ₹ 5,400 lakhs.

QUESTION 9: X Ltd. purchased Land costing ₹ 6,000 lakhs on 1.4.2014. This was financed by foreign currency loan (U.S. Dollars) payable in three annual equal instalments. Exchange rates were 1 Dollar = ₹ 57 and ₹ 62 as on 1.4.2014 and 31.3.2015 respectively. First instalment was paid on 31.3.2015. The company excercises the Option as per Para 46A . State, how these transactions would be accounted for?

ANSWER:

PROVISION OF PARA 46A OF THE COMPANIES (ACCOUNTING STANDARDS) RULES, 2012.

1. In case of **Long-term Foreign Currency Loans relating to Non-Depreciable Assets** Exchange Difference should be debited(in case of Exchange Loss) or credited (in case of Exchange Profit) to Foreign Currency Monetary Items Translation Difference A/c.
2. Such Exchange Difference should be transferred to Profit & Loss A/c in equal proportion over reporting periods ending on March 31,2020.
3. The Dr. or Cr. Balance of FCMITD A/c should be shown on the Equity & Liabilities side of the Balance Sheet under the head 'Reserves & Surplus'.

Exchange Difference

Foreign Exchange Loan = ₹ 6000 lakhs/140 = US $150 lakhs

Exchange Difference = US $150 lakhs × (₹ 62 – ₹ 57) = ₹ 750 lakhs

ACCOUNTING TREATMENT

1. Exchange Loss (₹ 750 lakhs) should be debited to Foreign Currency Monetary Items Translation Difference A/c.
2. Such Exchange Loss should be transferred to Profit & Loss A/c in equal proportion over reporting periods ending on March 31,2020. Hence ₹ 125 lakhs (i.e. ₹ 750 lakhs /6) should be transferred to Profit & Loss A/c on 31.03.2015.
3. The Dr. Balance of FCMITD A/c (i.e. ₹ 625 lakhs) should be shown on the Equity & Liabilities side of the Balance Sheet under the head 'Reserves & Surplus'.
4. Initially Land should be recognised at ₹ 6,000 lakhs.

QUESTION 10: X Limited, a newly incorporated company in India commenced its business from April 1, 2012. The Company purchased fixed assets costing ₹ 4,000 lakhs on 01-04-2012 and the same was fully financed by foreign currency loan (U.S. Dollars) payable in three annual equal installments. Exchange rates were 1 Dollar = ₹ 40.00 and ₹42.50 as on 01- 04-2012 and 31-03-2013 respectively. The company worked out foreign exchange loss as per AS 11 at ₹250 Lakhs and expensed the entire amount in the profit and loss account. The Managing Director of the company was worried about this heavy revenue loss and asked the accountant not to follow AS 11 issued by the ICAI for this particular transaction. The Accountant of the company, followed the instruction of the Managing Director and removed exchange loss from

the profit and loss account but then he added the entire exchange loss to the value of fixed asset and computed the depreciation thereon. As an Auditor of X Limited how you would deal with this particular transaction?

ANSWER:

PROVISION OF AS 11

As per new para 46A(1) of AS 11 "The Effects of Changes in Foreign Exchange Rates" inserted by Ministry of Corporate Affairs by way of notification, the exchange differences arising on reporting of long- term foreign currency monetary items in so far as they relate to the acquisition of a depreciable capital asset in respect of accounting periods commencing on or after the 1st April, 2011. Such exchange differences can be added to or deducted from the cost of the asset and shall be depreciated over the balance life of the asset, and in other cases, it can be accumulated in a "Foreign Currency Monetary Item Translation Difference Account" in the enterprise's financial statements and amortized over the balance period of such long term asset or liability, by recognition as income or expense in each of such periods.

ADVISE

X Ltd. has the choice to avail this option. However, the company should disclose the fact of such option and of the amount remaining to be amortized in the financial statements of the period in which such option is exercised and in every subsequent period so long as any exchange difference remains unamortized.

QUESTION 11: Explain briefly the Accounting Treatment needed in the following cases as per AS 11:

1. **Sundry Debtors include amount receivable from Ted of U.S., ₹ 5,00,000 recorded at the prevailing exchange rate on the date of sales, transaction recorded at $1 = 50.**
2. **Long term loan taken from a U.S. Company, amounting to ₹ 49,00,000. It was recorded at $1 = ₹49, taking exchange rate prevailing at the date of transactions.**

   Exchange rates at the end of the year were as under:

   $1 Receivable = ₹ 60

   $1 Payable = ₹ 61.

ANSWER:

PROVISION OF AS-11

AS 11 'The Effects of Changes in Foreign Exchange Rates' provides that exchange differences attributable to monetary items should be taken to Statement of Profit and Loss. In case the option under para 46A is exercised, the exchange differences arising on long-term foreign currency monetary items can be adjusted in the cost of the depreciable capital asset or in other cases transferred in Foreign Currency Monetary Item Translation Difference Account (FCMITD) and amortised.

ACCOUNTING TREATMENT

1. Exchange Gain = US $ 10,000 × (₹50 – ₹ 60) = ₹ 1,00,000 should be credited to Profit and Loss Account.
2. Exchange Loss = US $1,00,000 × (₹49 – ₹ 61) = ₹ 12,00,000 should be debited to Profit and Loss Account or transfer to FCMITD A/c and amortise.

QUESTION 12: X Ltd. borrowed US $5,00,000 on 31-12-2014 which will be repaid (settled) as on 30-6-2015. X Ltd. prepares its financial statements ending on 31-03-2015. Rate of exchange between reporting currency (Rupee) and foreign currency (US $) on different dates are as under:

31-12-2014	**1 US $ = ₹ 44.00**
31-03-2015	**1 US $ = ₹ 44.50**
30-06-2015	**1 US $ = ₹ 44.75**

(i) Calculate Borrowings in reporting currency to be recognised in the books on above mentioned dates and also show journal entries for the same.

(ii) If Borrowings were repaid (settled) on 28-2-2015 on which date exchange rate was 1 US $ = ₹ 44.20 than what entry should be passed?

ANSWER:

PROVISION OF AS-11

As per para 9 of As 11 "Changes in Foreign Exchange Rates", a foreign currency transaction should be recorded, on initial recognition in the reporting currency, by applying to the foreign currency amount the exchange rate between the reporting currency and the foreign currency at the date of the transaction.

As per para 11(a) of the standard, at each balance sheet date, foreign currency monetary items should be reported using the closing rate.

ACCOUNTING TREATMENT

Accordingly, on 31.12.2014 borrowings will be recorded at ₹ 2,20,00,000 (i.e., ₹ 5,00,000 × ₹ 44.00). Accordingly, on 31.12.2015, borrowings (monetary items) will be recorded at ₹ 2,22,50,000 (i.e., $ 5,00,000 × ₹ 44.50).

(I) JOURNAL OF X LTD.

Date	Particulars		Dr. (₹)	Cr. (₹)
31-12-2014	Bank A/c	Dr.	2,20,00,000	
	To Borrowings			2,20,00,000
31-03-2015	Profit & Loss A/c	Dr.	2,50,000	
	To Borrowings			2,50,000
30.06.2015	Borrowings A/c	Dr.	2,22,50,000	
	Profit & Loss A/c	Dr.	1,25,000	
	To Bank A/c			2,23,75,000

(ii) In case Borrowings were repaid before balance sheet date then the entry would be as follows:

(II) JOURNAL OF X LTD.

Date	Particulars		Dr. (₹)	Cr. (₹)
28-02-2015	Borrowings A/c	Dr.	2,20,00,000	
	Profit & Loss A/c	Dr.	1,00,000	
	To Bank A/c			2,21,00,000

Working Notes:

1. The exchange difference of ₹ 2,50,000 is arising because the transaction has been reported at different rate (₹ 44.50 = 1 US $) from the rate initially recorded (i.e., ₹ 44 = 1 US $) from the rate initially recorded (i.e., ₹ 44 = 1 US $).
2. The exchange difference of ₹ 12,500 is arising because the transaction has been settled at an exchange rate (₹ 44.75 = 1 US $) different from the rate at which reported in the last financial statement (₹ 44.50 = 1 US $).

(iii) The exchange difference of ₹ 1,00,000 is arising because the transaction has been settled at a different rate (i.e., ₹ 44.20 = 1 US $) than the rate at which initially recorded (1 US $ = ₹ 44.00).

QUESTION 13: X Ltd. of India purchased a machinery from U.S.A. at $ 1.5 million on 01/10/2014 by borrowing U.S $ 1 million from a foreign bank @10% p.a. when the exchange rate was ₹ 42 per dollar. If the loan was taken in India on the same conditions and term then the rate of interest would have been 15% p.a. The machinery is ready to put to use when purchased. This machinery is to be depreciated @ 10% on SLM basis. X Ltd. paid U.S. $ 1,00,000. to foreign bank towards principal and interest on 31/03/2015 when the exchange rate was ₹ 43.50 per dollar.. How these transactions are shown in the financial statements of X Ltd. for the year 2014 - 2015.

ANSWER

CALCULATION OF AMOUNT TO BE RECOGNIZED IN MACHINERY A/C, DEPRECIATION FOR THE YEAR AND CLOSING BALANCE OF THE MACHINERY ACCOUNT

Particulars	Amount
A. Cost of machinery	$ 15,00,000
B. Exchange rate per dollar existing on date of transaction	₹ 42.00
C. Cost of machinery to be recognized (A × B)	₹ 6,30,00,000
D. Depreciation for the Year (C × 10% × 0.5)	₹ 31,50,000
E. Closing balance of the machinery (C – D)	₹ 5,98,50,000

CALCULATION OF AMOUNT TO BE RECOGNIZED IN LOAN A/C, INTEREST FOR THE YEAR AND CLOSING BALANCE OF THE LOAN ACCOUNT.

Particulars		Amount
A. Loan borrowed from a foreign bank		$ 10,00,000
B. Loan to be recognized in the books of X Ltd. (₹ 42 × A)		₹ 4,20,00,000
C. Borrowing Cost as per AS – 16		
Amount borrowed	$ 10,00,000	
Add: Interest @ 10% p.a. for 6 months	$ 50,000	
Total:	$ 10,50,000	
Less: Payment received	$ 1,00,000	
Balance	$ 9,50,000	
Liability towards loan at year end due to interest and change in exchange rate		
Principal paid ($ 50,000 × 1.50)	₹ 75,000	
Interest paid ($ 50,000 × 43.50)	₹ 21,75,000	
Increase in closing liability ($ 9,50,000 × 1.50)	₹ 14,25,000	
Total (A)	₹ 36,75,000	
Interest that would have been payable if loan is taken in India (₹ 4.2 crores × 15% × 6/12) (B)		₹ 31,50,000
Borrowing cost (A) or (B) whichever is lower		₹ 31,50,000
D. Exchange difference (₹ 36,75,000 – ₹ 31,50,000)		₹ 5,25,000
E. Payment made ($ 1,00,000 × 43.50)		₹.43,50,000
F. Closing Balance (B + C + D – E)		₹ 4,13,25,000

6 AS 12 – ACCOUNTING FOR GOVERNMENT GRANTS

THEORETICAL BASE

QUESTION 1. State the Meaning of Government Grants as per AS 12.When to recognize Government Grants as per AS 12?

ANSWER:

MEANING OF GOVERNMENT GRANTS

Government grants are assistance by government in cash or kind to an enterprise for past or future compliance with certain conditions.

WHEN TO RECOGNIZE GOVERNMENT GRANTS?

1. Where there is reasonable assurance that the enterprise will comply with the conditions attached to them; and
2. Where such benefits have been earned by the enterprise and it is reasonably certain that the ultimate collection will be made.

   Note: Mere receipt of a grant is not necessarily a conclusive evidence that conditions attaching to the grant have been or will be fulfilled.

QUESTION 2. Explain the Treatment of Receipt and Refund of Government Grants related to Revenue as per AS 12.

ANSWER:

TREATMENT OF RECEIPT OF GOVERNMENT GRANTS RELATED TO REVENUE

Alternative 1	1. Treat as Income and Credit to Profit & Loss Account
Alternative 2	2. Deduct from the related expense while reporting.

TREATMENT OF REFUND OF GOVERNMENT GRANTS RELATED TO REVENUE

1. Reduce the balance of Unamortized Deferred Credit Balance
2. Charge excess refund to Profit & Loss Account
3. **Journal Entry:**

Grant A/c	Dr.	[with Unamortized Cr. Balance]
P&L A.c	Dr.	[With Excess of Refund over Unam-ortized Cr. Balance]
To Bank A/c		[with Refund]

QUESTION 3. Explain the Treatment of Receipt and Refund of Government Grants in the nature of Promoter's Contribution as per AS 12.

ANSWER:

TREATMENT OF RECEIPT OF GOVERNMENT GRANTS IN THE NATURE OF PROMOTER'S CONTRIBUTION

Government grants in the nature of Promoter's contribution should be credited to Capital Reserve and treated as a part of Shareholders' Funds.

TREATMENT OF REFUND OF GOVERNMENT GRANTS IN THE NATURE OF PROMOTER'S CONTRIBUTION

Reduce from the Capital Reserve.

Journal Entry:

Capital Reserve A/c Dr.
  To Grant A/c

QUESTION 4. Explain the Treatment of Receipt of Non-Monetary Grant from the Government as per AS 12.

ANSWER:

1. Asset received at a concessional rate.	It should be accounted for on the basis of its acquisition cost.
2. Asset received free of cost	It should be recorded at a nominal value.

QUESTION 5. Explain the Treatment of Receipt and Refund of Government Grants related to Specific Depreciable Fixed Assets as per AS 12.

ANSWER:

TREATMENT OF RECEIPT OF GOVERNMENT GRANTS RELATED TO SPECIFIC DEPRECIABLE FIXED ASSETS

1. **AS CAPITAL RECEIPT ALTERNATIVE**

   Show the grant as a deduction from the gross value of the asset concerned to arrive at book value. Where the grant related to a specific fixed asset equals the whole, or virtually the whole, of the cost of the asset, the asset should be shown in the balance sheet at a nominal value.

   Journal Entry: Grant A/c Dr.
   To Fixed Asset A/c

2. **AS DEFERRED INCOME ALTERNATIVE**

   1. Treat it as deferred income and recognize it in the Profit and Loss Statement on a systematic and rational basis over the useful life of the asset, in other words, Such Grants should be recognized as income over the useful life of the asset in the proportion in which depreciation on those assets is charged.
   2. Grant to recognised each year = [Depreciation for the year/Total Depreciation during useful life] x Total Grant =
   3. **Journal Entry:** Grant A/c Dr. [With Income Recognised]
      To P&L A/c
   4. Unamortized Deferred Income Balance should be disclosed separately in Financial Statements

TREATMENT OF REFUND OF GOVERNMENT GRANTS RELATED TO SPECIFIC DEPRECIABLE FIXED ASSETS

1. **UNDER CAPITAL RECEIPT ALTERNATIVE**
   1. Increase the book value of the asset
   2. Provide depreciation on the revised book value prospectively over the residual useful life of the asset.
   3. **Journal Entries:**

      (a) Fixed Asset A/c Dr. [With Refund]
      To Grant A/c

      (b) Grant A/c Dr. [With Refund]
      To Bank A/c

2. UNDER DEFERRED INCOME ALTERNATIVE

1. Reduce the balance of Unamortized Deferred Credit Balance
2. Charge Excess Refund to Profit & Loss Account
3. **Journal Entry:**

Grant A/c	Dr.	[with Unamortized Deferred Cr. Balance]
P&L A.c	Dr.	[With Excess of Refund over Unamortized Cr. Balance]
To Bank A/c		[with Refund]

QUESTION 6. Explain the Treatment of Receipt of Government Grants related to Specific Non- Depreciable Fixed Assets as per AS 12.

ANSWER:

IF GRANT RELATED TO NON -DEPRECIABLE DOES NOT REQUIRE FULFILLMENT OF CERTAIN OBLIGATIONS

1. It should be credited to Capital Reserve.
2. **Journal Entry:** Grant A/c Dr.
   To Capital Reserve A/c

IF GRANT RELATED TO NON-DEPRECIABLE REQUIRES FULFILLMENT OF CERTAIN OBLIGATIONS

1. It should be treated as deferred income and It should be credited to income over the same period over which the cost of meeting such obligations is charged to income.
2. **Journal Entry:** Grant A/c Dr. [With Grant Recognised as Income]
   To P&L A/c
3. The Unamortized Deferred Income Balance should be separately disclosed in the financial statements.

QUESTION 7. Explain in brief the treatment of Refund of Government Grants in line with AS 12 in the following three situations:

(i) When Government Grant is, related to revenue

(ii) When Government Grant is related to Specific Fixed Assets,

(iii) When Government Grant is in the nature of Promoter's contribution.

ANSWER: As per AS 12, refund to Government Grant is treated in the following manner:

(a) When Government Grant is related to Revenue:

(i) The amount of refund is first adjusted against any unamortized deferred credit balance still remaining in respect of the Grant

(ii) Any excess refund over such deferred credit balance or where no deferred credit exists, is immediately charged to Profit & Loss Account.

(b) When Government Grant is related to specific Fixed Asset:

(i) The amount of refund will increase the Book Value of the Asset, if at the time of receipt of Grant, the cost of asset was reduced by the amount of Grand.

(ii) If at the time of receipt, the Grant amount was credited to Deferred Grant Account, then the amount of refund will first reduce the unamortized balance of Deferred Grant Account, any excess refund will reduce the Capital Reserve.

(c) When the Government Grant is in the nature of Promoter's Contribution:

Capital Reserve will be reduced by the amount of refund.

QUESTION 8. State the Disclosure Requirements as to Govt. Grants.

ANSWER:

1. The Accounting Policy adopted for Government Grants, including the methods of presentation in the financial statements;
2. The nature and extent of Government Grants recognized in the financial statements, including grants of non-monetary assets given at a concessional rate or free of cost.

PRACTICAL QUESTIONS FOR PRACTICE

QUESTION 1. Explain the treatment of the following:

(a) ₹ 100 lakhs received from the Central Govt. as subsidy for setting up a Plant in backward area. Cost of Plant ₹ 500 lakhs

(b) ₹ 50 lakhs received from the State Govt. a Grant for setting up a Water treatment Plant. Cost of Plant ₹ 150 lakhs

(c) ₹ 25 lakhs received from the Local Authority for providing medical facilities to the employees.

(d) Received Land worth ₹ 100 lakhs free of cost from the State Govt.

ANSWER:

(a) As per AS 12, Government grants of the nature of promoters' contribution should be credited to capital reserve and treated as a part of shareholders' funds. In this case grant of ₹ 100 lakhs is in nature of promoters' contribution hence it should be credited to Capital Reserve which can neither be distributed as divided nor considered as deferred income.

(b) As per AS 12, the Grant relating to a specific fixed asset is shown as a deduction from the gross value of the asset concerned to arrive at book value. Grant of ₹ 50 lakhs will be deducted from the cost of the asset and the asset will be shown at ₹ 100 lakhs (i.e. ₹ 150 lakhs -₹ 50).

(c) As per AS 12, the Grant relating to revenue is credited to Profit & Loss A/c or deducted from the related expense. Grant of ₹ 25 lakhs will be credited to Profit & Loss A/c or deducted from the Medical Expenses.

(d) As per AS 12, Asset received free of cost should be recorded at a nominal value. Land should be recorded at a nominal value.

QUESTION 2: On 1.4.2013 TULSIAN Ltd. purchased a Fixed Asset for ₹ 5,50,000. The salvage value at the end of useful life of 5 years was estimated at ₹ 50,000. On the same date the company received Govt. Grant of ₹ 2,00,000. During 2014-2015 the company had to refund the Govt. Grant due to non-fulfillment of certain conditions. Show that accounting treatment in Journal and Balance Sheet upto 2014-2015 if the company decides to treat the Govt. Grant as Capital Receipt.

ANSWER:

JOURNAL

Date	Particulars		Dr. (₹)	Cr. (₹)
01.04.2013	Fixed Asset A/c	Dr.	5,50,000	
	To Bank A/c			5,50,000
	(Being the Fixed Asset purchased)			
01.04.2013	Bank A/c	Dr.	2,00,000	
	To Government Grant A/c			2,00,000
	(Being the Government Grant received)			

01.04.2013	Government Grant A/c To Fixed Asset A/c (Being the Government Grant credited to Asset A/c.)	Dr.	2,00,000	2,00,000
31.03.2014	Depreciation A/c To Fixed Asset A/c (Being the depreciation is calculated on the net book value of the asset) [(₹ 5,50,000 – ₹ 2,00,000 – ₹ 50,000)/5]	Dr.	60,000	60,000
2014 –2015	Fixed Asset A/c To Government Grant A/c (Being the Refund of Govt. Grant debited to Asset A/c)	Dr.	2,00,000	2,00,000
2014 –2015	Government Grant A/c To Bank A/c (Being the Govt. Grant refunded)	Dr.	2,00,000	2,00,000
31.03.2015	Depreciation A/c To Fixed Asset A/c (Being the depreciation provided on revised Book value) [(₹ 2,90,000 + ₹ 2,00,000 – ₹ 50,000)/4]	Dr.	1,10,000	1,10,000

AN EXTRACT OF BALANCE SHEET AS AT 31st MARCH 2014

Non-Current Assets		
Tangible Fixed Assets	5,50,000	
Less: Govt. Grant	(2,00,000)	
Balance	3,50,000	
Less: Depreciation	(60,000)	2,90,000

AN EXTRACT OF BALANCE SHEET AS AT 31st MARCH 2015

Non-current Assets		
Tangible Fixed Assets	2,90,000	
Add: Govt. Grant	2,00,000	
Balance	4,90,000	
Less: Depreciation	(1,10,000)	3,80,000

QUESTION 3: On 1.4.2013 TULSIAN Ltd. purchased a Fixed Asset for ₹ 5,50,000. The salvage value at the end of useful life of 5 years was estimated at ₹ 50,000. On the same date the company received Govt. Grant of ₹ 2,00,000. During 2014-2015 the company had to refund the Govt. Grant due to non-fulfillment of certain conditions. Show that accounting treatment in Journal and Balance Sheet upto 2014-2015 if the company decides to treat the Govt. Grant as Deferred Income.

ANSWER:

JOURNAL

Date	Particulars		Dr. (₹)	Cr. (₹)
01.04.2013	Fixed Asset A/c	Dr.	5,50,000	
	To Bank A/c			5,50,000
	(Being Fixed Asset purchased)			
01.04.2013	Bank A/c	Dr.	2,00,000	
	To Government Grant A/c			2,00,000
	(Being Government Grant received)			
31.03.2014	Depreciation A/c	Dr.	1,00,000	
	To Fixed Asset A/c			1,00,000
	(Being depreciation is calculated on the net book value of the asset) [(₹ 5,50,000 – ₹ 50,000)/5]			
31.03.2014	Government Grant A/c	Dr.	40,000	
	To P & L A/c			40,000
	(Being the Govt. Grant in proportion to Depreciation recognized as Income and T/f to P & L A/c)			
2014 –2015	Government Grant A/c	Dr.	1,60,000	
	Profit and Loss A/c	Dr.	40,000	
	To Bank A/c			2,00,000
	(Being the Govt. grant refunded)			
31.03.2015	Depreciation A/c	Dr.	1,00,000	
	To Fixed Asset A/c			1,00,000
	(Being depreciation is calculated on the net book value of the asset) [(₹ 5,50,000 – ₹ 50,000)/5]			

AN EXTRACT OF BALANCE SHEET AS AT 31st MARCH 2014

Reserves and Surplus:		
Government Grant:		
Received	2,00,000	
Less: T/f to P & L A/c.	(40,000)	1,60,000
Non Current Assets:		
Tangible Fixed Assets	5,50,000	
Less: Depreciation	(1,00,000)	4,50,000

A EXTRACT OF BALANCE SHEET AS AT 31st MARCH 2015

Tangible Fixed Assets	4,50,000	
Less: Depreciation	(1,00,000)	3,50,000

QUESTION 4. On 1st April, 2012. BHARAT TUSHAR Ltd. purchased a Fixed Asset worth ₹ 149.50 lakhs for which it got Government grant of ₹ 24.50 lakhs. The Salvage Value at the end of useful life of 4 years was estimated at ₹ 51.20 lakhs. X Ltd. decides to treat the Grant as Capital Receipt. During 2014-2015 the Grant has become refundable due to non-fulfilment of certain conditions.

Required: Calculate the amount of the Depreciation to be recognized every year in Profit and Loss Account during the useful life of the machinery if the company followed (a)Straight Line Method. (b) W.D.V Method.

ANSWER:

PROVISION OF AS 12

As per para 11.2 of AS 12 on Accounting Government Grants, the amount refundable in respect of a government grant related to a specific fixed asset is recorded by increasing the book value of the asset. Depreciation on the revised book value is provided prospectively over the residual useful life of the asset.

STATEMENT SHOWING THE BOOK VALUE, SLM DEPRECIATION CHARGED AND RECORDING OF REFUND OF GRANT

Particulars	[₹ Lakhs]
Cost of Fixed Asset	149.50
Less: Grant received	(24.50)
Net Cost of Fixed Asset	125
Useful life	4 years
Depreciation p.a. as per Straight Line Method [(125 – 51.20)/4]	18.45
Total Depreciation for 2 years (2012-2013 & 2013-2014)[18.45 × 2]	36.90
Book Value (as on 1.4.2014) [125-36.90]	88.10
Add: Grant refunded	24.50
Revised Book Value	112.60
Remaining useful life	2 years
Revised Annual Depreciation[(112.6 – 51.20)/2] for 2 years(2013-2014 & 2014-2015)	30.70

STATEMENT SHOWING THE BOOK VALUE, WDV DEPRECIATION CHARGED AND RECORDING OF REFUND OF GRANT

Particulars	₹ (in lakhs)
Cost of Fixed Asset	149.50
Less: Grant received	(24.50)
A. Net Cost of Fixed Asset	125.00
B. *Less:* Depreciation @ 20%	(25.00)
C. Book value of the machinery as on 31st March, 2013 (A – B)	100.00
D. *Less:* Depreciation @ 20%	(20.00)
E. Book value of the machinery as on 31st March, 2014 (C – D)	80.00
F. *Add:* Grant refunded	24.50
G. Revised Book Value	104.50
H. *Less:* Depreciation @ 30%	(31.35)
I. Book Value of Machinery as on 31st March, 2015 (G-H)	73.15
J. *Less:* Depreciation @ 30%	(21.95)
K. Book Value of Machinery as on 31st March, 2016 (I-J)	51.20

Working Note: Calculation of WDV Rate of Depreciation

(i) WDV Depreciation Rate (on 1.4.2012) = $1 - \sqrt[4]{\text{ResidualValue/NetCost}}$

$= 1 - \sqrt[4]{51.20 \text{ lakhs}/125 \text{ lakhs}}$

$= 1 - \sqrt[4]{0.4096} = 1 - 0.8 = 0.2$ or 20%

(ii) WDV Depreciation Rate (on 1.4.2014) $= 1 - \sqrt{\text{Residual Value/Revised Book Value}}$

$= 1 - \sqrt{51.20 \text{ lakhs}/104.50 \text{ lakhs}}$

$= 1 - \sqrt{0.49} = 1 - 0.7 = 0.3$ or 30%

QUESTION 5. On 1st April, 2012. BHARAT TUSHAR Ltd. purchased a Fixed Asset worth ₹ 125 lakhs for which it got Government grant of ₹ 36.90 lakhs. The Salvage Value at the end of useful life of 4 years was estimated at ₹ 51.20 lakhs. X Ltd. decides to treat the Grant as as Deferred Income.

Required: Calculate the amount of the Depreciation & Grant to be recognized every year in Profit and Loss Account during the useful life of the machinery if the company followed (a) Straight Line Method. (b) W.D.V Method.

ANSWER:

PROVISION OF AS 12

As per AS 12 on Accounting Government Grants, Deferred Income from grants is recognized in the Profit and Loss Account on a systematic and rational basis over the useful life of the asset in the proportion in which depreciation on those assets is charged. Unamortized and Deferred Grant Balance should be disclosed separately in financial statements.

(I) STATEMENT SHOWING SLM DEPRECIATION & GRANT TO BE RECOGNIZED IN P & L A/C

Year	Opening Balance	Depreciation	Closing Balance	Grant to be recognized every year
A	B	C	D = B – C	E = 36.9 lakhs × (C/ 73.8 lakhs)
2012-2013	125	18.45	106.55	9.225
2013-2014	106.55	18.45	88.10	9.225
2014-2015	88.10	18.45	69.65	9.225
2015-2016	69.65	18.45	51.20	9.225
		73.80		36.90

Depreciation p.a. as per Straight Line Method [(125 – 51.20)/4] = 18.45

(II) STATEMENT SHOWING WDV DEPRECIATION & GRANT TO BE RECOGNIZED IN P & L A/C

Year	Opening Balance	Depreciation	Closing Balance	Grant to be recognized every year
A	B	C = B × 20%	D = B – C	E = 36.9 lakhs × (C/ 73.8 lakhs)
2012-2013	125	25.0	100.0	12.5
2013-2014	100	20.0	80.0	10.0
2014-2015	80	16.0	64.0	8.0
2015-2016	64	12.8	51.2	6.4
		73.8		36.9

Working Note: *Calculation of WDV Rate of Depreciation*

WDV Depreciation Rate (on 1.4.2012) $= 1 - \sqrt[4]{\text{ResidualValue/NetCost}}$

$= 1 - \sqrt[4]{51.20 \text{ lakhs}/125 \text{ lakhs}}$

$= 1 - \sqrt[4]{0.4096} = 1 - 0.8 = 0.2$ or 20%

QUESTION 6. In Previous Question How you would deal with the refund of grant in the books of BHARAT TUSHAR Ltd if during 2014-2015 the Grant has become refundable due to non-fulfilment of certain conditions?

ANSWER:

Provision: As per AS 12 on Accounting Government Grants, the amount refundable in respect of a government grant related to a specific fixed asset is recorded by passing the following Journal Entry:

Deferred Grant A/c	Dr	[with Deferred Grant Balance]
Profit & Loss A/c	Dr	[with Deferred Grant already cr. to P& L A/c]
To Bank A/c		[with Grant Refunded]

During 2014-2015 the following Journal Entry will be passed:

(i) Deferred Grant A/c	Dr	Rs18.45 lakhs	
Profit & Loss A/c	Dr	Rs18.45 lakhs	
To Bank A/c			₹ 36.90 lakhs
(ii) Deferred Grant A/c	Dr	Rs14.40 lakhs	
Profit & Loss A/c	Dr	₹ 22.50 lakhs	
To Bank A/c			₹ 36.90 lakhs

QUESTION 7. Primus Hospitals Ltd. had acquire 40 units of Doppler Scan machines from Holiver USA at a cost of US$ 165,100 per unit in the beginning of financial year 2011-2012. The prevailing rate of exchange was ₹ 50 to 1 US$. The acquisition was partly funded out of a government grant of ₹ 5 crores. The grant relating to such machines was given with a rider that in the event of a change in management, the entity is bounded to return the grant. In April 2014, 51% control in the company was taken over by an overseas investor. The expected productive period of such an assets in normally reckoned at 5 years. The depreciation rate adopted was 20% p.a. on S.L.M. basis. The company had incurred expenditure of US $ 4,000 towards bank changes and ₹ 7,500 per unit as sea freight. You are also informed that neither capital reserve nor deferred income account has been maintained by the company. You are required to suggest the accounting treatment as a result of the return of the grant, in the light of the relevant AS.

ANSWER:

PROVISION OF AS 12

As per para 16 of As 6 'Depreciation Accounting', where the historical cost of a depreciable asset has undergone a change due to increase or decreases in long term liability on account of exchange fluctuations, price adjustments, changes in duties or similar factors, the depreciation on the revised unamortized depreciable amount should be provided prospectively over the residual useful life of the asset.

CALCULATION OF REVISED BOOK VALUE AS ON 1st APRIL, 2013

Particulars	(₹)
Acquisition of 40 Doppler Scan machines	
[US $ 165,100 × ₹ 50 × 40 machines]	33,02,00,000
Add: Bank charges paid ($ 4,000 × ₹ 50)	2,00,000
Add: Sea Freight on the above machines (₹ 7,500 per unit × 40 machines)	3,00,000
Total landed cost as on 1st April, 2011	33,07,00,000

Less: Government grant	(5,00,00,000)
Value of 40 Doppler Scan machines	28,07,00,000
Less: Depreciation @ 20% for 3 years of SLM basis (i.e., ₹ 28,07,000 × 20% × 3 years)	(16,84,20,000)
WDV at the beginning of the year 2014-2015	11,22,80,000
Add: Refund of Government grant	5,00,00,000
Revised Book value of 1st April, 2014	16,22,80,000

TREATMENT

1.On 1st April, 2014, the remaining useful life is only two years, i.e., 2014-2015 & 2015-2016. Hence the WDV of ₹ 16,22,80,000 is to be written off under SLM@ 50% each year i.e., ₹ 8,11,40,000 per year.

2.The Government grant of ₹ 5 crores that becomes refundable should be accounted for as an extraordinary item as per AS 12 , with related disclosure of the increase depreciation of ₹ 2.5 crores (i.e., ₹ 8,11,40,000 – ₹ 5,61,40,000) as a result of the return of such grant.

QUESTION 8. Grant Medicare Ltd. acquired 5 units of Brain Scan Equipment for US$ 5,00,000 in April 2013 incurring ₹ 20,00,000 on sea freight and US$ 12,000 per unit towards transit Insurance, bank charges etc. The purchase was partly funded out of the company's internal accruals and from Government Grant of ₹ 94 Lakhs. The prevailing exchange rate to the US$ was 50. The company estimated the useful life of the equipment at 4 years with an estimated salvage value of 13% (approx). The grant was considered as Deferred Income up to 2015-2016 and in April 2016 the company had to return the entire grant received due to non fulfillment of certain conditions. You are required to show the deprecation and the grant that is to be recognized in the Profit & Loss accounts for the period commencing, 2013-2014 onwards and also draw up the entry that is passed in April 2016 for the return of the Grant. The Company follows the written down value method for depreciating its assets.

ANSWER:

STATEMENT SHOWING ANNUAL DEPRECIATION AND AMOUNT OF GRANT TO BE RECOGNIZED IN P & L A/C

(Rupees in Lakhs)

Year	Value of asset	Depr.@40%	Closing Value	Deferred grant to be recognized 94 X dep. for the year/Total Depreciation
2013-2014	300.00	120.00	180.00	43.20
2014-2015	180.00	72.00	108.00	25.92
2015-2016	108.00	43.20	64.80	15.55
2016-2017	64.80	25.92	38.88	9.33
Total		261.12		94.00

The entries for depreciation & recognition of the grant will be as per the above table for the year 2013-2014, 2014-2015 & 2015-2016

The entry for the return of the Grant of ₹ 94 lakhs in April 2016 will be as under:

Deferred Grant A/c	Dr.	₹ 9.33	
Profit & Loss A/c (₹ 43.20 + ₹ 25.92 + ₹ 15.55)	Dr.	₹ 84.67	
To Bank A/c			₹ 94.00

(Being the return of the Grant received due to non-fulfillment of conditions)		

Working Note:

1. **Calculation of Revised Book Value of Machine as on 1st April, 2013**

Particulars	**(₹ in lakhs)**
Acquisition of 5 units of brain scan units [US $ 5,00,000 x ₹ 50]	250
Add: Sea Freight on the above units	20
Add: Transit insurance, Bank charges etc. paid ($ 12,000 x ₹ 50 x 5)	30
Total landed cost as on 1st April, 2013	300

2. **WDV rate of depreciation** = $1 - \sqrt[4]{39/300} = 40\%$

QUESTION 9. A company purchased on April 1, 2010 a special purpose machinery for ₹ 1 crore, and received Central Government subsidy for 25% of the price. Effective life of the machinery is 8 years. Explain the accounting treatment and quote the relevant AS.

ANSWER:

PROVISION OF AS 12

As per AS 12, two methods of presentation in financial statements of grants related to specific fixed assets are regarded as acceptable alternatives.

1. **Capital Receipt Alternative:** The grant is shown as a deduction from the gross value of the asset concerned in arriving at its book value. The grant is thus recognised in the profit and loss statement over the useful life of a depreciable asset by way of a reduced depreciation charge.
2. **Deferred Income Alternative:** Grants related to depreciabfe assets are treated as deferred income which is recognised in the profit and loss statement on a systematic and rational basis over the useful life of the asset. Such allocation to income is usually made over the periods and in the proportions in which depreciation on related assets is charged.

ADVICE

1. **Under Capital Receipt Alternative:** The cost of special purpose machinery will be recorded in trie books after reducing it by the amount of government subsidy of ₹ 25 lakhs. Thus the depreciable value of the machinery recorded in the books will be ₹ 75 lakhs (i.e. ₹ 1 crore – ₹ 25 lakhs). Depreciation of ₹ 9.375 lakhs (i.e. ₹ 75 lakhs/8 years) will be charged on it every year on straight line method.
2. **Under Deferred Income Alternative:** Machinery will be recorded in the books at ₹ 1 crore and depreciation will be charged on it for ₹ 12.5 lakhs (i.e. ₹ 1 crore/8 years) per year on straight line method. Government subsidy of ₹ 25 lakhs will be treated as deferred income and ₹ 13.125 iakhs (i.e. ₹ 25 iakhs / 8 years) will be recognized as income in the Statement of Profit and Loss every year.

QUESTION 10. X Ltd. acquired a fixed asset for ₹ 50,00,000. The estimated useful life of the asset is 5 years. The salvage value after useful life was estimated at ₹ 5,00,000. The State Givernment gave a grant of 20% to encourage the asset acquisition. At the end of the second year, the subsidy of the State Government became refundable. What is the fixed asset value after refund of grant/subsidy to the State Government but before amortising the asset value at the end of the second year?

ANSWER:

STATEMENT SHOWING THE CALCULATION OF FIXED ASSETS AT THE END OF THE SECOND YEAR

Particulars	₹
Original Cost of Fixed Assets	50,00,000
Less: State Government grant received	(10,00,000)
Less: Amount to be written off in the first year [(40,00,000 – 5,00,000)/5 years]	(7,00,000)
	33,00,000
Add: Refund of State Government grant Value of fixed assets, at the end of the second year, after refund of grant but before depreciation	10,00,000
	43,00,000

QUESTION 11. A Ltd. purchased a machinery for ₹ 40 lakhs. (Useful life 4 years and residual value ₹ 8 lakhs) Government grant received is ₹ 16 lakhs.Show the Journal Entry to be passed at the time of refund of grant in the begnning of 3rd year and the value of the fixed assets, if:

1. **the Grant is credited to Fixed Assets.**
2. **the Grant is credited to Deferred Grant Account.**

ANSWER:

JOURNAL OF A LTD. (AT THE TIME OF REFUND OF GRANT)

If the Grant is credited to Fixed assets:

I	Fixed Assets A/c	Dr. ₹ 16 lakhs	
	To Bank A/c		₹ 16 lakhs

II The balance of fixed assets after two years depreciation will be ₹ 16 lakhs and now it will become (₹ 16 lakhs + ₹ 16 lakhs) = ₹ 32 lakhs on which depreciation will be charged for remaining two years. Depreciation = (32 – 8)/2 = ₹ 12 lakhs p.a. will be charged for next two years.

If the Grant is credited to Deferred Grant Account:

As per para 14 of AS 12 income from Deffered Grant Account is allocated to Profit and Loss account usually over the periods and in the proportions in which depreciation on related assets is charged. Accordingly, in the first two years (₹ 16 lakhs/4 years) = ₹ 4 lakhs × 2 = ₹ 8 lakhs were credited to Profit and Loss Account and ₹ 8 lakhs was the balance of Deferred Grant Account after two years. Therefore, on refund in the 3rd year, following entry will be passed:

I	Deferred Grant A/c	Dr. ₹ 8 lakhs	
	Profit & Loss A/c	Dr. ₹ 8 lakhs	
	To Bank A/c		₹ 16 lakhs
	(Being Government grant refunded)		

II Deferred grant account will become Nil. The fixed assets will continue to be shown in the books at ₹ 24 lakhs and depreciation will continue to be charged at 8 lakhs per annum.

Working Notes:

(i) Balance of Fixed Assets after two years but before refund (under first alternative)
= (₹ 40 lakhs – ₹ 16 lakhs) – (₹ 4 lakhs × 2) = ₹ 16 lakhs

(ii) Balance of Fixed Assets after two years but before refund (under second alternative)
= ₹ 40 lakhs – (₹ 8 lakhs × 2) = ₹ 24 lakhs

Note: It is assumed that value of fixed assets is to be given after refund of government grant.

QUESTION 12. Z Ltd. Purchased a fixed assets for ₹ 75 lakhs, which has the estimated useful life of 5 years with the salvage value of ₹ 7,50,000. On purchase of the assets, government granted it a grant of ₹ 15 lakhs. Pass the necessary journal entries in the books of the company for first two years treating Grant as Capital Receipt.

ANSWER: As per AS 12 where Grant is treated as Capital Receipt, the grant is shown as a deduction from the gross value of the asset concerned in arriving at its books value as follows:

JOURNAL OF Z LTD.

Year	Particulars		Dr. (₹)	Cr. (₹)
1st	Fixed Asset A/c	Dr.	75,00,000	
	To Bank A/c			75,00,000
	(Being Fixed Asset purchased)			
	Bank A/c	Dr.	15,00,000	
	To Fixed Asset A/c			15,00,000
	(Being grant received from the government)			
	Depreciation A/c ₹(60,00,000 – 7,50,000)/5	Dr.	10,50,000	
	To Fixed Asset A/c			10,50,000
	(Being Depreciation charged on Straight line method)			
	Profit & Loss A/c	Dr.	10,50,000	
	To Depreciation A/c			10,50,000
	(Being depreciation transferred to Profit & Loss A/c)			
2nd	Depreciation A/c	Dr.	10,50,000	
	To Fixed Asset A/c			10,50,000
	(Being Depreciation charged on Straight line method)			
	Profit & Loss A/c	Dr.	10,50,000	
	To Depreciation A/c			10,50,000
	(Being depreciation transferred to Profit & Loss A/c)			

QUESTION 13. ABC Limited purchased a machinery for ₹ 25,00,000 which has estimated useful life of 10 years with the salvage value of ₹ 5,00,000. On purchase of the assets Central Government pays a grant for ₹ 5,00,000. Pass the journal entries with narration in the books of the company for the first year, treating Grant as deferred income.

ANSWER:

JOURNAL OF ABC LTD.

Year	Particulars		Dr. (₹)	Cr. (₹)
1st	Machinery A/c	Dr.	25,00,000	
	To Bank A/c			25,00,000
	(Being machinery purchased)			
	Bank A/c	Dr.	5,00,000	
	To Deferred Government Grant A/c			5,00,000
	(Being grant received from the government treated as deferred income)			

	Particulars		Dr.	Cr.
	Depreciation A/c (25,00,000 – 5,00,000)/10 To Machinery A/c (Being depreciation charge on straight line method)	Dr.	2,00,000	2,00,000
	Profit & Loss A/c To Depreciation A/c (Being depreciation transferred to P/L Account)	Dr.	2,00,000	2,00,000
	Deferred Government Grant A/c (5,00,000)/10 To Profit & Loss A/c (Being proportionate government grant taken to P/L Account)	Dr.	50,000	50,000

QUESTION 14. X Ltd. received a specific grant of ₹ 600 lakhs for acquiring the plant of ₹ 3,000 lakhs during 2011-2012 having useful life of 10 years. The grant received was credited to deferred income and shown in the balance sheet. During 2014-2015, due to non-compliance of conditions laid down for the grant the company had to refund the grant to the Government. Balance in the deferred income on that date was ₹ 420 lakhs and written down value of plant was ₹ 2,100 lakhs.

1. **What should be the treatment for the refund of the grant and the effect on cost of the fixed asset and the amount of depreciation to be charged during the year 2014-2015 in Profit and Loss Account? Assume that depreciation is charged on assets as per straight line method.**
2. **What should be the treatment of the refund if grant was deducted from the cost of the plant during 2011-2012?**

ANSWER: As per para 21 of AS 12, 'Accounting for Government Grants', amount refundable in respect of a grant related to revenue should be applied first against any unamortized deferred credit remaining in respect of the grant. To the extent the amount refundable exceeds any such deferred credit, the amount should be charged to the Statement of Profit and Loss.

1. 180 lakhs shall be charged to the Statement of Profit and Loss for the year 2014-2015. There will be no effect on the cost of the fixed asset and depreciation charged will be same as charged in the earlier years.
2. The book value of the assets will be increased by ₹ 600 and depreciation on the revised book value will be provided prospectively over the residual useful life of the asset. Depreciation charged during the year 2014-2015 shall be = (₹ 1680 + 600)/7 = ₹ 325.71.

QUESTION 15. Top & Top Ltd. has set up its business in a designated backward area, which entitles the company to receive from the Government of India a subsidy of 20% of the cost of investment. Having fulfilled all the conditions under the scheme, the company on its investment of ₹ 50 crores in capital assets, received ₹ 10 crores from the government in January 2015 (accounting period being 2014-2015). The company wants to treat this receipt as an item of revenue and thereby reduce the losses on profit and loss account for the year ended 31st March, 2015. Keeping in view the relevant Accounting Standard, discuss whether this action is justified or not.

ANSWERL

PROVISION OF AS 12

As per AS-12 "where the government grants are of the nature of promoter contribution i.e. they are given with reference to the total investment in an undertaking or by the way of promoters contribution towards its total capital outlay and no repayment is ordinarily expected in respect thereof the grants are treated as capital reserve, which can be neither distributed as dividend nor considered as deferred income".

ADVICE

The action of the Top & Top Ltd. is not justified in view of AS - 12. Therefore, it is inappropriate to recognize government grants in the Profit and Loss statement for the year ended 31st March, 2015. Since they are not earned but represent an incentive provided by government without related cost.

QUESTION 16. Samrat Limited has set up its business in a designated backward area which entitles the Company for subsidy of 25% of the total investment from Government of India. The Company has invested ₹ 80 Crores in the eligible investments. The Company is eligible for the Subsidy and has received ₹ 20 Crores from the Government in February 2015. The Company wants to recognize the said Subsidy as its Income to improve the bottom line of the Company. Do you approve the action of the Company in accordance with the Accounting Standards?

ANSWER:

PROVISION OF AS 12

As per AS 12 "Accounting for Government Grants", where the government grants are in the nature of promoters' contribution, i.e., they are given with reference to the total investment in an undertaking or by way of contribution towards its total capital outlay (for example, Central Investment Subsidy Scheme) and no repayment is ordinarily expected in respect thereof, the grants are treated as capital reserve which can be neither distributed as dividend nor considered as deferred income. The subsidy received by Samrat Ltd. for setting up its business in a designated backward area will be treated as grant by the government in the nature of promoter's contribution as the grant is given with reference to the total investment in an undertaking i.e. subsidy is 25% of the eligible investment and also no repayment is apparently expected in respect thereof.

ADVICE

Since the subsidy received is neither in relation to specific fixed assets nor in relation to revenue. Thus, the company cannot recognize the said subsidy as income in its financial statements in the given case. It should be recognized as capital reserve which can be neither distributed as dividend nor considered as deferred income.

QUESTION 17. Santosh Ltd. has received a grant of ₹ 8 crores from the Government for setting up a factory in a backward area. Out of this grant, the company distributed ₹ 2 crores as divided. Also, Santosh Ltd. received land free of cost from the State Government but it has not recorded it at all in the books as no money has been spent. In the light of AS 12 examine, whether the treatment of both the grants is correct.

ANSWER:

As per AS 12, when government grant is received for a specific purpose, it should be utilized for the same. So the grant received for setting up a factory is not available for distribution of dividend.

In the second case, even if the company has not spent money for the acquisition of land, land should be recorded in the books of accounts at a nominal value. The treatment of both the grants is incorrect as per AS 12.

QUESTION 18. X Ltd. received a revenue grant of ₹ 15 crores during 2012-2013 from Government for welfare activities to be carried on by the company for its employees. The grant prescribed the conditions for utilization.

However during the year 2014-2015, it was found that the prescribed conditions were not fulfilled and the grant should be refunded to the Government.State how this matter will have to be dealt with in the financial statements of X Ltd. for the year ended 2014-2015.

ANSWER:

PROVISION OF AS 12

As per AS 12, a grant that became refundable should be treated as an extra-ordinary item as per AS-5. The amount refundable in respect of a government grant related to revenue, is applied first against any unamortised deferred credit remaining in respect of the grant. To the extent that the amount refundable exceeds any such deferred credit, or where no deferred credit exists, the amount is charged immediately to Profit and Loss Statement.

ADVICE

Refund of grant of ₹ 15 crores should be charged to the Profit and Loss Account of the company as an extra-ordinary item during the financial year 2014-2015.

7 AS 16 – BORROWING COST

THEORETICAL BASE

QUESTION 1: State the meaning and components of Borrowing Costs.

ANSWER:

Meaning	Borrowing costs are interest and other costs incurred by an enterprise in connection with the borrowing.
Components	(a) Interest and commitment charges on bank borrowings and other short-term and long-term borrowings; (b) amortization of discounts or premiums relating to borrowings; (c) amortization of ancillary costs incurred in connection with the arrangement of borrowings; (d) finance charges in respect of assets acquired under finance leases or under other similar arrangements; and (e) exchange differences arising from foreign currency borrowings to the extent that they are regarded as an adjustment to interest costs.

QUESTION 2: State the meaning of Qualifying Asset. Name the Assets that are not considered as qualifying assets.

ANSWER:

Meaning	A qualifying asset is an asset that necessarily takes a substantial period of time (**ordinarily, a period of 12 months**) to get ready for its intended use or sale. Examples of qualifying assets are manufacturing plants, power generation facilities, inventories that require a substantial period of time to bring them to a saleable condition and investment properties.
Assets that are not considered as qualifying assets	1. Other investments and those inventories that are routinely manufactured or otherwise produced in large quantities on a repetitive basis over a short period of time. 2. Assets that are ready for their intended use or sale when acquired,

QUESTION 3: State the treatment of Borrowing Costs in case of Specifically borrowed funds.

ANSWER: The amount of borrowing costs eligible for capitalization on that asset should be determined as the actual borrowing costs incurred on that borrowing during the period *less* any income on the temporary investment of those borrowings.

QUESTION 4: State the treatment of Borrowing Costs in case of General borrowed funds.

ANSWER: The amount of borrowing costs eligible for capitalization should be determined by applying a capitalization rate to the expenditure on that asset. The capitalization rate should be the weighted average of the borrowing costs applicable to the borrowings of the enterprise that are outstanding during the period, other than borrowings made specifically for the purpose of obtaining a qualifying asset.

Note: *The amount of borrowing costs capitalized during a period should not exceed the amount of borrowing costs incurred during that period.*

QUESTION 5: State the Relevant Period for Capitalization of Borrowing Costs.

ANSWER:

Case	Relevant Period
1. When all the activities necessary to prepare the qualifying asset for its intended use or sale are in progress	Capitalization of borrowing costs should continue during the period in which active development is in progress.
2. When all the activities necessary to prepare the qualifying asset for its intended use or sale are interrupted.	Capitalization of borrowing costs should be suspended during extended periods in which active development is interrupted.
3. When all the activities necessary to prepare the qualifying asset for its intended use or sale are complete	Capitalization of borrowing costs should cease completion of active development.

QUESTION 6: How will deal with the Foreign Currency Borrowings.

ANSWER:

Case	Borrowing Costs as per AS 16	Exchange Difference to be treated as per AS 11
(a) ***If the difference between the interest on local currency borrowings and the interest on foreign currency borrowings is less than the exchange difference on the amount of principal of the foreign currency borrowings***	= Interest on Local Currency Borrowings	= Increase in liability towards principal amount of the foreign currency borrowings – (Interest on Local Currency Borrowings and Interest on Foreign Currency Borrowings)
(b) ***If the difference between the interest on local currency borrowings and the interest on foreign currency borrowings is equal to or more than the exchange difference on the amount of principal of the foreign currency borrowings***	= Interest on Foreign Currency Borrowings + Increase in liability towards principal amount of the foreign currency borrowings	NIL

QUESTION 7: State the Disclosure Requirements as per AS 16.

ANSWER:

1. The accounting policy adopted for borrowing costs; and
2. The amount of borrowing costs capitalized during the period.

PRACTICAL QUESTIONS FOR PRACTICE

QUESTION 1: BHARAT LTD. obtained a 14% loan from a bank for ₹ 120 lakhs on 1st June, 2014 to be utilized as follows:

Particulars	Amount (₹ in lakhs)
Construction of a Building (work was held up totally for 1 month during the year due to heavy rains)	50
Purchase of a Machinery	40
Working Capital	20
Advance for Purchase of Truck	10

Construction of Building was completed on 31.12.2014 but was put to use only on 01.04.2015 The machinery was installed on the same date. Delivery of truck was not received. During the year 2014-2015, the company had invested idle fund out of loan raised in banks' fixed deposit and had earned an interest of ₹ 2,00,000.

Required: **Show the treatment of Interest as per AS 16 and pass the Journal Entries relating to Interest on Loan.**

ANSWER:

PROVISION OF AS 16

1. According to para 6 of AS 16 "Borrowing Costs", borrowing costs that are directly attributable to the acquisition, construction or proiduction of a qualifying asset should be capitalised as part of the cost of that asset. Other borrowing costs should be recognised as an expense in the period in which they are incurred.

2. A qualifying asset is an asset that necessarily takes a substantial period of time (usually 12 months or more) to get ready for its intended use or sale. If an asset is ready for its intended use or sale at time of its acquisition then it is not treated as a qualifying asset for that purposes of AS 16.

3. The amount of borrowing costs eligible for capitalization on that asset should be determined as the actual borrowing costs incurred on that borrowing during the period *less* any income on the temporary investment of those borrowings.

Particulars	Nature	Treatment of Interest
1. Construction of a Building	Qualifying Asset	Interest to be capitalized As per
2. Purchase of Machinery	Not a Qualifying Asset*	Interest to be charged to P&L A/c
* On the basis that Plant & Machinery is ready for its intended use at the time of its acquisition/ purchase.		
3. Working capital	Not a Qualifying Asset	Interest to be charged to P&L A/c
4. Advance for Purchase of Truck	Not a Qualifying Asset	Interest to be charged to P&L A/c

Total Borrowing Cost = ₹ 120 lakhs × 14% × 10/12 = ₹ 14 lakhs

Eligible Borrowing Cost = ₹ 14,00,000 – ₹ 2,00,000 = ₹ 12,00,000

Qualifying Asset as per AS-16 = ₹ 50 lakhs (construction of a Building)

Borrowing Cost to be capitalized = 12 × 50/120 = ₹ 5 lakhs

Interest to be debited to Profit or Loss Account during 2014-2015 = ₹ (12 – 5) lakhs
= ₹ 7 lakhs

JOURNAL

Date	Particulars		Dr. (₹)	Cr. (₹)
31.03.2015	Interest on Loan A/c	...Dr.	14,00,000	
	To Loan A/c			14,00,000
	(Being the Interest on Loan accrued)			
	Land & Building A/c	...Dr.	5,00,000	
	To Interest on Loan A/c			5,00,000
	(Being the Interest on Loan capitalized)			
31.03.2015	P & L A/c	...Dr.	7,00,000	
	To Interest on Loan A/c			7,00,000
	(Being Interest on Loan charged to P&L Account)			

QUESTION 2: An industry borrowed ₹40,00,000 for construction of machinery on 1.6.2014. Interest on loan is 9% per annum. The machinery was put to use from 1.1.2015. Pass journal entries for the year ended 31.3.2015 to record the borrowing cost of loan as per AS 16.

ANSWER:

Particulars	₹
A. Interest upto 31.3.2015 (40,00,000 × 9% × 10/12 months)	3,00,000
B. *Less:*Interest relating to pre-operative period to be capitalized [3,00,000 × 7/10]	2,10,000
C. Amount to be charged to P & L A/c [3,00,000 × 3/10]	90,000

JOURNAL

Date	Particulars		Dr. (₹)	Cr. (₹)
31.03.2015	Interest on Loan A/c	...Dr.	3,00,000	
	To Loan A/c			3,00,000
	(Being the Interest on Loan accrued)			
	Machinery A/c	...Dr.	2,10,000	
	To Interest on Loan A/c			2,10,000
	(Being the Interest on Loan capitalized)			
31.03.2015	P & L A/c	...Dr.	90,000	
	To Interest on Loan A/c			90,000
	(Being Interest on Loan charged to P&L Account)			

QUESTION 3: X Ltd. purchased machinery from Y Ltd. on 30/09/2014. The price was 522.50 lakhs after charging 10 % VAT and giving a trade discount of 5 % on the quoted price. Transport charges were 0.25 % on the quoted price and installation charges come to 1% on the quoted price.

A loan of ₹500 lakhs was taken from bank on which interest at 15 % per annum was to be paid. Expenditure incurred on the trial run was: Material ₹50,000, wages ₹40,000 and overheads ₹30,000.

Machinery was ready for use on 01/12/2014. However, it was actually put to use only on 01/05/2015. Find out the cost of the machine and suggest the accounting treatment for the expenses incurred in the interval between the dates 01/12/2014 to 01/05/2015. The entire loan amount remained unpaid on 01/05/2015. X Ltd. does not intend to utilize the input tax paid on capital good.

ANSWER:

CALCULATION OF COST OF MACHINE AS PER AS 10

	Particulars		₹ in lakhs
A	Quoted Price of machine		500.00
B	Trade Discount @ 5 % on ₹ 500		(25.00)
C	Price after discount [A – B]		475.00
D	VAT @ 10 % on ₹ 475		47.50
E	Selling Price [C + D]		522.50
F	Transportation charges [0.25 % of ₹ 500]		1.25
G	Installation charges [1 % of ₹ 500]		5.00
H	Borrowing cost [₹ 500 lakhs × 15% × 2/12]		12.50
I	Expenditure on Trial Run		
	Material:	0.50	
	Wages:	0.40	
	Overheads:	0.30	1.20
J	Total Cost of the Machinery to be capitalized [E + F + G + H + I]		542.45

As per AS - 16, the capitalization of interest should cease when substantially all the activities necessary for intended use are completed. Therefore, interest for the period 01/12/2014 to 01/05/2015 should be expensed.

QUESTION 4: Southern Tower Ltd. purchased a plant from M/s. Tatamaco Ltd. on 30.09.2014 with a quoted price ₹ 180 lakhs. Tatamaco offer 3 months credit with a condition that discount of 1.25% will be allowed if the payment were made within one month. VAT is 12.5% on the quoted price. Company incurred 2% on transportation costs and 3% on erection costs of the quoted price, Preoperative cost amount ₹ 1.50 lakhs. To Finance the purchase of the machinery, company took a term bank loan of ₹ 125 lakhs at an interest rate of 14.50% per annum. The machine was ready for use on 31.12.2014; however, it was put to use only on 01-04-2015:

(i) Find out the original cost.

(ii) Suggest the accounting treatment for the cost incurred during the period between the date the machine was ready for use and the actual date the machine was put to use.

ANSWER:

(I) ORIGINAL COST OF THE MACHINE

Particulars	In lakhs	In lakhs
Quoted price	180.00	
Less: Discount @1.25%	2.25	177.75
Add: VAT@12.5%		22.50
Transportation @ 2%		3.60
Erection Cost @ 3%		5.40
Pre-operative Cost		1.50

Finance Cost (14.5% on ₹ 125 lakhs for the period 01.10.2014 to 31.12.2015)		4.53
Total		215.28

(ii) Cost incurred during the period between the date the machine was ready for use and the actual date the machine was put to use

Finance cost amounting to ₹ 4.53 lakhs (14.50% on ₹ 125 lakhs for the period 01.01.2015 to 31.03.2015) will be charged to Profit and Loss Account as per AS 16 "Borrowing Costs".

QUESTION 5: Suhana Ltd. issued 12% secured debentures of ₹ 100 Lakhs on 01.05.2014, to be utilized as under:

Particulars	**Amount (₹ in lakhs)**
Construction of factory building	**40**
Purchase of Machinery	**35**
Working Capital	**25**

In March 2015, construction of the factory building was completed and machinery was installed and ready for it's intended use. During the year 2014-2015, the company had invested idle fund out of money raised from debentures in banks' fixed deposit and had earned an interest of ₹ 2,00,000.

Show the treatment of interest under Accounting Standard 16 and also explain nature of assets.

ANSWER:

PROVISION OF AS 16

According to para 6 of AS 16 "Borrowing Costs", borrowing costs that are directly attributable to the acquisition, construction or proiduction of a qualifying asset should be capitalised as part of the cost of that asset. The amount of borrowing costs eligible for capitalisation should be determined in accordance with this Standard. Other borrowing costs should be recognised as an expense in the period in which they are incurred.

Also para 10 of AS 16 "Borrowing Costs" states that to the extent that funds are borrowed specifically for the purpose of obtaining a qualifying asset, the amoubnt of borrowing costs eligible for capiotalisation on that asset should be determined as the actual borrowing costs incurred on that borrowing during the period *less* any income on the temporary investment of those borrowings.

Decision: Eligible borrowing cost = ₹ 11,00,000 – ₹ 2,00,000 = ₹ 9,00,000

Sr. No.	Particulars	Nature of assets	Interest to be Capitalized (₹)	Interest to be charged to Profit & Loss Account (₹)
i.	Construction of factory building	Qualifying Asset	9,00,000 × 40/100 = ₹ 3,60,000	NIL
ii.	Purchase of Machinery	Not a Qualitfying Asset	NIL	9,00,000 × 35/100 = ₹ 3,15,000
iii.	Working Capital	Not a Qualifying Asset	NIL	9,00,000 × 25/100 = ₹ 2,25,000
	Total		₹ 3,60,000	₹ 5,40,000

SOLUTION

CALCULATION AND DISCHARGE OF PURCHASE CONSIDERATION

A. 10,000, Equity Shares to be issued [(20,000 × 1/2) × ₹ 15]	1,50,000
B. 480, 9% Pref. Shares to be issued [(50,000 × 120%)/125] × 125	60,000
C. Cash to Equity Shareholders [(20,000 × 1/2) × ₹ 1.86]	18,600
D. Total Purchase Consideration (A + B + C)	2,28,600

Note: *According to AS-14, the amount paid by purchasing Company to discharge the debentures holders and the liquidation expenses of Vendor Company are not considered as part of purchase consideration.*

ILLUSTRATION 2

Given below are the extracts from the Balance Sheets of B Ltd. as at 31.03.2015:

Particulars	*(₹ in lacs)*
Equity Share Capital of ₹ 100 each	75
12% Pref. Share Capital of ₹ 100 each	20
Reserves & Surplus	33
10% Debentures of ₹ 100 each	3
Current Liabilities	19
Tangible Fixed Assets	70
Current Assets	80

A Ltd. absorbs B Ltd.as on that date on the following terms:

(a) 10% Debentures of the transferor company are to be discharged by transferee company by issuing such number of its 15% Debentures of ₹ 100 each so as to maintain the same amount of interest.

(b) 12% Preference Shares of the transferor company are to be discharged by transferee company by issuing equivalent numbers of 15% preference Shares of ₹ 100 each at ₹ 150 each.

(c) The transferee company shall issue 4 equity shares of ₹ 10 each at ₹ 30 each for each equity share in the transferor company.

(d) The transferee company shall pay the cost of absorption which amounts to ₹ 1,00,000

Show the calculation and discharge of Purchase Consideration.

SOLUTION

CALCULATION OF PURCHASE CONSIDERATION

20,000,12% Preference Shares [(20,00,000/100) × ₹ 150]	30,00,000
3,00,000 Equity Shares [{(75,00,000/100) × 4} × ₹ 30]	90,00,000
	120,00,000

Note: *According to AS-14, the amount paid by purchasing Company to discharge the debentures holders and the liquidation expenses of Vendor Company are not considered as part of purchase consideration.*

ILLUSTRATION 3

Given below are the extracts from the Balance Sheets of Y Ltd. as at 31st March 2015:

Particulars	*(₹ in lacs)*
Equity Share Capital of ₹ 10 each	10.00
8% Pref. Share Capital of ₹ 100 each	2.00
Reserves & Surplus	3.00
12% Debentures of ₹ 100 each	1.00
Current Liabilities	2.20
Non-Current Assets	12.80
Current Assets	5.40

X Ltd. absorbs Y Ltd.as on that date on the following terms:

(a) 12% Debentures of Y Ltd. are to be discharged by X Ltd. by issuing such number of its 15% Debentures of ₹ 100 each so as to maintain the same amount of interest.

(b) The issue of such an amount of fully paid 9% Pref. Shares in X Ltd. at 125% as is sufficient to discharge 8% Pref. Shares in Y Ltd. at a premium of 20%.

(c) The Equity Shareholders of Y Ltd. will receive the requisite number of Equity Shares of X Ltd. The Equity Shares of X Ltd are to be of a nominal value of ₹ 10 each credited as ₹ 8 paid up and valued at ₹ 15 per share.

(d) The transferee company shall pay the cost of absorption which amounts to ₹ 1,00,000

Show the calculation and discharge of Purchase Consideration.

SOLUTION

CALCULATION OF PURCHASE CONSIDERATION

1920,9% Pref. Shares [(2,00,000 + 20%)/125) × ₹ 125]	2,40,000
1,00,000 Equity Shares [1,00,000 × 15]	15,00,000
	17,40,000

Note: *According to AS-14, the amount paid by purchasing Company to discharge the debentures holders and the liquidation expenses of Vendor Company are not considered as part of purchase consideration.*

ILLUSTRATION 4

Given below are the extracts from the Balance Sheet of V Ltd. as at 31st March, 2015:

Particulars	₹
Equity Share Capital of ₹ 10 each	2,00,000
8% Pref. Share Capital of ₹ 100 each	50,000
General Reserve	20,000
Profit & Loss A/c	16,100
Statutory Reserves	5,000
10% Debentures	50,000
Trade Payables	1,40,000
Tangible Assets	1,50,000

2,00,000	01/05/2014	8	16,00,000
3,00,000	01/7/2014	6	18,00,000
8,00,000	01/12/2014	1	8,00,000
		Total	96,00,000

Average carrying amount of Building during a period = 96,00,000/12 = 8,00,000

(iii) Interest to be capitalized = Average carrying amount of Building × Capitalization Rate
= ₹ 8,00,000 × 0.14 = ₹ 1,12,000

QUESTION 8: Axe Limited began construction of a new plant on 1st April, 2014 and obtained a special loan of ₹ 4,00,000 to finance the construction of the plant. The rate of interest on loan was 10%.

The expenditure that were made on the project of plant were as follows:

Particulars	**₹**
1st April, 2014	**5,00,000**
1st August, 2014	**12,00,000**
1st January, 2015	**2,00,000**

The company's other outstanding non-specific loan was ₹ 23,00,000 at an interest rate of 12%.

The construction of the plant completed on 31st March, 2015. You are required to:

(a) Calculate the amount of interest to be capitalized as per the provisions of AS 16 "Borrowing Cost".

(b) Pass a journal entry for capitalizing the cost and the borrowing cost in respect of the plant.

ANSWER:

TOTAL EXPENSES TO BE CAPITALIZED FOR BORROWINGS AS PER AS 16 "BORROWING COSTS".

Particulars	₹
Cost of Plant (5,00,000 + 12,00,000 + 2,00,000)	19,00,000
Add: Amount of interest to be capitalised	1,54,000
	20,54,000

JOURNAL

Date	Particulars		Dr. (₹)	Cr. (₹)
31.03.2015	Plant A/c	Dr.	20,54,000	
	To Bank A/c			19,00,000
	To Interest on Loan A/c			54,000
	[Being amount of cost of plant and borrowing cost thereon capitalized]			

Working Notes:

(i) *Computation of average Accumulated Expenses*

Particulars		₹
1st April, 2014	(₹5,00,000 × 12/12)	5,00,000
1st August, 2014	(₹12,00,000 × 8/12)	8,00,000
1st January, 2015	(₹2,00,000 × 3/12)	50,000
		13,50,000

(ii) *Amount of interest capitalised*

Particulars	₹
On specific borrowing (₹ 4,00,000 × 10%)	40,000
On non-specific borrowings (₹ 13,50,000 – ₹ 4,00,000) × 12%	1,14,000
Amount of interest to be capitalised	1,54,000

QUESTION 9: X Ltd. began construction of a new building on 1st January, 2015. It obtained ₹1 lakh special loan to finance the construction of the building on 1st January, 2015 at an interest rate of 10%. The company's other outstanding two non-specific loans were:

Amount	*Rate of Interest*
₹ 5,00,000	**11%**
₹ 9,00,000	**13%**

The expenditure that were made on the building project were as follows:

		₹
January	**2015**	**2,00,000**
April	**2015**	**2,50,000**
July	**2015**	**4,50,000**
December	**2015**	**1,20,000**

Building was completed by 31st December, 2015. Following the principles prescribed in AS-16

'Borrowing Cost,' calculate the amount of interest to be capitalized and pass one Journal Entry for capitalizing the cost and borrowing cost in respect of the building.

ANSWER:

1. COMPUTATION OF AVERAGE ACCUMULATED EXPENSES

Particulars	₹
₹ 2,00,000 × 12 / 12	= 2,00,000
₹ 2,50,000 × 9 / 12	= 1,87,500
₹ 4,50,000 × 6 / 12	= 2,25,000
₹ 1,20,000 × 1 / 12	= 10,000
	6,22,500

2. CALCULATION OF AVERAGE INTEREST RATE OTHER THAN FOR SPECIFIC BORROWINGS

Amount of Loan (in ₹) A	Rate of interest B	Interest (in ₹) C = A × B/100
5,00,000	11%	55,000
9,00,000	13%	1,17,000
		1,72,000

Weighted Average Rate of Interest = 12.285% (approx)

3. INTEREST ON AVERAGE ACCUMULATED EXPENSES

Specific borrowings (₹ 1,00,000 × 10%)	= 10,000
Non-specific borrowings (₹ 5,22,500* × 12.285%)	= 64,189
Amount of interest to be capitalized	= 74,189

4. TOTAL EXPENSES TO BE CAPITALIZED FOR BUILDING

Cost of building ₹ (2,00,000 + 2,50,000 + 4,50,000 + 1,20,000)	10,20,000
Add: Amount of interest to be capitalised	74,189
	10,94,189

5. JOURNAL ENTRY

Date	Particulars		Dr. (₹)	Cr. (₹)
31.12.2015	Building A/c	Dr.	10,94,189	
	To Bank A/c			10,20,000
	To Interest on Loan A/c			74,189
	(Being amount of cost of building and borrowing cost thereon capitalized)			

QUESTION 10: The borrowings profile of Santra Pharmaceutical Ltd. set up for the manufacture of antibiotics at Navi Mumbai is as under:

Date	Nature of borrowings	Amount borrowed ₹	Purpose of borrowings	Incidental expenses
1.1.2014	15% Demand loan	60 lakhs	Acquisition of Fixed Assets	8.33%
1.7.2014	14.5% Term Loan	40 lakhs	Acquisition of plant and Machinery	5%
1.10.2014	14% Bonds	50 lakhs	Acquisition of Fixed Assets	8%

The incidental expenses consist of commission and service charges for arranging the loans and are paid after founding off to the nearest lakh.

Fixed assets considered as qualifying assets are as under:	₹
Sterile Manufacturing shed	10,00,000
Plant and machinery (total)	90,00,000
Other fixed assets	10,00,000

The Project is completed on 1st January, 2015 and is ready for commercial production. Show the capitalization of the borrowing costs.

ANSWER:

(a) **Specific Borrowings**	
14.5% Term Loan for acquisition of Plant & Machinery	₹
Interest from 1.7.2014 to 31.12.2014 [₹ 40,00,000 × 14.5% × 6/12]	2,90,000
Incidental Expenses	2,00,000
Total	4,90,000
General Borrowings	

A. 15% Demand Loan	
Interest from 1.1.2014 to 31.12.2014 [₹ 60,00,000 × 15%]	9,00,000
Incidental Expenses	5,00,000
Total (A)	14,00,000
B. 14% Bonds	
Interest from 1.10.2014 to 31.12.2014 [₹ 50,00,000 × 14% × 3/12]	1,75,000
Incidental Expenses	4,00,000
Total (B)	5,75,000
C. Total General Borrowing Cost (A + B)	19,75,000
D. Total Average Outstanding Borrowings = [(60,00,000 × 12 + 50,00,000 × 3)/12]	72,50,000
E. Weighted Average Borrowing Cost = $\frac{\text{Total Borrowing Cost}}{\text{Total Average Outstanding}} \times \frac{19,75,000 \times 100}{72,50,000} = 27.24\%$	

ALLOCATION OF GENERAL BORROWING FUND

Item	Cost	Specific Borrowing	Net of specific borrowing
Sterile Manufacturing Shed	10,00,000	Nil	10,00,000
Plant & Machinery	90,00,000	40,00,000	50,00,000
Other Fixed Assets	10,00,000	Nil	10,00,000

Item	Expenditure on qualifying asset out of general	Capitalization Rate	Cost eligible for capitalization borrowing fund
Sterile Manufacturing Shed	10,00,000	27.24	2,72,400
Plant & Machinery	50,00,000	27.24	13,62,000
Other Fixed Assets	10,00,000	27.24	2,72,400

BORROWING COSTS TO BE CAPITALIZED

Asset	*Specific Borrowing Cost*	*General Borrowing Cost*	*Total*
Sterile Manufacturing shed	Nil	2,72,400	2,72,400
Plant & Machinery	4,90,000	13,62,000	18,52,000
Other Fixed Assets	Nil	2,72,400	2,72,400
Total	4,90,000	19,06,800*	23,96,800

QUESTION 11: RTP Ltd. has undertaken a significant expansion programme for its manufacturing facilities. The details are as follows:

1. **Details of Capital Expenditure:**

Facility	Amount (₹)	Remarks
Plant A	**68 crores**	**Specific borrowing to the extent of ₹48 crores**
Plant B	**40 crores**	**Specific borrowing to the extent of ₹ 12 crores**
Power generation facility at:		
Plant C	**8 crores**	**No specific borrowings**

Plant D	8 crores	No specific borrowings
Corporate Offices	16 crores	No specific borrowings
	140 crores	

2. **Facility expansion commenced on June 1, 2014 on all facilities. As of March 31, 2015, the status of completion of these facilities was as follows:**
   - **Plant A was completed as of December 31,2014**
   - **Plant B was competed as of November 30, 2014**
   - **Power generation facility at Plant C is still under construction as of March 31, 2015.**
   - **Plant D was completed as of February 28, 2015.**
   - **Corporate offices were still under construction as of March 31, 2015**
3. **Detail of Debts**
   - **₹40 crores 11% Secured Debentures raised on July 1, 2012 redeemable in four equal annual installments commencing from July 1, 2014.**
   - **₹ 30 crores Secured Working Capital 14% loan obtained on April, 1, 2014. This was partially repaid on December 31, 2014 in the amount ₹ 10 crores.**
   - **14% Loan from financial institutions amounting to ₹60 crores obtained for construction of Plant A and B, on May 1, 2014.**
   - **Foreign currency loans from financial institutions amounting to $ 12 million bearing interest at LIBOR Plus 2% obtained on June 1, 2014. The contracted LIBOR rate was 6% p.a. The exchange rate as of that date was US $ 1 = ₹ 43.00. The exchange rate as of March 31, 2015 was US $ 1 = ₹ 46.50. The average exchange rate during 2014-2015 was ₹ 45.00.**

None of the loans were repaid as of March 31, 2015.

***Required:* Calculate the amount of borrowing cost to be capitalized.**

ANSWER:

Step 1: Calculation of Average Unspecified Borrowings Outstanding during the year

	Particulars	₹ (in crores)
(i)	11% Secured Debentures (40 × 3/12) + (30 crores × 9/12)	32.50
(ii)	14% Secured Working Capital Loan [(30 × 9/12) + (20 × 3/12)]	27.50
(iii)	Foreign Current Loan [120 × 10/12 × ₹ 43]	43.00
		103.00

Step 2: Calculation of Average Interest on Unspecified Borrowings for the year.

	Particulars	₹ *(in crores)*
(i)	On 11% Secured debentures [(40 × 11% × 3/12) + (30 ×11% × 9/12)	3.575
(ii)	On 14% Secured working capital Loan [(30 × 14% × 9/12) + (20 × 14% × 3/12)]	3.85
(iii)	On Foreign Currency Loan (120 × 8% × 10/12 × ₹ 45)	3.60
		11.025

Step 3: Average Interest Rate for the year =

Step 4: Calculation of Average Interest on Unspecified Borrowing for the year.

	Particulars	₹ *(in crores)*
(i)	Plant A	
	On Specific Borrowing: (48 crores × 14% × 7/12)	3.9200

Non-Current Investments (₹ 1,00,000, 6% tax free G.P. Notes)	1,00,000	—
Inventories	1,90,000	2,20,000
Add: Undervaluation of Cl. Inventory	10,000	
Less: Overvaluation of Cl. Inventory		(20,000)
Other Current Assets	6,10,000	9,30,000
	57,00,000	27,00,000
Less: 15% Debentures	—	(8,00,000)
Less: Current Liabilities	(3,00,000)	(1,00,000)
Net Assets	54,00,000	18,00,000
No. of Shares	3,00,000	1,20,000
Intrinsic Value	18	15
No. of Equity Shares to be issued (1,20,000 × 15/18)		1,00,000
Share Capital [1,00,000 × ₹ 10]		10,00,000
Securities Premium [1,00,000 × ₹ 8]		8,00,000
Purchase Consideration		18,00,000

ILLUSTRATION 8

X Ltd. takes over Y Ltd. Given below are the extracts from the Balance Sheets of these companies at 31.03.2015:

Particulars	*X Ltd. (₹)*	*Y Ltd. (₹)*
Equity Share Capital of ₹ 10 each	30,00,000	12,00,000
Reserves & Surplus		10,00,000
15% Debentures	—	8,00,000
Current Liabilities	3,00,000	1,00,000
Tangible Block	24,00,000	18,00,000
Goodwill	—	1,50,000
Non-Current Investments (₹ 1,00,000, 6% tax free G.P. Notes)	1,00,000	—
Inventories	1,90,000	2,20,000
Other Current Assets	6,10,000	9,30,000

Additional Information:

Tangible Block	Understated by 20%	Overstated by 20%
Goodwill	17,90,000	70,000
Inventories	Understated by 5%	Overstated by 10%

X Ltd. to issue shares to share-holders of Y Ltd.at a price of ₹1 above the intrinsic value of its shares on the date of take-over.The market value of an equity share of X Ltd. at present is ₹ 100. The scheme of amalgamation was not supported by 100 shareholders of Y Ltd., and had to be paid ₹ 10 per share above their intrinsic value as consideration. The amount of the dissenting shareholders was borne by X Ltd.,Calculate Purchase Consideration and show the discharge thereof.

₹ 1,20,000 × 1/12	10,000
	6,22,500

2. CALCULATION OF AVERAGE INTEREST RATE OTHER THAN FOR SPECIFIC BORROWINGS

Amount of loan (in ₹)	Rate of interest	Ampount of interest (in ₹)
5,00,000	11%	55,000
9,00,000	13%	1,17,000
14,00,000		1,72,000
Weighted average rate of interest		12.285% (approx)

3. INTEREST ON AVERAGE ACCUMULATED EXPENSES

Particulars	₹
Specific borrowings (₹ 1,00,000 × 10%)	= 10,000
Non-specific borrowings (₹ 5,22,500 × 12.285%)	= 64,189
Amount of interest to be capitalized	= 74,189

4. TOTAL EXPENSES TO BE CAPITALIZED FOR BUILDING

Particulars	₹
Cost of building ₹(2,00,000 + 2,50,000 + 4,50,000 + 1,20,000)	10,20,000
Add: Amount of interest to be capitalised	74,189
	10,94,189

5. JOURNAL ENTRY

Date	Particulars		Dr. (₹)	Cr. (₹)
31.03.2015	Building account	Dr.	10,94,189	
	To Bank account			10,94,189
	(Being amount of cost of building and borrowing cost thereon capitalized)			

QUESTION 13: XYZ Ltd. has taken a loan of US$ 20,000 on April 1, 2014, for a specific project at an interest rate of 5% p.a., payable annually. On April 1, 2014, the exchange rate between the currencies was ₹ 40 per US$. The exchange rate, as at March 31, 2015, is ₹ 43 per US$.

Required: Calculate the amount of exchange difference arising from foreign currency borrowings to the extent that they are regarded as an adjustment to interest costs, if the corresponding amount could have been borrowed by XYZ Ltd. in local currency at an interest rate of (a)11% p.a. and (b) 13% p.a. as on April 1, 2014.

ANSWER:

CALCULATION OF THE AMOUNT OF EXCHANGE DIFFERENCE ARISING FROM FOREIGN CURRENCY BORROWINGS TO THE EXTENT THAT THEY ARE REGARDED AS AN ADJUSTMENT TO INTEREST COSTS

	Particulars	11%	13%
A	Increase in liability towards principal amount [USD 20,000 × (₹ 43 – ₹ 40)]	60,000	60,000
B	Interest on foreign currency borrowing (USD 20,000 × ₹ 43 × 5%)	43,000	43,000
C	Exchange differences on the amount of principal of the foreign currency borrowingsm (A + B)	1,03,000	1,03,000
D	Interest on local currency borrowings		
	(US$ 20,000 × ₹ 40 × 11%)	88,000	
	(US$ 20,000 × ₹ 40 × 13%)		1,04,000
E	Total borrowing costs as per AS 16 (C or D whichever is *less*)	88,000	1,03,000
F	Exchange difference to be treated as per AS 11 (C – D)	15,000	0

QUESTION 14: Sun Co-operative society Ltd has borrowed a sum of US $ 12.50 million at the commencement of the financial year 2014-2015 for its solar energy project at LIBOR (London Interbank offered rate of 1%) + 4%. The interest is payable at the end of the respective financial year. The loan was availed at the then rate of ₹ 45 to US dollar while the rate as on 31st March, 2015 is ₹ 48 to the US dollar. Had Sun Co-operative Society Ltd. Borrowed the Rupee equivalent in India, the interest would have been 11%. You are required to compute 'Borrowing Cost' also showing the amount of exchange difference as per prevailing Accounting Standards.

ANSWER:

CALCULATION OF THE AMOUNT OF EXCHANGE DIFFERENCE ARISING FROM FOREIGN CURRENCY BORROWINGS TO THE EXTENT THAT THEY ARE REGARDED AS AN ADJUSTMENT TO INTEREST COSTS

	Particulars	(₹ in lacs)
A	Increase in liability towards principal amount [USD 12.50 × (₹ 48 – ₹ 45)]	37.50
B	Interest on foreign currency borrowing [USD 12.50 × ₹ 48 × 5%]	30.00
C	Exchange differences on the amount of principal of the foreign currency borrowings (A + B)	67.50
D	Interest on local currency borrowings [USD 12.50 × ₹ 45 × 11%]	61.875
E	Total borrowing costs as per AS 16 (C or D whichever is *less*)	61.875
F	Exchange difference to be treated as per AS 11 (C – D)	5.625

8 AS 19 – LEASES

THEORETICAL BASE

QUESTION 1. State the areas to which AS 19 does not apply.

ANSWER:

1. Natural Resources such as oil, gas, timber, metal and other mineral rights;
2. Motion Picture Films, video recordings, plays, manuscripts, patents and copyrights;
3. Land.
4. Contracts for Services

QUESTION 2 State the meaning of the terms: Lease, Finance Lease and Operating Lease as per AS 19 .

ANSWER:

MEANING OF THE TERM 'LEASE'

A lease is an agreement between 2 parties where one person (called lessor)transfers the right to use an asset for an agreed period of time(Lease term) to another person(called lessee) for a Lease payment or series of Lease payments. For the purpose of accounting AS 19 'Leases' classify the lease into two categories: 'Finance Lease' and 'Operating Lease'.

MEANING OF THE TERM 'FINANCE LEASE'

A lease is classified as a finance lease if it transfers substantially all the risks and rewards related to ownership of an asset alongewith right to use an asset but not the legal ownership.

MEANING OF THE TERM 'OPERATING LEASE'

An operating lease is a lease other than a finance lease. It is lease, which does not transfer all the risks and rewards incidental to ownership.

QUESTION 3 State the Situations, which would normally lead to a lease being classified as Finance Lease as per AS 19.

ANSWER:

1. The lease transfers the ownership of the leased asset to the lessee by the end of the lease term.
2. The lessee has an option to buy the leased asset at the end of the lease term at price, which is lower than is its expected fair value at the date on which option will be exercised.
3. The lease term is for the major part of the economic life of the assets even if title is not transferred.
4. At the beginning of lease term, present value of minimum lease rental covers the initial fair value.
5. The leased asset is of specialized nature and can only be used by the lessee without major modification.

QUESTION 4. State the meaning of the terms: Inception of the Lease, Lease Term and Economic Life as per AS 19.

ANSWER:

Inception of the Lease	It is earlier of (a) date of the lease agreement and (b) the date of commitment by the parties to the principal provisions of the lease.
Lease Term	It is the non-cancelable period for which the lessee has agreed to take on lease the asset together with any further period for which the lessee has the option to continue the lease of asset, with or without further payment, and at the inception of the lease it is reasonably certain that this option will be exercised by the lessee.
Economic Life	It is either: (a) the period over which an asset is expected to be economically usable by one or more users; or (b) the number of production or similar units expected to be obtained from the asset by one or more users.

QUESTION 5. State the meaning of the terms: Minimum Lease Payments[MLP], Residual Value of the leased asset , Guaranteed Residual Value [GRV], Fair Value and Contingent Rent as per AS 19 .

ANSWER:

Minimum Lease Payments [MLP]	In case of the Lessee MLP= Agreed Lease Rentals + GRV of Lessee In case of the Lessor MLP = Agreed Lease Rentals + GRV of Lessor	
Residual Value of the leased asset	It is the estimated fair value of the leased asset at the end of lease term.	
Guaranteed Residual Value [GRV]	**In case of the Lessee**	that part of residual value which is guaranteed by the lessee or on behalf of the lessee (Higher of Two)
	In case of the Lessor	that part of residual value which is guaranteed by the lessee or on behalf of the lessee or an independent third party(Higher of Three)
Fair Value	It is the amount for which an asset could be exchanged or a liability settled between knowledgeable, willing parties in an arm's length transaction.	
Contingent Rent	It is that portion of lease payment that is not fixed in amount but is based on a factor other than just the passage of time (e.g. percentage of sales, amount of usage, price indices, market rate of interest).	

QUESTION 6 What is meant by the term "Interest rate implicit in lease"?

ANSWER: As per para 3 of AS 19 'Leases' the Interest Rate implicit in the lease is that discount rate at which at the inception of the lease ,

Aggregate Present Value of(a)the Minimum Lease Payments under a finance lease from the standpoint of the lessor; and (b) any Unguaranteed Residual Value accruing to the lessor, = Fair Value of the Leased Asset.

QUESTION 7. Explain the treatment of Finance Lease in Financial Statements of Lessee.

ANSWER: TREATMENT OF FINANCE LEASE IN FINANCIAL STATEMENTS OF LESSEE

For Asset taken on Lease	Asset on Lease A/c Dr [With Lower of Fair Value of Asset or PV of MLP from Lessee' view] To Lessor's A/c

For Depreciation	Depreciation A/c To Asset A/c		
For Finance Charges Due	Finance Charges A/c Dr [With Finance Charge] To Lessor		
For Payment	Lessor Dr [With Actual Lease Rental] To Bank A/c		
For T/F to P& L A/c	P& L A/c To Depreciation A/c To Finance Charges A/c		
Balance Sheet	**BALANCE SHEET**		
	Non-Current Liabilities		
	Long-term Borrowings (Lessor)		XXX
	Non-Current Assets		
	Fixed Assets:		
	Tangible Assets		
	Plant & Equipment on Lease	XXX	
	Less: Total Depreciation	(XXX)	XXX
Disclosure Requirements	1. Assets acquired under finance lease along with Depreciation, Total Depreciation & Net Carrying Amount at the Balance Sheet Date;		
	2. A Reconciliation between the total of minimum lease payments at the Balance sheet date and their present value as follows:		
	Period (Months)	**Absolute**	**PV**
	0 – 12	XXX	XXX
	12 – 60	XXX	XXX
	60 or more	XXX	XXX
	3. Contingent rents recognized as expense in the Statement of Profit and Loss for the period;		
	4. Sublease rentals received should be disclosed in P& L A/c		
	5. the total of future minimum sublease payments expected to be received under non-cancelable subleases at the Balance Sheet Date; and		
	6. a general description of the lessee's significant leasing arrangements including, but not limited to, the following:		
	(i) the basis on which contingent rent payments are determined;		
	(ii) the existence and terms of renewal or purchase options and escalation clauses; and		
	(iii) restrictions imposed by lease arrangements, such as those concerning dividends, additional debt, and further leasing.		
	7. Significant Leasing Policies		

QUESTION 8. Explain the Treatment of Finance Lease in Financial Statements of Lessor.

ANSWER:

TREATMENT OF FINANCE LEASE IN FINANCIAL STATEMENTS OF LESSOR

For Asset given on Finance Lease	Lease Receivable A/c Dr [With Net Investment] To Asset A/c (in case of a dealer)
	Notes: 1. Unguaranteed Residual Value of a leased [UGRV] = Residual Value of the asset – Guaranteed Residual Value (Lessor) 2. Gross Investment(GI) = MLP (Lessor)+ UGRV (Lessor). 3. Net Investment(NI) = PV of Gross Investment 4. Unearned Finance Income = Gross Investment(GI) – Net Investment(NI)
For Receipt of Lease Rental	Bank A/c Dr [With Actual Lease Rental] To Lease Receivable A/c [With Principal Amount i.e. Op.NI – Cl. NI] To Finance Income A/c [With Finance Income i.e.Balancing Figure]
For T/F to P& L A/c	Finance Income A/c Dr To P& L A/c
Balance Sheet	**BALANCE SHEET** **Non-Current Assets** ₹ **Other Non-Current Assets** Lease Receivable A/c [At Net Investment] XXX
Disclosure Requirements	1. A Reconciliation between the Total Gross Investment in the lease at the balance sheet date, and the Present Value of Minimum Lease Payments receivable at the balance sheet date as follows:

Period(Months)	Absolute	PV
0-12	XXX	XXX
12-60	XXX	XXX
60 or more	XXX	XXX

2. Unearned Finance Income;
3. the Unguaranteed Residual Values accruing to the benefit of the lessor;
4. the accumulated Provision for Uncollectible Minimum Lease Payments receivable;
5. Contingent Rents recognized in the Statement of Profit and Loss for the period;
6. a general description of the significant leasing arrangements of the lessor;
7. Accounting Policy adopted in respect of initial direct costs.
8. Significant Leasing Policies

QUESTION 9. Explain the Treatment of Operating Lease in Financial Statements of Lessee.

ANSWER:

TREATMENT OF OPERATING LEASE IN FINANCIAL STATEMENTS OF LESSEE

<table>
<tr><td>Provision of AS [Para 23]</td><td colspan="2">Lease payments (excluding costs for services such as insurance and maintenance) are recognized as an expense in the Statement of Profit and Loss on a straight line basis unless another systematic basis is more representative of the time pattern of the user's benefit, even if the payments are not on that basis.</td></tr>
<tr><td>For Rent Expense</td><td colspan="2">Rent Expense A/c Dr [on Straight Line Basis (i.e.Total Expense/ Lease Period)]
To Lessor</td></tr>
<tr><td>For Payment</td><td colspan="2">Lessor Dr [with Actual Payment]
To Bank A/c</td></tr>
<tr><td>For T/F to P& L A/c</td><td colspan="2">P& L A/c Dr
To Rent Expense A/c</td></tr>
<tr><td>Balance Sheet</td><td colspan="2">BALANCE SHEET</td></tr>
<tr><td></td><td>Other Current Assets</td><td>₹</td></tr>
<tr><td></td><td>Lessor A/c Ltd (Dr Balance)</td><td>XXX</td></tr>
<tr><td></td><td colspan="2">* Only one figure will appear.</td></tr>
<tr><td>Disclosure Requirements</td><td colspan="2">1. The total of future minimum lease payments under non cancellable operating leases for each of the following periods:</td></tr>
<tr><td></td><td>Period (Months)</td><td>Absolute</td></tr>
<tr><td></td><td>0-12</td><td>XXX</td></tr>
<tr><td></td><td>12-60</td><td>XXX</td></tr>
<tr><td></td><td>60 or more</td><td>XXX</td></tr>
<tr><td></td><td colspan="2">2. The total of future minimum sublease payments expected to be received under non-cancellable subleases at the balance sheet date;</td></tr>
<tr><td></td><td colspan="2">3. Lease Payments recognized in the Statement of Profit and Loss for the period, with separate amounts for minimum lease payments and contingent rents;</td></tr>
<tr><td></td><td colspan="2">4. Sub-Lease Payments received (or receivable) recognized in the Statement of Profit and Loss for the period;</td></tr>
<tr><td></td><td colspan="2">5. A General Description of the lessee's significant leasing arrangements including, but not limited to, the following:
(i) the basis on which contingent rent payments are determined;
(ii) the existence and terms of renewal or purchase options and escalation clauses; and
(iii) restrictions imposed by lease arrangements, such as those concerning dividends, additional debt, and further leasing.</td></tr>
</table>

QUESTION 10. Explain the Treatment of Operating Lease in Financial Statements of Lessor.
ANSWER :

TREATMENT OF OPERATING LEASE IN FINANCIAL STATEMENTS OF LESSOR

Provision of AS [Para 40]	Lease income (excluding receipts for services provided such as insurance and maintenance) from operating leases should be recognized in the Statement of Profit and Loss on a straight line basis over the lease term, unless another systematic basis is more representative of the time pattern in which benefit derived from the use of the leased asset is diminished.		
For Asset	Operating Lease Receivable A/c Dr [on Straight Line Basis To Lease Rental Income A/c (i.e.Total Expense/ Lease Period)]		
For Receipt of Lease Rental	Bank A/c Dr [With Actual Lease Rental] To Operating Lease Receivable A/c		
For Depreciation	Depreciation A/c Dr To Asset A/c		
For T/F to P& L A/c	Lease Rental Income A/c Dr To P& L A/c		
For T/F to P& L A/c	P& L A/c Dr To Depreciation A/c		
Balance Sheet	**BALANCE SHEET**		
	Other Current Liabilities	₹	
	Operating Lease		XXXX
	Receivable A/c (Cr Balance)		
	Non-Current Assets		
	Fixed Assets		
	Tabgible Assets		
	Plant & Equipment on Lease	XXXX	
	Less: Total Depreciation	(XXXX)	XXXX
	* Only one figure will appear.		
Disclosure Requirements	1. for each class of assets, the gross carrying amount, the accumulated depreciation and accumulated impairment losses at the balance sheet date; and (i) the depreciation recognized in the Statement of Profit and Loss for the period; (ii) impairment losses recognized in the Statement of Profit and Loss for the period; (iii) impairment losses reversed in the Statement of Profit And Loss for the period;		
	2. the future minimum lease payments under non-cancellable operating leases in the aggregate and for each of the following periods:		
	Period(Months)	Absolute	
	0-12	XXX	
	12-60	XXX	
	60 or more	XXX	

	3. total contingent rents recognized as income in the Statement of Profit and Loss for the period;
	4. a general description of the lessor's significant leasing arrangements; and
	5. accounting policy adopted in respect of initial direct costs.
	6. Significant Leasing Policies

QUESTION 11. Explain the Meaning and Treatment of Sale and Leaseback Transaction.

ANSWER:

Meaning	A sale and leaseback transaction involves the sale of an asset by the vendor and the leasing of the same asset back to the vendor.	
Accounting Treatment	Any difference between sales proceeds over the carrying amount should be deferred and amortized over the lease term in proportion to the depreciation of the leased asset.	
	Case	**Accounting Treatment of Profit/Loss**
	1. If Fair Value is more than the Carrying Amount	Profit should be recognised immediately.
	2. If Fair Value is less than Carrying Amount	Loss should be provided so as to bring down Carrying Amount to fair value.
	3. If Sale Price is more than Fair Value	Gain should be deferred and amortized in proportion to Lease Payments over the period for which the asset is expected to be used.
	4. If Sale Price is less than fair value	**(a) If Loss is not compensated through Reduced Lease Payments, Loss should be provided for immediately.** **(b) If Loss is compensated through Reduced Lease Payments, Loss should be deferred and amortized in proportion to Lease payments.**

PRACTICAL QUESTIONS FOR PRACTICE

CLASSIFICATION OF LEASE INTO OPERATING OR FINANCE LEASES

QUESTION 1. Classify the following into either operating or finance leases:

(i) Ownership of an asset gets vested to the lessee at the end of lease term.

(ii) Lessee has option to purchase the asset at lower than fair value, at the end of lease term.

(iii) Economic life of the asset is 6 years, lease term 5-1/2 years, but asset is not acquired at the end of lease term.

(iv) Present value (PV) of Minimum lease payments (MLP) = "X", Fair value of the asset is Y.

(v) Economic life is 6 years, lease term is 3 years, but the asset is of a special nature, and has been procured only for use of lessee.

ANSWER:

(i) Finance lease.

(ii) Finance Lease if it becomes certain at the inception of lease itself that the option will be exercised by the lessee.

(iii) Finance Lease, since a substantial portion of the life of the asset is covered by the lease term.

(iv) Finance Lease if X = Y, or where X substantially equals Y.

(v) Finance Lease, since the asset is procured only for the use of lessee.

QUESTION 2. Suraj Limited wishes to obtain a machine costing ₹30 lakhs by way of lease. The effective life of the machine is 14 years, but the company requires it only for the first 5 years. It enters into an agreement with Ashok Ltd., for a lease rental for ₹3 lakhs p.a. payable in arrears and the implicit rate of interest is 15%. The chief accountant of Suraj Limited is not sure about the treatment of these lease rentals and seeks your advise.

ANSWER:

PROVISION OF AS 19

As per AS 19, "Leases', a lease will be classified as finance lease if at the inception of the lease, the present value of minimum lease payment * amounts to at least substantially equal to of the fair value of leased asset.

ADVICE

1. The given lease agreement is an operating lease since:
   (a) the present value of minimum lease payment amounts[₹ 10.08 lakhs (i.e.₹ 3 lakhs x 3.36)] is substantially less than the fair value of leased asset (i.e ₹ 30 lakhs.)
   (b) the lease term (5 years) is substantially less than economic life of the asset (15 years)
2. Therefore, Lease payments under an operating lease should be recognized as an expense in the statement of profit and loss on a straight line basis over the lease term unless another systematic basis is more representative of the time pattern of the user's benefit.

QUESTION 3. A Ltd acquired machinery on lease from B Ltd on the following terms:

Lease Term	**5 Years**
Fair Value of Machinery (useful life 15 years)	**₹30 lakhs**
Annual Lease Rental payable at the end of each year	**₹5 lakhs, ₹4 lakhs, ₹3 lakhs, ₹2 lakhs, ₹1 lakh,**
Implicit Rate of Return (IRR)	**15%**

Required:

(a) State whether the Lease is Operating Lease or Finance Lease.

(b) Pass the necessary entries in the books of the Lessee & Lessor for the First year. Also prepare their Balance Sheets. Depreciation is provided on straight line basis @ 10% per annum.

ANSWER:

(a) The given Lease is Operating Lease since:

(i) Present Value of Minimum Lease Payment [MLP] is substantially less than the Fair Value of Machinery PV of MLP

$= (5 \times 0.8696) + (4 \times 0.7561) + (3 \times 0.6575) + (2 \times 0.5718) + (1 \times 0.4972) =$ ₹10.986

Fair Value of Machinery= ₹30 lakhs

(ii) Lease Term (5 years) is substantially less than the useful life of Machinery (15 years).

(B) JOURNAL OF B LTD

[₹in lakhs]

Date	Particulars		Dr. (₹)	Cr. (₹)
Ist Yr	Operating Lease Receivable A/c	Dr	3	
	To Lease Rental Income A/c			3
	(Being Operating Lease Receivable recorded-₹15 lakhs/5)			
Ist Yr End	Bank A/c	Dr	5	
	To Operating Lease Receivable A/c			5
	(Being Actual Lease Rental received)			
Ist Yr End	Depreciation A/c	Dr	2	
	To Asset A/c			2
	(Being Depreciation recorded-₹30 lakhs /15)			
Ist Yr End	Lease Rental Income A/c	Dr	3	
	To P & L A/c			3
	(Being the T/F of Lease Rental Income to P& L A/c)			
Ist Yr End	P& L A/c	Dr	2	
	To Depreciation A/c			2
	(Being the T/F of Depreciation to P& L A/c)			

AN EXTRACT OF BALANCE SHEET OF B LTD AT Ist YR END

Other Current Liabilities		₹
Operating Lease		2
Receivable A/c (Cr Balance)		
Non-Current Assets		
Fixed Assets		
Tabgible Assets		
Plant & Equipment on Lease	30	
Less: Total Depreciation	(2)	28

JOURNAL OF A LTD

[₹ in lakhs]

Date	Particulars		Dr. (₹)	Cr. (₹)
Ist Yr	Rent Expense A/c	Dr	3	
	To B Ltd			3
	(Being Rent Expense recorded-₹ 15 lakhs /5)			
Ist Yr End	B Ltd	Dr	5	
	To Bank A/c			5
	(Being Actual Rent Expense paid)			

Ist Yr End	P& L A/c Dr To Rent Expense A/c (Being the T/F of Rent Expense to P& L A/c)	3	3

AN EXTRACT OF BALANCE SHEET OF A LTD AT Ist YR END

Other Current Assets	₹
B Ltd (Dr Balance)	2

CALCULATION OF INTEREST RATE IMPLICIT IN LEASE

QUESTION 4. Calculate the interest rate implicit on lease from the following details:

Annual Lease Rent	**₹ 80,000 at the end of each year**
Lease Period	**5 Years**
Guaranteed Residual Value	**₹ 40,000**
Unguaranteed Residual Value	**₹ 24,000**
Fair Value at the inception of the lease	**₹ 3,20,000**

Discounted rates for the first 5 years are as below:

At 10% 0.909, 0.826, 0.751, 0.683, 0621

At 14% 0.877, 0.769, 0.675, 0.592, 0.519

ANSWER: Calculation of Interest rate Implicit on Lease.

PRESENT VALUE AT DISCOUNT RATE OF 10%

Year	Lease Payments (₹)	Disc. Factor (10%)	Present Value (₹)
1	80,000	0.909	72,720
2	80,000	0.826	66,080
3	80,000	0.751	60,080
4	80,000	0.683	54,640
5	80,000	0.621	49,680
5	40,000	0.621	24,840
5	24,000	0.621	14,904
	Total		3,42,944

PRESENT VALUE AT A DISCOUNT RATE OF 14%

Year	Liease Payments (₹)	Disc. Factor (10%)	Present Value (₹)
1	80,000	0.877	70,160
2	80,000	0.769	61,520
3	80,000	0.675	54,000
4	80,000	0.592	47,360
5	80,000	0.519	41,520
5	40,000	0.519	20,760
5	24,000	0.519	12,456
	Total		3,07,776

Interest Rate Implicit on Lease = 10% +[(14% –10%)/ (3,42,944 – 3,07,776)] × (3,42,944 – 3,20,000)

= 10% + 2.609% = 12.609% or say 12.61%

CALCULATION OF VALUE OF LEASE LIABILITY

QUESTION 5. S. Square Private Limited has taken machinery on lease from S.K. Ltd. The information is as under:

Lease term = 4 years

Fair value at inception of lease = ₹20,00,000

Lease rent = ₹6,25,000 p.a. at the end of year

Guaranteed Residual Value = ₹ 1,25,000

Expected Residual Value = ₹3,75,000

Implicit interest rate = 15%

Discounted rates for 1st year, 2nd year, 3rd year and 4th year are 0.8696, 0.7561, 0.6575 and 0.5718 respectively.

Calculate the value of the lease liability as per AS-19,

ANSWER:

PROVISION OF AS 19

As per AS 19 "Leases", the lessee should recognise the lease as an asset and a liability at an amount equal to the fair value of the leased asset at the inception of the finance lease. However, if the fair value of the leased asset exceeds the present value of the minimum lease payments from the standpoint of the lessee, the amount recorded as an asset and a liability should be the present value of the minimum lease payments from the standpoint of the lessee. In calculating the present value of the minimum lease payments the discount rate is the interest rate implicit in the lease.

CALCULATION OF PV OF MLP

Year	Minimum Lease Payment ₹	Internal rate of return (Discount/ate@5%)	Present value ₹
1	6,25,000	0.8696	5,43,500
2	6,25,000	0.7561	4,72,563
3	6,25,000	0.6575	4,10,937
4	7,50,000*	0.5718	4,28,850
Total	26,25,000		18,55,850

Present value of minimum lease payments ₹ 18,55,850 is less than fair value at the inception of lease i.e. ₹ 20,00,000, therefore, the lease liability should be recognized at ₹ 18,55,850 as per AS 19.

QUESTION 6.

Annual lease rent = ₹ 40,000 at the end of each year

Lease period = 5 years

Guaranteed Residual Value = ₹ 14,000

Fair value at the inception (beginning) of lease = ₹ 1,50,000

Interest rate implict on lease is 12.6%. The present value factors at 12.6% are 0.89, 0.79, 0.7, 0.622, 0.552 at the end of first, second, third, fourth and fifth year respectively.

Show the Journal entry to record the asset taken on finance lease in the books of the lessee.

ANSWER:

JOURNAL OF LESSEE

Date	Particulars	L.F.	Dr. (₹)	Cr. (₹)
	Asset A/c	Dr.	1,49,888	
	To Lessor			1,49,888
	(Being recognition of finance lease as an asset and			
	a liability)			

Working Note:

Year	Lease Payments ₹	Discounting Factor (12.6%)	Present Value ₹
1	40,000	0.89	35,600
2	40,000	0.79	31,600
3	40,000	0.70	28,000
4	40,000	0.622	24,880
5	40,000	0.552	22,080
5	14,000 (GRV)	0.552	7,728
			1,49,888

CALCULATION OF ANNUAL LEASE PAYMENT & UNEARNED FINANCE INCOME

QUESTION 7. B&P Ltd. availed a lease from N&L Ltd. The conditions of the lease terms are as under:

(i) Lease period is 3 years, in the beginning of the year 2015, for equipment costing ₹ 10,00,000 and has an expected useful life of 5 years.

(ii) The Fair market value is also ₹ 10,00,000.

(iii) The property reverts back to the lessor on termination of the lease.

(iv) The unguaranteed residual value is estimated at ₹1,00,000 at the end of the year 2013.

(v) 3 equal annual payments are made at the end of each year.

Consider IRR = 10%.

The present value of ₹ 1 due at the end of 3rd year at 10% rate of interest is ₹ 0.7513. The present value of annuity of ₹ 1 due at the end of 3rd year at 10% IRR is ₹ 2.4868. State whether the lease constitute finance lease and also calculate unearned Finance income.

ANSWER:

(I) COMPUTATION OF ANNUAL LEASE PAYMENT TO THE LESSOR

Particualrs	₹
Cost of equipment	10,00,000
Unguaranteed residual value	1,00,000
Present value of residual value after third year @10% (₹ 1,00,000 × 0.7513)	75,130
Fair value to be recovered from lease payments(₹ 10,00,000 – ₹ 75,130)	9,24,870
Present value of annuity for three years is 2.4868	
Annual lease payment = ₹ 9,24,870/2.4868	3,71,911.70

The present value of lease payment i.e., ₹ 9,24,870 equals 92.48% of the fair market value i.e., 10,00,000. As the present value of minimum lease payments substantially covers the initial fair value of the leased asset and lease term (i.e. 3 years) covers the major part of the life of asset (i.e. 5 years). Therefore, it constitutes a finance lease.

(II) COMPUTATION OF UNEARNED FINANCE INCOME

Particulars	₹
Total lease payments (₹ 3,71,911.70 × 3)	11,15,735
Add: Unguaranteed residual value	1,00,000
Gross investment in the lease	12,15,735
Less: Present value of investment (lease payments and residual value) (₹ 75,130 + ₹ 9,24,870)	(10,00,000)
Unearned finance income	2,15,735

QUESTION 8. WIN Ltd. has entered into a three year lease arrangement with Tanya sports club in respect of Fitness Equipments costing ₹ 16,99,999.50. The annual lease payments to be made at the end of each year are structured in such a way that the sum of the Present Values of the lease payments and that of the residual value together equal the cost of the equipments leased out. The unguaranteed residual value of the equipment at the expiry of the lease is estimated to be ₹ 1,33,500. The assets would revert to the lessor at the end of the lease. Given that the implicit rate of interest is 10% you are required to compute the amount of the annul lease and the unearned finance income. Discounting Factor at 10% for years 1, 2 and 3 are 0.909, 0.826 and 0.751 respectively.

ANSWER:

(I) COMPUTATION OF ANNUAL LEASE PAYMENT TO THE LESSOR

	₹
Cost of equipment	16,99,999.50
Unguaranteed residual value	1,33,500.00
Present value of residual value after third year @ 10% (₹ 1,33,500 × 0.751)	1,00,258.50
Fair value to be recovered from lease payments (₹ 16,99,999.50 – ₹ 1,00,258.50)	15,99,741.00
Present value of annuity for three years is	2.486
Annual lease payment = ₹ 15,99,741/ 2.486	6,43,500.00

(II) COMPUTATION OF UNEARNED FINANCE INCOME

	₹
Total lease payments (₹ 6,43,500 x 3)	19,30,500.00
Add: Unguaranteed residual value	1,33,500.00
Gross investment in the lease	20,64,000.00
Less: Present value of investment (lease payments and residual value) (₹ 1,00,258.50 + ₹ 15,99,741)	(16,99,999.50)
Unearned finance income	3,64,000.50

QUESTION 9. X Ltd. has leased equipment over its useful life that costs ₹ 7,46,55,100 for a three year lease period. After the lease term the asset would revert to the Lessor. You are informed that:

(i) The estimated unguaranteed residual value would be ₹ 1 lakh only.

(ii) The annual lease payments have been structured in such a way that the sum of their present values together with that of the residual value of the asset will equal the cost thereof.

(iii) Implicit interest rate is 10%.

You are required to ascertain the annual lease payment and the unearned finance income. P.V. factor @ 10% for years 1 to 3 are 0.909, 0.826 and 0.751 respectively.

ANSWER:

(I) CALCULATION OF ANNUAL LEASE PAYMENT

Cost of the equipment	7,46,55,100
Unguaranteed Residual Value	1,00,000
PV of unguaranteed residual value (₹ 1,00,000 × 0.751)	75,100
Fair value to be recovered from Lease Payment (₹ 7,46,55,100 – ₹ 75,100)	7,45,80,000
PV Factor for 3 years @ 10%	2.486
Annual Lease Payment (₹ 7,45,80,000 / PV Factor for 3 years @ 10% i.e. 2.486)	3,00,00,000

(II) CALCULATION OF UNEARNED FINANCE INCOME

	₹
Total lease payments [₹ 3,00,00,000 × 3]	9,00,00,000
Add: Residual value	1,00,000
Gross Investments	9,01,00,000
Less: Present value of Investments (₹ 7,45,80,000 + ₹ 75,100)	(7,46,55,100)
Unearned Finance Income	1,54,44,900

JOURNAL ENTRIES IN THE BOOKS OF LESSOR AND LESSEE

QUESTION 10. B Ltd acquired machinery on lease from A Ltd on the following terms:

Lease Term	**5 Years**
Fair Value of Machinery	**₹20 lakhs**
Annual Lease Rental at the end of each year	**₹5 lakhs**
Guaranteed Residual Value (GRV)	**₹1 lakh**
Expected Residual Value	**₹2 lakhs**
Implicit Rate of Return (IRR)	**15%**

Required:

(a) Calculate the Value of machine to be recognized by B Ltd

(b) Calculate the Net Investment in lease from the point of view of A Ltd.

(c) Calculate the Unearned Finance Income

(d) Calculate the Finance Charges for each year in the books of the Lessee.

(e) Pass the necessary entries in the books of the Lessee & Lessor for the First year. Also prepare their Balance Sheets. Depreciation is provided on straight line basis @ 10% per annum.

ANSWER:

(a) Value of Machine to be recognized by B Ltd

Value of machine to be considered B Ltd = Lower of Fair value or Present Value of MLP

PRESENT VALUE OF MLP

Particulars	Year	Amount	PV Factor	PV
Annual Lease Payments	1-5	5 lakhs	3.3522	16.761
Guaranteed Residual Value (GRV)	5	1 lakh	0.4972	.4972
Present Value of MLP			Total	17.2582

Value of machine to be considered B Ltd = ₹17.257 lakhs (being Lower of ₹20 lakhs or ₹17.2582 lakhs)

(b) Net Investment in lease from the point of view of A Ltd.

Net Investment (NI) = PV of Gross Investment

Gross Investment (GI) = MLP (lessor) + UGRV (lessor).

= (Agreed Lease Rentals + GRV of Lessor) + (Residual Value of the asset – Guaranteed Residual Value (lessor).

= [(₹5 lakhs × 5) + ₹1 lakh] + (₹2 lakh – ₹1 lakh)

= ₹27 lakhs

PRESENT VALUE OF GROSS INVESTMENT

Particulars	Year	Amount	PV Factor	PV
Annual Lease Payments	1-5	5 lakhs	3.3522	16.761
Guaranteed Residual Value (GRV)	5	1 lakh	0.4972	.4972
Unguaranteed Residual Value (UGRV)	5	1 lakh	0.4972	.4972
Present Value of GI			Total	17.7554

(c) Unearned Finance Income = Gross Investment(GI) – Net Investment(NI)

= ₹27 lakhs – ₹17.7554 lakhs

= ₹9.2446 lakhs

(d) Calculation of the Finance Charges

A Year	B OPENING BALANCE	C = B*15% FINANCE CHARGE	D LEASE RENT	E = B + C – D CLOSING BALANCE
1	17,25,820	2,58,873	5,00,000	14,84,693
2	14,84,693	2,22,704	5,00,000	12,07,397
3	12,07,397	1,81,110	5,00,000	8,88,507
4	8,88,507	1,33,276	5,00,000	5,21,783
5	5,21,783	78,217*	6,00,000	NIL

*The difference is due to approximation in computing the interest rate implicit in the lease.

(e) (i) Journal of B Ltd.

Date	Particulars		Dr. (₹)	Cr. (₹)
	At the inception of lease			
	Machinery A/c	Dr.	17,25,820*	
	To A Ltd.'s a/c			17,25,820*
	(Being lease of machinery recorded at present value of mlp)			
	At the end of the first year of lease			
	Finance Charges A/c	Dr.	2,58,873	
	To A Ltd.'s A/c			2,58,873
	(Being the finance charges for first year due)			
	A Ltd.'s A/c	Dr.	5,00,000	
	To Bank A/c			5,00,000
	(Being the lease rent paid to the lessor which includes outstanding liability of A/c. 2,41,127 and finance charge of rs. 2,58,873)			
	Depreciation A/c	Dr.	1,72,582	
	To Machinery a/c			1,72,582
	(Being the depreciation provided @ 10% p.a. on straight line method)			
	Profit and Loss a/c	Dr.	4,31,455	
	To Depreciation A/c			1,72,582
	To Finance Charges A/c			2,58,873
	(Being the depreciation and finance charges transferred to profit and loss account)			

AN EXTRACT OF BALANCE SHEET OF B LTD. AT THE END OF THE FIRST YEAR OF LEASE

Non-Current Liabilities		₹
Long-term Borrowings (Lessor)		14,84,693
Non-Current Assets		
Fixed Assets:		
Tangible Assets		
Plant & Equipment on Lease	17,25,820	
Less: Total Depreciation	(1,72,582)	15,53,238

(e) **(ii) JOURNAL OF A LTD.**

Date	Particulars		Dr. (₹)	Cr. (₹)
Ist Yr Beg	Lease Receivable A/c	Dr	17,75,540	
	To Machinery A/c			17,75,540
	(Being Finance Lease recorded at Net Investment)			
Ist Yr End	Bank A/c	Dr	5,00,000	

	To Lease Receivable A/c [₹17,75,540 – ₹15,41,860*]		2,33,680
	To Finance Income A/c [₹5,00,000 – ₹2,33,680] (Being Actual Lease Rental received)		2,66,320
Ist Yr End	Finance Income A/c Dr	2,66,320	
	To P& L A/c (Being the T/F of Lease Rental Income to P& L A/c)		2,66,320

AN EXTRACT OF BALANCE SHEET OF A LTD AT THE END OF THE FIRST YEAR OF LEASE

Non-Current Assets	
Other Non-Current Assets	
Lease Receivable A/c [At Net Investment]	15,41,860*

***PRESENT VALUE OF GROSS INVESTMENT AT THE END OF IST YEAR**

Particulars	Year	Amount	PV Factor	PV
Annual Lease Payments	1-4	5 lakhs	2.855	14.275
Guaranteed Residual Value(GRV)	4	1 lakh	0.5718	0.5718
Unguaranteed Residual Value (UGRV)	4	1 lakh	0.5718	0.5718
Present Value of GI			Total	15.4186

SEGREGATION OF FINANCE INCOME

QUESTION 11. Global Ltd. initiated a lease for 3 years in respect of an equipment costing ₹1,50,000 with expected useful life of 4 years. The asset would revert to Global Ltd. under the lease agreement. The other information available in respect of lease agreement is:

(i) The unguaranteed residual value of the equipment after the expiry of the lease term is estimated at ₹20,000.

(ii) The implicit rate of interest is 10%.

(iii) The annual payments have been determined in such a way that the present value of the lease payment plus the residual value is equal to the cost of asset.

Ascertain in the hands of Global Ltd.

(i) The annual lease payment

(ii) The unearned finance income

(iii) The segregation of finance income

(iv) Show how necessary items will appear in its Profit and Loss Account and Balance Sheet for the various years.

ANSWER:

(i) Annual Lease Payment

Presuming that lease payment is made at the end of the year

Discount factor for year 1, 2, 3 will be @ 10 %, 0.909, 0.826 and 0.751

As per the question

(P.V of lease payment + Residual Value) = 1,50,000

Let lease payment be X

(P.V of lease payment) = (0.909 + 0.826 + 0.751) = 2.486 X

P.V of residual value at the end of three years
0.751 X 20,000 = ₹15,020
As per the question -
2.486 X + 15,020 = 1,50,000
2.486 X = 1,34,980
X = 1,34,890 / 2.486 = 54,296
Say ₹54,300
Therefore, annual lease payment is ₹54,300

(ii) Unearned Finance Income
= Annual lease payments + Residual Value – P.V of Annual Lease Paymment
= 54,300 × 3 + 20,000 – 1,50,000 = 32,900

(III) SEGREGATION OF UNEARNED FINANCE INCOME

Year	Outstanding Amount	MLP	Finance charge	Principal Amount of Reduction
0	1,50,000	NIL	NIL	NIL
1	1,10,700	54,300	15,000	39,300
2	67,640	54,300	11,070	43,230
3	NIL	74,300	6,830*	67,470*
		1,82,900	32,900	1,50,000

* Balancing figure approximately

EXTRACT OF PROFIT AND LOSS ACCOUNT

(Amt. in ₹)

1st Year	To Finance Income	15,000
2nd Year	To Finance Income	11,070
3rd Year	To Finance Income	6,830

AN EXTRACT OF EXTRACT OF BALANCE SHEET AT THE END OF ...

Particulars	Ist year	2nd year	3rd year
Non-Current Assets			
Other Non-Current Assets			
Lease Receivable			
	1,10,700	67,470	Nil

QUESTION 12. Carrying amount of assets = ₹1,00,000
What will be the accounting treatment in each of the following cases?

Case ₹	Fair Value ₹	Selling Price
1.	**2,00,000**	**2,00,000**
2.	**2,00,000**	**1,50,000**
3.	**2,00,000**	**1,50,000** **Loss is compensated by reduced future lease payments**

4.	**2,00,000**	**2,50,000**
5.	**1,00,000**	**1,00,000**
6.	**1,00,000**	**70,000**
7.	**1,00,000**	**70,000** **Loss is compensated by reduced future lease payments**
8.	**1,00,000**	**1,40,000**
9.	**80,000**	**80,000**
10.	**80,000**	**50,000**
11.	**80,000**	**50,000** **Loss is compensated by reduced future lease payments**
12.	**80,000**	**1,00,000**

ANSWER:

Case

1. A profit of ₹1,00,000 (i.e. ₹2,00,000 – ₹1,00,000) on sales should be recognized immediately.
2. A profit of ₹1,00,000 (i.e. ₹2,00,000 – ₹1,00,000) on sales should be recognized immediately. But as selling price is less than the fair value a loss equal to ₹50,000 (i.e. ₹2,00,000 – ₹1,50,000) should be recognized immediately.
3. A profit of ₹1,00,000 (i.e. ₹2,00,000 – ₹1,00,000) on sales should be recognized immediately. But as selling price is less than the fair value there is a loss of ₹ 50,000 (i.e. ₹2,00,000 – ₹1,50,000). However, this loss is compensated through reduced lease payment. Hence loss of ₹ 50,000 should be deferred and amortized in proportion to lease payments.
4. A profit of ₹1,00,000 (i.e. ₹2,00,000 – ₹1,00,000) on sales should be recognized immediately. But as selling price is higher than the fair value a gain of ₹50,000 (i.e. ₹2,50,000 – ₹2,00,000) should be deferred and amortized over the period for which the asset is expected to be used.
5. As fair value equal to carrying amount of assets there is no profit or loss.
6. As fair value equal to carrying amount of assets there is no profit or loss. But as selling price is less than the fair value, a loss of ₹.30,000 (i.e. ₹1,00,000 – ₹70,000) should be recognized immediately.
7. As fair value equal to carrying amount of assets there is no profit or loss. But as selling price is less than the fair value, a loss of ₹30,000 (i.e. ₹1,00,000 – ₹70,000). However, this loss is compensated through reduced lease payments. Hence loss of ₹30,000 should be deferred and amortized in proportion to lease payments.
8. As fair value equal to carrying amount of assets there is no profit or loss. But as selling price is higher than the fair value a gain of ₹40,000 (i.e. ₹1,40,000 – ₹1,00,000) should be deferred and amortized over the period for which the assets is expected to be used.
9. Firstly a loss of ₹20,000 should be provided as so to bring down carrying amount of asset to the fair value of asset. But as selling price is equal to fair value no further treatment is required.
10. Firstly a loss of ₹20,000 should be provided as so to bring down carrying amount of asset to the fair value of asset. In this case as selling price is lower than fair value a further loss of ₹30,000 (i.e. ₹80,000 – ₹50,000) must be provided immediately.
11. Firstly a loss of ₹20,000 should be provided as so to bring down carrying amount of assets to the fair value of assets. But as selling price is less than the fair value there is a loss of ₹30,000 (i.e. ₹80,000 - ₹50,000). However, this loss is compensated through reduced lease payments. Hence loss of ₹ .30,000 should be deferred and amortized in proportion to lease payments.
12. Firstly a loss of ₹20,000 should be provided as so to bring down carrying amount of assets to the fair value of assets. But as selling price is higher than the fair value, a gain of ₹20,000 (i.e. ₹1,00,000 – ₹80,000) should be deferred and amortized over the period for which assets is expected to be used.

QUESTION 13. X Ltd. sold JCB Machine having WDV of ₹ 50 Lakhs to Y Ltd. for ₹ 60 Lakhs and the same JCB was leased back of Y Ltd to X Ltd. The lease is operating lease.

Comment according to relevant Accounting Standard if

- **(i) Sale price of ₹ 60 Lakhs is equal to fair value**
- **(ii) Fair Value is ₹ 50 Lakhs and sale price is ₹ 45 Lakhs.**
- **(iii) Fair value is ₹ 55 Lakhs and sale price is ₹ 62 Lakhs.**
- **(iv) Fair value is ₹ 45 Lakhs and sale price is ₹ 48 Lakhs.**

ANSWER: According to AS 19, follows will be the treatment in the given situations:

- (i) X Ltd. should immediately recognized the profit of ₹ 10 lakhs (i.e. 60 – 50) in its books.
- (ii) The loss of ₹ 5 lakhs (50 – 45) to be immediately recognized by X Ltd. in its books provided loss is not compensated by future lease payments.
- (iii) Profit of ₹ 5 lakhs (55 – 50) to be immediately recognized by X Ltd. in its books and balance profit of ₹ 7 lakhs (62-55) is to be amortised/deferred over lease period.
- (iv) The loss of ₹ 5 lakhs (50 – 45) to be immediately recognized by X Ltd. in its books and profit of ₹ 3 lakhs (48 – 45) should be amortised/deferred over lease period.

QUESTION 14. On April 2, 2014, Santa Ltd. sold equipment to Banta Ltd. for ₹6,14, 460. The carrying amount of the equipment on that date was ₹1,00,000. The sale was a part of the package under which Banta Ltd. leased the asset to Santa Ltd. for a ten-year term. The economic life of the asset is estimated at 10 years. The minimum lease rents payable by the lesser has been fixed at ₹1,00,000 payable annually beginning March 31, 2015. The incremental borrowing interest rate of Santa Ltd. is estimated at 10% per annum. Calculate the net effect on the Profit and Loss Account.

ANSWER:

PROVISION OF AS 19

As per para 48 of As 19 'Lasses', if a sale and leaseback transaction results in a finance lease, any excess of deficiency of sales proceeds over the carrying amount should not be immediately recognised as income or loss in the financial statements of a seller-lessee. Instead, it should be deferred and amortised over the lease term in proportion to the depreciation of the leased asset.

ADVICE

The PV of minimum lease payments at 10% discount rate: = ₹ 1,00,000 × 6.1446 = ₹6,14,460

Santa Ltd. should recognize the asset and the liability at ₹ 6,14,460.

The excess of sales proceeds over carry amount = ₹ 6,14,460 – ₹ 1,00,000 = ₹ 5,14,460

Therefore, assuming that Santa Ltd. has decided to charge depreciation on straight line basis, AS 19 requires Santa Ltd. to.

- (a) Recognize depreciation of ₹ 61,446 per annum for 10 years
- (b) Allocate excess of ₹ 5,14,460 over the lease term at the rate of ₹ 51,446 p.a.

The net effect is a debt of (₹ 61,446 – ₹ 51,446) ₹ 10,000 per annum to the Profit & Loss A/c for 10 years, as covered under the lease term.

Had there been no sale and lease back transaction, the Profit & Loss Account for each year covered in the lease term would have been changed by (₹ 1,00,000/10) or ₹ 10,000, towards depreciation. Thus, the sale and lease back transaction has no impact on profit or loss to be reported by the lessee (vendor in the sale transaction) over the lease period. The deferred income (excess) should be presented as a deduction from the carrying amount of the asset. Thus, the asset should be presented by Santa Ltd. in its Balance Sheet dated March 31, 2015 as follows:

	₹
Gross Block	6,14,460
Less: Accumulated depreciation	(61,446)

Net Block	5,53,014
Less: Deferred Income (5,14,460 – 51,446)	(4,63,014)
Net Block	90,000

In effect, the carrying amount of the equipment does not change with the sale and lease back transaction. In substance, the sale and lease lack transaction is a borrowing transaction resulting in recognition of a liability in the balance sheet and recognition of interest expense in the Profit and Loss Account.

MISCELLENOUS QUESTIONS

QUESTION 15. The following balances are extracted from the books of Ram Ltd. a real estate company on 31st March 2015:

	Dr. (₹in '000)	Cr. (₹in '000)
Lease hold premises	**42**	
Equipment, fixtures and fittings at cost on 1.4.2014	**264**	
Depreciation on equipments, fixtures on 1.4.2014		**164**

The following additional information's are also provided.

1. **Depreciation on equipment, fittings and fixtures is provided @ 15% on written down value.**
2. **On 1st October 2014, the company moved to a new premises. The premise is on a 12 years lease and the lease premium paid amounted to ₹42,000. The company used sub-contract labour of ₹40,000 and materials at cost of ₹38,000 in the reimburshment of the premises. These are to be considered as part of the cost of lease hold premises.**

   You are required to prepare the 'Notes to account including significant accounting policies forming part of the financial statements, for disclosure of above facts and information provided.

ANSWER: Since the implicit rate of interest is not mention the question it is assumed that value of lease premium paid along with the refurbishment cost is the fair value of the leased asset. Accordingly, question has been solved assuming the lease as finance lease.

Notes on Accounts for the year ended 31st March, 2015.

The cost of lease hold premises includes the cost of refurbishment to the extent of ₹ 78,000 (Materials ₹ 38,000 + Labour ₹ 40,000).

Working Notes:

		(₹ in 000)	
(a)	Fixed Assets:		
	Equipment, Fixtures & Fittings	264	
	*Lease hold premisses (42 + 40 + 38)	120	
		384	
(b)	Depreciation		
	Equipment, Fixtures & Fittings as on 1.4.2013	164	
	For the year 2013-2014	15	179
	*Cost to leasehold premises written off [(42 + 40 + 38) × 1/12 × 1/2)		5
			184

Significan Accounting Policies

1. Depreciation has been charged on equipment, fixtures & fitting on the basis of WDV Method year after year. Equipment, Fixtures & Fitting are shown at cost in the Balance Sheet & depreciation accumulated, thereon is shown on the liability side of the Balance Sheet.

2. **According to AS-19 leases, the lease has been classified as finance lease assuming that lessor has transfered substantially all the risks and rewards incident to ownership to Ram Ltd. At the inception of lease, asset under fiance lease is capitalized in the books of the lessee with the corresponding liability wherein lease payments are recognized as an expenses in the Profit & Loss Account on a systematic basis (i.e. straight line) over the lease term. The person lessor/lessee) presenting the leased asset in his Balance Sheet should also consider the additional requirements of AS 6 and AS 10.**

9 AS 20 – EARNINGS PER SHARE

THEORETICAL BASE

QUESTION 1. How is Basic Earning Per Share calculated?

ANSWER:

STEP 1. *Calculate Net Profit attributable to Equity Shareholder as follows:*

A. Net Profit before Tax (includes Prior Period and Extraordinary Items)

B. *Less:* Current Tax (including tax on Prior Period and Extraordinary Items) + Deferred Tax + Tax Pertaining to Earlier Years.

C. Net Profit after Tax [A – B]

D. *Less:* Pref. Dividend on Cumulative Preference Shares for Current Period only (whether or not provided in accounts).

E. *Less:* Pref. Dividend on Non-Cumulative Preference Shares for Current Period only (only if provided in accounts)

F. Net Profit attributable to Equity Shareholders [C – E – F]

STEP 2. *Calculate Weighted Average Number of Equity Shares Outstanding during the period as follows:*

The weighted average number of equity shares outstanding during the period is the number of equity shares outstanding at the beginning of the period, adjusted by the number of equity shares bought back or issued during the period multiplied by the time-weighting factor [i.e.Number of days/months for which the specific shares are outstanding as a proportion of the total number of days/months in the period]

Note: Partly paid equity shares are treated as a fraction of an equity share to the extent that they were entitled to participate in dividends relative to a fully paid equity share during the reporting period.

WEIGHTED AVERAGE NUMBER OF SHARES OUTSTANDING ON 31.03.2015

Date A	No. of Shares outstanding B	Weight Period (months) C	Product D = B × C
01.04.2015	5,00,000	12/12	5,00,000
01.06.2015	1,20,000	10/12	1,00,000
Weighted Average Number of Shares Outstanding			6,00,000
Add: Bonus issue in the ratio of 1:2			3,00,000
Weighted Average Number of Shares Outstanding			9,00,000

STEP 3. *Calculate Basic Earning Per Share as follows:*

= Net Profit or loss for the period attributable to Equity Shareholders

Weighted Average No. of Equity Shares O/S during the period

QUESTION 2. In the following list of Shares issued, for the purpose of calculation of Weighted Average Number of Shares, from which date weight is to be considered:

(a) Equity Shares issued in Exchange of cash,
(b) Equity Shares issued as a result of Conversion of Debt Instrument,
(c) Equity Shares issued in Lieu of Interest and/or Principal on other Financial Instrument,
(d) Equity Shares issued in Exchange for the settlement of Liability of the Enterprise,
(e) Equity Shares issued as consideration for the Acquisition of Asset other than in Cash.
(f) Equity Shares issued for rendering of Services to the Enterprise,
(g) Equity Shares issued in case of an amalgamation in nature of purchase
(h) Equity Shares issued in case of an amalgamation in nature of merger
(i) Equity Shares issued as Bonus Shares
(j) Equity Shares issued as a result of Share Split or Reverse Share Split

ANSWER:

When equity Shares are issued...	Included with effect from the...
(a) In exchange for Cash.	Date when cash is receivable.
(b) As a result of conversion of a Debt Instrument to Equity.	Date of conversion.
(c) In lieu of Interest or Principal on other Financial Instruments.	Date when interest careases to accrue.
(d) In exchange for the settlement of a liability of the Enterprise.	Date when settlement becomes effective.
(e) As consideration for acquisition of an asset other than cash.	Date on which the acquisition is recognised.
(f) For the rendering of services to the enterprise.	Date on which the service are rendered.
(g) In case of an amalgamation in nature of purchase .	Date of the acquisition.
(h) In case of an amalgamation in nature of merger.	From beginning of the reporting period.
(i) As Bonus Shares .	From beginning of the reporting period.
(j) Share Split or Reverse Share Split.	From beginning of the reporting period.

QUESTION 3. How is Adjusted Equity Shares Outstanding calculated in case of right issue?

ANSWER:

CALCULATION OF ADJUSTED EQUITY SHARES OUTSTANDING IN CASE OF RIGHT ISSUE

Step 1:	No. of Outstanding Shares prior to Rights
Step 2:	No. of Right Shares
Step 3:	No. of Outstanding Shares after Rights [Step 1 + Step 2]
Step 4:	Aggregate Fair Value of Shares prior to Rights = No. of Outstanding Shares prior to Rights Fair Value per Share
Step 5:	Preceeds from Rights = No. of Right Shares × Right Issue Price
Step 6:	Theoretical Ex-Right Fair Value Per Share = (Step 4 + Step 5)/Step 3
Step 7:	Adjustment Factor = Fair Value Per Share prior to Rights/ Theoretical Ex-Right Fair Value Per Share
Step 8:	Adjusted Equity Shares O/s = (No. of O/s Shares Prior to Rights × Adjustment Factor) × Period + (No. of O/s Shares after Rights × Period)

QUESTION 4. Define Restatement of Basic EPS. When is Restatement required? How is Adjusted Weighted Average No. of Equity Shares Outstanding for the prior period calculated?

ANSWER:

MEANING OF RESTATEMENT OF BASIC EPS

When the basic earning per share relating to prior periods presented in current period is adjusted, it is termed as restatement of basic earning per share.

WHEN IS RESTATEMENT REQUIRED?

When the number of equity shares outstanding increases as a result of bonus issue, right issue or share split or decreases as a result of reverse share split.

Calculation of Adjusted Weighted Average No. of Equity Shares Outstanding for the prior period

= No. of Shares O/S for the prior period × Bonus Issue Factor × Right Issue Factor × Share Split Factor x Reverse Share Split Factor

QUESTION 5 Define Potential Equity Share as per AS 20.When are Potential Equity Shares considered as: (a) dilutive (b) anti-dilutive?

ANSWER:

MEANING OF POTENTIAL EQUITY SHARE

As per AS 20 A Potential Equity Share is a Financial Instrument or other contract that entitles, or may entitle, its holder to Equity Shares. Some examples are:

(a) Debt Instruments or Preference Shares that are convertible into Equity Shares,

(b) Share Warrants convertible into equity shares

(c) Options including Employee Stock Option Plans (ESOP) under which Employees of an Enterprise are entitled to receive Equity Shares as part of their remuneration, and other similar plans, and

(d) Contingently Issuable Shares [i.e. Shares which would be issued upon the satisfaction of certain conditions resulting from contractual arrangements such as the acquisition of a business or other assets, or shares issuable under a Loan Contract, upon default of payment of principal or interest, if the contract so provides

WHEN ARE POTENTIAL EQUITY SHARES CONSIDERED AS DILUTIVE?

Potential Equity Shares are considered as dilutive when, and only when, their conversion to equity shares would decrease net profit per share from continuing ordinary operations

WHEN ARE POTENTIAL EQUITY SHARES CONSIDERED AS ANTI-DILUTIVE?

Potential equity shares are considered as anti-dilutive when their conversion to equity shares would increase earnings per share from continuing ordinary activities or decrease loss per share from continuing ordinary activities. The effects of anti-dilutive potential equity shares are ignored in calculating diluted earnings per share.

Note: Share application money that is pending allotment or any advance share application money as at balance sheet date, which is not statutorily required to be kept separately and is being utilized for the purpose of business shall be treated as potential equity shares and considered as dilutive.

Note: The most advantageous conversion rate or exercise price from the standpoint of the holder of the potential equity shares should be used for calculating the number of Equity shares to be issued on the conversion of dilutive potential equity shares

QUESTION 6. How is Diluted Earning Per Share calculated?

ANSWER:

STEP 1. *Calculate Adjusted Net Profit attributable to Equity Shareholder as follows:*

A. Net Profit or Loss for the period attributable to Equity Shareholders for Basic EPS

B. *Add:* Pref. Dividend saved on the conversion of the dilutive potential equity shares into equity shares

C. *Add:* Interest or Other Expenses (after tax) saved on the conversion of the dilutive potential equity shares into equity shares

D. *Less:* Income that will cease to accrue (after tax) on the conversion of the dilutive potential equity shares into equity shares

E. Adjusted Net Profit or Loss for the period attributable to Equity Shareholders [A + B + C – D]

STEP 2. *Calculate Adjusted Weighted Average Number of Equity Shares Outstanding during the period as follows:*

= Weighted Average No. of Equity Shares O/S for Basic EPS + Weighted Average No. of equity shares which would be issued on the conversion of potential equity shares into equity shares

STEP 3. *Calculate Diluted Earning Per Share as follows:*

= Adjusted Net Profit or loss for the period attributable to Equity Shareholders/ Adjusted Weighted Average No. of Equity Shares O/S during the period.

QUESTION 7. How is Ranking from Most Dilutive to Least Dilutive calculated?

ANSWER: In order to maximize the dilution of basic earnings per share, each issue or series of potential equity shares is considered in sequence from the most dilutive to the least dilutive. Where the earnings per incremental share is the least, the potential equity share is considered most dilutive and vice-versa.

STEP 1. *Calculate Increase in earnings for each issue or series of potential equity shares*

STEP 2. *Calculate Increase in number of Equity shares for each issue or series of potential equity shares*

STEP 3. *Calculate Earnings per incremental share for each issue or series of potential equity shares*

STEP 4. *Ranking from Most Dilutive to Least Dilutive*

QUESTION 8 How is most dilutive EPS calculated?

ANSWER:

STEP 1. *Calculate EPS for Most Dilutive Potential Equity Shares & Mark it as Dilutive(if less than Basic EPS) or Anti-dilutive(if more than Basic EPS)*

STEP 2. *Calculate EPS for Next Most Dilutive Potential Equity Shares & so on and Mark it as Dilutive(if less than Basic EPS) or Anti-dilutive(if more than Basic EPS)*

STEP 3: *Select the most dilutive EPS*

QUESTION 9 State the Disclosure Requirements as Basic and Diluted EPS as per AS 20.

ANSWER:

1. Present Basic and Diluted EPS on the face of the Statement of Profit and Loss for each class of Equity Shares even if the amounts disclosed are negative.
2. Amounts used as the numerators in calculating basic and diluted EPS, and a reconciliation of those amounts to the net profit or loss for the period;
3. Weighted Average Number of Equity Shares used as the denominator in calculating basic and diluted EPS, and a reconciliation of these denominators to each other; and
4. Nominal Value of Shares along with the earnings per share figures

PRACTICAL QUESTIONS FOR PRACTICE

EPS IN CASE OF PARTLY PAID-UP SHARES

QUESTION 1. In April, 2014, A Limited issued 18,00,000 Equity shares of ₹ 10 each, ₹ 5 per share was called up on that date which was paid by all the shareholders. The remaining ₹ 5 was called up on 1-9-2014. All the Shareholders (except one having 3,60,000 shares) paid the sum in September 2010. The net profit for the year ended 31-3-2015 is ₹ 33 lakhs after dividend on preference shares and dividend distribution tax of ₹ 6. 60 lakhs.

Compute the basic EPS for the year ended 31st March, 2015 as per AS 20.

ANSWER:

$$\textbf{Basic Earnings per share (EPS)} = \frac{\text{Net profit attributatble to equity share holders}}{\text{Weighted average no. of equity shares o/s during the year}}$$

$$= \frac{33{,}00{,}000}{13{,}20{,}000 \text{ Shares}} = ₹\ 2.5 \text{ per share}$$

Working Note: Calculation of Weighted Average Number of equity shares.

As per para 19 of AS 20 'Earnings Per Share', partly paid equity shares are treated as a fraction of equity share to the extent that they were entitled to participate in dividend relative to a fully paid equity share during the reporting period. Assuming that the partly paid shares are entitled to participate in the dividend to the extent of amount paid, weighted average number of shares will be calculated as follows:

Date	No. of Equity Shares	Amount paid per share	Weighted Average	no. of Equity Shares
1.4.2014	18,00,000	5	18,00,000 × 5/10 × 5/12	3,75,000
1.9.2014	14,40,000	10	14,40,000 × 7/12	8,40,000
1.9.2014	3,60,000	5	3,60,000 × 5/10 × 7/12	1,05,000
			Total shares	13,20,000

BASIC EPS AND ADJUSTED EPS IN CASE OF BONUS

QUESTION 2. Compute adjusted earning per share and basic earning per share based on the following information:

Net Profit 2013-2014	**₹ 11,40,000**
Net Profit 2014-2015	**₹ 22,50,000**
No of Equity Shares outstanding	**₹ 5,00,000**

Bonus issue on 1st January, 2015: 1 Equity Share for each equity share outstanding as at 31st December, 2014

ANSWER:

(a) Earning per share

Basic EPS 2013-2014 = ₹ 11,40,000/5,00,000 shares = ₹ 2.28

Basic EPS 2014-2015= ₹ 22,50,000/10,00,000 shares = ₹ 2.25

Adjusted EPS 2013-2014 = ₹ 11,40,000/10,00,000 shares = ₹ 1.14

Since the bonus issue is an issue without consideration, the issue is treated as if it has occurred prior to the beginning of the year 2013-2014, the earliest period reported.

BASIC EPS AND ADJUSTED EPS IN CASE OF BONUS, CONSOLIDATION & SPLIT

QUESTION 3. Compute Adjusted Earnings per share from the following information:

Net Profit during the year 2014 - 2015	**₹ 60,00,000**
No. of Equity Shares outstanding until 30th September, 2014	**10,00,000 shares of ₹ 1 each**
Bonus issue 1st October, 2014	**1 equity share for 5 equity shares outstanding at 30th September, 2014**
Consolidation of Shares on 1st January, 2015	**Into shares of ₹100 each**
Split up of shares on 31st March, 2015	**Into shares of ₹10 each**

ANSWER:

ADJUSTED EARNING PER SHARE

No. of equity shares outstanding until 30th September 2014	10,00,000 shares of ₹ 1 each
Shares issued as bonus shares on 1st October, 2014	10,00,000 shares / 5 = 2,00,000 shares
No. of equity shares outstanding on 31st December, 2014 before consolidation	(10,00,000 + 2,00,000) shares = 12,00,000 shares
Consolidation of shares on 1st January, 2015	12,00,000 shares / 100 = 12,000 shares
No. of equity shares outstanding on 31st March, 2015 before split of shares	12,000 shares
Split of shares on 31st March, 2015	12,000 shares x 100 / 10 = 1,20,000 shares
Adjusted Earning per share for the year 2014 - 2015	60,00,000 /1,20,000 = ₹50 per share

EPS IN CASE OF RIGHT ISSUE

QUESTION 4. Compute Basic EPS and Restated EPS for the previous year and Basic EPS for the current years from the following information:

Net Profit for the period 2013 - 2014	**₹22,00,000**
Net Profit for the period 2014 - 2015	**₹47,00,000**
No. of Shares outstanding prior to right issue	**10,00,000 shares**
Right issue	**2 New Shares for each 5 Shares outstanding**
Right issue price	**₹15**
Last Date to exercise rights	**31st December, 2014**
Response to Right Issue	**Fully Subscribed**
Fair Value of one equity share immediately prior to exercise of rights on 31st December, 2014	**₹22**

ANSWER:

STEP 1. No. of O/s Shares after Rights [10,00,000 + (10,00,000 × 2/5)] 14,00,000

STEP 2. Aggregate fair value of the shares prior to rights
=10,00,000 shares x ₹22 = ₹2,20,00,000

STEP 3. Proceeds from the exercise of the rights = 4,00,000 × ₹15 = ₹ 60,00,000

STEP 4. Theoretical ex-rights fair value per share

$$= \frac{\text{Aggregate fair value of the shares immediately prior to the exercise of the rights + Proceeds from the exercises of the rights}}{\text{Number of shares outstanding after the exercise of the rights}}$$

$$= \frac{2{,}20{,}00{,}000 + 60{,}00{,}000}{14{,}00{,}000} = ₹20$$

STEP 5. Adjustment Factor

$$= \frac{\text{Fair value per share immediately prior of the exercise of rights}}{\text{Theoretical ex-rights fair value per share}} = \frac{22}{20}$$

STEP 6. Adjusted Equity Shares outstanding during the year 2014 – 2015
= 10,00,000 shares x 1.10 x (9/12) + 14,00,000 shares x (3/12) = 11,75,000 shares

STEP 7. Adjusted EPS for current year = ₹ 47,00,000 / 11,75,000 shares = ₹ 4 per share
Basic EPS for Previous year = ₹22,00,000/10,00,000 = ₹2.20
Restated Basic EPS for Previous year = ₹22,00,000/(10,00,000 × 1.1) = ₹2.00

QUESTION 5. Compute Basic and Adjusted Earnings per share from the following information:

Net Profit for 2013-2014	**₹ 22 lakhs**
Net Profit for 2014-2015	**₹ 33 lakhs**
No. of shares before Rights Issue	**1,10,000**
Rights issue Ratio	**One for Every Four Held**
Rights Issue Price	**₹ 180**
Date of exercising Rights option	**31.7.2014 (fully subscribed on this date)**
Fair value of share before Rights Issue	**₹ 270**

All workings may be rounded off to two decimals.

ANSWER:

EPS for the year 2013-2014 as originally reported = ₹ 22,00,000/1,10,000 shares = ₹ 20

EPS for the year 2013-2014 restated for rights issue = ₹ 22,00,000/(1,10,000 shares × 1.07)
= ₹ 18.69

EPS for the year 2014-2015 including effects of rights issue
= 33,00,000/[(1,10,000 × 1.07 × 4/12)
+ (1,37,500 × 8/12)]
= 25.21

Working Note:

1. **Calculation of Theoretical Ex-rights Fair Value per share**

$$\frac{\text{Fair value of all outstanding shares immediately prior to exercise of rights + total amount received from exercise}}{\text{Number of shares outstanding prior to exercise + number of shares issued in the exercise}}$$

$$= \frac{(₹270 \times 1{,}10{,}000) + (₹180 \times 27{,}500)}{1{,}10{,}000 + 27{,}500} = \frac{3{,}46{,}50{,}000}{1{,}37{,}500} = ₹\ 252$$

2. **Calculation of Computation of adjustment factor:**

$$= \frac{\text{Fair value of shares immediately prior to exercise of rights}}{\text{Theoretical ex-rights value per share}} = \frac{₹270}{₹252} = 1.071$$

QUESTION 6. The following informatiion is available for AB Ltd.:

	₹
Net profit for 2013-2014	**22,00,000**
Net profit for 2014-2015	**30,00,000**

No of shares outstanding prior to right issue 10,00,000 shares.

Right issue: One new share for each five shares outstanding i.e. 2,00,000 shares.

Right issue: Right Issue price ₹ 25

Right issue: Last date to exercise right 31st July, 2014

Fair value of one equity share immediately prior to exercise of rights on 31.07.2014 is ₹ 32.

You are required to compute:

(i) Basic earnings per share for the year 2013-2014.

(ii) Restated basic earnings per share for the year 2013-2014 for right issue.

(iii) Basic earnings per share for the year 2014-2015.

ANSWER:

COMPUTATION OF BASIC EARNINGS PER SHARE

Particulars	Previous (₹)	Current (₹)
(i) EPS for the previous year as originally reported = Net profit for the year attributable to equity share holder/weighted average number of equity shares outstanding during the year [₹ 22,00,000/10,00,000]	2.20	
(ii) EPS for previous year restated for the right issue [₹ 22,00,000/10,00,000 shares × 1.04]	2.12	
(iii) EPS for the current year (including effect of right issue)	2.62	
{30,00,000/[(10,00,000 × 1.04 × 4/12) + (12,00,000 × 8/12)]}		

Working Notes:

1. Computation of theoretical ex-rights fair value per share

$$= \frac{\text{Fair value of all outstanding shares immediately prior to exercise of rights + total amount received from exercise}}{\text{Number of shares outstanding prior to exercise + number of shares issued in the exercise}} = ₹\ 30.83$$

$$= \frac{(₹32 \times 10,00,000) + (₹25 \times 2,00,000)}{10,00,000 + 2,00,000} = ₹\ 30.83$$

2. Computation of adjustment factor

$$= \frac{\text{Fair value of shares immediately prior to exercise of rights}}{\text{Theoretical ex-rights value per share}}$$

= ₹ 32/₹ 30.83 = 1.04 (approx.)

EPS IN CASE OF RIGHT & BONUS ISSUE

QUESTION 7.

Net Profit after tax for the year 2014 - 2015	**₹34,80,000**
Net Profit after tax for the year 2015 - 2016	**₹36,60,000**
No. of shares of ₹10 each outstanding as on 1st April, 2015	**₹1,00,000**
Right issue	**2 new shares for each 5 outstanding**
Right issue price	**₹30 per share**
Last date to exercise right	**31st December, 2015**
Fair Value of 1 equity share immediately prior to exercise of right on 31st December, 2015	**₹58 per share**
Bonus issue on 31st March, 2016	**1 Equity Share for 5 equity shares outstanding on 31st March, 2016**

Required: Calculate the Basic Earning Per Share for year 2015 - 2016 and restatement for the year 2014–2015.

ANSWER:

BASIC EARNING PER SHARE FOR THE YEAR 2015 - 2016

Particulars	₹
A. Net Profit after tax for the year 2015 - 2016	36,60,000
B. Weighted Average no. of equity shares outstanding during the period (As per W.N. 3)	1,46,400
C. Basic Earning per share for the year 2015 - 2016 (A / B)	25.00

RESTATEMENT OF BASIC EARNING PER SHARE RELATING TO YEAR 2014 - 2015

Particulars	₹
A. Net Profit after tax for the year 2014–2015	34,80,000
B. Weighted Average no. of equity shares outstanding during the period 2014–2015	1,00,000
C. Adjusted Weighted Average No. of Shares outstanding for the year 2014–2015 (As per W.N. 4)	1,39,200
D. Original basic earning per share for the year 2014–2015 (A / B)	34.80
E. Restated Basic Earning per share for the year 2014–2015 made in current year i.e. 2015–2016 (A/C)	25.00

Working Notes:

1. *Calculation of Theoretical ex-rights fair value per share and bonus element in right issue*

A.	Aggregate fair value of the share immediately prior to exercise of the rights (₹58 × 1,00,000)	58,00,000
B.	Proceeds from the exercise of rights [1,00,000 × (2/5) × ₹30]	12,00,000
C.	Total (A + B)	70,00,000
D.	Shares outstanding before right issue	1,00,000
E.	Right issue [(100000/5) × 2]	40,000

F.	Total no. of shares outstanding after right issue (D + E)	1,40,000
G.	Theoretical ex-rights fair value per share (C / F)	50
H.	Fair Value of Equity Share immediately prior to exercise of right	58
I.	Bonus Element in right issue (H / G)	1.16

2. *Calculation of bonus element in bonus issue made on 31st March, 2016* ₹

A.	No. of shares outstanding as on 31st March, 2016	1,40,000
B.	Bonus shares issued (A / 5)	28,000
C.	Total no. of shares outstanding after bonus issue (A + B)	1,68,000
D.	Bonus element (C / A)	1.20

3. *Calculation of Weighted Average no. of shares outstanding for the year 2015 - 2016* ₹

A.	No. of shares outstanding before right issue	100000
B.	Bonus element in right issue	1.16
C.	Shares outstanding before right issue [A x B x (9 months /12 months)]	87,000
D.	Shares outstanding after right issue (140000 x 3 months / 12 months)	35,000
E.	Shares outstanding before bonus issue (C + D)	1,22,000
F.	Bonus element in bonus issue	1.20
G.	Weighted average no. of equity shares outstanding during the period (E x F)	1,46,400

4. *Calculation of Adjusted Weighted Average No. of shares outstanding for the year 2014 - 2015* ₹

A.	No. of shares outstanding during the period 2014 - 2015	1,00,000
B.	Bonus element in right issue	1.16
C.	Bonus element in bonus issue	1.20
D.	Adjusted weighted average no. of shares outstanding for the year 2014–2015 (A × B × C)	1,39,200

QUESTION 8. Calculate the Basic Earning Per Share of X Ltd. for year 2014-2015 and restatement for the year 2013-2014:

Particulars	No. of Shares
Balance at the beginning of year	**10,000**
Issue of Shares for Cash	**2,400**
Issue of Shares to Underwriters	**120**
Buy - Back of Shares	**5,385**
Issue of Shares against Purchase of Building.	
(acquisition is recognized on the same day)	**600**
Issue of Shares in settlement of liability	**300**
X Ltd. purchased Y Ltd. on the basis of intrinsic value of	
shares of both the companies. The intrinsic value of shares	
of X Ltd. and Y Ltd. are ₹60 and ₹15 respectively	
Shares outstanding on 1st April, 2014 of Y Ltd. are 9600 .	
Split up of shares into shares of ₹10 each	

Net Profit after tax for the year 2013-2014	**₹34,80,000**
Net Profit after tax for the year 2014-2015	**₹36,60,000**
Right issue	**2 new shares for each 5 outstanding**
Right issue price	**₹30 per share**

Last date to exercise right	31st December, 2014
Response to Right Issue	Fully Subscribed
Fair value of 1 equity share immediately prior to exercise of right on 31st December, 2014	₹58 per share
Bonus issue on 31st March, 2015	1 equity share for 5 equity shares outstanding on 31st March, 2015

ANSWER:

Basic EPS for the year 2014-2015= $\frac{\text{Net Profit after tax for the year 2013-2014}}{\text{Weighted Average no. of equity shares outstanding during the period}}$

= ₹36,60,000/1,46,400 = ₹25

Restatement of Basic Earning per share relating to year 2013-2014

Basic EPS for the year 2013-2014 = ₹34,80,000/1,00,000 = ₹34.80

Restated Basic EPS for the year 2013-2014 = ₹34,80,000/1,39,200 = ₹25

Working Notes:

1. WEIGHTED AVERAGE NUMBER OF SHARES OUTSTANDING AFTER SPLIT OF SHARES ON 01.12.2014

Date A	No. of Shares outstanding B	Weight Period (months) C	Product D = B × C
01.04.2014	10000	12/12	10,000
01.06.2014	2400	10/12	2,000
01.07.2014	120	9/12	90
01.08.2014	(5385)	8/12	(3590)
01.09.2014	600	7/12	350
01.10.2014	300	6/12	150
01.11.2014	2400	5/12	1000
	[(9600 x ₹ 15) / ₹ 60]		
Weighted Average Number of Shares Outstanding during the period			10,000
Split of shares on 01.12.2014 [10,000 shares × 100 / 10]			= 1,00,000 shares

2. **Theoretical ex-rights fair value per share =** (Fair Value prior to Rights + Rights Issue Proceeds)/ No. of Shares outstanding after Right Issue = (₹58 × 1,00,000) + [1,00,000 × (2/5) × ₹30]/[100000 + (100000/5) × 2] = 50
3. **Bonus Element in Right Issue =** Fair Value of per Equity Share prior to exercise of right/ Theoretical ex-rights fair value per share = 58/50 =1.16
4. **Bonus Element in Bonus Issue =** 1 + 1/5 = 1.2
5. **Calculation of Weighted Average no. of shares outstanding for the year 2014-2015**

A.	No. of shares outstanding before right issue	100000
B.	Bonus element in right issue	1,16
C.	Shares outstanding before right issue [A × B × (9 months/12 months)]	87,000
D.	Shares outstanding after right issue (140000 × 3 months/12 months)	35,000
E.	Shares outstanding before bonus issue (C + D)	1,22,000
F.	Bonus element in bonus issue	1.20

G. Weighted average no. of equity shares outstanding during the period (E x F) 1,46,400

6. Adjusted Weighted Average No. of shares outstanding during Previous year = No. of shares outstanding during Previous year x Bonus element in right issue × Bonus element in bonus issue = 1,00,000 × 1.16 × 1.20 = 1,39,200

DILUTED EARNING PER SHARE IN CASE OF CONVERTIBLE DEBENTURES

QUESTION 9. "While calculating diluted earning per share, effect is given to all dilutive potential equity shares that were outstanding during that period." Explain. Also calculate the diluted earnings per share from the following information:

Net Profit for the current year	**₹ 85,50,000**
No. of equity shares outstanding	**20,00,000**
No. of 8% convertible debentures of 100 each	**1,00,000**
Each debenture is convertible into 10 equity shares	
Interest expenses for the current year	**₹ 6,00,000**
Tax relating to interest expenses	**30%**

ANSWER:

(a) "In calculating diluted earnings per share, effect is given to all dilutive potential equity shares that were outstanding during the period." As per para 26 of AS 20 'Earnings per Share', the net profit or loss for the period attributable to equity shareholders and the weighted average number of shares outstanding* during the period should be adjusted for the effects of all dilutive potential equity shares for the purpose of calculation of diluted earnings per share.

$$\text{Diluted EPS} = \frac{\text{Adjusted Net Profit for the current year}}{\text{Weighted Average Number of Equity Shares}}$$

ADJUSTED NET PROFIT FOR THE CURRENT YEAR

Particulars	₹
Net Profit for the current year (assumed to be after tax)	85,50,000
Add: Interest expense for the current year	6,00,000
Less: Tax relating to interest expense (30% of ₹ 6,00,000)	(1,80,000)
Adjusted net profit for the current year	89,70,000

WEIGHTED AVERAGE NUMBER OF EQUITY SHARES

Number of equity shares resulting from conversion of debentures

$$= \frac{1,00,000 \times 100}{10}$$

Weighted Average Number of Equity Shares used to compute diluted earnings per share

= [(20,00,000 × 12) + (10,00,000 × 9**)]/12

= 27,50,000 shares

$$\textbf{Diluted earnings per share} = \frac{89,70,000}{27,50,000 \text{ shares}}$$

Note: Interest on debentures for full year amounts to ₹ 8,00,000 (i.e. 8% of ₹ 1,00,00,000). However, interest expense amounting ₹ 6,00,000 has been given in the question. It may be concluded that debentures have been issued during the year and interest has been provided for 9 months.

QUESTION 10. From the information financial you are required to compute the Basic and Diluted EPS (earning per share) for accounting year 01-04-2014 to 31-03-2015 and adjusted EPS for the year 01-04-2013 to 31-03-2014.

Net Profit for year ended 31-03-2014	**₹75,50,000**
Net Profit for year ended 31-03-2015	**₹1,00,25,000**
No. of Equity shares as on 01-04-2014	**50,00,250**
Bonus issue on 01-01-2015	**1 share for every 2 held**
No. of 12% convertible Debentures of ₹100 each	**1,00,000**
Interest on Debentures	**₹3,00,000**
Conversion Ratio of Debentures	**10 shares per debenture**
Tax Rate	**30 percent**

ANSWER:

1. Basic EPS for Financial Year 2014-2015	
A. Net Profit for the Year	1,00,25,000
B. Weighted Average Shares Outstanding for FY 2014-2015 [50,00,250 + (50,00,250 × 1/2)]	75,00,375
C. Basic EPS [A/B]	1,337
2. Diluted EPS for Financial Year 2014-2015	
A. Net Profits for the year	1,00,25,000
B. After Tax Interest (1,00,000 Debentures × ₹ 100 Face Value × 12% × 3/12 × 0.70)	2,10,000
C. Adjusted Equity Earnings for the year [A + B]	1,02,35,000
D. Weighted Average Shares Outstanding for Basic EPS	75,00,375
E. *Add:* Potential Equity Shares (to be computed only from the date of issue) (1,00,000 Debentures × Conversion Ratio 10 × 3/12)	2,50,000
F. Adjusted Weighted Average Number of Equity Shares [D + E]	77,50,357
G. Diluted EPS [C/F]	1.32
3. Adjusted EPS for Financial Year 2013-2014	
A. Net Profits for the year	75,50,000
B. Adjusted Average Share Outstanding for FY 2013-2014	75,00,375
C. Adjusted EPS for [A/B]	1.01

DILUTED EARNING PER SHARE IN CASE OF ESOP

QUESTION 11. From the following information compute diluted earnings per share.

Net Profit for the year	**₹12,00,000**
Weighted average number of equity shares outstanding	**5,00,000 shares**
Average fair value of one equity share	**₹20**
Weighted average number of shares under option	**1,00,000 shares**
Exercise price per share under option	**₹15**

ANSWER:

COMPUTATION OF DILUTED EARNINGS PER SHARE

Particulars	Earnings (₹)	Shares	Earning per share (₹)
Net Profit for the year	12,00,000		
Weighted average number of equity shares outstanding		5,00,000	
Basic earnings per share (12,00,0000/5,00,000)			2.40
Weighted average number of shares under option		1,00,000	
Number of shares that would have been issued at fair value (1,00,000 x15.00)/20.00)	——*	(75,000)	——
Diluted earnings per share (12,00,0000/5,25,000)	12,00,000	5,25,000	2.29

*The earnings have not been increased as the total number of shares has been increased only by the number of shares (25,000) deemed for the purpose of computation to have been issued for no consideration.

QUESTION 12. X Ltd. has 30,000 Debentures outstanding of ₹10 each on 1st April, 2014. There are to be converted into Equity shares of ₹10 each at an exercise price, which would range between ₹40 to ₹50. What exercise price should be used for calculating diluted EPS?

ANSWER: Equity Shares to be issued if exercise price is ₹40 = (30,000 x ₹10) / 40 = 7,500 Equity shares Equity Shares to be issued if exercise price is ₹50 = (30,000 x ₹10) / 50 = 6,000 Equity shares According to AS - 20 exercise price which should be used for calculating diluted - EPS should be ₹40 because this exercise price is most advantageous from the standpoint of the holder of the potential equity shares.

DILUTED EARNING PER SHARE IN CASE OF CONVERTIBLE DEBENTURES & ESOP

QUESTION 13. Bharat Ltd. provides you the following information:

Weighted Average number of equity shares outstanding during the year 2014-2015	**4,00,000 shares**
Average fair value of one equity share during the year 2014-2015	**₹25.00**
Weighted Average number of shares under option during the year 2014-2015	**1,00,000 shares**
Exercise Price for shares under option during the year 2014-2015	**₹15.00**
Issued 32,000, 10% Convertible Debentures of ₹50 each. Each debenture is convertible into five equity shares.	
The tax rate applicable is 30%.	

Required: Compute Basic EPS & Diluted EPS in each of the following cases:

(a) If Net Profit before Interest & Tax for the year 2014-2015 is ₹81,60,000

(b) If Net Profit for the year 2014-2015 is ₹56,00,000

(c) If Convertible Debentures were issued on 01.01.2014 and Net Profit for the year 2013-2014 is ₹56,84,000

ANSWER:

(a) Net Profit after Interest & Tax = 70% (₹ ₹ 81,60,000 – ₹ 1,60,000) = ₹ 56,00,000

COMPUTATION OF BASIC EPS & DILUTED EPS
[Assumed Convertible Debentures were issued on 1.4.2013]

Basic EPS [₹56,00,000 / 4,00,000]	**₹14 per share**
Diluted EPS:	
Weighted average number of equity shares outstanding	4,00,000
No. of shares under option	1,00,000
No. of shares that have been issued at fair value [1,00,000 x 15 / 25]	(60,000)
Weighted number of equity shares after ESOP(4,00,000 + 1,00,000 – 60,000)	4,40,000
Weighted number of equity shares after the effect of ESOP & Convertible	
Debentures [(4,00,000 + 1,00,000 – 60,000) + (32,000 × 5)]	6,00,000
Adjusted Net Profit for the current year ₹ [56,00,000 +1,60,000 – 48,000]	57,12,000
Diluted EPS (₹ 57,12,000/6,00,000]	9.52

(b) Same ANSWER as in Case (a)

(c) Computation of Basic EPS & Diluted EPS

Basic EPS [₹56,84,000 / 4,00,000]	**₹14.21 per share**
Diluted EPS:	
Weighted average number of equity shares outstanding	4,00,000
No. of shares under option	1,00,000
No. of shares that have been issued at fair value [1,00,000 x 15/25]	(60,000)
Weighted number of equity shares after ESOP(4,00,000 + 1,00,000 – 60,000)	4,40,000
Weighted number of equity shares after the effect of ESOP & Convertible Debentures [(4,00,000 + 1,00,000-60,000)+(32,000 x 5 x 3/12)]	4,80,000
Adjusted Net Profit for the current year ₹ [56,84,000 + 40,000 – 12,000]	57,12,000
Diluted EPS (₹ 57,12,000/4,80,000]	11.90

QUESTION 14. Bharat Tushar (D) Ltd. provides you the following information:

Weighted Average number of equity shares outstanding on 1.4.2014	**4,00,000 shares**
Average fair value of one equity share during the year 2014-2015	**₹25.00**
Weighted Av.g number of shares under option during the year 2014-2015	**1,00,000 shares**
Exercise Price for shares under option during the year 2014-2015	**₹15.00**
On 01.04.2013 Issued 32,000, 10% Convertible Debentures of ₹50 each.	
Each debenture is convertible into five equity shares. These are converted into equity shares on 31.12.2014	
The tax rate applicable is 30%.	
Net Profit before Interest & Tax for the year 2014-2015	**₹81,20,000**

Required: Compute Basic EPS & Diluted EPS.

ANSWER:

(a) Net Profit after Interest & Tax = 70% (₹ ₹ 81,20,000 – ₹ 1,20,000) = ₹ 56,00,000

(b) Weighted average number of equity shares outstanding for Basic EPS = 4,00,000 + (1,60,000 x 3/12) = 4,40,000

COMPUTATION OF BASIC EPS & DILUTED EPS

Basic EPS [₹55,00,000/4,40,000]	**₹12.73 per share**
Diluted EPS:	
Weighted average number of equity shares outstanding for calculating Basic EPS	4,40,000
No. of shares under option	1,00,000
No. of shares that have been issued at fair value [1,00,000 x 15/25]	(60,000)
Weighted number of equity shares after ESOP (4,40,000 + 1,00,000 – 60,000)	4,80,000
Weighted number of equity shares after the effect of ESOP & Convertible Debentures [(4,40,000 + 1,00,000 – 60,000) + (32,000 × 5 × 9/12)]	6,00,000
Adjusted Net Profit for the current year ₹ [56,00,000 + 1,20,000 – 36,000]	56,84,000
Diluted EPS (₹ 56,84,000/6,00,000]	9.47

DILUTED EARNING PER SHARE IN CASE OF CONVERTIBLE PERF. SHARES & ESOP

QUESTION 15. Tushar Ltd. provides you the following information:

Weighted Average number of equity shares outstanding during the year 2014-2015	**4,00,000 shares**
Average fair value of one equity share during the year 2014-2015	**₹25.00**
Weighted Average number of shares under option during the year 2013-2014	**1,00,000 shares**
Exercise Price for shares under option during the year 2014-2015	**₹15.00**
Issued 32,000, 10% Convertible Pref. Shares of ₹50 each. Each Pref. Share is convertible into five Equity Shares.	
The tax rate applicable is 30%.	

Required: Compute Basic EPS & Diluted EPS in each of the following cases:

(a) If Net Profit before Pref. Dividend for the year 2014-2015 is ₹56,00,000

(b) If Net Profit after Pref. Dividend for the year 2014-2015 is ₹54,40,000

(c) If Convertible Pref. Shares were issued on 01.01.2015 and Net Profit after Pref. Dividend for the year 2014-2015 is ₹55,60,000

ANSWER:

(a) Net Profit after Pref. Dividend = ₹ 56,00,000 – ₹ 1,60,000 = ₹ 54,40,000

COMPUTATION OF BASIC EPS & DILUTED EPS

[Assumed Convertible Debentures were issued on 1.4.2013]

Basic EPS [₹54,40,000/4,00,000]	**₹13.6 per share**
Diluted EPS:	
Weighted average number of equity shares outstanding	4,00,000
No. of Shares under option	1,00,000
No. of Shares that have been issued at fair value [1,00,000 x 15 / 25]	(60,000)
Weighted Number of Equity Shares after ESOP 4,00,000 + 1,00,000 – 60,000)	4,40,000
Weighted number of equity shares after the effect of ESOP & Convertible Debentures [(4,00,000 + 1,00,000 – 60,000) + (32,000 x 5)]	6,00,000
Adjusted Net Profit for the current year .[54,40,000+1,60,000]	56,00,000
Diluted EPS (₹ 56,00,000/6,00,000]	9.33

(b) Same ANSWER as in Case (a)

(c) Computation of Basic EPS & Diluted EPS

Basic EPS [₹55,60,000/4,00,000]	**₹13.90 per share**
Diluted EPS:	
Weighted average number of equity shares outstanding	4,00,000
No. of Shares under option	1,00,000
No. of Shares that have been issued at fair value [1,00,000 x 15 / 25]	(60,000)
Weighted number of equity shares after ESOP (4,00,000 + 1,00,000 – 60,000)	4,40,000
Weighted Number of Equity Shares after the effect of ESOP & Convertible Debentures [(4,00,000 + 1,00,000-60,000) + (32,000 × 5 × 3/12)]	4,80,000
Adjusted Net Profit for the current year ₹[55,60,000 + 40,000]	56,00,000
Diluted EPS (₹ 56,00,000/4,80,000]	11.67

QUESTION 16. Bharat Tushar (P) Ltd. provides you the following information:

Weighted Average number of equity shares outstanding on 1.4.2014	**4,00,000 shares**
Average fair value of one equity share during the year 2014-2015	**₹25.00**
Weighted Average number of shares under option during the year 2014-2015	**1,00,000 shares**
Exercise Price for shares under option during the year 2014-2015	**₹15.00**
On 01.04.2014 Issued 32,000, 10% Convertible Pref. Shares of ₹50 each. Each Pref. Share is convertible into five Equity Shares. These are converted into equity shares on 31.12.2014	
The tax rate applicable is 30%.	
Net Profit before Interest, Tax & Pref. Dividend for the year 2014-2015	**₹81,20,000**

Required: Compute Basic EPS & Diluted EPS.

ANSWER:

(a) Net Profit after Pref. Dividend = [(70% of ₹ ₹ 81,20,000) – (₹ 1,60,000 × 9/12)] = ₹ 55,64,000

(b) Weighted average number of equity shares outstanding for Basic EPS = 4,00,000 + (1,60,000 x 3/12) = 4,40,000

COMPUTATION OF BASIC EPS & DILUTED EPS

Basic EPS [₹55,64,000/4,40,000]	₹12.65 per share
Diluted EPS:	
Weighted average number of equity shares outstanding for calculating Basic EPS	4,40,000
No. of shares under option	1,00,000
No. of shares that have been issued at fair value [1,00,000 x 15 / 25]	(60,000)
Weighted number of equity shares after ESOP (4,40,000 + 1,00,000 – 60,000)	4,80,000
Weighted number of equity shares after the effect of ESOP & Convertible Debentures [(4,40,000 + 1,00,000 – 60,000) + (32,000 × 5 × 9/12)]	6,00,000
Adjusted Net Profit for the current year .[₹ 55,64,000 + ₹ 1,20,000]	56,84,000
Diluted EPS (₹ 56,84,000/6,00,000]	9.47

MISCELLANEOUS QUESTIONS

QUESTION 17: From the following information of Beta Ltd. calculate Earning Per Share (EPS) in accordance with AS-20:

		Year 31.3.2014 (₹)	Year 31.3.2013 (₹)
1.	Net Profit before tax	3,00,000	1,00,000
2.	Current tax	40,000	30,000
	Tax relating to earlier years	24,000	(13,000)
	Deferred tax	30,000	10,000
3.	Profit after tax	2,06,000	73,000

4. Other information:
   (a) Profit includes compensation from Central Government towards loss on account of earthquake in 2014 ₹ 1,00,000 (non-taxable)
   (b) Outstanding convertible 6% Preference shares 1,000 issued and paid on. 30.9.2012. Face value ₹ 100, Conversion ratio 15 equity shares for every 7 preference share.
   (c) 15% convertible debentures of ₹ 1,000 each total face value ₹ 1,00,000 to be converted into 10 Equity shares per debenture issued and paid on 30.6.2012.
   (d) Total no. of Equity shares outstanding as on 31.3.2014, 20,000 including 10,000 bonus shares issued on 1.1.2014 face value ₹ 100.

ANSWER:

CALCULATION OF EARNING PER SHARE (EPS) OF BETA LTD.

	Particulars	Year ended 31.3.2014	Year ended 31.3.2013
1.	A. Earning after extra ordinary items (2,06,000 – 6,000), (73,000 – 3,000)	2,00,000	70,000
	B. No. of Equity Shares	20,000	20,000
	C. Basic Earnings Per share [A/B]	10.00	3.50

	A. Earning before extra ordinary items	1,00,000	70,000
	B. No. of Equity Shares	20,000	20,000*
	C. Basic Earnings Per share [A/B]	5.00	3.50
2.	Tax Rate applicable		
	(40,000 + 30,000)/2,00,000	35%	
	(30,000 + 10,000)/1,00,000	40%	
3.	A. Dividend on Weighted Average Preference Shares	6,000	3,000
	B. Incremental shares	15,000	7,500
	C. EPS on Incremental Shares [A/B]	0.40	0.40
		(dilutive)	(dilutive)
4.	Convertible Debentures		
	A. Increase in earnings		
	$\left(1,00,000 \times \frac{15}{100} \times 0.65\right)$	9,750	
	$1,00,000 \times \frac{15}{100} \times 0.60 \times \frac{9}{12}$		6,750
	B. Increase in shares	1,000	750
	C. Increase in EPS [A/B]	9.75	9.00
		(Anti dilutive)	(Anti dilutive)

" Since the bonus issue is without consideration, the issue is treated as if it had occurred prior to the beginning of the year 2013.

It is anti-dilutive as it increases the EPS from continuing ordinary operations (Para 39, AS 20)

Calculation of Diluted EPS	**Year ended 31.3.2014** ₹	**Year ended 31.3.2013** ₹
A. Profit from continuing ordinary activities before Preference Dividend	1,06,000	73,000
No. of ordinary equity shares	20,000	20,000
Adjustment for dilutive potential of 6% convertible pref. shares	15,000	7,500
B. Total no. of shares	35,000	27,500
C. Diluted EPS from continuing ordinary operations [A/B]	3.02	2.65
D. Profit including extra ordinary items	2,06,000	73,000
E. Adjusted No. of shares	35,000	27,500
F. Diluted EPS including extra ordinary items [D/E]	5.88	2.65

Disclosure of EPS in accordance with AS 20 in the Profit and Loss Account:

Earning per share (Face value ₹ 100)	31.3.2014 (₹)	31.3.2013 (₹)
Basic EPS from continuing ordinary operations	5.00	3.50
Diluted EPS from continuing ordinary operations	3.02	2.65

QUESTION 18. TULSIAN LTD provides you the following information:

Date	Particulars	No. of Shares
01.04.2015	**Balance at the beginning of year**	**5,00,000**
01.06.2015	**Issue of Shares for Cash**	**1,20,000**
01.07.2015	**Issue of Shares to Underwriters**	**6,000**
01.08.2015	**Buy - Back of Shares**	**2,69,250**
01.09.2015	**Issue of Shares against Purchase of Building. (acquisition is recognized on the same day)**	**30,000**
01.10.2015	**Issue of Shares in settlement of liability**	**15,000**
01.11.2015	**Tulsian Ltd. purchased Y Ltd. on the basis of intrinsic value of shares of both the companies. The intrinsic value of shares of Tulsian Ltd. and Y Ltd. are ₹ 60 and ₹ 15 respectively Shares outstanding on 1st April, 2015 of Y Ltd. are 4,80,000**	
01.12.2015	**Split up of shares into shares of ₹ 10 each**	
01.01.2016	**Bonus issue:1 share for every 2 held**	
No. of 12% convertible Debentures of ₹ 100 each		**1,00,000**
Interest of Debentures		**3,00,000**
Conversion Ratio of Debentures		**10 shares per debenture**
Net Profit for year ended 31-03-2015		**₹ 85,00,000**
Net Profit for year ended 31-03-2016		**₹ 1,10,00,000**
Tax Rate		**30%**
10% Cumulative Preference Shares		**₹1,00,00,000**
12% Non-Cumulative Preference Shares		**₹1,00,00,000**

Note: No dividend has been paid on Preference Shares for the last 3 years.

Required: Compute the Basic and Diluted EPS (earning per share) for accounting year 2015-2016 and Adjusted EPS for the year 2014-2015.

ANSWER:

Step 1.

CALCULATION OF NET PROFIT ATTRIBUTABLE TO EQUITY SHAREHOLDERS

Particulars	2014-2015 (₹)	2015-2013 (₹)
A. Net Profit after Tax	85,00,000	1,10,00,000
B. *Less:* 10 % Preference dividend on Cumulative Preference Shares	(10,00,000)	(10,00,000)
C. Net Profit for the period attributable to Equity Shareholders	75,00,000	1,00,00,000

Step 2.

WEIGHTED AVERAGE NUMBER OF SHARES OUTSTANDING ON 31.03.2016

Date outstanding C	No. of Shares (months) D = B × C	Weight Period A	Product B
01.04.2015	5,00,000	12/12	5,00,000
01.06.2015	1,20,000	10/12	1,00,000
01.07.2015	6,000	9/12	4,500
01.08.2015	(2,69,250)	8/12	(1,79,500)
01.09.2015	30,000	7/12	17,500
01.10.2015	15,000	6/12	7,500
01.11.2015	1,20,000	5/12	50,000
	[(4,80,000 x ₹ 15) / ₹ 60]		
	Weighted Average Number of Shares Outstanding		5,00,000
01.12.2015	Split of shares [5,00,000 shares × 100 / 10]		50,00,000
01.01.2016	Bonus issue: (50,00,000 × 1/2)		25,00,000
	Weighted Average Number of Shares Outstanding		75,00,000

1. Basic EPS for Financial Year 2015-2016
   - A. Net Profit for the Year — 100,00,000
   - B. Weighted Average Shares Outstanding for FY 2015-2013 [50,00,000 + (50,00,000 × 1/2)] — 75,00,000
   - C. Basic EPS [A/B] — 1.33
2. Diluted EPS for Financial Year 2015-2016
   - A. Net Profits for the year — 100,00,000
   - B. After Tax Interest (1,00,000 Debentures × ₹ 100 Face Value × 12% × 3/12 × 0.70) — 2,10,000
   - C. Adjusted Equity Earnings for the year [A + B] — 1,02,10,000
   - D. Weighted Average Shares Outstanding for Basic EPS — 75,00,000
   - E. *Add:* Potential Equity Shares (to be computed only from the date of issue) (1,00,000 Debentures × Conversion Ratio 10 × 3/12) — 2,50,000
   - F. Adjusted Weighted Average Number of Equity Shares [D + E] — 77,50,000
   - G. Diluted EPS [C/F] — 1.317
3. Adjusted EPS for Financial Year 2014-2015
   - A. Net Profits for the year — 75,00,000
   - B. Adjusted Average Share Outstanding for FY 2014-2015 [5,00,000 + (5,00,000 × 1/2)] — 7,50,000
   - C. Adjusted EPS for [A/B] — 10

Note: Interest on debentures for full year amounts to ₹ 12,00,000 (i.e. 12% of ₹ 1,00,00,000). However, interest expense amounting ₹ 3,00,000 has been given in the question. It may be concluded that debentures have been issued during the year and interest has been provided for 3 months.

QUESTION 19. From the following information relating to Y Ltd. Calculate Earnings Per Share (EPS):

	₹ in crores
Profit before V.R.S. payments but after depreciation	**75.00**
Depreciation	**10.00**
VRS payments	**32.10**
Provision for taxation	**10.00**
Fringe benefit tax	**5.00**
Paid up share capital (shares of ₹ 10 each fully paid)	**93.00**

ANSWER:

CALCULATION OF EARNINGS PER SHARE

Particualrs	**₹ in crores**
Profit after depreciation but before VRS payment	75.00
Less:	
VRS payments	(32.10)
Provision for taxation	(10.10)
Fringe benefit tax	(5.00)
Net Earnings	27.90
Number of Shares	9.30 crores
Earnings Per Share = 27.90/9.30 = ₹ 3 per share.	

QUESTION 20. [Determination of Dilutive/Anit-Dilutive]

Net Profit available to Equity Shareholders for the year 2014 - 2015	**₹48,00,000**
No. of Equity Shares Outstanding	**10,00,000**
15 % Preference Shares of ₹100 each convertible in 2015 - 2016 into Equity Shares of ₹10 each.	**10,000 Preference shares, Each Preference share is convertible into 10 equity shares.**
10 % Debentures of ₹100 each convertible in 2015 – 2016 into Equity Shares of ₹10 each	**1000 Debenturess, Each Debenture is convertible into 10 equity shares**
8% Debentures of ₹100 each convertible in 2015 - 2016 into Equity Shares of ₹10 each	**5000 Debenture, Each Debenture is convertible into 1 equity shares**
Tax Rate during the year 2014 - 2015	**40 %**

Determine whether these Potential Equity Shares are Dilutive or Anti-Dilutive.

ANSWER: Basic Earning per share = ₹ 48,00,000 / 10,00,000 = 4.80

Particulars	Increase in earnings	Increase in number of Equity shares	Earnings per incremental share	Ranking from Most dilutive to Least Dilutive
A	B	C	D = B / C	E
15 % Convertible Preference shares				
Increase in net profit [15% of (10,000 × ₹100)] attributable to Equity shareholders	1,50,000		1.5	II
Increase in number of shares (10,000 × 10)		1,00,000		
10 % Convertible Debentures				
Increase in net profit				
10% of (1000 × ₹100) 10,000				
Less: Tax @ 40 % 4,000	6,000		0.6	I
Increase in number of shares (1,000 × 10)		10,000		
8 % Convertible Debentures				
Increase in net profit				
8% of (5000 × ₹100) 40,000				
Less: Tax @ 40 % 16,000	24,000		4.80	III
Increase in Number of Shares (5,000 × 1)		5,000		

COMPUTATION OF DILUTED EARNING PER SHARE

Particulars	Net Profit Attributable (₹)	No. of Equity Shares	Net Profit attributable per share (₹)	
As reported	48,00,000	10,00,000	4.80	
10 % Convertible Debentures	6,000	10,000		
	48,06,000	10,10,000	4.76	Dilutive
15 % Convertible Preference shares	1,50,000	1,00,000		
	49,56,000	11,10,000	4.46	Dilutive
8 % Convertible Debentures	24,000	5,000		
	49,80,000	11,15,000	4.47	Anti -Dilutive

Since diluted earnings per share is increased when taking the 8 % Convertible Debentures into account (from ₹4.46 to ₹4.47), the 8 % Convertible Debentures are anti-dilutive and are ignored in the calculation of diluted earnings per share. Therefore, diluted earnings per share is ₹4.46

Note: Even if incremental earning pesr share is less than basic earning per share, it should be considered as anti-dilutive if its inclusion in calculation of diluted earning per share increased previously calculated diluted earning per share. The logic behind this is that the most dilutive earning per share shall be reported for the period.

10 AS 26 – INTANGIBLE ASSETS

THEORETICAL BASE

QUESTION 1. State the areas to which AS 26 is not applicable.

ANSWER:

1. Intangible assets held by an enterprise for sale in the ordinary course of business (AS 2, Valuation of Inventories, and AS 7,Accounting for Construction Contracts);
2. Deferred Tax Assets (AS 22,Accounting for Taxes on Income);
3. Leases that fall within the scope of AS 19, Leases; and
4. Goodwill arising on an amalgamation (AS 14, Accounting for Amalgamations) and goodwill arising on consolidation (AS 21, Consolidated Financial Statements).
5. Financial Assets;
6. Mineral Rights and expenditure on the exploration for, or development and extraction of, minerals, oil, natural gas and similar non-regenerative resources; and
7. Intangible Assets arising In Insurance Enterprises from contracts with policyholders.

QUESTION 2. State the Meaning and Essential Components of Intangible Asset as per AS 26.

ANSWER:

MEANING OF INTANGIBLE ASSET

An intangible asset is an identifiable non-monetary asset, without physical substance, held for use in the production or supply of goods or services, for rental to others, or for administrative purposes.

ESSENTIAL COMPONENTS OF INTANGIBLE ASSET

1. It must be Identifiable [i.e. the asset must be separable from other assets]
2. It must be controlled by the enterprise.
3. Future economic benefits must be associated with an intangible asset.

QUESTION 3. How will you record the intangible asset in each of the following cases:

1. **Intangible Asset acquired in exchange for share or other securities**
2. **An intangible asset acquired in an amalgamation in the nature of purchase**
3. **Intangible Asset acquired by way of Govt. Grant free of charge**
4. **Intangible Asset acquired by way of Govt. Grant for nominal consideration**
5. **An Intangible Asset acquired in exchange for another asset**
6. **If tangible element cannot operate without intangible element.**
7. **If tangible element can operate without intangible element**

ANSWER:

Case	Recording of Asset
1. Intangible Asset acquired in exchange for share or other securities	At its Fair Value, or the fair value of the securities issued, whichever is more clearly evident. **Note:** Fair value of an asset is the amount for which that asset could be exchanged between knowledgeable, willing parties in an arm's length transaction.
2. An intangible asset acquired in an amalgamation in the nature of purchase	As per AS 14
3. Intangible Asset acquired by way of Govt. Grant free of charge	At a Nominal Value
4. Intangible Asset acquired by way of Govt. Grant for nominal consideration	At the acquisition cost (including expenditure directly attributable to making the asset ready for its intended size)
5. An Intangible Asset acquired in exchange for another asset	As per AS 10
6. If tangible element cannot operate without intangible element.	Both elements should be treated as a fixed asset under AS-10.
7. If tangible element can operate without intangible element	• Tangible Element should be treated as a fixed asset under AS-10. • Intangible Element should be treated as Intangible Asset under AS-26.

QUESTION 4 State the meaning of Research and Components, Treatment and Disclosure Requirements of Research Costs as per AS 26.

ANSWER:

MEANING OF RESEARCH

Research is original and planned investigation undertaken with the prospect of gaining new scientific or technical knowledge and understanding.

COMPONENTS OF RESEARCH COSTS

1. Costs of materials and services used or consumed in research;
2. Costs of personnel directly engaged in research;
3. Overheads incurred on research
4. Any other expenditure that is directly attributable to research, such as fees to register a legal right and the amortisation of patents and licences that are used for research;

TREATMENT OF RESEARCH COSTS

Research Costs should be recognized as an expense when these are incurred.

DISCLOSURE REQUIREMENTS OF RESEARCH COSTS

Aggregate amount of research expenditure recognized as expense during the period should be disclosed.

QUESTION 5. State the meaning of Development and Components, Treatment and Disclosure Requirements of Development Costs as per AS 26.

ANSWER:

MEANING OF DEVELOPMENT

Development is the application of research findings or other knowledge to a plan or design for the production of new or substantially improved materials, devices, products, processes, systems or services prior to the commencement of commercial production or use.

COMPONENTS OF DEVELOPMENT COSTS

1. Costs of materials and services used or consumed in development;
2. Costs of personnel directly engaged in development;
3. Overheads incurred on development
4. Any other expenditure that is directly attributable to development, such as fees to register a legal right and the amortisation of patents and licences that are used for development;

TREATMENT OF DEVELOPMENT COSTS

Development Costs should be included in the cost of an intangible asset arising from development (or from the development phase of an internal project) **if, and only if, it meets the essential components of an intangible asset and** can demonstrate **all of the following conditions are satisfied** otherwise it have to be recognized as expense:

1. the technical feasibility of completing the intangible asset so that it will be available for use or sale;
2. its intention to complete the intangible asset and use or sell it;
3. its ability to use or sell the intangible asset;
4. how the intangible asset will generate probable future economic benefits. Among other things, the enterprise should demonstrate the existence of a market for the output of the intangible asset or the intangible asset itself or, if it is to be used internally, the usefulness of the intangible asset;
5. the availability of adequate technical, financial and other resources to complete the development and to use or sell the intangible asset; and
6. its ability to measure the expenditure attributable to the intangible asset during its development reliably.

Note: Recognized Amount should not exceed its recoverable amount as determinable in AS - 28 at each balance sheet date. If the amount exceeds the recoverable amount then immediately an impairment loss (i.e. Recognised Amount–Recoverable Amount) should be recognized.

DISCLOSURE REQUIREMENTS OF DEVELOPMENT COSTS

Aggregate amount of DEVELOPMENT expenditure recognized as expense during the period should be disclosed.

QUESTION 6. State the conditions for Recognition of Intangible Asset.

ANSWER: An intangible asset should be recognized if, and only if:

(a) It meets all the essential elements of an intangible asset;

(b) it is probable that the future economic benefits that are attributable to the asset will flow to the enterprise; and

(c) the cost of the asset can be measured reliably.

QUESTION 7. State the Treatment of Subsequent Expenditure on an intangible asset after its purchase or its completion.

ANSWER: Subsequent expenditure on an intangible asset after its purchase or its completion should be recognized as an expense when it is incurred unless:

(a) it is probable that the expenditure will enable the asset to generate future economic benefits in excess of its originally assessed standard of performance; and

(b) the expenditure can be measured and attributed to the asset reliably.

QUESTION 8. How should an Intangible Asset be amortised?

ANSWER: The depreciable amount (i.e.cost of an asset less its residual value of an intangible asset) should be allocated on a systematic basis (on straight-line basis unless some other pattern can be determined reliably) over the best estimate of its useful life (usually not exceeding 10 years from the date when the asset is available for use).

Note: The amortisation charge for each period should be recognized as an expense unless another Accounting Standard permits or requires it to be included in the carrying amount of another asset.

QUESTION 9. How should the Softwares & Websites , Goodwill arising under amalgamation in the nature of purchase and Patents, Copyright & Trade Mark be amortised?

ANSWER:

1. Amortise Softwares & Websites in 3-5 years,
2. Goodwill arising under Amalgamation in the nature of Purchase in 5 years (as per AS 14)
3. Patents, Copyright & Trade Mark in 10 years in the ratio of future economic benefits if can be reliably calculated, otherwise on straight-line basis

QUESTION 10. Should an Intangible Assets be assessed for impairment loss?

ANSWER: An intangible asset should be assessed for impairment loss as per AS - 28 since its initial recognition. It is not relevant whether asset has been put to use or not. An impairment loss is the amount by which the carrying amount of an asset exceeds its recoverable amount.

1. Disclose Intangible Asset in the Balance Sheet at Lower of Book Cost or Recoverable Amount (As per AS 28).
2. Recognize Impairment Loss (i.e. Excess of Book Cost over Recoverable Amount) as an expense & Charge to Profit & Loss A/c

QUESTION 11. State the Treatment of Retirements and Disposals of Intangible Asset.

ANSWER:

1. An intangible asset should be derecognized (eliminated from the balance sheet) on disposal or when no future economic benefits are expected from its use and subsequent disposal.
2. The difference between the net disposal proceeds and the carrying amount of the asset should be recognised as income or expense in the Statement of Profit and Loss.
3. An intangible asset that is retired from active use and held for disposal is carried at its carrying amount at the date when the asset is retired from active use.

QUESTION 12. Should Internally Generated Goodwill be recognized as an asset?

ANSWER: Internally generated goodwill ,brands, mastheads, publishing titles, customer lists should not be recognized as an asset.

QUESTION 13. State the Disclosure Requirements as to Intangible Asset.

ANSWER:

1. the Useful Lives or the Amortisation Rates used;
2. the Amortisation Methods used;
3. the Gross Carrying Amount and the Accumulated Amortisation (aggregated with accumulated impairment losses) at the beginning and end of the period
4. a Reconciliation of the carrying amount at the beginning and end of the period showing:
   (i) additions, indicating separately those from internal development and through amalgamation;

(ii) retirements and disposals;
(iii) impairment losses recognized in the statement of profit and loss during the period (if any);
(iv) impairment losses reversed in the statement of profit and loss during the period (if any)
(v) amortisation recognized during the period; and
(vi) other changes in the carrying amount during the period

5. Reasons for Amortisation of Intangible Asset over more than 10 years

PRACTICAL QUESTIONS FOR PRACTICE

QUESTION 1. TULSIAN Ltd. made the following payments during the year ended 31st March 2015:

(a) ₹ 60,00,000 to acquire a Software

(b) ₹ 60,00,000 to acquire a Website for a period of 8 years

(c) ₹ 60,00,000 to acquire a Copy right for a period of 15 years

(d) ₹ 60,00,000 to acquire Goodwill of a firm

(e) ₹ 60,00,000 to acquire Goodwill arising under Amalgamation in the nature of Purchase

(f) ₹ 60,00,000 to acquire a Patent for a period of 5 years. The net cash flows from the product during these 5 years are expected to be ₹ 36,00,000,₹ 46,00,000, ₹ 44,00,000, ₹ 40,00,000 and ₹ 34,00,000.

(g) ₹ 60,00,000 to acquire Stock Exchange Membership Rights

(h) ₹ 60,00,000 to the State Govt towards the cost of roads built in the vicinity of the project for the purpose of carrying materials to the site. The roads so built is the property of State Govt.

(i) ₹ 60,00,000 towards extensive special initial advertisement campaign for the new product.

(j) ₹ 60,00,000 to develop a Drug to treat Cancer but AS 26 criteria for capitalization was not met.

Required: Find out the Amortization Cost of each of the item to be charged to Profit & Loss A/c.

ANSWER:

(a) Amortization Cost of Software = ₹ 60,00,000/5= ₹ 12,00,000 (Since Maximum Amortization period of Software is 5 years)

(b) Amortization Cost of Website= ₹ 60,00,000/5= ₹ 12,00,000 (Since Maximum Amortization period of Website is 5 years)

(c) Amortization Cost of Copy right = ₹ 60,00,000/10= ₹ 6,00,000(Since Maximum Amortization period of Copy right is 10 years unless a higher period is justified with reasons in Notes to Accounts)

(d) Amortization Cost of Goodwill = ₹ 60,00,000/10= ₹ 6,00,000(Since Maximum Amortization period of Goodwill is 10 years unless a higher period is justified with reasons in Notes to Accounts)

(e) Amortization Cost of Goodwill arising under Amalgamation in the nature of Purchase = ₹ 60,00,000/5= ₹ 12,00,000 (Since Maximum Amortization period of such Goodwill is 5 years)

(f) Amortization Cost of Patent

Year	Net Cash Flows ₹	Amortization Ratio	Amortization Amount ₹
I	36,00,000	0.180	10,80,000
II	46,00,000	0.230	13,80,000
III	44,00,000	0.220	13,20,000
IV	40,00,000	0.200	12,00,000
V	34,00,000	0.170	10,20,000
	2,00,00,000	1.000	80,00,000

(g) Amortization Cost of Stock Exchange Membership Rights = ₹ 60,00,000/10= ₹ 6,00,000 Amortization period of Stock Exchange Membership Rights is 10 years unless a higher period is justified with reasons in Notes to Accounts)

(h) ₹ 60,00,000 to the State Govt towards the cost of roads should be charged to Profit & Loss A/c for the year ended 31st March 2015 unless Toll Rights are being owned by the company.

(i) ₹ 60,00,000 towards extensive special initial advertisement campaign for the new product should be charged to Profit & Loss A/c for the year ended 31st March 2015 .

(j) ₹ 60,00,000 to develop a Drug should be charged to Profit & Loss A/c for the year ended 31st March 2014 since AS 26 criteria for capitalization was not met.

QUESTION 2. Swift Ltd. acquired a patent at a cost of ₹ 80,00,000 for a period of 5 years and the product life-cycle is also 5 years. The company capitalized the cost and started amortizing the asset at ₹ 10,00,000 per annum. After two years it was found that the product life-cycle may continue for another 5 years from then. The net cash flows from the product during these 5 years were expected to be ₹ 36,00,000,₹ 46,00,000, ₹ 44,00,000, ₹ 40,00,000 and ₹ 34,00,000. Find out the amortization cost of the patent for each of the years.

ANSWER: Swift Limited amortised ₹ 10,00,000 per annum for the first two years i.e. ₹ 20,00,000. The remaining carrying cost can be amortized during next 5 years on the basis of net cash flows arising from the sale of the product. The amortisation may be found as follows:

Year	Net Cash Flows ₹	Amortization Ratio	Amortization Amount ₹
I	—	0.125	10,00,000
II	—	0.125	10,00,000
III	36,00,000	0.180	10,80,000
IV	46,00,000	0.230	13,80,000
V	44,00,000	0.220	13,20,000
VI	40,00,000	0.200	12,00,000
VII	34,00,000	0.170	10,20,000
Total	2,00,00,000	1.000	80,00,000

It may be seen from above that from third year onwards, the balance of carrying amount i.e., ₹ 60,00,000 has been amortized in the ratio of net cash flows arising from the product of Swift Ltd.

Note: The answer has been given on the basis that the patent is renewable and Swift Ltd. got it renewed after expiry of five years. It has been assumed that the company had amortized the patent at ₹ 10,00,000 per annum in the first two years on the basis of economic benefits derived from the product manufactured under the patent.

QUESTION 3 A company had deferred research and development cost of ₹ 150 Lakhs. Sales expected in the subsequent years as under:

Year	I	II	III	IV
Sales(₹ In Lakhs)	400	300	200	100

(a) You are required to suggest how should Research and Development cost is to be charged to Profit and Loss account.

(b) If at the end of the IIIrd year, it is felt that no further benefit will accrue in the IVth year, how the unamortized expenditure would be dealt with in the accounts of the Company?

ANSWER:

(a) Research and Development Cost should to be allocated in the ratio of Sales as follows:

Years	Research and Development cost allocation (₹ In Lakhs)
I	400 x150/1000= 60
II	300 x150/1000= 45
III	200 x150/1000= 30
IV	100 x150/1000= 15

(b) If at the end of IIIrd year the circumstances do not justify further deferral as given in QUESTION at the end of IIIrd year, ₹ 45 Lakhs is to be charged as an expense immediately as per AS - 26.

QUESTION 4. An enterprise acquired patent right for ₹400 lakhs. The product life cycle has been estimated to be 5 years and the amortization was decided in the ratio of estimated future cash flows which are as under:

Years	1	2	3	4	5
Estimated Future Cash Flows (₹ in lakhs)	200	200	200	100	100

After 3rd year, it was ascertained that the patent would have an estimated balance future life of 3 years and the estimated cash flow after 5th year is expected to be ₹ 50 lakhs each year. Determine the amortization under Accounting Standard 26.

ANSWER:

AMORTIZATION OF COST AS PER AS 26

Year	Net Cash Flows	Amortization Ratio	Amortization Amount ₹
1	200	.25	100
2	200	.25	100
3	200	.25	100
4	100	.40 (Revised)	40
5	100	.40 (Revised)	40
6	50	.20 (Revised)	20
			400

QUESTION 5. ABC Ltd. developed a know-how by incurring expenditure of ₹ 20 lakhs. The know-how was used by the company from 1.4.2008. The useful life of the asset is 10 years from the year of commencement of its use. The company has not amortised the asset till 31.3.2015. Pass Journal entry to give effect to the value of know-how as per Accounting Standard-26 for the year ended 31.3.2015.

ANSWER:

JOURNAL ENTRY

Particulars		Dr. (₹)	Cr. (₹)
Profit and Loss A/c (Prior period item)	Dr.	12,00,000	
Depreciation A/c	Dr.	2,00,000	
To Know-how A/c			14,00,000

QUESTION 6. Himalayas Ltd. is showing an intangible Asset at ₹ 72 lakhs as on 01.04.2015 and that item was required for ₹ , 96 lakhs on 01.04.2009 and that item was available for use from that date. Himalayas Ltd. has been following the policy of amortisation of the intangible asset over a period of 12 years on straight line basis. Comment on the accounting treatment of the above with reference to relevant accounting standard.

ANSWER:

PROVISION OF AS 26

As per AS 26, the depreciable amount of an intangible asset should be allocated on a systematic basis over the best estimate of its useful life. There is a rebuttable presumption that the useful life of an intangible asset will not exceed 10 years from the date when the asset is available for use. Amortisation should commence when the asset is available for use.

ADVICE

The Company has been following the policy of amortisation of the intangible asset over a period of 12 years on straight line basis. The period of 12 years is more than the maximum period of 10 years specified under AS 26. Accordingly, Himalayas Ltd. would be required to restate the carrying amount of intangible asset as on 1.4.2015 at ₹ 96 lakhs less ₹ 28.8 lakhs (₹ 9.6 lakhs × 3 years) = ₹ 67.2 lakhs. If amortisation had been as per AS 26, the carrying amount would have been ₹ 67.2 lakhs. The difference of ₹ 4.8 lakhs i.e. (₹ 72 lakhs – 67.2 lakhs) would be required to be adjusted against the opening balance of revenue reserves. The carrying amount of ₹ 67.2 lakhs would be amortised over 7 (10 less 3) years in future.

QUESTION 7: During 2014-2015, an enterprise incurred costs to develop and produce a routine, low risk computer software product, as follows:

	Amount (₹).
Completion of detailed programme and design	**25,000**
Coding and Testing	**20,000**
Other coding costs	**42,000**
Testing costs	**12,000**
Product masters for training materials	**13,000**
Duplication of computer software and training materials,	
from product masters (2,000 units)	**40,000**
Packing the product (1,000 units)	**11,000**
What amount should be capitalized as software costs in the books of the company, on Balance Sheet date?	

ANSWER:

PROVISION OF AS-26

As per para 44 of AS-26, costs incurred in creating a computer software product should be charged to research and development expense when incurred until technological feasibility/asset recognition criteria has been established for the product. Technological feasibility/asset recognition criteria has been established upon completion of detailed programme design or working model.

ADVICE

In this case, ₹ 45,000 would be recorded as an expense (₹ 25,000 for completion of detailed program design and ₹ 20,000 for coding and testing to establish technological feasibility/asset recognition criteria). Cost incurred from the point of technological feasibility/asset recognition criteria until the time when products costs are incurred are capitalized as software cost (₹ 42,000 + ₹ 12,000 + ₹ 13,000) ₹ 67,000.

QUESTION 8. A company acquired for its internal use a software on 28.01.2012 from the USA for US $ 1,00,000. The exchange rate on that date was ₹ 52 per USD. The seller allowed trade discount @ 5%. The other expenditure were:

(i) Import Duty: 20%

(ii) Purchase Tax: 10%

(iii) Entry Tax : 5% (Recoverable later from tax department)

(iv) Installation expenses : ₹ 25,000

(v) Profession fees for Clearance from Customs : ₹ 20,000

Compute the Cost of Software to be capitalized.

ANSWER:

CALCULATION OF COST OF SOFTWARE (INTANGIBLE ASSET) ACQUIRED FOR INTERNAL USE

Particulars	₹
Purchase cost of the software	$ 1,00,000
Less: Trade discount @ 5%	($ 5,000)
	$ 95,000
Cost in ₹ (US $ 95,000 × ₹ 52)	₹ 49,40,000
Add: Import duty on cost @ 20% (₹)	9,88,000
	59,28,000
Purchase tax @ 10% (₹)	5,92,800
Installation expenses (₹)	25,000
Profession free for clearance from customs (₹)	20,000
Cost of the software to be capitalised (₹)	65,65,800

Note: Entry Tax being a recoverable/refundable tax has not included as part of the cost of the asset.

QUESTION 9. An Enterprise has incurred expense for purchase of Technical Know-how for manufacturing a Moped. The Enterprise has paid ₹ 5 crores for the use of Know-how for a period of 4 years. The Enterprise estimates the production of mopeds as follows:

Year	No. of Mopeds
1	25,000
2	50,000
3	75,000
4	1,00,000

On going into production, at the end of the 1st year it achieved its targeted production, but considered to revise the estimates for the next 3 years as follows:

Year	No. of Mopeds
1	35,000
2	65,000
3	80,000

(a) How will the Enterprise amortise the Technical Know-how Fees as per AS-26.

(b) Whether this amortisation should be directly charged as an expense or should form part of Production Cost of the Mopeds.

ANSWER: Based on the revised estimate, total sales is 2,05,000 (i.e. 25,000 + 35,000 + 65,000 + 80,000) the first year charge should be a proportion of 25,000/2,05,000 on ₹ 5 crores, second year will be 35,000/2,05,000, and so on unless the estimates are again revised. If these estimates cannot be determined reliably it would be preferable to charge them off on a straight line basis, otherwise, as can be seen from the above example, significant amortisation amount is inappropriately postponed to later years. As already mentioned above, there will rarely, if ever, be persuasive evidence to support an amortisation method for intangible assets that results in a lower the given case, amortisation expense will be included as cost of inventory.

QUESTION 10. TULSIAN International Ltd. is developing a new production process. During the financial Year 31st March, 2014, the total expenditure incurred on this process was ₹ 100 lakhs. The production process met the criteria for recognition as an intangible asset on 1st Dec 2013. Expenditure incurred till this date was ₹ 44 lakhs.

Further expenditure incurred on the process for the financial year ending 31st March 2015, was ₹ 160 lakhs. As at 31-3-2015, the recoverable amount of know-how embodied in the process is estimated to be ₹ 144 lakhs. This includes estimates of future cash outflows as well as inflows.

You are required to work out:

(a) What is the expenditure to be charged to the Profit and Loss Account for the year ended 31st March 2014? (Ignore depreciation for this purpose)

(b) What is the carrying amount of the intangible asset as at 31st March 2014?

(c) What is the expenditure to be charged to the Profit and Loss Account for the year ended 31st March 2015? (Ignore depreciation for this purpose)

(d) What is the carrying amount of the intangible asset as at 31st March 2015?

ANSWER:

(a) ₹ 44 lakhs being the Cost incurred till the Date(1.12.2013) when Recognition Criteria met is to be charged to Profit & Loss A/c for the year ended 31st March 2014

(b) ₹ 56 lakhs being the Cost incurred since the Date(1.12.2013) when Recognition Criteria met shall be the Carrying amount as on 31-3-2014

(c) ₹ 72 lakhs being the Impairment Loss [i.e. Total Book Cost (56 + 160) – Recoverable Amount(144)] is to be charged to Profit & Loss A/c for the year ended 31st March 2015

(d) ₹ 144 lakhs being Lower of Book Cost or Recoverable Amount shall be the Carrying amount as on 31-3-2015

QUESTION 11. Shiva Ltd. is engaged in research on a new process design for its product. It had incurred an expenditure of ₹ 530 lakhs on research upto 31st March, 2014. The development of the process began on 1st April, 2014 and the Development Phase Expenditure was ₹ 360 lakhs upto 31st March, 2015. From 1st April, 2015 the Company will implement the new process design which will result in a after-tax cost saving of ₹ 80 lakhs per annum for the next five years. The Company's Cost of Capital is 10%. At what cost should the asset be recorded and what is its amortisation amount?

ANSWER:

Research Expenditure	As per Para 41 of AS-26, the expenditure on research ₹ 530 lakhs should be expensed in the year in which it is incurred. It is presumed that the entire expenditure of ₹ 530 lakhs is incurred in financial year 2013-2014. Hence, it should be written off as an expense in that year itself.	
Development Expenditure	As per para 44 of AS-26, the expenditure on development can be treated as an asset only if all the conditions listed in that paragraph are satisfied. It is presumed that the company has duly complied with this requirement.	
Cost of internally generated intangible asset	Para 53 specifies the items which can be included in the cost of an internally generated intangible asset, while Para 54 specifies the exclusions therefrom. It is presumed that the expenditure of ₹ 360 lakhs is determined in accordance with Para 53 and 54 of AS-26.	
Discounting Future Cash Flows	As per Para 30 of AS-26, fair value of an intangible asset can be estimated by discounting estimated future net cash flows. Even if this paragraph is primarily related to estimation of fair value of an intangible asset acquired in the course of amalgamation in the nature of purchase, the concept can be extended for internally generated intangible asset also.	
	Cost savings from the new process design for five years per annum	₹80 lakhs
	Company's Cost of Capital	10%
	Annuity Factor at 10% for five years (from the annuity tables)	3.7908
	Present Value of Future Cash Flows	₹80 x 3.7908
		₹303.264 lakhs
Recognition of Asset	Intangible Asset should be recognised at ₹ 303.264 lakhs being lower than the actual expenditure.	
Amortisation Amount and Period	The Company can amortise ₹ 303.264 lakhs over a five year period by charging ₹ 60.6528 lakhs per annum from the financial year 2015-2016 onwards.	
Treatment of Difference	₹ 56.736 lakhs (₹ 360 – ₹ 303.264 lakhs) should be charged to Profit and Loss Account.	

QUESTION 12. Refiners and Projects Limited is a company in the oil and gas sector, it undertakes extensive research and development work as part of its operations. It has till the end of the financial year 31 March, 2013 spent ₹ 592,23 crores on research expenses.

The development of a new process was completed in the accounting year 2013- 2014 after incurring an expenditure of ₹ 322.26 crores. In the accounting year 2014-2015 the company implemented the new process resulting in a post tax saving of ₹ 100 crores in the first year of operation and savings of ₹ 80 crores per annum thereafter for the next four years.

The cost of capital to the company is 12 per cent

Kindly indicate how you will, in the background of accounting standards prescribed, proceed to record the transactions in the books of accounts of the company.

You are given to understand that the research expenses shown above do not include any general or selling and administrative expenses.

The present value discounted at 12 per cent of a Rupee can be adopted at .893, .797, .712, .636 and .567 for the purposes of calculation.

ANSWER:

ACCOUNTING TREATMENT OF RESEARCH EXPENDITURE

Provision of AS 26	Accounting Treatment
As per AS 26 no intangible asset arising from research (or from the research phase of an internal project) should be recognised. Expenditure on research (or on the research phase of an internal project) should be recognised as an expense when it is incurred.	₹ 592.23 crores incurred on research till the end of financial year ended 31st March, 2013 cannot be capitalised and hence has to expensed in the year in which it is incrred. In case the same is still unexpensed it will have to be written off under 'Prior period Expenditure'.

ACCOUNTING TREATMENT OF DEVELOPEMENT EXPENDITURE

Provision of AS 26	Accounting Treatment
As per para 44 of the standard, an intangible asset arising from development (or from the development phase of an internal project) should be recognised if, and only if, an enterprise can demonstrate all of the conditions specified in the standard.	Development cost of ₹ 322.26 crores is eligible for capitalization assuming that the enterprise can demonstrate all the specified conditions.

ACCOUNTING TREATMENT OF CARRYING AMOUNT

Provision of AS 26	Accounting Treatment
As per AS 26, after initial recognition, an intangible asset should be carried at its cost less any accumulated amortization and any accumulated impairment losses.	Present value of future cash flows amounting ₹ 306.26 crores [(₹ 100 crores × 0.893) + (₹ 80 crores × 0.797) + (₹ 80 crores × 0.712) + (₹ 80 crores × 0.636) + (₹ 80 crores × 0.567)] is less than the cost incurred, it is prudent to carry the intangible asset at the discounted value of future cash flows (Rs. 306.26 crores). The excess of cost incurred over present values amounting ₹ 16 crores (₹ 322.26 – ₹ 306.26) has to be recognised as an impairment loss in the year 2013-2014.

ACCOUNTING TREATMENT OF DEPRECIATION AMOUNT

Provision of AS 26	Accounting Treatment
As per AS 26 depreciable amount of an intangible asset should be allocated on a systematic basis over the best estimate of its useful life. There is a rebuttable presumption that the useful life of an intangible asset will not exceed 10 years from the date when the asset is available for use. Amortization should commence when the asset is available for use.	The value of intangible asset should be amortized over a period of 5 years by following the straight line method. Therefore, an annual depreciatoon of ₹ 61.25 crores ₹ 306.26 (₹ 306.26 crores/5) should be charged for each year beginning with 2014-2015.

QUESTION 13. An intangible item is appearing in the Balance Sheet of A Ltd. ₹ 15 lakhs on 1-4-2015. The item was acquired for ₹ 25 lakhs on 1-4-2014. The enterprise has been following a policy of amortizing the intangible item over a period of 5 years on straight line basis. Applying paragraph 63 of AS 26 the enterprise determines the amortization period to be

8 years, being the best estimate of its useful life, from the date when the item was amiable for use i.e., April 1, 2014. Comment.

ANSWER: As per AS 26 the intangible asset was Acquired i.e. 1st April 2012, the revision of amortization period from 5 years to 8 years is a change in Accounting estimate and accordingly, para 78 of AS 26 would apply in this case. As per AS 26 if the expected useful life of the asset is significantly different from previous estimates, the amortisation period should be changed accordingly. AS 5 provides that in case of change in estimate, the effect should be given prospectively over the remaining useful life of the intangible asset i.e. 6 years.

Note: It is assumed that since the date of purchase of intangible item, the enterprise has been following a policy of amortizing the intangible asset over a period of 5 years on straight line basis by applying paragraph 63 of AS 26 i.e. being the best estimate of its useful life. On 1.4.2015, the company again reviewed the useful life of the intangible asset.

QUESTION 14. A Pharma Company spent ₹ 33 lakhs during the accounting year ended 31st March, 2015 on a research project to develop a drug to treat "AIDS". Experts are of the view that it may take four years to establish whether the drug will be effective or not and even if found effective it may take two to three more years to produce the medicine, which can be marketed. The company wants to treat the expenditure as deferred revenue expenditure. Comment.

ANSWER: As per para 41 of AS 26 'Intangible Assets', no intangible asset arising from research (or from the research phase of an internal project) should be recognized. Expenditure on research (or on the research phase of an internal project) should be recognized as an expense when it is incurred. Thus the company cannot treat the expenditure as deferred revenue expenditure. The entire amount of ₹ 33 lakhs spent on research project should be charged as an expense in the year ended 31st March, 2015.

QUESTION 15. M Ltd. launched a project for producing product A in Nov. 2013. The company incurred ₹ 30 lakhs towards Research and Development expenses upto 31st March, 2015. Due to unfavourable market conditions the management feels that it is not possible to manufacture and sold the product in the market for next so many years. The management hence wants to defer the expenditure write off to future years.

Required: Advise the company as per the applicable Accounting Standard.

ANSWER:

PROVISION OF AS-26

As per AS 26 expenditure on research should be recognised as an expense when it is incurred. An intangible asset arising from development (or from the development phase of an internal project) should be recognized if and only if, an enterprise can demonstrate all of the conditions specified in para 44 of the standard. An intangible asset (arrising from development) should be derecognised when no future economic benefits are expected from its use.

ADVICE

The management can not defer the expenditure write off to future years and the company is required to expense the entire amount of ₹ 30 lakhs in the Profit and Loss account of the year ended 31st March, 2015.

QUESTION 16. X Ltd is engaged in the business of newspaper and radio broadcasting. It operates through different brand names. During FY 2014-2015 it incurred substantial amounts on external trade, business communication and branding expenses by participation in various corporate social responsibility initiatives. The company expects to benefits by this expenditure by attracting new customers over a period of time and accordingly it has capitalized the same under brand development expenses and intends to amortize the same over the period in

which it expects the benefits to flow. As the statutory auditor of the company do you concur? Give reasons.

ANSWER:

PROVISION OF AS 26

As per AS-26 on "Intangible Assets", expenditure on an intangible item should be recognised as an expense when it is incurred unless it forms part of the cost of an intangible asset that meets the recognition criteria.

ADVICE

Since no intangible assets or other asset is acquired or created that can be recognized, the accounting treatment by the company to amortize the entire expenditure over the period in which it expects the benefits to flow is not correct and the same should be debited to the profit & loss account.

QUESTION 17. PQR Ltd. has acquired a Brand from another company for ₹ 100 lakhs. PQR Ltd. contends that since the said brand is a very popular and famous brand, no deprecation of amortisation needs to be provided.

ANSWER:

PROVISION OF AS 26

As 26 "intangible Assets" provides that an intangible asset should be measured initially at cost. After initial recognition, an intangible asset should be carried at cost less any accumulated amortization and any accumulated impairment losses. The depreciable amount of an intangible asset should be allocated on a systematic basis over the best estimate of its useful life. There is a rebuttable presumption that the useful life of an intangible asset will not exceed 10 years from the date when the asset is available for use. The auditor should satisfy himself that the value of brand is amortized in accordance with AS 26, as brand is considered to be intangible asset.

ADVICE

The contention of PQR Ltd. that Brand is very popular and famous, no depreciation of amortization needs to be provided, is wrong in view of the above and hence, the auditor will have to qualify in the report this matter and quantity, the amount of non-amortisation.

QUESTION 18. SAD Enterprises, a partnership firm, had purchased business of SWAD enterprises on 01.04.2014 and paid ₹ 50,000 towards goodwill. On 01.04.2015, SAD enterprises decided to admit W as partner and the goodwill was valued at ₹ 1,00,000 for the purpose.

Please explain with reasons, at what price goodwill can be shown in the books of account.

ANSWER:

PROVISION OF AS-26

As per AS 26 goodwill can be recorded in the books only when some consideration in money or moeny's worth has been paid for it. Therefore, only purchased goodwill should be recorded in the books.

ADVICE

Payment of ₹ 50,000 was made towards purchase of goodwill, hence to this extent goodwill can be recorded in the books. Additional goodwill of ₹ 50,000 is self generated goodwill, which should not be recorded. On admission, death or retirement of a partner, goodwill adjustmens can be carried can be carried out through capital accounts.

QUESTION 19. P, N and T are equal partners. The decided to change their profit sharing ratio into 5:4:3. They raised the goodwill in the books to the extent of ₹ 2,40,000 and it is to be written off immediately. Show Journal entries with narration to be passed for raising the goodwill and for its subsequent write off.

QUESTION 5. State the Meaning and Recognition Criteria of 29 ONEROUS CONTRACT as per AS 29.

ANSWER:

Meaning	An Onerous Contract is a contract in which the unavoidable costs of meeting the obligations under the contract exceed the economic benefits expected to be received under it. **Note:** The unavoidable costs are least of the following:- (i) cost of fulfilling contract and any compensation thereon or (ii) Penalties arising from failure to fulfill contract.
Same Recognition Criteria as for Provision	The amount of provision in respect of an onerous contract should be measured by applying the principles mentioned above for recognizing a provision.

QUESTION 6 How will you deal with the following situations so far as Recognition and Disclosure as per AS 29 are concerned?

(a) In case of present Obligation Outflow of Resources is probable & a reliable estimate can be made.

(b) In case of Possible Obligation Outflow of Resources is not probable

(c) In case of Possible Obligation Outflow of Resources remote

ANSWER:

SUMMARISED REQUIREMENTS AS TO PROVISION AND CONTINGENT LIABILITIEs

	Present Obligation	**Possible Obligation**	
	Outflow of Resources is probable & a reliable estimate can be made.	Outflow of Resources is not probable	Outflow of Resources is remote
Provision	Recognized	Not Recognized	Not Recognized
Disclosures	Required for the Provision	Required for the Contingent liability	Not Required

PRACTICAL QUESTIONS FOR PRACTICE

QUESTION 1. In the following cases, advise whether Present Obligation exists or not at the end of financial year 31st March, 2015.

Case 1	**Credit sales made to customers in year 2014–2015. However, from its previous experiences enterprise estimates that it shall not be able to collect 5% of the sales revenue.**
Case 2	**Sales made to customers in year 2014–2015. The warranty was given to all customers in year 2014–2015. The enterprise estimates that 10% of its customers will avail the warranty facility.**
Case 3	**A certain activity undertaken by the enterprise hitherto was license fee. However, from 1st January, 2015 it has become mandatory to obtain license for such activity otherwise the fines and penalties shall be attracted. Enterprise has not obtained any license till the end of financial year since it entails heavy initial cost.**
Case 4	**A suit is pending against the enterprise in the court. If suit goes against the enterprise, it shall entails heavy cost to the enterprise. However, as per the lawyer engaged by the enterprise suit will go in the favour of enterprise.**
Case 5	**A suit is pending against the enterprise in the court. If suit goes against the enterprise, it shall entails heavy cost to the enterprise. However, as per the lawyer engaged by the enterprise suit will go against the enterprise.**
Case 6	**The enterprise operates through a factory, which has contaminated the environment. Hitherto there is no law, which can restrict the enterprise. But from 1st January, 2015 a new law has come into operation which requires the damages caused by the factory of the enterprise to be rectified.**
Case 7	**The enterprise operates through a factory, which has contaminated the environment. Hitherto there is no law, which can restrict the enterprise but there is a possibility that a new law shall be enacted, which shall require the damages caused by the factory of the enterprise to be rectified.**

ANSWER:

DETERMINING WHETHER PRESENT OBLIGATION EXISTS OR NOT

Case	Advice
1	In this case, an obligating event was credit sales. If enterprise had not made such credit sales there was no question of any such credit risk. By making such credit sales, enterprise had created an event that result in obligating event hence, present obligation @ 5% exists on balance sheet date.
2.	In this case, an obligating event was, when sales are made with warranties. If enterprise had made sales without warranties, no such obligation exists in respect of warranties. Hence, by making such sales, an enterprise had created an obligating event that results in present obligation at balance sheet date @ 10%.
3	In this case, till the end of financial year the enterprise is not committed to obtain license. Hence, there is no question of making provision of initial cost of obtaining such license. But by operating three months without license the enterprise had created an obligating event which shall result in present obligation in the form of fines and penalties. Hence, a provision is required in respect of fines and penalties.
4	On the basis of evidence available, there is no present obligation as at balance sheet date, hence, there is no need of provision.

5	On the basis of evidence available, there exists a present obligation as at balance sheet date, hence, there is need of provision.
6	As environmental damages caused by the enterprise had lead to an obligation event hence, there exists a present obligation in respect of remedy of environment as at balance sheet date. Therefore, a provision is necessary in this case.
7	In this case, present obligation arises only when it is virtually certain that new law will be enacted. If this is a case then there is a need of provision otherwise not.

QUESTION 2. At the end of the financial year ending on 31st March, 2015 a company finds that there are twenty law suits outstanding which have not been settled till the date of approval of accounts by the Board of Directors. The possible outcome as estimated by the Board is as follows:

	Probability	Loss (₹)
In respect of five cases (Win)	**100%**	**—**
Next ten cases (Win)	**60%**	**—**
Lose (Low damages)	**30%**	**1,20,000**
Lose (High damages)	**10%**	**2,00,000**
Remaining five cases		
Win	**50%**	**—**
Lose (Low damages)	**30%**	**1,00,000**
Lose (High damages)	**20%**	**2,10,000**

Outcome of each case is to be taken as a separate entity. Ascertain the amount of contingent loss and the accounting treatment in respect thereof.

ANSWER:

PROVISION OF AS-29

According to AS 29 'Provisions, Contingent Liabilities and Contingent Assets', contingent liability should be disclosed in the financial statements if following conditions are satisfied:

1. There is a present obligation arising out of past events but not recognized as provision.
2. It is not probable that an outflow of resources embodying economic benefits will be required to settle the obligation.
3. The possibility of an outflow of resources embodying economic benefits is also remote.
4. The amount of the obligation cannot be measured with sufficient reliability to be recognized as provision.

ADVICE

In this case, the probability of winning of first five cases is 100% and hence, question of providing for contingent loss does not arise. The probability of winning of next ten cases is 60% and for remaining five cases is 50%. As per AS 29, we make a provision if the loss is probable. As the loss does not appear to be probable and the possibility of an outflow of resources embodying economic benefits is not remote rather there is reasonable possibility of loss, therefore disclosure by way of note should be made. For the purpose of the disclosure of contingent liability by way of note, amount may be calculated as under:

Expected loss in next ten cases = 30% of ₹ 1,20,000 + 10% of ₹ 2,00,000
= ₹ 36,000 + ₹ 20,000 = ₹ 56,000

Expected loss in remaining five cases = 30% of ₹ 1,00,000 + 20% of ₹ 2,10,000
= ₹ 30,000 + ₹ 42,000 = ₹ 72,000

To disclose contingent liability on the basis of maximum loss will be highly unrealistic. Therefore, the better approach will be to disclose the overall expected loss of ₹ 9,20,000 (₹ 56,000 × 10 + ₹ 72,000 × 5) as contingent liability.

QUESTION 3. X Ltd. has its financial year ended 31.3.2015, fifteen law suits outstanding, none of which has been settled by the time the accounts are approved by the directors. The directors have estimated that the probable outcomes as below:

	Probability	Amount of Loss ₹
For first ten cases:		
Win	**0.6**	**—**
Loss-low damages	**0.3**	**90,000**
Loss-high damages	**0.1**	**2,00,000**
For remaining five cases:		
Win	**0.5**	**—**
Loss-low damages	**0.3**	**60,000**
Loss-high damages	**0.2**	**1,00,000**

The directors believe that the outcome of each case is independent of the outcome of all the others. Estimate the amount of contingent loss and state the accounting treatment of such contingent loss.

ANSWER. As per AS 29 Contingent Liability should be disclosed in the financial statements if following conditions are satisfied:

1. There is a present obligation arising out of past events but not recognized as provision.
2. It is not probable that an outflow of resources emodying economic benefits will be required to settle the obligation.
3. The possibility of an outflow of resources embodying economic benefits is also remote.
4. The amount of the obligation cannot be measured with sufficient reliability to be recognized as provision.

In this case, the probability of winning first 10 cases is 60% and for remaining five cases is 50%. In other words, probability of losing the cases is 40% and 50% respectively. According to AS 29, we make a provision if the loss is probable. As the loss does not appear to be probable and the probability or possibility of an outflow of resources embodying economic benefits is not remote rather there is reasonable possibility of loss, therefore, disclosure by way of note of contingent liability amount may be calculated as under:

Expected loss in first ten cases = [₹ 90,000 × 0.3 + ₹ 2,00,000 × 0.1] × 10
= [₹ 27,000 + ₹ 20,000] × 10
= ₹ 47,000 × 10 = ₹ 4,70,000

Expected loss in remaining five cases = [₹ 60,000 × 0.3 + ₹ 1,00,000 × 0.2] × 5
= [₹ 18,000 + ₹ 20,000] × 5
= ₹ 38,000 × 5 = ₹ 1,90,000

Total Contingent Liability = ₹ 4,70,000 + ₹ 1,90,000 = ₹ 6,60,000.

QUESTION 4. An engineering goods compnay provides after sales warranty for 2 years to its customers. Based on past experience, the company has the following policy for making provision for warranties on the invoice amount, on the remaining balnce warranty period:

Less than 1 year: 2% provision

More than 1 year: 3% provision

The company has raised invoices as under:

Invoice Date	**Amount ₹**
19th January, 2013	**40,000**
29th January, 2014	**25,000**
15th October, 2014	**90,000**

Calculate the provision to be made for warranty under Accounting Standard 29 as at 31st March, 2014 and 31st March, 2015. Also compute amount to be debited to Profit and Loss Account for the year ended 31st March, 2015.

ANSWER:

A. Provision as at 31-3-2013 = ₹ 25,000 × 0.2 + ₹ 90,000 × .03 = ₹ 3,200

B. *Less:* Provision as at 31-3-2014 = ₹ 40,000 × 0.2 + ₹ 25,000 × .03 = ₹ 1,550

C. Amount debited to Profit and Loss Account (A – B) = ₹ 1,650

Note: No provision is to be made on 31-3-2015 in respect of sales amounting to ₹ 40,000 made on 19-01-2013 because the warranty period of 2 years has already expired.

QUESTION 5. A Co. Ltd. has not included in the Balance Sheet as on 31-03-2015 a sum of ₹ 3 crores being amount in the arrears of salaries and wages payable to the staff for the last 2 years as a result of successful negotiations which were going on during the last 18 months and concluded on 30-04-2015. The auditor wants to sign the said Balance Sheet and given the audit report on 31-05-2015. The auditor came to know the result of the negotiations on 15-05-2015. Comment.

ANSWER:

PROVISION OF AS 29 AND AS-4

As per As 4 "Contingencies and Events occurring after the Balance Sheet Date", adjustments to assets and liabilities are required for events occurring after the Balance Sheet date that provide additional information materially affecting the determination of the amounts relating to conditions existing at the balance sheet date. Similarly as per AS 29 "Provisions, Contingent liabilities and Contingent Assets", future events that may affect the amount required to settle an obligation should be reflected in the amount of a provision where there is sufficient objective evidence that the will occur.

ADVICE

The amount of ₹ 1.50 crores is a material amount and it is the result of an event, which has occurred after the Balance Sheet date. The facts have become known to the auditor before the date of issue of the Audit Report and Financial Statements.

The auditor has to perform the procedure to obtain sufficient, appropriate evidence covering the period from the date of the financial statements i.e., 31-03-2015 to the date of Auditors Report i.e., 31-05-2015. It will be observed that as a result of long pending negotiations a sum of ₹ 1.50 cores representing arrears of salaries of the year 2013-2014 and 2014-2015 have not been included in the financial statements. It is quite clear that the obligation requires provision for outstanding expenses as per AS 4 and AS 29.

So the auditor should request the management to adjust the same of ₹ 3 crores by making provision for expenses. If the management does not accept the request the auditor should qualify the audit report.

QUESTION 6. Mini Ltd. took a factory premises on lease on 1.4.2015 for ₹ 2,00,000 per month. The lease is operating lease. During March, 2015, Mini Ltd. relocates its operation to a new factory 'building. The lease on the old factory premises continues to be live upto 31.12.2014 The lease can not be cancelled and can not be sub-let to another user. The auditor insists that lease rent of balance 33 months upto 31.12.2014 should be provided in the accounts for the year ending 31.3.2015. Mini Ltd. seeks your advice.

ANSWER:

PROVISION OF AS-29 & ASI 30

As per AS-29 and ASI 30 'Applicability of AS 29 to Onerous Contracts', if an enterprise has a contract that is onerous, the present obligation under the contract should be recognized and measured as a provision.

ADVICE

In the given case, the operating lease contract has become onerous as the economic benefit of lease contract for next 33 months up to 31.12.2013 will be nil. However, the lessee, Mini Ltd., has to pay lease rent of ₹ 66,00,000 (i.e. 2,00,000 p.m. for next 33 months). Therefore, provision on account of ₹.66,00,000 is to be provided in the accounts for the year ending 31.03.2015. Hence auditor is right.

QUESTION 7. Sun Ltd. has entered into a sale contract of ₹ 5 crores with X Ltd. during 2013-2014 financial year. The profit on this transaction is ₹ 1 crore. The delivery of goods is to take place during the first month of 2014-2015 financial year. In case of failure of Sun Ltd. to deliver within the schedule a compensation of ₹ 1.5 crores is to be paid to X Ltd Sun Ltd. planned to manufacture the goods during the last month of 2013-2014 financial year. As on balance sheet date (31.3.2014), the goods were not manufactured and it was unlikely that Sun Ltd. will be in a position to meet the contractual obligation.

(i) Should Sun Ltd. provide for contingency as per AS 29 ?

(ii) Should provision be measured as the excess of compensation to be paid over the profit?

ANSWER:

(i) AS 29 "Provisions" Contingent Liabilities and Contingent Assets" provides that when f an enterprise has a present obligation, as a result of past events, that probably requires an outflow of resources and a reliable estimate can be made of the amount of obligation, a provision should be recognised. Sun Ltd. has the obligation to deliver the goods within the scheduled time as per the contract. It is probable that Sun Ltd. will fail to deliver the goods within the schedule and it is also possible to estimate the amount of compensation. Therefore, Sun Ltd. should provide for the contingency amounting ₹ 1.5 crores as per AS 29.

(ii) Provision should not be measured as the excess of compensation to be paid over the profit. The goods were not manufactured before 31st March, 2014 'and no profit had accrued for the financial year 2013-2014. Therefore, provision should be made for the full amount of compensation amounting ₹.1.50 crores.

QUESTION 8. An airline is required by law to overhaul its aircraft once in every three years. A company which operates aircrafts does not provide any provision as required by law in its final account. Discuss with reference to relevant Accounting Standard.

ANSWER:

PROVISION OF AS 29

As per AS 29. A provision should be recognised only when an enterprise has a present obligation as a result of a past event.

ADVICE

In-the given case, there is no present obligation, therefore no provision is recognized as per AS 29. The cost of overhauling aircraft is not recognized as a provision because it is a future obligation and the incurring of the expenditure depends on the company's decision to continue operating the aircrafts. Even a legal requirement to overhaul does not require the company to make a provision for the cost of overhaul because there is no present obligation to overhaul the aircrafts. Further, the enterprises can avoid the future expenditure by its future action, for example by selling the aircraft. However, an obligation might arise to pay fines or penalties under the legislation after completion of three years. Assessment of probability of incurring fines and penalties depends upon the provisions of the legislation and the stringency of the enforcement regime. A provision should be recognized for the best estimate of any fines and penalties if airline continues to operate aircrafts for more than three years.

QUESTION 9. You are an accountant preparing accounts of A Ltd., as on 31-03-2015. After year end the following events have taken place in April, 2015:

A suit against the company's advertisement was filed by a party claiming damage of ₹ 20 lakhs. Describe, how above will be dealt with in the account of the company for the year ended on 31-3-2015.

ANSWER: Suit filed against the company being a contingent liability must be disclosed with the nature of contingency, an estimate of the financial effect and uncertainties which may affect the future outcome must be disclosed as per AS-29

QUESTION 10. An enterprise operates an offshore oilfield where its licensing agreement requires it to remove the oil rig at the end of production and restore the seabed. Ninety per cent of the eventual costs relate to the removal of the oil rig and restoration of damage caused by building it, and ten per cent arise through the extraction of oil. At the balance sheet date, the rig has been constructed but no oil has been extracted. Analyse as per AS 29.

ANSWER: Present obligation as a result of a past obligating event. The construction of the oil rig creates an obligation under the terms of the licence to remove the rig and restore the seabed and is thus an obligating event. At the balance sheet date, however, there is no obligation to rectify the damage that will be caused by extraction of the oil.

An outflow of resources embodying economic benefits in settlement is Probable.

Conclusion: A provision is recognised for the best estimate of ninety per cent of the eventual costs that relate to the removal of the oil rig and restoration of damage caused by building it. These costs are included as part of the cost of the oil rig. The ten per cent of costs that arise through the extraction of oil are recognised as a liability when the oil is extracted.

QUESTION 11. A retail store has a policy of refunding purchases by dissatisfied customers, even though it is under no legal obligation to do so. Its policy of making refunds is generally known. Analyse as per AS 29

ANSWER: Present obligation as a result of a past obligating event .-The obligating event is the sale of the product, which gives rise to an obligation because obligation also arise from normal business practice, custom and a desire to maintain good business relations or act in an equitable manner.

An outflow of resources embodying economic benefits in settlement: Probable a, proportion of goods are returned for refund

Conclusion: A provision is recognised for the best estimate of the costs of refunds.

QUESTION 12. Under new legislation, an enterprise is required to fit smoke filters to its factories by 30 September 2015. The enterprise has riot fitted the smoke filters. Analyses under AS-29:

- **(a) At the balance sheet date of 31 March 2015**
- **(b) At the balance sheet date of 31 March 2016**

ANSWER:

(a) **Present obligation as a result of a past obligating event:** There is no obligation because there is no obligating event either for the costs of fitting smoke filters or for fines under the legislation.

Conclusion: No provision is recognised for the cost of fitting the smoke filters

(b) **Present obligation as a result of a past obligating event:** There is still no obligation for the costs of fitting smoke filters because no obligating event has occurred (the fitting of the filters). However, an obligation might arise to pay fines or penalties under the legislation because the obligating event has occurred (the non-compliant operation of the factory).

An outflow of resources embodying economic benefits in settlement: Assessment of probability of incurring fines and penalties by non-compliant operation depends on the details of the legislation and the stringency of the enforcement regime.

Conclusion: No provision is recognised for the costs of fitting smoke filters. However, a provision is recognised for the best estimate of any fines and penalties that are more likely than not to be imposed.

QUESTION 13. A company is in a dispute involving allegation of infringement of patents by a competitor company who is seeking damages of a huge sum of ₹ 900 lakhs. The directors are of the opinion that the claim can be successfully resisted by the company. How would you deal the same in the annual accounts of the company?

ANSWER:

PROVISION OF AS 29

As per para 14 of AS 29, 'Provision, Contingent Liabilities and Contingent Assets', a provision should be recognised when

(a) an enterprise has a present obligation as a result of a past event;

(b) It is probable that an outflow of resources embodying economic benefits will be required to settle the obligation; and

(c) a reliable estimate can be made of the amount of the obligation. If these conditions are not met, no provision should be recognised.

If these conditions are not met, no provision should be recognised.

ADVICE

Since the directors of the com pany are of the opinion that the claim can be successfully resisted by the com pany, therefore there will be no outflow of the resources. The company will disclose the same as contingent liability by way of the following note: "Litigation is in process against the company relating to a dispute with a competitor who alleges that the company has infringed patents and is seeking damages of ₹ 900 lakhs. However, the directors are of the opinion that the claim can be successfully resisted by the company."

QUESTION 14. X Ltd. (a Public Sector Company) provides consultancy and engineering services to its clients. In the year 2014-2015, the Government has set up a commission to decide about the pay revision. The pay will be revised with effect from 1-1-2013 based on the recommendations of the commission. The company makes the provision of ₹ 1000 lakhs for pay revision in the financial year 2014-2015 on the estimated basis as the report of the commission is yet to come. As per the contracts with the client on cost plus job, the billing is done on the actual payment made to the employees and allocated to jobs based on hours booked by these employees on each job.

The company discloses through notes to accounts

"Salaries and benefits include the provision of ₹ 1000 lakhs in respect of pay revision. The amount chargeable from reimbursable jobs will be billed as per the contract when the actual payment is made".

The accountant feels that the company should also book/recognise the income by ₹ 1000 lakhs in Profit and Loss Account as per the terms of the contract. Otherwise, it will be the violation of matching concept and understatement of profit.

ANSWER:

PROVISION OF AS 29

As per para 46 of AS-29, 'Provisions, Contingent Liabilities and Contingent Assets', where some or all of the expenditure required to settle a provision is expected to be reimbursed by another party, the reimbursement should be recognised when, and only when it is virtually certain that reimbursement will be received if the enterprise settles the obligation. The reimbursement should be treated as a separate assets. The amount recognised for the reimbursement should not exceed the amount of the provision.

Accordingly, potential loss to an enterprise may be reduced or avoided because a contingent liability is matched by a related counter-claim or claim against a third party. In such cases, the amount of the provision is determined after taking into account the probable recovery under the claim if no significant uncertainty as to its measurability or collectability exists.

ADVICE

In this case, the provision of salary to employees of ₹ 1000 lakhs will be ultimately collected from the client, as per the term so the contract. Therefore, the liability of ₹ 1000 lakhs is matched by the counter claim from the client. Hence the provision for salary of employees should be made reducing the claim to be made from the client. It appears that the whole amount of ₹ 1000 lakhs is recoverable from client and there is no significant uncertainty about the collection. Hence, the net charge to Profit & Loss Account should be NIL.

The opinion of the accountant regarding non-recognition of income of ₹ 1000 lakhs is not as per AS-29 and AS-9. However, the concept of prudence will not be followed if ₹ 1000 lakhs is simultaneously recognized as income. ₹ 1000 is not the revenue at present but only reimbursement of claim. However the accountant is correct to the extent as that non-recognition of ₹ 1000 lakhs as income will result in the under statement of profit.

QUESTION 15. Quick Ltd. is a company engaged in the trading of spare parts used in the repair of automobiles. The company has been regular in depositing the tax, as such there is no liability of Income Tax etc. for the Financial Year 2015-2016.

The figures for the year are as under:

Income chargeable to tax	**₹ 211.64 lakhs**
Total income after adjustments	**₹ 228.48 lakhs**
Tax thereon	**₹ 74.13 lakhs**
TDS deducted during the year	**₹ 30.45 lakhs**
Tax paid for the year	**₹ 43.68 lakhs**

The company has prepared its Balance Sheet as per above figures. However, during the assessment proceeding held before the finalization of the Balance Sheet the Income Tax Officer has issued demand of ₹ 7.52 lakhs, insisting that this amount of TDS has not been uploaded online and thus is not acceptable as deduction.

The company has in reply to the same filed a rectification with the Assessing Officer. The company is trying to collect the TDS certificates, but ₹ 2.39 lakhs deducted by XY LTD., is not traceable. The rectification is lying pending with the Assessing Officer.

Please suggest the treatment of ₹ 2.39 lakhs and ₹ 7.52 lakhs in Balance Sheet.

ANSWER:

PROVISION OF AS 29

As per para 10 of AS 29 ₹Provisions, Contingent Liabilities and Contingent Assets', a contingent liability is: (a) a possible obligation that arises from past events and the existence of which will be confirmed only by the occurrence or non-occurrence of one or more uncertain future events not wholly within the control of the enterprise; or (b) a present obligation that arises from past events but is not recognised because: (i) it is not probable that an outflow of resources embodying economic benefits will be required to settle the obligation; or (ii) a reliable estimate of the amount of the obligation cannot be made. An obligation is a present obligation if, based on the evidence available, its existence at the balance sheet date is considered probable, i.e., more likely than not.

ADVICE

TDS shall be allowed by the IT department on submission of duplicate TDS certificates. Since the company is making efforts and is hopeful for its ultimate collection, contingent liability will be made for ₹ 2.39 lakhs in the books of account.

Further as per para 15 of the standard, where it is more likely that no present obligation exists at the balance sheet date and the possibility of an outflow of resources embodying economic benefits is remote, no contingent liability is disclosed.

TDS certificates for ₹ 5.13 lakhs (₹ 7.52 lakhs less ₹ 2.39 lakhs) have been submitted and the company has filed a rectification with the Assessing Officer. Therefore, the possibility of an outflow of resources embodying economic benefits is remote; the company shall not disclose it as contingent liability. This amount should be disclosed by way of a note to the accounts.

Note: An alternative view can also be considered on the basis of the paragraph 14 of the standard which states that a provision should be recognised in the books when (a) an enterprise has a present obligation as a result of a past event; (b) it is probable that an outflow of resources embodying economic benefits will be required to settle the obligation; and (c) a reliable estimate can be made of the amount of the obligation.

Accordingly, in the given case, since there is a probability of outflow of resources and also the amount can be quantified on account of non-traceability of TDS certificates, a provision may be made for ₹ 2.39 lakhs in the books of account.

Regarding the balance amount of ₹ 5.13 lakhs (₹ 7.52 lakhs less ₹ 2.39 lakhs), since TDS certificated have been submitted, it is likely that the Income-tax Officer may accept the rectification filed by the assessee. However, since the TDS details have not been uploaded online because of which demand has been issued, there may be a possibility that the rectification may also not be accepted. Therefore, taking a conservative approach, ₹ 5.13 lakhs may be disclosed as a contingent liability.

SECTION – C

QUESTIONS BASED ON REVISED SCHEDULE III TO THE COMPANIES ACT, 2013

QUESTIONS BASED ON SCHEDULE III TO THE COMPANIES ACT, 2013

THEORETICAL BASE

SPECIMEN OF STATEMENT OF PROFIT & LOSS

NAME OF THE COMPANY.........................
STATEMENT OF PROFIT AND LOSS FOR THE YEAR ENDED ....

	Particulars	*Note No.*	*Figures for the Current Reporting Period*	*Figures for the Previous Reporting Period*
			₹	₹
I.	**Revenue from Operations**	1	xxx	xxx
II.	**Other Income**	2	xxx	xxx
III.	**Total Revenue [I + II]**		xxx	xxx
IV.	**Expenses:**			
	Cost of Materials consumed	3	xxx	xxx
	Purchases of Stock-in-Trade		xxx	xxx
	Changes in Inventories	4	xxx	xxx
	Employee Benefits Expense	5	xxx	xxx
	Finance Costs	6	xxx	xxx
	Depreciation and Amortization Expense	7	xxx	xxx
	Other Expenses	8	xxx	xxx
	Total Expenses		xxx	xxx
V.	**Profit before Tax(III–IV)**		xxx	xxx
VI.	**Exceptional Items**		xxx	xxx
VII.	**Profit Before Extraordinary Items and Tax (V – VI)**		xxx	xxx
VIII.	**Extraordinary Items**		xxx	xxx
IX.	**Profit before tax (VII – VIII)**		xxx	xxx
X.	**Tax Expense:**			
	(1) Current Tax		xxx	xxx
	(2) Deferred Tax		xxx	xxx
			xxx	xxx
XI.	**Profit (Loss) for the period**		xxx	xxx
XII.	**Earnings per Equity Share:**			

(1) Basic		xxx	xxx
(2) Diluted		xxx	xxx

Notes to Accounts:

NOTE 1: REVENUE FROM OPERATIONS

(a) From Sale of Products	xxx	xxx
(b) From Sale of Services	xxx	xxx
(c) From Other Operating Revenues [Trading Commission]	xxx	xxx
(d) *Less:* Excise Duty	(xxx)	(xxx)
	xxx	xxx

NOTE 2: OTHER INCOME

(a) Interest Income (in case of a company other than a finance company)	xxx	xxx
(b) Dividends From Subsidiary Companies	xxx	xxx
(c) Dividend Income From Companies other than Subsidiary Companies	xxx	xxx
(d) Net Gain/Loss on Sale of Investments [Gain – Loss)]	xxx	xxx
(e) Other Non-Operating Income (Net of Expenses directly attributable to such income) [Income – Expenses)]	xxx	xxx
(f) Net Gain on Foreign Currency Transaction of Translation (other than considered as Finance Cost)	xxx	xxx
	xxx	xxx

NOTE 3: COST OF MATERIALS CONSUMED

(a) Opening Stock of Materials	xxx	xxx
(b) *Add:* Purchases of Materials	xxx	xxx
(c) *Less:* Closing Stock of Materials	(xxx)	(xxx)
Cost of Materials consumed	xxx	xxx

NOTE 4: CHANGES IN INVENTORIES

Particulars	*Work-in-Progress* (₹)	*Finished Goods* (₹)	*Total*
Closing Stock	xxx	xxx	xxx
Less: Opening Stock	(xxx)	(xxx)	(xxx)
	xxx	xxx	xxx

NOTE 5: EMPLOYEE BENEFITS EXPENSE

Salaries and Wages	xxx	xxx
Contribution To Provident and Other Funds	xxx	xxx
Expense On Employee Stock Option Scheme (ESOP) and Employee Stock Purchase Plan (ESPP)	xxx	xxx

Staff Welfare Expenses	xxx	xxx
	xxx	xxx

NOTE 6: FINANCE COSTS

(a) Interest Expense	xxx	xxx
(b) Other Borrowing Costs	xxx	xxx
(c) Applicable Net Gain/Loss on Foreign Currency Transactions and Translation	xxx	xxx
	xxx	xxx

NOTE 7: DEPRECIATION AND AMORTIZATION EXPENSE

Buildings	xxx	xxx
Plant and Equipment	xxx	xxx
Vehicles	xxx	xxx
Office Equipment	xxx	xxx
Brands	xxx	xxx
Computer Software	xxx	xxx
	xxx	xxx

NOTE 8: OTHER EXPENSES

(a) Consumption of Stores and Spare Parts	xxx	xxx
(b) Power and Fuel	xxx	xxx
(c) Rent.	xxx	xxx
(d) Repairs to Buildings	xxx	xxx
(e) Repairs to Machinery	xxx	xxx
(f) Insurance	xxx	xxx
(g) Rates and Taxes [Excluding Taxes on Income]	xxx	xxx
(h) Miscellaneous Expenses	xxx	xxx
(i) Provisions for Losses of Subsidiary Companies	xxx	xxx
(j) Net Gain on Foreign Currency Transaction of Translation (other than considered as Finance Cost)	xxx	xxx
(k) Provisions, if material	xxx	xxx
(l) Withdrawl from Provisions, if material	xxx	xxx
(m) Expenditure on Corporate Social Responsibility (CSR)	xxx	xxx
(j) Payments to the Auditor as:		
(a) Auditor	xxx	xxx
(b) For Taxation Matters	xxx	xxx
(c) For Company Law Matters	xxx	xxx
(d) For Management Services	xxx	xxx
(e) For Other Services	xxx	xxx

(f) For Reimbursement of Expenses	xxx	xxx
	xxx	xxx

NOTE: SURPLUS I.E. BALANCE IN THE STATEMENT OF PROFIT AND LOSS TO BE TAKEN TO BALANCE SHEET

Opening Balance	xxx	xxx
Add: Profit for the period	xxx	xxx
Less: Transfer to Reserve	(xxx)	(xxx)
Less: Interim Dividend	(xxx)	(xxx)
Less: Proposed Preference Dividend	(xxx)	(xxx)
Less: Proposed Equity Dividend	(xxx)	(xxx)
Less: Dividend Distribution Tax	(xxx)	(xxx)
Closing Balance	xxx	xxx

Notes:

1. Any item of Income *or* Expenditure which exceeds **1% of the Revenue from Operations *or* ₹ 1,00,000, *whichever is higher*** is to be disclosed separately.
2. The Statement of Profit and Loss shall also contain by way of a note the following information, namely:

(a) **Value of imports calculated on C.I.F. basis** by the company during the financial year in respect of—

I. Raw Materials; II. Components and spare parts; III. Capital Goods;

(b) **Expenditure in Foreign Currency** during the financial year on account of royalty, know-how, professional and consultation fees, interest, and other matters;

(c) **Total Value of all imported raw materials, spare parts and components** consumed during the financial year and the total value of all indigenous raw materials, spare parts and components similarly consumed and the percentage of each to the total consumption;

(d) **The amount remitted during the year in Foreign Currencies** on account of dividends with a specific mention of the total number of Non-Resident Shareholders, the total number of shares held by them on which the dividends were due and the year to which the dividends related.

(e) **Earnings in Foreign Exchange** classified under the following heads, namely:—

I. Export of Goods calculated on F.O.B. basis;
II. Royalty, know-how, professional and consultation fees;
III. Interest and Dividend;
IV. Other Income, indicating the nature thereof.

FORM OF PREPARING A BALANCE SHEET OF A COMPANY

VERTICAL FORM OF BALANCE SHEET

Part I of Schedule III to The Companies Act, 2013 prescribes only vertical form of Balance Sheet.

GENERAL INSTRUCTIONS FOR PREPARATION OF BALANCE SHEET

1. Current Assets	An asset shall be classified as current when it satisfies any of the following **criteria**: (a) it is expected to be realized in, *or* is intended for sale *or* consumption in, the company's normal operating cycle; (b) it is held primarily for the purpose of being traded; *or*

	(c) it is expected to be realized within 12 months after the reporting date; or (d) it is cash *or* cash equivalent unless it is restricted from being exchanged *or* used to settle a liability for at least 12 months after the reporting date.
2. Non-Current Assets	All other assets shall be classified as non-current.
3. An Operating Cycle	An operating cycle is the time between the acquisition of assets for processing and their realization in cash *or* cash equivalents. Where the normal operating cycle cannot be identified, it is assumed to have a duration of 12 months.
3. Current Liabilities	A liability shall be classified as current when it satisfies **any of the following criteria:** (a) it is expected to be settled in the company's normal operating cycle; (b) it is held primarily for the purpose of being traded; (c) it is due to be settled within 12 months after the reporting date; *or* (d) the company does not have an unconditional right to defer settlement of the liability for at least twelve months after the reporting date. Terms of a liability that could, at the option of the counterparty, result in its settlement by the issue of equity instruments do not affect its classification.
4. Non-Current Liabilities	All other liabilities shall be classified as non-current.
5. Trade Receivable	A receivable shall be classified as a 'Trade Receivable' if it is in respect of the amount due on account of goods sold *or* services rendered in the normal course of business.
6. Trade Payable	A payable shall be classified as a 'Trade Payable' if it is in respect of the amount due on account of goods purchased *or* services received in the normal course of business.
7. Use of Prefix 'At' instead of 'On'	It may be noted that the prescribed form of Balance Sheet prefixes 'At' instead of 'On'. For example, if a Balance Sheet of X Ltd. is prepared on 31st march, then the date of the balance-sheet will be stated as 'At 31st March, 2015' and not as 'On 31st March, 2015. The word 'On' refers to the entire duration (which consists of 24 hours) of the day whereas the word 'At' refers to a specific point of time. Since the balance-sheet is prepared to represent the financial position of the concern at a particular point of time (viz. at the end of the day's business hours), it is **appropriate to use the word 'At' instead of 'On'.**

VERTICAL FORM OF SUMMARISED BALANCE SHEET [WITH MAJOR HEADINGS ONLY]

...NAME OF THE COMPANY...
BALANCE SHEET AS AT...

(Rupees in. ..)

Particulars	*Note No.*	*Figures for the Current Reporting Period*	*Figures for the Previous Reporting Period*
I. EQUITY AND LIABILITIES			
(1) Shareholders' Funds		xxx	xxx
(2) Share Application Money pending Allotment		xxx	xxx
(3) Non-Current Liabilities		xxx	xxx
(4) Current Liabilities		xxx	xxx
Total		xxx	xxx
II. ASSETS			
(1) Non-Current Assets		xxx	xxx
(2) Current Assets		xxx	xxx
Total		xxx	xxx

VERTICAL FORM OF DETAILED BALANCE SHEET

...NAME OF THE COMPANY...
BALANCE SHEET AS AT. ..

(Rupees in. ..)

Particulars	*Note No.*	*Figures for the Current Reporting Period*	*Figures for the Previous Reporting Period*
I. EQUITY AND LIABILITIES			
(1) Shareholders' Funds			
(a) Share Capital	1	....	....
(b) Reserves and Surplus [e.g. Debit Balance of Profit & Loss A/c as negative figure]	2	....	....
(c) Money received against Share Warrants		....	....
(2) Share Application Money pending Allotment		....	....
(3) Non-Current Liabilities			
(a) Long-term Borrowings [e.g. Bonds/ Debentures/Loans repayableafter 12 months]	3	....	....
(b) Deferred Tax Liabilities (Net)		....	....
(c) Other Long term Liabilities [e.g. Trade Payables to be settled after 12 months]		....	....

(d) Long-term Provisions [e.g. Provision for Employee Benefits to be settled after 12 months]		....	....
(4) Current Liabilities			
(a) Short-Term Borrowings [e.g. Loans repayable on demand *or* within 12 months]	4	....	....
(b) Trade Payables [e.g. Trade Creditors,Bills Payables to be settled within 12 months]	5	....	....
(c) Other Current Liabilities [e.g. Bank Overdraft,Unpaid Dividend/ matured Deposits/ matured Debentures, That portion of Long-term Borrowings repayable within 12 months, Interest accrued(whether due *or* not) on borrowings,Calls-in-Advance,Outstanding Expenses, Tax Payable]	6	....	....
(d) Short-Term Provisions [e.g. Provision for Tax, Proposed Dividend, Provision for Employee Benefits to be settled within 12 months]	7	....	....
Total		....	....
II. ASSETS			
(1) Non-Current Assets			
(a) Fixed Assets			
(i) Tangible Assets [e.g. Land, Buildings, Plant & Equipment]	8	....	....
(ii) Intangible Assets [e.g.Goodwill Purchased, Goodwill on Consolidation,Brands/Trademarks]	9	....	....
(iii) Capital Work-in-Progress [e.g. Building under construction]		....	....
(iv) Intangible Assets under Development [e.g. Computer Software under Development]		....	....
(b) Non-Current Investments [e.g. Investment in Property/Partnership Firms]	10	....	....
(c) Deferred Tax Assets (Net)		....	....
(d) Long-Term Loans and Advances [e.g. Capital Advances, Security Deposits, Loans & Advances receivable after 12 months]	11	....	....

(e) Other Non-Current Assets [e.g.Unamortised Expenses like Discount/Loss on issue of Debentures to be amortised after 12 months, Amalgamation Adjustment A/c]	12	....	....
(2) Current Assets			
(a) Current Investments	13	....	....
(b) Inventories [e.g. Raw- Materials, Work-in-Progress, Finished Goods,Loose Tools,Stores & Spares]	14	....	....
(c) Trade Receivables [e.g. Trade Debtors,Bills Receivables to be realized within 12 months, Provision for Doubtful Debts by way of deduction]	15	....	....
(d) Cash and Cash Equivalents [e.g. Cheques/Drafts on hand, Bank Deposits with more than 12 months maturity]	16	....	....
(e) Short-term Loans and Advances [e.g. Loans & Advances receivable within 12 months]	17	....	....
(f) Other Current Assets [e.g.Prepaid Expenses]	18	....	....
Total		....	....

Notes To Accounts:

NOTE 1: SHARE CAPITAL

Particulars	₹	₹
Authorised Capital		
..... Shares of ₹. .. each	xxx	xxx
Issued Capital		
..... Shares of ₹. .. each	xxx	xxx
Subscribed Capital and fully paid		
..... Shares of ₹. .. each ₹. .. per share paid up	xxx	xxx
*Subscribed Capital but not fully paid		
..... Shares of ₹. .. each ₹. .. per share paid up	xxx	xxx
Less: Calls unpaid:		
(a) by Directors & Officers	(xxx)	(xxx)
(b) by Others	(xxx)	(xxx)
Add: Forfeited Shares	xxx	xxx
	xxx	xxx

Notes:

1. For the period of 5 years immediately preceding the date as at which the Balance Sheet is prepared

(a) Aggregate Number and Class of **Shares** allotted as fully paid up pursuant to a contract **without payments being received in cash**

(b) Aggregate Number and Class of **Shares** allotted as fully paid up by way of **Bonus Shares**

(c) Aggregate Number and Class of Shares bought back

2. Shares in the company held by each shareholder holding more than 5% shares specifying the number of shares
3. Shares Reserved for issue under options and contracts/commitments for the sale of shares/ disinvestment, including the terms and amounts
4. Shares held by Holding Company/Ultimate Holding Company/Subsidiaries/Associates of Holding Company/Ultimate Holding Company.
5. **Reconciliation** of the No of shares outstanding at the beginning and at the end of the reporting period

Particulars	*Figures for the Current Reporting Period*	*Figures for the Previous Reporting Period*
A. Shares at the beginning of the year		
B. *Add:* Shares allotted as fully paid up pursuant to a contract without payments being received in cash		
C. *Add:* Shares issued on RIght/Preferential/Private Placement basis		
D. *Add:* Shares allotted as fully paid up by way of Bonus Shares		
E. *Add:* Shares Issued on exercise of Employee Stock Options		
F. *Add:* Shares Issued on conversion/surrender of Debentures/ Bonds/Term Loan.		
G. *Less:* Shares cancelled on buy back of Shares		
H. *Less:* Shares Foreited but not ressued during the current year		
I. Shares at the end of the year		

***Note:** *Subscribed and Paid up Share Capital will include Unpaid Amount on Shares subscribed by Subscribers to Memorandum of Association and such Unpaid Amount will be disclosed under the head* **'Current Assets' and sub-head 'Other Current Assets'**.

NOTE 2: RESERVES AND SURPLUS

Particulars	₹	₹
Capital Reserve		
Capital Redemption Reserve		
Securities Premium Reserve		
Debenture Redemption Reserve		
Revaluation Reserve		
Share Options Outstanding Account		
Other Reserves – (specify the nature and purpose of each reserve and the amount in respect thereof)		
General Reserve, Dividend Equalisation Reserve, Reserve for Contingent Liabilities, Reserve for bad debts, Tonnage Tax Reserve created under the Income-tax Act, 1961.		

Surplus i.e. Balance in Statement of Profit & Loss		
Opening Balance		
Add: Profit for the period		
Less: Transfer to Reserve		
Less: Used for Bonus Shares		
Less: Interim Dividend		
Less: Proposed Preference Dividend		
Less: Proposed Equity Dividend		
Less: Dividend Distribution Tax		
Closing Balance		

Notes:

1. Debit Balance of Profit & Loss A/c is to be shown as negative figure.
2. Similarly Debit Balance of Reserve & Surplus is shown as negative figure.
3. 'Fund' is to be used if Reserve is earmarked for specific purpose.

NOTE 3: LONG-TERM BORROWINGS

Particulars	₹	₹
Bonds/Debentures		
Term Loans from Banks		
Term Loans from Other Parties		
Deferred Payment Liabilities		
Deposits		
Loans and Advances from Related Parties		
Long term Maturities of Finance Lease Obligations		
Other Loans and Advances (specify nature)		

Notes:

1. Aggregate Amount of Secured Borrowings along with Nature of security.
2. Aggregate Amount of Unsecured Borrowings
3. Aggregate Amount of Loans guaranteed by Directors *or* Others under each head
4. Bonds/debentures (along with the Rate of Interest and particulars of redemption *or* conversion, as the case may be) in descending order of maturity *or* conversion, starting from farthest redemption *or* conversion date, as the case may be. Where bonds/debentures are redeemable by installments, the date of maturity for this purpose must be reckoned as the date on which the first installment becomes due.
5. Particulars of any Redeemed Bonds/Debentures which the company has power to reissue shall be disclosed.
6. Terms of Repayment of Term Loans and Other Loans
7. Period and amount of continuing default as on the Balance Sheet Date in repayment of Loans and Interest

NOTE 4: SHORT-TERM BORROWINGS

Particulars	₹	₹
Loans repayable on demand from Banks		
Loans repayable on demand from Other Parties		

Loans and Advances from Related Parties		
Deposits		
Other Loans and Advances (specify nature)		

Notes:

1. Aggregate Amount of Secured Borrowings along with Nature of security and Unsecured Borrowings.
2. Aggregate Amount of Unsecured Borrowings
3. Aggregate Amount of Loans guaranteed by Directors *or* Others under each head
4. Period and amount of continuing default as on the Balance Sheet Date in repayment of Loans and Interest

NOTE 5: TRADE PAYABLES

Particulars	₹	₹
Sundry Creditors		
Bills Payables		

NOTE 6: OTHER CURRENT LIABILITIES

Particulars	₹	₹
Current maturities of Long-term Debt		
Current maturities of Finance Lease Obligations		
Interest accrued but not due on Borrowings		
Interest accrued and due on Borrowings		
Income received in advance		
Unpaid Dividends		
Application Money received for allotment of securities and due for refund and interest accrued thereon.		
Unpaid matured Deposits and Interest accrued thereon		
Unpaid matured Debentures and Interest accrued thereon		
Other Payables (specify nature e.g.)		
Bank Overdraft		
Outstanding Expenses		
Calls-in-Advance		

NOTE 7: SHORT-TERM PROVISIONS

Particulars	₹	₹
Provision for Employees' Benefit		
Provision for Income Tax		
Provision for Dividend Distribution Tax		
Proposed Equity Dividend		
Proposed Preference Dividend		

NOTE 8: TANGIBLE ASSETS

Asset	*Original Cost in the beg*	*Additions*	*Disposal*	*Original Cost at the end*	*Total Depreciation in the beg*	*Depreciation for Current year*	*Depreciation on Asset Disposed off*	*Total Depreciation at the end*	*W.D.V at the end*
A	*B*	*C*	*D*	*E = B + C − D*	*F*	*G*	*H*	*I = F + G − H*	*J = E − I*
Land									
Building									
Plant & Equipment									
Furniture and Fixtures									
Vehicles									
Office Equipment									
Others (specify nature)									
Assets under Lease									

Notes:

1. Impairment Losses/Reversals
2. Every Balance Sheet subsequent to date of Capital Reduction/Revaluation must show the reduced *or* increased figures and must by way of a note also show the amount of the reduction *or* increase together with the date thereof for the first 5 years subsequent to the date of such reduction *or* increase.

NOTE 9: INTANGIBLE ASSETS

Asset	*Original Cost in the beg*	*Additions*	*Disposal*	*Original Cost at the end*	*Total Depreciation in the beg*	*Depreciation for Current year*	*Depreciation on Asset Disposed off*	*Total Depreciation at the end*	*W.D.V at the end*
A	*B*	*C*	*D*	*E = B + C − D*	*F*	*G*	*H*	*I = F + G − H*	*J = E − I*
Goodwill									
Brands									
Trademarks									
Computer Software									
Mastheads and Publishing Titles.									
Mining Rights.									
Copyrights, and Patents and Other Intellectual Property Rights, Services & Operating Rights.									

Recipes, Formulae, Models, Designs and Prototypes.									
Licenses and Franchise.									
Others (Specify Nature).									

Notes: Same as for Tangible Assets

NOTE 10: NON-CURRENT INVESTMENTS

Particulars	₹	₹
Trade Investments		
Investment in Property		
Investments In Equity Instruments		
Investments In Preference Shares		
Investments In Government *or* Trust Securities		
Investments In Debentures *or* Bonds		
Investments In Mutual Funds		
Investments In Partnership Firms		
Other Non-Current Investments (Specify Nature)		

Notes:

1. Basis for Valuation in case of Investments carried at other than at cost
2. Aggregate amount of Quoted Investments and Market Value thereof;
3. Aggregate amount of Unquoted Investments;
4. Aggregate Provision for Diminution in Value of Investments

NOTE 11: LONG-TERM LOANS AND ADVANCES

Particulars	₹	₹
Capital Advances		
Security Deposits		
Loans and Advances to Related Parties		
Other Loans and Advances (specify nature)		

Notes:

1. Amount of Secured Loans & Advances considered good
2. Amount of Unsecured Loans & Advances considered good
3. Amount of Loans & Advances considered Doubtful
4. Allowance for Bad and Doubtful on Loans and Advances
5. Loans and advances due by directors *or* other officers of the the company *or* any of them either severally *or* jointly with any other persons *or* amounts due by firms *or* private companies respectively in which any director is a partner *or* a director *or* a member

NOTE 12: OTHER NON-CURRENT ASSETS

Particulars	₹	₹
Long Term Trade Receivables (including trade receivables on deferred credit terms)		
Others (specify nature e.g.)		
Discount/Loss on Issue of Debentures		
Amalgamation Adjustment A/c		

Notes: Same as for Long-term Loans and Advances

NOTE 13: CURRENT INVESTMENTS

Particulars	₹	₹
Investments In Equity Instruments		
Investments In Preference Shares		
Investments In Government *or* Trust Securities		
Investments In Debentures *or* Bonds		
Investments In Mutual Funds		
Investments In Partnership Firms		
Other Current Investments (Specify Nature)		

Notes: Same as for Non-Current Investments

NOTE 14: INVENTORIES

Particulars	₹	₹
Raw- Materials		
Work-in-Progress		
Finished Goods		
Stock-in-Trade		
Stores & Spares		
Loose Tools		
Others (specify nature)		

Notes:

1. Goods-in-transit
2. Mode of Valuation

NOTE 15: TRADE RECEIVABLES

Particulars	₹	₹
Sundry Debtors		
Less: Provision for Doubtful Debts		
Bills Receivables		

Notes:

1. Aggregate amount of Trade Receivables outstanding for a period exceeding six months from the date they are due for payment
2. Other Notes Same as for Long-term Loans and Advances

NOTE 16: CASH AND CASH EQUIVALENTS

Particulars	₹	₹
Bank Balance		
Cheques/Drafts on hand		
Cash Balance		
Others (specify nature)		

Notes:

1. Earmarked balances with banks(for example for unpaid dividend)
2. Balances with banks to the extent held as margin money *or* security against the borrowings, guarantees, other commitments
3. Repatriation restrictions, if any, in respect of cash and bank balances
4. Bank deposits with more than 12 months maturity

NOTE 17: SHORT-TERM LOANS AND ADVANCES

Particulars	₹	₹
Loans and Advances to Related Parties		
Other Loans and Advances (specify nature)		

Notes: Same as for Long-term Loans and Advances

NOTE 18: OTHER CURRENT ASSETS (SPECIFY NATURE E.G.)

Particulars	₹	₹
Prepaid Expenses		
Unpaid Amount on Shares subscribed by Subscribers to Memorandum of Association		

NOTE 19: CONTINGENT LIABILITIES AND COMMITMENTS (TO THE EXTENT NOT PROVIDED FOR)

Particulars	₹	₹
(i) CONTINGENT LIABILITIES		
(a) Claims against the company not acknowledged as debt (e.g., Towards Excise, Customs, VAT, Service Tax, Income Tax, Suppliers, Customers)		
(b) Guarantees (e.g. to Banks on behalf of others)		
(c) Other money for which the company is contingently liable (e.g.Bills Discounted but not yet matured)		
(ii) COMMITMENTS		
(a) Estimated amount of contracts remaining to be executed on Capital Account and not provided for;		
(b) Uncalled Liability on Shares and Other Investments(e.g. Debentures) partly paid		
(c) Other Commitments (e.g. Arrears of Fixed Cumulative Dividends on Preference Shares)		

PRACTICAL QUESTIONS FOR PRACTICE

QUESTION 1: How will you disclose the following items while preparing the Balance Sheet of a company?

ANSWER:

Item	Major Head	Sub- Head	Sub- Sub- Head
Preference Shares whose redemption overdue	Shareholders' Funds *[As per ICAI's Guidance Note]*	Share Capital	
Share Application Money pending Allotment-Not exceeding Issued Capital and to the extent not refundable	Shareholders' Funds	Share Capital	
Share Application Money pending Allotment- to the extent refundable	Current Liabilities	Other Current Liabilities	
Debit Balance of Profit & Loss A/c	Shareholders' Funds	Reserves and Surplus *[As a Negative Figure]*	
Loans repayable after Operating Cycle	Non-Current Liabilities	Long-term Borrowings	
Loans repayable within Operating Cycle/12 months	Current Liabilities	Short-Term Borrowings	
Loans repayable on demand	Current Liabilities	Short-Term Borrowings	
Trade Payables to be settled after Operating Cycle	Non-Current Liabilities	Other Long term Liabilities	
Trade Payables to be settled within Operating Cycle/12 months	Current Liabilities	Trade Payables	
Interest accrued on Share Application Money	Current Liabilities	Other Current Liabilities	
Interest accrued and due on Long-term Borrowings	Current Liabilities	Other Current Liabilities	
Interest accrued but not due on Long-term Borrowings	Current Liabilities	Other Current Liabilities	
Outstanding Expenses	Current Liabilities	Other Current Liabilities	
Tax Payable	Current Liabilities	Other Current Liabilities	
Bank Overdraft	Current Liabilities	Other Current Liabilities	

Unpaid/Unclaimed Dividend	Current Liabilities	Other Current Liabilities	
Matured Deposits	Current Liabilities	Other Current Liabilities	
Matured Debentures	Current Liabilities	Other Current Liabilities	Current Maturities of Long-term Debt
That portion of Long-term Borrowings repayable within 12 months	Current Liabilities	Other Current Liabilities	
Provision for Tax	Current Liabilities	Short-Term Provisions	
Proposed Dividend	Current Liabilities *[**Note:** This treatment is as per ICAI's Guidance Note and AS 4]*	Short-Term Provisions	It may be noted that Revised Schedule VI requires merely the disclosure in **Notes to Accounts.**
Provision for Employee Benefits to be settled within 12 months	Current Liabilities	Short-Term Provisions	
Provision for Employee Benefits to be settled after 12 months	Non-Current Liabilities	Long-term Provisions	
Provision for Employee Provident Fund to be settled after 12 months	Non-Current Liabilities	Long-term Provisions	
Live Stock	Non-Current Assets	Fixed Assets	Tangible Assets
Brands	Non-Current Assets	Fixed Assets	Intangible Assets
Intellectual Property Rights	Non-Current Assets	Fixed Assets	Intangible Assets
Licenses and Franchise	Non-Current Assets	Fixed Assets	Intangible Assets
Building under construction	Non-Current Assets	Fixed Assets	Capital Work-in-Progress
Computer Software under Development	Non-Current Assets	Fixed Assets	Intangible Assets under Development
Investment in Property	Non-Current Assets	Non-Current Investments	
Capital Advances	Non-Current Assets	Long-Term Loans and Advances	
Security Deposits	Non-Current Assets	Long-Term Loans and Advances	
Deposits with Custom Authorities	Non-Current Assets	Long-Term Loans and Advances	
Loans & Advances receivable after 12 months	Non-Current Assets	Long-Term Loans and Advances	

Discount/Loss on issue of Debentures/Share Issue Exp. to be w/o after 12 months		Non-Current Assets	Other Non-Current Assets
Preliminary Expenses	As per Para 56 of AS 26, 'Intangible Assets', Preliminary Expenses are to be recognized as expenses as and when they are incurred. Hence, Preliminary Expenses are not to appear in the Balance Sheet.		
Work-in-Progress	Current Assets	Inventories	
Loose Tools	Current Assets	Inventories	
Stores & Spares	Current Assets	Inventories	
Trade Receivables to be realized within 12 months/ Operating Cycle	Current Assets	Trade Receivables	
Provision for Doubtful Debts	Current Assets	Trade Receivables [Shown by way of deduction]	
Cheques/Drafts on hand	Current Assets	Cash and Cash Equivalents	
Bank Deposits with more than 12 months maturity	Current Assets	Cash and Cash Equivalents	
Loans & Advances receivable within 12 months	Current Assets	Short-term Loans and Advances	
Prepaid Expenses	Current Assets	Other Current Assets	
Interest accrued on Investments	Current Assets	Other Current Assets	
Unpaid Amount on Shares subscribed by Subscribers to Memorandum of Association	Current Assets ***[Note:*** *Subscribed and Paid up Share Capital will include such Unpaid Amount]*	Other Current Assets	
Calls Unpaid on Shares (othe than those subscribed by Subscribers to Memorandum of Association)	**Notes to Accounts** *[**Note:** Subscribed and Paid up Share Capital will be net of Calls Unpaid]*		
Guarantees	Notes to Accounts	Contingent Liabilities and Commitments	Contingent Liabilities

Bills Discounted but not yet matured	Notes to Accounts	Contingent Liabilities and Commitments	Contingent Liabilities
Uncalled Liability on partly paid Shares held as Investments	Notes to Accounts	Contingent Liabilities and Commitments	Commitments
Uncalled Liability on partly paid Debentures held as Investments	Notes to Accounts	Contingent Liabilities and Commitments	Commitments
Arrears of Fixed Cumulative Dividends on Preference Shares	Notes to Accounts	Contingent Liabilities and Commitments	Commitments
Allocations and Appropriations such as Dividend, Bonus Shares and Transfer to/ from Reserves	Notes to Accounts	Reserves and Surplus	Surplus

QUESTION 2: State under which head these accounts should be classified in Balance Sheet, as per Schedule III to The Companies Act 2013:

(i) Share application money received in excess of issued share capital.
(ii) Share option outstanding account.
(iii) Unpaid matured debenture and interest accrued thereon.
(iv) Uncalled liability on shares and other partly paid investments.
(v) Calls unpaid.
(vi) Intangible Assets under development.
(vii) Money received against share warrant.
(viii) Long term maturity of finance lease obligation.

ANSWER:

CLASSIFICATION OF FOLLOWING ACCOUNTS FOR THE PRESENTATION IN SCHEDULE III TO THE COMPANIES ACT, 2013

Sl. No.	*Accounts*	*Head*
(i)	Share application money received in excess of issue share capital	Other Current Liabilities
(ii)	Share option outstanding account	Reserve & Surplus
(iii)	Unpaid matured debenture and interest accrued thereon	Other Current Liabilities
(iv)	Uncalled liability on shares and other partly paid investments	Contingent Liabilities and commitments-commitments to the extent not provided for
(v)	Calls unpaid	Share Capital
(vi)	Intangible Assets under development	Fixed Assets
(vii)	Money received against share warrant	Shareholder's Funds
(viii)	Long term maturity of finance lease obligation	Long Term Borrowings

QUESTION 3: State the disclose requirement of Proposed Dividend while preparing Financial Statements on company.

ANSWER:

Revised Schedule VI	The Revised Schedule VI, classifies 'Proposed Dividend' as commitments'.
AS 4	Paragraph 14 of AS 4 requires that "Dividends stated to be in respect of the period covered by the financial statements, which are proposed or declared by the enterprise after the Balance Sheet date but before approval of the financial statements, should be adjusted." Accounting Standards now have overriding impact over Revised Schedule VI. Therefore, unless Para 14 of AS 4 is changed, Proposed Dividend shall be adjusted.
ICAI Guidance Note	The ICAI Guidance Note on the Revised Schedule VI has clarified that the 'Proposed Dividend' is a provision.

QUESTION 4: How will you disclose the following items while preparing the Balance Sheet of a company?

1. **Trade Receivables**
2. **Trade Payables**
3. **Current Maturities of Long-term Debt**

ANSWER:

1. Trade Receivables are to be classified as Current Assets if Expected Realisation Period is either within the Operating Cycle Period or within the 12 Months Period.
2. Trade Payables are to be classified as Current Liabilities if Expected Payment Period is either within the Operating Cycle Period or within the 12 Months Period.
3. Current Maturities of Long-term Debt represents that portion of Long-term Borrowings which is due within 12 Months from the date of Balance Sheet or with in Operating Cycle Period. It appears under the head 'Current Liabilities' and sub-head 'Other Current Liabilities'. For Example, 12% Debentures of Reliance Ltd. ₹ 100 lacs [20% Redeemable within 1 year]. ₹ 20 lacs will appear as Current Maturities of Long-term Debt under the head 'Current Liabilities' and sub-head 'Other Current Liabilities' and ₹ 80 lacs will appear under the head 'Non-Current Liabilities' and sub head 'Long-term Borrowings'.

QUESTION 5: X Ltd. provides you the following information:

1. **Raw material stock holding period: 3 months**
2. **Work-in-progress holding period: 1 month**
3. **Finished goods holding period: 4 months**
4. **Debtors collection period: 6 months**

You are required to compute the operating cycle

ANSWER:

As per Schedule III "An operating cycle is the time between the acquisition of assets for processing and their realization in cash or cash equivalents".

Operating Cycle = Raw material stock holding period + Work-in-progress holding period + Finished goods holding period + Debtors collection period = 3 + 1 + 4 + 6 = 14 months.

QUESTION 6: State giving reason whether the Trade Receivables are Current Assets or Non-Current Assets as per Schedule III in the following cases:

Case	Operating Cycle Period	Expected Realisation Period
1.	11 Months	10 Months
2.	11 Months	12 Months
3.	11 Months	13 Months
4.	14 Months	13 Months
5.	14 Months	15 Months

ANSWER:

Case	*Current Assets or Non-Current Assets*	*Reason*
1.	Current Assets	Expected Realisation Period — is less than the Operating Cycle Period and — is within 12 Months.
2.	Current Assets	Expected Realisation Period is within 12 Months although it is more than the Operating Cycle Period
3.	Non-Current Assets	Expected Realisation Period is more than the Operating Cycle Period and 12 Months Period.
4.	Current Assets	Expected Realisation Period is less than the Operating Cycle Period although it is more than the 12 Months Period .
5.	Non-Current Assets	Expected Realisation Period is more than the Operating Cycle Period and the 12 Months Period .

QUESTION 7: State giving reason whether the Trade Payables are Current Liabilities or Non-Current Liabilities as per Schedule III in the following cases:

Case	Operating Cycle Period	Expected Payment Period
1.	11 Months	10 Months
2.	11 Months	12 Months
3.	11 Months	13 Months
4.	14 Months	13 Months
5.	14 Months	15 Months

ANSWER:

Case	*Current Assets or Non-Current Assets*	*Reason*
1.	Current Assets	Expected Payment Period — is less than the Operating Cycle Period and — is within 12 Months.
2.	Current Assets	Expected Payment Period is within 12 Months although it is more than the Operating Cycle Period.
3.	Non-Current Assets	Expected Payment Period is more than the Operating Cycle Period and 12 Months Period.
4.	Current Assets	Expected Payment Period is less than the Operating Cycle Period although it is more than the 12 Months Period .

5.	Non-Current Assets	Expected Payment Period is more than the Operating Cycle Period and the 12 Months Period .

QUESTION 8: PCT Ltd. is in the process of finalizing its accounts for year ended 31st March, 2015 and furnishes the following information:

(i) Finished goods normally are held for 1 month before sale.

(ii) Sales realization from Debtors usually takes 2 months from date of credit invoice.

(iii) Raw materials are held in stock to cover 1 month's production requirements.

(iv) Packing materials, being specifically made for the company and having lead time of 3 months is held in stock for 3 months.

(v) The holding period in respect of unfinished goods is 1 month.

(vi) Being a monopoly KAY Ltd. enjoys a credit period of 12.5 months from its suppliers who sometimes at the end of their credit period opt for conversion of their dues into long term debt of KAY Ltd.

You are required to compute the operating cycle of PCT Ltd. as per Schedule III of The Companies Act, 2013. As the suppliers of the company are paid off after a credit period of 12.5 months should this be part of Current Liability? Would your answer be the same if the creditors are settled in 330 days?

ANSWER:

Operating Cycle = 1 + 1 + 3 + 1 + 2 = 8 months

Classification of liability to suppliers: Schedule III provides that:

"A liability shall be classified as current when it satisfies any of the following criteria:

(i) it is expected to be settled in the company's normal operating cycle;

(ii) it is held primarily for the purpose of being traded;

(iii) it is due to be settled within 12 months after the reporting date; or

(iv) the company does not have an unconditional right to defer settlement of the liability for at least 12 months after the reporting date. Terms of a liability that could, at the option of the counterparty, result in its settlement by the issue of equity instruments and do not affect its classification."

(a) **When credit period is 12.5 months:** It will be treated as non-current liability since it is not due to be settled within 12 months after the reporting date.

(b) **When credit period is 330 days (i.e. 11 months approx.):** It will be treated as current liability since it is due to be settled within 12 months after the reporting date.

QUESTION 9: The management of X Ltd. contends that the work in process is not valued since it is difficult to ascertain the same in view of the multiple processes involved. They opined that the value of opening and closing work in process would be more or less the same. Accordingly, the management had not separately disclosed work in process in its financial statements. Comment in line with Schedule III.

ANSWER: Schedule III to the Companies Act, 2013 requires the disclosure of opening and closing WIP under broad heads by way of additional information [General Instructions 5 (iii)]. In addition, AS-2 also requires the valuation of WIP. Therefore, the non-disclosure in the financial statements by the company amounts to violation of Schedule III.

QUESTION 10: TULSIAN Ltd is having the following Fixed Deposit Receipts:

Bank	Date of FDR	Maturity Date	Amount
Yes Bank Limited	**01–Jan–2015**	**2–Jan–2016**	**30,00,000**
Bank of Baroda	**01–Jan–2015**	**31–Mar–2016**	**20,00,000**

State Bank of India	**28–Feb–2015**	**30–May–2015**	**10,00,000**
ICICI Bank	**1–Jan–2014**	**1–Apr–2016**	**40,00,000**

Prepare Notes to Accounts showing the above Deposits in accordance with the requirements of Schedule III as at the Balance Sheet date i.e. 31st March, 2015.

ANSWER:

NOTE 'X': CASH & BANK BALANCES AS AT 31.03.2015 (BALANCE SHEET DATE)

Particulars	₹
A. Cash in Hand	xxx
B. Balances with Bank	
(i) Less than or equal to 12 Months Maturity.	
– Cash Equivalent as per AS–3 (less than 3 Months Maturity) [SBI]	10,00,000
– Other Bank Balances [30,00,000 + 20,00,000]	50,00,000
(ii) More than 12 Months Maturity [ICICI]	40,00,000
	100,00,000

QUESTION 11: Z Ltd. has flexi deposit linked current account with various banks. Cheques are issued from the current amount and as per the requirements of funds, the flexi deposits are encashed and transferred to current accounts. As of 31st March 2015 certain cheques issued to vendors are not presented for payment resulting in the credit balance in the books of the company. The management wants to present the books overdraft under current liabilities and flexi deposits under cash and bank balances. Comment.

ANSWER:

Schedule III	Presentation of Bank Overdraft as per Schedule III: The instructions in accordance with which "Cash and Cash Equivalents" should be presented as per Schedule III to the Companies Act, 2013 are as follows: (i) Cash and Cash Equivalents shall be classified as: (a) Balances with banks; (b) Cheques, drafts on hand; (c) Cash on hand; (d) Others (specify nature). (ii) Earmarked balances with banks (for example, for unpaid dividend) shall be separately stated. (iii) Balances with banks to the extent held as margin money or security against the borrowings, guarantees, other commitments shall be disclosed separately (iv) Repatriation restrictions, if any, in respect of cash and bank balances shall be separately stated. (v) Bank deposits with more than 12 months maturity shall be disclosed separately.
Advice	It is evident that is substance the position is that the composite bank balance including the balance in flexi deposit accounts are positive, even though physical set-off has not been made as on the balance sheet date. Further the bank has got the right to set off of flexi deposits against the cheques issued and hence it would be more information and useful to the readers of the financial statements to disclosed the book credit balance as a set-off from the flexi deposit accounts. The disclosure of the said book credit balance as book overdraft under the head current liabilities as proposed by the management is not correct.

QUESTION 12: Is non-disclosure of source from which Bonus shares have been issued, a violation of Schedule III to the Companies Act, 2013?

ANSWER: No since Schedule III does not require such disclosure. Schedule III merely requires the disclosure of aggregate number and class of shares allotted as fully paid up bonus shares for a period of 5 years immediately preceding the Balance Sheet date in the Notes to Accounts.

QUESTION 13: X Ltd. paid ₹ 25 lakhs as advance to Y Ltd. towards the purchase of printing machinery on 15-01-2015 with delivery instruction to deliver the same in the last week of June, 2015. Further on 15-02-2015 X Ltd. purchased two diesel generator sets from Y Ltd. for ₹ 30 lakhs on 90 days Credit term. In the accounts for 2014-15, X Ltd. intends to adjust the advance paid against Credit purchase and show the net amount of ₹ 5 lakhs as due from them. As the statutory auditor, how would you deal with this?

ANSWER: Since X Ltd. has paid advance amount to the supplier of machinery to be used in the project, such advance amount should be grouped under the main heading 'Non-Current Assets' with the sub-head as Fixed Assets with a sub-classification as 'Capital Work-in-Progress.' This is as per requirement of Schedule III to The Companies Act, 2013 and the existing accounting practice.

If the advance is for purchase of other machinery, it should be grouped under a separate head – 'Long Term Loan and Advance' with a sub-classification as 'Capital advance' under the main heading 'Non-current Assets'. In view of the above, the proposal of X Ltd., to show the net balance in the personal account of Y Ltd. is not correct. Such proposal will conceal the two material items in the balance sheet – one, expenditure towards capital asset and the other current liability for purchase of the generator set.

Hence, the auditor should advice X Ltd., to show these tow items separately. If X Ltd. does not accept the advice, the auditor should qualify his report with suitable quantification of amount involved.

asset and the other current liability for purchase of the generator set.

Hence, the auditor should advice X Ltd., to show these tow items separately. If X Ltd. does not accept the advice, the auditor should qualify his report with suitable quantification of amount involved.

QUESTION 14: Y Ltd. purchased an existing bottling unit. The method of charging depreciation on machinery of the acquired unit was different from that followed by the company in its other units. The company wants to continue to charge depreciation for the acquired unit, in the method followed earlier by them and which was too consistent with their own method. Comment

ANSWER:

Guidance Note	Guidance Note on Accounting for Depreciation in companies issued by the Institute recommends that a company may adopt more than one method of depreciation. Therefore, it is permissible to adopt or follow different method of depreciation, for different types of assets, provided the same methods are consistently adopted every year in term of section 205(2) of the Companies Act, 1956. Also units in different geographical locations can follow different methods of depreciation on machinery provided the same are consistently followed.
Advice	Y Ltd. could continue to follow the previous method of charging depreciation for the acquired company, even if it is not in agreement with the method followed by Y Ltd. for their other units.

QUESTION 15: S Ltd. issued Bonds to the tune of ₹ 100 lacs and provided security to the tune of ₹ 80 lacs for the same. It insists that it will disclose the Bonds as "Secured" in the Balance Sheet of the Company. Comment.

ANSWER: Prima facie, the Bonds issued to the tune of ₹ 100 lacs are provided with security to the tune of ₹ 80 lacs i.e. neither fully secured nor unsecured. Guidance Note on the 'Terms used in Financial Statements" issue by ICAI, states "Secured Loans" as loan secured wholly or partly against tan asset. Hence the Bond should be classified under 'Secured Loans' for the purpose of disclosure in the balance Sheet. However the nature of security should be clearly specified.

QUESTION 16: The Balance Sheet of G Ltd is as under: Comment on the presentation in terms of Schedule III and Accounting Standards issued by NACAS.

BALANCE SHEET AS AT ... *(Rupees in ...)*

Particulars	Note No.	31.03.2015	31.03.2014
I. EQUITY AND LIABILITIES			
Share Capital	1	xxx	xxx
Reserves & Surplus	2	0	0
Employee stock option outstanding	3	xxx	xxx
Share application money	4	xxx	xxx
Non-Current Liabilities			
Deferred tax liability (Arising from Indian Income Tax)	5	xxx	xxx
Current Liabilities			
Trade Payables	6	xxx	xxx
Total		xxx	xxx
II. ASSETS			
Non-Current Assets			
Fixed Assets-Tangible	7	xxx	xxx
CWIP (including capital advances)	8	xxx	xxx
Current Assets			
Trade Receivables	9	xxx	xxx
Deferred Tax Asset (Arising from Indian Income Tax)	10	xxx	xxx
P & L Debit balance			
Total		xxx	xxx

ANSWER: Following Errors are noticed in presentation as per Schedule III:

(i) Share Capital & Reserve & Surplus are to be reflected under the heading "Shareholders' funds", which is not shown while preparing the balance sheet. Although it is a part of Equity and Liabilities yet it must be shown under head "shareholders' funds". The heading "Shareholders' funds" is missing in the balance sheet given in the question.

(ii) Reserve & Surplus is showing zero balance, which is not correct in the given case. Debit balance of statement of profit & Loss should be shown as a negative figure under the head 'Surplus'. The balance of 'Reserves and Surplus', after adjusting negative balance of surplus shall be shown under the head 'Reserves and Surplus' even if the resulting figure is in the negative.

(iii) Schedule III requires that Employee Stock Option outstanding should be disclosed under the heading "Reserves and Surplus"

(iv) Share application money refundable shall be shown under the sub-heading "Other Current Liabilities". As this is refundable and not pending for allotment, hence it is not a part of equity.

(v) Deferred Tax Liability has been correctly shown under Non-Current Liabilities. But Deferred tax assets and deferred tax liabilities, both, cannot be shown in balance sheet because only the net balance of Deferred Tax Liability or Asset is to be shown

(vi) Under the main heading of Non-Current Assets, Fixed Assets are further classified as under:
  (i) Tangible assets
  (ii) Intangible assets
  (iii) Capital work in Progress
  (iv) Intangible assets under development.

  Keeping in view the above, the CWIP shall be shown under Fixed Assets as Capital Work in Progress. The amount of Capital advances included in CWIP shall be disclosed under the sub-heading "Long term loans and advances" under the heading Non-Current Assets.

(vii) Deferred Tax Asset shall be shown under Non-Current Asset. It should be the net balance of Deferred Tax Asset after adjusting the balance of deferred tax

QUESTION 17: On 30th September, 2012 BHARAT Ltd. was incorporated with a Authorised Capital of ₹ 50 lakhs. It first accounts were closed on 31st March, 2013 by which time it had become a listed company with an issued, subscribed and paid up capital of ₹ 40 lakhs in 4,00,000 Equity Shares of ₹ 10 each.

The company started off with two lines of business namely 'Engineering Division' and 'Chemicals Division', with equal asset base with effect from 1st April, 2013. The 'Ceramic Division' was added by the company on 1st April, 2014. The following data is gathered form the books of account of BHARAT Ltd:

TRIAL BALANCE AS ON 31st MARCH 2015 *(₹ in 000's)*

Particulars	*Dr.*	*Cr.*
Engineering Division sales	—	**6,000**
Cost of engineering Division sales	**2,600**	—
Chemicals Division sales	—	**8,000**
Cost of sales of Chemicals Division	**4,300**	—
Ceramic Division Sales	—	**1,500**
Cost of sales of Ceramic Division	**900**	—
Administration cost	**2,000**	—
Distribution cost	**1,500**	—
Dividend-Interim	**1,200**	—
Fixed Asset at cost	**9,000**	—
Depreciation on Fixed Assets	—	**1,500**
Closing Stock	**400**	—
Trade Debtors	**440**	—
Cash at Bank	**160**	—
Trade Creditors	—	**500**
Equity Shares Capital is shares of ₹ 10 each	—	**4,000**
Retained Profits	—	**1,000**
	22,500	**22,500**

Additional Information:

(a) Administration costs should be split between the Divisions in the ratio 5 : 3 : 2.

(b) Distribution costs should be spread over the Divisions in the ratio 3 : 1 : 1.

(c) Directors have proposed Final Dividend of ₹ 800 thousands and transfer to reserve @10%.

(d) Some of the users of ceramics Division are unhappy with the product and have lodged claims against the company for damages of ₹ 750 thousands. The claim is hotly contested by the company on legal advice.

(e) Fixed Assets worth ₹ 3000 thousand were added in the Ceramic Division of 1.4.2014.

(f) Fixed Assets are written off over a period of 10 years on straight line basis in the books. However for Income tax purposes depreciation at 20% on written down value of the assets is allowed by Tax Authorities.

(g) Income tax rate may be assumed at 35% and Dividend Distribution Tax @ 16.2225%.

(h) During the year Engineering Division has sold to Alpha Ltd. goods having a sales value of ₹ 2500 thousands. Mr. BHARAT, the Managing Director of BHARAT Ltd. owns 100% of the issued Equity Shares of Alpha Ltd. The sales made of Alpha Ltd. were at normal selling price of BHARAT Ltd.

Required: Prepare Statement of Profit and Loss for the year ended 31st March, 2015 and the Balance Sheet as at the date as per Schedule III to The Companies Act, 2013. Your answer should include notes and disclosures as per Accounting Standards.

ANSWER:

BHARAT LTD.
PROFIT AND LOSS ACCOUNT FOR THE YEAR ENDING 31st MARCH 2015

Particulars	*Note No.*	*(₹ '000)*
I. Revenue from Operations (6,000 + 8,000 + 1,500)		15,500
II. Total Revenue		15,500
III. Expenses:		
Cost of Sales		7,800
Distribution costs		1,500
Administration costs		2,000
Total Expenses		11,300
IV. Profit before tax		4,200
V. Tax Expenses		
Current tax	1,239	
Deferred tax	231	1,470
VI. Profit or Loss for the period		2,730

BHARAT LTD.
BALANCE SHEET AS AT 31st MARCH, 2015

Particulars	*Note No.*	*(₹ '000)*
I. Equity and Liabilities		
(1) Shareholder's Funds		
(a) Share Capital	1	4,000.0
(b) Reserves and Surplus	2	1,187.8
(2) Current Liabilities		
Trade payable		500.0
Other Current Liabilities	3	1,573.2
Short term Provisions	4	1,239.0

	Total		8,500
II.	**Assets**		
	(1) Non-Current Assets		
	Fixed assets		
	Tangible assets	5	7,500
	(2) Current Assets		
	(a) Inventories		400
	(b) Trade Receivables		440
	(c) Cash and Cash Equivalents		160
	Total		8,500

Notes to Accounts: *(₹ '000)*

	Particulars	₹	₹
1.	**Share Capital**		
	Authorised Shares Capital		
	5,00,000 Equity Shares of ₹ 10 each		5,000
	Issued and subscribed		
	4,00,000 Shares of ₹ 10 each, fully paid up		4,000
2.	**Reserves and Surplus**		
	Retained Profit brought forward (₹ 1,000 – ₹ 210)		790.00
	Profit after tax of the current year	2,730	
	Amount transferred to General Reserve (10% of ₹ 2,730)	(273)	
	Amount transferred to CDT* (16.2225% of ₹ 2,000)	(324.45)	
	Dividends (₹ 1,200 + ₹ 800)	(2,000)	
	Profit for the years		132.55
	Total Profit		922.55
	Reserves		273.00
			1,195.55
3.	**Other Current Liabilities**		
	Proposed dividend	800.00	
	Dividend Distribution Tax	324.45	
	Deferred Tax Liability (₹ 210 + ₹ 231)	441.00	1,565.45
4.	**Short term Provisions**		
	Provision for tax		
5.	**Tangible Assets**		1,239
	Fixed Assets		
	Gross Block	9,000	
	Less: Depreciation	(1,500)	7,500

*The dividend distributed by an Indian Company is exempt from income tax in the hands of shareholders. However, the Indian company is liable to pay Dividend Distribution Tax (DDT) @ 16.2225% (i.e., inclusive of surcharge and eduction cess on such dividend).

Disclosures

1. SEGMENTS DISCLOSURE (BUSINESS SEGMENTS) *(₹ in '000)*

Particulars	*Engineering Division*	*Chemical Division*	*Ceramics Division*	*Total*
Sales	6,000	8,000	1,500	15,500
Cost of Sales	2,600	4,300	900	7,800
Administration Cost (5 : 3 : 2)	1,000	600	400	2,000
Distribution Cost (3 : 1 : 1)	9000	300	300	1,500
Profit/Loss	1,500	2,800	(100)	4,200
	6,000	8,000	1,500	15,500
Original cost of Assets (Equal Capital Base)	3,000	3,000	3,000	9,000
Depreciation @ 10% p.a.				
For the year ended 31.3.2014	300	300	NIL	600
For the year ended 31.3.2015	300	300	300	300

Note: Ceramic division is a reportable segment as per assets criteria.

2. SEGMENTS DISCLOSURE (BUSINESS SEGMENTS) *(₹ in '000)*

Particulars	*₹ in '000*
Opening Timing Difference on 1.4.2014	
WDV of fixed assets as per books	5,400
WDV of fixed assets as per Income Tax Act	4,800
Difference	600
Deferred Tax Liability @ 35% on ₹ 600	210
This has been adjusted against opening balance of retained profits.	
Current year (ended 31st March, 2015)	
Depreciation as per books	900
Depreciation as per Income Tax Act (₹ 480 + ₹ 480 + ₹ 600)	1,560
Difference	660
Deferred Tax Liability @ 35% on ₹ 660 (to be carried forward)	231

3. **Contingent Liabilities no provided:** Company is contesting claim for damages for ₹ 7,50,000 and as such the same is not acknowledged as debts.

4. **Related Party Disclosure:** Para 3 AS 18 lists out related party relationships. The includes individuals owning, directly or indirectly, an interest in voting power of reporting enterprise which given them control or significant influence over the enterprises, and relatives of any such individual. In the instant case, Mr. BHARAT as a managing director controls operating and financial actions of BHARAT Ltd. He is also owing 100% share capital of Alpha Ltd. thereby exercising control over it. Hence, Alpha Ltd. is related party as per para 3 of AS 18.

   Disclosure to be made:

   Name of the related party — Alpha Ltd.
   Nature of relationship — common director
   Nature of the transaction — Sale of goods at normal commercial terms
   Volume of the transaction — Sales to Alpha Ltd. worth ₹ 2500 thousands

Working Note:

TAX COMPUTATION

Particulars	₹
Profit before tax for the year ended 31.3.2015	4,200
Add: Depreciation provided in the books (₹ 300 + ₹ 300 + ₹ 300)	900
	5,100
Less: Depreciation as per Income Tax Act (₹ 480 + ₹ 480 + rs 600)	(1,560)
Taxable Income	3,540
Tax at 35% on ₹ 3,540	1,239